Special Edition Using Microsoft Visual Studio

A Complete Developer's Guide

MORE THAN JUST ANOTHER "TOOL" BOOK, this volume explores the reasons why you would use Visual Studio, the techniques professional developers employ when working with this tool suite, and the architectural underpinnings of leading-edge application development.

A major focus of this book is the use of COM, the Component Object Model, which is the centerpiece of Microsoft's architecture for distributed, component-based software development. This includes coverage of Distributed COM (DCOM) and ActiveX technologies.

Key Microsoft BackOffice tools are covered, including SQL Server, Microsoft Transaction Server (MTS), and the Microsoft Message Queue (MSMQ). These server-based applications have become key elements in Microsoft's Distributed Internet Applications Architecture (DNA), and they play a prominent role in the development and execution of leading-edge applications.

Full treatment is given to the use of Visual Basic, Visual C++, Visual J++ (Microsoft's implementation of the Java programming language), and the Visual InterDev environment for web-based development. Detailed coverage on Dynamic HTML is also included.

This book describes the widespread adoption of a component-based application architecture and the advantages it provides when building enterprise applications. It also covers both web-based development and advanced client/server architectures, including a wealth of material on distributed applications deployed in Wide Area Network (WAN) environments.

Many code examples are included to illustrate points made in the text. In addition, a sample application that demonstrates the principles and techniques described in the book is available on the web at **http://www.gasullivan.com/vs97book/**.

This book features a collection of material written by professional developers who actually use these tools every day and have successfully deployed large-scale applications built with Visual Studio.

Topics Covered

- Microsoft's object technologies (OLE, ActiveX, COM, and DCOM)
- Creating components with Visual Basic, Visual C++, and Visual J++
- Using ActiveX components for web-based and client/server applications
- Web-based techniques—using Dynamic HTML, ActiveX documents, and Visual InterDev
- Building distributed applications deployed across multiple servers in WAN environments
- Tools for software development teams—Visual SourceSafe, Visual Modeler, and the Microsoft Repository

Using

Special Edition

Using MICROSOFT® Visual Studio™

QUE®

Special Edition

Using

Using

MICROSOFT®

Visual Studio™

Don Benage and Azam A. Mirza

Special Edition Using Microsoft Visual Studio

Library of Congress Catalog Number: 97-80931

ISBN: 0-7897-1260-1

This book is sold *as is*, without warranty of any kind, either express or implied, respecting the contents of this book, including but not limited to implied warranties for the book's quality, performance, merchantability, or fitness for any particular purpose. Neither Que Corporation nor its dealers or distributors shall be liable to the purchaser or any other person or entity with respect to any liability, loss, or damage caused or alleged to have been caused directly or indirectly by this book.

2000 99 98 6 5 4 3 2 1

Interpretation of the printing code: The rightmost double-digit number is the year of the book's printing; the rightmost single-digit number, the number of the book's printing. For example, a printing code of 98-1 shows that the first printing of the book occurred in 1998.

All terms mentioned in this book that are known to be trademarks or service marks have been appropriately capitalized. Que cannot attest to the accuracy of this information. Use of a term in this book should not be regarded as affecting the validity of any trademark or service mark.

Screen reproductions in this book were created using Collage Plus from Inner Media, Inc., Hollis, NH.

Contents at a Glance

V Team Development with Visual Studio

Table of Contents

II Creating Controls and Components for Reuse

4 Using Microsoft's Object Technologies 89

IV Developing Scalable Distributed Applications

V Team Development with Visual Studio

Credits

EXECUTIVE EDITOR
Brad Jones

MANAGING EDITOR
Jodi Jensen

ACQUISITIONS EDITOR
Kelly Marshall

DEVELOPMENT EDITOR
Chris Nelson

PROJECT EDITOR
Dana Rhodes Lesh

COPY EDITORS
Susan Shaw Dunn
Margaret Berson

INDEXER
Christine Nelsen

TECHNICAL EDITORS
Ramesh Chandak
Keith Ballenger

SOFTWARE SPECIALIST
Andrea Duvall

BOOK DESIGNER
Ruth Harvey

COVER DESIGNER
Sandra Schroeder

PRODUCTION TEAM
Marcia Deboy
Michael Dietsch
Cynthia Fields
Maureen West
Trina Wurst

Composed in *Century Old Style* and *Franklin Gothic* by Que Corporation.

To Katarina, my wife and my blessing: I truly appreciate your strength of character, your tenderness, and your wisdom. Our life together has become an ever-improving adventure now that we're pushing the little red wagon in the same direction. Thanks for supporting me with my professional endeavors, for taking time to add "world-class mommy" to your professional credentials, and for making ordinary events exciting.

Cameron K. Beattie

To my wife, Diane.

Donald M. Benage

To my grandparents, Ruth and Sam Davidson, for your unconditional love.

Robert S. Black

To my beautiful wife, Rebecca, for all of your love and patience, and to my parents Don and Georgia for always believing in me.

Eric M. Brown

Dedicated to my love and best friend, Susan…thank you for all that you do in my life. Also to my father for showing me my first computer and my mother…for everything.

David Burgett

Thanks to my wife Connie and daughter Lauren for their incredible patience during this and all my projects.

J. "Eddie" Gulley

To my wife Amy, our parents, and the rest of our family who have all waited patiently with "honey-do" jobs. A big thanks to my little brother Jason, Bowl Haven, and the Alton Fantasy Baseball League for their support and patience.

David M. Kincade

To my wife, Anna, and six (yes, that's right, six) children. Thanks for putting up with me. To Mom and Dad. You taught me the principles by which I have always strived to live. Thank you.

John W. Leighton

Dedicated to teaching colleagues, past and present.

Joseph P. Lengyel

For Mom & Dad.

Larry D. Millett

To my lovely wife on our first anniversary—from a friend to a friend!

Azam A. Mirza

To my husband Bryan and son Jimmy: Thank you for your love and support. To my Mom and Dad and sisters: Thanks for putting up with me and loving me. In memory of my brother Chuck Vogt (1956-1987)—you are my greatest source of inspiration.

Angela Nielson

To my nephew Brian and niece Mary Kathryn who, by the time they're old enough to care about this dedication, will probably laugh at the technology covered in this book.

David O'Leary

A special thanks to my wife Renee who has always been loving and patient. Thanks to my daughter Allison for always being a source of inspiration.

J. Brad Rhodes

I want to dedicate my work on this book to my grandparents, W.T. and Elizabeth Slinkard, as well as to my mother Martha Eifert, my sister Laurie Glastetter, and my stepfather Bill Eifert.

Kevin D. Runnels

To my wife, Melissa, for her love and patience over the last several months. And to my dogs, Riley and Bailey, for someone to play with after a long day's work.

Jody C. Socha

Thanks to my wonderful wife Cindy and son Will for your patience during my researching and writing!

William F. Spencer V

For Robert and Christina. Thank you.

Chris Striker

To the employees, customers, partners, and vendors of G. A. Sullivan—your loyalty means everything to me.

Gregory A. Sullivan

To God be the glory; great things He has done. A special thanks to my wife Kim for all her love, support, and understanding.

Anthony J. Taylor

To my wonderful wife Pam, son Brad, and daughter Samantha. Thank you for all your patience and understanding in regards to my endeavors. I would never be able to attempt and accomplish such tasks without your inspiration and support.

Ronald W. Terry

A special thanks to my wife Tina for her love and patience. Thanks to my parents for the love and education.

Timothy A. White

To my dear husband Frank for your love, and to my friends Carol and Bill for your friendship.

Yanni Xiao

About the Authors

G. A. Sullivan is one of the fastest growing technology companies in the United States. The company was recently ranked as the 149th fastest growing private company in America according to *Inc.* magazine's 1997 *Inc.* 500 list of top companies. G. A. Sullivan is a noted leader in providing high-quality software development services through the application of leading edge information technology. The company specializes in developing core business solutions for its clients. As a Microsoft Solution Provider Partner, G. A. Sullivan is a recognized leader in the development of distributed client/server applications for I-net environments.

G. A. Sullivan provides a full range of service offerings including project management, high-level IT consulting, and staff augmentation. Consultants provide expertise in any area within the software development life cycle including project management, technical team leadership, system/business analysis, software development, database administration, and technical/user documentation.

G. A. Sullivan believes that technical leadership is a key component to continued success and thus participates in the industry through a variety of speaking and publishing engagements. In addition to writing technical publications, the company publishes a technical white paper series, writes articles for trade publications, and presents technical seminars, executive briefings, and informative roundtable discussions on leading edge technology topics at locations across the country.

For information, contact G. A. Sullivan at the following address:

G. A. Sullivan
55 West Port Plaza, Suite 100
St. Louis, Missouri 63146
Email: **corporate@gasullivan.com**
Web site: **www.gasullivan.com**
Phone: (314) 213-5600
Fax: (314) 213-5700

Cameron K. Beattie is a veteran information systems manager with over 11 years of experience applying his strategic vision, technical knowledge, and team leadership skills to manage the planning, design, development, operation, and maintenance of enterprisewide information systems.

Mr. Beattie earned a bachelor of science degree in mathematical & computer sciences from the University of Michigan, Ann Arbor, MI. Upon graduation, he was commissioned as a communications and computer systems officer in the U. S. Air Force. His exciting career began with extensive technical and management training, and from there he traveled to the Pentagon in Washington, D.C., where he served as program manager for the engineering and installation of secure computer systems. In following assignments, he served as operations manager for mainframe and PC services at Edwards Air Force Base (AFB) and then as the MIS director for the B-2 Stealth Bomber Combined Test Force at the Air Force Flight Test Center in California.

Most recently, he served as chief of transportation systems management for the information systems group of the Air Mobility Command (AMC) at Scott AFB in Illinois, where he managed computer systems support for logistics systems at over 140 airport locations. He directed a 14 million dollar budget, a management staff of 14, a team of over 50 programmers, and multiple contractor teams that all worked together to deliver, support, and improve the information systems that enable the world-wide tracking and management of military cargo and passengers. He also managed life cycle support for the mainframe-based accounting system that collected over $3.5 billion annually for airlift services provided by AMC and migrated that system from a DEC VAX to a Sun/Solaris (UNIX) based architecture on budget and on schedule. During his tenure at AMC, he diligently applied quality management and leadership principles that enabled his software development organization to achieve Software Engineering Institute (SEI) Capability Maturity Model (CMM) Level 2 certification.

When the time came for the next military assignment, the lure of private industry (and the desire to stop moving every few years) proved overwhelming, and Cameron and his wife, Katarina, chose to stay in the St. Louis area. Cameron now provides information systems development and management services for large St. Louis based firms as a consultant for G. A. Sullivan. Additional information on Cameron's experience and adventures can be found at his web site at **http://members.aol.com/CamBeattie.**

Donald M. Benage is an acknowledged information systems professional and Microsoft Certified Systems Engineer with more than 18 years experience applying leading technologies to complex business solutions. He has provided architecture strategy and technology assessments, as well as detailed systems and network designs, to numerous corporations in many different industries. This, coupled with his vast experience as a network administrator, has uniquely qualified him to handle information technology issues with major corporate clients from initial design through implementation.

Mr. Benage began his career as the personal computer burst into the market. He has since achieved a great deal of experience incorporating knowledge in management of computer support operations, hands-on software and hardware implementation, design of strategic systems for practical implementation, and network administration. Specific Microsoft product expertise was further enhanced by his employment with Microsoft Corporation for more than four years; he left their ranks as a senior systems engineer to pursue other challenges.

Mr. Benage is a frequent speaker at industry seminars and forums dedicated to understanding software development strategies and tools. As a director with G. A. Sullivan, he leads the day-to-day operations of the Technology Center, G. A. Sullivan's research and development facility. He is the lead author of *Special Edition Using Microsoft BackOffice*, Second Edition (a two-volume set) and *BackOffice Electronic Resource Kit*, both published by Que. Mr. Benage continues in a career filled with recognition for excellence in technical ability and client service.

Robert S. Black is a graduate of Washington University in St. Louis, Missouri, where he earned a bachelor of science in both computer science and system science and engineering. He currently develops software for client/server applications as a software consultant at G. A. Sullivan. Robert is a coauthor of Que's *Special Edition Using Microsoft BackOffice*, Second Edition.

Eric M. Brown is a Microsoft Certified Professional with G. A. Sullivan, specializing in applications development using object-oriented analysis and design techniques. Eric holds a bachelor of science in computer engineering and a bachelor of science in electrical engineering from the University of Missouri at Columbia. Eric has experience developing applications ranging from single-tier applications to client/server applications using various languages including Visual Basic, C, and C++. Eric can be reached by email at **ericb@gasullivan.com**.

David Burgett has been programming in various languages for 13 years and is experienced with many aspects of both software and hardware. He has worked on diverse projects ranging from video games to full-scale database applications. He also has experience with several operating systems and databases.

David is a Microsoft Certified Solution Developer (MCSD). He received a bachelor of arts in creative writing from the University of Kansas and spends most of his time either programming or writing, although he often has trouble telling the difference between the two. He is currently pursuing a published novel.

J. "Eddie" Gulley has a bachelor of science in business management and logistics and is almost finished with his master of science in computer science. He has over 14 years of experience applying information technology to business solutions. He applies particular focus to project management and database design. Eddie is currently exploring the world of decision support—as it once was known—or, more recently, data warehousing. He is a Microsoft Product Specialist, certified for Microsoft SQL Server.

As a G. A. Sullivan consultant, Eddie provides project management and database expertise for the implementation of distributed, client/server solutions to client needs. He can be reached by email at **eddieg@gasullivan.com**.

David M. Kincade has a bachelor of science degree in computer science from Southern Illinois University at Edwardsville. He has been working in the computer industry for nine years and has been in microcomputer application development for the last seven years. He has used Visual C++ and Visual Basic over the last five years and is certified in developing applications with Visual C++ and the Microsoft Foundation Classes.

As a G. A. Sullivan consultant, David provides technical skill and leadership for a variety of software projects. He lives in Alton, Illinois (northeast of St. Louis, MO) with his wife, three cats, and two fish. He can be reached by email at **davidk@gasullivan.com**.

John W. Leighton has been involved in the design and development of leading edge software systems for the past 12 years. These systems range from award-winning television and movie animation systems to controlling 48 axis machining centers to insurance agency management systems.

He has had extensive development experience in Windows, Windows NT, UNIX, and MS-DOS. He is well versed in the various database methodologies and technical software design. John is a strong advocate for the use of object-oriented technologies in software design and development.

John holds a bachelor of arts in mathematics from the University of Missouri, St. Louis.

He currently resides in the O'Fallon, MO, area with his wife and five of his children.

Joseph P. Lengyel began his career 11 years ago as a teacher. He is a well-qualified educator, experienced in teaching business and computer curriculums. With a bachelor of science in business administration from Fontbonne College, St. Louis, Missouri, and upon completing a master of science in computer information systems from Colorado State University, Fort Collins, Colorado, he began pursuing a dual career in teaching and applying technology to business and educational applications.

Joe's technical experience includes contributions in all aspects of the development effort, with particular emphasis on Windows NT Server–based applications. These experiences range from participation in business process reengineering engagements and designing detail object and data models to development tool evaluation and the practical application of leading edge technology through various development efforts.

Joe, who resides in the St. Louis area with his wife, Rosalie, is a consultant for G. A. Sullivan. He continues to maintain a presence in education, capitalizing on first-hand experience in industry and his technical leadership roles in the effective use of information technology.

Larry D. Millett, an experienced writer and developer, has worked with microcomputer networks for more than 10 years, consulting, training, and developing software for clients nationwide.

Larry has published widely. His efforts include the first and second editions of *Special Edition Using Microsoft BackOffice* for Que Corporation, white papers, technical articles, and commercial software. As a G. A. Sullivan consultant, Larry provides technical leadership for distributed multiplatform software projects. As director of technical services, he focuses on important enterprise software development technologies.

A Microsoft Certified Professional (MCP) and a member of ACM, Larry holds a master of science in computer science from Washington University, St. Louis, Missouri, and a bachelor of arts in philosophy from Harvard University. He lives in St. Louis with his wife and two sons.

Special thanks to Peter Reale.

Azam A. Mirza, a specialist in client/server software development and distributed systems architecture, is a strong proponent of using the Internet to help businesses meet today's challenges while positioning them to better compete in tomorrow's complex business environments.

As director of technology for G. A. Sullivan, Mr. Mirza significantly influences the direction business clients take in applying advanced solutions to their most complex business challenges. He routinely serves as the lead analyst and designer for an array of complex system development efforts across a wide range of industry disciplines. He is an expert in the design, development, implementation, and support of client/server applications in numerous operating system environments and on various hardware platforms. He has extensive software development experience in major software development languages and is well qualified in the field of Internet/intranet technologies.

Mr. Mirza's vast experience with Internet application design and development, coupled with his astute awareness of de facto standards and widely accepted guidelines for software development, has uniquely qualified him to author numerous standards documents on the consistent development of distributed applications. Publication efforts include the first and second editions of *Special Edition Using Microsoft BackOffice* for Que Corporation. Mr. Mirza has published a white paper on the emerging role the Internet is playing in the corporate world titled, "Intranets and the Internet: An I-net Introduction." He has also authored a white paper on the Microsoft Active Platform titled, "Using Active Platform to Enhance Your Web Site."

Mr. Mirza holds a bachelor of science in computer science from Washington University, St. Louis, Missouri, and a master of science in engineering management from the University of Missouri-Rolla.

Angela Nielson is a Microsoft Certified Professional specializing in client/server software development and relational database and data warehouse design using Microsoft SQL Server.

Angela resides in the St. Louis area and holds a bachelor of science in computer science from McKendree College, Lebanon, Illinois, and a master of science in distributed computing from Webster University, St. Louis, Missouri. As a consultant for G. A. Sullivan, Angela continues to leverage her knowledge with her considerable technical expertise to solve complex business problems and to develop new business opportunities for clients nationwide.

David O'Leary is a Microsoft Certified Professional who specializes in the design and development of object-oriented, pattern-based system architectures. David holds a bachelor of science in computer science from Loyola University in Louisiana.

J. Brad Rhodes is an experienced developer of client/server systems with an emphasis on systems architecture. Challenged by his involvement in large and medium business solutions, Brad has acquired a thorough understanding of client/server systems with a special emphasis on open systems technology. His leadership has helped many companies adopt new technologies including relational database management systems, distributed systems, and object-oriented programming and design.

This experience has led Brad to the position of vice president of technology at Hamilton and Sullivan, a leading provider of client/server solutions for the banking and financial industry. At Hamilton and Sullivan, Brad oversees the development of next-generation retail and commercial banking solutions.

Brad holds a bachelor of science in electrical engineering from Southern Illinois University at Edwardsville, Illinois, and has nearly completed a master of science in electrical engineering from Washington University in St. Louis, Missouri. Brad is also a Microsoft Certified Systems Engineer. He lives in the St. Louis area with his wife Renee and daughter Allison.

Kevin D. Runnels is a Microsoft Certified Solution Developer and a Microsoft Certified Systems Engineer with more than 10 years of experience in microcomputer programming, networking, and project management. Kevin has developed numerous systems for the accounting and financial services vertical markets and is a strong proponent of using computers as tools to expand business opportunities and markets as well as for traditional transaction processing. He is expert in the design and development of client/server applications and distributed computing, especially on the Microsoft Windows NT platform.

Kevin resides in the St. Louis area and has a bachelor of science degree in business administration from Southeast Missouri State University and an award in accounting from the University of California, Los Angeles. As a consultant for G. A. Sullivan, Kevin continues to leverage his practical business knowledge with his considerable technical expertise to solve complex business problems and to develop new business opportunities for clients nationwide.

Jody C. Socha has had seven years experience in systems development in project management, requirement analysis, and design roles. He is a graduate of Clemson University in South Carolina and was an officer in the U. S. Air Force for five years before joining G. A. Sullivan two years ago. He has worked on systems in a variety of fields ranging from transportation to banking to insurance.

William F. Spencer V, a senior program manager, designer, and architect, is leading the design of new multitier systems throughout St. Louis. He is an expert in assembling client needs into system requirements, user interface design, and system architectures, and is also an expert at major program management.

After extensive experience in embedded and scientific programming with Northrop Aircraft, he managed software development and test programs for the B-2 Bomber, through the end of the Cold War (with time out to program for Steve Wozniak's U.S. Festival). He is currently designing a multitier land management system as a G. A. Sullivan consultant to a major St. Louis natural resource company.

The programming he did for his last book, 1982's *Rubik's Revenge: The Simplest Solution* (William L. Mason, principal author) had to be done in BASIC on a DOS 1.0 PC. (Today's software does so much more, but takes the same amount of time...)

Mr. Spencer is currently completing a degree in fine art. He already holds degrees in electrical engineering (Purdue University), aerospace engineering (University of Southern California), and technical management (California Institute of Technology) and is a member of IEEE, Tau Beta Pi, and Eta Kappa Nu.

He enjoys winemaking, offshore sailing, and good coffee. He lives in St. Louis with his wife and son, and he can be reached by email at **bills@gasullivan.com**.

Chris H. Striker is a consultant with G. A. Sullivan. When not building nets of various sorts, he pounds percussion instruments into submission. Sometimes he uses sticks, and sometimes it sounds like music.

Gregory A. Sullivan, founder and president of G. A. Sullivan, has been an early proponent of many significant advances in software development, and over the years, he has amassed an impressive array of credentials.

Motivated by his enthusiasm for the personal computer revolution and how he believed it would ultimately impact the business community, Mr. Sullivan started G. A. Sullivan in 1982 shortly after receiving his bachelor's degree in systems science and mathematics from the Washington University School of Engineering and Applied Science, St. Louis, Missouri. He applied the simple computer tools available then in support of his personal commitment to the short- and long-term success of his clients. As the personal computer revolution exploded into the business community, he focused his energies on rapidly emerging new technologies.

Mr. Sullivan's recognized participation in the early design and developments of new technology advances were critical to establishing and maintaining an industry leadership role. He successfully established formal relationships and partnership agreements with technology leaders such as Microsoft. Additionally, he has established numerous personal affiliations with leading technical forums and organizations. Mr. Sullivan is an active member of the Association for Computing Machinery (ACM), the Institute of Electrical and Electronics Engineers (IEEE), and Tau Beta Pi. He is a member of the Washington University School of Engineering and Applied Science National Council, past president of the Alumni Advisory Council and cosponsor of the Stifel Jens Scholarship.

Anthony J. Taylor is a Microsoft Certified Professional with more than six years of extensive experience in software development and technical leadership. His experience includes contributions in all aspects of the development effort and in multiple technology environments.

Mr. Taylor's accomplishments have been in many industries and have required various degrees of knowledge about the specific characteristics of each. He played a vital role in the introduction of Internet-based applications to the corporate workplace. His utilization of quality standards and technical excellence has been a valuable asset and has created an outstanding reputation regarding his abilities.

Mr. Taylor holds an associate's degree in computer science from Longview Community College, Lee's Summit, Missouri. He graduated summa cum laude and was awarded departmental honors in computer science with a bachelor of science in management and computer information systems from Park College, Parkville, Missouri. He also has graduate-level and professional education in the application of project management standards to today's information technology environment.

Mr. Taylor resides in the Kansas City area with his wife, Kim, where he has played an instrumental role in the startup and growth of the G. A. Sullivan Kansas City office.

Ronald W. Terry holds a bachelor of science degree in aerospace engineering from the University of Missouri-Rolla, Rolla, Missouri, along with a master of science degree in mechanical engineering from Washington University, St. Louis. Ron, a proponent of seeking out and applying new technologies, has more than nine years of experience in developing systems using a variety of platforms and languages. His career began at a major military aircraft company where he developed real-time simulations of avionics systems with object-oriented methodologies and C++ in a UNIX environment. In addition, he participated in the development of various aircraft structural analysis related software applications in the FORTRAN and C programming languages on a VAX/VMS platform.

Since joining G. A. Sullivan, Ron has been involved in numerous client/server projects on the Windows NT and Windows 95 platforms, which include Visual Basic and Visual C++ development. It is on these projects that he has gained experience in technologies such as ActiveX, Remote Automation, and DCOM to provide distributed object solutions.

Ron, his wife Pam, son Brad, and daughter Samantha reside in St. Louis, Missouri, where he is a consultant for G. A. Sullivan.

Timothy A. White is a graduate of Southwest Missouri State University where he earned a bachelor of science in computer information systems. Tim has a broad range of experience as a DBA and client/server developer. Tim has worked on projects involving both distributed client applications and legacy integration efforts. Tim currently develops client/server applications as a software consultant at G. A. Sullivan.

Yanni Xiao is a senior consultant with G.A. Sullivan. She has a doctor of philosophy degree in geography specializing in geographic information systems (University of British Columbia, Vancouver), a master of science degree in remote sensing and mapping (Chinese Academy of Sciences), and a bachelor of science degree in computer science (Lanzhou University, China). Before she joined G.A. Sullivan, Dr. Xiao was an assistant professor at the University of Lethbridge in Canada from 1992–1995.

Dr. Xiao has over 10 years of experience with a variety of computer hardware, software, and software development tools in various industries including coal mining, travel, utility, and education. She has strong problem-solving skills and is particularly experienced in geospatial and statistical analysis, computer mapping and digital image processing, user interface development, database design, and user training.

Acknowledgments

A project of this size involves the hard work and dedication of many people. We would like to thank all the software developers, authors, editors, and their families for the hard work and support they contributed. To the many people at Microsoft who made this book possible and helped us along the way, our sincere thanks. To all the people at Que whose professionalism and effort helped us produce a quality product, thank you. And to the many other people—friends and customers of G. A. Sullivan who pitched in with assistance—we extend our sincere gratitude. Thank you for all your help.

In addition, we would like to thank the following people for their special efforts and assistance: Mark Sundt, Lizzie Parker, Stew MacLeod, Todd Warren, Chris Nelson, and Deana Woldanski.

We'd Like to Hear from You!

As part of our continuing effort to produce books of the highest possible quality, Que would like to hear your comments. To stay competitive, we *really* want you, as a computer book reader and user, to let us know what you like or dislike most about this book or other Que products.

You can mail comments, ideas, or suggestions for improving future editions to the address below, or send us a fax at (317) 817-7070. For the online inclined, the address of our Internet site on the World Wide Web is **http://www.quecorp.com**.

Thanks in advance—your comments will help us to continue publishing the best books available on computer topics in today's market.

Que Corporation
201 W. 103rd Street
Indianapolis, Indiana 46290
USA

Introduction

Special Edition Using Microsoft Visual Studio, a book written by professionals for professionals, is about Microsoft Visual Studio. Authored by a team of senior software developers and information system consultants, this book is designed to guide you through the complex implementation and development issues associated with Microsoft Visual Studio. The authoring team is comprised of software developers from G. A. Sullivan, a premier software development consulting company and Microsoft Solution Provider based in St. Louis, Missouri.

One of the most alluring features of this book is its up-to-date information. The authors worked hard to produce a time-critical, technically complete "how-to" book that offers in-depth coverage of the most important elements of the Microsoft Visual Studio suite of products, including the latest releases of Microsoft's development tool suite including Visual Basic 5.0, Visual C++ 5.0, and Visual InterDev. This book provides thorough coverage of how to use these products to create applications for modern client/server and Internet-enabled enterprise environments. It also includes sufficient notes, tips, and cautions to ensure you avoid common pitfalls and learn new techniques with a minimum of wasted time. ■

Who Should Use This Book?

This book is aimed at *software developers* of client/server and Internet/intranet (I-net) enabled applications who are responsible for creating and deploying applications by using the Microsoft development tool suite, and *information system managers* faced with planning issues. You'll learn how to design and develop applications and components by using Microsoft Visual Studio and its individual products. This book provides excellent advice for developers who must implement applications in a Microsoft BackOffice environment with Windows NT Server, Internet Information Server, SQL Server, and Microsoft Transaction Server. It also provides good advice for technical managers on how to use Microsoft products to build state-of-the-art systems that will improve their business footing and leverage their automated information systems to maximize return on investment.

With the variety of material presented in *Special Edition Using Microsoft Visual Studio*, coupled with its high quality of content, up-to-date material, level of detail, and easy-to-follow "how-to" format, this is the all-encompassing book you will quickly come to depend on to supply answers to your Microsoft Visual Studio questions. Although each product that makes up the Microsoft Visual Studio suite is described separately within the book, special attention is paid to integration issues and techniques. Also, portions of the book are devoted to providing background material to enhance your understanding of critical concepts, and how to be really effective with Microsoft Visual Studio in the enterprise.

How This Book Is Organized

This book is organized in a logical sequence, starting with a discussion of Microsoft Visual Studio basics, an overview of the product, and background material on creating database applications—a key area of concern for most developers. The chapters in Part II, "Creating Controls and Components for Reuse," focus on the important new techniques for creating component-based applications with Microsoft's object technologies such as COM and DCOM, and web-based technologies such as ActiveX and Java. Separate chapters are devoted to Visual Basic, Visual C++, and Visual J++, each an important language included in Visual Studio. Part II also includes chapters on using ActiveX components in I-net and client/server environments.

The chapters in Part III, "Developing Internet, Intranet, and Extranet Applications," are devoted entirely to the most active area of recent growth—that of applications designed to run in I-net environments. Detailed coverage is provided on both the client and server sides of these applications. This includes information on creating web browser-based applications and using Microsoft's addition to Internet Information Server known as Active Server Pages. The use of Visual InterDev, another major element of Visual Studio, is covered in detail, including the use of design-time controls. There is also coverage of Dynamic HTML, server-side scripting issues, and the techniques for integrating existing applications into an I-net infrastructure.

The chapters in Part IV, "Developing Scalable Distributed Applications," focus on the more traditional client/server development techniques, with a special emphasis on creating distributed applications by using multiple databases. Using Visual Basic with both RDO and ADO is covered. Also, two chapters are devoted exclusively to using Microsoft Transaction Server (MTS) to create scalable, transaction-based applications for hard-core, line-of-business use.

The final chapters of the book, in Part V, "Team Development with Visual Studio," deal with the tools that help teams of programmers work together. These tools include Visual SourceSafe, Visual Modeler, and the Microsoft Repository. Using each tool is described, in addition to background information on the rationale for using these powerful additions to the Visual Studio suite.

Part I: Application Development with Visual Studio

The chapters in Part I provide an introduction to the Visual Studio suite of products:

- Chapter 1, "An Inside Look at Visual Studio 97," introduces you to this suite of products. It describes what's in the box and why Visual Studio is an important addition to a developer's tool set. It also provides guidance on who can best use a tool suite such as Visual Studio and details some of the primary advantages it offers.
- Chapter 2, "Using Visual Studio to Create Applications," explores basic use of the Integrated Development Environment (IDE) known as Developer Studio, which is used by Visual C++ and Visual InterDev. It also introduces the IDE for Visual Basic and basic techniques for creating applications. Information on the debugging aids provided in Visual Studio is also supplied.
- Chapter 3, "Creating Database-Aware Applications with Visual Studio," provides important information on designing databases and database applications. It describes how to create and debug SQL stored procedures and the tools in Visual Studio that support these activities. It also introduces some concepts that are developed in more detail later in the book, such as multitier architectures, distributed databases, and partitioning client/server applications.

Part II: Creating Controls and Components for Reuse

The chapters in Part II explore Microsoft's object technologies and describe how to create applications with ActiveX controls and COM-based components:

- Chapter 4, "Using Microsoft's Object Technologies," discusses the object-oriented and object-based technologies that form the underlying infrastructure for creating modern applications. Many of the names and acronyms related to this area are defined and put into their historical perspective, clearing up the confusion that exists due to the changing meanings of some of these terms. A solid overview of the Component Object Model (COM) and the Distributed Component Object Model (DCOM) is provided. Also, a brief discussion of the competitive CORBA technology and its relationship to COM/DCOM is provided.
- Chapter 5, "Creating ActiveX Components with Visual Basic," covers the techniques used to build ActiveX controls. You are guided step-by-step as you create your first

control. Then more advanced controls are described, including constituent controls, aggregate controls, and user-drawn controls.

- Chapter 6, "Creating Components with Visual C++," explores the use of Visual C++ to create component-based software. Topics include the types of components that you can create, techniques for creating COM-based components, and the use of the Microsoft Foundation Classes (MFC) and Active Template Library (ATL) class libraries.
- Chapter 7, "Creating Components with Visual J++," examines the capabilities of Microsoft's implementation of Java, Visual J++. This chapter describes how to create applets and applications, the difference between the two, and how to use Visual Studio to debug your Visual J++ projects.
- Chapter 8, "Using ActiveX Client Components in an I-net Environment," describes how to use controls and components based on ActiveX technology in an environment based on web servers and clients. It also discusses the integration of ActiveX and Java.
- Chapter 9, "Using ActiveX Components in a Client/Server Environment," provides a detailed description of how to use ActiveX components in traditional client/server applications. The process of installing and registering components is covered, as are the utilities for configuring components to run on remote computers. Language-specific techniques for using ActiveX components with Visual Basic and Visual C++ are also described.

Part III: Developing Internet, Intranet, and Extranet Applications

The chapters in Part III provide detailed coverage on building applications for the Internet or private intranets and extranets:

- Chapter 10, "Clients, Servers, and Components: Web-Based Applications," provides a broad, conceptual look at the entire architecture of the typical I-net environment. A comparison is made with traditional client/server environments, and issues related to partitioning your application into client- and server-based components are discussed.
- Chapter 11, "An Inside Look at Web-Based Applications," provides an overview of many of the concepts developed later in this part of the book. Chapter 11 introduces the use of the web browser as an application framework and describes both client- and server-side issues when you're developing web-based applications. It also introduces the Visual InterDev tool for creating web applications.
- Chapter 12, "Creating Web Browser-Based Applications with Visual Basic," provides an in-depth discussion of a powerful new capability added to Visual Basic 5.0 that allows applications to be hosted in an ActiveX-compatible web browser. This chapter discusses design considerations and how to create ActiveX documents.
- Chapter 13, "An Inside Look at Active Server Pages and Internet Information Server," describes Microsoft's web server environment and its powerful capabilities for delivering dynamic web pages. The built-in Active Server objects are discussed in detail, and their purpose and usage are described.

- Chapter 14, "Developing Active Content with Visual InterDev," provides an in-depth introduction to Visual InterDev, the primary web development tool in Visual Studio. It describes the IDE and the various wizards provided to help you get your web development off to a good start. It also describes how to use both client- and server-side ActiveX components in your web-based development.
- Chapter 15, "Advanced Visual InterDev Concepts," describes advanced techniques you can use to build powerful web-based applications. It explores the use of client-side components and the Script Wizard for building client-based scripting. It also describes how to access ODBC-compliant databases and the Data Form Wizard. Team-based development with Visual InterDev is also described.
- Chapter 16, "Visual InterDev Design-Time Controls," describes a powerful feature of Visual InterDev known as *design-time controls*. This chapter describes some of the built-in design-time controls that allow you to manage database access more easily and format results from a web server, and the ability to include standard elements on multiple pages automatically.
- Chapter 17, "Server-Side Programming in an I-net Environment," explores key issues surrounding the use of code on the web server. In particular, it describes the pros and cons of locating code on the server, the techniques that are available to the programmer writing server-side scripts, and some of the pitfalls that you should avoid.
- Chapter 18, "Dynamic HTML," describes an important new development in the evolution of the Hypertext Markup Language (HTML). Dynamic HTML is based on an object model proposed by Microsoft to the World Wide Web Consortium (W3C) and adds both an exposed object model and comprehensive event model for developers to use when building advanced web-based applications.
- Chapter 19, "Enabling Existing Applications for I-net Environments," explores techniques for migrating existing applications into an I-net environment. It also discusses how to take advantage of component architectures by encapsulating existing applications as components that can be called from new front-end applications. Finally, it describes how to create ActiveX documents using the ActiveX Document Migration wizard.

Part IV: Developing Scalable Distributed Applications

The chapters in Part IV describe the tools and techniques you can use to build applications that use multitiered architectures and distributed databases:

- Chapter 20, "Clients, Servers, and Components: Design Strategies for Distributed Applications," continues the exploration of distributed applications. A number of important topics are discussed, including three basic strategies for implementing concurrent processing, the services paradigm, and two-tier versus three-tier client/server applications.
- Chapter 21, "Creating Distributed Applications," provides an overview of distributed applications—what it means to describe an application as *distributed*, the different types of distributed applications, and the tools that exist for creating them. The implications of I-net technologies for this type of application also are discussed.

- Chapter 22, "Building Client Front Ends with Visual Basic and RDO," explores classic two-tier client/server application development. Visual Basic is used to create a front-end application that connects to a back-end server running Microsoft's SQL Server database using Remote Data Objects 2.0 (RDO2).
- Chapter 23, "Building Client Front Ends with Visual Basic and ADO," is similar to Chapter 22 but discusses a different method of accessing data known as *ActiveX Data Objects*. This data access method isn't just for accessing structured relational database management systems (RDBMSs). It also can be used to access structured and unstructured data in a large variety of data types through a single interface.
- Chapter 24, "Deploying Distributed Applications," details how to use the Explorer administrative tool supplied with Microsoft Transaction Server (MTS) to package applications and implement them on remote computers installed on your network. It also describes how to monitor remotely executing applications by using the Microsoft Distributed Transaction Coordinator as a troubleshooting aid.
- Chapter 25, "Using Microsoft Transaction Server to Enable Distributed Applications," details what you must do to create applications for the MTS environment. The various statements you must add to your application so that it can take advantage of the power of MTS are described.

Part V: Team Development with Visual Studio

The chapters in Part V provide information on the additional tools in Visual Studio that allow groups of programmers to work together effectively:

- Chapter 26, "Using Visual SourceSafe," provides detailed guidance on how to use the SourceSafe source code management tool for source control and version tracking. This tool's various capabilities are described, as is how to perform different tasks by using the graphical interface provided.
- Chapter 27, "System Modeling and Microsoft Visual Modeler," provides an overview of the recently released Unified Modeling Language (UML) and the use of modeling as an aid to the development of good software. Microsoft Visual Modeler, as well as competitive and complementary tools (such as Rational Rose), is described. Code generation and reverse engineering also are described.
- Chapter 28, "The Microsoft Repository," reviews the capabilities of an important tool that only recently has been released—the Microsoft Repository, which stores models and source code in a single store.

Conventions Used in This Book

Special design features enhance the text material:

- Notes
- Tips

- Cautions
- Troubleshooting boxes

NOTE Notes explain interesting or important points that can help you understand the described concepts and techniques.

Tips are little pieces of information that help you in real-world situations. Tips often offer shortcuts or alternative approaches to make a task easier or faster.

CAUTION

Cautions alert you to an action that can lead to an unexpected or unpredictable result, including loss of data. The text provides an explanation of how you can avoid such a result. Pay careful attention to Cautions.

TROUBLESHOOTING

Troubleshooting boxes provide commonly asked questions about problems or challenges typically encountered by users. These troubleshooting tips are presented in the form of a commonly asked question and its answer.

Rather than have you wade through all the details relating to a particular function of an application in a single chapter or part before you progress to the next topic, this book provides special cross-references to help you find the information you need. These cross-references follow the material they pertain to, as in the following sample reference:

▶ **See** "Another Section or Another Chapter," **p. xxx**

This book also uses various typesetting styles to distinguish between explanatory and instructional text and text you enter. Onscreen messages, program code, and commands appear in a special `monospaced` font. Placeholders, or words that you replace with actual code, are indicated with *`monospace italic`*. Text that you are to type appears in **`monospace boldface`**.

When a line of code is too long to fit on one line of this book, it is broken at a convenient place and continued to the next line. A code continuation character (➥) precedes the continuation of a line of code. (You should type a line of code that has this character as one long line without breaking it.)

Key combinations that you use to perform Windows operations are indicated by joining the keys with a plus sign: Alt+F4, for example, indicates that you press and hold the Alt key while pressing the F4 function key.

PART I

Application Development with Visual Studio

CHAPTER 1

An Inside Look at Visual Studio 97

by Greg Sullivan

The Visual Studio 97 package

Learn about the individual components that make up Visual Studio 97 and how it is packaged and licensed.

Visual Studio system requirements

See how your computer must be configured to install and use Visual Studio 97.

Why Visual Studio 97 is important

Discover why Visual Studio 97 is important to software developers today and what its role is in the world of software development.

Who should use Visual Studio 97

Find out if Visual Studio 97 is right for you. Learn which tools apply to your work and why.

Mixed-language programming has been a way of life for many software developers for several decades. Until the acceptance of object-oriented software design and development techniques in recent years, the primary reason for mixed-language application development was to gain some advantage in performance. A good example of this is a video control function library written in assembler to display information on a monitor more efficiently (with respect to speed and memory) for an application written in a high-level language such as C or BASIC and for execution on a PC.

There are other reasons for using multiple languages for a development project. Support for the capability to call procedures written in other languages has become increasing available in most target environments (such as Windows 95), making the choice of language for a specific component more flexible. In a particular organization, the choice is sometimes dictated by the knowledge of those working on the project—with what language are they most comfortable? Sometimes one language offers a feature unavailable in other languages and might be the best choice for meeting a specific need. For example, Visual Basic's support for ActiveX documents, a new feature, makes it an attractive language for developing applications that must be hosted in a web browser. Integration with additional design tools can also be a factor. With the growing practice of implementing systems as a collection of components, the advantages of choosing different languages for various needs have never been greater.

▶ **See** "Understanding ActiveX Documents" **p. 334**

The need for mixed-language programming doesn't necessarily imply that you should be an expert in multiple programming languages. Some software engineers choose to possess *technical breadth*—knowledge of numerous tools or languages. Other software engineers prefer *technical depth*—being the most knowledgeable about a specific tool or language. Whether you're deep or broad technically, Visual Studio 97 is an important tool to use in creating software components or assembling software solutions. The most effective application development efforts are carried out by teams, with some software engineers *deep* in the selected languages and tools and others with *broad* knowledge of the selected languages and tools. ■

What Is Visual Studio 97?

Visual Studio 97 is a product bundle including most of Microsoft's most powerful software development tools for building modern-day applications and their associated software components. Similar to the way it has bundled desktop products in Microsoft Office for end users and server products in Microsoft BackOffice for network administrators, Microsoft has put together a suite of products in a package targeted at software developers.

ON THE WEB

Microsoft maintains a page on its corporate web site dedicated to Visual Studio 97, at **http://www.microsoft.com/vstudio**. You're encouraged to stay current with Visual Studio 97 developments and updates with frequent visits to this site.

Microsoft's package of software development tools is known as Visual Studio. The initial release of the complete package occurred in mid-1997 and is labeled Visual Studio 97 (see Figure 1.1). As with any initial release of a new software product, Visual Studio 97 has some identifiable shortcomings. A significant missing feature is a common front end shared by all tools, as the development tools don't yet share the Integrated Development Environment (IDE). Future plans for the product package include integrating each tool with a common user interface. Regardless of when this becomes available, Visual Studio 97 is a significant breakthrough in software development technology and should be given serious consideration for any application developed today in a client/server or I-net environment. (In this context, *I-net* refers to the use of Internet technologies to develop applications for the Internet or intranets.)

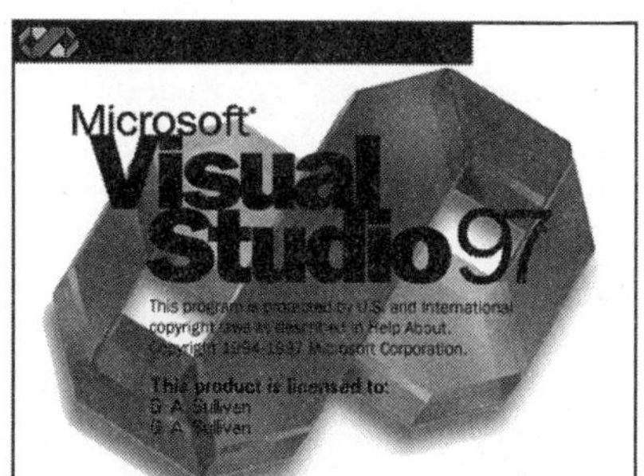

FIG. 1.1
Visual Studio 97 is the first development tool suite released by Microsoft.

The primary development tools that comprise the Visual Studio 97 package are

- Visual C++ 5.0
- Visual Basic 5.0
- Visual InterDev
- Visual J++ 1.1
- Visual FoxPro 5.0

You can buy each Visual Studio 97 product separately; however, if you're in a team environment developing an application that requires more than one of these languages, Visual Studio 97 offers several advantages:

- It's well suited to the mixed-language programming often required for distributed application development.
- It's specifically designed to accommodate team-oriented software development and contains many features supporting a team and its individual software engineers. The chapters in Part V, "Team Development with Visual Studio," explore this aspect of the product.
- Microsoft has priced the license fees for Visual Studio 97 so that the suite amounts to less than purchasing all the components individually. Depending on the licensing model used, the savings can be significant.

Visual Studio 97 is available in the Professional and Enterprise editions. Both editions are intended for use by serious application developers who are developing in a multitier, I-net application development environment. The Enterprise Edition adds products and tools that allow you to deal more effectively with database access and enterprise scalability issues.

What's in a Name?

Before providing a brief description of each product included with Visual Studio 97, bringing some clarity to the product names might be helpful. Microsoft now makes a practice of making product code names available to the public. Some products in Visual Studio 97 have had code names similar to actual product names (of other products), causing some confusion over which product is which.

Visual Studio 97—the entire product package and the focus of this book—was code-named *Boston*. One product included with Visual Studio 97 is Visual InterDev, originally code-named *Internet Studio*. Because this code name was widely used in industry press, some people confused *Internet* Studio with *Visual* Studio. As if the word *studio* wasn't overused enough, the name of the Visual Studio IDE is Developer Studio, so we now have Visual Studio (the entire product package) and Developer Studio (the IDE shared by some of the Visual Studio products) as officially released products. Internet Studio, simply a code name for Visual InterDev, is no longer valid.

Visual Studio 97 Professional Edition

The most basic version of Visual Studio 97 is the Professional Edition. This product package contains all the primary component-building and application-development tools available from Microsoft. It also contains an Integrated Development Environment for some of the products. The Professional Edition of Visual Studio 97 includes the following tools:

- *Visual C++ 5.0 Professional Edition.* Visual C++ is the most powerful development tool included with Visual Studio 97. Not surprisingly, it's also the most difficult in which to become proficient. Its most common use is in developing ActiveX software components, but it's also used to develop entire applications. Visual C++, which includes the Microsoft Foundation Class (MFC) library and the Active Template Library (ATL), is covered in detail in Chapter 6, "Creating Components with Visual C++."
- *Visual Basic 5.0 Professional Edition.* Of all the development tools included in Visual Studio 97, Visual Basic provides the best combination of power and flexibility. VB5 allows you to create ActiveX software components and assemble them into applications for deployment in client/server environments or on the Internet. Because Visual Basic is one of the most widely used tools in Visual Studio 97, it's covered throughout this book in great detail. In particular, detailed coverage is provided in Chapter 5, "Creating ActiveX Components with Visual Basic"; Chapter 12, "Creating Web Browser-Based Applications with Visual Basic"; and Chapter 22, "Building Client Front Ends with Visual Basic and RDO."
- *Visual InterDev.* A significant trend in software development today is the movement toward building client/server applications on Internet technologies, often referred to as *web-based software development*. Visual InterDev is the development tool included with Visual Studio 97 that specifically targets developers who create web-based applications. In contrast to Microsoft FrontPage, a web page development tool intended for desktop users, Visual InterDev is specifically targeted at application developers. The chapters in Part III, "Developing Internet, Intranet, and Extranet Applications," explore web-based application development and how to use Visual InterDev in this type of development activity.
- *Visual J++ 1.1.* Sun Microsystems has popularized the use of the Java programming language as an effective means for developing web-based applications. Although Microsoft and Sun compete in many ways, Microsoft has licensed the technology

from Sun and incorporated it into Visual J++. This tool helps you develop Java applets and applications in a Microsoft visual programming environment consistent with other development tool user interfaces. Visual J++ also can be extended to integrate Java with ActiveX. You can find more about using Visual J++ in Chapter 7, "Creating Components with Visual J++."

- *Visual FoxPro 5.0.* At its heart, Visual FoxPro is a relational database system. Based on the dBASE programming language, it has evolved from the FoxBase data management tool acquired by Microsoft several years ago. In its current form, Visual FoxPro has grown into a full object-oriented application development system that allows you to build client/server and Internet-based applications on top of the relational database system incorporated into the tool. Visual FoxPro is included as a product in Visual Studio 97; however, it isn't covered in this book. For additional information on the use of Visual FoxPro for database application development, see Que's *Special Edition Using Visual FoxPro 5*.

In addition to these development tools, Visual Studio 97 Professional Edition includes a special edition of the MSDN (Microsoft Developer Network) Reference Library in CD-ROM form. This edition of the reference library is geared specifically to Visual Studio 97 software developers, with an index and cross-reference of documentation associated with all the Visual Studio 97 products. It comes with Visual Studio 97 and includes interesting articles, samples of source code, text from reference books, and consolidated product documentation. A complete subscription to the MSDN library is available to Visual Studio 97 licensees for a special price. The MSDN library is an important tool for any software engineer developing software in a Windows environment with Microsoft tools; a complete subscription is highly recommended.

Visual Studio 97 Enterprise Edition

Visual Studio 97 Enterprise Edition includes the development tools contained in the Professional Edition; however, the Enterprise Editions of Visual C++ and Visual Basic are substituted for their Professional Editions. The Enterprise Editions contain enhancements designed to provide an improved environment for multitier client/server application development, I-net application development, and data management.

The Enterprise Edition of Visual C++ adds the following features:

- Visual Schema Designer allows you to design and build databases with Visual C++ Enterprise Edition.
- Remote Automation Technology and Distributed Component Object Model (DCOM) support are key to developing large-scale distributed applications.
- Remote Transact-SQL (T-SQL) Debugger enables debugging to step directly from C++ code directly into an SQL Server-stored procedure executing on another computer.

The Enterprise Edition of Visual Basic adds the following features:

- T-SQL Debugger enables interactive debugging for SQL Server-stored procedures and triggers.
- Application Performance Explorer (APE) allows you to test different scenarios for distributed application architectures through simulation and analysis.
- Visual Database Tools allows you to design and build logical and physical databases from a single tool.
- Resident RISC processor support improves application performance for applications designed and developed to run on RISC platforms.

The Enterprise Edition of Visual Studio 97 also includes other products and tools intended to extend the functionality of Visual Studio 97 Professional Edition, or to enhance support for software development in teams. Briefly, these products and tools are as follows:

- *SQL Server 6.5 Developer Edition.* This full version includes all the features of SQL Server 6.5, including relational database management, data replication, database administration tools, and an extensive stored procedure development environment. Although a full version of SQL Server 6.5 is provided with the Enterprise Edition of Visual Studio 97, its use is limited to software development activities such as building and testing applications. This Developer Edition of SQL Server 6.5 allows you to use test databases without disrupting users of live data in production databases. To learn more about how SQL Server 6.5 works with Visual Studio 97, see Chapter 3, "Creating Database-Aware Applications with Visual Studio."
- *Transaction Server 1.0 Developer Edition.* A full version of Transaction Server 1.0 is included, but with a license limiting its use to building and testing applications. When applications that use Transaction Server are implemented in a production environment, a full license for the product is required. Transaction Server is a set of tools and services that enables multiple operations to be linked into a single transaction. Transaction Server is built on Microsoft's Distributed Component Object Model (DCOM) and includes the Microsoft Distributed Transaction Coordinator (DTC). A complete coverage of Transaction Server 1.0 is in Chapter 25, "Using Microsoft Transaction Server to Enable Distributed Applications."
- *Visual SourceSafe 5.0.* Effective software development in a team environment requires a source control system. Microsoft now offers Visual SourceSafe for this purpose. It enables the control and management of the source files associated with any type of development project, including Visual Studio 97 projects. It also can be used to manage source files for web site development and end-user documentation. Visual SourceSafe is covered in Chapter 26, "Using Visual SourceSafe."
- *Microsoft Repository.* This new product from Microsoft allows you to organize software components for Visual Basic 5.0 and other development tools within and external to Visual Studio 97. It lets your development teams create a database of software

components and object models, along with the associated documentation. This tool accommodates a more efficient form of software reuse and represents an important step in the right direction with respect to efficient object-oriented software engineering. Microsoft Repository is based on a design specification jointly prepared by Microsoft and Texas Instruments Software. It's covered in detail in Chapter 28, "The Microsoft Repository."

- *Visual Modeler.* Visual Modeler is the new object-modeling tool from Microsoft. In its initial release, it works with Visual Basic, and future releases are planned for Visual C++. Visual Modeler is a component-based application design tool appropriate for designing client/server or Internet-based applications. This product is provided by Microsoft through its affiliation with Rational Software Corporation, a leading vendor of object-oriented design tools for many years. Visual Modeler is covered in detail in Chapter 27, "System Modeling and Microsoft Visual Modeler."
- *Remote Data Objects (RDO) 2.0.* RDO provides access to any database compliant with a 32-bit, Level II-compliant ODBC driver. It's a thin layer that sits over the ODBC driver and is designed to be an easy-to-use, high-performance interface to your databases from within an application-building tool such as Visual Basic or Visual C++. Extensive coverage of RDO is provided in Chapter 22.
- *Active Data Objects (ADO) 1.0.* Similar to RDO, ADO provides access to most of the popular relational database systems. It also provides access to a broader range of databases, including non-relational databases. Furthermore, ADO serves web-based database development more efficiently and effectively than RDO. Full coverage of ADO is provided in Chapter 23, "Building Client Front Ends with Visual Basic and ADO."

▶ **See** "ADO Versus RDO2: Which Access Method Should You Use?" **p. 664**

- *SQL Server 6.5 debugging tools.* The Transact-SQL Debugger allows you to debug SQL stored procedures interactively from within Visual C++ and Visual Basic.

▶ **See** "Using the T-SQL Debugger," **p. 68**

Microsoft likely will continue to extend the power of this product package by adding new tools to the Enterprise Edition, targeted at complementing the primary development tools included in the Professional Edition. The license fee for the Enterprise Edition is typically 50 percent to 100 percent more than the Professional Edition, depending on the type of pricing used.

Licensing

Visual Studio 97 is licensed per developer—that is, you must pay a license fee to Microsoft for each developer *seat* on your team. Although you may also license each Visual Studio 97 product individually, there's a pricing advantage to acquiring the Visual Studio 97 license as opposed to the individual licenses. The size of the advantage depends on current pricing of the entire package and the individual components, as well as the selection and number of tools required for your development effort.

Microsoft now offers licenses to Visual Studio 97 in three forms. First, there are license fees for the Professional and Enterprise editions at full price. Second, Microsoft offers a discount to full price if you're upgrading from certain previous versions of the primary development tools included in Visual Studio 97. Finally, to encourage more people to switch to Visual Studio 97, Microsoft offers a discount to those with certain competitive development products. The competitive and version upgrade discounts are typically available through rebate coupons provided by Microsoft.

ON THE WEB

Stay current with Microsoft pricing for Visual Studio, including competitive and version upgrade discounts, by checking its web site at **http://www.microsoft.com/vstudio**.

System Requirements

Visual Studio 97 requires a powerful computer with substantial amounts of hard disk space and memory. In fact, if all products are installed, the total hard disk space requirement can exceed 1GB. The minimum processor required to execute Visual Studio 97 is an Intel 486/66; however, an Intel Pentium 90 or higher is recommended.

Visual Studio 97 is available to operate on Windows 95 or Windows NT Workstation 4.0 or later. Components and applications developed with Visual Studio 97 might need to support execution on Windows 95 or Windows NT. If so, it's recommended to maintain a development computer with both operating systems for testing purposes. This increases the hard disk requirement, but the cost of storage is trivial compared with the cost of inconvenience to developers in testing software.

Minimum acceptable RAM for Windows 95 is 16MB. For Windows NT Workstation, the minimum acceptable RAM is 24MB. Microsoft recommends 32MB RAM; however, it's prudent to use at least 64MB RAM. Additional RAM is important when testing database applications with SQL Server 6.5 access on the same computer, in which case RAM in excess of 64MB is highly recommended.

In addition to these requirements, a CD-ROM is necessary. (Visual C++ and Visual J++ require a 32-bit CD-ROM driver.) It's possible to use a VGA monitor; however, a Super VGA monitor of at least 17 inches in size is highly recommended. A mouse or compatible pointing device is required, and additional tools and information are accessible on CD-ROM (189MB for the Professional Edition and 151MB for the Enterprise Edition).

Hard disk requirements vary, based on which edition of Visual Studio 97 is installed. It's possible to split installation across multiple drives (with the restriction that only the shared components can be separate—about 300MB without documentation). Also, it's possible to execute Visual Studio 97 from the installation CD-ROM with a minimal portion of it installed on your hard drive. Figure 1.2 shows *all* of Visual Studio 97 installed on a single drive. Table 1.1 depicts the minimum and maximum storage required for each product in Visual Studio 97 Professional Edition. Installing the individual products is optional.

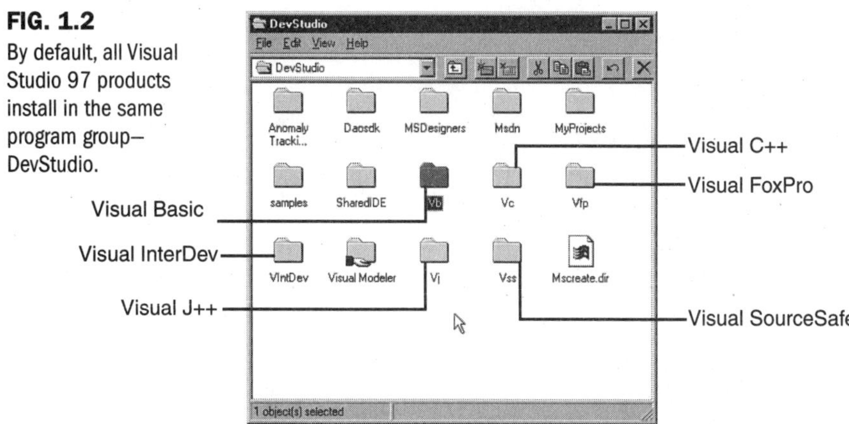

FIG. 1.2
By default, all Visual Studio 97 products install in the same program group—DevStudio.

Table 1.1 Storage Requirements for Visual Studio 97 Professional Edition

Tool	Minimum Disk Storage	Maximum Disk Storage
Visual C++ 5.0	120MB	500MB
Visual Basic 5.0	30MB	220MB
Visual InterDev	37MB	52MB
Visual J++ 1.1	35MB	55MB
Visual FoxPro 5.0	15MB	190MB
MSDN	10MB	1GB
Totals	**247MB**	**2.02GB**

In addition to more products, Visual Studio 97 Enterprise Edition includes larger versions of Visual C++ and Visual Basic, as shown in Table 1.2.

Table 1.2 Storage Requirements for Visual Studio 97 Enterprise Edition

Tool	Minimum Disk Storage	Maximum Disk Storage
Visual C++ 5.0	125MB	550MB
Visual Basic 5.0	35MB	345MB
Visual InterDev	37MB	52MB

continues

Table 1.2 Continued

Tool	Minimum Disk Storage	Maximum Disk Storage
Visual J++ 1.1	35MB	55MB
Visual FoxPro 5.0	15MB	190MB
SQL Server 6.5	80MB	95MB
Transaction Server 1.0	11MB	23MB
Visual SourceSafe 5.0	8MB	16MB
MSDN	10MB	1GB
Totals	**356MB**	**2.33GB**

SQL Server 6.5 is available only on Windows NT 3.51 or later, and Transaction Server 1.0 runs only on Windows NT 4.0.

The Role of Visual Studio 97 in Software Development

Software applications created with Visual Studio 97 are developed by assembling individual software components. The software engineers who "glue" software components together to form the entire solution are sometimes referred to as *solution developers*. Software engineers playing the role of *component builders* develop the software components used to build applications. These software components are purchased from industry vendors or are developed by component builders on your application development team.

NOTE Microsoft offers a Microsoft Certified Solution Developer (MCSD) certification for software engineers. Although the name *solution developer* seems to imply that this is intended only for those who assemble software components into applications, it can also apply to component builders. ■

Some software development tools are designed to develop components, whereas others are created for assembling components into solutions. Given the significance of this approach to software development, it's no surprise that Visual Studio 97 contains a combination of tools suited to one or the other purpose—or, in some cases, to both purposes. Moreover, in the world of multitiered application development, software components are needed in client-side application development and in server development. Again, Visual Studio 97 includes tools for both. Table 1.3 shows Visual Studio 97's development tools, with an indication as to whether they can create or assemble components. You can use *component producers* to create software components, and *component consumers* can assemble software components into applications.

Table 1.3 Visual Studio 97 Server Components and Client Components

	Server Components		Client Components	
Tool	**Producer**	**Consumer**	**Producer**	**Consumer**
Visual C++ 5.0	✔	✔	✔	✔
Visual Basic 5.0	✔	✔	✔	✔
Visual InterDev		✔		✔
Visual J++ 1.1	✔	✔	✔	✔
Visual FoxPro 5.0		✔		✔
SQL Server 6.5		✔		

As Table 1.3 shows, Visual C++ 5.0 and Visual Basic 5.0 can produce and consume software components. Visual InterDev and Visual FoxPro are available only to assemble software components into solutions. Visual J++ is designed to create software components in support of Java applet or application development. Finally, SQL Server 6.5 delivers the capability to use server-side software components through extended stored procedures.

To understand better the role of Visual Studio 97 in software development today, you need to examine some goals for the product. Clearly, the concept of integrating design, development, and development-management tools into one package can ease some of the burdens associated with software development, if the integration is implemented appropriately. Following is a review of some of the most important objectives set forth by Microsoft for Visual Studio 97:

- *Object-oriented software engineering.* Developing component-based software is the cornerstone of modern-day software development. Microsoft bases Windows development on its Component Object Model (COM); consequently, the need for a tool suite that integrates component development and application building is tremendous. Visual Studio 97 provides the capability to craft software components and glue them together into solutions in a cohesive and consistent development environment.
- *Internet development.* Using Internet technologies for commercial application development, whether exposed to the entire Internet or secured on an intranet, solves two of the biggest problems plaguing software development in recent years. One of the most perplexing problems in client/server application development in a Windows environment is software distribution. Another significant problem is computer

communications. Internet technologies minimize the impact of both problems. Consequently, the demand for a comprehensive tool suite for web-based application development is an important objective for Visual Studio 97.

- *Multiple-tier application development.* Client/server application development remains in high demand and works well with the incorporation of Internet technologies. Adding new tiers to applications allows you to isolate business rules and align them more closely with software in a fast-paced business environment. It's critical for Visual Studio 97 to support current multitier application development initiatives and to support additional techniques in the future.

▶ **See** "Client/Server Implementation Models," **p. 562**

- *Embrace and extend.* Industry vendors other than Microsoft have developed popular leading-edge technologies for software developers. Microsoft has announced publicly its intention to *embrace* certain of these technologies and *extend* them in the Windows environment. The best example of this is Microsoft's acceptance of Java technology introduced by Sun Microsystems. Visual J++ is Microsoft's implementation of Java for use in building web-based applications. As promised by Microsoft, Visual J++ embraces Java technology and extends it to operate effectively in Windows environments. (Its integration support for ActiveX and Java components is evidence of this.)
- *Mixed-language software development.* Using multiple programming languages for developing applications is desirable in many cases. Combining the most popular languages and development tools into Visual Studio 97 accommodates mixed-language software development.
- *Team software development.* Software developers work in teams made up of component builders, solution developers, object modelers, application architects, documentation specialists, end users, and others. An important goal of Visual Studio 97 is to provide a tool suite that allows each development team member to interact with development-related information in a manner consistent with that particular role. A perfect example of this is the versatility Visual SourceSafe offers in working with files created by members of the design team (the object or database model), the software development team (the source code), and the documentation team (the online and hard-copy documentation).
- *Tool integration.* Perhaps the most important objective for Visual Studio 97 is to provide a consistent user interface to each development tool. Now, only three development tools share the same user interface; the Developer Studio IDE is now operational for Visual C++ 5.0, Visual InterDev, and Visual J++ 1.1. The most glaring "miss" is that Visual Basic 5.0 doesn't support the Developer Studio IDE front end. This addition is anticipated for a future version of Visual Studio 97, as it remains one of the most important objectives; however, in the meantime, Visual Basic 5.0 possesses a very popular and widely used visual front end. In fact, some developers continue to prefer it over Developer Studio.

This is just a short list of some of the most important aspects of Visual Studio 97. With the introduction of Visual Studio 97, Microsoft has made it clear that it understands the needs of software developers and software development teams to have tools that work better together and take advantage of the most powerful technologies. Future versions of Visual Studio 97 and its associated products are expected to continue to enhance developer productivity.

Visual Studio 97 from Your Perspective

Visual Studio 97 represents a breakthrough in many ways to the world of software development. Although other development tool suites have existed before its introduction, this product varies in that it's backed by Microsoft's muscle. Microsoft is committed to improving the integration of Visual Studio 97 products and continuing to enhance the capabilities and efficiency of software development teams. Already, Visual Studio 97 means many things to many people.

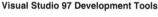

Software development teams faced with selecting tools often debate the relative merits of a given tool based on its power and flexibility versus its productivity. Typically, the most powerful and flexible software development tools are the most difficult to learn and the most inefficient because they're lower level in nature, require more in-depth knowledge of the underlying technology, and are more difficult to debug when problems arise.

On the other hand, the tools that tend to yield the shortest development times are usually less powerful or less flexible. Although throwing together a simple database application quickly is possible with a database tool such as Microsoft Access, it can't begin to match the performance or features of a full-blown implementation of the same database in SQL Server. This example is simply one of the trade-offs facing developers, administrators, and managers when selecting development tools (and production servers).

Many factors go into determining the best tool for a given job or portion of a job. An important factor is understanding—at least qualitatively—the relationship certain tools have to one another. Figure 1.3 suggests how the development tools included in Visual Studio 97 relate to each other in this regard.

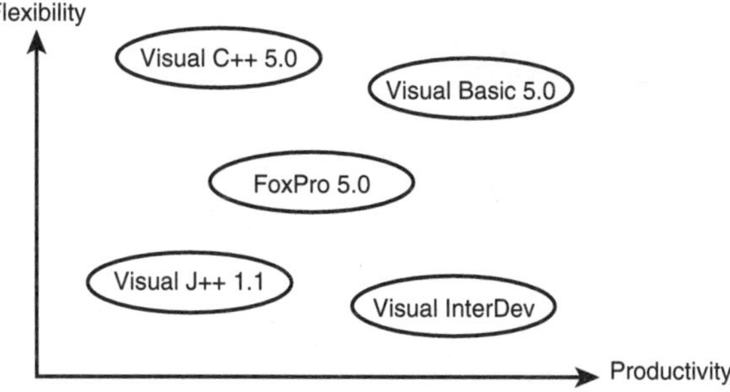

FIG. 1.3
It's helpful to understand how Visual Studio 97 products relate to one another with respect to flexibility and productivity.

This chart is intended to provide a basis for decision-making but isn't intended to be the definitive answer in tool selection. Its purpose is to support discussion about tool-selection decisions. The graph does bring to light the following points about the Visual Studio 97 tool suite:

- Visual Basic 5.0 is the best combination of flexibility (or power) and productivity (or efficiency), primarily because it can create and assemble software components into applications.
- Visual C++ 5.0 is a bit more powerful in that it offers better performance of executable code. It's far less efficient in terms of development time, however, because it's more difficult to learn than Visual Basic 5.0 and requires more knowledge of Windows programming.
- Visual J++ is shown to be less powerful, primarily because of its relative immaturity compared to the rest of the tools in Visual Studio 97. It's based on the Java software development language, which continues to undergo frequent updates. Also, because it's a programming language with constructs and syntax similar to C++, it's more difficult to learn.
- Although Visual InterDev is as efficient as Visual Basic 5.0 with respect to assembling components into web-based solutions, its capability is limited to this. The resulting lack of flexibility isn't a problem because Visual InterDev's intended purpose is to help build applications based on Internet technologies.
- Because Visual FoxPro isn't available for the development of software components, it's less powerful than Visual Basic and Visual C++. Moreover, it's intended first for development of standalone database applications, not fully scalable, multitier enterprise applications. Also, because it's based on a programming language (xBASE) that involves a learning curve, it's not as efficient to use in development as Visual InterDev.

As you contemplate Figure 1.3, keep in mind the continuous patching and updating of these individual products by Microsoft. An upgrade to one product can change its relationship to the others—in some cases, quite dramatically. A good example is the recent incorporation of a true compiler into Visual Basic, increasing its position with respect to flexibility. It's recommended to keep this type of graph current in development groups based on the opinions of those on the team.

As a Development Manager

The most appealing feature of Visual Studio 97 from the perspective of a development manager is the opportunity for a more organized development environment. The tools in Visual Studio 97 and their integration simplify the task of administering a complex development environment. This provides an opportunity to lower software development costs through more efficient coding practices and also by giving software engineers the tools to write code with fewer errors. Specifically, the Visual Studio 97 development environment offers the following benefits from the perspective of a development manager or development team leader:

- *Flexibility.* Because Visual Studio 97 includes development tools geared toward component builders and solution developers, it offers tremendous flexibility. Some tools, such as Visual Basic and Visual InterDev, are quick to learn and thus within the reach of the vast majority of the software development community. Others, such as Visual C++ and Visual J++, require a more in-depth knowledge of Windows programming concepts. Nevertheless, they're important tools for developing large-scale client/server and web-based applications.
- *Simplicity.* The introduction of development tool suites has changed development *tool* selection decisions to development *environment* decisions. This greatly simplifies the process of selecting the right tools for the job. To further simplify the process, Microsoft supports most of the important industry and de facto standards in software development (for example, Microsoft's support of Java from Sun Microsystems).
- *Consistency.* A common thread across most Visual Studio 97 development tools is the visual programming environment. This provides a high level of consistency as developers move from tool to tool over the course of their careers.
- *Support.* Visual Studio 97 includes a CD-ROM containing a version of the MSDN Library (see Figure 1.4). Owners of Visual Studio 97 also can register for the online version at **http://www.microsoft.com/msdn**. The combination of a local CD-ROM and the online service for MSDN is valuable for troubleshooting technical problems that arise during software development.

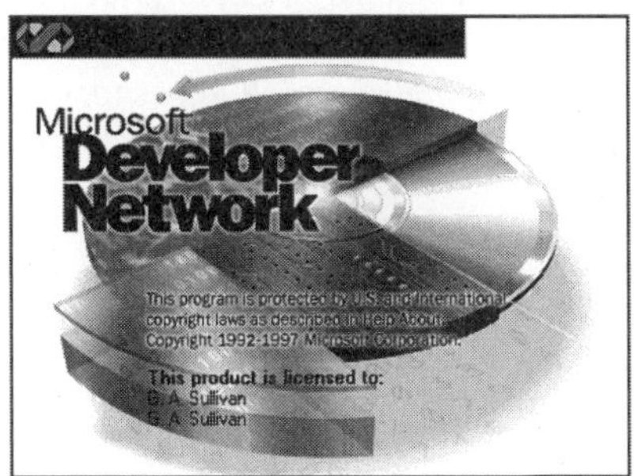

FIG. 1.4
The MSDN CD-ROM that comes with Visual Studio 97 is customized for software developers who use the product.

- *Integration.* One of the biggest reasons for moving your development environment to a complete tool suite is integration. The most obvious form of integration is in the user interface, which Visual Studio 97 offers in the Developer Studio IDE. Another important form of integration is the interaction of the tools with one another; for example, most of the files created with the design tools in Visual Studio 97 can be used by the development tools as well, greatly reducing the overhead associated with communication between design and development team members.

- *Team composition.* Software development teams in the Visual Studio 97 development environment can consist of individuals with various levels of experience and talent. This goes beyond the roles of component builder and solution developer. For example, non-programmers can work on the team in web page development with a straightforward tool such as Microsoft FrontPage 97, and their work can be integrated into Visual InterDev.
- *Control.* Controlling access to all files associated with a software development project is important for development managers and team leaders. This goes beyond controlling source code files to include documentation and design files. Visual SourceSafe 5.0 provides a safe way to control and monitor access to files in a team development situation (see Figure 1.5).

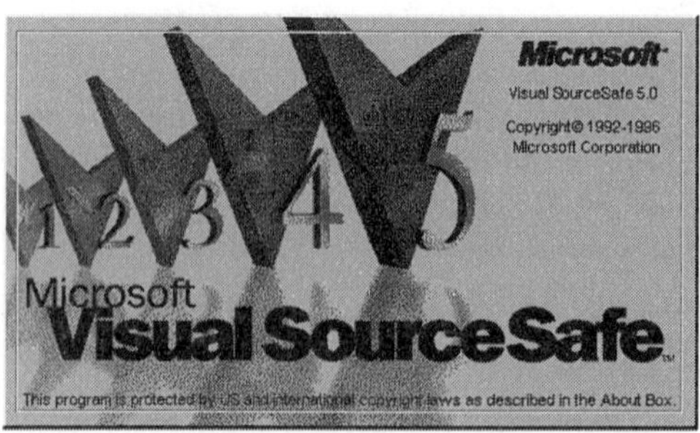

FIG. 1.5
Visual SourceSafe 5.0 is included with the Visual Studio 97 Enterprise Edition.

As an Application Architect

The biggest difference between the Professional and Enterprise editions of Visual Studio 97 is that the Enterprise Edition contains several tools pertaining to application design, including Visual Modeler (see Figure 1.6) and the Microsoft Repository. The best news is that application architects and object modelers now have tools for design purposes that integrate tightly with the development tools.

You can generate source code for Visual C++, Visual Basic, and Visual J++ from object models created in Visual Modeler. You can even extract source code from a source module and create an object model to import into Visual Modeler. This two-way interface is valuable for application architects and object modelers.

The other great news for Visual Modeler is that it supports the emerging standard for object modeling: Unified Modeling Language (UML). UML has been developed by several key object-oriented industry leaders employed by Rational Software Corporation, one of the leading object-modeling tool vendors, and has been licensed by Microsoft. At least 25 other leading vendors in the software industry support UML. This means that object models created in other tools that support UML can be imported into Visual Studio 97, and object models created by Visual Modeler can be exported to non-Visual Studio 97 tools that support UML.

▶ **See** "The UML Diagrams," **p. 752**

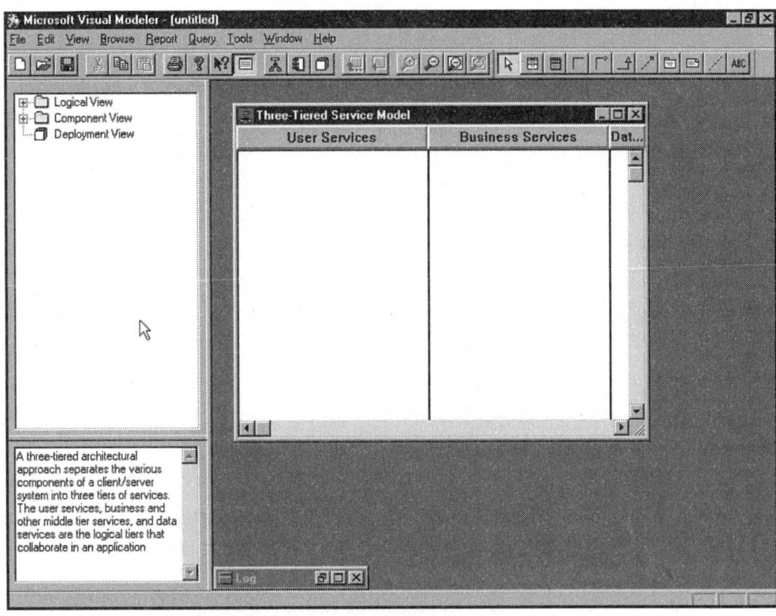

FIG. 1.6
Visual Modeler supports a variety of approaches to application design, including a traditional multitier model for client/server applications.

As a Component Builder

Developing software components to support COM has always been difficult and time-consuming. With the advent of ActiveX technology, the job became simpler in some respects and more complex in others. It remains possible to develop ActiveX components with Visual C++, but it's also now possible to develop these components with Visual Basic.

The advantage of developing ActiveX components in Visual Basic is that the developer is shielded from many of the complexities associated with COM. This simplifies the process of developing software components, makes the process of developing software components accessible to a broader group of developers, and—most important—reduces the cost of software development (by saving time) without a sacrifice to project quality.

> **CAUTION**
>
> That ActiveX components can now be developed with Visual Basic is no reason to avoid learning the fundamentals of COM and ActiveX technology.

You can use the development tools in Visual Studio 97 to develop several different types of software components. In particular, component builders can create Java applets, ActiveX controls, and Active Server components with Visual Studio 97. The purpose of the various components and details about building them is a topic to which an entire section of this book is dedicated. See the chapters in Part II, "Creating Controls and Components for Reuse," for a complete coverage of these components and important issues related to their construction and use.

Another advantage Visual Studio 97 provides to component builders is the Microsoft Repository, a tool that catalogs and stores software components. The Microsoft Repository can also store object models and documentation associated with the models and components. Because the Microsoft Repository supports UML, it's possible for other non-Visual Studio 97 tools to interoperate with Visual Studio 97 through the Microsoft Repository. If you accept UML as the standard by which your software components are designed and developed and by which your object models are created, the Microsoft Repository will prove to be a valuable tool regardless of which UML-based development tool suite you're using.

As a Solution Developer

Mixed-language development is a foregone conclusion in software development today, so software engineers will have some advantage if the user interface for the different languages is the same. Microsoft has recognized this need and delivered a common user interface called the Developer Studio IDE (see Figure 1.7).

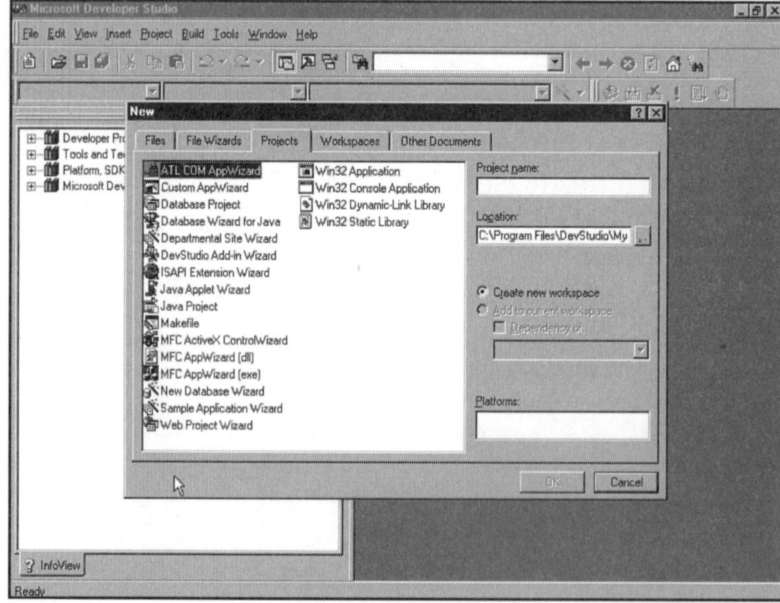

FIG. 1.7
The Developer Studio IDE supports Visual C++ 5.0, Visual InterDev, and Visual J++ 1.1.

Although all the visual programming tools included in Visual Studio 97 share similar user interfaces, it's advantageous for the IDE to provide access to each development tool. It's anticipated—although not absolutely guaranteed—that future versions of Visual Studio will add support for Visual Basic to the Developer Studio IDE.

Visual Studio 97 is available to host only on a 32-bit Windows platform—Windows 95 or Windows NT Workstation 4.0 or later. Out of the box, Visual Studio 97 targets the development of

32-bit Windows applications. Of course, these applications are available only for execution on Windows 95 and Windows NT operating platforms.

Although Microsoft is "nudging" software developers toward 32-bit application development, a large base of users remain in 16-bit Windows 3.1. It's possible to use Visual Studio 97 to create 16-bit Windows applications, but to do so you must order separate features from Microsoft. Another consideration in developing 16-bit applications is that only Visual Basic, Visual C++, and Visual FoxPro have versions that support this type of development. Clearly, the direction is toward 32-bit application development, even to the extent that adding 16-bit development can significantly increase overall development costs.

From Here...

In this chapter, you learned whom Visual Studio 97 is for and what it means to the various people involved in software development. You also saw what tools make up Visual Studio 97 and how Microsoft licenses the entire product package. Finally, you explored how Visual Studio 97 affects software development in today's world and its significance to software developers.

For more information on some of the topics addressed in this chapter and the steps to take next in your exploration of Visual Studio 97, see the following chapters:

- To learn about Microsoft's approach to object-oriented technology and how it affects software development, see Chapter 4, "Using Microsoft's Object Technologies."
- To learn how Visual Studio 97 can be used to develop applications for the Internet or your own intranet, see Chapter 11, "An Inside Look at Web-Based Applications."
- To learn the full power of using Visual Studio 97 to develop applications in a distributed computing environment, see Chapter 21, "Creating Distributed Applications."

CHAPTER 2

Using Visual Studio to Create Applications

by Don Benage

For years, Microsoft has had a goal to deliver a single Integrated Development Environment (IDE) for all its programming tools. Developers would learn how to use this environment and then write code in the language of their choice. They could even use multiple languages much more easily than if each language had its own unique IDE. Although Microsoft hasn't yet reached its ultimate goal, a huge step forward has been taken with Visual Studio.

This chapter covers some of the rudimentary tasks that you need to know to use Visual Studio. If you're an experienced developer who has already worked with a Microsoft language product, you may want to skip this chapter and proceed directly to the more advanced material in the rest of this book. If you're new to Microsoft's tool suite, this chapter will help you to get started. ■

Installing Visual Studio

Avoid pitfalls when installing this large suite of software development tools and utilities. Find out where to go on Microsoft's web site for the latest service patches.

Using Developer Studio

Learn about Developer Studio, the Integrated Development Environment (IDE) shared by Visual C++, Visual J++, and Visual InterDev. Discover how to use this powerful IDE used by most Visual Studio languages.

Using Visual Basic

Learn how to compile and debug applications in Visual Basic's powerful and friendly IDE. Find out why some people prefer this IDE over Developer Studio, and see how they compare.

Getting more help

Explore the many options you have for getting additional help with this powerful developer's suite. Discover the options you have within the products, on the CD-ROM, and on the World Wide Web.

Visual Studio Setup

Installing Visual Studio presents some special challenges due to the size of this large suite of tools. Most people probably won't need to install the entire suite. It would be a rare developer who had skills in using all the languages and tools that are part of Visual Studio. If you're sharing a system with several people who work at different times, however, or want to be able to experiment with the entire tool set, you may still want to install the entire product.

To install the entire system, you need more than 2GB of disk space. If you don't install all the online help files but instead run them from CD-ROM, you can save a substantial amount of space. However, the shared components alone require up to 300MB. You also should remove earlier standalone versions of any languages in the suite (for example, Visual Basic 4.0). Finally, you should allow plenty of time for the operation. Installation times vary widely depending on the speed of your computer's CD-ROM drive, hard disk(s), and internal clock; however, installation can easily take more than three hours to install everything.

Furthermore, Visual Modeler—a design and modeling tool described in Chapter 27, "System Modeling and Microsoft Visual Modeler"—isn't included on the CD-ROM set at the time of this writing and must be downloaded from Microsoft's web site. Also, a specialized tool called the Microsoft Repository (described in Chapter 28, "The Microsoft Repository") isn't included in the main installation menu that's offered by the CD-ROM's AutoPlay feature. You must manually locate and launch the individual setup program for this tool.

Finally, two service patches (SPs) for the Visual Studio product had been released as this book went to press, and undoubtedly additional SPs will be offered in the future. In general, Microsoft patches are always cumulative so that you'll require only the most recent one; you don't need to apply a series of patches in order (see the later section "Applying a Service Patch" for more information).

NOTE The second SP was offered in two forms: a core patch with fixes required by most users (approximately 34.6MB) and a complete patch with all fixes available at the time (87.8MB). Even with a relatively high-speed link to the Internet, downloading this patch is somewhat daunting. You may choose to download or order it on CD-ROM and have it shipped to avoid the time and connect charges you might incur. ■

All these potential hurdles notwithstanding, after you assemble the CD-ROMs and any appropriate SPs, uninstall any old versions, and check your hard disk to verify that you have enough space, you're ready to proceed. Although the process can be time-consuming, it's not difficult if you follow the basic guidelines offered in the following sections.

NOTE If you're installing multiple language products, you'll be asked to restart your machine after some of the individual products are installed. It's recommended that you take the time to restart your machine any time you're prompted to do so, even if you intend to install additional products. This isn't always required. If the setup program doesn't prompt you to restart, you may safely proceed with the next product without rebooting. ■

Installing Visual Studio

When you launch the setup program, as described shortly, you'll first be prompted with some Helpful Installation Hints. Although it generally doesn't matter in which order you install the various tools and languages, you should install the Microsoft Developer Network (MSDN) Library last, because this component checks to see which other components you've installed and adds support information for only those tools and languages it finds. To ensure that you have the support files for all the languages and tools you're using, install the MSDN Library after everything else is properly set up.

You'll also be prompted to upgrade your version of Internet Explorer (IE) to at least version 3.01. If you already have installed a later version of IE, you may safely ignore this request. Otherwise, you should install the upgrade to 3.01 from the CD-ROM or install an even more current version from the Microsoft web site before starting the installation program for other languages and tools.

To install Visual Studio, follow these steps:

1. Insert Disc 1 from the CD-ROM set into your CD-ROM drive.

NOTE The Master Setup program is available on all CD-ROMs in the box. If you know you want to begin with a product not on Disc 1 (such as Visual C++), you can start the Master Setup program with that CD-ROM and avoid the need to swap CD-ROMs as described later in step 7. If you're installing the entire suite, it's recommended that you proceed in the order in which the CD-ROMs are numbered. ■

2. Depending on your computer's configuration, the setup program may launch automatically via the AutoPlay feature of Windows NT 4.0 or Windows 95. Otherwise, you can manually launch the setup program by double-clicking the Setup.exe file in the root directory.
3. A Welcome dialog box with helpful hints appears. After ensuring that you've already taken care of everything on this short list, click the Continue button.
4. You're prompted to enter your User Name, Organization Name, and CD Key. You usually can find the CD Key on a yellow sticker attached to the back of one of the CD-ROM envelopes. Enter the requested information and click Continue.
5. The Master Setup menu appears (see Figure 2.1). You can select any of the tools or languages that you want to install, but remember to install MSDN last. For this example, the Visual C++ installation is shown.
6. Click Microsoft Visual C++ on the list of products. A secondary menu containing only those items pertinent to Visual C++ appears (see Figure 2.2).
7. Click Install Visual C++ 5.0. If you have the Enterprise Edition of Visual Studio (shown in Figure 2.2), it will be indicated on the menu. A dialog box prompting you to insert the appropriate CD-ROM appears. Replace the CD-ROM in your drive with the requested CD-ROM and click OK.

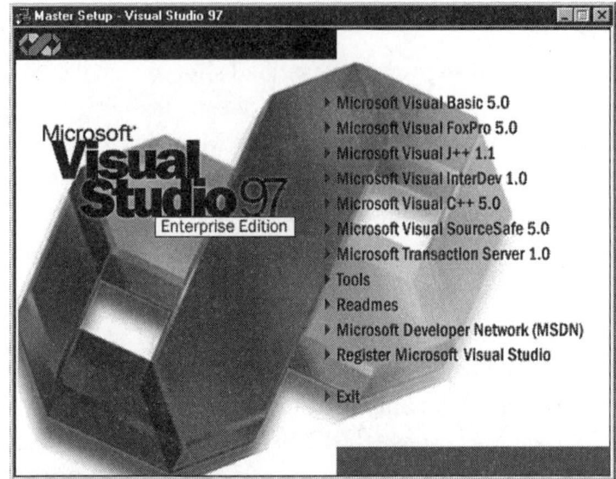

FIG. 2.1
The Visual Studio Master Setup menu allows you to begin the installation process for all languages and most of the add-on utilities.

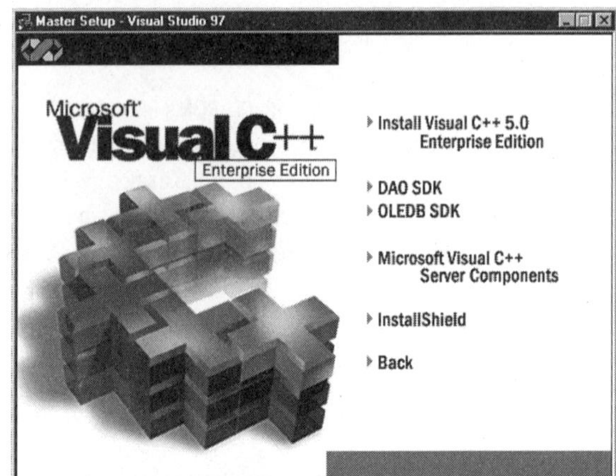

FIG. 2.2
The Visual C++ submenu contains the C++ language and additional companion products and Software Development Kits (SDKs).

8. A Welcome dialog box appears, informing you that this installation will take approximately 15 to 30 minutes and that you can always run setup again to add or remove items to your installation. Click the Next button.
9. The Microsoft License Agreement dialog box appears. You must click Yes to indicate that you agree to the terms of the license agreement, or the setup program will exit. The Installation Options dialog box then appears (see Figure 2.3).
10. Select the type of installation you want to perform: Typical, Minimum, CD-ROM, or Custom. The Typical selection is appropriate for most uses of the product. If you aren't sure, choose Custom and explore the dialog boxes detailing all the available options.
11. After you finish making and reviewing your selections, click Next. A series of progress boxes appears, along with a number of screens showing where you can find additional information on the Microsoft web site.

FIG. 2.3
The Installation Options dialog box shows you the disk space requirements for the files to be installed or those to be added if you're running setup at a later time to modify your original installation.

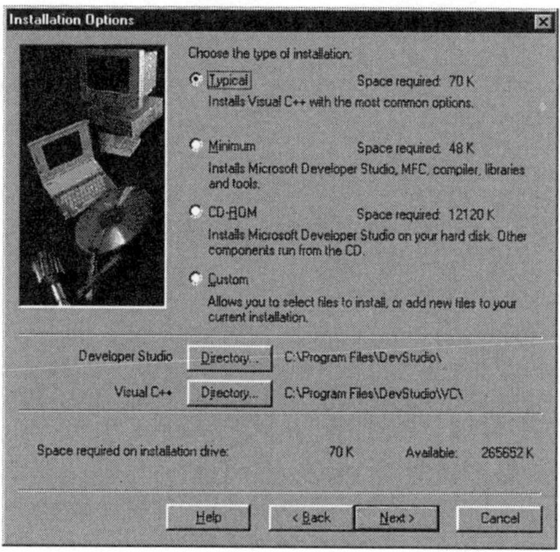

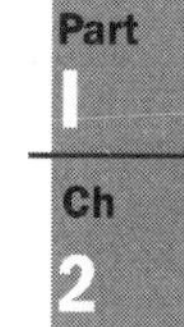

12. When the necessary files are copied to your hard disk, the Registry is updated, and the setup program is about to finish, a few important reminders are presented in a series of dialog boxes. The first describes how to install system symbol files to aid in debugging applications. Click OK.
13. The next dialog box describes how to register environment variables so that you can run build tools (to compile your source code) from the command prompt. Although most developers prefer to use the graphical Developer Studio environment for building applications, you may want to use the command line for a variety of special purposes (such as executing a lengthy build process automatically at a regularly scheduled time every night). This option is selected by default. Make your selection and click OK.
14. The final "reminder" dialog box describes how to enable SQL Server Debugging (see Figure 2.4). You can do this at any time. It doesn't need to be completed before you finish this installation process. Click OK.

FIG. 2.4
If you want to use Visual Studio to debug Transact-SQL statements as they're executed on your SQL Server database, follow the instructions to install the appropriate files on your SQL Server.

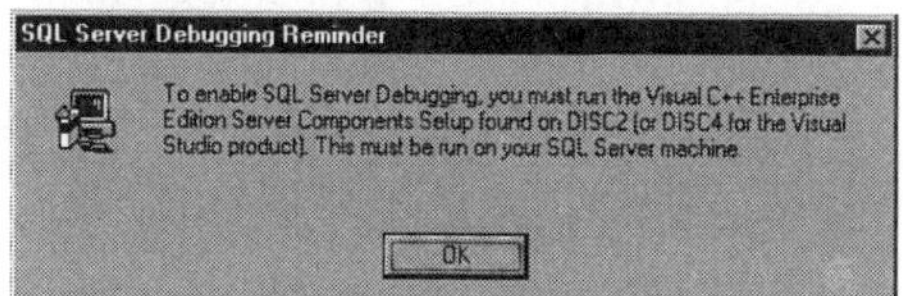

15. A Setup Complete dialog box appears. Click OK to return to the Master Setup menu for Visual Studio.

Repeat these steps with any remaining products or SDKs you want to install. Remember that if you're prompted to restart your machine, you should take the time to do so, and launch the Master Setup program again to continue. If you aren't prompted to reboot, you can continue with the next product immediately.

After you install all the languages, tools, and SDKs you plan to use, you're ready to apply any service patches that have been released. This important part of the installation process can save you hours of aggravation later. Although running your new tool suite may be tempting, it's a good idea to check the Microsoft web site if you haven't already done so, download any appropriate patches, and apply them at this time.

Applying a Service Patch

Microsoft provides *service patches*, which include a cumulative set of all bug fixes, for all products used for corporate information systems, including their operating systems.

ON THE WEB

Service patches are available at no charge (except connect time) on Microsoft's web site at **http://www.microsoft.com/vstudio/sp/**. The web page provides complete instructions for installing the latest patch. In general, installation requires nothing more than simply running a setup program, verifying that the default actions to be taken are acceptable, waiting for some files to be copied, and then rebooting your machine after the patch is applied.

In addition to the service patches is a wealth of troubleshooting information in Microsoft's *Knowledge Base*, an online database of problems and their fixes (see the later section "Where to Get More Help").

Using Developer Studio

Developer Studio is a powerful IDE that supports application development with Visual C++, Visual J++, and Visual InterDev. You also can use it to view much of the online information available to support your development efforts. The use of Developer Studio to view information is covered later in the section "Where to Get More Help," which provides a basic introduction to using the IDE for writing and debugging applications.

In this example, you'll create a blank project and workspace, open a sample application provided with Visual Studio, build the application, and use some basic debugging techniques. The language used is Visual C++. Similar features exist for other languages, although there are differences. The most powerful debugging is available with Visual C++, with reasonably good debugging features for Visual J++. There's substantially less assistance when debugging Visual InterDev at this stage in the product's development.

Loading a Sample Application

Most of the sample applications are distributed in compressed form. To prepare a sample application for use, follow these steps:

1. Launch Developer Studio if you haven't already done so. This can be done by choosing Programs, Microsoft Visual C++ 5.0, Microsoft Visual C++ 5.0 from the Start menu. (The first Visual C++ selects the program group; the second selects the Developer Studio IDE.)
2. Click the Search button on the far right of the Standard toolbar (with a pair of binoculars and a yellow question mark).

NOTE Don't confuse the Search toolbar button with the Find in Files button. Find in Files is represented by a pair of binoculars with a yellow file folder and is nearer the middle of the toolbar.

3. The Search dialog box appears (see Figure 2.5). On the Index page, enter **`Generic sample`** and click the List Topics button.

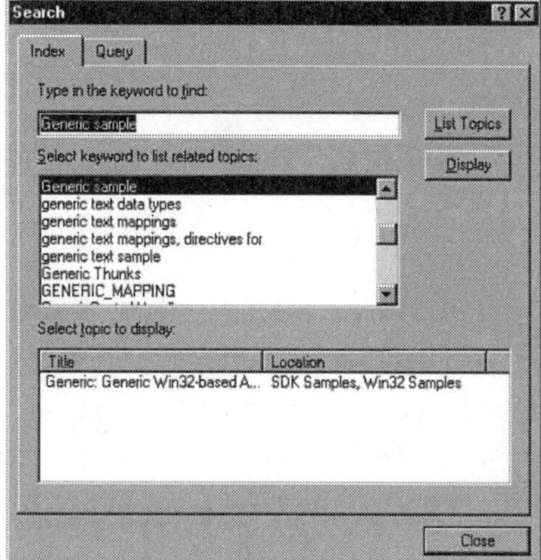

FIG. 2.5
The Search dialog box can be used with the index of topics or by using the Query tab to formulate a query.

4. When the topics appear in the scrollable list, select Generic Sample and click the Display button. A description of the Generic sample application will appear in the InfoViewer Topic window (see Figure 2.6).
5. Click the hot link Click to open or copy the Generic project files. A Sample Application dialog box appears. Click the Copy All button.
6. A Copy dialog box appears. In the To directory text box, enter the following location (or you may modify to suit your preferences):

   ```
   c:\program files\devstudio\samples\sdk\win32\generic
   ```

7. You're asked to confirm that you want to create the new sample directory. Click OK. The files are decompressed and copied to the specified directory. A dialog box informs you when the copy process is complete.
8. Click OK.

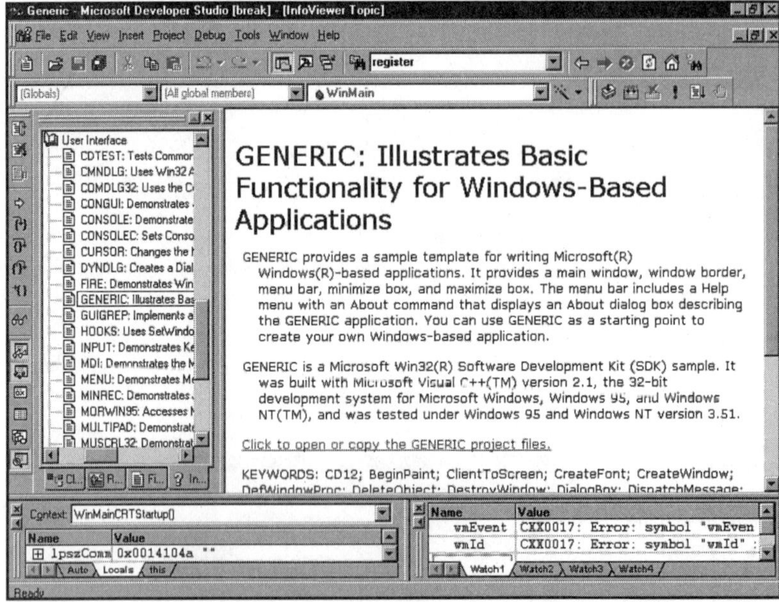

FIG. 2.6
The Generic application is a minimal Windows application with a main window, menu bar, and a Help menu with an About command that displays an About dialog box.

Using Projects and Workspaces

You're now ready to create a project and a corresponding workspace, load files into the project, change settings for your project, build the application, and do some simple debugging. To use Developer Studio for these tasks, follow these steps:

1. Choose File, New from the menu. In the New dialog box, click the Projects tab (see Figure 2.7).

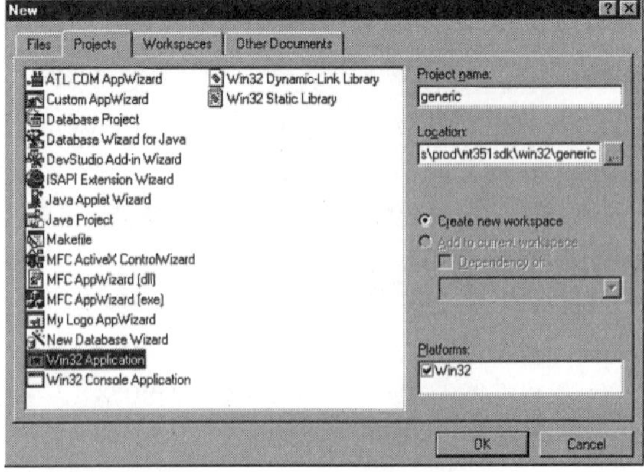

FIG. 2.7
The New dialog box allows you to create new workspaces, projects, applications, and other types of files and documents.

2. Select Win32 Application from the list. In the Project Name text box, enter a name for your new project (for example, **Generic**).
3. Select Create New Workspace to create a workspace that you can use to save the configuration of all the various windows you may create.
4. In the Location text box, enter a path for the folder where you want to store your project and workspace files. You can also click the ellipsis (...) button to browse for an appropriate location. Click OK.
5. At the prompt to confirm the creation of a new folder, click OK. Another dialog box confirms that your project and workspace are created. Click OK.
6. To copy the sample files into your project, choose Project, Add to Project, Files from the menu. The Insert Files into Project dialog box appears.
7. From the Files of Type drop-down list, select All Files.
8. Browse for the location of the folder where you copied the sample files from the distribution CD-ROM and select all the files. Click OK.
9. You can now try to build your application immediately, but one more detail must be taken care of. By reviewing the makefile included with the project, you can see the instructions that would be sent to the compiler if you launched a build from the command line. In particular, you can see that the library file Version.lib is required for this application to run (see Figure 2.8).

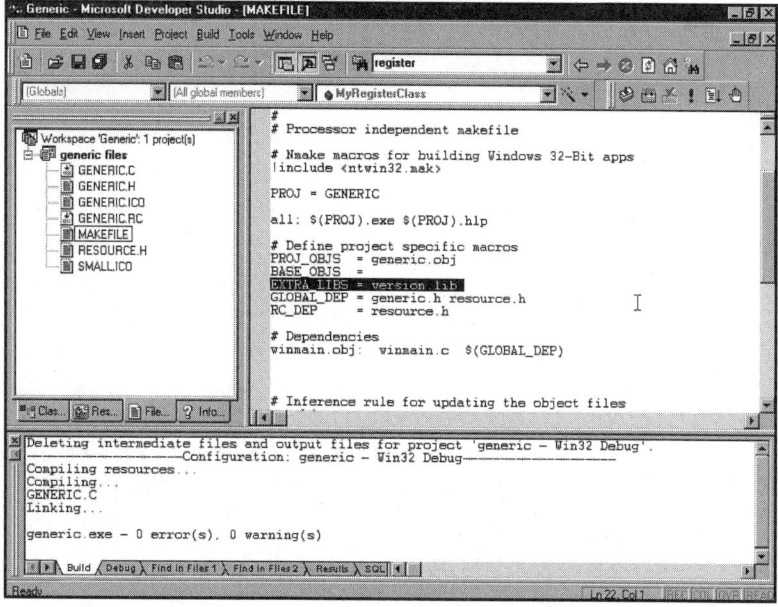

FIG. 2.8
The `EXTRA_LIBS` option is set to Version.lib in this makefile, indicating that the library file is needed for this application to build properly.

10. To make the equivalent setting in the graphical IDE, choose Project, Settings from the menu. The Project Settings dialog box appears.
11. Click the Link tab (see Figure 2.9).

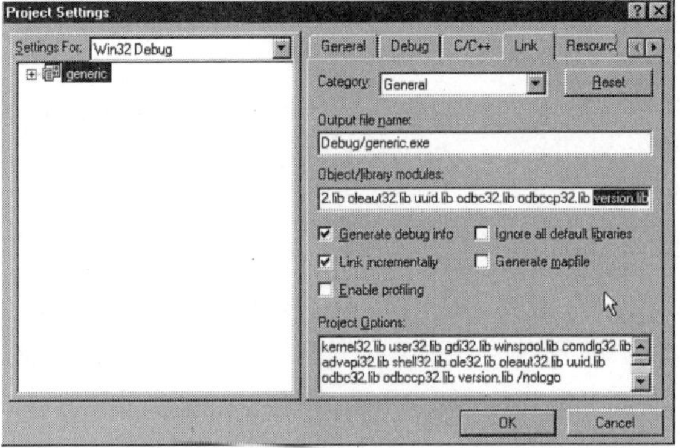

FIG. 2.9
The Project Settings dialog box allows you to make project-specific changes to the compiler and link options.

12. At the very end of the Object/Library Modules text box, insert **`version.lib`** to add this library to your project. Setting options in this dialog box when you're building applications within the IDE is the equivalent of using a makefile when you're building applications from the command line. Click OK.
13. To build the application, click the Build button (the second button from the left on the Build minibar) (see Figure 2.10). If you don't now have the Build minibar visible, right-click anywhere on the toolbar area and select it from the pop-up menu.

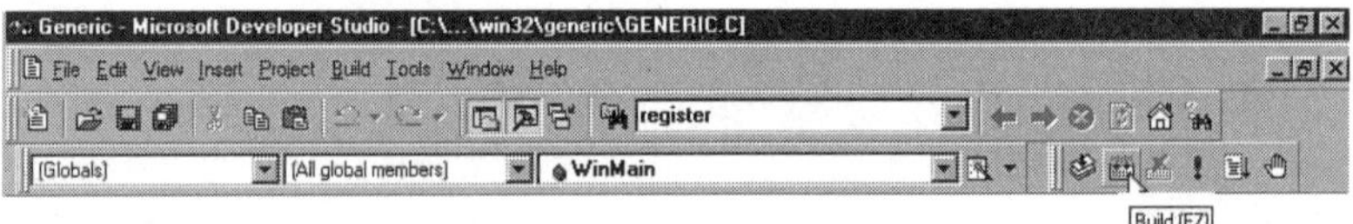

FIG. 2.10
The Build minibar has toolbar buttons that control the build and debug processes.

14. The results of your build process appears on the Build page of the output window at the bottom of the screen. (If the output window isn't visible, choose View, Output from the menu.)
15. Assuming that you had no (serious) errors (as should be the case if you've followed the example exactly), you can now run the application and experiment with some simple debugging techniques.

You've created a project and learned how to compile and link your application into an executable program or module. This rudimentary process is the basis for any build process you might run. But Developer Studio is used for more than just building applications. It's also a powerful debugging tool that helps you find any errors in your code and correct them.

Basic Debugging with Developer Studio

You'll now learn some rudimentary debugging capabilities offered by Developer Studio. These techniques are only the beginning. Many sophisticated techniques involve writing code specifically to aid the debug process and other skills beyond the scope of this book. This section will familiarize you with the basics and get you started. This example uses the results of the previous two procedures, which loaded and built the Generic sample application provided with Visual Studio.

To debug a Visual C++ application, follow these steps:

1. In the Workplace window at the left of the screen, double-click the Generic.C file to display its contents in the code window at the right. Scroll through the code until you find the `switch` statement and the `IDM_ABOUT` case statement just below that (see Figure 2.11).

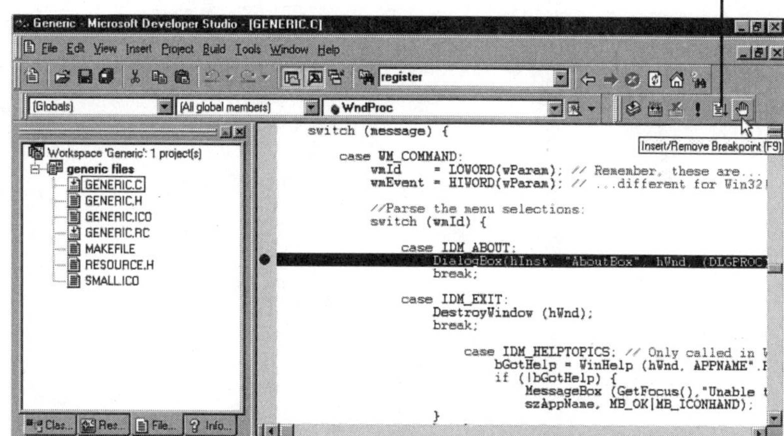

FIG. 2.11 A breakpoint is added at the statement that displays the About dialog box for this application.

2. Select the `DialogBox` statement, as shown in Figure 2.11. Click the Insert/Remove Breakpoint toolbar button (with the hand icon) to toggle a breakpoint on this line.
3. To run the application, click the Go toolbar button (with a page of code with a downward arrow to the right). The Generic application runs and displays its own window (see Figure 2.12).

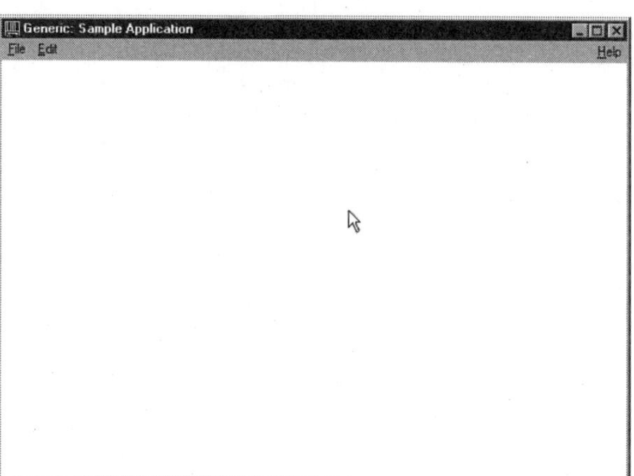

FIG. 2.12 The Generic application is only a shell. The only functionality that's provided is the About box and some very rudimentary behavior from menus, minimize buttons, and so forth.

4. Choose Help, About from the menu. The breakpoint should fire and the application will temporarily stop executing. Developer Studio will get focus and display the code window with the breakpoint highlighted.
5. If you haven't already turned on the Debug toolbar, do so now by right-clicking anywhere in the toolbar area and selecting it from the pop-up menu. In Figure 2.13, it's docked at the left edge of the code window.

FIG. 2.13
The Debug toolbar provides complete control over the debug process, allowing you to Step Into, Step Over, or Step Out of procedure calls.

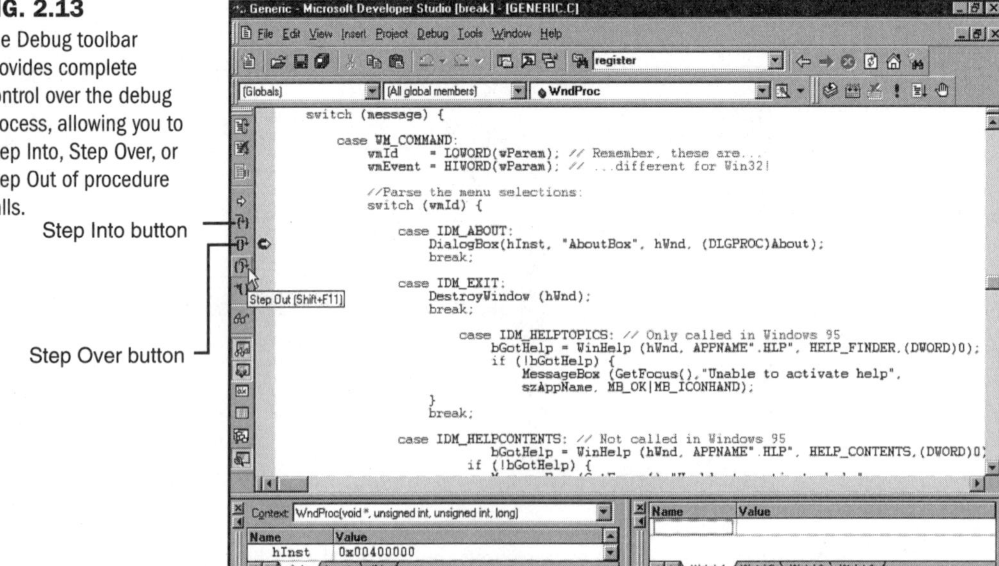

6. Highlight a variable or expression (such as `wmId`) and right-click the name. Choose QuickWatch from the pop-up menu. The QuickWatch window appears, containing the current value of the variable or expression you highlighted (see Figure 2.14).

TIP If you need only the value of a single variable, you don't even need the QuickWatch window. Simply select the variable and position the mouse pointer over the name. A tool tip will pop up over the name with the current value of the variable (see Figure 2.15).

7. Click the Step Into button on the Debug toolbar (refer to Figure 2.13). Execution continues with the next statement, which should display the About dialog box. Click OK to return to debugging at the next line of code.
8. You can continue to go line-by-line by using the Step Into button, skip ahead with the Step Over and Step Out buttons, or click the Go button to resume execution until the next breakpoint is encountered or execution is halted.

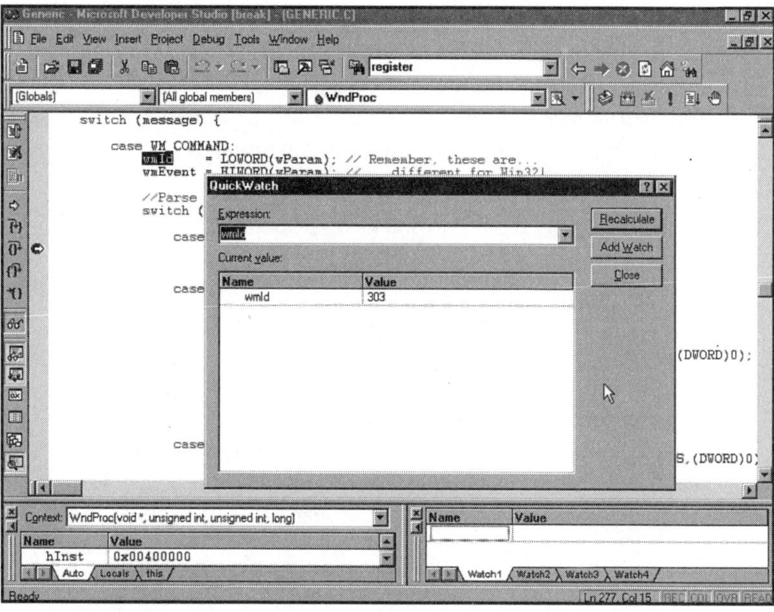

FIG. 2.14
The QuickWatch window is a fast and easy way to check the values of one or more variables or expressions.

FIG. 2.15
Using tool tips to display the value of a variable eliminates the need for watch windows if you need only one value and don't want to change anything.

```
switch (message) {

    case WM_COMMAND:
        wmId    = LOWORD(wParam); // Remember, these are...
        wm[wmId = 303]HIWORD(wParam); // ...different for Win32!

        //Parse the menu selections:
        switch (wmId) {
```

You've now had a little first-hand experience in using the Developer Studio debugging environment. You may want to explore other advanced features, such as viewing the contents of memory locations, checking the contents of CPU registers, viewing a disassembly of your C++ program into machine instructions, and others. Many of these features are accessed by simply clicking a toolbar button or making a menu selection. Feel free to try these out with the Generic sample or explore the other sample applications provided with Visual Studio.

Using Visual Basic's Development Environment

As already pointed out, Visual Basic doesn't share the Developer Studio IDE with Visual C++, Visual J++, and Visual InterDev. Microsoft will address this undesirable situation sometime in the future. In the meantime, the good news is that the IDE for Visual Basic is a powerful and friendly environment in its own right and offers some nice features not found in Developer Studio. Perhaps the best features of both environments will eventually be merged into a single, ultimate environment.

Until that goal is reached, many developers will be faced with learning how to use two different environments. Although this task isn't particularly difficult, it's at least annoying. And switching back and forth between the two inevitably causes moments of irritation as you try to use a feature from one environment while in the other. Be that as it may, this section introduces you to the main features of the Visual Basic environment and helps you become comfortable with its features.

To use the Visual Basic IDE, follow these steps:

1. Launch Visual Basic by choosing Programs, Microsoft Visual Basic 5.0, Visual Basic 5.0 from the Start menu. (The first Visual Basic menu selection is the Program Group; the second is the actual IDE.)
2. The Visual Basic IDE appears (see Figure 2.16).

   Depending on your preferences, you might also be presented with a New Project dialog box. If you don't want this dialog box automatically displayed in the future, select the Don't Show This Dialog in the Future checkbox. The various types of projects that you can create with Visual Basic appear in the dialog box.

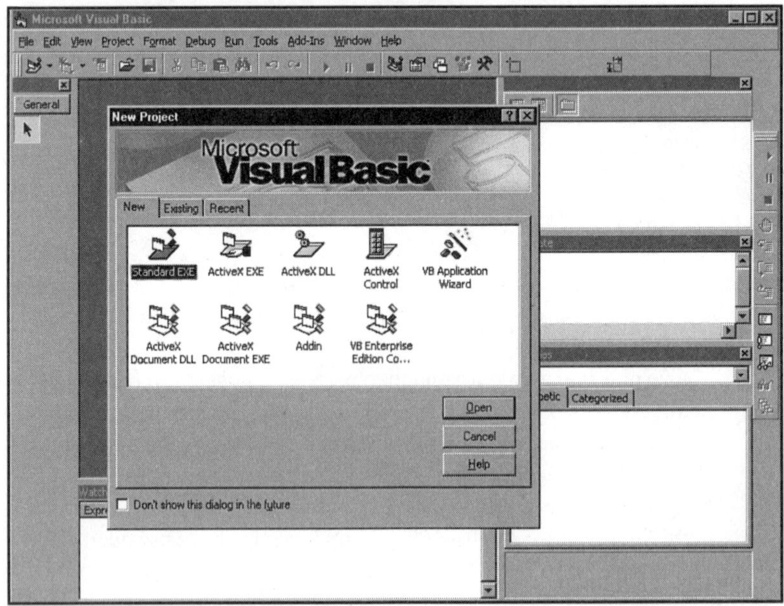

FIG. 2.16
The Visual Basic IDE is visible behind the New Project dialog box, which you can open at any time by choosing File, New Project from the menu.

3. For the purposes of this example, click the Existing tab in the New Project dialog box. You can browse the contents of your hard disk to find existing Visual Basic projects that you may be interested in modifying.
4. If you've loaded the sample applications provided with Visual Basic, you should find them in the folder C:\Program Files\DevStudio\Vb\samples, provided that you didn't change any of the defaults. In this example, the WinSeek sample application is loaded from the \Misc\FileCts subfolder.

NOTE The WinSeek sample application is a utility that searches for files based on a file specification you enter. You can use the ? and * wildcard characters in the specification. You can also use a simple tree control to select the folder in which to begin your search. Subfolders are automatically included in the search. The number of matching files is counted, and full pathnames to each are provided in a result window.

5. Find the project file named Winseek.vbp and double-click it to open the project.
6. The project's files appear in the project window in the upper right (see Figure 2.17). Click the plus sign to the left of the Forms folder to display the forms in this project. Double-click the name of a form to display it in the object window in the center of the screen.

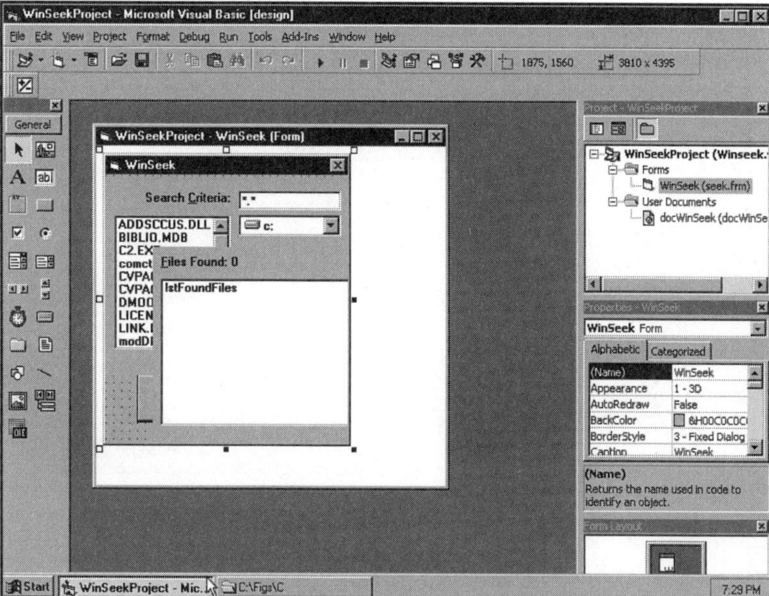

FIG. 2.17
The Visual Basic IDE with the WinSeek sample application loaded and the primary form visible.

7. Visual Basic can have separate code modules, which are stored in files that appear in the project window. Also, it's common to have code that's directly attached to a particular form as in this example. To display the code attached to a form, right-click the form name in the Project window and choose View Code from the pop-up menu (see Figure 2.18).
8. When the code appears, you're ready to debug the application. A common technique when troubleshooting an application error is to set a breakpoint at a particular line of code so that you can stop execution and investigate the current state of things. To toggle a breakpoint on a particular line of code, select the code by clicking the line in the code window and choose Debug, Toggle Breakpoint from the menu (see Figure 2.19). Set additional breakpoints, if you want.

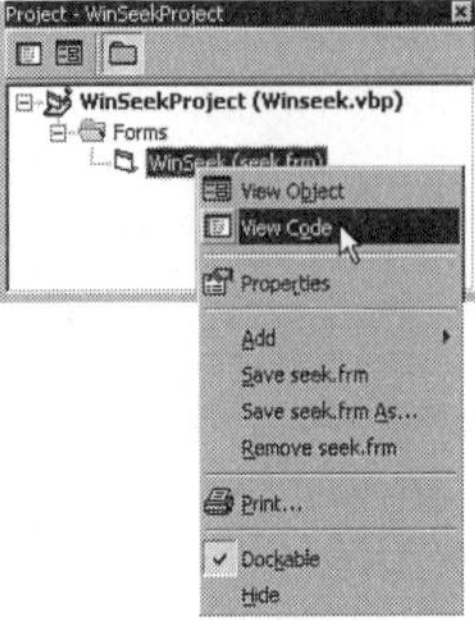

FIG. 2.18
Right-clicking most objects in the Visual Basic IDE displays a context-sensitive pop-up menu of appropriate actions you may want to take.

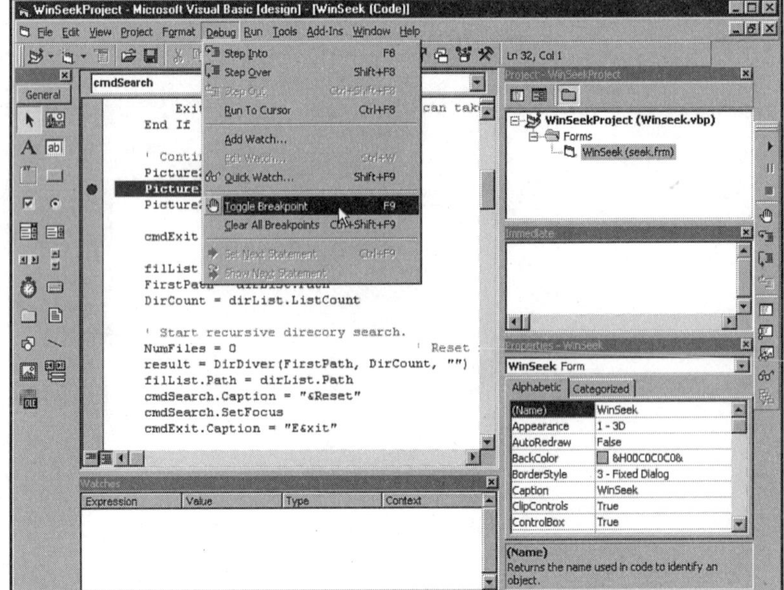

FIG. 2.19
A breakpoint is indicated by a circle in the left margin of the code window and by a different colored highlight.

9. To run the application, click the Run toolbar button, which shows a right arrow similar to the play button on most video cassette recorders (see Figure 2.20). You can also choose Debug, Run from the menu.

Depending on where you set your breakpoints, the application's main form will soon appear and the application is running.

You can use the application as you would normally, until you hit a breakpoint. At that time, the Visual Basic IDE will receive focus, and the code module now running appears with the current breakpoint highlighted (see Figure 2.20).

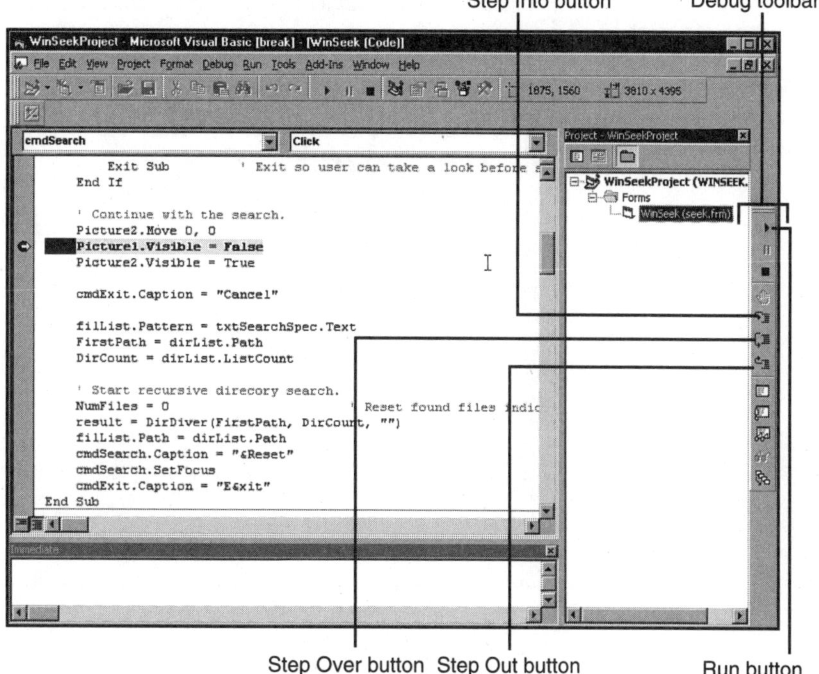

FIG. 2.20
The Visual Basic IDE allows you to dock toolbars on any edge of the window. (The Debug toolbar is shown at right.)

When you hit a breakpoint, you can use several techniques to investigate the current state of your running application:

- Use the watch window (choose View, Watch Window). To select any variable or property in the code window, highlight its name and then drag it into the watch window (see Figure 2.21). You also can add expressions to the watch window. After you add these elements, you can see the current value assigned (or that the expression evaluates to) in the Value column of the window.
- Use the Immediate window (choose View, Immediate Window). In the Immediate window, you can print an expression's current value, assign a new value, or execute most valid statements in Visual Basic. (You would not, for example, use the Immediate window to execute a `Select Case` statement or other advanced branching logic.) Simply enter the statement you want to execute directly into the Immediate window.

  As you enter a statement, Visual Basic will offer context-sensitive syntax help, just as it does in a code window. As you enter a command, a pop-up list box will offer the various alternatives available at certain points in the command-entry process (see Figure 2.22). This feature is known as *IntelliSense*. In this example, a simple print statement is used to display the `Caption` property of the `cmdExit` command button (see Figure 2.23).

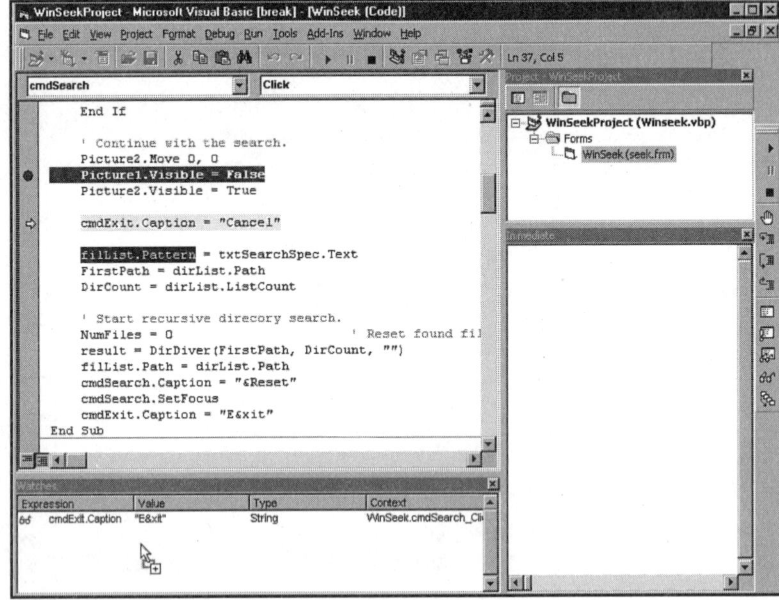

FIG. 2.21
You can add a variable or property to the watch window with a simple drag-and-drop operation.

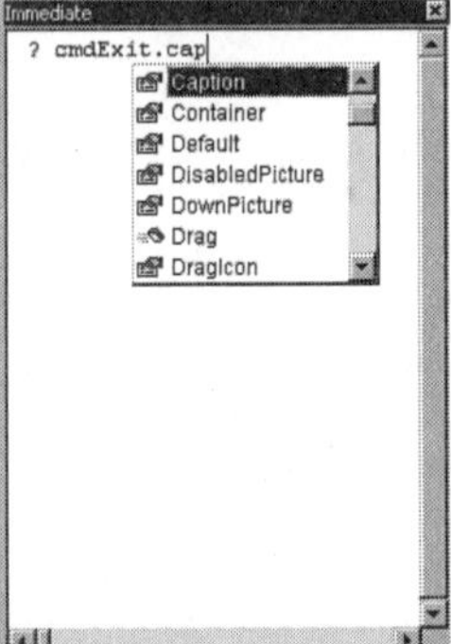

FIG. 2.22
To complete a command by using the syntax help feature, select the option you want from the menu and press Tab to continue.

When you're through investigating the current state of your application, you can continue execution in various ways. You can simply press the Run toolbar button again to continue execution until (and if) you hit another breakpoint. You can also use the Step Into, Step Over, and Step Out toolbar buttons (refer to Figure 2.20), which let you control whether to continue at the next statement within the current module, skip a module altogether, or continue execution at the first statement immediately following the current module.

Although this overview of the Visual Basic IDE is by no means exhaustive, it should provide you with a basic feel for its use and allow you to orient yourself so that you can continue exploration on your own. At any time while using the IDE, press the F1 key for help. The next section presents other sources of help.

FIG. 2.23
Printing a value in the Immediate window is sometimes a more expedient alternative than using the watch window.

Where to Get More Help

Each language product in Visual Studio has multiple options for getting help—some particular to the individual language and some shared across all Visual Studio products. In this section, you learn how to use various sources for additional information.

With the rapid rate of change that's now common among software development products, the tool many developers prefer to use first is Microsoft's web site. Microsoft has made a large and on-going investment in providing a wealth of background information, bug fixes, downloadable update files, and the latest news through **http://www.microsoft.com**.

Visual Studio's primary web page is at **http://www.microsoft.com/vstudio**. Go here for the latest news, pricing and upgrade information, frequently asked questions (FAQ), white papers, datasheets, evaluation guides, and ordering information.

You can download service patches from **http://www.microsoft.com/vstudio/sp**. Here you'll find not only the latest service patch itself, but also instructions for applying it, a list of the problems it fixes, frequently asked questions, and links to related Knowledge Base articles describing specific problem scenarios. You can download the appropriate patch directly or order a CD-ROM containing the patch because it may be quite large.

As mentioned earlier, the Microsoft Knowledge Base is a large database of known problems and their fixes. Although you can't always find your specific problem in the Knowledge Base, it's usually worth checking to ensure that the difficulty you're experiencing hasn't already been diagnosed and fixed. If you want to go directly to the Microsoft Knowledge Base, visit **http://www.microsoft.com/kb/default.asp**. This URL takes you to a query page where you can enter keywords related to your problem or question (see Figure 2.24).

In addition to the various online options, a wealth of information is on the Visual Studio CD-ROMs. Although this information is obviously not as up-to-date as the web site, it's available anytime and is a great source of background information and tutorial-type information that isn't subject to change frequently. During installation, you can choose to install this information directly to your hard disk or leave it on the CD-ROMs. If you have lots of hard disk space, it's clearly faster and easier to access this information directly from the hard disk. However, because of the vast amount of supporting information included in Visual Studio (more than 1GB), most people are willing to trade the moderate inconvenience of having to occasionally swap CD-ROMs for the savings in disk space.

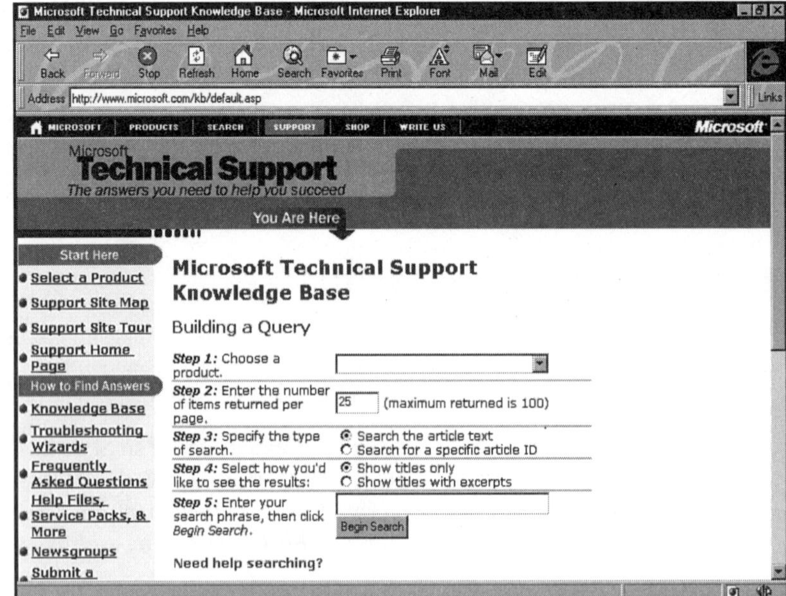

FIG. 2.24
The Microsoft Knowledge Base is an online database of problems and their fixes, complete with a query tool and search engine.

Two primary sources of information are available on CD-ROM in the Visual Studio product. The first is the Visual Studio edition of the MSDN Library CD-ROM. Also, the entire set of Visual Basic documentation is available in the form of Books Online and can be loaded independently of other reference materials.

You can view the MSDN Library CD-ROM directly in the Developer Studio IDE through the use of the InfoViewer. This application, designed as an integral component of Developer Studio, can be used to read the entire set of Visual C++ documentation. Also, you can use the built-in query capability to search for information on any topic. It can even be used to view HTML files, graphics files, Microsoft Word documents, Excel spreadsheets, and many other types of files.

Developer Studio includes multiple windows that you can dock, float, and resize as needed. *Docked* windows all share the same rectangular window and are separated by panes that you can drag to resize the various openings. *Floating* windows and toolbars exist as independent windows, which can be tiled, cascaded, or manually adjusted to facilitate viewing.

To use the InfoViewer, follow these steps:

1. If you haven't already done so, launch the Developer Studio IDE by choosing Programs, Microsoft Visual C++ 5.0, Microsoft Visual C++ 5.0 from the Start menu. You can also launch it by choosing Programs, Visual J++, Microsoft Developer Studio from the Start menu.

2. InfoViewer is most easily used with a combination of two windows: the Workspace and InfoViewer Topic windows. Depending on how you last used Developer Studio and what's now loaded, you may need to open these two windows. To open the Workspace window, choose View, Workspace from the menu or press Alt+0. To open the InfoViewer Topic window, choose View, InfoViewer Topic from the menu or press Alt+1.
3. The Workspace window may have multiple tabs visible near the bottom of the window. If so, be certain that you've selected the InfoView page (see Figure 2.25).

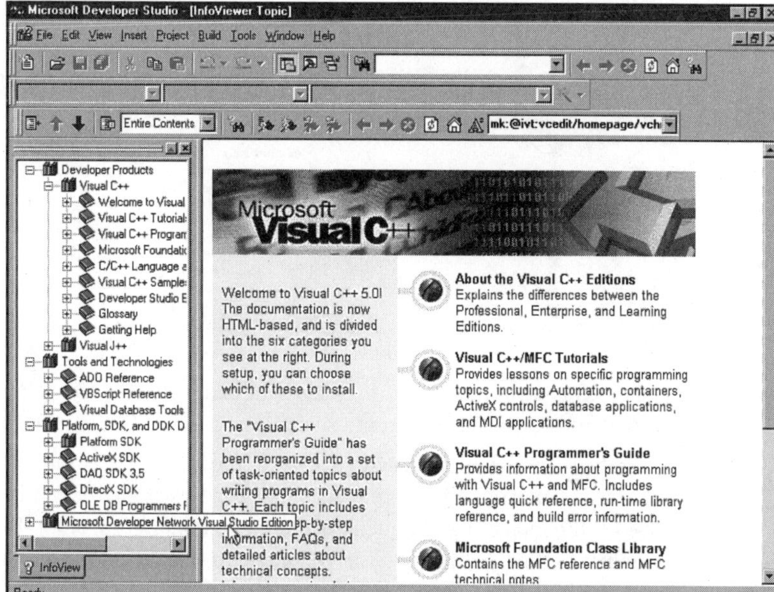

FIG. 2.25
The Developer Studio IDE includes a hierarchical folder directory in the Workspace window on the left that can be used to select a topic for viewing.

4. You can now use the list of contents in the Workspace window to select topics for viewing in the InfoViewer Topic window. Double-click a topic to open it for viewing.
5. In addition to using the folders in the Workspace window for navigating, you can click highlighted hot spots in the InfoViewer Topic window to jump to a new location for additional information on that topic, much as you would with a web browser.

Although the Visual Basic documentation hasn't been incorporated yet into the Developer Studio IDE, you can use it in a similar fashion by launching the Books Online application. While not integrated into the same workspace as your software development, Books Online is a convenient, easy-to-use application that lets you read the VB documentation onscreen or to search for specific information. You can also place electronic "bookmarks" to flag an important topic, making it easy to find and review later. To use Visual Basic Books Online, follow these steps:

1. Choose Programs, Microsoft Visual Basic 5.0, Books Online from the Start menu. The Books Online splash screen appears, and then the dual pane display window appears (see Figure 2.26).

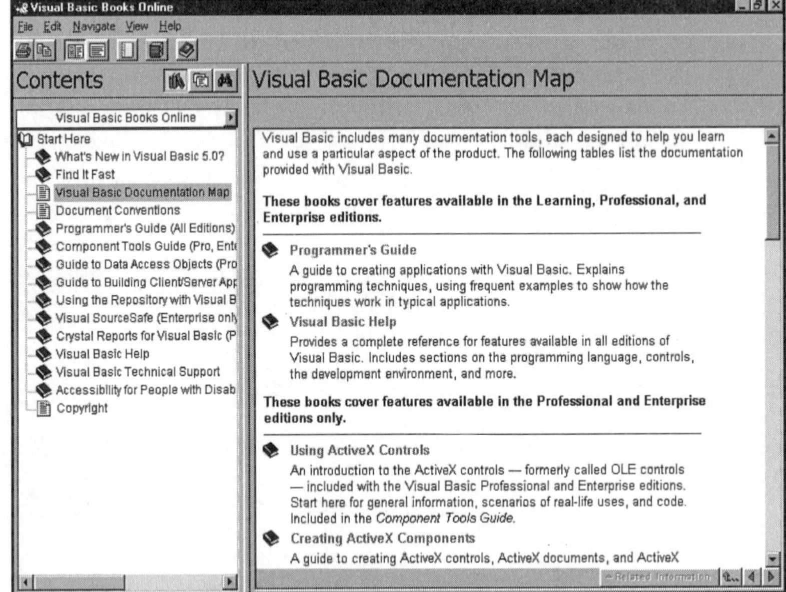

FIG. 2.26
Visual Basic Books Online uses a dual pane display window that you can resize or configure to your preferences.

2. The left pane of the display is called the Navigation window. The right pane is the Topic window. Use the View menu to select Navigation & Topic or Topic Only.
3. You have three options for the display in the Navigation window: Contents, Index, and Find. The name of the current selection appears at the top of the Navigation window just below the toolbar (or the menu bar, if the toolbar isn't visible). Use the three-button toolbar to the right of the displayed name to select a different option, if you want.
4. To find a particular topic, click the Find toolbar button.
5. Enter the keywords for which you want to search. For help on formulating your query, press the F1 key.

Entering two separate words in the Find box results in a search for one word or the other. If you want to search for a two-word combination (such as *ActiveX document*), enclose the phrase in quotation marks so that it will be treated as a single phrase rather than a group of individual words.

6. After you type in your text, press the Enter key. Books Online will find topics that match your request and display them in the Navigation window.
7. To select the topic you want, click its title in the Navigation window. It will appear in the Topic window.

You've learned about the primary web-based and CD-ROM–based resources available to Visual Studio users in search of additional information. These resources, combined with the information found in the rest of this book, should help make you an effective developer of applications with the latest techniques and designed to run in the sophisticated environments found in most organizations today.

From Here...

Although the goal of a single IDE for working in all languages still hasn't been attained, Microsoft has delivered a highly integrated and powerful multiple-language development tool suite with Visual Studio. This chapter touches on the highlights of its usage and should serve as a good beginning. Individual developers, however, usually have particular preferences as to how their environment should be configured. Microsoft has designed Developer Studio and the Visual Basic IDE to be highly customizable. As you work with the individual tools, you'll discover the methods and settings you find most effective and desirable. You can create the workspace most useful for you and automatically load those settings each time you use Visual Studio.

For more information on some of the topics addressed in this chapter and where to go next in your exploration of Visual Studio 97, see the following chapters:

- To learn about Microsoft's approach to object-oriented technology and how it affects software development, see Chapter 4, "Using Microsoft's Object Technologies."
- For further insight into the use of ActiveX components, see Chapter 8, "Using ActiveX Client Components in an I-net Environment."
- To learn how to use Visual Studio to develop applications for the Internet or your own intranet, see Chapter 11, "An Inside Look at Web-Based Applications."
- To explore the creation capabilities of Visual InterDev, see Chapter 14, "Developing Active Content with Visual InterDev."
- To learn how to tap into the full power of using Visual Studio to develop applications in a distributed computing environment, see Chapter 21, "Creating Distributed Applications."

CHAPTER 3

Creating Database-Aware Applications with Visual Studio

by J. Eddie Gulley

Modern development of multiple-tier (n-tier) client/server (CS) applications requires the orchestration of many different components. Often, these components have to be designed, developed, and tested separately from within many non-integrated tools. This lack of integration increases the learning curve, increases costs, and decreases productivity for developers.

Microsoft Visual Studio 97 finally brings together a complete toolkit for CS application developers. Included with Visual Studio 97 Enterprise Edition, the visual database tools provide database design and management support to developers through the Integrated Development Environment (IDE) implemented with Visual InterDev and Visual C++ and as an add-in for Visual Basic 5.0. These tools tightly integrate the project workspaces and Microsoft SQL Server for full life-cycle development of complex CS applications. ■

Using Visual Studio for SQL Server database design

Understand some of the issues involved in designing enterprise databases and discover the tools Visual Studio provides to address them. Discover why to use stored procedures for server-side logic.

Data modeling and SQL procedure development

Get an overview of the visual database tools in Visual Studio. Explore the Database Designer, T-SQL Debugger, and Source Editor.

Using Visual Studio for client/server design

See how Visual Studio provides the developer with a comprehensive toolkit for developing client/server (CS) systems.

Multiple-tier architecture

Learn how to partition client and server components in a multiple-tier architecture. Learn how Visual Studio enables you to develop multiple-tier distributed architectures.

I-net environments

Discover similarities between distributed computing and I-net architectures. Look at how Visual Studio lets you exploit Internet/intranet (I-net) environments.

Overview of SQL Server Design Issues

Before you dive into the design tools, you need to consider some of the issues involved in the design of a solid database on which your CS application will operate. These issues are as important to address as those involving language selection, overall system architectures, and other tasks required in the development of accurate, stable applications.

Some of the more important issues to consider in good database design are

- The logical and physical design of the database
- The location of server-side logic in SQL Server stored procedures versus middle-tier components

By not addressing these issues, you aren't providing your client/server project every chance at success. Worse, you could doom it to failure.

Necessity for Database Design

The importance of good logical and physical design in SQL Server is easy to underestimate. The necessity for appropriately capturing requirements early in the life cycle is important in all components of a CS application, but is perhaps more necessary in the context of the back-end database. The database in a CS architecture is normally much less resilient when changes are made later in the development cycle than other components. This is true because the database in the CS model is usually the foundation for the entire system.

Front-end applications have three functions: They allow data to be input by users, pass data to middle-tier business logic components for calculation or persistent storage in the database, and present results back to users. These requirements for user-services components create an inherent dependency on the middle-tier components and—even more important—on the data-services (RDBMS) components in the CS model. Thus, even minor changes to the database structure can flow throughout the CS model, causing even more changes to the dependent components. Changes to front-end graphical user interface (GUI) components usually don't require changes in other layers.

One accepted way of lessening the risk of changes to the database is to make a habit of documenting the structure of your database. A graphical method of doing this is entity relationship diagramming, which provides a picture of the tables and their relationships with other tables in the database (see Figures 3.1 and 3.2). Such a picture of the database allows developers and users to see database design decisions in an understandable format. Developers can easily walk through the diagram with end users to ensure that requirements are met. By being able to visualize the database design, you easily can see how data is stored and perhaps see problems inherent in a particular database design. It's beyond the scope of this book to teach you the intricacies of data modeling and design, but I highly encourage you to seek out other sources of instruction on this important development concept.

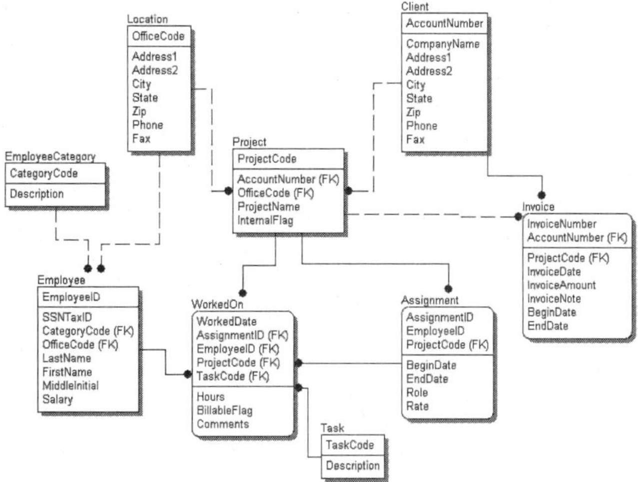

FIG. 3.1
The logical data model represents a process or processes in the context of the users or actors of that process.

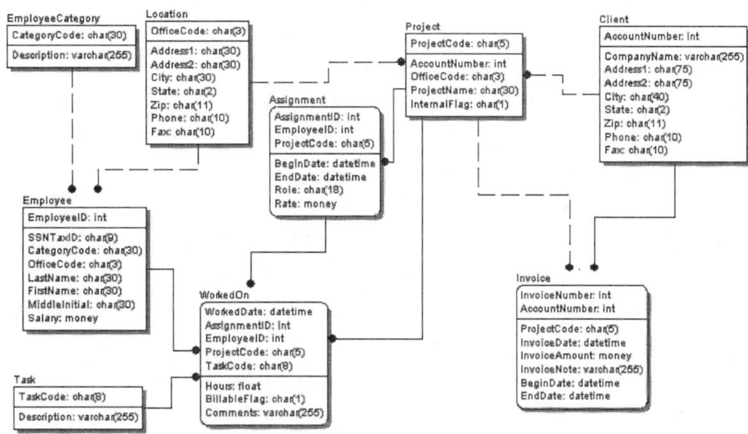

FIG. 3.2
The physical data model represents how a logical model is stored physically on a relational database.

A good entity relationship (ER) diagramming tool can serve to define the database at various levels of abstraction or models. A logical model of the database, in Figure 3.1, provides a method for communicating with and soliciting feedback from end users during the analysis phases of development. This logical view also provides end users and other database users with only the information they need for their purposes, and hides details important only to database designers and developers.

The physical model in Figure 3.2 provides a detailed view of the design of the database and provides for the actual representation of the schema applied to the database. The physical database schema consists of tables, columns, and relationships from the logical model and also individual column data types, defaults, table and column constraints, indexes, and tables constructs for resolving many-to-many relationships. With Visual Studio 97, designers can not only provide graphical representation of the database, but also can use that model as a means of creating the physical data structures within the relational database management system (RDBMS) through script generation and execution against a SQL Server database.

ON THE WEB

You can get more information about data modeling or entity relationship diagramming from web pages of computer-aided software engineering (CASE) tool vendors. For background on the concepts of and standards for entity relationship diagramming, visit the National Institute of Standards and Technology's (NIST) home page at **http://nemo.ncsl.nist.gov/idef**. Here, you can view or download Federal Information Processing Standard (FIPS) Publication 184 "Integration Definition for Information Modeling (IDEF1X)." IDEF1X, the NIST standard for data modeling, is implemented in most major database CASE tools.

SQL Stored Procedures for Server-Side Logic

CS systems that use a relational database management system such as SQL Server for data storage and retrieval often must integrate large amounts of Standard Query Language (SQL) statements into middle-tier components. These middle-tier components must allow the insertion, editing, deletion, and retrieval of data stored in the RDBMS. Often, much data-specific logic is required before these services can be fulfilled. For instance, the data may need to be validated from end-user entry before being inserted, or special business rules may need to be applied to the data before it's affected.

When the logic for data manipulation is placed into the middle tier, the full advantages of the RDBMS engine isn't realized. Middle-tier component languages usually aren't designed for manipulating large sets of data, but for processing of individual records at a time or for performing calculations on a few discrete values.

SQL is a mathematically based language designed for the manipulation and processing of large amounts of related data. By encapsulating the logic for data manipulation in stored procedures, the services necessary for fulfilling the data manipulation are performed in the same CS layer where that data is stored. Common sense tells you that this is a better partitioning of services within layers in the CS model and should provide better performance than SQL statements embedded in external language components. In most cases, the techniques used in external languages require multiple translations of the SQL string before its being sent to the SQL engine. These multiple translation layers come from the passing of SQL strings through data-access libraries such as ODBC and add overhead in the processing of the SQL commands.

Some of the more technical reasons why stored procedures are good choices for data-manipulation logic include performance and security. The main performance gain in using stored procedures is the location of the processing. Stored procedures are precompiled and executed within the context of the SQL Server engine. This negates network latency in execution speed, because the processes that manipulate data reside in the same memory and processing space as the data structures that store the data. In a networked environment, this can equate to large performance gains.

You can actually use stored procedures as a security tool. User permissions over database objects must be tightly controlled in a CS environment. Stored procedures can let you build up a distinct layer between the physical storage of data and the users of the data. Rather than give users permissions over all tables in which data is stored, you can restrict them to permissions over the execution of stored procedures. Users don't need to have select permissions on a table if they have permissions over a stored procedure that, after some validation logic, does the selection for them and returns a result set. In this model, rather than build an elaborate management scheme of a hierarchical groups-and-permissions structure on top of tables, you can give users permissions to execute a few stored procedures that act as a public interface to the underlying data storage.

NOTE Many other sources cover these concepts for stored procedure development. One good reference is Stephen Wynkoop's *Special Edition Using Microsoft SQL Server 6.5*, published by Que Corporation. ■

Visual Studio 97 Database Design Tools

The visual database tools encompass a full range of features to give you control over the physical database schema required for your Visual Studio 97 project. Four components make up the visual database tools:

- Database Designer
- Source Editor for SQL Server stored procedures and triggers
- Query Designer
- Data View

The Database Designer provides a graphical depiction of your database structure. Although not adhering to popular semantic and notational standards for entity relationship diagramming, the Database Designer provides a great tool for modeling and creating database structures without requiring you (the developer) to learn constructs of complex Database Definition Language (DDL). The Database Designer also allows you to experiment with the design of your SQL Server database without affecting the physical database until you're ready to do so. This capability to experiment lends itself well to the iterative development cycles popular today. The Database Designer also lets you make changes to a database while automatically migrating data to the changed structure if that data doesn't violate any rules of the changed structure.

The Source Editor for SQL Server provides a modern development environment for stored procedures and triggers. In traditional stored procedure development, you couldn't set breakpoints and step through code. You would try to compile the completed procedure and receive vague error messages—no line numbers, no ability to view the value of a variable. With Visual Studio's Source Editor, you have all these capabilities plus the ability to step into stored procedures and SQL statements embedded in your application. You can also set breakpoints and watch variables just like you can with almost all programming language Integrated Development Environments. It sure beats trial and error and the use of print statements to narrow down where in the source code errors are occurring.

The Query Designer allows you, graphically or in SQL, to create and execute queries against ODBC-compliant databases. Anyone familiar with the query-by-example (QBE) feature in Microsoft Access will welcome the ability to apply the same concept to more powerful CS databases.

The Data View component provides a graphical browser to a connected database. Data View resembles and acts as an explorer for your database. You can view database diagrams, tables, triggers, stored procedures, and views contained within your database from within your development environment. Without Data View, you often had to run a separate application, such as the MS SQL Server Enterprise Manager, to obtain an organized look at the objects in your database. Although this isn't necessarily a problem, having this capability built into your normal environment lets you view your entire system from within the same integrated development component.

The next section and the section "Stored Procedure Development with Visual Studio 97" provide more detail on how to use the Database Designer and the Source Editor for SQL Server stored procedures. These two components focus more on the design issues previously introduced and are newer additions to Microsoft's programming tools.

Data Modeling with Visual Studio 97

The purpose of this section isn't to teach you how to perform data modeling but to show you how to use the Data Designer to depict your database design graphically and create the database objects required to physically implement your design. Before you begin, you must create the necessary devices for storing your database and create a blank database to access through the Data Designer.

Creating and Connecting to Databases with the Database Designer

You can create devices and databases within SQL Server with the SQL Enterprise Manager or the ISQL interface provided with SQL Server. A developer's edition of SQL Server is included with Visual Studio 97 Enterprise Edition. Specific details on creating and managing devices and databases for SQL Server are found in the *SQL Server's Administrators Companion.* After you accomplish these tasks, follow these steps to start up the Database Designer and add a data connection:

1. You can access the Database Designer through Visual InterDev or Visual C++ 5.0, or through an add-in provided with Visual Basic 5.0. If you're using Visual Basic, you need to install the Visual Database Tools.

   You can install the Database Designer and the other Visual Database Tools as add-ins to Visual Basic 5.0 by choosing Add-Ins, Add-In Manager from the menu. Choose any add-ins you want to install by selecting from a list of available ones in the Add-In Manager.

2. To add a data connection to your project, in Visual Basic choose Add-Ins, Visual Database Tools from the menu (see Figure 3.3). Visual Basic uses the Developer's Studio

Integrated Development Environment for the Visual Database Tools. The Developer's Studio is the same IDE used for Visual C++, Visual InterDev, and Visual J++. After you access the Visual Database Tools in Visual Basic, the rest of the steps apply, regardless of which Developer Studio language you're working in.

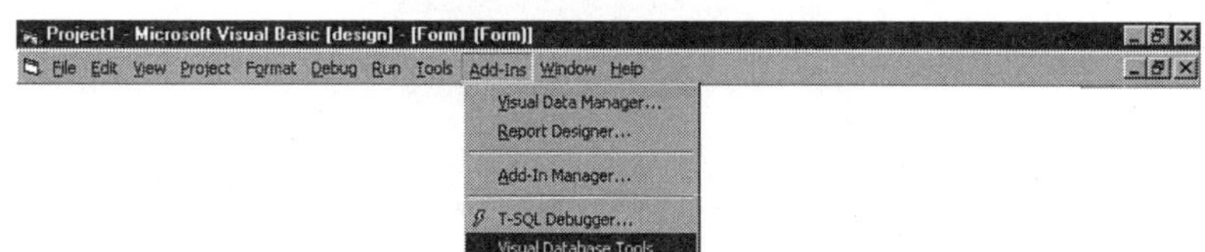

FIG. 3.3
The Visual Database Tools are an integrated part of Visual Basic.

3. At the prompt, you can select an existing data source or create a new one. You also can use a file- or system-type data source. When you use a file data source name (DSN), its configuration parameters are copied into your project. After the connection is created, the file DSN isn't needed anymore. A machine (system) DSN requires that to access the project, the DSN must be created on every machine requiring access. File DSNs are recommended for Visual InterDev projects because I-net projects inherently require many machines to share connections.
4. After you select or create a DSN for your project, the project attempts to connect to the appropriate SQL Server and database. If integrated security isn't used on the SQL Server or a trusted connection wasn't chosen when setting up the DSN, you're prompted to log in to the SQL Server database. The server, userid, and password you enter here must have been previously added to the SQL Server and given proper permissions.

Part I Ch 3

NOTE A little time spent learning the security model of SQL Server will greatly aid you in troubleshooting during development and when you begin integrated testing of large CS applications. SQL Server security knowledge can also boost your productivity when chasing down vague error messages that, at their root, are merely a matter of database object permissions.

The SQL Server security model is broken down into three modes: Integrated, Standard, and Mixed. With Integrated Security, SQL Server uses Windows NT's authentication services for login validation for all connections. Only trusted connections are allowed when using Integrated Security. Standard Security uses SQL Server's own login process. Mixed Security allows SQL Server to service login requests based on whether the requesting connection is trusted. Under Mixed Security, SQL Server uses Integrated for trusted connections and Standard for nontrusted connections.

Creating a Diagram with the Database Designer

Now that you've successfully created and connected to your database, it's time to create a diagram. The following steps outline how to create a database diagram from within the Developer's Studio IDE. The Developer's Studio is used for Visual C++, Visual InterDev, and Visual J++. All three language environments use the Developer's Studio for development and for the Visual Database Tools. Visual Basic also uses the Developer's Studio IDE for the Visual Database Tools.

1. Choose Insert, New Database Item from the menu.
2. At the prompt for the type of database item to add, select Database Diagram from the list and click OK (see Figure 3.4).

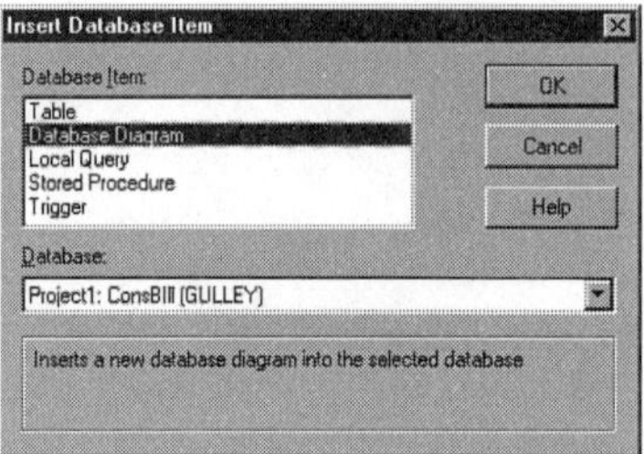

FIG. 3.4
You can add a database diagram to a specific database available through a project's data connection.

3. A blank database diagram is now open onscreen. You can work in full-screen mode or continue with your diagram in a frame within your IDE. To enable full-screen mode, choose View, Full Screen from the menu. It's often much easier to work with even small diagrams in full-screen view. The IDE consumes enough screen space that trying to navigate a diagram much larger than a table or two becomes quite time-consuming.

To begin creating tables in your diagram, follow these steps:

1. From the Database Diagram toolbar, select the New Table button.
2. At the prompt for the name of the new table, enter a name and click OK.
3. A blank table appears, in which you can begin entering column names and the necessary properties for your table. The Database Designer lets you choose the appropriate data type and precision for each column. By default, the columns are all set up to allow NULLs unless you deselect this option in the table designer.

Table 3.1 lists the properties you can set for each column with the Database Designer.

Table 3.1 Column Properties

Property Name	Definition
Column Name	Name you want to use for the column. All column names must be unique within a table and conform to SQL Server rules for database object identifiers.
Datatype	System- or user-defined datatype for the column.
Length	Used to specify the maximum number of characters for char types or digits for numeric types.
Precision	The total number of digits that can be stored on either side of a decimal point.
Scale	The total number of digits that can be stored on the right side of a decimal point. The scale value must be equal to or less than the precision for the column.

Property Name	Definition
Allow Nulls	Used to specify whether a column should allow NULL values. If NULLs are allowed, you can provide a default.
Default Value	Used to denote a default value for insertions. Defaults can be literal values or Transact-SQL function calls such as the `getdate()` function for returning the current system date and time. If a default isn't provided, columns that don't explicitly provide a value will be assigned NULL.
Identity	The identity property allows columns to contain auto-generated values to uniquely identify each table row. Identity columns are handy for sequential numbers as unique identifiers.
Identity Seed	Beginning value for future generations in an identity column. The next insertion into the table begins with this seed value. If not given, this value defaults to 1.
Identity Increment	Amount that an identity value increments from the previous record in the table. For instance, if the identity increment value is set at 10, each subsequent insertion adds 10 to the previous row's column value to generate the current identity value.

CAUTION

Before making a decision on the nullability of a column, make sure that you understand the consequences of multiple-value logic and SQL queries. Careful consideration given to this contentious issue can possibly prevent subtle logic errors from finding their way into your code. NULLs can be said to have multiple possible values, such as the attribute not applying to a particular record, the value may be unknown for a record, or the value known but not captured yet for a record. Queries that include columns containing NULLs must account for the possible logical meanings of the NULL values; also, care certainly should be taken to properly constrain such queries.

Figure 3.5 shows a completed table named Client represented in the sample client/server application demonstrated throughout this book. You can find the application at **http://www.gasullivan.com/vs97book/**.

The only thing left to do for this table is to denote the primary key(s) by following these steps:

1. Select any rows that represent a key field.
2. Select the appropriate column's record selector and then select the key button on the database diagram toolbar. The key icon on the key column's record selector column denotes a primary key for this table.
3. Choose to save your diagram or continue adding more tables. To save the table to the database, choose File, Save from the menu. At the prompt to enter a name for the diagram, enter an appropriate name and choose OK.

FIG. 3.5
The Database Designer can represent the logical or physical view of a database. Here is the physical view of the sample Client table.

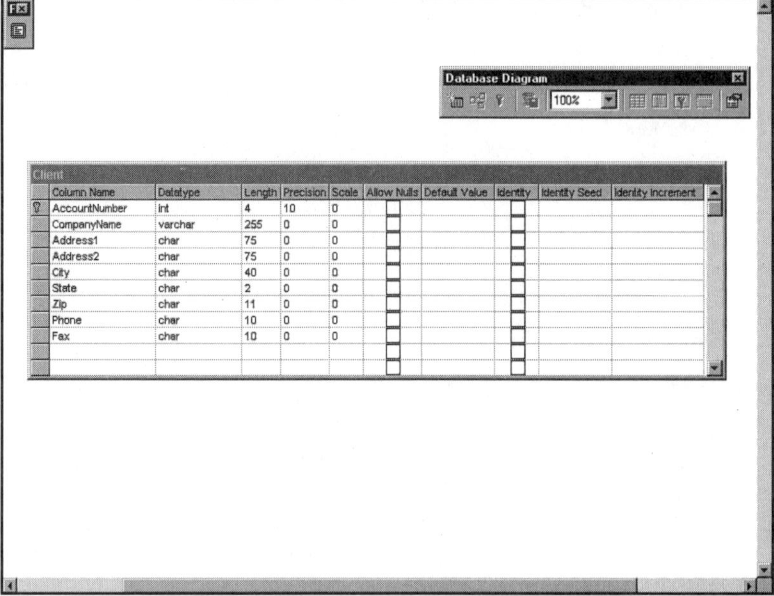

Column Name	Datatype	Length	Precision	Scale	Allow Nulls	Default Value	Identity	Identity Seed	Identity Increment
AccountNumber	int	4	10	0					
CompanyName	varchar	255	0	0					
Address1	char	75	0	0					
Address2	char	75	0	0					
City	char	40	0	0					
State	char	2	0	0					
Zip	char	11	0	0					
Phone	char	10	0	0					
Fax	char	10	0	0					

In more formal development shops, you might work under more guarded database access. In these cases, you'll want to save your diagram to a text script file, submit it to your database administrator (DBA) for review, and let him run the script against the database for object creation.

Creating Table Relationships with the Database Designer

After you create more than one table on the diagram, you might need to relate one or more tables. Table relationships are represented by foreign key constraints on dependent table columns. For instance, an invoice record might be related to a client record through a foreign key relationship on the AccountNumber column. This requires that any invoice record entered into the invoice table must reference through its AccountNumber column a valid Client record in the Client table.

To create foreign key relationships in a database diagram, click within the parent table's key columns and drag to the child table's foreign key column (see Figure 3.6). After you draw the required relationship, you're prompted to create the relationship, as shown in Figure 3.7.

The dialog box in Figure 3.7 defaults to an appropriate name for the foreign key constraint that will be created and allows you to verify that the correct columns in the parent and child tables are included in the constraint. By default, other options are also enabled, such as checking existing data, if any, against the new column constraint and checking the relationships for inserts and updates and for replication. Generally, you should accept the defaults unless your database requirements dictate otherwise.

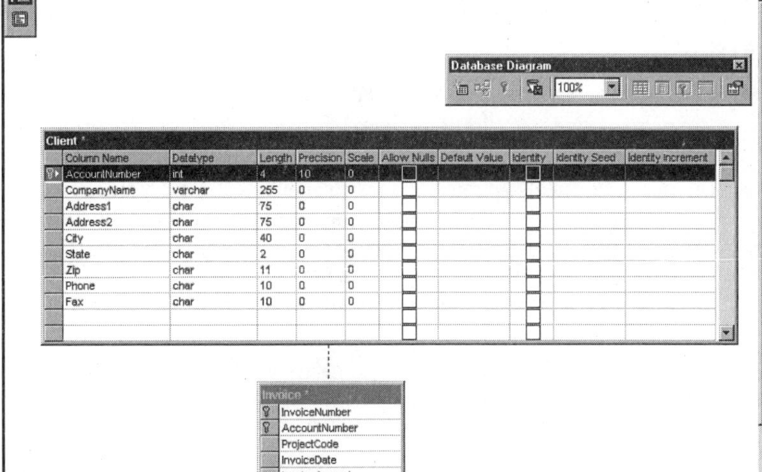

FIG. 3.6
A dashed line between two tables in a database represents foreign key relationships in progress.

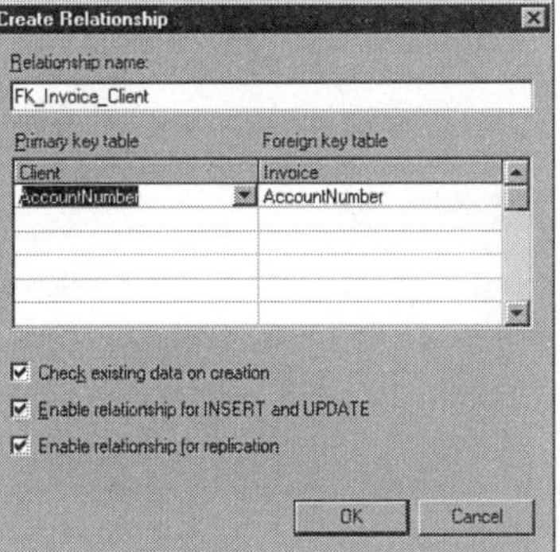

FIG. 3.7
You can access the properties of the selected relationship through the database diagram.

After the relationship is created, you see the related tables attached on the diagram through a three-dimensional bar with a key icon on the parent end and a double-link chain on the child end. This notationally represents a one-to-many relationship in entity-relationship diagramming.

Continue adding tables and relationships as necessary to complete the diagram of your database. After you finish, you can save all changes to the database immediately or generate a script file as noted earlier.

Navigating Database Objects and Diagrams with the Database Designer

You can also experiment further with the diagram. For instance, right-click any object to bring up menu options for different views of objects. You can view each table with full column names and parameters, just view the tables and key field columns, or just view tables with name spaces. You can also choose to view properties of any object on your diagram. By looking at the properties for a table, you can examine and alter indexes and other constraints for that object.

Figure 3.8 shows you the completed diagram for the sample application included at the site **http://www.gasullivan.com/vs97book/**.

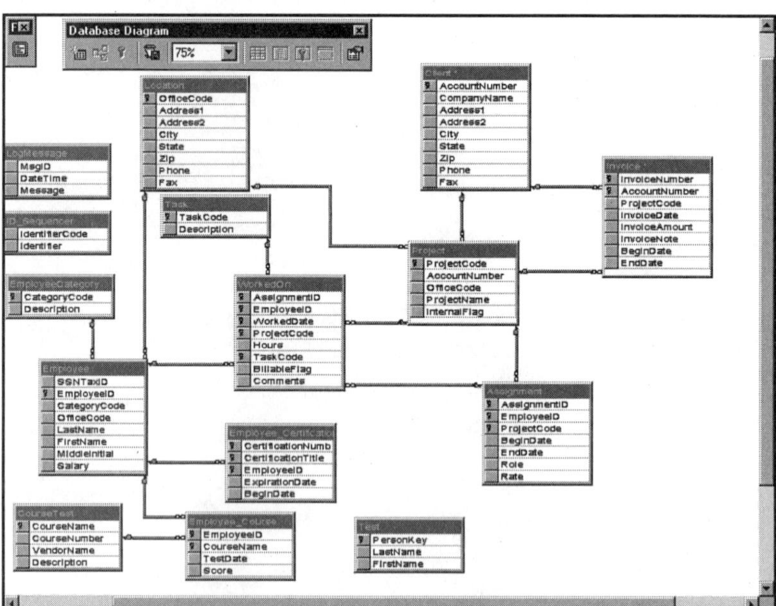

FIG. 3.8
The completed diagram for the same Time & Billing application.

The Database Designer also lets you create smaller views of a large diagram. This is often helpful in large CS projects where the database contains hundreds of tables and a developer is concerned only with a portion of the database dealing with a particular set of tables. You can create diagram views easily by inserting a new diagram and dragging the required tables from the data view to the blank diagram.

Another use for the diagramming tool is so that you can experiment with different layouts of tables and relationships without affecting the underlying database until the design is finished. You can accomplish this by creating a diagram, dragging existing tables to it, and altering their structure as desired. Just be sure to remember not to save the diagram to your database until you're sure that the design is what you want, or you lose any previously created structures.

With some experimentation and practice, you should be able to create complex databases with the Database Designer included with Visual Studio 97. This can bring more of an engineering approach to development projects and get developers and users interacting during the requirements phase for more successful projects.

Stored Procedure Development with Visual Studio 97

If you've ever had to develop stored procedures for SQL Server, you're aware of the lack of tools to support this development. Unlike application developers, SQL procedure programmers haven't historically had tools such as advanced editors, debugging facilities, or even good ways to test stored procedures. Often, you had to enter your procedure code into a text editor or directly into the ISQL interface provided with SQL Server. There was no on-the-fly syntax checking, color coding, or consistent indentation for procedure development. Debugging and testing were even worse—you often would submit your completed procedure to the SQL engine and receive error messages, which gave you only enough information to figure out the problem after a great deal of experience.

Debugging your procedures consisted of placing print statements at key points throughout to try to identify which areas were properly processed and which weren't. Testing stored procedures required you to set up the affected database objects with data to meet referential integrity requirements and then manually enter procedure calls with correct parameters. After that, you had to run select queries against affected tables to identify whether your procedure affected the underlying data correctly.

Visual Studio 97 brings the SQL developer into the modern age. Fairly complete support is provided in Visual Basic 5.0 as an included add-in and is integrated into the Visual InterDev and Visual C++ 5.0 IDE. You can now use your familiar editor for entering procedure code, with all the frills you're used to in your favorite development environments. Properly indented text, color coding, and syntax checking are all available in the editor.

Another new feature included with Visual Studio 97 is SQL stored-procedure debugging, using the same debugging components available with VC++ and Visual InterDev. VB has a separate Transact-SQL (T-SQL) debugger provided as an add-in, available automatically when testing your Remote Data Object (RDO) code or separately on demand.

If you're familiar with the Visual C++ IDE and debugging facilities, you'll be up and running fairly quickly with procedure development and debugging. If you're familiar with VB, you'll soon learn about the Transact-SQL debugger and see how you can apply the same productivity to your SQL development as to the rest of your application code tasks.

Installing T-SQL Debugger

Begin by ensuring that T-SQL debugger is installed. If you chose to install all the enterprise tools when you installed Visual Basic 5.0, you should have a new option, T-SQL Debugger, on the Add-Ins menu. If not, you'll need to repeat the setup process, choosing a custom install and opting to Select All for the enterprise tools selection.

In addition to installing the T-SQL debugger on your client machine, you need to ensure that your database installation is SQL Server 6.5 and is running at least Service Pack 1. Then you need to run the Sdi_nt4.exe setup program on your SQL Server machine. You can find the Sdi_nt4.exe application on the client machine on which you installed VB 5.0 in the \CliSrv\Tsql directory.

NOTE To verify the server installation, ensure that SDI.DLL is resident in your \MSSQL\BINN directory on a Windows NT installation of SQL Server, or \MSSQL\BIN on a MS-DOS, 16-bit Windows, or Windows 95-based client.

Using the T-SQL Debugger

You can access the T-SQL Debugger via one of several methods: explicitly during procedure-design time, implicitly by stepping through Visual Basic code that make calls to your stored procedures, or explicitly from within a Visual Basic `UserConnection` object.

NOTE To automatically step into a stored procedure, make sure that you've selected Automatically Step Into Stored Procedures in the T-SQL Debugger options. You can access the T-SQL Debugger options by choosing Tools, T-SQL Debugger Options from the Visual Basic menu.

You can explicitly invoke the debugger during design time by choosing Add-Ins, T-SQL Debugger from the menu. This brings up the Batch T-SQL Debugger dialog box (see Figure 3.9).

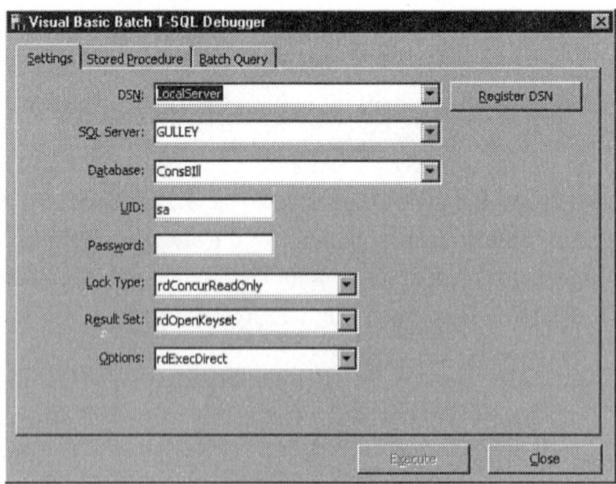

FIG. 3.9 The T-SQL Debugger settings properties allow you to set the parameters for your debugging session.

On the first tabbed page, enter information pertaining to the data source name with which you want to access the database. Available sections include

- DSN
- SQL Server name
- Database

- UserID
- Password
- Lock Type
- Result Set

The Lock Type property in the T-SQL Debugger dialog box refers to the type of concurrency control the debugging session should have over the resultset being affected. The named items in the listbox refer to Remote Data Objects (RDO) constants that refer to specific values which can be assigned to the `LockType` property of RDO resultset objects. Table 3.2 describes the available lock types.

Table 3.2 Available Lock Types

Lock Type	Description
`rdConcurReadOnly`	Resultset is read-only. No modifications can be made to the data.
`rdConcurLock`	The resultset locks all associated data pages. Pessimistic in that it assumes that no other users will need the same data.
`rdConcurRowVer`	Optimistic lock type in that it assumes that no other user will attempt to change the affected data, so it doesn't lock any of the affected pages. Requires row identifier to be compared against the record in the resultset. If the identifiers match, the modification takes place; if not, an error is generated.
`rdConcurValues`	Version of optimistic lock where no data pages are locked. Requires row-by-row comparison of values before changes can be committed.
`rdConcurBatch`	Optimistic locking where no locks are held but where each change is accumulated in a batch. When the batch is applied, each record is modified according to rules of a lower-level parameter. Status values of each record in a batch are returned.

The Result Set parameter on the T-SQL Debugger refers to the type of cursor to use with the RDO resultset object in the debugging session. Table 3.3 describes the available resultset types.

Table 3.3 Available Resultset Types

Resultset	Description
`rdOpenKeyset`	Dynamic type cursor where you can still see records changed by other users but not those added by others. You also can't access records deleted by another user.

continues

Table 3.3 Continued

Resultset	Description
`rdOpenForwardOnly`	Static type cursor in which you can see records only as they were when you retrieved the recordset. You can't see records added, modified, or deleted by others since you opened your cursor. You can only scroll forward with this cursor type.
`rdOpenStatic`	Similar to forward-only cursor, except that you can scroll forward or backward.
`rdOpenDynamic`	All data additions, modifications, or deletions made to the data in your open cursor are visible. Scrolling in any direction is enabled.

The Options selection for the T-SQL Debugger session refers to how the session should present its SQL statements to the SQL Server: either directly through the `SQLExecDirect` Open Database Connectivity (ODBC) API function when `rdExecDirect` is selected or by preparing a stored procedure for each statement when `rdNone` is selected.

After the DSN information is entered, you can change to the Stored Procedures page, which is very helpful in the debugging and testing process. This page allows you to

- Select stored procedures already in the database
- Show the actual call string with parameter values
- Set input parameters
- Insert parameters into the call string

After you select your stored procedure and enter values for any input parameters, you can click the Execute button.

CAUTION

Stored procedures are designed to manipulate or alter data in your database. It's strongly suggested that you select the Use Safe Mode (transaction rollback) for Stored Procedure Calls option in the T-SQL Debugging options. This way, any changes a stored procedure might make can be rolled back on completion of the debugging/testing session.

Now you should be in the T-SQL Debugger interface itself (see Figure 3.10). The interface is made up of a code window (for viewing the actual procedure code being debugged), a local variable watch window, a global variable watch window, and a procedure output window. The simple toolbar gives you ready access to all the debugging options available.

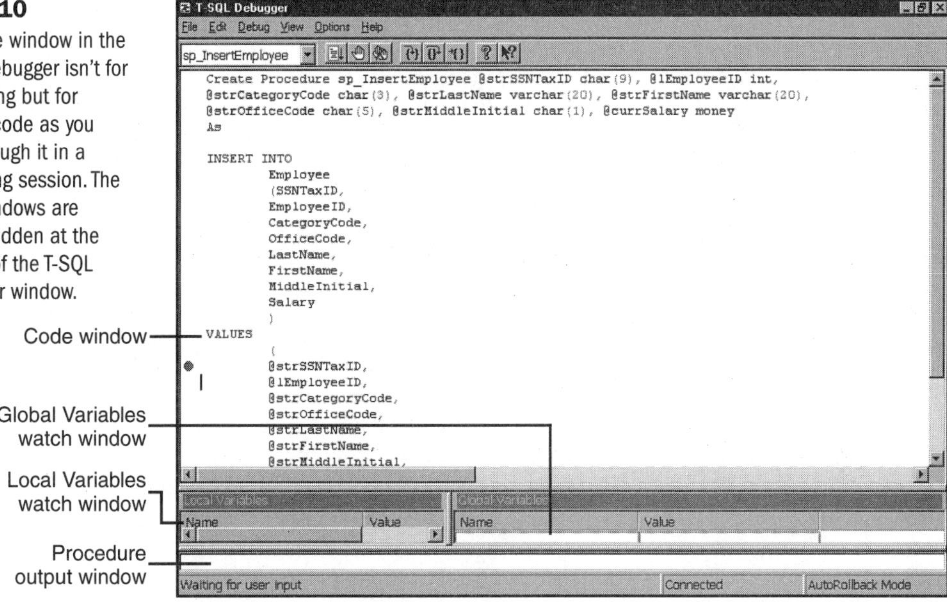

FIG. 3.10
The Code window in the T-SQL Debugger isn't for developing but for viewing code as you step through it in a debugging session. The other windows are mostly hidden at the bottom of the T-SQL Debugger window.

The debugging options available in the T-SQL Debugger are as follows:

- Run
- Ability to set and clear breakpoints
- Step to subexpressions
- Step into subexpressions
- Step over subexpressions
- Run to cursor
- Result Set
- Stop
- Restart

You also can invoke a separate Call Stack window and a temporary table dump window for viewing the related output. Experienced SQL procedure developers will definitely recognize these features as ones long awaited. If you take time to learn the features well, you should benefit from increased productivity.

Creating and Editing SQL Server Stored Procedures

In addition to the debugging facilities provided, Visual Studio 97 allows you to create new stored procedures or edit existing ones from within the Microsoft Developer Studio IDE. Data View provides a graphical hierarchy of all database objects for the database related to the data source you have in your project.

To create a new stored procedure, follow these steps:

1. Right-click the Stored Procedure folder.
2. Select New Stored Procedure from the pop-up menu to bring up a code page with a simple `Create Procedure` statement already entered (see Figure 3.11). You need to add a name for your procedure on the procedure name placeholder.

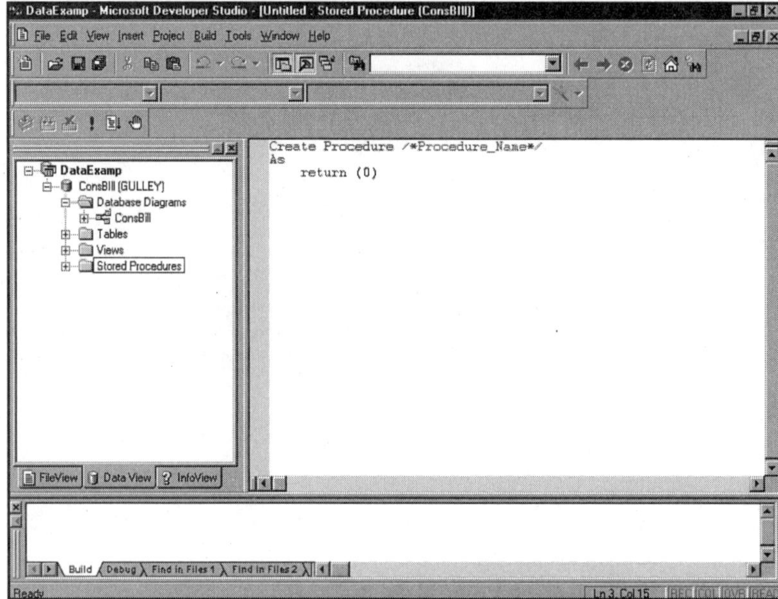

FIG. 3.11
Stored procedures are written by using the Visual Studio source editor.

3. Add any necessary input parameters and begin entering any necessary declare statements for local variables. A simple return statement is added for you, but you'll need to develop any serious error-handling or output parameters.

   As you enter procedure code, notice that SQL keywords are blue and your own identifiers are black. These simple but effective visual indicators are great debugging tools for anyone familiar with developing procedures with the old tool sets. It's pretty easy to notice an error in a keyword when it's not the appropriate color. When everything is black text on white, subtle errors are almost impossible to see.

TIP As you write your procedure code, having a printed copy of your data model close by is often handy so you can look up identifier name spellings, data types, and table keys and indexes. Or, you can use the Data View explorer from within the same IDE to explore the properties of tables and columns as you write your procedures.

After you enter your procedure code, compile it into the SQL Server database. One of the more common errors you might run into is that objects referenced by the procedure aren't already in the database. With the Data View Explorer just a mouse click away, you can quickly inspect referenced objects and pick out misspellings or invalid datatypes from your procedure code.

4. To run a stored procedure after you develop it, just right-click the procedure code window. As shown in Figure 3.12, you can run the procedure (which, for a new procedure, means compiling it) or debug it. Either selection submits the procedure to the SQL Server for compilation and error checking.

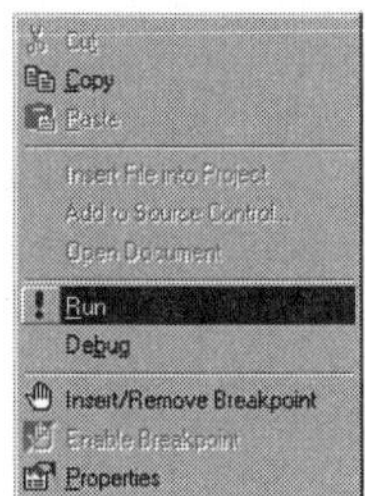

FIG. 3.12 The context menu available by right-clicking within the Developer Studio Code window allows you to run or debug your stored procedure.

5. After the procedure is compiled, the application prompts you to enter any input parameter values and run the procedure. Resultsets and other SQL Server output (such as rowcounts) and any error conditions are displayed in the output window along the bottom of the IDE (see Figure 3.13).

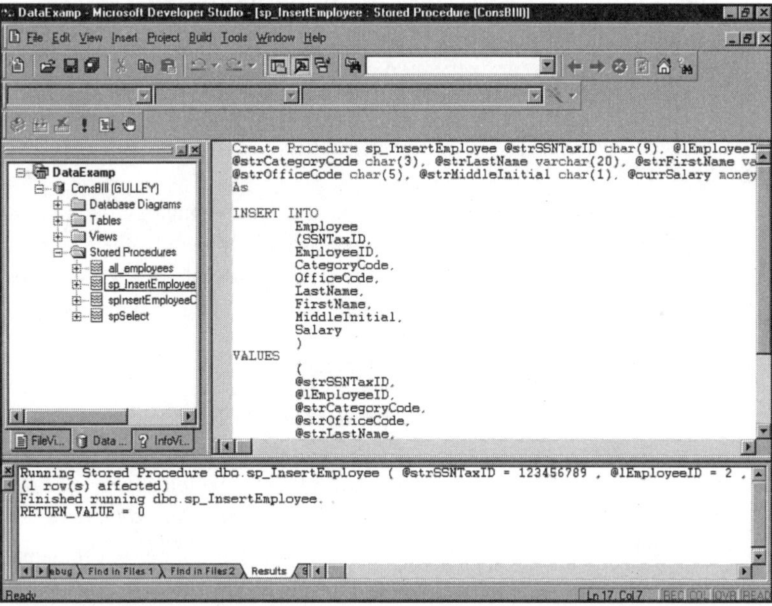

FIG. 3.13 Stored procedure output varies according to the statements and parameters of your procedure itself. In this case, the return value indicates success in the insert of the employee record.

After your procedure is successfully compiled and run, notice that it's added to the Data View hierarchy. It's also ready to be debugged, which you can do either during your application debugging inline with application code, or from the code window by right-clicking the procedure code window and selecting Debug from the pop-up menu.

As you can see, Visual Studio 97 has added some great SQL Server database design and development tools to the CS developer's toolkit. With a little work and experimentation, you should become a more productive database developer with these tools.

Distributed Computing: An Overview

Today's systems are often a mix of architectures and technologies. What most of them have in common is that they're of a distributed nature. A *distributed system* is a dynamic collection of computers linked by a network, running software designed to provide an integrated computing environment to users. Distributed systems can range from single-purpose applications that support business processes to full-service computing facilities that service a broad range of users with a broad range of resources.

Given these complex tasks, a distributed system must be designed and developed in levels of abstraction or architectures. Two main design paradigms have emerged to support distributed architectures:

- Client/server computing
- Multiple-tier architectures

The following sections will help you understand what client/server and multiple-tier architectures are and how Visual Studio 97 helps in the development of distributed systems. You'll also gain an understanding of how the Internet and intranets (I-nets) are just extensions or alternate design paths for distributed computing, which sit on top of the CS and multitier architectural foundations.

Client/Server Computing

CS computing is at the heart of the Information Technology (IT) industry today. As organizations have moved from a centralized computing environment to client/server, the very description of client/server computing continues to evolve. Generally speaking, client/server computing is the splitting of processes into two or more parts, the client and the server:

- The *client* is the requestor of services in the CS mix. The best example of client processing is today's GUI interfaces. Most business systems development projects have as a chief component the development of a GUI to accept user input and interface with server-side processes for persistent data support, process-intensive tasks, or retrieval of server-managed data. This requesting role often allows the tag *user services* to be attached to the processing that takes place on the client end of the CS mix.
- The *server* is on the receiving end of this mix. The server accepts client requests for processing or data retrieval. This processing usually involves enforcement of business-rule logic, provision of an interface to a persistent data store such as a relational database server, or communications with other resource managers to fulfill the client's request.

The server is often labeled as the "business services" or "data services" layer in the CS mix.

As shown in Figure 3.14, function calls implement communication between the client and the server. The client component calls a server function. The client passes parameters (param) to the server function arguments (args). The server processes the request and then returns success/failure codes or provides requested data. The client in turn receives the return from the server and acts on any errors, returns success to its client application, or displays data back to users.

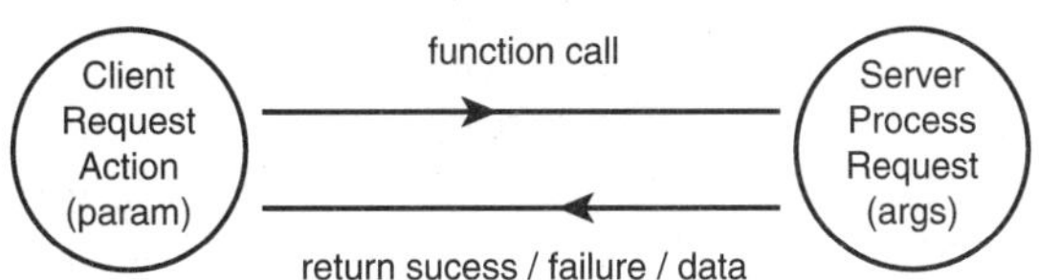

FIG. 3.14
In the client/server mix, two processes cooperate to perform a system service. One (the client) invokes a function, which takes arguments (args) by passing parameters to the server process.

To facilitate communication between the client and server across a network, client components must be able to locate and invoke functions on server components. They must also be able to map parameter values to native datatypes. Different machine architectures require that this interprocess communication be able to marshal or translate data from one architecture to another to provide for correct parameter value representation on the client and server.

In reality, any component in a CS environment can act as a server and a client. Often, a component might act as a client to other servers and as a server to other clients. These client and server components can exist within the context of a single machine, but they usually operate in a multiuser environment (see Figure 3.15).

Figure 3.15 shows a typical distributed system. Users are connected to a local network and share network resources, such as file and print services. Applications share data from an RDBMS. Modern business systems increasingly extend this local distributed model by integrating web and other Internet access with the local resources, as well as opening up access to external networks for geographically separated business units or for integration with customer or supplier systems. This orchestration of disparate components and resources creates unique design issues and goals, which you must address in the distributed system.

Client/Server Design

Distributed CS components have unique issues and goals, which must be addressed in their design. Some of these goals and issues are

- Support for resource sharing
- Concurrent processing
- Scalable processing

- Openness
- Fault tolerance
- Transparency

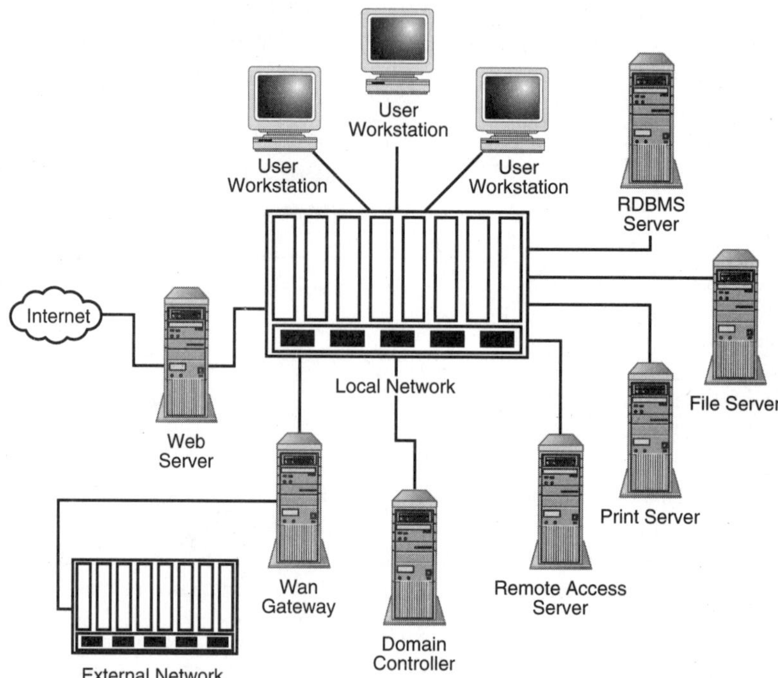

FIG. 3.15
In the simple distributed system model, clients (workstations) request services and resources from network servers hosting services such as file and print and database services.

Some of the earliest implementations of distributed systems included sharing of print and file services on a local network. Most network operating systems provide for this level of resource sharing by providing such services as standard naming, location directory, and file-handling functions. More recent developments in resource sharing include opening up resources beyond the local boundaries, wide area network (WAN) integration and access to enterprise data, and I-net and remote users.

With the opening up of local networks in distributed computing, concurrent processing and scalability issues increase in importance. *Concurrency* indicates the need for multiple users or user processes to request the same services and the need for server processes to execute in parallel to fulfill all requests in an efficient manner. *Scalability* is concerned with the ability of resource managers to service multiple requests simultaneously on an increasingly more frequent basis as larger numbers of users or clients are added to a distributed system.

Openness as a design goal is the capability of a distributed system to remain extensible across disparate user platforms and components. This requirement often requires resources to operate over multiple protocols and provide standard access facilities. The rapid acceptance of standards for database access—such as a common interface for RDBMS servers in the form of the SQL language—is a good example of openness across distributed systems.

Fault tolerance is the capability of systems to recover from failure. Distributed systems must provide hardware redundancy and software recovery features to provide a fault-tolerant environment. Fault tolerance is also related to the capability of a distributed system to provide the necessary high availability of shared resources. Very few businesses could operate without a high degree of systems availability, a need increased by the interrelated demands of a distributed system.

Transparency in distributed systems is the distributed environment's capability to isolate users from the complexities of the distributed implementation. Users shouldn't need to concern themselves with how data is accessed across local or wide area environments. For maximum productivity and efficiency, the distributed system needs to have the appearance of a single system to the user. Transparency is also an important abstraction technique for developers. Developers shouldn't need to know implementation details of shared resource managers, but should be provided with standard interfaces to integrate their components with others.

Distributed CS Technologies in Visual Studio 97

Visual Studio 97 provides many tools and development technologies to support the requirements of distributed CS systems. In this section, you'll see how the technologies and tools in Visual Studio 97 support the development of systems that support the major design issues and goals.

With Visual Studio 97, you can design and develop distributed client/server systems by taking advantage of standard integrated tools and technologies. Visual Studio 97 supports the following:

- Concurrency and scalability, which are supported with COM and DCOM and allow you to take advantage of MTS and RDBMS through standard ODBC interfaces.
- Openness, which is provided through the use of ODBC and OLE DB as a standard interface to data providers. COM and DCOM act as an open interprocess communication mechanism to allow client and server processes to communicate in a distributed environment.
- Fault tolerance, which is provided with the integration of technologies within the operating system and SQL Server engine and with transaction capabilities built into MTS. SMP support for multithreaded applications also provides process-level fault tolerance.
- Transparency, which is provided through the use of object-oriented language features of the development languages included in Visual Studio 97. VB and VC++ provide for COM and DCOM support in isolating developers from external implementations.
- Resource sharing, which is directly supported for the development team by the inclusion of Visual SourceSafe as a team development tool for managing the version control and configuration management of source code. SQL Server is also a major player in the

resource-sharing requirements. Data-access technologies allow you to build a common database for multiple applications built with different application development tools so that they can access the database and interface with common procedures and business logic services.

Multiple-Tier Architectures

One concept that seeks to address some of the major issues involved in the design of distributed systems is multiple-tier architectures. A *multiple-tier architecture* is an abstraction of processes into distributed objects or components that communicate across multiple machines in a networked environment.

Partitioning Components in Multiple-Tier Architectures

The partitioning of components can be logical or physical. Logically partitioned tiers consists of two or more processes—such as a GUI application and a shared object library DLL—cooperating to fulfill user requests. The processes are located on and execute on the same machine in a logical partition. Logically partitioned applications have many advantages, not the least of which is the capability to change the implementation of components internally without affecting component users. As long as a component's interface remains the same, component developers are free to change or optimize the internal workings of components.

Physically partitioned tiers meet the same definition, but the processes are executed on different machines. A typical example of a physically partitioned tier is a direct link between a Data Entry GUI application and the RDBMS to which it directs transactions to on a networked database server. The server-side logic executes within the RDBMS server through the use of stored triggers or procedures for business rule logic and data validation. Well-designed server procedures provide a well-planned interface for applications to request data services from the RDBMS.

Beyond the two-tier model, multiple-tier systems can exist with many complex structures. Figure 3.16 shows a common three-tier configuration. Additions to this three-tier model are common. The main source of additional tiers comes in the form of specialized "middleware," a component or components that provide program-to-program or program-to-data communication.

Program-to-program communication is the concept of two processes—the client and the server—communicating across a network. The calling of remote functions on server components involves program-to-program communication. Program-to-data communication deals with the use of interface APIs on data stores such as SQL Server. The SQL language enables program communication to access persistent data storage. Open Database Connectivity (ODBC) is an example of middleware implemented in the Windows environment. ODBC allows client applications (or middle-tier business objects) to communicate with an ODBC-compatible data source via SQL.

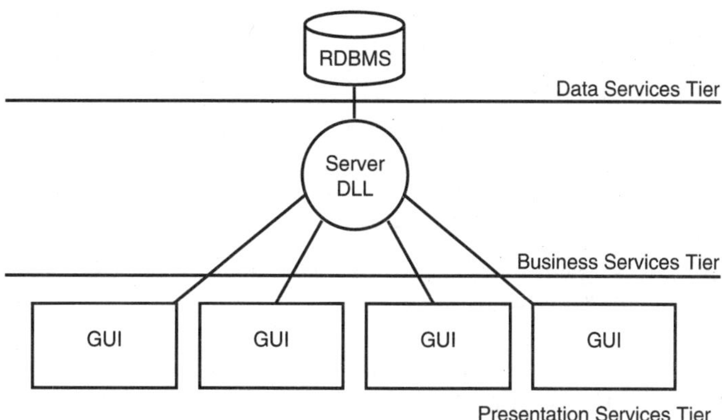

FIG. 3.16
Multiple-tier architectures come in a variety of different configurations.

In the three-tier model shown in Figure 3.16, you see the architecture typically intended when developers discuss multitier architectures. With this three-tier model, a clear distinction exists over the types of processes handled by each tier. The GUI application is responsible for interacting with users. Typical requirements at the presentation tier are to

- Allow your users to enter and edit data
- Perform analytical functions against data retrieved from the data services tier
- Create reports from data retrieved from the data services tier

The business services tier often serves many functions. In the preceding model, it would typically be responsible for

- Providing data validation and business-rule enforcement over data going to and from the data services tier
- Maintaining connections to the database
- Providing for concurrent processing of multi-user requests against the database
- Providing user connections on a one-for-one basis or include complex resource-pooling services

The middle tier must also provide transaction control. *Transaction control* is usually a cooperative process between the business services and data services tiers. A business component provides for transaction control by using the RDBMS transaction commit and rollback protocols against changed data. If the business component doesn't get to complete a transaction with the RDBMS before losing the client connection, it might have to roll back any data changes made on the RDBMS. Likewise, the business component must provide for data commits to take place after a transaction is completed successfully and client feedback is provided.

The data services tier in the preceding model is typically represented by a standard RDBMS. The RDBMS provides for several interfaces, which the middle-tier components can use to maintain a connection to the RDBMS server and to provide for data-manipulation functions. The key requirement at this level is standard interfaces to allow SQL calls to be made to the RDBMS server.

Multiple-tier architectures build on the client/server computing model by providing for the communication of components at different tiers through the normal client/server model. You've seen how components interact in the three-tier model. Other numbers of tiers may also be found in client/server systems. Systems using more than three physical or logical tiers are usually doing so for load-balancing purposes. Rather than have all middle-tier software components on one middle-tier application server, they may have some components on one application server and others on other servers. You can also use multiple middle-tier application servers run the same middle-tier components and better balance the load among many users in high-volume systems.

NOTE The middle-tier components often act as client *and* server. Server behavior is necessary when handling the request for validation from the GUI, and client behavior when executing the SQL request from the database server.

Why multiple-tier architectures? This question is perhaps one of the hardest to answer when it comes to distributed computing. It's better to ask what advantages are gained by going with distributed computing.

Multiple-tier architectures can allow for the processing of computing tasks to take place where it's best used. Users have gained processing power on their desktops and are gaining the know-how to take advantage of it. Applications designed to take advantage of client computing power can distribute loads across networks to scale processing requirements. The presentation processes are moved off the server to better enable cheaper servers to handle the same load.

Middle-tier business components allow errors to be corrected and rules to be enforced before they're passed to database servers. These types of middle-tier components allow fewer erroneous transactions to consume database resources and enable the resources to better serve good ones. By distributing this logic to other machines on the network for all users to share, business-rule enforcement can be better designed to remain common among several applications, thus providing a more stable enterprise architecture for computing.

Placing the data services tier on a separate database server enables much better availability and fault tolerance in distributed systems. The database server can handle a higher transaction load if it doesn't also have to handle file and print services. It will also be highly unlikely that failures in one machine will migrate to other machines. This capability to isolate system failure to components on different machines is a great strength in distributed computing.

In extremely high-volume data or transaction environments, the data services and business tiers can themselves be replicated to other servers and act as mirror processes either to serve large numbers of users or to support the geographical separation of users. The failure of one process isn't likely to cause the failure of another, thereby ensuring application availability to at least a portion of the user community.

Designing Multiple-Tier Architectures

The main goal in designing multitier systems is to provide for scalability. Scalability across large-scale networking or internetworking environments often brings many more issues to deal with as a developer than process-intensive client two-tier applications. In the two-tier model, the database does most of the work. Application front ends make direct database SQL calls and handle all the business logic with process-intensive client applications or database procedures.

The burden for scalability is on the database. The maximum number of user connections or the number of transactions the system can handle is up to the database server. Client applications in two-tier models support one user and have little to do with system performance. Performance is a database issue.

With the design of multitier applications, more and more pressure is on the middle tier to handle scalability to a certain extent. Following is a list of additional requirements for the middle tier:

- Management of connectivity with the database for multiple clients
- Security
- Performance
- Scalability
- System availability
- Allocation of workload to allow multiple simultaneous users to perform system functions and access data
- Authentication of user requests
- Optimization of database and network access
- Handling failures of server resources and client applications to ensure that data in process is left in a consistent state

With the requirements that come with multitier systems, the level of complexity involved in developing multitier applications increases. Applications developers must become more familiar with lower-level functions on local and network operating systems. The margin for error also decreases as multitier systems scale to enterprisewide mission-critical applications.

Designing Multiple-Tier Architectures with Visual Studio 97

Visual Studio 97 provides technologies and tools to deal with the complexity of multitier applications. One of the more visible additions to Visual Studio 97 is Microsoft Transaction Server (MTS). MTS simplifies multitier application development by providing much of the infrastructure development preassembled, thus freeing you to concentrate on the business logic of your multitier system.

In addition to providing the transaction-processing functions implied by its name, MTS provides much of the infrastructure processing requirements necessary with multitier applications. MTS takes over the control of the middle tier, taking advantage of Microsoft's Component Object Model (COM) and ActiveX technology. COM provides the glue that enables remote connectivity, interface specifications, and communication mechanisms for networked, distributed components.

MTS takes advantage of COM and ActiveX technology by providing directory services for clients to locate server components and by providing messaging constructs to pass data between application components. The developer is isolated from the details of distributed component communication and just references the appropriate server code. Server code is referenced by instantiating the appropriate server component libraries in the client application. The rest is treated just like local procedure calls.

The directory services that allow COM and ActiveX components to be located and resolved are implemented by the Registry in Windows 95 and Windows NT. Appropriate naming and class lookup routines allow for the registering of process IDs for server components that any client can reference. As the developer, you don't need to worry about these details, but you do need to become familiar with appropriately referencing and calling server components.

MTS also provides Windows NT-level security for multitier applications. MTS extends Windows NT's user- and group-based login permission structures to accommodate the implementation of access control over the public interfaces of COM and ActiveX components. You also can extend MTS security.

MTS provides many features for managing performance and scalability in distributed systems. Specifically, MTS provides thread and process management, maintains database connection pools, and provides support for distributed COM (DCOM).

MTS components provide a thread pool for middle-tier components. When a request is made of a middle-tier ActiveX component, MTS allocates a thread. It then uses that thread to communicate with the ActiveX component, and takes care of deallocating the thread when the process completes. To gain true scalability, you would have to write all this process and thread code yourself. MTS takes this work away from you and allows you to concentrate on more critical business logic in satisfying user demands, which translates into more scalability with less effort on your part.

MTS frees database resources for more scalable solutions by maintaining a similar pool of preconnected database connections. This alleviates the overhead of establishing and de-establishing database connections on a one-for-one basis in response to every data request. As clients are idle, connections can be reassigned to handle other requests—definitely an improvement in resource usage. Again, you're free from having to code your application to handle the complexity of connection pooling for scalability.

MTS can also distribute database transactions across SQL Servers, which is helpful if you need to update more than one database in a single transaction and maintain data integrity with transaction control. MTS does this by providing a common interface to address multiple SQL Servers or resource managers via Microsoft's Distributed Transaction Coordinator (DTC). A resource manager can be any ODBC-compliant relational database.

As you can see in Figure 3.17, MTS doesn't change the look of the multitier model much, but it does provide less complexity for application developers and some basic services that address the design issues involved with multitier architecture design. You're shielded from the complexity of implementing infrastructure-type software components for such tasks as security, transaction control, remote component resolution and location, database connection pooling, and multithreaded control over processes.

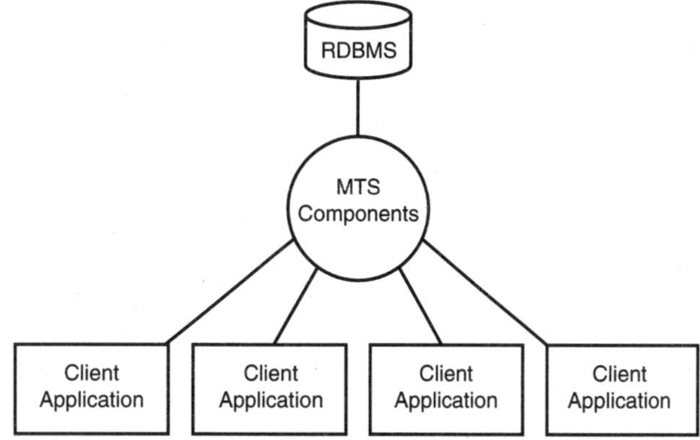

FIG. 3.17
This example of a multitier architecture using Microsoft Transaction Server illustrates the typical multitier model.

I-net Environments and Distributed Computing

With the advent of Internet/intranet (I-net) computing, the development world seems to have been taken by surprise. What is I-net and how does it mix with modern distributed computing? How do developers leverage their experience with CS and multitier development to take advantage of I-net as a computing environment? The following sections answer some of these questions and show how your experience in CS development can be leveraged for I-net development.

What Is an Internet/Intranet Environment?

The *Internet* is a large network of networks. Relatively unmanaged, the Internet is a collection of networks, internetworked together to provide for rapid communication and data sharing over a geographically dispersed area. Today, that geographical area just happens to be nearly the entire computing world. It's safe to say that millions of computers are linked via the Internet, and millions of users are taking advantage of the computing resources made available by the Internet.

An *intranet* is an internal network of a common organization, usually a business or government group, used to share information and facilitate communication among users. Intranets also may be geographically dispersed and vary from the Internet in that only specified users or networks are allowed access. Intranets are distinguished from other internal network systems by their reliance on a Hypertext Transport Protocol (HTTP) or "web–based" application user interface.

Combined, the I-net represents one of the fastest areas of growth today in computing resources and in the development of business systems. Unfortunately, with this growth come even more design issues and questions that must addressed when developing I-net–enabled applications.

When most people think of I-net, the World Wide Web (the web) comes to mind. The web is a client/server-based technology that allows users to access a seemingly endless variety of information from I-nets. The web uses HTTP to request information or services from a web server. Other I-net services implemented as interface protocols are File Transfer Protocol (FTP), used to browse remote file storage and save or retrieve files from remote computers; Telnet, a protocol used to remotely perform processing on a remote computer; and many other protocols for retrieving, sending, or manipulating digital data or processing power on a remote computer.

Most of the Internet-related press today focuses on software developers creating protocols responsible for the transmission of digital information in every form. Java and ActiveX implement a transmission and execution environment for applets and components across I-net environments. Other technologies are concerned with such information services as digitized audio and video.

It's important for you, the developer, to understand that the real action is on the server. As with any other client/server environment, the Internet must provide for scalable performance, standard information access (not just relational data), fault tolerance, and security.

With the cross-platform requirements placed on web browsers, many of these mission-critical requirements must be handled by the server. With I-net applications potentially being required to scale to many thousands of users, handling these issues on the server is perhaps the only answer.

Typically, the client or browser in an I-net environment must only interpret a data stream through the use of a protocol and display the data in the correct format. The server, however, must be able to field requests from potentially thousands of users for a wide variety of information represented by a wide range of media. Text-type data from databases, images from file systems and databases, and other digital multimedia information from a variety of sources must be handled in a responsive manner by the server.

Figure 3.18 shows a typical I-net application architecture. As with any client/server system, I-nets must take advantage of multiple tiers, even more so with the demands for performance and scalability across sometimes unproven network bandwidth.

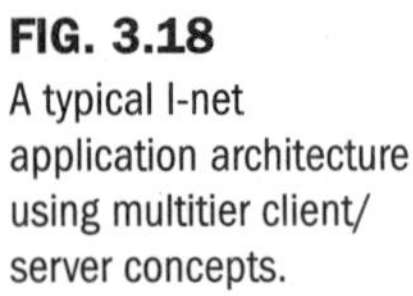

FIG. 3.18
A typical I-net application architecture using multitier client/server concepts.

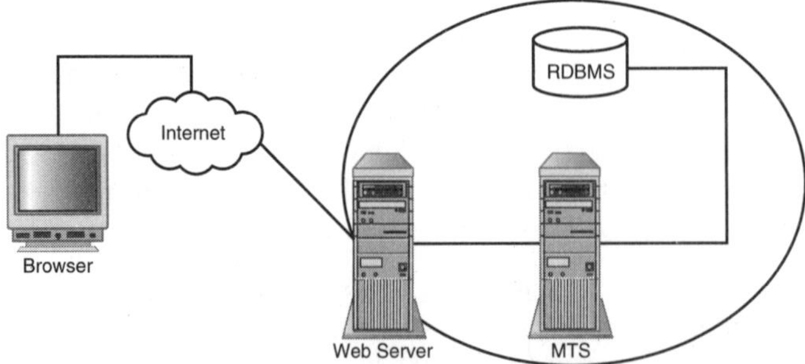

When the Internet and the web took us all by storm, most of us were just getting into multiple-tier architectures. A closer look at what an I-net application is and how it works will show you that you can use what you already know for I-net development.

In Figure 3.18, the client application (GUI) has been replaced by a web browser. Web browsers, at their simplest, translate Hypertext Markup Language (HTML) pages requested from a web server and display their contents. Most of you have seen this at work. Some browsers also provide an execution environment for language-code execution (for example, a Java virtual machine for hosting runtime support for applets to execute on any platform). Others provide plug-in support for any number of non-standard protocols used to transmit and display or play all types of multimedia content.

I-net applications are beginning to move beyond the static content popular in the beginning. Corporate IS staffs are being asked to I-net–enable existing applications for broader availability across a broader user base. With the need to open up enterprise data stores and provide legacy system functionality to I-net users, a good solid architecture must be in place. Multitier architectures can be and are being used successfully to provide data access and application functionality via I-net protocols.

With I-net applications, you don't have to retool your servers and throw out your components. With multitier architectures, you can just add the browser as another data user in the client/server mix. With standards, you can allow your HTML pages to interact with server components to provide database access and other server functions. Common business object middleware still can be used to validate data entered by a remote I-net user. Often, the same code used to develop your GUI can be reused in the development of I-net applications implemented on the browser.

At the site **http://www.gasullivan.com/vs97book**, you'll see an example of common middle-tier objects serving a traditional client/server application and a more modern Active Server Pages (ASP) front end from a SQL Server. Both front-end applications will use the same ActiveX control for client-side processing—proof that multitier architectures, when properly implemented, can provide flexible, distributed solutions.

Visual Studio 97 and I-net

Visual Studio 97 brings I-net application development into the mainstream. In a typical I-net application, the browser downloads a static HTML document. That browser must support any HTML contained in the document, including any required scripting or unique display rules for the hypertext. One challenge in developing I-net applications this way is making sure that your HTML document can support the widest range of browser features. This is becoming increasingly impossible as vendors rush to add new features to their browsers, and the technology is moving faster than standards can be adopted.

For developers who want to serve as large a user base as possible, this war of browser features can be bewildering and confusing as to the latest standard for tables or another HTML content type. With ASP and Internet Information Server 3.0, Microsoft seems to have solved the browser feature problem by moving the main intelligence in I-net development to the server. (More detailed information concerning ASP and IIS 3.0 can be found in Chapter 13, "An Inside Look at Active Server Pages and Internet Information Server.")

IIS 3.0 supports server-side scripting of HTML for dynamic content generation at access time. ASP is the name of the technology that allows you to develop active HTML components on the server to execute any required code before streaming HTML to the client. ASP remains compatible with almost all browsers, even text-based ones. The dynamic content is interpreted on the server before being pushed to the requesting client. ASP is distinguished from Dynamic HTML in that it's interpreted and generated on the server rather than something that the client web browser must support. Chapter 18, "Dynamic HTML," provides more information about Dynamic HTML.

Before ASP, if you needed to enhance your web site to display enhanced graphics or text, there was no good way of doing it that would be supported by every browser. Now with ASP, you can run scripts on the server to handle the nuances of your special requirements and send the resulting HTML to the browser. With client-side scripting, you can provide dynamic web sites that interact with your users.

The technology behind ASP is simple. You embed scripts inside HTML documents, which in turn are executed by IIS whenever a request is made for that document. The server then generates HTML, based on criteria between the user session and the script included on the page. With IIS 3.0, you can develop Active Server Pages with JScript or VBScript—another opportunity to leverage your existing development knowledge.

From Here...

In this chapter, you learned about the importance of good database design and how it affects the effectiveness of your application development projects. You learned how to use the tools provided in Visual Studio 97 to help design databases, and got an overview of distributed computing and multitier architectures.

For more information on the topics covered in this chapter, see the following chapters:

- To learn more about object-oriented development and the tools Microsoft has developed to enable application development in the enterprise, see Chapter 4, "Using Microsoft's Object Technologies."
- For further insight into the use of ActiveX components, see Chapter 8, "Using ActiveX Client Components in an I-net Environment."
- For further information on developing applications for I-net environments, see Chapter 11, "An Inside Look at Web-Based Applications."
- To explore the creation capabilities of Visual InterDev, see Chapter 14, "Developing Active Content with Visual InterDev."
- To obtain additional information on distributed applications, see Chapter 17, "Server-Side Programming in an I-net Environment."

PART II

Creating Controls and Components for Reuse

CHAPTER 4

Using Microsoft's Object Technologies

by Cameron K. Beattie

In the early days of personal computing, programmers diligently wrote procedural code to create character-based PC applications, knowing that individual users would run separate copies of the program on their own machines. Programmers rarely needed to be concerned about how a program would communicate with other code running on the local machine, let alone worry about how their program would interact with other programs running on a remote machine.

Times change quickly. Today, the computing power available from a typical desktop computer can well exceed the computing power of room-size computers of the early days. It's now commonplace for Internet-enabled computers to browse data from hundreds of thousands of computers interconnected around the globe. Now that computers can readily connect to each other, programmers need the tools and a unified architecture that allows them to write modular programs to communicate in a standard, organized fashion. Object technology provides the power to deliver this functionality, and Visual Studio 97 gives you powerful tools to implement it. This chapter gives you a broad overview of the object technology foundation Microsoft has made available to you for developing Windows applications with Visual Studio.

Object technology basics

Gain a basic understanding of the terms and concepts behind object-oriented programming (OOP) and learn about current technologies used to implement OOP.

The roots of Microsoft's object technologies

See where Microsoft's object technology came from, where it is today, and what's planned for tomorrow.

Selecting an object model

See where Microsoft's object technologies fit in today. Examine the competition, and know what factors are important when selecting an object model for your projects.

COM architecture basics

Get a language-neutral overview of some of the most important elements of Microsoft's Component Object Model (COM) and the objects you can create with it.

Network objects that use Java technologies

Gain an understanding of the strengths and weaknesses of Java, the latest I-net technology phenomenon.

Practical strategies for implementing COM objects

Explore procedures and techniques for implementing and integrating objects with legacy applications, new applications, and I-net applications.

Object technologies need an underlying framework that can allow complex and interrelated programs to work together in harmony. The object architecture that Microsoft created—called the Component Object Model or simply COM—is the foundation underlying OLE and ActiveX technologies and is Microsoft's solution for providing object-to-object communication. With the enhancements of the Distributed Component Object Model (DCOM), this technology even provides communication services across networks to objects physically located on different machines. ■

Object Technology Basics

No matter which Visual Studio programming language you select for your projects, a basic understanding of COM, OLE, and ActiveX is vital for your success. You can still use Visual Studio programming languages to create procedural code, and sometimes that's necessary and appropriate, but doing so can limit the benefits of using an object-oriented design. This chapter focuses on object-oriented foundations shared by all the Visual Studio development languages, and subsequent chapters in this book provide detailed implementation strategies specific to each language.

Benefits of Object-Oriented Programming

Users of custom corporate computer applications continue to demand more functionality from their aging systems, and they're becoming less patient about waiting for new functions to be implemented. Because legacy computer systems tend to be monolithic collections of original code, maintenance code, integration code, and lingering "quick-fix" code, these applications have become dramatically more difficult and costly to maintain. Changing key sections of these fragile constructions to add new features is fraught with peril, especially if these applications are part of a mission-critical system. To make matters worse, such applications might be documented only sparsely (if at all), and only rarely are any members of the original programming team still working for the company. If you've ever been faced with the task of extending the life of such an application, you know there must be a better way to build and maintain enterprise-wide computer systems. Fortunately, there is.

Suppose that your company, like many companies, has a legacy application that might give unpredictable results for dates beyond the year 1999. Suppose that rather than be a single massive collection of procedural code, this application was built from functional modules. Each module has a very specific purpose, and calling that module is the only way for the application to perform that specific task. Thus, in this scenario, one dedicated code module has the task of performing all date calculations, and any other module in the entire application relies on that module for any and all date calculations. To test this program's capability to handle dates beyond the year 2000, you have to test only that date-calculation module to see what happens. If it needs repair, you can change the implementation inside that module, test it, and then plug it back into the program to complete your task. If the date storage and retrieval module also poses a problem, you can use a similar procedure to test, repair, and restore that module. Instead of this scenario, however, most companies are paying staggering costs to update hundreds of thousands of lines of legacy code, in some cases line by line.

With the pace of change in today's business world, companies can no longer afford to create systems that can't be updated easily. This modular approach is available now, and you can implement it today by using the programming tools in Visual Studio.

These magic little modules are known abstractly as *objects*. You can implement computer-modeled objects in software as discrete components that you can create, modify, or reuse as building blocks for complex, enterprisewide applications. Rebuilding existing functionality from scratch is admittedly quite costly and time-consuming. After the foundation is in place, however, you no longer have to start over repeatedly from scratch to create each new application, because a large portion of your desired functionality can be constructed from previously built components.

Imagine how long it would take for new computers to be developed if computer hardware manufacturers had to start from scratch every time they wanted to build a new computer. Many of the components of a new computer don't require changes since the last model was released, so existing components (such as power supply, video card, network interface card, or modem) are simply reused. Eventually, when new designs are implemented, the new item can easily replace the previous model, with perhaps a modification of that particular interface but without having to redesign the entire computer.

After the computer is sold to a user, upgrading a component is also simplified by this modular approach. Suppose that you want to upgrade to a faster modem. You can select your new modem from a variety of vendors, and any modem supported by your operating system will work just fine. You don't need to worry whether the modem will work, because modems have become a commodity with standard interfaces and communication protocols.

Software developers now seek the tremendous advantages of component architecture that hardware developers have enjoyed for years. By using component-based software architectures, you can implement object-oriented designs yet maintain a large degree of language neutrality. This way, corporations can use existing programming talent in any language supported by the object model implemented on their computer platforms. This language neutrality is accomplished by using programming tools that create components compatible at the binary level. This process allows programmers around the globe to independently develop components or entire applications that will properly communicate together, as long as the interfaces defined between them remain consistent. These components might originally be created for internal applications, but they can then be shared within the company or even marketed to other companies with similar needs.

If you aren't already familiar with object-oriented programming, you likely need to invest some time to learn how to implement this new technology effectively. The effort you spend now to become proficient with this technology will reward you with increased productivity, job satisfaction, and job security.

After your development team invests the initial time and energy required to implement object-oriented development, the advantages to your company are also worth noting:

- You can reuse many of the objects representing standard business functions, reducing the time required to build new programs and the overall cost of maintaining them.

- When maintenance is required, you can easily replace older versions of individual objects with new versions without breaking the application.
- As needs change, you can relocate new objects transparently to new platforms and even to other computers across the network, still without breaking the applications.
- Large and complex programming projects that would seem nearly impossible with other techniques can now be conquered much more easily.
- The time and expense required to integrate existing applications with new applications and to perform emergency repairs on applications will gradually decline as more objects are implemented.
- The recovered programmer hours can be redirected toward backlogged projects and new initiatives.

You might be wondering if your favorite programming language can support object-based application development. A major benefit of COM is that it defines a common binary standard. This means that COM defines an interface as a low-level binary API based on a table of memory pointers, which then allows code modules from different COM-compliant compilers to operate together. Theoretically, you can build a COM-compatible compiler for any programming language that can create memory structures by using pointers and can call functions through pointers. Within Visual Studio, Visual C++ and Visual Basic both include COM-compatible compilers.

The result for Visual Studio users is that client objects implemented in Visual Basic can call on the services of server objects written Visual C++, and vice versa. Each language has certain advantages when creating COM objects, but when used together, they are a powerful combination with which you can tackle nearly any programming challenge you encounter.

A Quick Review of Object-Oriented Programming Terms and Notation

Object-oriented programming (OOP) presents a revolutionary improvement in the architecture and tools used to build and maintain computer applications. You can choose from various object-oriented methodologies, and most are named after the individuals who proposed them. If you want to investigate them in detail, today's leading object-oriented methodologies include Booch, Coad-Yourdon, Jacobsen, Martin-Odell, Rumbaugh, Shalaer-Mellor, and Wirfs-Brock. Despite this wide variety of methodologies, the underlying OOP concepts are essentially the same. To preclude any confusion over the meaning of the OOP terms used in this book, the following sections give you a brief review of common terms and notation used in object-oriented programming.

Objects You can think of an OOP *object* as a programming entity that in many ways resembles a physical object. OOP objects typically have properties that describe their attributes and methods that specify their behavior. Properties of OOP objects can be much like properties of physical objects, describing attributes such as color, cost, or size. You can set and lock these properties when designing the program, or you can make them available to users to change during runtime. Methods are the named functions or actions that an object is programmed to accomplish when called. Methods are invoked by referencing the object and the method's name. When called, the object behaves as defined by the method to obtain, manipulate, or destroy program data, without any requirement to reveal how these tasks are accomplished.

Objects are *portable*, which is to say that they can be used without modification in any environment where they're supported. Objects are *reusable*, because you can use the same object to perform the same task in different programs. Better yet, you can use objects other people have created if you want to quickly add a standard service or function to one of your own programming projects.

For the purpose of object-oriented programming, an individual object is a particular *instance* created from a particular *class* of objects. A *class* is a set of objects that you define to have the same attributes and behavior. Classes can be very specific or very general, depending on your needs. For example, you could define a class that encompasses all writing implements, or you could define a class that represents only wooden yellow pencils with No. 2 lead. The *class structure* defines a generic blueprint or model of a new object of that class. Every OOP object belongs to a class and is completely defined by its class structure. To actually bring an object to life in the computer, a specific *instance* of the object must be *instantiated*, which means that a new member of the class is created in memory.

▶ **See** "Objects," **p. 756**

When you define a class in code, you must define all the object's methods, data structures, and interfaces. By default, the methods and data are reserved for the object's exclusive use and are declared as *private*. If you want to make methods and data available for direct manipulation by other objects, you can declare them as *public* when you define them in the class structure. Typically, you would define any methods and data you want exposed for clients or used by the user interface as public, and define the internal elements that implement those services as private.

NOTE C++ programmers have been programming with object classes for years, but the class structure is a relatively new addition to Visual Basic. Support for object classes began with Visual Basic 4 and is further expanded in Visual Basic 5. As more wizards, integration options, and powerful C++ features (such as classes) have been added to Visual Basic, the stigma against using early versions of VB for anything but simple projects has vanished. Visual Basic is now quite suitable for creating robust and reliable enterprisewide applications. ■

OOP purists remind us that for an object to qualify as a "true" OOP object, it must support the characteristics of encapsulation, polymorphism, and inheritance. These distinctions are discussed in detail later in the section "OOP Advanced Topics."

An object that provides services to another object is acting as a *server*. The object using those services is referred to as the *client*. An object can be a client and a server at the same time—that is, it can request the services of one object while providing services to yet another object. For clarity, it's usually best to focus on a single relationship between two objects at a time, and denote one as the client and the other as the server.

Object Relationships When you're trying to design objects, it's handy to have a common method for representing these programming objects graphically. You can use the syntax `object.method` to denote invoking a particular method of the server object. There are many variations, but Figure 4.1 shows the typical way to represent an object graphically.

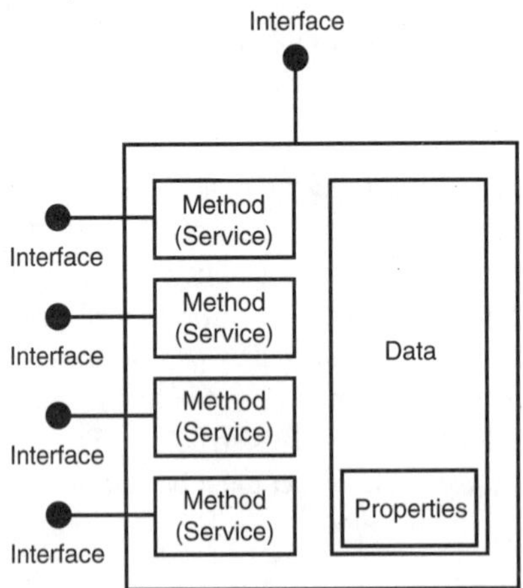

FIG. 4.1
A COM object contains all the methods, properties, and data required by that object.

In Figure 4.1, the object and its contents are shown as rectangles. The interface nodes are shown as circles connected to the object by a straight line extending from the object. Connections to the interfaces are implemented by using memory pointers, which can be drawn as arrows extending from the client object to the interface node of the server object.

When the client and server are operating in the same process space in the computer, the server is referred to as being *in process*, or as an *in-process server*. In-process servers provide the fastest possible service to the client. They are typically objects in the same program, or objects loaded into the same process space ahead of time from an external source such as a dynamic link library (DLL) file. Figure 4.2 shows the relationship between a client and an in-process server.

It's also possible for the server object to operate on the same computer as the client object but in a separate process space. In this situation, the server is called a *cross-process* or *out-of-process server*. Because there are two ways to have an out-of-process server, however, it's more specific to refer to this as a *local server*. For example, your spreadsheet becomes a local server to your word processor when you copy a table of numbers from the spreadsheet and paste it into your word processor. Figure 4.3 shows this relationship.

The other way an out-of-process server occurs is when the client and server are on different computers. This once-rare situation is rapidly gaining in popularity as objects are distributed across computer networks. The out-of-process object providing the service in this case is called a *remote server*. Performance is typically slower than with in-process or local servers, but the gains in functionality and scalability can be revolutionary, as is highlighted later in the discussion on distributed computing. Figure 4.4 shows the remote server relationship.

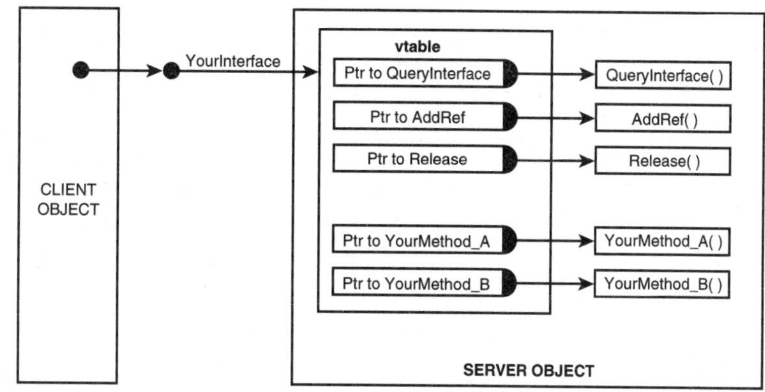

FIG. 4.2
This client object has obtained the services of a server object on the same computer and in the same process space. In this relationship, this server is a local, in-process server.

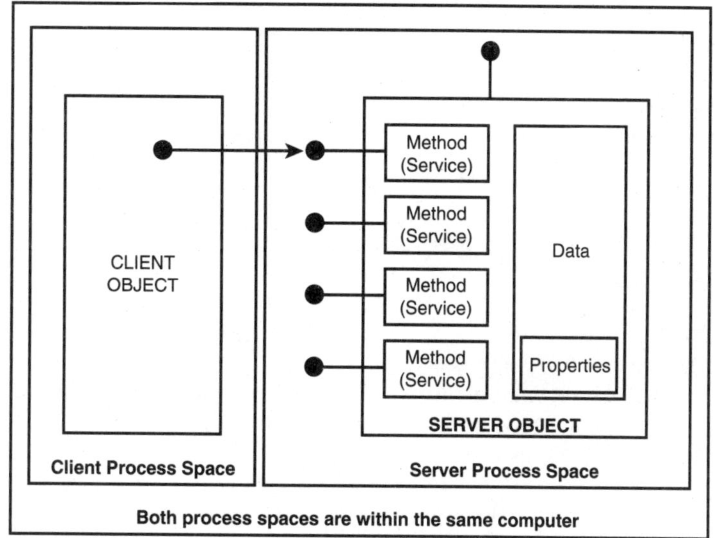

FIG. 4.3
This client object has obtained the services of a server object on the same computer, but outside its process space. In this relationship, this server is a local, out-of-process server.

You can conveniently group in various ways objects that perform very specific tasks. These object-grouping techniques are effective ways to reuse objects and minimize maintenance.

Perhaps the most straightforward way is to create a new object to act as a container in which you place the reused objects. This method is referred to as *object containment*, because the outer object completely contains the inner objects. The interfaces of the inner objects are visible only to the outer object and can't be accessed directly by external objects. Figure 4.5 depicts this relationship.

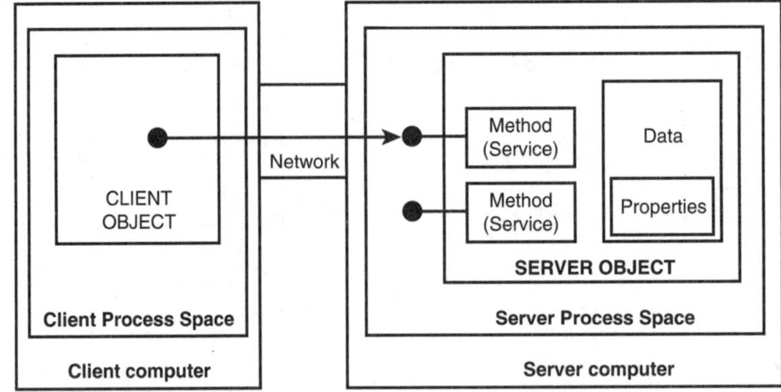

FIG. 4.4
This client object has obtained the services of a server object on another computer on the network. In this relationship, this server is a remote, out-of-process server.

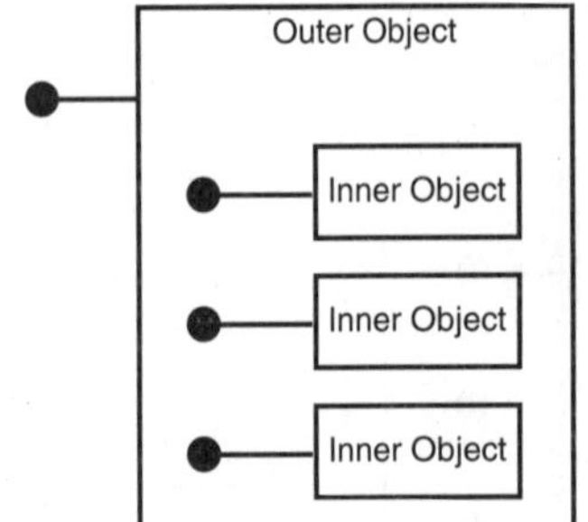

FIG. 4.5
This outer object completely contains the interfaces and services of the inner objects, a collection of reused and new objects that clients can access via communication with the new outer object.

A related grouping method is created by starting with a containment relationship but allowing the outer object to pass along or *delegate* the connecting pointer from the client object directly to the inner object needed to implement the desired function. Referred to as *object delegation*, this relationship is illustrated in Figure 4.6.

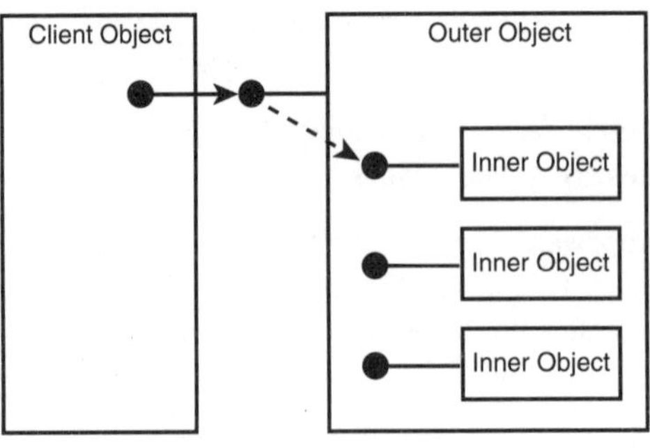

FIG. 4.6
With object delegation, the client object first obtains a pointer to the external interface of the server. The server then provides the address of the inner object that can provide the requested service, and the client connects directly to the inner object.

Finally, objects can be collected together, or *aggregated*, by an outer object that allows the inner objects to expose their interfaces directly to client objects. This is perhaps the most complicated case to implement because the clients of the inner objects don't directly see the relationships between the inner and outer objects. This relationship, referred to as *object aggregation*, is shown in Figure 4.7.

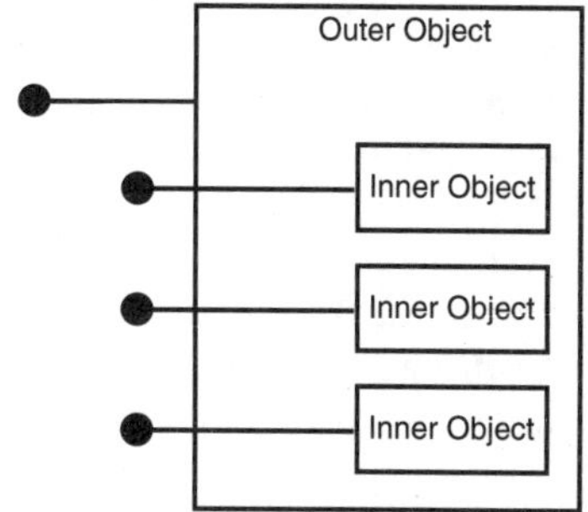

FIG. 4.7 With object aggregation, the client object can directly access the exposed interfaces of each inner object in the server's collection.

Object-Oriented Versus Procedural Programming

Procedural programming is an approach where you determine the steps needed to solve a problem and implement them by creating the algorithms in code that act on the data and store the resulting output separately from the algorithms. Object-oriented programming is an approach where you can group a code module's related data and implementation code into a unified structure, and it acts together in response to requests from other objects. SmallTalk and C-based software development languages have provided this OOP capability for years but are extremely cumbersome for all but dedicated experts. Today, with Visual Studio 97, you can use Visual C++, Visual Basic, and Visual J++ separately or in combination to create robust, enterprisewide object-oriented applications.

OOP Advanced Topics

In object-oriented programming, a discrete combination of code and data must represent each programming object. OOP also requires a way for client objects to dynamically create new instances of objects based on a given class and to create and destroy server objects as needed while the application is operating. Because some languages accomplish OOP objectives more completely than others, many people distinguish between *object-oriented* languages and *object-based* languages. Object-based languages implement as many of the modular features of object-oriented programming as possible within design constraints that enable simplicity or backward compatibility for that language. For example, although object-based languages such as earlier versions of Visual Basic allowed you to create object-like structures in code, creating another similar object required that you create it at design time, perhaps cutting and pasting code from the first object.

To qualify as a true OOP object, the programming structure must support the characteristics of encapsulation, polymorphism, and inheritance. Entire books have been devoted to this topic, but for the purposes of this chapter, a brief explanation and some simple examples will suffice to illustrate the basic concepts.

Encapsulation

Encapsulation occurs when the desired services and data associated with an object are made available to the client through a predefined interface without revealing how those services are implemented. The client uses the server object's interfaces to request desired services, and the object performs on command without further assistance. Suppose that you're developing a Domestic Simulator application. You might want to create a `spouse` object class where you define methods for common household tasks, such as methods called `WashDishes` and `MowTheLawn`. If a client object (perhaps even another `spouse` object) determines that it's time to invoke `WashDishes`, it can make that request via the interface you've appropriately named `IWashDishes`. The desired result might be that any instantiated `Dishes` object with a `Clean` property value now set to `False` would be cleaned and set to `True`.

How this method is accomplished is irrelevant to the client. The `WashDishes` method can be performed with the time-honored `Wash in Sink` procedure or with any version of the popular `Automatic Dishwasher` procedure, but the end result will be the same. Similarly, the interface `IMowTheLawn` would be used to invoke the `MowTheLawn` method. In this case, the server object might be programmed to trim all `Grass` objects with a `length` property of greater than 3 inches down to an even 3 inches. This `MowTheLawn` method can use the slow but reliable `Rotary Mower` procedure, the faster `Power Mower` procedure, or the coveted `Riding Mower` procedure, but the end result will be the same. In each case, the simulated grass will be an acceptable length, and the client will have no need or desire to know how it got that way.

Objects can even encapsulate their own data from all other objects. By default, an object's data is considered *private*, and clients must call one of the object's methods to manipulate data or report data values. It's sometimes practical or necessary to expose the data for direct manipulation by client objects, which is accomplished by adding the `public` declaration when you define the object's class structure.

COM fully supports encapsulation, as COM permits a client object to access a server object only through its well-defined interfaces.

Polymorphism

Polymorphism is the capability for different kinds of objects to respond appropriately and differently to the same stimulus. In OOP, you can see polymorphism as the capability for client objects to access the services of different server objects in the same syntactic manner, even when dealing with different object types.

An illustration will help clarify this concept. Returning to the Domestic Simulator example, suppose that to make the program more realistic, in addition to the `Spouse` class of objects, you also define object classes representing `Child` and `Dog`. Suppose that you have your program instantiate a spouse object called `Katarina`, a child object called `BabyAlex`, and a dog object called `Rover`. Still trying to make it realistic, you can individually define methods for each object to appropriately simulate the behaviors of walking, eating, sleeping, and speaking. You can then have your program make a call to `Rover.Speak` and compare that result with a call to `Rover.Eat` to see whether Rover's bark is worse than his bite. However, asking the spouse object to speak by making a call to `Katarina.Speak` should give you a dramatically different result than the one produced when you call the dog object to speak. Asking the child object to speak by using `BabyAlex.Speak` might give little or no result until the Domestic Simulator has run for a sufficient amount of time. Although all these requests are made in exactly the same way—by using the syntax *`ObjectName`*`.Speak`—the request produces different results, depending on the object type. This is polymorphism in action.

COM supports polymorphism by allowing different classes of objects to support interfaces with the same name, while allowing these objects to implement the interfaces differently.

Inheritance

Inheritance is the capability to define increasingly more specific objects, starting with the existing characteristic definitions of general objects. Thus, when a more specific class of objects is desired, you can begin the definition by first inheriting all the characteristics of another defined class and then adding to them. Again, an example is useful to help explain this concept.

In the Domestic Simulator program, you can first define a class of objects called `Animal` to represent the common attributes of all animals in your simulation. Suppose that the `Animal` class includes characteristics such as breathing and eating. From the `Animal` class, you can create subclasses for `Wild_Animal` and `Pet_Animal`. These two objects will automatically know how to eat, but now you can define that `Pet_Animal` objects will eat only from their food bowls, whereas `Wild_Animal` objects will eat food wherever they find it, including your simulated garden and simulated trash containers. By adding specific characteristics in addition to the common characteristics of the `Pet_Animal` class, you can create classes for `PetDog`, `PetCat`, and any other kind of pet you want to share the house with in your simulation. With all this additional behavior defined in higher level classes, your previously mentioned polymorphic pet `Rover` can now be instantiated from the `PetDog` class, having completely inherited all the common characteristics you defined for a `Pet_Animal` and for `Animal` objects in general.

COM supports *interface inheritance*, the capability for one interface definition to inherit characteristics from another interface. COM, however, doesn't support *implementation inheritance*, the capability for one object to inherit the actual implementation code from another object. Implementation inheritance makes sense when an entire application is compiled in the same language. Because COM is standardized at the binary level and not the language level, passing the actual implementation code between objects would produce unpredictable and potentially disastrous results. This subtle but important difference has sparked an ongoing debate about whether COM truly supports inheritance. For comparison, the CORBA specification doesn't require implementation inheritance either, but some CORBA implementations have supported it for certain special cases. In practice, being able to integrate objects created from different development languages is extremely useful and greatly outweighs this one concession to theoretical OOP purity.

In the long run, the debate over whether a language is truly object-oriented becomes merely an academic exercise. What matters to you, the programmer, is which characteristics you need for a particular programming project, and what language or combination of languages provides the easiest, fastest, and most efficient way to implement them. With Visual C++, Visual Basic, and

Visual J++, Visual Studio provides a complete set of object-oriented tools that can accommodate the most simple to the most complex object programming projects.

Progressive Development of Microsoft Object Technologies

In recent years, incredibly rapid progress has been made in advancing the techniques and technologies used for object-oriented programming and modular program communication. These new and improved technologies, with all their new names and integration requirements, have also brought their share of confusion to the programming community. A brief look at the incremental steps that brought us to our current state of the art should help clear away some of that lingering confusion.

Microsoft Windows

In the 1980s, if you wanted to do some serious object-oriented programming, you could use SmallTalk or C, but programming in those languages was extremely tedious. With the release of the Windows operating system, Microsoft introduced a graphical user interface for the personal computer that used a visual object metaphor but didn't fully qualify as object-oriented. The early versions were slow and unstable, but they succeeded in greatly simplifying program-to-program communication via the Windows Clipboard. Users could run more than one program at a time, each in a separate window. You could even move files and directories simply and easily by dragging and dropping them to new locations.

Although we now take it for granted, being able to copy and paste by using the Clipboard was (and still is) a remarkably handy way to copy data from one document to another without retyping. Using the Clipboard was also a convenient way to move images from one document to another without requiring a separate process to translate the graphics format.

Compound documents were easily created in this manner; unfortunately, it was often difficult to modify the result after the transfer of an image or document. Because usability of PC applications would be improved if the pasted parts could be edited by using the interfaces from their native application environments, Microsoft created the Dynamic Data Exchange (DDE) protocol, which exchanged data by sending commands between applications. This was an improvement but was very slow, very difficult to implement, and less robust than if this capability could be provided as a direct service of the operating system.

OLE 1.0

In 1991, Microsoft improved the object-enabling concept by introducing a technology called Object Linking and Embedding (OLE 1.0). OLE was a slight improvement to DDE but was still slow and prone to problems due to an underlying architecture that was still a messaging system between applications. On the positive side, OLE-enabled software gave users a more convenient way to store and maintain portions of documents (or entire documents) in a container document. The documents could be from different programs, as long as all the programs were

OLE 1.0-enabled. It was now possible, by double-clicking the embedded portion, to open the document and edit it in its native program's controls without leaving the program used for the container document. For example, you could use OLE 1.0 to place an Excel spreadsheet within the text of a Word document and edit it within Word. OLE 1.0 also allowed you to link files so that updates to the original file would be propagated to the linked copies in other documents. OLE 1.0 became well known, well used, and fairly well understood.

Although this embedding capability was extremely useful, OLE 1.0 still didn't qualify as a truly object-oriented technology, because the data was only referenced from a source file and not encapsulated. If you happened to rename the source data file or move it to a new location on disk, you would also unknowingly render all related OLE links unusable. Perhaps the biggest accomplishment of OLE 1.0 was that it popularized the idea that documents should act as containers for functional components of other programs.

This modular component strategy also proved quite useful in the development of applications. Microsoft introduced their first version of Visual Basic not so much to pursue the goals of object technology as to simplify application development for the Windows operating system. Visual Basic succeeded in introducing a vast number of programmers to the graphical user interface paradigm, but early Visual Basic programs tended to be more experimental than useful. Early versions were acceptable for creating small, specialized programs for single users or small user groups on local area networks, but didn't provide the performance or scalability required for building large, mission-critical applications.

VBX Components

Visual Basic did have one critical capability that most other programming languages lacked. Programmers could buy an ever-increasing variety of specialty plug-in components off the shelf from third-party developers. These components, also known as *widgets*, saved tremendous amounts of programmer time and development dollars because programmers could buy (rather than build) many necessary functional pieces for corporate programming projects. It could even be argued that it was the diversity and quality of the secondary add-on component market—not the quality of the base product—that steadily increased the user base and pushed the continuous improvement of Visual Basic.

Because add-on components extended the capability of Visual Basic, they were assigned the .vbx (Visual Basic extension) filename extension and were commonly referred to as VBXs. Although not true OOP objects, VBX components worked extremely well in providing off-the-shelf, modular functionality. Although the performance of a VBX component was often disappointingly slow, these modular widgets represented solid progress on the road to better object technologies. As a testament to the versatility and popularity of these widgets, you can still find in use today various niche applications relying heavily on specialized VBX components.

NOTE You shouldn't try to use VBX controls with Visual Studio. VBX controls are 16-bit and aren't compatible with the COM-enabled, 32-bit architecture of Visual Studio languages. However, you can still use VBX controls for applications development for Windows 3.1 by using Visual Basic 3.0 (which is 16-bit) and the 16-bit version of Visual Basic 4.0.

COM and OLE 2.0

In 1993, Microsoft created the Component Object Model (COM) and laid the technical foundation that has dramatically improved object communication in the Windows environment. COM provided the technical specifications for creating compatible objects and the communication "plumbing" in the Windows operating system required to make it work. The first use of this new programming model came when Microsoft completely rebuilt the OLE functionality by using the new COM architecture. Rather than use a messaging protocol built on top of the operating system (such as DDE or OLE 1.0), COM provided interprocess communication (IPC) directly as a service of the operating system. Although it was a very different product and approach, Microsoft kept the OLE name, dubbing it OLE 2.0. OLE 2.0 eventually provided all the existing features of OLE 1.0, plus a few more.

With the COM communication architecture, OLE 2.0 could now connect objects outside the process boundaries of an application and could instantly support new versions of objects without changing the source code of the applications that used them. This approach connected binary components actively running in various process spaces. To differentiate this new technology, Microsoft stopped proclaiming that "OLE stands for Object Linking and Embedding" and declared that OLE was no longer an abbreviation; the word *OLE* was the entire name for the technology. OLE is still spelled with all capital letters but is commonly pronounced *Oh-LAY* instead of *Oh-el-EE*.

NOTE With the framework in place to create reusable designs independent of the implementations, COM and OLE 2.0 architecture can accommodate any new features and technologies without changing the architecture itself. Many subsequent developments have been built under the OLE banner, but due to the extensible nature of the OLE 2.0 architecture, theoretically no technical reason exists for Microsoft to develop a technology that could properly be named OLE 3.0. For that reason, any subsequent mention of OLE in this book without a version number will refer to the OLE 2.0 set of technologies.

OCX Components

While the OLE developments were occurring, competition in the visual programming tool arena was heating up. Borland released the Delphi programming environment, which provided some serious competition for Visual Basic in the category of simple but powerful graphical user interface development tools. Despite this game of technical leapfrog with the competition, Microsoft continued to gain market share through an improving product line, brand loyalty from its growing dominance in the desktop suite market, and a highly effective marketing team. Visual Basic advanced from version 3 to version 4, and the 16-bit VBX components were succeeded by OLE-based 32-bit components called *OLE Controls*. Naturally, OLE Controls needed a new name to distinguish them from their 16-bit VBX predecessors. Microsoft assigned OLE Controls the .ocx file extension, and these components became known as OCXs.

OCX components provided modular, 32-bit functionality to all the popular visual programming languages, including Microsoft Visual C++ and Microsoft Visual Basic. Although OCX components are used in the Visual Basic toolbox just like VBX components had been, OCXs are actually full-fledged COM objects. The process of converting developers from VBX components to OCX components started gaining significant momentum about the same time that Microsoft decided to expand the use of the OLE terminology.

The Expanding World of OLE

OLE Controls made up one member of a whole family of COM-based technologies renamed under the OLE banner. Here are the highlights:

- *OLE Clipboard.* The OLE technology that provides the cut, copy, and paste editor functions in the Windows Clipboard.
- *OLE Visual Editing.* The OLE technology that allows you to edit, while remaining in your current compound document, an object originally created in a different application by using the interface and services of that different application. This concept was first known as *in-place editing* and later called *in-place activation*, before Microsoft renamed it *Visual Editing* and obtained a trademark for the term.
- *OLE Drag-and-Drop.* The OLE technology that allows you to select an object from one application in the Windows environment, use the mouse to drag it over another object, and then drop it onto that object. Depending on the behavior defined for the target object, the dropped object can be copied, moved, linked, or discarded by using this technique.
- *OLE Automation.* The Microsoft technology that allows one component to control or *automate* another application or control. Thus, rather than receive input through the user interface, the component is operated programmatically by another code module. One typical example is allowing your component to access predefined mathematical functions available from an OLE-enabled spreadsheet program such as Microsoft Excel, rather than program them yourself. As do the rest of the OLE components, OLE automation uses the COM architecture to communicate. Of course, the helper program must be installed and available on the user's PC for the OLE Automation in your program to function properly.
- *OLE Remote Automation.* An interim solution for extending OLE Automation capability so that it can control objects across machine boundaries. DCOM has encompassed OLE Remote Automation.
- *Network OLE and Distributed OLE.* The names given to the OLE technology that allowed OLE-compatible software components to communicate directly over a network. You could have used Distributed OLE to perform time-consuming or processor-intensive functions on a network server to relieve the burden on a user's PC. Extensive searches against large databases or complex calculation problems were good candidates for this technology. The idea remains today, but these names and technologies have been encompassed by DCOM.

The confusion over the OLE names was beginning to diminish just about the same time Microsoft realized that the Internet was a much bigger phenomenon than it had anticipated.

Microsoft decided to realign its naming conventions again and return OLE to its roots. The OLE banner was officially removed from all but the original set of technologies related to the linking and embedding of objects into OLE container documents. These three technologies are now grouped into a category called *OLE Documents* and are individually named *Linking*, *Embedding*, and *In-Place Activation*.

Microsoft's Embrace of the Internet: OCX to ActiveX

In 1995, the Internet revolution spurred Microsoft's technical (and marketing) ingenuity into high gear. Microsoft originally underestimated the importance of the Internet revolution, but within about a 90-day period in late 1995, Bill Gates completely realigned the Microsoft corporate strategy to include Internet support into almost everything the company was producing.

To boldly signal its entry into the booming I-net revolution, Microsoft created a new high-tech *Active* brand name for present and future I-net related technologies. The company decided to market the remaining OLE technologies as *ActiveX*, which is easier to pronounce than OLE but much harder to define. Because ActiveX is essentially a brand name, expect the collection of technologies in this category to mutate over time. Microsoft further marked its I-net intentions by declaring that its new I-net architecture for the PC would be named the *Active Platform*. At present, the following technologies are included under the Active Platform umbrella:

- *Active Desktop* allows the PC desktop to act as an integrated COM container that can hold COM objects such as ActiveX components, provide all the functionality now associated with web browsers, and connect to I-net broadcast channels. The goal is to completely integrate local PC resources with I-net–based resources into a single, unified user interface. This capability, available in Internet Explorer 4.0, will become a standard part of the operating system with the release of Windows 98.
- *Active Server* provides a consistent server-side component programming environment.
- *ActiveX technologies* are COM-based technologies that allow components written in different languages on different operating systems to communicate consistently and robustly.

All the ActiveX technologies are all built to use COM. Not all COM-based technologies fit under the ActiveX umbrella, however—for example, MS Office software and Windows operating systems are COM-enabled but aren't considered part of ActiveX.

In late September 1997, Microsoft introduced the Windows Distributed Internet Applications Architecture (Windows DNA). Windows DNA describes the collection of Microsoft technologies that allow you to integrate client/server and I-net programming. The foundation of Windows DNA is still COM, but COM itself will soon have some new enhancements and be called *COM+*. This new, improved COM isn't available yet, but the anticipated features are discussed later in the section "Objects over the Horizon: COM+."

Today, probably more confusion exists than ever among developers over the various names for Microsoft-produced technologies. At this point, understanding the underlying concepts is far more important than keeping up with the current naming conventions. If you're curious what the names were in late 1997 when this chapter was written, Figure 4.8 shows the relationship of some of these OLE/ActiveX technologies to the COM foundation.

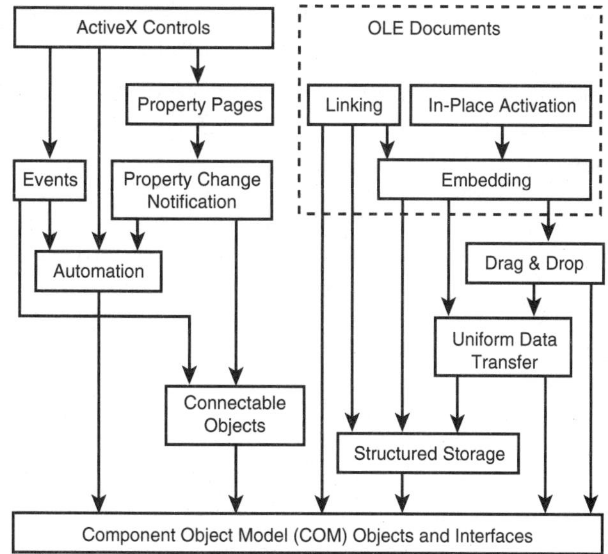

FIG. 4.8
The ActiveX and OLE technologies all have a common foundation in COM.

The proud tradition of naming confusion with OLE Controls was continued in March 1996, when Microsoft used the Active brand to rename these components as *ActiveX controls*, allowed them to operate as COM-compliant components, and dedicated their use to the Internet. Sure, you can still use these controls as widgets in the design-time toolbox of your development language, but now all the promotion and commotion revolves around using ActiveX controls to make spectacular web pages and web-enabled applications.

Microsoft's web-centric focus also spurred the company's aggressive push to develop or enhance its other I-net–related technologies. These products and technologies included Active Server Pages, VBScript, Visual J++, and Visual InterDev, which are all included or supported in Visual Studio. COM will continue to provide the underlying architecture designed to integrate all this new technology seamlessly. This is the brave new computing world your Visual Studio 97 programs will be operating in.

Remote Objects: ORBs and DCOM

For objects to interact between computers and across networks, they must have a common way of communicating. This is accomplished by using an *Object Request Broker (ORB)*, which you can think of as a very intelligent switchboard providing directory and connection services between client and server objects. Various ORBs and ORB-like technologies are now available, and considerable debate has raged over which one is, or should be, the universal standard.

One early entry in this technology category was the Distributed Computing Environment (DCE) from a technology consortium called the Open Group. DCE encompasses an evolving suite of technologies available for various platforms. A wide array of system vendors distributed this DCE technology, including Bull S.A., Cray Research, Data General, Digital, Fujitsu, Hewlett-Packard, Hitachi, IBM, NEC, Siemens Nixdorf, Sony Silicon Graphics, Stratus, and Tandem Computers. Various DCE technologies have been used as a foundation for other technologies released by IBM, DEC, and, yes, even Microsoft.

Another development was the Common Object Request Broker Architecture (CORBA) from the Object Management Group (OMG). The CORBA specification, developed in the early 1990s, has now gained the support of more than 20 major technology vendors, including Apple, Sun, and IBM. OMG has achieved a very impressive membership of more than 700 companies, including Adobe, Apple, Computer Associates, Digital Equipment, Hewlett-Packard, Netscape, Novell, Oracle, Silicon Graphics, Symantec, Texas Instruments, Unisys, and Xerox. Despite this apparently overwhelming show of support, OMG won't be able to ensure CORBA's status as the single industry standard without the cooperation of the most globally influential company in software today, Microsoft. Unfortunately for OMG, CORBA compliance doesn't fit into Microsoft's plans.

ON THE WEB

For more history about CORBA and the Object Management Group, visit OMG's web site at **http://www.omg.org**.

Back at Redmond, Microsoft diligently created its own full-fledged object request broker specifically for the Windows set of operating systems. After years of development rumors, this technology was officially released in 1996 as the Distributed Component Object Model (DCOM). DCOM extended the COM architecture to provide object communication services at the binary level between computers that use a COM-compatible operating system and are connected via a network.

NOTE For general discussions about the technology, the term *COM* is commonly used to denote the COM and DCOM technologies. ■

Objects over the Horizon: COM+

COM and DCOM deliver much functionality, but Microsoft is working to make COM even better. In October 1997, Microsoft announced a unified and improved version of COM and DCOM called *COM+*, which is due to be released in late 1998. COM+ promises to provide faster performance and improved capabilities, but the main thrust will be to relieve you from having to program the object housekeeping details, which Microsoft colorfully refers to as the *grungy stuff*. Microsoft describes COM+ improvements as an "auto-everything" approach to using objects. You can still program the grungy stuff if you want, but with COM+ the system will do it for you if you choose not to. Because COM+ isn't ready for prime time yet, however, you still need to know and use the basic techniques needed to implement COM objects by using Visual Studio. According to Microsoft, all properly constructed COM objects built now will work equally well or better under the enhancements of COM+.

What would Microsoft innovation be without new names? In the COM+ world, Microsoft's COM ORB will be known as *COM Runtime*, and the name DCOM will simply refer to the DCE Remote Procedure Call protocol that connects distributed COM objects. COM+ will also provide a new Services layer that provides transaction handling, data binding, load balancing, security, and an event infrastructure. COM+ will integrate tightly with Microsoft Transaction Server (MTS) to provide a full-featured and robust computing environment to host any Windows-based, object-oriented system you can imagine and develop.

▶ **See** Chapter 24, "Deploying Distributed Applications," **p. 667**

▶ **See** Chapter 25, "Using Microsoft Transaction Server to Enable Distributed Applications," **p. 691**

With the announcement of COM+, Microsoft has made its intention clear that now and in the future, the road to Windows-based, object-oriented software is paved with COM.

ON THE WEB

To keep up with the latest news on COM+, visit Microsoft's COM home page at **http://www.microsoft.com/COM/**. For more information on Microsoft Transaction Server, visit Microsoft's MTS home page at **http://www.microsoft.com/transaction/**. At press time, the Windows DNA announcement and answers to frequently asked questions about DNA was posted at **http://www.microsoft.com/sitebuilder/DNA/**.

Object Technologies Today

COM is Microsoft's way to connect objects, but it isn't the only way. The industry is now grappling with the choice of designing programs to communicate by using a designated open standard (such as CORBA) or to communicate by using COM, the emerging object communication technology that's the de facto standard for Windows-based computing.

COM/DCOM Compatibility with Other Object Technologies

CORBA-based technologies are the most significant competing object models you'll encounter when supporting enterprisewide integration of your programs created with Visual Studio. For example, IBM provides a CORBA-compliant object architecture for mainframe systems in its System Object Model (SOM) and also in its Distributed System Object Model (DSOM).

ON THE WEB

If your company has IBM-supported mainframe or workstation equipment, you probably want to become more familiar with SOM/DSOM. For more information, visit IBM's home page at **http://www.ibm.com** and perform a site search for **SOM** or **DSOM**.

Other popular CORBA-based ORB offerings are available from Visigenic and IONA. Both companies have also created technologies that help you integrate COM and CORBA objects, and both are discussed further in the following section.

COM Versus CORBA: Standard, Stand-Off, Integration, or Assimilation?

CORBA-based solutions are still the main competitors to COM. CORBA has been available much longer and was created from the start to be a non-proprietary or "open" standard, backed by OMG and its alliance of technology firms. COM was created as a proprietary Microsoft development. During October 1996, in an effort to diffuse concerns about it being proprietary, Microsoft announced the creation of The Active Group to guide the evolution of ActiveX and the underlying COM technology. The Active Group was formed under the auspices of The Open Group, another organization dedicated to supporting standards in the software industry.

ON THE WEB

For more information about The Open Group, visit its web site at **http://www.opengroup.org**. For an interesting observation about "Who Owns ActiveX," see David Chappell's cover story from the September 1997 edition of *Byte* magazine. This article also can be found on the web at **http://www.byte.com/art/9709/sec5/art7.htm**.

Although this appeared to be a positive step toward opening the architecture to the rest of the industry, the track record suggests that Microsoft will retain the deciding vote on any significant changes proposed for COM.

The industry track record also indicates, however, that Microsoft is an extremely tough contender in any market it enters. Microsoft can be counted on to be particularly aggressive in promoting and implementing its object technology, because this area is absolutely critical to the advancement of personal computing. In cooperation with Microsoft, Software AG has ported COM and ActiveX support to the Sun Solaris and UNIX family of operating systems with a product called DCOM for the Enterprise (DCOM FTE). Microsoft is working diligently to ensure that every major operating system will soon have COM support. Hence, using Visual Studio to create COM-compliant objects for Windows and UNIX platforms is a safe bet now, and COM objects will have even more utility in the future as COM support spreads to other platforms.

ON THE WEB

For more information on COM and ActiveX support for UNIX-based operating systems, visit Software AG at **http://www.sagus.com**.

There's still a great debate over which object model you should use: COM or CORBA. It would be nice if these two models were compatible, but because that's unlikely to happen in the foreseeable future, you have to make a choice. Despite all the hype, your choice should be based on what you consider better for your own purposes.

If you're creating applications for the PC desktop, the Object Request Broker de facto standard for Windows-based development is COM, and COM is built right into the operating system. Similarly, COM is the clear choice for homogeneous Windows-based programs used across Windows NT-based computer networks.

If, however, your programs need to operate in a network environment that contains a mix of operating systems, including various flavors of UNIX, you might need to integrate your programs by using CORBA-compliant ORB software. In that case, it's wise to standardize with products from a single CORBA-compliant vendor because integration between CORBA-based products has sometimes proven to be very difficult. Other ORBs may find niche markets where they can survive, but for enterprises where most users have PCs on their desks, the initial standoff between COM and CORBA will likely give way to integration and then finally to assimilation by COM.

ON THE WEB

The Object Management Group maintains a concise set of links to CORBA-related web sites at **http://www.omg.org/new/corbkmk.htm**.

Perhaps you're wondering if programs created in Visual Studio 97 (which uses COM) are compatible with CORBA. Such integration isn't yet available out of the box, but third-party tools are now available to help you with this integration.

Visigenic is a growing provider of CORBA-compliant technology and has licensed its VisiBroker ORB product to an increasing number of companies, including Netscape, Novell, Oracle, Sybase, and Silicon Graphics. Visigenic also offers a product called VisiBridge, which provides technology that allows COM objects on Windows platforms to communicate with CORBA objects on UNIX and mainframe operating systems.

ON THE WEB

For more information on VisiBroker, VisiBridge, and other Visigenic products, visit the company's web site at **http://www.visigenic.com**.

Another popular CORBA-compliant object broker is Orbix from Iona. Orbix also provides a bridging technology that allows application integration between COM-based Windows platforms and CORBA-based UNIX platforms.

ON THE WEB

More information on Orbix and other Iona products is available at **http://www.iona.com**.

These and other products to bridge the compatibility gap between COM and CORBA are very useful, and will be necessary until the two competing standards either can communicate directly or are merged into a unified standard. Bridging technology provides valuable integration capability; unfortunately, however, as you increase the number of communication layers, the complexity of your programs and the risk for functionality and performance problems also increases. Because COM is quickly being ported to nearly every major computing platform, it might not be long before native COM support is available in all common platforms and Visual Studio programmers will have much less need for a COM-to-CORBA interface layer.

Assimilation has also begun under the market pressure of the COM/OLE technologies. In late 1993, a coalition of technology companies—including Apple, IBM, Novell, Oracle, SunSoft, Taligent, and Xerox—backed a compound document architecture standard called *OpenDoc* from Component Integration Laboratories (CILabs). This technology provided some promising competition for Microsoft's COM/OLE technology and prompted a great deal of interest and discussion from the industry, but generated only a meager amount of market share. Being "open" and "standard" was just not enough for the OpenDoc alliance to overcome the growing market success of COM-based technologies. OpenDoc's battle to survive amid the growing dominance of OLE technologies was short-lived. The battle concluded in May 1997, when CILabs essentially surrendered by announcing it was discontinuing support of the OpenDoc architecture.

ON THE WEB

CILabs has since been dissolved by its board of directors. At the date of this writing, the company's farewell greetings were posted at **http://www.cilabs.com**.

The battle between CORBA and COM to become the generally accepted ORB standard is nowhere near over. Netscape Communications Corporation is including a CORBA-compliant object request broker and support for the Internet Inter-Orb Protocol (IIOP)—the CORBA-compliant Internet protocol from OMG—in its Enterprise 3.0 server and Communicator 4.0 browser. This means Netscape's browsers can use IIOP to connect with remote objects across the I-net. The incompatibility gap between Microsoft's Internet Explorer and Netscape Navigator/Communicator is widening, but Microsoft is trying to make this a moot point by using Active Desktop as a preemptive strike to essentially eliminate the need for—and ultimately even the existence of—all competing browsers. Microsoft's Active Desktop concept integrates all the functions of traditional browser technology directly into the desktop of all future Windows operating systems. Hence, if the PC-using public embraces this new version of Windows, the PC browser battle will essentially be over and Microsoft's COM-based technologies will be the de facto standard.

ON THE WEB

Microsoft maintains web pages dedicated to OLE and COM topics at **http://www.microsoft.com/oledev/** and **http://www.microsoft.com/com/**.

The Scoop on Java-Based Technologies

Still another battleground for Microsoft's object technologies is in the I-net arena. This battle has become more intense as a result of the explosive increase in I-net usage and the increasing desire to use I-net for mission-critical, distributed corporate applications.

Sun Microsystems has created a phenomenon of its own with the creation of the Java programming language. Originally created to be a small but powerful means to program applications for small computing devices, it found popularity as a means to create quickly downloadable applets for I-net web pages. As Java's popularity expanded, so has the scope of what developers are attempting to create by using Java and Java-related technologies.

Microsoft's mixed position on this situation is easily misunderstood. Microsoft considers Java to be a great object-oriented programming language and has created the Visual J++ product to provide Java programmers a rich development environment. However, Microsoft considers Java-related technologies to be a very poor choice as an operating system. On all but the smallest computing platforms, the Java virtual machine (JVM) that contains and executes the Java applets is essentially an operating system or operating environment built on top of the native operating system. Because Java and Java-related technologies are attempting to be a cross-platform solution, the Java language and the JVM must limit themselves to the lowest common denominator in terms of platform-specific features. Thus, important capabilities available from operating systems (such as Windows) are essentially unavailable to programmers writing "pure" Java code. The platform-specific implementations of the JVM also introduce the opportunity for incompatibilities, as does the variety of Java development environments. Even if you think you've developed the most "pure" Java applets or even full-fledged Java applications, you should still test them extensively to make sure that they work correctly on all desired platforms.

With Visual Studio, Visual J++ gives you the option of writing "pure" Java applets, or you can use the new J/Direct interface to allow your applets to access the entire range of Windows-specific APIs. Java purists have panned this flexibility for developing Java applets for the PC. Nonetheless, as a programmer supporting Windows-based users, you're faced with a choice: use "pure" Java to create slower and less functional applets that may or may not work on other platforms, or optimize your code to work in Windows.

JavaBeans, another Java-related technology that's not very popular with Microsoft, is a technology that Sun and IBM have developed to give Java applications the same compound document capabilities that ActiveX provides. JavaBeans can be visual components that you can add to forms in visual development tools, or they can be non-visual components that accomplish background tasks. JavaBeans are also designed to be cross-platform–compatible, but the current reality is that you still need to test your Java and your JavaBeans on each combination of platform and Java virtual machine represented in your user community.

Looking further into Java's relationship to the I-net, Sun actively supports the CORBA specification and has pledged to integrate Java with IIOP, the CORBA-compliant Internet protocol from OMG. Java's existing Remote Method Invocation (RMI) protocol will be integrated to use IIOP across the I-net. Hence, Sun has joined other industry powerhouses such as Netscape, Oracle, and IBM in support of IIOP. Despite such a powerful alliance among giants in the industry, they can still be considered underdogs when compared to Microsoft and its rapidly growing ActiveX/COM/DCOM strategy for I-net development.

Microsoft hopes that as COM gains further acceptance and use throughout the industry, the importance of CORBA and other architectures will diminish along with their market share. If that happens quickly, Microsoft will have assimilated another major layer of the desktop computing architecture. If not, CORBA will remain as a viable, competing distributed object architecture for the desktop and the I-net, and will need to be accounted for when you're integrating and supporting enterprisewide systems.

ON THE WEB

Microsoft's web site provides various information about its position on these technologies. An easy way to find the most recent update is to do a keyword search at Microsoft's search page at **http://www.microsoft.com/search/**. A good starting point to locate more information on CORBA is the Object Management Group's web site at **http://www.omg.org**.

COM Outside Windows

Although COM was originally a Windows-only technology, Microsoft and its partners are porting it to every other major computing platform and operating system, including Solaris, MVS, Macintosh, and UNIX. This time the integration rumors are backed by dollars, because in addition to its internal efforts, Microsoft has negotiated outside contracts to port COM to some of these other platforms. As mentioned previously, COM is native to Windows, and Software AG has already ported COM and ActiveX to the Sun Solaris family of operating systems. By the end of 1998, you also can expect to see COM support released for HP/UX, IBM MVS 5.2.2 (OS 390), IBM OS/400, Digital UNIX 4.0 (Alpha), Digital Open VMS, Siemens Nixdorf SINIX, Linux 2.0, and SCO UnixWare. Hence, if COM isn't yet supported on your computer system of preference, you probably won't have to wait long until it is.

ON THE WEB

To get the most recent information and beta versions of COM ports for these other operating systems, visit Software AG's web site at **http://www.sagus.com**.

COM/DCOM Architecture Basics

This section takes a closer look at the common implementation requirements of Microsoft's object technologies, while still maintaining language neutrality. It provides a quick introduction to COM-related terms and concepts, which are then explained in greater depth in subsequent chapters with language-specific implementation guidance.

Interfaces

The COM infrastructure is built to support communication through object interfaces. In COM, you can think of an *interface* as the communications link between two different objects, and the set of functions available through that link. Interface names conventionally begin with a capital `I` to denote their status as an interface, and the remaining text describes the function or service being exposed. For example, in the Domestic Simulator program mentioned earlier, you might name an interface `ISpeak`, which would be read aloud as *I-Speak* or *Interface Speak*.

▶ **See** "Interfaces," **p. 182**

A COM interface is actually implemented as a memory structure called a *VTable*, which contains an array of function pointers. Each element of the VTable array contains the address of a specific function implemented by the object. It's conventional to say that a COM object exposes its interfaces to make its functions available to clients. The object also can contain the data manipulated by the methods, and you can choose to keep this data hidden from the client object. Figure 4.9 shows this structure.

FIG. 4.9
You could define a COM interface called `ISample`, which is implemented in memory with pointers to the standard COM methods and to your custom defined methods.

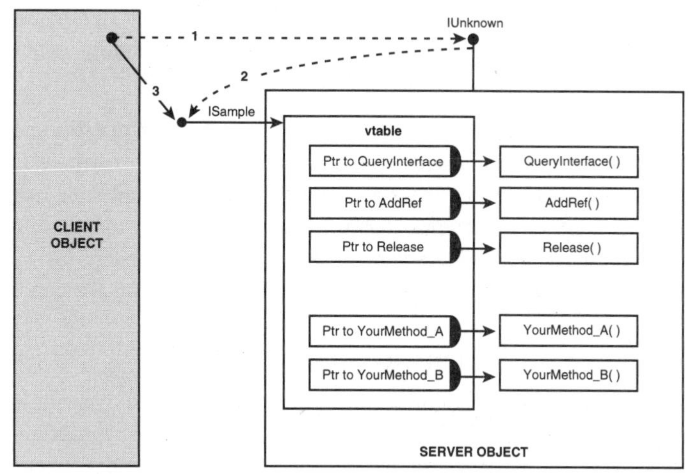

IUnknown One of the most basic rules of the COM specification is that all COM objects must support a specific interface named `IUnknown`. This interface is the standard starting point for referencing any other interface that the COM object might contain. The COM specification arbitrarily dictates this structure, but it makes sense if you consider that a client object doesn't know what other interfaces are exposed by a server object until the client requests this information by using this predefined interface designed to reveal what interfaces are "unknown." A more technical way of stating the relationship is that an object's interfaces must directly or indirectly inherit from `IUnknown` to be valid under the COM specification. You, the programmer, are responsible for implementing the `IUnknown` interface for your objects; however, because this operation is so routine, Microsoft programming tools accomplish most of this work in the background or allow you to customize some basic example code. Figure 4.9 also shows how a client must request a pointer from `IUnknown` to access an object's interfaces.

QueryInterface The object's `IUnknown` interface must also implement a function named `QueryInterface`, which reports back to the client whether a requested interface is supported and, if so, provides a means to access it. A successful call to `QueryInterface` provides the client with a pointer to the requested interface.

Globally Unique Identifiers

Every COM component class and interface must be uniquely identified. This is accomplished by providing a means for you to generate and assign a unique number called the *globally unique identifier* (GUID). A GUID (pronounced as *goo-i-d* or *gwid*) is a 128-bit integer virtually guaranteed to be unique across space and time until about 3400 AD, because of the algorithm used to create it. You can create a new GUID whenever you need to by using the

GUID-generation tools (GUIDGen and UUIDGen) provided in Visual Studio. To create your new GUID, the algorithm uses the current date and time, a clock sequence, an incremented counter, and the IEEE machine identifier. The odds against any two people ever creating the same GUID are astronomical. After you create a GUID, you can use it to identify your programming objects and interfaces uniquely. When used to identify an interface, this GUID number is referred to as an *interface identifier* (IID). When used to identify an object, the GUID number is called a *class identifier* (CLSID).

After a particular interface is defined, numbered with a unique IID, and published, it must not be changed; thus, the interface is said to be *immutable*. When you want to update the features of an interface, you must define, number, and publish an additional interface to supplement the older version, retaining any previous versions within the component. If you don't include these previous versions, you'll create version incompatibility problems for your users. You'll see an example of this later in the section "Binary Compatibility and Version Control."

Registering Your Components

After you have a GUID to identify your new object, you must register it with the host system. For machines running Windows, you do this by adding the appropriate information to the Windows Registry, a special system file containing that machine's hardware and software configuration information. When you create and distribute components, you should build your installation program to update the Registry without requiring manual assistance from users. After a component is registered, the operating system will know how and where to access that particular object.

NOTE According to the current definition, any self-registering OLE component that fully implements `IUnknown` can be correctly called an ActiveX control. OLE Automation servers and most of the widget-type controls from a visual development toolbox are included under the ActiveX controls banner.

Binary Compatibility and Version Control

With the ability for developers around the globe to create objects that must work together, you need to be able to update your objects without causing the failure of existing objects that still depend on your previous version. COM requires that client objects specify the exact server interface they want by using that interface's assigned GUID (as described in the next section). Each version must have a different identifier, and `QueryInterface` returns a pointer to the version the client specifically asks for.

COM allows objects to have multiple interfaces, so any number of versions can be supported simultaneously. When all versions are retained by an object and made available to clients, the old and new clients always work appropriately. When you create a new version of an interface, it's a good practice to change the name or add a version number after the name to avoid any confusion. With proper versioning, you can safely support old and new objects on either side of the client/server relationship. Figure 4.10 shows this concept, using objects from the Domestic Simulator example.

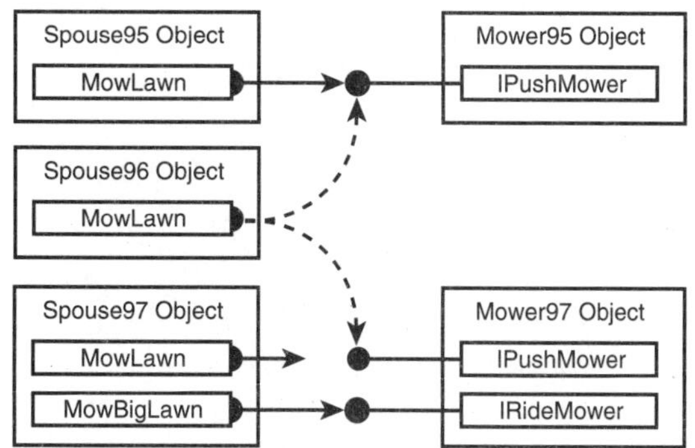

FIG. 4.10
Mower objects from different vendors will still get the grass cut as long as COM versioning rules are followed.

Suppose that you purchased the Domestic Simulator described earlier. `Spouse95` objects created by SimWare are designed to call the PushMower interface (`IPushMower`) in the `Mower95` object when the simulated lawn needs to be cut. Eventually, LawnSoft releases a new version of its mower object, called `Mower97`, that's the envy of the simulated neighborhood. Some people buy it to upgrade their simulation, but because it's more expensive and not that much better than the mower object everybody started with, most don't buy it. Furthermore, for your simulator to take advantage of this new type of mower, your `Spouse` object must know that the new mower exists and must know the identifier of the new interface to access it. To allow spouses to be able to use this new variety of mowers, SimWare upgrades its `Spouse` object and releases the `Spouse97` version. The `Spouse97` object now has two ways to mow the lawn: Use the `MowLawn` object to call the old PushMower interface or use the new `MowBigLawn` object to call the new RideMower interface.

The whole point of this exercise is that because the versioning was done correctly and each object supported prior interfaces, any combination of spouse and mower objects could successfully mow the lawn. If not, when you drop in a replacement object, you risk breaking the existing object relationships and your application will no longer function correctly. Make it a habit to ensure that your objects fully support your prior interface definitions as well as any new interface definitions in a given object, and your objects will always work together properly.

Creating COM Objects

Clients can create a new instance of an object by making an appropriate call to the object-creation services provided by the COM Library. How this is accomplished depends on the language, but the call always needs to provide the GUID for the class identifier (CLSID) of the desired object.

At the completion of the creation process, the client gets a memory pointer to the new object. It can then use that pointer to ask the object directly for pointers to any other services provided by the object.

COM Library Services

Each platform that supports COM provides a COM Library, which implements a group of functions that supply basic COM services to objects and their clients. The first and foremost service is the means to create a COM object on request. One way to accomplish this is as follows:

1. The client asks the COM Library to create an object of a specific CLSID.
2. The COM Library uses a system utility called the Service Control Manager (SCM) to find the CLSID information in the system Registry, locate the correct server for this class of object, and start it.
3. The COM Library uses the server to create a generic instance of the object and passes an interface pointer to the client.
4. The client asks the object to initialize itself, thus loading any persistent data associated with the object.

Class Factories

If you want to create more than one object at a time, you could repeat the previous creation process, but a more efficient way is to implement and use a class factory. A *class factory* is a service component whose only purpose is to create new components of a particular type, as defined by a single CLSID. The standard interface used for this purpose is appropriately called `IClassFactory`. It's up to the component programmer to provide the class factory for each class but, fortunately, implementing the `IClassFactory` interface is simple and straightforward. If you want to add licensing capabilities to your class factory, you can opt to use Microsoft's newly defined `IClassFactory2` interface, which requires the client object to pass the correct key or license to the class factory before it will create the new instance of the desired class.

Monikers

Another way to accomplish the creation of an object is by using a moniker. A *moniker* is a special type of COM object built to know how and where to instantiate another specific object and to initialize that object with its persistent data. Each moniker can identify exactly one instance of an object. If you want more than one instance of a given class of objects, you need to use a different moniker for each object, because each object might have its own unique data.

Suppose that in the human resources application at your firm, employees and their histories are stored as COM objects. If you use monikers, a separate moniker would be needed for every single employee in the company. If your employee object, for example, were needed by the system, the system would call up your particular moniker. Your moniker would then create your employee object in memory, load your history information from the persistent data storage, hand the pointer for the employee object back to the requester, and then unload itself from memory.

You can also create a *composite moniker* that activates a group of other monikers. *Absolute monikers* point to OLE documents instead of objects.

Where COM Objects Live

After it's created, a COM object requires a place in memory where it can exist, deliver the services requested by clients, and then unload itself from memory when all the clients report that they're finished with it. To have this existence, a computer object must live within a *process* or *process space* with a defined area in the system memory, some instruction code, perhaps some associated data, and some resources for interacting with the system.

A *thread* is the name given to the action of serially executing a specific set of machine code instructions within a particular process space. Computers with processors and operating systems that can execute more than one thread in each process are said to be *multithreaded*. A process capable of multithreading must always have at least one main thread, called the *primary thread*, but can also have many others. In Windows, *user-interface threads* are associated with each window and have message loops that keep the screen display active and responsive to new user input. Meanwhile, Windows uses *worker threads* to accomplish other computing tasks in the background. After a thread is initiated, it executes its code until it finishes, is terminated by the system, or is interrupted by a thread with higher priority.

COM supports multithreading by putting objects in the same process space into their own groups, referred to as *apartments*. The purpose and function of *apartment threads* are comparable to those of the user-interface threads described previously. Similarly, COM uses the term *free threads* to describe what were previously called worker threads. Regardless of the terminology, COM makes multithreaded development easier by handling the communication between these threads and between the various objects.

COM Objects Communicating Together

COM objects must be designed to be well-behaved neighbors. You want to ensure that any COM objects you create correctly implement the rules that enable consistent behavior and reliable communication with other objects. The following sections discuss the most basic rules your COM objects must live by.

Reference Counting

After an object is created, it can take on a life of its own. Because more than one client might be using its services at any one time, each object needs to keep track of its clients so that it doesn't close itself down before all the clients are finished with it. When a client begins using the services of an object, it has the responsibility to call the `AddRef` method to increment the server object's reference counter. Similarly, when the client has finished, it has the responsibility to notify the server object by calling the `Release` method to decrement the reference counter. When all clients have released themselves from the object, the reference counter goes to zero. The object then knows its work is completed and can safely save any persistent data and self-destruct by unloading itself from memory. If a client subsequently needs the object, the object is created again and the reference counting process is repeated.

You must implement the methods for `AddRef` and `Release` as part of the `IUnknown` interface. Because all interfaces inherit from `IUnknown`, the `AddRef` and `Release` methods are then automatically available through any interfaces you define for your object.

COM Objects Across Process and Network Boundaries

COM objects need to be able to communicate with their local neighbors on the same machine, as well with distant COM objects residing on machines located on the other side of the world. Considerably more complexity is involved with the latter process, but you need to understand both processes to create objects that comply with the COM specification.

Remote COM Servers Remote COM servers (also known as *cross-process* or *out-of-process servers*) are COM objects providing service from a physically separate computer usually connected via a network. Both computers must be operating with COM-enabled operating systems for this process to work correctly. Remote COM servers typically provide slower performance than their in-process cousins, but they can deliver all the advantages explained earlier for generic OOP remote servers, and COM remote servers can provide compatibility between 16-bit and 32-bit clients.

Transparent Connections: Marshaling, Proxies, and Stubs In COM, a *proxy* is a small binary component activated in the client's process space, which acts as an in-process connector to the server interface, regardless of the server's physical location. A *stub* is a small binary component activated in the server's process space, which acts as an in-process connector to the proxy in the client. With this arrangement (see Figure 4.11), the COM client doesn't need to know where the server object is located because COM creates a proxy or stub as needed, making all servers appear to be in the same process space.

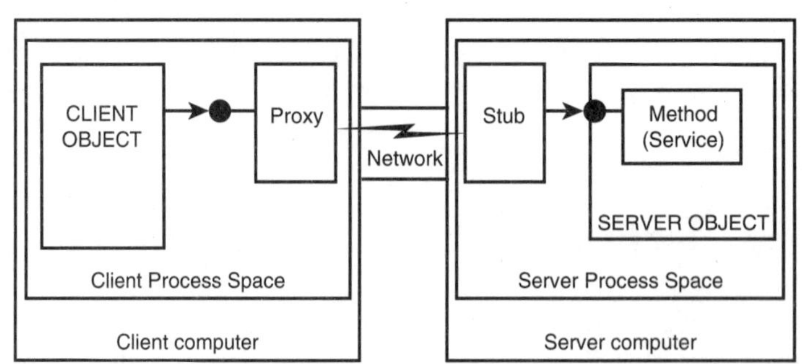

FIG. 4.11 COM proxies and stubs provide each remote object with an in-process communication link to other objects across a network.

While a great deal more overhead is necessary to communicate with out-of-process objects than in-process objects, no additional effort is necessary for the client. With this architecture, all objects are made available to clients uniformly and transparently.

Some extra work needs to happen behind the scenes to make this communication process transparent to the objects. For an in-process server, the client can simply use a pointer to the server, but out-of-process clients have only a pointer to the proxy, and COM must support interprocess communication such as Remote Procedure Calls (RPC) to reach the stub, which then communicates through a pointer to reach the server. *Marshaling* is the name given to this process of packaging interface data into an appropriate format for delivery across process or network boundaries. The code module that performs these tasks is called a *marshaler*. For the return trip to the client, the process to unpackage this data is called *unmarshaling*.

Object Automation If you want to create an object that can be programmed or automated by another object, your object will expose this capability through a specially defined standard interface called `IDispatch`. This interface, also called a *dispatch interface* or *dispinterface*, must implement a standard method called `Invoke` that acts as a channel to receive automation commands from clients. Dispatch interfaces allow you to expose functions and data as methods and properties, which are combined in logical units called *Automation objects*. An application or component that exposes Automation objects is called an *OLE Automation server*. An application or component that uses the services of an Automation server is called an *OLE Automation client*. Used by OLE Automation servers, the `IDispatch` interface is generic across programming languages.

COM Object Data

COM objects, much like traditional applications, need to be able to store their data. A COM object can store its data through persistent storage of object data, uniform data transfer, and connectable objects.

A COM object that can store its data by using a fairly permanent medium (such as in a database on a disk drive) is said to have *persistent* data. Persistent storage is accomplished natively in COM by means of a structure formerly called *OLE structured storage*, now called *Compound Storage*. This structure essentially implements its own independent file system, and the whole thing is stored within a single traditional file on the host machine.

Compared with the traditional file structures, the directories are called *storages*, and the data is stored in file-like structures called *streams*. In much the same way that files contain data specially formatted for the program that created it, streams can hold data in any format designated by the object that creates it. The *Root Storage* can contain any number of additional storages, also called *substorages*, and any number of streams. Each substorage can also contain any number of additional substorages and streams, with the only limit being the amount of space available on the disk. This entire structure is then physically stored as a single conventional file on the system's disk drive. Figure 4.12 compares the familiar DOS/Windows file structure and the COM Compound Storage system.

Historically, there have been many ways to exchange data between programs. You could import a data file or copy and paste from the Clipboard, or perhaps a program might read an initialization file. COM has defined a common approach for moving data between objects called *Uniform Data Transfer*. Again, a standard interface, `IDataObject`, is defined to accomplish this functionality. By calling the `IDataObject` interface, one COM object (an ActiveX control, for instance) can quickly and easily request data from another object any time new data is needed.

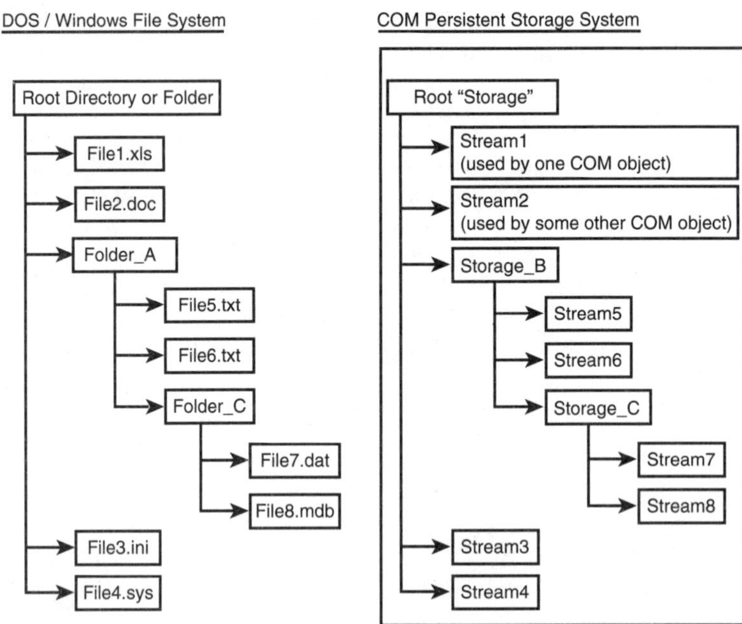

FIG. 4.12
The COM Structured Storage architecture closely resembles the DOS/Windows file system architecture but is stored on a single file on the host system.

When one object needs data from another object based on data changes, timers, or other spontaneous events, a better technology called *Connectable Objects* can be used to pass the data between objects. The idea behind connectable objects is to set up dedicated incoming and outgoing interfaces used exclusively for interobject communication. Each connection is instantiated with its own *Connection Point* object within the server object. The client instantiates an internal object called a *sink*, which receives the incoming communication. Standard interfaces defined for this purpose are named `IConnectionPointContainer` and `IConnectionPoint`. The implementation details for implementing these COM interfaces in Visual Basic and Visual C++ are explored in greater detail in subsequent chapters.

Strategies for Using Object Technology with Legacy Applications

For most large organizations, the issue is no longer whether your firm should move to client/server, object-oriented, and distributed computing models, but when and how. Most organizations would like to begin this transition immediately, especially for any new applications, because the benefits of building applications by using object technology are compelling. However, creating new OOP systems of significant size and complexity typically requires additional training for the programming staff, a large investment of funds, and months or years to complete. During that time, all the existing applications built with traditional methods still need to be maintained and updated. Furthermore, new and old systems usually have to interoperate during the transition, because instant transitions involving multiple systems are rarely possible.

This task is indeed daunting, but the sooner your organization determines its strategy for making the transition, the better prepared you can be for implementing it.

When your company is committed to begin the transition, the issue is then how you can economically and sensibly accomplish it. Because aging systems still provide a great deal of functionality, and changing them is getting more expensive every day, many businesses have focused on more urgent problems and secretly hoped for some technical breakthrough to come along and save them before it's too late. Object technologies are no magic bullet, but they can help you solve many of the challenges in creating new systems and updating old ones while maximizing your existing investment in your company's legacy code base.

For most large companies, it isn't wise, practical, or even possible to simply discard the existing mission-critical applications and quickly rebuild them by using object technologies. If this is your situation, you need an incremental strategy that allows you to selectively redevelop, reengineer, and repackage your legacy systems, blending the old processing models with new ones that can all share the same communication framework. COM object technologies can provide that framework.

Each corporate situation presents unique challenges that must be addressed individually, but when you're dealing with these challenges, some common themes emerge. Although there are many variations and combinations, this section explores four basic strategies for applying object technology to the challenge of supporting your legacy computer systems:

- Keep your old systems and interoperate with newly created systems.
- Create new objects around old code to wrap or encapsulate the functions of legacy applications.
- Reengineer legacy applications, using objects to create new multitiered, distributed applications.
- Create object-oriented browser-based interfaces to your legacy data.

Interoperating with Legacy Systems

Many mission-critical legacy systems are stable, reliably do exactly what they're supposed to, and require very little maintenance. Perhaps this claim sounds amazing, but these applications allow your business to continue another day while you and your teammates diligently resolve the most recent crisis or create that "rush job" application desperately required by your more vocal users.

Sometimes there's a compelling reason to change the status quo: the business process changes dramatically, the cost for support becomes unacceptable, or the program could no longer be supported if a serious modification were required or if the language or platform were no longer supported by your company. In such a case, you'll want to start planning the transition and focus on the new system. Because this process will require a great deal of your already scarce programming resources, why not hedge your bets and make use of the legacy system as long as it's practical?

Situations involving this approach would include the following:

- *You have a legacy system that's not yet obsolete, but you anticipate it will be within the next 18 months.* Or perhaps you're planning a change to your business processes that will require a completely different system. Rather than continue to implement short-term fixes on the old system, spend your time and energy to adequately and completely prepare for and implement the new system. The users might accept this approach more readily if you involve them in the requirements, development, and delivery process. Keep the user community updated on your progress in implementing the new system, ask some key users to help test it, and then offer training sessions as soon as practical to ease anxiety about transitioning to the new system.
- *You have a legacy system that manipulates a separate database.* In this case, the old system and the new system can be designed to operate safely while simultaneously using the shared database, and the phase-out can happen gradually as functionality is added to the new system. Users can use either system safely during the transition period.
- *You have a mission-critical system that simply can't go down until a replacement system has proven itself.* In this case, a completely separate system must be implemented and tested extensively over time to ensure that it performs to corporate expectations. Both systems must be operated independently until users are fully trained and the new system is trusted. Then a simple and well-publicized transition plan should be implemented to coordinate the movement of all live data and all users to the new system.
- *You have a monolithic system that's extremely costly to modify, and complete replacement would be so cost-prohibitive that it isn't even an option.* This situation is perhaps the most difficult to deal with, as the old system must be maintained in its legacy state for the foreseeable future. Perhaps your best move here would be to encourage your company to take all reasonable steps to retain the legacy programmers. Also, you might want to start a divide-and-conquer plan, in which you explore business-reengineering options to begin to move separable business functions onto new systems and away from the great monolithic system.

Object Wrappers for Legacy Code

Another approach is to take existing code modules and imbed them inside a new object that acts as a wrapper, completely isolating the legacy code while retaining its functions. This wrapper can encapsulate any or all of the old interfaces—including screen displays, API calls, database interactions, and any other communication elements—exposing them as appropriate COM interfaces. As time, funding, and priorities permit, you can then progressively design and implement new objects to replace the wrapped modules from the legacy application.

There are several specific ways to use this wrapper approach. A *database wrapper* accesses and encapsulates just the legacy data, completely bypassing legacy code. A *service wrapper* encapsulates legacy system services, such as printers and communications devices. An *application wrapper* encapsulates the code and data of a legacy system application. Application wrappers can provide the object-oriented equivalent of traditional "screen-scraping" programs, which emulate the interaction of users on character-based terminals and provide that data through a new graphical user interface. Visual C++ is probably the most common choice for creating these wrappers, but you can also use Visual Basic or Visual J++.

Although wrappers can be a fantastic method for leveraging your legacy programming investments, this approach has a major downside because the old, inflexible legacy code is still hiding inside the object wrapper. The effort to replace the wrapped legacy code with a newly constructed, reverse-engineered object will likely be seen as a very low priority among the users, because they have already received the new functionality and now feel comfortable with it. From their point of view, maintaining the new functionality is your problem, not their problem. Replacing a functioning wrapper object might also be a tough sell to management, which probably has a huge list of higher priority new initiatives and maintenance projects that need your immediate attention. With this in mind, it's usually wise to build object wrappers with great care and attention to detail, as they might need to last until the underlying function is obsolete to the business, or until a completely new system replaces it.

Reengineering with Objects to Create Multitiered, Distributed Applications

Functions performed by existing monolithic architectures can be reengineered or broken down into a multitiered, object-oriented architecture that's more maintainable, scalable, flexible, and reusable.

The first step is to divide functions into three logical groups representing user services, business services, and data services. This analysis can be more challenging than it sounds:

- The user services group includes all the functions that support interaction with the user, such as forms, menus, controls, and other visual displays. User interfaces on the old system might be simple text-based screens, whereas the new system probably needs a considerably more elaborate graphical user interface.
- The business services group includes the functions that implement the business tasks and rules of the organization. If your company is typical, many of the business rules are undocumented, yet still buried deep within the legacy applications, and must be derived by analyzing procedures and even individual lines of legacy code. When you've discovered them, the business rules contained in the old system must be compared to the rules you want for the new system and adjusted accordingly.
- The data services group includes all the functions related to the storage and manipulation of data. Legacy data storage might be implemented with a flat-file data structure, whereas the new system might need to use a relational database.

This logical design might need to be revised as the business needs change, but after the initial implementation is accomplished, subsequent iterations of this cycle are much faster and easier. After this logical division of tasks is accomplished, you can design the physical location of the components.

This process can become quite complicated, but fortunately an object modeling tool called Visual Modeler can be downloaded from Microsoft's web site and used with Visual Basic 5.

Visual Modeler provides the basic features needed to construct and document your object classes and relationships, and it can save you a tremendous amount of time.

▶ **See** Chapter 27, "System Modeling and Microsoft Visual Modeler," **p. 745**

In most organizations, the legacy system can't be shut down while the new system is under construction. Where possible, use an incremental development process to allow the programming team to deliver a series of small victories instead of an ever-more-anxious period of waiting (and hoping) for the success of one enormous project release.

The first components to build are the ones supporting the lowest level functions of the system. Resist the urge to start with the user interface, because you'll quickly become frustrated trying to design interfaces for functions not yet implemented. These low-level functions include such things as data-access components, networking services, and services for hardware and peripherals. Because these functions are potentially needed by any application on the system, migration of these services to reusable components will provide the fastest benefit for other projects that also require these services.

The next components to build are those that support time-consuming computer processes that can be more efficiently accomplished in a separate process space. Performance of the main system can be enhanced greatly by implementing these slower processes as components that can operate in a separate process on the same machine or on a separate, more specialized machine. Functions that fit this category might include fax processing, database report generation, credit-card validation, and computing of numeric solutions by using complex algorithms. When these components are moved onto a separate processor, asynchronous processing can be used by any application on the system modified to take advantage of it.

After these two groups of components are built, tested, and operational, you've formed the foundation that can support a cycle of continuous improvement. Each of the following projects should provide the remaining components to one major subsystem of the legacy application. Attempting to complete all the remaining components at one time is a risky endeavor that should be avoided if possible for two reasons:

- The users and management of most organizations like to see steady progress for all the money they're investing in your programming projects. The smaller the scope of the project, the less likely you are to encounter problems that require significant schedule delays.
- Because this technology is still relatively new, it's likely that your programming team will be gaining valuable experience during this process, and schedules are rarely built to accommodate many "experience-building" mistakes. By taking the path of incremental improvement, team members can gain experience as they deliver a steady stream of system enhancement on time and on budget.

Browser-Based Interfaces for Legacy Data

One of the fastest and most exciting approaches capitalizes on the recent explosion in the use of I-net technology. You can create object-oriented interfaces for your legacy data by porting the functionality of your legacy applications to a browser-based implementation. The larger your organization, the more promising the benefits, as long as your company already has the equipment and infrastructure in place to facilitate it. If access to local area networks, wide area networks, and the Internet from each desktop is commonplace at your organization, this might be your fastest, least expensive, and most flexible option for transitioning away from your legacy systems.

If your company doesn't yet have the infrastructure in place, the benefits of this approach can be so compelling as to become a cost-justifiable reason to start investing in the infrastructure.

This I-net approach relies on the browser on each user's desktop to act as the client container for your interfaces and data. The browser and an I-net connection to the company I-net server computers are the only additions required at the user's computer. With this approach, as soon as you change the content delivered by the central server computer, everyone can use the most recent version.

Visual Studio is particularly well suited to support development of object-oriented browser-based systems. Because DCOM provides your object communication framework, you need to have a DCOM-enabled container for your objects at the user's machine. Your best choice for this container today would be Internet Explorer; when Windows 98 is released, it would be the new Windows 98 Active Desktop. If you're planning to write all your servers by using Visual J++, your user platform options would then include the so-called Network Computer (NC) or WebPC machines that are sparsely equipped network client computers running a standard Java Virtual Machine and little else. Because all your server objects will be accessed across the I-net, that's all that needs to be done at the user's machine.

Visual Studio gives you an even greater degree of flexibility on the server side. Your ultimate goal is to encapsulate all desired services associated with the legacy system into a new set of COM server objects. You can use any of the encapsulation strategies discussed previously, and you can implement it by using COM objects you've created by using any combination of Visual C++, Visual Basic, or Visual J++. Then you can use Visual InterDev to include those objects in a set of active server pages that serves as new the user interface. After your objects and interface pages are developed and tested, you can release them by posting them to a production server platform. Unlike conventional installs (where you interrupt users to make an install), with this approach you must notify your users by other means before you can expect them to start using the new system. But like conventional systems, it's a good idea to train the users before unleashing them on mission-critical data systems.

Suppose that your firm's existing inventory database resides on a legacy mainframe computer and is accessed from PCs by using a terminal emulator. You can implement replacement with new browser-based graphical user interfaces by incrementally creating Active Server Pages to suit the needs of each user group (sales, order fulfillment, finance, and so on). These pages can be delivered from an internal I-net server that was also connected across the network to the legacy mainframe. COM objects created to run on the server provide services by making database calls to the legacy database and delivering the results to the objects operating in the user's browser container. Both the legacy system and your net I-net system can operate simultaneously until all the user groups are provided new interfaces. When the legacy database is migrated to a new system, the calls to the legacy database can be modified and redirected to any standard Structure Query Language (SQL) enterprise database product. If your database product is COM-compatible (such as Microsoft's SQL Server), your task is even easier.

The benefits of this I-net approach can be downright exciting to an IS department trying to support a large user base. Gone are the hassles of software version control, trying to physically install or upgrade individual copies of your corporate software on hundreds or thousands of geographically separated computers, or trying to use network install utilities to accomplish these tasks. You can at least expect the following benefits from this I-net approach:

- The programming tools allow much greater flexibility and much faster delivery of minor changes than conventional software development cycles.
- As users become more familiar with the browser interface, training can become less of a challenge, compared with teaching a new interface with every program.
- Specialized hardware connections and leased circuits to mainframe computers can be redirected just to corporate I-net servers, or the mainframes can be modified to become I-net servers themselves, thus facilitating the standardization of the communication infrastructure.
- The data shared and services provided within the company can be easily and selectively extended to business partners and existing customers, and advertised online to new customers.

The list of benefits goes on, but even these few things are enough to illustrate the advantages to large organizations with a geographically dispersed user base.

Although this approach has numerous benefits, it does have some significant drawbacks that need to be considered before you commit to it. As with any centralized system, if the network goes down, the entire user community might suddenly lose service. This can be somewhat mitigated by operating mirrored servers at separate locations, so if one server can't be accessed by a given user, that user might be able to establish a connection to the alternate server. Even with mirrored servers, the fragile state of the global I-net communication backbone does pose a significant risk to mission-critical systems. If this risk is unacceptable, you need to stick with more traditional approaches.

Security is also a factor when considering any I-net–based approach. Secure protocols are now available but have yet to gain universal trust. However, many corporate information systems can be operated safely with the minor degree of risk now associated with I-net communication methods.

▶ **See** the chapters in Part III, "Developing Internet, Intranet, and Extranet Applications," **p. 292**, for more information about browser-based interfaces for legacy data.

Strategies for Implementing Object Technologies for New Applications

The first order of business for creating new applications is to gather and document as many project requirements as you can. This step can't be overemphasized. Object-oriented programming allows a great deal of flexibility in designing and adjusting the solution to a given programming problem, but an entire project design might have to be scrapped if a critical requirement is omitted during design and then discovered during user testing.

Use every resource at your disposal to ensure that you've captured all the requirements of the user's business process. Rapid prototyping is especially helpful when you're trying to present a new graphical user interface paradigm. By presenting a live demonstration of a sample graphical user interface option for a business process solution, you can often unlock creativity and innovation from users during the design phase before formal development begins. This is a dual-edged sword, however, as user expectations and requirements may also rise significantly. The risk is worth it, because you should be able to reveal and solve any existing problems with the business processes rooted only in limits imposed by a previous automation system. After you document a comprehensive set of business requirements, you can begin creating an object-oriented design.

When designing an application from scratch, the procedural programming strategy typically uses a mixture of two related approaches:

- *The top-down approach to programming.* Divide large tasks into smaller tasks until each task is simple enough to be implemented directly.
- *The bottom-up approach to programming.* Write procedures that implement basic tasks, and combine them into progressively more complicated structures until you've created the desired functionality.

The suggested approach for OOP design draws on the top-down and bottom-up approaches. First, examine your problem description from the top, and look for the items, descriptions, and actions described. The nouns will become the object classes, the adjectives will become the properties, and the verbs will become the methods. Then you can start the design process by establishing the classes and associating each method with the class most responsible for that action. From this starting point, you can concentrate on the bottom-level tasks, adding the properties and further refining your design.

This process is simplified significantly by using modeling software. As mentioned previously, you can use Microsoft's Visual Modeler for no charge, or you may want to purchase the more full-featured version called Rational Rose. Regardless of your choice of modeling tool, learn your modeling software well before attempting to use it to build an object-oriented system from scratch. The development time and money saved by effective use of a modeling tool will make it well worth your effort.

▶ **See** Chapter 27, "System Modeling and Microsoft Visual Modeler," **p. 745**

ON THE WEB

For more information about Rational's object modeling tools, visit its web site at **http://www.rational.com**.

When your preliminary design is acceptable to you and your colleagues, repackage it as a presentation and walk through it with your most supportive user representatives. Even the most elegant object-oriented designs are worthless if they don't satisfy the users' needs. Rapid prototyping is also a valuable tool for testing ideas, to ensure that programmers and users are communicating effectively and to reveal and facilitate the discussion of any hidden assumptions buried in the individual requirements.

When your most supportive users are happy, test a basic prototype with your least supportive users. Working with these "difficult" users might not be comfortable, but it will likely yield two very important benefits:

- These more hostile users will tend to make a more determined effort to find the flaws in your project and your logic. Although some portion of this feedback might simply be frivolous griping, many of the comments will reveal places for significantly improving the project. Making peace with hostile users early in the process by negotiating these improvements into the initial design of the project is a much better strategy than avoiding these users and their opinions until you're forced to face them during full-scale user testing.
- After these initially hostile users become part of the development process, they might join you in feeling some personal ownership in the project, subsequently defending the project to ensure that "their" project becomes a success. Requirements definition and preliminary design are critical phases of the development process where changes can be made easily and cheaply, so don't waste the opportunity to capture as many changes as you can while fostering a positive spirit of support among the users.

After you and your users agree on a preliminary object design, resist the urge to immediately begin coding. As a rule, it's cheaper and faster to buy an object than it is to write it yourself, so now start looking for prebuilt objects. First look in your own organization. If your organization doesn't have a well-organized object repository, now is the time to start one. Next, look outside your organization for objects that can be obtained from other parts of the same company or from commercial sources. Remember that ActiveX components are COM objects, and you have thousands of commercially distributed ActiveX components to choose from. Only after you truly exhaust your options for reuse should you pass out the coding assignments.

Now that you're ready to begin writing the code, Visual Studio provides you and your team with enormous flexibility. You may need to use any or all of the approaches mentioned previously, depending on the requirements of your project. Language-specific implementation guidance is provided in subsequent chapters for each Visual Studio tool.

After your objects are developed, tested, and put into production, you need to determine who will support them. The project team that originally created the objects for a specific project will likely move on to other tasks, but the objects they put into the corporate inventory will eventually need maintenance. As many other projects reuse your objects, the responsibility for maintenance of a given object can become quite diluted. To avoid abandoning these valuable objects inadvertently, the objects themselves and the repository should be assigned to a project-neutral focal point or team. Perhaps some of the resources saved by reusing objects can be applied to the task of maintaining the object inventory, and should be budgeted independently from the budget lines of the projects that created them.

One final caution: Invest the time needed to prevent the nearly universal problem of poorly documented applications. Properly and fully document your objects, and then include that documentation and the objects in the corporate object repository. You may even need to reuse or maintain some of these objects yourself someday, so take the time to document them appropriately the first time around.

From Here...

Now that you have a general understanding of object-oriented programming and Microsoft's object technologies, it's time to get some language-specific instructions on how to create a few of those versatile COM objects known as ActiveX components:

- To learn how to create ActiveX components with Visual Basic, see Chapter 5, "Creating ActiveX Components with Visual Basic."
- To learn how to create ActiveX components with Visual C++, see Chapter 6, "Creating Components with Visual C++."
- To learn how to create ActiveX components with Java, see Chapter 7, "Creating Components with Visual J++."

CHAPTER 5

Creating ActiveX Components with Visual Basic

by David Burgett

The most important enhancement of Visual Basic 5.0 over previous versions is its capability to create reusable ActiveX controls. ActiveX controls allow you to encapsulate business rules with functionality in a single package that you can distribute easily by conventional means or by automatic download from an I-net site. You can incorporate ActiveX components into any ActiveX-enabled browser (including Microsoft Internet Explorer), Office 97 applications, Visual C++, and, of course, Visual Basic. With the addition of simple ActiveX control creation to the tool set, Microsoft has poised Visual Basic as a necessary part of any large, I-net–aware development effort.

Several versions of Visual Basic support ActiveX control creation. In addition to the usual retail versions, Microsoft has released a Control Creation Edition of Visual Basic 5.0 that can be downloaded without charge at **www.microsoft.com/vbasic**. Although this limited version can't make executables and lacks most of the advanced features of the full development environment, it does include all the standard Visual Basic controls and provides an inexpensive opportunity to explore Visual Basic's new capabilities. Of course, with this new functionality comes a

Your first ActiveX control

Learn about the three basic types of ActiveX controls. The easiest to create is the subclassed control, which adds new properties or functionality to an existing control.

Constituent controls

Understand the difference between constituent controls and the ActiveX control itself. Clearly understanding this difference is imperative before you can effectively expose the appropriate properties and methods for your ActiveX control.

Aggregate controls

Learn about the aggregate ActiveX control, which consists of several existing constituent controls and greatly extends their potential. Create two controls by using the ActiveX Control Interface Wizard.

Property pages

Understand how to create property pages for your ActiveX control to give it a consistent, professional look your users will quickly come to expect.

User-drawn controls

Create a user-drawn ActiveX control. With user-drawn controls, you create the user interface programmatically, giving you complete control at the expense of more complicated programming.

new level of development and knowledge. To develop an effective control for use by applications and browsers, you must ensure that all necessary functionality is exposed to users. You must also ensure that all errors are handled properly, either silently by the control or by passing the error back to the calling application. Care must also be taken to ensure that the control, if visible, displays properly in many different environments and responds to resizing events, if applicable.

These new concerns are well worth the added development time. By using self-sufficient controls in your applications, you separate the optimization and enhancement of your program into small, easily managed sections. Suppose that you use a sorted listbox control written by another developer in your program. The original developer then improves the sort routine, reducing by 10 seconds the time necessary to sort a long list of items. With no changes to your application, you gain the same 10-second improvement simply by downloading and registering the new control.

You also can use ActiveX controls to enhance your existing Microsoft Excel and Word documents, your company Internet presence, or even your desktop with the recent release of Internet Explorer 4.0. To gain these benefits, you must first understand the nature and purpose of your proposed control and the options available for creating it. To prepare for the exercises in this chapter, you should review the history and definition of OLE and ActiveX technologies in Chapter 4, "Using Microsoft's Object Technologies." ■

Introducing ActiveX Controls

The three basic ways to create an ActiveX control with Visual Basic are separated by your use of preexisting controls:

- The simplest method involves *subclassing* an existing control, adding new functionality or default properties.
- To add a degree of complexity, you can choose to create a new type of control by combining multiple existing, constituent controls into a single package, commonly called an *aggregate control.*
- To expand the possibilities and, thus, the complexity, you can choose to create a new control completely from scratch, obligating yourself to the visual display in addition to the functionality.

The easiest control to create is the simple subclassed control. Subclassed controls often serve only as a measure of convenience in reducing your workload, but don't underestimate the power a simple enhancement can have.

The most basic subclassed control is one that simply has new default properties set for it. For example, the default value of a checkbox in Visual Basic is `0 - Unchecked`. You can easily create a control with all the functionality and appearance of a normal checkbox, but set the default value to `1 - Checked`. This might sound like a great expense for little benefit, but it can actually be a great time saver if you use checkboxes regularly. After you're acquainted with creating ActiveX controls, you can create this example easily in just a few minutes. Suppose that you could cut your development time by just five seconds per checkbox. This very simple example would pay for itself in time and energy within a relatively small number of forms.

Building a Simple ActiveX Control: The Logo Control

In this section, you'll build an ActiveX control that's more functional than the checkbox example. You'll subclass the existing image control to create one that provides a consistent look and feel throughout applications, web pages, and documents and which saves you time by simplifying their creation. The new control, Logo, is used to display a company logo for splash screens, letterheads, or web pages (see Figure 5.1). After you complete the control, your corporate logo will be available in your toolbox right next to your other tools.

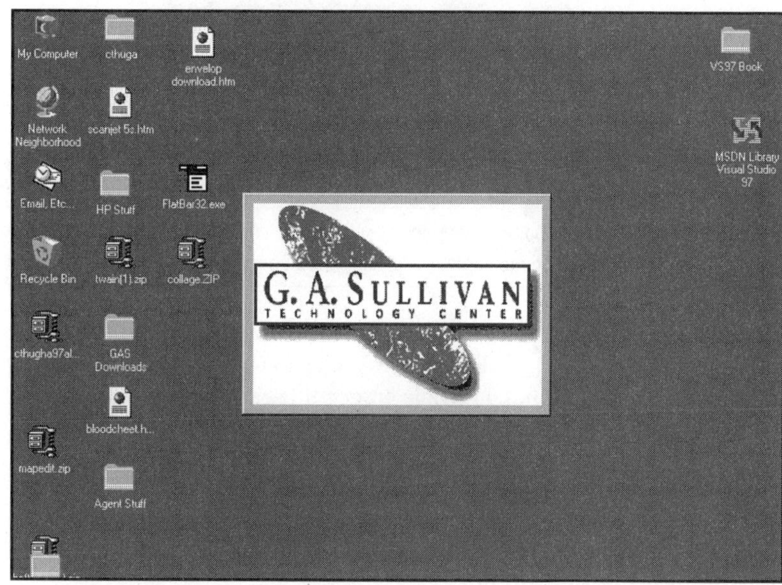

FIG. 5.1 The Logo control makes creating splash screens, letterheads, and web pages as easy as dragging and dropping.

Creating the Corporate Logo Control

To start creating your corporate logo, open a new ActiveX control project by following these steps:

1. Open Visual Basic or choose File, New if Visual Basic is already running.
2. Select ActiveX Control from the New Project dialog box (see Figure 5.2).

In addition to the new ActiveX control (OCX), you can create ActiveX EXEs, DLLs, and ActiveX Documents. EXEs and DLLs are helper files that make the control available to a container, but there is an important distinction. An EXE is run in a separate process, making one copy available to multiple containers that can share data. A DLL is run in the same process and the same container, making communication between the control and the container much faster at the expense of shared variables and additional memory.

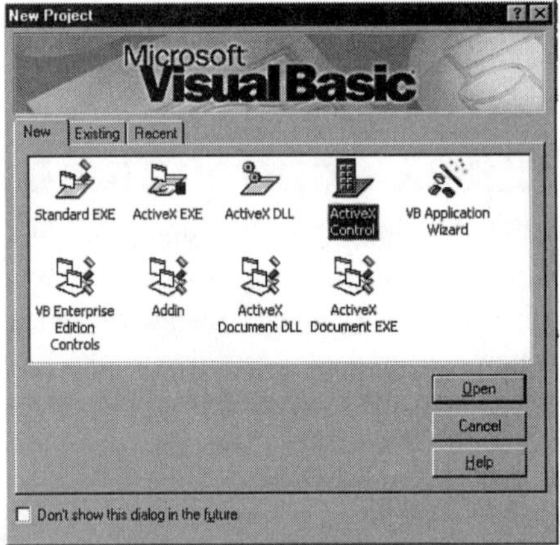

FIG. 5.2
Visual Basic 5.0 adds many types of projects you can create by using its tool set.

An ActiveX Document is different from EXEs and DLLs in that rather than be a support file offering a control to a container, the ActiveX Document is similar to other documents, having the capability to save and copy its data to other containers.

For more information on the differences among these control types, see the Books Online articles "Creating ActiveX Components" and "Building Code Components."

The first difference you'll notice between your ActiveX control project and other Visual Basic projects is the form you'll use to design your control. This form, called a UserControl, isn't a true form in that it has no visible border, title bar, or control boxes (see Figure 5.3). The reasons for this will become clear as you develop the control.

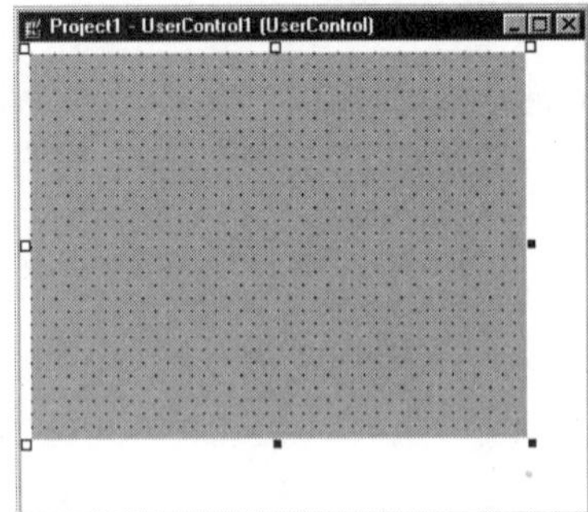

FIG. 5.3
The UserControl form is very similar to a standard Visual Basic form, but without a title bar or border. These minor differences are very important in differentiating an ActiveX control from a standard EXE form.

Next, notice the new format of the Project Explorer (see Figure 5.4).

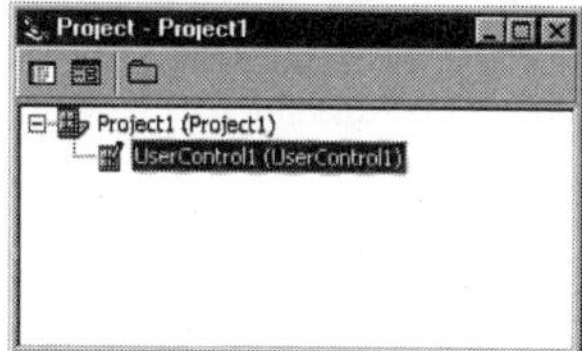

FIG. 5.4
The Project Explorer is now a tree hierarchy instead of a simple list. This new format helps you locate a particular element quickly, and it more clearly represents the relationships between the elements.

The new tree hierarchy of the Project Explorer will help you keep track of which controls, forms, and classes belong to a given project, which can be a challenge while trying to debug a control. Multiple projects are now supported, allowing you to maintain ActiveX controls and their test forms in separate projects. Each project is listed with the filename (if specified) in parentheses.

You should provide easily understood names for the UserControl and project. The name you supply for the UserControl is the one developers and end users will see. Also, it will become the default name within the Visual Basic development environment, with a number appended to it to create a unique control name.

To set the control properties, follow these steps:

1. Right-click the UserControl and choose Properties.
2. Change the `Name` property to Logo.
3. Choose Project, Project1 Properties.
4. Change Project Name to `GASLogo` (see Figure 5.5).

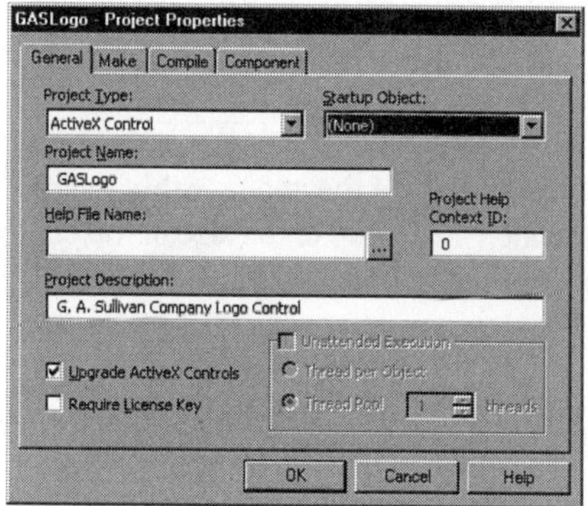

FIG. 5.5
The General page of the Project Properties dialog box allows you to set the name, description, and help file for the control. On the other pages, you can determine how the control will actually be created, including settings for version information and compatibility, optimization, and conditional compilation arguments.

You can't use the same value for the UserControl name and the Project name. Remember to set the UserControl name to something succinct and memorable that describes the control clearly, because this is the name that will appear to developers when the control is added to a form.

Adding Constituent Controls to the ActiveX Control

Because you'll enhance a control, the first step is to add the preexisting control to the new UserControl. Double-click the image control in the toolbox to create a small image control in the center of your UserControl for displaying the G. A. Sullivan corporate logo. For the Logo control to act in the desired manner, you must set the properties of the image control as follows:

1. Click the Image control and press F4 or choose Context, Properties.
2. Set the `Name` property to `imgLogo`.
3. Set `Stretch` to `True`.
4. Set `Picture` to the G. A. Sullivan corporate logo (or the image of your choice).
5. Set `Left` to 0.
6. Set `Top` to 0.

NOTE The choice of an image control rather than a PictureBox control clearly determines the destiny of your new control. The image control lacks many of the methods and properties of the PictureBox control, including a Windows handle to allow manipulation of the control through the Windows API. In return for this lack of functionality, the Image control uses significantly fewer system resources, allowing it to repaint more quickly.

It doesn't matter where the image resides when you set the `Picture` property of the Image control. Visual Basic stores the data within the control itself, allowing you to distribute the control as a single file.

The `Stretch` property determines the state of the image within the control. If it's set to `False`, the image is displayed with its defined size, despite the size of the control. As a result, only part of the image might be displayed, or the entire image might be visible with a blank area around it. When set to `True`, the image size is altered to conform to the control. For the corporate Logo control, it will be important to be able to resize the logo, based on the container. If the control is used in a letterhead, for example, it probably needs to be smaller than if it's used within an application's splash screen.

You must remember the distinction between the UserControl you're creating and its constituent controls. The UserControl is the interface your end user will see and use. The constituent controls used to create the UserControl (the Image control in the Logo example) are visible only to you as you develop the control. Any properties of the constituent controls that need to be exposed to a developer who uses your control will need to be mapped to related properties of the UserControl, as demonstrated later in this chapter. The confusion between these two items will probably cause most of your debugging headaches as you learn to create ActiveX controls in Visual Basic.

With this in mind, you might now understand that simply setting the `Stretch` property of the Image control doesn't complete the resizing of the Logo control. Developers using this control will be able to resize only the UserControl, not the Image control within the UserControl; therefore, you need to attach the `Resize` event of the UserControl to the Image within code as follows:

1. Right-click the UserControl (anywhere outside the boundary of the Image control) and choose View Code from the shortcut menu.
2. Enter the following code:

```
imgLogo.height=UserControl.scaleheight
imgLogo.width=UserControl.scalewidth
```

This code allows the Logo to be resized with the UserControl in the design and runtime environments. The differences between these two environments and the methods for writing conditional code based on the environment are discussed later in the chapter.

Your first control is now ready to use. Before loading your web site or opening your company letterhead, you should first test the control from the Visual Basic design environment.

Testing the Logo Control

The control you're developing can exist only within a container, such as an executable form, a web browser, or a Microsoft Word document. To test your control, therefore, you must create a container for it by adding a new project to your project group with an executable. This new concept for Visual Basic users will become second nature when the difference between controls and containers is clear.

▶ **See** Chapter 8, "Using ActiveX Client Components in an I-net Environment," **p. 239**

▶ **See** Chapter 9, "Using ActiveX Components in a Client/Server Environment," **p. 253**

To add a test container to your project group, choose File, Add Project and then select Standard EXE from the New page of the Add Project dialog box. Your Project Explorer should now look like the one in Figure 5.6.

Because the new project is to be used only for testing, you don't need to supply names or change properties for it. To test the new control, you add it to the form just like any other control.

The Logo control will be the lowest control in the right-most column of the toolbox. You can rest the mouse pointer over it for a moment to confirm this.

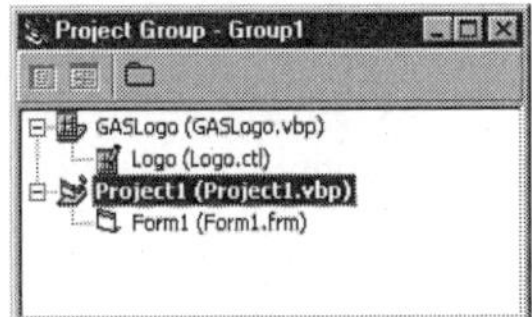

FIG. 5.6
The project group, new to Visual Basic, holds multiple projects, allowing you to create and test ActiveX controls within a single development environment.

NOTE If the UserControl development window is still open, the Logo control will be grayed out and inaccessible. Because Visual Basic must compile and run the control to display it on a form, you can't use the control development window and the form that uses the control at the same time. If the logo is grayed out, close the window in which you developed the Logo control.

Add a Logo control to the new form by double-clicking it in the toolbox. Notice immediately that the Logo is much larger than in the previous window. This increase in size is caused by the code you supplied in the control's `Resize` event. When you added the control to the form, the event was fired, and the code was executed, expanding the image to the size of the control (see Figure 5.7).

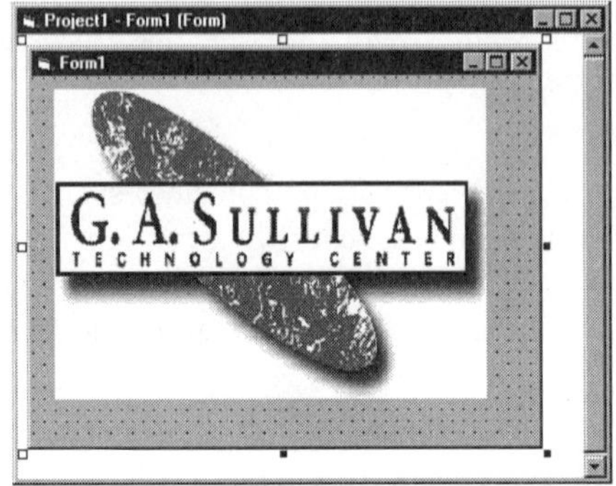

FIG. 5.7
The control is placed in a form container, and the image is automatically resized to fill the control. This automatic resizing is critical to the usability of the control, allowing it to be used in a wide variety of containers.

You can resize the Logo control to ensure that the image is the desired size. The Logo control can now be used like any other. You can manipulate the properties and code the events as usual.

For the control to be distributed, you must create an OCX file by choosing File, Make GASLogo.ocx.

You're now ready to use and distribute your Logo control to create splash screens, documents, and web pages (see Figure 5.8). The OCX file containing the control is the only file you must distribute.

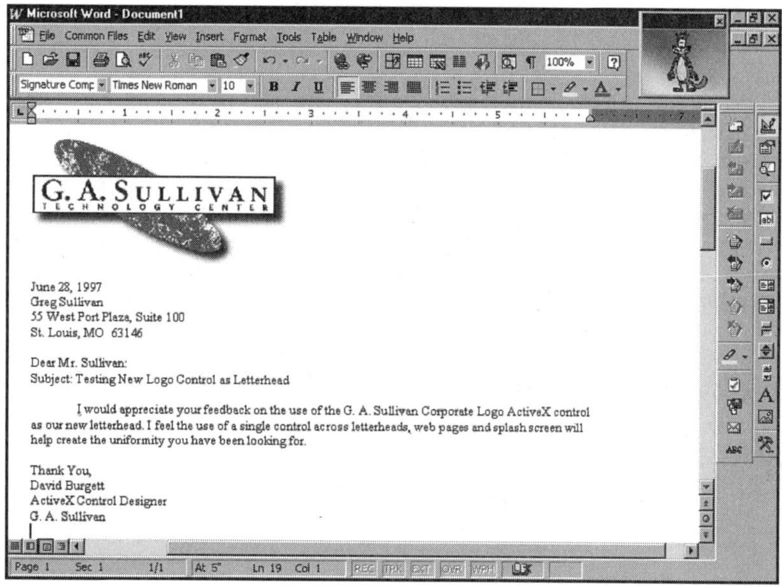

FIG. 5.8
Insert the Logo control into a Microsoft Word document to create a professional-looking letterhead. Because the control retains its automatic sizing capability, you can use it in multiple documents by resizing it as necessary.

TIP The .oca files accompanying your .ocx files are cache files created and maintained by the operating system. They're updated whenever necessary, so their date and file size might change frequently.

Creating an Aggregate Control: The Framed Text Box

The second type of ActiveX control you can build with Visual Basic is an *aggregate control* consisting of multiple existing controls needed for a particular task. The constituent controls used to build an aggregate control can be those included with Visual Basic, third-party controls, or your own ActiveX controls. When the aggregate is complete, the constituent controls work as a single control and appear as such to users.

You can create aggregate controls for specific applications, such as a Personal Information control with text boxes to hold a user's name, address, telephone number, and other personal information (see Figure 5.9). Creating such a control means you have to create the control only once for use in multiple applications or web pages. The business rules applied to entering information, such as allowing only numeric entries in the phone number field, are all part of the control, so they don't add to the complexity of the application that uses the control. Use of a single control wherever user information is required also provides consistency between your applications and familiarity for users.

A Personal Information control example is easy to implement because it consists only of text boxes and labels to define the text boxes. Next, you'll create a slightly more challenging aggregate control that incorporates several different types of controls, implements unique properties and methods, and has a custom property page.

FIG. 5.9
This sample form accepts personal user information through six default FramedText controls. You can resize the finished FramedText control to leave visible only the desired amount of text in a single line or across multiple lines.

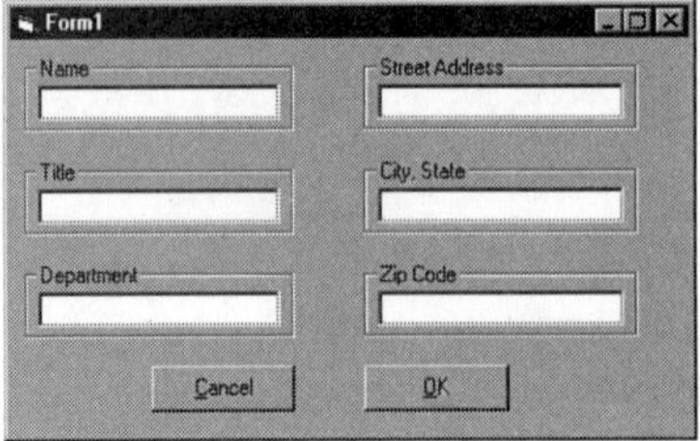

Building Your Aggregate Control

To understand the creation of aggregate controls, you'll create a commonly used combination of a text box surrounded by a frame. You've probably used or created an application that uses this technique. A frame control is placed on a form, and a text box control is placed within the frame. The frame's caption is then set to show users the purpose of the text box. This can lead to very user-friendly forms easily understood by even the most novice users.

Creating visual consistency between the forms in your applications or across different applications is easy when using this type of framed text control on every data entry page. The problem with this technique is the added difficulty involved in creating and maintaining two controls for each data entry field. Each time you need to resize any entry field, you have to resize the frame control and the text box itself. Also, the text box—not the frame—holds the data you're interested in. The text box control is a child control of the frame, not the form, creating additional work if you use any routines that cycle through all the controls on a form.

You can greatly simplify this ritual of creating and maintaining the combination frame and text box control by creating a single FramedText ActiveX control. Begin by following these steps:

1. Open Visual Basic or choose File, New Project.
2. Choose New ActiveX Control.
3. Name the UserControl `FramedText`.
4. Name the project `FramedTextProject`.

You need to add a frame and TextBox control to the UserControl form:

1. Double-click the Frame control in the Visual Basic toolbox. Size isn't important.
2. Click the TextBox control in the Toolbox. Draw the text box within the frame control.
3. Set the following properties for the Frame control:

```
Name        "frmFrame"
Left        0
Top         0
Caption     "FramedText"
```

4. Set the properties for the TextBox control:

`Name`	`"txtText"`
`Left`	`120`
`Top`	`240`
`MultiLine`	`True`

5. To ensure that the constituent controls always fill the aggregate control, add the following code to the `UserControl_Resize` event:

```
frmFrame.Width = UserControl.ScaleWidth
frmFrame.Height = UserControl.ScaleHeight
txtText.Width = frmFrame.Width - 2 * txtText.Left
txtText.Height = frmFrame.Height - 1.5 * txtText.Top
```

6. Choose File, Save FramedText.ctl.
7. Close the UserControl design window.

Add an EXE as you did for the Logo control to test the FramedText control. Add the FramedText control to the form in your EXE. If you notice immediately the time you saved in drawing only a single control, you'll appreciate this time savings more each time you resize the control or set the properties. Resize the control on the form to verify that your code is working as expected.

NOTE The values given for placement of the text box within the frame and multipliers are just guidelines. Feel free to experiment with these values to create the look you want.

Using the ActiveX Control Interface Wizard to Create Properties for Your Control

Now that you have a FramedText control on the form, notice that the new control lacks many of the properties you need—most important, text and caption properties. You first might think to treat the text box as a property of the control and access its `Text` property accordingly. Remember, however, that constituent controls are private members of the UserControl. As the developer using the control, you have access only to the UserControl and its exposed properties.

You've probably realized that there must be some way to create a new property for the UserControl and to connect that property to the `Text` property of the text box. Indeed, there is a way—the ActiveX Control Interface Wizard.

Starting the ActiveX Control Interface Wizard To create the `Text` property and the others you need, use the ActiveX Control Interface Wizard included with all levels of Visual Basic. To begin, choose Add-Ins, ActiveX Control Interface Wizard.

If the ActiveX Control Interface Wizard doesn't appear on your Add-Ins menu, place it there by following these steps:

1. Choose Add-Ins, Add-In Manager.
2. Select the VB ActiveX Control Interface Wizard checkbox.
3. Click OK.

The first dialog box of the wizard details its benefits. As the dialog box explains, this wizard helps you create your ActiveX control by providing choices about which properties and methods will be available to the developer and writing the basic code necessary to support them. You can disable the introductory dialog box as shown in Figure 5.10. If you don't see this dialog box, click the Back button to display it.

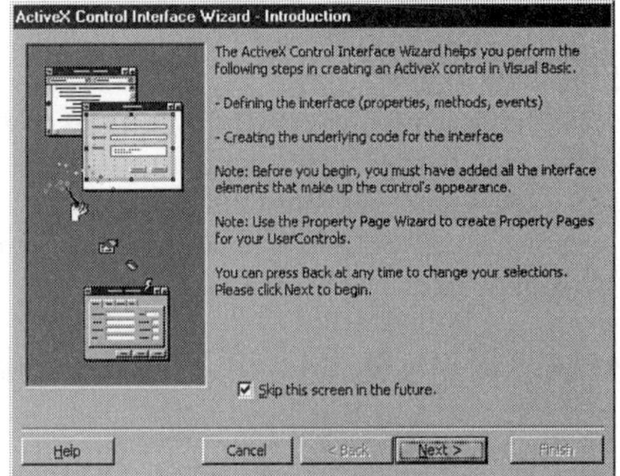

FIG. 5.10
To skip the first dialog box of the ActiveX Control Interface Wizard in the future, select the Skip This Screen in the Future checkbox.

The introduction includes two important notes concerning interface design and property pages. The note about property pages simply reminds you to use the VB Property Page Wizard to create them more easily. The note about interface design informs you that it's necessary to add all constituent controls to the UserControl before running the wizard. This requirement is based on the manner in which the ActiveX Control Interface Wizard creates the code for your control. If you add additional constituent controls to your UserControl after running the wizard, these controls might not behave well or might have incorrect property or method assignments. Choosing the constituent controls should be the first task of every ActiveX control design, so this constraint shouldn't hinder your development.

Click Next to move to the Select Interface Members dialog box of the wizard.

Choosing Among Default Properties, Methods, and Events In the Select Interface Members dialog box, you determine which available properties, methods, and events you'll expose in your ActiveX control (see Figure 5.11). Two lists in the dialog box show the available names and the currently selected names.

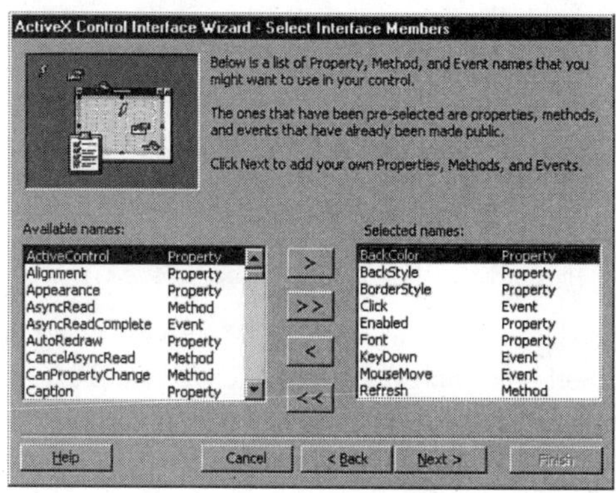

FIG. 5.11
You can choose which standard properties, methods, and events to include in your control. Visual Basic selects those already present and gives you all the standard options, as well as those of your own creation.

The list on the right shows the properties, events, and one method defaulted to all visible ActiveX controls. As you examine the list, notice several useful properties Visual Basic provides for you, such as `BackColor`, `Enabled`, and `Font`. Visual Basic also includes several useful events, such as `Click`, `KeyDown`, and `MouseMove`. The single method provided for you is `Refresh`, which is useful for all visible controls.

In addition to these useful elements, Visual Basic suggests two properties that aren't useful to the FramedText control. The first of these properties is `BackStyle`, which can be set to opaque or transparent, based on the control in question. To decide whether to include `BackStyle` in the FramedText control, you must again understand the difference between the ActiveX control and its constituent controls. Your first thought might be to include the property so that users can place a FramedText control over other controls (such as a background image), allowing the buried controls to show through the frame. Because `BackStyle` isn't a standard property of the frame control, however, it's always opaque and will completely cover the UserControl, so users will find the `BackStyle` property useless and confusing.

It's possible to create a FramedText control with an applicable `BackStyle` property, involving little additional difficulty. As an additional exercise, consider redesigning the FramedText control to use four line controls and a label control in place of the frame.

The second property not useful for the FramedText control is `BorderStyle`. `BorderStyle` could be applied to the frame control, allowing developers to turn off the frame border and thus the FramedText control. Because you're designing the control to specifically have a frame, however, including the `BorderStyle` property would be counterproductive.

To remove the `BackStyle` and `BorderStyle` properties, highlight both properties and click the < button.

Adding New Properties and Methods Now that you've pared the list down to the bare necessities offered by Visual Basic, it's time to enhance the functionality and usability of the FramedText control by adding additional properties and methods. As noted before, the properties most prominently lacking from the FramedText control are `Text` and `Caption`.

Highlight the following items from the Available Names list and move them to the Selected Names list:

- Properties: `Caption`, `hWnd`, `MousePointer`, `MultiLine`, `PasswordChar`, `SelLength`, `SelStart`, `SelText`, `Text`, `ToolTipText`, `WhatThisHelpID`
- Methods: `PopupMenu`, `Cls`
- Events: `Change`, `InitProperties`, `ReadProperties`, `Resize`, `WriteProperties`

Click Next > to move to the Create Custom Interface Members dialog box, in which you can define unique properties, methods, and events for which Visual Basic will create the necessary base code (see Figure 5.12). Although you don't need to add any custom interface members for this simple FramedText example, most ActiveX controls require many custom members in order to be useful, as you'll see in the next example.

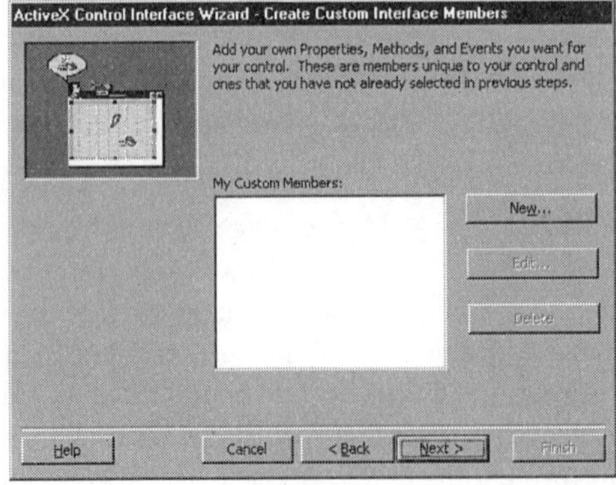

FIG. 5.12
In the Create Custom Interface Members dialog box, you can define your own properties, methods, and events. This dialog box includes any custom interface members previously created manually.

Click Next > to move to the Set Mapping dialog box of the wizard.

Mapping Interface Members The Set Mapping dialog box is the most critical in the wizard because it allows you to map the properties, methods, and events of the UserControl to the constituent controls (see Figure 5.13). Although Visual Basic suggests default mappings, the functionality you want might require a different mapping. If you don't map the interface members to their appropriate controls correctly, your ActiveX control won't function correctly.

Consider the `Text` property of the FramedText control you're creating. This property should refer to the text box constituent control, not the user control itself. You'll map the `Text` property of the FramedText control to the `Text` property of the text box, connecting the two to ensure that a change in one is mirrored in the other. As a result, when the `Text` property of the FramedText control is changed programmatically or at runtime, Visual Basic automatically passes the specified value through to the constituent text control. Because this process is invisible to developers and end users, the `Text` property appears to be a simple property like any other.

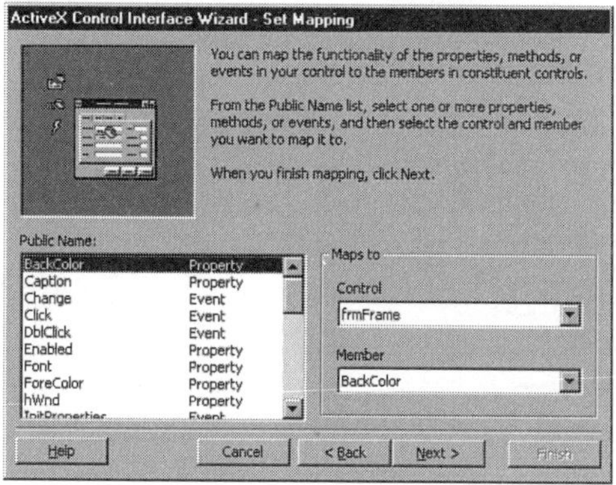

FIG. 5.13
In the Set Mapping dialog box of the wizard, you can map the properties, methods, and events defined in the previous two dialog boxes to their appropriate constituent controls.

To map the `Text` property, follow these steps:

1. Choose `Text` Property from the Public Name list.
2. Choose txtText from the Maps to…Control drop-down list. Visual Basic automatically inserts the `Text` property in the Maps to…Member listbox.
3. Map the rest of the properties, methods, and events to the specified UserControl or constituent controls as listed:

UserControl	`hWnd`, `InitProperties`, `PopupMenu`, `ReadProperties`, `Refresh`, `Resize`, `WriteProperties`
frmFrame	`BackColor`, `Caption`, `Click`, `DblClick`, `MouseDown`, `MouseMove`, `MousePointer`, `MouseUp`, `ToolTipText`, `WhatsThisHelpID`
txtText	`Change`, `Enabled`, `Font`, `ForeColor`, `KeyDown`, `KeyPress`, `KeyUp`, `PasswordChar`, `SelLength`, `SelStart`, `SelText`

CAUTION

You must understand the limitations of the properties you're selecting. The `MultiLine` property, for example, is read-only. Although you can add a `MultiLine` property to the UserControl and map it to the text control, the property will remain read-only; trying to change it will cause an error.

4. Click Next to move to the Finished dialog box of the wizard.

Finishing the ActiveX Control Interface Wizard In the Finished dialog box, you can choose to view a summary report. Ensure that the checkbox is selected and click Finish. The summary report gives you an overview of the work left to be done to make your control effective and stable (see Figure 5.14).

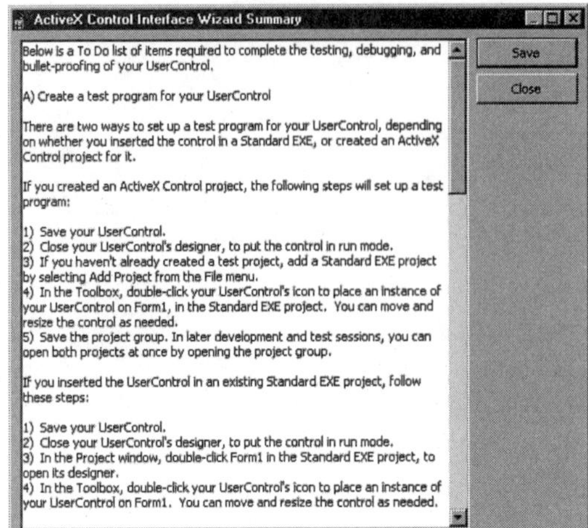

FIG. 5.14
The Wizard Summary text suggests tasks yet to be completed, as well as tips for creating fully functional controls. Pay close attention to Section C of the summary; it offers excellent advice for making your control look and act professional.

Some of the items listed are familiar ones, such as adding an EXE to your project to test the control. Others might be new to you, such as mapping properties to multiple constituent controls, which you'll want to do for properties such as `BackColor`, which you previously mapped to the frmFrame control. For example, you might decide to map `BackColor` to the txtText control, as well, to ensure the same back color for the frame and text box. To do this, add the following line to the public property `Let BackColor`:

```
txtText.BackColor() = New_BackColor
```

You can easily add another property to the FramedText control to allow users to specify separate colors for the frame and the text box. Simply add a new property (as demonstrated later in this chapter), call it `TextBackColor`, and map it to the text control.

Completing the Control with Manually Created Properties and Events

As a Visual Basic programmer, you've no doubt spent many hours setting properties for each control on your forms. If you are a more advanced programmer, you've probably created your own properties for forms and class modules. Now it's time for you to create properties for your own ActiveX controls.

In the preceding section, you used the ActiveX Control Interface Wizard to map the properties of the UserControl to the constituent controls. By examining the code Visual Basic creates for you, you can understand how a property is created (see Figure 5.15).

FIG. 5.15
The ActiveX Control Interface Wizard creates the code necessary for the `Text` property, including a call to the `PropertyChanged` procedure, notifying Visual Basic when the property has changed.

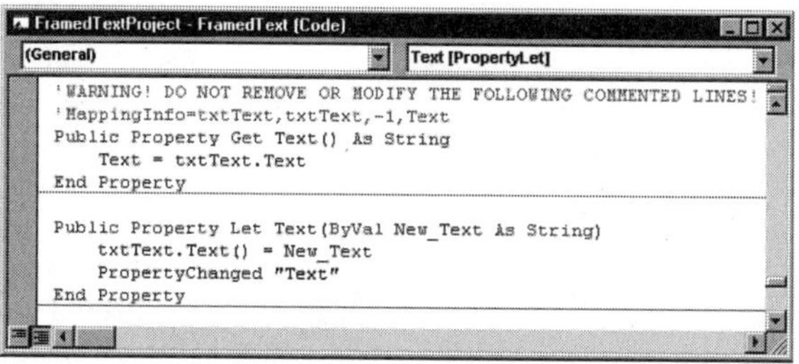
FramedTextProject - FramedText (Code)
(General)
Text [PropertyLet]
'WARNING! DO NOT REMOVE OR MODIFY THE FOLLOWING COMMENTED LINES!
'MappingInfo=txtText,txtText,-1,Text
Public Property Get Text() As String
Text = txtText.Text
End Property
Public Property Let Text(ByVal New_Text As String)
txtText.Text() = New_Text
PropertyChanged "Text"
End Property

CAUTION

As the comments suggest, the `MappingInfo` line contains internal information for Visual Basic and shouldn't be altered or deleted.

The code created for the `Text` property has two routines: a `Property Get` and a `Property Let`. The word *property* differentiates these routines from normal methods and procedures. The third type of `Property` procedure that you need to know about is `Property Set`, which works similarly to `Property Let` except that it defines a reference to an object rather than the value of one of the standard variable types. Use `Property Let` as you would use `Let`, with standard variables (such as integer or string), and use `Property Set` as you would use `Set`, with objects (such as forms or controls).

The `Property Get` function is straightforward. Whenever the program needs to know the value of the UserControl `Text` property, this function returns the value of the txtText control.

The `Property Let` procedure is nearly as simple as you might expect. It accepts a string parameter that holds the new value for the UserControl `Text` property. The procedure updates the `Text` property of the txtText control each time the `Text` property of the UserControl is altered.

TIP

You can pass extra parameters to your own custom `Property` procedures as long as the parameter list in the `Get` and the `Let/Set` declarations agree. Simply define the parameters you want and add to the end of the list the parameter holding the value passed into a `Let/Set` procedure.

The function of an extra line in the `Property Let` text procedure might not be immediately clear. The call to the `PropertyChanged` procedure tells Visual Basic that the property has changed, so VB can update its internal recordkeeping and store the new value. The design-time and runtime versions of the controls are actually different instances of the running program. If Visual Basic doesn't save the new property value internally, the runtime instance of the control won't reflect property changes made at design time.

Visual Basic handles these property value changes through an object called `PropertyBag`. The ActiveX Control Interface Wizard creates all necessary calls to `PropertyBag` for you in the `ReadProperties` and `WriteProperties` methods of the UserControl. `PropertyBag` has two methods—`ReadProperty` and `WriteProperty`—to move values from the internal storage to the actual control.

The `ReadProperty` method has a required `DataName` and an optional `DefaultValue` parameter. `DataName` refers to the property being read; `DefaultValue` is used if no entry is in `PropertyBag`. Similarly, `WriteProperty` takes required `DataName` and `Value` parameters and an optional `DefaultValue` parameter. The `Value` parameter specifies the value to place in `PropertyBag` in the section defined by the `DataName` parameter. `DefaultValue` works a bit differently in `WriteProperty`, in that `WriteProperty` writes information to `PropertyBag` only if the `Value` specified is different from the `DefaultValue`.

For example, the `ReadProperty` method might be called for the FramedText control with a `DataName` of `"Text"`. This returns the value of the `Text` property in `PropertyBag`, or the `DefaultValue` if the `Text` property is empty. Similarly, the `WriteProperty` method, when passed a `DateName` of `"Text"`, saves the value passed in the `Value` or `DefaultValue` in the `Text` property of `PropertyBag`.

By comparing the `Value` and `DefaultValue` and saving only when necessary, Visual Basic conserves file space. Thus, you should use `DefaultValue` whenever possible.

Raising events in your control is just as easy as mapping properties. By calling the `RaiseEvent` method, you can force Visual Basic to respond to any event you choose. For example, in the ActiveX Control Interface Wizard, you specified that the `Click` event should be mapped to the `frmFrame_Click` event. Thus, when users click the frame in the runtime environment, the code in the developer's `FramedText_Click` event is executed.

The problem with this is that the `Click` event for the FramedText control is fired only when users click the frame portion of the control; it doesn't fire when users click the text box. This disparity demonstrates the individual nature of the constituent controls, rather than the desired unity.

Fortunately, correcting this problem is simple. From the `txtText_Click` event, call `RaiseEvent Click` to force Visual Basic to fire the appropriate `Click` event. You could call the `frmFrame_Click` event instead, but this would add an unnecessary extra level of procedural calls. If you need to include additional internal code in response to the `Click` event, you want to call the frame's `Click` event directly.

To complete the FramedText control, create `RaiseEvent` calls in the txtText control for the following events: `DblClick`, `MouseDown`, `MouseMove`, and `MouseUp`.

NOTE For the `Mouse` events, be sure to copy the `RaiseEvent` call from the frmFrame control to ensure that you include the correct parameters.

The FramedText control is now ready to use like any other Visual Basic control. It's manipulated in the design environment and referred to programmatically like all other controls. Test the executable to ensure that it works as it should. You can now use it in place of the standard text box whenever you want to draw special attention to an entry field.

Creating a More Complex Aggregate Control: The TimeSheet Control

To see an even more complex aggregate control, create a TimeSheet control to provide end users with a means of entering billable hours via a company intranet (see Figure 5.16).

▶ **See** "Creating a Java Applet or Application," **p. 221**

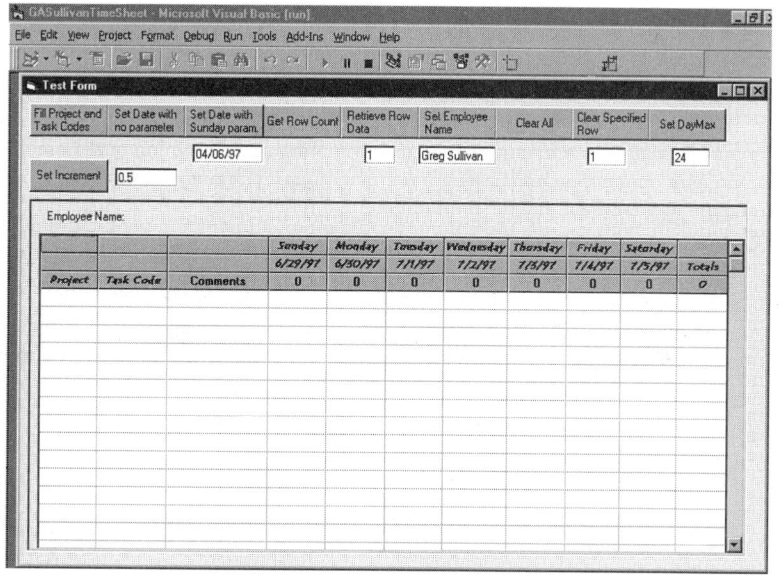

FIG. 5.16 The TimeSheet control can be used in a standalone application, as seen here, or on a company intranet page. By using a single TimeSheet control in all potential browsers, you can ensure that all data entry conforms to the same set of business rules.

End users will be able to choose a Project Code and Task Code from a list of acceptable options, enter hour amounts for those projects and tasks, and enter any comments about the tasks. The control itself needs to make the acceptable Project and Task codes available, verify and correct all data entered, and provide automatic totaling for all values entered. The control also should accept a project description for every code and display this description in a ToolTip when users pause over the specified row of time values.

NOTE Visual Basic's Control Creation Edition doesn't include the MSFlexGrid control necessary for the TimeSheet example. Although you could use a control array of text boxes or a third-party grid control instead, neither is necessary to follow the example. ■

This single control can easily be made available to all employees, in house and on site, with business rules built into the control, thus helping ensure that no erroneous time sheets are submitted. This example shows how ActiveX controls can improve efficiency and accuracy while expanding accessibility. This TimeSheet control will become an integral part of the G. A. Sullivan Billing Project created throughout this book and included at **http://www.gasullivan.com/vs97book/**.

Building the TimeSheet Control

To begin your control, open Visual Basic and a new ActiveX control as before. Edit the project properties to set the Project Name to `GAS TimeSheet`. Set the `Name` property of the UserControl to `TimeSheet`.

NOTE Remember to make these names clear and suggestive, as developers will see the names when they try to add a reference to your ActiveX control. ■

To design the control, first decide its functionality and choose which preexisting controls to use. The TimeSheet control should look and function like any typical time sheet. The design will be a common grid, with columns of dates under which times can be entered into the appropriate rows. The rows represent the projects and tasks consultants can work on in any given week.

To display the time sheet information in rows and columns, use the Microsoft Flexible Grid control included with Visual Basic. The MSFlexGrid isn't a part of the standard toolbox items, so you'll have to tell Visual Basic where to find it by adding a reference to MSFlxGrd.OCX. (The file extension shows that the MSFlexGrid is itself an ActiveX control.) This example shows the extensibility of ActiveX controls—you're using an ActiveX control as the basis for a new ActiveX control.

Follow these steps to add a reference to the MSFlexGrid control:

1. Choose Project, Components from the menu.
2. Select Microsoft FlexGrid Control 5.0.

NOTE If Microsoft FlexGrid Control 5.0 isn't an option on the Components list, you'll have to find the file yourself. Click Browse and locate the MSFlxGrd.OCX file, which should be in the \Windows\System directory. ■

3. The MSFlexGrid control is now available in your toolbox. Double-click its icon to place the default MSFlexGrid on your UserControl (see Figure 5.17).
4. By default, the MSFlexGrid has two columns and two rows, with one of each *fixed*. Your time sheet will have 11 columns—seven for days and one each for project code, task code, comments, and total hours. Base the total row number in the time sheet on how many different projects and tasks any particular employee works on in a given week. As an initial estimate, you can choose 48 as the maximum. You should also set the other necessary setup properties for the MSFlexGrid now, as follows:

Property	Setting
`Name`	`grdTimeSheet`
`Cols`	11
`Rows`	48
`FixedCols`	0
`FixedRows`	3
`Left`	0
`Top`	0

Resize the UserControl to the largest convenient size. Resize the MSFlexGrid to fill the UserControl.

5. Like the GASLogo control created earlier in this chapter, you want the TimeSheet control to resize to fill the entire UserControl. Add the following code to the `UserControl_Resize` event:

```
grdTimeSheet.height=UserControl.scaleheight
grdTimeSheet.width=UserControl.scalewidth
```

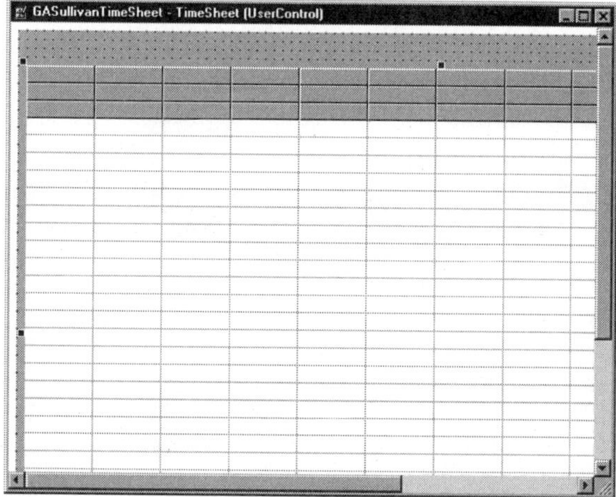

FIG. 5.17 The MSFlexGrid is the main component of the TimeSheet control. The example here has three fixed rows at the top to serve as headers.

Using Constituent Controls to Enhance the TimeSheet Control's Functionality

Now that the basic grid is in place for your TimeSheet control, you need to add the constituent controls that will add functionality to the TimeSheet control. One major drawback of the MSFlexGrid is that users can't type directly into the grid. Because the grid is designed to be bound to a database, there's no way to type directly into the control as into a text box control.

That said, you might guess that the next control to add to the TimeSheet control is a text box control for data entry. When users type an entry into the TimeSheet, the actual text manipulation takes place in the text control, with the final value being placed into the grid.

When examining the MSFlexGrid, you probably noticed that it supports `KeyDown`, `KeyPress`, and `KeyUp` events, which can be used for text manipulation. Because so much code is necessary to support all the text-manipulation functions a text box inherently handles, it's worthwhile to tackle the difficulty of incorporating the text box into the control. You'll still have to write code to handle different `KeyPress` events in the grid control for determining whether to display the text box or another control. By using the text box, you give users full editing functions, including cut, copy, and paste.

Follow these steps to create a text box with the appropriate properties:

1. Add a TextBox control to the TimeSheet control. (Size and placement aren't important.)
2. Set the `Name` property of the TextBox control to `txtTime`.
3. Set `BorderStyle` to `0 - None`.
4. Set `Visible` to `False`.

Ideally, users of your aggregate ActiveX control should never see its constituent controls as separate controls; the aggregate controls should always appear and work as a single control. For the TimeSheet control, the text box should be invisible to users—they should have a sense that they're editing their text directly in the TimeSheet control itself. For this reason, set the `BorderStyle` of the text box to none, forcing it to be invisible (see Figure 5.18).

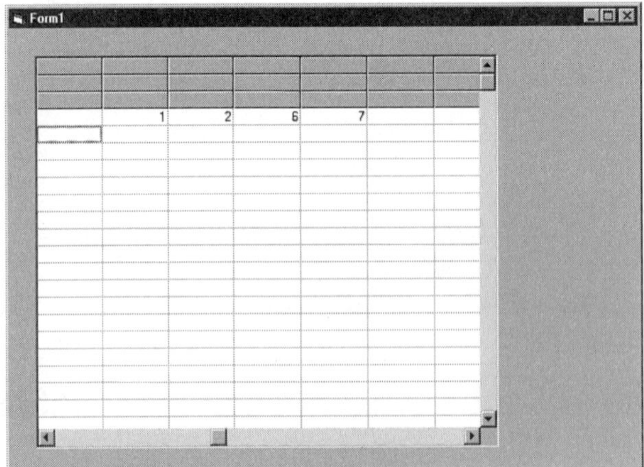

FIG. 5.18 The invisible text box allows you to enter text into the grid seamlessly. By ensuring that the user can't differentiate between the constituent controls, you create a professional-looking, complete control.

To make the txtTime control fully invisible to the user, you need to place it in the appropriate area of the TimeSheet and size it to match the cell being edited. To enable this, place the following code in the `KeyPress` event of `grdTimeSheet`:

```
txtTime.Top = GrdTimeSheet1.CellTop + GrdTimeSheet1.Top
txtTime.Left = GrdTimeSheet1.CellLeft + GrdTimeSheet1.Left
txtTime.Width = GrdTimeSheet1.CellWidth
txtTime.Height = GrdTimeSheet1.CellHeight
```

NOTE The assignment statements for the `Top` and `Left` properties will work without adding an associated `grdTimeSheet` property because the top and left of the grid control have been set to 0. This code will be necessary later in the chapter when you move the grid control to allow room for other controls.

Whenever users press a key, txtTime appears inside the cell invisibly and accepts their input. Before this process is useful, however, you need to add four more lines of code immediately below the preceding code:

```
txtTime.text = chr(KeyAscii)
txtTime.setstart=len(txtTime.text)
txtTime.setfocus
txtTime.visible=true
```

The first line passes the character selected by users to the `Text` property of txtTime, offering the appearance that users are typing directly into the grid. The TimeSheet control won't be very user-friendly if users have to press a dummy key before they can start entering data. The second and third lines set the focus to txtTime and place the cursor at the end of the word, so users can continue typing immediately. Again, this helps make the transition between grid and text box seamless, enhancing the illusion that the TimeSheet is a single control.

To test your TimeSheet control, add an EXE to your project, place a TimeSheet control on the default `Form1`, and run the application. Use the mouse or arrow keys to select a cell and then begin typing. The text you type will seem to appear directly in the grid itself, lining up within the current cell. Notice that if you type too many characters to fit in the cell, the text automatically scrolls, just as anyone would expect. This is another benefit of using the TextBox control.

Now that users can enter data into the TextBox control, you must ensure that the data can be transferred from the text box to the grid after it's entered. Users can signify completion with one of two keys: Enter to accept the data or Esc to cancel any changes and stop data entry.

In the `KeyPress` event, enter the following code:

```
Select Case KeyAscii
Case Is = 13:
grdTimeSheet.Text = txtTime.Text
txtTime.Visible = False
      Case Is = 27:            txtTime.Visible = False
End Select
```

Try the code again in the executable. You can now enter text into any non-fixed cell on the grid.

Lifetime of a UserControl and the Associated Events

Now that users can enter text into the grid, you need to provide column headers so that they know which data belongs in each cell. These headers should be created within the TimeSheet itself and be visible in the design-time environment. Before you can write the code to accomplish this, you should understand the five most important events in the lifetime of an ActiveX control.

An ActiveX control begins its life cycle when the first instance of it is created within a system. This includes creation within a running application, a web page, or a design-time environment. When an instance of the control is created, the `UserControl_Initialize` event is fired, giving programmers a chance to set any setup variables necessary.

NOTE The `Initialize` event is equivalent to the `Form_Load` event found in regular forms.

Immediately after the `Initialize` event, the `InitProperties` or `ReadProperties` event fires as the control populates its properties. The difference between the two events is chronological. The first time a control is created, the `InitProperties` event fires, both setting up the properties and filling them. When that instance of the control is re-created, the `ReadProperties` event fires, simply filling in the appropriate values.

For example, when you place a TimeSheet control on your executable's form, first the `Initialize` event fires, and then `InitProperties`. When you run the application, the control actually ends and restarts. Because this is the second creation of this particular instance of the control, the `ReadProperties` event fires after the `Initialize` event.

Two events are associated with destroying the control: `WriteProperties` and `Terminate`. `WriteProperties` occurs only when the control needs to save its current data back to the control container. The most common occurrence of this is when a control is deleted from the form in the design-time environment.

The `Terminate` event fires when any instance of the control stops. This includes ending an application, closing a web page, deleting a control within the design-time environment, or switching between runtime and design time. (The distinction will become more important later in the chapter when you use the `Ambient` property of the UserControl.) The `Terminate` event is used to process any clean-up code before the control is destroyed, such as closing the database for data-bound controls.

Now that you're familiar with the events fired at creation and destruction of your ActiveX control, you can use that knowledge to create column headers for the TimeSheet control. The column headers for a G. A. Sullivan time sheet are as follows:

- *Project.* The code of the project to which the consultant is assigned.
- *Task.* The code of the specific project task to which this time is billable.
- *Comments.* Any consultant or client comments.

- *Days of the Week.* Seven columns for specifying the days of the week, the date, and the total hours worked for that day.
- *Total.* Total hours billed to the specified Project and Task.

When you first added the MSFlexGrid control to the TimeSheet control, you set the `FixedRows` property to 3. In the grid control, fixed rows appear at the top of the grid, are light gray in color, and never scroll off the page. These rows are to be filled with the column headers.

The lowest of the three fixed rows will contain the main headers and the day totals. The top and middle rows will hold the day of the week and the date, respectively. Add the code in Listing 5.1 to the `UserControl_Initialize` event. These values represent the static grid headings; the dynamic grid headings are determined at runtime.

Listing 5.1 Values for Static Grid Headings

```
Dim iCounter as integer
With grdTimeSheet
    .TextMatrix(2, 0) = "Project Code"
    .TextMatrix(2, 1) = "Task Code"
    .TextMatrix(2, 2) = "Comments"
    .TextMatrix(0, 3) = "Sunday"
    .TextMatrix(0, 4) = "Monday"
    .TextMatrix(0, 5) = "Tuesday"
    .TextMatrix(0, 6) = "Wednesday"
    .TextMatrix(0, 7) = "Thursday"
    .TextMatrix(0, 8) = "Friday"
    .TextMatrix(0, 9) = "Saturday"
    .TextMatrix(1, 10) = "Totals"
End With
```


Close the UserControl design window and examine the form in the executable. The column headers now appear in the design-time environment and at runtime as well (see Figure 5.19).

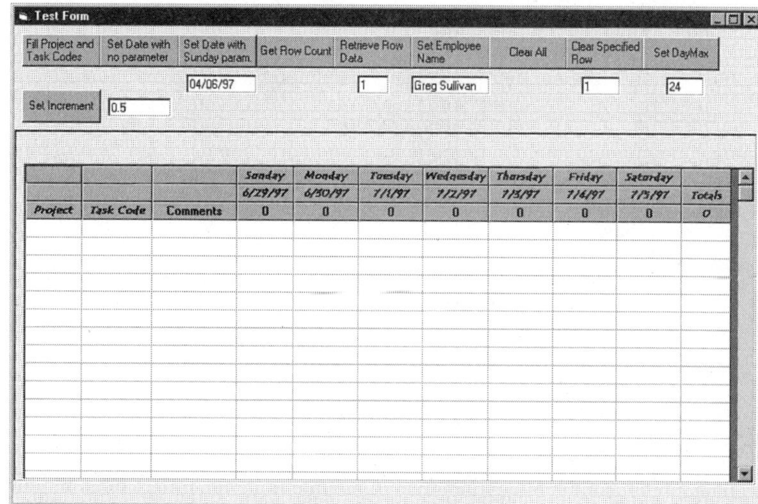

FIG. 5.19 With all column headers in place, the TimeSheet control now resembles a typical time sheet. Setting the default date headers to the current week gives the TimeSheet control an automated look and feel.

Considering Private Versus Public Methods

To fill in the rest of the column headers, you need to write two subroutines that can be called at initialization and any time during the control's life. When writing ActiveX controls, you need to plan carefully which portions of the control should be exposed to future developers and which should be guarded to ensure that they aren't abused. Remember that future developers not only include anyone who uses your control, but also, because controls can be subclassed, anyone who uses any child of your control.

When you define a function or subroutine in an ActiveX control, you must tell the Visual Basic compiler whether it's private or public. If you declare it as public, it will be compiled as a normal method of the control and can be called in the form of `Control.MethodName` just like the `clear` method of the ListBox control. If you declare the subroutine as private, it's available only to other routines within the same module. If you try to call a private subroutine from outside the control, you get a `Method or Data Member Not Found` compiler error.

To display the day totals in the third row, create a private subroutine that you can call anytime a new number of hours is entered into the TimeSheet. Because this is an internal bookkeeping subroutine, making it available to the control's users isn't necessary. Users should never have to call a routine explicitly to update the totals; the control will handle it implicitly.

Add the code in Listing 5.2 to your TimeSheet control.

Listing 5.2 The *RecalcTotals* Procedure

```
Private Sub RecalcTotals()
   Dim x As Integer
   Dim y As Integer
   For x = 3 To 9
      GrdTimeSheet1.TextMatrix(2, x) = "0"
   Next
   For x = 2 To GrdTimeSheet1.Rows - 1
      GrdTimeSheet1.TextMatrix(x, 10) = ""
   Next
   For x = 3 To GrdTimeSheet1.Rows - 1
      For y = 3 To 9
         If Val(GrdTimeSheet1.TextMatrix(x, y)) > 0 Then
            GrdTimeSheet1.TextMatrix(2, y) = Val(GrdTimeSheet1.TextMatrix(2, y))
            ➥+  Val(GrdTimeSheet1.TextMatrix(x, y))
            GrdTimeSheet1.TextMatrix(x, 10) = Val(GrdTimeSheet1.TextMatrix
            ➥(x, 10)) +  Val(GrdTimeSheet1.TextMatrix(x, y))
         End If
      Next
   Next
   GrdTimeSheet1.TextMatrix(2, 10) = Val(GrdTimeSheet1.TextMatrix(2, 3)) + _
      Val(GrdTimeSheet1.TextMatrix(2, 4)) + _
      Val(GrdTimeSheet1.TextMatrix(2, 5)) + _
      Val(GrdTimeSheet1.TextMatrix(2, 6)) + _
      Val(GrdTimeSheet1.TextMatrix(2, 7)) + _
      Val(GrdTimeSheet1.TextMatrix(2, 8)) + _
      Val(GrdTimeSheet1.TextMatrix(2, 9))
End Sub
```

Add a call to `RecalcTotals` to the end of the `UserControl_Initialize` event, and your TimeSheet control will have hour totals across the third fixed row. Next, add another call to the subroutine in the `txtTime_KeyPress` event at the end of the code for `KeyAscii=13`. Test the application; it should now accept and total numeric input in the grid.

Adding the Rest of the Constituent Controls to the TimeSheet Control

Most of the basic functionality has now been implemented for the time sheet. The columns are labeled and totaled appropriately, and users can enter values into the grid. The only major functions still missing from the TimeSheet control are the capability to choose project and task codes for a row and the capability to enter comments.

You might have noticed that at this point you can actually enter numeric data in the Comments column by using the txtTime control; however, using this control for comment entry limits the comments column by the same business rules applied to the time column, which, when the control is complete, will accept only numeric data. It's possible—and not difficult in code—to determine which column is now accepting the data and apply the business rules accordingly; unfortunately, that reduces the readability of the code and complicates debugging. A better solution is to add another text control to accept alphanumeric data for the Comments column.

Set the properties for txtComments identical to those of txtTime, with the exception of the `MultiLine` property, which should be set to `True` to allow users to enter multiple lines of text in a text box only one line high. The event procedures should be similar as well; you can simply copy most of the code to the new control. For the multiline capability of the text control to be useful, you have to make the control more than one line of text high; therefore, you should adjust the size of the txtComments control to be twice the height of the cell being clicked in the `grdTimeSheet_Click` event. Although the text will be squeezed back into a single line when it's placed into the grdTimeSheet control, it will be easier to enter long text when more is visible.

> **CAUTION**
>
> Make sure that all references to txtTime are changed to txtComments, and if you add any additional code that references a specific cell of the grid control, be sure to edit the values accordingly. The Visual Basic compiler can't catch these types of errors, and debugging them can be quite difficult.

To complete the TimeSheet control, you need to add to it two combo boxes to hold the list of acceptable project and task codes. Combining lists into one listbox control creates the list as it's required and saves a small amount of memory; however, it also diminishes the control's performance speed by forcing it to re-create the list at runtime.

Accordingly, add two combo box controls to the TimeSheet control and name them `lstProjectCodes` and `lstTaskCodes`. You need to add to the TimeSheet control two public methods, `SetProjectCodes` and `SetTaskCodes`, which will accept an array of strings containing the appropriate data. This array of strings will be used to fill the Project Descriptions combo box, which means end users can choose only from valid projects. The same technique is used for the Task Descriptions combo box. Because the control expects to have a list of project descriptions, the array passed containing the project codes is actually a two-dimensional array that also holds the descriptions (see Figure 5.20).

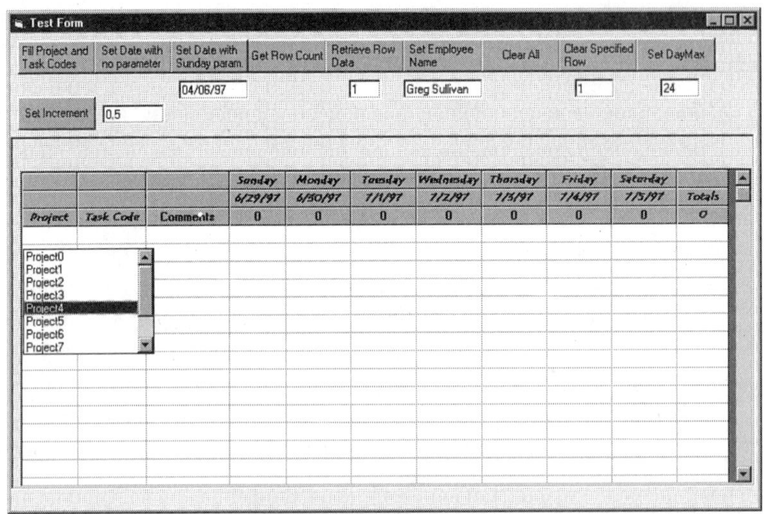

FIG. 5.20
The first listbox displays the appropriate project codes for this time card, ensuring that only a valid project code is used. You should always define appropriate business rules for a control before doing any actual coding.

If you've never passed an array to a Visual Basic procedure, don't worry—it's easier than it might seem. Simply declare the parameter as you would for any variable-length array in the procedure declaration, as follows:

```
Public Sub SetProjectCodes(codes() As String)
```

To determine the number of elements passed into the procedure, use the `Ubound()` function and work with the array as you would any locally defined one.

Carefully Considering Exposed Properties to Make a Control Complete and Useful

The default properties of the combo box control should work fine for the TimeSheet as well. The only property that stands out as one that could be changed is `Sorted`. The TimeSheet control would probably seem more user-friendly if the Project and Task codes were displayed in alphabetical order, so this might be your initial impulse.

Before you do this, however, you should consider your end users' needs. Perhaps the project codes for a given company are customarily in a particular order but not necessarily alphabetical. If users are accustomed to a specific list order, altering that order might actually make the control more difficult to use.

The ideal solution is to allow users to decide whether to sort the combo boxes; however, the `Sorted` property of combo boxes is read-only at runtime, making such a property very difficult to implement.

If you want to explore the option of letting users decide, consider either maintaining two combo boxes for each list or using the Windows API to design the combo box from scratch in code. To use the API, start with `CreateWindowEx`, any good book on the Win32 API, and a lot of elbow grease, and you should be on your way.

Some properties are easy to create and useful to the control. Because you've seen how the ActiveX Control Interface Wizard can create the properties for the control, you'll create a property manually to help you understand the internal mechanics involved. You'll create a `DayMax` property for the TimeSheet control to establish one of the business rules applied to the data entered into the TimeSheet. The `DayMax` property gives developers a way to control the maximum number of hours that can be entered for any given day. This way, the maximum number of working hours can be set to 8 or some other valid value between 1 and 24, helping to decrease data entry mistakes.

A `UserControl` property is nothing more than a publicly defined variable, a designated value that the outside world can see. You might decide, therefore, to define a public module-level integer variable for the TimeSheet control and name it `DayMax`. This way, any program using the TimeSheet control can set or read `TimeSheet.Daymax` as any valid integer value. Although this method would work, it offers the control no protection from being set to a negative value or a nonsensical value, such as 10,000. What you need is a way to call a procedure anytime the value changes. Visual Basic properties give you just that, and more.

CAUTION

Be sure to remove any declarations you've made for `DayMax` before implementing it as a property. If you attempt to define a property and a module variable with the same name, the compiler will stop with an `Ambiguous Name detected` error.

Recall the syntax for property declaration:

```
Public Property Get PropertyName() as PropertyType
Public Property Let/Set PropertyName(PropertyValue as PropertyType)
```

Define the procedures for the `DayMax` property. Now that you know how to define the property to the world, you need to create an internal integer variable that holds the value of the public variable. Define `m_DayMax` as a module-level public integer. The `m_` stands for *member* to help you remember that the variable is an internal member of the control. Create the property by entering the code in Listing 5.3.

Listing 5.3 The Code Behind a Control Property After Sufficient Error Checking Is Included

```
Public Property Get DayMax() As Integer
   DayMax = m_DayMax
End Property
Public Property Let DayMax(ByVal New_DayMax As Integer)
   If New_DayMax >= 1 And New_DayMax <= 24 Then
      m_DayMax = New_DayMax
   End If
End Property
```

Now close the code window and open the executable form. Select the TimeSheet control and examine its properties. The `DayMax` property appears in the Property Browser like any Visual Basic–defined property and is set to the default value for integers of zero (see Figure 5.21).

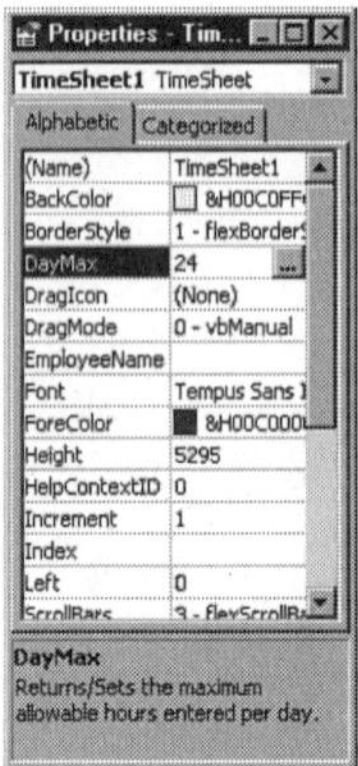

FIG. 5.21
The `DayMax` property appears in the standard Visual Basic property window with a brief description in the Help pane. Note that clicking the ... button to the right of the DayMax line opens the property page containing the `DayMax` property.

To make the `DayMax` useful, you must set its default value to a valid value, such as 24. This is accomplished in the `UserControl_InitProperties` event, setting `m_DayMax` to 24 and allowing the property to read this value when it's created.

Using the ActiveX Control Interface Wizard's Set Attributes Dialog Box

Finish adding the constituent controls to the TimeSheet control by adding a `lblEmployeeName` label and an associated label captioned `Employee:` just above the MSFlexGrid control.

Now that all constituent controls have been placed on the TimeSheet control and you've added the `DayMax` property manually, start the ActiveX Control Interface Wizard to complete the following list of custom interface members:

- `EmployeeName` property: String; mapped to `lblEmployeeName.caption`.
- `Increment` property: Single; no mapping.

- `RowCount` method: Returns the current number of rows filled with data.
- `RowData` method: Returns an array filled with the data from the specified row.
- `SetDate` method: Sets the column headers based on the date passed in or based on the current week.

ON THE WEB

The entire code for the TimeSheet control is available at **http://www.gasullivan.com/vs97book/**.

Use the ActiveX Control Interface Wizard to map the `EmployeeName` property directly to the associated label. No further work on this property is necessary for now. The `EmployeeName` property would be extremely useful in a more advanced version of the TimeSheet control that updates a centralized database or automated payroll.

The `Increment` property is a single value used to round data values entered to the nearest increment specified. For example, if you want to allow your employees to enter time in 15-minute segments, set the `Increment` property to .25. Now all values entered will be rounded to the nearest quarter hour automatically.

Because the `Increment` property is non-visual, don't map it to any of the constituent controls. Having a non-mapped interface member will bring up the wizard's Set Attributes dialog box (see Figure 5.22). This dialog box defines settings for any non-mapped properties. You can define the return type and the arguments to simplify method declaration or the data type, default value, and read/write privileges to simplify property declaration.

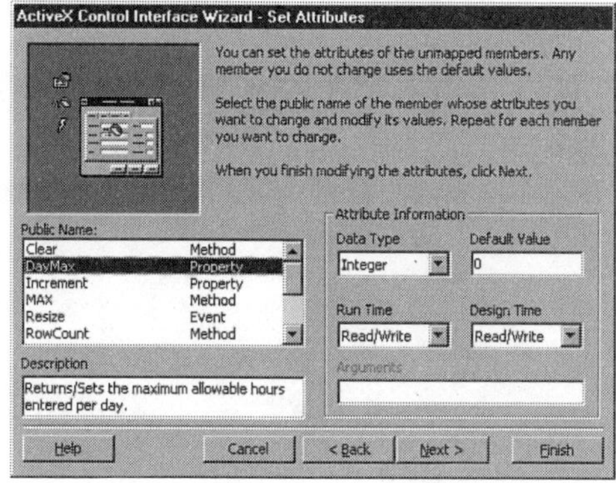

FIG. 5.22
The Set Attributes dialog box of the ActiveX Control Interface Wizard allows you to set read/write access, default values, data types, and help descriptions. Appropriate default property values speed development time and make a control user-friendly.

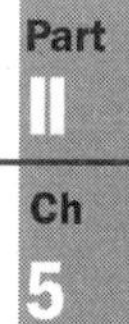

You can also use the Set Attributes dialog box to define a description for each unmapped property, method, and event. This description will be available to developers via the Visual Basic Object Browser and the property window, as seen in the last section of this chapter. If you plan to distribute your control for development use, you should always define a clear, helpful description—other developers will appreciate it.

Notice that the ActiveX Control Interface Wizard includes `DayMax` in the list of properties. This demonstrates the capability to run the wizard multiple times, even after property or method definitions change. As noted before, it's important to have all constituent controls in place before running the wizard, but code changes won't have an adverse effect.

NOTE If you run the wizard multiple times on a single control, you'll probably encounter Visual Basic's odd way of dealing with multiple declarations. Rather than replace an old declaration with the newly defined one, Visual Basic simply comments out the old code. While this is excellent for recovering from mistakes made within the wizard, it makes for messy code. Removing these extra comments will make your code more readable. ■

Set a description and the appropriate values for each custom interface member and then finish the wizard. Copy the code for the three new methods and test it in the executable. You should be able to change the employee name, view automatic rounding of all hour data entered, and retrieve information about the data in the grid.

Using the *AmbientProperties* Object

As explained previously, one major difference between ActiveX controls and normal executables is that you create ActiveX controls to run in two distinct states: design time and runtime. The control developers manipulate in the design environment (for example, Visual Basic or C++) is a running application, the same application that executes in the runtime environment. As the control developer, you must have a way to determine which state the control is being run in so that it can react appropriately. The `AmbientProperties` object holds this information and much more (see Figure 5.23).

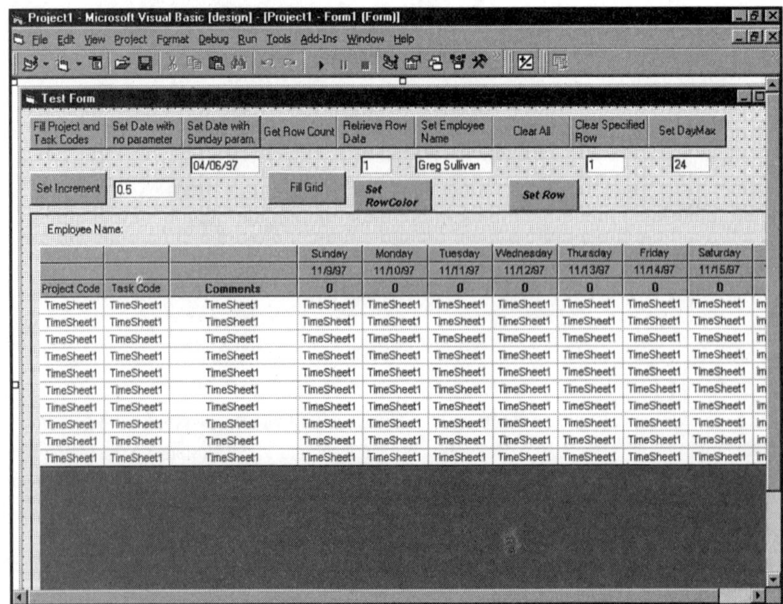

FIG. 5.23 By using the `Ambient.UserMode` property, you can fill the grid with the control name at design time only. Use discretion with the `UserMode` property; overuse or misguided use will only confuse your users.

Every container that can support an ActiveX control provides an `AmbientProperties` object (called simply `Ambient`) with which you can determine this. Visual Basic defines 16 read-only properties within the object, allowing you access to important container values such as `BackColor`, `DisplayName`, `Font`, and `UserMode`.

`UserMode` is a Boolean value that determines whether the control is being executed for end users or developers. If end users are using the application containing the control, `UserMode` is `True`; otherwise, it's `False`. This property allows you to design controls with different design-time and runtime interfaces, such as the Common Dialog, Timer, and Wizard controls.

To demonstrate use of the `UserMode` property, add code to the TimeSheet control to display the name of the control in each non-fixed cell of the TimeSheet at design time only. Add the code in Listing 5.4 to the `UserControl_Show` event. The `Ambient` object's most useful property for creating ActiveX controls is the `UserMode` property, which allows you to determine whether the controls are being used in design- or runtime mode.

Listing 5.4 Adding a Creative Finishing Touch with the *Ambient* Property

```
If Ambient.UserMode = False Then
   Dim x As Integer, y As Integer
   For x = 3 To MSFlexGrid1.Rows - 1
      For y = 0 To 10
         MSFlexGrid1.TextMatrix(x, y) = Ambient.DisplayName
      Next
   Next
End If
BackColor = Ambient.BackColor
MSFlexGrid1.ForeColor = Ambient.ForeColor
```


Now examine the control placed on the executable form, noticing that each cell contains the name `TimeSheet1`, the default name for the TimeSheet control. The final two lines blend the control into its container by setting the control's color scheme to match that of the container. Thus, if you set the `BackColor` of the executable form to another color, close the form, and then redisplay it, the frame around the grid portion of the TimeSheet control reflects the color change as well. This technique works very well if the TimeSheet is used with no border (`BorderStyle = 0`). Run the executable to ensure that the `DisplayName` is filled in only at design time.

You probably noticed the problem with this code when you had to close the executable form and reopen it to display the name changes. The code to fill the grid with `Ambient.DisplayName` executes only when the control is drawn on the form. Thus, the `DisplayName` in the grid doesn't update when you change the control's properties. To account for this, the UserControl has an `AmbientChanged` event, which fires whenever one of the ambient properties of the control container is changed. The list of ambient properties includes, in addition to those used previously, properties that let you determine that your control is the default for the form, the palette being used to paint the control, and even the local language being used by Windows.

To use the `AmbientChanged` event, copy the code from the `UserControl.Show` event and paste it into the `UserControl.AmbientChanged` event. Delete the three final lines from the `Show` event to ensure that the colors used to paint the TimeSheet control will change only when the related colors of the container change. Leave the code to display the `Ambient.DisplayName` at design time in both events to ensure that the grid is filled when the form is displayed and updated when the control name is changed.

To further optimize your control, use the `PropertyName` parameter passed into the `AmbientChanged` event. You can build a `Select Case` statement to execute only the code necessitated by the property that changed, rather than execute all code each time.

NOTE The `AmbientProperties` object is container-specific. In other words, different containers might have different `AmbientProperties` objects and, thus, different ambient properties. For example, `BackColor` is a standard property of the form's `AmbientProperties` object, but not necessarily of a custom container. Your completed control should therefore include code to handle any situation where the control is placed on a nonstandard container that doesn't support the properties you're trying to read.

Now that you have all your properties created and set appropriately, you might be wondering how developers will keep track of them all. Another new feature of Visual Basic 5.0 is its capability to group properties together into logical groups on property pages.

Creating Property Pages

In using Visual Basic, you've probably used a control that contains a custom property page. In fact, you've used one to create the TimeSheet control, the MSFlexGrid. In the ActiveX control designer, right-click MSFlexGrid1 and choose Properties. Rather than bring up the usual Visual Basic Properties window, the MSFlexGrid displays its own custom property page (see Figure 5.24).

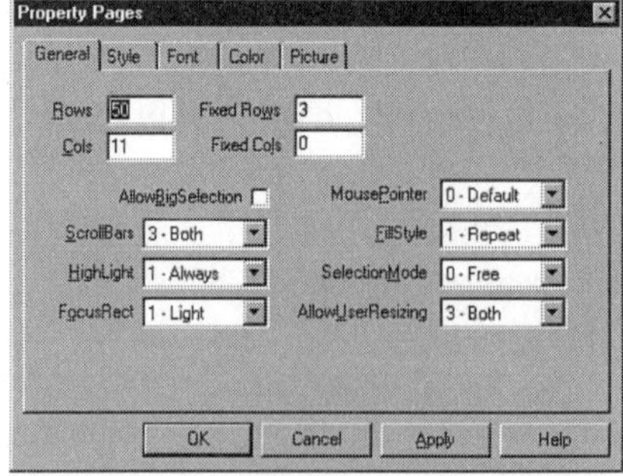

FIG. 5.24
The MSFlexGrid's custom property page groups the control's properties into five convenient pages.

The benefit of using a custom property page is ease of use and understanding for developers. The custom property page lets you group properties onto tabbed pages, making their purpose more readily understood. The property page for the MSFlexGrid divides its properties into five tabs devoted to General, Style, Font, Color, and Picture properties. On the General page, developers can see at a glance the number of fixed and standard rows and columns without having to scan up and down a typical Properties window. Likewise, with all font-related properties grouped on a single page, developers can see them all quickly and even view a sample based on the current settings.

Creating Property Pages with the Wizard To add a property page to the TimeSheet control, you use the Property Page Wizard to construct the basic page. Choose Add-Ins, Property Page Wizard from the menu.

If the Property Page Wizard doesn't appear on your Add-Ins menu, you can place it there by following these steps:

1. Choose Add-Ins, Add-In Manager from the menu.
2. Select the checkbox next to VB Property Page Wizard.
3. Click OK.

The first dialog box of the wizard is an introduction, which can be turned off by selecting the checkbox. The second dialog box of the wizard, Select the Property Pages, shows you a list of the property pages Visual Basic suggests you include. Three default property pages are included with Visual Basic: StandardFont, StandardColor, and StandardPicture. These same pages are included in the custom property page for the MSFlexGrid.

Visual Basic has already suggested that you use the StandardFont and StandardColor pages by adding them to the list of available pages. Select both and click Add to add a new page. Name the page General when prompted and move to the next screen. Choose General at the bottom of the list and click the up-arrow button twice to move it to the top of the list (see Figure 5.25).

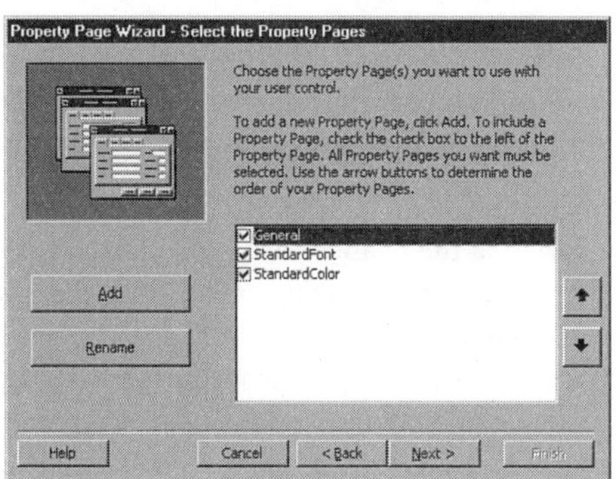

FIG. 5.25
Visual Basic suggests StandardFont and StandardColor property pages, to which you'll add a General property page as shown here. Additional pages are only a click away.

In addition to the Font, Color, and Picture pages, Visual Basic includes any property pages (.pag files) you have in your project. By adding existing pages to your project, you can reuse property pages for many different controls, with only minor modification.

Ensure that all three pages are selected and advance to the next dialog box, Add Properties. In this dialog box, you can decide which properties belong together on a single page. On the left is the list of Available Properties, and on the right are tabbed listboxes for each selected property page. With the General tab selected, choose >> to move the three available properties into the General listbox (see Figure 5.26).

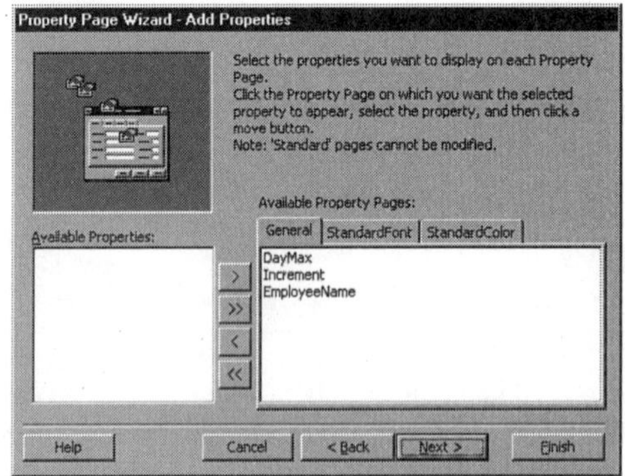

FIG. 5.26
The three available properties for the TimeSheet control should be moved onto the General property page. In more complicated controls, it's important to place similar properties together to help users understand their purpose.

NOTE The StandardFont and StandardColor pages are maintained directly by Visual Basic; thus, you can't add properties to these pages.

Choose Next > to move to the final page of the Property Page Wizard. Choose to view the summary report and select Finish. If you've just created the General property page, Visual Basic issues a confirmation that it was created. Respond to the confirmation and examine the summary report closely—it contains a plethora of tips on how to test, bulletproof, and accessorize your property pages.

Close the summary report and open the executable form. Right-click the TimeSheet control and notice a new entry titled Properties. Select this entry to view the custom property page for the TimeSheet control (see Figure 5.27).

Test the property page to ensure that the changes are applied back to the control. Close the property page and return to the ActiveX control designer. Notice that the General property page now resides in your project window. Double-click the page to view it. Property pages are designed like all ActiveX controls. You can use the property page design window to modify the page any way you like. For example, to personalize the page to your company, you could add a background image of your company logo. You can also locate the controls where you want them on the page.

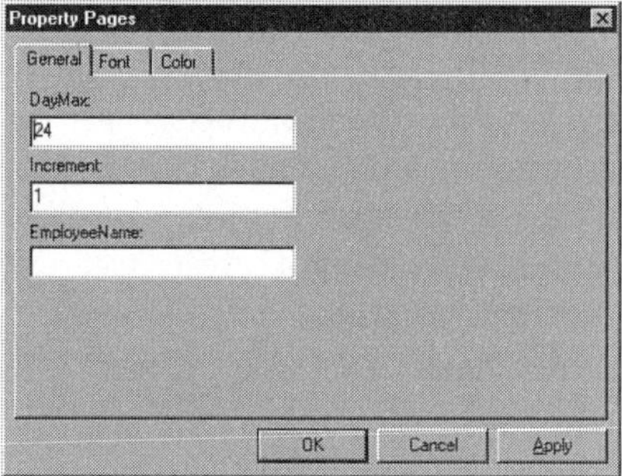

FIG. 5.27
The custom property page for the TimeSheet control is complete in just a few minutes with the Property Page Wizard. This small amount of work can pay large rewards in ease of use and readability for users.

NOTE You'll probably be inclined to resize the General property page to conserve space, but this isn't necessary. When the custom property page is displayed, Visual Basic will create a uniform interface by forcing all forms to the size of the largest form.

Creating Property Pages from Scratch At some point, you'll probably find it easier to create your own property pages from scratch than to use the wizard. Start by choosing Project, Add Property Page to create the page. When the page is created, save the form and examine the properties for the ActiveX control. The `PropertyPages` property maintains a list of all included property pages. Check the box next to your new page to include it in the list.

To make a designed-from-scratch page functional, you would have to write the code the Property Page Wizard creates for you. Examine the code in the General property page. You'll notice the `PropertyPage` object has two new events in addition to the usual events for forms:

- `ApplyChanges` is called by the Apply and OK buttons and by a change to another property page. Its purpose is to apply all property changes made on the page back to the control. As you would expect, this is accomplished by simply assigning to the control properties the values specified in the text boxes or listboxes on the property page.
- `SelectionChanged` fires when the property page is displayed and when the array of selected controls changes.

The standard Properties window in Visual Basic allows you to select multiple controls, displaying only common properties and values for which the value is the same for each selected control. Examination of the basic code created by the Property Page Wizard shows that your new property page doesn't support this. The created code in `SelectionChanged` fills the property page with the values from only the first of the selected controls.

The same limitation exists for the `ApplyChanges` event; although the Visual Basic property window can set a property for multiple selected controls, the default code created by the Property Page Wizard applies the changes to only the first selected control. To alter the code to apply the changes to all controls, create a loop and alter the property value for each control in the `SelectedControls` array.

TIP For additional information, see the "Creating Property Pages for ActiveX Controls" and "Property Page Wizard" sections in Books Online.

The TimeSheet control is now complete. This control is a bit different from the previous two controls—the Logo control and the TextBox control—in that it's not a control you're likely to keep in your toolbox permanently. The TimeSheet control has been created to serve a specific purpose on the company intranet page, but don't overlook the other possibilities for this control. It could easily be integrated into a Word document with VBA code to create automated reports and graphs or modified to hold other kinds of spreadsheet-related data, such as expense reports, inventory records, or financial data.

▶ **See** "Components of a Dynamic Web-Based Application," **p. 322**

Creating User-Drawn Controls

Now that you've written both simple subclassed and aggregate controls, you need to learn about the third type of ActiveX control—*user-drawn*. User-drawn controls are the most complex, because you're required to code not only the functionality, but also the interface. Common user-drawn controls include representations of common objects (such as business cards or a deck of playing cards) as well as images created at runtime to demonstrate the drawing process.

To see the creation of user-drawn controls, you'll create a StarBurst control that will draw a simple 16-point star filling the control (see Figure 5.28). The creation of the control is straightforward, with a single routine drawing each line in rapid succession to create the star. You easily can modify this routine to change colors after drawing each line, to pause for a specified amount of time between lines, or to draw continuously with random colors until some event occurs.

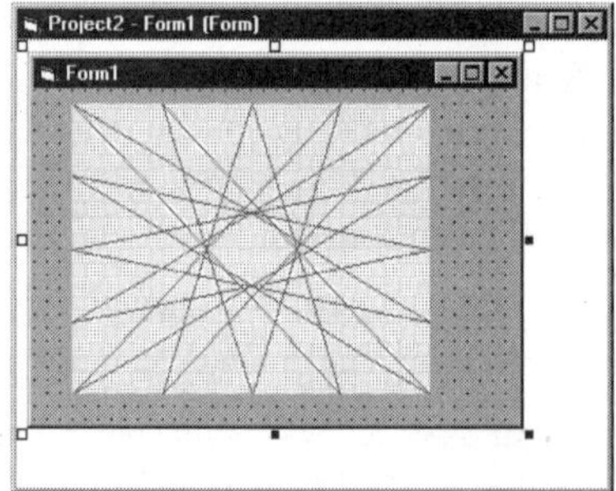

FIG. 5.28
The StarBurst control redraws itself with any `ForeColor` and `BackColor` you specify. Also, you might add `DrawMode` and `TimerInterval` properties to create a constantly changing design.

Follow these steps to create the StarBurst control:

1. Create a new ActiveX control and name it `StarBurst`.
2. Name the project `StarBurstProject`.
3. Add the code in Listing 5.5 to the `UserControl.Resize` event. This simple code becomes very flexible through its use of the UserControl's width and height properties.

4. Adding the code to the `Resize` event ensures that the StarBurst will always fill the entire control. To ensure that the control is always redrawn correctly, the `Paint` event needs to include a call to the `Resize` event.
5. Change the `ControlContainer` property of the control to `True` to allow the control to contain other controls.
6. Test the control by adding an EXE and placing a StarBurst control on the form. It will draw the starburst and maintain its aspect ratio as you resize the control.

Listing 5.5 A Simple User-Drawn Control

```
Dim ix As Integer, iy As Integer

UserControl.Cls
ix = UserControl.Width
iy = UserControl.Height
Line (ix / 4, iy)-(ix / 2, 0)
Line -(ix / 4 * 3, iy)
Line -(0, 0)
Line -(ix, iy / 4 * 3)
Line -(0, iy / 2)
Line -(ix, iy / 4)
Line -(0, iy)
Line -(ix / 4 * 3, 0)
Line -(ix / 2, iy)
Line -(ix / 4, 0)
Line -(ix, iy)
Line -(0, iy / 4)
Line -(ix, iy / 2)
Line -(0, iy / 4 * 3)
Line -(ix, 0)
Line -(ix / 4, iy)
```


Try adding another control to the form, within the StarBurst container. Move the StarBurst control to ensure that the container control is actually contained.

If you double-click a control in the toolbox, Visual Basic adds the control to the form by default. To add a control inside the StarBurst container, single-click the control in the toolbox and draw an outline of the control within the container.

Run the ActiveX Control Interface Wizard and remove all properties, methods, and events except `BackColor`, `BorderStyle`, `Click`, `Enabled`, `ForeColor`, and `Refresh`. You don't need any custom interface members, and the mapping for all six items is to the UserControl.

Because the BackColor and ForeColor are already mapped to the UserControl and the Line function draws in the ForeColor of the form, most of the work has been done for you. You only need to add a call to the Resize event in both Property Let procedures to ensure that the control is redrawn immediately. Enabled, Click, and Refresh need no additional code.

If you look at the properties you've placed on the executable form for the StarBurst control, notice that you can't choose from the standard BorderStyle types. To make the StarBurst control conform to other Visual Basic controls with a BorderStyle property, you must create an enumerated type to assign to the property.

NOTE An *enumerated type* is simply a way to keep two sets of related constants mapped to one another. Suppose that the developer would like to see None and FixedSingle as BorderStyle options, and Visual Basic expects to see a numeric value. Creating an enumerated type allows both sides to see what they want and agree on what that means.

In the declarations section of the control, add the following enumeration code:

```
Enum BorderStyleEnum
    None = 0
    FixedSingle = 1
End Enum
```

This code defines the values you'll allow for BorderStyle. To force BorderStyle to allow only these two values, you must change the type definition in the Property Let and Get procedures. They should be the same as shown in Listing 5.6.

Listing 5.6 Adding a Professional Look to Your Control's Properties

```
'WARNING! DO NOT REMOVE OR MODIFY THE FOLLOWING COMMENTED LINES!
'MappingInfo=UserControl,UserControl,-1,BorderStyle
Public Property Get BorderStyle() As BorderStyleEnum
    BorderStyle = UserControl.BorderStyle
End Property

Public Property Let BorderStyle(ByVal New_BorderStyle As BorderStyleEnum)
    UserControl.BorderStyle() = New_BorderStyle
    PropertyChanged "BorderStyle"
End Property
```

If you now examine the BorderStyle property of the control on the executable form, you should see the familiar choices of None and FixedSingle (see Figure 5.29).

TIP Be sure to define all color properties for your control as OLE_COLOR, not Long, if you want users to be able to choose the color from the palette rather than enter a long integer.

The StarBurst control now has fully operational properties that act and appear just like the properties for any standard Visual Basic control.

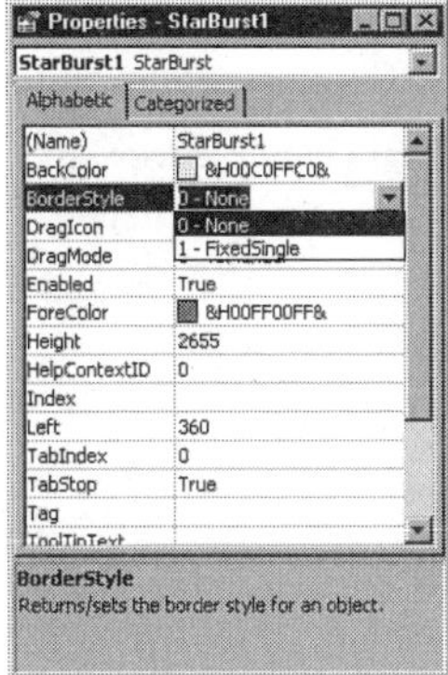

FIG. 5.29
The enumerated types for `BorderStyle` appear in the Visual Basic Properties window as a drop-down list. Creating control properties that act just like Visual Basic's controls takes only a few lines of code.

From Here...

By using Visual Basic to create ActiveX controls, you can easily create a single interface for standalone applications as well as web browsers and documents. This single-control approach greatly reduces development time and encourages consistency across multiple formats and applications.

The growth of the Internet in the last few years has been phenomenal and shows no signs of slowing. Add to this the increasing popularity of corporate intranets and the integration of Internet Explorer 4.0 into the operating system, and it becomes clear the web browser is quickly taking its place as a necessary piece of software on every computer. With online software purchases on the rise, the ability to issue updates and bug fixes only for the necessary controls (instead of the entire application) becomes important. ActiveX controls give you this capability by automatically downloading and updating themselves when appropriate. Usually, end users need to do no more than confirm the download, making application maintenance a breeze across an intranet and simplifying downloads over the Internet.

In addition to these benefits, the capability to add ActiveX controls directly into Microsoft Word and Excel documents changes the entire face of document handling. No longer will documents be static; with ActiveX controls embedded in them, documents can be more responsive, more informative, and more user-friendly—all with very little additional development work.

With the advent of ActiveX control creation and many other advanced features available in version 5.0, Visual Basic takes its place as a premier development language suited to projects of any size and complexity.

Refer to the following chapters for more information relevant to ActiveX controls:

- To gain essential background information for understanding and using object-oriented controls, see Chapter 4, "Using Microsoft's Object Technologies."
- To learn how to create controls with Java instead of ActiveX, see Chapter 7, "Creating Components with Visual J++."

- To understand the details behind the creation of web pages that contain ActiveX components, see Chapter 8, "Using ActiveX Client Components in an I-net Environment."
- To focus on using components in a traditional client/server environment, see Chapter 9, "Using ActiveX Components in a Client/Server Environment."
- To understand all web-based technologies and how they can be used together, see Chapter 11, "An Inside Look at Web-Based Applications."

CHAPTER 6

Creating Components with Visual C++

by Brad Rhodes and Dave Kincade

C++ has become one of the most powerful and complete programming languages available. Microsoft's Visual C++ extends the C++ programming environment by providing you with a feature-rich development environment and a vast array of extension libraries. Visual C++ follows C++'s design principle by providing you with higher levels of programming extraction without taking away any lower-level access to the computer or operating system. C++'s power is offset by the learning curve that you need to overcome to be effective in Visual C++.

Simpler applications will rarely tap into the power of the Visual C++ environment, yet complex applications will quickly demand the power of the C++ language. Several factors determine an application's complexity:

Using Visual C++

Learn about using Visual C++ to create component software and using MFC as a development tool, and explore new Visual C++ enhancements.

Overview of MFC

Understand MFC history and enhancements added to each version release. Learn about document/view architecture to establish structures to hold, retrieve, store, and change data on request. See how utility classes help in the development of component software.

Creating COM components with MFC

See COM and DCOM from a C++ programmer's perspective. Learn about the interface concept and how to build COM objects by using Visual C++ and MFC.

Using OLE Automation with MFC

Gain an understanding of OLE Automation and see how simple it is to create and use OLE Automation objects with Visual C++ and MFC.

Creating COM components with ATL

Learn how you can use the Active Template Library (ATL) to create components in the Visual C++ environment.

- *Distribution model.* Widely distributed production applications are developed primarily in C++—for example, Microsoft Word and Lotus Notes.
- *Robustness.* Servers developed to support hundreds of users over long periods of time are developed typically in C++. Examples include Netscape's and Microsoft's web servers and the database servers from Oracle, Microsoft, and Informix.
- *Maintenance life cycle.* When a product is developed to be maintained over a long period of time, it has a long maintenance life cycle. Such products benefit from C++'s natural promotion of code reuse and support for library and DLL packaging of code.
- *Throughput.* Applications that need to optimize machine usage or use multithreading to increase throughput will benefit from C++'s power. Such applications include data warehousing tools.

Flexibility is what gives Visual C++ an edge over other development tools. The more complicated the application, the more it's beneficial to use Visual C++ as the development tool. This flexibility comes from the basis that C++ is the language used to develop most of the Windows NT and Windows 95 operating systems. The APIs for these systems are designed for use from C++.

The recent additions to Visual Basic allowing access to OLE components will greatly improve Visual Basic's capability to access components in the operating system and third-party packages. Visual C++ has access to all the components available to Visual Basic developers and many tools and components that aren't available to VB developers.

In addition to providing a world-class C++ compiler, the Visual C++ development environment delivers a number of reusable components, including the Microsoft Foundation Class (MFC) library and the Active Template Library (ATL). Visual C++ integrates these extension libraries into the development environment and uses wizards to greatly simplify the use of MFC and ATL classes. ■

Using Visual C++, an Object-Oriented Language

Because Visual C++ uses the C++ object-oriented programming language, it's well suited to helping you create reusable component objects. These benefits have to do with the language's structure and are independent of the development platform and development tool used. Some specific features account for the advantages of using Visual C++:

- Strong type checking
- Reusability
- API access
- Exception handling
- Standard library

▶ **See** "Object Technology Basics," **p. 90**

Strong Type Checking

C++ is a *strongly typed* programming language, meaning that it's designed specifically to provide you with compiler error messages whenever you misuse a variable. (First-time programmers find strongly typed languages more difficult to learn because they must be more precise in specifying how a data type is to be handled.) The C++ additions to the C language allow you to take precise control over the use of data types.

Weakly typed languages allow a sloppier approach. In a weakly typed system, the compiler often tries to fix any misuse of a variable by implicitly converting from one type to another. The problems with weakly typed languages begin when the code base is fairly large. After the compiler goes through several layers of software, with each layer potentially going through a type conversion, the data type can easily be mishandled. When this happens, determining the source of the problem is extremely difficult. Strong typing in the language prevents this scenario from ever happening.

Reusability

A key concept of the C programming language was the separation of a module's definition from a module's implementation. In C, a module's definition is placed in a header file (.h), and its implementation is placed in the C file (.c). The header file contains all the externally available interfaces, fully defined. C++ inherits from C this concept of module implementation separate from module definition.

The implementation of a software module can be packaged in an object (.obj) or library (.lib) file. You can reuse a packaged software module over and over again. To use a common module, you include the definition file and link in the implementation. The dynamic link library further propagates this concept by allowing the packaged modules to be linked together at runtime.

C++ enhances the production of componentized software modules by introducing the concepts of *inheritance*, *polymorphism*, and *encapsulation*. These mechanisms provide software components with a more manageable means of extending and enhancing the individual components. The Component Object Module (COM) and Distributed Component Object Module (DCOM) further enhance the production of binary compatible software components.

▶ **See** "COM and OLE 2.0" **p. 102**

The MFC class library is a great example of an extendible software component library. You can leverage MFC to produce new software components or applications. You can possibly extend any part of MFC so that the software library can be custom-tailored to the requirement.

Later, this chapter shows how you can use Visual C++ to create software components. You'll create a reusable software component with MFC and then create the same reusable software component by using the Active Template Library (ATL).

API Access

C++ was designed to extend the C programming language without cutting off any access to system resources that C contained. Most modern operating systems are written in C or Assembler. The best possible access to a machine's resources is through direct API calls. The C++ language and most of the libraries written for C++ allow you to work at the C++ object level without cutting off access to C's API calls.

Exception Handling

C++ provides many powerful and flexible features. The introduction of *exceptions* provides a framework for you to create a highly structured error-trapping mechanism. It's only natural that in a component-based application, components are used to perform much of the work. When a component encounters an error condition, the component may not have enough information about the context of the action to provide appropriate error recovery. Exceptions provide a path for the component to communicate back to the application that something unexpected has happened.

Suppose that you have a component used for serial port communications or network communications. If you assume there's a user interface and begin putting up user-interface messages, you'll greatly decrease the component's flexibility. A Windows NT service that runs only in the background can no longer use such a component.

For this reason, exceptions allow the component to detect errors and throw the error condition back out to the higher-level code that's using the component. This higher-level code can catch the error and either put up a user interface message or make an error-log entry. In some cases, a higher-level piece of code may be able to continue despite the error, perhaps after taking corrective action.

Standard Library

C++ provides the standard library. The ANSI specification for this library is the combination of the older C standard library and the new standard template library. These two libraries combine to provide a powerful base of reusable code.

Creating Components with Visual C++

The Visual C++ development environment offers numerous approaches to developing componentized software. You can take these different approaches to develop different component types. Each approach includes a number of positives and negatives, depending on the type of component being developed. It's advantageous to view the different approaches to creating components from a high level before getting into the details of implementing the components.

The first type of componentized software is the development of libraries. Libraries have been used for years to divide up software development efforts. The concept of using software libraries has been extended by the addition of the dynamic link library (DLL). A DLL is very similar to a traditional software library except that DLLs are loaded by an operating system-provided runtime linker rather than statically linked into the executable.

Another type of software component is a *class framework* or class library. A good example of a class library is the MFC class library described later in the section "Using MFC." A class library is very similar to a normal C library, except that the header file for the class library contains C++ class definitions.

A third type of software components are COM components, which include ActiveX components. COM components extend the binary specification laid out in the DLL concept to include multiple interfaces grouped into classes. Building COM-based components is possible by using just raw C function specifications, the MFC class framework, or the Active Template Library (ATL).

▶ **See** "COM/DCOM Architecture Basics," **p. 112**

You could build COM components by writing straight to the C API and hand-coding the Interface Definition Language (IDL) files. Thankfully, Visual C++ provides MFC and the ATL class libraries and wizards to greatly simplify the creation of components. Given the availability of MFC and ATL, there's no reason to implement a component by using the straight C API.

The MFC and ATL class libraries are at complete opposites of the design spectrum. The MFC library is a more monolithic group of classes. Implementing classes that extend parts of the library is often difficult without getting involved with other classes in the library. When developing relatively small standalone components, using the MFC library causes quite a bit of overhead. You must statically or dynamically link the MFC implementation modules into your component for a complete delivery. Regardless of your component's size, you need to ship the approximately 1MB mfc42.dll file—a lot of overhead for a small component.

When developing large components with a lot of functionality, the overhead of the MFC library begins to be marginalized. The component may include support for a user interface, drag-and-drop activation, ActiveX document support, and Windows printing. This component type takes advantage of a large amount of the MFC class library. Many of these features would be difficult to implement without MFC. Also, many of these types of components will be used in MFC-developed applications.

Part II Ch 6

Compared with the MFC, the ATL takes a minimalist approach to providing support for component creation. You include only the parts of the ATL that you need. All of the ATL is implemented in header files, and there's no need to link any DLL or static library. For the most part, the ATL components compile down to a very small piece of code that's very near the hand implementation that would be done by writing straight to the C library.

The downside of the ATL is that this is the first version. It doesn't have anywhere near the support or stability that MFC enjoys. Many features aren't yet available in ATL. As with everything in C++, however, it's possible to use the ATL and MFC libraries in combination, taking advantage of ATL's capability to implement COM interfaces and using MFC for more high-level constructs.

Using MFC

By selecting the MFC class library as the basis for a project, you've made the development of Windows-based components an easier job. MFC provides a number of classes that encapsulate most of the conceptual objects used in Windows programming.

Most objects in the MFC world are derived from the abstract base class `CObject`. It contains the basic reusable functionality built on by other MFC classes. `CObject` contains the template to access runtime type information (`GetRuntimeClass()` and `IsKindOf()`), perform some diagnostic functions (`AssertValid()` and `Dump()`), and perform serialization (`IsSerializable()` and `Serialize()`).

`CObject` also contains the capability to dynamically create an instance of an object just by having the runtime type information for that object. This functionality is important to COM because server objects are created dynamically at the client's request. Recent versions of MFC have been enhanced to encapsulate most of the COM concepts.

A Brief History of MFC

In 1989, Microsoft pulled together a number of its brightest minds from many varied areas to form a development group that became known as the application framework development group (AFX). AFX's task was to develop a set of libraries that developers could use as a tool in the development of GUI programs.

The initial design of the AFX class framework contained a deep class inheritance tree, a type of design considered advantageous by object-oriented programmers. The problem is that programmers transitioning from a very flat C API programming environment find it overwhelming to transition to deeply nested class frameworks. Microsoft's later Win32 group was charged with delivering the AFX framework to developers. The Win32 group wanted to protect its investment in the Win32 API and help developers transition to the AFX class library.

The Win32 group took the AFX class framework and flattened the architecture. In some of the inheritance trees, this flattening went from eight classes deep to three classes deep. The resulting version of the framework much more represented a heavy wrapper of the Windows APIs. This new attempt was released in 1992 and was called the Microsoft Foundation Classes (MFC) version 1.0.

With the release of Visual C++ 1.0 in April 1993, Microsoft included the new and improved MFC 2.0, in which you could add popular new features such as context-sensitive help, toolbars, and status bars. It also allowed you to easily conform to Microsoft user-interface standards. Because many developers were worried about having to rewrite applications that used MFC 1.0, Microsoft made MFC 2.0 backward-compatible with version 1.0. This was also the first version of MFC that could be used with Windows NT.

Late in 1993, Microsoft released Visual C++ 1.5 and MFC 2.5. This upgrade added support for OLE 2.0 and ODBC. In late 1994, Microsoft's big addition to MFC version 3.0 was thread safety. With the release of MFC 3.0, Microsoft dropped support for Windows 3.1. The latest version, 5.0, adds substantial new support for the development of COM objects.

Application Framework

The application framework in MFC is a complex yet easy-to-use set of objects that encapsulate everything needed to create the shell of a Windows component. This shell works very well if you're creating an OLE Automation object, a COM object with multiple interfaces, an ActiveX control, or a full standalone Windows application.

The application framework handles all the complexities of writing a Windows component. When a new project is created, Visual C++ builds a new class, derived from the appropriate type, to handle the project type. Then the ClassWizard lets you create new classes or customize existing classes. From a component-development standpoint, the ClassWizard is extremely useful in the creation of OLE Automation components but is somewhat lacking when it comes to creating COM objects not derived from `IDispatch`.

Document/View Overview The document/view architecture was initially developed in the SmallTalk object-oriented programming language. This application architecture is based on the concept that you should always separate modules into distinct and well-defined sections. The document/view architecture provides an object-oriented mechanism for separating view-related processing from document-related processing.

This is best understood when talking about an application, such as Microsoft Word. View processing is primarily concerned with drawing the representation of a document onscreen and would use the display environment to present the data. For Word, view processing includes drawing the text, scrolling the window, highlighting text, boldfacing text, and so on.

Document processing involves those operations that affect the in-memory representation of the document, such as inserting paragraphs, saving the file, and opening the file. This includes moving the representation to and from the desktop. Many operations that change the representation of the document in memory will result in view changes. The document can always call the view to display the required changes.

As you can see, the document/view architecture is a powerful way of separating modules of a software system. The problem with this architecture, however, is that it's non-intuitive, and working with it the first time is extremely confusing. But after you pass the learning curve, the document/view architecture provides a powerful mechanism for implementing well-defined systems.

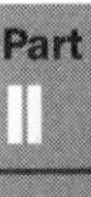

This transition can be likened to the transition from a DOS-based programming environment to a Windows-based programming environment. It's a paradigm shift. There's a transition from the traditional concept of having data and displaying it by using the document/view architecture.

The document/view concept is relatively simple: One object (the document) should hold the data, and another object (the view) should know how to display it. The document should have structures to hold the data, know how to retrieve and store the data, and know how to change the data on request. The view should know how to display the data, allow the application's user to modify the data, and tell the document about the changes to the data.

With this architecture, multiple views can display the same data in different ways. For example, a spreadsheet's application document would keep the spreadsheet data in a two-dimensional array. The first view would display the data as a traditional spreadsheet with the data in rows and columns; the second view would display the data as a graph.

Single Document Interface (SDI) In a Single Document Interface (SDI) application, only one document can be alive at a time. This document can have only one view active at a time but have multiple views defined and allow users to switch between them. A good example of an SDI application is Notepad provided with Microsoft Windows 95 and Windows NT.

When it comes to creating component software, SDI can have some advantages. If the component being built is an out-of-process component, by using SDI you can set up the component in a way that each client will create its own instantiation of the component server.

Multiple Document Interface (MDI) In a Multiple Document Interface (MDI) application, multiple document types can be alive simultaneously, multiple instances of each type of document can be alive simultaneously, and multiple views for each document (regardless of type) can be visible onscreen—all within the same application. Microsoft Word is an example of an MDI application.

When creating a component based on the MDI architecture, you can create different interfaces for each document and have one server running that handles multiple clients. Each client would have its own document to hold its data. The data wouldn't cross from one client to another client, unless that functionality was programmed into the server component.

Utility Classes

MFC provides a number of utility classes that can help in the development of a component, application, or any other type of project. These utility classes fall into a number of categories, including file handling, arrays, lists, maps, complex data structures, and data types.

Multithreaded Applications

Because C++ is at a low enough level, it can support the process of creating multiple processing threads in one application. When an application starts executing, a single process thread is running the application. If you need to perform multiple tasks simultaneously, it becomes a simple task to create a second worker or interface thread that will perform any tasks necessary.

On a single-processor machine, a multithreaded program will probably run faster because the computer system has many components. Each component—primarily the CPU and the disk—can become a bottleneck. A multithreaded program can use more resources more efficiently by better using components that aren't bottlenecked. For instance, while one thread waits for the disk to perform an I/O operation, the second thread can use the processor.

On a multiprocessor machine, however, the computation time-saving escalates quite quickly. One processor may be performing the processing for the main application thread while a second processor is performing the computation tasks for the second thread of the application.

Many times, developers let the main process thread continue to monitor the application message loop while the child threads monitor other hardware, perform time-expensive computations, read and write files to a disk, or draw objects onscreen.

In multithreading terminology are two types of child (nonprocess) threads: worker and user interface.

Worker threads are designed to perform a task and then terminate at the end of the task. The worker thread and the main application process thread can have two-way communications. They also can use concepts such as semaphores, mutexes, critical sections, events, and locks to perform thread synchronization.

Often, programs are written by using multithreaded techniques to increase throughput. To increase throughput, threads can be moved to separate CPUs, or, on a single-CPU system, one thread can use the CPU while a second thread is stalled, waiting for a read operation on the disk. Threads often need to communicate with each other to coordinate their activities. For instance, two threads processing all the rows in a database would need to communicate which rows they're processing so that each row gets processed only once.

An example of this type of communication is the *semaphore*, which allows one thread to lock a chunk of memory while it's changing the data. This way, other threads are prevented from reading that memory chunk until it's valid.

User-interface threads enter into their own message loop. In the Windows programming environment, the message loop is the part of the API that allows software to communicate with the operating system that's ready for the next piece of user input. These types of threads are very useful if the application needs to implement multiple top-level windows that are independent of each other.

Using COM

Over the past few years, component software has become a hot topic. With the rapid change in technology, the concept and terminology of component software has changed almost as rapidly as the development tools used to create them. Luckily, the development tools' implementation of COM has been slow enough not to get caught in the changing definitions.

Definition of COM

Chapter 4, "Using Microsoft's Object Technologies," discusses the Component Object Model in detail. As a quick review, COM is the specification of how application components should communicate and control each other in a Windows environment. COM is supported and facilitated by the operating system and is the basic concept in which OLE and ActiveX technology now reside.

The main focus of object-oriented and component-based design is the packaging of code behind a well-designed interface. If a component's user adheres to the interface specification, the component should behave predictably.

An analogy in real life of the importance of good interface design is the electrical outlet. You don't need to concern yourself with much beyond identifying that the electric outlet is a standard electrical outlet before plugging in your computer. The two sides to this commitment are that the electrician commits to wire the outlet only for common voltage and amps, and you commit to plug in only common electrical appliances. A 220-volt electrical outlet purposely has a different interface.

▶ **See** "COM/DCOM Architecture Basics," **p. 112**

Interfaces

To be direct, an *interface* is a group of functions that supports one common concept for an object and can be referenced by a GUID (global unique ID). All interfaces start with a capital `I`. After an interface is designed and published, it can't be changed. If an interface needs to be changed, a new interface must be created and a new GUID assigned.

As a simple example, imagine that you have a bowling ball object and an interface into the bowling ball object called `IBowlingBall`. This interface can have functions like `Aim()`, `SetSpeed()`, `SetRotation()`, and `Throw()`. All the functions in the interface would control the bowling ball object.

Now imagine that you have a spaceship object. You might want to have an interface to control the navigation, another interface to control the weapons system, and a third interface to cook food in the galley. Each interface would control only part of your object, but some of the underlying functionality would probably overlap. Maybe your spaceship couldn't engage its warp drive if the shields were raised. Maybe your microwave and lasers are on the same circuit and would blow a fuse if you tried to fry an egg and tried to fry some egg-shaped aliens at the same time. The spaceship object handles these relationships; the interfaces just provide access to the spaceship object.

IUnknown Already, a number of interfaces have been published. The most important interface already published is `IUnknown`, which every COM object must implement. The `IUnknown` interface contains two functions for reference counting (`AddRef()` and `Release()`), and one function that allows other applications to access your specific interface (`QueryInterface()`).

Think of an office building as an object and each company in the building as an interface. The `IUnknown` interface is the guard in the lobby who counts the number of people entering the building (`AddRef`) and the number of people leaving the building (`Release`). He also knows the location of every company with an office in the building (`QueryInterface`). If you ask for a company (an interface) that doesn't exist in the building, he tells you that it's not in the building (not supported). On the other hand, if you asked for a company that did exist in the building, he would tell you its location.

Because every COM object implements the `IUnknown` interface, Visual C++ has created the C++ definition of the interface and included it with the software, in the Unknwn.H include file (see Listing 6.1).

Listing 6.1 *IUnknown,* the Standard Set of Interfaces From Which All COM Objects Derive

```
interface IUnknown
{
public:
    BEGIN_INTERFACE
    virtual HRESULT STDMETHODCALLTYPE QueryInterface(
        /* [in] */ REFIID riid,
        /* [iid_is][out] */ void __RPC_FAR *__RPC_FAR *ppvObject) = 0;

    virtual ULONG STDMETHODCALLTYPE AddRef( void) = 0;

    virtual ULONG STDMETHODCALLTYPE Release( void) = 0;

    END_INTERFACE
};
```

NOTE You can find the Unknwn.H file in your Visual C++ Include directory.

Other Interfaces A number of other interfaces have been defined. Remember that as soon as they're defined, however, they must remain the same forever. If you need to make any change to the interface, you must create a new interface. On the other hand, you can change the underlying implementation and still keep the existing interface, as long as the interface itself doesn't change.

If you look in the help file for Visual C++ (specifically, in Platform, SDK, and DDK Documentation\Platform SDK\Object Services\COM\Reference\Interfaces), you'll see a number of other interfaces defined in the Visual C++ header files. Many of these interfaces will become common to component designers, and others will remain as special-use cases.

One interface, `IDispatch`, doesn't show up in the help file's list of COM interfaces because it's a special implementation of a COM interface used with OLE Automation. That interface is covered in detail later when OLE Automation is discussed in the section "Using Automation."

Visual C++'s Implementation of COM

Because COM is the method for components to communicate, MFC has gone to great lengths to reduce the amount of typing required to get an interface off the ground. The MFC implementation centers around the use of a number of macros, abstract base classes, and inheritance. MFC takes the concept of message maps used for Windows event communication and extends it to implementing COM interfaces.

In MFC, you shouldn't think of an interface as more then a struct or class of virtual functions. Object-oriented designs often include a base class that's nothing but pure virtual functions.

MFC provides a couple of macros to help clean up the definition of interfaces—the `STDMETHOD_(method)` and `STDMETHOD_(type, method)` macros found in the objbase.h header file:

```
#define STDMETHOD_(method)
  //virtual HRESULT STDMETHODCALLTYPE method
#define STDMETHOD_(type, method)
  //virtual type STDMETHODCALLTYPE method
```

With these macros, re-create a simple version of the `IUnknown` interface. Listing 6.2 shows the code that creates the new `IUnknown` interface.

Listing 6.2 How the *STDMETHOD* Set of Macros Are Used

```
struct IUnknown
{
    STDMETHOD_(ULONG, AddRef) () = 0;
    STDMETHOD_(ULONG, Release)() = 0;
    STDMETHOD(QueryInterface) (REFIID iid, void** ppvObject) = 0;
};
```

You might have noticed that all functions of the `IUnknown` interface are pure virtual functions because such functions are part of the definition of the interface. It's up to the implementation to determine how the functions actually work.

Now it's time to create your own interface. Because every interface must implement the `IUnknown` interface, your interfaces will be derived from `IUnknown` (refer to Listing 6.1). Listing 6.3 shows the interfaces for the spaceship example discussed earlier in the section "Interfaces."

Listing 6.3 Spaceship Object Interfaces

```
struct INavigation : public IUnknown
{
    STDMETHOD_(void, SetDirection) (int x, int y, int z) = 0;
    STDMETHOD_(void, SetSpeed)     (int speed) = 0;
    STDMETHOD_(void, EngageWarp)   () = 0;
};
struct IWeapons : public IUnknown
{
    STDMETHOD_(int,  GetShieldStrength) () = 0;
    STDMETHOD_(void, SetShieldStrength) () = 0;
    STDMETHOD_(void, FireLaser) (int x, int y, int z, int power) = 0;
};
struct IGalley : public IUnknown
{
    STDMETHOD_(void, SetMicrowavePower) (int power) = 0;
    STDMETHOD_(void, SetMicrowaveTime)  (int time) = 0;
    STDMETHOD_(void, StartMicrowave)    () = 0;
};
```

As you can see, all Listing 6.3 does is derive the interfaces from the `IUnknown` interface, which means that the interfaces include the pure virtual function definitions for `AddRef()`, `Release()`, and `QueryInterface()`.

NOTE Structure definitions are always derived from the `IUnknown` structure, which provides your classes with the default `IUnknown` interfaces: `QueryInterface()`, `AddRef()`, and `Release()`. ■

All that's left to do is to create a GUID for each of the preceding three interfaces, implement a class that contains and uses these interfaces, and compile. These steps will be outlined more in the following examples.

Example 1: An InProc COM Server

This InProc COM server is a standard 52-playing-card server that will simulate having a deck of 52 cards (ace through king of all four suits). It has two interfaces:

- `ICardDeck`, which enables the client application to shuffle the deck, get the top card, get a count of the number of used cards, and get the text name of any card
- `ICheat`, which enables the client application to look at the card anywhere in the deck and put any card at any position in the deck

The following sections outline how to create this application.

Running AppWizard to Generate the InProc Server To generate the InProc server, follow these steps:

1. Choose File, New from the menu.
2. On the Projects page, select MFC AppWizard (dll) (see Figure 6.1).

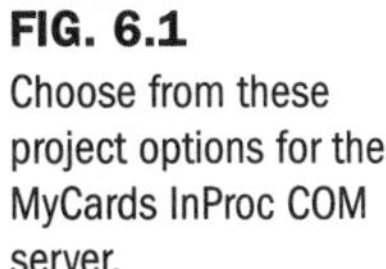

FIG. 6.1
Choose from these project options for the MyCards InProc COM server.

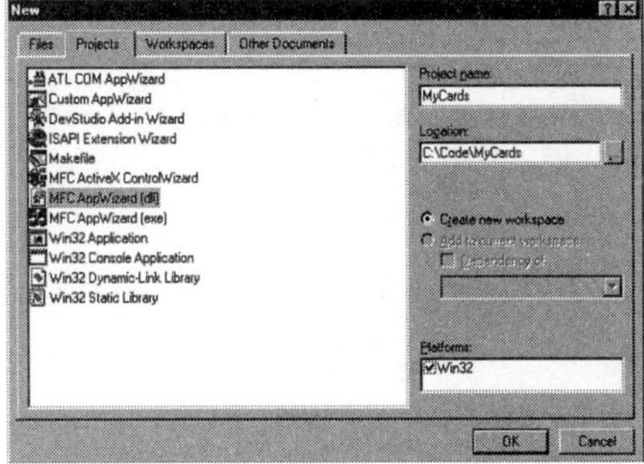

3. In the Project Name text box, enter **`MyCards`**.
4. Set the proper directory in the Location combo box.
5. When all the options are set correctly, as in Figure 6.1, click OK. The MFC AppWizard – Step 1 of 1 dialog box appears (see Figure 6.2).

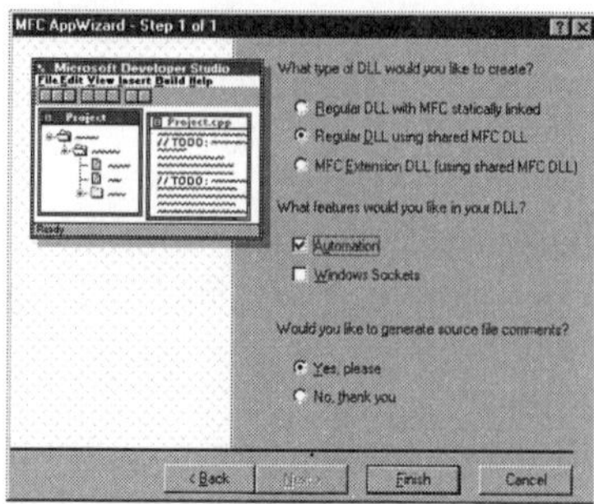

FIG. 6.2
The MFC AppWizard – Step 1 of 1 dialog box for the `MyCards` InProc COM server.

6. Make sure that the Regular DLL Using Shared MFC DLL option and the Automation checkbox are selected, and then click the Finish button.

The New dialog box in Figure 6.1 has several options. The first area controls how the MFC libraries are linked to your project. You can statically link the MFC libraries in their entirety to your DLL, but that adds nearly a megabyte to the size of executable. You can link the MFC libraries as another DLL. Or you can choose to make your DLL an extension to the MFC. (You would used this option when you're extending certain classes from MFC for use by other developers.)

The dialog box in Figure 6.2 includes a second set of options that allows you to include certain MFC extensions in your DLL. MFC supports OLE Automation and Windows sockets, but not all DLLs built will need to access OLE Automation and Windows sockets extensions to the core MFC functionality. Because we're talking mostly about COM objects here, however, you want the support for OLE Automation.

Creating the CardInterface.h Interface Header File The CardInterface.h file contains all the information about the `ICardDeck` and `ICheat` interfaces. Any application (including the COM server) can use this file because it contains only the abstract definition of the interfaces. Follow these steps to create this file:

1. Create a new text file called CardInterface.h and add the code shown in Listing 6.4.
2. Save the file with the filename CardInterface.h.

Listing 6.4 The Interface Definition File for the *ICardDeck* and *ICheat* Interfaces

```
// CardInterface.h - File containing all the information about the ICardDeck and
//                   ICheat Interfaces.
#if !defined( __CARDINTERFACE_H__ )
#define __CARDINTERFACE_H__
// Constants for the ICardDeck Interface
const int SUIT_NONE    = 0;
const int SUIT_HEART   = 1;
```

```
const int SUIT_DIAMOND = 2;
const int SUIT_CLUB    = 3;
const int SUIT_SPADE   = 4;
const int CARD_NONE    = 0;
const int CARD_ACE     = 1;
const int CARD_TWO     = 2;
const int CARD_THREE   = 3;
const int CARD_FOUR    = 4;
const int CARD_FIVE    = 5;
const int CARD_SIX     = 6;
const int CARD_SEVEN   = 7;
const int CARD_EIGHT   = 8;
const int CARD_NINE    = 9;
const int CARD_TEN     = 10;
const int CARD_JACK    = 11;
const int CARD_QUEEN   = 12;
const int CARD_KING    = 13;
// ICardDeck Interface
struct ICardDeck : public IUnknown
{
    STDMETHOD_(void, Shuffle) () = 0;
    STDMETHOD_(void, GetNextCard) (int* pnSuit, int* pnCard) = 0;
    STDMETHOD_(int,  GetUsedCount) () = 0;
    STDMETHOD_(BSTR, GetCardName) (int nSuit, int nCard) = 0;
};
// ICheat Interface
struct ICheat : public IUnknown
{
    STDMETHOD_(int,  GetCurrentPosition) () = 0;
    STDMETHOD_(void, SetCardAtPosition) (int nPos, int nSuit, int nCard) = 0;
    STDMETHOD_(void, LookAtPosition) (int nPos, int* pnSuit, int* pnCard) = 0;
};
#endif        // #if !defined( __CARDINTERFACE_H__ )
```

Creating New GUIDs for the Two Interfaces Now you'll use the GUIDGen utility to generate GUIDs for the `ICardDeck` and `ICheat` interfaces. This generic utility is supplied with Microsoft Developer Studio. There are four types of GUIDs you can generate with GUIDGen (see Figure 6.3):

- `IMPLEMENT_OLECREATE{...}` is used by the MFC `IMPLEMENT_OLECREATE` macro. This macro may be inserted into your code by one of the Visual C++ AppWizards.
- `DEFINE_GUID{...}` is an older format of the `IMPLEMENT_OLECREATE` macro.
- `static const struct GUID = {...}` creates a GUID that's properly defined for the statically allocated GUID.
- `Registry Format({xxxxxxxx...xxx})` creates a properly formatted GUID for the developer to hand enter a GUID into the Registry. This would allow the developer to register his control by hand.

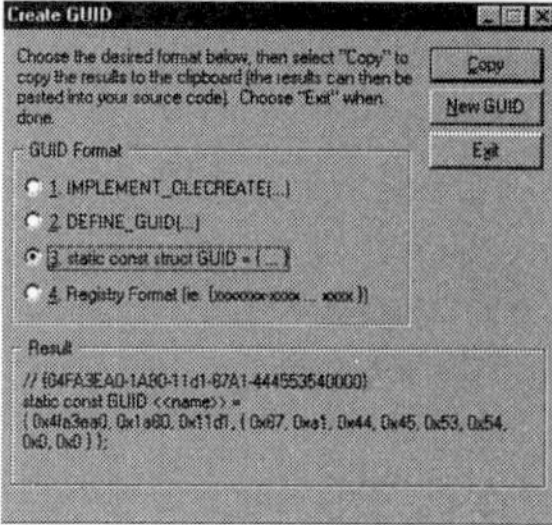

FIG. 6.3
Use the GUIDGen utility to create GUIDs for the COM server.

Follow these steps:

1. Run the GUIDGen utility, which you can find in your Visual C++ Bin directory.
2. Select the `static const struct GUID = {...}` format and click the Copy button.
3. In the CardInterface.h file, insert the copied text just below the `const` for `CARD_KING`.
4. Change the text `<<name>>` to **`IID_ICardDeck`**.
5. Click the New GUID button and then repeat steps 2 through 4 for the `IID_ICheat` interface.

Listing 6.5 shows the text added to CardInterface.h with output from the GUIDGen utility.

Listing 6.5 Text Added to CardInterface.h

```
...
const int CARD_QUEEN    = 12;
const int CARD_KING     = 13;
// GUID for the ICardDeck Interface
// {35AB55A0-005B-11d1-87A1-444553540000}
static const GUID IID_ICardDeck =
{ 0x35ab55a0, 0x5b, 0x11d1, { 0x87, 0xa1, 0x44, 0x45, 0x53, 0x54, 0x0, 0x0 } };
// GUID for the ICheat Interface
// {35AB55A1-005B-11d1-87A1-444553540000}
static const GUID IID_ICheat =
{ 0x35ab55a1, 0x5b, 0x11d1, { 0x87, 0xa1, 0x44, 0x45, 0x53, 0x54, 0x0, 0x0 } };
// ICardDeck Interface
struct ICardDeck : public IUnknown
...
```

Creating the *CCOMCards* Class To create the `CCOMCards` class, you need to start with a template generated by the ClassWizard, remove the OLE Automation code (as it's not used), and then include the common set of defines in the CardInterface.h file.

To generate the basic COM component template, follow these steps:

1. Choose View, ClassWizard from the menu to start the ClassWizard.
2. Click the Add Class button and select New from the drop-down menu.

3. In the Class Information section, type **CCOMCards** in the Name text box and select the Base Class of `CCmdTarget`.
4. In the Automation section, select Creatable by Type ID and use the default type ID of `MyCards.COMCards` (see Figure 6.4).

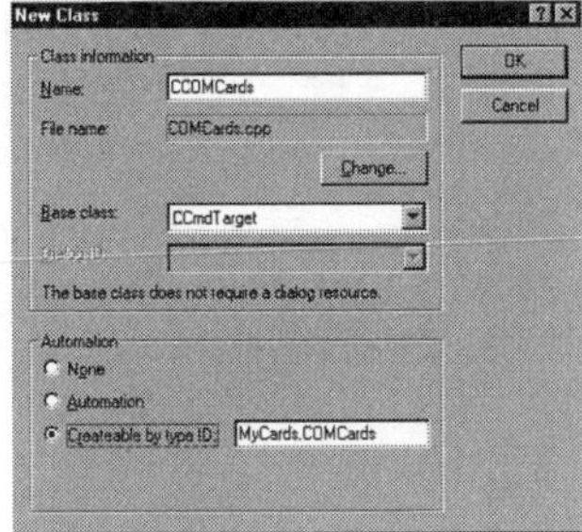

FIG. 6.4
The Creatable by Type ID option allows the Automation client to instate the object by name.

5. Click OK.

These steps create the class that will implement the `ICardDeck` and `ICheat` interfaces. The class is derived from `CCmdTarget` because it has some default implementation that will help you implement the `IUnknown` interface.

Although you selected that you wanted to use OLE Automation, you don't really want to use it. Choosing to create by type ID does three things:

- It creates a GUID for this class that you can use for the COM object.
- It inserts some necessary MFC macros in the header and implementation files that you'll use.
- It places some macros in the header and implementation files that you'll want to remove because you really aren't doing Automation.

Now remove the following OLE Automation code from COMCards.h:

```
// Generated OLE dispatch map functions
//{{AFX_DISPATCH(CCOMCards)
    // NOTE - the ClassWizard will add and remove member functions here.
//}}AFX_DISPATCH
DECLARE_DISPATCH_MAP()
```


Add the `CardInterface` common header to the file by using the boldface code shown in Listing 6.6.

Listing 6.6 The *CardInterface* Common Header

```
#if !defined(AFX_COMCARDS_H__C293A3D6_0059_11D1_87A1_444553540000__INCLUDED_)
#define AFX_COMCARDS_H__C293A3D6_0059_11D1_87A1_444553540000__INCLUDED_
#if _MSC_VER >= 1000
```

continues

Listing 6.6 Continued

```
#pragma once
#endif // _MSC_VER >= 1000
// COMCards.h : header file
//
#include "CardInterface.h"
/////////////////////////////////////////////////////////////////////////////
// CCOMCards command target
class CCOMCards : public CCmdTarget
{
    DECLARE_DYNCREATE(CCOMCards)
    CCOMCards();           // protected constructor used by dynamic creation
// Attributes
public:
// Operations
public:
// Overrides
    // ClassWizard generated virtual function overrides
    //{{AFX_VIRTUAL(CCOMCards)
    public:
    virtual void OnFinalRelease();
    //}}AFX_VIRTUAL
// Implementation
protected:
    virtual ~CCOMCards();
    // Attributes
    int         m_nUsedCardCount;
    int         m_nCurrentPosition;
    // The card array where entry contains a number representing a card
    // (0-12 Hearts, 13-25 Diamonds, 26-38 Clubs, 39-51 Spade)
    int         m_aCardArray[52];
    // Generated message map functions
    //{{AFX_MSG(CCOMCards)
        // NOTE - the ClassWizard will add and remove member functions here.
    //}}AFX_MSG
    DECLARE_MESSAGE_MAP()
    DECLARE_OLECREATE(CCOMCards)
    BEGIN_INTERFACE_PART(CardDeck, ICardDeck)
        STDMETHOD_(void, Shuffle) ();
        STDMETHOD_(void, GetNextCard) (int* pnSuit, int* pnCard);
        STDMETHOD_(int,  GetUsedCount) ();
        STDMETHOD_(BSTR, GetCardName) (int iSuit, int iCard);
    END_INTERFACE_PART(CardDeck)
    BEGIN_INTERFACE_PART(CardCheat, ICheat)
        STDMETHOD_(int,  GetCurrentPosition) ();
        STDMETHOD_(void, SetCardAtPosition) (int nPos, int nSuit, int nCard);
        STDMETHOD_(void, LookAtPosition) (int nPos, int* pnSuit, int* pnCard);
    END_INTERFACE_PART(CardCheat)
    DECLARE_INTERFACE_MAP()
};
/////////////////////////////////////////////////////////////////////////////
//{{AFX_INSERT_LOCATION}}
// Microsoft Developer Studio will insert additional declarations
// immediately before the previous line.
```

```
#endif // !defined(AFX_COMCARDS_H__C293A3D6_0059_
➥11D1_87A1_444553540000__INCLUDED_)
```

Take a quick look at some of the macros used in Listing 6.6: `DECLARE_OLECREATE`, `BEGIN_INTERFACE_PART`, `STDMETHOD`, `STDMETHOD_`, `END_INTERFACE_PART`, and `DECLARE_INTERFACE_MAP`. The first macro, `DECLARE_OLECREATE`, has the definition

```
#define DECLARE_OLECREATE(class_name) \
public: \
    static AFX_DATA COleObjectFactory factory; \
    static AFX_DATA const GUID guid; \
```

This macro, with the accompanying `IMPLEMENT_OLECREATE` macro used in the implementation file, allows this object to be dynamically created when the client component requests a new object.

The next four macros—`BEGIN_INTERFACE_PART`, `STDMETHOD_`, `STDMETHOD`, and `END_INTERFACE_PART`—all work together to integrate the interfaces into the class. Listing 6.7 shows their definitions.

Listing 6.7 Common Macros Used in COM Objects

```
#define BEGIN_INTERFACE_PART(localClass, baseClass) \
    class X##localClass : public baseClass \
    { \
    public: \
        STDMETHOD_(ULONG, AddRef)(); \
        STDMETHOD_(ULONG, Release)(); \
        STDMETHOD(QueryInterface)(REFIID iid, LPVOID* ppvObj); \
#define STDMETHOD(method)        virtual HRESULT STDMETHODCALLTYPE method
#define STDMETHOD_(type,method) virtual type STDMETHODCALLTYPE method
#define END_INTERFACE_PART(localClass) \
    } m_x##localClass; \
    friend class X##localClass; \
```

These macros create a nested class inside the `CCOMCards` class that includes the functions in the `IUnknown` interface. This nested class is then given access to all the protected and private members of the `CCOMCards` class through a `friend` statement. Listing 6.8 shows the complete `ICardDeck` interface.

Listing 6.8 The *ICardDeck* Interface

```
class XCardDeck : public ICardDeck
{
public:
    virtual ULONG   STDMETHODCALLTYPE AddRef();
    virtual ULONG   STDMETHODCALLTYPE Release();
```

continues

Listing 6.8 Continued

```
    virtual HRESULT STDMETHODCALLTYPE QueryInterface(REFIID iid, LPVOID*
      ➥ppvObj);
    virtual void STDMETHODCALLTYPE Shuffle();
    virtual void STDMETHODCALLTYPE GetNextCard(int* pnSuit, int* pnCard);
    virtual int  STDMETHODCALLTYPE GetUsedCount();
    virtual BSTR STDMETHODCALLTYPE GetCardName(int iSuit, int iCard);
} m_xCardDeck;
friend class XCardDeck;
```

The last macro is `DECLARE_INTERFACE_MAP`. This macro, along with the `BEGIN_INTERFACE_MAP`, `INTERFACE_PART`, and `END_INTERFACE_MAP` macros in the implementation file, allows the `CCmdTarget` derived class (`CCOMCards`) to access the proper interface's information when the `QueryInterface` function of the `IUnknown` interface is called.

The final step in creating the `CCOMCards` interface definition is to remove the unneeded OLE Automation code. Remove the code shown in Listing 6.9 from the CCOMCards.h file.

Listing 6.9 Lines to Remove from the CCOMCards.h File

```
BEGIN_DISPATCH_MAP(CCOMCards, CCmdTarget)
    //{{AFX_DISPATCH_MAP(CCOMCards)
        // NOTE - the ClassWizard will add and remove mapping macros here.
    //}}AFX_DISPATCH_MAP
END_DISPATCH_MAP()
// Note: we add support for IID_ICOMCards to support typesafe binding
//  from VBA. This IID must match the GUID that is attached to the
//  dispinterface in the .ODL file.
// {C293A3D4-0059-11D1-87A1-444553540000}
static const IID IID_ICOMCards =
{ 0xc293a3d4, 0x59, 0x11d1, { 0x87, 0xa1, 0x44, 0x45, 0x53, 0x54, 0x0, 0x0 } };
BEGIN_INTERFACE_MAP(CCOMCards, CCmdTarget)
    INTERFACE_PART(CCOMCards, IID_ICOMCards, Dispatch)
END_INTERFACE_MAP()
```

Adding the COM Implementation Code to the *CCOMCards* Class Edit the COMCards.cpp file to add the boldfaced code in Listing 6.10. The first item to add is a call to shuffle the deck of cards when this object is first constructed. The next lines to add are the `INTERFACE_MAP` entries. The last set of code is the implementation of the object's interfaces.

Listing 6.10 COM Implementation Code

```
// COMCards.cpp : implementation file
//
#include "stdafx.h"
#include "MyCards.h"
#include "COMCards.h"
#ifdef _DEBUG
#define new DEBUG_NEW
```

```
#undef THIS_FILE
static char THIS_FILE[] = __FILE__;
#endif
/////////////////////////////////////////////////////////////////////////////
// CCOMCards
IMPLEMENT_DYNCREATE(CCOMCards, CCmdTarget)
CCOMCards::CCOMCards()
{
    EnableAutomation();
    // To keep the application running as long as an OLE automation
    // object is active, the constructor calls AfxOleLockApp.
    AfxOleLockApp();
    // Shuffle the cards
    m_xCardDeck.Shuffle();
}
CCOMCards::~CCOMCards()
{
    // To terminate the application when all objects created with
    // with OLE automation, the destructor calls AfxOleUnlockApp.
    AfxOleUnlockApp();
}

void CCOMCards::OnFinalRelease()
{
    // When the last reference for an automation object is released
    // OnFinalRelease is called. The base class will automatically
    // delete the object. Add additional cleanup required for your
    // object before calling the base class.
    CCmdTarget::OnFinalRelease();
}

BEGIN_MESSAGE_MAP(CCOMCards, CCmdTarget)
    //{{AFX_MSG_MAP(CCOMCards)
        // NOTE - the ClassWizard will add and remove mapping macros here.
    //}}AFX_MSG_MAP
END_MESSAGE_MAP()
BEGIN_INTERFACE_MAP(CCOMCards, CCmdTarget)
    INTERFACE_PART(CCOMCards, IID_ICardDeck, CardDeck)
    INTERFACE_PART(CCOMCards, IID_ICheat,    CardCheat)
END_INTERFACE_MAP()
// {C293A3D5-0059-11D1-87A1-444553540000}
IMPLEMENT_OLECREATE(CCOMCards, "MyCards.COMCards",
    0xc293a3d5, 0x59, 0x11d1, 0x87, 0xa1, 0x44, 0x45, 0x53, 0x54, 0x0, 0x0)
/////////////////////////////////////////////////////////////////////////////
// CCOMCards message handlers
/////////////////////////////////////////////////////////////////////////////
// Interface functions for the ICardDeck Interface
STDMETHODIMP_(ULONG) CCOMCards::XCardDeck::AddRef()
{
    TRACE("CCOMCards::XCardDeck::AddRef()\n");
    METHOD_PROLOGUE(CCOMCards, CardDeck)
    return( pThis->ExternalAddRef() );
}
```


continues

Listing 6.10 Continued

```
STDMETHODIMP_(ULONG) CCOMCards::XCardDeck::Release()
{
    TRACE("CCOMCards::XCardDeck::Release()\n");
    METHOD_PROLOGUE(CCOMCards, CardDeck)
    return( pThis->ExternalRelease() );
}
STDMETHODIMP CCOMCards::XCardDeck::QueryInterface(REFIID iid, LPVOID* ppvObj)
{
    TRACE("CCOMCards::XCardDeck::QueryInterface()\n");
    METHOD_PROLOGUE(CCOMCards, CardDeck)
    return( pThis->ExternalQueryInterface(&iid, ppvObj) );
}
STDMETHODIMP_(void) CCOMCards::XCardDeck::Shuffle()
{
    // Get the pThis pointer
    METHOD_PROLOGUE(CCOMCards, CardDeck)
    // Reset the count and position variable
    pThis->m_nUsedCardCount   = 0;
    pThis->m_nCurrentPosition = 0;
    // Prepare the bool structure to order the cards
    int  nCardsPicked = 0;
    bool bSelectedCards[52];
    for( int i = 0; i < 52; ++i )
    {
        bSelectedCards[i] = false;
    }
    // Reset the random number generator
    srand( (unsigned)time( NULL ) );
    // Select the 52 cards
    while( nCardsPicked < 52 )
    {
        // Get a card
        int nCard = int(rand() / double(RAND_MAX) * 52);
        // See if that card is used
        if ( !bSelectedCards[nCard] )
        {
            bSelectedCards[nCard] = true;
            pThis->m_aCardArray[nCardsPicked] = nCard;
            ++nCardsPicked;
        }
    }
}
STDMETHODIMP_(void) CCOMCards::XCardDeck::GetNextCard(int* pnSuit, int* pnCard)
{
    // Get the pThis pointer
    METHOD_PROLOGUE(CCOMCards, CardDeck)
    // See if we have cards left
    if ( pThis->m_nUsedCardCount >= 52 )
    {
        *pnSuit = SUIT_NONE;
        *pnCard = CARD_NONE;
    }
    else
    {
```

```
        *pnSuit = (pThis->m_aCardArray[pThis->m_nCurrentPosition] / 13 + 1);
        *pnCard = (pThis->m_aCardArray[pThis->m_nCurrentPosition] % 13 + 1);
        ++(pThis->m_nUsedCardCount);
        ++(pThis->m_nCurrentPosition);
    }
}
STDMETHODIMP_(int) CCOMCards::XCardDeck::GetUsedCount()
{
    METHOD_PROLOGUE(CCOMCards, CardDeck)
    return( pThis->m_nUsedCardCount );
}
STDMETHODIMP_(BSTR) CCOMCards::XCardDeck::GetCardName(int nSuit, int nCard)
{
    METHOD_PROLOGUE(CCOMCards, CardDeck)
    CString sCardName;
    // Get the card number
    switch( nCard )
    {
    case CARD_ACE:    sCardName = "Ace";     break;
    case CARD_TWO:    sCardName = "Two";     break;
    case CARD_THREE:  sCardName = "Three";   break;
    case CARD_FOUR:   sCardName = "Four";    break;
    case CARD_FIVE:   sCardName = "Five";    break;
    case CARD_SIX:    sCardName = "Six";     break;
    case CARD_SEVEN:  sCardName = "Seven";   break;
    case CARD_EIGHT:  sCardName = "Eight";   break;
    case CARD_NINE:   sCardName = "Nine";    break;
    case CARD_TEN:    sCardName = "Ten";     break;
    case CARD_JACK:   sCardName = "Jack";    break;
    case CARD_QUEEN:  sCardName = "Queen";   break;
    case CARD_KING:   sCardName = "King";    break;
    default:          sCardName = "Unknown";
    }
    sCardName += " of ";
    // Get the suit
    switch( nSuit )
    {
    case SUIT_DIAMOND: sCardName += "Diamonds";  break;
    case SUIT_HEART:   sCardName += "Hearts";    break;
    case SUIT_CLUB:    sCardName += "Clubs";     break;
    case SUIT_SPADE:   sCardName += "Spades";    break;
    default:           sCardName += "Unknown";
    }
    // Return a BSTR (the client will need to free the BSTR)
    return( sCardName.AllocSysString() );
}
///////////////////////////////////////////////////////////////////////////////
// Interface functions for the ICheat Interface
STDMETHODIMP_(ULONG) CCOMCards::XCardCheat::AddRef()
{
    TRACE("CCOMCards::XCardCheat::AddRef()\n");
    METHOD_PROLOGUE(CCOMCards, CardCheat)
    return( pThis->ExternalAddRef() );
}
```

Part II

Ch 6

continues

Listing 6.10 Continued

```
STDMETHODIMP_(ULONG) CCOMCards::XCardCheat::Release()
{
    TRACE("CCOMCards::XCardCheat::Release()\n");
    METHOD_PROLOGUE(CCOMCards, CardCheat)
    return( pThis->ExternalRelease() );
}
STDMETHODIMP CCOMCards::XCardCheat::QueryInterface(REFIID iid, LPVOID* ppvObj)
{
    TRACE("CCOMCards::XCardCheat::QueryInterface()\n");
    METHOD_PROLOGUE(CCOMCards, CardCheat)
    return( pThis->ExternalQueryInterface(&iid, ppvObj) );
}
STDMETHODIMP_(int) CCOMCards::XCardCheat::GetCurrentPosition()
{
    METHOD_PROLOGUE(CCOMCards, CardCheat)
    return( pThis->m_nCurrentPosition );
}
STDMETHODIMP_(void) CCOMCards::XCardCheat::SetCardAtPosition(int nPos,
➥int nSuit, int nCard)
{
    METHOD_PROLOGUE(CCOMCards, CardCheat)
    // Check the validity of the position
    if ( nPos >= 0 && nPos < 52 )
    {
        // Compute the card number
        int nCardNumber = (nSuit - 1) * 13 + (nCard - 1);
        // Put the new card at the specified position
        pThis->m_aCardArray[nPos] = nCardNumber;
    }
}
STDMETHODIMP_(void) CCOMCards::XCardCheat::LookAtPosition(int nPos,
➥int* pnSuit, int* pnCard)
{
    METHOD_PROLOGUE(CCOMCards, CardCheat)
    if ( nPos < 0 || nPos >= 52 )
    {
        *pnSuit = SUIT_NONE;
        *pnCard = CARD_NONE;
    }
    else
    {
        *pnSuit = (pThis->m_aCardArray[nPos] / 13 + 1);
        *pnCard = (pThis->m_aCardArray[nPos] % 13 + 1);
    }
}
```

Almost every function in Listing 6.10 uses the `METHOD_PROLOGUE` macro and the `pThis` pointer. The `METHOD_PROLOGUE` macro actually creates the `pThis` pointer. The definition of `METHOD_PROLOGUE` is found in the AFXDISP.H header file in the MFC include directory:

```
#define METHOD_PROLOGUE(theClass, localClass) \
    theClass* pThis = \
        ((theClass*)((BYTE*)this - offsetof(theClass, m_x##localClass))); \
...
```

Because the interfaces are actually nested classes, the `this` pointer points to the interfaces themselves, not the `CCOMCards` object. The `METHOD_PROLOGUE` macro computes the offset of the specified object into the `CCOMCards` object and subtracts that from the `this` pointer provided. `pThis` is a new pointer into the `CCOMCards` object that allows you to access the member variables found in the `CCOMCards` class.

The code in Listing 6.10 also uses three `CCmdTarget` functions: `ExternalAddRef()`, `ExternalRelease()`, and `ExternalQueryInterface()`. `CCmdTarget` provides these functions so that you don't have to do all the reference counting and interface tracking every time you create a component. Just be sure to derive your component from `CCmdTarget`, and the functionality is provided for you.

Compiling and Registering the New InProc COM Server Compile the project to produce MyCards.dll and run the command `REGSVR32 MYCARDS.DLL` to register the COM server. This command calls your DLL to determine the objects and their GUIDs. It then makes entries in the system's Registry so that other programs can use this object.

Example 2: A COM Client That Uses the InProc Server

This example is the client application that would use the preceding COM server and both its interfaces. This example won't need as many tricks and macros as the preceding example. The implementation is rather simple but must have a fair amount of error checking.

Follow these steps to create the CcardClient application:

1. Choose File, New from the menu.
2. Set the options in the New dialog box similar to those shown in Figure 6.5. Click OK to start the AppWizard.

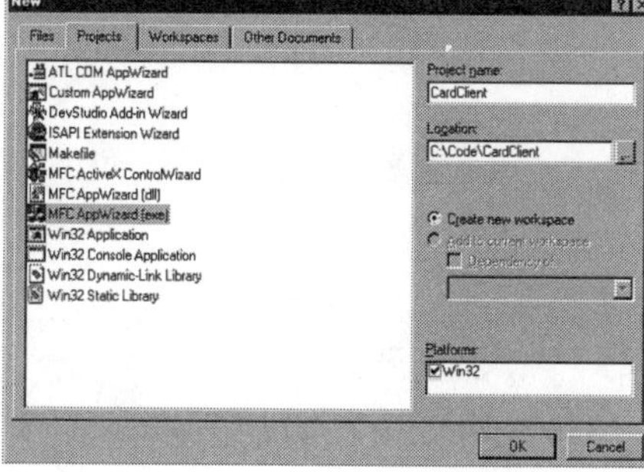

FIG. 6.5
Start setting up your application in the New dialog box.

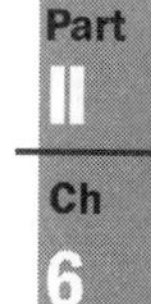

3. In the MFC AppWizard – Step 1 dialog box, change the application type to Single Document Type.
4. In the Step 2 dialog box, leave the database support set to none and accept the defaults for the rest of the AppWizard buttons by clicking the Finish button. Figure 6.6 shows the results of the CcardClient AppWizard settings.

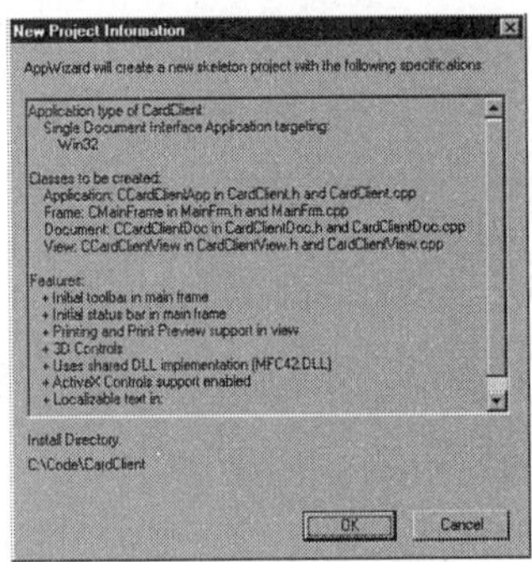

FIG. 6.6
These settings are used for the CcardClient application sample.

5. Edit the stdafx.h file and add the boldfaced line shown in Listing 6.11.

Listing 6.11 Code to Be Added to the CcardClient Application's stdafx.h File

```
// stdafx.h : include file for standard system include files,
//  or project specific include files that are used frequently, but
//      are changed infrequently
//
#if !defined(AFX_STDAFX_H__C4D43FC7_006B_11D1_87A1_444553540000__INCLUDED_)
#define AFX_STDAFX_H__C4D43FC7_006B_11D1_87A1_444553540000__INCLUDED_
#if _MSC_VER >= 1000
#pragma once
#endif // _MSC_VER >= 1000
#define VC_EXTRALEAN          // Exclude rarely-used stuff from Windows headers
#include <afxwin.h>         // MFC core and standard components
#include <afxext.h>         // MFC extensions
#include <afxdisp.h>        // MFC OLE automation classes
#include <afxole.h>
#ifndef _AFX_NO_AFXCMN_SUPPORT
#include <afxcmn.h>               // MFC support for Windows Common Controls
#endif // _AFX_NO_AFXCMN_SUPPORT

//{{AFX_INSERT_LOCATION}}
// Microsoft Developer Studio will insert additional declarations
// immediately before the previous line.
#endif //
!defined(AFX_STDAFX_H__C4D43FC7_006B_11D1_87A1_444553540000__INCLUDED_)
```

6. Edit `CcardClientApp::InitInstance` to initialize COM (see the boldfaced line in Listing 6.12).

Listing 6.12 The Code That Adds COM Initialization

```
BOOL CcardClientApp::InitInstance()
{
    AfxOleInit();
    AfxEnableControlContainer();
    // Standard initialization
    // If you are not using these features and wish to reduce the size
    //  of your final executable, you should remove from the following
    //  the specific initialization routines you do not need.
#ifdef _AFXDLL
    Enable3dControls();            // Call this when using MFC in a shared DLL
#else
    Enable3dControlsStatic();      // Call this when linking to MFC statically
#endif
...
```

7. Add a menu item to the application. Open the resource editor and double-click the `IDR_MAINFRAME` menu.
8. Add the PopUp menu item named Cards.
9. To the PopUp menu Cards item, add one menu item called Test. This menu should now look like Figure 6.7.

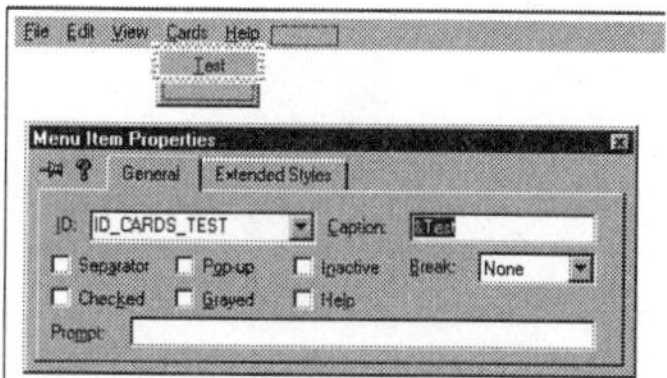

FIG. 6.7
The Test menu item allows you to test the Card COM object.

10. Start the ClassWizard by choosing View, ClassWizard from the menu.
11. In the Object IDs list select `ID_CARDS_TEST`, select `COMMAND` from the Messages list, and then click Add Function to create the command handler for this message. Figure 6.8 shows the ClassWizard as it's ready to create the command handler.

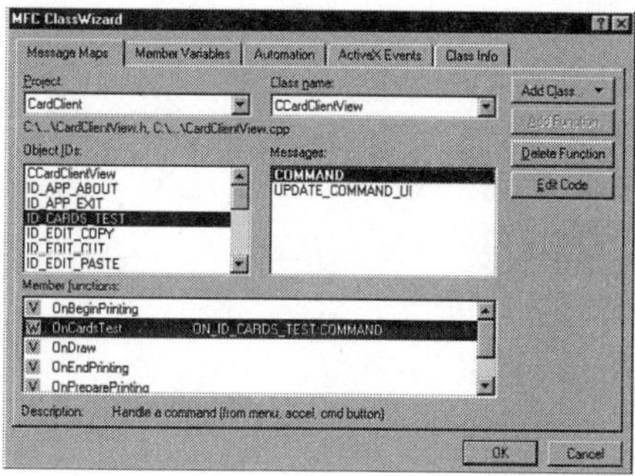

FIG. 6.8
The ClassWizard is ready to create a command handler in the view class for the `ID_CARDS TEST` command.

12. Add the CardInterface.h header file from Listing 6.13.

Listing 6.13 All the Information About the *ICardDeck* and *ICheat* Interfaces

```
// CardInterface.h - File containing all the information about the ICardDeck and
//                   ICheat Interfaces.

#if !defined( __CARDINTERFACE_H__ )
#define __CARDINTERFACE_H__

// Constants for the ICardDeck Interface
const int SUIT_NONE    = 0;
const int SUIT_HEART   = 1;
const int SUIT_DIAMOND = 2;
const int SUIT_CLUB    = 3;
const int SUIT_SPADE   = 4;

const int CARD_NONE    = 0;
const int CARD_ACE     = 1;
const int CARD_TWO     = 2;
const int CARD_THREE   = 3;
const int CARD_FOUR    = 4;
const int CARD_FIVE    = 5;
const int CARD_SIX     = 6;
const int CARD_SEVEN   = 7;
const int CARD_EIGHT   = 8;
const int CARD_NINE    = 9;
const int CARD_TEN     = 10;
const int CARD_JACK    = 11;
const int CARD_QUEEN   = 12;
const int CARD_KING    = 13;

// GUID for the ICardDeck Interface
// {35AB55A0-005B-11d1-87A1-444553540000}
static const GUID IID_ICardDeck =
{ 0x35ab55a0, 0x5b, 0x11d1, { 0x87, 0xa1, 0x44, 0x45, 0x53, 0x54, 0x0, 0x0 } };

// GUID for the ICheat Interface
// {35AB55A1-005B-11d1-87A1-444553540000}
static const GUID IID_ICheat =
{ 0x35ab55a1, 0x5b, 0x11d1, { 0x87, 0xa1, 0x44, 0x45, 0x53, 0x54, 0x0, 0x0 } };

// ICardDeck Interface
struct ICardDeck : public IUnknown
{
    STDMETHOD_(void, Shuffle) () = 0;
    STDMETHOD_(void, GetNextCard) (int* pnSuit, int* pnCard) = 0;
    STDMETHOD_(int,  GetUsedCount) () = 0;
    STDMETHOD_(BSTR, GetCardName) (int nSuit, int nCard) = 0;
};

// ICheat Interface
struct ICheat : public IUnknown
{
```

```
    STDMETHOD_(int,  GetCurrentPosition) () = 0;
    STDMETHOD_(void, SetCardAtPosition) (int nPos, int nSuit, int nCard) = 0;
    STDMETHOD_(void, LookAtPosition) (int nPos, int* pnSuit, int* pnCard) = 0;
};

#endif        // #if !defined( __CARDINTERFACE_H__ )
```

13. Edit the CcardClientView.cpp file to add the boldfaced line shown in Listing 6.14.

Listing 6.14 Adding the CardInterface.h *#include* Statement

```
// CcardClientView.cpp : implementation of the CcardClientView class
//
#include "stdafx.h"
#include "CcardClient.h"
#include "CcardClientDoc.h"
#include "CcardClientView.h"
#include "CardInterface.h"
#ifdef _DEBUG
#define new DEBUG_NEW
#undef THIS_FILE
static char THIS_FILE[] = __FILE__;
#endif
...
```

14. Modify the `CcardClientView::OnCardsTest()` function to add the boldfaced code shown in Listing 6.15.

Listing 6.15 Completing the CcardClient Application

```
void CcardClientView::OnCardsTest()
{
    // Get the ClassID for the Card COM object
    CLSID clsid;
    HRESULT hResult;
    hResult = ::CLSIDFromProgID(L"MyCards.COMCards", &clsid);
    if ( hResult != NOERROR )
    {
        TRACE("Could not get the Class ID!\n");
        return;
    }
    // Get the class factory's pointer
    LPCLASSFACTORY pClassFactory;
    hResult = ::CoGetClassObject(clsid,
        CLSCTX_INPROC_SERVER, NULL, IID_IClassFactory, (void**)&pClassFactory);
    if ( hResult != NOERROR )
    {
        TRACE("Could not get the class factory pointer!\n");
        return;
    }
```

Part II
Ch 6

continues

Listing 6.15 Continued

```
// Create a CCOMCards object (on the server) and get its IUnknown pointer
LPUNKNOWN pUnknown;
if (pClassFactory->CreateInstance(NULL, IID_IUnknown, (void**)&pUnknown) !=
➥S_OK)
{
    TRACE("Could not get the IUnknown pointer!\n");
    pClassFactory->Release();
    return;
}
// Get a pointer to the ICardDeck interface
ICardDeck* pCardDeck;
if ( pUnknown->QueryInterface(IID_ICardDeck, (void**)&pCardDeck) != S_OK)
{
    TRACE("Could not get the ICardDeck pointer!\n");
    pUnknown->Release();
    pClassFactory->Release();
    return;
}
// Get a pointer to the ICheat interface (could also use pUnknown)
ICheat* pCheat;
if ( pCardDeck->QueryInterface(IID_ICheat, (void**)&pCheat) != S_OK)
{
    TRACE("Could not get the ICheat pointer!\n");
    pCardDeck->Release();
    pUnknown->Release();
    pClassFactory->Release();
    return;
}
// Test everything out
int nSuit;
int nCard;
while( pCardDeck->GetUsedCount() < 52 )
{
    int nSuit;
    int nCard;
    pCardDeck->GetNextCard(&nSuit, &nCard);
    BSTR bCardName = pCardDeck->GetCardName(nSuit, nCard);
    TRACE("%s\n", LPCSTR(CString(bCardName)));
    ::SysFreeString(bCardName);
}
// Reshuffle
pCardDeck->Shuffle();
// Stack the deck for a two handed game of poker
TRACE("\nTIME TO PLAY POKER\n");
pCheat->SetCardAtPosition(1, SUIT_DIAMOND, CARD_ACE);
pCheat->SetCardAtPosition(3, SUIT_DIAMOND, CARD_KING);
pCheat->SetCardAtPosition(5, SUIT_DIAMOND, CARD_QUEEN);
pCheat->SetCardAtPosition(7, SUIT_DIAMOND, CARD_JACK);
pCheat->SetCardAtPosition(9, SUIT_DIAMOND, CARD_TEN);
// Deal the poker hands
TRACE("YOU                   ME\n");
while( pCheat->GetCurrentPosition() < 10 )
{
```

```
        // Get your card
        pCardDeck->GetNextCard(&nSuit, &nCard);
        BSTR bCardName = pCardDeck->GetCardName(nSuit, nCard);
        CString sYourCard(bCardName);
        ::SysFreeString(bCardName);
        // Get my card
        pCardDeck->GetNextCard(&nSuit, &nCard);
        bCardName = pCardDeck->GetCardName(nSuit, nCard);
        CString sMyCard(bCardName);
        ::SysFreeString(bCardName);
        // Display what we got
        TRACE("%-20.20s %-20.20s\n", LPCSTR(sYourCard), LPCSTR(sMyCard));
    }
    // Release everything (order does not matter)
    TRACE("\nReleaseing everything\n");
    pCheat->Release();
    pCardDeck->Release();
    pUnknown->Release();
    pClassFactory->Release();
    // Let the user know we are done
    AfxMessageBox("Done processing ... successfully!");
}
```

Here are a few notes about the code in Listing 6.15:

- The function `CLSIDFromProgID` returns a GUID given the string name for the class by looking in the Registry.
- The function `CoGetClassObject` locates and loads (if necessary) the object specified by the GUID. In this case, it's retrieving the `IID_IClassFactory` object, which is an object that automatically generates an instance of the `CCOMCards` class on request.
- The class factory's `CreateInstance` function creates an instance of the class and returns a pointer to the `IUnknown` interface. The interface `QueryInterface` function is called to gain access to the `ICardDeck` and `ICheat` interfaces.

Finally, after the application is compiled and tested, the output shown in Figure 6.9 appears.

Using Automation

After seeing the implementation of interfaces that use COM in the preceding examples, you may be looking for something a little simpler. That simplicity comes by the way of Automation. Automation is one of the easiest types of COM to implement, especially because Visual C++ does most of the work for you.

Automation supports the concept of *late binding*. Normally, DLLs and COM objects are first linked into your application before your application ever runs. This is an *early binding* mechanism. In late binding, you can query an object for the types of methods that it supports and what those methods may take as arguments. This way, a client can work with servers that it may not fully know about.

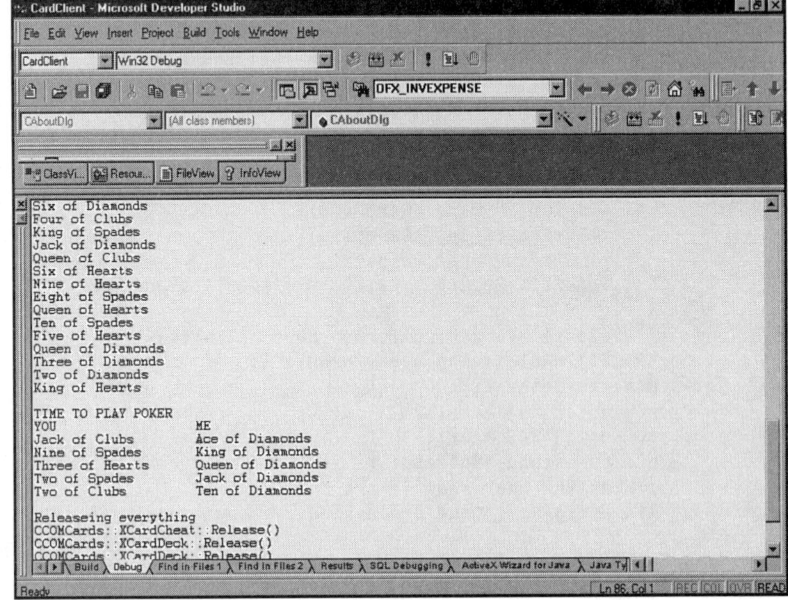

FIG. 6.9
The final output of the CcardClient application.

Definition of Automation

Automation is the answer to the late-binding issue. The key to Automation is the `IDispatch` interface, which has four functions: `GetTypeInfo`, `GetTypeInfoCount`, `GetIDsOfNames`, and `Invoke`. The most import function, `Invoke`, performs late binding. When a client application wants to call a function on the server, it provides information to `Invoke` to tell the server which function to execute and what parameters to use when it executes. Listing 6.16 shows the `IDispatch` interface definition. Although the definition looks complicated, just remember that Visual C++ hides quite a bit of this complexity when it helps you implement Automation.

Listing 6.16 The *IDispatch* Portion of the OAIDL.H File

```
interface IDispatch : public IUnknown
    {
    public:
        virtual HRESULT STDMETHODCALLTYPE GetTypeInfoCount(
            /* [out] */ UINT __RPC_FAR *pctinfo) = 0;

        virtual HRESULT STDMETHODCALLTYPE GetTypeInfo(
            /* [in] */ UINT iTInfo,
            /* [in] */ LCID lcid,
            /* [out] */ ITypeInfo __RPC_FAR *__RPC_FAR *ppTInfo) = 0;

        virtual HRESULT STDMETHODCALLTYPE GetIDsOfNames(
            /* [in] */ REFIID riid,
            /* [size_is][in] */ LPOLESTR __RPC_FAR *rgszNames,
            /* [in] */ UINT cNames,
```

```
            /* [in] */ LCID lcid,
            /* [size_is][out] */ DISPID __RPC_FAR *rgDispId) = 0;

        virtual /* [local] */ HRESULT STDMETHODCALLTYPE Invoke(
            /* [in] */ DISPID dispIdMember,
            /* [in] */ REFIID riid,
            /* [in] */ LCID lcid,
            /* [in] */ WORD wFlags,
            /* [out][in] */ DISPPARAMS __RPC_FAR *pDispParams,
            /* [out] */ VARIANT __RPC_FAR *pVarResult,
            /* [out] */ EXCEPINFO __RPC_FAR *pExcepInfo,
            /* [out] */ UINT __RPC_FAR *puArgErr) = 0;

    };
```

The first two functions, `GetTypeInfoCount` and `GetTypeInfo`, combine to form one method of informing the client applications of the functions supported by each specific implementation of the `IDispatch` interface. Because Visual C++ and MFC support the other method—building an Object Description Language (ODL) file and compiling it into a Type Library File (TLB)—this chapter doesn't look in depth at these two functions.

The third function, `GetIDsOfNames`, translates a number of function names to the IDs that must be used when the functions are called through `Invoke`. To save time, you can retrieve multiple function IDs in one call to `GetIDsOfNames`.

After the information to translate a function name to an ID is retrieved, you can use this information in the call to `Invoke`. The other information supplied has to do with the parameters to be passed to the function, the return value from the function, and exception-handling information. We won't go into any more detail about the `Invoke` parameters because all this information is nicely encapsulated in MFC.

MFC's Implementation of Automation

When implementing an Automation server or client in Visual C++ and MFC, the system takes care of almost everything except calling and implementing the functions for you. It uses a number of macros to hide the implementation details, but you need to look at how to implement the macros. Because MFC's implementation of Automation is so simple, look at the implementation in the following example.

Example 3: An OutOfProc Automation Server

The following sample program shows how to implement an OutOfProc (DLL) Automation server, taking full advantage of Visual C++ and MFC's encapsulation of Automation. This server creates an Automation class that performs basic math functions.

Creating the InProc Automation Server Use the AppWizard to create the new Visual C++ project:

1. Choose File, New from the menu.
2. On the Projects page, select MFC AppWizard (DLL).

3. In the Project Name text box, enter **AutoMath**.
4. Set the proper directory in the Location edit box. When all the options are set correctly, click OK.
5. The MFC AppWizard – Step 1 of 1 dialog box appears. Make sure that the Regular DLL Using Shared MFC DLL option and Automation checkbox are selected, and then click the Finish button.

Creating the *CMath* Class By using the ClassWizard, follow these steps:

1. Click the Add Class button and select New.
2. In the Class Information section, type **CMath** in the Name text box and select the Base Class of `CCmdTarget`.
3. In the Automation section, select Automation and then click OK.

Selecting the Automation option means that the ClassWizard will do most of the work for you. It will insert a number of macros in the header and implementation file that sets up for the insertion of Automation functions.

Because Automation uses the `IDispatch` interface, it will have to implement the `IUnknown` interface just like all other interfaces. For this reason and some `IDispatch` function implementation reasons, this new class is again derived from `CCmdTarget`.

Adding the Automation Functions to the *CMath* Class Now add the interface definitions that cover the automation portion of the `CMath` class. Follow these steps:

1. Select the `CMath` class.
2. On the Automation page, click the Add Method button and type **Add** in the External Name drop-down combo box.
3. Select long as the Return Type.
4. Add two parameters, 11 and 12, with the type of long. Your Add Method dialog box should look the one in Figure 6.10.

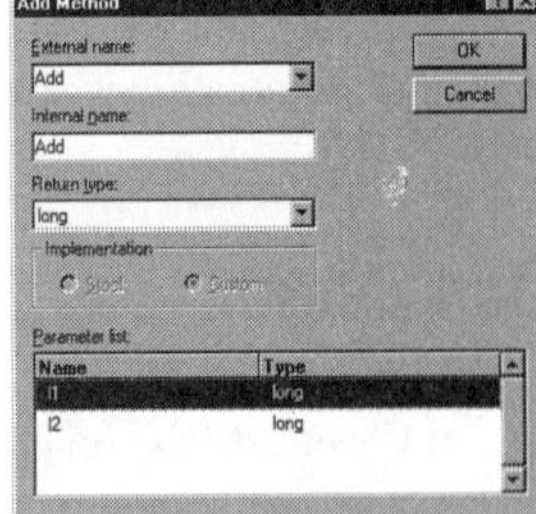

FIG. 6.10
Use the ClassWizard to add the `Add()` Automation function to the `CMath` class in the InProc Automation server.

5. Click OK.
6. Repeat steps 2–5 to create the `Subtract()` function, which takes two longs as parameters and returns a long.

7. Click the Add Property button and type **AddCorrect** as the External Name.
8. Select a Type of BOOL.
9. In the Implementation section, click Get/Set Methods and add a parameter named `bAddCorrect` as a Boolean. Figure 6.11 shows what the dialog box should look like.

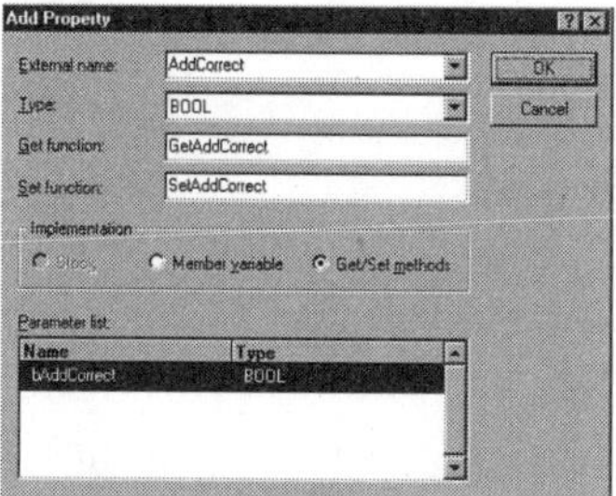

FIG. 6.11
Use the ClassWizard to add the `AddCorrect` property to the `CMath` class in the InProc Automation server.

10. Click OK. This property determines whether the `Add` method returns the correct value.
11. Again, click the Add Property button. Type **SubtractCorrect** as the External Name.
12. Select a Type of BOOL.
13. Change Variable Name to `m_bSubtractCorrect` so that your dialog box looks like the one in Figure 6.12.

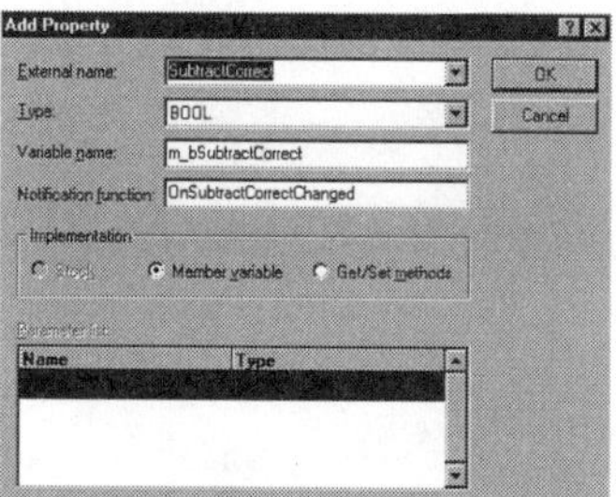

FIG. 6.12
Use the ClassWizard to add the `SubtractCorrect` property to the `CMath` class in the InProc Automation server.

14. Click OK. This property will determine whether the `Subtract` method returns the correct value.
15. Click OK in the ClassWizard dialog box when finished adding Automation methods and properties.

The ClassWizard adds some declarations to the header file and the code shown in Listing 6.17 to the implementation file for the `CMath` class.

Listing 6.17 Code for the New *CMath* Class

```
BEGIN_DISPATCH_MAP(CMath, CCmdTarget)
    //{{AFX_DISPATCH_MAP(CMath)
    DISP_PROPERTY_NOTIFY(CMath, "SubtractCorrect",
        m_bSubtractCorrect, OnSubtractCorrectChanged, VT_BOOL)
    DISP_PROPERTY_EX(CMath, "AddCorrect", GetAddCorrect, SetAddCorrect, VT_BOOL)
    DISP_FUNCTION(CMath, "Add", Add, VT_I4, VTS_I4 VTS_I4)
    DISP_FUNCTION(CMath, "Subtract", Subtract, VT_I4, VTS_I4 VTS_I4)
    //}}AFX_DISPATCH_MAP
END_DISPATCH_MAP()
```

This dispatch map is how MFC keeps track of which function should be called when the Automation server's `Invoke` function is called.

Also, the ClassWizard has been updating a file called AutoMath.ODL (Object Description Language), which contains the external information needed to be able to interface with this Automation server. When you compile, the ODL file is also compiled and a Type Library file (.tlb) is generated. The .tlb file helps an Automation client properly use this Automation server.

Adding the *m_bAddCorrect* Member Variable You need to add a Boolean variable that verifies that your class is adding correctly. Follow these steps:

1. Add a Boolean member variable called `m_bAddCorrect` to the protected section of the `CMath` header file.
2. Add the boldfaced code in Listing 6.18 to the constructor of the `CMath` class in the implementation file.

Listing 6.18 Modifications for Adding the *m_AddCorrect* Variable

```
CMath::CMath()
{
    EnableAutomation();
    // To keep the application running as long as an OLE automation
    //     object is active, the constructor calls AfxOleLockApp.
    AfxOleLockApp();
    m_bAddCorrect      = TRUE;
    m_bSubtractCorrect = TRUE;
}
```

Adding the Implementation Code for the *CMath* Object Modify the code to the `CMath` implementation file so that it resembles the code in Listing 6.19.

Listing 6.19 Implementation of the *CMath* Class Functions

```
...
long CMath::Add(long l1, long l2)
{
```

```
    if ( m_bAddCorrect )    return(l1 + l2);
    else                    return(l1 * l2);
}
long CMath::Subtract(long l1, long l2)
{
    if ( m_bSubtractCorrect )   return(l1 - l2);
    else                        return(l1 / l2);
}
BOOL CMath::GetAddCorrect()
{
    return m_bAddCorrect;
}
void CMath::SetAddCorrect(BOOL bNewValue)
{
    m_bAddCorrect = bNewValue;
}
void CMath::OnSubtractCorrectChanged()
{
    // We won't do anything here, but we could detect the
    // value changing by placing code in this function.
}
```

Compiling and Registering the New InProc Automation Server Compile the project to produce AutoMath.dll and run the command `REGSVR32 AUTOMATH.DLL` to register the Automation server.

Example 4: An Automation Client That Uses InProc and OutOfProc Servers

Now that you've developed an Automation server, all you need is an Automation client that uses it. Building an Automation client is much easier than building the Automation server (which really wasn't hard at all). Again, MFC and its macros hide all the complicated COM stuff.

In the new version of Visual C++, smart pointers and the `#import` preprocessor statement have come on the scene for Automation. In this sample Automation client, you will be using both features.

Smart pointers wrap the pointer to an OLE or COM object. Smart pointers use some advance C++ programming techniques to automatically call the `AddRef()` and `Release` functions when using an interface. This keeps you from explicitly calling these functions yourself.

The import preprocessor statement saves a step when you're developing a client that uses a COM server. Before having the `#import` preprocessor statement, you would have to obtain an Interface Definition Language (IDL) or an Object Definition Language (ODL) file to include in your project. These files would define the interfaces for your C++ code. The `#import` directive allows you to include the Type Library (TLB) file directly. There used to be a tool to create the IDL or ODL file from the TLB; now you just include the TLB directly.

Creating the Automation Client Application By using the AppWizard, follow these steps:

1. Create an MFC SDI application, using the settings shown in Figure 6.13.

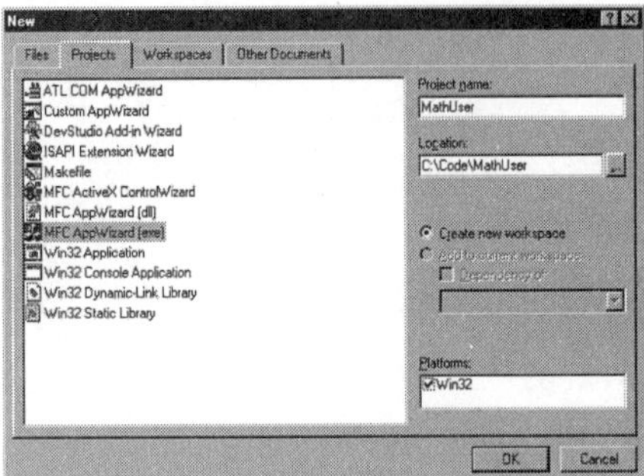

FIG. 6.13 In the AppWizard, use these settings to create the MathUser Automation client application.

2. In the Step 3 of 6 dialog box, select Automation support. Use the default settings for the rest of the selections. Figure 6.14 shows the proper settings for Step 3.

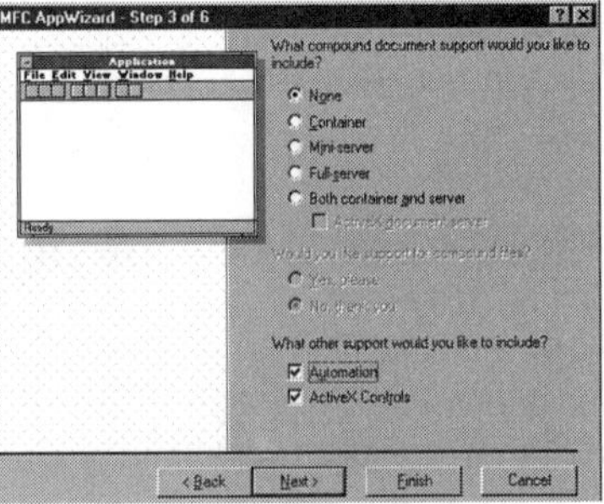

FIG. 6.14 Your settings for the Step 3 of 6 dialog box should match these.

Editing the StdAfx.h File Edit the StdAfx.h file to add the `#import` directive by adding the boldfaced lines shown in Listing 6.20.

Listing 6.20 Code to Be Added to the StdAfx.h File in This Project

```
...
#define VC_EXTRALEAN          // Exclude rarely-used stuff from Windows headers
#include <afxwin.h>         // MFC core and standard components
#include <afxext.h>         // MFC extensions
#include <afxdisp.h>        // MFC OLE automation classes
#ifndef _AFX_NO_AFXCMN_SUPPORT
#include <afxcmn.h>               // MFC support for Windows Common Controls
#endif // _AFX_NO_AFXCMN_SUPPORT
#import "../AutoMath/Debug/AutoMath.tlb"
using namespace AutoMath;
...
```

The `#import` directive, when compiled, creates two files in the Debug directory: AutoMath.tlh and AutoMath.tli. The .tlh (Type Library Header) and .tli (Type Library Implementation) files implement an interface to the Automation server. The advantage of using the `#import` directive instead of the old method of creating a class based on a type library is that if the type library file changes, the `#import` directive rebuilds the files on the next compile. Under the old way, the class based on the type library file had to be regenerated.

If you look at the contents of the newly created files, notice some strange-looking code. What this code is doing is creating a smart pointer to the Automation server. It's also implementing all the functions of the Automation server as inline calls to `Invoke` (through the `_com_dispatch_method` function implemented by Visual C++).

You may have also noticed that both properties created in the Automation server are implemented both ways in the smart pointer. You'll exploit that advantage when you implement your testing function.

Adding a Menu Item to Allow Testing With the resource editor, edit the `IDR_MAINFRAME` menu. Add a `POPUP` menu item named Math and add one menu item called Test. The menu should look like Figure 6.15.

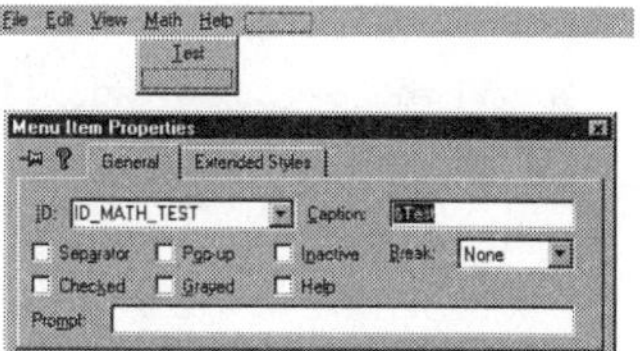

FIG. 6.15
Use a menu item for testing the `AutoMath` Automation object.

Adding a Command Handler for the *ID_MATH_TEST* Command ID By using the ClassWizard, create a command handler for the `ID_MATH_TEST` command in the `CMathUserView` class.

Adding Test Code to the Command-Handler Function Modify the `CMathUserView::OnMathTest()` function and add the code shown in Listing 6.21. This test function uses both methods of changing the two Boolean properties: the `Put...` functions and the direct set method.

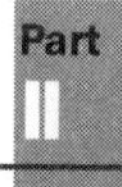

Listing 6.21 The New *CmathUserView::OnMathTest* Implementation

```
void CMathUserView::OnMathTest()
{
    // Create the "smart pointer" to the math object
     IMathPtr pMath;
    if ( pMath.CreateInstance(__uuidof(Math)) != S_OK )
    {
        AfxMessageBox("Could Not Create Instance!");
        return;
    }
```

continues

Listing 6.21 Continued

```
    // Test the math functions
    long lResult;
    lResult = pMath->Add(25, 5);
    TRACE("Add(25, 5) = %ld\n", lResult);
    lResult = pMath->Subtract(25, 5);
    TRACE("Subtract(25, 5) = %ld\n", lResult);
    // Start messing up
    TRACE("Changing the correct flags\n");
    pMath->AddCorrect = FALSE;
    lResult = pMath->Add(25, 5);
    TRACE("Add(25, 5) = %ld\n", lResult);
    pMath->SubtractCorrect = FALSE;
    lResult = pMath->Subtract(25, 5);
    TRACE("Subtract(25, 5) = %ld\n", lResult);
    // Start doing it right again
    TRACE("Doing it right again\n");
    pMath->PutAddCorrect(TRUE);
    lResult = pMath->Add(25, 5);
    TRACE("Add(25, 5) = %ld\n", lResult);
    pMath->PutSubtractCorrect(TRUE);
    lResult = pMath->Subtract(25, 5);
    TRACE("Subtract(25, 5) = %ld\n", lResult);
    // Display done message
    AfxMessageBox("Test Complete. Check the output window.");
}
```

Implementing Components with ATL

ATL is a template-based library designed to provide developers with the tools to quickly build COM objects, Automation servers, and ActiveX controls. Rather than derive from a class to extend the functionality of the class, you create a new class from the template. Typically, when creating this new class, you pass in a class type that the template uses to construct a new type. The template is then seen as an extension of your class.

What ATL Provides to COM Developers

ATL provides standard implementations for `IUnknown`, `IClassFactory`, `IClassFactory2`, and `IDispatch` to aid in the creation of COM objects. In addition to these classes, ATL includes support for a window class, which is used to create ActiveX objects.

One area where MFC and ATL vary is that MFC doesn't use multiple inheritance to implement COM interfaces. ATL uses a lot of multiple inheritance, due to the template-based architecture of the library. This means that ATL must do its reference counting at the class level. When you're using multiple inheritance, which base class should do the reference counting isn't clear. MFC does its reference counting at the interface level. Per-interface reference counting is more flexible than per-object.

Reference counting allows the same object to be instantiated and used by multiple clients. The first client calls `AddRef()` to access the interfaces and calls `Release()` when it's done. When the reference count of the object goes down to zero, the object can be removed from memory. There are two schemes for implementing reference counting:

- Implementing a reference count per interface.
- Implementing a reference count per object. The object is a group of interfaces.

Per-interface reference counting is good because each interface is tracked in memory by itself. However, per-interface reference counting is expensive because the client must call `QueryInterface`, `AddRef`, and `Release` for each function to be called. Per-object reference counts allow a group of interfaces to be made available with one `QueryInterface`, `AddRef`, and `Release` set of calls.

MFC implements only the per-interface reference counting. ATL, by default, implements the per-object reference counting. For ATL to support lighter weight interfaces, its implementors have chosen to provide *tear-off interfaces*, which allow ATL interfaces to be reference counted at the interface level.

Like MFC, ATL implements COM interfaces by inheriting from classes that contain pure virtual functions. Unlike MFC, ATL does this by inheriting from template classes. The code snippet in Listing 6.22 shows how the `ATLCard` class is constructed.

Listing 6.22 An Example of an ATL-Derived COM Interface Definition

```
...
 class ATL_NO_VTABLE CATLCard :
     public CComObjectRootEx<CComSingleThreadModel>,
     public CComCoClass<CATLCard, &CLSID_ATLCard>,
     public IDispatchImpl<IATLCard, &IID_IATLCard, &LIBID_ATLCSRVLib>,
     public IDispatchImpl<IATLCheat, &IID_IATLCheat, &LIBID_ATLCSRVLib>
{
...
```

Here, the `CATLCard` class inherits the `AddRef()` and `Release()` pure virtual functions from the base class of `CComObjectRootEx<>`, `IUnknown`. ATL actually implements `AddRef` in `CComObjectRootEx`. The `IDispatchImpl` template classes define the functions necessary for the interfaces, including the `Invoke` and `GetTypeInfo` interface definitions.

Example 5: An InProc COM Server with ATL

This example will implement the in-process server for the standard 52-playing-card deck (thc same as Example 1 implemented earlier). Implementing this sample in ATL will help you see the differences between component development in MFC and ATL.

Constructing an InProc Server Start the project by using the ATL COM AppWizard to construct an in-process server:

1. Choose File, New from the menu.
2. On the Projects page, select ATL COM AppWizard.
3. In the Project Name text box, enter **ATLCSrv**.
4. Set the proper directory in the Location text box. When all the options are set correctly (see Figure 6.16), click OK.

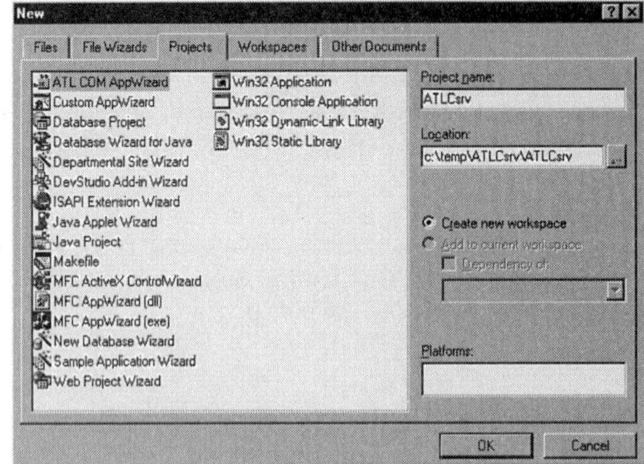

FIG. 6.16
These project options for the ATLCSrv InProc COM Server reflect how your dialog box should look.

5. The ATL COM AppWizard – Step 1 of 1 dialog box appears (see Figure 6.17). Set the Server Type to Dynamic Link Library (DLL). Leave Allow Merging of Proxy/Stub Code and Support MFC deselected.

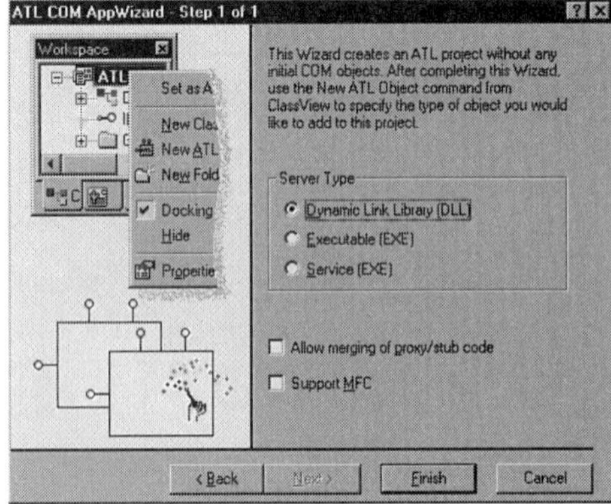

FIG. 6.17
Use these settings for the ATL COM AppWizard - Step 1 of 1 Options dialog box for the ATLCSrv InProc COM server.

6. Click OK when the New Project Information dialog box appears.

Now that you've constructed the project, you can begin creating the component.

Creating the ATL COM Component To create the ATL COM component, you use the ATL Object wizard, which allows you to select the type of object you want to create. For instance, if you're creating an object that will be used in Internet Explorer, select the Internet Explorer option to create an object template that includes the calls Internet Explorer will call. The Simple Object is the most basic set of COM interfaces. The Add-In object creates an ATL object that extends the Windows 95 user shell, a shell extension object. The Active Server Component option creates an object for use in Active Server Pages. The MS Transaction Server option creates a Transaction Server-ready object. The Component Registrar object provides just the mechanisms for placing values into the Registry.

Follow these steps to create the ATL COM component:

1. Choose Insert, New ATL Object from the menu to open the ATL Object Wizard (see Figure 6.18).

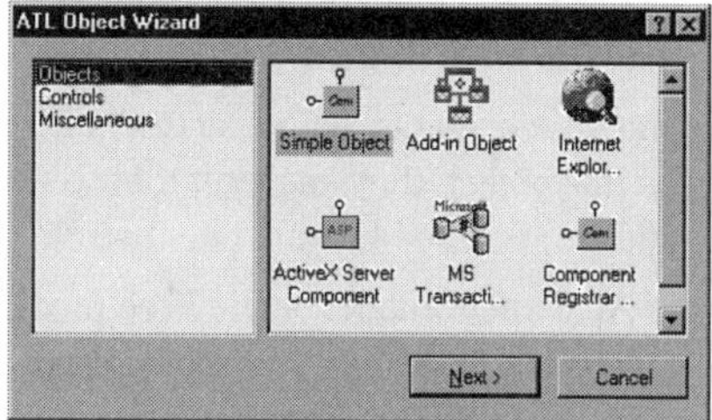

FIG. 6.18
Use this dialog box to create ATL objects and controls.

2. Select Objects in the left pane and Simple Object in the right pane.
3. Click Next to open the ATL Object Wizard Properties dialog box (see Figure 6.19).

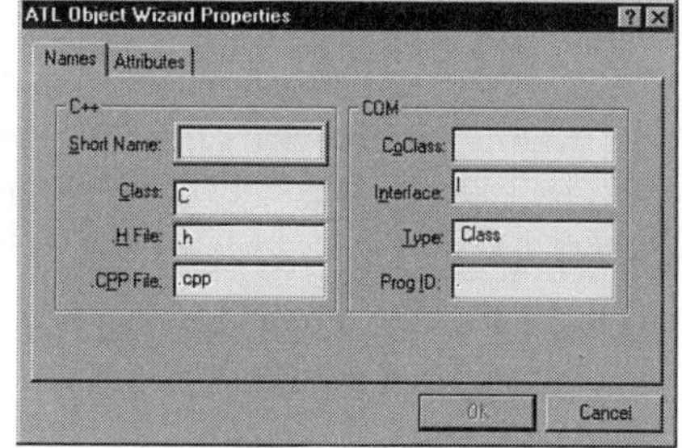

FIG. 6.19
With this dialog box, you specify the properties for your new ATL object.

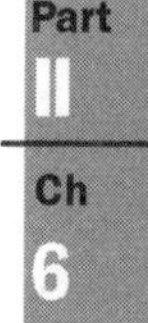

4. Enter the class name **`ATLCards`** in the Short Name text box and then let the wizard generate the other fields in the dialog box.
5. Select the Attributes tab (see Figure 6.20).

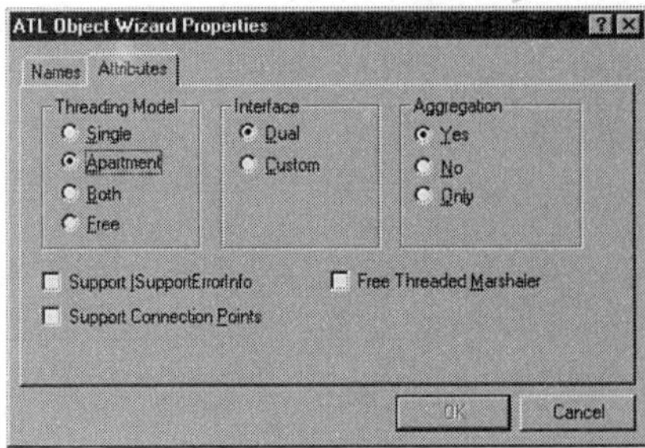

FIG. 6.20
The ATL Object Wizard Properties dialog box's Attributes page sets more technical aspects of the object.

For the simple object, the Attributes page includes three major sections: Threading Model, Interface, and Aggregation. The Threading Model settings are as follows:

- *Single* specifies this object to be single threaded. If two objects call this object at the same time, one is completely blocked while the first finishes execution. This isn't very useful in a multiuser application.
- *Apartment* specifies that this object is in an apartment threading model. When multiple clients access this object, they each get their own copy of the object. Each individual object should be accessed by only one thread.
- *Both* specifies that the Apartment model or the Free model can be supported.
- *Free* specifies that the object is completely thread safe. Multiple clients running multiple threads at the same time can access the object.

6. Leave the default settings for this example and click OK to create the class.

These steps create the class `CATLCards` and the first interface `IATLCards`. You'll put the standard card-handling functions into the `IATLCards` interface and then create a new interface to create the `Cheat` functions implemented earlier.

Creating the *ICheat* Interface You need to add the new interface to the existing `CATLCards` class. Unfortunately, the ATL class wizards don't provide support to add an interface to the existing class. This limitation does give you an opportunity to investigate what the wizards are doing by going ahead and implementing the interface by hand. Follow these steps:

1. Add the interface definition to the IDL file, shown in Listing 6.23. (Note that the `uuid` is generated by using the GUIDGen utility in the bin directory of Visual C++.)

Listing 6.23 Adding the *ICheat* Interface to the CATLCards.idl File

```
...
    [
        object,
        uuid(685BB54E-16EA-11D1-8375-000000000000),
        dual,
        helpstring("IATLCard Interface"),
        pointer_default(unique)
    ]
```

```
    interface IATLCard : IDispatch
    {
    };
    [
         object,
         uuid(54207220-16F1-11d1-8375-000000000000),
         dual,
         helpstring("IATLCheat Interface"),
         pointer_default(unique)
    ]
    interface IATLCheat : IDispatch
    {
         [id(1), helpstring("method GetCurrentPosition")]
         ➥HRESULT GetCurrentPosition
([out]int *iCurrentPos);
         [id(2), helpstring("method SetCardAtPosition")]
         ➥HRESULT SetCardAtPosition
([in] int nPos, [in] int nSuit, [in] int nCard);
         [id(3), helpstring("method LookAtPosition")] HRESULT LookAtPosition
([in] int iPos, [out] int * pnSuit, [out] int * pnCard);
    };
[
    uuid(685BB541-16EA-11D1-8375-000000000000),
    version(1.0),
    helpstring("atlcsrv 1.0 Type Library")
]
...
```

2. Notice in Listing 6.23 that the methods in the `IATLCard` interface haven't been defined yet. This listing goes ahead and defines the methods that define the `IATLCheat` interface.
3. Add the code in Listing 6.24, which derives the implementation object from the `idl` definition.

Listing 6.24 Code to Derive Implementation Object

```
...
class ATL_NO_VTABLE CATLCard :
    public CComObjectRootEx<CComSingleThreadModel>,
    public CComCoClass<CATLCard, &CLSID_ATLCard>,
    public IDispatchImpl<IATLCard, &IID_IATLCard, &LIBID_ATLCSRVLib>,
    public IDispatchImpl<IATLCheat, &IID_IATLCheat, &LIBID_ATLCSRVLib>
{
public:
    CATLCard()
    {
    }
DECLARE_REGISTRY_RESOURCEID(IDR_ATLCARD)
BEGIN_COM_MAP(CATLCard)
    COM_INTERFACE_ENTRY(IATLCard)
    COM_INTERFACE_ENTRY(IATLCheat)
    COM_INTERFACE_ENTRY2(IDispatch, IATLCheat)
END_COM_MAP()
```


continues

Listing 6.24 Continued

```
// IATLCard
public:
     STDMETHOD(LookAtPosition)(/*[in]*/ int iPos, /*[out]*/ int * pnSuit,
     ➥/*[out]*/ int * pnCard);
     STDMETHOD(SetCardAtPosition)(/*[in]*/ int nPos, /*[in]*/ int nSuit,
     ➥/*[in]*/ int nCard);
...
```

You've made two changes to the ATLCard.h file. The addition of the `IdispatchImpl` template instantiation in the inheritance of `CATLCard` implements the interface. Adding the two entries to the `COM_MAP` allows the new interface to be referenced by the `QueryInterface` functions.

4. Implement the functions in the ATLCard.cpp file. These changes are straightforward and identical to the implementations earlier in Example 1.

Adding the Methods to the *IATLCards* Interface Now that the cheat interface is complete, you can go back to using the ATL COM wizards to implement the methods that make up the `IATLCards` interface. This section covers creating one of the interfaces; the others are created in the exact same fashion. Follow these steps:

1. Add the `GetCardName` method by right-clicking the `IATLCard` interface in the Class View window. Select Add Method from the pull-down menu to open the Add Method to Interface dialog box (see Figure 6.21).

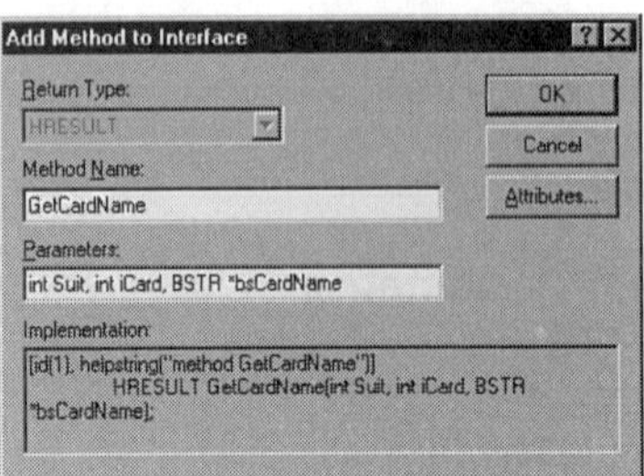

FIG. 6.21
Use the Add Method to Interface dialog box to define methods on an interface.

2. Notice the proper use of the `[in]` and `[out]` variable declarations in Listing 6.24 of the preceding section. These let COM properly define the inbound and outbound variables for the method. Entering these correctly in the Add Method to Interface dialog box will propagate these to the three places that need this information and save you time.

3. Implement `GetCardName`. This implementation is essentially the same as the version in Example 1, with one main difference: Because you're using the ATL to implement the COM object, you want to avoid using MFC altogether. The code in Example 1 makes effective use of the `CString` object to implement the string handling. You can use the string class provided in the Standard Template Library (STL) to get the same effective string handling.

Listing 6.25 shows the changes made to the CATLCard.cpp file.

Listing 6.25 Changes to the CATLCard.cpp File

```
...
STDMETHODIMP CATLCard::GetCardName(int iSuit, int iCard, BSTR * bsCardName)
{
    // Get the card number
     std::string sCardName;  // temporary string put our local result in.
    switch( iCard )
    {
          case CARD_ACE:     sCardName = "Ace";      break;
          case CARD_TWO:     sCardName = "Two";      break;
          case CARD_THREE:   sCardName = "Three";    break;
          case CARD_FOUR:    sCardName = "Four";     break;
          case CARD_FIVE:    sCardName = "Five";     break;
          case CARD_SIX:     sCardName = "Six";      break;
          case CARD_SEVEN:   sCardName = "Seven";    break;
          case CARD_EIGHT:   sCardName = "Eight";    break;
          case CARD_NINE:    sCardName = "Nine";     break;
          case CARD_TEN:     sCardName = "Ten";      break;
          case CARD_JACK:    sCardName = "Jack";     break;
          case CARD_QUEEN:   sCardName = "Queen";    break;
          case CARD_KING:    sCardName = "King";     break;
          default:           return S_FALSE;
    }

     sCardName += " of ";
     switch( iCard )
     {
         case SUIT_DIAMOND: sCardName += "Diamonds";  break;
          case SUIT_HEART:   sCardName += "Hearts";    break;
          case SUIT_CLUB:    sCardName += "Clubs";     break;
          case SUIT_SPADE:   sCardName += "Spades";    break;
          default:           return S_FALSE;
     }
     // Copy our result to a BSTR string.
     CComBSTR cbstrCardStr( sCardName.data() );
     *bsCardName = cbstrCardStr;
     return S_OK;
}
...
```


Listing 6.25 shows the `BSTR()` conversion operation being called, which automatically does `SysAllocString` and returns the proper `BSTR` pointer that you need to return from the function.

The ATL component is designed to have the same functionality as the original MFC component. This way, you can test the ATL component by using the CcardClient application from Example 2. Because the component behaves the same as the MFC component, the output of CcardClient will be identical.

From Here...

In this chapter, you learned how Visual C++ can be a very powerful tool in component development. In particular, you explored many of the issues in creating components by using Visual C++, MFC, and ActiveX.

- To learn about Microsoft's approach to object-oriented technology and how it affects software development, see Chapter 4, "Using Microsoft's Object Technologies."
- To understand how Visual Basic creates components, see Chapter 5, "Creating ActiveX Components with Visual Basic."
- To understand how components can be used in a client/server environment, see Chapter 9, "Using ActiveX Components in a Client/Server Environment."
- To learn how you can use Visual Studio to develop applications for the Internet or your own intranet, see Chapter 11, "An Inside Look at Web-Based Applications."
- To understand how to develop large, highly scalable applications, see Chapter 20, "Clients, Servers, and Components: Design Strategies for Distributed Applications."
- To learn the full power of using Visual Studio 97 to develop applications in a distributed computing environment, see Chapter 21, "Creating Distributed Applications."

CHAPTER 7

Creating Components with Visual J++

by Azam A. Mirza

- **Building Java applets with Visual J++**

  Learn about creating Java applets and applications with Visual J++. Learn about creating projects, building individual modules, building the applet, and using user interface elements.

- **Testing your Java applet**

  Learn about testing your application with Internet Explorer or another Java-compliant browser. Understand the differences between applications and applets.

- **Debugging your Java applet**

  Learn to how to debug a Visual J++ applet using the Visual Studio integrated debugging environment and how to make changes and enhancements to your applets.

- **Using Visual J++ wizards**

  Learn how you can use the Applet Wizard and the Resource Wizard to create a template for your projects that you can work from and customize to your needs.

The Microsoft Visual J++ environment is an Integrated Development Environment (IDE) for building Java applets and applications. Visual J++ shares the Developer Studio IDE with Visual C++ and Visual InterDev. The Developer Studio IDE provides a one-stop shop for building, testing, and debugging Visual J++ programs.

The Visual J++ system not only leverages the IDE to provide a visual environment for building Java applets, but it also includes a very fast compiler, a powerful debugging mechanism, a resource editor, and wizards to get you productive with the least amount of overhead. The Visual J++ environment uses the concept of a project workspace to organize development efforts. You work by creating and adding files to the project that houses the program.

This chapter is not a discussion of the Java language, but instead an introduction to using the Visual J++ language to create Java applets that can be used to enhance your web development efforts. This chapter assumes that you, the developer, are familiar with the Java language specification and have a basic understanding of software development principles and concepts.

It is possible to build a Visual J++ applet and use it in a Visual InterDev project, all within the same workspace.

NOTE If you would like to learn about the Java language, refer to the Java Language Specification or the Java Application Programming Interface included in the online documentation provided with Visual J++. You can also use the sample applications and applets provided with Visual J++ to familiarize yourself with the Java language and the Visual J++ environment.

Creating a Java Applet or Application

Visual J++ can create two kinds of Java programs: an *applet* or an *application*. The primary difference between an applet and an application is that an applet runs in the context of an HTML page inside a Java-capable browser, such as Microsoft Internet Explorer, whereas an application can run on its own using a standalone Java language interpreter. In terms of developing an applet or application, there are a few differences that must be kept in mind when working with Visual J++. These differences include the following:

NOTE A Java-capable browser is one that provides support for interpreting the Java language through a Java virtual machine. Examples include Internet Explorer and Netscape Navigator.

- An applet class must be derived from the Java `Applet` class. An application class does not need to be derived from the `Applet` class but can be.
- An application class must include a `main()` function as its starting point. An applet class does not require a `main()` function. The browser that is hosting the applet will control its execution.
- An applet is graphical by default because a graphical browser hosts it, whereas an application is text-based by default.

You can provide a graphical front end for an applet that runs as an application by deriving the application class from the `Frame` window class in addition to the `Applet` class. The `Frame` window class is used only when an applet is run as a standalone application.

To create an applet using Visual J++, you must first create a project that will host the development. You can then create, add, and modify project files that host the class modules, the resource files, and even the HTML file that might host the Java applet. The following sections discuss each of these activities in further detail.

Creating the Project Workspace

As stated earlier, the Visual J++ environment uses project workspaces to keep track of the class files in a project. To create a project in Visual J++, take the following steps:

1. Start Visual J++ and select New from the File menu.
2. The New dialog box appears. Click the Projects tab, as shown in Figure 7.1.

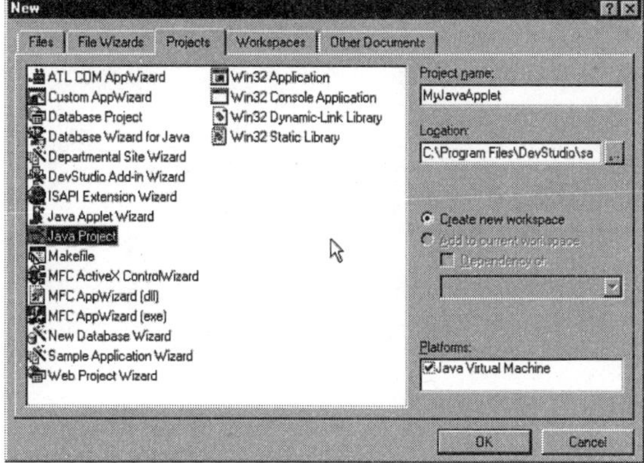

FIG. 7.1
The New tabbed dialog box is part of the Visual Studio shared IDE that can be used to create files of various types.

3. Select Java Project.
4. Provide a name for your project in the Project Name box.
5. In the Location text box, provide an alternative location for the project directory or select the default location.
6. Click OK. Visual J++ will create a new project in the directory specified.

The IDE provides two Explorer-style views into the Visual J++ project:

- *Class View*—Provides a view of the project organized around Java classes defined in the project
- *File View*—Provides a view of the project organized around the files included in the project

▶ **See** "Using Developer Studio," **p. 36**

When you create a project using the method described in the preceding six steps, the system creates a project that is used to create a single Java applet or application. The system by default creates a scenario for building two kinds of Java applets, a debug version and a release version.

Adding Files to the Project

After you have created the project, you will have a skeleton workspace with just the project defined in it. You can now create files in the project or add files from other Java projects by using file drag-and-drop techniques.

To add a new file to the project, take the following steps:

1. Select New from the File menu and click the Files tab. The Files dialog box appears, as shown in Figure 7.2.

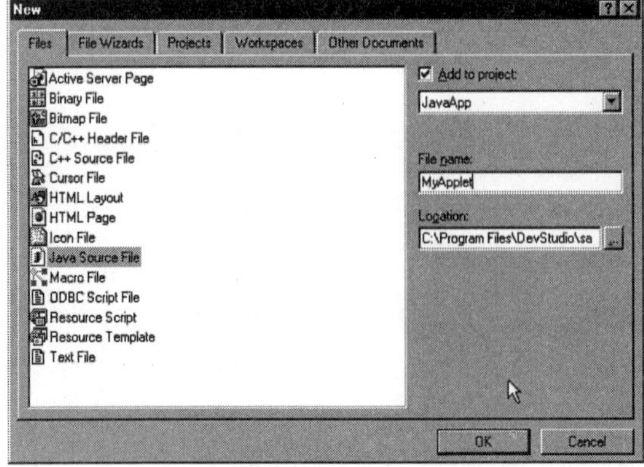

FIG. 7.2
You can create a Java file by selecting the Java Source File or the Text File option from the list.

2. Select Java Source File from the list.
3. Provide a name for the Java Source File in the File Name text box.
4. Click OK. Visual J++ will create and add an empty text file to the project.

Now that you have added a source file to the project, you can add code to the file to build your Java applet.

Building the Applet

A Java source file is a text file that you can edit in the Visual Studio source editor. Try creating a simple Java applet that displays the famous "Hello World" caption in a web page as a Java applet. To build the Java applet and run it in a browser, take the following steps:

1. Double-click the Java source file in the FileView Explorer to open it in the source editor.
2. After the file is open in the source editor, add the following lines of code:

```
import java.awt.Graphics;
public class HelloWorld extends java.applet.Applet
{
    public void paint( Graphics g )
    {
        g.drawString( "Hello Java World.", 10,20 );
}
}
```

3. After you have typed the code, save the file by selecting Save from the File menu.
4. To run the applet, select Execute from the Build menu. The Information For Running Class dialog box will appear, as shown in Figure 7.3.
5. Type the class filename as **`HelloWorld`** and click OK. The class filename must exactly match the class name you declare within the code, or the applet will not run.
6. Visual J++ will launch Internet Explorer and display the Java applet in an HTML file that it creates for testing purposes, as shown in Figure 7.4.

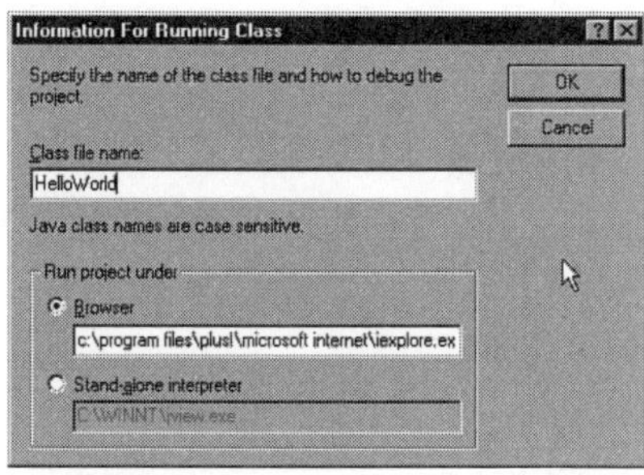

FIG. 7.3
The class filename tells the Visual J++ compiler which class you are trying to execute.

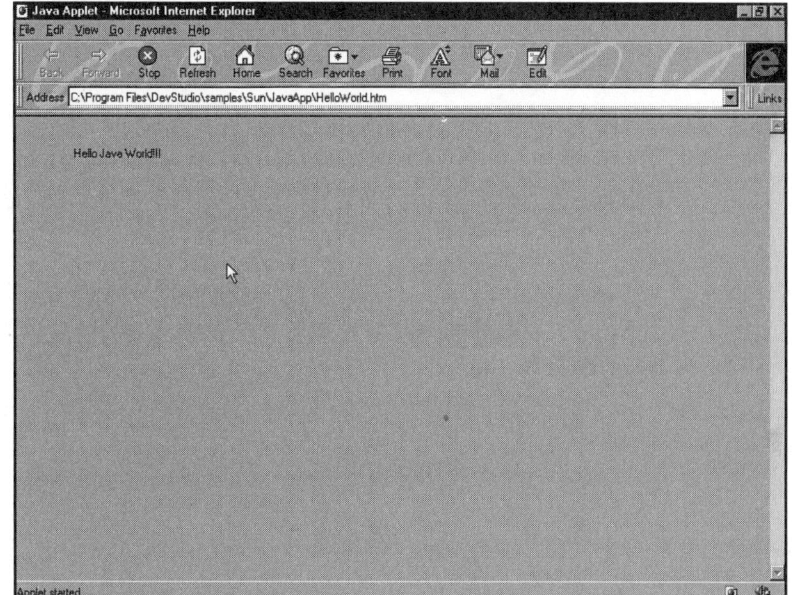

FIG. 7.4
You can use any Java-compliant browser, such as Internet Explorer, to test the Java applet.

To change the default browser from Internet Explorer to another browser, go to the Debug tab in the Project Settings dialog box, select the Category of Browser, and change the Browser path to the executable file for the new browser.

7. View the applet and then close the browser and return to Visual J++.

You can also create your own HTML file for testing purposes. To create your own sample HTML testing file, complete the following steps:

1. Select New from the File menu.
2. Select HTML Page from the Files tab and type **`HelloWorld`** as the filename in the text box, as shown in Figure 7.5.

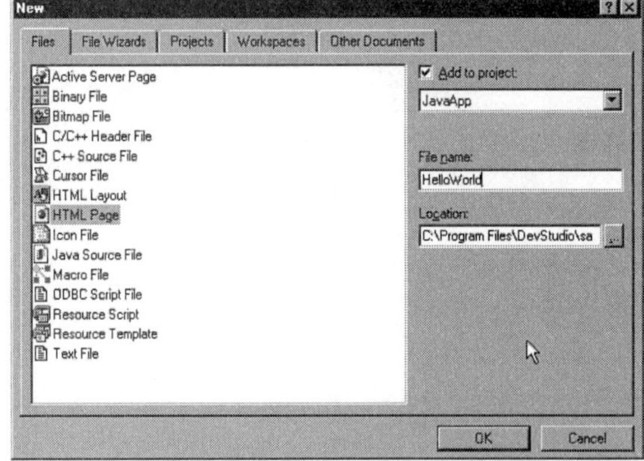

FIG. 7.5
The integrated environment allows you to easily add an HTML file to a Visual J++ project.

3. Click OK and a sample HTML file will be added to your project.
4. Double-click HelloWorld.htm to open it in the source editor and add the following lines of code where it says, `<!-- Insert HTML here -->`:

```
<applet code="HelloWorld.class" WIDTH=200 HEIGHT=50>
</applet>
```

   In the preceding code lines, the code tag identifies the Java class file to run for the applet. The height and width properties define the size of the applet in the web page.
5. Save the HTML page.
6. From the Project menu, select the Settings menu option. The Project Settings dialog box displays.
7. From the Debug tab, select Browser in the Category drop-down listbox (see Figure 7.6).

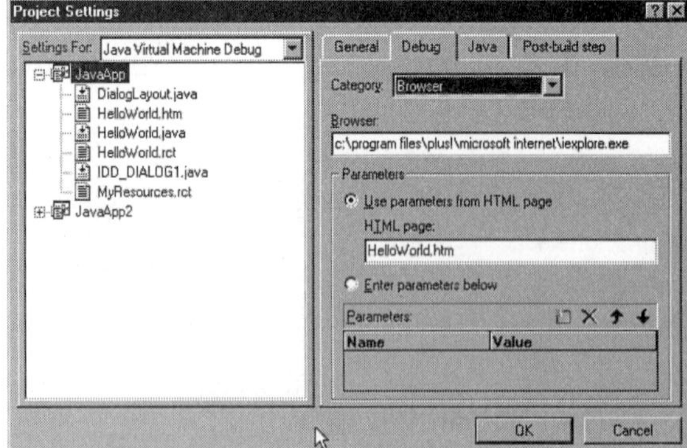

FIG. 7.6
The Project Settings dialog box is used to set various options for your Visual J++ project.

8. Select Use Parameters from HTML Page and enter **`HelloWorld.htm`** in the HTML Page text box.
9. Click OK to continue. Now the HelloWorld.htm file is set as the default HTML page to run the Java applet.

10. Execute the project again. The selected browser will start and load HelloWorld.htm as the test page and load the HelloWorld.class Java applet.

NOTE Just as in C/C++, names of functions, variables, and class files are case sensitive.

Using the Java Applet Wizard

Rather than creating a Java applet project from scratch, you can also use the Java Applet Wizard to generate a skeleton project. If you have worked with Visual C++ or Visual Basic, you are familiar with the concept of using wizards to automate the most common and mundane tasks associated with creating applications.

However, it should be noted that the wizard is only good for very simple applications. For complex applications, the wizard provides a good starting point, and then you can add your own code to modify the application to your own needs.

The Java Applet Wizard is a similar beast. It automates the task of getting started with creating a Java applet in Visual J++. The sample HelloWorld applet can also be created using the Applet Wizard. To use the Applet Wizard, complete the following steps:

1. Select New from the File menu to open the New dialog box.
2. From the Projects tab, select Java Applet Wizard and provide a name for your project, as shown in Figure 7.7.

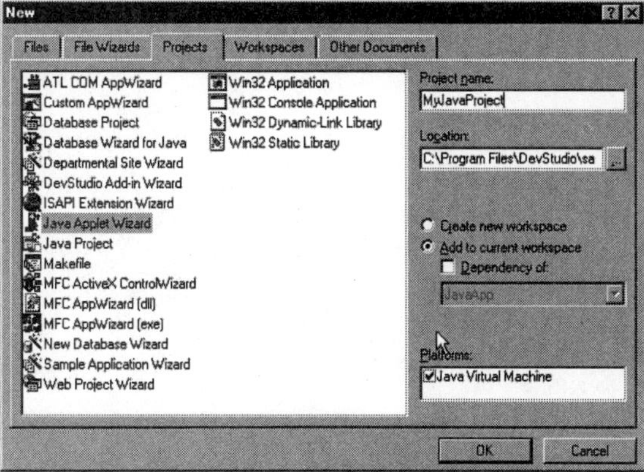

FIG. 7.7
You can add the new project to the current workspace or create a new one.

3. Click OK. The Java Applet Wizard will begin, as shown in Figure 7.8.
4. Select the As an Applet Only option and provide a name for your applet; then click Next to continue.
5. Select the option for creating a sample HTML file and specify the applet width and height, as shown in Figure 7.9.

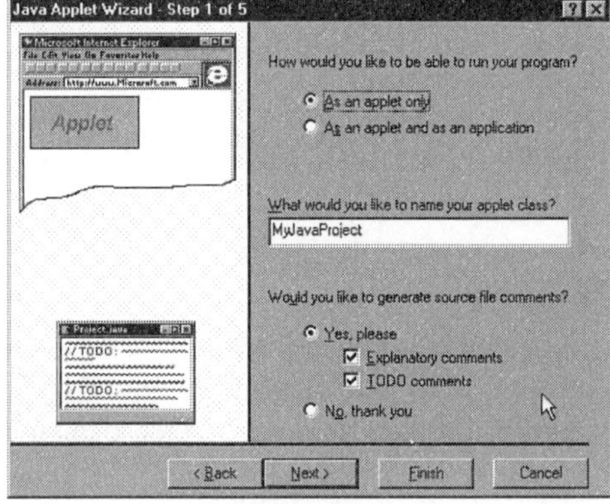

FIG. 7.8
The Java Applet Wizard can create an applet or an application.

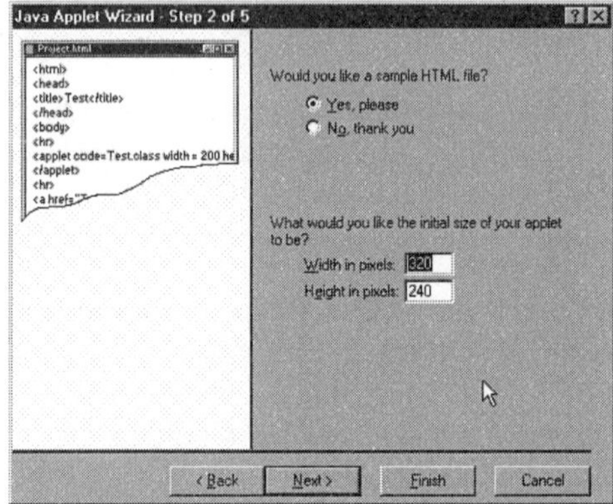

FIG. 7.9
A sample HTML file can provide a convenient mechanism for testing your applet during development.

6. Click Next to continue. Step 3 of the wizard will be displayed, as shown in Figure 7.10.

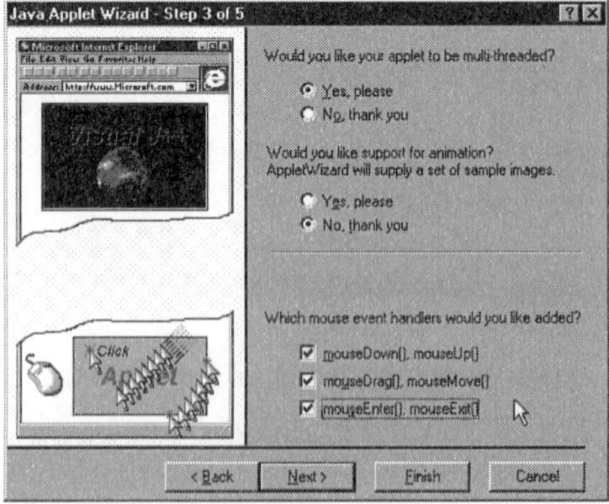

FIG. 7.10
You can add sample event handlers for handling mouse events.

7. Select Yes to make the applet multithreaded. Select No, Thank You to disable animation options. Select all three event handlers to provide support for different mouse movements for the applet. A multithreaded applet can cede control to the system while it is loading and allows better performance in page loading and viewing.
8. Click Next to continue. The applet parameter screen will be displayed, as shown in Figure 7.11.

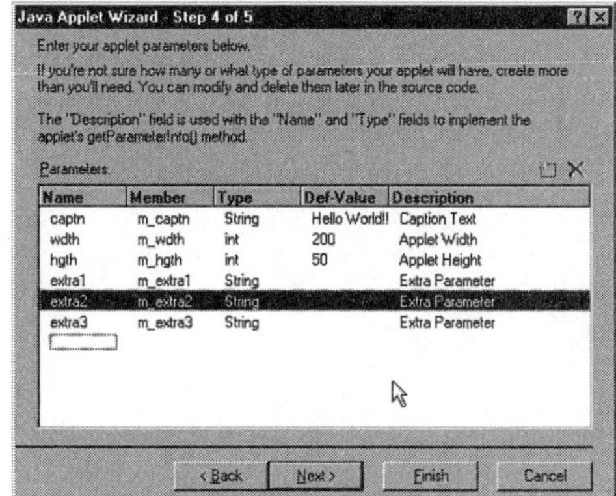

FIG. 7.11
You can always specify extra parameters and have the wizard create them.

9. Specify the following three applet parameters on the parameter screen:

Name	Member	Type	Def-Value	Description
`captn`	`m_captn`	string	Hello World	Text Caption
`wdth`	`m_wdth`	int	200	Applet Width
`hgt`	`m_hgt`	int	50	Applet Height

10. Click Next to continue. In the last step, enter the information you want the applet to return when queried for applet information. Enter the information as specified in Figure 7.12.
11. Click Finish to continue. The wizard will display an information screen. Click OK and the wizard will create the necessary files and add them to your project.
12. Two files will be added to your project, the HelloWorld2.htm file and the HelloWorld2.java class file. You can now work with these files and customize your applet as you like.

NOTE To add the HelloWorld applet code from before, just add the lines in the `paint` function to the `paint` function created by the wizard.

This section describes a simple Java applet but introduces you to some of the most common tasks involved in creating a Java applet. The process is fairly simple and straightforward, especially when using the Java Applet Wizard. The following section introduces you to the concept of using user interface elements, such as dialog boxes and menus, as part of your Java applet. In the next few sections, you will learn some of the more advanced techniques such as using resources and adding event handlers to your applets.

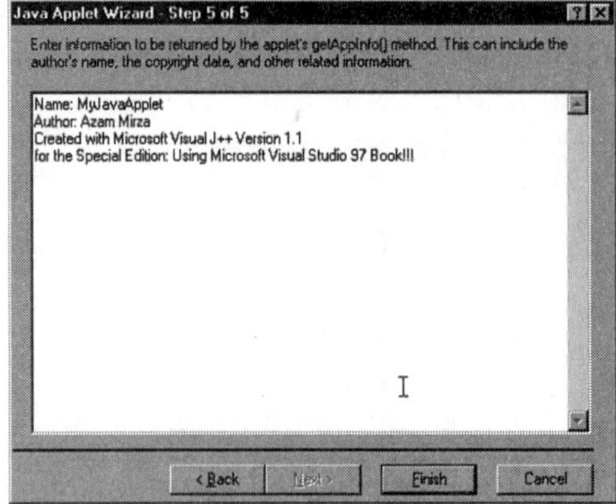

FIG. 7.12 The `getAppInfo()` method will return the information entered here to the querying application.

Adding Resources

Resources include such user interface elements as menus and dialogs. Under typical Windows development environments, most developers are very familiar with using resources such as menus, text boxes, lists, and so on. However, the Java language uses a different mechanism for handling resources. Java uses the Abstract Window Toolkit (AWT) to interpret source code to specify user interface elements, rather than using resource files and templates.

For that purpose, Visual J++ utilizes the Visual Studio resource editor to create resource files and templates and then uses the Resource Wizard to convert these resource files into Java classes. The following sections describe creating resource files for your Java projects and then converting them to Java classes using the Resource Wizard.

Creating Resources

Resources are created using the menu and dialog editors included with Visual Studio. Resources can be created from scratch, or you can import resources from other projects by using the Visual Studio file drag-and-drop capabilities. To create a resource template file for your Visual J++ project, open the project and then complete the following steps:

1. Select New from the File menu.
2. On the Files tab, select Resource Template and provide a name for the template, as shown in Figure 7.13.
3. Click OK. A HelloWorld.rct file will be added to the project.
4. Double-click the file and the source editor will open the resource template folder with an empty resource folder.

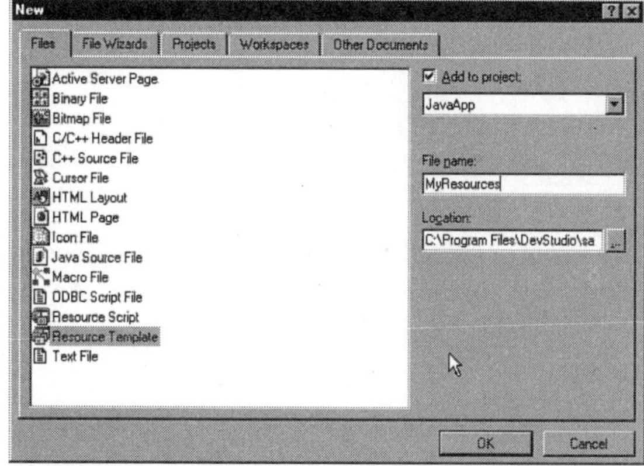

FIG. 7.13
Resource Template is a special folder that holds all your resource files in a project.

5. To add a resource to the template, select Resource from the Insert menu. The Insert Resource dialog box appears, as shown in Figure 7.14.

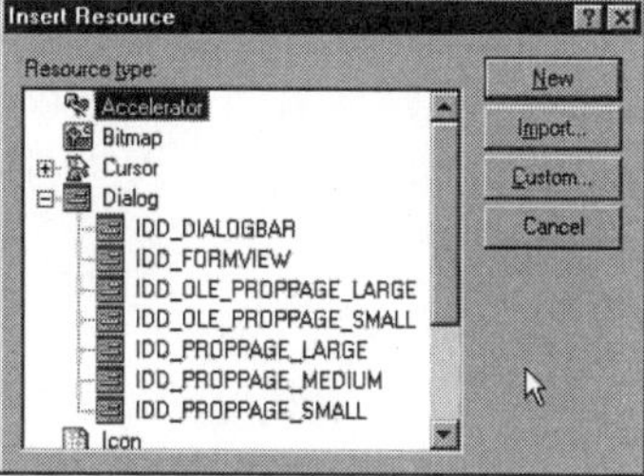

FIG. 7.14
Valid resource types for all Visual Studio 97 products are listed in the Insert Resource dialog box.

6. Select Dialog from the list and click New. A new dialog will be added, and the dialog editor will start, as shown in Figure 7.15.

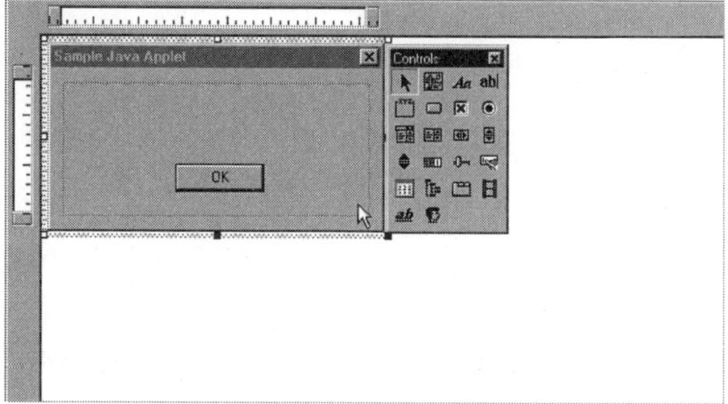

FIG. 7.15
A default dialog with an OK and a Close button is added by the Insert Resource dialog box.

7. Double-click the dialog box to open the Dialog Properties dialog box, as shown in Figure 7.16.

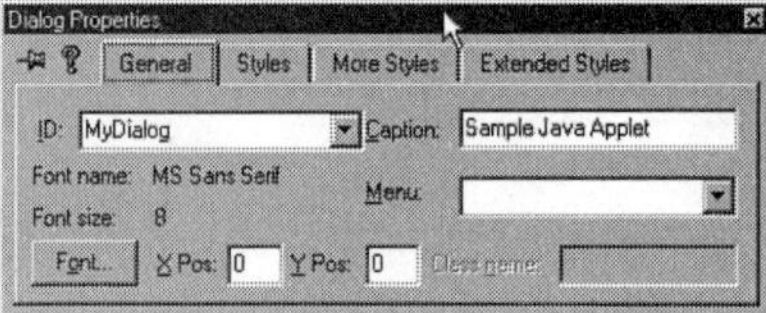

FIG. 7.16 The Dialog Properties box can be used to specify various properties such as caption and font style.

8. Change the ID and the caption of the dialog box to an appropriate name and caption for your dialog box.
9. Add controls to the dialog box by dragging controls from the Controls Toolbox palette to the dialog resource.
10. Close the dialog editor by clicking the Close icon and save your changes.

You have just created a resource template for your project with a dialog resource. You can now convert your resource template to a Java class file by using the Resource Wizard. However, the Java language only supports a subset of Windows resources. Any resource used in a resource template that does not have a Java counterpart is ignored during the creation of the Java resource class.

NOTE Although the Dialog editor allows you to place all the controls in the Controls toolbox on your dialog template, only those supported by the Resource Wizard will be converted to Java GUI components by the Resource Wizard. ■

The following resource types are supported by the Java AWT:

- Label
- Text box
- Command button
- Checkbox
- Radio button
- Listbox
- Combo box
- Horizontal scrollbar
- Vertical scrollbar

Running the Resource Wizard

The Resource Wizard converts the templates and resource files created by the resource editor into Java class files. To convert a resource template using the wizard, take the following steps:

1. Select Java Resource Wizard from the Tools menu.
2. The wizard will start, as shown in Figure 7.17.

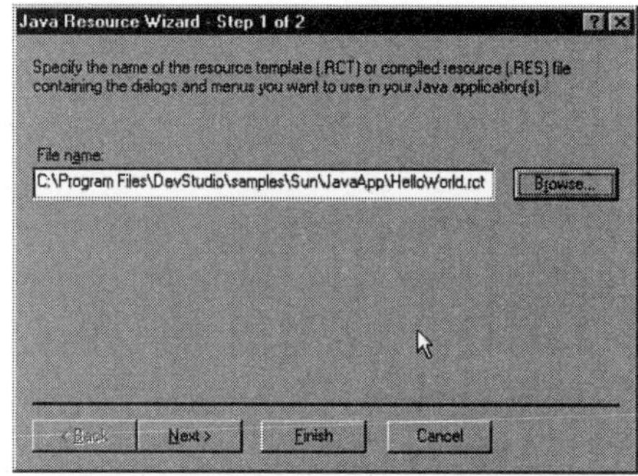

FIG. 7.17
The wizard can convert either resource template files (.rct) or compiled resource files (.res).

3. Provide a filename or select Browse to select a file from an open dialog box.
4. Click Next to continue. The resources available for conversion will be displayed, as shown in Figure 7.18.

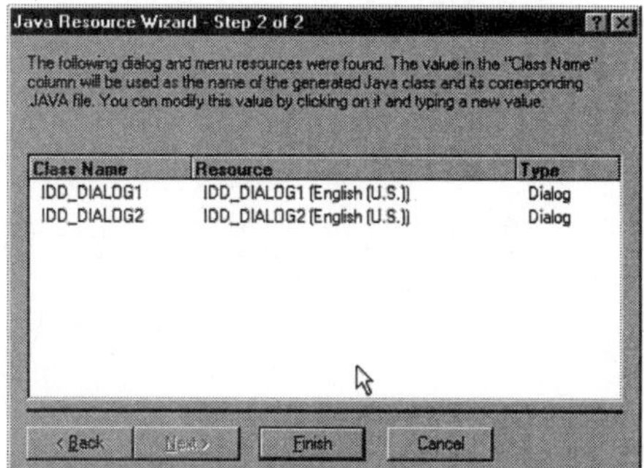

FIG. 7.18
Only dialog and menu resources are listed in the listbox.

5. Select the resources to convert and click Finish.
6. The wizard will list the files that will be created. Click OK.
7. The files will be created and placed in the project root directory. You can add the files to the project now by using file drag-and-drop techniques.

Using the Resource Wizard Generated Files

Once you have created the Java class files for the resources and added them to your project, you can use the resources in these files as a part of your Java applet. To use the Java dialog class in your project, complete the following steps:

1. Open the Java applet file, HelloWorld.java, and add the following code to the beginning of the file:

```
import java.awt.*;
import java.applet.*;
import MyDialog;
```

2. In the applet class declaration, add the following line:

   ```
   MyDialog dlg;
   ```

3. Add an `init()` method to your applet, as shown in the following:

   ```
   public void init()
   {
   dlg = new MyDialog(this);
   dlg.CreateControls();
   }
   ```

4. Comment out the call to the `drawString` method in the `paint` function.
5. Now add the following code at the end of the applet class declaration. This code toggles the button text when the button is clicked:

   ```
   public boolean action(Event evt, Object arg)
   {
         if(evt.target instanceof Button)
         {
         String str = dlg.IDC_TEXT1.getText();
               if (str == "Hello World")
               {
                     dlg.IDC_TEXT1.setText("Hello Java World");
               }
               else
               {
                     dlg.IDC_TEXT1.setText("Hello World");
               }
                     return true;
         }
         return false;
   }
   ```

6. Save the file. Select Execute from the Build menu to run the applet.
7. An applet will be displayed with a single button that you can click to change its label from OK to Clicked! and back.

Adding Event Handling

The `action` function, defined in the preceding section, is an event handler that is called every time the controls on the applet generate an event. Take a look at that function again:

```
public boolean action(Event evt, Object arg)
{
      if(evt.target instanceof Button)
      {
String str = dlg.IDC_TEXT1.getText();
            if (str == "Hello World")
            {
                  dlg.IDC_TEXT1.setText("Hello Java World");
            }
            else
            {
```

```
                    dlg.IDC_TEXT1.setText("Hello World");
               }
                    return true;
          }
          return false;
     }
```

The action function checks to see if a button generated the event. If there were more than one button on the dialog, you would need to determine which one generated the event. In this case, there is only one button, so you can be sure that it generated the event. The function then checks the value of the button label and toggles it appropriately.

The Java specification includes an Event class for providing event handlers for events such as mouseUp, mouseDown, and so on. The component class included with the Java language specification provides support for handling events. You can override the events provided with the component class by writing your own event handlers for the events handled in the component class.

Debugging Your Applets

Debugging is the process of finding errors and mistakes in your application code. Visual J++ includes an integrated debugger that simplifies the task of finding errors in your applications and correcting them.

Before you can debug your application in Visual J++, you must set up the project and the environment for debugging. Visual J++ uses different methods for debugging applications and applets. When you are debugging an application, your program runs in a standalone interpreter; when you're debugging an applet, your program runs in a browser.

To set up the environment to debug a Java application, complete the following steps:

1. Select Settings from the Projects menu. The Project Settings dialog box appears.
2. Select the Debug tab, as shown in Figure 7.19.

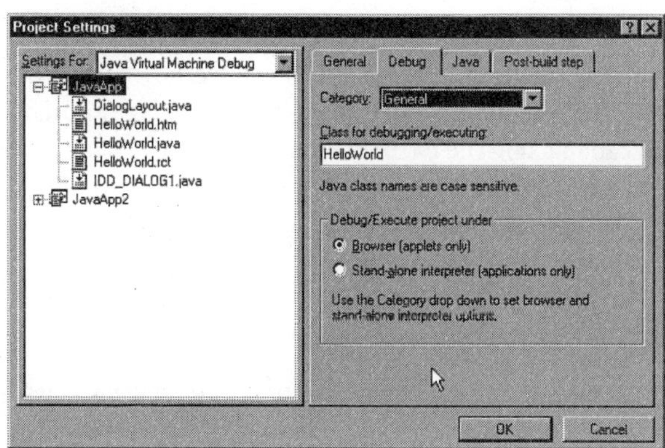

FIG. 7.19
The Project Settings dialog box provides a one-place setup of all environment options for a Visual J++ project.

3. In the Class for Debugging/Executing text box, type the name of the class that contains the application's `main()` method.

NOTE A Java application must contain a `main()` method. It is the function the Java virtual machine uses to start the application.

4. Click the Stand-alone Interpreter option.
5. Click OK. You are now ready to debug your application.

To set up the environment to debug a Java applet, follow the same procedure, but in step 3, provide the name of the applet's `init()` class instead.

NOTE A Java applet does not need a `main()` method. However, applets do include the `init()` method, which is the function first called when an applet is starting.

Once you have set up the project environment for debugging, you can use the debugger to control the execution of your program by setting breakpoints and examining the status of your applet. The debugger also provides support for debugging multithreaded programs.

The most common kinds of errors encountered by developers are the syntax errors that prevent a program from being compiled. The Output window displays errors that prevent a program from being built and provides the filename, line number, and error number. The Output window behaves like a source window; you can copy and print information from the window. If the status bar is displayed, it gives a summary of the current error.

TIP You can get help on any error by moving the insertion point to the error number and pressing the F1 key. The online help information will be displayed.

To fix a compile-time error, simply double-click the error line in the Output window, and the source editor will open the appropriate file and place the cursor at the line where the error happened.

The exception-handling facility in Java allows programs to handle abnormal and unexpected situations in an orderly, structured manner. When a method detects an exception that must be handled, it notifies the exception handler using the `throw` method. The exception handler receives the notification using the `catch` method. For a more detailed discussion of these methods and of Java in general, check out these books:

- *Special Edition Using Java 1.1*, 3rd Edition, ISBN 0-7897-1094-3, Que Corporation
- *Visual J++ 1.1 Unleashed*, 2nd Edition, ISBN 1-57521-356-7, Sams Publishing
- *Developing Enterprise Apps with Visual J++*, ISBN 1-57169-085-9, Sams Publishing

If no catch handler exists for an exception, the program typically causes the Java interpreter to print an error message, print a stack trace, and exit. If you are debugging a program in Visual J++, however, the debugger notifies you that the exception was not caught.

NOTE Developers familiar with the C++ exception-handling mechanisms will immediately recognize the `throw` and `catch` methods used by Visual J++ as a comparable mechanism. ■

From Here...

In this chapter, you learned about creating Java applets and applications using the Visual J++ development environment. You learned about creating projects to build Java applets, about building and testing your applets using the integrated environment and web browsers, and about using the integrated debugging capabilities of the Developer Studio 97 IDE. In addition, you learned about using the wizards provided with Visual J++ for getting a jump start on your development efforts.

- To understand the details behind technologies such as COM/DCOM, ActiveX, and Java, see Chapter 4, "Using Microsoft's Object Technologies."
- To learn about creating components with Visual Basic, see Chapter 5, "Creating ActiveX Components with Visual Basic."
- To learn about creating components with Visual C++, see Chapter 6, "Creating Components with Visual C++."
- To learn about the Visual Studio development environment, see Chapter 2, "Using Visual Studio to Create Applications."

CHAPTER 8

Using ActiveX Client Components in an I-net Environment

by Azam A. Mirza

Web development using ActiveX controls

Learn about the techniques for using ActiveX controls in web development tools. This chapter discusses different scenarios for using ActiveX controls on client machines and on the server side, and the impact of each approach.

Using ActiveX controls with Internet Explorer

Learn how Internet Explorer takes advantage of ActiveX controls and how it handles issues such as licensing, authentication, and downloading of controls.

ActiveX controls and Visual J++

Learn about the interaction of ActiveX components with Java code. Learn how ActiveX controls can be used from within Visual J++ projects.

The centerpiece of Microsoft's ActiveX strategy is *ActiveX controls*—streamlined versions of OCX controls designed specifically for I-net environments. They provide packaged functionality in a binary format that you can use to build component-based applications.

A key advantage of ActiveX controls over other comparable technologies is their capability to be used in a wide variety of development tools and programming languages. ActiveX controls aren't used exclusively for web development. Thousands of business and commercial client/server applications also take advantage of ActiveX controls. For example, Microsoft Internet Explorer uses ActiveX controls to enhance your web pages with sophisticated formatting features and animation.

This chapter, however, is devoted to using ActiveX controls in I-net environments. I'll discuss techniques for incorporating ActiveX components in your web sites with the Visual InterDev and FrontPage 97 development tools. I'll also discuss the issues involved in using ActiveX components with Internet Explorer and how ActiveX and Java work together in Visual J++. ■

Using ActiveX Controls in Web Sites

ActiveX is a set of technologies that help you create interactive content for your web sites. With ActiveX, you can incorporate multimedia, interactive objects, and sophisticated applications that come together to create a truly dynamic experience. ActiveX provides the functionality that brings all this together to create truly energized web sites.

▶ For more information about ActiveX technologies, **see** Chapter 13, "An Inside Look at Active Server Pages and Internet Information Server," **p. 363**.

A strong point for ActiveX is its integration of existing technologies with the new web-based technologies such as Java and HTML. By leveraging tried-and-true and mature technologies such as OLE and COM/DCOM, ActiveX builds on stable and standards-based technologies for providing functionality in the I-net environment.

▶ For more information about COM/DCOM, **see** Chapter 4, "Using Microsoft's Object Technologies," **p. 89**.

ActiveX provides a multitude of benefits for developers embracing World Wide Web technologies, including

- The capability to create rich and interactive content. By leveraging the power of desktop technologies, combined with web-based technologies, ActiveX provides you with a rich environment and technologies to create great and exciting web content (see Figure 8.1).

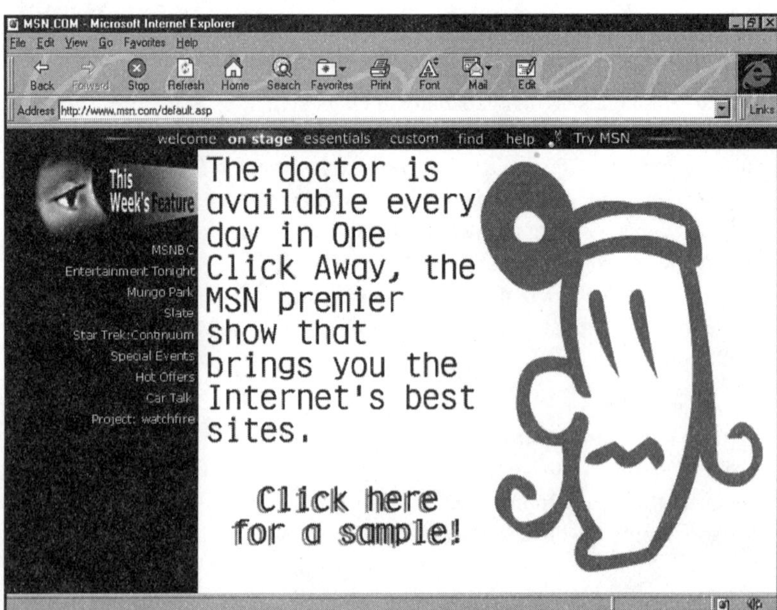

FIG. 8.1
The Microsoft Network's web site is an example of using ActiveX components to create a dazzling web experience.

- Thousands of ActiveX controls now available for use in web applications. New ones are being released every day.
- Open, standards-based and cross-platform support. ActiveX supports widely used web technologies such as HTTP, Java, TCP/IP, and others.
- Support on multiple platforms, including Microsoft Windows, Macintosh, and UNIX.
- Support for the two most widely used browsers: Internet Explorer and Netscape Navigator.

ON THE WEB

To use ActiveX controls with Netscape Navigator, you must use the ActiveX plug-in for Netscape, ScriptActive, from NCompassLabs, available at NCompassLabs's web site at **http://www.ncompasslabs.com**.

- Creation tools such as Delphi, Visual C++, and Visual Basic. Not only can you create ActiveX controls with these tools, but you can also develop component-based applications by using these tools with ActiveX controls and technologies playing a central role.

Understanding Techniques for Using ActiveX Components

ActiveX is an open platform for I-net software development. Figure 8.2 shows how ActiveX technologies encompass all aspects of the web, from clients to servers to development tools to authoring tools to networking technologies.

On the server side, Active Server Pages and Active Server Components provide support for ActiveX functionality. On the client side, ActiveX controls and the client platforms that support hosting of ActiveX controls provide ActiveX functionality.

▶ For more information about using Active Server Pages, **see** Chapter 13, "An Inside Look at Active Server Pages and Internet Information Server," **p. 363**.

Microsoft has released two development products that allow you to take advantage of these ActiveX technologies on the client and the server by making it possible to use ActiveX controls as part of the development environment. These products include Visual InterDev and FrontPage 97; the next two sections discuss using ActiveX controls in these tools.

▶ For more information about using Visual InterDev to create web content, **see** Chapter 14, "Developing Active Content with Visual InterDev," **p. 389**.

ActiveX Components and Visual InterDev

This section doesn't discuss how to develop web pages with Visual InterDev. It's more a discussion of the techniques to employ in using ActiveX controls when doing Visual InterDev development.

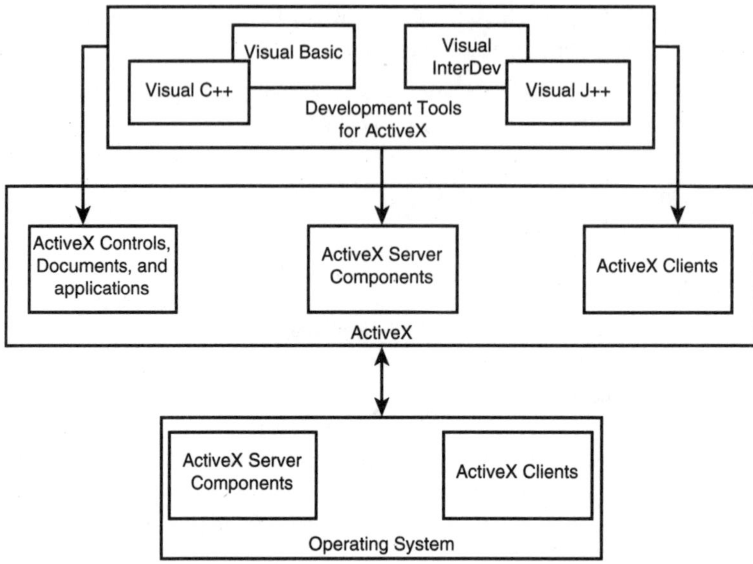

FIG. 8.2
Microsoft provides a comprehensive set of products for taking advantage of ActiveX technologies.

Visual InterDev is a powerful development environment that provides support for using ActiveX technologies on the server and the client. On the server side, Visual InterDev leverages the power of Active Server Pages to provide support for building and using Active Server Components. Figure 8.3 shows how Visual InterDev interacts with Active Server Pages and Active Server Components.

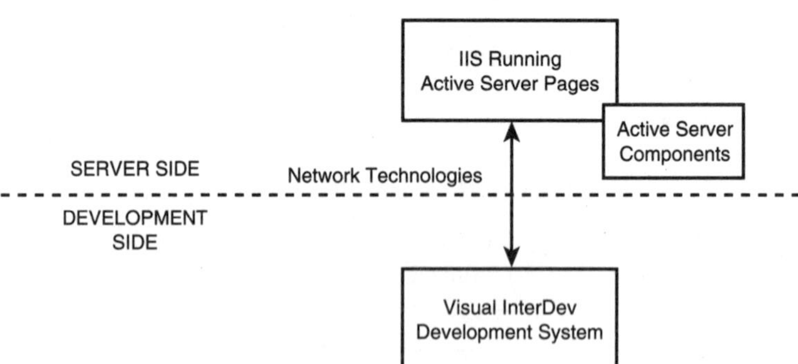

FIG. 8.3
Visual InterDev provides a rich programming environment for using Active Server Components.

Active Server Components are actually ActiveX controls without any user interface elements. Active Server Components, also referred to as server-side ActiveX controls, are used to provide two kinds of functionality:

- To gain access to operating systems services
- To encapsulate business rules as part of an application to perform specific tasks such as tax calculations

Tools such as Visual Basic and Visual C++ provide full support for creating Active Server Components. The choice of tool selected for creating Active Server Components depends on your familiarity with the tool and the functionality being developed. As obvious, Visual C++ is a great tool for building components requiring speed and performance. On the other hand, Visual Basic provides a rapid development environment for building components. To get a feel for how Active Server Components work, look at the components provided with Active Server Pages, such as the TextStream component.

▶ **See** "ActiveX Server Components Included with Visual InterDev," **p. 410**

On the client side, ActiveX controls provide packaged functionality for building dynamic web sites. Visual InterDev provides full support for building web sites that incorporate ActiveX controls for accomplishing various tasks, such as using command buttons, text boxes, and grids. The main distinction between ActiveX controls and Active Server Components is that ActiveX controls employ user interface elements to enhance the look, feel, and functionality of your web application.

Visual InterDev provides support for using any ActiveX control. It also includes an extensive collection of controls for taking advantage of most Windows graphical elements, such as labels, text boxes, and image controls.

The most common method of using client-side ActiveX controls in Visual InterDev is to include them in Active Server Pages when you develop web applications. When a client browser such as Internet Explorer accesses an Active Server Page with an ActiveX control, the control is downloaded to the client machine and then executed as part of the web page. Figure 8.4 shows the relationship between ActiveX controls, Active Server Pages, and client browsers.

▶ **See** "Using Client-Side ActiveX Components," **p. 424**

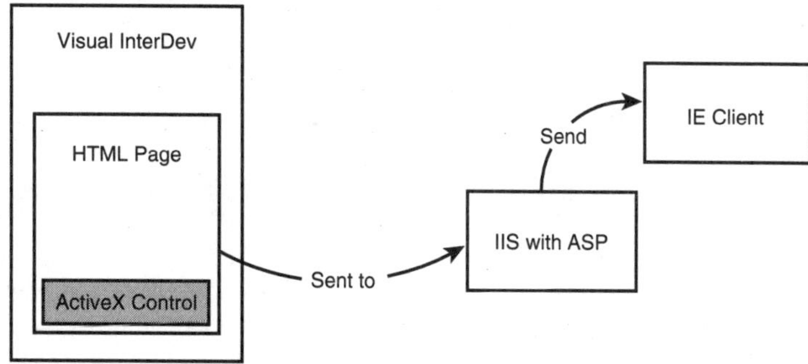

FIG. 8.4
Active Server Pages execute on the server and generate an HTML script that's sent to the browser along with any needed ActiveX controls.

NOTE If you try to access a page that uses client ActiveX controls with Netscape Navigator, the page will load without the ActiveX control, and no errors will be generated. ■

ActiveX Components and FrontPage 97 (Visual InterDev Edition)

FrontPage 97 is a graphical HTML development tool that helps you build web pages in a visual environment. Visual InterDev includes a version of FrontPage 97 called FrontPage 97 Visual InterDev Edition. The stripped-down version of FrontPage 97 in Visual InterDev doesn't include support for some advanced functions such as WebBots. One main difference between Visual InterDev and FrontPage 97 is that the latter allows you to insert ActiveX controls into HTML pages in WYSIWYG (What You See Is What You Get) mode. When FrontPage 97 displays a control in the page, you can drag and drop it within the HTML text. Figure 8.5 shows an HTML page in FrontPage 97 with an ActiveX control placed on it.

▶ **See** "The FrontPage 97 HTML Editor," **p. 407**

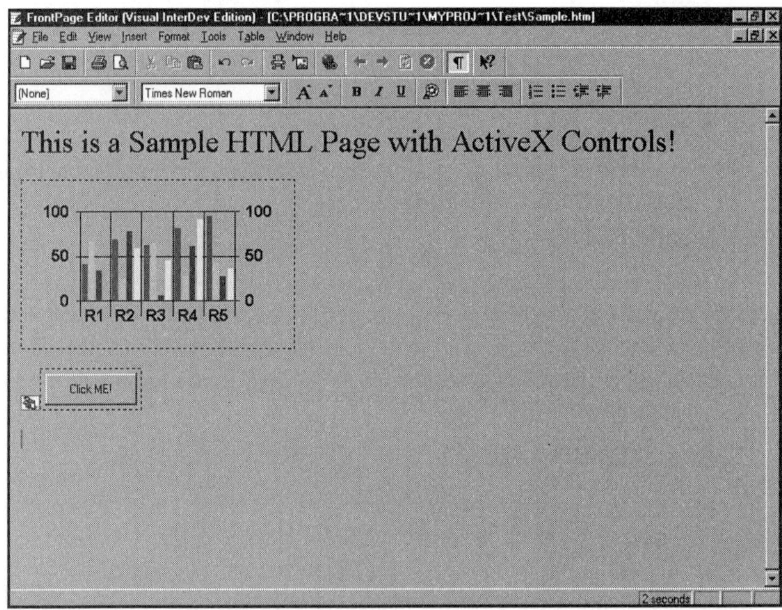

FIG. 8.5
The WYSIWYG nature of FrontPage 97 makes it easy to place controls precisely where you want them to appear.

Using ActiveX Components with Internet Explorer

If you've used Internet Explorer to surf the World Wide Web, you've surely come across sites that incorporate ActiveX controls to provide powerful functionality. Internet Explorer is a container application that supports hosting ActiveX controls, Active documents, and so on. Figure 8.6 shows how Internet Explorer interacts with ActiveX control-enabled web pages.

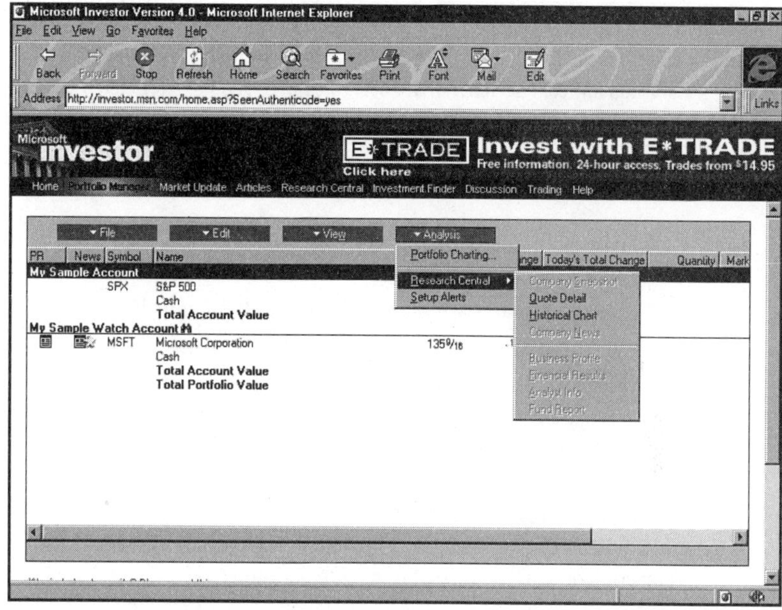

FIG. 8.6
As a container application, Internet Explorer handles downloading, displaying, and executing ActiveX controls.

As a container application, Internet Explorer takes care of many administrative tasks associated with using ActiveX controls in web pages. Specifically, Internet Explorer takes care of

- Making sure that the developers have properly signed and marked their ActiveX controls. If an unsigned control is being loaded, Internet Explorer tells the user of a possible security breach and, based on user response and the security settings, takes the appropriate actions.
- Downloading and installing the ActiveX control and all supporting files onto the client machine.
- Periodically checking to determine whether an updated version of the control is available. If so, the browser automatically downloads the newer version and updates the client machine.

The following sections discuss how you can make sure that your controls are appropriately signed and packaged for downloading to client machines and how Internet Explorer handles control updates.

Signing and Marking ActiveX Controls

If you've installed Internet Explorer on your machine and tried to navigate to a web site that uses an unsigned ActiveX control, you're familiar with the security dialog boxes that inform you about possible security problems. The easiest way to get around these dialog boxes is to properly sign and mark your ActiveX controls before deployment.

When installed, Internet Explorer defaults to the High security setting, with the idea that it's safe to have more security than less when going to unknown web sites. The High setting won't allow you to download any controls that haven't been properly signed and registered by the web site. You can change the security setting by using the Internet Options dialog box (View, Internet Options).

The signing and marking of controls refer to two distinct operations:

- Developers have registered the controls with an appropriate digital certificate-issuing authority.
- The certificates are incorporated into the controls.

ON THE WEB

VeriSign is the certificate-issuing authority used to obtain digital certificates for ActiveX controls. You can reach VeriSign at **http://www.verisign.com**.

Signing a control assures that the control's developer is positively identified and that the control hasn't been changed in any way since it was signed. If you make any changes to your control, you must re-sign it. The signature on a control is checked only once when the control is first downloaded. After that, Internet Explorer doesn't recheck the signature on the control.

However, signing the control isn't enough by itself. You must also mark your controls safe for initialization and safe for scripting. What this means is that the control has been marked as safe to be initialized by Internet Explorer and the scripts included with the control are safe for execution. If you mark your control as safe for initializing, you're asserting that no matter what values are used to initialize your control, it won't do anything that would damage a user's system or compromise the user's security. If you mark your control as safe for scripting, you're asserting that your control won't do anything to damage a user's system or compromise security regardless of how your control's methods and properties are manipulated by the web page's script. In other words, it has to accept any method calls (with any parameters) or property manipulations in any order without doing anything bad.

During development, you can do some things to make sure that a control is safe for marking. Make sure that the control

- Doesn't manipulate the file system
- Doesn't modify the Registry except to register and unregister itself
- Initializes all arrays and indexes correctly
- Doesn't misuse memory and releases all memory used
- Validates all input and ensures that the initialization values are within valid limits

Downloading and Updating ActiveX Controls

When Internet Explorer encounters a web page with an ActiveX control (or multiple controls), it first checks users' local system Registries to find out whether that component is available on their machines. If it is, Internet Explorer displays the web page and activates the control. If the control isn't already installed on the users' computers, Internet Explorer automatically finds and installs the component over the web, based on a location specified by the developer creating the page.

The web page developer provides this information by setting the control's CODEBASE property, which specifies an URL location or set of locations where the control can be found and downloaded on the Internet. Internet Explorer then uses this information to locate the control and download the component automatically.

Before a component is downloaded, Internet Explorer displays a message notifying users of the download. Users can choose to cancel the download or proceed. If the control is digitally signed, a digital certificate provides the name of the software vendor supplying the control and verifies that the control hasn't been tampered with. Figure 8.7 shows a digital certificate displayed for an ActiveX control before it's downloaded.

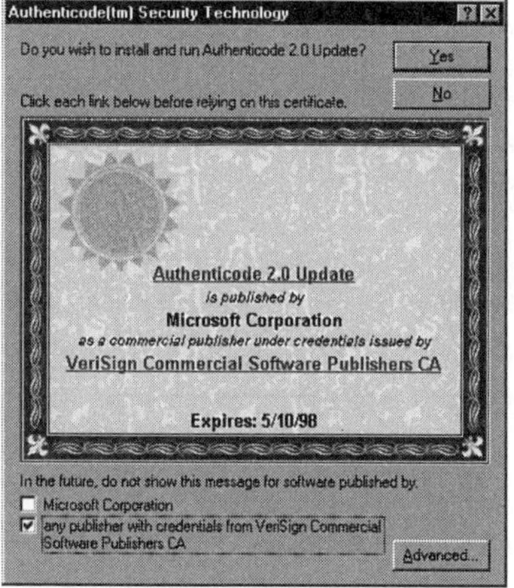

FIG. 8.7 The digital certificate identifies the control's publisher and the digital certification authority that signed it.

The information is carried by the control itself, so the digital certificate will be displayed automatically before downloading with no development work required by the person who uses that control on a web page.

NOTE By default, controls are downloaded into an ActiveX control cache located in the \windows\occache directory.

The Component Download Service in Internet Explorer supports versioning, so new versions of the control can be detected and automatically downloaded as required.

ActiveX controls include a mechanism to prevent the unlicensed use of controls in web pages. The licensing mechanism works by allowing controls to be distributed with a developer license or a runtime license. Under a developer license, developers can use the control for development purposes in tools such as Visual Basic, Visual C++, and Visual InterDev. Under a runtime license, users can only view the control within an existing application or web page, but can't insert the control into a tool for further development purposes.

Most controls include a binary file with the .lic extension that includes information about the license. Development tools use this file to determine whether a control can be used in the development environment.

Using ActiveX Controls with Visual J++

Visual J++ is the Java development tool that allows you to take full advantage of the technology. Visual J++ provides full support for the Java virtual machine (VM) on the Win32 platform. The Java VM supports the integration between Java and the Component Object Model (COM), which is the underlying technology for ActiveX. To take advantage of the integration between Java and COM, you must use Visual J++.

The integration of ActiveX and Java allows you to take advantage of the full breadth of options available for developing web applications. As a Visual J++ developer, you can take advantage of ActiveX controls as part of your Java development efforts to gain access to resources such as the system services. Figure 8.8 shows the integration between Java and ActiveX.

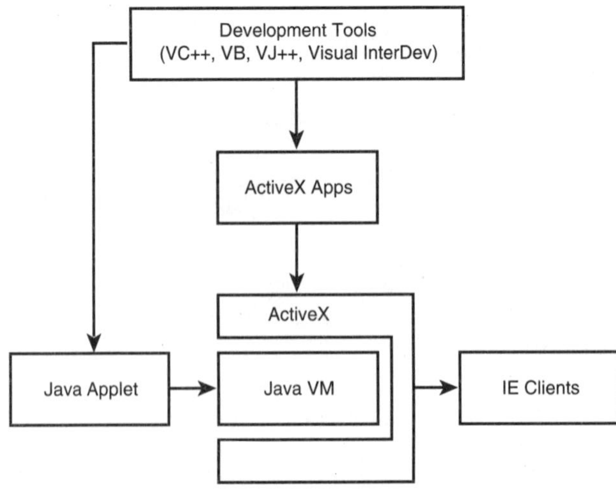

FIG. 8.8 Microsoft's extension of Java to include support for ActiveX results in a rich environment for developers and users.

NOTE If you're a Java developer, you can leverage the thousands of available ActiveX controls in your applications by using ActiveX and Java integration in Visual J++. However, this makes your application Win32 specific, and you lose the cross-platform benefits of Java applications.

Because the Visual J++ compiler supports the integration between Java and ActiveX, you can refer to ActiveX controls directly from your Java source code. To use this facility, you must first import the ActiveX control into a Java class in Visual J++. Visual J++ includes the Java Type Library Wizard for this purpose.

The Java Type Library Wizard

The Java Type Library Wizard in Visual J++ imports the type information stored in ActiveX controls into a Java class file. The wizard imports the type library information into a directory with the same name as the type library. To use the wizard, follow these steps:

1. Choose Tools, Java Type Library Wizard from the menu. The Java Type Library Wizard dialog box appears (see Figure 8.9).

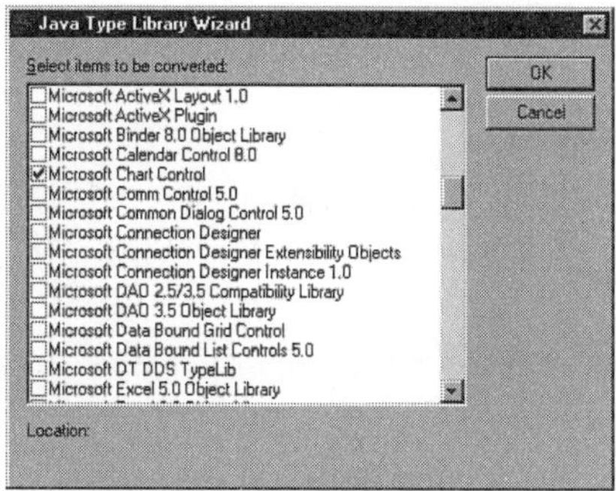

FIG. 8.9 The Java Type Library Wizard dialog box displays all the controls registered on the system.

2. Choose the controls you want to import and click OK. The wizard imports the control and creates a summary.txt file, the path to which appears in the wizard output window in Developer Studio.
3. Double-click the file path in the output window to open the summary.txt file in the editor (see Figure 8.10).

After you run the wizard and create the imported classes, you can use the `import` statement in your Java code to refer to the classes as shown here:

```
// import the classes in package named importedclass
import importedclass.*;
```

▶ For more information about using ActiveX controls in Visual J++, **see** Chapter 7, "Creating Components with Visual J++," **p. 221**.

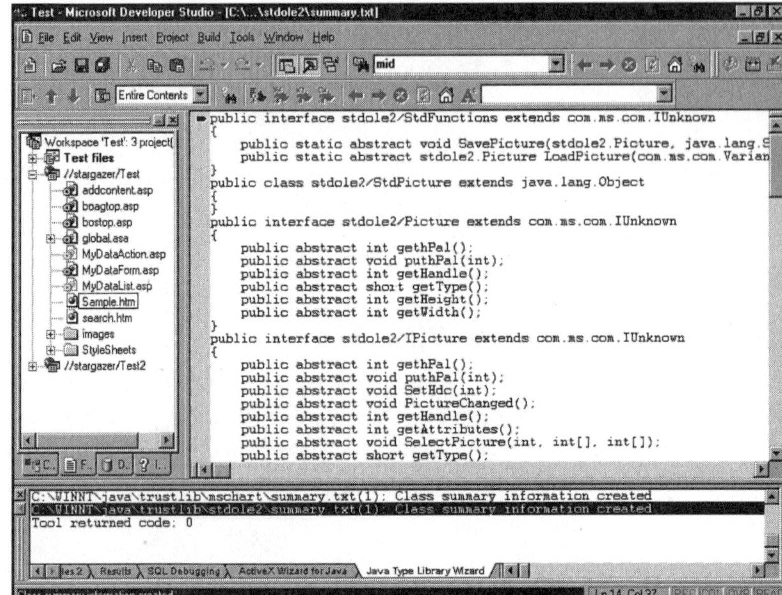

FIG. 8.10
The summary.txt file lists the Java signatures of all the methods for the ActiveX control.

The OLE/COM Object Viewer

The OLE/COM Object Viewer included with Visual J++ is used to browse the methods and properties exposed by ActiveX components. To use the OLE/COM Object Viewer, follow these steps:

1. Choose Tools, OLE/COM Object Viewer from Developer Studio's menu. The OLE/COM Object Viewer appears (see Figure 8.11).
2. From the Explorer pane on the left, select an object to browse. The corresponding interface and object information is displayed in the right pane.
3. To view the Type Library information on a control, right-click the control's name and choose View Type Information from the pop-up menu. The ITypeLib Viewer appears, as shown in Figure 8.12.
4. Close the OLE/COM Object Viewer when finished.

The Object Viewer is a simple but powerful tool that's very helpful in determining the functionality provided by an OLE/COM object such as an ActiveX control. You can browse through properties and methods of various objects to determine the correct calling procedures and the number of arguments required by an object.

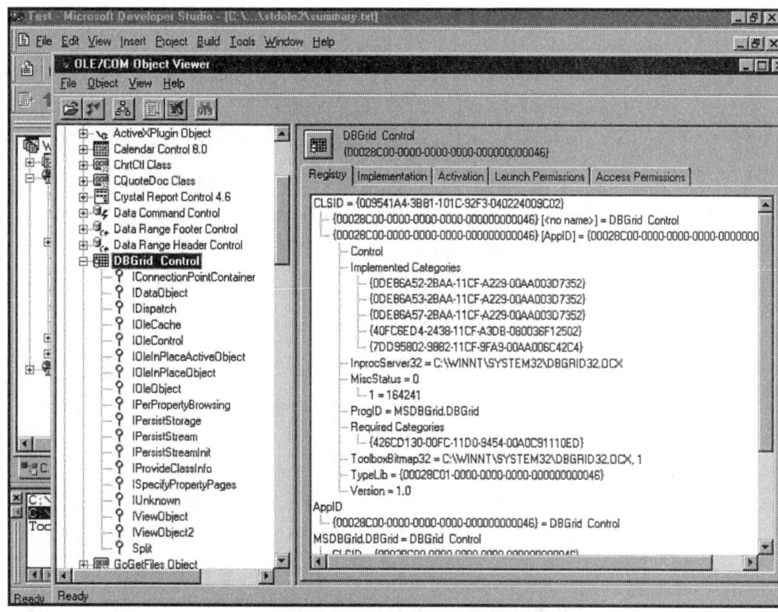

FIG. 8.11
The OLE/COM Object Viewer is a graphical tool for browsing ActiveX control properties and methods.

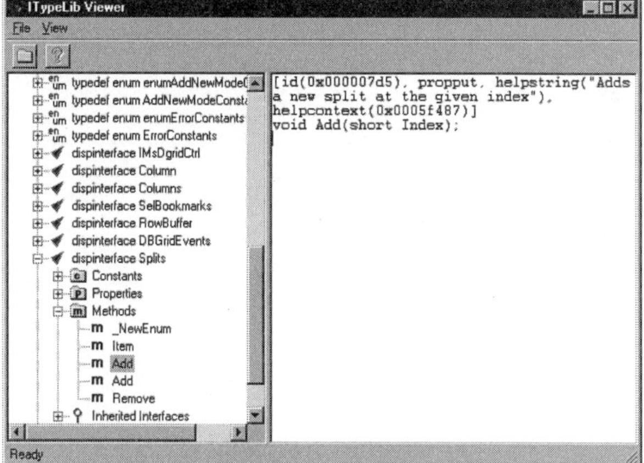

FIG. 8.12
The ITypeLib Viewer provides a graphical display of all properties, methods, and interfaces defined for the control.

From Here...

This chapter discusses the use of ActiveX controls in various aspects of I-net environments. You learned about the various issues involved with using ActiveX controls with Internet Explorer and about the security issues involved with ActiveX control usage. ActiveX controls are an integral part of web-based development with tools such as Visual InterDev or FrontPage 97.

For more information, see these chapters:

- To learn about the Visual Studio development environment, see Chapter 2, "Using Visual Studio to Create Applications."
- To understand the details behind technologies such as COM/DCOM, ActiveX, and Java, see Chapter 4, "Using Microsoft's Object Technologies."
- To learn about creating components with Visual Basic, see Chapter 5, "Creating ActiveX Components with Visual Basic."
- To learn about creating components with Visual C++, see Chapter 6, "Creating Components with Visual C++."
- To learn about creating components with Visual J++, see Chapter 7, "Creating Components with Visual J++."
- To learn about concepts associated with web-based application development, see Chapter 11, "An Inside Look at Web-Based Applications."
- To learn about Active Server Pages and their capabilities, see Chapter 13, "An Inside Look at Active Server Pages and Internet Information Server."
- To learn about getting started with Visual InterDev, see Chapter 14, "Developing Active Content with Visual InterDev."
- To learn about advanced concepts associated with Visual InterDev development, see Chapter 15, "Advanced Visual InterDev Concepts."

CHAPTER 9

Using ActiveX Components in a Client/Server Environment

by Ronald W. Terry

Based on the Component Object Model, an ActiveX component exposes its objects for use by another unit of executable code. This implies a client/server relationship in that a client requests objects from the ActiveX server, which in turn performs services for the client. The client itself can be an ActiveX component, which in turn acts as a server and exposes objects to another client.

This relationship can be carried out on a single machine where the client and the server reside locally, or the client and server can be on separate machines in which the server is called a remote server.

Deployment of ActiveX components

Learn about the different types of ActiveX components typical in an n-tier client/server environment, where they're most effective, and how they're installed and registered.

Remote automation

Read about the utilities available to configure ActiveX components to run on remote machines by using the Remote Automation or DCOM transports.

ActiveX components and Visual Basic

Become familiar with the techniques in using ActiveX components with the Visual Basic development tool.

ActiveX components and Visual C++

Learn the procedures for incorporating ActiveX components in a Visual C++ application.

This chapter discusses the techniques of using the various types of ActiveX components in a client/server environment with the two most prominent client/server development tools today: Visual Basic and Visual C++. Visual Basic has been a highly successful front-end development tool dealing with capturing and displaying information for users. Although Visual C++ can equally develop the forms and dialog boxes that comprise a user interface, its niche in the client/server development environment has been in the business rules tier. This tier is comprised of objects with little or no user interface and with the primary task of performing the computationally intensive algorithms for data transformations. ■

Understanding Techniques for Using Components

ActiveX components come in a wide variety of functionality that seems to be limited only by component developers' imaginations. From user interfaces that capture and display data in an elegant manner to complex behind-the-scenes business calculations, an ActiveX component can become a versatile building block in developing client/server applications.

As with any building block—whether it's a brick for a building or an object for a software application—it's not as important for you to learn the innermost workings or how the building block was produced to be an effective user. Instead, learning the behavior and limitations of the building block, along with being proficient with the techniques and tools used to adhere multiple blocks together, is of utmost importance in producing an effective composite structure.

The following sections focus on the different types of ActiveX components typical in a client/server application, their key characteristics, and in which tier they're most effective. The techniques of installing and registering components are also covered. How the component is registered in the Windows Registry determines where the component is located and the security factors involved for client access. You also see how to access remote components (executed on a separate machine) by using the Remote Automation and DCOM transports.

Component Types in a Client/Server Environment

You can categorize components used in a client/server environment into three types: ActiveX controls, ActiveX documents, and ActiveX code components. Figure 9.1 shows a typical three-tiered client/server application depicting where each type normally would be incorporated. The front-end or user-interface tier would be composed of forms and dialog boxes consisting of ActiveX controls. These controls would capture or display data for the user and pass/retrieve it to the business tier. The components on the business tier massage the data, perform calculations, and provide results back to the components in the user interface tier. Also, the business components can pass the data to the data tier. Components in the data tier contain the necessary logic to set and retrieve data from the database.

These components can all reside on the client machine, creating what's known as a *fat client*, or be distributed among many machines. For instance, the user-interface tier would reside on the client machine, the business-tier objects would reside on a dedicated machine chosen for performance, and the data-tier objects would reside on the same machine as the database engine.

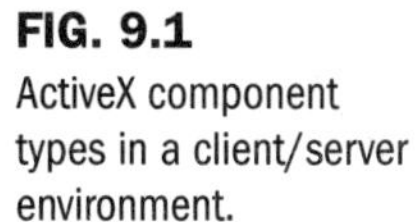

FIG. 9.1
ActiveX component types in a client/server environment.

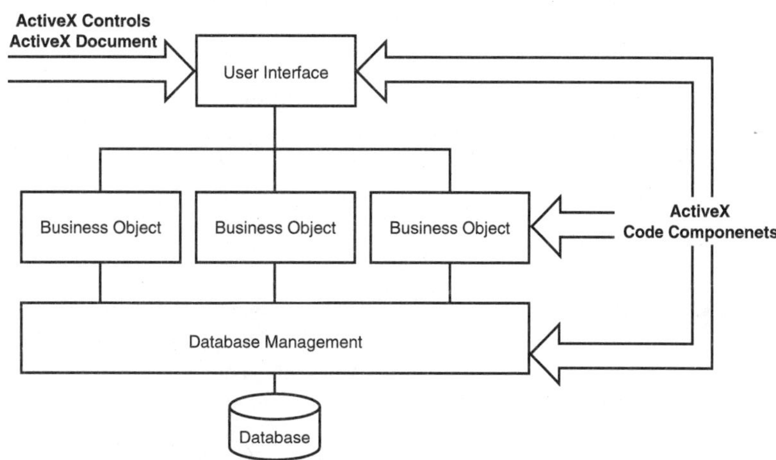

Deciding how the components will be distributed involves trade studies based on the environment in which they'll be used. Consider these key issues when distributing components:

- *Maintenance.* If component maintenance is an overwhelming factor, locate the business and data components on a separate machine that all clients can access. By doing so, making updates to business and data components is localized to only one machine. When the components are updated, all the clients that access them are accessing the updated ones. If the components were installed on client machines, the tedious task of updating every client machine would have to be undertaken.
- *Network traffic.* As components get distributed across machines, the network traffic inherently increases. If your distributed application's performance is starting to suffer due to high network traffic, you may want to move some of the most frequently called components to the client machines.
- *Client access.* If the client machine has no access to the network, all components need to be installed on the client.
- *Machine performance.* Identify the computational-intensive components and locate them on a machine with the most horsepower.
- *User interface.* Components consisting of some sort of user interface need to be located on the client machine.

The following sections explain in more detail the three different categories of ActiveX components and their uses. A how-to guide in installing and registering components for use by clients locally or remotely follows.

ActiveX Controls *ActiveX controls* are components that provide some form of interface between users and the application, such as a text box or a command button. ActiveX controls are assembled on forms or dialog boxes and are part of the user-interface tier. They expose properties that can be set at design time to adjust the look and feel of the control. Properties can also be accessed at runtime, as well as the controls' methods and events, which allows controls to respond to different needs of the application as it's executing.

ActiveX controls are the most common components. Although they're easily created with any of the Visual Studio development tools (as you've seen in earlier chapters), they're more commonly provided by third-party developers. ActiveX controls are in-process servers that are compiled into files with the extensions of .ocx (most common) or .dll. These files are copied to the client machine hard drive and expose functions that enable the control to register itself through the use of special utilities.

ActiveX Documents *ActiveX documents* are special components hosted in document containers such as a web browser, Microsoft Office Binder, Visual Basic 5.0 IDE, or a container that you created. Through an additional set of interfaces supported by the ActiveX document, containers can provide a view port into the document's data.

Unlike ActiveX controls, documents are displayed full frame in their host (see Figure 9.2) and can take control of their host to some extent. When a document is viewed, the document menus are merged with those of the containers to give users the impression that they're working with an application rather than a container.

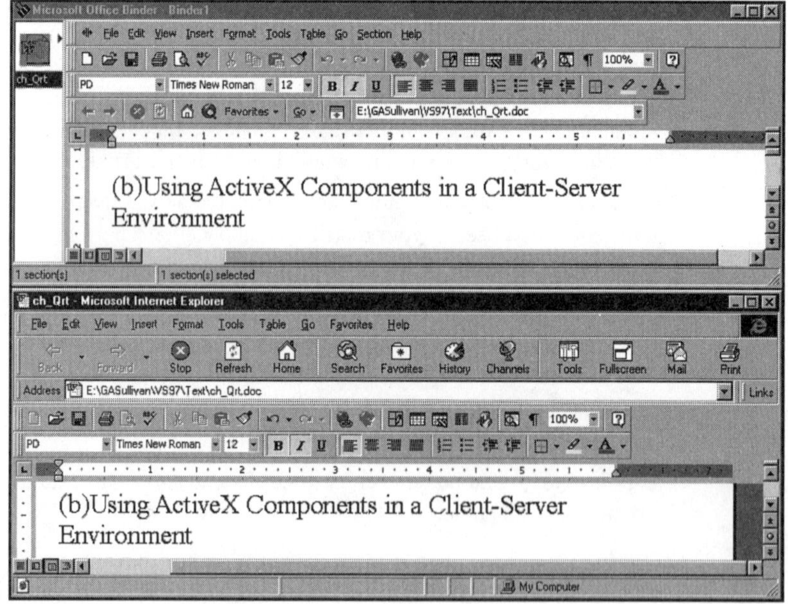

FIG. 9.2 ActiveX documents can reside in many different containers. As shown here, a Word document can reside in Internet Explorer or Office Binder.

With the popularity of web-based applications, it's no wonder that the focus of implementing ActiveX documents was placed on web browsers. Although a container can be easily created by using the SHDOCVW.DLL file installed by Internet Explorer 4.0, working with documents is addressed in Chapter 11, "An Inside Look at Web-Based Applications," where ActiveX components in the Internet environment are addressed.

ActiveX Code Components *ActiveX code components*, formerly referred to as *OLE Automation servers*, have little or no user interface. Code components are used primarily to implement business rules behind the scenes and can reside in all tiers of a client/server application.

Client applications use objects created from the classes exposed by the components and manipulate them through the properties, methods, and events provided. Through the properties, methods, and events exposed to the client—collectively called the *class interface*—components are "glued" together to produce an application.

ActiveX code components can be packaged as in-process or out-of-process servers, with the former residing in files with the .dll extension and the latter in .exe files. Like ActiveX controls, code components expose self-registration functions and are accompanied by a type library (.tlb) file. Visual Basic and Visual C++ development tools use this type library file to obtain information on the components interface at design time.

How Components Are Installed and Registered

ActiveX components are normally installed by a setup program, provided with the application that uses the component, and placed in the System32 directory. If a component isn't associated with any setup program, simply copy the file containing the component to the hard drive. Locating files containing ActiveX components in one location (such as the System32 directory) is a good idea.

According to ActiveX standards, ActiveX components must be self-registering, which, for an in-process control or code component, means implementing and exporting the `DllRegisterServer` and `DllUnregisterServer` functions. If the components were installed with an application such as Visual Basic or Visual C++, they most likely were placed in the \Windows\System or System32 directory by their respective setup program and registered with the system Registry behind the scenes.

If the in-process component was developed locally or copied to the local machine without a setup program, the component will need to be registered manually. This is accomplished with the Regsvr32.exe command-line utility located in the \Windows\System or \System32 directory. Regsvr32 takes advantage of several command-line arguments (see Figure 9.3).

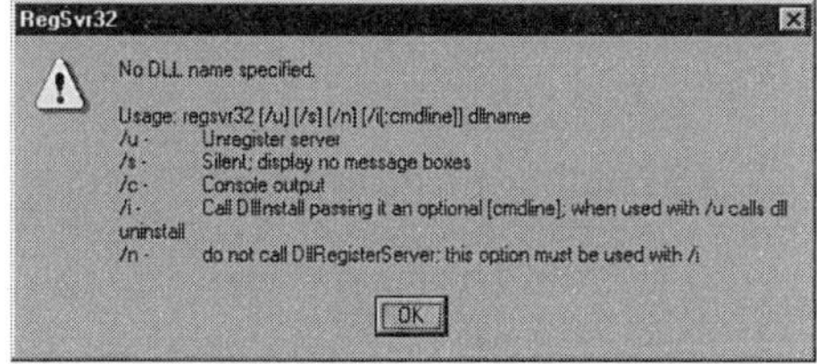

FIG. 9.3
The Regsvr32 utility's command-line arguments.

To register an ActiveX in-process component, simply choose Run from the Start menu and enter the following:

```
Regsvr32.exe <DLL or OCX File Name>
```

Similarly, to unregister the component, enter the following:

```
Regsvr32.exe <DLL or OCX File Name> /u
```

If you're registering in-process ActiveX components often, associate DLL and OCX files with the Regsvr32 utility. By doing so, you can just double-click a DLL or OCX file in Explorer to automatically launch the Regsver32 utility with the file as the command-line argument.

To associate a DLL or OCX with the Regsvr32 utility, locate the file in Explorer. Right-click the file, and then choose Open With. In the dialog box that appears, click Other and select Regsvr32 to open the component file with the Regsvr32 utility and subsequently register the component. If the Always Use This Program to Open This File checkbox is selected, all files with the same extension are associated with the utility.

For out-of-process servers, the components are automatically registered by executing the server.

Components and Remote Automation

ActiveX clients and out-of-process ActiveX servers communicate via a proxy/stub mechanism automatically supplied by COM. Distributed COM (DCOM) extends this mechanism across a network, allowing the out-of-process code component to be instantiated and executed on a remote machine and thus distributing the computational load across multiple machines.

DCOM shipped with Windows NT 4.0, and a service pack is available to provide DCOM for Windows 95. For machines not running Windows NT 4.0 or Windows 95 with the DCOM upgrade, Remote Automation is available to provide the same functionality as DCOM. Remote Automation was introduced before DCOM and shipped with Visual Basic 4.0. Although DCOM is slowly taking over the role Remote Automation held, Remote Automation is still supported by Visual Basic 5.0's Enterprise Edition for backward compatibility and for situations in which the client process resides on a 16-bit machine.

The following steps are necessary to implement a remote server. Use of DCOM is assumed and, where different, Remote Automation is indicated.

1. Install and register the server on the remote machine (the remote server must be an out-of-process ActiveX code component) by simply copying the executable to the server machine and executing it.
2. Configure the access and launch privileges for the component that uses the Racmgr32.exe or dcomcnfg.exe (DCOM only) utility. (Both utilities are discussed later in this section.)
3. Register the server on the client machine by copying the executable to the client machine and executing it. At this point, however, the component is configured as a local server.
4. On the client machine, configure the remote component to run remotely by using the Racmgr32.exe or dcomcnfg.exe (DCOM only) utility.

5. Install and register Autprx16.dll or Autprx32.dll on the client and server machines (Remote Automation). These files are located in the \Windows\System or \System32 directory of the development machine and were installed with Visual Basic.
6. Install and run the Automation Manager (Autmgr32.exe) on the server machine (Remote Automation). This file was also installed in the \Windows\System or \System32 directory with Visual Basic.
7. Run the client application.

Figure 9.4 shows the Racmgr32 utility, which is found in the Visual Basic program group. The Remote Automation Control Manager window consists of a list of the classes in your Windows Registry as potential ActiveX components. Two tabbed pages appear on the right: one to configure client access, and the other to configure server connection. The Client Access page is for configuring the remote server's access privileges, which is performed on the server machine.

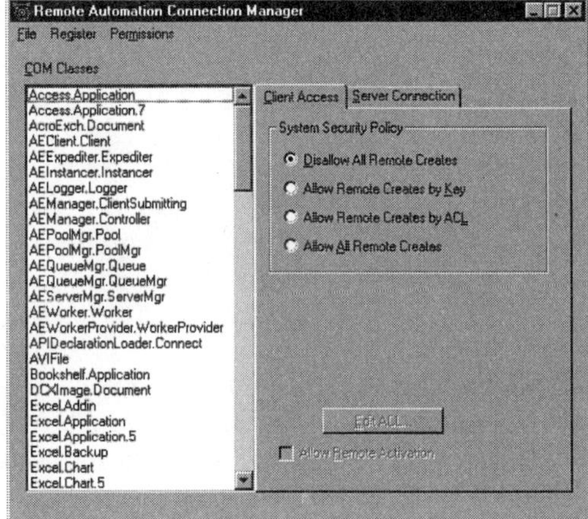

FIG. 9.4
The Racmgr32 utility is used on the server machine to configure client access to remote components.

Remote Automation provides four levels of access security:

- Selecting Disallow All Remote Creates disables the selected class from remote access by clients.
- Selecting Allow Remote Creates by Key enables the Allow Remote Activation checkbox at the bottom of the page. This security level allows objects to be created from the selected class by remote clients as long as the Allow Remote Activation checkbox is selected.
- Selecting Allow Remote Creates by ACL enables remote access from clients specified in an Access Control List (ACL), a list of users or user groups with various levels of access privileges assigned to them. By selecting Allow Remote Creates by ACL, only those users in the ACL will have access to the component and are further limited by their assigned access privilege. To edit the ACL, click the Edit ACL button.

- Selecting Allow All Remote Creates allows any object to be created from the selected class.

When invoking the Remote Automation Control Manager on the client machine, click the Server Connection tab. The Server Connection page has two option buttons and three drop-down boxes that you can use to configure the network connection (see Figure 9.5). When you're selecting a class for the first time, the connection icon toward the top of the page will indicate Local. To change this to Remote, right-click the class or the icon and select Remote. However, the type of remote transport and network connection still needs to be configured.

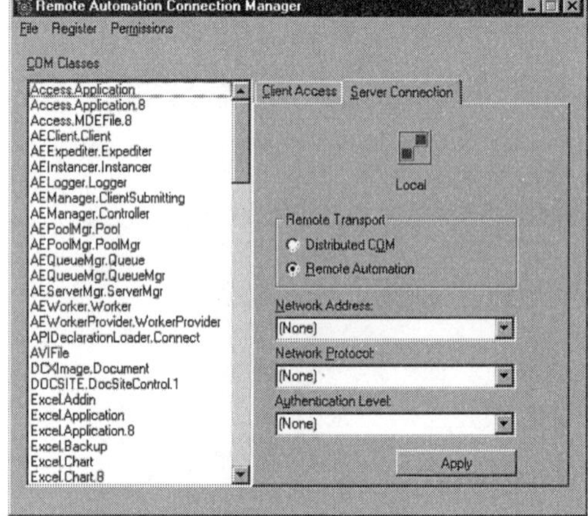

FIG. 9.5 The Server Connection page of the Racmgr32 utility is used on the client machine to configure the connection to out-of-process ActiveX components.

In the Remote Transport section, choose Distributed COM or Remote Automation. If you choose DCOM, notice that only the Network Address drop-down box is enabled (DCOM uses its own network protocol and security). All three drop-down boxes become enabled with the Remote Automation selection. Figure 9.6 shows a sample entry for the selected remote server by using Remote Automation.

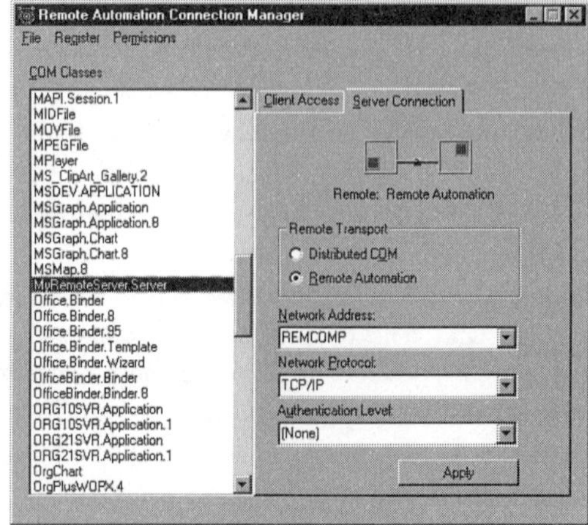

FIG. 9.6 The `MyRemoteServer.Server` connection. This component will be accessed on the network machine named REMCOMP with the TCP/IP protocol.

Because the Racmgr32.exe utility is extremely easy to use, you can quickly configure component servers. You can select the local connection and run the client application, and the local component will be used. Then select Remote along with Remote Automation, and the component will be accessed from the specified network machine by using Remote Automation. Finally, keep the selection at Remote and select DCOM, and the component will be accessed on the remote machine by using the DCOM protocol. It's as easy as that.

Another utility is provided for DCOM-enabled machines (Windows NT 4.0 and Windows 95 with DCOM upgrade) that facilitates configuring DCOM access. You can find this utility, dcomcnfg.exe, in the Windows \System32 directory. Executing this application displays the dialog box shown in Figure 9.7.

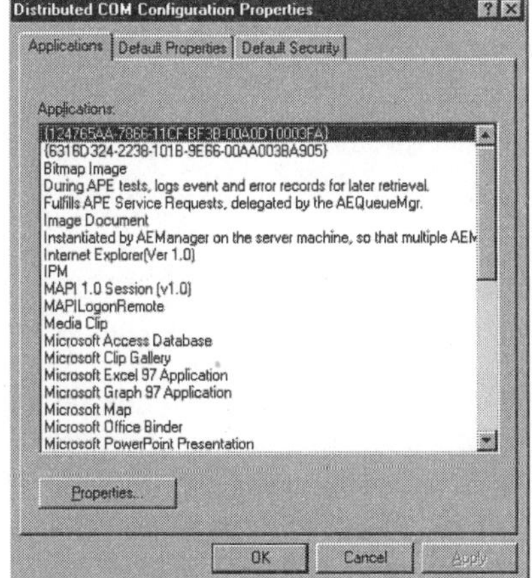

FIG. 9.7
The dcomcnfg.exe utility is used to configure the properties and security of components running under DCOM.

This dialog box consists of three tabbed pages:

- Applications, which lists the applications registered as ActiveX servers. Use this page to configure a component by selecting the server and clicking the Properties button.
- Default Properties, which allows you to enable or disable DCOM on the local machine and set default communication properties.
- Default Security, which allows you to identify which clients have access to running components, to launch servers on the local machine, and to change Registry settings for components.

Use dcomcnfg.exe to configure a component to run on a remote machine with the DCOM transport.

NOTE Make sure that the component is installed and registered on the remote machine and registered on the local machine.

Follow these steps:

1. From the Applications page, select the component you want to run remotely and click Properties.
2. Click the Location tab.
3. Select the Run Application on the Following Computer checkbox and provide the machine name of the remote server.
4. Choose OK twice to save the configuration and exit the utility.

Likewise, to configure a remote server, follow these steps with the dcomcnfg utility:

1. From the Applications page, select the server component you want to configure and click Properties.
2. Make sure that the Run Application on This Computer checkbox is selected on the Location page.
3. Use the Security page if you want the component to have a different security configuration from the default (as defined on the Default Security page of the Distributed COM Configuration Properties dialog box).
4. Use the Identity page to set the account under which the component will run.
5. Choose OK twice to save the configuration and exit the utility.

Now that you've seen the different types of components and how they're installed and registered, it's time to cover how they're glued together into a working application. For client/server applications, the most popular tools for performing this task are Visual Basic and Visual C++, both part of the Visual Studio suite. The rest of this chapter is devoted to using ActiveX components with these two development tools.

To learn the techniques of using ActiveX controls and code components, you'll develop a simple dialog box-based application first with Visual Basic and then with Visual C++. This application will prompt for an URL and, on the user's request, navigate to the web site and display the associated web page. The following controls and components (installed on your machine when the Visual Studio development tools were installed) will be used:

- Microsoft Rich Text Box (RICHTX32.OCX)
- Sheridan 3-D Command Button (THREED32.OCX)
- Internet Explorer (SHDOCVW.DLL)

The two controls, Microsoft Rich Text Box and Sheridan 3-D Command Button, will be discussed first in the "ActiveX Controls" section. Then, the Internet Explorer Automation object will be incorporated to provide the web-navigation capability that will be covered in the "ActiveX Code Components" section.

Using Components with Visual Basic

After you use an ActiveX component within Visual Basic, you'll come to appreciate the ease at which you can rapidly build component-based applications with this highly successful development tool. What's more, after you work with a particular component and become familiar with the basic steps of incorporating one into a Visual Basic project, using other components will become second nature to you.

You use ActiveX controls by selecting the control from the toolbox and placing it on a form. You can set the control's design-time properties to adjust the look and feel. Properties and methods can also be accessed programmatically. Event-handler functions are incorporated into the form's code to provide logic that needs to be executed in response to a particular event from a control.

Using ActiveX code components requires declaring a variable that's an object of the component. When a call is made to instance the object, properties and methods can then be accessed.

These procedures are discussed in detail in the following sections. Now create a project for the sample application. With Visual Basic running, choose File, New Project from the menu, and select Standard exe.

ActiveX Controls

Using an ActiveX control involves these general steps, explained in more detail in the following sections:

1. Load the control into the current project.
2. Access the control's properties and methods.
3. Handle events fired by the control.

Loading the Control To use an ActiveX control in a project, you need to add the control to the toolbox. Choose Project, Components from the menu to open the Components dialog box. In the list of controls registered with the Windows Registry, select a control and click OK. An icon representing the control appears in the toolbox.

If the control you're interested in doesn't appear in the list box but the .ocx file is installed on your machine (the control may not be registered), click the Browse button on the Components dialog box. In the Add ActiveX Control dialog box, locate the .ocx file and select it to load the control into the project. With the control added to the toolbox, you can use it just like any other control provided with Visual Basic.

Follow these steps to load the Microsoft Rich Textbox and Sheridan 3D Command Button controls into your sample application:

1. Choose Project, Components from the menu to open the Components dialog box.
2. Select the Microsoft Rich Textbox Control 5.0 item.
3. Select the Sheridan 3D Controls item.

4. Click OK. Six new icons appear in the toolbox. Five of the icons represent the Sheridan 3D controls (of which the Command Button is a member); the sixth one represents the Microsoft Rich Textbox (see Figure 9.8).

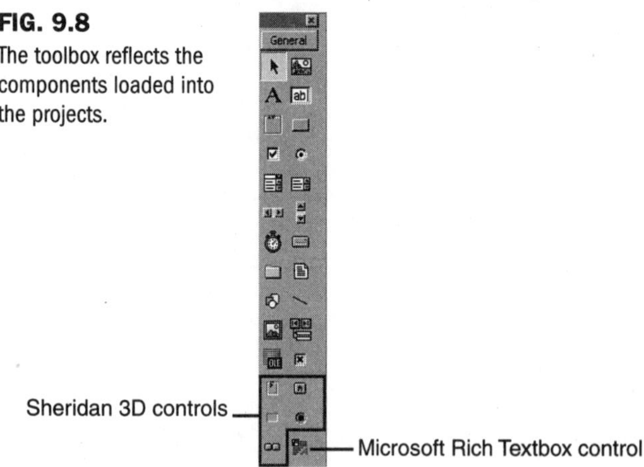

FIG. 9.8 The toolbox reflects the components loaded into the projects.

You can now assemble the controls on your form.

Place a Microsoft Rich Textbox and a Sheridan 3D Command Button on the form of your sample application. Also place a common label control next to the text box. Your project should look like Figure 9.9.

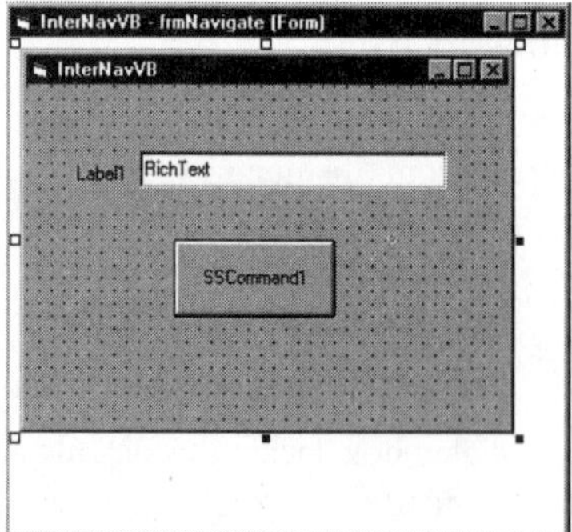

FIG. 9.9 The Microsoft Rich Textbox and Sheridan 3D ActiveX controls positioned on the main form.

Accessing Properties and Methods With the control loaded, the properties and methods exposed by the component are most easily viewed with the Object Browser (see Figure 9.10). The list on the left contains the classes or components that are part of the type library selected in the top drop-down box. Selecting the component will cause its properties, methods, and events to appear in the right list. The pane at the bottom of the dialog box displays information about the item selected in either list—a convenient way to familiarize yourself with a component before using it in code.

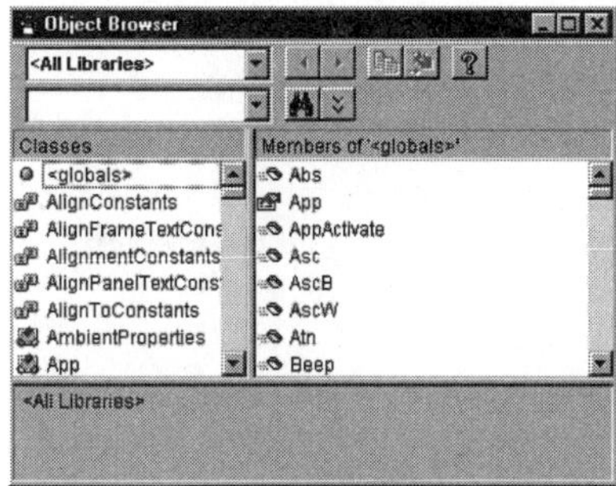

FIG. 9.10 Use the Object Browser to review an ActiveX component's properties and methods.

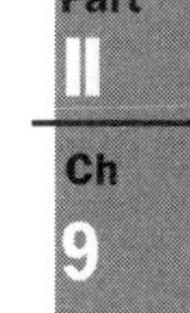

Another way to display control properties that are available at design time is through the Properties window, which normally appears between the Project and Form Layout windows at the right of the IDE. You can use the Properties window to set component properties at design time. Selecting the property displays information about it in the bottom pane of the window. With the property selected, the value can be entered in the column directly to the right of it.

For the example, you'll want to set the `Caption` properties for the Label and CommandButton controls. Also, you'll need to set the `Text` property of the TextBox control to a blank string:

1. Select the Label control on the form. In the Properties window, locate the `Caption` property and change the value from `Label1` to `URL:`.
2. In a similar fashion, change the CommandButton's `Caption` property to `Navigate`.
3. Select the Rich Textbox control and remove the `Rich Text` string from the `Text` property in the Properties window. Your project should now resemble Figure 9.11.

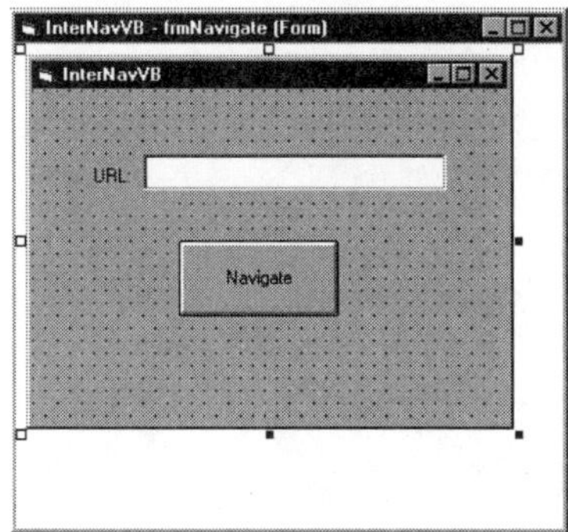

FIG. 9.11 The final appearance of the sample application with the appropriate properties set.

Properties and methods of an ActiveX control can be accessed programmatically. An object of a control is identified by the `(Name)` property in the Properties window. For example, to obtain the text value of the Rich Textbox identified by the name `RichTextBox1`, the following code segment would be added:

```
Dim sText As String
sText = RichTextBox1.Text
```

Setting the text value is accomplished with this statement:

```
RichTextBox1.Text = "Hello World"
```

Methods are accessed in the same manner. For example, if you wanted to invoke the `LoadFile` function of the Rich Textbox, the following code would be inserted:

```
Dim sFile As String = "MyFile.rtf"
RichTextBox1.LoadFile(sFile)
```

This code would load an .rtf file into a RichTextBox control.

Run the sample application. Notice that the only operation that can be performed is entering text into the text box. What you really want to happen is the application navigating to the entered URL at the user's command. You'll use the click event fired by the Sheridan 3D Command Button to tell the program to access the text in the text box and navigate to the URL. This leads to a discussion of handling events from ActiveX controls with Visual Basic.

Handling Events ActiveX controls will fire events predefined by the control's developer, notifying the client process of important events. ActiveX controls provided by vendors usually provide information to be displayed with Visual Basic help documenting what events they fire.

You can view exposed events from a control loaded into the project in various ways:

- Use the Object Browser. Along with the control's properties and methods, the events raised are displayed with a brief description. Figure 9.12 shows a good example, where the Object Browser is showing the Command Button control. As shown in the dialog box, an event called `Click` is raised by the Command Button control, and a description of how this event gets fired is provided in the bottom pane of the dialog box.

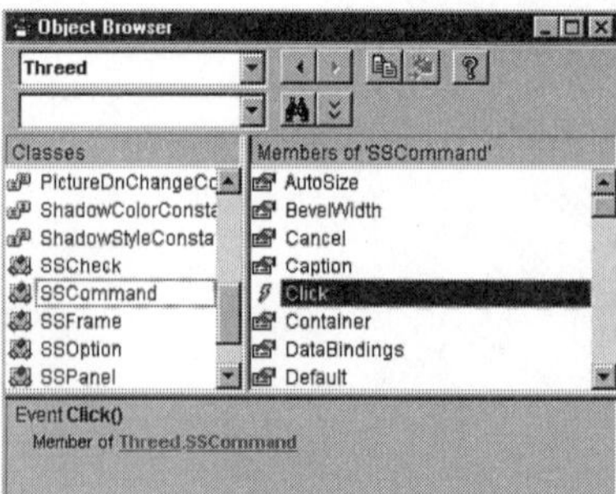

FIG. 9.12 Viewing the Sheridan 3D Command Button's `Click` event.

- View the form's code in the Code window. From the left drop-down list, you can select a control or code component to associate code with. The right drop-down list provides the events raised by the component. Selecting an event provides an event prototype in the code section of the form (as seen for the Command Button's `Click` event in Figure 9.13). It's within this subroutine you provide the necessary logic to be executed when this event is fired.

FIG. 9.13
The Command Button event handler prototype inserted into the form's code.

Returning to the sample application, enter the bold line of code in the Command Button `Click` event:

```
Private Sub SSCommand1_Click()

        MsgBox RichTextBox1.Text

End Sub
```

Run the application, type some text into the text box, and click the Navigate button. Did the text in the text box appear in the message box?

You'll now want to add web-navigation capability to your application via the Internet Explorer component. Using ActiveX code components is the next topic of discussion.

ActiveX Code Components

Using ActiveX code components involves the following steps, which are covered in more detail in the following sections:

1. Load the component into the current project.
2. Instantiate an object of the component class.
3. Access properties and methods of the component.
4. Handle events raised by the component.

Loading the Code Component Code components aren't child windows like controls. Subsequently, they're not dropped onto forms from the toolbox. However, you can load code components into the project, similar to a control. This pulls the type library information into the project, allowing you to view the component's properties and methods.

To add a code component, choose Project, References from the menu. The list box in the References dialog box contains ActiveX components registered with the Windows Registry. Selecting a component allows its properties and methods to be accessed at design time.

If the component doesn't appear in the list box, click the Browse button to open the Add Reference dialog box. Locate the file containing the type library information and select it to register the type library with the Registry and provide access to the properties and methods exposed by the component.

Follow these steps to load the Internet Explorer code component into your sample project:

1. Choose Project, References from the menu.
2. Select the Microsoft Internet Controls item to load the type library from the shdocvw.dll file.
3. Click OK.

Accessing Properties and Methods With the code components type library loaded, the properties and methods exposed by the component are most easily viewed through the Object Browser, the same as for ActiveX controls. To view the Internet Explorer code component properties and methods, do the following:

1. Choose View, Object Browser from the menu.
2. From the top drop-down list, select the SHDocVw library.
3. In the left list box, select the InternetExplorer item. The properties, methods, and events appear in the right list box.
4. Note the class name in the bottom pane. You'll need this, along with the `Application` property, when making a call to create a running object.

ActiveX components are created and manipulated programmatically. These are the basic steps in using a code component within Visual Basic code:

1. Declare a variable of type `Object`.
2. Create and return a reference to the ActiveX object.
3. Access properties and methods with the . member selector.
4. Release the reference to the object by setting the object variable to `Nothing`.

To incorporate the Internet Explorer component into your example, follow these steps:

1. With the form's code displayed in the Code window, add the following to the declarations section:

   ```
   Dim m_oInternetExplorer As Object
   ```

2. In the form's load event handler, insert the following:

   ```
   Private Sub Form_Load()

       Set m_oInternetExplorer = CreateObject("InternetExplorer.Application")

   End Sub
   ```

3. In the command button's click event, add this code:

```
Private Sub SSCommand1_Click()

    m_oInternetExplorer.Navigate (RichTextBox1.Text)
    m_oInternetExplorer.Visible = True

End Sub
```

4. In the form's unload event, insert the necessary code to release the reference to the object:

```
Private Sub Form_Unload(Cancel As Integer)

    Set m_oInternetExplorer = Nothing

End Sub
```

5. Make an executable file by choosing File, Make <project name>.exe.
6. Make sure that Internet service is up and running. Run the application, type a valid URL, and click Navigate. You should see the Internet Explorer launch with the appropriate web page displayed.

Handling Events Some ActiveX code components will raise events similar to ActiveX controls. Visual Basic allows you to provide event handling for ActiveX components with the `WithEvents` keyword used in the dimension statement. This tells Visual Basic up front that you want to handle events exposed by the component.

To see how to use the `WithEvents` keyword, handle the `Quit` event from Internet Explorer and place the reference releasing code there, as follows:

1. Change the declaration statement to read as follows:

```
Dim WithEvents m_oInternetExplorer As InternetExplorer
```

   This tells Visual Basic that you want to handle the events raised by the `InternetExplorer` class.

2. Notice the `m_oInternetExplorer` item in the left drop-down list. Select it to list all the events raised by the `InternetExplore` component in the right drop-down list.
3. Select the `Quit` event from the right drop-down list.
4. In the `Quit` event-handler function, add the following message box and relocate the object release code:

```
Private Sub m_oInternetExplorer_Quit(Cancel As Boolean)

    m_oInternetExplorer.Visible = False

    MsgBox "Exiting Internet Explorer"

    Set m_oInternetExplorer = Nothing

End Sub
```

5. Relocate the object creation code to the command button's click event:

```
Private Sub SSCommand1_Click()

    Set m_oInternetExplorer = CreateObject("InternetExplorer.Application")

    m_oInternetExplorer.Navigate (RichTextBox1.Text)
    m_oInternetExplorer.Visible = True

End Sub
```

6. Make an executable, and run the application as before.

Distributing Applications

You would create an executable of your application that uses ActiveX components as you would for any application. Your application, however, will require the .ocx and .dll files that package the components used to be distributed and registered on the target machine. Just as Visual Basic uses the registered .ocx and .dll files, your application also will use them and will generate a runtime error if the file isn't found. Therefore, your application's installation procedure should copy all files that package the components as well as automatically register them.

NOTE If you're using components obtained from a third party, consulting the accompanying documentation regarding distribution licenses is always a good idea.

When you're ready to distribute your application, you should use Visual Basic's Application Setup Wizard to create the installation program.

NOTE If your application will use remote server components and you want the servers registered without copying the executable to the target machine, ensure that a .vbr file exists for each server. A .vbr file is created when the server project (ActiveX executable) is compiled with the Remote Server Files option selected on the Component page from the Project Properties dialog box (Project, Project Properties).

To create an installation program, follow these steps:

1. Start the Setup Wizard by choosing Start, Programs, Microsoft Visual Basic, and Application Setup Wizard. Click Next in the first setup dialog box.
2. The next dialog box prompts for the project for which to build a setup application (see Figure 9.14). Complete this dialog box as follows:
    - Enter the path for the project file, or click Browse to locate it.
    - By selecting Rebuild the Project, the Setup Wizard will rebuild the project for you.
    - Select Create a Setup Program to create a program for setting up your application on separate machines. If your application is to be distributed over the Internet, choose Create Internet Download Setup (available only for ActiveX controls and ActiveX EXE and DLL projects with public classes).

FIG. 9.14
The Select Projects and Options dialog box of the Setup Wizard.

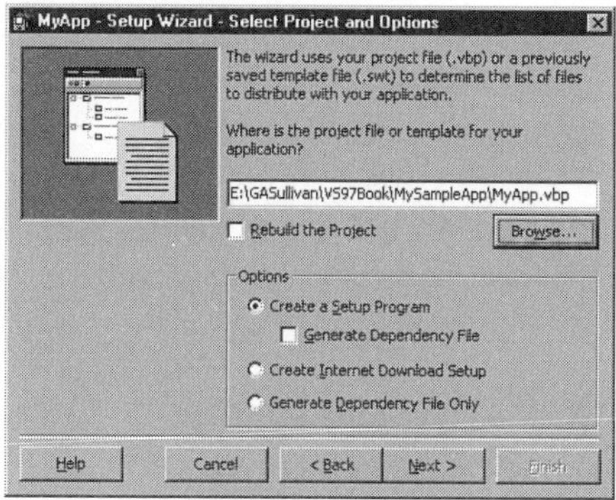

3. Click Next.
4. If your project references a type library (.tlb) file, the Setup Wizard asks whether this refers to a Remote Automation sever (see Figure 9.15). In this case, the MyRemoteServer.TLB file does in fact represent a remote server, so choose Yes. You're then reminded to manually add the .vbr file to the ActiveX Server Components list (which you'll see shortly).

FIG. 9.15
When the Setup Wizard finds reference to a type library file, it asks whether this refers to a Remote Automation component.

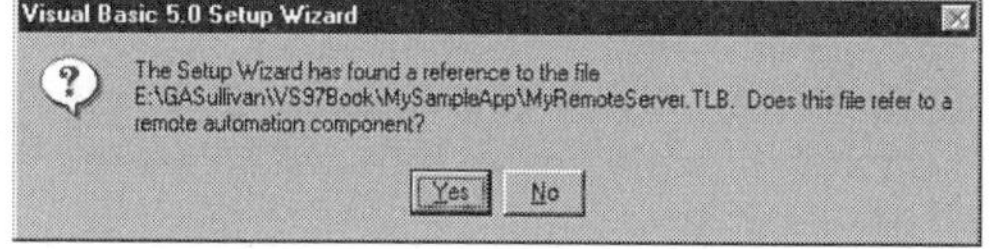

5. In this example, the Setup Wizard found two files with no dependencies (see Figure 9.16). Select the files that you're certain have no dependent files and click Next.

FIG. 9.16
If the Setup Wizard finds files with missing dependencies, it asks for verification that no dependency information is available.

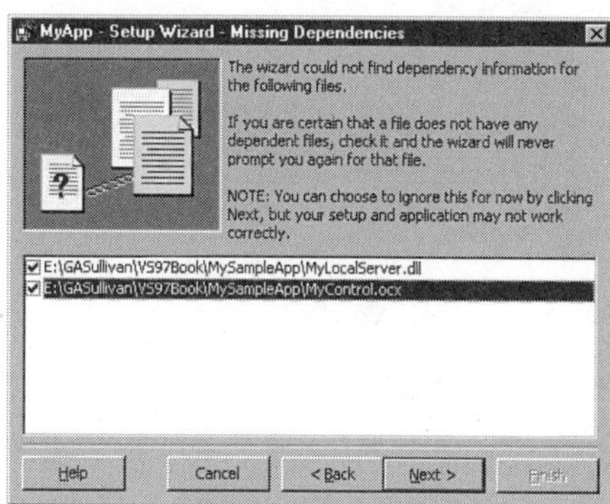

6. The next screen in the Setup Wizard provides a means to select the method of distribution, be it a floppy disk, single directory, or disk directories. In this example, the Single Directory option is selected. Click Next; the Setup Wizard asks for the directory.
7. Provide the directory location and click Next again.

   A dialog box appears, listing the ActiveX servers that the Setup Wizard has determined are used in your application. As shown in Figure 9.17, only the local server is listed. Recall from step 3 that you need to add the remote server manually.

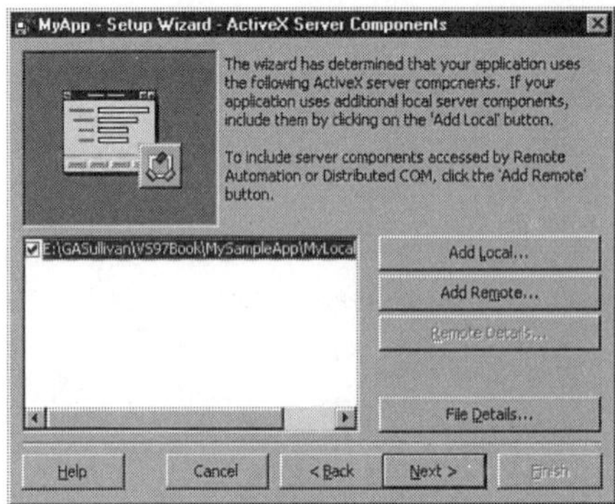

FIG. 9.17 The Setup Wizard's ActiveX Server Components dialog box provides the means to add remote servers to the setup program.

8. Click the Add Remote button to bring up a dialog box that lets you search for the .vbr file containing the registration information for your remote server. After locating the file, the wizard prompts for required information for Remote Automation or DCOM access. In this example, DCOM is selected and the name of the computer where the remote server will be executed is provided (see Figure 9.18).

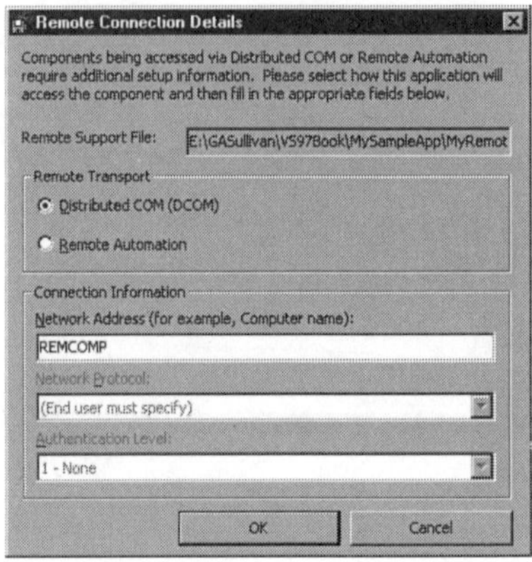

FIG. 9.18 The Setup Wizard's Remote Connection Details dialog box prompts for the necessary remote transport and connection information.

NOTE Selecting DCOM as the remote transport disables the Network Protocol and Authentication Level drop-down boxes because DCOM has its own protocol and security. If you use Remote Automation, however, you would have to supply this information.

9. Enter the required information and click OK. The remote server appears in the ActiveX Server Components list box (see Figure 9.19). Click Next.

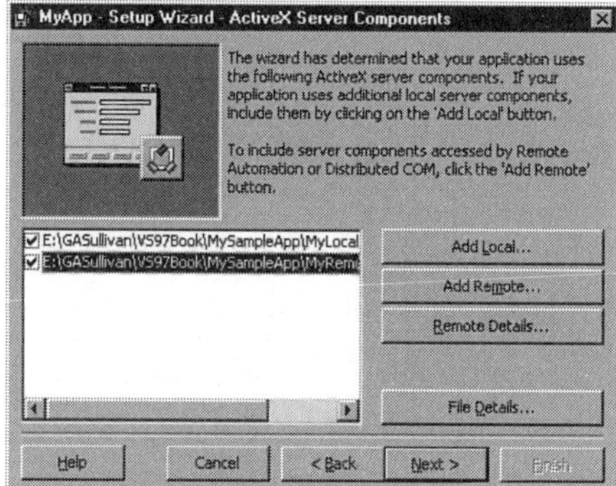

FIG. 9.19
The ActiveX Server Components dialog box, showing the addition of a remote server.

10. You're now asked to confirm the dependency on any ActiveX controls. Ensure that the files shown are the ones used in the application and select their checkboxes. Click Next.
11. A summary appears of all the files that should be shipped with your application. You can include additional files by clicking Add, or remove files from the distribution by deselecting their checkbox. Click Next.
12. The Setup Wizard has all the necessary information it needs to create a setup program. You're asked if you want to save this setup as a template to be run again on this project. Click Finish; the wizard copies the files to the distribution directory, compresses them, and creates the Setup.exe file that will be invoked on the client machine.

Using Components with Visual C++

As mentioned earlier, when you become comfortable with using one component, using others of the same type becomes second nature. Using ActiveX components with Visual C++ is no exception. After you use an ActiveX control with the resource editor or use a code component programmatically, you'll use the same techniques repeatedly with each and every ActiveX component you use.

Using ActiveX controls in Visual C++ is similar to that of Visual Basic when you become familiar with Visual C++'s resource editor. With the control loaded into the project, an icon representing the control appears on the editor toolbar for "dropping" onto dialog boxes and forms in a similar manner. Visual C++ exposes design-time tools that enable viewing and setting control properties, as well as a test container that allows a control to be tested and its behavior monitored before you incorporate it into applications.

ActiveX code components, on the other hand, are incorporated a little differently in Visual C++ in that they aren't loaded into the project for early binding, as was the case in Visual Basic. To use an ActiveX code component, a container class must be created to encapsulate the interface provided by the component. Before Visual C++ 5.0, this was accomplished by the ClassWizard, which created source code that was included into your project that implemented the container class. With Visual C++ 5.0, special support for COM has been added to the compiler. By using the new `#import` directive to import a type library, the preprocessor generates the C++ header file describing the interface and a second file containing the implementation, thus eliminating the need to maintain container source code as before.

Creating an MFC Application with ActiveX Support

Now is a good time to open the project in which you'll be working with the components. You'll be developing the same sample application as you did with Visual Basic in the earlier discussion. Follow these steps to create a dialog box-based MFC application:

1. Choose File, New from the menu to open the New dialog box.
2. From the Projects page, select MFC AppWizard (exe). Provide the project name and location in the text boxes on the right. Click OK.
3. Select the Dialog Based option and default on the Language drop-down list. Click Next.
4. In the MFC AppWizard – Step 2 of 4 dialog box, select Automation Support and ensure that ActiveX Controls Support is also selected. By selecting Automation support, your application can use Automation objects exposed by other programs or expose its own Automation objects to other ActiveX clients. With the ActiveX Controls support selected, your application is created with the necessary logic to be an ActiveX controls container. Click Next.
5. Accept the default options on MFC AppWizard – Step 3 of 4 dialog box. Allowing the AppWizard to generate source file comments is helpful if you're new to developing in Visual C++. These comments indicate where in the source code you'll need to provide some form of functionality. By choosing to link to the MFC library dynamically (the second set of options on the dialog box), your program will make calls to the MFC library at runtime. This selection minimizes the size of your executable. Click Next.
6. The last AppWizard dialog box appears (see Figure 9.20). You should have three classes in the list box. Selecting a class in the list displays in the text boxes information regarding the base class and the associated implementation files that will be generated. Click Finish to have the AppWizard create the project and insert the implementation files. You're then presented with a dialog box summarizing the project. Click OK.
7. Now you can compile your application, even though it has no functionality. Choose Build, Build <project name>.exe from the menu. After the project finishes compiling, choose Build, Execute <project name>.exe from the menu. You should see a dialog box similar to the one shown in Figure 9.21. Because no functionality has been added yet, clicking either command button will halt the execution and return the developer studio to design mode. Click one of the buttons.
8. Your sample application won't need the two command buttons or the TODO caption supplied by the AppWizard. Invoke the resource editor by double-clicking the dialog box resource file in Resource View. You should see the contents of Figure 9.22 onscreen.

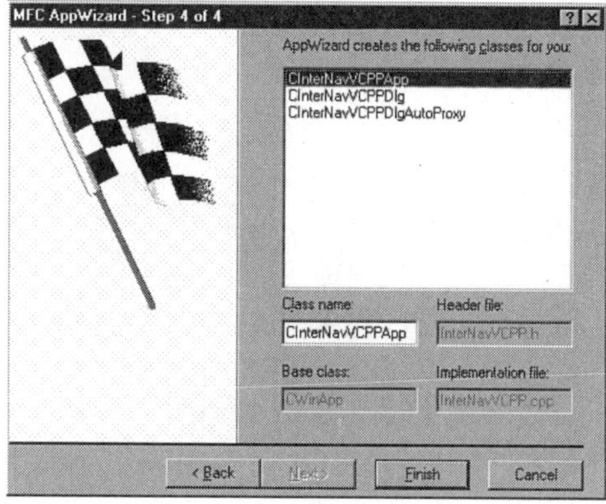

FIG. 9.20
The last dialog box of the MFC AppWizard summarizes the classes that will be added to your project.

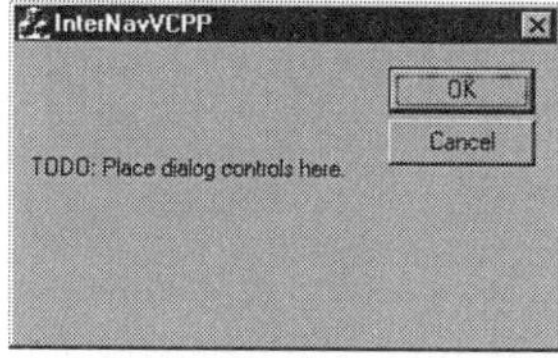

FIG. 9.21
Execution of the skeleton project.

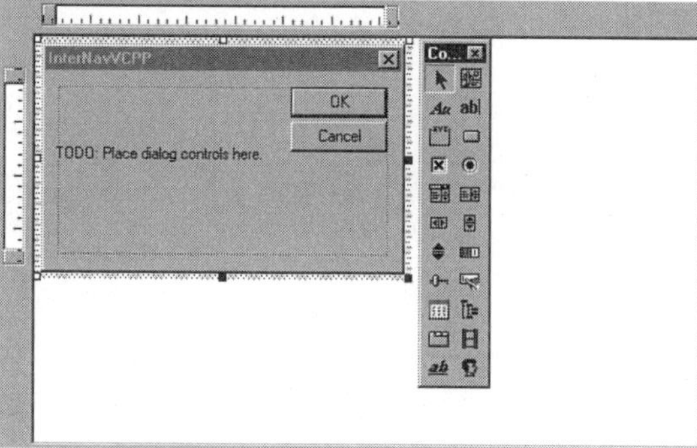

FIG. 9.22
Editing the dialog box resource with the resource editor.

9. Remove the two command buttons and the caption by selecting them and pressing Delete.

You're now ready to proceed with adding the ActiveX controls that will be used in the application. Save your project.

ActiveX Controls

Using an ActiveX control within Visual C++ involves the following steps, which are discussed in detail in the following sections:

1. Load the control into the project by creating a class to wrap the control's interface.
2. Identify the control's properties and methods, and set the design-time properties.
3. Establish a member variable representing an object of the control's wrapper class.

Loading the Control To load a control into a project, use the Component Gallery (choose Project, Add to Project, Components and Controls from the menu). The Component Gallery stores shortcuts as well as Registry information about registered controls.

If you've installed and registered an ActiveX control and it doesn't appear in the Component Gallery, you must create the shortcut yourself. In Explorer, use the right mouse button to drag the .ocx file containing the control to the Registered ActiveX Controls folder. Choose Create Shortcut(s) Here from the pop-up menu.

To load the two ActiveX controls into your application, follow these steps:

1. Choose Project, Add to Project, Components and Controls from the menu to bring up the Component Gallery dialog box. Double-click the Registered ActiveX Controls folder to display its contents.
2. Locate and select the Microsoft Rich Text control (version 5.0).
3. Click Insert, and then click OK in the message box that asks you to verify your selection.
4. The Confirm Classes dialog box appears, listing all the classes (with their implementation files) associated with the ActiveX control that will be inserted into your project. Click OK.
5. Repeat steps 1 through 4 for the Sheridan 3D Command Button control.
6. If you now view the resource editor (as in Figure 9.23), notice the addition of two icons on the resource editor's toolbar.

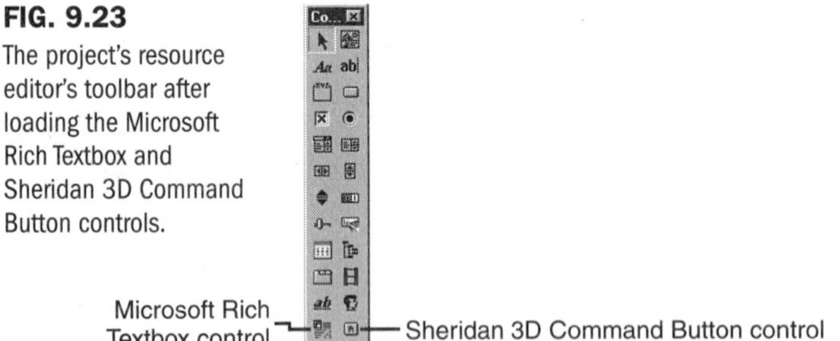

FIG. 9.23 The project's resource editor's toolbar after loading the Microsoft Rich Textbox and Sheridan 3D Command Button controls.

7. Select the Microsoft Rich Textbox control from the toolbar and place it on the dialog box.
8. Select the Sheridan 3D Command Button control and place it on the dialog box. Your dialog box should look like Figure 9.24.

NOTE The label control to the left of the text box is placed on the dialog box in the same way. You can change the label's caption by right-clicking the label and then choosing Properties. On the General page, enter the new caption in the appropriate text box.

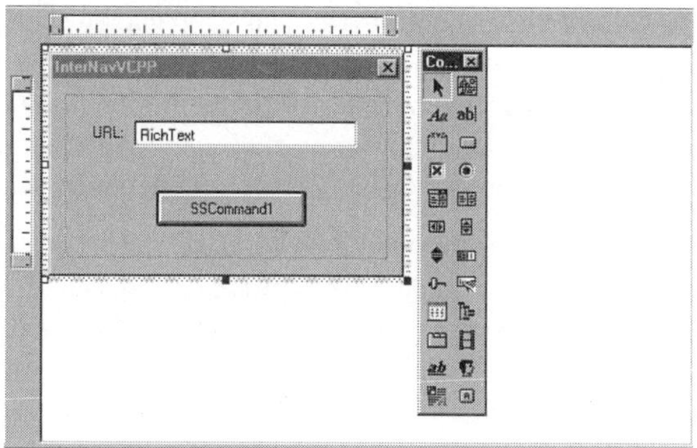

FIG. 9.24 The dialog box resource after placing the Microsoft Rich Textbox and Sheridan 3D Command Button controls on it.

TIP To reposition controls in the dialog box, drag them with the mouse or, with the control selected, use the arrow keys. Likewise, you can resize the control with the arrow keys while holding down the Shift key.

With the ActiveX controls loaded into the project and placed in the dialog box resource, you now can use the properties, methods, and events exposed by each.

Accessing Properties and Methods The ActiveX control's developer designated certain properties to be accessed at design time. You can view these properties and set their values from the control's property page displayed by the resource editor. To access the property page of the Sheridan 3D Command Button control in your application, do the following:

1. With the resource editor in view, right-click the Command Button control. Choose Properties; a dialog box such as the one in Figure 9.25 appears.

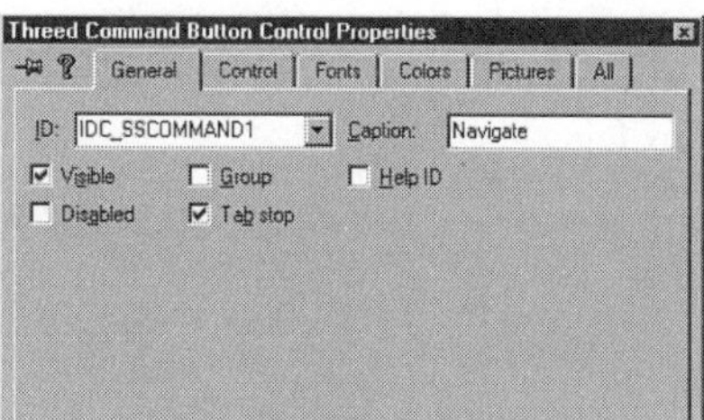

FIG. 9.25 The property sheet for the Sheridan 3D Command Button.

2. The properties are grouped into categories on each page. Display each page to get a feel for what properties the control's developer exposed at design time. Notice that you also can access all properties from the different categories on the All page.
3. On the General page, change the Caption property to `Navigate`. Play around with the other properties to see how creative you can get with this control's appearance.

The properties for the Microsoft Rich Text control are accessed in the same way. It's a good idea to go ahead and view what properties are exposed by this control for future reference, but you won't need to change any values for this application. You will, however, need to access the `Text` property of the Microsoft Rich Text control at runtime.

If you remember back to when the controls were inserted via the Component Gallery, several classes were generated and placed into your project. These ***wrapper classes*** wrap the interfaces to the controls and have member functions for all properties and methods. You can view these member functions through the Class View or by editing the class implementation file. To view the member functions for the Microsoft Rich Text control wrapper class, follow these steps:

1. With the Class View page displayed in the left pane of the Developer Studio, expand the view of the `CRichText` class. You'll see a complete list of all member functions that can be used to communicate with the control. You can see a subset of these member functions that begin with the prefixes `Get` and `Set`, which are accessor and modifier functions, respectively, that allow you to retrieve and set the control's property values at runtime.
2. Locate the `GetText()` member function from the expanded list in the Class View. Right-click the function and choose Go To Definition. The implementation file (RichText.cpp) containing the definition (or implementation) of this particular accessor function opens. You should now be viewing the following code in the right pane of the developer studio:

   ```
   CString CRichText::GetText()
   {
       CString result;
       InvokeHelper(DISPID_TEXT, DISPATCH_PROPERTYGET, VT_BSTR, (void*)&result,
   NULL);
       return result;
   }
   ```

   You'll call this function later in the sample application to obtain the `Text` property from the text box.

To make use of the properties and methods exposed by an ActiveX control at runtime, the dialog box class needs a data member that's an object of the control's wrapper class. The ClassWizard provides the support for adding data members of type <control wrapper class> to the dialog box class. You'll want to add a data member of type `CRichText` to your dialog box to have access to the text property by following these steps:

1. With the dialog box resource in view, right-click the Microsoft Rich Text control and choose ClassWizard.
2. On the Member Variables page is a list of control IDs and their respective data member names, if any (see Figure 9.26). Select the `IDC_RICHTEXTCTRL1` ID and click the Add Variable button.
3. Complete the member variable name in the Add Member Variable dialog box. You use this name in your code to reference the object of the control's wrapper class. Click OK to display the data member assigned to the `IDC_RICHTEXTCTRL1` ID. Click OK again, and the ClassWizard will add the boldface lines of code to the dialog box class's interface file (see Listing 9.1).

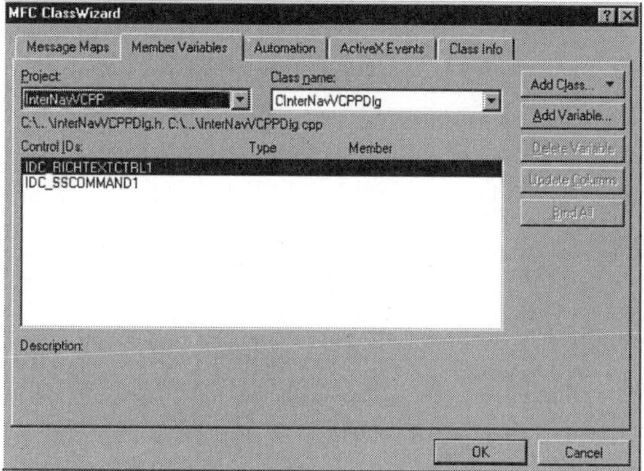

FIG. 9.26 Adding member variables with the MFC ClassWizard.

Listing 9.1 Adding a Member Variable

```
// InterNavVCPPDlg.h : header file
//
//{{AFX_INCLUDES()
#include "richtext.h"
//}}AFX_INCLUDES

#if
➥!defined(AFX_INTERNAVVCPPDLG_H__FF98D69A_FFDE_11D0_83C1_000000000000__INCLUDED_)
#define AFX_INTERNAVVCPPDLG_H__FF98D69A_FFDE_11D0_83C1_000000000000__INCLUDED_

#if _MSC_VER >= 1000
#pragma once
#endif // _MSC_VER >= 1000

class CInterNavVCPPDlgAutoProxy;

/////////////////////////////////////////////////////////////////////////////
// CInterNavVCPPDlg dialog

class CInterNavVCPPDlg : public CDialog
{
    DECLARE_DYNAMIC(CInterNavVCPPDlg);
    friend class CInterNavVCPPDlgAutoProxy;

// Construction
public:
    CInterNavVCPPDlg(CWnd* pParent = NULL);    // standard constructor
    virtual ~CInterNavVCPPDlg();

// Dialog Data
    //{{AFX_DATA(CInterNavVCPPDlg)
    enum { IDD = IDD_INTERNAVVCPP_DIALOG };
```

continues

Listing 9.1 Continued

```
    CRichText m_oRichText;
    //}}AFX_DATA

    // ClassWizard generated virtual function overrides
    //{{AFX_VIRTUAL(CInterNavVCPPDlg)
    protected:
    virtual void DoDataExchange(CDataExchange* pDX);    // DDX/DDV support
    //}}AFX_VIRTUAL

.
.
.

#endif //
➥!defined(AFX_INTERNAVVCPPDLG_H__FF98D69A_FFDE_11D0_83C1_000000000000__INCLUDED_)
```

The ClassWizard also adds the following boldface line of code to the implementation file:

```
void CInterNavVCPPDlg::DoDataExchange(CDataExchange* pDX)
{
    CDialog::DoDataExchange(pDX);
    //{{AFX_DATA_MAP(CInterNavVCPPDlg)
    DDX_Control(pDX, IDC_RICHTEXTCTRL1, m_oRichText);
    //}}AFX_DATA_MAP
}
```

4. Invoke the `GetText()` member function (or any another function, for that matter) of the Microsoft Rich Text control and obtain the value of the text property:

```
CString strText;

strText = m_oRichText.GetText();
```

Handling Events The ClassWizard maps an ActiveX control's events to dialog box class handler functions. The wizard displays all the events that the control can fire. By selecting the events you want your dialog box class to handle, the ClassWizard will place the class into an event sink map that connects the event to its handler function.

If you went ahead and compiled and executed the sample application, you would see the dialog box appear and be able to enter an URL into the text control. But that's about all the functionality the application has at this point. What you really want the program to do is navigate to the URL when you click the Navigate button. Clicking the Command Control button fires an event. The dialog box class handles the event by providing a member function that gets invoked when the event is fired. It's within this member function that you'll want to incorporate the necessary logic to retrieve the text from the text control and navigate to the URL.

Because the navigation logic will be handled by the Internet Explorer component (which is covered later in the "ActiveX Code Components" section), an intermediate step will be followed. When the event is handled, logic is put into place to receive the text from the text control and display it in a message box.

To handle the click event, follow these steps:

NOTE This procedure is the same for mapping all events for all ActiveX controls.

1. With the dialog box resource in view, right-click the button control and choose Events to display a dialog box containing all the event types the control can fire (see Figure 9.27).

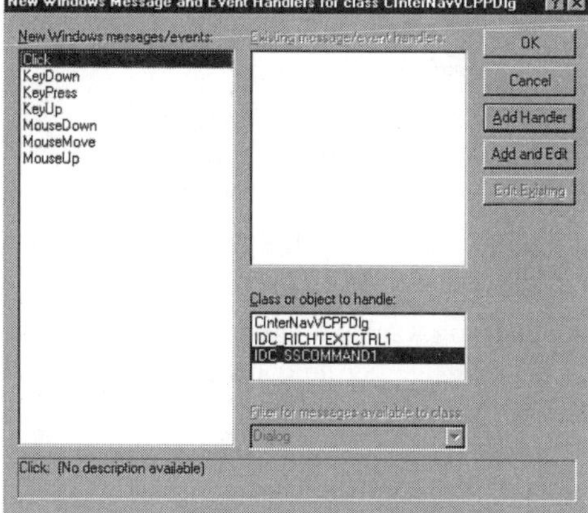

FIG. 9.27 The events fired by the Sheridan 3D Command Button.

2. Select the `Click` event from the left list, and then click the Add and Edit button. You're prompted for the name of the member function that will be mapped to the event. Click OK to accept the default name.
3. You're launched into the implementation file where the handler function prototype has been created by the ClassWizard. Enter the following code inside the function:

```
void CInterNavVCPPDlg::OnClickSscommand1()
{
    CString sDisplay;

    sDisplay = "The URL You Entered: " + m_oRichText.GetText();

    AfxMessageBox(sDisplay);

}
```

4. Compile and run the program. Type any text into the text box and click Navigate. The message box should display what was typed.

You also can view and directly maintain the message/event map through the ClassWizard dialog box. Follow these steps:

1. Choose View, ClassWizard from the menu. On the Message Maps page, you should see what's shown in Figure 9.28. The two side-by-side list boxes in the middle of the dialog box contain the objects and events for the class displayed in the upper-right drop-down list.

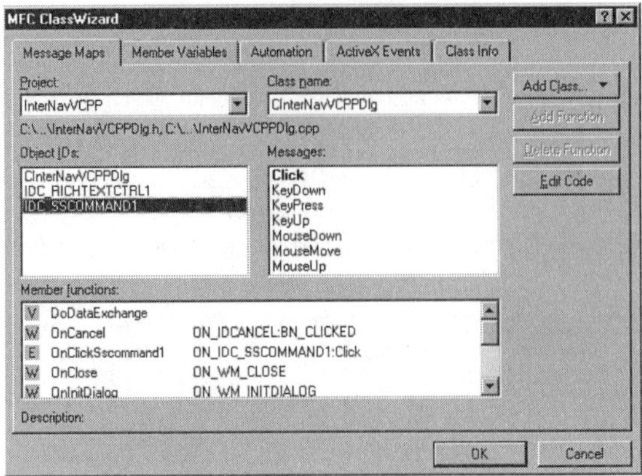

FIG. 9.28
The MFC ClassWizard's Message Maps page is used to add and maintain event handlers.

2. Select the command button's ID (`IDC_SSCOMMAND1`) in the Object IDs list. The events for this control appear in the list on the right.
3. Select the event for which you want to add a handler function and click the Add Function button. Accept or change the handler function name and proceed to add logic into the function's implementation.

ActiveX Code Components

Using an ActiveX code component in a Visual C++ project is similar to using ActiveX controls in that a class that wraps the components interface is inserted into a project. It's this wrapper class in which the rest of your application accesses the properties and methods the component developer exposed. What's different is that the ActiveX code component isn't inserted into the project through the Component Gallery, and the component isn't visually edited with the resource editor.

Various techniques are available for loading and using ActiveX code components within Visual C++. To learn these techniques, you'll add the Internet Explorer Automation object to the sample application that you created earlier in the "ActiveX Controls" section to provide the web navigation functionality this application needs.

Now is a good time to become familiar with the interface to the Internet Explorer component. To obtain information about the component (or any registered component), use the OLE/COM Object Viewer utility provided with Visual C++. This utility will display Registry as well as type library information about the selected component. To view the Internet Explorer component, do the following:

1. Choose Tools, OLE/COM Object Viewer from the menu.
2. From the left list, expand the Automation Objects folder and locate the Internet Explorer entry. Select the entry to see the Registry information (see Figure 9.29).

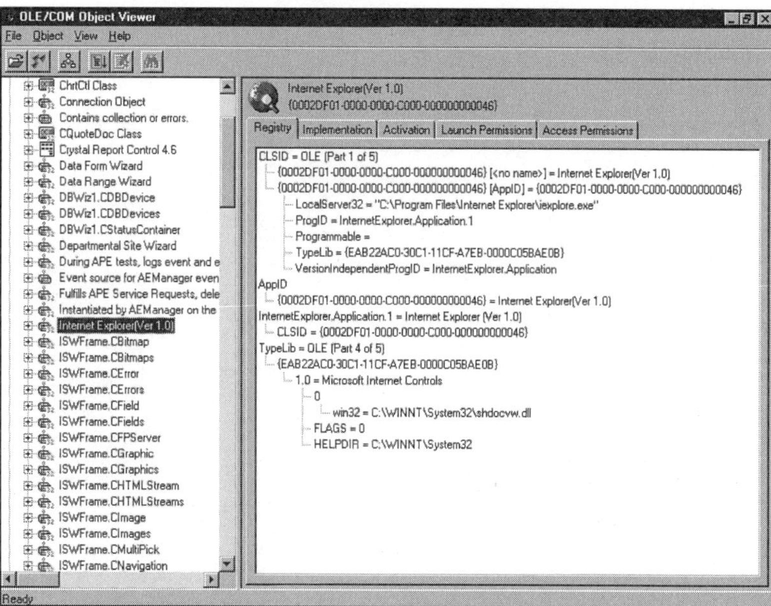

FIG. 9.29 The Internet Explorer automation object's Registry entry as viewed by the OLE/COM Object Viewer.

3. The most pertinent information to obtain from this is the `ProgID` entry. You'll use this value (`InternetExplorer.Application.1`) in your code to create a running object. Also, the location of the type library is found in the TypeLib/{CLSID}/1.0/0/win32 entry, which for this case is C:\WINNT\System32\shdocvw.dll.
4. In the OLE/COM Object Viewer window, choose File, View TypeLib from the menu and locate the type library file (C:\WINNT\System32\shdocvw.dll).
5. Expand the `interface IWebBrowserApp` entry in the left pane to see all the member functions implemented in the interface in the right pane (see Figure 9.30). It's these member functions that you'll create support for in the wrapper class inserted in your project.

There are two ways to create and insert a wrapper class for an ActiveX code component in Visual C++:

- Use the ClassWizard, which will create and insert source code into the project for a class based on the ActiveX code components type library.
- Use a new feature for Visual C++ 5.0—the `#import` directive. The `#import` directive is used to import the type library of the component into the implementation file of the class that will use the object. The compiler will read the type library and build the wrapper class for you. This way, there's no source code to maintain in the project.

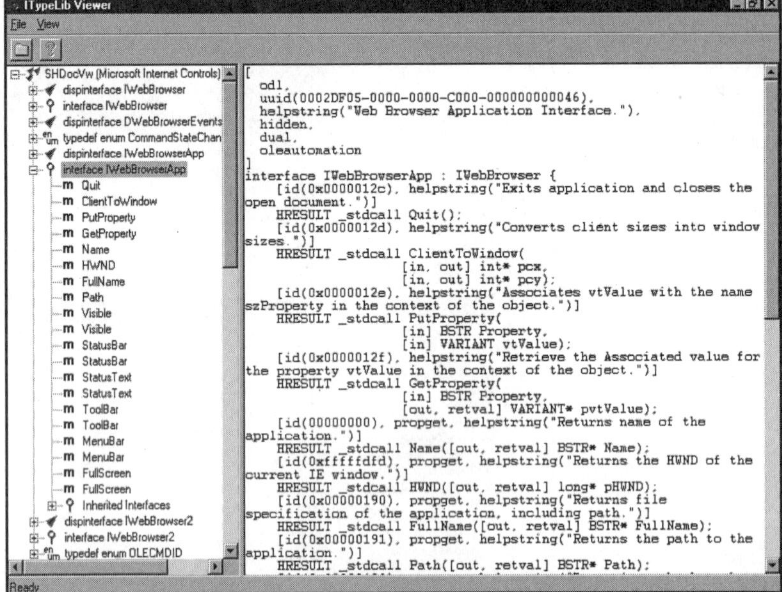

FIG. 9.30
The `IWebBrowserApp` interface implementation.

The ClassWizard Provided an ActiveX code component's type library, the ClassWizard will generate a class that encapsulates each interface listed in the library. The member functions of these classes are tailored to access each property and method included in the library. To create and insert a class for the Internet Explorer component, follow these steps:

1. Choose View, ClassWizard from the menu. Click the Add Class button and select the From a Type Library option.
2. Locate and open the type library file (in this case, C:\WINNT\System32\shdocvw.dll). You should be presented with the Confirm Classes dialog box, which lists the classes that the ClassWizard will generate.
3. Select only the `IWebBrowserApp` class and click OK.
4. Click OK again to exit the ClassWizard. Notice an `IWebBrowserApp` class in the Class View, along with the shdocvw.h and shdocvw.cpp files in the File View that contain the implementation.

The *#import* Directive A new feature introduced with Visual C++ 5.0 is compiler support for COM. By using the `#import` directive with a type library file, the preprocessor generates two header files: one describing the interface to the wrapper class and the other containing the implementation. What's nice is that no source code is added to your project, which subsequently means less code to maintain. The syntax for using the `#import` directive is

```
#import <filename> [attributes]
using namespace <library name>;
```

<*filename*> is the name of the file containing the type library information. This file can be any of the following or any other file format that the `LoadTypeLib` API can understand:

- A type library file (.tlb or .olb)
- An executable file (.exe)
- A dynamic link library file (.dll) containing a type library resource
- A compound document holding a type library

NOTE Refer to Visual C++'s online documentation for a description of all the available attributes.

To prevent name collisions between the imported component and your existing code, the compiler defines a namespace identified by the type library name. A ***namespace*** is a declarative region that attaches an additional identifier to any names declared inside it. To identify a member of a namespace, the scope resolution operator is used:

```
<namespace>::<member>
```

To avoid typing the scope resolution throughout your code, the `using namespace` line directly after the `#import` line is incorporated and includes the library name.

To incorporate the Internet Explorer component into your application by using the `#import` directive, follow these steps:

1. Insert the following lines of code into the dialog box class's header file:

```
#import "C:\WINNT\System32\shdocvw.dll" rename("tagREADYSTATE",
➥"tagIEREADYSTATE")
using namespace SHDocVw;
```

NOTE You need to rename `tagREADYSTATE` to `tagIEREADYSTATE` to prevent a name collision inside the compiler-generated implementation files.

2. In the class declaration section, declare the following data member:

```
IWebBrowserAppPtr m_oIWebBrowserAppPtr;
```

This creates an object of the smart pointer class that encapsulates the interface.

Classes Created by the ClassWizard If you used the ClassWizard to incorporate the code component into your project, you'll be creating an object of the class that was derived from the `COleDispatchDriver` class. Member functions inherited from this class provide the means of instantiating the COM object and retrieving and releasing its dispatch interface. The following are the basic steps of using a class derived from `COleDispatchDriver`:

NOTE Assume that `IChildClass`, a class created by the ClassWizard, exists for these steps.

1. Declare a data member of type `IChildClass`.
2. Call the `COleDispatchDriver::CreateDispatch` function to load the server program and retrieve the `IDispatch` pointer. This increments the object's reference count by 1.
3. When you're finished with the component, release `IDispatch` and decrement the reference count by calling the `COleDispatchDriver::ReleaseDispatch()` function.

In the sample application, the ClassWizard created and inserted `IWebBrowserApp` into your project. You use the Internet Explorer component in your application as follows:

1. In the header file for the dialog box class (InterNavVCPPDlg.h, in this case), insert the three boldface lines of code shown in Listing 9.2.

Listing 9.2 Adding the Internet Explorer Component as an *IWebBrowserApp Object*

```
// InterNavVCPPDlg.h : header file
//
//{{AFX_INCLUDES()
#include "richtext.h"
//}}AFX_INCLUDES

#include "shdocvw.h"     //Contains the declaration of the IWebBrowserApp class

#if
➥!defined(AFX_INTERNAVVCPPDLG_H__FF98D69A_FFDE_11D0_83C1_000000000000__INCLUDED_)
#define AFX_INTERNAVVCPPDLG_H__FF98D69A_FFDE_11D0_83C1_000000000000__INCLUDED_

.
.
.

// Implementation
protected:
    CInterNavVCPPDlgAutoProxy* m_pAutoProxy;
    HICON m_hIcon;

    VARIANT vDummy;                       //Argument for
                                          //IWebBrowserApp::Navigate()
    IWebBrowserApp m_oInternetExplorer;   //Declaration IWebBrowserApp object

    BOOL CanExit();

.
.
.

#endif //
➥!defined(AFX_INTERNAVVCPPDLG_H__FF98D69A_FFDE_11D0_83C1_000000000000__INCLUDED_)
```

2. In the implementation file for the dialog box class, insert the following boldface lines into the dialog box class's constructor:

```
CInterNavVCPPDlg::CInterNavVCPPDlg(CWnd* pParent /*=NULL*/)
: CDialog(CInterNavVCPPDlg::IDD, pParent)
{
    //{{AFX_DATA_INIT(CInterNavVCPPDlg)
        // NOTE: the ClassWizard will add member initialization here
    //}}AFX_DATA_INIT
    // Note that LoadIcon does not require a subsequent DestroyIcon in Win32
    m_hIcon = AfxGetApp()->LoadIcon(IDR_MAINFRAME);
    m_pAutoProxy = NULL;

    //Initial the dummy argument that will be passed to the
    //IWebBrowserApp::Navigate function
    vDummy.vt = VT_EMPTY;

    //Create an instance of the InternetExplorer.Application object
    //and retrieve its dispatch interface
    m_oInternetExplorer.CreateDispatch("InternetExplorer.Application.1");

}
```


3. Insert the following boldface line of code into the dialog box class's destructor:

```
CInterNavVCPPDlg::~CInterNavVCPPDlg()
{
    // If there is an automation proxy for this dialog, set
    //  its back pointer to this dialog to NULL, so it knows
    //  the dialog has been deleted.
    if (m_pAutoProxy != NULL)
        m_pAutoProxy->m_pDialog = NULL;

    //Release the dispatch interface and decrement the object's
    //reference count
    m_oInternetExplorer.ReleaseDispatch();

}
```

4. Change the code inside the command button's click event handler function to call the `IWebBrowserApp::Navigate` and `IWebBrowserApp::SetVisible` member functions:

```
void CInterNavVCPPDlg::OnClickSscommand1()
{

    m_oInternetExplorer.Navigate(m_oRichText.GetText(),
                                 &vDummy,
                        &vDummy,
                        &vDummy,
                        &vDummy);

    m_oInternetExplorer.SetVisible(TRUE);

}
```

5. Compile and run the application, making sure that you have Internet service provided to you. Type a valid URL in the text box and click the Navigate button. Internet Explorer should be launched and the respective web page brought into view.

Classes Created by the *#import* Directive If you've used the `#import` directive to create your dispatch interface wrapper class, you'll be using the `_com_ptr_t` template class to access the component's members. `_com_ptr_t`, known as a *smart pointer*, encapsulates a raw interface pointer and handles the creating, reference adding, and releasing of the component object automatically. The `_com_ptr_t` class is hidden in the `_COM_SMARTPTR_TYPEDEF` macro located in the .tlh file created by the `#import` directive. For example, in the shdocvw.tlh file, the following macro is found for the `IWebBrowserApp` interface:

```
COM_SMARTPTR_TYPEDEF(IWebBrowserApp, __uuidof(IWebBrowserApp));
```

This will get expanded by the compiler to the following:

```
typedef _com_ptr_t<_com_IIID<IWebBrowserApp, __uuidof(IWebBrowserApp)>
    IWebBrowserAppPtr;
```

You'll use this class, `IWebBrowserAppPtr`, in your code to use the Internet Explorer component.

Returning to the sample application, follow these steps to incorporate the Internet Explorer component:

1. In the header file for the dialog box class (InterNavVCPPDlg.h, in this case), insert the four boldface lines of code shown in Listing 9.3.

Listing 9.3 Adding the Internet Explorer Component as an *IWebBrowserAppPtr Object*

```
// InterNavVCPPDlg.h : header file
//
//{{AFX_INCLUDES()
#include "richtext.h"
//}}AFX_INCLUDES

#import "C:\WINNT\System32\shdocvw.dll" rename ("tagREADYSTATE",
➥"tagIEREADYSTATE")
using namespace SHDocVw;

#if
!defined(AFX_INTERNAVVCPPDLG_H__FF98D69A_FFDE_11D0_83C1_000000000000__INCLUDED_)
#define AFX_INTERNAVVCPPDLG_H__FF98D69A_FFDE_11D0_83C1_000000000000__INCLUDED_

 .
 .
 .

// Implementation
protected:
    CInterNavVCPPDlgAutoProxy* m_pAutoProxy;
    HICON m_hIcon;

    VARIANT vDummy;                           //Argument for
                                              //IWebBrowserApp::Navigate()
    IWebBrowserAppPtr m_oInternetExplorer;    //Declaration IWebBrowserApp object

    BOOL CanExit();
```

```
.
.
.
n
//{{AFX_INSERT_LOCATION}}
// Microsoft Developer Studio will insert additional declarations immediately
//before the previous line.

#endif //
!defined(AFX_INTERNAVVCPPDLG_H__FF98D69A_FFDE_11D0_83C1_000000000000__INCLUDED_)
```


2. In the implementation file for the dialog box class, insert the following boldface lines into the dialog box class's constructor:

```
CInterNavVCPPDlg::CInterNavVCPPDlg(CWnd* pParent /*=NULL*/)
: CDialog(CInterNavVCPPDlg::IDD, pParent)
{
    //{{AFX_DATA_INIT(CInterNavVCPPDlg)
        // NOTE: the ClassWizard will add member initialization here
    //}}AFX_DATA_INIT
    // Note that LoadIcon does not require a subsequent DestroyIcon in Win32
    m_hIcon = AfxGetApp()->LoadIcon(IDR_MAINFRAME);
    m_pAutoProxy = NULL;

    //Initial the dummy argument that will be passed to the
    //IWebBrowserApp::Navigate function
    vDummy.vt = VT_EMPTY;

    //Create an instance of the InternetExplorer.Application object
    //and retrieve its dispatch interface
    m_oInternetExplorer.CreateInstance("InternetExplorer.Application.1");
}
```

NOTE When an object of the `_com_ptr_t` class leaves scope, the `Release` method of the interface pointer is called automatically. There's no need to explicitly release the reference as was the case for the class derived from `COleDispatchDriver`.

3. Change the code inside the command button's click event handler function to call the `IWebBrowserApp::Navigate` and `IWebBrowserApp::SetVisible` member functions:

```
void CInterNavVCPPDlg::OnClickSscommand1()
{

    m_oInternetExplorer ->Navigate((LPCSTR)m_oRichText.GetText(),,
                                    &vDummy,
                             &vDummy,
                             &vDummy,
                             &vDummy);

    m_oInternetExplorer ->PutVisible(TRUE);
}
```

4. Compile and run the application.

From Here...

In this chapter, you've been introduced to the types of ActiveX components typical in a client/server environment. Also, you've learned the techniques to install and register ActiveX components to be accessed on a local or remote machine. You've also seen the steps necessary in incorporating ActiveX components into Visual Basic and Visual C++ applications.

- For information on COM and ActiveX technologies, see Chapter 4, "Using Microsoft's Object Technologies."
- For information on creating ActiveX components, see Chapter 5, "Creating ActiveX Components with Visual Basic"; Chapter 6, "Creating Components with Visual C++"; and Chapter 7, "Creating Components with Visual J++."
- For information on where to locate functionality in a client/server environment, see Chapter 20, "Clients, Servers, and Components: Design Strategies for Distributed Applications."

PART III

Developing Internet, Intranet, and Extranet Applications

CHAPTER 10

Clients, Servers, and Components: Web-Based Applications

by Azam A. Mirza

Client or server?

Learn about the issues involved in client-side versus server-side functionality in terms of system performance, security, ease of maintenance, and future upgradeability.

Software development evolution

Learn about the evolution of software development from the mainframe-based large monolithic systems to the distributed client/server paradigm to the I-net environment.

The I-net architecture

Understand the concepts of I-net application development and the similarities between the I-net architecture and traditional client/server environments.

Client components

Explore the various components that make up the client side of the I-net architecture.

Web-enabling the data warehouse

Learn how the web server can be utilized as a single point of entry into the enterprise data warehouse and the other server components that provide functionality in I-net environments.

The last two years or so have been an exciting time to be a software engineer. The Internet has had a profound effect on the computing world. Not only have we seen a shift in the way we perceive computers and how they affect our lives, but we have witnessed a transformation in the way organizations view their core businesses and how computers and the Internet play a role in bringing them into the information age.

The Internet has brought a number of technologies, tools, and languages to the forefront of the computing world. For example, the TCP/IP protocol has become the de facto standard for networking across the globe. The HTTP and HTML protocols have been widely accepted and embraced as the mechanisms for information dissemination across the World Wide Web. The SMTP protocol is fast becoming the standard for global communications through electronic mail. The list goes on and on.

The software development principle has not been insulated from the sweeping changes being experienced by the computing world. The World Wide Web has changed the way we design, build, deploy, and use applications.

The web has made it necessary for programmers to pay attention to the client browser and the web server as important and necessary ingredients when developing future applications.

This chapter discusses the issues involved with client/server development in I-net environments and the evolution of application development from the mainframe-based monolithic applications, to the various flavors of client/server architectures, to the newly introduced I-net application development paradigm. This chapter explores the pieces that together provide a solution for building I-net applications and how each piece of the puzzle fits into the application development process. ■

Client or Server?

Deciding what software to put on the client system and what to put on the server is crucial for the success of an I-net project. Performance, security, and upgradeability are three of the key areas that affect software placement. Additionally, if you want to store user preferences, you need to decide where to put the functionality, on the client or the server.

Performance

The response time of the system to the user can be important in having effective software. Putting unnecessary elements on the server will slow the speed of the response by virtue of sending data through network traffic, waiting for the server to validate the data, and then sending a response. Validating data on the client system whenever possible can save much in the response time of the system. This does not mean validating passwords, but rather checking to make certain that all required data is present and maybe doing some simple computations. For example, if you were designing a system where the user can purchase goods, perhaps you would have the client software compute the total and display it to the user without ever going to the server. The user can make a more informed decision more quickly, and the server does not have to continually receive data, do simple processing, and send the data back.

Keeping the database on the server side is a logical way and, most of the time, the only way to design a system. Sending the client a copy of the database would be time-consuming, and it would be difficult to keep the client copy of the database in sync with the server copy.

This scheme for preserving the performance of the system also helps to conserve server resources by reducing the server load. Additionally, it is important to curb the traffic over the network.

Security

By the same token, it is best for some processing to be done on the server. Anything requiring password validation should always be done on the server. Password validation on the client would be impractical and dangerous. The client machine would have to have access to viable passwords, and an unscrupulous user could gain unauthorized access to the server.

In addition, servers provide a physically secure location for storing sensitive user data and important files. It is much easier to isolate a server in a secure location than to do so for a lot of client machines.

Upgradeability

One other area to consider when designing a system is the upgradeability of the system for the future. Putting certain components on the client machine can cause the need to upgrade every client machine when a software change needs to be made. For example, if you decide that every machine needs to have an ActiveX control to handle certain processing, then the control needs to be downloaded or installed on every machine. Later, when you decide that the control is not meeting requirements and needs to be changed, the control again must be installed on every computer. If you had put the processing on the server, you would need to update the software in only one place.

The following are some guidelines summing up where the functionality should be placed, on the client or the server.

For the client:

- Validate user-entered data, such as making certain that required fields are not blank.
- Simple processing and display, such as computing the total cost that a customer has spent.

For the server:

- Access to the database, files, or libraries stored on the server
- Password validation
- Managing client sessions
- Processing of data where the algorithm is confidential

User Preferences

User preferences are settings that allow a web page to be tailored to a specific desire. For example, if you are browsing a page displaying the current stock market prices, perhaps only the stocks that you are interested in are displayed.

Where to store the information concerning user preferences can be an important and difficult decision. There are two main choices to make: Either the user has to log in, or the data has to be kept on the client computer.

The Yahoo! Finance web site (**quote.yahoo.com**) uses a server-side database to store user preferences and portfolio information. It requires users to set up a login ID and password to access the user preference information.

If the user is required to log in to the system, user preferences could be stored in a server-side database. This is particularly crucial if the information should be restricted to only particular users. For example, in a corporate intranet, the president of the company could have a page tailored to show confidential information, and another employee would not have access to the same information.

You can set up client-side preferences in two ways: You could write a client-side component, or, more commonly, you could use magic cookies.

If the security of the data is not an issue, magic cookies can be a solution to custom-tailoring web pages. The type of user preferences considered here are the layout of the web page and what non-confidential data should be displayed. Magic cookies or cookies are information that can be stored on the client machine. The following are some problems with cookies that developers should be aware of:

Cookie files typically reside on the user's system in the directory c:\<*Systemroot*>\Cookies, for example, c:\winnt\cookies. A cookie file is a data file usually with the .DAT extension that stores information in a binary format.

- Each browser on a computer has its own cookie file. That means a user will not get consistent information accessing the same site from the same computer using different browsers.
- Different users on the same machine get the same information if using the same browser.
- The same user on a different computer will not get the same information.
- A cookie file can hold at maximum 300 cookie entries with arbitrary deletion, meaning that entries can be deleted and added without any kind of restrictions after the 300-entry maximum is reached.
- A cookie file can hold at maximum 20 cookie entries for a particular IP address.
- A user is free to delete or modify cookie files.
- A user can prevent a cookie from being set or sent.

With all these problems with cookies, why should you use them? The typical user will use a single browser on a single computer and will not edit cookie files. Cookies are extremely useful in maintaining state.

Cookies can be comfortably used to maintain information about where the user has accessed information. For example, when a user accesses **http://ESPN.SportsZone.com/nfl/index.html**, a survey is often displayed. When the user fills out the page, a cookie is set, and then the page is reloaded. Instead of displaying the survey, the new page displays the results. If you had blocked the cookie from being set, the original page would be displayed. No severe damage would occur to the user or the web site. Similar results would occur if the user deleted, modified, or otherwise interfered with the cookie file. Clearly no confidential information should be stored with cookies.

The Evolution of Application Development Processes

Client/server computing has long been viewed as a plausible solution for building line-of-business applications. The main benefits of client/server computing were its distributed nature, the utilization of system resources in a more practical manner, and the cheaper cost of deployment compared to the older mainframe environments.

A single mainframe machine meant a single point of failure and inefficient use of system resources. Users performing unrelated tasks were forced to share the same system resources. Scalability was an issue because reaching the limits of the mainframe processing power resulted in upgrades to a costlier and bigger machine. Figure 10.1 shows the typical architecture of a mainframe environment.

FIG. 10.1
The mainframes handled all processing chores, and the clients used terminals to access online resources.

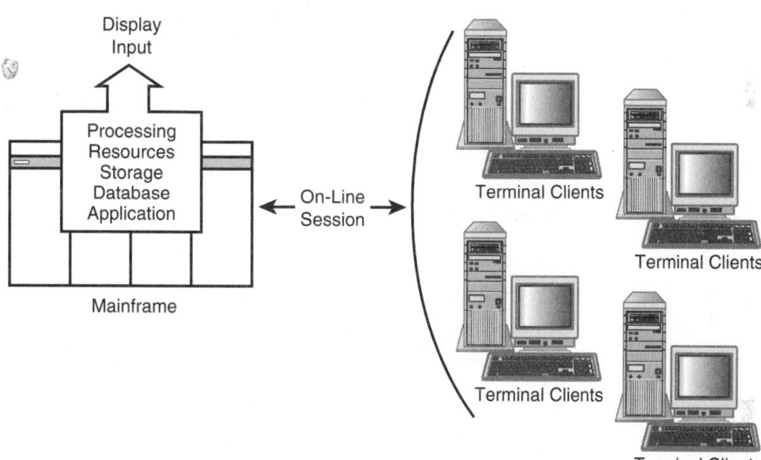

In contrast, client/server computing provides a flexible architecture for building a corporate infrastructure. By breaking up the processing chores between several smaller server machines, it is possible to better utilize the resources and processing power of the system as a whole. In addition, the clients are more than just dumb terminals; they are capable of handling many processing and user needs, such as running word processing software, without needing the server to accomplish their tasks. Figure 10.2 shows a typical client/server environment model.

However, client/server computing has its own pitfalls. In many cases, the deployment of multiple server machines within the enterprise resulted in a management nightmare. Rather than deploying and viewing the servers as a single logical unit, they were deployed and used as single, standalone machines, each working individually. Also, client/server environments demanded more sophistication on the part of the users. Users looking for a particular resource not only had to know where the resource was located but also had to know how to connect to it and use it. The client/server environment, for all its flexibility and power, was also a more difficult environment to learn and use.

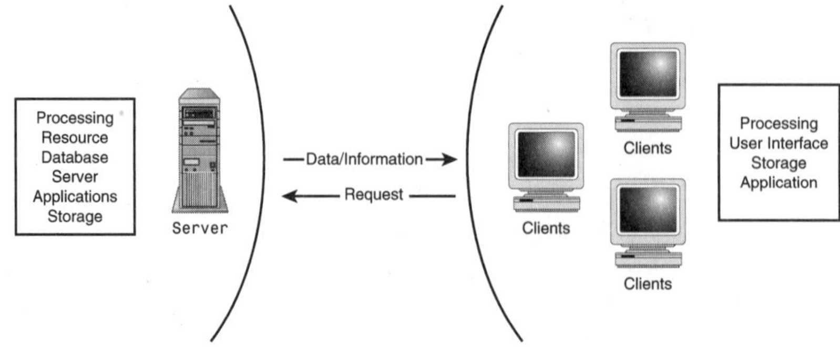

FIG. 10.2 Client/server computing places a larger burden on the user to determine where a particular resource is located.

For software developers, the jump from mainframes to client/server software development was just as difficult. In the mainframe world, applications were developed, compiled, and executed on the mainframe. The client's purpose was to provide a session into the mainframe system that could be used to execute applications. Figure 10.3 shows the software development life cycle as it exists in the mainframe world.

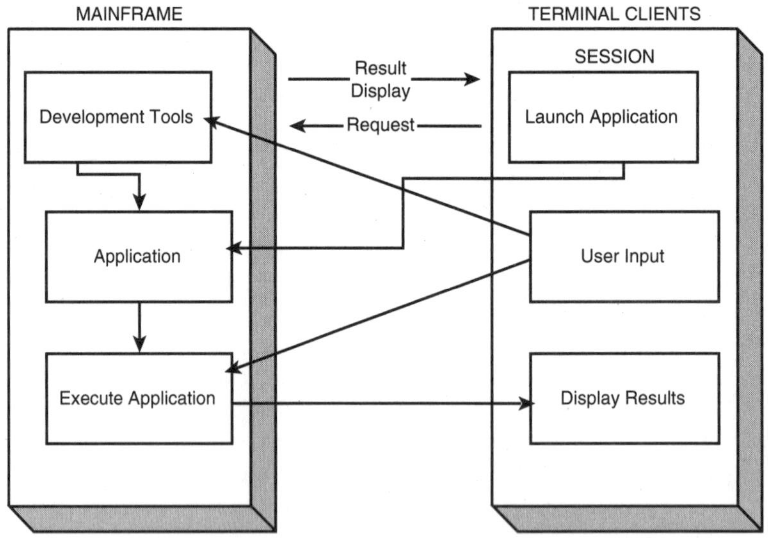

FIG. 10.3 The mainframe provides the development and the execution environment for applications accessed through the client.

With the popularity of the client/server environment, software development became more complex and difficult. Processing was now divided between client machines and server machines. Software developers have to decide where to put the functionality. Application development has become more than just writing code. Developers have to understand the concepts of application partitioning, user interface design, and networking protocols. Deciding where to put the functionality has become just as important as writing the code to implement it. Decisions have to be made to best utilize the processing power of the clients and the servers.

NOTE For example, an important decision that a developer faces in client/server environments is where to put the database query logic. Should it be implemented using stored procedures or should it be implemented using client-side SQL queries? The correct decision is usually based on the needs and design requirements of the application.

The complexity and difficulty of building client/server applications is offset by the awesome flexibility and power afforded by such an environment. Figure 10.4 illustrates the development life cycle for client/server environments.

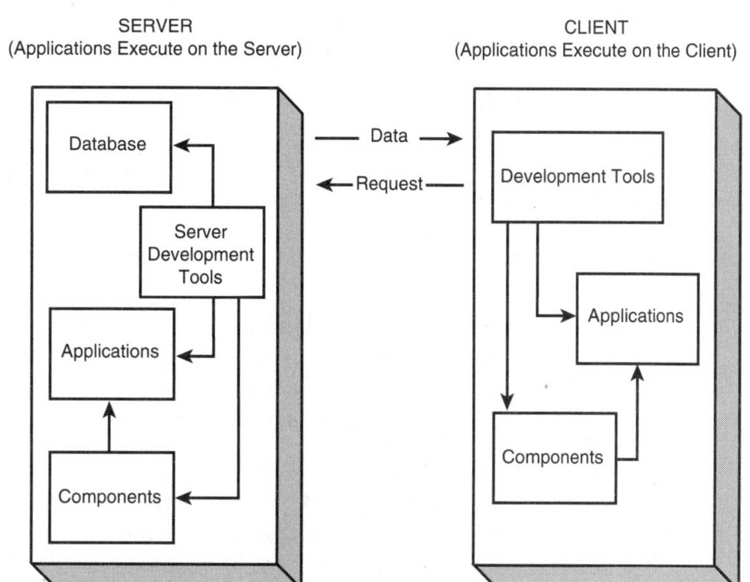

FIG. 10.4 Building client/server applications requires making decisions about where to put the functionality.

Typical client/server development projects include development efforts for building a client user interface and business logic and building and programming a database server. The common term for building database-enabled applications in such a setup is *two-tier client/server.* Figure 10.5 illustrates the two-tier client/server architecture.

Recent advancement in client/server computing has separated the business logic from the user interface. This is referred to as *three-tier client/server architecture.* The business logic units are modules that are independent of the client and the server and run on their own, providing a communication mechanism between the database and the client. This separates the client from having to handle logic processing and also insulates the client-side developers from having to program database-specific logic into their programs. Figure 10.6 illustrates the concept of three-tier client/server computing.

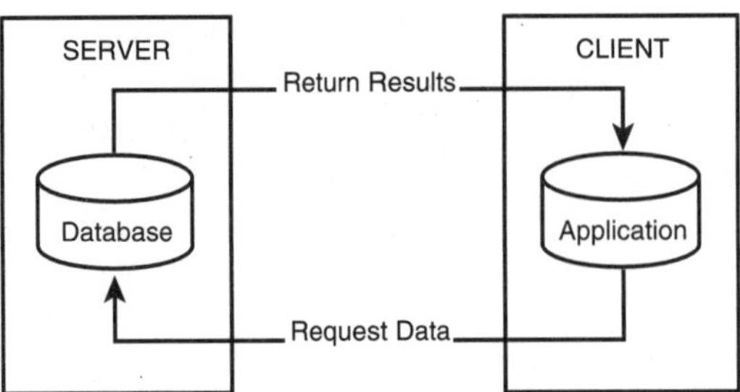

FIG. 10.5
Two-tier client/server architecture draws the line between the database server and the client component.

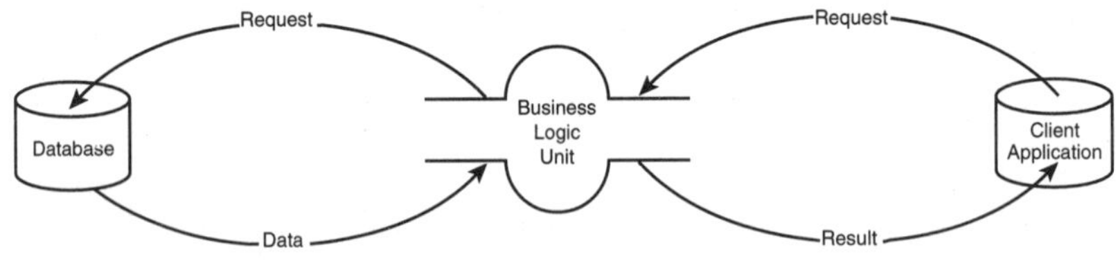

FIG. 10.6
The business logic unit takes care of connecting to the database server and obtaining data that can then be passed to the client machine for presentation to the user.

Three-tier client/server architectures afford developers more flexibility in building applications. Client-side developers need to worry only about interfacing with the business logic unit and not worry about the functionality of the database back end and how to query the database. They are assured of getting the pertinent data in a format they can handle.

The business logic unit handles formulating the appropriate database queries in response to client requests and talking to the database. Modifications can easily be made to each individual part of the system without having to change any of the other pieces in the system. The main benefit of business logic units is their ability to be developed and deployed once and then accessed multiple times from throughout an enterprise using client machines. The OLE Automation mechanism within the Windows operating system environment provides a mechanism for deployment of business logic units.

The logical extension of three-tier architectures is to develop applications that span multiple tiers. The most common example is the use of component-based software development mechanisms to break down an application's business logic units into multiple pieces that can be distributed throughout an enterprise and provide very specific functionality. Figure 10.7 illustrates the concept of distributed, multitier client/server environments.

By distributing components throughout machines in an enterprise, multitier architectures better utilize the processing power available. In addition, upgrades and enhancements to a particular component within an application can be carried out without having to reinstall the whole application on every client machine. Developers can replace the one instance of the component wherever it resides on the network, and all client machines using the component will instantly receive the upgraded functionality.

▶ **See** Chapter 21, "Creating Distributed Applications," **p. 575**

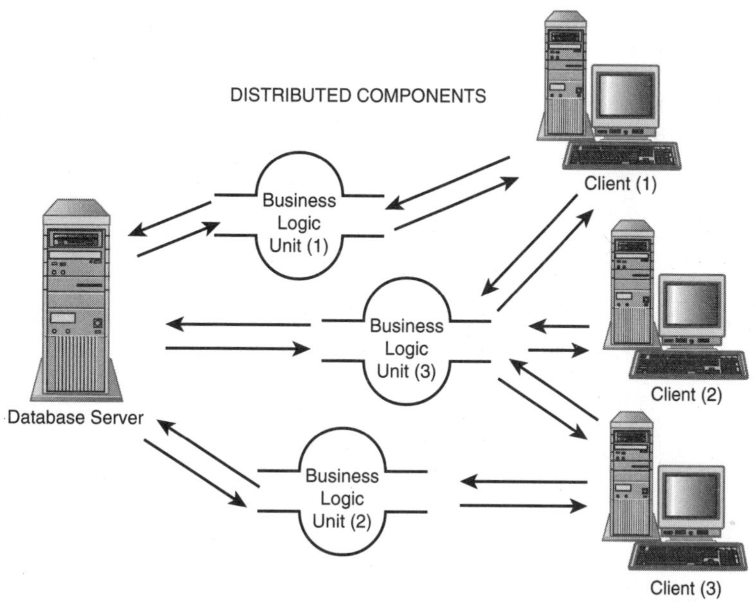

FIG. 10.7
Distributed client/server environments place processing needs where they can best utilize the available processing power.

The I-net architecture model takes the client/server concept to the next level. I-net is just another form of client/server computing that uses the web browser as the client and a web server as the back end in its most basic form. However, the I-net architecture provides significant benefits over client/server computing in terms of application development, deployment, and ease of use. The following section discusses the I-net architecture in more detail.

The I-net Architecture

As the world races to connect to the Internet, an unexpected phenomenon is taking place. Corporations trying to figure out profitable and beneficial uses for this emerging global network have found a way to enhance the power and usefulness of their own internal networks as well. The intranet, a younger and more contained sibling of the Internet, has emerged. The intranet is a scaled-down version of the Internet, not in functionality or features, but in size and scope. Figure 10.8 presents a sample intranet architecture.

Intranets are internal, corporatewide networks based on technology used for the Internet. Whereas the Internet provides corporate networks with connectivity to the global network of networks, intranets enable corporations to build internal, self-contained networks that have important advantages over existing network technologies.

NOTE I-net is a collective term that refers to the Internet, intranets, and extranets. *Extranets* are a collection of interconnected intranets. ■

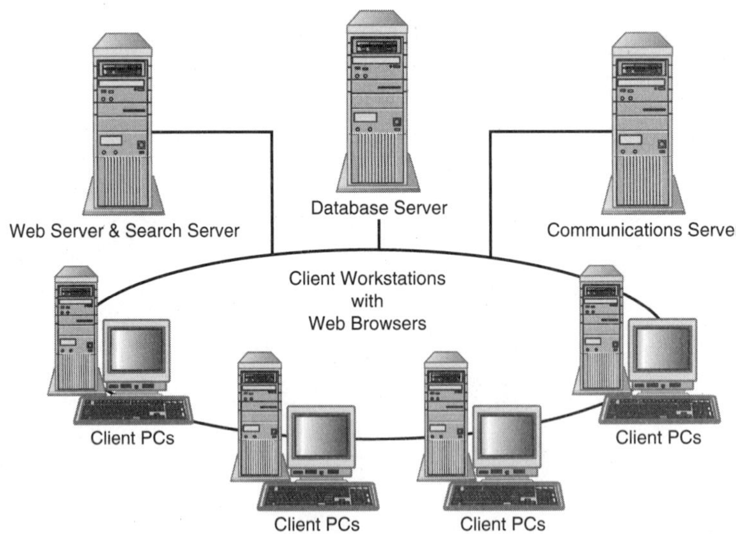

FIG. 10.8
An intranet can utilize existing resources within an enterprise to provide an I-net based client/server environment.

The I-net process model, and its network connectivity architecture, holds several major advantages over traditional networking architectures. First and foremost, companies are realizing the cost-effectiveness of the I-net architecture. It is relatively inexpensive to set up an internal I-net environment. The technologies at the core of an internal I-net setup are open, standards-based, and widely implemented. The server software for setting up a World Wide Web (WWW) server, often referred to as a *web server*, is available from a multitude of vendors such as Microsoft and Netscape. The client workstations use inexpensive and easy-to-use *web browser* software for connecting to the web server. The networking infrastructure needed for setting up a basic I-net is already in place in most corporations. In addition, with the integrated Internet Explorer browser in the upcoming Windows 98, the familiarity and intuitiveness of this model will increase on the user side.

NOTE A rapidly growing intranet might eventually place extensive demands on an existing infrastructure in terms of hardware and networking resources and might necessitate upgrades.

Second, I-nets implement a hybrid architecture that brings together the best features of the client/server process model with those of the host-based process model. The I-net architecture is geared towards ease of deployment, centralized control of information, and simple administration of resources. In the I-net process model, the server is responsible for providing information and requested data to the intended users. In addition, the server holds the key to the graphical user interface presented to the user through the client browser software. Client workstations (typically desktop PCs) use web browser software to display information sent by the server. The server controls the layout and content of the information. This makes management and administration of information very reliable because it is centralized.

However, the client is not just a dumb terminal. It does perform operations such as information caching and local storage of information downloaded by the user. In other words, the I-net architecture is a process model that takes the best from the client/server world and combines it with the best attributes of the traditional host-based architecture employed by mainframes and minicomputers.

Finally, an important advantage of I-nets is their ability to bring together heterogeneous systems into a common interoperable network. The corporate world has spent millions of dollars and many years trying to connect disparate and incompatible systems into a seamless network. The results have not been completely satisfactory. Because the I-net architecture was developed from the ground up to be able to connect disparate systems together, it lends itself well to the corporate culture in most organizations where different systems such as PCs, Macs, and UNIX-based workstations must coexist.

In terms of software development, the most important and significant benefit of using an I-net environment for building and deploying applications is the capability to create cross-platform applications without the cost of creating and distributing multiple versions of the application. Applications that use the web browser on the client and use the web server as an interface between the browser and the application server, or database server, on the back end generate HTML output that can be viewed by users on any platform that supports a web browser. Figure 10.9 illustrates the concept.

FIG. 10.9
The web server provides a single point of entry for all access to back-end application and database servers.

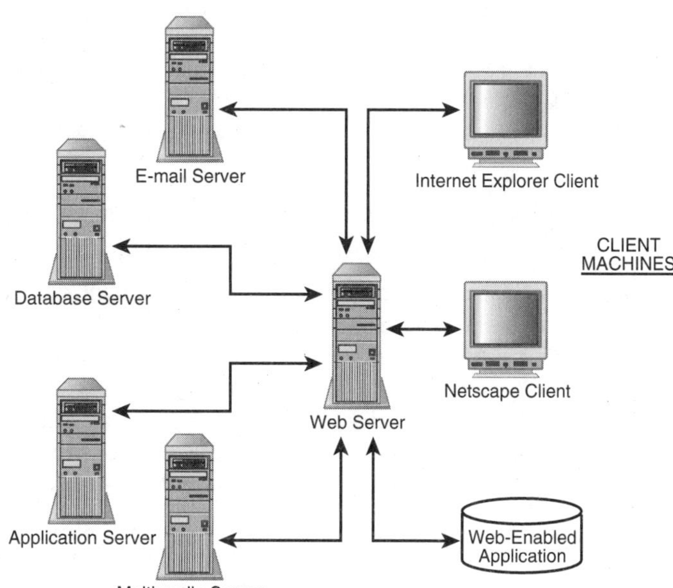

The centralized maintenance and administration of I-net–based applications is another important benefit. The cost of maintenance and enhancements to distributed client/server applications is much greater than the cost of maintenance of I-net applications. Changes made to web-based applications on the server take effect immediately for all users, eliminating the need for individual changes to each and every client machine. I-net applications that take advantage of client-side components such as Java applets or ActiveX controls can utilize the automatic download capabilities of the browser to get a newer version of the component when it becomes available.

NOTE Microsoft Internet Explorer is an example of a web browser that automatically checks to see if a newer version of a client-side component is available for download and upgrades the component on the client machine. The browser does give the user a chance to either accept or reject the upgrade.

The following sections discuss the various components that come together to provide the functionality for building applications in an I-net environment.

The Client

In a typical I-net environment, client workstations use a networked environment to connect to servers that facilitate requests for information and data. At its most basic level, an I-net requires a single web server, a network infrastructure based on the TCP/IP networking protocol, and client workstations running a web browser. At the other end of the spectrum, an I-net can consist of hundreds of web servers and thousands of client browsers located all around the world, connected through a complex array of networking components.

Client workstations can comprise a multitude of machines and operating systems in a large, heterogeneous corporate environment. I-nets provide a means for bringing all these disparate systems together into a cohesive and interoperable network.

In the I-net world, hardware has become a less important factor, with greater emphasis being placed on the software systems running on client machines. Due to companies such as Netscape providing web browsers for multiple platforms, it is not as important to worry about hardware conformity across the organization when dealing with I-net technology. The use of traditional applications and tools should govern client hardware choices. As far as I-net connectivity is concerned, hardware issues have so far been confined to maximizing network throughput through faster connections and the speed and capabilities of the graphical subsystem.

The software components that enable client workstations to connect to and use an I-net environment are

- Web browsers
- Communication tools
- Components

The following sections discuss these client software components, which are used in most I-net implementations.

Web Browsers

The web browser is the most basic and common client tool used for accessing web servers. The web browser displays the information retrieved from web servers on client workstations. The web browser has become an important piece of the web software puzzle. The idea of developing applications independent of client considerations has become a reality with the concept of the web browser and web server paradigm. The web browser extends the concept of clients to the next level by providing a standards-based mechanism for accessing information. It uses the hypertext protocol and standard networking mechanisms to accomplish its tasks.

Browsers are clever programs that can interpret information sent by the user in a multitude of ways. They can format and display textual information based on web server directives. In addition, browsers can render graphics, video, and audio information.

Most browsers also have the capability for add-on tools and extensions to be installed and integrated, such as video players, audio players, file and graphics viewers, discussion group and chat facilitators, email clients, and other tools to enhance the basic functionality of the browser.

The marketplace for browsers is heavily crowded with entries from numerous vendors. However, the two most widely used web browsers currently available are Netscape Navigator and Microsoft Internet Explorer. Both browsers are solid products that offer high performance, extensive features, support for industry standards, and in the case of Netscape Navigator, availability on 16 different operating system platforms.

NOTE With its release of version 4.0 of the Internet Explorer product, Microsoft has significantly closed the gap between the two products. However, Internet Explorer 4.0 is available only on Windows 3.1, Windows 95, and Windows NT, with UNIX and Macintosh support forthcoming. For organizations looking to implement I-net solutions in diverse and heterogeneous environments, Netscape Navigator currently provides the most flexibility.

Communication Tools

In addition to the web browser, a client workstation will have tools installed for communications purposes. Most common among these are tools for email messaging systems and for reading and posting to discussion groups. In addition, tools are becoming available for using the multimedia hardware on client workstations (speakers and microphone) to provide digital phone facilities over the Internet. Users can speak to each other using their computers rather than a traditional telephone. There are also tools for providing live feeds of television and radio broadcasts.

These tools can be effectively used to provide users with I-net–based digital phone capabilities, the ability to bring seminars, presentations, and educational training to user desktops, and the ability to provide video-conferencing facilities for users in different geographic locations.

Components

Browsers such as Navigator and Internet Explorer support plug-in additions for enhancing their functionality with third-party tools. Both companies have published specifications for supporting plug-ins. This capability is a powerful mechanism that allows developers to add custom functionality to the browsers.

The Internet Explorer web browser components can be compared to Microsoft's VBX/OCX controls that were introduced through Visual Basic and Visual C++. Microsoft's components are referred to as ActiveX controls, and they are the next generation of OCX controls specifically designed for use in an I-net environment.

▶ **See** Chapter 8, "Using ActiveX Client Components in an I-net Environment," **p. 239**

In addition to ActiveX controls, both Internet Explorer and Navigator support Java language applets, which are plug-in components, based on the Java language developed by Sun Microsystems. In the short time since their introduction, these two control-building methods have started generating the same kind of industry support that resulted in the huge third-party market for VBX custom controls for Visual Basic.

The Server

Although the client has garnered the lion's share of attention in the development community because of its emphasis on the web browser, the Java language, and the support for applets and controls, the most critical component of any I-net infrastructure is the server hardware platform and operating system. The selection criteria for server platforms include the following:

- High performance
- Scalability (the ability to expand as needs change)
- Powerful operating system administration and management tools
- High throughput hardware systems for both networking and storage media
- Strong security features

Due to the graphical nature of information being handled by I-net–based networks, performance capabilities of the server hardware are an important consideration. In particular, the hard disk subsystem and the network interface must provide good throughput and reliable operation.

The server platform will house a variety of software components to provide various services to I-net users. Some of the major server components of an I-net architecture are

- The World Wide Web server
- The database server
- The communication server
- The search server

- The multimedia services server
- The proxy server

The following sections describe these server components in more detail. Each of these services can be installed on a single machine or can be spread across multiple machines for better performance and manageability.

The World Wide Web Server

The basic software component that brings together the power of I-nets is the web server software. Web server software allows client machines access to information by facilitating information publishing, application execution, and data retrieval.

Most web server software packages such as Microsoft's Internet Information Server (IIS), various Netscape server products, and O'Reilly's WebSite provide a comprehensive set of setup, management, and administration facilities. In many cases, a basic and functional web server can be installed, set up, and made operational within an hour. In addition, all server packages include sophisticated system administration utilities such as the Server Manager utility included with Microsoft Internet Information Server.

Until recently, most web servers stored static information for access by clients. With the introduction of technologies such as Java applets, ActiveX controls, and database access tools, web servers have become more than just repositories for publishing static information. Web servers are now capable of providing such powerful capabilities as user authentication, connectivity to database servers, dynamic web page creation based on user actions, database query resolution, and data encryption. This list is not exhaustive, but is intended to provide an indication of the advances that have been made in the last year or so in the capabilities of web server software.

Microsoft's IIS deserves special mention due to its integration with the Windows NT Server operating system, and with the security subsystem in particular. Because of this tight integration, IIS offers the following capabilities:

- IIS can use the built-in Windows NT Server security model for user authentication and password validation.
- Authenticating users against the Windows NT domain user account database can control user access to the I-net.
- File and directory access from an intranet can be controlled by setting permissions for user groups through the usual Windows NT permissions mechanisms.
- Traffic analysis and performance monitoring can be performed using the Windows NT Performance Monitor utility.
- Logging can be performed using the Windows NT Event Log.

▶ **See** Chapter 13, "An Inside Look at Active Server Pages and Internet Information Server," **p. 363**

The Database Server

The database server is a recent addition to the I-net phenomenon. Most web implementations were using flat files or proprietary systems for storing data and information. However, because most organizations already have large databases installed and operational, it was an obvious choice to use the database as a repository for information being published on the web.

In addition, corporations provide users access to corporate data through applications written to access the databases. If most data resides in existing relational database systems and an organization wants to replace its proprietary applications with I-net–based applications, mechanisms are needed to facilitate the flow of information to and from the database servers and the web server.

Extensions to standards such as ODBC (Open Database Connectivity) and the introduction of standards such as ISAPI (Internet Server Application Programming Interface) have made it possible for web servers to connect to database servers and access corporate data. The connectivity between web servers and database servers provides a means for making corporate data available to users. The traditional client/server database applications are being replaced by web-based database applications. In the years to come, database servers will become an integral part of the I-net infrastructure as more and more database-enabled applications are implemented for use on the I-net platform.

Microsoft provides support for building database-enabled applications with a product such as Microsoft Access or Microsoft SQL Server. Access is a workgroup database designed for small and medium-sized applications with a few megabytes of data at most and a small user base. SQL Server is designed to be the database for the enterprise that can handle large volumes of data and a large number of users. Typical SQL Server database sizes range from a few hundred megabytes to a terabyte with hundreds or thousands of users.

NOTE Visual Studio 97 includes a Developer's Edition of SQL Server 6.5 for use as part of database-enabled development efforts. This edition is only restricted in the number of client connections it supports from the full retail version. ■

The Communication Server

Communication servers facilitate information exchange between users. They provide functionality for

- *Electronic mail (email)*—A messaging system for exchanging information between users
- *Bulletin boards*—A "sticky notes" system for disseminating information to a group of users
- *Discussion groups*—A forum for exchanging ideas and engaging in discussions on various topics
- *Chat rooms*—A place where users can interactively "talk" to each other
- *Remote access*—Allows users remote connection to the I-net through dial-up networking

Communications servers work in conjunction with web servers to provide a seamless means for users to interact with the I-net and with each other. Communications servers also provide secure connectivity through email gateways to the outside world. Users can send and receive email messages to people all around the world using their web browser or other email software package.

Microsoft Exchange Server is the centerpiece of the communication server strategy Microsoft is pursuing. It is a full-blown workgroup, collaboration, email, and discussion group system that scales very well to large amounts of data and user bases.

The Search Server

Search servers, also called *search engines*, implement powerful search and indexing mechanisms to provide users with a means for finding information. Over time, an I-net site can become a large and complex collection of published information, structured data, and applications. A well-developed I-net site must enable users to do searches on the information in the system based on their own criteria. Most available search servers allow users to search the system using multiple criteria and to define the scope of their search.

Search servers accomplish their task by cataloging and indexing the information being published on the web site. As new information is added to the web site, a search engine will update its indices to reflect these changes.

The most critical aspect of search mechanisms is the ability to provide search results in a fast, efficient, and error-free manner. Speed becomes an important issue as the size of a web site grows. A well-designed search engine can handle large, complex searches and enhance the usefulness of the information.

NOTE Search servers are different than search engines such as Yahoo! and Lycos, which provide a searching mechanism for the entire Internet. Search servers are specifically used to catalog a particular web site. For example, the search button on the Microsoft web site uses a search server for user queries.

ON THE WEB

For more information about the Microsoft Search Server, refer to the Microsoft web site at **www.microsoft.com**.

The Multimedia Services Server

Multimedia servers provide support for high speed streaming media such as video and audio. Multimedia servers use high-speed links to provide corporate customers access to live or prerecorded multimedia content.

One of the most compelling applications for multimedia servers is to provide support for live audio and video communications. Users can interact with each other through sight and sound rather than using text-based messages.

Another application for multimedia servers is to make it possible for corporations to allow users access to computer-based training classes using audiovisual mechanisms. Users can access video catalogs of seminars and training classes and view them using their browser software or other multimedia clients.

Microsoft NetShow provides support for enabling multimedia capabilities as part of your web site. Microsoft NetShow allows you to develop and present multimedia presentations and live video feeds as part of your web site. The NetShow client is needed to view content developed and broadcast with the NetShow Theater Server.

ON THE WEB

For more information about Microsoft NetShow, visit **www.microsoft.com/netshow/**.

Proxy Server

Proxy servers allow clients connecting to a corporate network to access the global Internet. Proxy servers provide a high-performance, secure, and reliable means for users to gain access to the Internet from within the corporate intranet.

Proxy servers also control access to web servers and other I-net resources. They support mechanisms for providing access to the WWW, FTP, Telnet, and other common Internet protocols. In addition, proxy servers also restrict access to an intranet from the Internet world. In effect, a proxy server is a security tool that polices the bidirectional flow of information between I-net networks.

Microsoft Proxy Server provides support for adding firewall and content-caching abilities as part of a web connection. If you are setting up an Internet connection, Microsoft Proxy Server can provide a secure and cost-effective solution for establishing a secure presence on the Internet.

ON THE WEB

For more information on the Microsoft Proxy Server, visit **www.microsoft.com/proxy**.

From Here...

This chapter looks at I-net architecture and how you can utilize I-net technologies to build applications that take advantage of the web browser and web server concept. I-net development is an extension of the traditional client/server environment that utilizes standard protocols and communications mechanisms to store, publish, and disseminate information.

- To learn about the database features and tools included with Visual Studio, see Chapter 3, "Creating Database-Aware Applications with Visual Studio."
- To learn about creating components using Visual Basic, see Chapter 5, "Creating ActiveX Components with Visual Basic."
- To learn about creating components using Visual C++, see Chapter 6, "Creating Components with Visual C++."
- To learn about creating components using Visual J++, see Chapter 7, "Creating Components with Visual J++."
- To learn about concepts associated with web-based application development, see Chapter 11, "An Inside Look at Web-Based Applications."
- To learn about the Visual Studio development environment, see Chapter 2, "Using Visual Studio to Create Applications."
- To learn more about strategies for application development in the enterprise, see Chapter 4, "Using Microsoft's Object Technologies."
- For a discussion of applications for client/server environments, see Chapter 20, "Clients, Servers, and Components: Design Strategies for Distributed Applications."
- For a more general discussion of distributed applications, see Chapter 21, "Creating Distributed Applications."

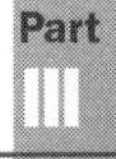

CHAPTER 11

An Inside Look at Web-Based Applications

by Anthony J. Taylor

As the face of business continually changes, organizations are attempting to respond to the new technology transitions as cost-effectively as possible while maintaining their present software solutions. Many are focusing their approach to making their information interactive and are concentrating on creating or improving web-based applications as the solution for the distribution of critical corporate information.

The current trend in distributing corporate information is the increase of web-based applications as corporate intranets. Dynamic web sites are truly distributed applications and have the following benefits, which companies are beginning to realize: content-centric design, low bandwidth access, ease of distribution, low maintenance cost, and cross-platform applications.

This chapter explores web-based applications and issues related to their development. It then discusses the use of Active Server Pages and the technologies behind them. Finally, it explains how these technologies fit into the Microsoft InterDev environment and how this new Integrated Development Environment (IDE) will enable successful creation of web-based applications.

The web browser as a client framework

See how the web browser functions as a client framework, and discover the differences between static and Dynamic HTML for the creation of web-based applications.

Internet Information Server with Active Server Pages

Learn about the functionality of Active Server Pages (ASP) and understand how database connectivity occurs through IIS.

Components of a dynamic web-based application

Learn how to apply the technologies described to create a dynamic web-based application.

InterDev's involvement in the web-based application environment

See how you easily can use Microsoft Visual InterDev to develop web-based applications.

The Web Browser as a Client Framework

The use of web browsers has evolved dramatically in the web-based environment. Now web browsers are used not only to access the static data housed on a web server, but also to change web content interactively. Before the development of recent technologies, the flow of data was from the server to the client only. Now, however, the application client and application server have a bidirectional flow of control (see Figure 11.1).

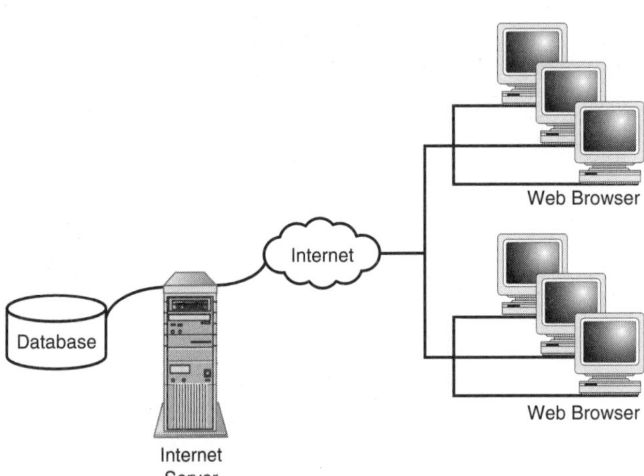

FIG. 11.1
The bidirectional flow of control in the web-based environment is possible because an operation is defined in a library class but implemented in a subclass in the application.

There are many benefits now that the web browser can be used as a client framework. Some benefits of a client framework include

- Reuse of design, saving time and effort
- More functionality because of the bidirectional flow of control
- Less code needed, making updating easier

Many companies have eagerly modified their existing applications to achieve these benefits. Web users no longer are disappointed to find stale information; they can view custom web content that responds interactively to their responses, whether they click the mouse or press a key.

As web browsers have evolved for usability as a client framework, other progressions have also occurred. The following sections briefly discuss the changes pertaining to application architecture and the transitions web developers must make.

The Evolving Application Architecture

As the application development environment evolves, the architecture needed for the new development arena has also progressed. Figures 11.2, 11.3, and 11.4 illustrate the evolution of the application architecture.

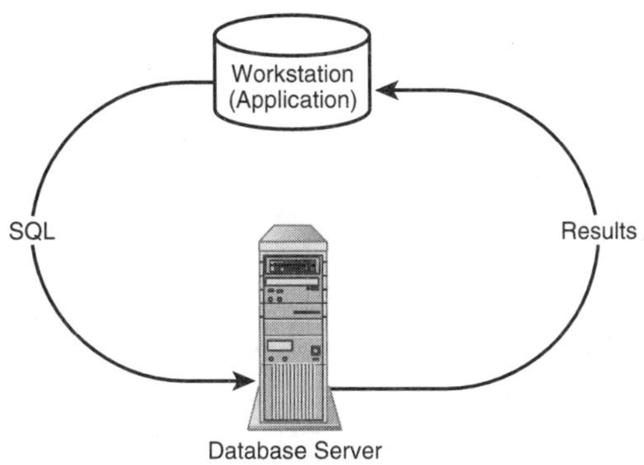

FIG. 11.2
The traditional client/server development platform was only a two-tiered environment structure.

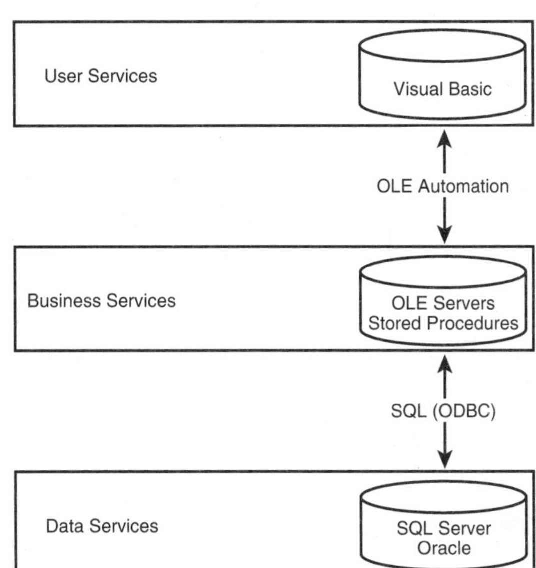

FIG. 11.3
Multiple user interfaces, security for business processes, and distributed processing are a few of the many advantages to multiple-tier architecture.

Web files can not only communicate on a local network, but also can be transferred via a global network to a web browser, making management of server-side scripts and component files more difficult. Although browser-based applications appear to be the solution to client-centric information, this new environment has its pros and cons, especially with the "standards wars" taking place.

Of the many proprietary web browsers, Microsoft Internet Explorer and Netscape Navigator are the current leaders. Many Application Programming Interfaces (APIs) also are on the market today—Microsoft ISAPI, Netscape NSAPI, WebSite WSAPI, and WebSTAR W*API, just to name a few. With so many vendor products in the marketplace, delivering universally readable HTML pages with features becomes difficult.

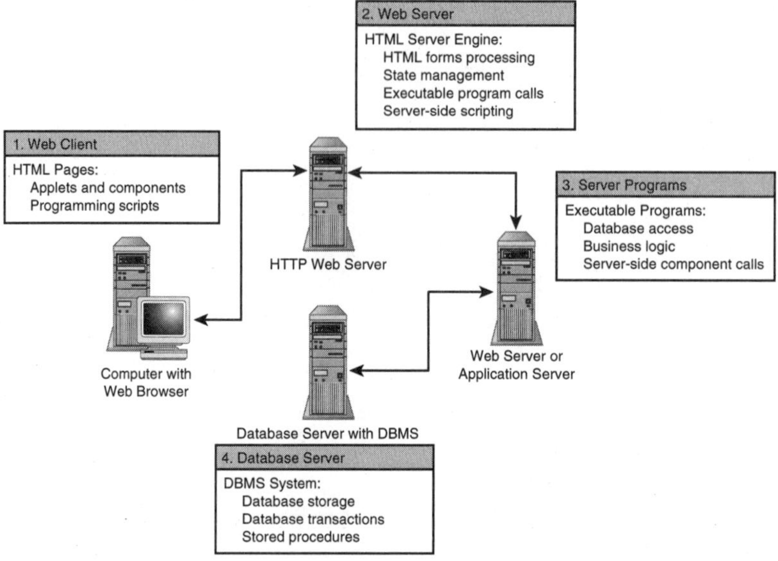

FIG. 11.4 The web development environment uses a complex assortment of hardware.

NOTE Despite the push for the convergence of web-based technology standards, we're beginning to see exactly the opposite. For example, Dynamic HTML standards have diverged between Microsoft and Netscape.

How can you resolve the problem, for example, of having a video file on an HTML page whose full-motion features many browsers can't view? Do you force one browser to be the standard by which every component is compatible, or do you create alternative images and file types for every web browser ever used to view a web page? These and other issues must be addressed when determining global standards for HTML, Java, Cascading Style Sheets (features and options to specify style, color, and font for HTML development), and other web-based technologies.

New Challenges for Developers

As a web-based application programmer, you face many issues. This paradigm is different. The new browser-based environment uses the connectionless Hypertext Transfer Protocol (HTTP), which makes maintaining state a challenge.

State is the capability to retain information. To assist with state, cookies offer some help but aren't the end-all solution. A *cookie* is a token file sent to a client browser but not stored on the client computer's hard disk; instead, it resides on the server. Some browsers don't support cookies, so objects that use cookie files must be supported for the browser as well.

Control logic might begin to make sense to you, but you should approach known event-driven functions differently from in the traditional client/server development arena. You also use different tools, which are sometimes more primitive in the web environment than in traditional programming environments.

Controls might be needed to perform services for web users. When developing web-based applications, you must answer these questions before using controls within your applications:

- Which control should you use?
- Are custom controls needed? If so, should you purchase or create them?
- Which web-development technologies are best for the application at hand?
- How do the developed applications use existing technologies?

Suppose that you want to test a web page before deployment. How would you ensure quality when the audience (possibly the global marketplace) could be using any of a variety of technology architectures? It's impossible to benchmark applications with an almost infinite amount of connectivity combinations possible.

It's clearly evident that today you must stay abreast of the web-based application environment and the technologies used. Change occurs continually, and smart programmers will be those who maintain a current knowledge of the skills necessary for web-based application development.

Static Versus Dynamic HTML: The Old Way Versus the New Way

Hypertext Markup Language (HTML) is the method used to mark up or *tag* a document so that it can be distributed on the web. HTML that's not modified based on user input is referred to as *static HTML.*

Static HTML files that reside on the web are only as new as when the files were published. This method is fine for files that seldom change, such as annual tax statements or monthly sales reports; however, when new data is needed, the HTML files need to be published again so that web users can view the updated material. Listing 11.1 is an example of a simple HTML document.

NOTE To create a simple HTML document, you can use your choice of many various text editors. For Listing 11.1, Microsoft Notepad was used.

Listing 11.1 A Simple HTML Document

```
<HTML>
<HEAD>
<TITLE>Accounting Software Support</TITLE>
</HEAD>
<BODY>
<CENTER>
<H1>Software Support Services</H1>
<HR><H3>At Jones & Jones CPA, we provide quality installation, training,
and customized reporting for the following accounting software packages:</H3>
<BR><TABLE ALIGN=CENTER BORDER=0 WIDTH=70%><TR><TD>
<A HREF="http://www.jones.com/default.htm"><IMG SRC="icon1.gif"
ALT="Jones CPA Software" ALIGN="CENTER" HEIGHT=100 WIDTH=125 HSPACE=20 BORDER=0>
```

continues

Listing 11.1 Continued

```
<A HREF="http://www.cpasoft.com/index.html"><IMG SRC="icon2.gif"
ALT="CPASoft Solutions" ALIGN="CENTER" HEIGHT=100 WIDTH=125 HSPACE=20
BORDER=0></TD></TR></TABLE>
</CENTER>
</BODY>
</HTML>
```

ON THE WEB

For a listing of the available HTML tags, visit the World Wide Web Consortium site at **http://www.w3.org** or **http://www.w3.org/markup/**. The Microsoft Site Builder Workshop at **http://www.microsoft.com/workshop/author/newhtml/default.htm** might also be helpful.

As the demand for delivery of dynamic information on the web has increased, so has the technology used in web-based application development. Many web site developers are being approached to publish content on the web that can be created on demand to meet web users' expectations. Web users want content fresh, exciting, up-to-date, and tailored to their personal information needs. This new expectation requires a new web-development method—Dynamic HTML.

Microsoft Dynamic HTML is a feature of Internet Explorer 4.0 and was developed in collaboration with the World Wide Web Consortium (W3C). Figure 11.5 shows the anatomy of a web application with Dynamic HTML.

The old way—static HTML—is fine for data that changes as part of a regular business cycle, but today's web is extremely interactive and changes continually. To update web content as the data changes, you must use the new way—Dynamic HTML.

You can author truly dynamic web applications by using Dynamic HTML. You can change any text or graphic element on a web page without a return trip to the server by using Dynamic HTML—even if the web page has already been loaded. Web sites will be more inviting due to this flexibility.

Document Object Model (DOM) is the object model provided for HTML by Dynamic HTML. All elements in a web page are exposed as objects. You can change the look and feel of these objects at any time by modifying their attributes or applying methods. You can also state specifically how you want the positioning and style of page elements by using Cascading Style Sheets (CSS). You can use each x- and y-coordinates and z-order to position each element precisely.

CAUTION

If Dynamic HTML isn't used for a substantial change to web content, extremely slow performance will occur when an additional round-trip to the server is made to display the new text.

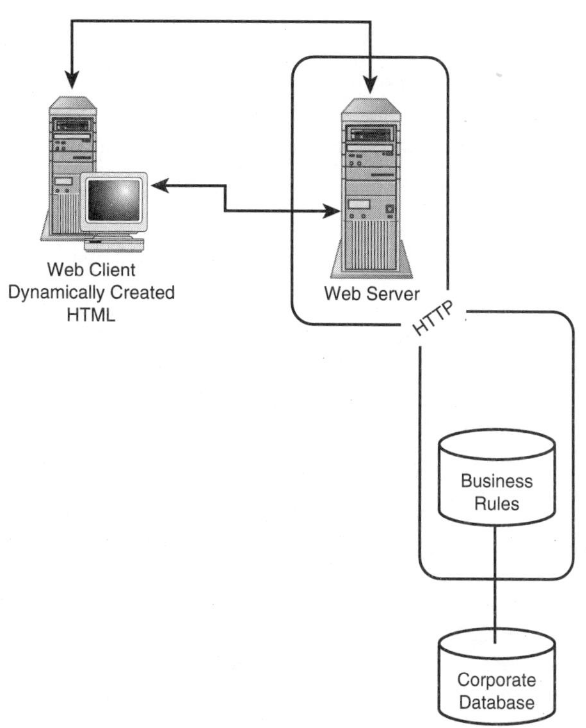

FIG. 11.5
Dynamic HTML gives users customized views of data from the database.

Download times with Dynamic HTML are actually shorter than with static HTML. You can even avoid trips to the server by using Dynamic HTML's data-binding feature. Dynamic HTML also gives you more efficiency with the use of animation and graphics. You can decide the allocation for bandwidth consumption between fetches, the consumption of bandwidth packaging, and the elements of design to optimize the users' experiences.

See Chapter 18, "Dynamic HTML.," **p. 487**, to learn more about Dynamic HTML.

Internet Information Server with Active Server Pages

Microsoft Internet Information Server (IIS) is designed to expand the I-net by providing a development platform where you can perform secure, high-speed information publishing. IIS is Microsoft's web server and a product of the Windows NT Server package. Active Server Pages (ASP) allows server-side scripting and the capability to add interactivity to the standard HTML file.

ASP files allow you to develop web-based applications in virtually any language. ASP also offers you an opportunity to create web solutions independent of the type of web browser used.

The mixture of IIS and ASP might be the solution you've searched for. For additional detailed information on the combination of these two technologies, see Chapter 13, "An Inside Look at Active Server Pages and Internet Information Server."

An Overview of Active Server Pages

With ASP, you can execute scripts on the server side versus the client side, which allows the web server to do all the script's processing work. Because the script is generated on the server side, the usual worry of capabilities on the client-side server is now eliminated.

An ASP is basically a text file with an extension of .asp. When requested by a web browser, an ASP script instance is generated. The server then reads and executes the commands from top to bottom. The result of the browser request is personalized content, formatted on the server and then sent to the browser.

The primary benefits of ASP are as follows:

- Extensibility
- Browser independence
- Integration with existing HTML files
- Easier and less time-consuming creation, with no manual compiling or linking

Figure 11.6 shows the anatomy and use of ASP in a web-based application environment. You can find more information on the use of ASP in Chapter 13.

As you see in Figure 11.6, ASP files are used to create dynamic content with Microsoft's COM platform. Third-party controls (or your own controls) can be used to extend the web-based application functionality. In Figure 11.6, when the client connects to a site containing an ASP file, the web server takes the web client request and dynamically interprets the Active Server Page objects and scripting into HTML, which is then presented to the client. The significance of the default.asp file is that it's the home web page for the web site being requested.

To create an ASP file, you first create a static HTML page. For example:

```
<HTML>
<BODY BGCOLOR="#ffffff">
 <H1>Hello!</H1>
</BODY>
</HTML>
```

Next, change the extension of the file from .htm to .asp, so the page will be recognized by the ASP engine on the server as a scripting page to be parsed. Then, add the ASP scripting as shown in boldface in the following listing. The variable `=Now` will display the current time in the output of the following example:

```
<HTML>
<BODY BGCOLOR="#ffffff">
 <H1>Hello!</H1>
 <H1>The Time is: <% =Now %> </H1>
</BODY>
</HTML>
```

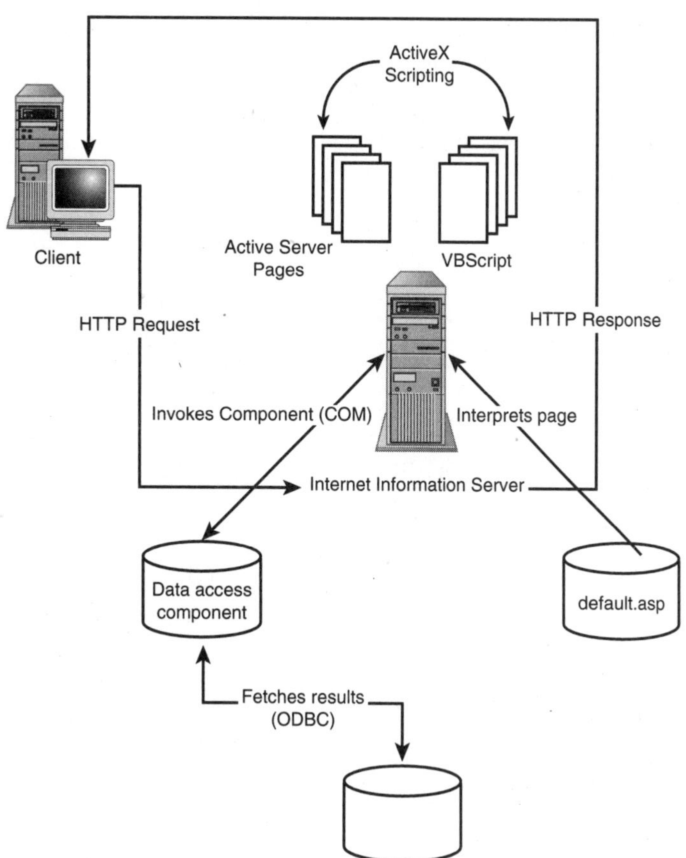

FIG. 11.6
With Active Server Pages, companies can mix ActiveX scripting and ActiveX Server Components for the creation of web-based applications.

Database Connectivity Through IIS

Providing useful, organized information to web users can differentiate a company from its competitors. Information can be a powerful tool, and by allowing web access to important information and presenting it so that users can easily understand it, organizations can leverage this power. For example, companies that provide web users access to a database of parts, a sales catalog, or information on a legacy system will have a strong advantage over companies that don't.

Today's web users want access to all data, as well as the capability to combine different types of data. This is desirable, of course, but information systems department leaders want to meet this need without relocating the data from its original source.

IIS provides database connectivity by using ActiveX Data Objects (ADO), an ASP component. ADO provides access to any data source compatible with Open Database Connectivity (ODBC). Some popular databases include Microsoft Access and SQL Server, as well as Sybase, Informix, and Oracle. If you're already familiar with DAO/RDO, you'll find a short learning curve for ADO. Another benefit of ADO is the capability to use ADO with any development language (C/C++, Visual Basic, VBScript, Java, and more).

ADO provides high-level, language-neutral programming objects, and OLE DB (object linking and embedding database) is the component architecture that allows all types of data to be accessed with no need to relocate the data. OLE DB interfaces expose resident functionality and don't force data to be in a relational database format. Figure 11.7 shows the use of ADO and OLE DB interfaces.

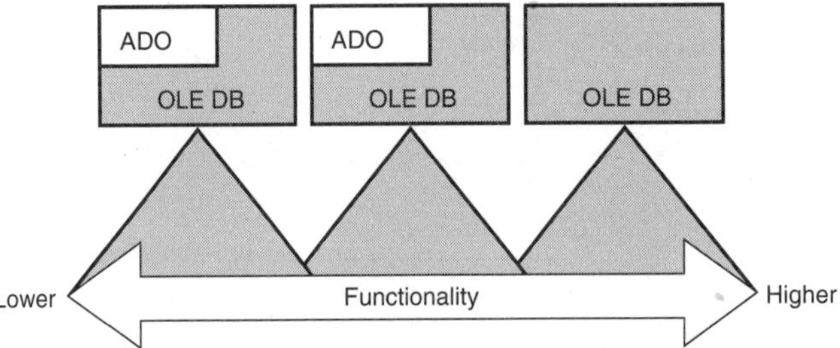

FIG. 11.7
When you use a combination of ADO and OLE DB interfaces, data access can be simple and functional.

Notice in Figure 11.7 that OLE DB offers a higher degree of functionality. Depending on the functionality desired, however, a combination of ADO and OLE DB might be suitable. An example of this would be the use of OLE DB to access nonrelational data, such as spreadsheets or electronic mail, and the use of ADO for accessing relational data, such as SQL Server. OLE DB is the cornerstone of Microsoft's Universal Data Access strategy.

ON THE WEB

For more information on database connectivity, the following URLs might be helpful:

- See **http://www.microsoft.com/ado/** for information on ActiveX Data Objects.
- Visit **http://www.microsoft.com/data/** to see what the industry is doing in the area of OLE DB. It's also possible to download the v1.1 SDK and register as an OLE DB Developer.
- For ODBC information, refer to **http://www.microsoft.com/odbc/**.

The Usenet newsgroups at **microsoft.public.oledb** and **microsoft.public.odbc** also might be beneficial.

Components of a Dynamic Web-Based Application

Components, or *objects*, have altered the method of software development and use of systems forever. A business problem can be solved now by reusable software components. Any object can be modified without altering the other objects contained in a framework, or the interaction between them. Initial programming efforts remain intact and can be reused repeatedly in various ways.

Web components vary in their ease-of-use and application. Each has specific attributes for a particular function, and it's important to match the correct technology with the task needed.

It's not enough to have components themselves. They must exist in a distributed, open environment that permits their execution in a plug-and-play fashion—an environment that truly enables the reality of dynamic reengineering.

To insert a component into a standard HTML document, you use the `<OBJECT>` tag. Here is a brief example:

```
<OBJECT CLASSID="" DATA=""
CODEBASE="" ID="" TYPE="">
<PARAM NAME=" " VALUE=" ">
</OBJECT>
```

Companies are migrating to a component-based environment—not just for the sake of using new technology, but because they see component use and reuse as a solution to their critical business problems. Components are suited for the distributed systems environment because both the data and business logic are housed within objects, allowing them to be located anywhere within a distributed network.

When you're creating interactive web-based applications, many components are available to assist you. The following sections describe several of the available technologies.

ActiveX

ActiveX is a group of technologies provided by Microsoft that allows you to create active content for the World Wide Web. ActiveX makes interactive web creation faster and easier. Using ActiveX technology will make the Internet more productive and useful.

ActiveX is a product of the Microsoft object linking and embedding (OLE) technology. Some might wonder if ActiveX is a new name for OLE because they're both based on the Component Object Model (COM). Although they appear similar, they provide different services to web developers.

OLE refers only to the technology that allows users to build multiple documents through object linking and embedding. OLE is optimized for desktop application integration and end-user usability, whereas ActiveX is optimized for size and speed to allow controls to respond interactively to events by being embedded in a web-based architecture. All ActiveX and OLE technologies are built on the COM-provided foundation.

▶ **See** Chapter 4, "Using Microsoft's Object Technologies," **p. 89**, for more information on ActiveX technologies and COM.

COM is the method that allows two separate software application components to access each other's services. With COM, a software application component applies its functionality as one or more COM objects. Each COM object supports one to many interfaces, which in turn might support one to many methods.

The elements of ActiveX include client and server technologies, as follows:

- *ActiveX controls* are the objects in web-based applications that make a web site come alive with user-controllable functions. ActiveX controls are limited only by your imagination. Literally thousands of ActiveX controls are available for functions ranging from a simple timer to a complete word processor. ActiveX controls are plug-and-play components that you can use in any application, similar to those included in Internet Explorer 4.0 (see Table 11.1).
- *ActiveX scripting* enables control from the browser or server of ActiveX controls and Java applets as they function in the integrated environment. VBScript and JScript are two scripting languages discussed later in this chapter. ActiveX scripting allows the creation of standard language runtimes by enabling a host to compile scripts, acquire and call entry points, and maintain the available namespace for you.
- *ActiveX document support* allows web users to view non-HTML documents (such as Word, Excel, and PowerPoint files) through a web browser.
- *Java virtual machine* allows the integration and execution of Java applets with ActiveX controls by any ActiveX-supported web browser.
- *ActiveX server framework* provides several web server-based services, including database access, security, and others.

Table 11.1 ActiveX Controls Used in Internet Explorer

Control	Description
Animated Button	Uses the Microsoft Windows animation common control to display various frame sequences of an AVI, depending on the button state.
Chart	Enables drawing of various chart types with different styles.
Gradient	Shades the area with a range of colors, displaying a transition from one specified color to another.
Label	Displays given text at any specified angle. It can also render the text along user-defined curves.
Marquee	Scrolls, slides, or bounces uniform resource locators (URLs) within a user-defined window.
Menu	Displays a menu button or a pull-down menu. This control acts like a tri-state button when no menu items are specified or displays a pull-down menu when one or more menu items are specified. It can also display a pop-up menu if the Pop-up method is used.
Pop-up Menu	Displays a pop-up menu whenever the Pop-up method is called and fires a click event when a menu item is selected.
Pop-up Window	Displays specified HTML documents in a pop-up window. You can use this control to provide ToolTips or previews of links.

Control	Description
Preloader	Downloads the specified URL and puts it in the cache. The control is invisible at runtime and starts downloading when enabled.
Stock Ticker	Continuously displays changing data. The control downloads the URL specified at regular intervals and displays that data. The data can be in text or XRT format.
Timer	Invokes an event periodically. It's invisible at runtime.
View Tracker	Generates `OnShow` and `OnHide` events whenever the control falls within or out of the viewable area.

ON THE WEB

For information about additional ActiveX controls, visit **www.microsoft.com/activex/gallery**.

Java Applets

Microsoft Internet Explorer 3.0 and higher supports Java applets. Of the many variations of IDE tools for Java development, Visual Studio 97's Visual J++, Sun Microsystems' Java JDK, and Borland's Latte are a few of the development environments available on the web.

▶ **See** Chapter 7, "Creating Components with Visual J++," **p. 221**

ON THE WEB

For more information on the Java development environments mentioned in this chapter, see these web sites:

- Borland Latte: **http://www.borland.com/jbuilder/latte/**
- Microsoft Visual J++: **http://www.microsoft.com/visualJ/**
- Sun's Java JDK: **http://www.sun.com/software/Dev-progs/PR/JDK.html**

A platform-specific program called a *virtual machine* executes an applet. The Microsoft Virtual Machine—available on 32-bit Windows, Macintosh, and Windows 3.1—has been highly acclaimed by the media and developers as the safest, fastest, most functional, and most reliable pure Java on the market.

Java also works with ActiveX, which opens up a vast number of combinations between the two technologies. By extending Java with ActiveX, you can create reusable components. Also thanks to ActiveX technology, you can enhance Java applets with multimedia effects, highly tune performance, and use a wide variety of objects, including ActiveX controls, ActiveX documents, and ActiveX scripting. You can use these applets as building blocks for web applications.

Java is an object-oriented language that you can integrate with the existing client/server infrastructure. Java is similar to the C++ programming language, except that it doesn't have pointers, contains a different method for garbage collection, and is extremely strict regarding its object orientation. Sun Microsystems developed Java to be independent of the platform being used.

When using Java class libraries, you can create specific use-class libraries or purchase commercially developed class libraries.

To call a Java applet, you use a simple HTML tag:

```
<APPLET CODE="Name.Class"
 HEIGHT=500 WIDTH=500>
</APPLET>
```

Java applets from earlier alpha versions might not execute on newer Java-supporting web browsers. Check the HTML source code to determine whether the applet will execute. The older Java versions used the <APP> tag; newer versions use the <APPLET> tag.

VBScript

Visual Basic, Scripting Edition (VBScript) is a fast, small, lightweight interpreted language used in web browsers and applications designed to work with ActiveX controls and other embedded objects in HTML documents. Although it's a direct subset of Microsoft Visual Basic, VBScript doesn't include the capability of directly accessing or performing file input/output (I/O) with the underlying operating system.

NOTE Now, only Microsoft Internet Explorer fully supports VBScript.

ActiveX objects are crucial to productive VBScript coding. When VBScript authors use these controls, web applications provide a quality appearance to web users.

VBScript authors can dynamically manage the outcome of an ActiveX control placed directly on the web page. Code that responds to animate object events can now be created with VBScript.

VBScript procedures are coded either between the <HEAD> and </HEAD> tags or between the <BODY> and </BODY> tags. The code must always be wrapped in <SCRIPT> tags. To ensure that the browser correctly executes the code as VBScript and not another language, make sure that the LANGUAGE indicator is set to equal either VBScript or VBS.

The use of VBScript within an HTML document file is given in the following example, with the actual VBScript code in boldface:

```
<HTML>
<HEAD>
<TITLE></TITLE>
<SCRIPT LANGUAGE = "VBScript">
<!--
VBScript code is inserted here
-->
</SCRIPT>
</HEAD>
<BODY>
<SCRIPT LANGUAGE = "VBS">
```

```
<!--
VBScript code can also be inserted here.
-->
</SCRIPT>
</BODY>
</HTML>
```

When including your VBScript code within the <BODY> section, always embed the source with HTML comment tags (<!-- and -->) to ensure that the code is hidden from browsers that aren't compatible with VBScript.

ON THE WEB

For more information about VBScript, visit **www.microsoft.com/vbscript**.

JScript

Microsoft's JScript is a scripting language similar to VBScript in its use. Like VBScript, JScript is used to add interactivity and intelligence to web-based documents and doesn't produce standalone applets. Now, only Microsoft Internet Explorer fully supports JScript.

JScript resembles the programming language Java but has a few exceptions, as are obvious from the following comparisons:

JScript is	Java is
An interpreted language	Compiled to bytecode before execution on client
Object-based, lacks classes and inheritance	Object-oriented, uses classes with inheritance
Embedded code in HTML	Applet codes separate from HTML
Loose typing with variable data types not declared	Strong typing with variable data declared
Object references checked at runtime	Object references must exist at compile time
Secure, can't write to hard disk	Secure, can't write to hard disk

Because Internet Explorer programmers can code in JScript or VBScript, you must use the LANGUAGE parameter to specify which language is used. In the following example, HTML is extended to enable the dispatching of an event to a JScript user-defined function by the name of callthis():

```
<INPUT TYPE=BUTTON NAME=mybutton VALUE="Click on Me"
onclick="callthis();"LANGUAGE="JavaScript">
```

Another alternative is to extend the `<SCRIPT>` tag itself, as in the following example:

```
<FORM>
...
<INPUT TYPE=BUTTON NAME=mybutton VALUE="Click on Me">
<SCRIPT FOR="mybutton" EVENT="onClick" LANGUAGE="JavaScript">
alert("Hello");
</SCRIPT>
...
</FORM>
```

With the addition of the `FOR` and `EVENT` attributes in the preceding example, Internet Explorer developers can bind a script to a defined object (here, the `mybutton` button), which is the source associated with an event (in this case, the `onclick` event). The result of the example would be an *alert* or pop-up window that displays the word `Hello` when users click the `mybutton` button.

ON THE WEB

For additional assistance with JScript, visit **www.microsoft.com/jscript**.

Other Server-Based Components: CGI and ISAPI

Although many server-based components have already been discussed in this chapter, two others are worth mentioning: Common Gateway Interface (CGI) and Internet Server Application Programming Interface (ISAPI). You can create these two server-side extensions in many ways, depending on the programming language and extension used.

Common Gateway Interface (CGI) CGI has maintained its long-standing place as a standard in web interactivity. CGI scripts allow the creation of applications in many different languages. Although web users can view only the CGI submission, many processes take place to produce the result:

1. Input is passed to the web server by the web browser.
2. The input is then passed to a CGI script by the server.
3. After the CGI script processes the input, the input is routed (if necessary) to another application, and then the CGI script sends the output to the web server.
4. The web server passes the output back to the browser. This final CGI script output can vary from a newly generated document based on user input to a database's search results.

You can create CGI applications in any executable or interpreted programming language that allows access to operating system environment variables: standard input (`stdin`) and standard output (`stdout`). History shows the Perl language is popular for this purpose; however, many other languages, such as C, awk, and REXX, have also been used in the creation of CGI applications.

NOTE If an interpreted language is used, the corresponding interpreter must be available when IIS starts the CGI extension application.

If server-side extensions are created by using Perl, there's now an alternative to implementing them as CGI applications. An independent software vendor and HIP, Inc., have combined to create an interpreter for Perl that's available as an ISAPI application. Legacy and Perl scripts can now be executed without the CGI spawning process, which eliminates much overhead.

ON THE WEB

For more information on Perl, visit HIP's web site at **http://www.HIP.com.**

Internet Server Application Programming Interface (ISAPI) ISAPI extensions are filters and applications that you can use to create active web-based applications. An *Internet filter* is a dynamic link library (DLL) that resides on an HTTP server to filter the data traffic that travels to and from the server. You can activate additional processes, such as clicking HTML links or completing an HTML form, by implementing ISAPI extensions into a web page. These extensions are DLL applications that an HTTP server can load and call. ISAPI applications vary from CGI applications in that they have access to the same resources as the server and are executed in the identical address space as the HTTP server. Figure 11.8 shows the relationship between ActiveX server-side extensions and IIS.

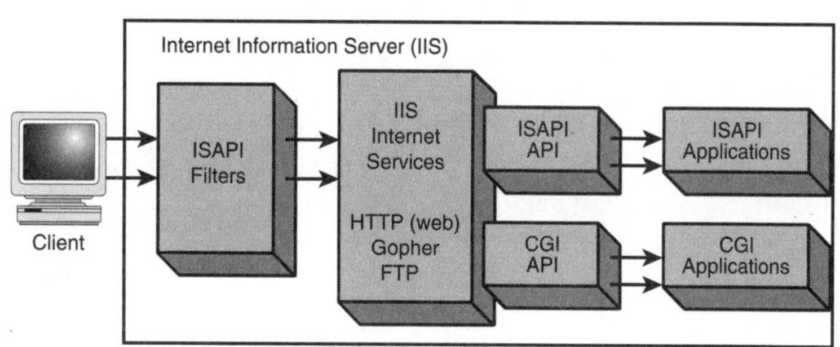

FIG. 11.8
The overhead with ISAPI extensions is much lower than with CGI applications because ISAPI extensions can be preloaded, can unload DLLs that haven't been called for a period of time, and don't require the creation of additional processes.

ISAPI filters are templates that you can use to request data dynamically. There can be a level of complexity with ISAPI filters versus ISAPI applications. ISAPI filters require knowledge of the underlying technology executing the template request. With ISAPI applications, however, little or no previous knowledge of the underlying technology is required because the application is used to dynamically create the content.

With ISAPI applications, you're limited by the functionality provided. The trade-off between ISAPI filters and applications depends on the primary reason for their utilization—ease-of-use versus flexibility. The filter is an in-process control, whereas the application is out-of-process and requires more overhead than a DLL.

InterDev and Its Involvement in the Web-Based Application Environment

Visual InterDev is an IDE that allows you to create web-based applications by using multiple and varied development languages and technologies. You can build I-net applications with the visual development and database tools and features included in Visual InterDev.

Microsoft created Visual InterDev in response to the generally immature web-application development tools and utilities, which often consist merely of text editors. A typical Visual InterDev-created web-based application consists of server-side scripts developed by using VBScript or any ActiveX-scripting-supported language. The scripts, which use server-side runtime ActiveX components, sometimes perform complex processing but usually provide system services or implement business rules.

Visual InterDev might or might not provide all the design tools and features you want, but it's extensible. This means that design-time controls (ActiveX controls that have been extended with a new COM-based interface) can be used for the design of the web-based application, but when the application is executed from a script, users don't view the control. Users view only the output, produced in the form of HTML text and script code.

Visual InterDev allows the use and sharing of projects and components from multiple development tools. Visual InterDev allows the creation of web-based applications that integrate components and business processes that use not only simple server-side scripts, but also Visual C++, Visual FoxPro, Visual Basic, Visual J++, and a multitude of third-party development tools that integrate with Visual InterDev.

Visual InterDev contributes web-to-database connectivity and high-end visual database design tools. Database components in Visual InterDev include the following:

- Database wizards
- Database design-time ActiveX controls
- The Query Designer
- Integrated Data View
- The Stored Procedures editor
- The Database Designer

Visual InterDev provides database wizards that direct you through the creation of data-bound HTML forms. The Data Form Wizard automatically generates the required complex HTML and ActiveX server scripting to bind a web page to the database.

Various design-time controls for database access are also included in Visual InterDev. An example of a design-time control is the Microsoft Data Command control. With this control, an ODBC database connection is selected, and the Visual InterDev Query Designer then visually builds a query against that database connection.

The Query Designer helps you by working with any ODBC data source and visually constructing complex SQL statements. It helps you generate the correct DML (Data Manipulation Language) code for `INSERT`, `UPDATE`, `SELECT`, and `DELETE` queries.

In addition to providing a live connection to each database, Data View depicts each connection used by the web-based application, enabling you to work directly with the connections within the Visual InterDev IDE. Detailed information—such as objects and their properties within each database, field types, key structures, stored procedures, and table definitions—are provided through Data View, which works with the Query Designer and Database Designer to provide the administration, maintenance, and development of databases.

You can use Database Designer and Database Administrator to create new SQL Server 6.5 databases and to modify the properties and structure of existing databases. With a couple of clicks, you can perform difficult database administration tasks. You use a syntax-colored source editor when editing SQL Server and Oracle stored procedures.

Visual InterDev provides integrated source management for users of Microsoft Visual SourceSafe 5.0. This is extremely helpful when multiple developers are working on web applications in a team-based setting, as explicit check-in and check-out procedures are used for all files in the application environment.

Visual InterDev includes a set of wizards to perform a variety of common tasks, such as creating web projects and data-bound HTML forms. The wizards can be a starting point from which you can customize the finished web application.

CAUTION

If you make changes to a wizard-created application and then execute the wizards again, your initial changes will be lost.

In addition to the developer tools, a basic set of multimedia management and editing tools are included in Visual InterDev. Microsoft Media Manager allows you to manage and track content, Microsoft Music Producer enables you to create custom audio tracks for web pages, and Microsoft Image Composer allows you to manipulate and edit images.

▶ **See** Chapter 14, "Developing Active Content with Visual InterDev," **p. 389**

▶ **See** Chapter 16, "Visual InterDev Design-Time Controls," **p. 449**

ON THE WEB

For more information on Visual InterDev, visit the Microsoft Visual InterDev web site at **http://www.microsoft.com/vinterdev**.

From Here...

In this chapter, you learned about web-based applications and the technologies that create and deploy them. You also saw a diagram of a sample web-based application and the components used. Also, you learned how easy it can be to apply Active Server Pages to your I-net applications by using the features available in the newly introduced IDE by Microsoft: Visual InterDev.

No matter which technologies and methods you choose for your web-site creation, one fact remains: The dynamic content you develop will increase the effectiveness of your web-based applications and allow the right information to be delivered to the right users.

For more information on web-based application topics covered in this chapter, see the following chapters:

- For more insight into the use of ActiveX components, see Chapter 8, "Using ActiveX Client Components in an I-net Environment."
- For more help on the use of ASP with IIS, see Chapter 13, "An Inside Look at Active Server Pages and Internet Information Server."
- To explore the creation capabilities of Visual InterDev, see Chapter 14, "Developing Active Content with Visual InterDev."
- For more information on server-side programming in an I-net environment, see Chapter 17, "Server-Side Programming in an I-net Environment."
- To learn more about the new way in web page development, see Chapter 18, "Dynamic HTML."

CHAPTER 12

Creating Web Browser-Based Applications with Visual Basic

by Joe Lengyel

The ever-changing landscape of software development is increasingly focusing on the Internet, intranets, and the active platform. The promises inherent in ubiquitous information and communication presents serious challenges for information systems professionals of all types. Similarly, software vendors shoulder the task of providing tools and utilities for software artisans.

Visual Basic is arguably the most widely used application development toolkit available. More lines of Visual Basic code are written today than any other programming language. Furthermore, increasing numbers of software developers—novice and professional—are building applications with Visual Basic.

To meet the challenges of the active platform while building on the sizable base of experienced programmers, Visual Basic offers ActiveX documents. This chapter shows you how to harness the power of this new technology. ■

Overview of ActiveX documents

Gain insight into ActiveX document technology. Learn the impact this paradigm will have on information systems development environments.

ActiveX document design considerations

Understand the considerations that accompany designing ActiveX documents. Compare how this differs from standard form development.

Building and testing an ActiveX document

In a detailed step-by-step discussion, learn how to build an ActiveX document composed of UserDocument objects, controls, forms, and code. Test this application in Internet Explorer.

Using the ActiveX Document Migration Wizard

Learn how to use the ActiveX Document Migration Wizard for converting standard forms to ActiveX documents. Gain an understanding of how to use this tool to leverage existing enterprise applications.

Understanding installation and platform issues

In a detailed discussion, learn about installation and configuration issues. Gain an understanding of how various platforms affect both development and deployment.

Understanding ActiveX Documents

ActiveX documents, the new building block featured in Visual Basic 5.0 (VB5), allow you to build applications that merge with and enhance the elements of I-net (Internet or intranet) sites. Similar to VB forms, ActiveX documents provide a variety of conventional and I-net capabilities, including functionality using the hyperlink object. Although web development has been possible with VB in the past, ActiveX technology introduced in VB5 accomplishes the following:

- Leverages the knowledge base of the VB development community to the Internet process model
- Becomes a web-development enabler for a larger pool of information systems personnel
- Facilitates the promotion and reuse of existing enterprise VB applications
- Provides the capability to view and modify existing documents in their resident applications within the browser window

A real-world example of an intranet scenario will illustrate the benefits of ActiveX documents. Suppose that Company ABC has a traditional client/server application built in VB. This application manages and administrates all aspects of the company's business, including order entry, inventory, product lists, and so forth. The company has a SQL database that supplies data to the user interface through a Remote Data Object. When enhancements are made to the application, the VB project is recompiled and rebuilt, and a new copy of the executable is placed on each user's machine.

Now consider that Company ABC plans to expand its operations and open a second office in another region of the country. The company requires use of the same corporate application previously described. This is where ActiveX documents can be very useful. Information systems professionals can migrate the existing VB application to become an ActiveX document application, which can be deployed on a web server. Users in both company locations can visit the application via their client web browser. Enhancements to the application will appear seamlessly because the web browser determines the runtime requirements of the application and downloads these components to each user's machine.

This is an example of a web-enabled application built with VB. Many of the screens and program logic are reused from the existing corporate application. The ActiveX document can contain the regular assortment of controls in the VB toolbox, as well as any other ActiveX controls that the company is licensed to use. This example shows that ActiveX documents are a web-development alternative to technologies such as HTML and scripting languages such as JScript and VBScript.

Developing on the ActiveX platform presents a host of new challenges and features for application architects. One difficult function is blending the best components of existing software with new and improved components built with the latest tools.

What Is an ActiveX Document?

An *ActiveX document* can be any particular display of information, such as a word processing document, a data grid, or a chart. You can associate this display of information with a browser because the browser is the tool with which these active viewports of information can be seen. For this chapter, an ActiveX document consists of a `UserDocument` object, code, and one or more controls from the toolbox placed on the `UserDocument`.

`UserDocument`, a new feature of VB5, is the base object of an ActiveX document you develop in Visual Basic. Although the ActiveX document concept isn't new, building an ActiveX document with `UserDocument` objects in VB5 is new and unique. The `UserDocument` object is the ActiveX equivalent of a standard VB form, but you need to know the differences that you'll encounter almost immediately.

Development of a standard VB project often begins with a standard form, which becomes the home to various buttons, labels, and code. Development is very similar with an ActiveX document application. You begin with one `UserDocument`, and similar types of buttons, labels, and code can be added; however, you'll encounter differences in the properties and methods of the `UserDocument`, as well as in other application-specific features, such as navigating between ActiveX documents. Furthermore, the deployment platform is different because client/server development is fundamentally distinctive from I-net development. The distinctions aren't trivial.

You aren't limited to using only `UserDocuments` in an ActiveX document application. You can add standard forms and modules to your project, as you might to any standard project. An ActiveX document application (an executable or DLL) can consist of numerous `UserDocument` objects, as well as the regular assortment of forms, controls, and so on. As the full force of development focuses on I-net applications, the standard features of applications that exist today will gradually fade away. This migration ability is a positive attribute, however, because it means that the logic and functionality of existing components are reusable.

You first should familiarize yourself with the `UserDocument`'s properties and methods. Press F4 to peruse the properties list; double-click anywhere on the `UserDocument` to review the methods.

Understanding ActiveX Document Topology

You can think of ActiveX document technology in terms of three layers:

- *Documents.* The `UserDocument` objects containing controls and code.
- *Containers.* Browsers, such as Internet Explorer.
- *Servers.* The VB application housing the ActiveX document(s).

An ActiveX document is made available through a server, which can be a VB executable or DLL. A *server* is a component that provides the ActiveX document to an ActiveX container such as Internet Explorer. The ActiveX document is served to the browser viewport by the executable or DLL.

The capability to deploy applications for use in browsers allows you to extend your current client/server solutions throughout I-nets. A typical scenario today involves a VB application consisting of a visual front end for presenting data and reporting options to the enterprise users, and a DAO or RDO connection to a database for piping data to controls such as text boxes, grids, and listboxes. These applications typically feature reporting functions to provide documentation to customers and executives.

Administrative efforts needed for providing these reports, along with supporting application end users, isn't insignificant. Annual maintenance and support are large portions of enterprise budgets. As development technology focuses more on I-nets, the separate distribution and maintenance costs for customers and enterprise users will gradually merge. As customers use vendor web sites more to retrieve account information, schedules, product lists, and the like, application development will no longer be split between traditional client/server applications and web applications. Instead, all applications will be browser-based or web applications, and the support and development costs for information systems departments will assume this focus. A single application will serve customers and enterprise users alike and be used within a browser. The components in VB5 contribute to the existing available development tools to make this reality bigger each day.

Selecting a Project Type

VB offers you four types of projects in which to build ActiveX documents:

- ActiveX document EXE
- ActiveX document DLL
- ActiveX EXE
- ActiveX DLL

Major differences exist between projects of the type EXE and those that are DLL. The differences between document EXEs and component EXEs are explained later in this section.

▶ **See** Chapter 5, "Creating ActiveX Components with Visual Basic," **p. 131**

An ActiveX component can be built as an out-of-process component (an .exe file) or an in-process component (a .dll file) with respect to the use of ActiveX objects. Historically, DLLs have served as building blocks in a reusable component capacity. For example, each new application that needs a network security check can use a DLL that facilitates a network logon. A DLL is an in-process component that runs in the process space of the application that uses it. An in-process component performs more quickly than its counterpart out-of-process component, an EXE, because no cross-process navigation is required; therefore, the performance of a DLL will exceed the performance of the same component compiled as an EXE. In-process components do have drawbacks. A natural security breach occurs whenever calls are made from a calling program to an external file. This type of breach might corrupt a program, so you should take special care to make sure that establishment of connections and passing of parameters are done properly.

NOTE When the host application is Internet Explorer, trying to show a modeless form from a DLL fires an error condition. *Modeless* forms and dialog boxes allow the focus to be shifted to other forms and dialog boxes. *Modal* forms and dialog boxes must be closed before other actions can be taken. A dangling modeless process creates the error condition within Internet Explorer. ■

EXEs are out-of-process components that run outside the address space of the client application and within their own process. Most applications that you use, such as those in Microsoft Office, are executables. One benefit of out-of-process components is the asynchronous performance achieved as a consequence of the separate client and component processing. In other words, EXEs do multitasking.

One large danger area of ActiveX EXEs is the potential for data disruption. Although this can depend on the distribution method, a single server installation of an EXE functions as a single application being used by many users. In this context, no components are installed on the users' machines. In essence, only one ActiveX application process is taking place, with containers creating separate instances of that process. As a consequence, separate container sessions can simultaneously make transactions, rendering data for one session of the container unexpectedly modified due to changes made through the second container session. Naturally, this problem is an issue within certain contexts. It's not insurmountable—developers deal with these issue types daily—but the volume and scope are larger when an I-net is involved.

The performance for an out-of-process component will be slower than a DLL because of an executable's incapability to make references directly between the client and the component. For example, referrals between a client and a component can't be made by reference. Instead, a copy of the data must be made in the component, which is a slower process than passing by reference.

ActiveX EXEs are COM objects and can be used in applications that support COM. This means executables created with VB will appear, without any special effort on the developer's part, in the list of available object references. When you create a project and designate it as an ActiveX EXE, you're essentially telling VB one of two things:

- This standalone component will be reused in the future as a tool to build new applications.
- This component will be used as a feature of an application—possibly an ActiveX document application.

ActiveX components are web-enabled and can be used on ActiveX documents or elsewhere. Knowing the interaction of the two can be beneficial because the same programming approach and tactics can apply to both. Just remember that if you want to present an interactive interface for an application that will be deployed in an I-net environment, you should create an ActiveX document EXE; otherwise, create your components with an ActiveX EXE.

▶ **See** Chapter 4, "Using Microsoft's Object Technologies," **p. 89**

Setting Up Project Files

The file set that makes up an ActiveX document application varies from that of a standard application. When you save a form in a standard VB application, two files usually are created for the one form. The form object is stored in a plain text file, which contains the source code and property values. This file gets an .frm extension. Controls on the form that can't be stored as plain text are stored in .frx files. If you've ever accidentally deleted or misplaced an .frx file, you know the form has to be virtually re-created.

Similarly, the source code and property values of `UserDocument` objects and the code behind the document are stored in plain text files. These files receive a .dob file extension. Controls that can't be stored in .dob files because of their graphical elements are stored in .dox binary files. VB also creates a `UserDocument` document file when the project is compiled, which receives a .vbd extension and is placed in the same directory as the other project files. The .vbd file is the address file for the application to the container. The sample application that you build later in this chapter shows the significance and use of the .vbd file.

After you compile your ActiveX document, you can change the extension of the .vbd file—for example, Players.vbd can become Players.nfl. With this capability, users can make the name of the ActiveX document an intuitive mnemonic of the functionality of the application.

Building an ActiveX Document

The general process of creating an ActiveX document is like creating any other project. The following list gives an overview of the steps to take:

1. Start a new project.
2. Select a project type, either an ActiveX document EXE or an ActiveX document DLL. By default, these template projects contain a single `UserDocument`. Each `UserDocument` is the core object for an ActiveX document.
3. Add any desired controls to the `UserDocument`(s).
4. Add other forms, code modules, or more `UserDocument` objects to the project.
5. Compile and make the project.
6. Deploy the project.
7. View the project in a container.
8. Test and debug the project.

▶ **See** Chapter 22, "Building Client Front Ends with Visual Basic and RDO," **p. 603**

In the first exercise, you make an ActiveX document from scratch; the exercise for migrating forms to `UserDocuments` comes later. As you go along, remember the design issues discussed so far.

ON THE WEB

Bear in mind that this exercise requires the use of Internet Explorer. If you haven't installed Internet Explorer, do so now. You can obtain a free copy at **http://www.microsoft.com/ie/**.

Reviewing Design, Development, and Implementation Issues

Before you build an ActiveX document, review some design, development, and implementation issues:

- An executing ActiveX document isn't a standalone application and can only be viewed in a container. When you execute this chapter's sample ActiveX document application in the IDE, you know the application is running only because the Start button is disabled. This can make debugging and testing a challenge.
- Containers vary, and it isn't always possible to know the capabilities and limitations of the environment in which your ActiveX document will be deployed. You can establish a minimum set of capabilities across containers and environments and work toward that environment. Another alternative is to establish a target container and then program defensively to handle inadequacies with all others. Test your application in a few containers to get an idea of how the ActiveX documents look and operate in the container's viewport. See the later section "Understanding Integration Issues" for a more detailed discussion on this topic.
- Navigating from one ActiveX document to another can vary by container and platform. The performance you achieve in Internet Explorer, for example, might vary from what Netscape Navigator and other browsers can achieve. This is especially important if you have to support a heterogeneous browser environment. Understand the different methods available and the container for which each is designed. Some troubleshooting might be needed in this area.
- You can merge menus developed for individual ActiveX documents with the menu of the host container. This means the exclusive menu items of the application will remain and common menu items will default to the container's version.
- Be sure to indicate clearly to users what they're using and where they're located, as you don't want them to be unclear about the location or intent of the web site in their browser. When in doubt, spell this information out plainly. This can be done effectively on the container title bar with labels on each page and with an About box to give users a mnemonic for remembering the site, as well as some contextual relevance for the site. For example, you'll never be unsure that you've arrived at the Microsoft home page (**http://www.microsoft.com/**).

Creating the Grape Vine Application

In this section, you create an executable ActiveX document and view it in a container. The exercise doesn't guide you through the creation of a rigorous application development, but you place numerous controls onto a `UserDocument`, write some basic routines, compile and execute the project, and use the application in a container. Nothing you do will be different from what you've probably already done. Your ability to leverage your investment in the VB learning curve will pay dividends here; in fact, as the scope of your web development gets serious, this exercise will prepare you to handle the greater challenges of I-net development.

ON THE WEB

You can find in digital format all the code bits described in this chapter at **http://www.gasullivan.com/vs97book/**. Save time by performing cut-and-paste operations on the code for the how-to sections in this chapter.

Building the Framework To build a new ActiveX document, follow these steps:

1. Open a new ActiveX document EXE project. Remember, this project type automatically creates the first `UserDocument` object for you, which can be found in the project explorer in the User Documents folder. The project explorer is your window to all the objects within the project, such as modules, classes, forms, and so forth. Because VB lets you have multiple projects open simultaneously, the project explorer also organizes your access to all open projects.
2. In the project explorer, select the new `UserDocument` and activate it by choosing the View Object button located on the toolbar. Press F4 to activate the Properties list for the `UserDocument` and assign properties to the objects in the project. In step 5, you save the objects as files. These are distinct steps that serve exclusive purposes.
3. Provide the new object with the name `FirstUserDoc` in the `Name` property of the Properties list. The name should now appear in the title bar of the object, followed by `(UserDocument)`. The project has no name at this time.
4. Supply a name for the project by choosing Project, Project1 Properties from the menu. Type **`AxGrapeVine`** in the space available for the Project Name and click OK. This name now appears in the title bar of the `UserDocument`; each new `UserDocument` in the project will bear this name as well. The `Ax` indicates that this is an ActiveX document project.
5. Save the project by choosing File, Save. When you're asked to save the `UserDocument`, use the default name FirstUserDoc. (VB provides the default .dob document object file extension for the `UserDocument`.)
6. Provide the name `AxGrapeVine` for the project and save it. The project should receive a .vbp file extension.

7. Activate the toolbox and add a command button to FirstUserDoc. Name the command button `cmdSommelier`. Type **`Sommelier`** for the `Caption` property of the control. Add a second command button, named `cmdAbout`, and type **`About`** for its `Caption` property.

8. Add a label control. Type the following text in the `Caption` property of the label:

   `Welcome! You have located The Grape Vine home page. This site provides assistance with selecting an appropriate wine for your next meal or party. Click the Sommelier button at the bottom to review the Options page.`

9. To spice up the home page, add an image control. You can set the `Picture` property to any bitmap (.bmp) or metafile (.wmf) you choose.

   The ActiveX document should now appear like the one in Figure 12.1.

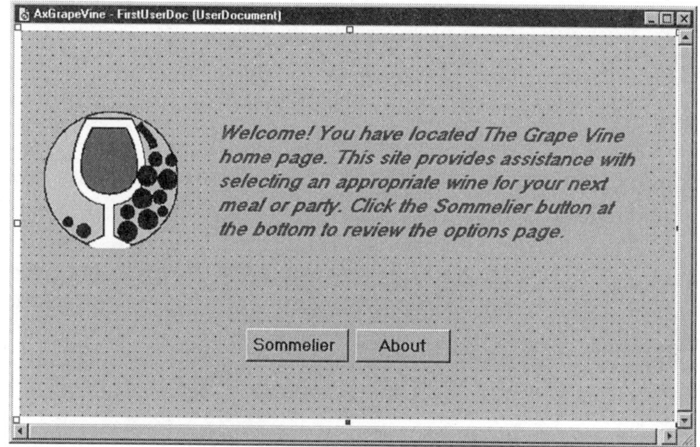

FIG. 12.1
The `AxGrapeVine` project after addition of OLE controls to the FirstUserDoc `UserDocument` object.

10. Modify the `Click` event of `cmdSommelier` to resemble the following code segment:

```
Private Sub cmdSommelier_Click()
    OptionsPage.Show vbModal
End Sub
```

11. Modify the `Click` event of `cmdAbout` to resemble the following code segment:

```
Private Sub cmdAbout_Click()
    frmAbout.Show vbModal
End Sub
```

12. Add a form to the project. Choose Project, Add Form from the menu. In the Add Form dialog box, choose the blank Form item. Choose Open. A new blank form should now reside in the Forms folder of the Project window.

13. Provide the new form with the name `OptionsPage`. The name should now appear in the title bar of the object, followed by `(Form)`.

14. Modify the `Caption` property of `OptionsPage` by typing the following text:

    `Choose one or more items from the list boxes; click the Suggest button at any time.`

15. Add a command button named `cmdSuggest` to `OptionsPage` and type **`Suggest`** for its `Caption` property. Add a second command button named `cmdHome` and type **`Home`** for its `Caption` property.
16. Add one label control for each of the following `Caption` properties: Appetizers, Cheeses, Soups, Salads, Pasta, Red Meat, Chicken, Other Meat, Seafood, and Miscellaneous.
17. Add one combo box control for each of the following `Name` properties: `cboAppetizers`, `cboCheeses`, `cboSoups`, `cboSalads`, `cboPasta`, `cboRedMeat`, `cboChicken`, `cboOtherMeat`, `cboSeafood`, and `cboMiscellaneous`.
18. Change the `Style` property of each combo box to `2 - Dropdown List`.
19. Add one text box control for each of the following `Name` properties: `txtAppetizers`, `txtCheeses`, `txtSoups`, `txtSalads`, `txtPasta`, `txtRedMeat`, `txtChicken`, `txtOtherMeat`, `txtSeafood`, and `txtMiscellaneous`.
20. Save the application. The `OptionsPage` form should now appear as shown in Figure 12.2.

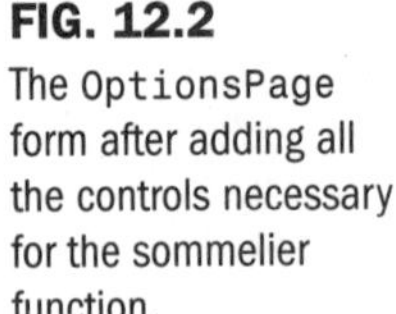

FIG. 12.2
The `OptionsPage` form after adding all the controls necessary for the sommelier function.

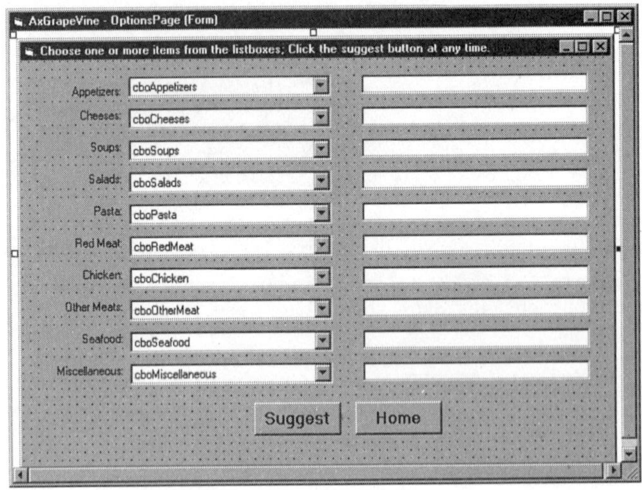

Adding the Code Now you add the bulk of the logic for the application. Remember, the code can be cut from the site **http://www.gasullivan.com/vs97book/** and pasted where you need it.

1. Add the code in Listing 12.1 to the `Load` event of `OptionsPage`.
2. Add the code in Listing 12.2 to the `Click` event of `cmdSuggest`.

3. Add the code in Listing 12.3 to the `Click` event of `cmdHome`.
4. Create a new procedure and supply it with the name `LoadListBoxes`. Add the code in Listing 12.4 to the new procedure.

Listing 12.1 The Form's *Load* Event to Center the Form on the Monitor

```
Private Sub Form_Load()
     Me.Left = (Screen.Width - Me.Width) / 2
     Me.Top = (Screen.Height - Me.Height) / 2
     LoadListBoxes
End Sub
```

Listing 12.2 Determining an Appropriate Wine for Each Food Item Selected

```
Private Sub cmdSuggest_Click()
'routine to suggest wines based on selections in combo boxes
MousePointer = vbHourglass
If cboAppetizers.ListIndex <> -1 Then
     Select Case cboAppetizers.ListIndex
        Case 0
            txtAppetizers.Text = "Light-bodied red wines or whites"
        Case 1
            txtAppetizers.Text = "Semi-dry or sweet wines; light, fruity," _
                                 & "young reds"
        Case 2
            txtAppetizers.Text = "Medium or full-bodied reds"
     End Select
End If
If cboCheeses.ListIndex <> -1 Then
     Select Case cboCheeses.ListIndex
        Case 0
            txtCheeses.Text = "Fruity reds"
        Case 1
            txtCheeses.Text = "Full-bodied reds"
        Case 2
            txtCheeses.Text = "Sweet wines"
        Case 3
            txtCheeses.Text = "Full-bodied reds; fruitier wines"
        Case 4
            txtCheeses.Text = "Creamy whites; champagne; sparkling wines"
     End Select
End If
If cboSoups.ListIndex <> -1 Then
     Select Case cboSoups.ListIndex
        Case 0
            txtSoups.Text = "Medium-bodied reds"
        Case 1
            txtSoups.Text = "Light white wine"
```

continues

Listing 12.2 Continued

```
            Case 2
                txtSoups.Text = "Full-bodied reds"
            Case 3
                txtSoups.Text = "Light-bodied whites"
            Case 4
                txtSoups.Text = "Fruity reds"
        End Select
    End If

    If cboSalads.ListIndex <> -1 Then
        Select Case cboSalads.ListIndex
            Case 0
                txtSalads.Text = "No wine recommended"
            Case 1
                txtSalads.Text = "High-acidic wines"
            Case 2
                txtSalads.Text = "Dry whites"
            Case 3
                txtSalads.Text = "Fruity reds or whites"
        End Select
    End If
    If cboPasta.ListIndex <> -1 Then
        Select Case cboPasta.ListIndex
            Case 0
                txtPasta.Text = "Light, fruity reds and blush wines"
            Case 1
                txtPasta.Text = "Full-bodied reds"
            Case 2
                txtPasta.Text = "Light-bodied reds; dry whites"
            Case 3
                txtPasta.Text = "Dry white wine"
        End Select
    End If
    If cboRedMeat.ListIndex <> -1 Then
        Select Case cboRedMeat.ListIndex
            Case 0
                txtRedMeat.Text = "Medium- or robust-bodied reds"
            Case 1
                txtRedMeat.Text = "Robust full-bodied reds"
            Case 2
                txtRedMeat.Text = "Fruity young reds"
            Case 3
                txtRedMeat.Text = "Full-bodied reds"
        End Select
    End If
    If cboChicken.ListIndex <> -1 Then
        Select Case cboChicken.ListIndex
            Case 0
                txtChicken.Text = "Medium-bodied reds; white wines"
            Case 1
                txtChicken.Text = "Roses; blush wines"
```

```
        Case 2
            txtChicken.Text = "Crisp, oaky-flavored wines"
        Case 3
            txtChicken.Text = "Full-bodied reds"
     End Select
End If
If cboOtherMeat.ListIndex <> -1 Then
     Select Case cboOtherMeat.ListIndex
        Case 0
            txtOtherMeat.Text = "Medium-bodied reds"
        Case 1
            txtOtherMeat.Text = "Light reds; roses, blush wines"
        Case 2
            txtOtherMeat.Text = "Full-bodied reds"
        Case 3
            txtOtherMeat.Text = "Full-bodied reds; dry whites"
        Case 4
            txtOtherMeat.Text = "Full-bodied, robust reds"
     End Select
End If

If cboSeafood.ListIndex <> -1 Then
     Select Case cboSeafood.ListIndex
        Case 0
            txtSeafood.Text = "Crisp, light whites"
        Case 1
            txtSeafood.Text = "Light reds; crisp, young whites"
        Case 2
            txtSeafood.Text = "Full-bodied whites"
        Case 3
            txtSeafood.Text = "Full-bodied reds"
        Case 4
            txtSeafood.Text = "Full-bodied whites"
        Case 5
            txtSeafood.Text = "Champagne; sparkling wines"
        Case 6
            txtSeafood.Text = "Medium-bodied reds"
        Case 7
            txtSeafood.Text = "Champagne; sparkling wines"
        Case 8
            txtSeafood.Text = "Delicate whites"
     End Select
End If
If cboMiscellaneous.ListIndex <> -1 Then
     Select Case cboMiscellaneous.ListIndex
        Case 0
            txtMiscellaneous.Text = "Dry white wines; champagne"
        Case 1
            txtMiscellaneous.Text = "Beaujolais; fruity reds; blush whites"
        Case 2
            txtMiscellaneous.Text = "Sweet wines; champagne"
     End Select
End If

MousePointer = vbDefault
End Sub
```

Listing 12.3 Unloading the Current Form and Returning Users to the Home Page

```
Private Sub cmdHome_Click()
Unload Me
End Sub
```

Listing 12.4 Loading All Listbox Controls with Items from Which Users Can Select

```
     Public Sub LoadListBoxes()
'fill the Appetizers cbo
     cboAppetizers.AddItem "Antipasto"
     cboAppetizers.AddItem "Pate"
     cboAppetizers.AddItem "Toasted ravioli"
'fill the Cheeses cbo
     cboCheeses.AddItem "Mild"
     cboCheeses.AddItem "Strong/aged"
     cboCheeses.AddItem "Blue cheese, Saga"
     cboCheeses.AddItem "Goat cheese"
     cboCheeses.AddItem "Brie/creamy cheese"
'fill the Soup cbo
     cboSoups.AddItem "Hearty soup"
     cboSoups.AddItem "Lighter soup"
     cboSoups.AddItem "Stew"
     cboSoups.AddItem "Clam chowder"
     cboSoups.AddItem "Cheese soup"
'fill the Salad cbo
     cboSalads.AddItem "Vinegar dressing"
     cboSalads.AddItem "Herb dressing"
     cboSalads.AddItem "Creamy dressing"
     cboSalads.AddItem "Sweet dressing"
'fill the Pasta cbo
     cboPasta.AddItem "Primavera/vegetable sauces"
     cboPasta.AddItem "Hearty tomato sauces"
     cboPasta.AddItem "Shellfish sauces"
     cboPasta.AddItem "Cream/white sauces"
'fill the Red Meat cbo
     cboRedMeat.AddItem "Barbeque"
     cboRedMeat.AddItem "Game"
     cboRedMeat.AddItem "Grilled or roasted"
     cboRedMeat.AddItem "Steak"
'fill the Chicken cbo
     cboChicken.AddItem "Roasted or grilled"
     cboChicken.AddItem "Chicken salad"
     cboChicken.AddItem "Chicken with cream sauce"
     cboChicken.AddItem "Duck"
'fill the Other Meat cbo
     cboOtherMeat.AddItem "Veal"
     cboOtherMeat.AddItem "Ham"
```

```
    cboOtherMeat.AddItem "Pork roast"
    cboOtherMeat.AddItem "Pork chops"
    cboOtherMeat.AddItem "Lamb"
'fill the Seafood cbo
    cboSeafood.AddItem "Grilled"
    cboSeafood.AddItem "Full-flavored fish"
    cboSeafood.AddItem "Swordfish/tuna"
    cboSeafood.AddItem "Fish in cream/butter sauce"
    cboSeafood.AddItem "Lobster"
    cboSeafood.AddItem "Salmon"
    cboSeafood.AddItem "Smoked fish"
    cboSeafood.AddItem "Sole"
'fill the Miscellaneous cbo
    cboMiscellaneous.AddItem "Fruit"
    cboMiscellaneous.AddItem "Cold cuts"
    cboMiscellaneous.AddItem "Dessert"
End Sub
```

Creating an About the Grape Vine Box As discussed earlier, a good feature of a web page is to have an About box. Users can refer to this useful tool for understanding the whereabouts and purpose of the web site, as well as other useful application-pertinent facts. To add an About box to the Grape Vine application, follow these steps:

1. Choose Project, Add Form from the menu.
2. In the Add Form dialog box, select the About Box item and choose Open. A new About Box template form now resides in the Forms folder of the Project window.
3. Change the text property for each label control on the form, using the following example text as a guide:
   - `lblTitle` = The Grape Vine
   - `lblVersion` = Version 1.0
   - `lblDescription` = The Grape Vine is an online sommelier that suggests wines according to choices made from various food lists. The program can suggest wines for one or more selections. Users should make the final decision on the wine that best complements their tastes.
   - `lblDisclaimer` = Warning: This program protected by copyright laws.
4. Create a new procedure that will center `frmAbout` when it's loaded. Add the code in Listing 12.5 to the `Load` event of the form `frmAbout`.

   The form `frmAbout` should appear as shown in Figure 12.3.
5. Compile the project and correct any syntax errors that occur. Save the project again.
6. Create an EXE by choosing File, Make AxGrapeVine.exe from the menu.

Listing 12.5 Centering the Form Onscreen

```
Private Sub Form_Load()
     Me.Left = (Screen.Width - Me.Width) / 2
     Me.Top = (Screen.Height - Me.Height) / 2
End Sub
```

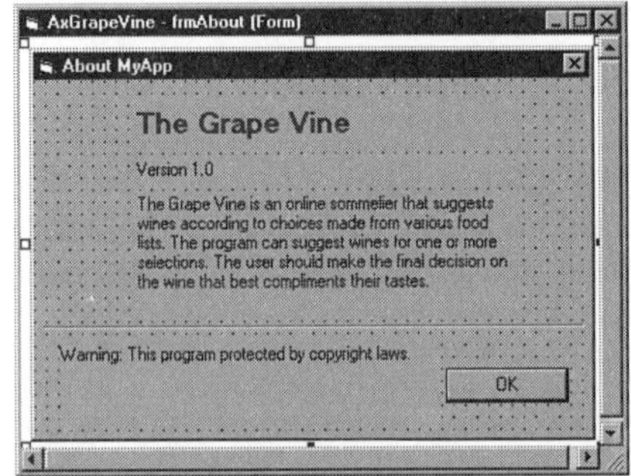

FIG. 12.3
An About box is a useful mechanism for conveying location and context to visitors of a web site.

Testing the Grape Vine

You can now execute the application, but remember that this application can't be viewed in the IDE as a standalone application. You must view and debug the application with the aid of a container. To do this, follow these steps:

NOTE The `CreateToolWindow` method, in this context, allows you to create a dockable window in the IDE for the purpose of debugging an ActiveX document. The process of opening a browser window for each test of the application can become tedious. `CreateToolWindow` partially sidesteps this hassle by facilitating everything in the IDE.

1. Run the project by choosing Run, Start from the menu or by pressing F5.
2. Start Internet Explorer. If you aren't online, Internet Explorer will present you with an error message similar to the one in Figure 12.4. It's not a problem—click OK.

The message means Internet Explorer attempted to connect to the Microsoft home page, Internet Explorer's default URL, and an online connection didn't exist. To prevent this type of message from occurring, make a local URL the default startup page for the browser. After you choose OK, Internet Explorer resorts to loading a local HTML page into the container until you supply a new URL. The URL for the generic local HTML page shown is C:\windows\system\blank.htm.

FIG. 12.4
Internet Explorer provides feedback when an URL address can't be located.

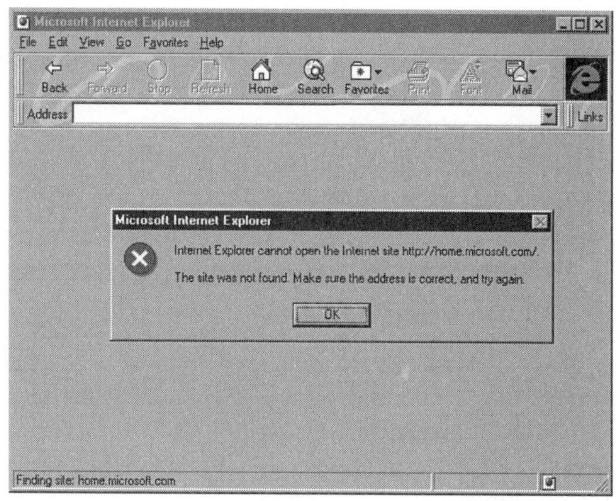

3. In the address box of Internet Explorer, enter the path and name of the ActiveX document now executing (the path on your machine might not be the same as this one):

```
D:\VSD\ActiveXExe\FirstUserDoc.vbd
```

FirstUserDoc.vbd loads and appears in the container window (see Figure 12.5).

FIG. 12.5
Viewing the startup page of the `AxGrapeVine` project in the Internet Explorer container.

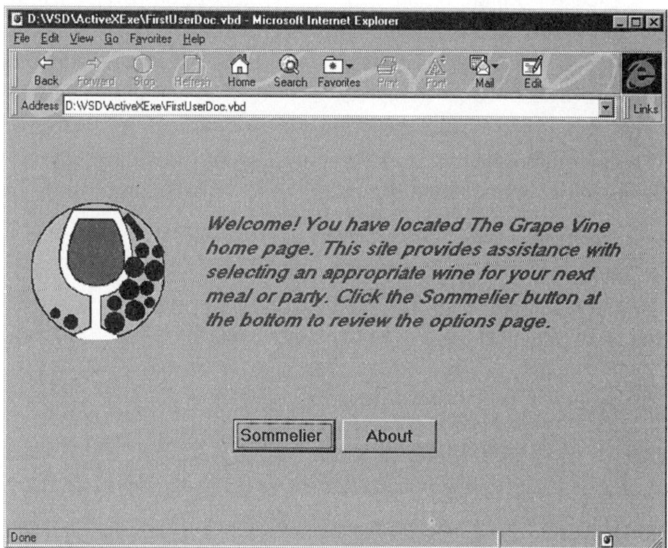

4. Before doing anything more, add the URL address to your Favorites list by choosing Favorites, Add to Favorites from the container menu. For debugging purposes, having the URL predefined to a mouse click saves you time and patience.
5. Click the buttons to observe the functionality. Click the About button to make the About box appear. Click the Sommelier button to open the `OptionsPage` form (see Figure 12.6).

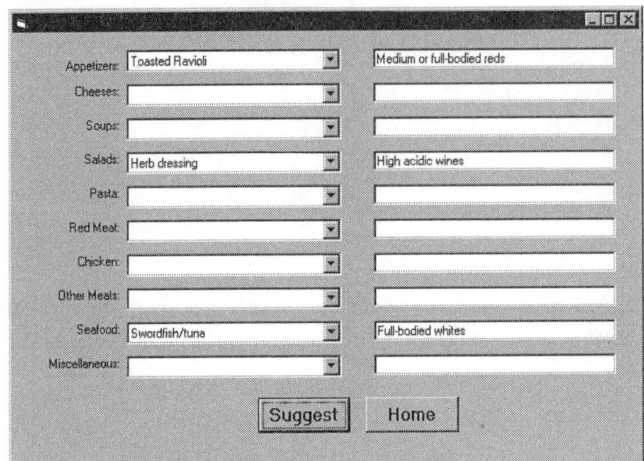

FIG. 12.6
The container viewport while using the Sommelier feature of the Grape Vine ActiveX document.

The application should remain running in the IDE; however, each time you make a change in the application, you must stop and restart Internet Explorer to clear its list. This is where the Favorites entry comes in handy. Depending on the sophistication of the application, the debugging process can be simple or difficult. You might try developing the application as a standard VB project first and migrate it afterward to an ActiveX application, so you can use the debugging talents you've honed during development of standard VB applications. You'll become more accomplished at debugging ActiveX documents with time and experience.

Working with Menus

Now you need to add a menu to the `UserDocument`. In this exercise, the menu calls up the About box in the container viewport. You create this menu for the About box in the VB development environment. If the Grape Vine application is still running, stop it now. To create the menu, follow these steps:

1. Bring up the menu editor by right-clicking the `UserDocument`.
2. In the menu editor, add entries for `mnuHelp` and `mnuAbout`.
3. Add the caption `Help` to the menu item `mnuHelp`. Add the caption `About The Grape Vine` to the menu item `mnuAbout`. Make `mnuAbout` a submenu of `mnuHelp` by selecting the right arrow in the middle of the dialog box.

4. Your completed entries should appear as in Figure 12.7. Click OK to close the menu editor and save the menu entries.

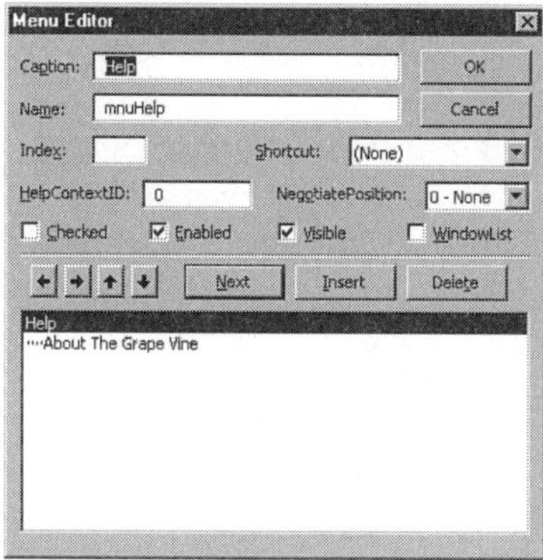

FIG. 12.7
The Menu Editor depicts the items added to the menu of the ActiveX document.

5. Add the following code to the `On_Click` event of `mnuAbout`:

```
frmAbout.Show vbModal
```

6. Save the project and create a new executable.
7. Press F5 to execute the project.

The menu items added in these steps should now appear on the container's menu bar. To test the menu items, open the About box. From here, you can augment and enhance the application.

TROUBLESHOOTING

My container menus are not displaying. Containers won't exhibit their menus correctly unless the ActiveX document successfully merges the application's Help menu with the container's Help menu. The jump from the .htm file to the .vbd file interrupts any chance of having this merge occur successfully. The workaround for this is to have the .vbd file load directly. Menu merging is still an infant capability and a trial-and-error process.

Looking at Installation and Configuration Concerns

You've created an ActiveX document and are ready to deploy. This means, in all likelihood, you need to use the Application Setup Wizard that comes with VB5. Although you can create a custom setup wizard, the version VB offers is robust and about what most installations need. The VB setup kit is configurable through the user interface (UI), and even more so for the experienced developer.

CAUTION

Be careful when modifying any features of the VB setup kit–the fault tolerance for overwriting an important file at a user's desktop might be zero.

You'll find that installing an ActiveX document is a lot different than installing a standard VB application. You no longer need heaps of floppies or even a CD-ROM with runtime and dependency files. Certain steps associated with Internet setup are made easier, but others—including heterogeneous platform issues—make deployment much more challenging. You might be deploying an application for the known world to view, not just the end users down the hall.

Using Internet Download Setup

The setup utility, with your interaction, builds an installation program for deploying the application on clients and servers across LANs, WANs, and I-nets. Although VB5 still possesses the standard setup program option, the Professional and Enterprise Editions include a new feature for creating an Internet download setup. This way, you can create a setup for ActiveX projects, including projects that contain `UserDocuments`. The wizard facilitates the installation and use of an application in one of two ways:

- By creating a standard installation setup, installing the application to a network server, and allowing users to contact the application over a network connection
- By creating an Internet download setup, allowing users to contact the application via I-net, and installing the application for use on the client

Which method you choose has everything to do with the target location you have in mind during requirements planning and development. In other words, it's about scope. Know your audience. You should use the Internet Download Setup for any I-net–based application.

Understanding Browser-Initiated Installation

By far the biggest paradigm shift you'll encounter when deploying active applications is the installation. In the past, software was installed at each client or network share point. Internet setups work much differently. As you build the setup, the wizard collects necessary files and places them in a specified location, which can be a web server or a network server. (Eventually the files need to be placed in a location that the I-net can access.) There they will sit, waiting to be reached by the next browser.

The next time the URL address of the application is specified by some browser out in the ether, the application will be installed at the client computer—that is, the browser drives the installation. As the browser attempts to load the default ActiveX document screen, it compares the application requirements and the resources of the local computer. The browser then downloads and registers any differences identified by the comparison. Although the browser handles this workload, it does so objectively, and any missing components prevent the proper installation and subsequent use of the ActiveX application.

▶ **See** Chapter 10, "Clients, Servers, and Components: Web-Based Applications," **p. 293**

Stepping Through the Setup

In this section, you step through the process of creating an Internet download setup, installing the application, and viewing the application in a container. First, start the Application Setup Wizard. After reading the Introduction dialog box information, click Next to proceed to the Select Project and Options dialog box (see Figure 12.8).

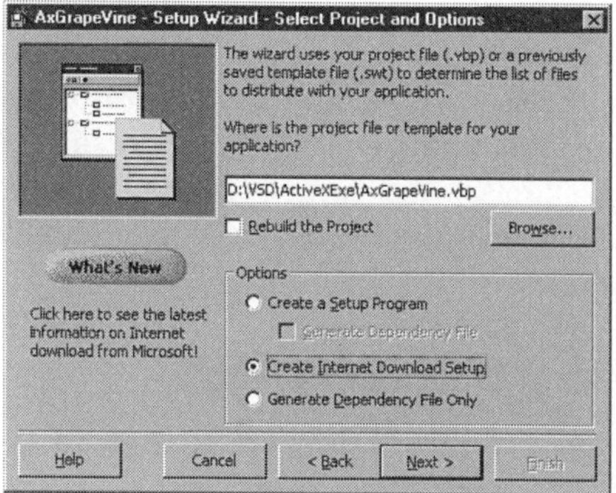

FIG. 12.8
The Select Project and Options dialog box lets you choose the project file and specify setup program options.

Click the Browse button and locate the AxGrapeVine.vbp project file. Select the Create Internet Download Setup option. Choosing the Rebuild the Project option recompiles the project and builds a new executable. You've performed these tasks already, so leave the checkbox for this option clear and click Next to continue.

NOTE In general, you won't have much need for the Rebuild the Project option. Having a cleanly compiled and built executable before using the setup program is best.

ON THE WEB

The Select Project and Options dialog box features a hyperlink to information on Internet download from Microsoft. The link takes you to **http://www.microsoft.com/vbasic.icompdown**, where you can find web-development content for Visual Basic.

The Internet Distribution Location dialog box requires you to specify a path where the download files will be placed (see Figure 12.9). At this time, select any location your computer has been mapped to; in the future, bear in mind that you must choose a location accessible via an HTTP transaction by users who might have guest permissions or less.

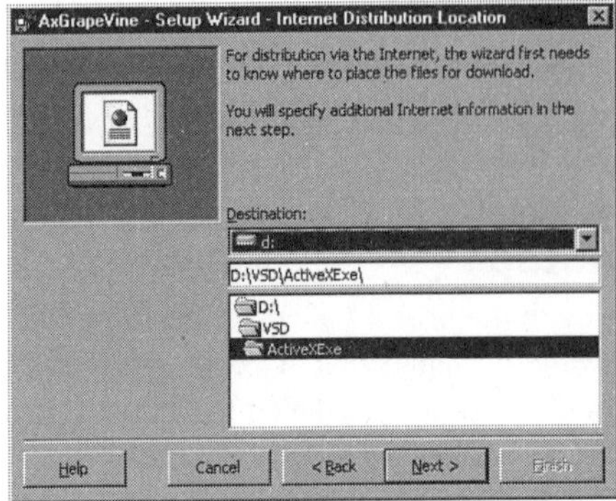

FIG. 12.9
The Internet Distribution Location window allows users to specify a source location where the wizard can install the application files.

The Internet Package dialog box, shown in Figure 12.10, allows you to specify whether parts of your distributed application will be located at a Microsoft web site and linked to the remaining components. The setup wizard creates a primary cabinet (.cab) file and encloses in it items such as ActiveX controls, EXEs, documents, and DLLs. For ActiveX-based projects, one or more additional .cab files are created to store all additional controls and referenced objects (such as RDO 2.0).

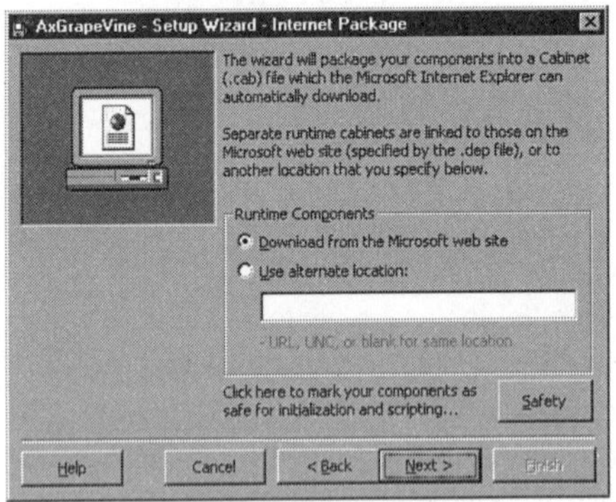

FIG. 12.10
The Internet Package dialog box allows users to specify a source for component download.

If you're distributing this application across the Internet, it's advisable to choose Download from the Microsoft Web Site. If you're distributing this application across your intranet, choosing the Use Alternate Location option is more appropriate. For example, an intranet application in an environment with no Internet access can still support ActiveX documents if the necessary .cab files are placed in the setup directory. All the .cab files are available at the Microsoft web site or on the Visual Basic CD-ROM and can be copied to the network server and used by the application. Each method has its benefits, but generally you want to consider speed, security, and version management. Most important, know the objectives you want to achieve for the application and the enterprise, and choose your installation method accordingly.

Choose the Use Alternate Location option for this exercise. Leave the text box blank to default to the previously selected setup location.

Click the Safety button to personally indicate project components you decide are safe for the user environment. The options Safe for Initialization and Safe for Scripting are available only for Internet installations. Exercise caution when assigning either option unless you're absolutely sure of these assertions. Furthermore, your .cab files must be fully signed before you can make complete use of these features. Click Cancel to close the Safety dialog box and then click Next to continue.

NOTE *Signed* refers to a digital signature applied to distributed software components to indicate who created the component. It's an assurance by the creator that the component won't damage the user's computer. Signing doesn't completely ensure that an installed component won't damage a user's system, but it does create a path from the user to the creator in case the software harms the system. Developers can be held liable in some instances when installed components cause damage.

In the ActiveX Server Components dialog box, you can specify local or remote ActiveX server components, such as ActiveX EXEs, DLLs, or OCXs (see Figure 12.11). The selection of these components might seem daunting, but it isn't—the hard part is planning and developing local or remote server components. Suppose that you develop a remote ActiveX EXE for the Grape Vine to function as a data-collection agent. A single server can collect data from disparate, geographically dispersed data sources, perform aggregations on the data, and serve the data back to a client application. You can position this server remotely and benefit from single-point maintenance, improving network performance by eliminating the need to pass large volumes of raw data across a LAN or WAN. Conversely, if a screen refresh is most important, locally positioned components are more advantageous. You should rely on the local default option at this time because no server components are involved in the Grape Vine application. Click Next to continue.

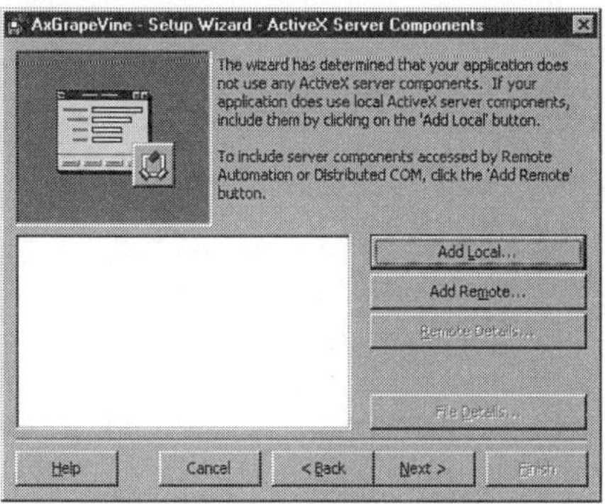

FIG. 12.11 The Active Server Components dialog box allows users to select local or remote application servers.

The File Summary dialog box gives you a chance to review or add runtime files to be distributed with the application. This step usually requires you to make some file additions to the list. Knowing which files to include requires an exhaustive understanding of the support files that must accompany all components, third-party or otherwise, in your application. Third-party vendors often include runtime distribution lists with their products. You should always build your install set and test it on a clean machine—that is, a machine without the runtime components that you're distributing—to ensure that you won't have problems after the fact. Don't expect the setup wizard to include all the necessary files by default (it won't), and you'll experience iterations of building, testing, and troubleshooting before you meet with success.

Figure 12.12 shows the File Details dialog box, in which you can exert significant control over the execution of the setup program. In this dialog box, you can view or change where files will be installed on the end user's machine. For example, an option exists to install the selected component as a shared file. As this implies, other applications will have use of the component. If a series of installs will be made, each requiring the use of the file in question, this option is useful, but you should exercise caution and modify this file option only if you're sure of your actions. If a shared ActiveX component is installed to different folders, removing one file instance might result in removal of the Registry information that makes the remaining copies accessible, rendering the remaining components inaccessible. You definitely want to test any changes you make to the default settings. For this installation of the Grape Vine, all default settings are appropriate. Click Next to accept the current list of runtime files.

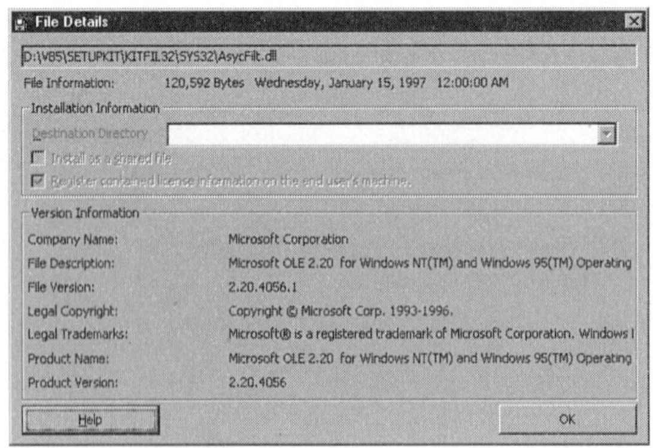

FIG. 12.12
The File Details dialog box allows users to view and change the installation information for files to be delivered with your I-net application.

You can click Save to store the setup template for future use. Remember to choose an appropriate location and assign a useful mnemonic name.

NOTE You can modify the setup template in any common text editor. Current VB documentation cautions strongly against this unless you're a very experienced developer. In reality, it isn't that serious. Your first installation should be on a test server, anyway. Be sure to make a copy of the setup file before modifying it. If the setup doesn't go as you want it to, you can compare the two files to see where you might have erred.

Select the Finish button to complete the setup process. The setup program will be built in short order.

The setup program creates several files to manage the installation and execution of the application:

- The .htm file is a generated web page that automatically installs and registers .cab files on the user's machine and then opens the initial .vbd file in the viewport.
- The .inf setup-information reference file is used during installation of the application.
- The Setup Wizard uses the .ddf project file to create the .cab file.
- The .dep file is a dependency file used by the Setup Wizard.
- The .swt file is a Setup Wizard template for the application. You can customize this file.

Testing the Setup

Internet Explorer visits the .htm file to install the application. The other files act in a support capacity during the installation process. To test the setup program, follow these steps:

1. Start Internet Explorer.
2. Choose File, Open from the menu.
3. In the Open dialog box, choose the Browse button.
4. Locate and select the AxGrapeVine.htm file. Choose the Open button. The text box in the Open dialog box fills with the AxGrapeVine.htm file and path.
5. Choose OK.

The installation of the application begins. Almost immediately a warning message appears, explaining that one or more of the components to be installed isn't verifiably safe. This happens because the safety checks weren't selected during the setup process. Be sure to heed the admonitions of this message. If you're not sure of the security implications, you should cancel the setup.

TROUBLESHOOTING

Certain components consistently fail to download. At this writing, browsers won't download components successfully with the browser security level set above medium. You probably need to take security completely off for some components to work at all. Because this can compromise the security directives of your enterprise, understand how component download affects the development effort. Also bear in mind that most users choose to cancel download operations from web sites they have arrived at as visitors or guests. Communicate the download process effectively to all those intended users so that they'll know exactly what to expect and how they are to respond.

The application installation completes in short order, and the FirstUserDoc ActiveX document appears in the browser window.

Test the setup program on a machine that now doesn't contain either a VB IDE or any of the ActiveX components in the project. Test the installation on multiple operating systems and environments to ensure success.

Understanding Integration Issues

Serious development always leads to a stage when software integration and implementation become necessary. A basic part of development involves understanding the environment in which the application will be deployed. ActiveX technology developed in VB5 isn't different from other development tools. Some platforms are well suited for VB5 applications; others clearly aren't ready to be the target platform. Various client/server and I-net development technologies exist because of the diverse platforms on which enterprises and end users function. With that in mind, a discussion about platform capabilities is beneficial here.

Although some development tools are supported on multiple platforms, Visual Basic isn't one of them. Simply put, when you develop in VB, it's done on a PC. You can use a distributed VB application on various platforms, although all-encompassing, cross-platform deployment isn't the primary charge of VB; however, users on various platforms with different browsers can visit an executing ActiveX VB application. VB does allow you to create an Active Server Page (ASP), making the functionality accessible by all browsers, whether running with Windows, Apple Macintosh, or UNIX operating systems. Also, Visual Basic completely supports ODBC, making ODBC databases on any platform accessible through common, object-oriented data-access mechanisms. For these reasons, it's important to understand and appreciate the concerns that arise in cross-platform environments (see Figure 12.13).

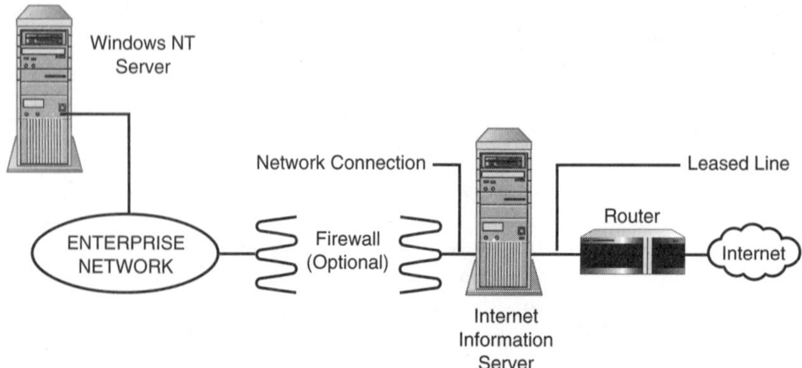

FIG. 12.13
An Internet connectivity scenario. Although the type of technology can vary, such as a network operating system, the topology is pretty standard.

Platforms

Imagine that the web server in Figure 12.13 can be a Windows NT or UNIX server; the NOS can be Windows NT, Novell, Banyan Vines, or UNIX; and clients on the network can include Windows NT, Windows 95, Windows 3.1, Macintosh, UNIX, or OS/2. The collection of technology assembled to achieve enterprise I-net connectivity can be quite diverse, making development a conceptually daunting challenge. Business or organization demands often pair combinations of platforms that seem mutually exclusive. For developers, supporting the concept can be withering. At the same time, developers demand the programming tools that allow them to assemble open applications to meet these needs. Your biggest concerns as a developer should be the browsers, the installation platform, data access (if any), and security.

The trend in I-net access is to integrate browsing facilities into nearly every facet of enterprise information systems. Content creators and developers are beginning to retire the notion of anything standalone, beginning to think instead of a whole new online application environment where browsers offer omnipotent control to users. This not only provides a more seamless end-user experience, but also enables a new class of exciting I-net development.

Many developers have a significant investment in knowledge, tools, and components based on a particular language. Thus, the browser must provide broad support for the creation of ActiveX controls or other software components in popular languages such as VB, Java, and C++. Customers—specifically, developers and webmasters—are demanding more from browser architecture. Consider that developers want an open browser architecture that supports all available programming languages and is consistent among various user environments, such as Windows and Macintosh. Customers also want tools that support rapid application development, with the capability to integrate operating systems and browsers to their proprietary software solutions.

ON THE WEB

Although it isn't necessary, some corporate intranets feature a customized browser. Many intranets are strictly internal and are used with a corporate-established browser. Many organizations want to create and distribute a web browser that reflects the specific needs of their organization and end users. In this context, the target for an application is predefined, and development is easier for that reason. You can develop a customized corporate browser with a tool such as Internet Explorer Administration Kit. You can find more information about Internet Explorer's Administration Kit at **http://www.microsoft.com/ie**.

Browsers

The dominant browsers of the day include

- Internet Explorer
- Netscape Navigator
- Mosaic

NOTE Check with your software vendor for available Internet Explorer versions per platform. Each new version becomes more sophisticated and offers greater support of ActiveX and HTML technology. Understand the demands that will be placed on your enterprise browser before making any decisions.

Internet Explorer is a family of products that supports a broad range of platforms and is produced in many languages. Microsoft offers Internet Explorer for the Macintosh, Windows 95, Windows 3.1, and Windows NT platforms. It's built to take advantage of the strengths of each major platform, thereby providing increased capabilities without burdening users with a new learning curve. Because of UI consistency, end users can take advantage of key operating-system features while easily changing platforms. Invariably, developers find the broadest range of capabilities by targeting Internet Explorer as a browser.

The merits and demerits of the other browsers won't be discussed, but you can expect the other products to require a special plug-in or added capability before they can host an ActiveX document.

The only server platform that readily accepts a VB ActiveX document installation is Windows NT Server. Although this seems limiting, consider the market share and inroads Windows NT Server has achieved in recent years. Numerous administrative and security characteristics make Windows NT Server an excellent server platform. Because VB and Windows NT are products of the same vendor, the marriage is very comfortable.

The PC is the most widely used desktop platform. Although you can't install a VB application directly to a Macintosh or UNIX workstation, these platforms can use a VB ASP in a browser.

Security

If you're worried about security, that's good. If you aren't sure that your environment is secure, that's bad. Most important is to have a security plan and to monitor, revise, and update your security plan and implementation periodically. In this realm are database security, network security, and application security. Database security is discussed more in the next section.

Network security can be discussed from the standpoint of Internet users and intranet users. The presence of an Internet server and network firewall by themselves offers good security. Internet users navigate to a web site by using a public URL, and an Internet server translates that address into an internal address, hidden to anyone outside the enterprise. Effective Internet server administration and management built on a foundation of solid security measures can provide rigorous protection to the network.

ON THE WEB

You can obtain more information about Internet security on the Internet. A simple query, using a search engine such as Yahoo! or AltaVista with the words `security` AND `internet`, will return plenty of information and links on the subject. If you want a more organized source, find a book that discusses the Internet and its numerous topics, including security. You'll find many Internet books at **http://www.mcp.com/que**.

If contemplated and developed correctly, applications can be quite secure. The important point is to establish a series of protective firewalls that accomplish the following:

- Encapsulate in a generic wrapper the processes with which the browser interacts, to hide server and program name details
- Encrypt all passwords
- Develop the application to make bookmarking web pages inside the verification process impossible

Data Access

Your application very likely will interact with a data source. Applications that interact with a database expose developers to a whole new set of issues:

- Database security
- Data corruption
- Data integrity
- Presentation capabilities
- Interfaces

A serious and legitimate concern for database administrators is protecting enterprise databases from unauthorized access and tampering. Protecting data viewed and used by enterprise users is much less of a concern than exposing corporate data to the world via web sites. Many Internet users preoccupy themselves by hacking into secure databases and corrupting or illegally using data. People find a way to breach security, even on the most protected networks and databases, so the concern administrators have about protecting the privacy and integrity of enterprise data is very real.

Consider a financial institution that makes account information available to customers through a web site. Administrators must provide a secure system to prevent unauthorized access to private account data. Implementing the right topology and architecture greatly reduces the threat of a security breach. It's important to position the components to hide specific names and paths of servers, executables, databases, and files. This means privileged information shouldn't be readily available by viewing the HTML source code through the browser's View menu. Because ActiveX documents are based on `UserDocument` objects and not HTML specifically, source code is encapsulated and hidden from end users.

As with any application, data needs to be protected from accidental user corruption. The ability to corrupt data is a function of the privileges users are given. Obviously, users with read-only permissions have virtually no chance of directly polluting data through the UI, as long as the interface is developed correctly. Many users, however, are given desktop tools and database access with CRUD (create, read, update, and delete) permissions, in the interest of productivity. This type of user, wielding a database access tool, can cause damage if left unsupervised. Give enterprise users the minimum of permissions. Don't be too quick to give additional authorization to users who appear more savvy and want to be more productive. This is exactly the type of user who might take chances and make mistakes at the expense of valuable data.

The biggest fear is unauthorized remote users. No one can do much about unauthorized users with legitimate passwords. You can hope such a user's access will tip itself off eventually, at which time the password can be changed. Keep close tabs on remote users. Never give remote users more than read privileges unless absolutely necessary. Business processes that require more permissions should be heavily scrutinized. Remember, inadequate database security not only jeopardizes confidentiality of data, but also your ability to maintain database integrity. It's a cost any enterprise can ill afford.

Understand the demands a web site places on the database, the network, and the company infrastructure. Today's users don't have patience with slow throughput, so determine your expected user volumes, peak demand periods, and appropriate hardware resources accordingly. Optimize the cost benefit of hardware resources. Often, departments can lease time and web space from company web and database servers. The benefits of this arrangement include maintenance off load and cost savings.

Will the application share data between documents and forms? If so, particular care must be taken when developing variables and variable scope. Understand these types of implications when targeting for a multicontainer distribution. Take particular care in reviewing forms that have been migrated by using the Migration Wizard; these forms can be prime candidates for data-integrity violations.

From Here...

A time and place will come when all applications will have been ported to enterprise intranets and new development will be only Active in format. New development will be targeted specifically to I-net solutions and built with ActiveX technology. This chapter discussed how to implement ActiveX documents. You built an ActiveX document application and migrated objects from existing standard applications into your ActiveX application. For more information on some of the topics addressed in this chapter, see the following chapters:

- For a thorough overview of web-based application technology, see Chapter 11, "An Inside Look at Web-Based Applications."
- To learn how to web-enable existing applications, see Chapter 19, "Enabling Existing Applications for I-net Environments."
- For information on building applications for a distributed environment, see Chapter 20, "Clients, Servers, and Components: Design Strategies for Distributed Applications."

ON THE WEB

For a look at multimedia creation tools for I-net applications, see "Web Content Creation Tools and Utilities" on the web page at **http://www.gasullivan.com/vs97book/**.

CHAPTER 13

An Inside Look at Active Server Pages and Internet Information Server

by Azam A. Mirza

The Active Platform

Learn about the strategy behind the Active Platform and the underlying technologies that bring the power of client/server computing to the World Wide Web.

Active Server Pages

Learn about the features that make ASP such a powerful and flexible mechanism for creating dynamic, feature-rich Web sites.

Active Server objects

Gain an understanding of the built-in Active Server objects that provide powerful functionality as part of ASP. A detailed discussion of their usage and purpose is provided.

Active Server scripting

Learn about the Active Server scripting mechanisms. See how to build powerful web sites by harnessing the power of server-side scripting intermixed with HTML.

The basic software component that brings together the power of I-nets is the World Wide Web server software. Web server software gives clients access to corporate information and data by facilitating information publishing, application execution, and data retrieval.

Most web server software packages—such as Microsoft Internet Information Server (IIS), various Netscape server products, and WebSite—provide a comprehensive set of setup, management, and administration facilities. In most cases, a basic and functional web server can be installed, set up, and made operational within an hour. Also, all server packages include sophisticated system administration utilities, such as the Server Manager utility included with IIS.

Until recently, most web servers stored static information for access by clients. With the introduction of technologies such as Java applets, ActiveX controls, and database-access tools, web servers have become more than just facilitators for publishing static information. Web servers now can provide powerful capabilities, such as user authentication, connectivity to database servers, dynamic page creation based on user actions or database queries, and data encryption. The list isn't exhaustive, but is intended to provide a measure of advances that have been made in the last year or so in terms of the capabilities of web server software.

Microsoft's Internet Information Server deserves special mention due to its tight and robust integration with Windows NT Server and the security subsystem in particular. This tight integration allows IIS to use the built-in Windows NT Server security model for user authentication and password validation. User access to the web can be controlled by authenticating users against the Windows NT domain user lists. Files and directory access from the web can be controlled by setting permissions for user groups through the Windows NT security mechanisms. Traffic analysis and performance monitoring can be performed by using the Windows NT Performance Monitor utility, and logging can be performed by using the Windows NT event log.

Microsoft has also provided additional functionality to the core web server product through add-on products and tools. This chapter discusses these tools and technologies in further detail. ■

The Active Platform

As part of its strategy to deliver components that enable Microsoft BackOffice as the backbone of Internet technologies, Microsoft has added a high-level component to IIS that delivers cross-platform support, open standards, and a tightly integrated set of tools for delivering dynamic web content to users.

Active Platform is an open architecture based on industry standards for creating web sites and web-enabled applications for I-nets. Active Platform provides a means for developers to create web content that can be used across hardware platforms and operating systems.

ON THE WEB

Microsoft's web site, **http://www.microsoft.com**, contains extensive information about Active Platform and other Internet technologies. Visit the site periodically for the latest information about Microsoft tools and products.

Active Platform leverages such technologies as HTML, scripting mechanisms (such as VBScript and JScript), Microsoft Component Object Model (COM), Java support, and the underlying operating system services to deliver dynamic, interactive, and customizable content to client desktops on the Internet and intranets.

By providing a high-level platform that sits atop IIS and the operating system, Microsoft has created a platform that frees you, the web developer, from worrying about underlying details and operating system idiosyncrasies. You can build web sites that conform to Active Platform specs and not worry about the hardware platform and operating system the site will run on.

Active Platform not only brings uniformity to the server side for web-enabled applications, it also encompasses the client side with the same open architecture to deliver a cohesive means of displaying content residing on Active Platform servers.

Three main parts to Active Platform make it possible to create, deploy, and use powerful web-enabled applications for the Internet and intranets:

- ActiveX technologies
- Active Desktop
- Active Server Pages

Figure 13.1 shows the relationship among the various Active Platform components, which are based on Microsoft's Active Platform technologies. The following sections describe these technologies and the other components in more detail.

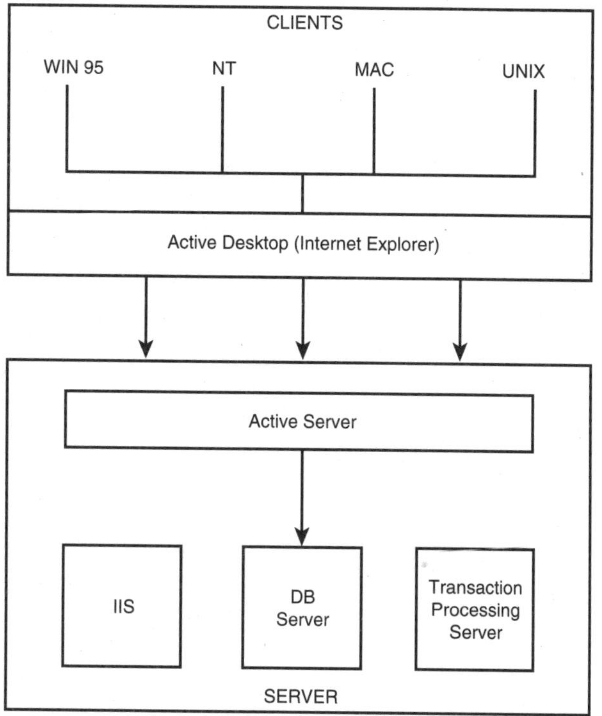

FIG. 13.1 Active Platform technologies underlie the Microsoft Internet initiative that enables active connections between multiple platforms and servers.

ActiveX Technologies

The term *ActiveX technologies* refers to the tools and standards that work together to bring dynamic, interactive content to your web site. ActiveX technologies are software standards, components, and tools that work on various operating systems and heterogeneous networks to enable Active Platform. Some of the technologies included in the ActiveX standard are as follows:

- *Dynamic HTML.* This extension to HTML technology allows you to create dynamic, on-the-fly web pages. Dynamic HTML pages are created in response to the completion of an ActiveX application and display the results to users. For example, an ActiveX database access object might query a relational database, obtain the resultset, create a dynamic HTML page to display the resultset, and send the dynamic HTML page to the client browser for display to the user.

▶ **See** Chapter 18, "Dynamic HTML," **p. 487**, for more information about developing content with Dynamic HTML.

ON THE WEB

For more information about Dynamic HTML, refer to Microsoft's web site at **http://www.microsoft.com/workshop/author/dhtml/default.htm**.

- *Language-independent scripting support.* Full support is provided for scripting mechanisms, such as VBScript and JScript. ActiveX supports open scripting standards that provide scripting support in various languages and on all supported platforms. You can execute scripting on the client browser and on the web server components through the use of an ActiveX scripting engine.

NOTE IIS 3.0 supports compilation-free execution of server-side scripts.

- *System services.* ActiveX provides access to operating system services through its component architecture model. Active Platform can access operating system services on supported platforms, such as Windows, Macintosh, and the various UNIX flavors that will be supported through various third-party vendors in the near future.
- *Development tools.* Support for ActiveX is incorporated into all Microsoft development tools for creating ActiveX components. These include Microsoft's Visual InterDev, Visual C++, and Visual Basic. ActiveX components can be written in any language that supports the creation of such components.
- *Java support.* ActiveX technologies provide full support and interoperability for the Java technology and Java applets. The Microsoft Java virtual machine (JVM) and the Visual J++ development tool provide support for accessing ActiveX objects from Java applets. This provides support for building Java applets that can interface with operating system services through an ActiveX object. For example, the Java specification doesn't allow for applets to gain access to file system services. By building an ActiveX object that works as a bridge between the operating system and the Java applet, however, you can gain access to these resources from the Java world.

NOTE Future versions of Visual Studio tools will provide support for the J/Direct interface, which makes the interaction between Java applets and Windows services very easy and seamless.

NOTE Active Server Pages, discussed later in the "Active Server Pages" section, include the Microsoft Java virtual machine for running Java applets and applications.

- *ActiveX Data Objects (ADO).* ActiveX provides a new mechanism for accessing databases by using ODBC (Open DataBase Connectivity). ADO is similar to DAO (Data Access Objects) and RDO (Remote Data Objects) used by Visual C++ and Visual Basic, and provides developers with a means to access the data stored in corporate relational databases. Developers can create HTML pages with scripts that take advantage of ADO constructs to access databases or create data-aware ActiveX controls.

NOTE Microsoft Visual Basic 5.0 and Visual C++ 5.0 are two of the Visual Studio products that you can use to create data-aware ADO controls.

These ActiveX technologies and tools encompass the entire Active Platform on the client and server sides. Some are implemented as standalone tools for enhancing the Active Platform environment, whereas others implement specific functions on the client and server sides.

Active Desktop

Active Desktop is the client component of the Active Platform environment. Active Desktop enables the creation of applications that run on the client systems under a multitude of operating systems and hardware platforms.

Active Desktop provides you with a means of writing applications to a common interface to ensure the capability to run on multiple operating systems and hardware platforms. It includes support for language-independent scripting, dynamic HTML, system services, and ActiveX component technology. Active Desktop provides the following advantages over proprietary solutions:

- A single delivery mechanism for providing user interface objects
- Support for language-independent, client-side scripting capabilities
- Support for the Dynamic HTML technology
- Support for client-side ActiveX components and controls created with such tools as Visual Basic 5.0
- Support for Java applets through the Java virtual machine, the Java runtime compiler, and the Java JIT (Just-In-Time) compiler

Active Desktop is fully integrated with Microsoft Windows 95 and Windows NT. It provides full support and access to the extensive set of APIs available for Windows. The main delivery mechanism for Active Desktop is Microsoft's Internet Explorer web browser.

NOTE Internet Explorer 4.0 provides a look at the first steps of integration between the Windows GUI shell and the Internet Explorer browser through the use of Active Desktop.

Figure 13.2 shows an example of a web site that uses ActiveX components and which is being accessed through the Internet Explorer Active Desktop.

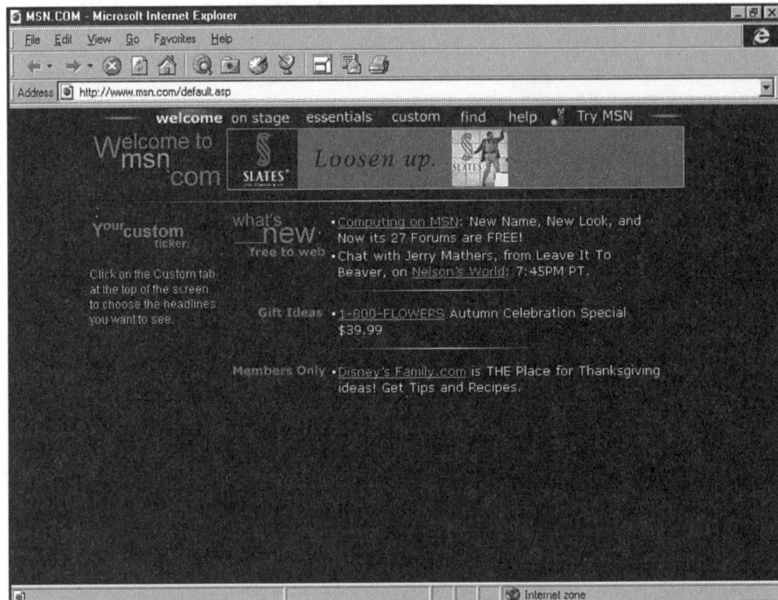

FIG. 13.2
The Microsoft Network web site provides an ActiveX-enabled web experience.

Active Server Pages

IIS 3.0 includes components for enabling your web site for Active Platform. The component that provides server-side ActiveX functionality is called Active Server Pages (ASP), which is nothing more than an HTML page with embedded server-side scripts written in VBScript or JScript. The script is executed on the web server. A pure HTML page is generated as a result of the script execution, and that page is sent to the browser. Figure 13.3 shows how ASP works on the web server.

NOTE *Active Server Pages* denotes the product that was previously referred to as ActiveX Server and code-named Denali. ■

Because an ASP page is nothing more than an HTML page with an .asp extension, all HTML tags are allowed in the ASP file. ASP files also provide the capability to dynamically generate HTML tags on the server before the page is sent to the client browser.

ASP is a high-level component that takes advantage of the scalable, high-performance capabilities of Windows NT Server to provide you with a rich environment for creating server-side web applications. ASP includes full support for Windows NT Server system services, database access, transaction processing, and message queuing. In particular, ASP provides support for the following key functionality:

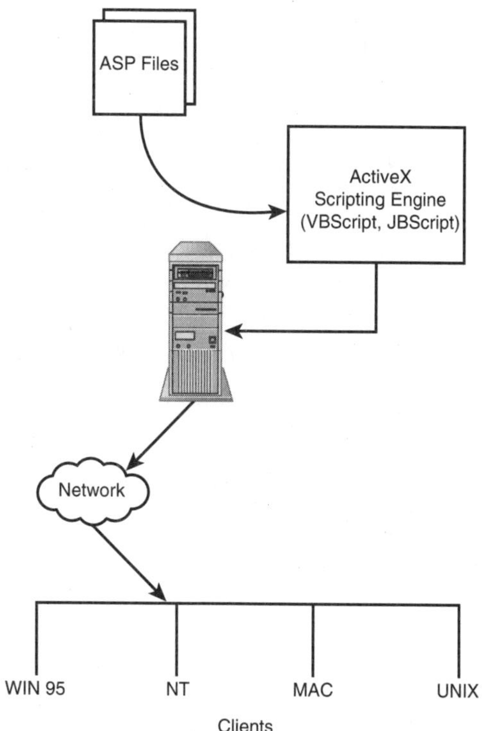

FIG. 13.3
The web server parses the .asp file. Only the generated HTML is sent to the client browser.

- *Active Server Objects.* ASP provides support for hosting component objects commonly referred to as *ActiveX components*. Development tools such as Visual C++, Visual Basic, Visual J++, and PowerBuilder provide support for building reusable components for use by ASP. Active Server Objects are different from ActiveX controls in one respect: They don't have any user interface elements because they run only on the server machine.
- *Active Server Scripting.* ASP provides support for executing scripts on the server. ASP can parse scripts written in VBScript, JScript, Perl, or any other supported scripting language.
- *State Management.* ASP adds support for state management to the World Wide Web. HTTP is a stateless protocol that provides no capabilities for tracking and managing application, user, and web-server states.
- *Database Connectivity.* ASP provides support for connecting your web site to a relational database system through the use of Active Data Objects (ADO) and server-side scripting.

The following sections provide information about installing ASP, as well as using and creating ASP components and applications.

Installing Active Server Pages

ASP is provided as an add-on component to IIS 2.0 or higher. To install ASP, you must have the following software components already in place:

- Windows NT Server 4.0 with Windows NT Server 4.0 Service Pack 1 or higher
- Support for TCP/IP installed as part of the Windows NT Server setup
- Internet Information Server 2.0 or higher

ON THE WEB

You can download ASP from Microsoft's web site at **http://www.microsoft.com/iis/default.asp**.

To install ASP, follow these steps:

1. Choose Start, Run from the menu.
2. In the Run dialog box, type ***path*:\asp.exe**, where ***path*** is where asp.exe resides. The Active Server Pages Setup Wizard launches to install the software.
3. Read the displayed license agreement and click I Agree to Continue. The welcome screen appears.
4. Click Next to continue.
5. If any IIS services are running, the Setup Wizard asks you to stop these services (see Figure 13.4). Click Yes to stop the running IIS services.

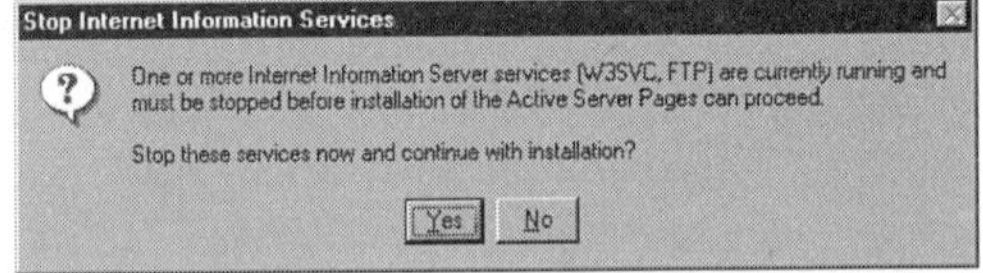

FIG. 13.4
IIS services must be stopped before Active Server Pages can be installed.

6. The Select Options dialog box appears (see Figure 13.5).

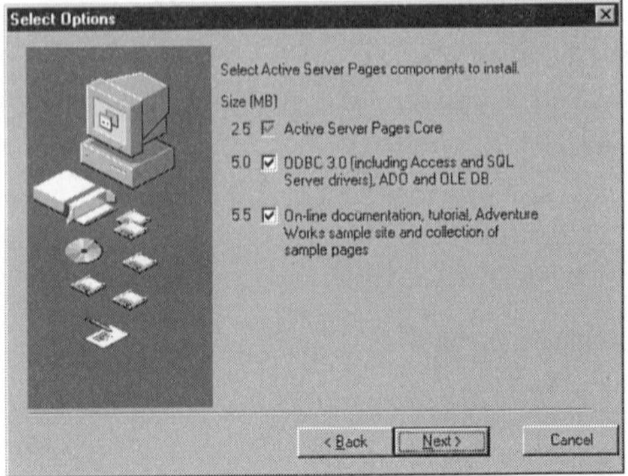

FIG. 13.5
The Select Options dialog box allows you to install additional Active Platform components, such as ODBC support.

By default, all options are selected:

- *Active Server Pages Core.* This option can't be cleared. It installs the core ASP component files needed to provide support for ASP.
- *ODBC 3.0.* This option installs support for ODBC 3.0, the driver for accessing Microsoft Access and Microsoft SQL Server databases for use with ODBC, and support for ADO (Active Data Objects) and OLE DB.

▶ **See** "Universal Data Access and OLE DB," **p. 642**

▶ **See** "Active Data Objects," **p. 644**

- *Documentation and Samples.* This option installs the online documentation and the examples used to illustrate ASP technology.

7. Select the components you want to install and click Next.
8. The Setup Wizard prompts for a location for the samples and documentation files (see Figure 13.6). Click Next to accept the default (or Browse to change the location) and install the samples and documentation files in the specified directory.

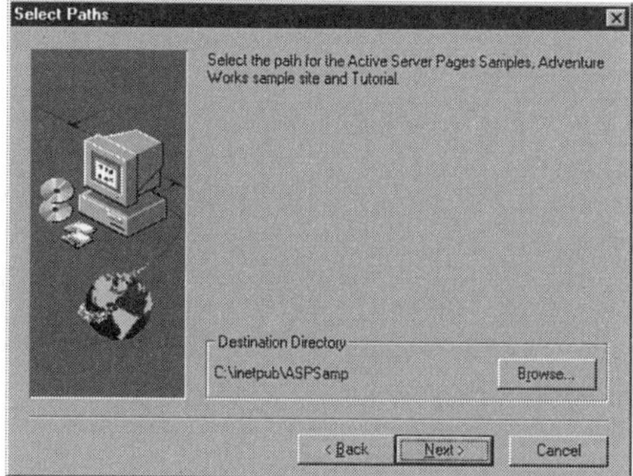

FIG. 13.6
You can install samples and documentation files on a different drive and directory than the server components.

9. The Setup Wizard installs the files necessary for ASP. After setup is complete, the wizard displays a dialog box showing the installed components (see Figure 13.7).

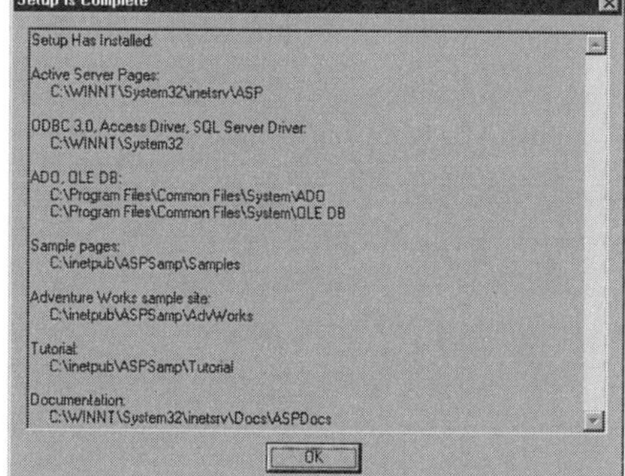

FIG. 13.7
A summary of installation results appears for your review.

10. Click OK to complete the setup of ASP.

As part of the installation process, additional entries are added to the Microsoft Internet Server program group. The Active Server Pages Roadmap entry is particularly useful—it provides a set of HTML documents, including samples for Active Server implementation and online documentation.

After ASP is installed, you're ready to develop content for your web site to take advantage of ASP functionality. The following sections describe how you can use this functionality to bring a new level of sophistication and performance to your web site.

ActiveX Server Objects

ASP provides support for five server objects. These objects are unusual because they're built in to ASP and don't need to be created before being used in Active Server scripts:

- `Application`
- `Session`
- `Request`
- `Response`
- `Server`

The *Application* Object

The `Application` object is used to store and share web-based application-specific information between users. The variables you define as part of the `Application` object are available to all instances of a particular web application and to all users accessing that application.

NOTE In ASP parlance, an *application* is defined as a collection of .asp pages stored within the same virtual web directory and all its subdirectories. A *virtual web directory* is an alias for a physical location of a web site directory. For example, the virtual directory alias \MyWeb might be used to define a physical path such as \\MyServer\InetPub\wwwroot\MyWeb\Production.

The `Application` object supports the following methods:

- The `Lock` method prevents other users from accessing and modifying the `Application` object properties and variables while a particular user is accessing it.
- The `Unlock` method releases a locked `Application` object for use by other users. If `Unlock` isn't explicitly invoked on a locked object, the object is automatically unlocked when it times out or script execution ends.

You can use the Application object to create variables and store values available to all instances of the application. For example, the following code snipped provides a counter that's incremented every time users access the particular .asp page that includes the given script:

```
<%
Application.Lock
Application("Counter") = Application("Counter") + 1
Application.Unlock
%>
```

This code provides a sample mechanism for keeping track of the number of times a certain web page has been accessed. The Lock and Unlock methods ensure that two users don't access the same variable simultaneously.

NOTE If an attempt is made to modify a locked object, the request will be queued until the object becomes available or the web page times out. A web page timeout can be set as part of the page definition, or a global timeout can be used that's set on the web server itself and applies to all web pages by default. For example, a page may have a timeout value of 300 seconds. If a user accessing the page does nothing for more than five minutes after the initial page load, the page will be reloaded from the server rather than the local cache when the user tries to refresh it.

All variables declared within the context of the Application object are discarded when the application ends. The data stored within the Application object variable must be saved to persistent storage if it's to be used later. The VBScript procedure code sample in Listing 13.1 provides an example of storing and tracking the number of page hits to a text file on the server.

Listing 13.1 Storing and Tracking Page Hits on the Server

```
<SCRIPT LANGUAGE=VBScript RUNAT=Server>
Sub SavePageHits()
   SET f = Server.CreateObject("MS.TextStream")
   f.CreateTextFile
   Server.MapPath("/") + "\count.txt", 2, TRUE, FALSE
   f.WriteLine(Application("Counter"))
   f.CloseTextFile
End Sub
</SCRIPT>
```


NOTE Application object variables must be saved to disk if they're to be used between different application sessions.

The Application object also provides support for two special events, OnStart and OnEnd, which are declared in the global.asa file and are executed when the application starts and ends. These events are used to initialize variables at application startup and to clean up when an application ends. Listing 13.2 provides usage examples for the two events.

▶ **See** "The Global.asa File," **p. 422**

Listing 13.2 Using the *Application_OnStart* Event to Initialize Database Connectivity Options

```
<SCRIPT LANGUAGE=VBScript RUNAT=Server>
Sub Application_OnStart
   Application("DataConn_ConnectionString") =
               "DBQ=C:\IntraGAS\ei3.mdb;DefaultDir=C:\IntraGAS;
               Driver={Microsoft Access Driver (*.mdb)};  DriverId=25;
               FIL=MS Access; ImplicitCommitSync=Yes;MaxBufferSize=512;
               MaxScanRows=8;PageTimeout=5; SafeTransactions=0;Threads=3;
               UID=admin;UserCommitSync=Yes;"
   Application("DataConn_ConnectionTimeout") = 15
   Application("DataConn_CommandTimeout") = 30
   Application("DataConn_RuntimeUserName") = "admin"
   Application("DataConn_RuntimePassword") = ""
End Sub
</SCRIPT>
```

The *Session* Object

Unlike the `Application` object, which holds information across multiple instances of the same application and across multiple users, the `Session` object stores state information about a single user. It provides scope for saving user variables. Despite its narrower scope, the `Session` object is very similar to the `Application` object in functionality and usage.

`Session` variables are similar to traditional application global variables. They're available to an application throughout; however, each instance of the application gets its own set of `Session` object variables.

The `Session` object supports the following method and properties:

- The `Abandon` method is used to destroy all `Session` object variables and release their memory. If `Abandon` isn't called explicitly, the variables are destroyed when the `Session` object times out. Calling `Abandon` within the context of a web page doesn't destroy the `Session` object until the page is processed fully and all scripts on the page are executed. The following code sample illustrates the use of the `Abandon` method:

```
<%
Session.Abandon
Session("Counter") = Session("Counter") + 1
Reponse.Write(Session("Counter"))
%>
```

- The `SessionID` property is a `LONG` data type that returns the unique identity assigned to the current user session. The server automatically generates the `SessionID` when a new session is started.

CAUTION

Don't use SessionIDs as unique keys. When a web server is restarted, the SessionID counter is also reinitialized.

- The Timeout property specifies the period in minutes before a Session object is destroyed. If users don't refresh or request a page within the timeout period, the session ends.

In addition to these properties and the Abandon method, the Session object supports the OnStart and OnEnd events. These events are identical in functionality to the Application object events, except their scope is limited to the current user session.

The *Request* Object

The Request object is used to query information from the client browser. The information is passed from the client to the server through an HTTP request. The server, to retrieve the information from the HTTP message, uses the Request object.

You can pass five types of variables to a server application from the client by using the Request object. Each variable has its own collection within the Request object. The Request object contains these collections:

- QueryString
- Form
- Cookies
- ServerVariables
- ClientCertificate

The syntax for accessing the variables stored within the Request object collections is very simple:

```
Request[.Collection](Variable)
```


The collection name is optional and may be omitted. If the collection isn't specified, all the collections within the Request object are searched in the order the collections are listed earlier. The following sections discuss the Request object collections in more detail.

The *QueryString* Collection The QueryString collection provides a parsing mechanism for the QUERY_STRING HTTP tag. It provides access to the HTTP string contained after the question mark, as in the following example:

```
http://www.gasullivan.com/user.asp?id=azamm&name=azam
```

The HTTP string can be retrieved by using the Request object's QueryString collection:

```
ID = Request.QueryString("id")
Name = Request.QueryString("name")
```

If more than one value is assigned to the same variable, the variable is stored as an array. By using an optional `index` parameter, you can access the multiple values:

```
Request.[QueryString]("variable")[.index]
```

To determine the number of values stored within a variable array, use the optional count property:

```
Request.[QueryString]("variable")[.index ¦ .Count]
```

The `index` parameter can have any value between 1 and `Request.[QueryString]("variable")[.index ¦ .Count]`.

To access multiple values stored within the same collection variable, use a numeric index after specifying the variable:

```
Name1 = Request.QueryString("name").(1)
Name2 = Request.QueryString("name").(2)
```

Finally, if you need to access unparsed `QueryString` data, you can gain access to it by using `Request.QueryString` without any parameter values.

The *Form* Collection The `Form` collection is used to retrieve values posted to an HTTP request by an HTML form, using the `POST` method. A form is a part of the HTML standard and supported by all browsers. Web sites use forms to collect user information by using text boxes, checkboxes, radio buttons, and list boxes. Usually, a form has a submit button, which is used to trigger the `POST` method (see Figure 13.8). The `POST` method passes the entered information back to the server in an HTTP `Request` object.

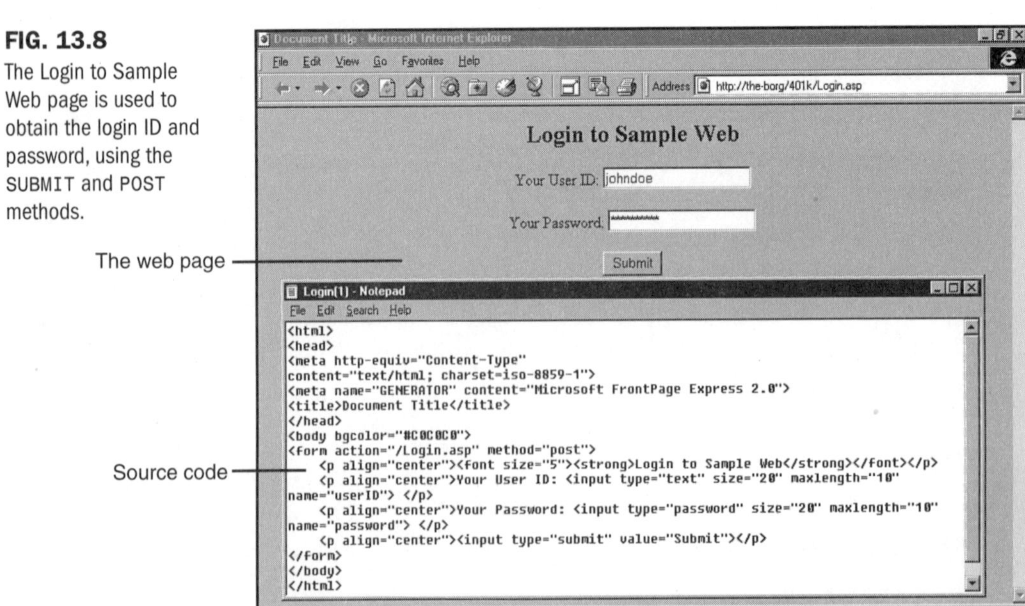

FIG. 13.8
The Login to Sample Web page is used to obtain the login ID and password, using the `SUBMIT` and `POST` methods.

The user registration page used by most web sites is an example of an HTML page that uses a `Form` collection along with the `POST` method to collect user data.

The `Form` collection has the following syntax:

```
Request.Form(parameter)[(index)¦.Count]
```

The `Request` object allows access to the data from a form within the Active Server Page. The *`parameter`* value specifies the name of the form element from which the values are to be retrieved.

The optional *`index`* value allows access to multiple values within a parameter. It can have values between 1 and `Request.Form(`*`parameter`*`).Count`.

Consider the following form, which is used to collect user ID and password information from users logging on to a web site:

```
<FORM ACTION = "/scripts/login.asp" METHOD = "post">
<P>Your User ID: <INPUT NAME = "userID" SIZE = 30>
<P>Your Password: <INPUT NAME = "password" SIZE = 30>
<p><INPUT TYPE = SUBMIT>
</FORM>
```

This form will generate a request of the following type:

```
userID=azamm&password=pass
```

By using the `Form` collection, you can access the login information and validate the user. The validation routine can look something like

```
UserID = Request.Form("userID")
Password = Request.Form("password")
```

where the values are retrieved from the `Form` collection and assigned to local variables for validation.

The *Cookies* Collection The `Cookies` collection is used to retrieve the cookies sent via the HTTP request. A *cookie* is synonymous to an .ini file or Registry entries in the sense that it's used to store preferences, user information, and other pertinent user data. Any information can be stored, passed, and accessed through a cookie.

By definition, cookies are stored on the client machine for fast retrieval at a later time. For example, cookies are used to provide personalized web content to users. User preferences and tastes are stored in cookies on the client machine to customize the content being displayed to the users each time they log on to a web site.

The `Cookies` collection of the `Request` object is used only to read cookies from a client machine. The `Response` object mentioned later in this chapter is used to write cookie information to a client machine.

The syntax for requesting cookie information is

```
Request.Cookies(cookie)[(key)¦.attribute]
```

where

- *cookie* specifies a cookie whose value should be read.
- *key* is an optional parameter used to retrieve subkey values from a cookie.
- *attribute* is a read-only parameter that specifies information about the cookie itself. The *attribute* parameter can have the following values:

Value	Description
`Expires`	This write-only value specifies the date on which the cookie expires.
`Domain`	If specified, this write-only value is used to send cookies only to requests within this domain.
`Path`	The cookie is sent only to requests to this path. If this write-only attribute isn't set, the application path is used.
`Secure`	This write-only parameter specifies whether the cookie is secure.
`HasKeys`	This read-only parameter specifies whether the cookie contains keys.

To determine if a cookie is a *cookie dictionary* (whether the cookie has keys), use the following script:

```
<%= Request.Cookies("myCookie").HasKeys %>
```

If `myCookie` is a cookie dictionary, the preceding value evaluates to `True`. Otherwise, it evaluates to `False`.

You can use a loop to cycle through all the cookies in the `Cookie` collection, or all the keys in a cookie as shown in Listing 13.3. Iterating through keys on a cookie that doesn't have keys won't produce any output.

Listing 13.3 Iterating Through Keys on a Cookie Without Keys

```
<%
For Each cookie in Request.Cookies
  If Not cookie.HasKeys Then
%>
   <%= cookie %> = <%= Request.Cookies(cookie)%>
<%
  Else
        For Each key in Request.Cookies(cookie)
%>
   <%= cookie %> (<%= key %>) = <%= Request.Cookies(cookie)(key)%>
<%
   Next
  End If
Next
%>
```

The *ServerVariables* Collection The `ServerVariables` collection is a set of predefined server variables used to read information about the server, the operating environment, and the client browsers. Generally, most `ServerVariables` collection items are read-only. The syntax for the `ServerVariables` collection is

```
Request.ServerVariables(variable)
```

The following environment variables are accessible through the `ServerVariables` collection:

- `AUTH_TYPE`. The authentication method used by the web server to validate users when they try to access a protected web page. The three methods allowed include the clear-text password validation, encrypted password validation, and the Windows NT domain validation.
- `CONTENT_LENGTH`. The length of the content provided by the client.
- `CONTENT_TYPE`. The data type of the content provided by the client, used by HTTP requests that have information attached to them, such as the `POST` method.
- `GATEWAY_INTERFACE`. The revision of the CGI specification used by the server. The format is `CGI/revision`.
- `HTTP_`*`HeaderName`*. The value stored in the header *`HeaderName`*. Any header other than those listed must be prefixed by `HTTP_` for the `ServerVariables` collection to retrieve their value. The server interprets any underscore (_) characters in *`HeaderName`* as dashes in the actual header. For example, if you specify `HTTP_MY_HEADER`, the server searches for a header sent as `MY-HEADER`.
- `LOGON_USER`. The Windows NT domain login account name being used by the user.
- `PATH_INFO`. Extra path information provided by the client. Scripts residing on the server can be accessed by using their virtual path and the `PATH_INFO` variable. If the `PATH_INFO` information is obtained from an URL, the server decodes it before the variable is passed to scripts.
- `PATH_TRANSLATED`. A translated version of `PATH_INFO` that takes the path and performs any necessary virtual-to-physical path mapping.
- `QUERY_STRING`. Another method of accessing the query information stored in the string following the question mark (`?`) in the HTTP request.
- `REMOTE_ADDR`. The IP address of the remote host making the HTTP request.
- `REMOTE_HOST`. The IP hostname of the remote host making the HTTP request. If the remote host doesn't have an IP hostname defined, the server leaves this field empty.
- `REQUEST_METHOD`. The method used to make the HTTP request. Examples include `GET`, `POST`, and `PUT`.
- `SCRIPT_MAP`. Provides the base portion of the URL.
- `SCRIPT_NAME`. A virtual path to the script being executed. This is used for self-referencing URLs.
- `SERVER_NAME`. The server's hostname, DNS alias, or IP address as it would appear in self-referencing URLs.
- `SERVER_PORT`. The server port number the HTTP request was sent to.

- SERVER_PORT_SECURE. A string that provides information about the port handling the HTTP request. This variable can have a value of 0 or 1. If the port handling the request is a secure port, the value is set to 1; otherwise, it's set to 0.
- SERVER_PROTOCOL. The name and revision number of the request information protocol. The format is protocol/revision.
- SERVER_SOFTWARE. The name and revision number of the server software honoring the request and running the gateway. The format is name/revision.
- URL. The base portion of the URL.

The following code uses a loop to cycle through the ServerVariables collection:

```
<TABLE>
<TR><TD><B>Server Variables</B></TD><TD><B>Value</B></TD></TR>
<% For Each name In Request.ServerVariables %>
<TR><TD> <%= name %> </TD><TD> <%= Request.ServerVariables(name) %> </TD></TR>
</TABLE>
<% Next %>
```

The *ClientCertificate* Collection The ClientCertificate collection is used with the SSL (Secure Sockets Layer) protocol to provide certification information to the web server from the client browser.

To determine whether you're connecting to a web browser that uses SSL, examine the prefix of an URL. Instead of an **http://** tag, an SSL web site URL starts with **https://**. Secure Sockets Layer (SSL) is an industry standard, first introduced by Netscape, that allows web sites to create, store, and display secure, encrypted information to users. Content stored on SSL-enabled web sites is encrypted before being transmitted to the client browser, and vice-versa. Your browser must support SSL for enabling a secure connection to the web server.

When a user connects to a secure server, the server requests certification, and the browser responds by sending the certification fields. If no certificate is sent, the ClientCertificate collection returns EMPTY.

The syntax for retrieving client certificate information is

```
Request.ClientCertificate(Key[SubField])
```

where

- *Key* specifies the name of the certification field to retrieve.
- *SubField* is an optional parameter you can use to a retrieve an individual field in the Subject or Issuer key. This parameter is added to the *Key* parameter as a suffix.

The *Key* field can have the following possible values:

- Subject. A list of values that contains information about the subject of the certificate. Subkeys extract the individual pieces of information from the Subject key.
- Issuer. A list of values that contains information about the issuer of the certificate. Subkeys extract the individual pieces of information from the Subject key.

- `ValidFrom`. A valid VBScript date that indicates when the certificate becomes active.
- `ValidUntil`. A valid VBScript date that indicates when the certificate expires.
- `SerialNumber`. A string that represents the serial number in a series of hexadecimal bytes separated by hyphens.
- `Certificate`. A string containing the entire certificate in binary format.
- `Flags`. A set of flags that provides additional client certificate information. The following flags may be set:

Flag	Description
`ceCertPresent`	A client certificate is present.
`CeUnrecognizedIssuer`	The last certification in this chain is from an unknown issuer.

NOTE To use these flags, you must include the client-certificate include file on your ASP page. If you're using VBScript, include Cervbs.inc; if you're using JScript, include Cerjavas.inc. These files are in the \Inetpub\ASPSamp\Samples directory on your web server.

The *`SubField`* parameter can have the following values:

- `C` specifies the name of the country of origin.
- `O` specifies the company or organization name.
- `OU` specifies the name of the organizational unit.
- `CN` specifies the user's common name. This *`SubField`* is used with the `Subject` key.
- `L` specifies a locality.
- `S` specifies a state or province.
- `T` specifies the title of the person or organization.
- `GN` specifies a given name.
- `I` specifies a set of initials.

The following code illustrates a loop that cycles through `ClientCertificate` collection values:

```
<%
For Each key in Request.ClientCertificate
  Response.Write( key & ": " & Request.ClientCertificate(key) & "<BR>")
Next
%>
```


The *Response* Object

The `Response` object sends HTML output to the client browser from an Active Server Page. For example,

```
<% Response.Write("Hello World!"%>
```

results in a display of the text on a web page on the client browser.

The `Response` object has the following syntax:

```
Response.collection|property|method
```

The *`collection`* parameter contains only a single collection, `Cookies` (defined earlier in the `Request` object section).

The `Response` object supports the following properties:

- `Buffer` indicates whether page output is buffered. When buffered output is specified, the server doesn't send any output to the client until all the scripts on the page are processed or the `Flush` or `End` method is called. The call to `Response.Buffer` should be the first line of the .asp file.
- `ContentType` specifies the HTTP content type for the response. The default content type is `text/HTML`.
- `Expires` specifies the length of time before a page cached on a browser expires. The time is given in minutes. A value of 0 means immediate expiration of the cached page.
- `ExpiresAbsolute` specifies the date and time on which a page cached on a browser expires. The default value for date is the day the script is run; the default value for time is midnight.
- `Status` is the value of the status line returned by the server. Status values, defined in the HTTP specification, consist of a three-digit number and a textual description.

The `Response` object also supports the following methods:

- `AddHeader` sets the HTML header name to *`value`*.
- `AppendToLog` adds a string to the end of the web server log entry for this request. The string must not contain any commas and must not be more than 80 characters. Multiple calls to this method append the strings to the existing entry.
- `BinaryWrite` writes the given information to the current HTTP output without any character-set conversion. This method is most useful for writing binary information required by a custom application.
- `Clear` erases any buffered HTML output.
- `End` stops processing the .asp file and returns the current result.
- `Flush` sends buffered output immediately.
- `Redirect` sends a redirect message to the browser, causing it to attempt to connect to an alternative URL.
- `Write` writes a variable to the current HTTP output as a string. The variable can be data of any type as defined by the VBScript `variant` data type.

The *Server* Object

The `Server` object provides methods and properties that allow interaction with the web server. The methods and properties provided by the `Server` object serve very useful purposes. The

Server object gives you access to the OLE automation mechanism through the use of Active Server Components.

▶ **See** "Server-Side ActiveX Components," **p. 409**

The Server object supports the ScriptTimeout property, which sets the amount of time a script can run before it times out. The property has a default value of 90 seconds.

The Server object also supports the following methods:

- CreateObject creates an instance of a server component and provides the capability to create OLE server objects in the web application. These objects can be written in any language, such as Visual Basic or Visual C++.

▶ **See** "ActiveX Server Components Included with Visual InterDev," **p. 410**

- HTMLEncode applies HTML encoding to the specified string.
- MapPath maps the specified virtual path—the absolute path on the current server or the path relative to the current page—into a physical path.

NOTE A *virtual path* defines an alias to a physical path on the web server. For example, the absolute physical path c:\myweb\data\images\ may be defined as a virtual path with an alias of \images. Virtual paths can be defined by using the Internet Service Manager included with Internet Information Server. ■

- URLEncode applies URL encoding rules, including escape characters, to the string.

Active Server Scripting

Server-side scripting can be used to create dynamic web content. You can use scripting languages such as VBScript or JScript to write applications that can respond to user-supplied information, user queries, or conditional logic. Server-side scripting allows you to customize the content of a web page to different scenarios and display a different version of a web page every time a client browser accesses it.

Server-side scripting also allows you to customize your web pages based on the capabilities of the client browser being used. For example, certain browsers might not support ActiveX controls. In such scenarios, you can develop a page that displays without using the controls.

Until recently, most web content was static in nature, with a small amount of interactivity and dynamism provided by CGI scripts. CGI scripts are complex and inflexible by nature. By using Active Server Pages and VBScript or JScript, you can produce dynamic web content more easily and quickly.

NOTE In addition to VBScript or JScript, which are supplied with ASP, third-party scripting engines can also be developed and plugged into ASP to provide support for other scripting languages. ■

As evidenced by the installation process for ASP, Internet Information Server provides the hosting environment for the Active Server Scripting Engine. An ASP scripting engine is nothing more than an ISAPI (Internet Server Application Programming Interface) application loaded by IIS at startup.

NOTE ASP isn't a scripting language, but merely an environment for parsing script commands based on the scripting engine being used.

When IIS encounters a request for an ASP file, it compiles and executes the scripts in the file on-the-fly. The output produced is an HTML page sent to the client browser. This compile-free environment is one of ASP's greatest advantages.

The default scripting language for ASP is VBScript, but you can switch freely among various scripting languages. To switch easily among installed scripting engines, use the following script:

```
<SCRIPT LANGUAGE=VBScript RUNAT=Server>
```

or

```
<SCRIPT LANGUAGE=JScript RUNAT=Server>
```

As should be obvious, scripts are programming languages. As such, you must use a specific syntax and follow certain requirements when producing applications with them. The following sections discuss some of the constructs and syntax requirements enforced by the ASP scripting engine.

Delimiters

Delimiters differentiate HTML tags from plain text and mark the beginning and end of a script unit. HTML uses the < and > characters to mark HTML text. ASP uses `<%` and `%>` as a variation on the HTML delimiters to designate sections of ASP scripts. For example,

```
<% name = "John Smith"%>
```

assigns the value `John Smith` to the variable `name`. ASP uses the delimiters `<%=` and `%>` to enclose output expressions. For example,

```
<%= name %>
```

sends the value `John Smith` to the browser in the preceding example.

Statements

A *statement* is a complete scripting unit that expresses an action, declaration, or assignment. The `For...Next` loop construct and the `If...Then...Else` conditional construct are examples of statements. Statements can also contain HTML code. For example, in Listing 13.4, HTML code is freely mixed with VBScript, because ASP supports the mixing of different scripting languages and HTML code.

Listing 13.4 Mixing Different Scripting Languages and HTML

```
<%
Loop
If tRangeType = "Table" Then Response.Write "</TABLE>"
If tPageSize > 0 Then
  If Not fHideRule Then Response.Write "<HR>"
  If Not fHideNavBar Then
    %>
    <TABLE WIDTH=100% >
    <TR>
      <TD WIDTH=100% >
        <P ALIGN=<%= tBarAlignment %> >
        <FORM <%= "ACTION=""" & Request.ServerVariables("PATH_INFO") &
              ➥stQueryString & """" %> METHOD="POST">
          <INPUT TYPE="Submit" NAME="<%= tHeaderName & "_PagingMove" %>" VALUE=
              ➥"  &lt;&lt;  ">
          <INPUT TYPE="Submit" NAME="<%= tHeaderName & "_PagingMove" %>" VALUE=
              ➥"  &lt;  ">
          <INPUT TYPE="Submit" NAME="<%= tHeaderName & "_PagingMove" %>" VALUE=
              ➥"  &gt;  ">
          <% If fSupportsBookmarks Then %>
            <INPUT TYPE="Submit" NAME="<%= tHeaderName & "_PagingMove" %>"
              ➥VALUE="  &gt;&gt;  ">
          <% End If %>
          <% If Not fHideRequery Then %>
            <INPUT TYPE="Submit" NAME="<% =tHeaderName & "_PagingMove" %>"
              ➥VALUE=" Requery ">
          <% End If %>
        </FORM>
        </P>
      </TD>
      <TD VALIGN=MIDDLE ALIGN=RIGHT>
        <FONT SIZE=2>
        <%
        If Not fHideNumber Then
          If tPageSize > 1 Then
            Response.Write "<NOBR>Page: " & Session(tHeaderName & "_
              ➥AbsolutePage") & "</NOBR>"
          Else
            Response.Write "<NOBR>Record: " & Session(tHeaderName & "_
              ➥AbsolutePage") & "</NOBR>"
          End If
        End If
        %>
        </FONT>
      </TD>
    </TR>
    </TABLE>
  <%
  End If
End If
%>
```

Script Tags

ASP supports VBScript as the default scripting language. The expressions, commands, and procedures used within script delimiters must be valid for VBScript; however, other scripts can be used freely within ASP through the use of the `<SCRIPT>` and `</SCRIPT>` tags. By using the `RUNAT` and `LANGUAGE` attributes within these tags, you can change the scripting language and use any other script commands freely. The following code switches to JScript by using script tags:

```
<SCRIPT RUNAT=SERVER LANGUAGE=JSCRIPT>
 function MyFunction ()
 {
   Response.Write("MyFunction Called")
 }
</SCRIPT>
```

Procedures

A *procedure* is a collection of script commands organized and executed together. Primary scripting language procedures can be defined freely within an ASP file. You can even mix and match different scripting language procedures by using the `<SCRIPT>` and `</SCRIPT>` tags.

Visual InterDev and IIS use VBScript as the primary scripting language, as defined by the ASP DLL supplied by Microsoft. However, you can change to a different scripting language as your primary scripting language by using the syntax

```
<SCRIPT LANGUAGE=JScript RUNAT=Server>
```

at the beginning of your ASP page.

Procedures can be defined within the scripting delimiters `<%` and `%>`, as long as they're written in the primary scripting language. Procedures can be contained within the same file they're called from, or they can be placed in a separate ASP file and included within the calling file by using the server-side `<!--#INCLUDE FILE=...>` construct.

To call procedures, include the name of the procedure in a command. For VBScript, you can also use the `Call` keyword when calling a procedure. If the procedure you're calling requires arguments, however, the argument list must be enclosed in parentheses. If you omit the `Call` keyword, you must also omit the parentheses around the argument list. If you use `Call` syntax to call any built-in or user-defined function, the function's return value is discarded. If you're calling JScript procedures from VBScript, you must use parentheses after the procedure name; if the procedure has no arguments, use empty parentheses.

Procedures can be invoked by using various methods based on the scripting language being used. Listing 13.5 illustrates creating and calling procedures by using two different scripting languages (VBScript and JScript).

Listing 13.5 Creating and Calling Procedure in Two Different Scripting Languages

```
<HTML>
<BODY>
<TABLE>
<% Call Echo %>
</TABLE>
<% Call PrintDate %>
</BODY>
</HTML>

<SCRIPT LANGUAGE=VBScript RUNAT=Server>
Sub Echo
 Response.Write _
 "<TR><TD>Name</TD><TD>Value</TD></TR>"
 Set Params = Request.QueryString
 For Each p in Params
 Response.Write "<TR><TD>" & p & "</TD><TD>" & _
 Params(p) & "</TD></TR>"
 Next
End Sub
</SCRIPT>

<SCRIPT LANGUAGE=JScript RUNAT=Server>
function PrintDate()
{
 var x
 x = new Date()
 Response.Write(x.toString())
}
</SCRIPT>
```

From Here...

In this chapter, you learned about Internet Information Server and Active Server Pages. You learned about Microsoft's Active Platform strategy and how ActiveX controls, ActiveX server objects, and ActiveX scripting mechanisms work together to provide an environment for developing rich and powerful web-enabled applications. Refer to the following chapters for information related to building web sites and web-based applications with ASP and IIS:

- To learn about the Visual Studio development environment, see Chapter 2, "Using Visual Studio to Create Applications."
- To learn about the database features and tools included with Visual Studio, see Chapter 3, "Creating Database-Aware Applications with Visual Studio."
- To learn about creating components with Visual Basic, see Chapter 5, "Creating ActiveX Components with Visual Basic."

- To learn about creating components with Visual C++, see Chapter 6, "Creating Components with Visual C++."
- To learn about creating components with Visual J++, see Chapter 7, "Creating Components with Visual J++."
- To learn about concepts associated with web-based application development, see Chapter 11, "An Inside Look at Web-Based Applications."
- To learn about getting started with Visual InterDev, see Chapter 14, "Developing Active Content with Visual InterDev."
- To learn about using design-time controls, see Chapter 16, "Visual InterDev Design-Time Controls."
- To learn about server-side programming with Active Server Pages, see Chapter 17, "Server-Side Programming in an I-net Environment."
- To learn about Dynamic HTML and its advantages, see Chapter 18, "Dynamic HTML."
- To learn more about using Visual SourceSafe with Visual InterDev, see Chapter 26, "Using Visual SourceSafe."

CHAPTER 14

Developing Active Content with Visual InterDev

by Azam A. Mirza

Microsoft Visual InterDev is a next-generation development tool designed for building dynamic web applications and enterprisewide Internet and intranet web sites. Until recently, web development was predominantly a matter of writing static HTML pages for viewing through a browser; however, the popularity of the web has created a need for building web sites and applications that can deliver dynamic and user-specific content.

Visual InterDev leverages the power of two of Microsoft's key Internet technologies to deliver an environment for building dynamic web sites. It uses the Microsoft Internet Information Server (IIS) as an integral back-end web server for hosting web sites.

The Visual InterDev IDE

Learn about the IDE used by Visual InterDev and how it is used to create workspaces, projects, and files for developing a web site.

Wizards

Learn about using the wizards to create projects and files. Get an understanding of the various wizards and how they can help you get a jump on web application development.

Content creation tools

Learn about the content creation tools supplied with Visual InterDev, including the Visual InterDev source editor and FrontPage 97 HTML editor.

ActiveX server components

Learn about creating, using, understanding, and distributing ActiveX server components. Learn about the server components supplied with Visual InterDev.

ActiveX client components

Learn about using client-side ActiveX components and Java applets in your web sites.

In addition, it uses Active Server Pages (ASP) technology for delivering dynamic web pages to client browsers.

▶ **See** Chapter 13, "An Inside Look at Active Server Pages and Internet Information Server," **p. 363**

The HTML- and HTTP-based nature of the web makes traditional client/server tools less useful for building web applications. In addition, the HTML interface is not a mature environment and lacks many of the GUI features taken for granted when doing client/server development. For example, the standards supported by the various browsers differ widely, with some browsers supporting only Java and others supporting both Java and ActiveX.

NOTE Netscape Navigator doesn't include native support for displaying ActiveX controls. However, you can access web sites that use ActiveX controls by downloading the ActiveX plug-in for Netscape, called *ScriptActive* from NCompass Labs for Windows 95 and Windows NT, from the NCompass Labs web site (**http://www.ncompasslabs.com/**). ■

A critical component of dynamic web application development is database connectivity. A truly dynamic web site is invariably dependent on a back-end database to provide the content. The web environment presents interesting twists and challenges to maintaining database connections and providing users access to pertinent data.

Microsoft Visual InterDev was designed to address these issues and various others when tackling web application development. It provides a mating of traditional client/server development methodologies, tools with web-based technologies, and tools for building robust web applications. The following sections discuss in detail the Visual InterDev development environment and how you can use it to build great dynamic web sites.

NOTE To use Visual InterDev, you must be using Microsoft Internet Information Server with Active Server Pages and the Microsoft FrontPage Server Extensions. Visual InterDev needs FrontPage Server Extensions to communicate with the web server. ■

Visual InterDev Integrated Development Environment

Microsoft Visual InterDev uses the Microsoft Developer Studio as its Integrated Development Environment (IDE). Developer Studio is the IDE used by two other products included as part of Visual Studio 97—Visual C++ and Visual J++.

Users familiar with either Visual C++ or Visual J++ will feel instantly at ease with the Visual InterDev IDE. Developer Studio is a very user-friendly and highly productive IDE that serves as a kind of "one-stop shop" for all development-process tasks.

▶ **See** Chapter 2, "Using Visual Studio to Create Applications," **p. 31**

When using the Developer Studio IDE for building web applications, the developer is actually working against a live web site. During development, the parts of the web site being modified are copied to the local developer workstation. When the developer has finished making modifications, Visual InterDev automatically uploads the latest versions of the modified files to the web server.

NOTE Typically, developers work against a web server that acts as the staging server for Visual InterDev development. A *staging server* is analogous to a development machine that is used to develop, debug, and test web sites before moving the content to a production server. As content is developed, it can be uploaded to the staging web server and debugged for errors during the development process.

After a web site has been fully developed and debugged, it can be moved to the production server for use. Visual InterDev provides a simple and powerful mechanism for moving a web site from the development stage to the production stage.

Visual InterDev includes a unique and powerful mechanism for graphically displaying the topology of a web site, called the Link View. From the Tools menu, select View Links on WWW and provide the URL of a web site to explore its topology.

▶ **See** "Link Repair and Link View," **p. 444**

The following sections highlight the key features of Visual InterDev that are used to build powerful, dynamic, database-enabled web applications and sites.

Working with Workspaces

When working within the Visual InterDev IDE, developers work in the context of a workspace. A workspace is the hosting place for various Visual InterDev, Visual C++, and Visual J++ projects. A developer can have any number of projects open within a workspace, depending on the amount of memory available on the machine.

The Developer Studio IDE can host Visual C++, Visual J++, and Visual InterDev projects within the same workspace, thus enabling developers to work on an ActiveX control in Visual C++ or a Java applet in Visual J++ at the same time as they work on a web site in Visual InterDev. The developers can develop the components and test them on the web site from within a single IDE.

To create a workspace in Visual InterDev, perform the following steps:

1. Select New from the File menu. The New dialog box appears.
2. Click the Workspaces tab and select the Blank Workspace option.
3. Enter a name for the workspace you are creating. The Location box automatically updates to display the location where the workspace will be created. By default, Visual InterDev stores all workspaces in the directory <root>\Program Files\DevStudio\MyProjects on the local workstation and in the \inetpub\wwwroot\ directory on the server.

CAUTION

Make sure the workspace name you provide is unique because the system will attempt to create a directory with that name in the default location for creating Visual InterDev projects. Alternatively, you can provide a different location for creating the workspace.

4. Click OK to create the new workspace. The Visual InterDev IDE updates to display the newly created workspace with no projects attached.

The next section outlines the procedures for creating web projects within Visual InterDev.

Creating Projects

The first step in creating a web site is to create the project that will host the web site. A workspace within Visual InterDev IDE hosts the project. You can have multiple projects within a workspace; however, only one project can be the active project at any given time.

To create a web project, follow these steps:

1. Select New from the File menu. The New dialog box is displayed.
2. Click the Projects tab to display the various project options that can be selected, as shown in Figure 14.1.

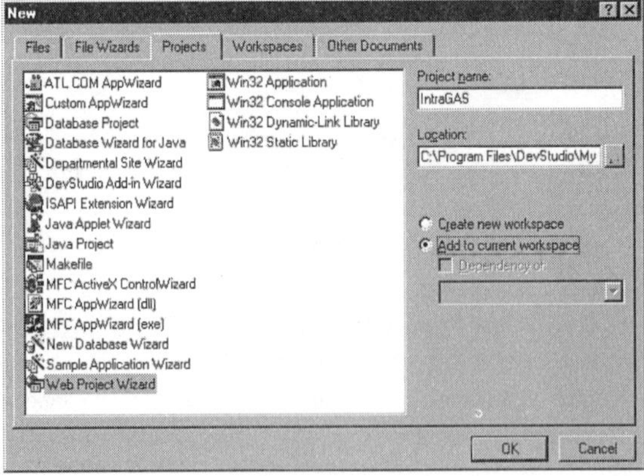

FIG. 14.1 Visual InterDev enables you to create projects by using the project wizards.

NOTE Because Visual C++ and Visual J++ share the Visual InterDev IDE, the New dialog box also displays possible choices for the other two environments. Select the appropriate choice from the displayed list.

3. Select the project type you want to create. For creating web sites, you can choose the Web Project Wizard or the Departmental Site Wizard.

NOTE The Web Project Wizard enables you to generate a skeleton web site that you can work from. The Departmental Site Wizard is geared towards creating a sample departmental site for use within corporate intranets.

4. Provide a name for your project. The location box is updated automatically to display the location for creating the new project.
5. You can opt to create the project in a new workspace or choose Add to Current Workspace.
6. Click OK to create the project.

After you click the OK button in the New dialog box, the Project Wizard starts. The following section discusses the various Visual InterDev project wizards in greater detail.

Project Wizards

By using the project wizards, you get a head start on your web-development efforts. The wizards are included primarily to provide a starting point and to automate some of the more mundane tasks involved with developing web applications with Visual InterDev.

Although it is possible to create a site manually, using one of the wizards as a starting point and then working from the files it creates is a lot faster.

Wizards are available throughout Visual InterDev for expediting routine tasks. The next section discusses the various project wizards.

The Web Project Wizard You can use the Web Project Wizard to create a simple startup web site. By default, the project created with this wizard will be stored in the publishing root directory of your web server at \inetpub\wwwroot\<project name> directory.

You can start the Web Project Wizard by using the steps outlined in the "Creating Projects" section earlier in this chapter and selecting the Web Project Wizard from the project list in the New dialog box. After the Web Project Wizard starts, follow the steps outlined here:

1. Provide the name of the web server this web project will be connected to. As shown in Figure 14.2, the wizard tries to locate the web server when you click the Next button.
2. The Specify Your Web dialog box appears, as shown in Figure 14.3. Select the appropriate option for creating a new web by providing a name for the web project in the appropriate text box.
3. To provide for search capabilities as part of your web site, select the checkbox next to Enable Full Text Searching for Pages in This Web.
4. Click the Finish button to create the web site.

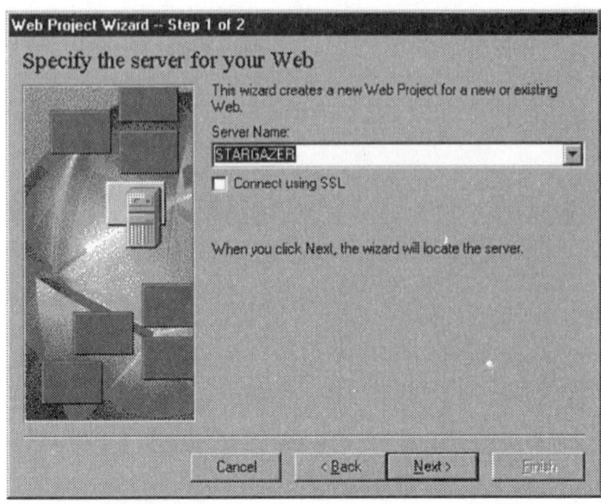

FIG. 14.2
The Specify the Server for Your Web dialog box is used to specify a web server to host the project being created by the Web Project Wizard.

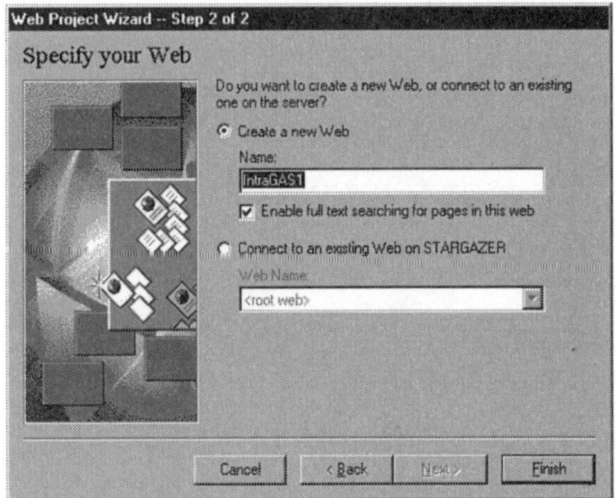

FIG. 14.3
The Specify Your Web dialog box is used to create a new web or to connect to an existing web site for making modifications and changes.

At this point you are ready to start working with your web site project and add additional files as needed. The search.htm file provides basic functionality for doing full text searches of HTML files within a web site. The first thing you can do is to customize the home page to look like what you need and then add additional HTML pages that can be accessed from the hyperlinks on the home page.

▶ **See** "The Global.asa File," **p. 422**

The Departmental Site Wizard The Departmental Site Wizard provides templates for creating an intranet site designed to display departmental information. To create a departmental site, create a new project (as described in the "Creating Projects" section) by selecting the Departmental Site Project. Then follow these steps:

1. Select a web server to host the web site as shown earlier in Figure 14.2. Then click Next to continue.
2. Specify a name for the web site as shown earlier in Figure 14.3. Then click Next to continue.

3. Select the pages that will be a part of your departmental web site. Figure 14.4 shows the choices available to you. Make the appropriate selections and click Next.

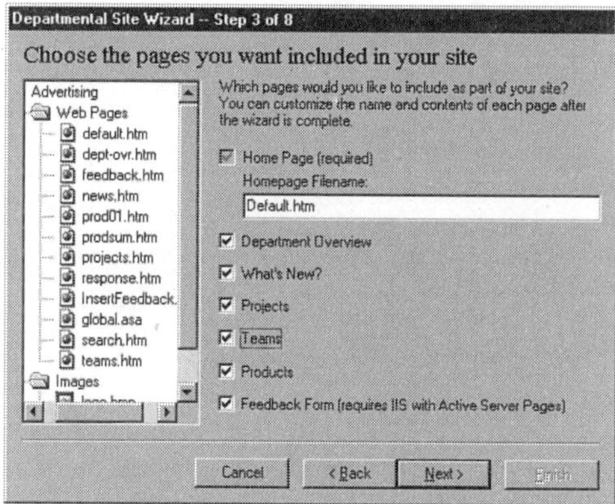

FIG. 14.4
The web page choices provide a starting point for various aspects of a typical departmental web site.

4. As shown in Figure 14.5, you provide a name for the department and, optionally, a path to a departmental logo file. Select the other options as appropriate and then click Next.

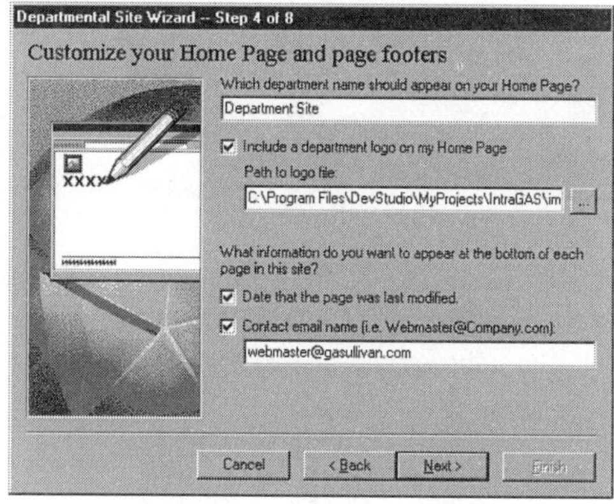

FIG. 14.5
In Step 4 of the wizard, you can customize the home page to include information such as the last modification date.

5. The Add a Navigation Bar dialog box provides options for Navigation bar placement. The Navigation bar enables users to move between various pages on a web site easily. Select the placement option you want—at the top of each page or at the top and bottom of each page.
6. You can customize a feedback page, as shown in Figure 14.6, for getting feedback from users on various aspects of your web site.
7. To store the feedback obtained from users, the wizard creates a feedback table in a database, as shown in Figure 14.7. Specify a table name and then select a Data Source Name (DSN) by clicking the Select DSN button.

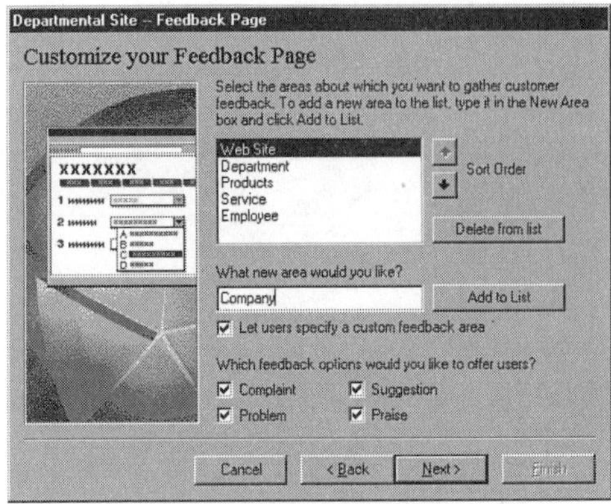

FIG. 14.6 The feedback page can be used to collect useful information from users about how they perceive the web site.

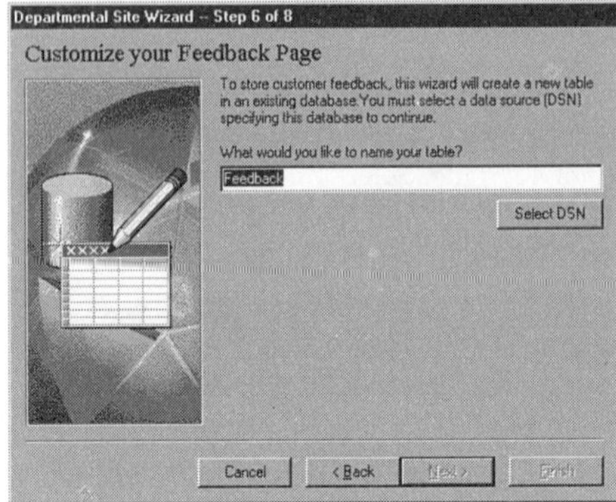

FIG. 14.7 The feedback table must reside in an ODBC-compliant database such as Microsoft Access or SQL Server.

8. The Select DSN button starts the ODBC administrator so that you can define a DSN for connecting to the database where the feedback table will reside. Figure 14.8 shows the main ODBC setup screen.

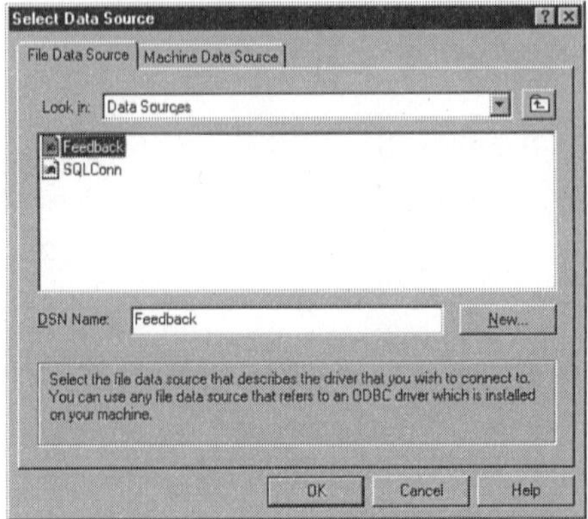

FIG. 14.8 In the ODBC Select Data Source dialog box, you can select a predefined data source or create a new one.

9. Click Next to display the theme selection page, as shown in Figure 14.9. Select an appropriate theme and click Next to continue.

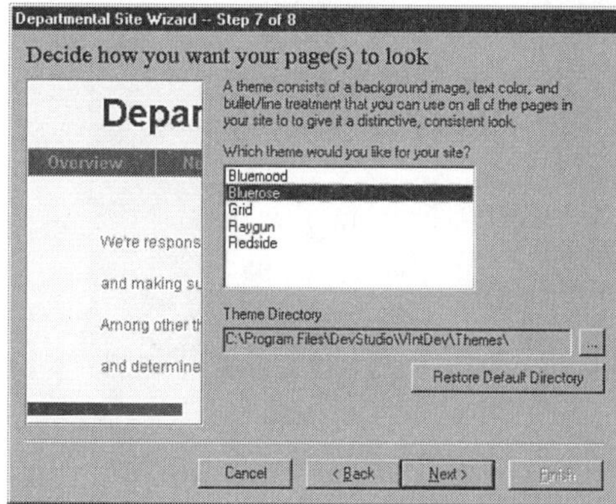

FIG. 14.9
The wizard provides predefined themes for configuring the look and feel of your web site pages.

10. At this point, the wizard is complete, and you can click Finish to close the wizard and allow it to create the files needed to create the web site.

After the web site is created, you can run and view the site by opening the startup page, or any other page, in a web browser. You can do so from the Visual InterDev IDE by right-clicking the filename in Explorer and selecting Preview in Browser from the pop-up menu.

Sample Application Wizard The Sample Application Wizard provides a convenient mechanism for installing Visual InterDev sample applications provided by Microsoft on the Visual InterDev CD-ROM or on the Microsoft web site.

To install applications by using the Sample Application Wizard, follow these steps:

1. Select New from the Visual InterDev File menu. The New dialog box appears.
2. Select the Projects tab and then the Sample Application Wizard. Provide a name for the sample application and click OK to continue.
3. The Sample Application Wizard starts and displays the dialog box shown in Figure 14.10.
4. Select a Visual InterDev sample application to install from the list and click Next to continue.

NOTE Visual InterDev includes two sample applications. These include the Dos Perros Chile Company sample application that demonstrates an Internet web site for doing order entry and catalog browsing. The 401(k) sample application demonstrates a sample intranet application used to track employee benefits information. Other sample applications can be downloaded from the Microsoft web site.

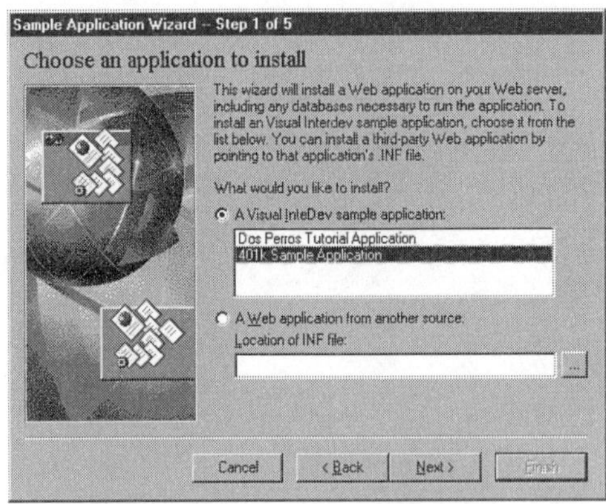

FIG. 14.10 The Sample Application Wizard can also be used to install third-party web applications.

NOTE The Sample Application Wizard installs all components, such as database tables, needed for installing and running the provided sample web sites.

5. In the Specify a Web Server dialog box, shown in Figure 14.11, supply a name for the web server where the application will be hosted and a name for the application itself. The default choices are usually appropriate. Click Next to continue.

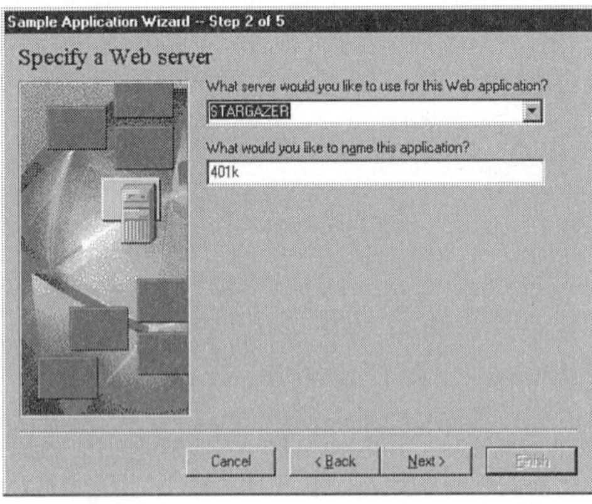

FIG. 14.11 The wizard installs the sample application on the selected web server, where it becomes part of the specified project workspace.

6. If the sample application requires a database, the wizard displays a dialog box for selecting the database, as shown in Figure 14.12.
7. Select a shared location where both the web server and the development clients can access the database, as shown in Figure 14.13. Click Next to continue.
8. Click the Finish button to install the sample application.

To run the sample applications, load the start page in Microsoft Internet Explorer and navigate the application pages. Both applications are fairly straightforward and easy to navigate.

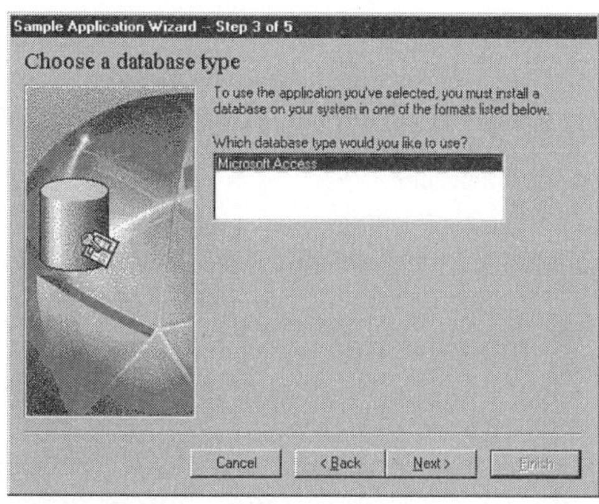

FIG. 14.12
The database listbox lists the types of databases that can be used to install the sample application tables.

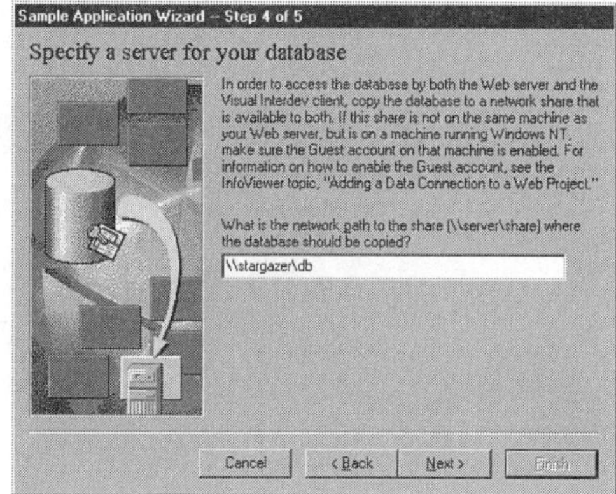

FIG. 14.13
The shared database directory must reside on a network drive where both the web server and the development client have access permissions.

Adding Content to a Project

After you have created a Visual InterDev project, either manually or by using a wizard, you are ready to add site-specific content to your web site. The Visual InterDev IDE provides a Windows Explorer-style File View for navigating through your newly created web site project. Figure 14.14 shows the Visual InterDev file viewer.

Several methods are available for adding content to a project. The following sections describe each of these methods in detail.

Creating New Files or Folders

Adding new files or folders in Visual InterDev is quite simple. You can create files of various types, including

- *Active Server Page*: An .ASP file that will contain server scripts
- *HTML Page*: A typical .HTM or .HTML file used by most web sites

- *HTML Layout*: An .ALX HTML Layout control file
- *Macro File*: A .DSM file used by the Developer Studio environment
- *ODBC Script File*: A .SQL file that contains SQL commands
- *Text Files*: Simple .TXT text files

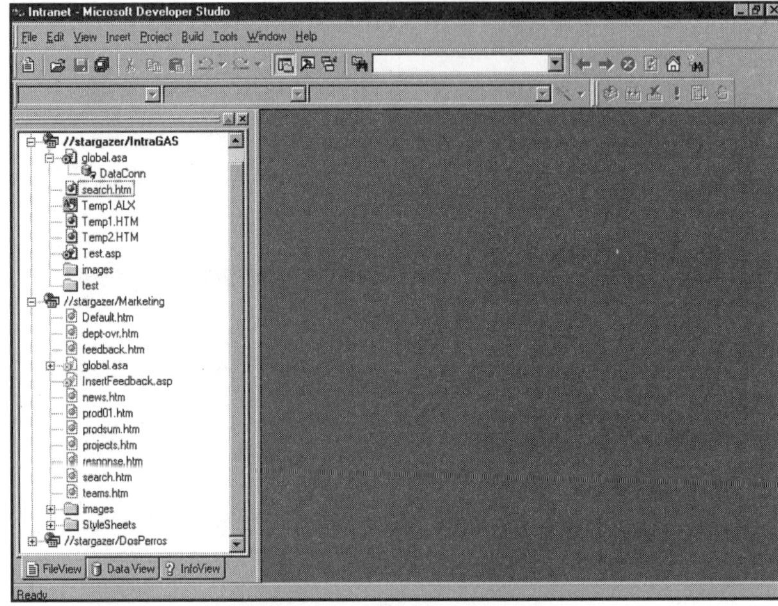

FIG. 14.14
The File View shows your web site files and folders in a tree-like structure.

To create a new file or folder for a project, follow these steps:

1. Select New from the File menu or right-click the project or folder name and choose New Folder.

NOTE The New Folder menu option displays a dialog box where you enter the name of the new folder.

You can create a new folder as a subfolder of an existing folder by right-clicking that existing folder and selecting New Folder.

2. If you are creating a new file, the New dialog box will be displayed. Select a file type from the Files tab, the File Wizards tab, or the Other Documents tab and provide a name for the file in the text box.
3. Click the Add to Project checkbox to add the file to the current project or a different project.

4. Specify a path to the file location if it is different from the default path displayed.
5. Click OK to create a new file and add it to the root level of the project.

After a file is created, you can move it to a subfolder within the project by dragging and dropping it on the intended destination folder.

Adding Existing Files or Folders to a Project

To add an existing file to a Visual InterDev project, follow these steps:

1. From the File View, right-click the project name or folder to which you want to add the file or folder. Figure 14.15 shows the shortcut menu that pops up.

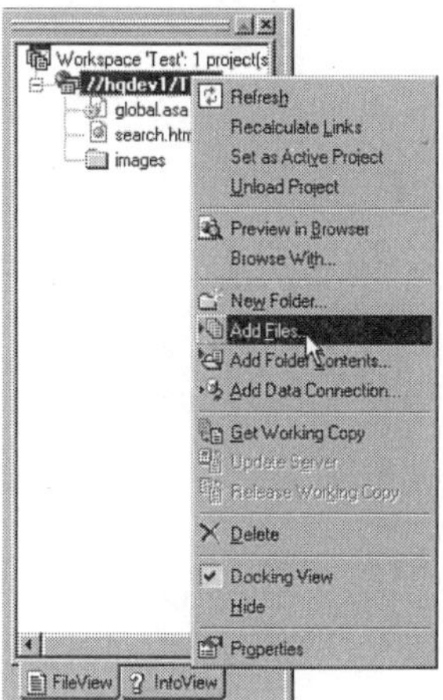

FIG. 14.15
The right-click shortcut menu provides access to the most commonly used Visual InterDev commands.

2. Select Add Files from the menu.
3. Select the files to add to the project and click OK to continue.

To add an existing folder to a project, follow these steps:

1. From the File View tab, right-click the project name or folder to which you want to add the folder.
2. From the shortcut menu, select Add Folder Contents.
3. From the ensuing dialog box, select the folder to add. The contents of the folder are added to the project or folder you selected in step 1.

Using Drag and Drop

The File View Explorer supports full drag-and-drop capabilities. To add files or folders through drag and drop, follow these steps:

1. Click a folder or file in the Windows Explorer and drag it to the File View Explorer in Visual InterDev.
2. Drop the file or folder at the location where you want to add it, and the file or folder is added to the project.

NOTE The drag-and-drop process copies the files to the web server and creates a working copy on the local workstation.

Using File Wizards

Visual InterDev provides a couple of file wizards for adding special files to a project. The following file wizards are provided with Visual InterDev:

- *Data Form Wizard*: A wizard for creating .ASP files that tie into a database on the back end
- *Template Page Wizard*: A wizard for creating web page templates

The following sections discuss these wizards in further detail.

The Data Form Wizard The Data Form Wizard is used to create an .ASP file that connects to a database on the back end for displaying dynamic web content on a web page with full search, list, update, delete, and input capabilities. To create a database-enabled file by using the wizard, follow these steps:

1. Select New from the File menu and select the File Wizards tab from the new dialog box.
2. Select the Data Form Wizard and provide a name for your file. Then click Next to start the Data Form Wizard, as shown in Figure 14.16.

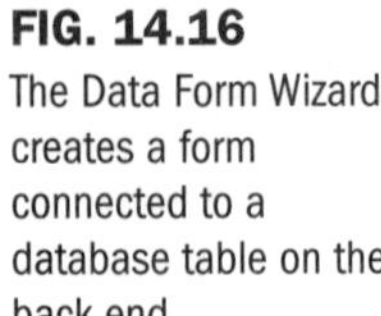

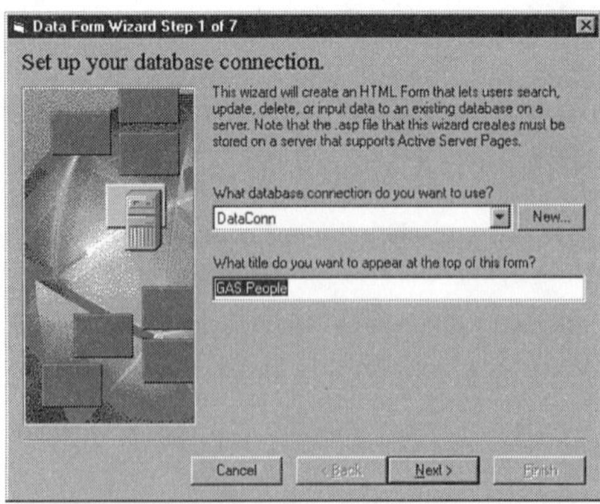

FIG. 14.16 The Data Form Wizard creates a form connected to a database table on the back end.

3. In the Data Form Wizard dialog box, select the name of an existing DSN, or create a new one by selecting the New button.
4. Provide a title for the web page and click Next.
5. On the record source page, select the source for your data from the choices provided, as shown in Figure 14.17.

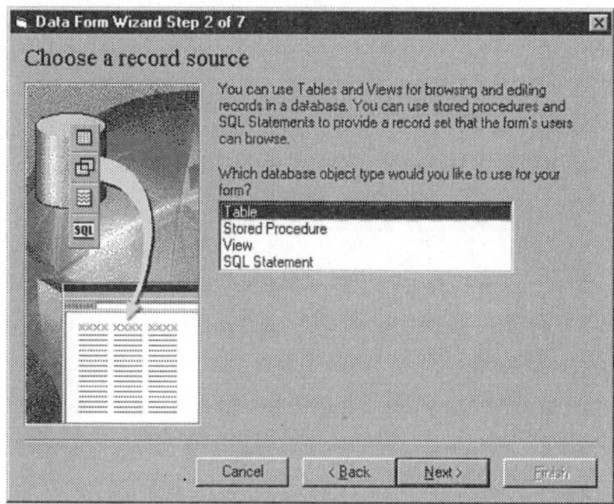

FIG. 14.17 With the Data Form Wizard, you can create a web page based on a table, a stored procedure, a table view, or a SQL statement.

6. In the next step, you choose the source for your data and the fields to be displayed on the page, as shown in Figure 14.18.

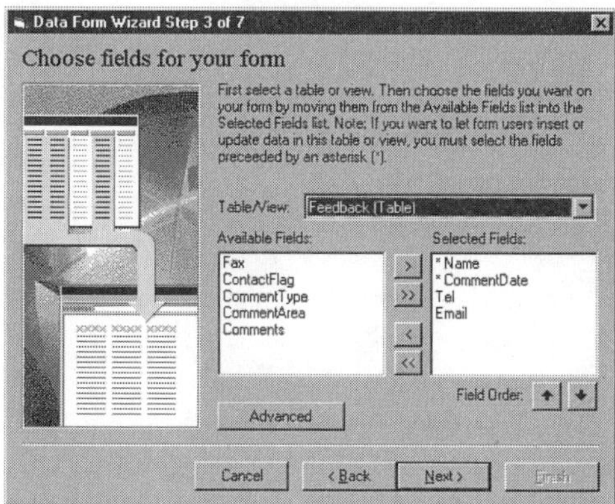

FIG. 14.18 From the Table/View drop-down list, you can select the source for your data and the order of the fields.

7. Click the Advanced button to display the dialog box shown in Figure 14.19. In the Advanced Options dialog box, you can provide custom labels for your fields and specify lookup tables for certain fields that derive their display content from other tables in the database. When you have finished with the Advanced Options dialog box, click OK to continue.

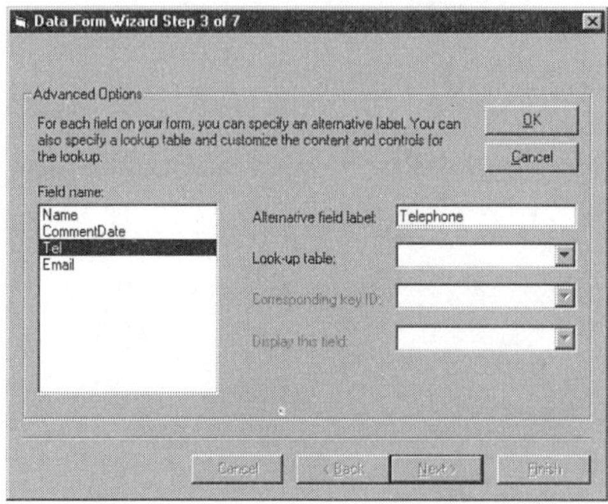

FIG. 14.19
The Advanced Options dialog box allows you to further customize the data presentation of your web page.

NOTE A lookup table is used to derive the display values for a particular field in a table. For example, you might have a lookup table with a customer name and customer ID. Another table might just store the customer ID and use the first table to look up the corresponding customer name.

8. Use the Field Order arrows to rearrange the field display order on the page. Then click Next to continue.
9. Specify the options for editing and displaying your web page, as shown in Figure 14.20. The page can be a display-only page, or it can support add (insert), update (modify), and delete capabilities. Select the appropriate options and click Next to continue.

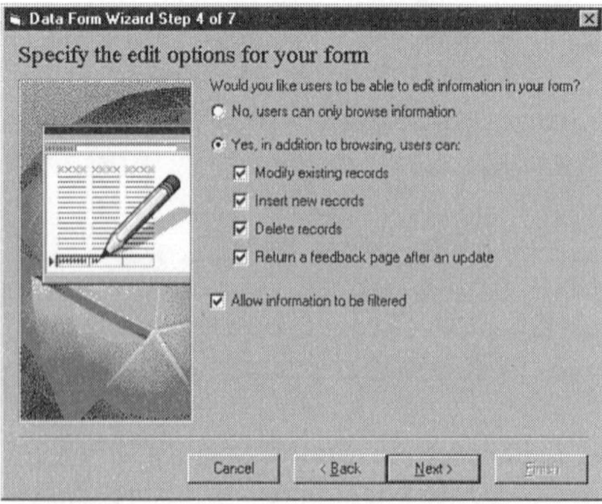

FIG. 14.20
The Edit Options box enables you to set up whether users can modify information in your form.

10. Select the data display options for your web page, as shown in Figure 14.21. The List View allows you to display a predetermined number of records per page. Select the appropriate options and click Next.

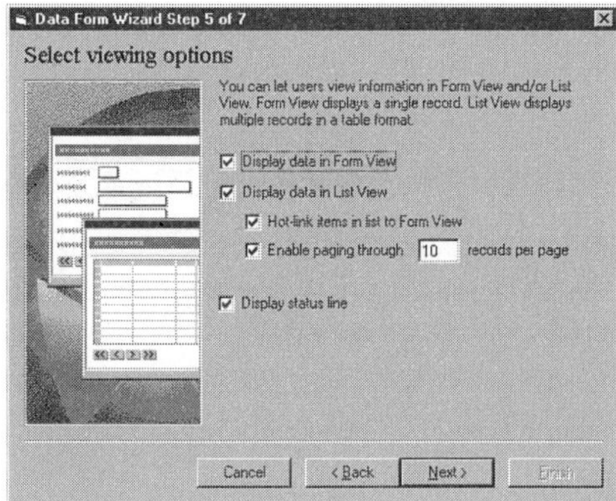

FIG. 14.21 The data can be displayed in Form View or List View.

11. Select the display theme for your page from the options provided and click Next to continue.
12. Click the Finish button to end the wizard and create your web pages. If you select both List and Form View, three different files will be created by the wizard—one for the List View, one for the Form View, and one to include functions for handling data display and other tasks.

▶ **See** "Exploring the Data Form Wizard," **p. 439**

The Template Page Wizard The Template Page Wizard is used to create web pages based on a predesigned template, a starting point from which you can customize the web pages. To use the Template Page Wizard, follow these steps:

1. Select New from the File menu and select the Template Page Wizard from the File Wizards page. Provide a name for the page and click OK to start the Template Page Wizard, as shown in Figure 14.22.

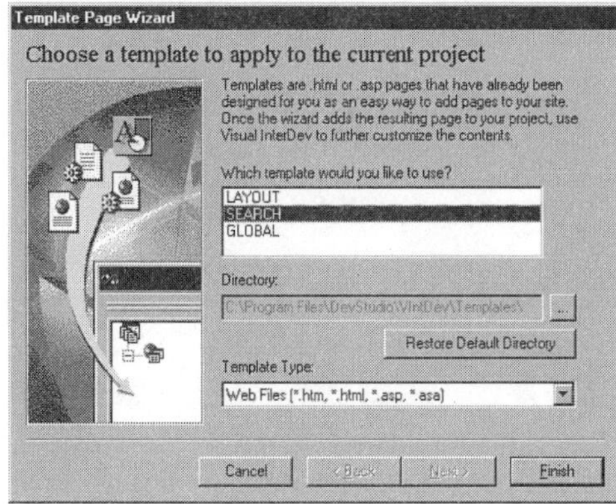

FIG. 14.22 The Template Page Wizard can create web pages based on predefined templates.

2. Select the template you want to use and click the Finish button. The wizard creates the appropriate page and adds it to the project.

Visual InterDev Content Development Tools

Visual InterDev provides several content development tools designed to simplify the task of building dynamic web sites. The tools are designed to transfer the focus from the development *environment* to the development *process* and include these tools, discussed in detail in the following sections:

- Visual InterDev Source Editor
- FrontPage 97 HTML Editor
- Other tools

Visual InterDev Source Editor

The Visual InterDev Source Editor is in actuality the integrated IDE editor used by all other Visual Studio 97 tools. The Source Editor is similar to other Windows text editors in usability features. Figure 14.23 displays the main Visual InterDev Source Editor.

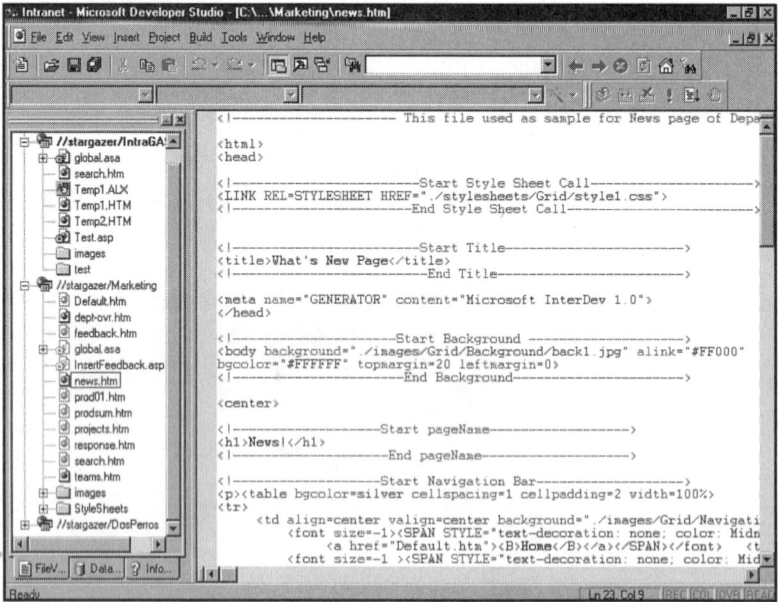

FIG. 14.23 The Visual InterDev Source Editor is a powerful editor for building applications.

The Source Editor includes functionality designed specifically to make the development process as smooth as possible. Some of these features are

- Support for source file creation for Visual C++, Visual J++, Visual InterDev, and simple text files
- Support for macros for automating various tasks
- Syntax coloring for support for different source files
- Support for BRIEF and EPSILON text editors
- Support for editing features such as bookmarks, search-and-replace, and find mechanisms
- Support for drag-and-drop editing

In addition, the source editor provides a right-click shortcut menu for access to the most commonly used commands.

The source editor enables you to open an Internet address from within the editor by using the Open command on the right-click menu while holding the cursor over an Internet address.

In the Visual InterDev environment, the most common use for the source editor is to edit Active Server Pages files.

The FrontPage 97 HTML Editor

Visual InterDev includes a special edition of the Microsoft FrontPage 97 HTML editor. The FrontPage 97 editor is a WYSIWYG (What You See Is What You Get) HTML editor that makes it easy to build sophisticated layouts and web pages. Figure 14.24 shows the main screen of the FrontPage 97 HTML editor.

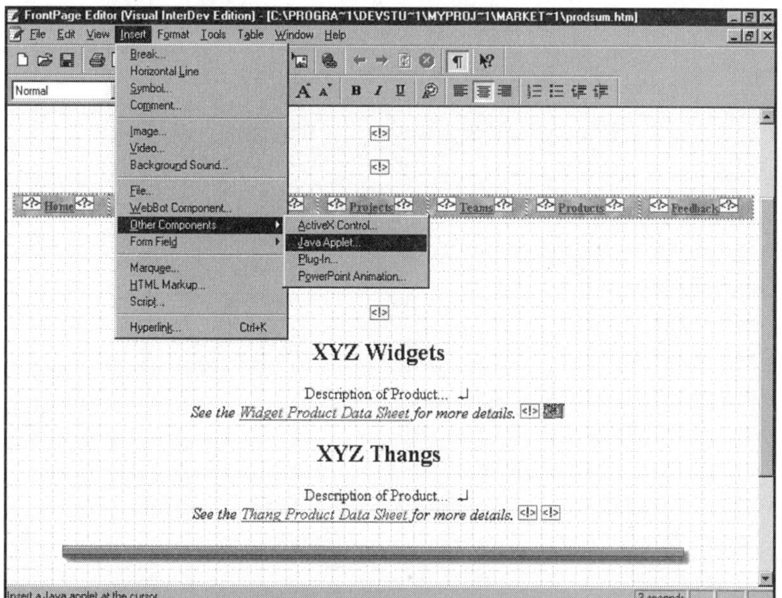

FIG. 14.24 The FrontPage 97 HTML editor provides support for ActiveX objects, Java applets, and HTML.

The FrontPage 97 HTML editor is best suited for editing pure HTML files. Do not use it to edit template files or .ASP files. The design-time versions of these files include many scripts that cannot be interpreted by the FrontPage 97 editor.

CAUTION

If you do edit an .ASP file with FrontPage 97, make sure that you do not make changes to the exclamation point areas used to designate scripts, unsupported controls, and such objects. If you double-click the exclamation point, FrontPage 97 attempts to display the code or control designated by that exclamation point.

You can set the FrontPage 97 editor as the default editor for all HTML files. To do this, follow these steps:

1. Create a project that includes an HTML file.
2. Right-click the HTML file to display the shortcut menu and select Open With.
3. In the Open With dialog box, select FrontPage 97 Editor from the list.
4. Click the Set as Default button to set FrontPage 97 as the default editor for all HTML files.

You can set any third-party editor as the default editor for HTML files by using the Add button in the Open With dialog box.

Other Tools

In addition to the two content-development tools described in the previous sections, the Visual Studio environment includes other tools that play a pivotal role in developing useful web sites. These include

- *Microsoft Internet Explorer*: Used for viewing web pages as they are being developed. Internet Explorer is the default browser used by Visual InterDev for displaying web pages for development debugging.
- *Microsoft Image Composer*: Enables creation of images and animation for use as part of a web site. Image Composer supports a multitude of image formats for maximum flexibility and ease of use.
- *Microsoft Music Producer*: A tool for producing music files for use in a web site. Music Producer uses very sophisticated techniques and algorithms and includes sample instruments for creating music even if you're not a music expert.
- *Microsoft Media Manager*: A tool for managing the large number of multimedia files that are part of a big web site. It provides strong cataloging and indexing features for managing sound, image, video, and animation files.

Server-Side ActiveX Components

Visual InterDev includes a facility for utilizing ActiveX components in the server environment. These are ActiveX components that execute on the server and provide a means to integrate web applications with traditional client/server applications. Server-side ActiveX components are utilized by the Active Server scripting mechanism to provide productivity gains by encapsulating business rules into components.

▶ **See** "Using Server-Side Scripting with Visual InterDev," **p. 477**

NOTE An ActiveX Server component is nothing more than an OLE Automation Server that can be created by using any tool that supports OLE Automation Server creation. Such tools include Visual C++, Visual Basic, Delphi, and PowerBuilder.

One of the most important benefits of server-side ActiveX components is their capability to provide a wrapper mechanism around existing legacy and client/server applications. ActiveX server components are most easily created by using tools such as Visual Basic. After being created, the components can be used in Visual InterDev to integrate into a web application.

NOTE An ActiveX server component is distinct from an ActiveX client component in that it does not include any graphical user-interface elements.

ActiveX servers provide a reuse mechanism for commonly used code. A variety of applications and tools are coming out that provide support for ActiveX server components by exposing their properties and methods as packaged components.

Using ActiveX Server Components in Visual InterDev

Visual InterDev provides scripting support for creating and instantiating ActiveX server components as part of Active Server Page scripts. The following sample code uses a server-side component called `UserInfo` to display information from a database about the user connected to the web server.

▶ For more information about creating ActiveX server components, **see** Chapter 5, "Creating ActiveX Components with Visual Basic," **p. 131**.

```
Set UserInf = Server.CreateObject("UserInfo.UserInfo")
If Not UserInf.Status Then
      display error code and exit
Else
UserInf.GetUserInformation
End If
```


The preceding sample code performs a variety of tasks through the use of the `UserInfo` ActiveX server component. The `CreateObject` method instantiates the `UserInfo` object and establishes a connection to the database that is verified by the `Status` property being set to

True. After a user connects to the web server, the GetUserInformation method obtains the user info from the database and displays it by using the Response object to write the results to the client.

▶ **See** "The Response Object," **p. 381**

Distributing Components by Using DCOM

The DCOM specification provides mechanisms for distributing objects across the network on different machines. This is a powerful concept that enables you to run your ActiveX components on machines other than the web server, possibly because the ActiveX server component is nothing more than an OLE Automation Server.

DCOM provides a powerful means of distributing load and processing power across multiple machines within an enterprise; however, the utility (dcomcfg.exe) used to distribute ActiveX server components over different machines can do this only for out-of-process servers.

▶ **See** "COM Objects Across Process and Network Boundaries," **p. 118**

NOTE The Active Server Pages (ASP) must be enabled to use out-of-process components by setting the following Registry key to 1:

```
HKEY_LOCAL_MACHINE\SYSTEM\CurrentControlSet\Services\W3SVC\ASP\Parameters\
➥AllowOutOfProcCmpnts
```

You can use regedt32.exe to change the Registry setting manually. ■

A more powerful method of distributing server components is to leverage the power of the Microsoft Transaction Server for distributing in-process and out-of-process server components.

▶ For more information about distributing and managing server components through Microsoft Transaction Server, **see** Chapter 25, "Using Microsoft Transaction Server to Enable Distributed Applications," **p. 691**.

ActiveX Server Components Included with Visual InterDev

Microsoft supplies prebuilt ActiveX server components with Visual InterDev to accomplish some common and frequently used tasks. These include

- Advertisement Rotator
- Browser Capabilities
- TextStream
- Content Linking

The following sections describe these components in further detail.

Advertisement Rotator The Advertisement Rotator component automatically cycles through advertisements displayed on a page, based on a predetermined sequence. The main purpose of the Advertisement Rotator component is to provide a mechanism for web sites to display advertisements for revenue generation.

The Advertisement Rotator component uses the Rotator Schedule File to determine the sequence and schedule for displaying various advertisements. The component uses the following files for implementing its functionality:

- *Adrot.dll*: The Advertisement Rotator Component file.
- *Redirection File*: An optional ASCII text file used to implement redirection of users to advertiser sites. It also records the number of users who click an advertisement.
- *Rotator Schedule File*: An ASCII text file that contains the display schedule for advertisements and how long each advertisement will be displayed. This is a required file that must be present in the specified virtual directory on the server. Refer to the Visual InterDev documentation for the properties and methods supported by the Rotator Schedule File.

The Advertisement Rotator component supports the following properties and methods:

- `Border`—Property that specifies the border size around an advertisement
- `Clickable`—Property that specifies whether an advertisement is a clickable hyperlink
- `TargetFrame`—Property that specifies the target frame that will be used to display the advertisement
- `GetAdvertisement`—Method that determines the next advertisement to display, gets the information from the associated Rotator Schedule File, and formats it as HTML

The following code sample shows how the preceding methods can be used to display an advertisement on a web page:

```
<% Set ad = Server.CreateObject("MSWC.AdRotator")
ad.Border(0)
ad.Clickable(FALSE)
ad.TargetFrame(Frame1)
%>
<%
ad.GetAdvertisement("/scripts/adrot.txt")
%>
```

The preceding code sample sets the advertisement properties and then displays the advertisement, using the `GetAdvertisement` method.

Browser Capabilities The Browser Capabilities component provides information on the features supported by a client browser. By knowing the capabilities of a user's browser, developers can tailor their HTML content to more closely match the browser's feature set.

The Active Server Pages provide a file called browscap.ini, which includes information about the capabilities of various browsers. When a browser requests a page from a web server, the HTTP header sent by the browser also includes information about itself. The

Browser Capabilities component then compares the information in the HTTP header against the browscap.ini file and sends the information to the server.

NOTE The browscap.ini file is located in the c:\winnt\system32\intesrv\ASP\cmpnts directory. The browscap.dll component file also resides in the same directory.

The format of the browscap.ini file is similar to any other .INI files included with Windows. The file includes separate sections for various browsers, which define the properties of the respective browsers. The following listing shows a few sections of the browscap.ini file:

```
;;;;;;;;;;;;;;;;;;;;;;;;;;
;;; Microsoft Browsers ;;;
;;;;;;;;;;;;;;;;;;;;;;;;;;

[Microsoft Internet Explorer/4.40.308 (Windows 95) ]
browser=IE
version=1.0
majorver=#1
minorver=#0
frames=FALSE
tables=FALSE
cookies=FALSE
backgroundsounds=FALSE
vbscript=FALSE
javascript=FALSE
javaapplets=FALSE
platform=Windows95

[IE 1.5]
browser=IE
version=1.5
majorver=#1
minorver=#5
frames=FALSE
tables=TRUE
cookies=TRUE
backgroundsounds=FALSE
vbscript=FALSE
javascript=FALSE
javaapplets=FALSE
beta=False
Win16=False

[Mozilla/1.22 (compatible; MSIE 1.5; Windows NT)]
parent=IE 1.5
platform=WinNT

[Mozilla/1.22 (compatible; MSIE 1.5; Windows 95)]
parent=IE 1.5
platform=Win95
```

```
;;ie 2.0
[IE 2.0]
browser=IE
version=2.0
majorver=#2
minorver=#0
frames=FALSE
tables=TRUE
cookies=TRUE
backgroundsounds=TRUE
vbscript=FALSE
javascript=FALSE
javaapplets=FALSE
beta=False
Win16=False
```

The Browser Capabilities component can be used in an .ASP file to determine the capabilities of a browser, as shown in the code listing that follows:

```
<%@ LANGUAGE="VBSCRIPT" %>
<HTML>
<HEAD>
<META NAME="GENERATOR" Content="Microsoft Visual InterDev 1.0">
<META HTTP-EQUIV="Content-Type" content="text/html; charset=iso-8859-1">
<TITLE>Document Title</TITLE>
</HEAD>
<BODY>
<%Set brows = Server.CreateObject("MSWC.BrowserType")%>
Browser <%= brows.browser%>
Version <%=brows.version%>
</BODY>
</HTML>
```

The preceding code sample instantiates a Browser Capabilities object and uses some of its properties to determine the browser name and version information.

NOTE The Browser Capabilities component does not have any methods associated with it.

TextStream The TextStream component, together with the `FileSystem` object, is used to create, open, read, and write to text files. The `FileSystem` object is used for the simple purpose of creating and opening text files. It has no properties and includes two methods:

- `CreateTextFile`—Creates a text file with the specified filename
- `OpenTextFile`—Opens a text file with the specified filename

The following code illustrates the use of a `FileSystem` object:

```
Set FSO = Server.CreateObject("Scripting.FileSystemObject")
Set txtfile = FSO.CreateTextFile("c:\test.txt", True)
txtfile.WriteLine("This is a test.")
txtfile.Close
```

In the preceding sample, the `CreateObject` method creates a `FileSystem` object. The `FileSystem` object's `CreateTextFile` method is then used to instantiate a `TextStream` object. The `TextStream` object uses the `WriteLine` and `Close` methods to write to the text file.

The `TextStream` object has the following properties and methods:

- `AtEndOfLine`—Property returns `True` if the file pointer is at the end of a line. This property is read-only.
- `AtEndOfStream`—Property returns `True` if the file pointer is at the end of a TextStream file. This property is read-only.
- `Column`—Property that returns the column number of the current character in a TextStream file. This property is read-only.
- `Line`—Property that returns the current line number in a TextStream file. This property is read-only.
- `Close`—This method closes a TextStream file.
- `Read`—This method reads a specified number of characters from a TextStream file.
- `ReadAll`—This method reads a TextStream file from start to finish and returns it as a string.
- `ReadLine`—This method reads an entire line except for the newline character from a TextStream file.
- `Skip`—This method skips over a specified number of characters when reading a TextStream file.
- `SkipLine`—This method skips an entire line when reading a TextStream file.
- `Write`—This method writes the specified string to the TextStream file.
- `WriteLine`—This method writes a specified string and a newline character to a TextStream file.
- `WriteBlankLines`—This method writes a specified number of newline characters to a TextStream file.

Content Linking The Content Linking component provides a mechanism for creating a table of contents for your web site. It accomplishes this task by using a Content Linking list file. The Content Linking list file is a simple ASCII text file that includes entries for page URLs and their descriptions.

A sample Content Linking list file is presented following:

```
---LINKLIST.TXT---
default.htm   Home Page
about.htm   About the Company
Marketing.htm   Marketing Department Web Page
Acct.htm   Accounting Department Web Page
```

The Content Linking component supports the following methods:

- `GetListCount`—Counts the total number of items in the Content Linking list file
- `GetNextURL`—Gets the URL of the next page listed in the Content Linking list file
- `GetPreviousDescription`—Gets the description line of the previous page listed in the Content Linking list file
- `GetListIndex`—Returns the index of the current page in the Content Linking list file
- `GetNthDescription`—Gets the description of the nth page listed in the Content Linking list file
- `GetPreviousURL`—Gets the URL of the previous pages listed in the Content Linking list file
- `GetNextDescription`—Gets the description of the next page listed in the Content Linking list file
- `GetNthURL`—Gets the URL of the nth page listed in the Content Linking list file

The following example demonstrates the building of a table of contents based on a Content Linking list file named linklist.txt in the /scripts virtual directory:

```
<%@ LANGUAGE="VBSCRIPT" %>
<HTML>
<HEAD>
<META NAME="GENERATOR" Content="Microsoft Visual InterDev 1.0">
<META HTTP-EQUIV="Content-Type" content="text/html; charset=iso-8859-1">
<TITLE>Document Title</TITLE>
</HEAD>
<BODY>
<% Set CL = Server.CreateObject ("MSWC.NextLink") %>
<% count = CL.GetListCount ("/scripts/linklist.txt") %>
<% I = 1 %>
<ul>
<% Do While (I <= count) %>
<li><a href=" <%= CL.GetNthURL ("/scripts/linklist.txt", I) %> ">
<%= CL.GetNthDescription ("/scripts/linklist.txt", I) %> </a>
<% I = (I + 1) %>
<% Loop %>
</ul>
</BODY>
</HTML>
```

Client-Side Components

Client-side components are ActiveX controls or Java applets that are integrated into an HTML page and downloaded to a client computer before they can be used by the browser. For the client-side component to run in the browser, both the browser and the operating system must support it.

Visual InterDev provides support for using and incorporating client-side components into the web page through the source editor and the FrontPage 97 editor. The following sections describe how the Visual InterDev environment can be used to leverage the power of client-side components for building exciting web sites.

ActiveX Controls

ActiveX controls are compiled components that provide specific functionality. Thousands of ActiveX controls for performing a variety of tasks are available for use in application-building tools such as Visual InterDev, Visual Basic, Visual C++, Delphi, PowerBuilder, and many others.

NOTE Currently, ActiveX controls are supported on the Windows and Macintosh platforms, with support for UNIX slated in the near future.

Because ActiveX controls are platform-specific, they are not portable from environment to environment, and a different compiled version must be supplied for each supported platform. However, the platform dependence allows ActiveX controls to take advantage of platform-specific features and functionality.

Using ActiveX controls in Visual InterDev is very simple and straightforward. You can use either the Visual InterDev Source Editor or FrontPage 97 to automate the insertion of ActiveX controls in web pages.

To use ActiveX controls on an HTML or ASP page, follow these steps:

1. Open the HTML or ASP page on which the control will be placed.
2. Place the cursor where you want to insert the control and right-click to get to the shortcut menu, as shown in Figure 14.25.
3. Select the Insert ActiveX Control from the menu to display the Insert ActiveX Control dialog box, shown in Figure 14.26.
4. Select the control to insert, and click OK to display the control's image and Properties dialog box, as shown in Figure 14.27.
5. Close the control page. The HTML for the control is displayed in the Visual InterDev Source Editor.

In addition, you can use FrontPage 97 to insert controls into HTML pages in WYSIWYG mode. The controls can even be inserted by using drag and drop. The object editor used in FrontPage 97 is the same as the one used in Visual InterDev Source Editor.

Java Applets

Java applets, like ActiveX controls, are software programs that can be inserted into HTML pages. Java applets are available for creating anything from user interface elements to games and full-blown applications.

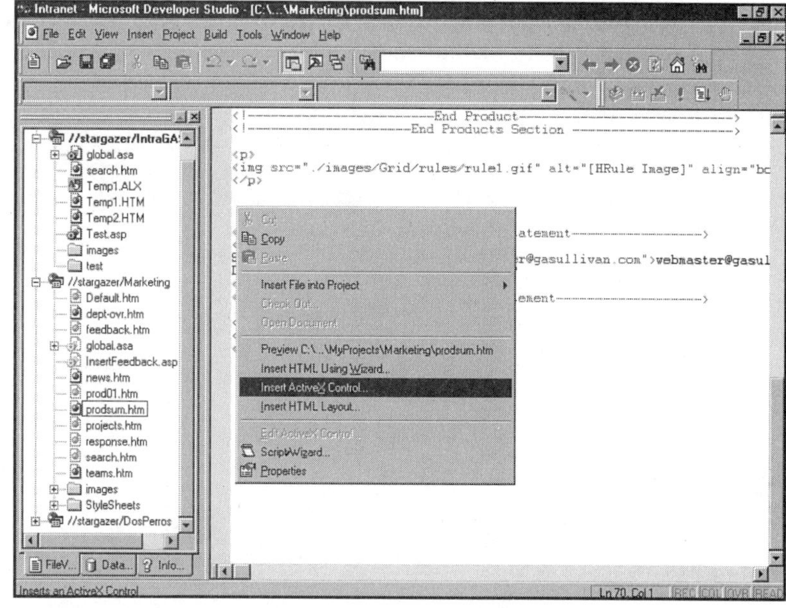

FIG. 14.25
The Insert options can be used to place various controls into the current page.

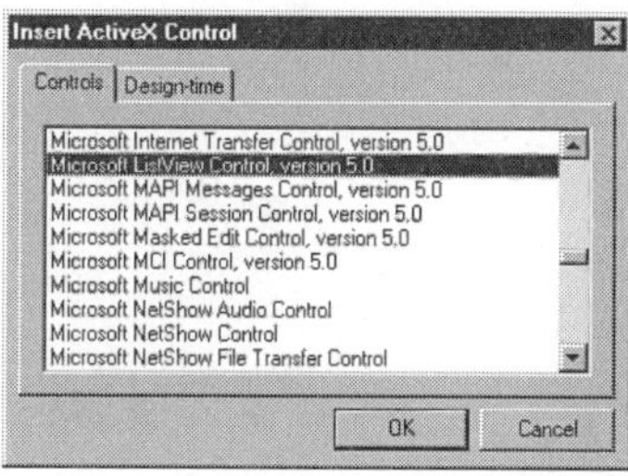

FIG. 14.26
The Insert ActiveX Control dialog box lists all the registered controls on your machine.

FIG. 14.27
Set the initial values for the various control properties by using the Properties dialog box.

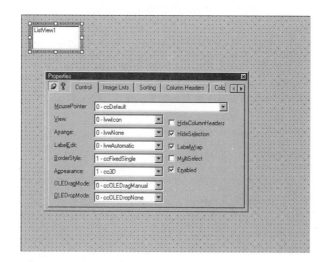

Java applets are unique in that they are platform-independent. Any platform that has a Java virtual machine can run Java applet code with no need to recompile for different platforms.

CAUTION

The platform-independent nature of Java applets makes them unsuitable for utilizing platform-specific functionality. Java applets adhere to the "least-common-denominator" philosophy of cross-platform support.

The easiest way to insert a Java applet into an HTML page is to use the FrontPage 97 editor. Follow these steps:

1. Open the HTML page in FrontPage 97.
2. From the Editor menu, choose Insert, Other Component, Java Applet.
3. The Java Applet Properties dialog box appears, as shown in Figure 14.28.

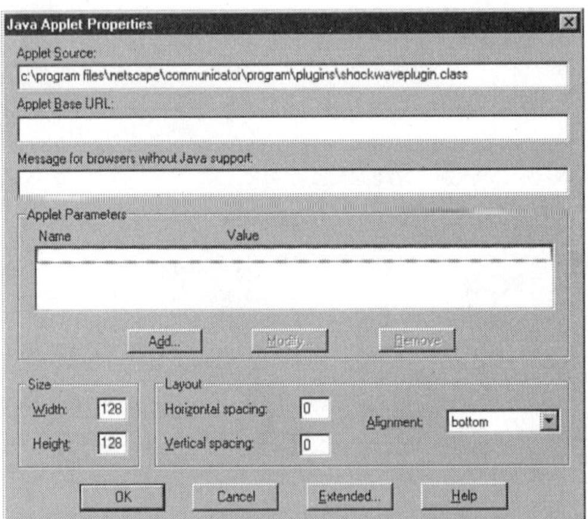

FIG. 14.28
The Java Applet Properties dialog box can be used to set runtime properties for your applet.

4. Provide the .Class filename with the full path to the object in the Applet Source text box. The .Class file is the object file that contains the compiled Java applet runtime.
5. In the Applet Base URL text box, supply the URL to the Java .Class file. This defines where the Java applet file is stored on the web server.
6. In the Message for Browsers Without Java Support text box, provide an HTML message for browsers that do not support Java applets.
7. Add the values for each parameter you want to pass to the Java applet.

NOTE Because Java provides no means for displaying properties and their associated values for applets, you will have to consult the applet documentation for the correct parameters and values.

8. In the Layout property area, specify the display properties for the Java applet.
9. Click OK to close the Properties dialog box and insert the Java applet into your HTML source.

Besides using FrontPage 97 to insert Java applets into web pages, Java applets can also be hosted by Visual J++ within the same workspace as Visual InterDev in the Visual Studio 97 IDE.

From Here...

In this chapter, you learned about some of the basic features and functionality of Visual InterDev. You learned how to use the Visual Studio IDE to create Visual InterDev projects, how to add content to those projects, and how to use wizards to maximize your efforts. You also learned about using and incorporating server-side and client-side components into your projects.

Refer to the following chapters for information related to building web sites and web-based applications using Visual InterDev:

- To learn about Active Server Pages, see Chapter 13, "An Inside Look at Active Server Pages and Internet Information Server."
- To learn about the advanced features of Visual InterDev, see Chapter 15, "Advanced Visual InterDev Concepts."
- To learn about the Visual Studio development environment, see Chapter 2, "Using Visual Studio to Create Applications."
- To learn about creating ActiveX controls, see Chapter 5, "Creating ActiveX Components with Visual Basic."
- To learn about creating components with C++, see Chapter 6, "Creating Components with Visual C++."
- To learn about creating components with J++, see Chapter 7, "Creating Components with Visual J++."
- To learn about the Visual InterDev design-time controls, see Chapter 16, "Visual InterDev Design-Time Controls."

CHAPTER 15

Advanced Visual InterDev Concepts

by Azam A. Mirza

In Chapter 14, "Developing Active Content with Visual InterDev," you learned about some of the basic features provided by Visual InterDev, and in Chapter 16, "Visual InterDev Design-Time Controls," you will learn about the ActiveX controls that can help you build database-aware web pages. Now you are ready to learn about some of the exciting advanced features provided by Visual InterDev. This chapter introduces you to developing client-side features into your web sites, using client-side components and scripting.

Visual InterDev is designed to be *the* development tool for building dynamic and powerful web sites. To accomplish this task, it leverages the power of relational database systems for storing, managing, and producing data to be displayed to users. Most of the world's client/server applications use a database on the back end to provide support for data storage and retrieval, and the dynamic web world is no different. Visual InterDev includes powerful database connectivity, management, and development tools for building database-aware web sites.

In this chapter, you learn about some of these advanced features in greater detail and learn how you can leverage the power of Visual InterDev to energize your web site development effort. ■

The starting point

Learn about the Global.asa file that provides a starting point for all Visual InterDev web applications.

Web applications

Learn about client-side components and how to use them to enhance your web site. Learn about using the Script Wizard to build client-side scripts. Gain an understanding of the differences between Java applets and ActiveX controls and how they are used in Visual InterDev when building web applications.

Database tools

Learn about the database tools provided with Visual InterDev for enabling application building, using ODBC-compliant databases on the back end.

The Data Form Wizard

Explore the advanced features and inner details of the Data Form Wizard and the files it creates.

Web development

Gain an understanding of the complete and comprehensive solution Visual InterDev provides for web development, including support for team development, staging and publishing, and site diagramming.

The Global.asa File

The Global.asa is a special file automatically generated by the Visual InterDev project wizards to hold global functions and variables for the web application. Global.asa is also the place where global event handlers for the application and a particular user session are placed. Listing 15.1 lists the bare-bones Global.asa file that is created initially by Visual InterDev. The Global.asa file is where the `Application` and `Session` object event handlers are stored.

The Global.asa file resides in the root directory of your web application on the web server.

Listing 15.1 The Global.asa File

```
<SCRIPT LANGUAGE="VBScript" RUNAT="Server">

'You can add special event handlers in this file that will run
'automatically when special Active Server Pages events
'occur. To create these handlers, just create a subroutine with
'a name from the list below that corresponds to the event
'you want to use. For example, to create an event handler for
'Session_OnStart, you would put the following code into this
'file (without the comments):
'Sub Session_OnStart
'**Put your code here **
'End Sub

'EventName          Description
'Session_OnStart     Runs the first time a user runs any page in your application
'Session_OnEnd      Runs when a user's session times out or quits your application
'Application_OnStart  Runs once when the first page of your application is run
                     'for the first time by any user
'Application_OnEnd  Runs once when the web server shuts down

</SCRIPT>
<SCRIPT LANGUAGE=VBScript RUNAT=Server>
Sub Session_OnStart
   '==Visual InterDev Generated - DataConnection startspan==
'--Project Data Connection
   Session("DataConn_ConnectionString") = "DBQ=C:\ProgramFiles\DevStudio\
➥MyProjects\IntraGAS\Data\ei3.mdb;DefaultDir=C:\Program Files\DevStudio\
➥MyProjects\IntraGAS\Data;Driver={Microsoft Access Driver (*.mdb)};
➥DriverId=25;FIL=MS Access;ImplicitCommitSync=Yes;MaxBufferSize=512;
➥MaxScanRows=8;PageTimeout=5;SafeTransactions=0;Threads=3;UID=admin;
➥UserCommitSync=Yes;"
   Session("DataConn_ConnectionTimeout") = 15
   Session("DataConn_CommandTimeout") = 30
   Session("DataConn_RuntimeUserName") = "admin"
   Session("DataConn_RuntimePassword") = ""
'==Visual InterDev Generated - DataConnection endspan==
End Sub
</SCRIPT>
```

▶ **See** "The Application Object," **p. 372**
▶ **See** "The Session Object," **p. 374**

The Global.asa file is executed whenever a web application is accessed for the first time and whenever the application ends. The application starts when the first user accesses the application and ends when the last user exits the application. Each individual user access is regarded as a separate session.

NOTE The Global.asa file is not displayed to the user. It is a file that is executed on the server without any output being sent to the client browser.

The Global.asa file must be stored in the root directory of the application, and every application can have only one Global.asa file.

In addition, the Global.asa file is used to declare objects that have global scope within the application. Use the `<OBJECT>` tag to declare objects in the Global.asa file. The syntax for using the `<OBJECT>` tag in the Global.asa file is

```
<OBJECT RUNAT=Server SCOPE=Scope ID=Identifier
➥{PROGID="progID"¦CLASSID="ClassID"}>
```

- *`Scope`*—Identifies the scope of the object. In the context of the Global.asa file, scope is the application or the individual session.
- *`Identifier`*—Defines a unique name for the object.
- *`progID`*—An identifier associated with the class identifier. The format for *`progID`* is `[`*`Vendor`*`.]`*`Component`*`[.`*`Version`*`]`.
- *`ClassID`*—Specifies a unique OLE object. Either *`progID`* or *`ClassID`* must be specified for every object declared.

Listing 15.2 provides an example of an object declaration in the Global.asa file.

Listing 15.2 Using Application Object Variables to Store Information

```
<OBJECT RUNAT=Server SCOPE=Session ID=MyConn
PROGID="ADODB.Connection">
</OBJECT>
```

The Global.asa file can also include scripts written in any supported scripting language. To include scripts in the Global.asa file, use the `<SCRIPT>` and `</SCRIPT>` tags. If you include script that is not enclosed by the script tags, the server generates an error.

▶ **See** "Script Tags," **p. 386**

Using Client-Side ActiveX Components

A powerful feature of dynamic web sites is their ability to incorporate client-side components. An example of client-side components is the use of Java applets or ActiveX controls to perform various tasks such as animations, scrolling marquees, and advertisements. Figure 15.1 illustrates a web site that uses ActiveX controls to provide highly powerful web-based application functionality.

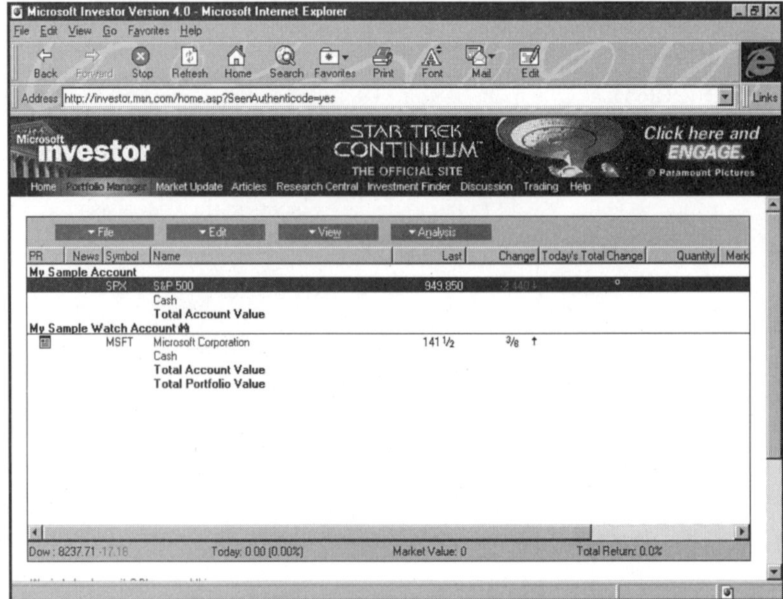

FIG. 15.1
The Microsoft Investor web site uses client-side ActiveX controls to provide portfolio tracking functionality.

Visual InterDev supports two kinds of client-side components. These include

- ActiveX controls
- Java applets

In addition, developers can also include scripts in their web pages that execute on the client side. Visual InterDev includes a powerful tool, the Script Wizard, for building client-side scripts.

There are multitudes of ways to use client-side components within your web applications. The following sections describe the ways these components can be incorporated to enhance your web applications.

ON THE WEB

You can download a large number of freeware and shareware ActiveX controls from a variety of web sites on the Internet. A good place to start is the Microsoft web site (**www.microsoft.com**) or a shareware web site such as the c|net's **www.shareware.com**.

ActiveX controls are compiled client-side components that perform specific tasks. To use ActiveX controls, your operating system and the client browser must support ActiveX controls. Currently, Microsoft Internet Explorer is the only major browser that supports ActiveX controls. In addition, ActiveX controls are supported on the Windows and Macintosh platforms with support for UNIX in the development stages.

NOTE ActiveX controls are the result of the evolution of Microsoft OLE Custom Controls (OCXs) into web-aware objects that are streamlined for use across the Internet technologies.

As stated, ActiveX controls are compiled objects that are downloaded to the client machine for execution. For that reason, different versions of compiled ActiveX controls are required for various platforms. Their platform-specific nature enables ActiveX controls to take advantage of operating-system–specific features and capabilities. Most of the ActiveX controls available today are for the 32-bit Windows systems, Windows 95 and Windows NT. These controls can be developed in a variety of languages, such as Visual Basic, Visual C++, and Borland Delphi.

ON THE WEB

To build ActiveX controls for the Macintosh environment, you need to use the MetroWerks Code Warrior SDK, available for the Macintosh environment. For more information, visit **www.metrowerks.com**.

▶ **See** Chapter 5, "Creating ActiveX Components with Visual Basic," **p. 131**

▶ **See** Chapter 6, "Creating Components with Visual C++," **p. 173**

If you are familiar with Visual Basic Custom Controls (VBXs) or OLE Custom Controls (OCXs), you will have no problem adapting to ActiveX controls. Visual InterDev and FrontPage Editor both provide easy mechanisms for incorporating ActiveX controls in your web applications. Starting with Visual Studio 97, Visual Basic and Visual C++ are also capable of using ActiveX controls as part of traditional client/server applications.

TIP Other development environments such as Delphi, PowerBuilder, and Lotus Notes also provide support for using ActiveX controls.

ActiveX Controls in HTML Pages

ActiveX controls can be incorporated into HTML pages by using the `<OBJECT>` tag. The script for the ActiveX control has to be enclosed within the `<OBJECT>` and `</OBJECT>` tags and can be scripted in either VBScript or JScript. Figure 15.2 illustrates the script used to insert a sample ActiveX control in an HTML page.

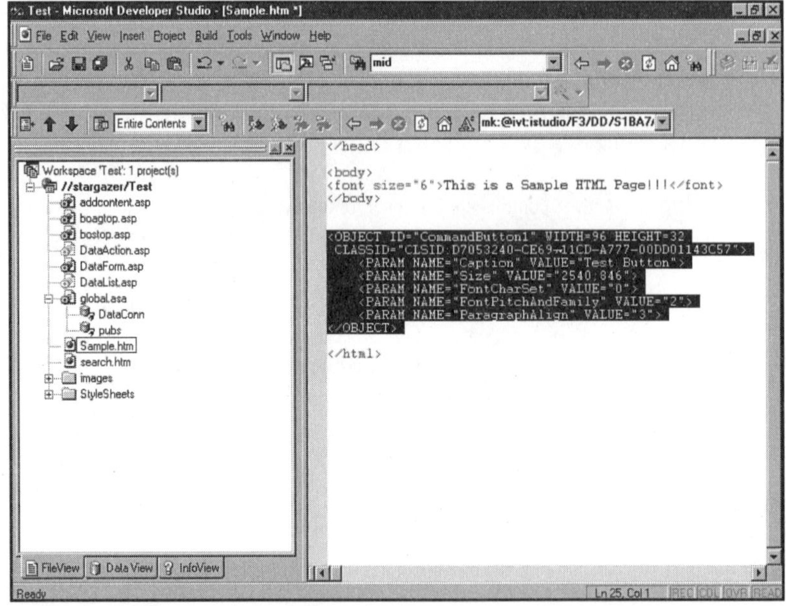

FIG. 15.2
ActiveX controls can be placed anywhere within an HTML page by using the <OBJECT> tag.

NOTE ActiveX controls are different from Active Server Objects in that they include user interface elements.

The syntax of the object tag is as follows:

```
<OBJECT>
ID=identifier
ALIGN=LEFT¦CENTER¦RIGHT
BORDER=n
CLASSID=url
CODEBASE=url
CODETYPE=codetype
DATA=url
DECLARE
HEIGHT=n
HSPACE=n
NAME=url
SHAPES
STANDBY=message
TYPE=type
USEMAP=url
VSPACE=n
WIDTH=n>
```

- `ID`—Specifies the name used to identify the ActiveX control, for example, `ID="txtName"`.
- `ALIGN`—Specifies the alignment property used to place the control on a page, for example, `ALIGN=LEFT`.
- `BORDER`—Specifies the width of the border if the object is defined to be a hyperlink.

- `CLASSID`—Identifies the object implementation. The syntax depends on the object type; for example, for registered ActiveX controls, the syntax is `CLSID:`*`class-identifier`*.
- `CODEBASE`—Identifies the code base for the object. The syntax depends on the object.
- `CODETYPE`—Specifies the Internet media type for code.
- `DATA`—Identifies data for the object. The syntax depends on the object.
- `DECLARE`—Declares the object without instantiating it. Use this when creating cross-references to the object later in the document or when using the object as a parameter in another object.
- `HEIGHT`—Specifies the height of the object.
- `HSPACE`— Specifies the horizontal spacing. This is the space between the object and any text or images to the left or right of the object.
- `NAME`—Sets the name of the object when submitted as part of a form.
- `SHAPES`—Specifies that the object has *shaped hyperlinks*. Shaped hyperlinks are image areas that are not text-based or do not have a simple rectangular shape.
- `STANDBY`—Sets the message to show while the object is being loaded.
- `TYPE`—Specifies the Internet media type for data.
- `USEMAP`—Specifies the image map to use with the object.
- `VSPACE`—Specifies the vertical spacing. This is the space between the object and any text or images above or below the object.
- `WIDTH`—Specifies the width of the object.

In addition, you can define and set property settings for ActiveX controls by using the `<PARAM>` tags within the `<OBJECT>` and `</OBJECT>` tags.

The syntax for the `<PARAM>` tag is as follows:

```
<PARAM NAME=propertyname VALUE=value>
```

- `NAME`—Specifies the name of the property to be initialized. For example, most ActiveX controls define a caption property.
- `VALUE`—Specifies the value for the property.

You can define as many `<PARAM>` tags as necessary within the `<OBJECT>` tags to initialize values for properties. Most properties are optional, however, and do not need to be set in the web page.

Visual InterDev also provides built-in tools that automate and simplify the process of inserting ActiveX controls into web pages. To insert an ActiveX control into a web page, open a project in Visual InterDev that includes an HTML file and then complete the following steps:

1. Open the HTML file in the Visual InterDev editor by double-clicking the file in the File View Explorer, as shown in Figure 15.3.

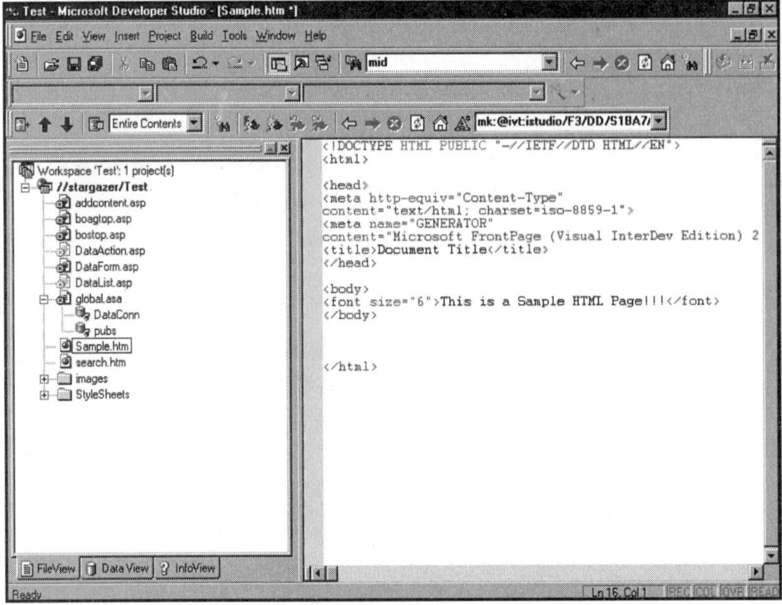

FIG. 15.3
The File View Explorer provides a tree-style view of the files in your current Visual InterDev project.

2. Place the mouse pointer at the location where you want to insert the ActiveX control in the HTML file, and right-click to show the shortcut menu seen in Figure 15.4.

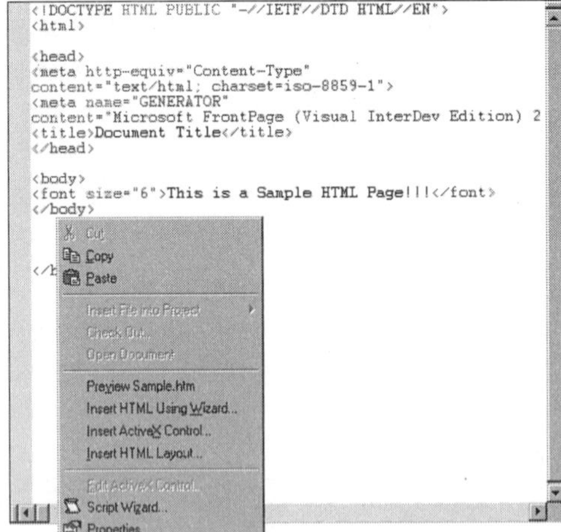

FIG. 15.4
The shortcut menu provides access to the most commonly used Visual InterDev commands.

3. Choose Insert ActiveX Control from the shortcut menu.
4. Choose the control to insert from the list of ActiveX controls displayed in the Insert ActiveX Control dialog box.
5. Click OK to insert the control and display its image in the Properties dialog box, as shown in Figure 15.5.

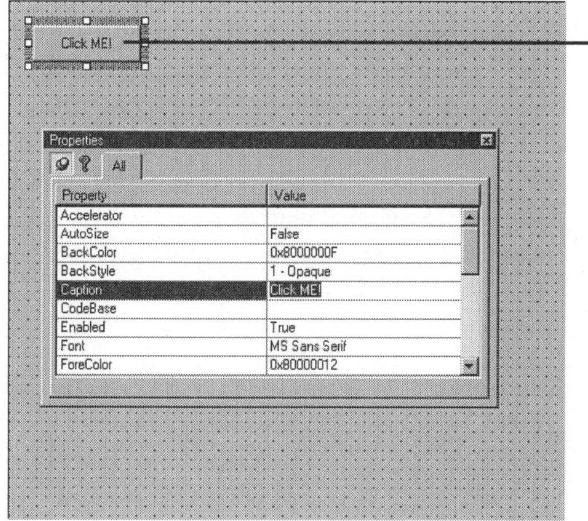

FIG. 15.5
The Properties dialog box enables you to set values for the ActiveX control properties.

6. After you have set the properties the way you want, close the Properties dialog box and size the control the way you want. Then close the control page.
7. The HTML for the control is written into the HTML page automatically, as shown in Figure 15.6.

```
<!DOCTYPE HTML PUBLIC "-//IETF//DTD HTML//EN">
<html>

<head>
<meta http-equiv="Content-Type"
content="text/html; charset=iso-8859-1">
<meta name="GENERATOR"
content="Microsoft FrontPage (Visual InterDev Edition) 2
<title>Document Title</title>
</head>

<body>
<font size="6">This is a Sample HTML Page!!!</font>
</body>

<OBJECT ID="CommandButton1" WIDTH=96 HEIGHT=32
 CLASSID="CLSID:D7053240-CE69-11CD-A777-00DD01143C57">
    <PARAM NAME="Caption" VALUE="Click ME!">
    <PARAM NAME="Size" VALUE="2540;846">
    <PARAM NAME="FontCharSet" VALUE="0">
    <PARAM NAME="FontPitchAndFamily" VALUE="2">
    <PARAM NAME="ParagraphAlign" VALUE="3">
</OBJECT>

</html>
```

FIG. 15.6
The ActiveX Insert tool automates the process of adding the <OBJECT> tags to the HTML page for the ActiveX control.

Using the Visual InterDev ActiveX control insertion and editing tool is a lot easier than writing the <OBJECT> tag script into the HTML page.

NOTE The FrontPage 97 Editor provides a similar tool for inserting and editing ActiveX controls in HTML files.

ActiveX Controls in ASP Pages

Using ActiveX controls in ASP pages is identical to using them in HTML pages; however, ASP provides a powerful mechanism for dynamically setting the properties of a client-side ActiveX control at runtime. By using server-side scripting, you can dynamically set property values for ActiveX controls; for example, you can set the values of a listbox by getting the values from a database table. The job is accomplished by using `<%=varname%>` or a similar expression within the appropriate `<PARAM>` tags for the ActiveX control in the ASP page. Listing 15.3 illustrates the method.

Listing 15.3 Dynamic Setting of Client-Side ActiveX Controls

```
<% dim lblCaption
lblCaption = "User Name:"
%>
<OBJECT ID="Label1" WIDTH=132 HEIGHT=24
 CLASSID="CLSID:978C9E23-D4B0-11CE-BF2D-00AA003F40D0">
  <PARAM NAME="Caption" VALUE=<%=lblCaption%>>
  <PARAM NAME="Size" VALUE="3493;635">
  <PARAM NAME="FontCharSet" VALUE="0">
  <PARAM NAME="FontPitchAndFamily" VALUE="2">
</OBJECT>
```

The `CLASSID` is a special parameter that is used to uniquely identify the ActiveX control. Every ActiveX control must have a uniquely generated `CLASSID`. If you recompile or re create your ActiveX control, a new `CLASSID` will be generated. At that point, you must update the `CLASSID` in your HTML code with the new `CLASSID`.

The Script Wizard

The Script Wizard is a tool included with both Visual InterDev and the FrontPage 97 Editor. The Script Wizard makes it possible to program handlers for events, methods, and properties for ActiveX controls. It also provides support for building client-side VBScript or JScript code.

The ActiveX Control Pad also includes the Script Wizard. It is a separate product that can be downloaded from the Microsoft web site (**www.microsoft.com**).

NOTE The Script Wizard is used to generate client-side scripts only. It cannot generate server-side scripts. ■

ActiveX controls generate events when executed. You can write VBScript or JScript code to handle these events and provide functionality for performing various tasks in response to the generated events. In addition, the Script Wizard provides access to the browser events, methods, and properties to give you control over the client browser.

TIP You can easily change the default scripting language for the Script Wizard by choosing Tools, Options in Visual InterDev. The Options dialog HTML tab shows options for changing the default Script Wizard language between VBScript and JScript.

Now you will see how to use the Script Wizard and learn about its capabilities. Open an HTML page in the Visual InterDev source editor and insert an ActiveX button control, using the methods defined earlier in the "ActiveX Controls in HTML Pages" section. Follow these steps to add code for handling the `Click` event for the command button on the HTML page:

1. Open the HTML file in the Visual InterDev source editor and right-click anywhere in the file to display the shortcut menu. Choose Script Wizard from the menu options.
2. The Script Wizard dialog box is displayed, as shown in Figure 15.7.

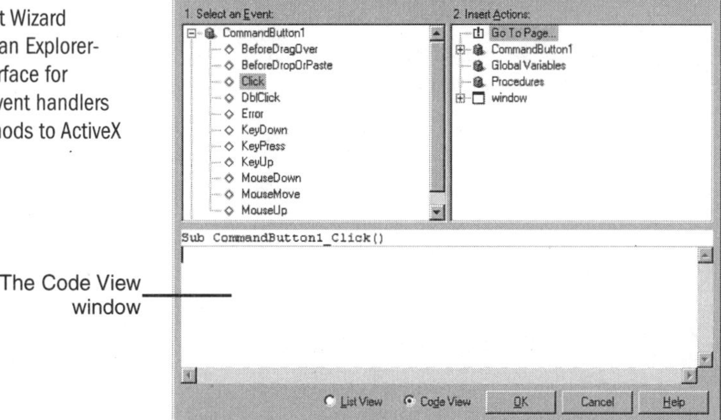

FIG. 15.7 The Script Wizard provides an Explorer-style interface for adding event handlers and methods to ActiveX controls.

NOTE The Script Wizard is smart enough to recognize the presence of the ActiveX control on the page and, accordingly, displays the events and properties for that control.

3. Expand the command button event tree by clicking the plus sign next to the command button name in the left pane.
4. Select the `Click` event in the left pane. Make sure the Code View option button at the bottom of the dialog box is selected.
5. Type in the VBScript code displayed in the bottom window of the dialog box, as shown in Figure 15.8.

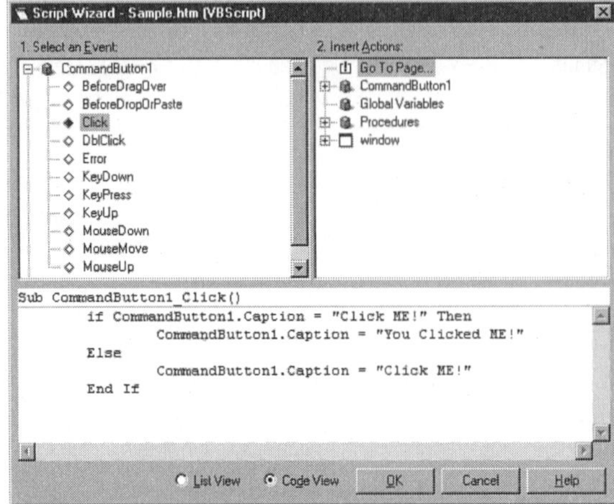

FIG. 15.8
The Code View window provides full support for scripting in the default scripting language.

6. Click OK to close the Script Wizard dialog box. The procedure you just entered is displayed in the HTML page, as shown in Figure 15.9.

FIG. 15.9
The Script Wizard adds the client-side procedures in the HTML page, close to the control they are written for.

7. Display the HTML page in a browser by choosing the Preview feature of Visual InterDev from the shortcut menu.
8. With the page displayed, use the View Source option of the browser to display the source behind the HTML page. You should see the `CommandButton1_Click` event handler as part of the HTML page, as shown in Figure 15.10.

FIG. 15.10
The View Source feature of Internet Explorer allows you to view the source being used to generate the HTML page.

Sample.htm - Notepad

File Edit Search Help

```
<title>Document Title</title>
</HEAD>
<BODY>
<font size="6">This is a Sample HTML Page!!!</font>
</BODY>
<SCRIPT LANGUAGE="VBScript">
<!--
Sub CommandButton1_Click()
        if CommandButton1.Caption = "Click ME!" Then
                CommandButton1.Caption = "You Clicked ME!"
        Else
                CommandButton1.Caption = "Click ME!"
        End If
end sub
-->
</SCRIPT>
<OBJECT ID="CommandButton1" WIDTH=96 HEIGHT=32
 CLASSID="CLSID:D7053240-CE69-11CD-A777-00DD01143C57">
    <PARAM NAME="Caption" VALUE="Click ME!">
    <PARAM NAME="Size" VALUE="2540;846">
    <PARAM NAME="FontCharSet" VALUE="0">
    <PARAM NAME="FontPitchAndFamily" VALUE="2">
    <PARAM NAME="ParagraphAlign" VALUE="3">
</OBJECT>
```

Client-side procedure

One of the important features of the Script Wizard is its capability to expose the events, properties, and methods associated with an ActiveX control. This powerful feature comes in handy when you are trying to figure out the functionality provided by an ActiveX control.

TIP The Script Wizard is similar in its capability to the Visual Basic Object Browser for exposing control properties, events, and methods.

Java Applets

Java applets are programs that can be integrated into HTML pages to provide a variety of functions, including animations, applications, sound, graphics, and audio. Java applets are actual applications written in the Java language, which can be programmed to perform any task imaginable.

▶ **See** Chapter 7, "Creating Components with Visual J++," **p. 221**

ON THE WEB

Thousands of Java applets are available as shareware on the Internet. You can use any of these applets as part of your Visual InterDev applications. For more information, visit **www.javaworld.com**.

Database Development Tools

Visual InterDev provides strong support for building applications that rely on relational databases to provide interactivity and dynamic content. For that reason, Visual InterDev provides tools and features not only for developing database-enabled web applications, but also for managing back-end databases.

Visual InterDev database features include

- Support for creating and managing ODBC data sources
- Support for database connectivity by using ODBC in web applications
- Visual tools for managing data directly by using the Visual InterDev IDE Data View
- Support for design-time ActiveX controls for building data-aware web applications
- The Advanced Query Designer for building complex database queries

▶ **See** Chapter 16, "Visual InterDev Design-Time Controls," **p. 449**

The tools for core database management and development functionality provided by Visual InterDev are referred to as the Microsoft Visual Database Tools. The Visual Database Tools are not exclusive to Visual InterDev and are shared across other Visual Studio development tools, such as Visual C++ Enterprise Edition and Visual Basic Enterprise Edition. The database tools within Visual Studio, however, are based on ODBC connectivity to the database, and you must have ODBC-compliant drivers available for the database you are trying to use, such as Microsoft SQL Server, Microsoft Access, or Oracle databases. The Visual Development tools include

- The Integrated Data View—Provides a view into the currently selected database
- The Database Designer—A designer for creating, managing, and administering ODBC-compliant databases
- The Advanced Query Designer—Used for building SQL queries to be used in database applications

The following sections discuss these features of the Visual Database Tools in more detail, including a discussion of database connectivity using ODBC.

Using ODBC Data Sources

An ODBC data source defines how an application connects to a back-end database. Visual InterDev includes support for the ODBC 3.0 database connectivity tools. ODBC services are provided by a driver supplied by the database manufacturer or a third-party vendor. ODBC provides connectivity for both client/server databases, such as SQL Server, and shared file databases, such as Microsoft Access.

NOTE Visual InterDev includes ODBC drivers for Microsoft Access, FoxPro, SQL Server, and Oracle. Other database drivers are available through third-party developers. ■

The ODBC driver provides a logical software connection to the database and uses a defined data source to determine the location of the database, how to connect to it, the login information, and the parameters common to all query operations.

ODBC 3.0 supports two kinds of database connections. These include

- The method of storing database information in the system Registry under user and system Data Source Names (DSNs)
- The new method of storing data sources as text files, referred to as the File DSN

Both methods provide the same functionality; however, Registry-based DSNs are machine-specific, whereas file-based DSNs can be shared across multiple machines. The file DSNs provide a very useful method for sharing DSNs across an enterprise by saving the DSN files on a shared network drive.

It is possible to create ODBC DSNs through the Visual InterDev development environment; however, it is important to remember that both the web server and the Visual InterDev development workstation need an ODBC DSN to connect to the database. The web server needs the DSN to provide runtime access to the database while users are browsing the web site. The development workstation needs the DSN for connectivity to the database during development and testing.

It is a good idea to use file DSNs and store them on a shared directory on the web server to provide access to these file DSNs from the development workstations.

To set up a shared ODBC file DSN on the web server, take the following steps:

1. Log on to the web server and start the ODBC Administrator utility from the Control Panel.
2. Choose the File DSN tab and click Add to start the New Data Source Wizard.
3. From the list of database drivers, choose the driver for which you want to create the DSN and click Next.
4. Provide a name for the data source and then click Next. Make sure that you provide a full UNC path (\\servername\sharename\dsnname) to the DSN file location on a shared drive on the web server.

NOTE A UNC (Universal Naming Convention) path refers to a network location using the server name and directory tree, for example, \\MyServer\MyDirectory\MySubDirectory.

5. Click the Finish button to close the New Data Source Wizard.
6. If the DSN you have set up requires additional information, a dialog box is displayed, as shown in Figure 15.11.

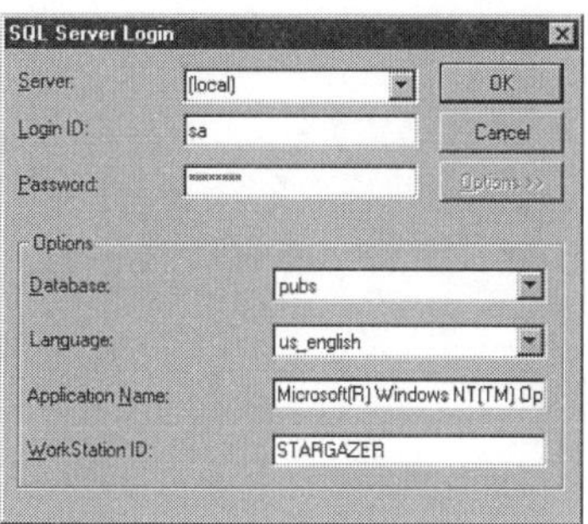

FIG. 15.11
The SQL Server Login dialog box is displayed to obtain login information for the DSN.

7. Provide the login information and click OK to return to the ODBC Administrator utility.
8. Click OK to close the ODBC Administrator utility.

Now that you have added an ODBC DSN, you can use that DSN to add database connections within your Visual InterDev projects. To add a database connection to a project, take the following steps:

1. Open the project in Visual InterDev and right-click the project name to display the shortcut menu. Choose Add Data Connection to display the Select Data Source dialog box.
2. Choose the file DSN you created previously. If necessary, a login dialog box is displayed for the database being accessed, as shown in Figure 15.12.

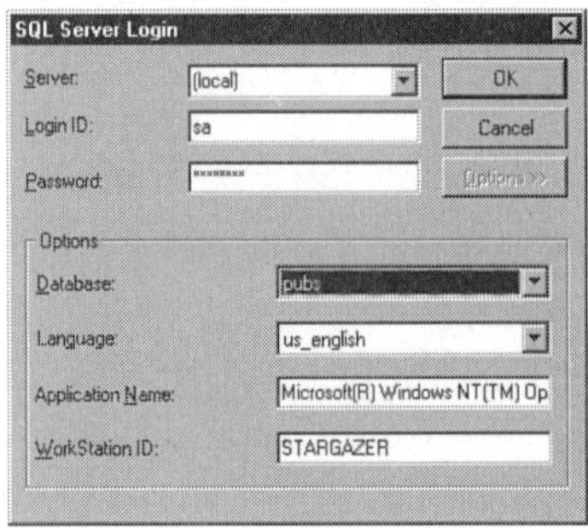

FIG. 15.12 Provide a valid login for the database and choose the database name from the list.

3. Click OK to continue. A database connection is added to the project, as shown in the File View in Figure 15.13.

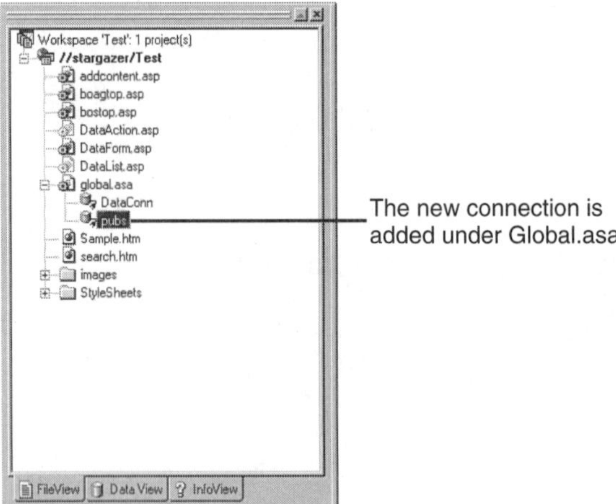

FIG. 15.13 The database connection allows access to all the tables, queries, and views within the database.

After you have set up a connection to a database within your project, you can use the various Visual Database Tools to manage the database, build queries, and perform tasks required for doing database application development.

The Integrated Data View

The Integrated Data View is used to provide a live view into the ODBC data sources being used in a web application. The Data View is a powerful tool with which you can manage ODBC databases, including support for adding, deleting, and updating of database tables and records. Figure 15.14 illustrates the Data View within the Visual InterDev IDE.

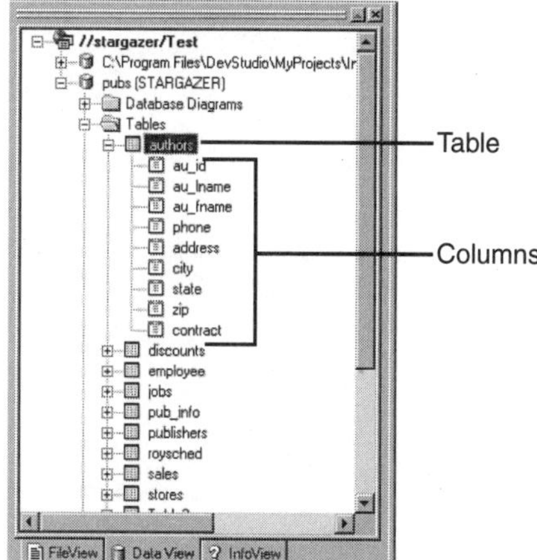

FIG. 15.14
The Data View uses the familiar Explorer-style IDE to provide access to database objects and properties.

The Data View lists the database tables, views, and stored procedures defined within the database. You can view, edit, add, update, or delete anything from this view into the database. The Data View is fairly similar to the SQL Server Enterprise Manager in its capabilities and user interface.

Figure 15.15 illustrates the various views that can be obtained into the database and the data stored in the tables. Double-click a table to display in the right pane the data stored in that table. Use the pop-up database utilities toolbar to toggle between views.

▶ **See** "Visual Studio 97 Database Design Tools," **p. 59**

Right-click any object in the Data View Explorer to get to the Properties menu to display the properties of the object.

The Database Designer

The Database Designer brings visual ease of use and flexibility to creating and managing remote SQL Server 6.5 databases. The Database Designer is integrated into the Data View and provides the following two key elements for creating and managing SQL Server 6.5 databases:

- *Table Design Mode*—Used to define, create, and manage SQL Server table definitions
- *Database Diagrams*—Used to define foreign keys, constraints, and relationships between tables

▶ **See** "Visual Studio 97 Database Design Tools," **p. 59**

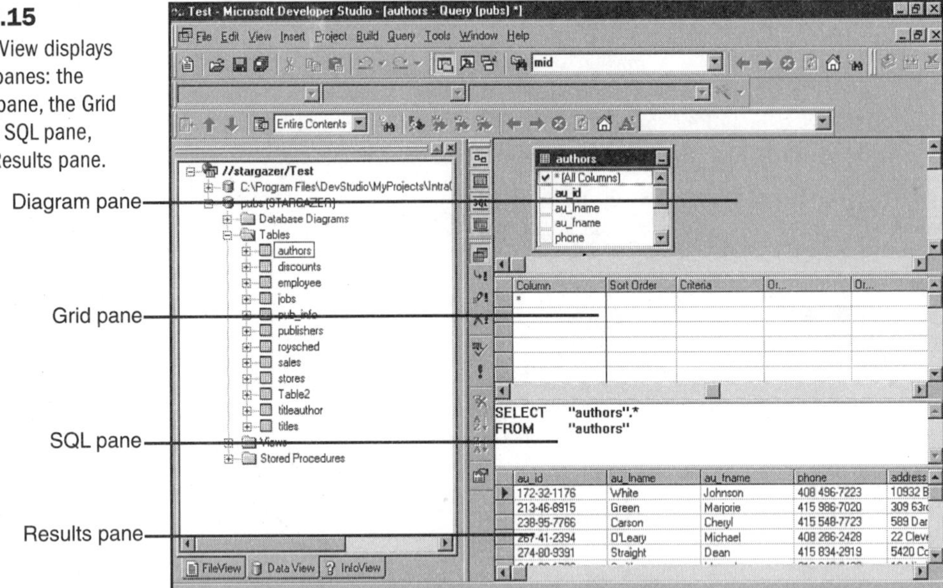

FIG. 15.15
The Data View displays multiple panes: the Diagram pane, the Grid pane, the SQL pane, and the Results pane.

The Advanced Query Designer

The Advanced Query Designer is a familiar tool that has its roots in the old Microsoft Query and the query designer built into Microsoft Access. If you have used either of these tools, you will feel right at home with the Advanced Query Designer. Figure 15.16 illustrates the Advanced Query Designer.

To use the Advanced Query Designer to create queries, take the following steps:

1. Double-click a table in the Data View Explorer to open the table in the right pane.
2. Click the Diagram pane, the Grid pane, and the SQL pane to display the various data views from the Query toolbar.
3. Select any other tables you want to use in the query and drag them to the Diagram pane.
4. Select columns to include in the query by clicking the checkbox next to the column name. As you select the columns, notice that the Grid and SQL panes update to reflect the changes.
5. Click the Run (!) button in the Query toolbar to run your query and display the data in the Results pane.
6. When you have finished, close the Advanced Query Designer. When you are asked to save the query, provide an appropriate name and location and save the query. You can now use the query in your application.

▶ **See** "Visual Studio 97 Database Design Tools," **p. 59**

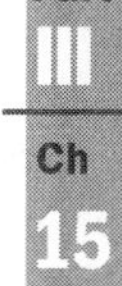

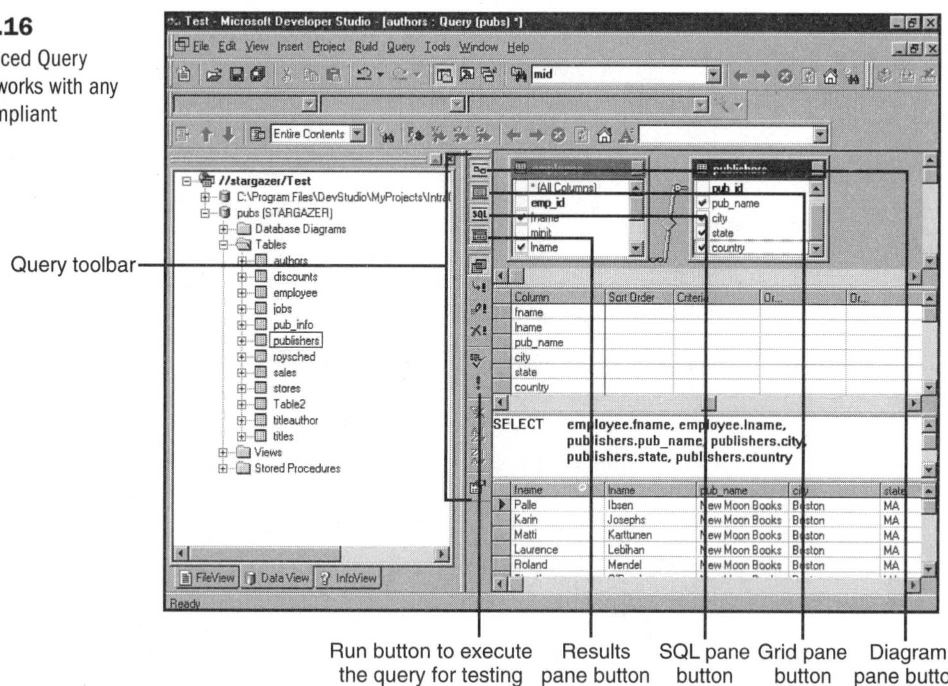

FIG. 15.16
The Advanced Query Designer works with any ODBC-compliant database.

Exploring the Data Form Wizard

The Data Form Wizard is a powerful tool for creating database-aware web pages. It provides an advanced set of features for creating list- and form-based pages for displaying data to users. Web pages created with the Data Form Wizard can be used to view, edit, add, update, or delete information from tables in an ODBC database.

▶ **See** "Using File Wizards," **p. 402**

The Data Form Wizard has an Advanced Options dialog box in which you can control the appearance and behavior of the data being displayed. Figure 15.17 shows the Advanced Options dialog box for the Data Form Wizard.

To set advanced options, follow these steps:

1. Select the field name in the Field Name listbox.
2. Enter the new field label in the Alternative Field Label box. The alternative label is used instead of the default label generated by Visual InterDev if it is specified.
3. If the field is based on a lookup table, select the lookup table in the Look-up Table drop-down box.
4. Select the `ID` field from the Corresponding Key ID drop-down box and the `Display` field from the Display This Field drop-down box.

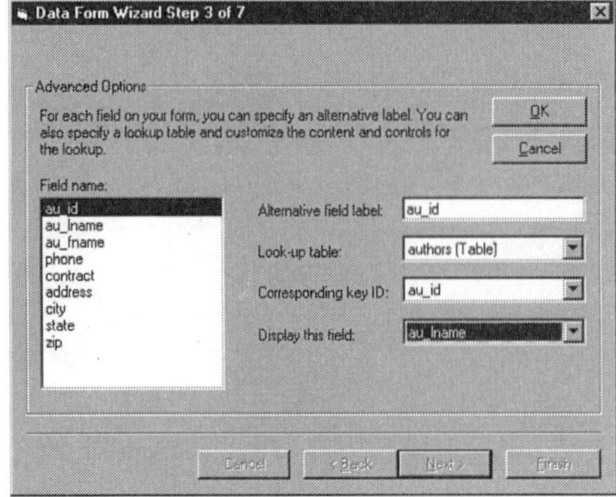

FIG. 15.17
The Advanced Options dialog box is used to specify field and label properties.

5. Repeat the procedure for all pertinent fields in the Field Name listbox.
6. Click OK to close the Advanced Options dialog box.

A lookup table enables the selection of a field, the contents of which will be used to populate a drop-down listbox. Users will then be limited to selecting only from the options available in the drop-down listbox.

The Data Form Wizard generates three .ASP files, complete with source code and design-time control references. The filenames of these files are based on a table-name–based prefix and a wizard-assigned suffix. The suffixes generated by the wizard are List.asp, Form.asp, and Action.asp. The files generated include

NOTE The two design-time controls used are the Data Range Header control and the Data Range Footer control.

▶ For more information about design-time ActiveX controls, **see** Chapter 16, "Visual InterDev Design-Time Controls," **p. 449**.

- *name*List.asp—Displays the contents of the database in List View. Figure 15.18 provides an illustration of a List View page.
- *name*Form.asp—Displays the contents of the database in Form View. Figure 15.19 provides an illustration of a Form View page.
- *name*Action.asp—A nondisplayed file that contains the server-side script for handling filter, update, insert, and delete commands from the Form View.

Each of the three generated files includes variable and procedure declarations for the file, along with a large number of HTML formatting codes for displaying the page appropriately in the web browser.

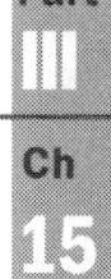

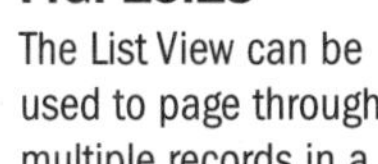

FIG. 15.18
The List View can be used to page through multiple records in a grid format.

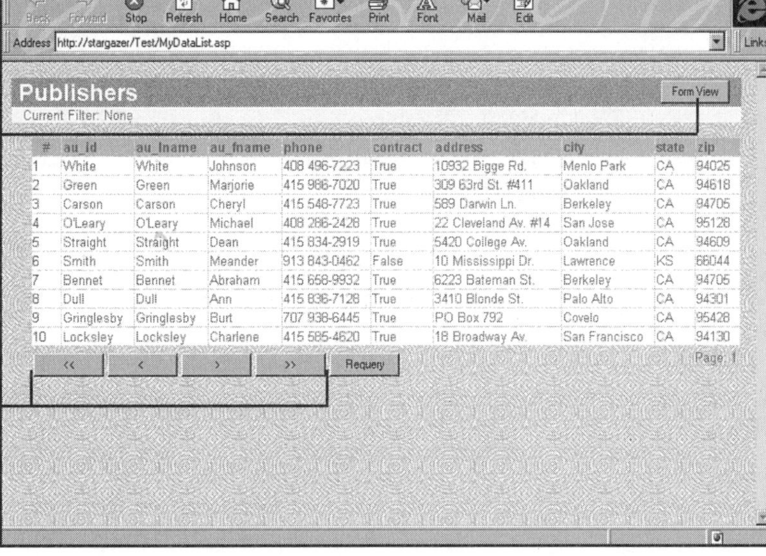

FIG. 15.19
The Form View provides buttons for Update, Delete, New, Filter, and List View.

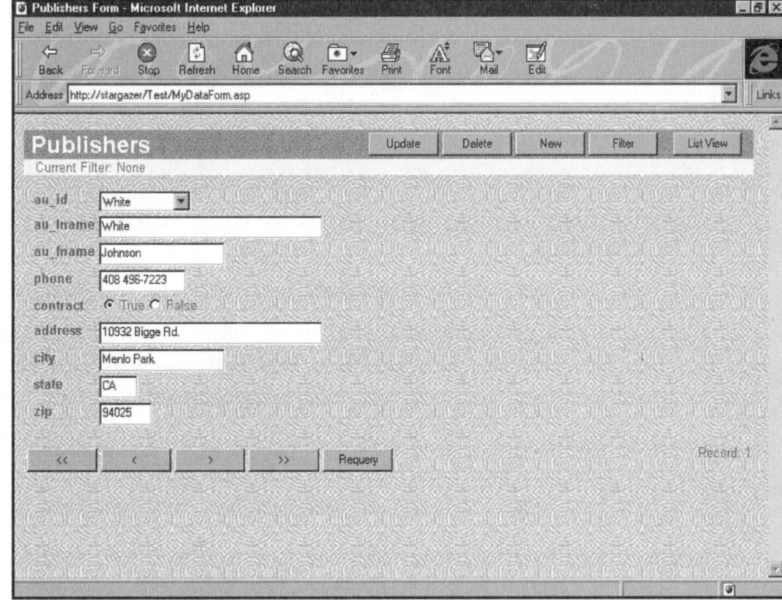

The List.asp file includes the following procedures:

- `ConvertNull`—Trims spaces from the input string and substitutes Empty for Null values.
- `QuotedString`—Adds bracketing codes around the input string and returns the result.
- `IsURL`—Tests the input string to see if it is a URL by checking for prefixes such as HTTP:// and FTP://. Returns True if the string is a URL.
- `ShowField`—Displays the field on the page, based on its data type, attributes, and advanced option settings.

In addition to the preceding items, the Form.asp file includes the following procedure:

- `CanUpdateField`—Tests to determine if the specified field is updateable. The function returns True if the field is updateable.

The Action.asp file includes the following procedures:

- `RestoreNull`—Changes an Empty value to a Null.
- `RaiseError`—Raises an error based on the `Err.Raise` method. The error is based on the input parameter passed to the procedure.
- `ConvertToString`—Converts the filed input to a string.
- `IsEqual`—Returns True if the input variables are equal.
- `IsRequiredField`—Returns True if the input field is a required field in the recordset.
- `CanUpdateField`—Tests to determine if the specified field is updateable. The function returns True if the field is updateable.
- `InsertField`—Updates a recordset field during an insert operation. Returns True if successful.
- `UpdateField`—Updates a recordset field. Returns True if successful.
- `FilterField`—Creates a filter field based on user input. Filters display records based on the filter field.
- `PrepFilterItem`—Builds a name and value pair for a SQL `Where` clause.
- `feedbackField`—A display field involved in a database operation for feedback. This subroutine uses the `Response.Write` method to create HTML dynamically to send the results of a database operation to the client browser.

In addition to the procedures described in the preceding lists, the Data Form Wizard generates a lot of supporting script. It generates scripts for creating the database connection and for checking the recordset status and code for handling lookup table functionality.

The Data Form Wizard generates files complete with script code and design-time ActiveX controls. If the code generated by the Data Form Wizard requires any modifications, you must make them manually.

▶ For more information about utilizing the ActiveX design-time controls, **see** Chapter 16, "Visual InterDev Design-Time Controls," **p. 449**.

Managing Visual InterDev Projects

A great deal of functionality is provided by Visual InterDev and its associated tools and utilities for building powerful web applications. In addition, Visual InterDev includes a set of utilities to provide ancillary functions, such as support for team development, staging and publishing of web sites, working on multiple projects, and other project management issues. The following sections discuss these functions in further detail.

Team Development

Visual InterDev provides strong support for team development through Visual SourceSafe. Visual SourceSafe is integrated into the Visual Studio 97 IDE and provides source management for the products included in Visual Studio 97.

▶ For more information about using Visual SourceSafe, **see** Chapter 26, "Using Visual SourceSafe," **p. 715**.

SourceSafe provides source management, version control, and file check-in and check-out capabilities that work seamlessly within Visual InterDev to manage large team-development efforts. Visual SourceSafe works with any type of file, including text files, HTML files, and binary image and graphics files.

Visual SourceSafe integration for web projects is server-based. The web server administrator needs to install a copy of Visual SourceSafe on the server. No Visual SourceSafe components need to be installed on Development workstations.

Because Visual SourceSafe works on the server, the file check-in and check-out operations work over HTTP. They can work across firewalls and proxy servers and can span the Internet.

Developers can install client versions of Visual SourceSafe on their workstations to take advantage of other source-management capabilities, such as File Compare and File Merge.

To use Visual SourceSafe with Visual InterDev, take the following steps:

1. Install Visual SourceSafe on the machine running the web server. Make sure the Enable Integration option is activated during setup of Visual SourceSafe.
2. Configure the user database on SourceSafe to provide access for two special user types: the Anonymous Internet account for the web server and the user IDs for web developers who need access to the source control system.
3. Start Visual InterDev and open the project for which you want to enable source control.
4. Choose Project, Enable Web Source Control.
5. Provide the name of the source control database to use with the project.
6. Click OK to continue.

Staging and Publishing Web Sites

The File View Explorer within Visual InterDev is a powerful tool that not only provides a view into the contents of a web site, but also enables you to create, delete, rename, and move files and folders. The support for drag and drop makes it very easy to move files between folders and projects.

Because a single workspace can contain multiple projects in the File View Explorer, you can easily move files between distinct remote web servers. This allows you to host multiple versions of a web site on different servers and move back and forth between them easily, with simple drag and drop.

For example, you can have two projects open within a single workspace that connects to two different servers. One server can be the staging server, where you do most of your development and testing of web sites. The other server can be the production server, where users connect to browse the web site. By using drag and drop, you can easily move content from the staging server to the production server and publish your web site to the user community. Figure 15.20 shows a workspace with two web projects in one space, where developers can move content back and forth.

FIG. 15.20
The File View Explorer allows drag-and-drop publishing of a web site.

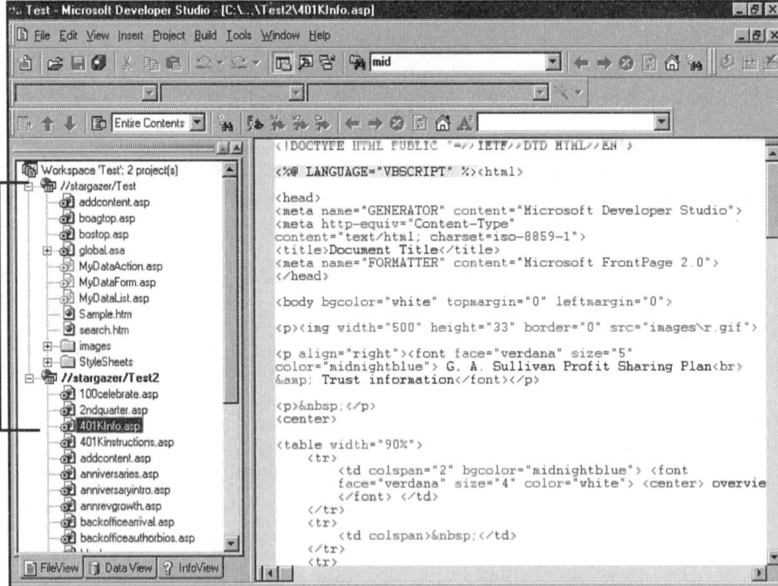

Link Repair and Link View

The ease of use Visual InterDev affords in terms of file manipulation automates many aspects of web site management, so you can move files and folders with ease. However, when files are moved from one folder to another, the HTTP links within these files might no longer work.

Visual InterDev includes a Link Repair option that automatically repairs links to elements within a web site as files are moved. By default, this option is turned off in Visual InterDev. You can turn on the option by right-clicking the project in the File View and choosing Properties. In the Properties dialog box, activate Link Repair by clicking On.

CAUTION

Be careful with Link Repair. While parsing the files to repair links, Visual InterDev might mess up the spacing of text in HTML files, making them difficult to read in the Visual InterDev source editor.

Visual InterDev also includes a great tool for managing a web site. Called the Link View, this tool provides a graphic representation of a web site. Link View can work on any web site, providing a graphic representation of all the pages within the web site and the links between them. Figure 15.21 illustrates the Link View produced for the G. A. Sullivan web site.

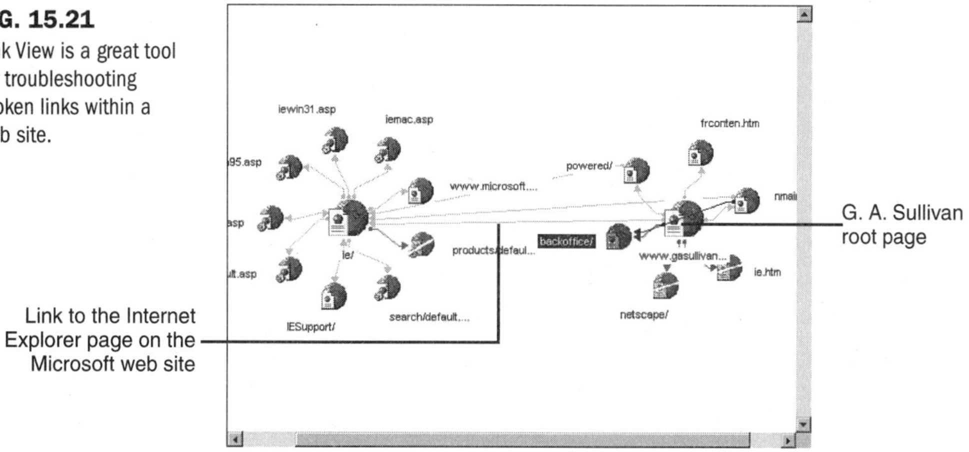

FIG. 15.21
Link View is a great tool for troubleshooting broken links within a web site.

Link to the Internet Explorer page on the Microsoft web site

G. A. Sullivan root page

To use Link View, take the following steps:

1. Choose Tools, View Links on WWW.
2. In the View Links on WWW dialog box, provide the URL for the site you are trying to map, as shown in Figure 15.22.

FIG. 15.22
The URL can be of any web site accessible from the machine on which Link View is running.

3. The root page is displayed in the middle, surrounded by pages the root page provides a link to.
4. To display the links for any page, right-click on the page and choose View Links from the shortcut menu.

The arrows shown between the objects in a site are color-coded to indicate the status of the link. The link colors are based on the following scheme:

- *Blue*—Designates links to currently selected objects
- *Gray*—Designates links to unselected objects
- *Red*—Broken links that cannot be resolved for some reason

A view of the links to and from an object can be displayed by clicking the object. This method provides a quick view of all the links to and from a particular web page. To zoom the Link View in and out, choose View, Zoom or use the Zoom listbox on the Link View toolbar.

From Here...

In this chapter, you learned about some of the advanced features and functionality of Visual InterDev. You learned about using client-side components and scripting, the Visual Database Tools supplied with Visual InterDev, and project management facilities.

Refer to the following chapters for information related to building web sites and web-based applications using Visual InterDev:

- To learn about getting started with Visual InterDev, see Chapter 14, "Developing Active Content with Visual InterDev."
- To learn about Active Server Pages, see Chapter 13, "An Inside Look at Active Server Pages and Internet Information Server."
- To learn about Dynamic HTML and its advantages, see Chapter 18, "Dynamic HTML."
- To learn about using design-time controls, see Chapter 16, "Visual InterDev Design-Time Controls."
- To learn about server-side programming using Active Server Pages, see Chapter 17, "Server-Side Programming in an I-net Environment."
- To learn about the database features and tools included with Visual Studio 97, see Chapter 3, "Creating Database–Aware Applications with Visual Studio."
- To learn about creating components with Visual Basic, see Chapter 5, "Creating ActiveX Components with Visual Basic."
- To learn about creating components with Visual C++, see Chapter 6, "Creating Components with Visual C++."
- To learn about creating components with Visual J++, see Chapter 7, "Creating Components with Visual J++."

- To learn about concepts associated with web-based application development, see Chapter 11, "An Inside Look at Web-Based Applications."
- To learn more about using Visual SourceSafe with Visual InterDev, see Chapter 26, "Using Visual SourceSafe."
- To learn about the Visual Studio development environment, see Chapter 2, "Using Visual Studio to Create Applications."

CHAPTER 16

Visual InterDev Design-Time Controls

by Chris H. Striker

One of the more tedious tasks you'll undertake when developing dynamic, database-driven web pages is writing the code that connects to a database, generates HTML from retrieved data, and provides interactivity with the database. Fortunately, Visual InterDev contains a handful of design-time ActiveX controls to make this task considerably easier; in fact, the combination of some of these controls takes nearly all the work out of the task. With the Data Command control or the Data Range Header and Footer controls (together making up the Data Range controls), most of the grunt work of incorporating database access in web pages is done for you.

You use the design-time controls in very much the same way you use other ActiveX controls—they're inserted in pages as objects, have parameters and properties you can set, and are accessible via scripting. As opposed to other ActiveX controls, which run on the client, design-time controls reside and function on the server; also, they're available only in your development environment (Visual InterDev). For example, the Include control, the other design-time control included in Visual InterDev, inserts the contents of another file into your web page. This happens when the page is requested—the server looks through the contents of the page, sees the Include control object, and replaces the object with the contents of the file specified by the control. The page with the inserted contents is then sent down to users. ■

The Data Command control

This general-purpose control is good for accessing your web project's data connection, as well as for defining database and recordset objects to be used via scripting.

The Data Range controls

The Data Range Header and Data Range Footer controls echo the functionality of the Data Command control but go a step further: They automate the process of presenting the data in your recordsets on web pages by generating the HTML and scripting necessary to do the job.

The Include control

Don't let this control's size or simplicity fool you. By providing a way to include the contents of other pages within your page, you can easily standardize HTML elements and scripts across your site.

NOTE This chapter assumes that you're comfortable with Active Server Pages (ASP), server-side scripting, and ActiveX controls.

▶ **See** Chapter 8, "Using ActiveX Client Components in an I-net Environment," **p. 239**, for information on ActiveX controls.

▶ For information on Active Server Pages, **see** Chapter 13, "An Inside Look at Active Server Pages and Internet Information Server," **p. 363**, and Chapter 14, "Developing Active Content with Visual InterDev," **p. 389**.

▶ **See** Chapter 17, "Server-Side Programming in an I-net Environment," **p. 467**, for information on server-side scripting.

Setting Up a Data Connection

Before you incorporate the Data Command, Data Range Header, or Data Range Footer controls in your pages, you must first define a data connection. Visual InterDev makes this easy. Open your web project in Visual InterDev and look at the global.asa file, which contains the code for the data connection.

NOTE The database used for the following example, as well as successive examples throughout the chapter, is the Northwind database that ships with Microsoft Access. (This database is included with Microsoft Office 97 Professional Edition.)

Follow these steps to establish a data connection for your web project:

1. Right-click the global.asa file.
2. From the drop-down menu, choose Add Data Connection (see Figure 16.1).

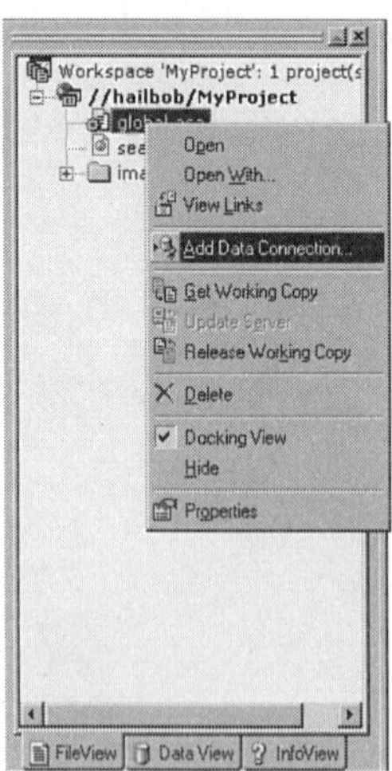

FIG. 16.1
Throughout Visual InterDev, context-sensitive menus appear with a right-click. Here, you're presented with the option to add a data connection because Visual InterDev recognizes that you've right-clicked the global.asa file.

3. In the Select Data Source dialog box, you can set up a file data source for the database you want to use. Select New.

4. In the Create New Data Source dialog box, select the Microsoft Access Driver at the top of the list (or the driver for the data source you want to use) and click Next.
5. Enter the name of your new data source and click Next.

Step 5 saves the data source file in the default location for your machine. If you want to specify another location, you can browse to the location and select it.

6. Enter the name of your new data source and click Next. Then click Finish in the Create New Data Source dialog box.
7. In the ODBC Microsoft Access 97 Setup dialog box, choose Select.
8. Browse to the location of the Northwind.mdb file (or another database you want to associate with the data source file you just specified) and click OK.
9. Click OK in the ODBC Microsoft Access 97 Setup dialog box.
10. Your new data source should be listed in the Select Data Source dialog box at this point (see Figure 16.2). Select it and click OK.

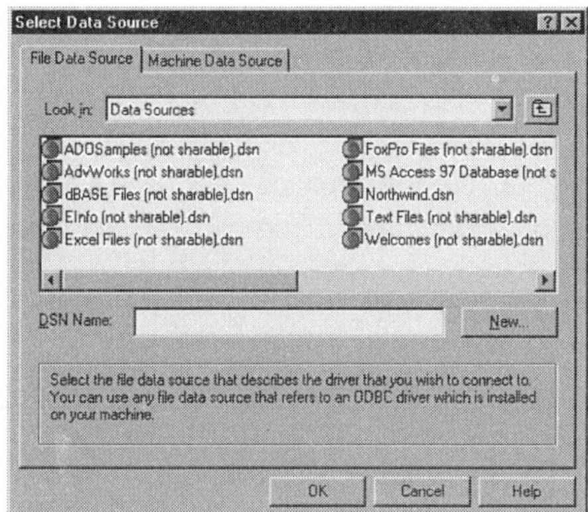

FIG. 16.2
After you select your data source here, Visual InterDev inserts the code necessary to build the data connection in your global.asa file.

11. Check the properties in the General and Run-Time tabs of the Data Connection Properties dialog box. The defaults should be fine, but you have the opportunity here to alter the `ConnectionTimeout`, `CommandTimeout`, `ConnectionString`, `Name`, `UserName`, and `Password` properties.

This procedure specifies a data connection for your web project. Notice that the global.asa file now features an expansion plus sign next to it in the File View in Visual InterDev. If you expand the global.asa file, you can see the data connection. When you open the global.asa file, you should see code similar to the following:

```
<SCRIPT LANGUAGE=VBScript RUNAT=Server>
Sub Session_OnStart
     Visual InterDev Generated - DataConnection startspan==
     Project Data Connection
          Session("DataConn_ConnectionString") = "DBQ=D:\VISUAL STUDIO 97\
          ➥DESIGN TIME CONTROLS\Northwind.mdb;DefaultDir=D:\VISUAL STUDIO 97\
```

```
        ➥DESIGN TIME CONTROLS;Driver={Microsoft Access Driver (*.mdb)};
        ➥DriverId=25;FIL=MS Access;ImplicitCommitSync=Yes;MaxBufferSize=512;
        ➥MaxScanRows=8;PageTimeout=5;SafeTransactions=0;Threads=3;UID=admin;
        ➥UserCommitSync=Yes;"
        Session("DataConn_ConnectionTimeout") = 15
        Session("DataConn_CommandTimeout") = 30
        Session("DataConn_RuntimeUserName") = "admin"
        Session("DataConn_RuntimePassword") = ""
    Visual InterDev Generated - DataConnection endspan==
End Sub
</SCRIPT>
```

Notice that Visual InterDev has set several session properties:

- `DataConn_ConnectionString`
- `DataConn_ConnectionTimeout`
- `DataConn_CommandTimeout`
- `DataConn_RuntimeUserName`
- `DataConn_RuntimePassword`

Now that the data connection is defined, you can use the database tools included with Visual InterDev. Switch to the data view of the workspace window or double-click the `DataConn` object below the global.asa file in the File View of the workspace window. Notice that the objects in your database are exposed. Expand the tables section and double-click one of the tables. The table opens and the Query toolbar appears (compare your screen to Figure 16.3). With these tools, you can write SQL by hand or build statements with the visual tool (by dragging and marking fields), and you can test the statements. You'll use these tools to build the SQL used by the Data Range control to return recordsets.

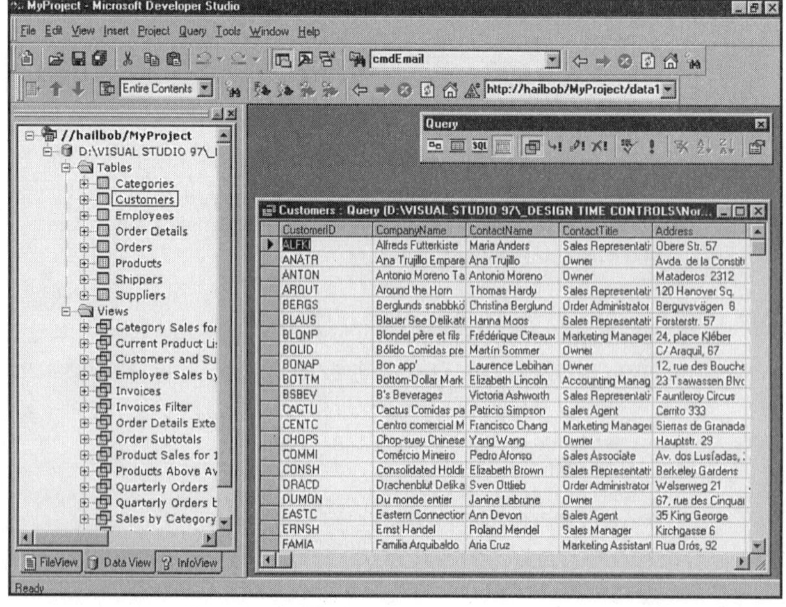

FIG. 16.3
Visual InterDev provides a fairly comprehensive set of tools with which to work with data. Here, the Customers table of the database is opened, displaying its contents.

Using the Data Command Control

The Data Command control provides an easy way to generate the server-side code necessary to connect to a database and to define your data objects. If you're developing a web page that accesses a database and want to maintain control over the interactivity with the database (filtering, sorting, and so on) and the generation of HTML to display content, you'll probably want to use the Data Command control. This control generates the code necessary to establish the connection, passes the SQL needed to generate a recordset for your use, and defines the returned recordset object.

Properties

The properties listed in the following sections determine the functionality of the Data Command control. As with most properties, they're displayed on your Active Server Page as parameters (specified by the `<PARAM>` tag) within the `<OBJECT>` element for your control. Keep in mind that many of the properties for the Data Command control are also used by the Data Range Header control.

The *CommandText* Property This property is the command/SQL to be issued against the database specified in your data connection. You can set this property by any of the following three methods:

- Selecting an item (such as a table) from the drop-down list
- Typing a SQL statement
- Automatically generating SQL via the SQL Builder

The `CommandText` property works with the `CommandType` property described later. If you set the `CommandType` property to SQL, the SQL Builder button is enabled, and you can enter your own SQL into the `CommandType` property text box or use the SQL Builder to generate the SQL. If the `CommandType` property is set to Table, View, or Stored Procedure, the drop-down list is populated with these objects from your database.

The *CommandTimeout* Property The `CommandTimeout` property indicates how many seconds ADO should wait for a command to execute against the database before terminating the command and generating an error. The default for this value is 30 seconds; ADO waits indefinitely if you set this property to 0.

NOTE ADO, or ActiveX Data Objects, is the newest of the data-access methods Microsoft offers. It's slated to succeed DAO (Data Access Objects) and RDO (Remote Data Objects).

The *CommandType* Property This property indicates what type of command is being passed by the `CommandText` property: SQL, Stored Procedure, Table, or View. See the discussion on the `CommandText` property for more information.

The *CursorType* Property The `CursorType` property indicates the type of cursor used with the recordset returned by the control. A Forward Only cursor allows only forward movement through the recordset (via the `MoveNext` method); this is the default `CursorType`. The Keyset cursor allows forward and backward movement, fixes membership, and reflects the current state of the database. A Dynamic cursor allows forward and backward movement and dynamic membership; it reflects the current state of the database, and new rows inserted by other users appear automatically. The Static cursor type allows forward and backward movement, but the recordset is a snapshot. It doesn't necessarily reflect the current state of the database and isn't automatically refreshed to indicate changes by other users.

NOTE *Fixed membership* means that the data in the returned recordset is valid for the moment at which the recordset is built; changes to the database won't be reflected in the recordset. *Dynamic membership* means that the recordset reflects changes to the database since the recordset was created.

The *DataConnection* Property This property indicates which data connection the control should use when building recordsets. The list of data connections is built from the connections that already have been added to your web project (typically in the global.asa file).

The *ID* Property The `ID` property is the standard identification property used for all ActiveX controls; it's the handle by which controls are referenced via scripting. You can change this property although it's assigned a unique value derivative of the type of control when you insert the control. A valid ID has the following characteristics:

- Must begin with an alphabetic character
- Can't contain an embedded period
- Must not exceed 255 characters
- Must be unique in the scope in which it's declared

Examples of valid `ID`s are `DataCommand1`, `dcOne`, `dc_Two`, and `txtBox`.

The *LockType* Property The `LockType` property indicates the type of locking to be used when updating or inserting. The default value depends on the provider but is typically Read-Only, which allows no modifications. Pessimistic tells the provider to do as much as necessary to ensure successful updates, Optimistic doesn't lock records until they're actually updated, and BatchOptimistic is the required `LockType` for batch update mode.

The *MaxRecords* Property With this property, you can limit the number of records returned in your recordset. This property is set to 0 (all records) by default.

The *Prepared* Property This property indicates whether you want a prepared version of your command before execution. Although this doesn't make the speed of the first issuance of the command faster, it does speed successive executions. Keep in mind that not all providers support prepared statements.

Using the Control

In this example, you add the Data Command control to a new Active Server Page. You also build a short VBScript routine to display the contents of the recordset returned by the Data Command control. This is the most flexible means of accessing data via Visual InterDev's design-time controls. As is usually the case, however, flexibility comes with a price; it's up to you to provide a means of displaying and interacting with the data.

1. Select File, New from the menu.
2. In the New dialog box, select Active Server Page from the list in the left window. Type the name of your new file in the File Name text box and click OK to close the dialog box.
3. Your new page opens automatically in Visual InterDev. Notice that it includes, and has highlighted, the line <!-- Insert HTML here -->. Right-click this line and then select Insert ActiveX Control from the drop-down list to open the Insert ActiveX Control dialog box.
4. Select the Controls tab and see the display of all the ActiveX controls registered on your system.
5. Select the Design-Time tab to display a subset of these controls (just the design-time controls on your system). You should see the Data Command control, the Data Range Header and Footer controls, and the Include control. (There might be others.) Select the Data Command control.

   The control opens and its Properties dialog box appears—the control itself hasn't yet been embedded in the page. Your dialog box should look similar to Figure 16.4.

FIG. 16.4
Properties dialog boxes are available for nearly every object you'll use in Visual InterDev. Typically, they provide an easy means of access to all properties exposed by the object.

6. On the Control page of the Properties dialog box, select the data connection established in the global.asa file from the Data Connection drop-down list.
7. Select Table from the Command Type drop-down list (review the CommandType property discussed earlier). In the Command Text drop-down list, select a table to access. At this point, your dialog box should look similar to the one in Figure 16.5.

   Notice that the SQL Builder button is now disabled. In this example, you've chosen to access a table, which the control knows how to access without your helping it build the SQL.

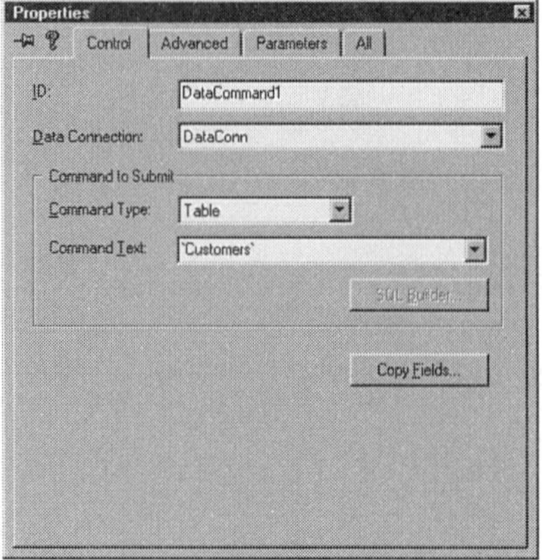

FIG. 16.5
When possible, Visual InterDev attempts to make things easier on you. In this case, Visual InterDev knows to populate the Data Connection drop-down list with the connections specified in your global.asa file.

8. Select the Advanced tab of the Properties dialog box. Here you have access to more properties: `CursorType`, `LockType`, `CacheSize`, `Prepared`, `CommandTimeout`, and `MaxRecords`. (These properties were discussed earlier.) For this example, leave these properties alone.

If you click the All tab of the Properties dialog box, you get a list of all properties for the control in one place, presented in the list format common to all controls. If you feel more comfortable setting properties in this format, you can do so from the All tab.

9. Close the properties window and the control itself. Visual InterDev inserts the HTML for the `<OBJECT>` element specification, including parameters for all the properties you set. Visual InterDev also includes the server-side script that makes the data objects available.

Try previewing your page by first saving it (choose File, Save) and then right-clicking anywhere on the page. Select to Preview <Page>. Notice that nothing shows up. Go back to the code for the page and look—nothing shows up because there's no code to access the contents of the recordset you directed the Data Command control to provide. The Data Command control establishes the connection to the data source and provides a recordset for your use, but that's all it does. Accessing the recordset and presenting its data on your page is up to you.

Clearly, this provides the most flexibility but requires the most work. A quick and dirty way to get the content on the page is to follow the closing `<METADATA>` tag that Visual InterDev inserts with this server-side script:

```
<%
Dim holdField
Do Until DataCommand1.EOF
     For Each holdField In DataCommand1.Fields
          Response.Write holdField.Value & "<BR>"
     Next
     DataCommand1.MoveNext
Loop
%>
```

This code loops through the recordset and writes the contents of each field in the fields collection to the page, using the `Write` method on the `Response` object. Try this and then preview your page again. This time you should see all your data appear on the page (but in a format you probably wouldn't want to present to a user).

ON THE WEB

You can check your code against the file datacommand.asp, which you can find at **http://www.gasullivan.com/vs97book**.

Using the Data Range Header Control

The Data Range Header control is similar to the Data Range Command control in that it also establishes connection and recordset objects for your use. The similarity ends there, however. The Data Range Header control, with the Data Range Footer control, provides you with an easy way to use the returned recordset to generate HTML that displays the data from a database, as well as the navigation controls necessary to move through pages of the data (if configured to do so). This process isn't fully automatic—you still need to weave the contents of the returned recordset object into your HTML—but the process is greatly simplified.

You need to be familiar with a few concepts in using the Header control (and the Footer control). First, keep in mind what you're building. Typically, you'll set up an HTML table structure to hold data contained in a recordset object. You'll want to set up the table first, preceding the data row of the table with the Data Range Header control and following with the Data Range Footer control. The code generated by these two controls includes a `Do...Loop` structure, so the row is repeated for each record in the recordset, thus generating the HTML for repeated rows.

Another key concept is *paging*. Without the use of paging, every record returned in a recordset is displayed on the web page. This could be a very large number of records, causing performance to suffer considerably. The page is built on the server in its entirety before it's sent to the client. If the page contains a table with hundreds or thousands of rows, users might have to wait for an unacceptable length of time.

By using paging, you can set up a page that returns a fixed number of records from the recordset at a time and provides controls that allow access to other pages. This increases performance considerably, especially for recordsets with large numbers of records.

Properties

The `CommandText`, `CommandTimeout`, `CommandType`, `CursorType`, `DataConnection`, `ID`, `LockType`, and `MaxRecords` properties for the Data Range Header control are the same as the ones for the Data Command control. The Data Header control also exposes the `BarAlignment`, `CacheSize`, `PageSize`, and `RangeType` properties.

The *BarAlignment* Property This property lets you specify whether you want the navigation bar to be left-justified, centered, or right-justified on your page. Keep in mind this applies only if you're using paging; otherwise, all records display on your page and a navigation bar isn't necessary.

The *CacheSize* Property This property allows you to set the size of the cache in which records from a recordset are stored locally. For Forward Only cursors, the default value is 1; for other types, the default is 10. No error is generated if the returned number of records is less than the cache size. A cache size of 0 isn't allowed.

The *PageSize* Property With the `PageSize` property, you can specify how many records you want to appear on a page when using paging. If you set this property to 0, paging is disabled, all records in the recordset appear on one page, and the navigation bar doesn't appear.

The *RangeType* Property With this property, you can control the placement of the navigation bar in the generated server-side script, as well as the output of the Copy Fields dialog box. If the `RangeType` property is set to Table, the navigation bar is placed outside the table element. If the property is set to Text or Form, the navigation bar is placed inside the table.

If the property is set to Text or Table, the output of the Copy Fields dialog box is of the form

```
<%=DataRangeHdr("FieldName")%>
```

The server replaces this value with the contents of this field. However, if you set the `RangeType` property to Form, the Copy Fields dialog box provides code like this:

```
<INPUT TYPE="Text" SIZE=25 MAXLENGTH=60 NAME="FieldName" VALUE="<%=
DataRangeHdr("FieldName") %>"><BR>
```

In this case, the output surrounds the contents of the field with the HTML necessary to define the element as an HTML-intrinsic input control for a form.

Using the Control

Follow the same procedure you used earlier to create another Active Server Page in your web project. This time, rather than insert the Data Command control in your page, use the Data Range Header and Data Range Footer controls. Before inserting them, however, you need to create a table structure in which to place the controls.

Find the place on the page where this line appears:

```
<!--Insert HTML here -->
```

Highlight the line and replace it with this rudimentary table structure:

```
<TABLE>
     <TR>
          <TD>Company Name</TD>
          <TD>Contact Name</TD>
          <TD>Order Date</TD>
     </TR>
```

In this table, the row displays the names of the fields. The second row (to be added shortly) displays the contents of the actual fields themselves. You'll need a server-side looping structure wrapped around the second row so that the server will send HTML for repeated rows of the table to the client, one row for each record in the recordset. Perform the following steps to create this structure:

1. Place the cursor after the `</TR>` tag and press Enter. This is the location for the Data Range Header control.
2. Select Insert, Into HTML, ActiveX Control.
3. In the Insert ActiveX Control dialog box, select the Design-Time tab. Then select the Data Range Header control and click OK.
4. You should be familiar with the next dialog box that appears; it's very similar to the one you saw when inserting the Data Command control. In the Control tab, select your data connection from the Data Connection drop-down list.
5. For the previous control, you selected 2 – Table from the Command Type drop-down list. This time, leave Command Type set to the default, 0 – SQL. This leaves the Command text box empty—you have to write your own SQL or use the SQL Builder to build the statement. Click the SQL Builder button.

Your screen should now look similar to the one in Figure 16.6. (You might want to expand the Query Builder window so that you'll have more space within which to work.) If your Query Builder window isn't showing all the panes visible in Figure 16.6, enable them from the Query toolbar. The first four buttons on the toolbar are for the Diagram Pane, the Grid Pane, the SQL Pane, and the Results Pane. The Diagram Pane is the space into which you drag tables and columns; the Grid Pane gives you another graphical view of the SQL you're building; the SQL Pane is where you can view and alter the SQL you're building; and the Results Pane is where you can see what your SQL returns.

Notice that the Workspace view has changed from File View to Data View as a result of your having opened the SQL Builder. Here you should see your tables, views, and other objects for the database specified in your data connection (in the global.asa file). As you continue, this chapter assumes that you're working with the Northwind database. Following these steps, finish building your SQL statement:

1. Click the Customers table and drag it to the Diagram Pane of the Query Builder window. A window for the table appears in the Diagram Pane, and a partial SQL statement appears in the SQL Pane.
2. In the Customers table window, mark the checkbox next to (All Columns). Your screen should look similar to the one in Figure 16.7.

   Notice that several things happen. The Grid Pane indicates all columns from the Customers table have been selected for output. Also, the SQL is completed in the SQL Pane. Click the Run button (with the exclamation point) on the Query toolbar to check the query. In the Results Pane, you should see the results of the query (the complete Customers table, in this case). If this were all you wanted to do with the SQL, however, you could simply have selected 2 – Table from the Command Type drop-down list in the

Data Range Header Control Properties dialog box. You selected 0 – SQL because you wanted a recordset based on a more complicated query.

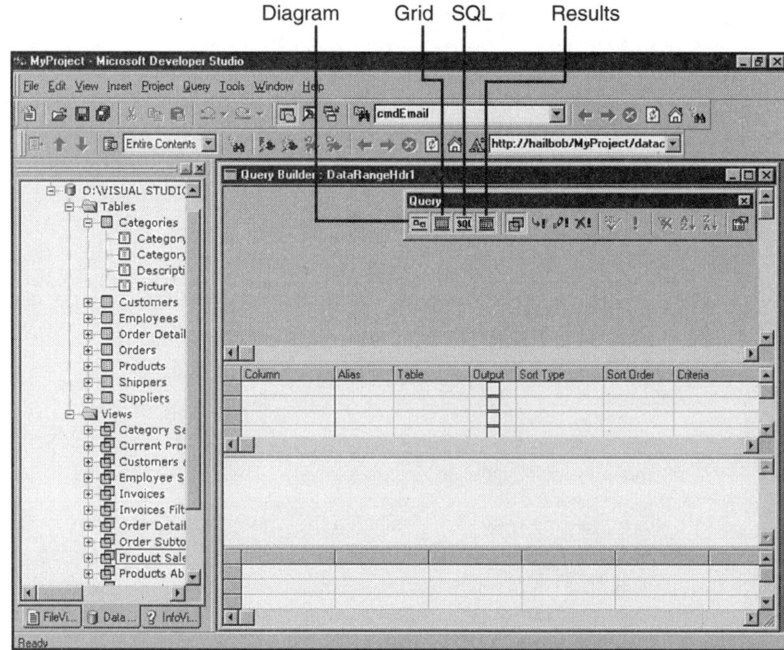

FIG. 16.6
One of the most useful database-oriented features of Visual InterDev is the Query Builder, which provides a visual environment in which you can build and test SQL statements.

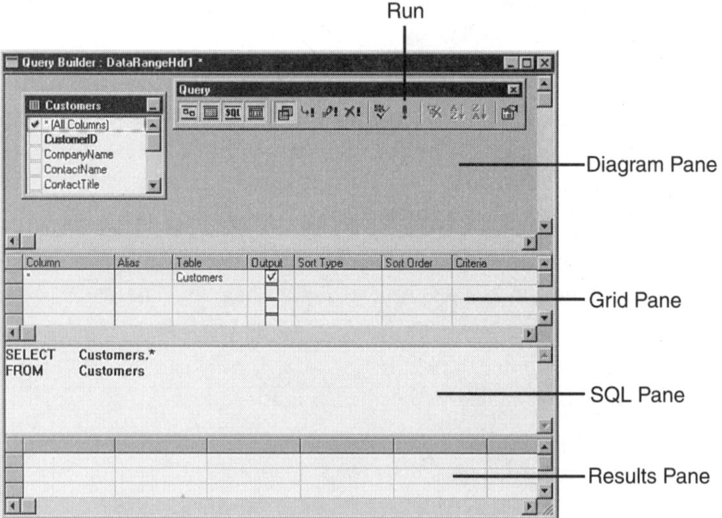

FIG. 16.7
The panes in the Query Builder communicate with each other—a change made in one pane is immediately reflected in all other affected panes.

3. Go back to the Data View of the Workspace window and drag the Orders table to the Diagram Pane of the Query Builder window.
4. Deselect the (All Columns) box in the Customers window. At this point, your screen should look similar to the one in Figure 16.8.

FIG. 16.8
Be sure to fully explore the Query Builder. For instance, the Query toolbar has buttons that provide the framework for insert, update, and delete queries automatically.

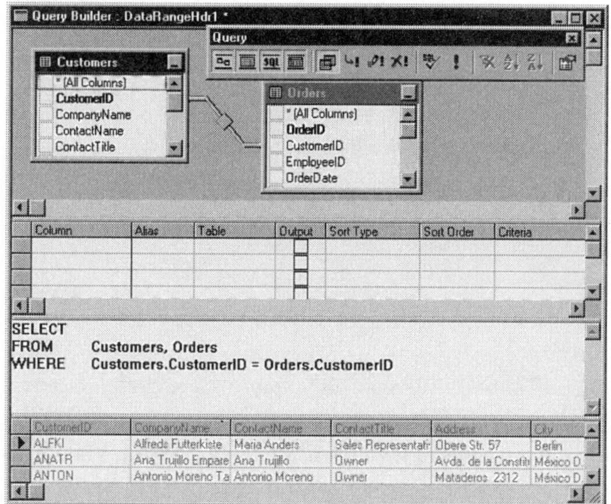

A few things have happened here. First, in the Diagram Pane is a graphical representation of the relationship between the CustomerID field in the Customers table and the CustomerID field in the Orders table.

You can change the nature of the join by right-clicking the join indicator and selecting properties.

Also, the SQL in the SQL Pane has changed to indicate the join on these two fields. As you add fields to your query, watch the SQL Pane and Grid Pane change to reflect your additions.

5. Click the checkboxes for the CompanyName and ContactName fields in the Customers table. They both appear in the Grid Pane and are reflected in the `SELECT` clause of the SQL.
6. Drag the Order Date field from the Orders table to the first empty row in the Grid Pane (another way of adding a field, as opposed to clicking its checkbox).
7. Click the Run button again on the Query toolbar. The Results Pane displays the results of your new SQL statement. Compare your results to the ones in Figure 16.9.

This is just the beginning of what you can do with your SQL. To sort on the Order Date, for example, click the Sort Type drop-down list in the Grid Pane for the Order Date field and select Ascending. Run the Query again and notice that the results are now sorted in ascending order by the Order Date.

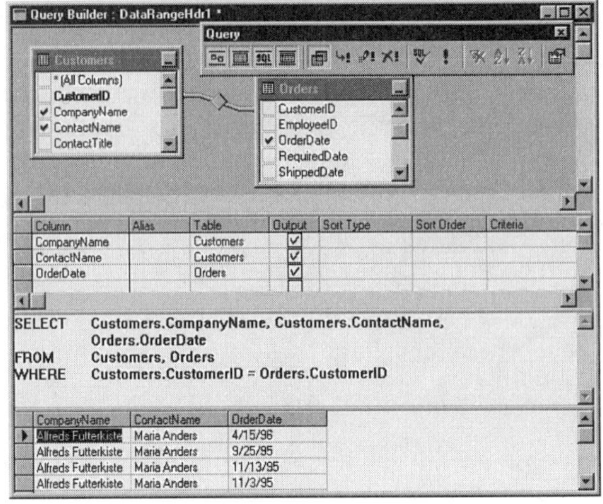

FIG. 16.9
Remember to test your SQL before closing the Query Builder. It's much easier to ensure that your SQL is valid and that you're retrieving the data you want here than in your web page.

Notice that the Query Builder indicates it's building the SQL for the Data Range Header control. Everything you've been doing in this window is just to prepare the SQL for the control. You can close the Query Builder window at this point. When Visual InterDev asks whether you want to update the Data Range Header control, respond yes. If the Properties dialog box for the control isn't open, right-click the control itself and choose Properties. Notice that the SQL you built in the SQL Builder now appears in the Command Text box. Compare your dialog box to Figure 16.10.

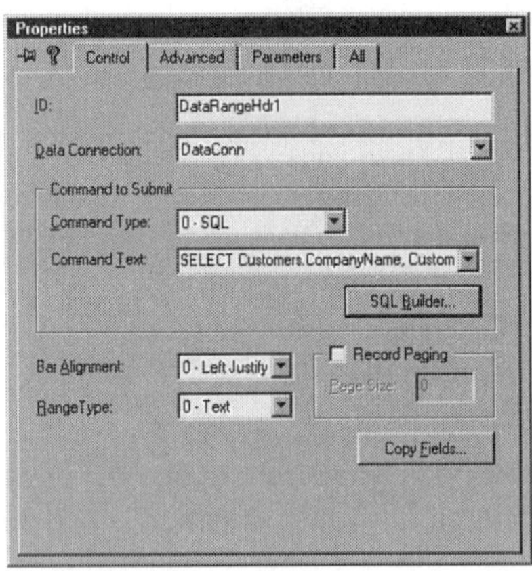

FIG. 16.10
Properties for the Data Range Header control, after building the SQL for the `CommandText` property in the SQL Builder.

In the Control tab of the Properties dialog box, check the box for Record Paging. Notice that Visual InterDev won't allow this yet because the default `CursorType` is Forward Only. Record Paging requires a cursor to be selected that enables forward and backward movement through the recordset. Select the Advanced tab of the Properties dialog box and change the Cursor Type to 1 – Keyset. Go back to the Control tab and try turning on Record Paging again. This time, the setting is accepted. You can now change the Page Size setting if you want (for this sample, leave it at 10).

You need to set two other properties at this point. On the Control tab, change Bar Alignment to 2 – Centered and RangeType to 2 – Table. The Data Range Footer control responds to these settings to determine how to position the buttons that navigate through pages in your recordset and to close off your table correctly after the rows for the table are generated.

NOTE If you want, you can adjust other properties, such as CacheSize; refer to the earlier property information for the Data Range Header control for more details.

Before you close the Data Range Header control, click the Copy Fields button on the Control tab to copy to the Clipboard the code you need to specify the fields in your table cells. In the Copy Fields dialog box, move all three fields to the right-hand list. Click OK and close the control.

Place your cursor after the closing <METADATA> tag and choose Edit, Paste to insert the server-side code for the fields you copied from the Data Range Header Properties dialog box into your page. The code should look similar to this:

```
<%= DataRangeHdr1("CompanyName") %><br>
<%= DataRangeHdr1("ContactName") %><br>
<%= DataRangeHdr1("OrderDate") %><br>
```

Position your cursor at the beginning of the first of these lines and enter **<TR>**. Then wrap each line with <TD> and </TD> tags to place each in its own cell. At this point, your code should look like this:

```
<TR>
<TD><%= DataRangeHdr1("CompanyName") %><br></TD>
<TD><%= DataRangeHdr1("ContactName") %><br></TD>
<TD><%= DataRangeHdr1("OrderDate") %><br></TD>
```

You've completed the first part of the Data Range control structure. Next, you need to add the Data Range Footer control.

Using the Data Range Footer Control

The Data Range Footer control is used only with the Data Range Header control; it provides the server-side code necessary to complete the looping structure that pulls data from your recordset, as well as the navigation controls required when using paging. If you set the properties for the Data Range Header control so that it's not using paging, you don't need the footer control—you simply need to write the server-side code that completes the loop. (Keep in mind that performance will deteriorate considerably as the number of records returned in the recordset grows.)

Properties

No properties are associated with the Data Range Footer control because this control works only with the Data Range Header control. All the functionality of the Data Range Footer control is controlled by the property settings for the Data Range Header control.

Using the Control

Go back to the file you were creating, using the Data Range Header control. Find the following code:

```
<TR>
<TD><%= DataRangeHdr1("CompanyName") %><br></TD>
<TD><%= DataRangeHdr1("ContactName") %><br></TD>
<TD><%= DataRangeHdr1("OrderDate") %><br></TD>
```

Position your cursor at the beginning of the line following this code and then follow these steps:

1. Choose Insert, Into HTML, ActiveX Control.
2. Select the Design-Time tab in the Insert ActiveX Control dialog box, select the Data Range Footer control, and click OK.
3. You don't need to set other properties here, so just close the control. The control adds the server-side code to close off the table (by adding the `</TABLE>` tag) and the code to complete the loop.

You can check your code against the file datarange.asp on the web site at **http://www.gasullivan.com/vs97book/**.

Preview the page and experiment with the controls provided for paging through the records. Clearly, the presentation isn't pretty; you can change the HTML on your own to make the pages more attractive.

Using the Include Control

The Include control is a bit different than the other design-time controls included with Visual InterDev. Unlike the others, this control doesn't provide any sort of database functionality; it provides a means by which you can tell a web server to include the content of another file (typically, an .inc file) in a page that the users have requested.

This control is very useful. If you have a large number of pages that share common HTML elements (for example, navigation elements, header or footer elements, or style sheets), you can put together files that contain only these elements and reference the files on all pages that need them by using the Include control. Also, you can prepare include files that contain scripting functions you want available on multiple pages in your web project. This makes administering, maintaining, and modifying your site much easier; each page is less complex because it contains only code unique to that page, and any changes to common elements in your site need to be made only in the files included via the Include control.

Properties

The only property for the Include control is `Source`, which specifies the file to insert into the page containing the control. The syntax for the path to the control is the same as you would use in referencing all other files within your web page (virtual and relative paths, the ../ construct for referencing files in the directory above the current directory, and so on).

NOTE A path to an include file might read /includes/sampleinclude.inc if the sampleinclude.inc file is in a subdirectory under the current page's directory; it might read sampleinclude.inc if the sampleinclude.inc file is in the same directory as the current page; and it might read ../sampleinclude.inc if the sampleinclude.inc file is in a directory immediately above the current page's directory. ■

Using the Control

Add a new HTML file called footer.htm to your web project. Replace the HTML in the file with the following:

```
<center>
<font face = "verdana" size = 1 color = midnightblue>
______________________________<BR>
copyright(c) 1997 My Company all rights reserved
</font></center>
```

Close the file. Generally, include files end with an .inc extension so that tracking which files are include files and which are files that reference (include) include files is easier. Rename your footer.htm file to footer.inc. To do so, right-click the file in the File View of the Workspace window. Select Release Working Copy. Right-click the file again and select Rename. Change the name of the file from footer.htm to footer.inc.

NOTE The .inc extension isn't required for the Include control to function. However, it's generally a good idea—and standard practice—to use the .inc extension to differentiate these files from the others in your web project. It takes a little extra work, but as your project grows, you'll find it's worth the extra steps. ■

Now add a new Active Server Page called home.asp to your web project. It's to this file that you'll add the Include control with a reference to the footer.inc file. Follow these steps:

1. After you add the page, highlight the comment `<!-- Insert HTML here -->`, right-click it, and then select Insert ActiveX Control.
2. Click the Design-Time tab in the Insert ActiveX Control dialog box. Select the Include Control and click OK.
3. In the Source text box, enter the name of the file you want to include (**`footer.inc`**, in this case).
4. Close the control and save the Active Server Page.

When you preview the page, notice that the contents of the footer.inc file appear in the Active Server Page. You can put whatever you want in a file to be included via the Include control, and you can include any number of files anywhere you want within an Active Server Page. The only caveat here is that you can't dynamically provide the value of the source property through scripting. The following HTML code specifies the Include control; notice that the method Visual InterDev uses to indicate the footer.inc file doesn't allow for dynamic inclusion.

```
<!--METADATA TYPE="DesignerControl" startspan
    <OBJECT ID="Include1" WIDTH=151 HEIGHT=24
     CLASSID="CLSID:F602E725-A281-11CF-A5B7-0080C73AAC7E">
        <PARAM NAME="_Version" VALUE="65536">
        <PARAM NAME="_ExtentX" VALUE="3969">
        <PARAM NAME="_ExtentY" VALUE="635">
        <PARAM NAME="_StockProps" VALUE="0">
        <PARAM NAME="Source" VALUE="footer.inc">
    </OBJECT>
-->
<!--#INCLUDE FILE="footer.inc"-->
<!--METADATA TYPE="DesignerControl" endspan-->
```

From Here...

In this chapter, you worked a bit with the design-time controls included with Visual InterDev. The Include control is a solid utilitarian control that you'll find extremely useful. The data-related controls can be considered decent starting points; they don't generate fully developed code, nor do they construct attractive interfaces, but they do take a good deal of the grunt work out of building data-driven web pages. By using them, you can focus your energies on fleshing out your application and applying finishing touches.

- Chapter 13, "An Inside Look at Active Server Pages and Internet Information Server," discusses the use of Active Server Pages on Internet Information Server and shows you how to use ASP.
- Chapter 14, "Developing Active Content with Visual InterDev," shows how to use Visual InterDev to create dynamic web sites.
- Chapter 15, "Advanced Visual InterDev Concepts," describes some of the more advanced features of Visual InterDev.
- Chapter 17, "Server-Side Programming in an I-net Environment," shows you more about writing code for use with Active Server Pages.
- Chapter 18, "Dynamic HTML," covers the new specification for Dynamic HTML and shows you how to use many of the new features.

CHAPTER 17

Server-Side Programming in an I-net Environment

by Robert S. Black

Knowing which programming language to use

Learn how to decide what language you should use based on various factors, including leveraging existing resources and what platform the software will run.

Connecting to the server

Consider what software you should use to connect to the server, such as CGI, WinCGI, ISAPI, NSAPI, and Active Server Pages, and their relative strengths and weakness.

Scripting with Visual InterDev

Learn to quickly create a dynamic web site by scripting with Visual InterDev.

Using different tools

Follow a demonstration of the use of WinCGI, Active Server Pages, Visual Basic, style sheets, and HTML.

Connecting to the database

Learn how to connect to the database by using Active Server Pages and Visual Basic.

Using server-side components

Follow an actual three-tier connection example.

The need for data fuels the prevalence of information systems in the workplace and the Internet for everyone to use. Servers are required to parcel out data efficiently to handle the many requests. Programming for the server takes a great deal of care. Many issues—such as security, speed, and future functionality—weigh heavily in what software to use and how to implement the best server for internal I-net use (an intranet) and external I-net use (the Internet).

When picking the correct way to implement a server, many considerations should be taken into account. What's the purpose? Are you boxing yourself into future problems? Can you get the information to those who need it quickly and efficiently? Is access to the data restricted sufficiently so that unauthorized users can't view or edit the data? This chapter deals with these issues, as well as looks at what processing should take place on the server. What languages, software, and protocols should be used? How should different components be integrated?

This chapter is designed as an overview to look at the big picture in server-side programming. Many of the other chapters provide a greater in-depth knowledge of particular areas, such as Chapter 10, "Clients, Servers, and Components: Web-Based Applications"; Chapter 14, "Developing Active Content with Visual InterDev"; Chapter 15, "Advanced Visual InterDev Concepts"; and Chapter 16, "Visual InterDev Design-Time Controls." ■

Deciding on a Language

Deciding what language in which to write your system is a function of your requirements and design. More specifically, scalability, portability, time to produce, the use of current resources, and whether this language can carry out certain functions should be paramount in deciding what language or languages to use.

Keep in mind that it doesn't matter to the client what languages are used on the server. If the client is using the Netscape Navigator browser, it will work fine with all Microsoft software on the server. The only time the client is affected is with the scripting language or components on the client.

Because deciding what language to use depends on a given situation, it's difficult to give explicit rules governing language selection. Therefore, this area will be covered briefly here, but the remaining sections of this chapter discuss factors that influence language decisions.

You need to take current resources into consideration when designing a system. Whether it's with existing software or personnel, the correct design should take these factors into account:

- *Personnel.* Because there's a great flexibility on how processing can occur on the server, you should base your decisions on what languages to use on the current skill set of the staff. If your current staff consists of expert Visual Basic programmers, use VBScript in your Active Server Pages or write server-side ActiveX components with Visual Basic. If your staff has been using JavaScript or JScript in the client-side web pages, use JavaScript or server-side Java applets that take advantage of the Java programming language. If the staff has Java experience, they should be using Java on the server.
- *Existing software.* Using existing software can be key in keeping development costs down and having a more rapid development of software. Often, a company has an object that can be used to access data in the database. Typically, the methods to this object are independent of the items in the database, so you can use the same object to access the database via your I-net. This provides several advantages—most importantly, you don't have to rewrite the existing code. Also, when you make changes to the database, you have to change the code in only one place for your entire information system; separate changes don't need to be made for each system. (Database objects are covered more in-depth later in the section "Using Server-Side Components.") Finally, you could build multiple user interfaces with the same underlying structure.

NOTE More software than database objects can be reused for I-net purposes. Database objects are ideal for reuse because of the features mentioned. Other software, such as data-processing components, also could be reused. This software could be called from a web page instead of traditional client software. Other objects share in the benefit that existing code can continue to be used. ■

- *Portability.* The issue of portability comes up repeatedly in the corporate computing world. The problem doesn't so much exist on the server side as it does when dealing with client machines. Most corporations have heterogeneous computing environments with multiple desktop environments running on Windows-, Macintosh-, and UNIX-based clients. In the traditional client/server world, creating applications and deploying them on multiple client platforms has always been the biggest obstacle to uniformity of systems within a corporation. The I-net makes it possible, for the first time, to develop applications that can truly be independent of the client machines. By using the client web browser mechanism and writing applications that take advantage of server-side processing, you can build and deploy applications that can be independent of client-side operating systems.

CAUTION

Keep in mind that client browsers, even though they might support the common mechanisms, are no longer identical in their functionality. Over the years, Internet Explorer and Navigator have diverged from each other in critical areas such as support for Dynamic HTML and the version of the Java SDK being supported. However, the web browser still presents the closest thing we have today to a client-independent computing environment.

Deciding How to Connect to the Server

When a user request is made to a server, the server attempts to handle the request. If the request is for a static HTML document, the server software returns the document at the location the user requested. If you want to do processing on that request, many decisions need to be made, such as how you connect to the server and what software you use to do the processing.

Deciding how to connect to the server can be one of the biggest decisions in creating a successful I-net project. Ignoring certain needs could cause tremendous problems for the future of your project. Some key trade-offs to consider in the design of a system are performance, portability, scalability, leveraging existing resources, and security.

It's important to recognize that there's no one solution for every problem. You should weigh heavily all the trade-offs and design a system that works best for your situation and that minimizes your risk.

Possible choices on how to connect to the server include using the Common Gateway Interface (CGI) or Windows Common Gateway Interface (WinCGI), using proprietary application program interface (API) calls, or using proprietary software to connect. Each choice has distinct advantages and disadvantages. With each choice are more decisions to make, such as which API or proprietary software should you use. The following three sections discuss connections with CGI, WinCGI, proprietary APIs, and web application development tools.

Connecting to the Server with Common Gateway Interface

CGI is a standard for the interface between external programs and web servers. In a nutshell, CGI is a specification that allows external programs to communicate and respond to queries from web clients through the web server. When a client makes a request to a web server for a CGI program execution, the web server executes the CGI program and passes the execution parameters it received from the client to the CGI program. The request and the accompanying parameters are sent as an HTTP request. The CGI program parses the parameter list, executes the program, compiles the results, and sends them back to the client through the web server.

Advantages and Disadvantages of CGI

As with any connection method, CGI has its advantages and its disadvantages. Using CGI has numerous advantages:

- It can be developed in virtually any language as a compiled program or as a script with environment variable access. It can do input and output with `stdin` and `stdout`.
- Almost all web server software on the market uses CGI, so it's entirely portable from one server to another.
- Because it has been the main way to interface programmatically between a web browser and server, a great amount of existing code is written in CGI.
- It's relatively easy to program with CGI compared to the proprietary APIs that have been developed, because single processes are easier to debug.
- It's virtually impossible to crash the server that a CGI process is running on. A bad CGI program will just crash the process.

The two key disadvantages of CGI are its performance and security problems:

- When a new client calls the server, a new process is spawned. This means that for each new client, there's another process on the server, which can cause a heavy server load.
- CGI lets a client run a process on the web server outside a firewall. This capability can pose serious security problems if the proper precautions aren't taken. Users could gain access to an unauthorized part of your system.

CGI Solutions

Some solutions to deal with CGI's problems include using proprietary APIs, special development tools, or a site monitoring and performance tool. Coverage of proprietary APIs and special development tools are presented later in the sections "Connecting to the Server with Proprietary APIs" and "Connecting to the Server with Web Application Development Tools."

Programming with CGI

Although writing a primitive CGI program is simple, writing usable software that has all the necessary functionality and meets the security needs of a system isn't.

ON THE WEB

You can find a wealth of information to explain and demonstrate how to implement CGI in various languages. Two sites with links to CGI information are **http://www.progsource.com/cgi.html** and **http://www.Stars.com/Software/CGI**.

You can develop CGI programs in Visual C++ or Visual Basic. To develop CGI programs in Visual Basic, you must use the WinCGI programming interface provided by Microsoft at its web site. WinCGI is a mechanism that uses INI files to replicate the `stdin` functionality used by the CGI standard to pass parameters to the program.

NOTE Some web servers don't support WinCGI.

When a request is made to a CGI program, the web server passes a filename as a command-line argument. The CGI program takes data from this file to determine what information was requested and where the output should be sent, among other data. This temporary file is generated for each CGI request. The CGI program then makes necessary computations and returns the appropriate data. The WinCGI class in Listing 17.1 demonstrates retrieving INI entries from a profile file to be used by the CGI program.

Listing 17.1 A Generic WinCGI Class

```
Option Explicit
Private Const MAX_BUFFER_SIZE = 4096
Private m_sRequestMethod As String
Private m_sOutputFileName As String
Private m_iOutputFileNumber As Integer
Private m_sProfileFile As String
Private m_sQueryString As String
Private m_colArguments As New Collection

'Win32 API call to get data from a file that is in an INI format
Private Declare Function GetPrivateProfileStringA Lib "kernel32" _
   (ByVal lpApplicationName As String, ByVal lpKeyName As Any, _
    ByVal lpDefault As String, ByVal lpReturnedString As String, _
    ByVal nSize As Long, ByVal lpFileName As String) As Long

'Does the initialization of the object
Public Function Initialize() As Long

On Error GoTo Handle_Error
```

continues

Listing 17.1 Continued

```
    Set m_colArguments = GetArguments
    m_sProfileFile = m_colArguments(1)

'Gets the data sent, request method and file which to write the results
    m_sQueryString = GetProfile("CGI", "Query String")
    m_sRequestMethod = GetProfile("CGI", "Request Method")
    m_sOutputFileName = GetProfile("System", "Output File")

'Gets the next available filenumber for output
    m_iOutputFileNumber = FreeFile
    Open m_sOutputFileName For Append As #m_iOutputFileNumber

Handle_Error:
    Initialize = Err
End Function

'Gets data from the profile file
Private Function GetProfile(ByVal sSection As String, ByVal sKey As String)
➥As String
    On Error GoTo Handle_Error

    Dim lResult As Long
    Dim sBuffer As String * MAX_BUFFER_SIZE

    lResult = GetPrivateProfileStringA(sSection, sKey, "", _
                sBuffer, MAX_BUFFER_SIZE, m_sProfileFile)
    If lResult = 0 Then
        GetProfile = ""
    Else
        GetProfile = Left$(sBuffer, lResult)
    End If

    Exit Function
Handle_Error:
    GetProfile = ""

End Function

'Returns a collection of Command line arguments
'The first one is the filename of the Profile file
Private Function GetArguments() As Collection

    Dim sCommand As String
    Dim colTemp As New Collection
    Const SPACE = " "
    Dim s As String
    Dim x As Long

    sCommand = Trim$(Command)
    x = 1
    While sCommand <> "" And x <> 0
        x = InStr(sCommand, SPACE)
        If x <> 0 Then
            s = Left(sCommand, x)
        Else
```

```
            s = sCommand
        End If
        sCommand = Trim$(Right(sCommand, Len(sCommand) - x))
        colTemp.Add s
    Wend

    Set GetArguments = colTemp
    Set colTemp = Nothing
End Function
Public Sub Send(ByVal s As String)
    Print #m_iOutputFileNumber, s
End Sub

'Terminates the class
Private Sub Class_Terminate()

Set m_colArguments = Nothing
Close #m_iOutputFileNumber

End Sub

'Returns the data sent to the CGI program
Public Property Get QueryString() As String

QueryString = m_sQueryString

End Property

'Returns the request method such as GET or POST
Public Property Get RequestMethod() As String

RequestMethod = m_sRequestMethod

End Property
```


To use the class in Listing 17.1, save it with the class name of `CCGI`. For an example of how to use this class, Listing 17.2 is a program that returns a web page containing the favorite color submitted by the user.

Listing 17.2 The Favorite Color WinCGI

```
Sub Main()

Dim oCGI As New CCGI
Dim sQuery As String

On Error GoTo CheckError

'Initialize the CGI object
oCGI.Initialize

'Get the query string
sQuery = Trim$(oCGI.QueryString)
```

continues

Listing 17.2 Continued

```
'Parse the query string to get the color
sQuery = Mid(sQuery, InStr(sQuery, "=") + 1)
oCGI.Send ("")

Select Case UCase$(oCGI.RequestMethod)
    Case "GET"
        Select Case sQuery
            Case "Red"
                oCGI.Send ("My favorite color is Red.")
            Case "Blue"
                oCGI.Send ("My favorite color is Blue.")
            Case "Yellow"
                oCGI.Send ("My favorite color is Yellow.")
            Case Else
                oCGI.Send ("I don't have a favorite color.")
        End Select
    Case Else
        oCGI.Send ("Unable to complete request.")
End Select
Set oCGI = Nothing

Exit Sub
CheckError:
oCGI.Send ("")
oCGI.Send ("Error main " & Err & ": " & Err.Description)

End Sub
```

To use the code in Listing 17.2, place it in the same project as the class in Listing 17.1, compile it as cgitext.exe, and put it in the cgi-win directory of your web server. Run your web server and make calls to the program with the HTML in Listing 17.3 in a web page.

Listing 17.3 Favorite Color HTML

```
<FORM ACTION="http://localhost/cgi-win/cgitest.exe" method="GET">
<table width=600>

<tr><td align=center valign=top><input type=submit name="cmdSubmit"
    value="Blue"></td></tr>
<tr><td align=center valign=top><input type=submit name="cmdSubmit"
    value="Red"></td></tr>
<tr><td align=center valign=top><input type=submit name="cmdSubmit"
    value="Yellow"></td></tr>
<tr><td align=center valign=top><input type=submit name="cmdSubmit"
    value="None"></td></tr>

</table>
</form>
```

Connecting to the Server with Proprietary APIs

Other solutions to the security and performance problems of CGI come in the form of proprietary APIs. This type of API also adds functionality to server connections, but introduces new problems.

Specifically, this section refers mainly to Microsoft's Internet Server Application Program Interface (ISAPI) and Netscape Communication Corporation's Netscape Server Application Program Interface (NSAPI). ISAPI is supported by Microsoft's full line of web server products, including Internet Information Server (IIS). NSAPI is supported by all Netscape web servers (Communications, Commerce, FastTrack, and Enterprise), as well as versions 2.0 and 2.5 of Netscape Proxy Server.

Advantages and Disadvantages of Proprietary APIs

Proprietary APIs vary from CGI in many ways. These differences lead to some key advantages and disadvantages of using proprietary APIs over CGI.

Programming with ISAPI and NSAPI has distinct advantages, the biggest being the speed and fewer resources required. Because these APIs spawn new threads instead of new processes, the server has significantly less load. The time it takes to generate a new thread instead of a new process is greatly reduced, so users will have a much greater response time when using this system.

ISAPI and NSAPI also can further break down Hypertext Transfer Protocol (HTTP) so that more functionality can be achieved with security validation.

One obvious disadvantage of proprietary APIs is their proprietary nature. If you decide to switch servers entirely, new software needs to be written.

Another less obvious but potential problem is the increased complexity of programming. Multithreaded applications, by nature, are more difficult to design and harder to debug than single-threaded applications. Also, developers have to deal with cleaning up data in memory.

ISAPI and NSAPI also have a greater potential in crashing a web server. Because they use in-process DLLs, a mistake in the code could bring down the entire server instead of a single process.

ISAPI Versus NSAPI

ISAPI and NSAPI are two competing APIs developed by Microsoft and Netscape, respectively. Both APIs are designed to accomplish essentially the same task—that is, to allow developers to write applications that can run on a web server. As competing APIs, they accomplish this task in different ways and are obviously incompatible with each other. As is always the case in such scenarios, the individual APIs work best with the development tools and products from the respective vendor. However, you must consider some issues when making a decision about which API to use.

ISAPI is a Microsoft standard that works with Microsoft server products and the Visual Studio development tools. However, it's a Windows NT-only solution that can't be ported to UNIX or other platforms. NSAPI, on the other hand, works best with Netscape server products and is available on a multitude of platforms, including various flavors of UNIX and Windows NT. ISAPI's strong integration with Microsoft tools gives it a distinct advantage on the Windows NT platform and, if you're developing for a Windows-only environment, probably makes it a more flexible and robust choice.

NSAPI can be written in C and C++, whereas ISAPI can be written in C, C++, and Pascal. As an API, NSAPI can be used with Visual C++. However, most notable from a Visual Studio perspective is Visual C++'s ready support of ISAPI application development through the use of a supplied wizard. The wizard makes it very easy to get started with building an ISAPI application and provides the initial framework necessary to develop more complex applications.

Connecting to the Server with Web Application Development Tools

Connectivity between the client and server can be more easily developed with special web application development tools. These tools typically provide a connection between the client and the server, and an easy manner to connect to a database.

Web application development tools include Netscape's LiveWire (**http://www.netscape.com**), Allaire's Cold Fusion (**http://www.allaire.com**), NetDynamics (**http://www.netdynamics.com**), and Microsoft's Visual InterDev (**http://www.microsoft.com**). All these development tools allow for special scripts to be used to develop the interactivity between the client and the web server, and the web server and the database. You can use scripting as the glue to hold together various components to complete tasks necessary for a web site. The following sections cover Visual InterDev in more depth because it's part of the Visual Studio suite of tools.

Advantages and Disadvantages of Web Application Development Tools

Like with connecting with any other method, this approach has advantages and disadvantages. Using web application development tools has several advantages over developing all the code yourself. The speed at which you can develop software is greatly increased. You can maintain a consistent look and feel for your entire web site. You can manage overall control of your web site, such as the order in which pages are presented to users.

Some disadvantages of web application development tools include the following:

- The tools typically are vendor-specific, so code isn't portable between servers, unless the vendors support multiple web server products. Typically, third-party vendors—companies without their own web server products—support various web servers.

- Developers might have to use a new scripting language instead of a language they're already familiar with, although scripting is typically easier to learn than CGI or API programming. Also, oftentimes, the scripting language used is common, so developers might have already used it before.
- You can't reuse the access to the database. For example, if a company wrote an intranet personnel program, it would write code for database access in the script in the development tool. If the company had a previous need or foresaw future needs to access the database, it possibly would have to duplicate the code to access it. Now it's possible to make calls to outside database access components from scripts in web application development tools.

Alternative Development Tools

This section explains what languages and servers each development tool uses; the next section provides detailed coverage of actual implementation with Microsoft Visual Studio's Visual InterDev.

Netscape's LiveWire uses a modified JavaScript as its scripting language. Additional functions are added to JavaScript to make it more useful on the server. For example, several URL manipulation functions wouldn't be required on the client. LiveWire can run on UNIX, Windows NT, and Macintosh, and the scripts can run on any Netscape server.

Allaire's Cold Fusion uses its own scripting language, the Cold Fusion Markup Language (CFML). The software can run on Windows NT and Windows 95 and can use Microsoft IIS and Netscape Enterprise Server.

NetDynamics, Inc.'s NetDynamics 3.1 uses Java instead of a scripting language. This means that you can write software for it by using Microsoft's J++, Symantec's Visual Café, or JavaSoft Java Development Kit (which comes with NetDynamics). NetDynamics runs on Windows NT, Windows 95, and various UNIX machines. NetDynamics can use any CGI web server, any NSAPI 2.0-enabled web server, or an ISAPI-enabled web server.

▶ For more information in developing with Java, **see** Chapter 7, "Creating Components with Visual J++," **p. 221**.

Visual InterDev is part of Microsoft's Visual Studio suite. The scripts run as Active Server Pages (ASP) and will run on Microsoft IIS. Developers can use JScript or VBScript. The following section demonstrates the use of server-side scripting with Visual InterDev.

Using Server-Side Scripting with Visual InterDev

Scripting with Visual InterDev provides users with an easy way to quickly create a dynamic web site. You can use scripting to link separate components as well as make calls to the database.

▶ For a more complete look at Visual InterDev, **see** Chapter 14, "Developing Active Content with Visual InterDev," **p. 389**; Chapter 15, "Advanced Visual InterDev Concepts," **p. 421**; and Chapter 16, "Visual InterDev Design-Time Controls," **p. 449**.

VBScript or JScript?

JScript, Microsoft's implementation of JavaScript, and VBScript, Microsoft's scripting language, are the two scripting languages featured in Visual InterDev. VBScript and JScript will run as Active Server Pages on a server with Internet Information Server. They both can makes calls to OLE objects. And with the key exception that VBScript has error trapping whereas JScript doesn't, they both have similar functionality. (See "Connecting to the Database" later in this chapter for more information on error trapping.)

Because VBScript and JScript have similar functionality, deciding whether to use VBScript or JScript on the server depends mainly on personal preference. If the project developers know Visual Basic, VBScript would be an ideal choice because it's a subset of VB. If developers are using JScript on the client side, JScript on the server makes sense so that developers have to use only one scripting language and can become familiar with it.

Both scripting languages have similar functionality, so a decision can be made from a personal point of view rather than a technical one. Portability isn't an issue because I'm talking about only server-side scripting here.

Visual InterDev ActiveX Objects

Objects native to Visual InterDev are used on the server and can be called with JScript or VBScript. These objects allow developers to easily access the database, access information on the server, and provide protocols to interface with the client. The following sections deal with some of these objects. A more thorough handling of this material is provided with the Visual InterDev documentation, but these sections will help highlight and give a good overall understanding of the material.

Rather than create special functions in VBScript or JScript, Microsoft includes various classes in Visual InterDev and allows developers to call these classes from either scripting language.

Two of these classes, `Server` and `Application`, contain methods to perform miscellaneous functions that make programming on the server easier. The `Server` class, in addition to having HTML and URL manipulation as well as other functions, has a `CreateObject` method. `CreateObject` creates an instance of one of several objects:

- An `Ad Rotator` object, which can change the advertisement on the page each time a user requests the same page
- A `Browser Capabilities` object, which can find the capabilities of the browser being run by the client
- The ActiveX Database Object (ADO), discussed later in this chapter

The `Application` class can set variables of all users of a particular application. This class deals with windowing (size, state, which one is active). It has events that allow developers to write code for when an event occurs, such as the `BeforeApplicationShutDown` event, which saves information before the application is shut down.

Interface Between the Client and Server Visual InterDev uses two ActiveX objects to interface between the client and the server. The `Request` and the `Response` objects enable interaction between the client and server.

The `Request` object gives developers access to all the information passed with an HTTP request. This information includes items from a form, query parameters, client certificates, and cookies passed from a client browser. The following requests a cookie named `ExampleCookie` from the client and returns a collection:

```
<%= Request.Cookies("ExampleCookie") %>
```

The `Response` object allows developers to pass information to the client browser. There are various properties and methods—for example, `Expires` and `Write`, which set how many minutes the web page has to be refreshed when it's requested and which can dynamically write HTML scripts to the client, respectively.

To set the `ExampleCookie` to the string `"Hello World!"`, use the following code:

```
<% Response.Cookies("ExampleCookie") = "Hello World!" %>
```

Setting `Response.Expires` to zero minutes prevents web browsers from caching the web page. This can be useful for keeping track of the number of times a user accesses a particular web page on your web site or for changing the advertisement every time the page is requested.

Managing Client State In many instances, keeping track of where a user is in your site is important. For example, if a user has to fill out a form before being presented with other information, you must make certain that the form is complete before the rest of the information is presented. To do so, you must keep track of the user's state. Storing information on the client computer can be done in the form of a cookie with the help of the `Session` object or by storing information directly on a web page.

You can use the `Session` object to help administer a user session. The `Session` object includes the `SessionID` and `Timeout` properties. `SessionID` provides a unique identifier for a user and can repeat when the web server is restarted. `Timeout` is the number of minutes a session can remain idle before disconnecting the user.

The `Session` object has an explicit way in which to keep state. You can store information in the `Session` object as such:

```
<% Session("lastpage") = 37
   Session("username") = "adb" %>
```

This information is actually stored by using a cookie. These methods won't work with browsers where cookie support has been disabled by users.

Rather than trust cookies on the client machine to keep track of user state information, you could put that functionality directly on the client's web page. This way, your pages can work with browsers that don't support cookies. It also would ensure that users can't block the cookie from being received. It wouldn't prevent users from altering the `SessionID` sent, but you can take measures to reduce the risk to virtually zero. To do this, you can create a random string generator on the server that would supply each new logon with a `SessionID` value. Then store this value on the web page in the following manner, where the `SessionID` is in single quotes after `value=`:

```
<input type=hidden name='SessionID' value='A"Z@vqiAV7D.&od=q?Sg'>
```

This data is returned to the server much like a Submit button submits data to the server, but the control is hidden from users' visibility. Store the `SessionID` string in the database with other characteristics of the user session. As well as for managing a client's state, you can use the data stored in the database for keeping a history of user logons and expiring a user session. This gives you similar functionality to the `Session` object without relying on cookies.

NOTE A user would have a hard time generating a string that matches another user's `SessionID`. If you generate a string 20 characters long with 80 possibilities per character, the chances of matching an existing string are one in 80 to the 20th power.

Connecting to the Database Visual InterDev uses ActiveX Data Objects (ADO) to connect to a database from a scripting language. The main advantage of using ADO is convenience. For other ideas on connecting to a database, see "Using Server-Side Components" later in this chapter.

One big problem with using scripting languages in Visual InterDev to connect to the database is the lack of error-handling capabilities. JScript has no error-handling functions, whereas VBScript has only `On Error Resume Next`. You shouldn't connect to the database without being able to trap errors due to the frequency in which errors are generated when interacting with a database.

`On Error Resume Next` tells the program to continue to the next line when an error is encountered. One way to handle errors is with the code in Listing 17.4.

Listing 17.4 Inline Error Handling

```
On Error Resume Next
... ' your own code
... ' your own code
'Line which may generate error
If Err <> 0 Then
   Msgbox "Error " & Err & " : " & Err.Description
   Err.Clear
End If
...
```

You need to make many determinations in connecting to the database, such as the database, the data source, and what type of connection you want to open. The code in Listing 17.5 helps you connect to the database, although building the connect string depends on the specifics for your system.

Listing 17.5 Connecting to the Database with ADO and VBScript

```
'Create the database connection
Set adoDB = Server.CreateObject("ADODB.Connection")

'Open session with using the connect string
'adoDB_DBConnectString is stored in your projects inf file
'the connection string can include user name and password
aboDB.Open Session("adoDB_DBConnectString")

'Create the Command Object
Set cmdQuery = Server.CreateObject("ADODB.Command")

'Create the resultset
Set ars = Server.CreateObject("ADODB.Recordset")

'Set up the query
cmdQuery.CommandText = "SELECT * FROM ExampleTable "
cmdQuery.CommandType = 1

'set the active connection to the command object
Set cmdQuery.ActiveConnection = DBConn

'open the resultset
ars.Open cmdTemp, , 0, 1
```


The following code loops through a result set and sends the data to the web browser:

```
Do While Not ars.Eof
    Response.Write ars("ExampleColumn")
    ars.MoveNext
Loop
```

NOTE If you want to use ADO-defined constants rather than hard-code the numbers in your code, include the location of the file that stores this information—ADOJAVAS for JScript and ADOVBS for VBScript:

```
<!--#include virtual="/ASPSAMP/SAMPLES/ADOVBS.INC"-->
```

An `#include` directive allows you to include an external file as part of your ASP page code. It's similar to the `#include` directive used in C/C++. ■

Using Server-Side Components

Using server-side components can be great for code reuse and portability of software. Even if you choose a proprietary solution instead of a more generic one, if you design your software with a component-based architecture, future modifications and additions to your system can be much easier and cost-effective. Also, if you're connecting to the database, you have much more error-handling capability than using scripting.

▶ More information on using server-side components is available in Chapter 6, "Creating Components with Visual C++," **p. 173**; Chapter 9, "Using ActiveX Components in a Client/Server Environment," **p. 253**; and Chapter 10, "Clients, Servers, and Components: Web-Based Applications," **p. 293**.

This section demonstrates an actual three-tier example. The modMain.bas is the main program that makes calls to the Billing.CLS or Billing2.CLS component, which in turn interfaces with the database.

NOTE After changing the database, the code in the main program remains the same by simply calling Billing2.CLS. The interface for the second class doesn't change at all from the first—just the implementation changes. Changing the middle tier can prevent code changes in the interface and allows all applications that use the database to make calls to a single program.

The ACME Billing Company wants to provide a customer balance, the date the balance is due, and the address to which to send the balance. The company already has an ActiveX DLL that other software calls to generate a bill.

NOTE This example is greatly simplified for demonstration purposes.

Tables 17.1 and 17.2 list the columns, their types, and descriptions for the Customer and Region MS-Access Database tables.

Table 17.1 Customer Database Table Structure

Column Name	Type	Explanation
ID	AutoNumber	Identity
LastName	Text	Customer's last name
FirstName	Text	Customer's first name
Balance	Currency	Customer's balance
EmailAddress	Text	Customer's unique email address
Region	Number	Foreign key to region

Table 17.2 Region Database Table Structure

Column Name	Type	Explanation
ID	AutoNumber	Identity
Name	Text	Region's name
Address1	Text	1st line of billing address
Address2	Currency	2nd line of billing address
Day	Text	Day of the month which the bill is due

Listing 17.6 is the Visual Basic code for an ActiveX DLL that returns the appropriate data to a calling program. This code uses a Microsoft Access database.

Listing 17.6 Billing Class Interface to the Database

```
Option Explicit

'Directory where the database is found
Const DBPath = "c:\Billing.mdb"

'Error Codes
Const NO_RECORD_FOUND = 1234
Const ILLEGAL_VALUE_NAME = 1235

'Connection to the database
Private m_DB As Database

'Given an identifier and the name of the data that you wish to retrieve
'GetValue will return an error code and set vValue to the value of the
'data requested
Public Function GetValue(ByVal sIdentifier As String, ByVal sValueName As
                        ➥String, ByRef vValue As Variant) As Long

'String used to hold a SQL statement
Dim sQuery As String

'the returned recordset
Dim rs As Recordset

On Error GoTo CheckError

'set return value to successful
GetValue = 0

'Check the desired value name
'if it is valid then execute the appropriate SQL statement
'otherwise return an error code
Select Case sValueName

    Case "Balance"
        sQuery = "SELECT Balance FROM Customer WHERE EmailAddress =
                 ➥'" & sIdentifier & "' "
    Case "Day"
        sQuery = "SELECT Day FROM Region, Customer WHERE EmailAddress =
                 ➥'" & sIdentifier & _
                 "' AND Customer.Region = Region.ID "
    Case "Address1"
        sQuery = "SELECT Address1 FROM Region, Customer WHERE EmailAddress =
                 ➥'" & sIdentifier & _
                 "' AND Customer.Region = Region.ID "
    Case "Address2"
        sQuery = "SELECT Address2 FROM Region, Customer WHERE EmailAddress =
                 ➥'" & sIdentifier & _
                 "' AND Customer.Region = Region.ID "
```

continues

Listing 17.6 Continued

```
    Case Else
        GetValue = ILLEGAL_VALUE_NAME

End Select

'if the value name is valid then continue
If GetValue = 0 Then

    'get the value
    Set rs = m_DB.OpenRecordset(sQuery, dbOpenSnapshot)
    If Not rs.EOF Then
        vValue = rs(0)
    Else
        GetValue = NO_RECORD_FOUND
    End If
End If

Exit Function
CheckError:

GetValue = Err

End Function

Private Sub Class_Initialize()

Set m_DB = OpenDatabase(DBPath)

End Sub

Private Sub Class_Terminate()

Set m_DB = Nothing

End Sub
```

To test this code, include it in a project with a module that has the code from Listing 17.7. Put an MDB (Access database) file with the above database structure (refer to Tables 17.1 and 17.2) in the same directory where your Visual Basic project files reside. Make certain that you have some entries in the database. The message box returns the error code and if successful the desired data. Set `sEmail` to a value in the database.

Listing 17.7 Main Program That Calls Billing.CLS

```
Sub Main()

Dim oBilling As New CBilling
Dim lCode As Long
Dim x As Variant
Dim sEmail As String
Dim sValueName As String
```

```
sEmail = ""
sValueName = "Address2"
lCode = oBilling.GetValue(sEmail, sValueName, x)
MsgBox lCode & " " & x
End Sub
```

The head of ACME Billing Information Systems decides that Address2 is too restrictive and the column needs to be broken into three columns: City, State, and ZipCode. If ACME had written separate code to interface to the database in its billing system and web page, both systems would need to be rewritten and tested, as would any another system that interfaced with those tables. Fortunately, ACME used a single DLL, so only one component needs to be rewritten and tested.

Listing 17.8 contains the code that needs to be modified to accommodate the new database structure.

Listing 17.8 Billing Class Interface to the Database with the New Database Scheme

```
Case "Address2"
        sQuery = "SELECT City, State, ZipCode FROM Region, Customer WHERE
                 ➥EmailAddress = '" & sIdentifier & _
                 "' AND Customer.Region = Region.ID "
    Case "City"
        sQuery = "SELECT City FROM Region, Customer WHERE EmailAddress =
                 ➥'" & sIdentifier & _
                 "' AND Customer.Region = Region.ID "
    Case "State"
        sQuery = "SELECT State FROM Region, Customer WHERE EmailAddress =
                 ➥'" & sIdentifier & _
                 "' AND Customer.Region = Region.ID "
    Case "ZipCode"
            sQuery = "SELECT ZipCode FROM Region, Customer WHERE EmailAddress =
                     ➥'" & sIdentifier & _
                     "' AND Customer.Region = Region.ID "
    Case Else
        GetValue = ILLEGAL_VALUE_NAME

End Select

'if the value name is valid then continue
If GetValue = 0 Then

    'get the value
    Set rs = m_DB.OpenRecordset(sQuery, dbOpenSnapshot)
    If Not rs.EOF Then
        If sValueName <> "Address2" Then
            vValue = rs(0)
```

continues

Listing 17.8 Continued

```
        Else
            'special case for Address2
            vValue = rs!City & ", " & rs!State & " " & rs!ZipCode
        End If
    Else
        GetValue = NO_RECORD_FOUND
    End If
End If
```

The new database structure is masked by the ActiveX DLL for the existing system, while additional functionality is provided for future needs. Notice that if you pass `Address2` to the `GetValue` function, the correct result is still returned. Also, you could pass `City`, `State`, or `ZipCode` and get only the desired information.

From Here...

This chapter explains the uses and advantages of server-side programming. You've learned what should go on to the client and what to the server. This chapter also explains some of the advantages of using various languages and software. It illustrates the advantages of using a component between the web server and database server. To learn more about server-side programming, see the following chapters:

- If you're interested in software development, you might want to examine Microsoft's compilers in Chapter 6, "Creating Components with Visual C++," and Chapter 7, "Creating Components with Visual J++."
- For more in-depth information on what software should go on the server and what should be on the client, see Chapter 10, "Clients, Servers, and Components: Web-Based Applications."
- For information on Visual InterDev, see Chapter 14, "Developing Active Content with Visual InterDev"; Chapter 15, "Advanced Visual InterDev Concepts"; and Chapter 16, "Visual InterDev Design-Time Controls."

CHAPTER 18

Dynamic HTML

by Chris H. Striker

As the number of World Wide Web users has increased, developers of web-based content have struggled to provide content that approximates the functionality, ease-of-use, and flexibility of traditional software applications. This has been no small task; the web's nature challenges the fundamental structure of application development. Over the years, various technologies have been introduced that help developers come closer to their goals: new HTML standards, Java applets, ActiveX controls, scripting, and so on. Nevertheless, because a fully exposed object model didn't exist, these technologies necessarily remained only partial solutions at best.

With Dynamic HTML, the landscape has changed. Web-based development is about to take a significant leap forward. Based on the Document Object Model that Microsoft proposed to the World Wide Web Consortium (W3C), Dynamic HTML offers to developers a comprehensive, fully exposed object model. Via Dynamic HTML, developers can create content that maximizes speed while maximizing interactivity—these are no longer necessarily mutually exclusive. Developers can create content that changes in response to user input without having to access the server. Ultimately, many restrictions to web-based development have been removed. ■

Dynamic HTML object model

The exposed object model, with the comprehensive event model, allows you to control every aspect of your pages.

Accessing document content

Not only can you control the elements of your pages, you can control the actual content of your pages.

Data binding

You now can bind HTML elements to data sources via new data controls, create tables that automatically generate rows for each record of a data source, and exploit on-the-fly HTML regeneration based on sorts and filters, all without additional trips to the server.

A sample page

Follow the instructions to create a sample page that demonstrates all the key features of Dynamic HTML.

Overview of Dynamic HTML Features

In this chapter, you have an opportunity to create a single page that demonstrates all the key features of Dynamic HTML: dynamic content, dynamic styles, absolute positioning, multimedia effects, and data binding. To do so, you need to have installed Internet Explorer 4.0 for Windows 95 or Windows NT 4.0. This chapter also assumes that you're familiar with HTML 3.2 and VBScript.

ON THE WEB

Keep in mind that this chapter is a small tip of a relatively large iceberg; to fully take advantage of Dynamic HTML, you need to familiarize yourself with the contents of the Internet Client SDK. For a full treatment of the technologies discussed in this chapter, and especially for complete documentation regarding scripting with Dynamic HTML, refer to the Internet Client SDK from Microsoft at **http://www.microsoft.com/workshop/prog/inetsdk/**.

Dynamic Content

One chief restriction of web-based development has been that offering content to users is a one-shot deal. Users request a page, the web server processes the request and offers the page to users, users read the page and send further requests. Change to the page's content was severely limited; with the exception of objects embedded in the HTML (such as Java applets), the content was necessarily static. New content had to come as another page sent by the server. With Dynamic HTML, this has changed; developers can author pages that dynamically change their content in response to any of the events exposed by the event model, all without going back to the server. Dynamic HTML elements, as well as the information contained in elements, can be removed, added, or modified on-the-fly.

Dynamic Styles

Styles are specified by using Cascading Style Sheets (CSS) or as element attributes. With Dynamic HTML, developers can alter style information at runtime via scripting. Any attribute or property specified in a style can be altered—such as color, size, position, and visibility—all in response to any events exposed by the event model. Internet Explorer 4.0 supports "intelligent recalculation" so that the rest of the page responds to any changes; if a change to a particular section of the page forces other elements to move, Internet Explorer handles the moving.

Absolute Positioning

Another main difficulty that web developers have had to grapple with is the limit on the layout and design of pages. The positioning of elements on a page was restricted to the options offered by traditional HTML. Given this context, web developers made creative use of tables, frames, and other HTML constructs to present the illusion that their designs broke the boundaries of HTML. In the process, however, these developers spent considerable amounts of time and introduced unnecessary levels of complexity to "outsmart" HTML.

With absolute positioning, a page's layout is free from old limitations. You can now create attractive designs and user interfaces with the degree of flexibility programmers have come to expect from visual tools such as Visual Basic, Delphi, or Visual C++. The first step toward absolute positioning was taken by Microsoft with its HTML Layout Control—within the confines of the HTML Layout objects, developers were free to position objects anywhere on a 2D plane. Absolute positioning in Dynamic HTML represents the effort to move this capability to HTML itself, via an open standard. It allows positioning on x-y coordinates and z-planes, as well as with scripting animation.

Multimedia Effects

As a sort of "extra," Microsoft has offered developers a set of controls with Dynamic HTML that provides multimedia effects to HTML elements and demonstrates some of the eye-catching potential that Dynamic HTML affords. The following is a list of the controls and their descriptions:

- The Mixer control lets you control multiple .wav files, as well as which files play in response to particular user actions.
- The Path control lets you animate elements on the page by using ticks provided in a fashion similar to a Timer control. The Path control can interpolate positions within ranges of time (specifying position for each tick isn't necessary).
- The Sequencer control allows you to time and sequence other controls, scripts, and intrinsic functions. This control can access and manipulate the timed behavior of other ActiveX controls and intrinsic HTML controls, manipulate ActiveX methods and properties, and call scripts.
- The Sprite control allows you to present slide-show animations with graphic images.
- The Structured Graphics control lets you use vector-based images on web pages, as well as the functionality that vector-based art implies: rotating, scaling, animating, translating, transforming, and so on. Because vector-based images are mathematical descriptions of shapes rather than the bitmap information contained in raster images, overhead is small and speed is improved dramatically.
- The Transitions control lets you use any of several special effects over a range of time to display and hide page elements.
- The Visual Filters control allows you to use any of several filters (such as shadow or spotlight) to enhance the display of visual elements on a page.

Data Binding

Web pages have traditionally been a fairly weak means of accessing databases. Although developers have used CGI scripts and other means to provide some of the functionality users have come to expect from true client/server applications, many key elements have been absent. Every distinct view of data required a new request to a server, and there was no means of binding elements on web pages to a database. Also, users had to wait until a server built and sent an entire page containing data before they could view any of the contents. Finally, generating the HTML to present the data to users was often needlessly time-consuming and sometimes arduous.

Dynamic HTML addresses all the aforementioned limitations via several new data controls. When a page is accessed, Dynamic HTML knows how to regenerate content on-the-fly based on sorting and filtering user input without accessing the server. You can bind HTML elements and form fields to records or fields in records, allowing updates to data sources. You can write pages that begin displaying data as soon as the client receives the first record. Also, by linking HTML elements to a data control via `DATASRC`, `DATAFLD`, and `DATAFORMATAS` attributes, Dynamic HTML allows for automatic generation of table rows from data records. In short, Dynamic HTML provides a new level of database connectivity within the context of the web.

Now, Microsoft has plans for three data controls to be used with Dynamic HTML: the Tabular Data control (which accesses delimited text files), the Advanced Data control (which allows access to ODBC-compliant databases), and the JDBC control (which allows access to JDBC-compliant databases). Microsoft has indicated, as has been the case with ActiveX controls in general, that it expects other parties to develop data controls.

ON THE WEB

For the latest information about the Advanced Data control, visit Microsoft's site at **http://www.microsoft.com/adc**.

The Dynamic HTML Object Model

What makes all the preceding features possible is the exposed object model. Before Dynamic HTML, only a limited set of elements was available to developers for programmatic control. Only a small number of the attributes of HTML elements were available, as well as a limited number of events. With the introduction of Dynamic HTML, all elements on a web page are exposed to developers, as well as all attributes and a comprehensive set of events.

NOTE The object model works with whatever scripting language you want to use, be it VBScript, JScript, or any other model-compliant language. Also, pages that use Dynamic HTML still display reasonably well in older browsers that don't support the proposed standard.

Dynamic HTML Object Model Tree

The hierarchy shown in Figure 18.1 in the Dynamic HTML Object Model exposes the highest-level objects in Internet Explorer. The highest-level object is the `window` object, which is the highest-level parent object to all other objects and elements within Internet Explorer. Via these objects, developers have what might be considered meta-level control of the browser relative to the actual content displayed.

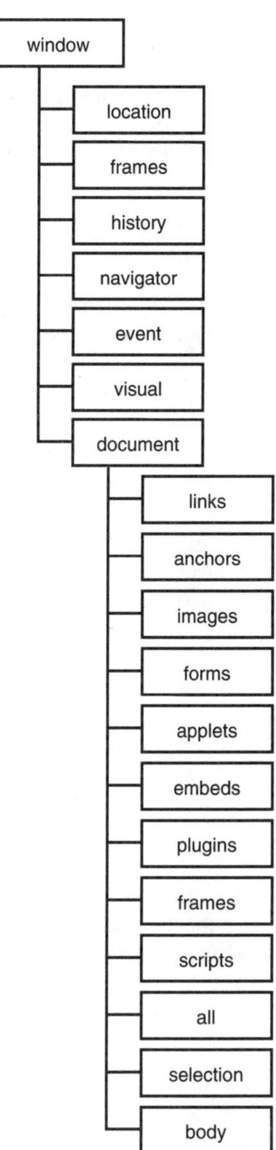

FIG. 18.1
The top levels of the object model exposed by Internet Explorer for use with Dynamic HTML. The items in the object model are accessed by specifying the hierarchy; for example, to get at the `links` collection of the current document, you might use code such as `window.document.links`.

The `location` property references the address to which the browser points. By manipulating this object, the browser can be set to point to a different address. For instance, the following VBScript code sends the browser to the Microsoft home page:

```
window.location.href = "http://www.microsoft.com"
```

The `history` object represents the list of addresses the browser has recently visited. Via scripting, you can send user browsers backward or forward through the list, or take action based on the list's contents.

The `navigator` object, representing the browser, allows you to do a host of useful things. For instance, you can grab the name of the browser, the version of the browser, or the state of the Alt key; you also can check whether users have cookies enabled or Java enabled.

The read-only `event` property returns the event being addressed.

The `visual` object allows you to gather information about the users' viewing capabilities/preferences. With this object, you can determine the color depth at which users are viewing your page, the horizontal resolution, and the vertical resolution.

The `document` object addresses the actual contents of whatever page is loaded in the browser. Under the `document` object are collections for the following items:

```
links                    embeds
anchors                  plugins
images                   frames
forms                    scripts
applets
```

Other items of particular note are

- The `all` collection, which is a collection of all objects on the page. Via this collection, you can gain access to every element, no matter what collection it resides in.
- The `selection` object, which references whatever users have selected onscreen at a moment in time.
- The `body` property, which allows access to what may be considered meta-level information within the context of the document. Via this object, you can access and manipulate document-wide properties, methods, and events.

Element Class and Collection

Within a page, every element is available for programmatic manipulation. Dynamic HTML exposes an element model through which all properties, methods, and events are made accessible to scripts. This access is facilitated by the organization of HTML elements. Since the earliest HTML standards, document tags have been arranged in a hierarchical structure. Consider this HTML code:

```
<HTML>
        <HEAD>
                <TITLE>Sample Page</TITLE
        </HEAD>
        <BODY>
                <H1>Section One</H1>
                <H2>Section Two</H2>
                <P><I>Sample Content</I></P>
        </BODY>
</HTML>
```

Here, the hierarchy is clear from the structure of the HTML itself. The `<HEAD>` and `<BODY>` tags are directly subordinate to the `<HTML>` tag. The `<TITLE>` tag is subordinate to the `<HEAD>` tag, the `<H1>` and `<H2>` tags are subordinate to the `<BODY>` tag, and so on.

The actual elements are made available to you via collections. Earlier, you read that all elements on a page are exposed through an `all` collection. To use the `all` collection via scripting, you might use code similar to this:

```
dim holdItem
holdItem = document.all(1)
```

This code would set the `holdItem` variable to the second element on the page.

NOTE Keep in mind that an index for a collection always begins with zero and ends with `(`*`collection`*`.length) - 1`. The `length` property specifies how many members are in the specified collection. ■

Another way to grab elements via script is to grab an element by using the tag itself to access a subset of the `all` collection:

```
holdElement = document.all.tags("P").item(0)
```

This line grabs the first `<P>` element on the page.

NOTE The `item` method is the default for a collection; you can specify it if you want, but the code works the same way if you omit `item`. ■

You can also use the name of the element, as specified in the `id` attribute for the element. If you wanted to grab this element,

```
<P id = "firstelement">Here is some sample code</P>
```

you might use VBScript like this:

```
holdElement = document.all.item("firstelement")
```

The `all` collection may be considered a good general-purpose tool; however, you can access particular sets of HTML elements via the aforementioned collections (`links`, `anchors`, `images`, `forms`, `applets`, `embeds`, `plugins`, `frames`, and `scripts`). Most are self-explanatory. The `links` collection allows access to the `<A>` elements that contain `href` attributes and the `<AREA>` elements. The `anchors` collection accesses the `<A>` elements containing `name` attributes. The `images` collection refers to the `<IMG>` elements; the `forms` collection accesses all `<FORM>` elements on a page. The `applets`, `embeds`, and `plugins` collections access their respective HTML elements. The `frames` collection addresses a page's frame structure, and the `scripts` collection accesses a page's `<SCRIPT>` elements.

Table 18.1 shows the properties available for every element. (There might be others for specific elements.)

Table 18.1 Element Properties Accessible to Scripts

Property	Access	Description
`parentElement as Element`	read-only	Returns the containing element in the structural tree.
`tagName as String`	read-only	Returns the tag name represented by the element. The tag name is returned uppercased.
`ClassName as String`	read/write	Returns the class specified for the element. `Class` is uppercased to avoid conflict with the reserved class name.
`id as String`	read/write	Returns the ID identifier for the element.
`style as Style`	read-only	Returns a style object representing the inline style for the element.
`document as Document`	read-only	Returns the document object containing the element.
`left as Long`	read-only	Returns the calculated position of the element in coordinates relative to the window.
`top as Long`	read-only	Returns the calculated position of the element in coordinates relative to the window.

Table 18.2 shows the methods available. (Again, there might be others for specific elements.)

Table 18.2 Element Methods Accessible to Scripts

Method	Return Value	Description
`scrollIntoView (start as Boolean)`	none	Scrolls the element to the first or last line of the display
`contains(element as Element)`	Boolean	Returns whether the supplied element is contained within the element's subtree
`getMember (attribName as String)`	String	Returns the persisted value for the specified attribute
`setMember (attribName as String, value as Variant)`	none	Sets the persisted value for the specified attribute
`removeMember (attribName as String)`	none	Causes the attribute to be removed and not persisted into the HTML document

The Event Model

The exposed event model is the last piece of the puzzle. Via the event model, you can create pages that respond to user actions. As was the case with the object model, a limited set of events has been available to developers in the past. With Dynamic HTML, the event model is fully fleshed out.

One of the most significant features of the event model is *bubbling*. As the event model adheres to the hierarchical nature of the object model, events bubble up through the hierarchy until they reach a handler that addresses them. This means you can write generic code that will handle `onmouseover` events for every element on the page, for instance. In the past, you would have had to specify the handler explicitly for every element individually.

Regarding bubbling, remember a couple of key points:

- As events bubble automatically, you need a way to prevent further bubbling.
- Some elements have default actions associated with them (to follow the value for the `href` attribute is the default action of the `<A>` element). You need a way to override the default action if that's your intention. You can handle both scenarios via the event object, which provides a `cancelBubble` method and allows you to determine whether you're overriding the default action.

Suppose that you have an image (specified with the `<IMG>` tag) that you've given the ID parameter `Image1`. You might want a handler for the `onclick` event for the document as a whole, but a different handler that executes only when users click the `Image1` image. In this case, you need to make certain that after the handler specific to the `Image1` element fires, the event doesn't bubble up to the main document `onclick` handler. You can manage this with code such as the following:

```
<script language = "VBScript" for="document" event="onclick()">
     ElementID = window.event.srcElement.id
     Msgbox("This was processed by the document-wide handler.")
</script>
<script language = "VBScript" for "Image1" event = "onclick()">
     msgbox("This was processed by an element-specific handler.")
     event.cancelBubble = true
</script>
```

In binding events to scripts, you have three options:

- You can specify the script to run within the HTML tag itself:

  ```
  <A onmouseover = "processrollover"language = "VBScript">
  ```

- You can specify the event information in the script tag (the language independent method):

  ```
  <SCRIPT FOR=... EVENT=... IN=... LANGUAGE=...>
  ```

- With VBScript only, you can specify the object in the name of the handler:

  ```
  <SCRIPT language = "VBScript">
  Sub object_onmouseover
  ```

```
...
End Sub
</SCRIPT>
```

At this point, to take full advantage of scripting for Dynamic HTML, you need to delve deeper into the event object itself. Tables 18.3 through 18.7 contain detailed information on the `event` object, standard events, and element-specific events.

ON THE WEB

You also can find the information in Tables 18.3 through 18.7 in Microsoft's Internet Client SDK at **http://www.microsoft.com/workshop/prog/inetsdk/**.

Table 18.3 Event Object Properties

Property	Permissions	Description
`altKey as Boolean`	read-only	Returns whether the Alt key is pressed at the time of the event.
`contains (element as Element)`	read-only	Returns bitmask indicating which mouse buttons are pressed at the time of the event: 0 for none, 1 for left, 2 for right, 3 for both.
`cancelBubble`	read/write	Sets or returns whether the event should continue to bubble up through the containership hierarchy. True value on return from a handle cancels further event bubbling for only that event.
`ctrlKey as Boolean`	read-only	Returns whether the Ctrl key is pressed at the time of the event.
`fromElement as Element`	read-only	Returns the element that the mouse is coming from for the `onmouseover` and `onmouseout` events.
`keyCode as Integer`	read/write	Returns a standard numeric ASCII keycode for key events; if set by `onkeypress`, changes the character sent to the object.
`returnValue as Variant`	read/write	Sets or returns a return value to the event, a language-neutral way to return values to events, as some languages may not support event notifications as functional routines.
`shiftKey as Boolean`	read-only	Returns whether the Shift key was pressed at the time of the event.
`srcElement as Element`	read-only	Returns an element object representing the element that first received the notification before it started to bubble.

Property	Permissions	Description
`toElement as Element`	read-only	Returns the element that the mouse is going to for the `onmouseover` and `onmouseout` events.
`x as Long`	read-only	Returns the horizontal position of the mouse with respect to the origin of the document's physical location at the time of the event.
`y as Long`	read-only	Returns the vertical position of the mouse with respect to the origin of the document's physical location at the time of the event.

Table 18.4 Keyboard Events

Event Name (Parameters)	Return Value	Description
`onkeydown (keycode as integer, shift as htmlShift)`	none	Fired when a key goes down.
`onkeypress (keyCode as integer)`	Change `keyCode` to 0 to cancel	Fired when a key is pressed. Changing `event.keyCode` or integer return value changes the character.
`onkeyup (keyCode as integer, shift as htmlShift)`	none	Fired when a key goes up. Note that for a shift key, the key is up and so shift state is off accordingly.
`onhelp`	none	Occurs when help key (F1) is pressed.

Table 18.5 Mouse Events

Event Name (Parameters)	Return Value	Description
`onmousedown (button as htmlButton, shift as htmlShift, x as long, y as long)`	none	Fired when the left mouse button goes down over the element.

continues

Table 18.5 Continued

Event Name (Parameters)	Return Value	Description
`onmousemove (button as htmlButton, shift as htmlShift, x as long, y as long)`	none	Fired when the mouse moves over the element.
`onmouseup (button as htmlButton, shift as htmlShift, z as long, y as long)`	none	Fired when the left mouse button goes up over the element.
`onmouseover`	none	Fired when the mouse enters the element.
`onmouseout`	none	Fired when the mouse exits the element.
`onclick`	`false` to cancel default action	Fired when users left-click the element. A click event can also occur when Enter is pressed on a focusable element. The click event follows the `onmouseup` event when it occurs as a result of a mouse button. For a mouse with one button, the button is considered the left mouse button.
`ondblclick`	none	Fired when users double-click the element. The system determines the timing between what constitutes two click events or a click and a double-click.

Table 18.6 Focusable Element Events

Property Name (Parameters)	Return Value	Description
`onfocus`	none	The element is receiving the focus.
`onblur`	none	The element is losing the focus.

Table 18.7 Element-Specific Events

Event Name (Parameters)	Supported Object(s)	Return Value	Description
`onabort`	`<IMG>`	none	Occurs if users abort the download of the image. To abort an image, click a link, click the stop button, and so on.
`onbounce (side as String)`	`<MARQUEE>`	none	Occurs when marquee with behavior equal to alternative text hits edge, `"bottom"`, `"left"`, `"right"`, or `"top"`.
`onchange`	`<INPUT TYPE = CHECKBOX>`, `<INPUT TYPE = FILE>`, `<INPUT TYPE = RADIO>`, `<INPUT TYPE = TEXT>`, `<SELECT>`, `<TEXTAREA>`	none	Occurs when the contents of the object change. This event is fired when the contents are committed, not while the value is changing. For example, for a text box, this event isn't fired while users type, but rather when they commit their changes by pressing Enter or leaving the text box's focus. This code is executed before the code specified by `onblur`, if the control is also losing the focus.
`onerror`	`<IMG>`	none	Occurs when an error happens when loading an image element.
`onfinish`	`<MARQUEE>`	none	Occurs when motion is complete.
`onload`	`<IMG>`, document window	none	Occurs when the element is completely loaded.
`onreadystatechange`	`<APPLET>`, `<EMBED>`, `<FRAME>`, `<IFRAME>`, `<IMG>`, `<OBJECT>`, `<SCRIPT SRC=...>`, document	none	Occurs whenever the state of the element changes. This is a more detailed version of the `onload` event. Check the `readyState` property for the element. The different states causing this event to be fired occur when the element is loading, when the element is

continues

Part III Ch 18

Table 18.7 Continued

Event Name (Parameters)	Supported Object(s)	Return Value	Description
			still loading but is now firing events and can be interacted with, and when the element is completely loaded.
onreset	<FORM>	none	Occurs when users reset a form. The onreset event handler executes code when a reset event occurs.
onscroll (scrollParam as scrollObject)		none	Fired on elements that have an overflow mechanism specified through the overflow CSS attribute. Occurs when the element is scrolled; event doesn't bubble.
onselect	<INPUT TYPE = PASSWORD>, <INPUT TYPE = TEXT>, <TEXTAREA>	none	Occurs when the text selection on a text element changes.
onsubmit	<FORM>	none	Occurs when a form is about to be submitted (the onsubmit event default action is to submit the form). Event can be overridden by returning false in the event handler. Purpose is to allow client-side validation.
onunload	window	none	Occurs immediately before the page being unloaded.
onselectionchange	document	none	Fires on the document when the user's selection changes.
onzoom (zoomPercent as integer)	document	Return integer to override the percent of the zoom	Fires on the window whenever the window is zoomed.

Accessing Document Content

To Dynamic HTML, the content of a page is a single stream of text that begins and ends with the <BODY> tag. The textRange object representing this stream can be manipulated to alter the content on the page. Very few pages, however, offer a stream of text between <BODY> tags with no other elements in between. This is good news for you if you want to manipulate the actual content of a page. The elements between <BODY> tags provide an easy way to break down that stream into easily manipulated component parts.

Keep in mind that the textRange object doesn't automatically exist—you need to create it explicitly by using the createTextRange method. After you create a textRange, methods exist with which you may change the start and end positions, search, or modify all or part of the range. The most basic way to create a text range containing the entirety of a page (everything between the opening and closing <BODY> tags) is a line of VBScript such as

```
Set newRange = document.body.createTextRange()
```

The textRange object itself exposes five properties and a number of methods, as shown in Tables 18.8 through 18.11.

Table 18.8 *textRange* Object Properties

Property Name	Description
end	Sets or returns the end-character position in relation to the entire stream. If this is set less than the start value, start is also set equal to this value.
start	Sets or returns the start-character position in relation to the entire stream. If start is greater than end, end is also set equal to this value.
htmlSelText	Returns the raw HTML for the selected text.
htmlText	Returns the valid HTML fragment for the text.
text	Sets and returns the text for the range without any of the HTML markup.

Table 18.9 *textRange* Object Methods

Method	Description
CommonParentElement	Returns the common parent element for the range.
executeCommand (cmdID as long, value as Variant)	Executes a command on the range—for example, changing the text formatting. The following methods provide information when executing command IDs: queryCommandState, queryCommandEnabled, and queryCommandText.

continues

Table 18.9 Continued

Method	Description
`duplicate`	Returns a copy of the current range.
`isEmbed ([cp as Integer]) as Boolean`	Returns a Boolean that represents whether the specified character is an embedded object. If true, the `parentElement` method can be used to access the embedding.
`parentElement ([cp as Integer]) as Element`	Returns the parent node for the specified character. The character position is scoped to the current range.
`inRange (compareRange as Range) as Boolean`	Returns whether the specified range is within or equal to the current range.
`isEqual (compareRange as Range) as Boolean`	Returns whether the specified range is equal to the current range.
`scrollIntoView (start as Boolean)`	Scrolls the range into view.

Table 18.10 *textRange* Object Range Movement Methods

Method Name	Description
`collapse (start as Boolean) as long`	Allows you to create an empty range at the beginning or end of the current range.
`expand (unit as htmlUnit) as long`	Expands the range so that partial units are completely contatined.
`move (unit as htmlUnit, [count as Variant]) as long`	Changes the text the range spans over. Doesn't move any text, but instead is used to change what text the range is over.
`moveEnd (unit as htmlUnit, [count as Variant]) as long`	Causes the range to grow or shrink from the end of the range.
`moveStart (unit as htmlUnit, [count as Variant]) as long`	Causes the range to grow or shrink from the beginning of the range.
`setRange (begin as long, end as long)`	Sets the range to the ordinal offsets specified by the method. The offsets are within the scope of the current range.

Table 18.11 *textRange* Object: Inserting Text

Method Name	Description
`pasteHtml (string)`	Pastes HTML into the current range. The HTML is forced to fit the current context of the document.

Two more methods are particularly useful when working with `textRanges`: `rangeFromText` and `rangeFromElement`.

rangeFromText

The `rangeFromText` method is used in this fashion:

```
document.rangeFromText(text as String, Optional count as Long, Optional flags,
➥range as Object) as TextRange
```

This method is useful for creating text ranges based on a search through the content of a page for a specific known string of text. Table 18.12 lists the parameters.

Table 18.12 *rangeFromText* Parameters

Parameter Name	Default If Not Supplied	Description
`count`	Search forward	The string to search for
`Flags`	No flags	`>0` to search forward, `<0` to search backward, `=0` to search only within the supplied range or selection if no range is supplied
`Range`	Start from current insertion point	The range to search in

rangeFromElement

The `rangeFromElement` method creates a text range from the contents of a known element. The method takes only one parameter—the element to be searched for. If you had an element with a specified ID such as

```
<strong id=firstelement>Sample Text</strong>
```

and wanted to create a `textRange` object that contained `Sample Text`, you could use the `rangeFromElement` method like this:

```
Set holdRange = document.body.rangeFromElement(document.firstelement)
```

Data Binding in Dynamic HTML

As mentioned earlier in the overview of Dynamic HTML features, data binding is accomplished via the use of new data controls and three new attributes: DATASRC, DATAFLD, and DATAFORMATAS.

The New Attributes

The DATASRC attribute specifies the data control to which HTML elements are being bound by referencing the ID of the data control. It applies to only the TABLE, SPAN, DIV, OBJECT, PARAM, INPUT, SELECT, TEXTAREA, IMG, and MARQUEE elements. If you have a data control with an ID attribute of dcOne on your page, you can bind a table to it with HTML like this:

```
<TABLE DATASRC="#dcOne">
```

NOTE Remember that in using the DATASRC attribute for tables, you need to put a number sign in front of the ID. ■

The DATAFLD attribute specifies the field in a record to which an HTML element is being bound. It applies only to the SPAN, DIV, OBJECT, PARAM, INPUT, SELECT, TEXTAREA, IMG, and MARQUEE elements. If you want to specify a cell in a table to which to bind a field in a record from a data source, you could specify it as follows:

```
<TD><SPAN DATAFLD="CompanyName">
```

where "CompanyName" is the name of the field.

The DATAFORMATAS attribute specifies what kind of data is being bound. You can specify "html" for data to be considered a string of HTML, "text" for data to be considered text, and "none" if the data is to be taken in raw format. It applies only to the SPAN, DIV, and MARQUEE attributes.

The Data Consumers

Data consumers are the HTML elements that support current record binding (referred to as the elements to which the preceding attributes apply). The following list provides descriptions of the data consumers, with indications as to whether they support editing:

NOTE Now, only the Advanced Data Connector supports editing; the Tabular Data Control used in the Sample Page later in the chapter doesn't. ■

- The DIV element doesn't support editing. It displays a block of plain text or HTML text. It re-renders when underlying value in column changes or current record changes.
- The SPAN element doesn't support editing. It displays a block of plain text or HTML text. It re-renders when underlying value in column changes or current record changes.
- The SELECT element supports editing and supplies functionality similar to a list box or a combo box. Binding is supported only for the selected item; multiple selections aren't supported. It works with <OPTION> tags and the index into the <OPTION> group of tags.

- The RADIO type INPUT element supports editing and is used to select a single value from a group of options.
- The CHECKBOX type INPUT element supports editing. It is considered individual Boolean selections.
- The TEXT type INPUT element supports editing. It's a textbox.
- The HIDDEN type INPUT element doesn't support editing and is accessible for read-only operations.
- The TEXTAREA element supports editing. It's a multicolumn textbox.
- The MARQUEE element doesn't support editing.
- The IMG element doesn't support editing. The bound value should contain only an URL to an image.
- The OBJECT element doesn't support editing. Binding to the default value of an OBJECT is allowed; DATASRC and DATAFLD specify attributes of the <OBJECT> tag. The OBJECT element also can bind to <PARAM> tags of the <OBJECT> tag.
- The APPLET element doesn't support editing. Binding is to the <PARAM> tag corresponding to property name being bound. You can now bind only one <PARAM> tag.

The Data Events

To allow for modifications and updates to data, you need a way to perform client-side validation before the data control sends information to the data source. To cancel an event (for events that can be canceled), you need only to return FALSE by the handler. What follows is a description of the various events:

- `onbeforeupdate(can_cancel)` fires when the element loses the focus or the page is attempted to be unloaded. Fires only if the value in the element has changed since the element received focus. Fires before the `onafterupdate()` event and the `onchange` event. One caveat is that `onbeforeupdate()` fires immediately at the change for the CHECKBOX input type element, the RADIO input type element, the SELECT element, and OBJECTs with an immediate bind flag set.
- `onafterupdate()` fires following the transfer of data from the element to the data source. Fires only in instances where `onbeforeupdate` fired. Won't fire if the value is set from script. This event can't be canceled.
- `onrowexit()` fires just before the data source control changes the current record. Allows for record-level validation before changing records. Boolean value is passed to indicate whether event can be canceled. Also fires when page or the browser is shutting down.
- `onrowenter()` fires when the current record changes (meaning that new values are available to the control). Allows for preprocessing of the new data. This event can't be canceled.

Building a Sample Page

In this section, you'll build a page that demonstrates most key features of Dynamic HTML: the absolute positioning of various elements on the page, the application of a transition to a graphic element, the dynamic change of a page's content and styles, the display and hiding of content sections, the response to user events on HTML elements, the control of HTML with scripting via the object model, and the access to a data source via the Tabular Data control.

While building this page, keep in mind that before Dynamic HTML, you typically would have to build several pages to provide the same degree of functionality and content. What's more, users would have to request these pages one at a time from a web server, slowing the process considerably.

Step 1: Starting the Project

Before you begin creating your Dynamic HTML page, you need to be set up to work within a web project in Visual InterDev. You must have access to a computer running Personal Web Server (on computers running Windows 95), Peer Web Services (on computers running Windows NT Workstation) or IIS 3.*x* (on machines running Windows NT Server). The computer must have the FrontPage Server Extension installed. As you develop your web further, you may find that you need Active Server Pages installed as well. You can install the various web servers from your operating system installation discs and the FrontPage extensions and Active Server Pages from the Visual InterDev setup.

You also will need to have Internet Explorer 4.0 installed. There are several installation options, but everything in the sample page you'll build will work with any of the installations.

If you've already created a web with Visual InterDev, you can use that web to develop, test, and implement your Dynamic HTML page. If this is the case, start Visual InterDev and open your web project. Otherwise, follow these steps to create a new web project on your web server:

1. Start Visual InterDev.
2. Choose File, New from the menu.
3. Select the Projects tab in the New dialog box.
4. Select the Web Project Wizard to create a new web project.
5. Enter the name for your new web project in the Project Name text box.
6. Click OK.
7. Enter the name of your web server in the Server Name combo box.
8. Select the option to Create a New Web.
9. Select the option to Enable Full Text Searching for pages in the web.
10. Ensure that the name for your web has been entered in the Name text box.

After you open a web project in Visual InterDev, you need to create a new HTML file:

1. Choose File, New from the Visual InterDev menu.
2. Select the Files table in the New dialog box.

3. Select HTML Page.
4. Select Add to Project.
5. Ensure that the path to your web is entered in the drop-down box.
6. Enter the name for your new HTML file in the File Name box.
7. Click OK.

At this point, you have a new HTML file defined in your web. Your screen should look similar to the one in Figure 18.2.

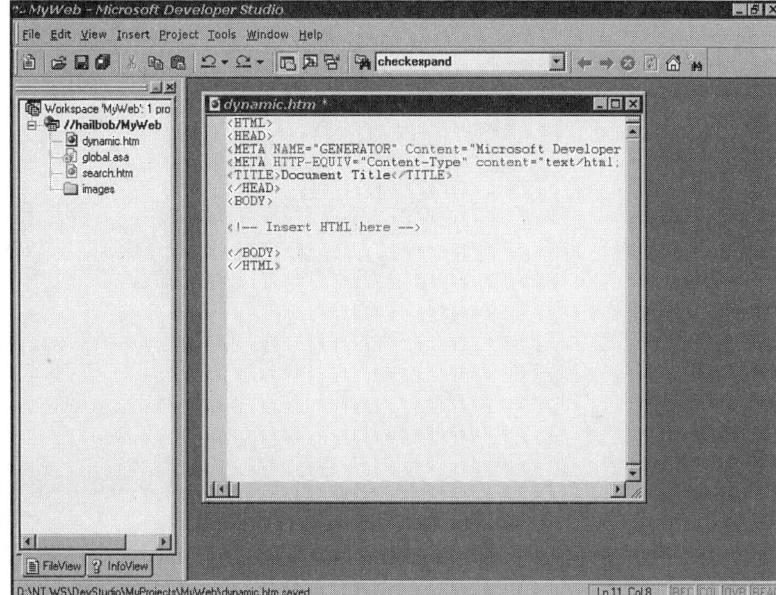

FIG. 18.2 The Visual InterDev environment with a new HTML file open for editing. Notice that Visual InterDev has created a global.asa file, a search.htm file, and an images directory for your new web.

Step 2: Adding the Template

To facilitate building your Dynamic HTML page, replace the comment `Insert HTML here` with the placeholder comments in Listing 18.1.

Listing 18.1 Dynamic HTML template

```
<!-- HTML for logo -->
<!-- Transition Object -->
<!-- HTML for menu -->
<!-- HTML for sections -->
<!-- HTML for popup window -->
<script language = "VBScript">
'page-level section array variable
'routines to call transition filter upon window load
'routines to process mouseover and mouseout events
```

continues

Listing 18.1 Continued

```
'routine to display/hide sub-menu items upon click event
'routine to display content layers upon click event
'routines to handle popup window upon mouseover and mouseout events
'routine to sort table contents via tabular data control
</script>
```

At this point, the HTML for your page should resemble Figure 18.3.

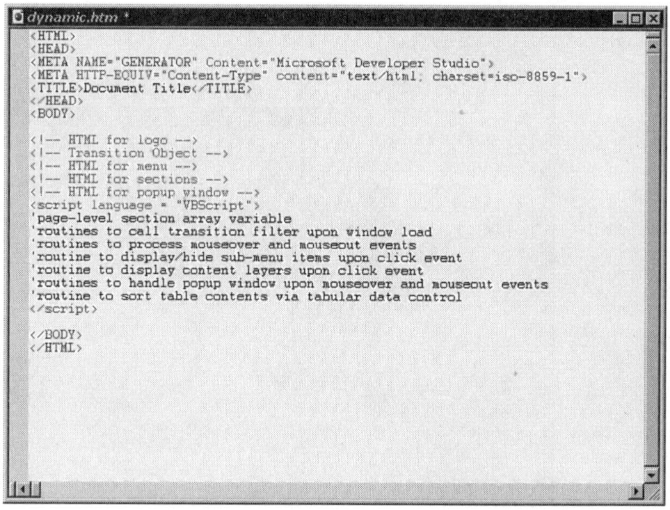

FIG. 18.3
HTML with placeholder comments. As you build the sample page, you may want to leave the comments in so that you have placeholders marking the various sections of HTML and VBScript.

```
dynamic.htm *
<HTML>
<HEAD>
<META NAME="GENERATOR" Content="Microsoft Developer Studio">
<META HTTP-EQUIV="Content-Type" content="text/html; charset=iso-8859-1">
<TITLE>Document Title</TITLE>
</HEAD>
<BODY>

<!-- HTML for logo -->
<!-- Transition Object -->
<!-- HTML for menu -->
<!-- HTML for sections -->
<!-- HTML for popup window -->
<script language = "VBScript">
'page-level section array variable
'routines to call transition filter upon window load
'routines to process mouseover and mouseout events
'routine to display/hide sub-menu items upon click event
'routine to display content layers upon click event
'routines to handle popup window upon mouseover and mouseout events
'routine to sort table contents via tabular data control
</script>

</BODY>
</HTML>
```

After adding the template, add the following attributes to the `<BODY>` tag:

- `bgcolor = "white"`
- `topmargin = "20"`
- `leftmargin = "20"`

Step 3: Adding the Graphic

As you build your page, you'll replace the placeholder comments with HTML code and VBScript code. The first task is to place the HTML for the image at the top of the page. Replace the comment `HTML for logo` with the HTML in Listing 18.2.

Listing 18.2 HTML for the Logo Graphic

```
<img id = "logo" src = "logo.gif" alt="Arcadia Bay"
style="visibility: hidden;" border=0>
```

Replace the logo.gif filename with a file of your own choosing. If the file you want to use doesn't reside in the same physical directory as your HTML page, you'll need to specify the path to your file (for instance, images/mylogo.gif).

At this point, you can view the page as you develop it by opening the file in Internet Explorer or by previewing it in Visual InterDev. To preview the page in Visual InterDev, right-click anywhere in the file editing window and then choose Preview <filename> from the context-sensitive menu.

This will open the InfoViewer Topic window, which acts as Internet Explorer in this case. This window lets you view and use your page from within Visual InterDev just as you would in a separate instance of Internet Explorer.

Notice that nothing appears on the page, because the style attribute in the `<img>` tag for the graphic specifies `visibility: hidden`. If you aren't already familiar with styles, you may want to review the specification for Cascading Style Sheets and their use with Internet Explorer. To view the graphic, remove the style attribute altogether (remember to replace it if you do so).

Step 4: Adding the Transition to the Graphic

The method you used to include a graphic on your page is fairly standard. It's also boring. Traditionally, web designers have used techniques such as animated GIFs, Java applets, and Shockwave objects to spice up their pages; Dynamic HTML dramatically expands the available options. With the new multimedia ActiveX controls (included with Internet Explorer and installed automatically during setup), you have a wide range of effects to choose from.

Here, you'll apply a transition filter to the graphic so that it dissolves into view when the page is accessed. Replace the comment `Transition Object` with the HTML in Listing 18.3.

Listing 18.3 HTML for the Transition Object

```
<OBJECT ID="dissolvein"
CLASSID="CLSID:F0F70103-6A8F-11d0-BD28-00A0C908DB96">
<PARAM NAME="Transition" value="12">
<PARAM NAME="RESTOREBITS" VALUE="0">
</OBJECT>
```

You've specified the Visual Transition ActiveX control for inclusion on the page. However, if you view your page now, you'll notice that nothing has changed; your graphic doesn't dissolve into view because nothing on the page links the graphic to the control. To create the link that tells the control to direct the display of the graphic, you need to use scripting.

NOTE The choice of VBScript, JavaScript or another scripting engine is up to you if your target platform includes only the Microsoft browser. Because the object models for Internet Explorer and Dynamic HTML are open, you can choose any engine you like that can address the models. The examples here are presented in VBScript; feel free to translate into another language if you feel more comfortable doing so. ■

To link the Visual Transition ActiveX control to the graphic, replace the comment `routines to call transition filter upon window load` with the VBScript in Listing 18.4.

Listing 18.4 VBScript Routines to Handle Transition

```
Sub Window_onLoad()
      logo.style.visibility = "hidden"
      call dissolveLogo()
end sub
sub dissolveLogo
      logo.stopPainting(dissolvein)
      logo.style.visibility = ""
      logo.startPainting(1500)
end Sub
```

If you preview the page now, you should see the graphic dissolve into view. You can control the rate at which the dissolve occurs by changing the parameter for the `startPainting` method in the `dissolveLogo` routine.

In Internet Explorer 3.*x*, a degree of control over the presentation of HTML was available to programmers via scripting. Because the object models weren't fully exposed, this control was necessarily limited. This is no longer the case. Here, VBScript code is accessing the graphic via the ID specified in the `<img>` tag (`logo`). Later, you'll see how to use the object model hierarchy to access HTML elements on the page without specifying their ID attributes explicitly. For now, notice that the VBScript routines you just added reference the element with the ID `logo`, clear the `visibility: hidden` style setting, and run the graphic through the `startPainting` method of the Visual Transition ActiveX control. This wouldn't be possible without the object model that Dynamic HTML exposes.

Step 5: Adding the Menu

The next step is to add a menu with items that highlight when the mouse rolls over them to your page. To add the menu structure, replace the comment `HTML for menu` with the HTML code in Listing 18.5.

Listing 18.5 HTML for the Menu Layer

```
<div id = "menu" style = "position:absolute;left:20;top:75">
<font face = verdana size = 2 color = midnightblue>
<!-- onclick events will go within the a tags below shortly -->
<a id = "one" onmouseover = "processover" onmouseout = "processout"
language = "VBScript">Company History</a><br>
<a id = "two" onmouseover = "processover" onmouseout = "processout"
language = "VBScript">Consultants</a><br>
<!-- insert the html for the submenu here -->
<a id = "three" onmouseover = "processover" onmouseout = "processout"
language = "VBScript">Partners</a><br>
</font>
</div>
```

Notice that the entire structure begins and ends with `<div>` tags, which mark the contained HTML as a separate chunk of elements that can be positioned independent of the rest of the items on the page. As you build this page, notice that the remaining HTML falls within `<div>` tags as well. This way, you can control which chunks of HTML are displayed at any given time.

The opening `<div>` tag contains the information Internet Explorer 4.0 needs to position the menu on the page. The style attribute specifies absolute positioning with pixel locations for the left and top edges. By changing these settings, you can force the menu to appear anywhere on the page.

If you previewed your page at this point, the menu would appear but simply sit there. This is another point at which developers traditionally had to turn to a Java applet or similar technique to provide feedback to users. Again, by exposing the HTML object model, developers can achieve the same result with much less work. Notice that the `<a>` tags enclosing the menu items contain `id` parameters and references to routines that handle the `onmouseover` and `onmouseout` events. You'll now add these routines. Replace the comment `routines to process mouseover and mouseout events` with the VBScript routines in Listing 18.6.

Listing 18.6 VBScript Routines to Handle Highlights

```
Sub processover
     heldID = window.event.srcElement.id
     set heldObj = document.all(heldID)
     heldObj.style.color = "limegreen"
End Sub
Sub processout
     heldID = window.event.srcElement.id
     set heldObj = document.all(heldID)
     heldObj.style.color = "midnightblue"
End Sub
```


Preview your page again. This time, roll the mouse pointer over the menu items. Notice that they provide feedback by highlighting when the mouse is over them. This is precisely the sort of feedback that was far more difficult to achieve before Dynamic HTML. Make sure that your page looks similar to Figure 18.4.

Look at the routines that provide this functionality—`processover` and `processout`. Recall that the routine that handled the link between the graphic and the Visual Transition ActiveX control referenced the `<img>` tag explicitly by its `id` attribute; notice that these routines don't, although they work for each of the three menu items. This is possible because of the event model and the `all` collection.

When an event fires, it's sent up through the event model hierarchy until it reaches a handler or reaches the top level without having found a handler, at which point it disappears. In this case, the `onmouseover` and `onmouseout` events have handlers specified in the `<a>` tags. Within the handlers, the first line of code grabs the ID for the element on the page that fired the event. The construct `window.event.srcElement.id` references the ID for the element that fired the event that's traveling up the event hierarchy in the current window. The next line sets an object variable (`holdObj`) to the element that has that ID by looking through the `all` collection for the document (the `all` collection can be considered a list of all the elements on the page). When the routine sets the object, it sets the color property through the style collection.

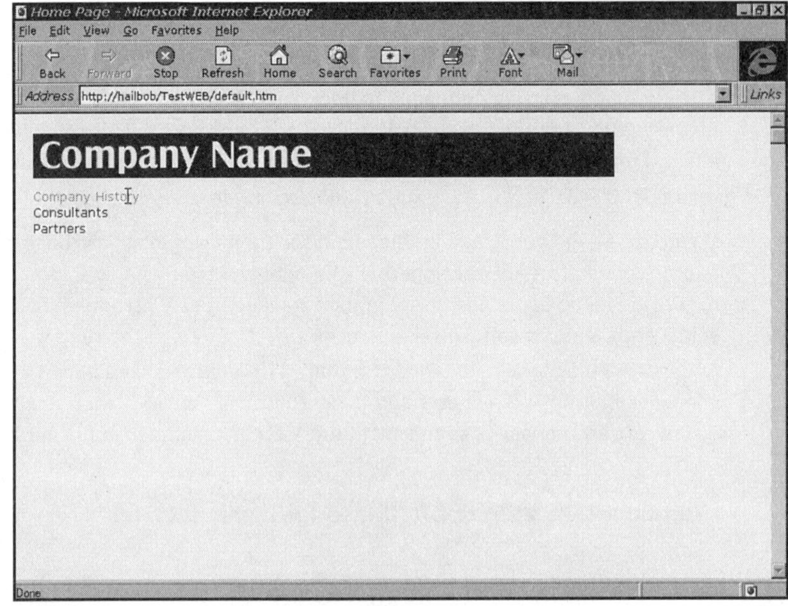

FIG. 18.4 Page with logo and menu in Internet Explorer, with a menu item highlighted. Feel free to play with various fonts, colors, and graphics as you build the sample.

Step 6: Adding the Submenu

Designing navigation structures for web sites has always been tricky—especially for larger sites. Developers have made innovative use of frames, tables, Java applets, ActiveX controls, and other objects in their quest for flexible, intuitive navigation. Dynamic HTML makes the process of developing such structures far easier. In this step, you'll add code for a submenu to your existing menu.

To begin, add the HTML for the submenu itself to your page. Replace the comment `insert the html for the submenu here` with the HTML in Listing 18.7.

Listing 18.7 HTML for the Submenu

```
<div id = "twochild" style = "display:none">
<font size = 1>
<a id = "four" onmouseover = "processover" onmouseout = "processout"
language = "VBScript">  capabilities</a><br>
<a id = "five" onmouseover = "processover" onmouseout = "processout"
language = "VBScript">  directory</a><br>
<font size = 2>
</div>
```

Notice that this chunk of HTML is contained within a `<div>` tag that has an `id` of `"twochild"`. The `"twochild"` ID is arbitrary—you can name it anything you want. In this case, the name makes it easy to address this element when the element with the ID `"two"` is clicked. The `<a>` tags contain references to the same `onmouseover` and `onmouseout` events that you used before; the items on the submenu will highlight the same as the elements on the main menu. Last, notice that the display style attribute is set to none. When you first view the page, the submenu won't show up.

Now add the code that makes the submenu work. First, replace the comment `routine to display/hide sub-menu items upon click event` with the VBScript routine in Listing 18.8.

Listing 18.8 VBScript Routine to Display/Hide the Submenu

```
Sub expandit
     heldID = window.event.srcElement.id & "child"
     set heldObj = document.all(heldID)
     if heldObj.style.display = "none" then
          heldObj.style.display = ""
     else
          heldObj.style.display = "none"
     end if
End Sub
```

Next, add a reference to the `expandit` routine that you just added to the page. You want the routine to be called when users click the second top-level menu item. Change the `<a>` tag with the ID `"two"` so that it reads as in Listing 18.9.

Listing 18.9 Addition of *onclick* Event Reference to HTML <a> Tag

```
<a id = "two" onclick = "expandit" onmouseover = "processover"
onmouseout = "processout" language = "VBScript">
```

Preview your page. Try clicking the second menu item. You should see the submenu appear and the items highlight when you pass the mouse pointer over them (check your screen against Figure 18.5). Note the method by which the `expandit` routine gets the ID for the submenu—it gathers the ID of the element on which users clicked and appends `child` to the ID. It then looks through the `all` collection for that new ID. This way, you can handle submenu items for each item on the top-level menu, submenu items for each item on the submenus, and so on, all with the same script. Because the submenu is contained within `<div>` tags nested inside the `<div>` tags for the top-level menu, when the submenu displays, the rest of the menu moves down automatically (Dynamic HTML handles this for you).

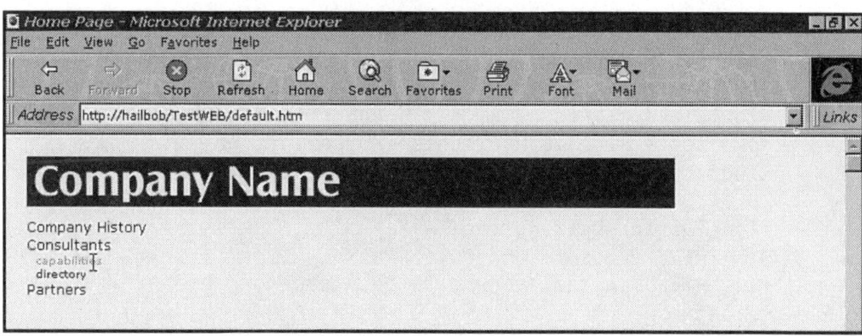

FIG. 18.5
The submenu visible on the page, with an item highlighted. As you build the sample, think of ways to further customize your page. For instance, you might want to make it so that the top-level items stay highlighted when expanded.

Step 7: Adding the Content Layers

Now that your navigation structure is complete, you need to add the content layers that will display when you click their respective menu items, as well as the functionality that controls their display. To begin, replace the comment `HTML for sections` with the HTML in Listing 18.10.

Listing 18.10 HTML for Main Content Layers

```
<div id = "partone"
style = "position:absolute;left:180;top:75;visibility:hidden;width:440">
<font face = verdana size = 4 color = midnightblue>
<p align = right>Company History<br>
<font size = 2>
<p align = left>
Placeholder for information about the company<p>
</font>
</div>
<div id = "partthree"
style = "position:absolute;left:180;top:75;visibility:hidden;width:440">
<font face = verdana size = 4 color = midnightblue>
<p align = right>Partners<br>
<font size = 2>
<p align = left>
Placeholder for general information about partnerships.
Sample partner program:<br>
<ul>
<li>
<!-- surround the following line with <a> tag to trigger popup -->
<font color = indianred>Microsoft<font color = midnightblue>
Solutions Provider Channel
</ul>
</font>
</div>
<div id = "partfour"
style = "position:absolute;left:180;top:75;visibility:hidden;width:440">
<font face = verdana size = 4 color = midnightblue>
<p align = right>Consultants - Capabilities<br>
<font size = 2>
<p align = left>
Sample information about consultant capabilities<p>
</font>
</div>
<div id = "partfive"
style = "position:absolute;left:180;top:75;visibility:hidden;width:440">
<font face = verdana size = 4 color = midnightblue>
<p align = right>Consultants - Directory<br>
<font size = 2>
<p align = left>
<!-- Tabular Data Control -->
<!-- HTML for sort controls -->
<!-- HTML for table bound to data source -->
</font>
</div>
```

Observe that the IDs for the sections you just added correspond to the items in your menu structure. They appear when their respective items are clicked and are hidden when other items are clicked. Also notice that the HTML you just added contains new comments, which will be replaced as you add more functionality to your page. Now add the rest of the code that displays the content layers.

First, you need to change the `<a>` tags referenced in Listing 18.11 to include the `processclick() onclick` event.

Listing 18.11 Changing the Menu Item *<a>* Tags to Add a *processclick()* Event Reference

```
<a id = "one" onclick = "processclick(1)" onmouseover = "processover"
onmouseout = "processout" language = "VBScript">

<a id = "three" onclick = "processclick(3)" onmouseover = "processover"
onmouseout = "processout" language = "VBScript">

<a id = "four" onclick = "processclick(4)" onmouseover = "processover"
onmouseout = "processout" language = "VBScript">

<a id = "five" onclick = "processclick(5)" onmouseover = "processover"
onmouseout = "processout" language = "VBScript">
```

Part III Ch 18

Notice that the calls to the `processclick()` routine include an index into an array. You need to add VBScript code to your page that provides the values for this array. What's more, this array and its contents need to be accessible to the entire page, as opposed to being accessible to just the routine you're calling (the array needs to have page-level scope). Replace the comment `page-level section array variable` with the VBScript code in Listing 18.12.

Listing 18.12 VBScript Code for a Page-Level Section Array Variable

```
Dim section(5)
section(1) = "one"
section(2) = "two"
section(3) = "three"
section(4) = "four"
section(5) = "five"
```

Finally, you need to add the actual `processclick()` routine itself. Replace the comment `routine to display content layers upon click event` with the VBScript routine in Listing 18.13.

Listing 18.13 VBScript Routine to Handle Menu Item Click Events

```
Sub processclick(num)
     for x = 1 to 5
          if x <> num and x <> 2 then
```

continues

Listing 18.13 Continued

```
                set holdObj = document.all("part" & section(x))
                holdObj.style.visibility = "hidden"
            end if
        next
        set holdObj = document.all("part" & section(num))
        holdObj.style.visibility = "visible"
End Sub
```

The `processclick()` routine loops through the index values into the section array. It grabs the ID for each element that wasn't clicked, appends `part` to the beginning, and sets the visibility to `hidden`. If the index number is 2 or the index clicked, the routine skips it (there's no "parttwo" content section, and you don't want to hide the one users clicked). The routine then grabs the ID for the one users did select, adds `part` to the beginning of the ID, and sets the visibility to `visible` for the section referenced by that ID alone. Try viewing the page to confirm that the content sections are displaying appropriately (check your page against Figure 18.6).

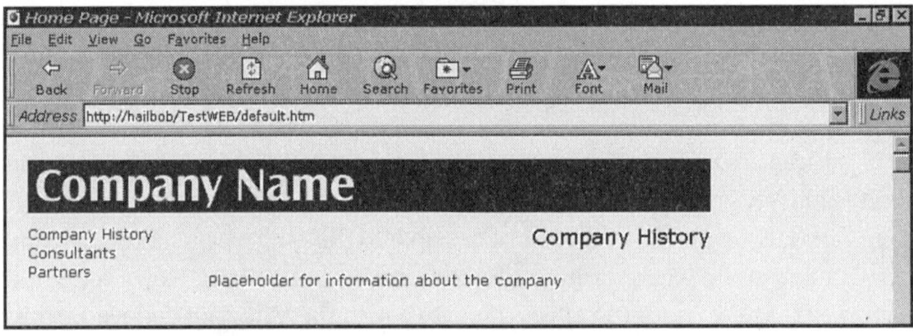

FIG. 18.6 A content layer exposed on the page. Again, this might be a good place for customization. You might want to make *Company History* remain highlighted so that you wouldn't need the title in the actual content layer.

Step 8: Adding the Pop-Up Window

Another challenge that web developers have had to face is the display of what can be a great deal of information. Users generally don't like to have to scroll through unwieldy amounts of information to get to what they want to see. Users also don't like to have to jump from page to page repeatedly to avoid scrolling. Dynamic HTML offers developers an easy way to design pages that get around both problems. In this step, you'll add a pop-up window that will appear when users pass the mouse pointer over a particular page section. To get started, replace the comment `HTML for popup window` with the HTML in Listing 18.14.

Listing 18.14 HTML for the Pop-Up Window Layer

```
<div id = "popup"
style = "position:absolute; left:50; top:305; visibility:hidden;width:550">
<center>
<table width = 550 border = 4 rules = none
bordercolor = midnightblue cellspacing = 0
```

```
cellpadding = 10 bgcolor = cornsilk>
<tr><td>
<font face = verdana size = 1 color = midnightblue>
<p id = "popuptext">sample text</p>
</font></td></tr>
</table></center>
</div>
```

Again, the code begins and ends with <div> tags. The opening <div> tag contains the same sort of absolute positioning information that you've used with other sections. Remember, you can change all these items programmatically; in this example, however, you'll be leaving the positioning attributes alone.

Next, you need to add the VBScript routine that displays and hides the pop-up window. Replace the comment `routines to handle popup window upon mouseover and mouseout events` with the VBScript code in Listing 18.15.

Listing 18.15 VBScript Routines to Display/Hide Pop-Up Layer

```
Sub processpopup(whichone)
     Set popupElement = document.rangeFromElement(popuptext)
     If whichone = "microsoft" Then
          holdText = "Some info about Microsoft Solution Provider Partners."
     End If
     popupElement.pasteHTML(holdText)
     popup.style.visibility = "visible"
End Sub
Sub wipepopup
     popup.style.visibility = "hidden"
End Sub
```


Finally, locate this HTML that follows the comment `surround the following line with <a> tag to trigger popup`:

```
<font color = indianred>Microsoft 
<font color = midnightblue>Solutions Provider Channel
```

Add the <a> tag so that it reads as in Listing 18.16.

Listing 18.16 HTML After Modification to Include Calls to Event Handlers to Handle the Pop-Up Window

```
<a onmouseover = "processpopup('microsoft')" onmouseout = "wipepopup"
language = "VBScript"><font color = indianred>Microsoft
<font color = midnightblue> Solutions Provider Channel</a>
```

The `processpopup()` routine first creates a text range from the <p> tag within the HTML for the pop-up window itself. The routine then takes the parameter that's passed when the routine is called and assigns the correct message to a variable. The routine then uses the `pasteHTML` method to change the text within the text range to the new text. Keep in mind you can paste HTML as well as plain text into the element. Finally, the routine displays the pop-up window. The `wipepopup` routine simply hides the window when the mouse exits the area that called the `processpopup` routine. Preview your page and check it against Figure 18.7.

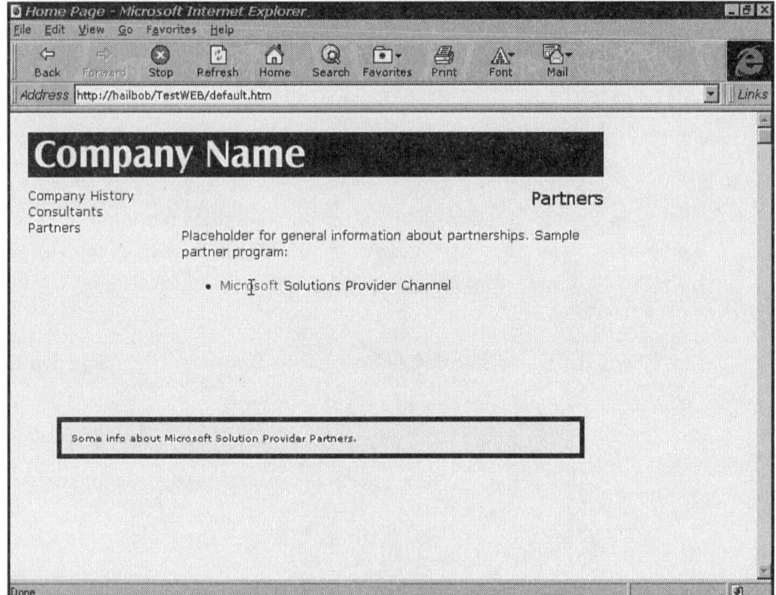

FIG. 18.7
The pop-up window. Another idea for customization is to make the pop-up window remain onscreen after the mouse moves off *Microsoft*, but allow users to drag it any place in the browser and click it to make it disappear.

Step 9: Adding the Data Connection and Bound Data Fields

Web pages become truly useful when they can access data on a server. For quite a while, developers used CGI scripts to access data. More recently, various technologies have been introduced to allow for database connectivity, such as Microsoft's Internet Database Connector and ActiveX Data Objects (ADO). These technologies required round trips to the server to get new data based on the application of filters, sorts, and queries.

With Dynamic HTML, Microsoft has introduced two new controls with which to access data via completely different means. With the Tabular Data control and the Advanced Data Connector, developers can bring down entire sets of data in one request from the server. Furthermore, page elements can now be bound to the data. By using these controls, developers can create pages that grab data once, present controls to users with which to select and sort subsets of the data, and redraw the page to reflect changes, all without returning to the server. Developers can also allow updates and additions to data sources via the bindings. These capabilities represent a fundamental change in the context of the web; in the near future, the line between web sites and applications that had previously been so distinct will fade away altogether.

ON THE WEB

The Advanced Data Connector and its use is beyond the scope of this chapter. See Microsoft's web site at **http://www.microsoft.com/adc** for information on the ADC.

In this example, you'll use the Tabular Data control; it's far easier to use quickly and is sufficient to demonstrate the principles of binding and refreshing without returning to the server. You'll build a table bound to a data source that will display when users click the directory submenu item. First, you need to ensure that your data source is in place. Make a file called data.txt from the comma-delimited text in Listing 18.17.

Listing 18.17 Data File for the Data Source

```
FirstName,LastName,Address,City,State,Zip,Phone,Fax,EMail
Chris,Stevens,102 NE Bernard Street,St.Louis,Missouri,63102,555-9348,555-9283,
➥cstevens
Lud,Mises,1 Chicago Avenue,St. Louis,Missouri,63182,555-3849,555-2893,lmises
Maxwell,Roach,383 Waltz Street,Cincinnati,Ohio,83728,555-2938,555-8827,mroach
Ray,Snyder,83 First Street,Kansas City,Kansas,77363,555-8837,555-8837,rsnyder
```

Part III Ch 18

Ensure that the data file is in the same directory as your page. Next, you need to place the Tabular Data control object. Replace the comment `Tabular Data Control` with the HTML in Listing 18.18.

Listing 18.18 HTML for the Tabular Data Control Object

```
<OBJECT ID=TDC1 CLASSID="clsid:333C7BC4-460F-11D0-BC04-0080C7055A83" WIDTH=0
➥HEIGHT=0>
<PARAM NAME=DataURL Value="Data.txt">
<PARAM NAME=TextQualifier Value=",">
<PARAM NAME=UseHeader Value=True>
</OBJECT>
```

The `DataURL` parameter specifies your data source, the `TextQualifier` parameter specifies what character is being used to delimit your data, and the `UseHeader` parameter specifies whether the first line of your data source contains field names. Next, you need to add the HTML for the table itself. Replace the comment

```
HTML for table bound to data source
```

with the HTML in Listing 18.19.

Listing 18.19 HTML for a Table with Cells Bound to the Tabular Data Control

```
<center>
<TABLE ID=Table1 DATASRC=#TDC1 border = 0 width = 440>
<TBODY>
```

continues

Listing 18.19 Continued

```
<TR><TD width = 440 colspan = 2 bgcolor = midnightblue>
<font face = verdana size = 2 color = white>
<strong><SPAN DATAFLD=FirstName></SPAN>
 <SPAN DATAFLD=LastName></SPAN></strong>
</TD></tr>
<tr><TD width = 220>
<font face = verdana size = 2 color = midnightblue>
<SPAN DATAFLD=Address></SPAN></TD>
<TD width = 220>
<font face = verdana size = 2 color = midnightblue>
Phone: <SPAN DATAFLD=Phone></SPAN>
</TD> </TR>
<tr><TD>
<font face = verdana size = 2 color = midnightblue>
<SPAN DATAFLD=City></SPAN>, 
<SPAN DATAFLD = State></SPAN> 
<SPAN DATAFLD=ZIP></SPAN></TD>
<TD><font face = verdana size = 2 color = midnightblue>
Fax: <SPAN DATAFLD=Fax></SPAN>
</TD></TR>
<tr><TD>
<font face = verdana size = 2 color = midnightblue>
 
</TD><TD>
<font face = verdana size = 2 color = midnightblue>
EMail: <SPAN DATAFLD=EMail></SPAN>
</TD></TR>
</TBODY>
</TABLE>
</center>
```

Preview the page and select the directory submenu item. Check your file against Figure 18.8.

Now look back at the HTML for the table. Notice that the HTML specifies only table cells for a single record from the data source. When a table is bound to a data source with the `DATASRC` attribute (in the `<TABLE>` tag), Dynamic HTML knows to repeat the contents of the table enough times to display all the data in the data source. The actual fields in the data source are referenced with the `DATAFLD` attributes in the `<SPAN>` tags. The `<SPAN>` tag tells Internet Explorer that it contains a distinct unit; the `DATAFLD` attribute within the tag indicates that this field will be acquired from the data source specified by the `DATASRC` attribute in the `<TABLE>` tag. Aside from these additions, the rest of the code for the table is standard HTML. Note that the HTML that defines the table is contained within the `<DIV>` tags for the section with the ID `partfive`.

Step 10: Adding Sort Capability to the Data Presentation

At this point, the display of data is static; it allows no user interactivity. The last step is to add controls that allow users to sort the data. Typically, this is when you would have to assume a trip back to the server; with Dynamic HTML, this trip is no longer necessary. First, add the table that contains the sort controls. Replace the comment `HTML for sort controls` with the HTML in Listing 18.20.

FIG. 18.8
A table containing bound data. Here, you might make the email field a link that users could click to send email automatically.

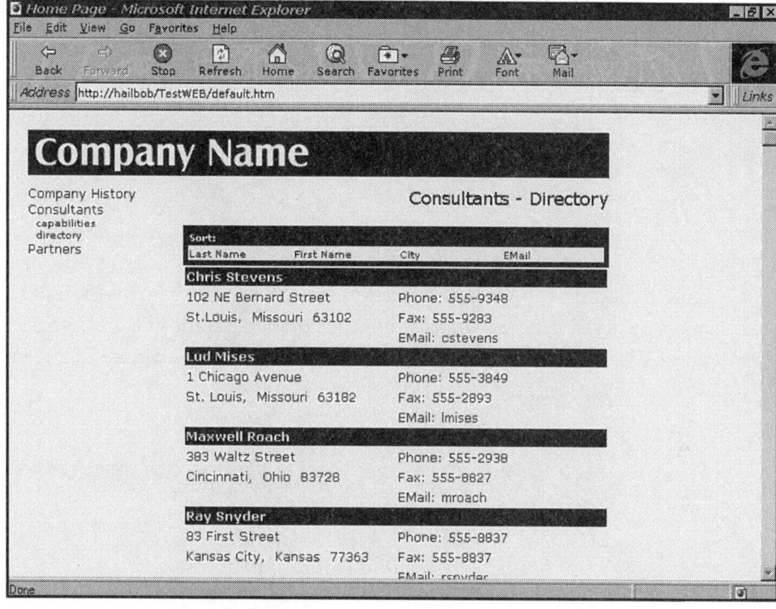

Listing 18.20 HTML for a Table Containing Sort Controls

```
<table width = 440 border = 4
bordercolor = midnightblue rules = none
cellspacing = 0>
<tr><td valign = top bgcolor = midnightblue
colspan = 4>
<font face = verdana size = 1 color = white>
<strong>Sort:</strong>
</font></td></tr>
<tr><td valign = top bgcolor = cornsilk width = 110>
<font face = verdana size = 1 color = midnightblue>
<span id = "lastname" onclick = "applysort"
onmouseover = "processover"
onmouseout = "processout" language = vbscript>
Last Name</span></td>
<td valign = top bgcolor = cornsilk width = 110>
<font face = verdana size = 1 color = midnightblue>
<span id = "first" onclick = "applysort"
onmouseover = "processover"
onmouseout = "processout" language = vbscript>
First Name</span></td>
<td valign = top bgcolor = cornsilk width = 110>
<font face = verdana size = 1 color = midnightblue>
<span id = "city" onclick = "applysort"
onmouseover = "processover"
onmouseout = "processout" language = vbscript>
City</span></td>
```

continues

Listing 18.20 Continued

```
<td valign = top bgcolor = cornsilk width = 110>
<font face = verdana size = 1 color = midnightblue>
<span id = "email" onclick = "applysort"
onmouseover = "processover"
onmouseout = "processout" language = vbscript>
EMail</span></td></font></tr>
</table>
```

Notice that the `<SPAN>` tags contain references to the same handlers for the `onmouseover` and `onmouseout` events, as well as a new `applysort` handler for the `onclick` event. Next, add the `applysort` handler by replacing the comment `routine to sort table contents via tabular data control` with the VBScript code in Listing 18.21.

Listing 18.21 Handling Data Sorting in the Tabular Data Control

```
Sub applysort
     heldID = window.event.srcElement.id
     set heldObj = document.all(heldID)
     if heldID = "lastname" then
         TDC1.SortAscending=true
        TDC1.SortColumn="LastName"
        TDC1.Reset
     elseif heldID = "first" then
          TDC1.SortAscending = true
          TDC1.SortColumn = "FirstName"
          TDC1.Reset
     elseif heldID = "city" then
          TDC1.SortAscending = true
          TDC1.SortColumn = "city"
          TDC1.Reset
     elseif heldID = "email" then
          TDC1.SortAscending = true
          TDC1.SortColumn = "EMail"
          TDC1.Reset
     End If
End Sub
```

Preview the page and go to the section that contains the table; check your page against Figure 18.9. Click the fields in the new sort control table at the top of the page. You'll see the data in the table sort in accordance with the field you clicked. This happens without a trip back to the data source.

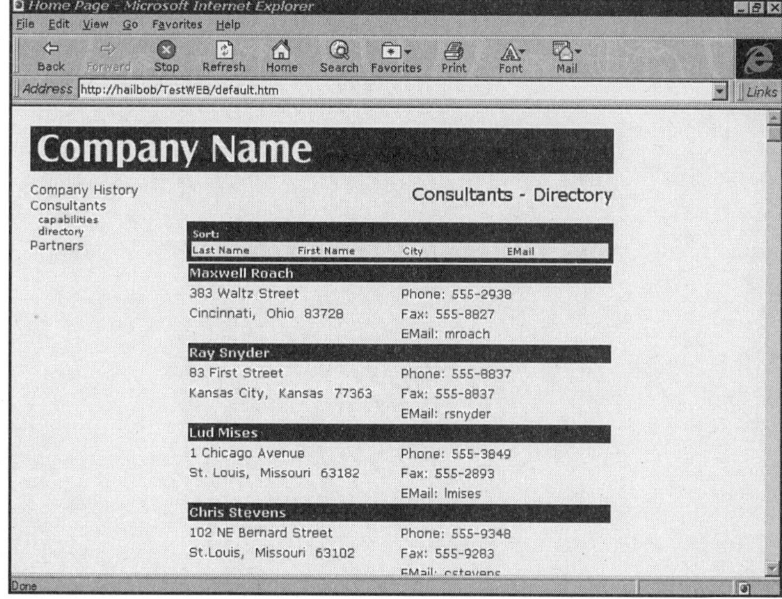

FIG. 18.9
The table containing bound data after the city sort is applied. A good idea for this type of page is to provide filtering as well as sorting capability.

From Here...

As you've probably surmised, web development has taken a dramatic step forward with the advent of Dynamic HTML. The range of possibilities available to web developers dwarfs the limited set of options that came before; combined with Active Server Pages, server-side objects and scripting, and so forth, the day is fast approaching when the line between traditional development and web development dissolves altogether.

- Chapter 13, "An Inside Look at Active Server Pages and Internet Information Server," discusses the use of Active Server Pages on IIS and shows you how to use ASP.
- Chapter 14, "Developing Active Content with Visual InterDev," shows you how to use Visual InterDev to create dynamic web sites.
- Chapter 15, "Advanced Visual InterDev Concepts," describes some of the more advanced features of Visual InterDev.
- Chapter 16, "Visual InterDev Design-Time Controls," discusses the design-time controls that ship with Visual InterDev (the Data Command, Data Range, and Image controls), and their use in Web pages.
- Chapter 17, "Server-Side Programming in an I-net Environment," shows you more about writing code for use with Active Server Pages.

CHAPTER 19

Enabling Existing Applications for I-net Environments

by Azam A. Mirza

Traditional software development and I-nets

Learn about the differences between traditional systems and the new component-based architecture. See how you can leverage the power of components to build I-net applications that take advantage of the latest technologies.

ActiveX documents

Understand the ActiveX document concept. See how to build ActiveX documents and understand their features and limitations.

Application migration issues

Learn about Visual Basic's capabilities and resources for migrating existing applications to the I-net environment.

ActiveX Document Migration Wizard

See how the ActiveX Document Migration Wizard converts existing Visual Basic applications into I-net applications.

The three years since the Internet revolution started have radically changed the landscape for software development. Just when client/server technology was taking hold in the enterprise, the World Wide Web and its technologies have introduced a new metaphor for building, deploying, and using applications.

With its support for standards-based component software such as Java applets and ActiveX controls, its standards-based client user interface through the web browser, and its standards-based communications protocols, the web is an exciting opportunity for building applications that can be truly heterogeneous across the enterprise. By standardizing the least important aspects of software development, the web takes the focus away from delivery and presentation and puts it in the content being presented. As a developer, you don't have to worry about how to transport the content or how to fashion the user interface; instead, you can devote your efforts to building the application logic that best handles a given scenario. However, content delivery and a compelling user interface are also very important to the creation of a successful web site.

The World Wide Web also presents an enormous amount of risk for enterprises moving into Internet-based software development. The rapid pace of technology change and the unending stream of product and standards upgrades makes it difficult to stay current and relevant.

Most organizations today have a large number of applications and existing systems running in the enterprise. These systems range anywhere from "old" legacy systems, such as COBOL and FORTRAN programs, to "new" legacy systems, such as Visual Basic and C applications. The last few years have seen a push to move from legacy systems to the client/server environment. Organizations have spent a considerable amount of time, money, and resources in updating their old systems for the 21st century, only to find out that the Internet has rendered their best-laid plans obsolete.

Few organizations are willing to embark on reengineering their systems from scratch again. Instead, they're looking for ways to leverage their existing applications for the Internet. Microsoft's strategy for Internet development is simple and has followed a clear path since day one: leverage the tools and technologies of today and Internet-enable them for the future. Microsoft has web-enabled its entire line of server, client, productivity software, and development tools over the last two years. It also has filled the gaps in its product line by introducing web tools such as FrontPage, Visual InterDev, and Internet Explorer to provide a comprehensive and complete solution.

Rather than retrain software professionals, you can use the existing expertise of your developers in tools such as Visual C++ and Visual Basic to make them successful web developers. The following sections discuss how to identify existing applications as candidates for migration to the Internet and how to follow a step-by-step method for doing so regardless of what development tool the applications were written in. Lastly, this chapter tackles the migration issues in the light of the Visual Basic development environment and how Microsoft provides tools and techniques for Internet-enabling your existing VB application. ■

Migrating Existing Systems to Component Architectures

The concepts of components and multitier architectures have been the main focus of software development recently. Most software developers recognize the potential and benefits of the component-based software development approach. However, most organizations have a large installed base of legacy applications that have no concept of componentization or multitier architectures. To move into the Internet world, organizations have to rewrite or move their existing applications to the web.

The ease or difficulties of moving your existing applications to the I-net environment depend largely on the languages these applications are written in and the platforms they run on.

Legacy Applications

Traditional legacy applications are still the most widely deployed and used environment. Legacy code isn't defined by the language used or the platform being supported, however—it's identified by the method used to develop the applications. Most legacy code is written in COBOL or FORTRAN but can also include procedural programs written in C and BASIC. Most legacy applications run entirely on the server side and use the client only for display and user input. Figure 19.1 depicts a typical legacy application environment.

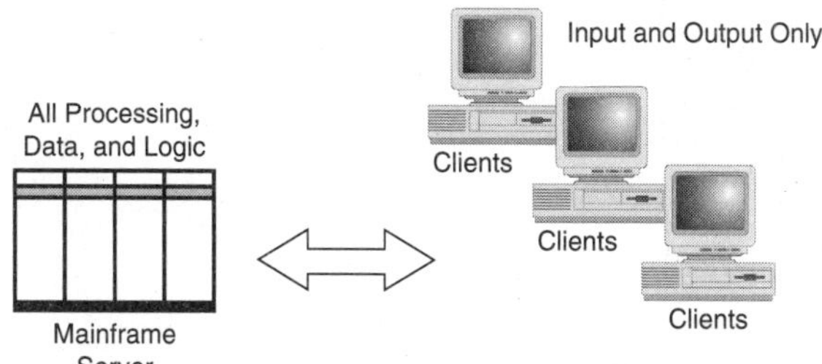

FIG. 19.1
Legacy systems typically placed all processing logic on the server side.

For applications written in legacy environments with third-generation languages such as COBOL or FORTRAN, it's usually a simple matter of converting the business logic into modules that can be encapsulated into components or accessed through a wrapper built by using a language such as Visual C++. A lot of work is being done in developing connectivity mechanisms for web-enabling old legacy platforms.

This discussion does beg the question, why use legacy applications and languages? Millions of lines of legacy code are in production environments, and millions more are added each year. Organizations have spent considerable time and resources building and deploying these systems and training professionals in these technologies. It's not practical or possible to throw away all that effort and expertise. For that reason, it's best to leverage these applications—by developing methods to move them into the new environment, and by building wrappers around them to provide access to the built-in logic and at the same time provide a means for moving into the latest tools and technologies. Figure 19.2 shows a sample scenario for leveraging the power of existing legacy applications in the World Wide Web environment.

As mentioned earlier, a large number of organizations are still engaged in maintaining or enhancing legacy applications. If these organizations were to move completely away from developing any new applications with legacy tools, there would still be a need to maintain current production systems. Usually, the current developers are entrusted with the task of doing maintenance work, although most developers aren't happy doing just maintenance work. They can integrate their skills and knowledge of the existing systems into the migration efforts to new systems by working with the new development teams.

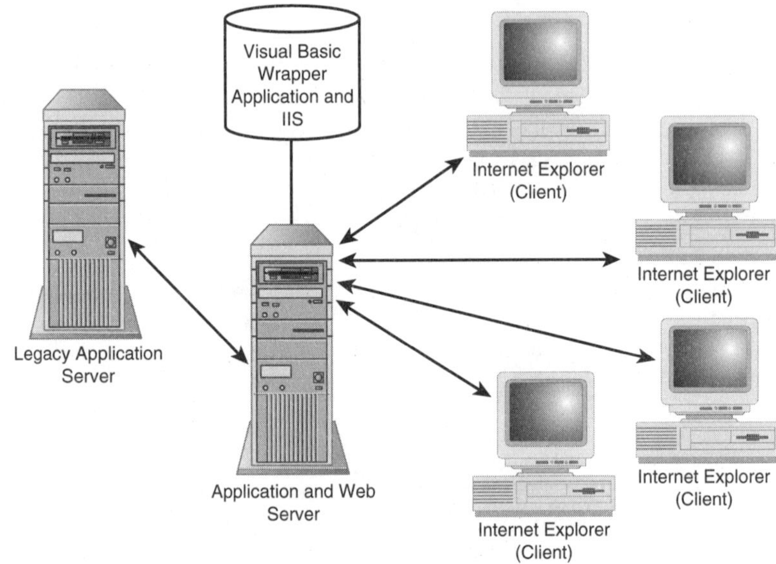

FIG. 19.2
You can use Visual Basic to build wrapper DLLs around legacy code for access from a web browser.

Traditional Client/Server

With the advancement in computer technology and the advent of personal computers, computer systems have moved away from the mainframe legacy model toward the networked client/server approach. In client/server systems, processing isn't limited to the servers on the back end, but is distributed among the client machines and the server machines. Figure 19.3 shows the traditional client/server environment.

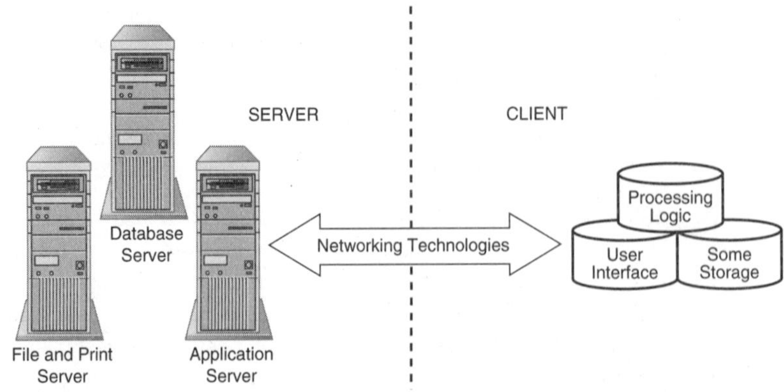

FIG. 19.3
In traditional client/server architectures, clients usually encapsulate the bulk of the processing logic, and the server stores the data.

The client/server process takes the work away from the server and distributes it more judiciously by using software components that communicate with each other with well-defined interfaces and networking protocols. The client/server approach also allows you to take advantage of the platform on which the various components will be deployed. The client/server approach requires a major shift in the development thinking process. Rather than build large, monolithic, standalone systems, you have to begin thinking in terms of components and modules that individually provide various functionality and combine to make a complete system.

The development of each component in the client/server environment can be viewed as a small standalone project independent of other projects.

Multitier Systems

Multitier systems extend the traditional client/server concept. A *multitier design* is one in which an application's implementation is divided into three distinct areas: user interface, business logic, and database system. These three components were initially referred to as *three-tier client/server*. However, the extension of three-tier in multitier is a simple matter of distributing the business logic and database systems across multiple machines in the enterprise in the form of components that perform specific tasks.

Figure 19.4 shows a sample multitier client/server architecture. This division of services allows you to logically separate the application and introduce a layer of abstraction between the enterprise data and the clients that access it.

FIG. 19.4
The multitier client/server architecture allows component-based units to provide different functionality.

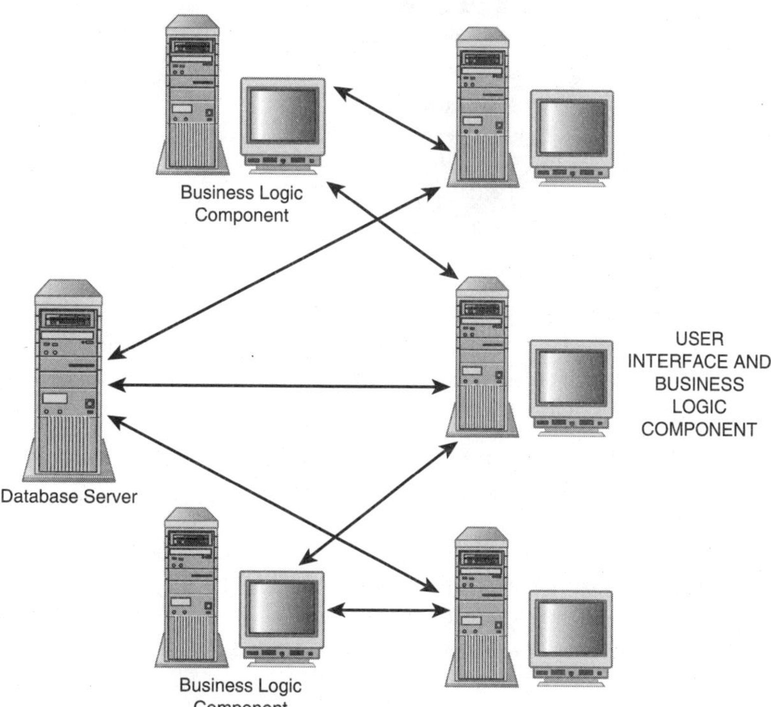

User Interface The user interface is the visual part of a multitier architecture responsible for generating output on client machines and obtaining user input. It usually resides on client machines and is responsible for displaying data to users, allowing users to manipulate the data and communicating with the business logic components to validate or generate appropriate data. The forms, controls, menus, and messages displayed on user machines are all part of the user interface.

In client/server systems, developers built from scratch user interface elements. In the web-enabled environment, however, the web browser acts as a container for user interface elements. Figure 19.5 shows a typical user interface for a multitier web-enabled application.

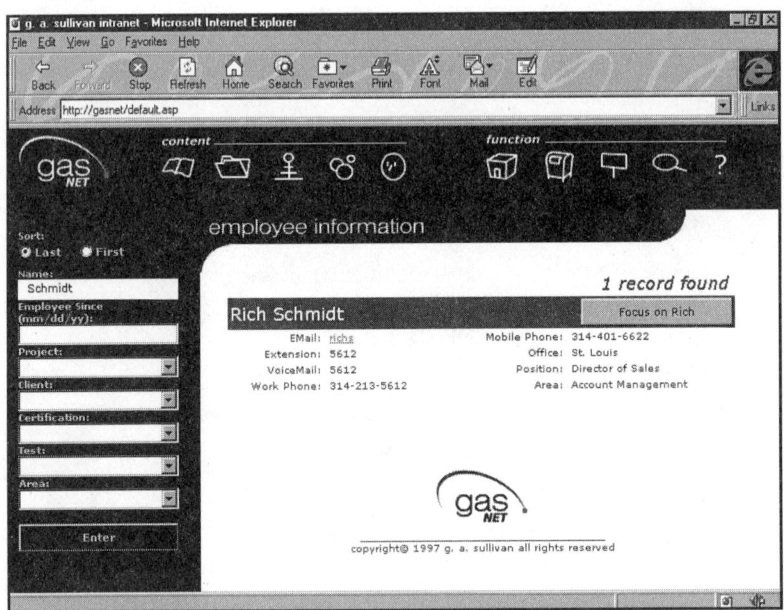

FIG. 19.5
Internet Explorer acts as the client component in web applications.

Business Logic The business logic component of a multitier architecture houses the business-specific rules. *Business rules* are components designed to interact with the database to retrieve and present data to the user based on defined rules. Typical examples of business logic components include

- Data-validation routines, such as validating user input data
- Calculation routines such as calculating the sales tax on goods sold
- Business-specific functions such as faxing documents

Business logic components are nonvisual, don't have any user interface elements such as menus and text boxes, and usually reside on distributed machines across the enterprise. OLE Automation servers (also referred to as ActiveX Server Components) are examples of a mechanism used for distributing business logic.

TIP Visual Basic Enterprise Edition includes samples that illustrate the use of business logic components in a real-world application. Refer to the Visual Basic documentation on how you can install and run these samples.

Database System The database system is primarily responsible for storing and providing data. Typical examples include the Relational Database Management Systems (RDBMS) and other storage media. The database is responsible only for data storage, recovery, validity, integrity, and replication. You can use multiple database systems within a single system, each handling the data requirements for a specific purpose. Database systems are true back-end systems that don't include any user interface or business logic systems.

Database systems hold a very prominent place in the Internet-enabled application arena. As the World Wide Web moves from static content to a dynamic, ever-changing applications-based environment, more and more emphasis will be placed on using back-end databases to store data and information being supplied to users. The tight integration between Microsoft SQL Server and Internet Information Server is a good indicator of how important database systems will be in the Internet world. Also, tools such as Visual InterDev, Visual Basic, and Visual C++ provide numerous powerful methods for accessing data stored in corporate databases from web-enabled applications. These methods include the tried-and-true ODBC (Open Database Connectivity) method and the DAO (Data Access Objects), RDO (Remote Data Objects), and ADO (ActiveX Data Objects) methods.

▶ **See** Chapter 3, "Creating Database-Aware Applications with Visual Studio," **p. 55**

▶ **See** "Database Development Tools," **p. 433**

Component-Based Systems in I-net Environments

The component-based approach to software development splits the development process into a bunch of small projects geared toward building each individual component. The concept is to be able to share these components across multiple applications, providing the much-coveted reuse of the services provided by the components. The task of building a business solution from these components is what results in a standalone application.

NOTE The concept of sharable, reusable components for building applications was first introduced with Visual Basic in the form of VBXs (Visual Basic Custom Controls). OCXs (OLE Custom Controls), ActiveX controls, and OLE Automation Server are all enhancements of the original idea adapted to provide compatibility with emerging technologies such as the World Wide Web.

Components are usually compiled binary objects that provide runtime reuse and sharing of objects. The component-based approach provides a multitude of advantages over traditional software development methods, including the following:

- Reusable components can be written in many languages, including Borland Delphi, Visual Basic, Visual C++, and Visual J++. This provides a great deal of flexibility in terms of development tool selection and vendor independence. Organizations can best use the expertise of their developers by leveraging the tool they're most familiar and comfortable with.

- Components can be deployed across an enterprise in a distributed fashion. This allows for maximum use of resources in terms of CPU processing power, network bandwidth, and highest performance. An application can use components residing on various database servers, business logic servers, and client machines to accomplish its tasks.
- By building reusable generic components, organizations can take advantage of a high level of reuse by using these components across multiple applications.
- Developers can specialize in whether they want to be component builders or component users to build business solutions.

As noted, the component-based software development methodology has been in existence since Visual Basic was first introduced. With the World Wide Web's popularity, Microsoft has moved quickly to adapt its component architecture to embrace the web. With the introduction of ActiveX and the embracing of Java technology through the introduction of Visual J++, Microsoft provides a strong suite of solutions for building component-based web applications. Figure 19.6 illustrates the ActiveX strategy for building component solutions for the web-based environment.

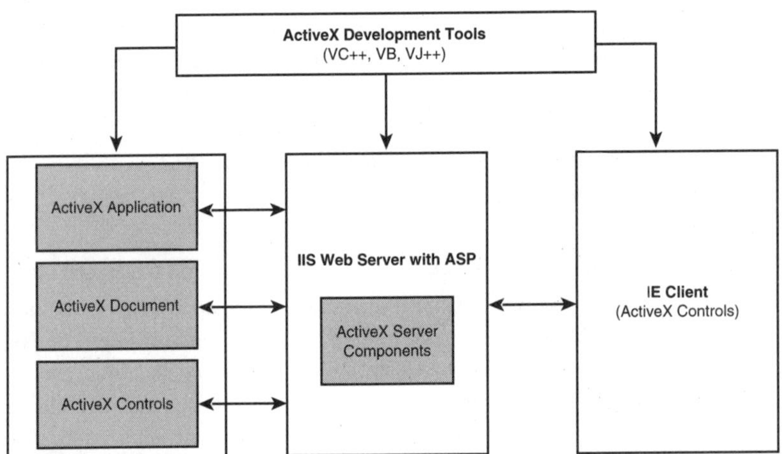

FIG. 19.6
ActiveX is a set of technologies that let you build applications for the I-net environment.

You can develop ActiveX components in any number of tools (including Visual C++, Visual Basic, and Visual J++) and can run them on a number of platforms (including Microsoft Windows 95, Windows NT, Macintosh, and UNIX). Combining Java and OLE, ActiveX provides promising capabilities for building I-net applications while extending and enhancing the capabilities of existing tools and environments.

ActiveX allows developers to freely mix and match controls created in different development environments on clients and servers. For example, you can develop an ActiveX control in Visual Basic that provides charting capabilities on the client, an ActiveX server component that calculates the sales growth rates for the company in Visual C++, and use Visual InterDev to use both of these two components as part of a web-based application.

▶ **See** Chapter 5, "Creating ActiveX Components with Visual Basic," **p. 131**

▶ **See** Chapter 6, "Creating Components with Visual C++," **p. 173**

▶ **See** Chapter 14, "Developing Active Content with Visual InterDev," **p. 389**

Web applications based on ActiveX components and Java provide benefits for all aspects of software development. End users benefit by gaining dynamic, content-rich applications for I-nets through the use of a single client interface such as Internet Explorer. You can leverage existing expertise and knowledge of tools such as Visual Basic and Visual C++ to build powerful components and applications for use in the I-net environment. Organizations gain the benefits of an open, standards-based environment and technologies, retain the investments in existing systems, and are able to build new applications with the exciting new technologies.

Migrating Visual Basic Applications to the I-net Environment

The first steps in migrating Visual Basic applications to the I-net environment involves identifying and targeting the project candidates for such an undertaking. The following are some guidelines that you can use to determine the most appropriate migration method:

- *ActiveX control.* Identify modules that perform a specific function as part of a DLL or executable and convert them to an ActiveX control (.ocx file). For example, a standalone form that displays a graph of information can be converted into an ActiveX control that you can use as a client-side control as part of your web applications. Figure 19.7 shows a custom ActiveX control usage scenario.

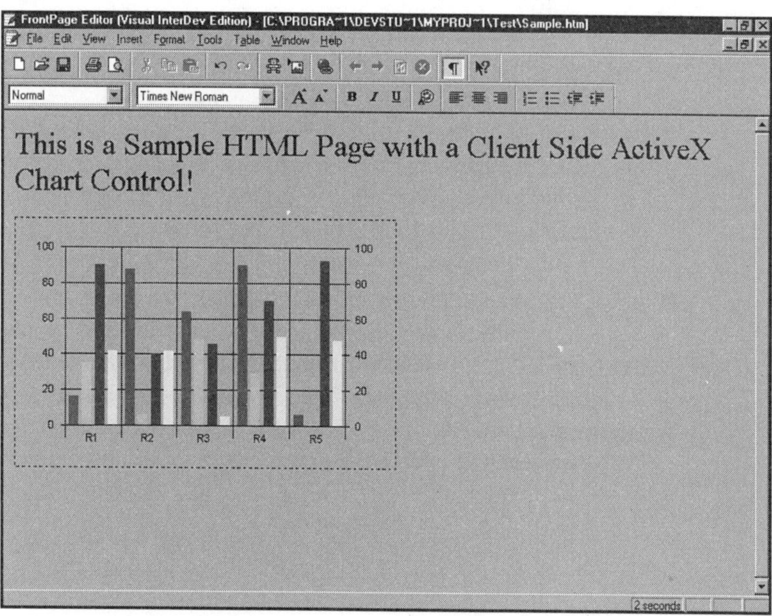

FIG. 19.7
You can use FrontPage 97 to incorporate ActiveX controls in your applications.

This method isn't exclusive to Visual Basic and can just as easily be applied to Visual C++ or other tools. However, other tools can't match the ease associated with doing it in Visual Basic.

▶ **See** Chapter 5, "Creating ActiveX Components with Visual Basic," **p. 131**

- *ActiveX DLL.* An ActiveX DLL is nothing more than an in-process OLE server that runs in the same address space as the client that invokes it. For example, if you have a Visual Basic class or module that provides database functions, it can be converted to an in-process ActiveX DLL to be run in the address space of a calling application that can use it to communicate with the database server. Figure 19.8 shows how an in-process ActiveX component communicates with a client application or another in-process component.

▶ **See** "COM Objects Across Process and Network Boundaries," **p. 118**

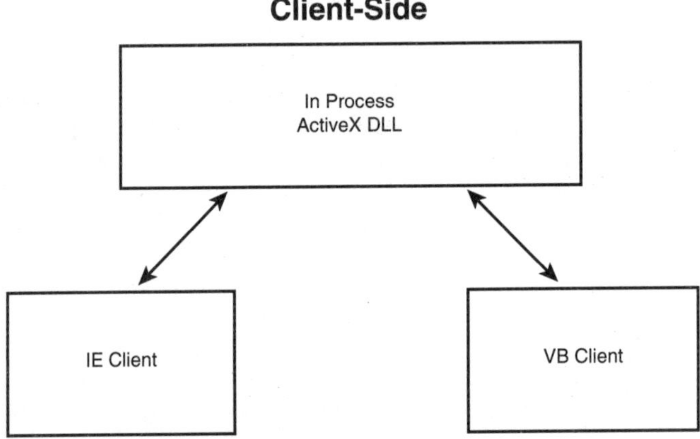

FIG. 19.8
An ActiveX DLL can encapsulate a set of common business rules that can be loaded as part of an application.

- *ActiveX EXE.* An ActiveX EXE is an out-of-process OLE server that runs in its own address space on the client machine, on the server, or on a remote machine in a distributed network environment. For example, a remotely installed ActiveX EXE can provide the functionality for calculating the premiums for a given automobile insurance policy. The EXE can run on a single machine and service premium calculation requests from a bunch of client applications. Figure 19.9 illustrates the out-of-process mechanism.
- *ActiveX documents.* An ActiveX document is a component that can be contained within an ActiveX container. A document is actually a fully functional application with data persistence and storage capabilities. For example, a Microsoft Word document is an ActiveX document that's created and subsequently accessed through a container application, namely Winword.exe. However, a Word document also can be accessed through other containers, such as Internet Explorer. Figure 19.10 illustrates the ActiveX document concept.

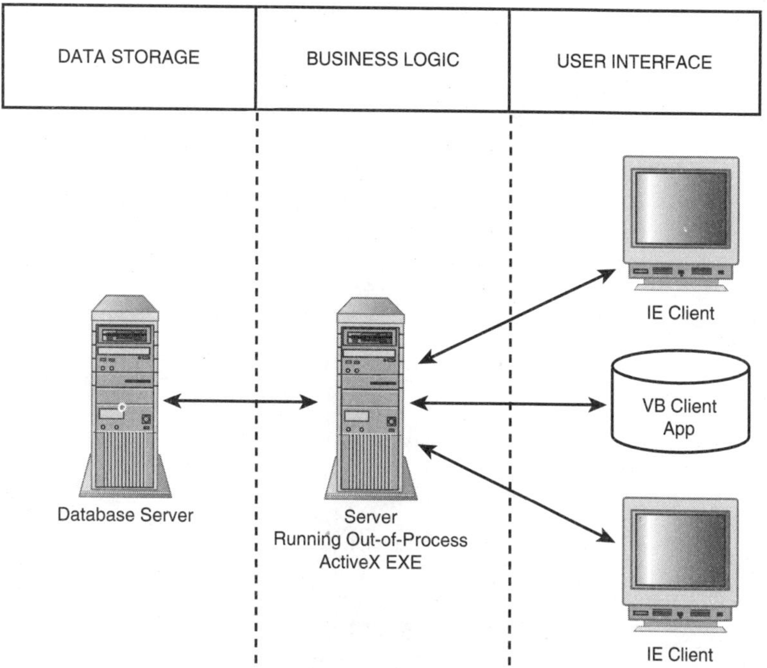

FIG. 19.9
An out-of-process ActiveX component can provide server-side processing functionality.

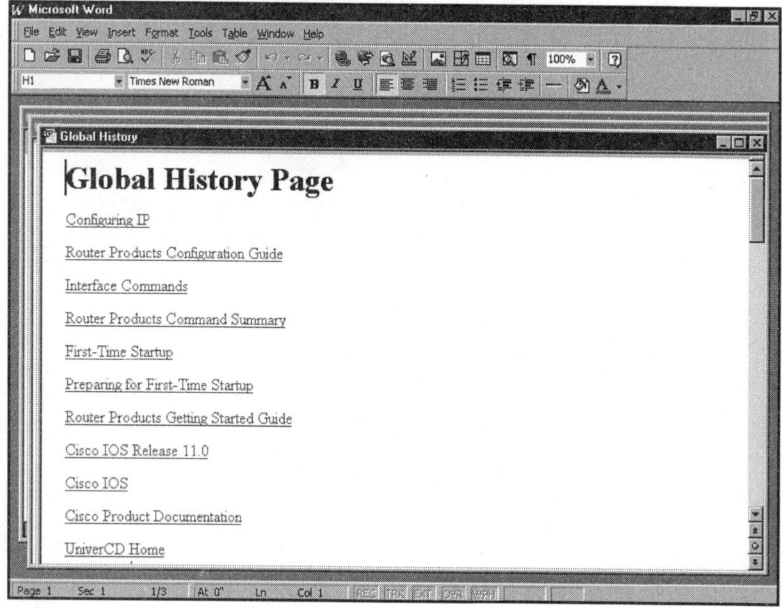

FIG. 19.10
Microsoft Word documents are an example of an ActiveX document and container application concept.

The rest of this chapter concentrates specifically on the ActiveX documents concepts and how you can use them to migrate your entire applications over to the I-net environment.

ActiveX Documents

ActiveX documents are the oldest concept from the original OLE specification. All Microsoft products, such as Word and Excel, are based on the Document View architecture. Visual Basic ActiveX documents take the Microsoft Word metaphor to a new level and really blur the line between a *document* and an *application*. Visual Basic ActiveX documents are truly applications that behave like documents. Figure 19.11 shows an ActiveX document within the Internet Explorer environment.

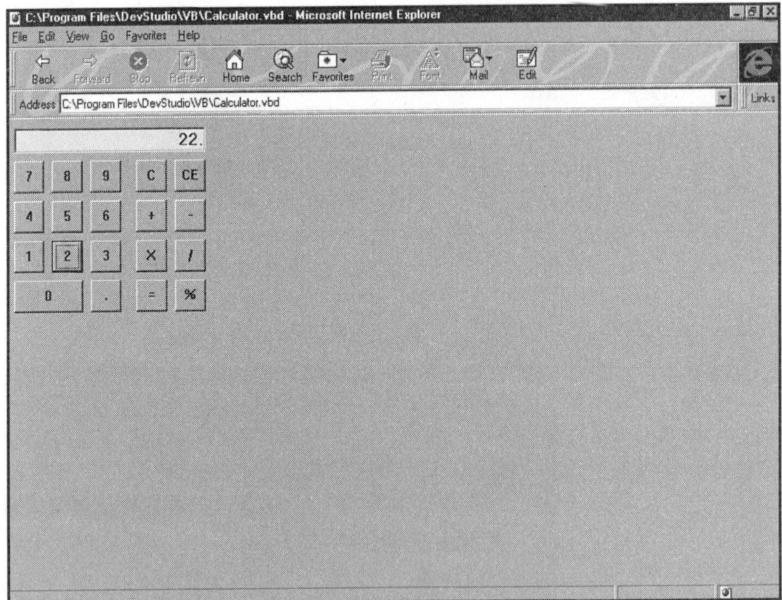

FIG. 19.11
You can contain Visual Basic ActiveX documents in an ActiveX container such as Internet Explorer.

When you create an ActiveX document-based project, you're creating a Visual Basic document that can be contained within a container. When you compile a Visual Basic ActiveX document project, a Visual Basic document file (.vbd) and its corresponding container/server (an ActiveX DLL or EXE) are created. The document file and the DLL or EXE file are similar to the Word .doc file and the Winword.exe application relationship. The .vbd file provides the document, and the DLL or EXE provides the objects that allow another ActiveX container such as Internet Explorer to host, view, and activate the document.

Several advantages to using ActiveX documents as a means of migrating your current applications to the I-net environment include the following:

- You can leverage the knowledge of Visual Basic developers within your organization. Your developers don't have to learn another programming language, such as HTML, CGI, or Java.

- The full Visual Basic development environment is available to you, including the Visual Basic code window, debugger, and compiler.
- You can create ActiveX documents that run in Internet Explorer.
- The ActiveX component can contain all the necessary code to deliver the functionality of a particular business function from a single location in the form of a component object.
- The visual nature of the Visual Basic development allows you to create document layouts with extreme ease and speed. In contrast, coding an HTML document without the help of GUI tools such as FrontPage 97 takes practice and guesswork.
- Support for the `Hyperlink` object allows an ActiveX document to request that the container (if it's `Hyperlink`-aware) navigate to another ActiveX document or a web site.
- Support for the `AsyncRead` method is available. The method begins an asynchronous transfer of data, allowing other code to execute while the data is retrieved. This method is useful in allowing the application to process other code while the page is loading into the browser window. For example, the page might be retrieving data from a database during initial load. With the `AsyncRead` method, you can load the rest of the page while the application retrieves the data from the database.

The following section discusses the details of creating an ActiveX document by using Visual Basic 5.0.

Creating ActiveX Documents The process of creating an ActiveX document is like creating any other project in Visual Basic. To create an ActiveX document project, follow these steps:

1. Start a new ActiveX document EXE project. By default, these template projects contain a single UserDocument, which is the integral part of an ActiveX document.
2. Add controls to the UserDocument and code for the controls just as you would when creating a regular Visual Basic form or dialog box. Figure 19.12 shows a UserDocument with various controls placed on it.

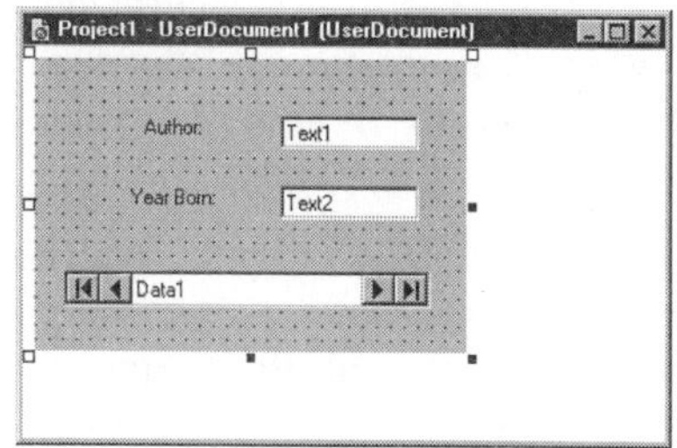

FIG. 19.12 An ActiveX document can contain other ActiveX controls to provide required functionality.

3. You can add more forms, code modules, or UserDocument objects to the project.
4. Test and debug your project by running the application and viewing the document in the target container such as Internet Explorer.

   To test your document, run the project, start Internet Explorer, and open the .vbd file created that's stored in the Visual Basic root directory (C:\Program Files\DevStudio\VB). The document will then be loaded within Internet Explorer.

Figure 19.13 shows Internet Explorer with the document loaded.

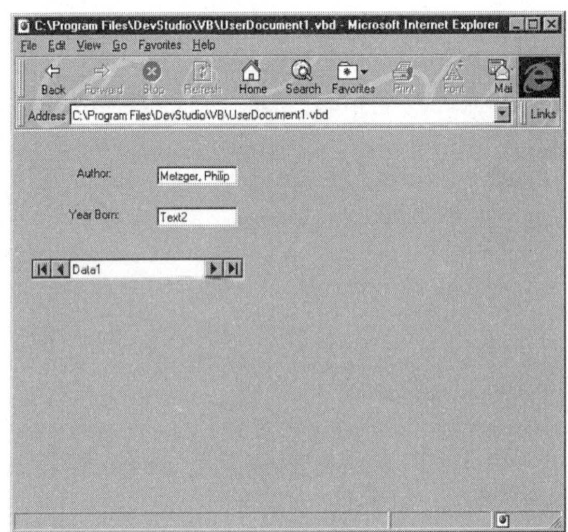

FIG. 19.13 Internet Explorer functions as the container that hosts the ActiveX document.

5. After you debug the project, compile it to create the document file (.vbd) and the in-process (.dll) or out-of-process (.exe) component.
6. When finished, you can deploy the ActiveX document for use by your applications.

▶ **See** "Registering Your Components," **p. 114**

The .exe or .dll file contains the actual compiled code. Initially, the .vbd file contains the class ID of the .exe or the .dll file. If you choose to allow users to save data (using `PropertyBag`), the data will also be stored in the .vbd file. Users can view your ActiveX document by opening the .vbd file in a host application.

Anatomy of an ActiveX Document The basic parts of an ActiveX document include the `UserDocument` objects, accompanying code, standalone code modules, and controls placed on the `UserDocument` and its associated code. Figure 19.14 shows a sample ActiveX document and its parts.

Similar to Visual Basic forms, document files are also stored as .dob text files and also include a supporting .dox file for storing binary objects such as bitmaps, similar to the .frx file associated with Visual Basic forms. The .dob and .dox files define the document's properties, methods, and user interface elements.

The accompanying compiled files include the .dll or .exe server component and the document file with the .vbd extension. Figure 19.15 shows what happens when you compile an ActiveX document project.

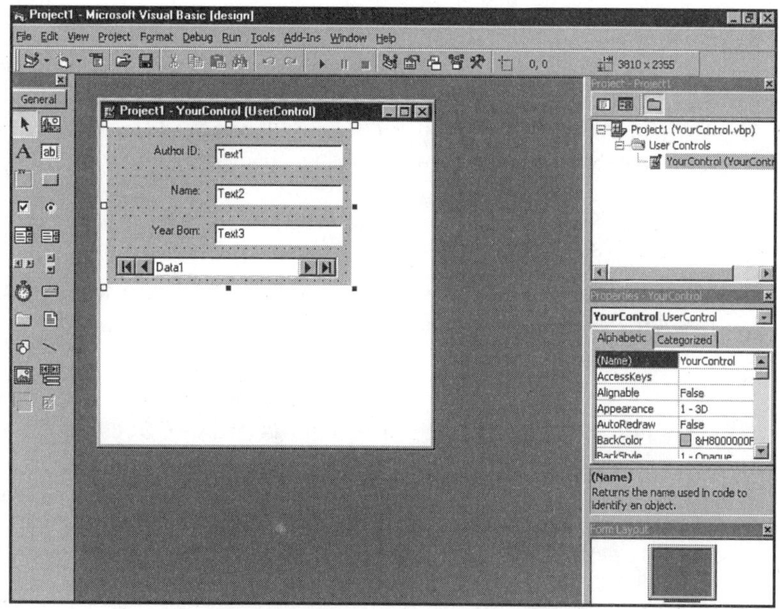

FIG. 19.14
Visual Basic provides a comprehensive development environment for ActiveX documents.

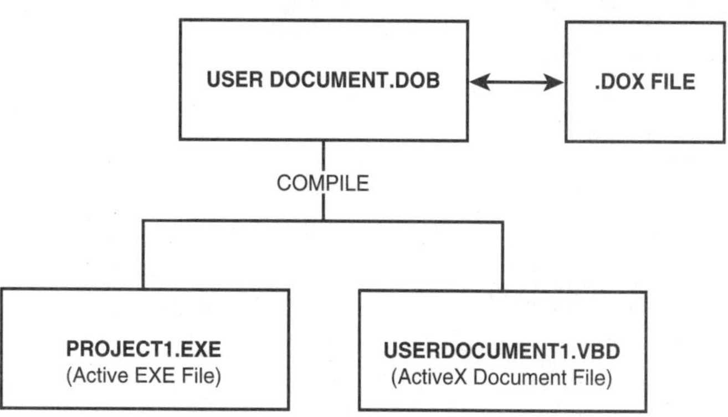

FIG. 19.15
The compiled project produces two files for the ActiveX document.

TIP After you compile your ActiveX document, you can rename the .vbd file to any extension—for example, from MyDoc.vbd to MyDoc.htm.

Using Internet-Specific Features in ActiveX Documents ActiveX documents allow you to take advantage of the Internet through the use of two supplied mechanisms:

- `Hyperlink` *object.* By using the properties and methods of the `Hyperlink` object supplied with Visual Basic, your application can request that Internet Explorer jump to a given URL. Suppose that you have onscreen a image that, when clicked, allows users to jump to a given web site. You can add the following code to the `Click` event of the image control to provide the `Hyperlink` functionality:

  ```
  Private Sub img1_Click()
       UserDocument.Hyperlink.NavigateTo "http://www.gasullivan.com"
  End Sub
  ```

- `AsyncRead` *method.* Asynchronously download data by using the `AsyncRead` method with the `AsyncReadComplete` event. Listing 19.1 shows a bitmap loaded on an ActiveX document.

Listing 19.1 Loading a Bitmap on an ActiveX Document

```
Private Sub UserDocument_InitProperties()
   'Place this code in the InitProperties event of the UserDocument
   UserDocument.AsyncRead "c:\images\gaslogo.bmp", _
      vbAsyncTypeFile, "GASLogo"
End Sub

Private Sub UserDocument_AsyncReadComplete (AsyncProp As VB.AsyncProperty)
' Check to see if the call has been made to load the picture and then do so.
   Select Case AsyncProp.PropertyName
      Case "GASLogo"
         Picture1.Picture = _
            LoadPicture(AsyncProp.Value)
   End Select
End Sub
```

Migrating a Standard VB Application

As stated earlier, one very important feature of Visual Basic 5.0 is the capability to migrate an existing standard VB form to a `UserDocument` object. This is done by using the ActiveX Document Migration Wizard. This wizard offers great potential because large applications written in VB4, for example, can be migrated with minimal effort.

If you're concerned about version conflicts, take comfort in portability features. You can configure the Migration Wizard to disable nonportable code automatically, meaning that the wizard will flag code that's inconsistent with the properties and methods of the `UserDocument` object.

Most exceptions encountered during migration involve invalid form properties in `UserDocuments`. Let the wizard disable the code so that you can locate and replace it at a later time. Make sure that all form controls are included in the current project and referenced appropriately.

Migration Overview

Converting a form to a `UserDocument` can occur in one of the following ways:

- Within a standard project
- Within an ActiveX document EXE project
- Within an ActiveX EXE project

CAUTION

In any case, the form to be converted must be an object in the current Project Explorer. If it's not, you must add the form through the Project menu, but be sure to back up the form before you attempt any migration. If you're developing in an environment that uses Visual SourceSafe or another similar version control package, undo the form checkout and use the local copy of the form in case the conversion doesn't go as you want it to.

Bear the following in mind when converting a form:

- During the migration, `Form` properties are copied to a new `UserDocument` as cleanly as possible—but if you don't expect a perfect migration, you won't be disappointed.

NOTE Events present on a form that aren't found on the `UserDocument` include `Activate`, `Deactivate`, `LinkClose`, `LinkError`, `LinkExecute`, `LinkOpen`, `Load`, `QueryUnload`, and `Unload`. Events present on the `UserDocument` but not found on a form object include `AsycReadComplete`, `EnterFocus`, `ExitFocus`, `Hide`, `InitProperties`, `ReadProperties`, `Scroll`, `Show`, and `WriteProperties`.

- Menu items are preserved; however, `UserDocuments` don't display menus in the same format as forms. `UserDocument` menus merge with the container menus, and the `UserDocument` menu and the container menu appear in the browser.
- The wizard copies all controls from the form to the `UserDocument`. You might have trouble migrating out-of-date controls or controls not in the project toolbox. If you're successful, the controls will appear in the same location, with the properties and name preserved.
- The wizard converts form event handlers as they're being copied. Event-handler names are renamed appropriately for `UserDocuments`. The wizard also copies the code behind the form (CBF). The Migration Wizard lets you choose to have nonsupported code and event handlers commented out during the migration process. Otherwise, any items migrated but not supported will produce compile errors. Other unsupported code and event handlers not flagged by the Migration Wizard also produce compile errors. It's recommended that you disable unsupported code. Each line will be preceded with the prefix `AXDW`, so during the cleanup of disabled code, you can search for this string to prevent the possibility of overlooking code portions you need to find.

- The wizard doesn't support OLE objects that have been inserted into your forms, such as Paintbrush pictures or Word documents, and informs you that these controls aren't supported. If you need to have OLE controls in your application, don't migrate the form. This alternative is acceptable until such time that OLE embedded objects are supported or another option becomes available on `UserDocuments`.

NOTE Because the `UserDocument` object doesn't support embedded OLE objects, the OLE control in the toolbox is disabled whenever a `UserDocument` is active in the IDE.

Activating the ActiveX Document Migration Wizard

Before you can migrate a form to a `UserDocument`, you have to activate the migration tool. You must activate the ActiveX Document Migration Wizard, included as an add-in to VB5, before you can use it. After it's activated, the wizard is available for every project.

To activate the wizard, choose Add-Ins, Add-In Manager from the menu. In the Add-Ins Manager dialog box, select the VB ActiveX Document Migration Wizard from the list of available entries and click OK. From this point, the Migration Wizard option will be found under the Add-Ins menu.

Using the ActiveX Document Migration Wizard

Visual Basic's Professional and Enterprise Editions include the ActiveX Document Migration Wizard, which is designed to help you convert your existing forms into ActiveX documents for use in I-net environments.

NOTE The ActiveX Document Migration Wizard converts forms to ActiveX documents but doesn't create an ActiveX document-based application from your form-based project.

The following tasks are performed when you convert a regular form to an ActiveX document:

- Form properties are copied to a new `UserDocument`. The `UserDocument` is created by the wizard and uses the same name as the form being converted.
- Menu items are also copied over. If you don't want your form menu to appear in the browser, you must manually remove them from the form before running the wizard. The exception is the Help menu, which is merged between the container and the ActiveX document.
- The controls are copied exactly from the form to the new `UserDocument`. The properties, methods, and layouts of the controls are retained.
- OLE-embedded objects aren't converted into the new `UserDocument`. If you've used the OLE `Container` object (an OCX control in Visual Basic), it won't be migrated to the `UserDocument`. Forms with OLE `Container` controls on them can't be migrated with the wizard.

- The events are converted from the form to the corresponding `UserDocument` events. Event handlers are renamed appropriately, and events without any ActiveX document counterparts are moved to the general code section as normal routines that can be called from the code.
- All the code is copied over. Code that isn't relevant in the context of ActiveX documents (such as `Show` and `Hide` methods) is commented out.

To use the ActiveX Document Migration Wizard to convert a form, follow these steps:

1. Open the project you want to convert.
2. Choose Add-Ins, Add-In Manager from the menu. The Add-In Manager dialog box appears.
3. Click the VB ActiveX Document Migration Wizard checkbox (see Figure 19.16), and then click OK. The wizard is added to the Add-Ins menu.

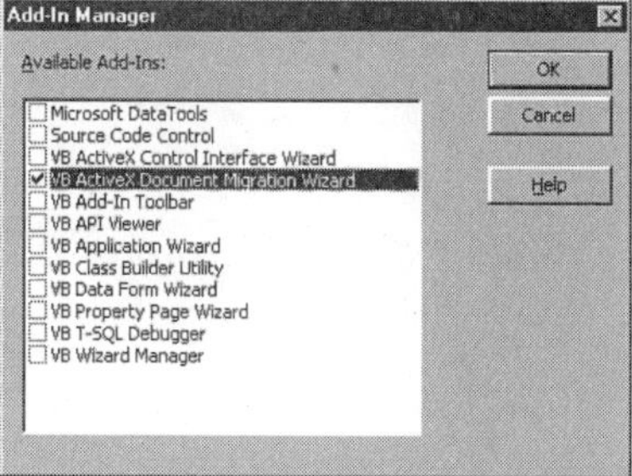

FIG. 19.16
The Add-In Manager allows you to add various productivity applications to your Visual Basic development environment.

4. Choose Add-Ins, ActiveX Document Migration Wizard from the menu. The ActiveX Document Migration Wizard appears.
5. Click Next to continue. The Form Selection dialog box is displayed, as shown in Figure 19.17.

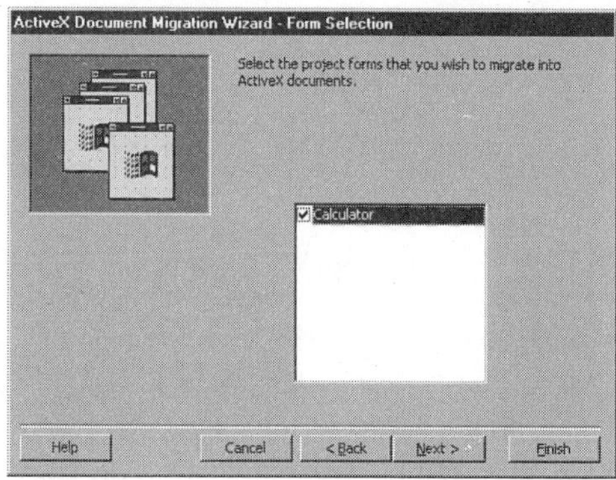

FIG. 19.17
Select the forms you want to convert to ActiveX documents from the list.

6. Select the forms you want to convert, and then click Next to continue.
7. In the Options dialog box that appears, you can comment out invalid code by selecting the appropriate option (see Figure 19.18). Also, if your application type isn't an ActiveX DLL or EXE, you have to choose one of the two options for converting to the appropriate type.

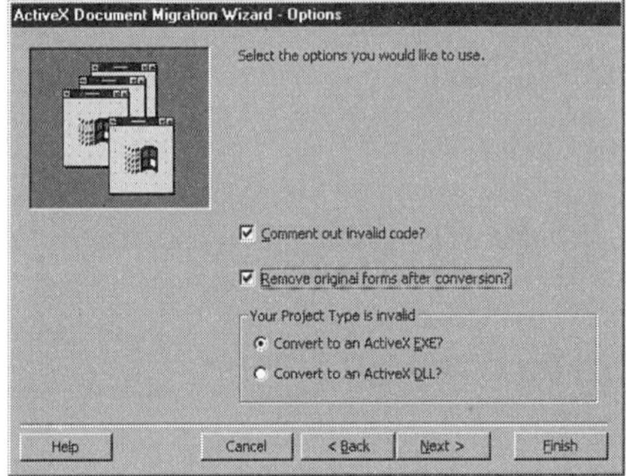

FIG. 19.18 You can remove your old forms from the project by selecting the appropriate checkbox.

8. Click Next to continue. In the Finished! dialog box that appears, you can select to have the wizard display a summary screen of the steps it performs and how you can test your document (see Figure 19.19).

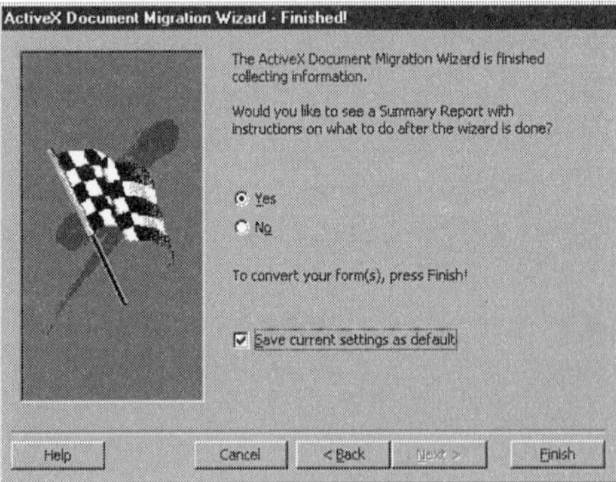

FIG. 19.19 Use the Save Current Settings as Default option to save your wizard options.

9. Click Finish to close the wizard and start the migration process. A dialog is displayed to inform you that the wizard is finished. A summary window appears if you selected the summary option in the Finished! dialog box, as shown in Figure 19.20.
10. Click Close to close the summary report and return to your project.

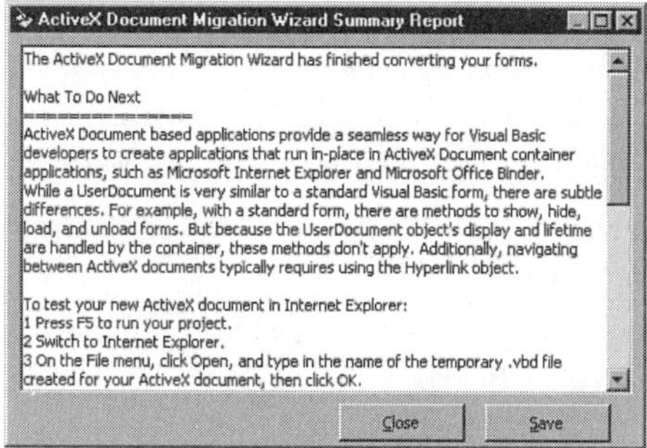

FIG. 19.20
You can save the summary report for later reference by using the Save button.

The project window now includes the new `UserDocument`. You can test the ActiveX document by running the application, launching Internet Explorer, and then opening the UserDocument.vbd file.

The Summary Report window provides detailed steps for testing and debugging the ActiveX documents with Internet Explorer.

From Here...

In this chapter, you learned about some of the current software-development technologies and how they relate to the Internet and Internet-enabled application development efforts. You also were introduced to the features built into Visual Basic for migrating traditional applications to the I-net environment. You learned about ActiveX documents and how they provide a powerful mechanism for encapsulating existing applications in the Internet framework. Other chapters in this book provide a detailed look at some of the other components of Visual Studio that allow you to take full advantage of all of Microsoft's technologies for building and leveraging the I-net environment:

- To learn about the Visual Studio development environment, see Chapter 2, "Using Visual Studio to Create Applications."
- To understand the details behind technologies such as COM/DCOM and ActiveX, see Chapter 4, "Using Microsoft's Object Technologies."
- To learn about creating components with Visual Basic, see Chapter 5, "Creating ActiveX Components with Visual Basic."
- To learn about creating components with Visual C++, see Chapter 6, "Creating Components with Visual C++."
- To learn about creating components with Visual J++, see Chapter 7, "Creating Components with Visual J++."

- To learn about concepts associated with web-based application development, see Chapter 11, "An Inside Look at Web-Based Applications."
- To learn about Active Server Pages and their capabilities, see Chapter 13, "An Inside Look at Active Server Pages and Internet Information Server."
- To learn about getting started with Visual InterDev, see Chapter 14, "Developing Active Content with Visual InterDev."
- To learn about advanced concepts associated with Visual InterDev development, see Chapter 15, "Advanced Visual InterDev Concepts."

PART IV

Developing Scalable Distributed Applications

CHAPTER 20

Clients, Servers, and Components: Design Strategies for Distributed Applications

by Larry Millett

The services paradigm

View an application as a set of services provided by interacting components. This paradigm transcends two-tier, three-tier, or multitiered implementation architectures.

Design objectives for a distributed system

Although all applications must fulfill specific business requirements, distributed applications as a class have several common design objectives.

Distributed system design constraints

Identify common constraints that limit design choices in a distributed application.

Concurrent processing strategies

Review the three basic strategies for concurrent processing: parallel, pipeline, and asynchronous.

Client/server implementation models

Compare the traditional two-tier client/server approach with the three-tier approach. Consider when each model might be most appropriate.

A design strategy for distributed applications

Read about a strategy for designing distributed applications.

Every year on the Fourth of July, the Boston Pops Orchestra plays a free concert at the Esplanade, culminating in the 1812 Overture. Tchaikovsky's score includes church bells and cannons, rendered by a number of churches in Boston and an artillery detachment at Bunker Hill. Because of their distance from the Esplanade, the cannons must fire and the bells must ring several seconds before the orchestra reaches that point in the score. In fact, because the churches and guns are at varying distances, each is subject to a different delay. Gun crews and bell ringers watch the orchestra on television, and when the performance reaches a predetermined point, each plays their part. Listeners at the Esplanade hear bells ringing all together and cannons firing right on cue with the orchestra.

You can consider the 1812 Overture a distributed application, with the orchestra, the artillery, and each belfry as components. As is typical with most distributed software, success depends greatly on component interaction. It all works well together because the constraints are simple (the tempo of the performance, the speed of sound, and the relative distances) and roles and interactions are well defined. The bells and cannons do not try to play in time or in close harmony with the orchestra; rather, they aim for subsecond accuracy in their timing. So long as each component performs well and the timing is correct, the bells and cannons produce a delightfully bombastic effect.

Like the 1812 Overture, a distributed application integrates the actions of many components. Distributed application design must focus not only on the details of individual parts, but also on making the distributed components work smoothly together in concert.

This chapter begins with a brief review of design objectives for a distributed system and a review of constraints that sometimes make the objectives difficult to achieve. The balance of the chapter presents design strategies. ■

Design Objectives for a Distributed Application

A properly designed application fulfills a well-defined business need. In addition, the best distributed applications exhibit several desirable features:

- *Performance*—High throughput and fast response times.
- *Efficiency*—Effective, frugal use of available computing resources.
- *Scalability*—Orderly growth to accommodate increased processing volume and complexity.
- *Security*—Appropriate access for authorized users.
- *Verifiability*—A structured quality assurance (QA) effort can verify that the application correctly implements specific business requirements.
- *Reliability*—Infrequent failures and graceful degradation on failure of one or more components.
- *Maintainability*—Ease of deployment, operation, and enhancement.

Achieving all these properties for any application requires substantial application of talent, discipline, and experience throughout the development process. Achieving these properties in a distributed application requires careful and sophisticated design, with particular attention to the interactions between components.

The following sections discuss these design objectives in more detail.

Performance

Application performance is the number one criterion for system quality. System design, architecture, and implementation may be flawless, but if users spend too much time waiting for results, they will be dissatisfied. Applications may perform quite differently in production than in a development environment, due to different network configurations and loads.

It's important to identify specific criteria for application performance (usually in a requirements document). Without objective criteria, performance will be judged subjectively. Important criteria include response time (time to complete one operation), apparent response time (time a user must wait after executing an operation), and throughput (data processed per unit time). Ideally, separate performance criteria should address the best case (no other application active on the network, single user) and the worst case (very heavy network and application loads, many users). Performance criteria should always be stated for the common case (typical application and network loads).

Several studies have shown that people perceive response time under one-fifth of a second as instantaneous. Studies also show that response time over one second can have a negative effect on attitude and productivity. Sometimes, application constraints make subsecond response time simply unattainable; often, asynchronous processing can improve apparent response time.

Overall performance for a distributed application depends as much on component interactions as on individual component performance. Communication delays and resource sharing will require special attention.

Efficiency

A distributed application typically uses resources on several computers, as well as network resources. Each individual component must use local resources effectively; the application as a whole must use network resources frugally. Ultimately, inefficiency will manifest as poor performance or poor scalability.

It's important to pursue the right efficiencies. Processor time and memory are cheap and abundant; bandwidth from Europe to North America is typically scarce and expensive. The anticipated growth path for the application will motivate tradeoffs.

Scalability

For a successful application deployed in a successful business, processing demands—number of users, transaction volume, database size—tend to increase. However, this volume typically grows chaotically. A well-designed application grows in an orderly manner to accommodate disorderly growth in demand. The growth plan may include deploying additional instances of some components, adding additional database storage, or redistributing processing tasks.

The best applications also scale down for cost-effective use by organizations with smaller processing demands (and fewer resources). For example, an order processing system designed for a corporate headquarters might use SQL Server for data management; branch offices might use a scaled-down version with a FoxPro database.

It's important to understand the relationship between resource usage and processing volume. Ideally, resource requirements should increase linearly with volume: If volume is n and usage for a particular resource is r, you would like to have $r = kn$, for some constant k. If for some resources $r = kn^2$ or worse, scalability is at risk.

NOTE For some applications, linear resource usage ($r = kn$) is inherently unattainable. In those cases, load distribution through parallel processing (discussed later in this chapter) will improve scalability. If the processing load is divided among three instances of the application, resource usage for the three instances ($a^2 + b^2 + c^2$) will be less than resource usage for a single instance $(a + b + c)^2$. ■

Security

Because a distributed application crosses system boundaries, security becomes more important and more difficult. Generally, each component will execute under a local account context. Remote components, however, need to connect and be provided or denied services as appropriate.

When a distributed application runs entirely within a Windows NT network, Windows NT's integrated security is the best solution. More comprehensive security solutions may include certificate servers or the distributed security service of Microsoft Transaction Server.

ON THE WEB

You can find information on programming with the Microsoft Certificate Server at **http://premium.microsoft.com/msdn/library/sdkdoc/appprog_8vjm.htm**.

▶ **See** "MTS Component Integration Services," **p. 696**

Fault Tolerance

Components in a distributed application must cope not only with local failures, but also with failures in remote components. The number of potential errors mounts up in a frighteningly exponential way. A well-designed distributed application must degrade gracefully in the event of errors; the best distributed applications automatically recover. A well-designed component manages the effects of a fault locally, rather than propagate the error to other parts of a system.

For efficient administration, a distributed system should pursue a consistent error notification strategy. For example, several components might share a common log file. The Windows NT Event Log is another excellent resource for error notification.

TIP Microsoft Visual Basic 5.0 (VB5) includes a new feature for easy insertion of entries to the Windows NT Application Log: the `LogEvent` method of the App object. However, `App.LogEvent` only works in a compiled application; in debug mode, it will appear to have no effect.

Search VB5 help for the `LogEvent` method of the App object.

NOTE For more information about the Windows NT Event Logs, see *Special Edition Using Microsoft BackOffice*, Volume 1, from Que, ISBN 0-7897-1142-7, Chapter 5, "Checking the Logs," on p. 151. ■

Verifiability

Testing a distributed system is far more complex than testing a monolithic application. Effective quality assurance (QA) requires participation from the earliest stages of the development process. Effective testing requires a parallel test environment that matches as closely as possible the production environment.

The most important design features for verifiability are clear separation of services and well-documented component interfaces. Separation of services is discussed later in the section "Designing a Distributed Application." Microsoft's Visual Basic help files provide a good example of well-documented interfaces. For example, see the documentation for the TextBox control.

Quality assurance (QA) for distributed applications is more complex than for traditional applications. QA staff should participate in the application design process so that they can develop an effective application test plan.

Maintainability

Changes in business result in changes to software, and the pace is accelerating. In a well-designed application, a change to a business requirement results in a change to a single component. To achieve this goal, however, you must encapsulate business logic in middle-tier components.

A complete design must address initial system deployment, ongoing operation, and distribution of updates. As components become more widely distributed, update distribution becomes more difficult to coordinate.

A component-based design is one of the best approaches for long-term maintainability. See the discussion of "The Services Paradigm" later in this chapter.

Design Constraints for a Distributed Application

Constraints are factors in the application environment that limit design choices. It's important to address these constraints in the application design. The 1812 Overture operated under constraints of geographic distribution, subsecond timing, and the speed of sound. Distributed software must operate under a number of common constraints:

- *Platform*—Hardware, networks, physical plant, and operating systems
- *Bandwidth*—Communications speed and reliability between components
- *Resource sharing*—Cooperative access to shared resources
- *Availability*—Allowable down time
- *Audience*—Target users and administrators
- *Legacy*—Interaction with existing systems
- *Political*—Organizational and personal relationships

Take a look at each type of constraint in more detail.

Platform

Typically, components of a distributed application must run on a variety of existing hardware under a number of existing operating systems connected by a patchwork of networks. Each component must perform well locally and interact correctly with remote components.

Target platform constraints also include support (or lack thereof) for interprocess communication (IPC), remote procedure calls (RPC), and object request broker (ORB) services. IPC provides local communication between applications running on a single computer; RPC allows an application running on one computer to interact with an application running on another computer. ORB services include object allocation, deallocation, and invocation. For applications running on Windows NT 4.0 or later (or Windows 95 with an update), Microsoft's Component Object Model (COM) and Distributed COM (DCOM) provide all three services. In fact, DCOM provides a good degree of location transparency; in many cases, components can be deployed locally or remotely with no code changes required.

If some components must run on non-Windows platforms, some extra effort will be required. Basically, you will have three choices:

- Implement DCOM on the target platform. To date, COM has been implemented on Windows NT, Windows 95, MacOS, some versions of MVS, and several UNIX platforms. However, it is a well-documented binary standard and could certainly be implemented on other platforms. While implementing COM and DCOM is a major undertaking, this might be the best approach for some very large projects (on the scale of a nationwide tax processing application for the IRS).
- Use a COM alternative such as Common Object Request Broker Architecture (CORBA). Microsoft does not currently support CORBA on Windows, though third-party implementations are available. Leaving aside the technical merits of COM versus CORBA, this approach would result in better platform independence. However, Visual Studio is very tightly integrated with COM, and a lot of powerful features will be lost. For example, VB has built-in support for COM in its `CreateObject()` and `GetObject()` methods; VB has no support for CORBA components.

▶ **See** "COM Versus CORBA: Standard, Stand-Off, Integration, or Assimilation?" **p. 108**

ON THE WEB

Detailed information on CORBA can be found on the Object Management Group's web site at **www.omg.org**.

- Use a more primitive mechanism, such as Distributed Computing Environment (DCE) RPC or TCP/IP sockets. As with the CORBA approach, the application becomes more vendor-neutral. However, a non-object–based mechanism (like sockets) provides program-to-program communication, not object-to-object communication. This might seem to be a subtle distinction, but the bottom line is more lines of code.

Microsoft is working to expand the alternatives available for interaction with non-Windows components. This is one of the primary objectives for their Universal Data Access initiative.

Technologies nearing release include Cedar (LU 6.2 interface to IMS and CICS transaction programs), OLE DB/DDM (access to VSAM and AS400 data sets) and Host Data Replicator (SQL Server replication to DB2).

▶ **See** "Cedar," **p. 585**

▶ **See** "The OLE DB/DDM Driver," **p. 584**

▶ **See** "The Host Data Replicator (Cakewalk)," **p. 580**

ON THE WEB

For the latest information on Microsoft's Universal Data Access technologies, go to **http://www.microsoft.com/data**.

Bandwidth

A distributed application is, by definition, a communicating application. Good design must take into account the speed and reliability of available communications links. For different cases, available bandwidth may vary from a few bits per minute (voice interactive response) to a few megabits per second (function calls to an in-process DLL).

During application design, it's important to consider patterns of bandwidth availability on the target network. For example, gigabit Ethernet backbone may connect servers, whereas European users connect through a congested 56K connection. Some client machines might have a permanent network connection; others might connect infrequently by dial-up connections. It's especially important to consider bandwidth constraints when partitioning an application into components (see "Designing a Distributed Application" later in this chapter).

▶ **See** "Limited Bandwidth Strategies," **p. 589**

Resource Contention

Sharing resources between processes is one of the fundamental problems in computing. At the most basic level, processes compete for processor time, memory, disk, and network resources. At a higher level, shared resources include rows in database tables and services provided by other components.

Because database servers provide effective resource-sharing mechanisms, some developers tend to discount this problem in application design. However, resource contention can be an obstacle to scalability, so every effort must be made to minimize resource sharing. Where sharing cannot be eliminated, try to make it nonexclusive.

Availability

An application that must be available 24 hours a day, 7 days a week, without interruptions requires much more thorough design than a batch job system. Not all applications require long periods of uninterrupted availability; those that do present several special design challenges. First, some method must be found to maintain the system: apply patches and updates, install new devices, defragment disk space, and so on. Second, you must ensure that all resources required by the system (databases, routers, electricity, and so forth) are available on the same uninterruptible basis.

High-availability applications require attention to infrastructure details (backup power supply, redundant network paths), hardware details (redundant storage, hot standby, failover switches), and application features (automatic restart, administrator alert). The most important element in design of a high-availability application, however, is a careful analysis of possible failures and recovery options.

Audience

The audience for an application includes its users, its support staff, and its administrators. Design decisions must take into account the needs of each. For example, users might be working in a high-volume call center where extra seconds waiting for data may cost the enterprise thousands of dollars. This case requires special attention to response time. Consider also users' overall comfort level working with computers: A cashier in a shoe store has different expectations than a developer.

IT support staff require accurate, up-to-date user documentation. Trainers may also need access to requirements and design documents to develop a curriculum.

System administrators need to understand how to install, maintain, and operate the application. For example, they might need to maintain a remote installation by dial-up connections. This case requires attention to performance with limited network bandwidth. Administrators are often neglected when gathering application requirements; remember that the success of an application depends in large part on successful administration.

An application has at least three audiences: end users, support staff, and system administrators. End users require an appropriate user interface and snappy performance. Support staff require accurate user documentation. System administrators require compliance with security policies, predictable behavior, accurate system documentation, and straightforward installation.

Political

A distributed system often crosses organizational boundaries as well as system boundaries. Different organizations have different priorities and different expectations for the application. For example, an application developed in Department A may need access to a database owned by Department B. The application may be a crash priority for Department A but an annoying distraction for Department B. The project manager might win Department B's cooperation by developing a reusable component for looking up supplier information.

Compromises may be required in the use of existing components, design of reusable new components, or use of an enterprise data model. For example, the proposed database schema for a new application might duplicate some information already available in an enterprise database. Database administrators might insist on a modified schema. This may seem a compromise for the application at hand, but can ensure data consistency for the enterprise.

Political give and take is a soft skill often disdained by developers. Usually, it's simply a matter of listening carefully to other parties' priorities and finding a way to make your own priorities consistent. By showing respect for other points of view, you can gain respect for your own. Once you've earned some trust and respect, you can usually bypass political gamesmanship.

The Services Paradigm

The Component Object Model (COM) is fundamental to Microsoft's strategies for operating systems and tools. COM applications consist of *services* provided by *components*. A service is a group of related functions (an interface) that implements a business requirement; a component is an executable unit of software (EXE or DLL) that implements one or more services. Software design in this model consists of defining services and packaging them into components. Software development consists of building components and integrating them into applications. In documentation for Visual Studio 97 (VS97), Microsoft uses the terms *services model* and *component-based* interchangeably.

The services model provides an approach for turning business requirements into software components. Central to this approach is the idea of a three-tiered framework:

- *Presentation Services* provide interaction with users of the application, typically a graphical user interface (GUI).
- *Business Services* apply common business policies to users' interaction with data.
- *Data Management Services* provide durable storage and retrieval of business information.

The three-tiered framework does not imply any physical implementation; a three-tier application may consist of seven components installed on two computers. Three-tier architecture is a modeling framework, a way of thinking about the services in an application. Grouping all three types of services into a single component results in a monolithic application. The traditional two-tier client/server approach generally *does* imply a physical implementation: a database component and a desktop component.

The services paradigm is particularly well suited to the development of distributed applications and can result in several benefits:

- Encapsulation of complex business logic
- Programming language independence
- Component reuse
- Reduced project risk

Implementing a service in one component simplifies maintenance when business requirements change. Code changes may often be limited to a single component. So long as the original interface for a service does not change, developers may add new functions or change the implementation of existing functions without breaking other components.

Because COM is a binary standard, it is language-neutral. So long as a component implements its services as advertised, it matters very little whether a component is built with Visual Basic (VB), Visual C++ (VC), Delphi, or Symantec C++.

The services approach generally results in components of a good granularity for reuse, particularly in the business services layer. Separating common business policies from application-specific user interactions makes the business services components more generic and better suited to reuse. Effective reuse, however, requires careful component design and developer awareness (developers seldom reuse code they don't know about). Also, a thriving ActiveX control market makes available a wide variety of shrink-wrap components.

Numerous studies have documented that complexity grows exponentially with the size of an application. The services paradigm results in smaller modules with well-defined interfaces. The reduced complexity of each module results in more effective quality assurance. Component reuse also reduces project risk.

Concurrent Processing Strategies

Concurrency can improve performance in a distributed application by putting multiple processors to work on a problem. Coordinating the processes requires some additional overhead, however, and adds design complexity. Few applications benefit from a degree of concurrency greater than about four processes. Still, even limited concurrency, judiciously applied, can greatly improve overall performance.

Two concurrency strategies improve throughput: *parallel processing* and *pipelines*. In parallel processing, multiple instances of the same application attack a common task. A pipelined application divides a task into stages and processes the different stages concurrently. The two strategies are quite compatible, often combined in processor designs. Intel's Pentium, for example, implements a five-stage pipeline architecture with parallel integer processing pipelines. Although a typical instruction requires several clock ticks to execute, pipelining allows the chip to complete one instruction at each clock cycle. The parallel architecture actually allows the Pentium to complete two instructions per clock cycle, under ideal conditions.

Asynchronous processing can be a very effective way to improve apparent user response time. The key is to recognize that response time often means time for a *user* to complete a task, rather than time for the *system* to complete a task. The general approach is for the user process to generate a request and place it into a queue for a separate background process. This type of processing is asynchronous because processes run concurrently without synchronization.

Parallel Processing

The classic example of parallel processing is matrix multiplication: A separate process computes each row in the result matrix (see Figure 20.1). This technique, known as *vector processing*, is the basis of a number of supercomputer designs.

Parallel processing can work well when a problem decomposes into a number of virtually identical independent tasks. In fact, the general problem of executing computer programs subdivides into parallel tasks, a practice known as *symmetric multiprocessing*.

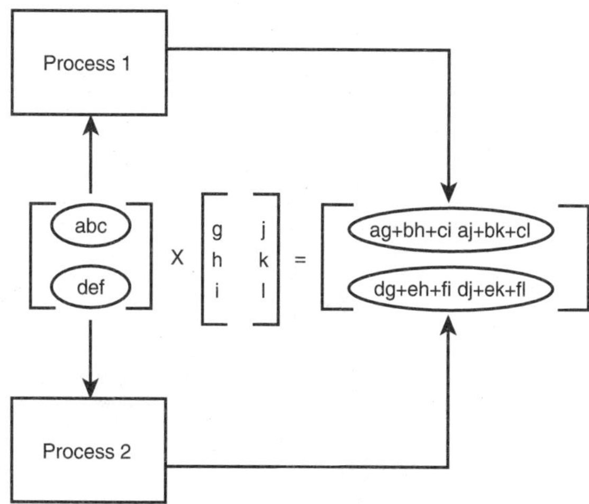

FIG. 20.1
Matrix multiplication with parallel processes.

Parallel processing also works well for a problem that decomposes into a number of relatively independent tasks. Examples include background spell-checking in Microsoft Word and flight control systems where a number of parallel processes monitor different instruments.

NOTE Concurrent processing adds overhead to application execution. When several processors are available (multiple CPUs in one machine, or multiple machines), the performance gain justifies the overhead. With a single processor, concurrent processing can still improve performance for I/O-intensive tasks.

In Visual Studio, Visual C++ provides the best support for multithreaded programming. However, concurrency can also be achieved by running multiple instances of an application, by using out-of-process ActiveX components, and by running components on multiple computers.

The chief design problems for parallel architectures are resource sharing and synchronization. Identical by definition, parallel tasks often require access to the same resources (memory locations, database rows, I/O streams). Coordinating use of these resources adds design complexity and execution overhead. As a side effect of resource sharing, execution times can vary for each parallel subtask. Synchronizing task completion and the start of each new task adds even more overhead and complexity.

Pipeline Processing

A pipeline works like an assembly line: Each stage brings a task nearer to completion and passes it to the next. Work proceeds concurrently on each stage. If the pipeline has *n* stages, and each stage takes one second, the first task will finish in *n* seconds. One additional task will complete every second thereafter. Figure 20.2 illustrates a pipelined application.

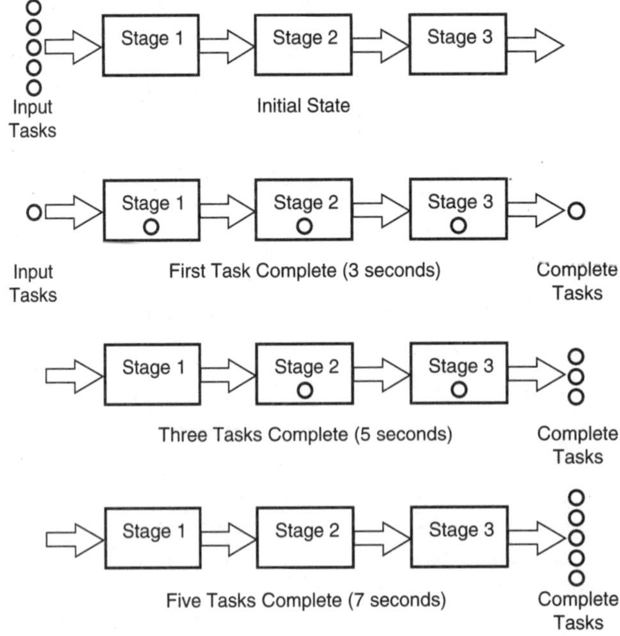

FIG. 20.2
A three-stage pipelined application in which throughput will be one task per second.

The chief design problem for pipeline architectures is dividing tasks into stages that require approximately equal processing time. Queuing theory states that for an *n*-stage pipeline where the longest time to process any stage is *t* seconds, total time to process one item will be *nt* seconds. If you define throughput as number of tasks completed per second, overall throughput for the pipeline is limited to the throughput of the slowest stage. Slower stages become bottlenecks and require additional synchronization to keep the pipeline operating smoothly. Often, parallel processing at one or more stages can improve throughput. Figure 20.3 illustrates a pipeline with one parallel stage. Stage 1 and Stage 3 each require one second per task; Stage 2 requires 2 seconds per task. Two parallel instances yield an effective throughput of one task per second for Stage 2.

NOTE It's important to distinguish throughput from response time. For the pipeline in Figure 20.3, throughput (tasks completed per second) will be one task per second. However, response time (time to complete one task) will be four seconds.

One simple example of a parallel/pipeline architecture is a printer pool. Often, printing is the last stage in a series of document processing tasks. Printers are rather slow devices, and an efficient document processing pipeline might easily overwhelm a single printer. By attaching several printers in a pool so that jobs are arbitrarily assigned to the first available printer, you implement a parallel stage in a pipeline.

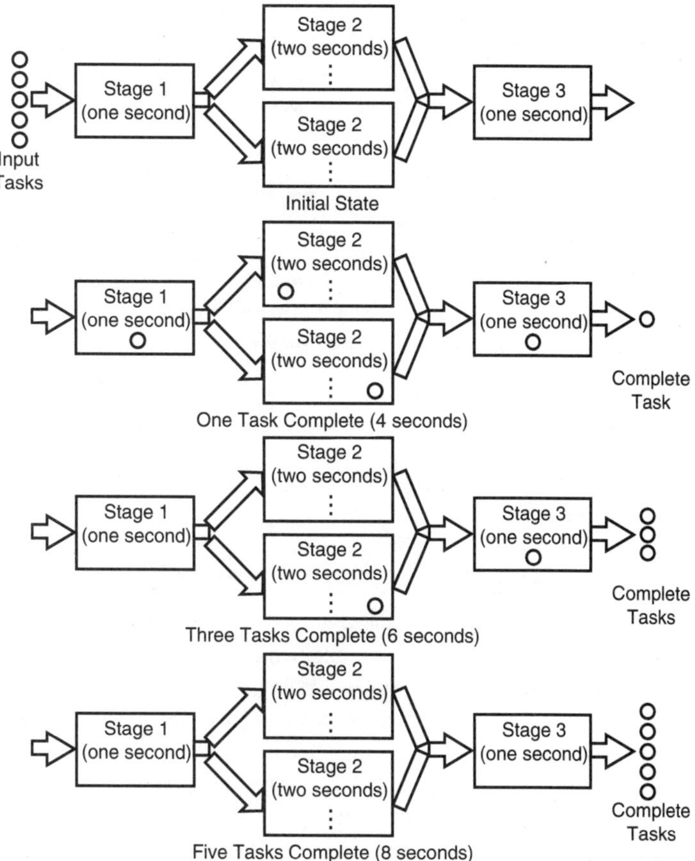

FIG. 20.3
A hybrid parallel/pipeline architecture.

Asynchronous Processing

The background printing feature of Microsoft Word is an excellent example of asynchronous processing. If a document prints at six pages per minute, a 30-page report would require five minutes. By spinning off the printing as a separate task, control returns to the user almost immediately.

The primary design problem for asynchronous processing is error handling. First, the background process has to notify the user process that an error has occurred. Second, and more problematic, by the time an error occurs, the state of the user process has usually changed significantly. In Microsoft Word, for example, a user might have made a substantial number of revisions since printing. It's generally impractical to return to the state at the time of the original request and retry. For a Word user, it's probably acceptable to just print again from the current state of the document.

For client/server applications, database access is an obvious opportunity for asynchronous processing. For example, a background query can retrieve needed data while a user works on a startup dialog. Avoid asynchronous database updates: If the update fails, it may be impossible to return the user to the pre-update context.

Client/Server Implementation Models

Distributed applications generally fall into two categories: cooperating peers or client/server. In the cooperating peers model, several instances of the same application cooperate to generate a result. In the client/server model, several distinct applications cooperate to generate a result. The client/server approach allows for efficient division of labor and has become the dominant model.

Within the client/server model, two approaches have become popular:

- Traditional (two-tier)
- Three-tier (or multitier)

The Traditional (Two-Tier) Client/Server Model

In a traditional client/server application, a database server implements data management functions, and a client application implements other functions. Business logic often is divided between the client application and database-hosted stored procedures and triggers. For example, a report might use a stored procedure to perform currency conversions on data access and retrieval based on a conversion date computed in the report program. The business logic for determining the conversion date is implemented in the client program; business logic for looking up and applying the exchange rate is implemented in a stored procedure.

A traditional client/server model can be implemented fairly quickly because it requires less up-front design. User response time may also be better than in more complex client/server models. The two-tier model is a good choice for an application with a small number of users and a clearly limited scope.

Two-tier applications usually don't scale well to large numbers of users. Implementation of substantial business logic in stored procedures results in database contention as the number of users increases. Also, the client almost always requires a high bandwidth connection to the database server, so two-tier is not a good choice for remote users. Update distribution can be tricky, as changes in the client component must be carefully coordinated with changes in the server component.

The Three-Tier Model

In the three-tier model, a database server implements data management functions, a mid-tier application implements common business logic, and a presentation component provides a user interface. When several applications access the same data, it makes sense to encapsulate related business logic in a separate component. For example, a human resources (HR) department will probably have many applications that access personnel data. For all these applications, business policy might state that all HR staff have access to basic information about employees (name, address, department, supervisor, and so forth), but only supervisors have access to compensation and benefits information, and only managers have access to disciplinary information. A single mid-tier application can retrieve data from the database, apply the access limitations, and pass it along to client applications. As access policies change, only the mid-tier component will require maintenance.

Business data is often subject to integrity rules that cannot be enforced properly by a database server. For example, the database server could enforce the rule that a new order can be created only for an existing customer (a referential integrity constraint). However, the server could not efficiently enforce the rule that a customer with a 90-day past due balance may not place new orders. Although a developer could write an insert trigger or stored procedure to implement the rule, this approach has several shortcomings. First, a trigger would result in longer execution times for inserts, resulting in increased database contention. Second, a trigger or stored procedure enforces the rule *after* the user has filled in all the blanks to create an order. A better approach would be to encapsulate customer information, including available credit, into a mid-tier component for access by the user interface component. Then the application can check customer credit when the user *begins* to create an order.

Components that enforce business rules on data may require a high bandwidth connection to the database server where that data resides. Database response time is typically the largest factor by far in response time for the business object. Where the business rules component in turn serves many other components, those components should be located together on the same server, or on a group of servers with high bandwidth connections. Mid-tier components can also be used to overcome bandwidth limitations by caching data from the database. This approach works well with nonvolatile data.

Sometimes the middle tier will include services that are not strictly business services (graphics processing, transaction management, numerical analysis). Such applications are sometimes called *multitier*. The same design principles apply, however, so this chapter will not discuss multitier applications separately.

Three-tier applications generally scale much better than two-tier. Implementing business logic in a middle tier component rather than triggers or stored procedures greatly reduces the number of database queries, and thus reduces database contention. When database operations pass through a middle tier, user response time can suffer. However, while mid-tier initialization may slow the first operation, subsequent operations may be much faster. Also, not all database operations need to pass through a middle tier. For simple database lookups where the data is unlikely to be used again, direct access from the user interface to the database is appropriate.

Two-Tier Versus Three-Tier: An Example

Consider a sample application: consultant time-sheet submission. First, examine the components for a two-tier implementation. The database server might implement the following services:

- Tables for consultants, clients, assignments, and hours
- Stored procedures to retrieve data for a consultant, a client, current assignments for a consultant, and hours for a specified period
- Referential integrity constraints
- Insert and update triggers to ensure that all hours entered apply to an active consultant, client, and assignment
- Insert and update triggers to ensure that no consultant bills more than 24 hours in one day
- Insert and update triggers to ensure that no consultant enters hours for a prior month later than the fifteenth of the following month

The desktop component might implement the following services:

- Database login
- User interface for hours entry (read-only for prior months)
- Timesheet data structures
- Invoke database stored procedures to look up consultant, assignments, clients, and hours for a specified period
- Range checking (no more than 24 billable hours/day)
- Generate and execute SQL statements to update database
- Error handling for database operations (for example, a trigger rejects an update)

This division of labor capitalizes on the strengths of both the database server and the desktop platform. The design can be implemented fairly quickly by a single developer using Microsoft SQL Server and Visual Basic. Initial deployment should be relatively simple: install database components on the database server, and distribute an install kit to consultants for the desktop component. Subsequent updates, however, will require careful coordination of database changes with distribution of the modified desktop application.

As the business grows, however, one thousand consultants update timesheets within a three-hour period every Monday morning. The implementation of range checking and business policies in triggers results in longer-running updates and inserts and substantial database contention. Contention results in failed database operations (timeouts), resulting in retries, additional contention, more failed operations, and ultimately unhappy consultants. A hardware upgrade might improve the situation, but it's an expensive solution for a problem that occurs only on Monday mornings.

Consider now a three-tier approach. Data services look very much the same, except for the omission of triggers:

- Tables for consultants, clients, assignments, and hours
- Stored procedures to retrieve data for a consultant, a client, current assignments for a consultant, and hours for a prior period
- Referential integrity constraints

The presentation services might include the following:

- User interface for database login
- User interface for hours entry
- Interact with business services

The presentation layer is quite simple and might be implemented as a Visual Basic application, or as a web application with scripting and ActiveX or Java components.

The business services layer might include the following services:

- Database login
- Invoke database stored procedures to lookup consultant, assignments, clients, and prior hours
- Timesheet data structures
- Range checking (no more than 24 billable hours/day)
- Enforce no updates to prior months
- Generate and execute SQL statements to update database
- Error handling for database operations (for example, a trigger rejects an update)

This architecture is substantially more complex than the two-tier implementation. Development will probably take longer simply due to the problems of integrating the separate components. Initial deployment requires installation of database components, distribution of user components, and installation of mid-tier components.

The three-tier model is more complex, but it's also substantially more scalable and flexible. Because triggers do not enforce business logic, inserts and updates are fast and efficient, and the database server can handle heavier loads with less contention.

Now suppose that the consulting company opens branch offices in four cities and that copies of the database are maintained in each city. As consultants enter hours, the entries must update both the local database and the central database at world headquarters. For each implementation, each database would require distributed transaction support. You'll also require integrated account management so that a consultant requires a single login for all databases to which he has access.

The two-tier implementation would require the following changes to the desktop component:

- Configuration parameters to determine which databases to use
- Implement login to multiple databases
- Generate and execute SQL for distributed inserts and updates
- Implement more complex error handling

The updated desktop component would have to be distributed to all consultants, and distribution would have to be carefully coordinated with database changes. This is a nontrivial problem when dealing with a thousand consultants in five cities. Also, database administrators must ensure that the same version of each trigger and stored procedure is installed on each database. As consultants enter hours, triggers fire separately on each database to enforce business logic. In fact, the 24-hours/day constraint is enforced separately in the desktop application and in insert triggers and update triggers on each database.

Now consider changes to the three-tier application. The presentation layer requires no changes. Mid-tier components require the same changes as the desktop application in the two-tier approach:

- Configuration parameters to determine which databases to use
- Implement login to multiple databases
- Generate and execute SQL for distributed inserts and updates
- Implement more complex error handling

The updated mid-tier components must be distributed and installed on application servers at world headquarters and at each branch location, and rollout must be coordinated with database updates. However, coordinated rollout requires cooperation among only a handful of system administrators.

Although a two-tier implementation results in a simpler design and simpler initial deployment, the three-tier model offers superior long-term scalability and flexibility.

Designing a Distributed Application

The first step in designing any application is to identify the business objectives for the system, and the constraints under which it must operate: the requirements. One of the most effective approaches to requirements gathering is the *use case* approach, developed by Ivar Jacobson and others. To oversimplify a bit, a use case is a scenario that describes a business problem to be solved by software. Use cases are very effective tools for identifying the business objectives for a system. Unfortunately, this tool was omitted from Microsoft Visual Modeler. Use-case diagrams are included in Rational Rose 4.0 (Visual Modeler is a subset of the Rational Rose tool).

▶ **See** "What Is Visual Modeler?," **p. 746**

ON THE WEB

For information about Rational Rose 4.0 (including a free demo version), visit the Rational software web site at **http://www.rational.com**.

Once the initial requirements are clear, a design process should include the following steps:

- Model business objects and their interactions
- Define services and interfaces
- Identify dependencies among business objects and services
- Partition the application into components
- Target components onto platforms

Typically, this will be an iterative process: decisions in one stage will require changes to an earlier stage.

Model Business Objects and Their Interactions

Top-down structured analysis and design techniques are *algorithm-oriented*: they focus on the steps required to produce a result. These techniques work well for small to medium monolithic applications. Object-oriented (OO) approaches are *interaction-oriented*: they focus on interactions between components. Because OO techniques focus on the most critical aspect of a distributed system design, they are by far the best choice for distributed system design.

To derive an object model from use cases, remember your high school grammar. Nouns from the use cases will show up as classes in the object model; verbs will show up as interactions between objects. Ideally, the object model should result in several diagrams: class diagrams showing classes and relations (specialization, aggregation, association), and sequence diagrams showing the sequence of interactions for each use case. Figure 20.4 shows a sample class diagram, which uses the Unified Modeling Language (UML) notation. Figure 20.5 shows a sample sequence diagram.

FIG. 20.4
This class diagram shows that Automobile, Truck, and Motorcycle are specializations of Vehicle; a Fleet is an aggregation of Vehicles; and a Vehicle is associated with a Road.

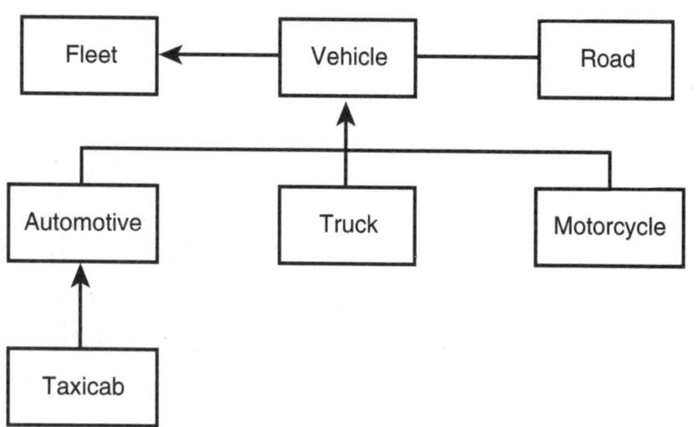

The object interactions identify services for the service-based design approach. The objective for this stage of design is to define in detail the services that the application will implement. A detailed definition of a service is basically a function definition and should include the name of the function, a detailed definition of the formal parameters, and possible return values.

The object model for the application will be a work in progress throughout the life of the application. As requirements change or become clarified through subsequent steps, the model will change. At some point in every project, it becomes necessary to "baseline" the object model—identify a specific version as the design for the current release.

Define Services and Interfaces

The object interactions are the services for the service-based design approach. The objective for this stage of design is to define in detail the ways in which the application will invoke services. The invocation details of a service comprise its *interface*. A detailed definition of an interface is basically a function definition. It should include the name of the function, a detailed definition of the formal parameters and possible return values, and any preconditions for invoking the service.

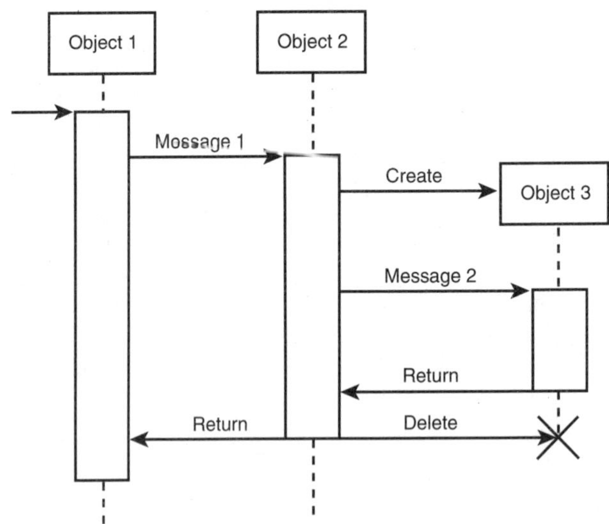

FIG. 20.5 This UML sequence diagram shows Object 1 sending Message 1 to Object 2, which in turn creates Object 3 and sends it Message 2. After Message 2 returns, Object 2 deletes Object 3, and returns Message 1.

An interface definition should be considered a contract for provision of a service. Early publishing of an interface definition allows developers to treat the service as a black box so that implementation of services can proceed in parallel. Once published, however, an interface should not change. This is quite difficult to achieve early in a project, but the alternative is chaos. If a service is used by a number of objects, the ripple effect will be widespread. That's why it's important to baseline the object model.

This stage of design is a good time to look for reuse opportunities. Obvious candidates include data management (SQL Server) and transaction management (MTS). You may find that important business logic has already been implemented in a prior project's mid-tier component. Often, a little research will identify a commercial product (ActiveX component or class library) that provides services closely matching project requirements.

Opportunities for software reuse generally fall into three categories:

- Component reuse
- Class library reuse
- Cut and paste miracle

Component reuse means binary reuse. An existing component will be incorporated into the new application without access to source code. Good examples include ActiveX controls and the database server. Use of a non-COM dynamic link library (DLL) is slightly less effective because it requires some source code (header files for C++; function DECLARE statements in VB), and because the interface is subject to change.

Class library reuse is structured source code reuse. An existing well-designed set of source code that addresses a specific problem domain can be incorporated into your project. Examples include the Microsoft Foundation Classes (MFC) and other shrink-wrap class libraries such as Rogue Wave's dbtools.h++. Often, an organization will have an internally developed class library addressing company-specific problem domains. A well-implemented and well-documented class library can save a lot of design and implementation time.

The *cut-and-paste miracle* occurs when a department manager remembers an application vaguely similar to the one under development, and deletes several weeks from the implementation schedule because the new project can just reuse most of that code. For small, complex functions that have been correctly implemented once before, the cut-and-paste miracle may save a few hours. Unfortunately, the time saved is usually offset by time spent searching through legacy code for the reusable bits, and time spent melding that code into the new application. The cut-and-paste miracle rarely works as well as expected.

Finally, pause to identify services implemented in the new application that might be useful in subsequent projects. Planning for subsequent reuse does require additional design and implementation time in the schedule.

Identify Relationships Among Business Objects and Services

Software engineers define *coupling* as relationships between software components and *cohesion* as relationships within a component. Generally, cohesion is good, and coupling is bad. A certain degree of coupling, however, is inevitable, and a reasonable goal is for cohesion to be substantially stronger than coupling.

Relationships among business objects and services take a variety of forms. An `Invoice` object, for example, presupposes a `Customer` object; a `ComputeTotal` service for the invoice may depend on a `ComputeTaxes` service. The best tool for identifying relationships is the object model. Relationships between objects will appear in the class diagram as aggregation, association, or specialization relations. Sequence diagrams will show dependencies between services.

An aggregation relation is a *part-of* relation. A taxicab may be part of a fleet; a fleet aggregates vehicles. A specialization relation is a *type-of* relation. A taxicab is a type of automobile, which is a type of vehicle, so a taxicab has a specialization relation to automobile and to vehicle. An association relation is a *uses* relation. A vehicle uses roads, so a vehicle has an association relation to roads. The sample class diagram in Figure 20.4 earlier in the chapter illustrates these relations.

Generally, specialization and aggregation relations show much stronger coupling between objects than association relations. Objects with a specialization relationship should always be implemented in the same component. Objects with an aggregation relation should be implemented in the same component, unless one or more objects add value as a reusable independent component.

Sequence diagrams show the strength of association relations. The more messages exchanged between a pair of objects, the stronger the relation. The message sequence diagram shows the number of types of messages passed; design should also consider the frequency of each message type. Figure 20.5, earlier in the chapter, shows a sample sequence diagram.

Dependencies also show where requirements changes are likely to have ripple effects. Sometimes, a minor design change can isolate objects or services that are likely to change frequently.

Partition the Application into Components

Partitioning a distributed application is the most challenging part of the design process. Object boundaries, application tiers, dependencies, and deployment issues must all be considered and balanced. A few general guidelines apply:

- *Minimize services implemented in the presentation layer.* A minimalist presentation layer is easily reimplemented on a new platform such as an X terminal or a web browser.
- *Minimize the number of communications between components.* Each discrete interaction between components introduces round-trip communication delay. Prefer a single complex procedure call to a series of simpler procedure calls. Stated differently, *maximize the ratio of work to connect time.*
- *Minimize coupling between components.* The term *coupling* refers to functional dependencies between components. For example, a mid-tier component might depend on a presentation component to validate a database login. This would require that *every* application that uses the mid-tier component must also use the presentation component for database login.
- *Group services based on the resources they interact with.* This strategy addresses bandwidth constraints. When several objects share a common set of resources, package them in a single component that can be deployed with good access to the needed resources. For example, several mid-tier services might make heavy use of a database; combine those services in a component and deploy it on an application server with a fast connection to the database. Stated differently, *maximize locality of reference.*
- *Use a simulation tool to validate your design.* The Application Performance Explorer (APE) included with Visual Basic 5.0 can provide useful insights into architectural alternatives (see Figure 20.6).

One very effective strategy for partitioning a three-tier application is to classify the services provided by each object as presentation, business, or data. The object and layer boundaries give a good first cut at a partition. Each object will be partitioned into three subcomponents (assuming that it provides services in each tier). Then, within each tier, group subcomponents based on interactions and dependencies within that layer. This same approach works for a two-tier or multitier application.

Include closely related objects in one component to improve performance and maintainability. However, expect the strength of interactions to vary markedly across tiers. Two objects may be strongly related in the data layer but quite distinct in the presentation layer.

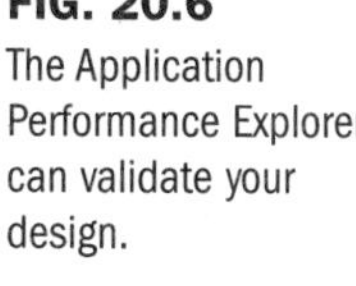

FIG. 20.6
The Application Performance Explorer can validate your design.

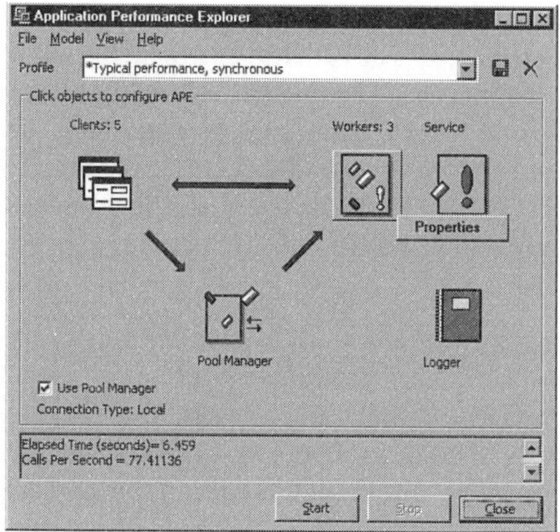

Select an Implementation Model for the Application

After creating an object model and incorporating reusable components, select an implementation model. Obviously, reuse decisions will play a substantial role in this decision. The organization's level of experience with client/server computing will also play an important role: groups with less experience tend to develop primarily two-tier applications. Sometimes, an application will have very few business services and just works better as two-tier.

A traditional client/server application presents relatively few partitioning decisions. The database server will provide data management services, and a client application will implement business logic and the user interface. In some cases, business logic could be implemented through triggers and stored procedures, or in client code. Generally, stored procedures minimize the number of database calls, improve scalability, and simplify deployment.

For data used by more than one application, or data subject to significant business rules, the three-tier model supports encapsulation of important business logic. Usually, three-tier applications scale more effectively to large numbers of users. Reuse decisions may also motivate a decision for three-tier.

Target Components onto Platforms

In this final design stage, emphasis shifts from abstraction to implementation. Business requirements implemented in the object model must now be reconciled with constraints imposed by the computing environment. Sometimes, partitioning decisions will have to be revised.

Often, external factors dictate a particular platform for both the database server and the GUI. For instance, the department database server might run Sybase System 11 on a multiprocessor UNIX system, and target users might run Windows 3.11 on 486-66 machines. Beyond available hardware, platform constraints also include IPC/RPC mechanisms and hosting for other required services such as transaction management.

Presentation Layer Components For most applications, the presentation layer platform is predefined: whatever sits on the user's desk today. Typically, this will include a range of performance and capabilities. Usually, management exerts substantial pressure to support all existing hardware; however, this may lead to unnecessary compromises in the application. It's always a mistake to hobble a new application to support old hardware. The issue is especially important if DCOM support is at stake. Probably the most important issue is appropriate network bandwidth. A component that makes excessive demands on network resources will perform poorly and may be unstable.

It's generally a good idea to define a minimum platform and a recommended platform. The platform specification should include processor type and speed, memory, available disk space, operating system, and network bandwidth and protocols. As a rule of thumb, when a relatively small number of target users (fewer than 20%) have subminimum systems, the hardware upgrade costs will usually be less than the cost to reengineer the application. This is especially true for the transition from 16-bit Windows to 32-bit Windows. If a majority of users have equipment that does not comply with the recommended platform, application performance is at risk.

Limit functionality in the presentation layer to session management (showing windows in the proper order, enabling and disabling controls) and very basic input validation. More complex validation belongs in the middle tier. This generally means that inputs are validated in groups rather than a field at a time. Identifying these validation groups is an important step in designing both the presentation layer and the middle tier.

Business Services Layer Components that enforce business rules on data require a high-bandwidth connection to the database server where that data resides. Database response time is typically the largest factor by far in response time for the business object. Where the business rules component in turn serves many presentation components, it may make sense to deploy closer to the user.

The business services layer offers deployment flexibility that may not be available for data services or presentation services. Consider whether concurrent processing (pipeline, parallel, or asynchronous) is appropriate. Remember, these three approaches are mutually compatible. Choosing a concurrency strategy may result in modifications to the object model.

When a problem decomposes functionally into a series of sequential tasks, consider a pipeline. Try to design the pipeline for similar processing time at each stage. The design should include a state transition diagram depicting the state of a task as it passes through each stage of the pipeline. This diagram will often identify resource conflicts and processing bottlenecks.

When a problem consists of a number of small uniform tasks, consider a parallel architecture. Parallel processing provides enhanced fault tolerance as well as enhanced throughput. Design should include a state transition diagram for the process.

When a problem includes independent subtasks, consider asynchronous processing. Design should include a state transition diagram for the asynchronous task.

Sometimes, data services may be distributed across multiple databases. When data services require coordinated operations against two or more databases, the application will require distributed transaction support. Microsoft Transaction Server provides good support for distributed transactions, particularly when all databases are hosted on Microsoft SQL Server 6.5.

Data Services Layer Most often, an existing database server will provide data management services. If the enterprise has been using the three-tier approach for some time, there should be some opportunity for reuse at both the data services and business services layers.

At the data services layer, it's very important to maximize the amount of work performed per query. For example, inexperienced developers will sometimes write an application to query the database individually for each row in a result set. VS97 includes several database access classes (Remote Data Objects, Active Data Objects, Data Access Objects) for more effective management of result sets. Most database servers support stored procedures, another way to maximize work per query. There is a tradeoff, however: stored procedures are often difficult to debug and don't fit well into most configuration management tools.

Use Data Access Objects (DAO) with desktop databases such as Paradox, FoxPro, and especially Access. Remote Data Objects (RDO) can provide much more efficient access to a database server on the local area network, providing extended access to database errors, and return codes and output parameters for stored procedures. Active Data Objects (ADO) can also provide efficient access to database servers, with fewer advanced features than RDO. All three libraries use ODBC; Microsoft is nudging developers toward ADO.

See "ADO Versus RDO2: Which Access Method Should You Use?" **p. 664**

ON THE WEB

For a comparison of DAO, RDO, and ADO, see **http://www.microsoft.com/data/whatcom.htm**.

The data services layer is often a hot spot for resource contention. Take care to implement services so as to minimize locking. Avoid cursors, use the minimum workable locking level, and avoid long-running transactions. In particular, no database transaction should require user input or confirmation. (The users might decide to go to lunch.)

From Here...

In this chapter, you looked at the problem of designing a client/server application on a traditional network, beginning with Microsoft's strategic services paradigm. Then you looked at some of the factors that influence a design. After reviewing common design objectives and constraints, you learned about concurrent processing approaches, with a comparison of the two-tier and three-tier client/server application models. Finally, you saw all the pieces pulled together into a comprehensive design strategy.

- To learn more about Microsoft's strategies for application development in the enterprise, see Chapter 4, "Using Microsoft's Object Technologies."
- See Chapter 10, "Clients, Servers, and Components: Web-Based Applications," for a discussion of applications for I-net environments.

- For a more general discussion of distributed applications, see Chapter 17, "Server-Side Programming in an I-net Environment."
- Chapter 3 provides a detailed discussion of "Creating Database-Aware Applications with Visual Studio."

CHAPTER 21

Creating Distributed Applications

by Timothy A. White

The landscape of corporate America is and has been undergoing significant change, partly in response to the dramatic pace at which technology has evolved. Technology is enabling organizations to realize the potential of distributed business environments, pushing services and products to customers around the globe. Technology allows business to transpire regardless of location. As this evolution occurs, businesses shift from the old data processing (host-based) paradigm to the newer client/server paradigm. With this shift, many of the legacy applications that have served them well are either rewritten or scrapped.

This chapter explores some of the available technologies that allow organizations to utilize these existing legacy assets and to combine them with the power of client/server computing. Many of the features of Visual Studio, as described in this book, can be coupled with the techniques discussed in this chapter to further leverage corporate assets. Not only does this save an organization money and time, but it also can uncover vast quantities of valuable data that has been hidden deep in the bowels of legacy systems. As you read this chapter, let your mind remain open to new ideas. The overworked phrase "thinking out of the box" applies here.

What is a distributed application?

Gain an understanding of distributed applications and where they fit in the corporate application development environment.

Key technologies

Discover some of the key components that Microsoft has delivered for creating and integrating distributed applications.

Coping with limited bandwidth

Review strategies for coping with variable or limited network availability in a distributed environment.

Intranet/Internet alternatives

Get an overview of some alternatives to the connected and disconnected client approaches using intranet and Internet applications.

This chapter discusses distributed applications from two perspectives. The first perspective looks at internally distributed applications running on a variety of platforms, distributing tasks across the enterprise. The second perspective views remote user applications that free workers from the confines of the office and place them in the best possible position to create positive value for the organization. These methods are not mutually exclusive; in fact, many organizations will realize significant benefits from a derivative of the two. ■

What Is a Distributed Application?

A *distributed application* is one that has multiple components running on different machines. In today's business environment, the creation of distributed applications is an evolutionary process. The boundaries of distributed applications are constantly being expanded and stretched as the world of technology changes to keep up with the business needs of corporate America. Corporate information technology (IT) staffs are looking for ways to not only balance budgets and deliver timely solutions, but also to leverage their existing legacy systems while developing new systems using newer, more flexible client/server technologies.

This chapter is not intended to provide step-by-step "how to" instructions on developing distributed applications, but to raise your level of awareness of the technologies and tools available for such endeavors. It also strives to point out some of the pitfalls in building and implementing distributed solutions.

Distributed applications reflect the distributed nature of many large organizations. Organizations that can take advantage of distributed environments, leveraging all their information assets, can gain a real advantage in the marketplace. Demographic data, managed properly and used to produce timely indications of changes or shifts in a business environment, can produce significant positive results. Many organizations have demographic data stored in a variety of places throughout the organization. Using older techniques of gathering this information and crunching it into usable formats can take weeks, months, or even years. With this long turnaround time, many opportunities that this data can create are lost due to poor responsiveness. In this area, distributed applications, and specifically the ability to link disparate data stores, can provide tangible results for many organizations.

Distributed applications take on many forms. Some are fairly easily understood, such as the two-tier client/server model. Others are far more complex, requiring the efforts of many developers and potentially years to build and implement. As the pace of technological evolution quickens, several challenges confront corporate IT staffs. Two of these challenges are the need to leverage legacy systems and the push towards departmentalized computing.

Legacy Integration

Legacy integration is not a new concept, but one that is growing in popularity. This is largely due to necessity, but also to the tools now available to developers and integrators. Literally billions of lines of legacy application code are in use today, most of it working fairly well. Many of these applications will still be in use well into the next century. The data stored on legacy systems also represents a potential competitive advantage for many organizations. By making better use of this resource, organizations can realize increased synergy and profits. With the evolution of many organizations, the legacy systems that once supported all their needs might no longer suffice. This is not to say that all the pieces of these legacy systems are fundamentally flawed, but rather that some key components need to be reengineered to meet changing business needs. So, given these business needs for new or advanced functionality, the question becomes: integrate or rebuild? Organizations looking for that something to put them over the top might find it in the form of increased efficiency in the use of their legacy systems and data. Legacy integration can also improve delivery time of key applications and better utilization of resources.

It is fairly common to hear someone say, "We should just rewrite it in *xyz*," with *xyz* representing any number of client/server development tools. This sounds great because as a developer, you always want to use the latest and greatest development tools, but for the business this might have little or no positive financial impact. In other words, rewriting these applications can be a tough sell. The impact of rewriting a legacy system typically trickles through the entire systems development environment. Rewriting one system can have a monumental impact on other systems, which then must be changed or rewritten. In today's environment, leveraging the current investment is probably the more prudent course of action, unless there are significant financial incentives for rewriting applications.

In the eyes of many corporations, these legacy applications represent a tremendous investment—not only in hardware and software, but also in business logic that might not be easily defined or reengineered. It becomes difficult to justify rewriting something that is working, proven, and providing positive benefits to the business. If it is not a total change of direction in business processes, integrating with existing systems can ease the development effort. It does so not only by reducing costs and time associated with the development, but also by reducing the number of business processes that need to be defined or redefined—which can mean many hours spent in meetings discussing the actual and theoretical business processes.

The development of quality applications, regardless of tools and expertise, takes time. Quality solutions require you to take time for design, development, good business analysis, and definition of user and system requirements. Add to this the time to rewrite legacy code, and the deliverable time frame might outlast the useful life of the application. Today's business environment can change dramatically in a short period of time. If application development staffs are not responsive and flexible to the business needs, the business opportunities at hand might be missed. This not only alienates the business, but the perceived unresponsiveness will do little for IT's stance within the organization.

One way to quicken the process of rewriting legacy applications is to talk to the developers of the original system. By picking their minds about what business processes drove key areas of application functionality, you can quickly discern needed functionality from unneeded functionality in a new system. Because many legacy systems are 10 to 20 years old or older, these individuals might no longer be an available resource. Project managers might also have a difficult time assembling a development team that is equally qualified to look at legacy code, reverse-engineer the business rules, and build client/server applications. Once again, the factor of timeliness comes into play: Is it worth the time to reverse-engineer the legacy process, or should it be integrated with the new applications or functionality? As stated earlier, with the rapidly changing business environment, the more prudent approach might be integration.

Many opportunities can exist in integrating with legacy applications, but many challenges will also be faced. Integration raises some of the more difficult questions. Problems such as dealing with disparate hardware, operating systems, and communication protocols come to mind immediately. There is also the question of various data storage mechanisms. How are data stores, such as VSAM and SQL Server, integrated? Another challenge is in building the right mix of developer talents. Both advanced technology and legacy systems experts will be required, and the proper mix will make the integration efforts a lot smoother. Not many IT shops have developers or systems specialists that have attempted these types of development efforts. Confidence, persistence, willingness to listen, openness to new tools and technologies, and sheer durability will go a long way toward conquering these challenges.

Departmentalized Applications

A departmentalized application is typically characterized by a small set of users. Hardware might be dedicated to a particular user community, and the application fulfills a single, departmentally specific purpose. This single purposefulness coincides with the corporate definition of a department, which typically is designed around a single business purpose or function. Departmental applications are typically more cost-effective to develop in the short term. There are, however, some inherent problems with this approach, primarily the sharing of data. These silos of data can increase the costs of departmental applications in the long term.

Departmentalized applications make sense for several reasons. Typically it is more cost-effective to develop applications that have a smaller scope and a smaller set of users. This allows for a smaller development team, which eliminates some management overhead. The user community is focused on one business goal—whatever it is that their department does. And it is easier to manage response time and scalability on the departmental level, not having to worry about scaling to extremely large user communities and so forth.

Departmentalization does come at a cost. Typically the information is not shared across departments, which takes away from the synergy and responsiveness of an organization. This is one reason for the use of corporate data warehouses and data marts, which provide the ability to gather information from multiple sources and store it centrally for all to access. The data warehouse or data mart concept works fine for a scenario in which the departmental data is used for analysis that is not "real-time" sensitive. In some situations, however, departments within an organization will demand real-time data from other departments.

You can overcome the challenge of distributed data by using distributed transaction processing. This approach consists of applications that make use of and manipulate multiple databases or data stores. Managing distributed transactions—making sure that they process successfully—is the central issue faced in this approach. You would not want to risk data integrity by updating one database and not the other. Another issue is the availability of either local or remote databases. You might not want to stop processing in the application because a distributed database is unavailable. These issues, as you will see later in this chapter, can be handled by using a reliable and durable transaction-processing architecture.

The following sections introduce you to an array of technologies that exist to help you build distributed and integrated applications. Examples are also presented for how to overcome many of the challenges mentioned here. The first section covers some of the technologies that are available for developing solutions for these situations.

▶ For more information about design strategies for distributed applications, **see** Chapter 20, "Clients, Servers, and Components: Design Strategies for Distributed Applications," **p. 549**.

Key Technologies

Microsoft has amassed an array of tools and technologies that allow you to build distributed applications and to integrate these applications with each other and with legacy systems. Some of these tools are used primarily for moving data to multiple data stores, whereas others are concerned with sharing data and processes between disparate environments. As mentioned earlier in this book, Microsoft tends to use catchy code names. Some of the tools described in this section are referred to by their code names, and some are listed with the production name and the code name.

The following technologies are discussed in this section:

- Replication
- The Host Data Replicator
- The Microsoft Transaction Server
- The OLE DB/DDM driver
- Cedar
- The Microsoft Message Queue

The technologies presented here have a common goal. They strive to allow you, as the developer, to focus on business issues and worry less about the back-office issues. The role of the developer is to focus on the business issues and problems at hand, design solutions, and then select the proper tools for the implementation of these solutions. Microsoft has sought to provide you with a rich tool set for nearly all the situations that can arise during the implementation of these solutions. Some of these tools are designed to help you build distributed client/server applications that can be integrated with legacy applications. Others are designed for distributed applications that must make use of multiple databases or handle remote users.

ON THE WEB

The following technologies and tools are presented in cursory fashion. For more details on these and any of the Microsoft products, it is recommended that you visit its web site, **www.microsoft.com**. Be prepared to spend a significant amount of time locating information; a wealth of technical documentation is provided on each of these tools.

You will also find some hints on finding information regarding each tool or topic at the end of each topic's section of this chapter.

Replication

As an organization grows and its data becomes more specialized and departmentalized, it is often necessary for applications to share data. Organizations stand to gain competitive advantages through synergy and responsiveness. The sharing of data between departments is paramount in developing this synergy. For situations where real-time consistent data is not necessary and loosely synchronized data will suffice, replication provides you with a valuable tool.

Replication is a process by which data is propagated from one database to another, maintaining a consistent view. This propagation can be transaction based, scheduled, or on demand. *Transaction-based replication* of data is based upon a database transaction occurring. This model presents near real-time distributed transactions. Transaction-based replication is slowed by transaction size, transaction volume, and network traffic. *Scheduled replication* is more widely used in situations where the data is not as time-sensitive or transaction volume does not make it possible or practical to use transactional replication. One common use for scheduled replication is in data warehousing, where data can be gathered for decision support based on the previous day's events. *On-demand replication* is typically used for data security functions, such as taking copies of distributed databases for point-in-time disaster recovery.

Replication, as described by Microsoft, uses *publishing* databases, which publish data to *subscribing* databases. Publishing databases can publish data to one or many subscribers. Microsoft SQL Server will support replication by means of ODBC to Microsoft Access or Oracle databases, which can be very beneficial for organizations with disparate data stores. Subscribers to replication see a point-in-time consistent view of the publishing database. In other words, replication does not guarantee that at every instant in time all copies of a data element will be identical.

SQL Server replication supports partitioning of replicated data. Data might be horizontally partitioned, vertically partitioned, or a combination of the two. *Horizontal partitioning* publishes only specific rows of data to a subscribing database. *Vertical partitioning* publishes only specific columns of data to a subscribing database. *Combination replication*, involving both horizontal and vertical partitioning, replicates only selected columns from selected rows. Combination partitioning truly grants you flexibility in the implementation of replication and the solutions you are able to provide. This functionality is useful for systems that might need only specific pieces of data from a department.

For more information regarding Microsoft SQL Server replication, developers can refer to *Special Edition Using Microsoft BackOffice*, Volume 2 from Que, ISBN 0-7897-1130-3, and the documentation provided with the SQL Server software. For other RDBMSs, refer to the manufacturer's documentation for the specifics regarding replication.

The Host Data Replicator (Cakewalk)

Many companies that have existing host-based legacy environments use DB2. To answer the call for data transparency with these systems, Microsoft has developed the Host Data

Replicator, code-named Cakewalk. The Host Data Replicator allows replication of database tables between DB2 and SQL Server. It also allows bidirectional replication, in which an entire table is refreshed with a snapshot from the source environment. The Host Data Replicator uses Microsoft's SNA version 3.0 for the connectivity to the host environment, while all of the processing resides on the NT server on which the Host Data Replicator is installed. The Host Data Replicator supports a variety of replication scenarios, types, and DB2 products.

The Host Data Replicator supports a myriad of replication scenarios that allow for flexibility and transparency of data between SQL Server and DB2 systems. Replication scenarios supported are horizontal, vertical, and combination partitioning, as discussed previously. The Host Data Replicator also supports the use of derived columns, allowing for the calculation of fields during replication. The Host Data Replicator also provides the ability to use Structured Query Language (SQL) to alter data before or after replication and the ability to manipulate the data type or column order of replicated data.

The Host Data Replicator supports the following replication features:

- *Vertical partitioning*—Replication of only selected columns
- *Horizontal partitioning*—Replication of only selected rows
- *Combined partitioning*—Replication of only selected columns from selected rows
- *Derived columns*—Calculated from source data
- *SQL*—Ability to use SQL expressions to alter data before or after replication
- *Data manipulation*—Ability to manipulate the data to fit the target's data type or column order

The Host Data Replicator provides for three replication time frames. The first is on-demand replication. This can be implemented through a programmatic interface to provide quasi-transaction-based replication. The next is scheduled replication, which is very useful if hour-, day-, or week-old data is sufficient for the business purposes it is intended to serve. The last is recurring scheduled replication. This is very similar to scheduled replication, usually set to occur at a specific time or times of the day and over a given period of time.

The Host Data Replicator supports a variety of DB2 flavors. Some organizations might have multiple DB2 environments, but the transparency provided by the Host Data Replicator can be used with one or more of these DB2 environments and Microsoft SQL Server. This also allows the same set of application code to work using any of the supported DB2 platforms. By writing applications to use the Host Data Replicator, you can free the dependence of the application on a specific DB2 platform. This allows scalability on the DB2 legacy side of the development environment without changing the code to access it.

Host Data Replicator supports the following versions of DB2:

- DB2 for MVS
- DB2/VM

- DB2/400 for AS/400
- DB2/2 for OS/2
- DB2/6000 for RS6000
- DB2/2 for Windows NT

For IT shops that have an install base of DB2, it has become much easier to share information with SQL Server databases. This will reduce development time for new client/server applications by allowing developers to share data between environments without sacrificing development time providing middleware solutions.

ON THE WEB

For more information on the Host Data Replicator, visit the Microsoft Developer Network web site at **www.microsoft.com/MSDN** and search on *Cakewalk* or *Host Data Replicator*.

The Microsoft Transaction Server

The Microsoft Transaction Server (MTS) is a set of components that provide specific pieces of functionality for creating, deploying, and managing distributed applications. MTS allows for the packaging and distribution of application components and logic. A key component of MTS is the Distributed Transaction Coordinator (DTC) for managing distributed transactions.

MTS manages packages of components, which are either purchased or developed in-house. These components are pulled together to form application units. MTS also manages a shared pool of Open Database Connectivity (ODBC) data connections. These data connections can allow application access to a variety of data stores, ranging from SQL Server database tables to mainframe VSAM files.

MTS can also be used to deploy mid-tier logic implemented in the form of ActiveX components. These ActiveX objects receive requests from client applications, apply business logic to the request, and then call the appropriate resource manager to fulfill the request. Collections of these ActiveX components form packages, which can be released to a Windows NT server to act as a linkage between clients and the shared resources they want to access. This functionality typically forms the middle tier in a three-tiered client/server system.

Using MTS packages has the following advantages:

- *Scalability*—Applications can be scaled from one server to many clustered servers to handle larger volumes.
- *Distributed*—Applications can be written as if for a single user but run as distributed components using MTS.
- *Multiuser*—MTS provides thread and memory management.
- *Resource pooling*—MTS provides object pooling and database connection pooling.
- *Atomicity*—MTS ensures through the use of the Distributed Transaction Coordinator that work is either done completely or not done at all.

As stated earlier, one component of MTS is the Distributed Transaction Coordinator (DTC). The DTC allows for preservation of the ACID (Atomicity, Consistency, Isolation, and Durability) properties of transactions. These transactions can be either managed by the DTC or resolved by an administrator in the case of problem transactions. DTC also provides an Application Programming Interface (API) based on the Component Object Model (COM) to aid in the development of distributed applications. This API enables C++ developers to create transaction objects. These objects can then be instantiated and processed using the transaction resource managers and transaction coordinators.

▶ **See** "What Is a Transaction?," **p. 670**

Atomicity of transactions means that either a transaction completes successfully or no part of the transaction completes successfully. Under DTC, transactions are all or nothing. DTC ensures this by using the two-phase commit (2PC).

In the 2PC, an `update` statement is submitted to each SQL Server. The data is updated but not committed. In this state, the server is *prepared* to commit. Once the DTC is notified that both updates occurred and that both databases are prepared, the DTC sends a `commit` instruction to both, and the databases commit the transaction. Should a failure, like a power outage, occur during this process, the DTC maintains a log of state information regarding the transaction. When both databases are back online, the log is checked, and both databases return the last known state regarding the transaction. They either go ahead and commit a prepared transaction, or roll back the entire transaction. With this level of fault tolerance, you can keep your databases consistent and clean, while using distributed transactions.

At times you will have transactions that don't behave properly; these are said to be *in-doubt transactions*. DTC will resolve these transactions by communicating with other DTC services involved in the transaction. Based on that communication, the transaction is either rolled back or committed. It is also possible for system administrators to monitor the DTC for in-doubt transactions and resolve them by using the SQL Enterprise Manager. Manually resolving in-doubt transactions does take some level of expertise, specifically in knowing how the results might affect the business processes that have been created or are using the transaction.

Another welcome feature to DTC is the COM-based API. This makes it much easier for you to develop applications that take full advantage of the services that DTC offers. It also frees you from the complexities of developing middleware solutions. This allows you to focus more time on the business processes at hand, which will lead to better applications for the business user. In the eyes of the business user, your development efforts will also seem more timely and responsive.

▶ For additional information on the Distributed Transaction Coordinator, **see** "The Role of the DTC in Transaction Processing," **p. 677**.

▶ For additional information on the Microsoft Transaction Server, **see** "Managing Transactions in MTS," **p. 692**.

For more information regarding the Microsoft Transaction Server or the Distributed Transaction Coordinator, see *Special Edition Using Microsoft BackOffice*, Volume 2 from Que, ISBN 0-7897-1130-3, or the documentation provided with the SQL Server software.

The OLE DB/DDM Driver

The OLE DB/DDM driver, code-named Thor, gives you the ability to integrate legacy data with more current relational database systems, such as SQL Server. The OLE DB/DDM driver makes use of two data access methods: Microsoft's OLE DB and IBM's Distributed Data Management (DDM). OLE DB/DDM opens up the world of legacy data files, such as VSAM and OS/400 files, to the client/server application developer, you. This enables you to leverage a tremendous resource within many organizations, their legacy data.

OLE DB is a major component of Microsoft's Universal Data Access initiative. This allows for data stored in any form to be accessed through a common set of interfaces. This means that corporate data stored in spreadsheets, relational databases, flat files, or email systems is accessible to the application, greatly simplifying your job as the application developer. This is accomplished by the data stores exposing common interfaces to the data.

OLE DB partitions the database functionality into logical components and allows for these components to communicate by event processing. An OLE DB component can be created to present data in a tabular format while allowing for complex application logic to be processed within the component. OLE DB provides a COM-based API for developing robust database applications using any number of data stores and for a variety of platforms. Support for OLE DB falls on the shoulders of the data provider, that is, Microsoft Excel, Microsoft Project, or ODBC SQL-oriented data. OLE DB resides above the data store and below the application, allowing the application developer to interface with the OLE DB APIs without worrying about the underlying data store. It is worth noting that OLE DB is not a replacement for ODBC, but rather allows OLE DB data consumers to utilize ODBC data providers.

IBM's Distributed Data Management (DDM) protocol is a standard access method to row-oriented legacy data files, such as VSAM. DDM is available for most host environments. The OLE DB/DDM driver requires no host-side software from Microsoft.

The OLE DB/DDM driver allows you to access VSAM data set members much as you would access files on a Windows NT server. Because you can not only view the VSAM data set member, but also have record-level I/O access, you can utilize this data without first performing costly conversions to SQL Server or other RDBMS formats. The OLE DB/DDM driver also allows access to both fixed and variable record length records, with full data set navigation. Other features of OLE DB/DDM are file locking, record locking, and record attribute preservation of VSAM files. OLE DB/DDM truly is a single solution for accessing multiple data storage types on multiple disparate platforms.

The following is a list of VSAM file types supported:

- Key-sequenced data set
- Entry-sequenced data set
- Relative record data set
- Partitioned data set

▶ **See** "Universal Data Access and OLE DB," **p. 642**

ON THE WEB

For more information regarding the OLE DB/DDM driver, visit the Microsoft Developer Network web site at **www.microsoft.com/msdn** and search on *Thor* or *OLE DB/DDM*.

Cedar

Cedar, as code-named by Microsoft, allows you to create distributed client/server applications using legacy mainframe applications as functional components. Cedar's program-to-program interoperability allows organizations to leverage their existing mainframe applications in a distributed COM-based client/server environment. Using the tools that come with Cedar, you can quickly create Distributed COM (DCOM) components using legacy systems. These components can communicate and interoperate to form very robust applications. Cedar allows for atomic, transaction-based client/server applications to use business logic that is already in place rather than having to rewrite or reengineer legacy business logic. Companies can utilize their existing investments in mainframe programming tools and developers while taking advantage of the more flexible COM- and DCOM-oriented technologies and tool sets to extend legacy systems.

An example of this flexibility is extending a mainframe-based record look-up utility. You could incorporate this functionality into a new Windows-based application, tying it to a pushbutton, allowing the mainframe component to find information, based on a name, and supplying this data to your Windows application.

These DCOM components created by Cedar can be used by and run on any DCOM-compliant platform, such as MVS. Developers can use these components in creating client/server distributed applications, which can consist of components running locally, on middle-tier servers, and on the mainframe, passing data between them from a variety of data stores. As in the previous example, a program or utility running on MVS could be created as a DCOM component and utilized by your Windows application.

You can create Cedar components by using the Cedar Interface Builder. The Interface Builder allows you to define the methods and I/O parameters for the host application. This process includes specifying the location and name of the mainframe program and specifying any default data type mappings. The last step in this process is the creation of the Cedar type library and registering it with MTS. The Cedar components will reside on the Windows NT server, not on the legacy host system, and must be registered on any client platforms that they will be called from.

Cedar works by intercepting object method calls and redirecting them to the appropriate mainframe program. Cedar uses the definition, built during the creation of the component, to convert the method call into the appropriate format for the target platform and sends the method call to the host platform. The connection to the host environment is provided by Microsoft SNA Server 3.0. Once the mainframe component processes the method call and returns the results, Cedar converts the results from the native host format to a format understandable by the calling object. The results are then sent back to the calling object.

Cedar is a component of MTS, discussed earlier. This allows Cedar to interact and make use of the MTS transaction functionality. Cedar, working with MTS components such as DTC and using the OLE DB/DDM database connectivity, can provide two-phase commit functionality between different database systems running on different platforms. This empowers you, as the developer, to create synergistic applications that make full use of legacy assets while delivering the flexibility and functionality that the organization desires.

Cedar-defined objects can be used with any development tool that supports automation objects. Such tools include Visual Basic 5.0 and Visual C++. You can view these objects using the standard object browser once the object library is added to the application.

ON THE WEB

For more information on Cedar, visit the Microsoft Developer Network web site at **www.microsoft.com/msdn** and search on *Cedar*.

The Microsoft Message Queue

Today's business environment often requires individuals within different departments to communicate with each other to reach a common business goal. In much the same way, business requirements are also forcing applications running on different systems to communicate with each other in support of common business goals. With disparate data stores, machines, network protocols, and applications, this might seem a daunting task. One answer is to rebuild existing applications and homogenize them and the networks on which they run. This start-from-scratch mentality is a difficult sell in the "do more with less" IT environment of today. A more reasonable solution is to allow applications to communicate with each other regardless of platform or language. Allowing new applications to communicate with existing applications across disparate technologies, passing state and transactional information from application to application, becomes the ideal method of merging technologies quickly and efficiently.

The answer to the merging of heterogeneous technologies comes in the form of messaging. Microsoft has answered this need with the Microsoft Message Queue (MSMQ), code-named Falcon. Message queuing provides reliable communication between applications that could possibly be running on varying platforms across heterogeneous networks. Messaging can be real-time or occur at periodic intervals. MSMQ provides guaranteed delivery and offers a variety of response types. MSMQ is also an ideal tool for a remote client architecture, where users can be at any location at any time. Using the Windows NT framework for security and offering a Software Development Kit (SDK) and API, MSMQ becomes an invaluable part of many distributed application projects.

MSMQ conducts either synchronous or asynchronous messaging with guaranteed message delivery. MSMQ uses a *store-and-forward* format, meaning that messages are written to intermediate queues and then if possible are transferred to either another intermediate queue or the destination queue. At each leg of this journey, the messages are removed from the intermediate queue only after they have reached their target queue. Should a target queue be unavailable, the message will remain in the intermediate queue until it can be delivered or removed from the queue manually. In this way MSMQ provides guaranteed message delivery regardless of network or system problems.

Building on the philosophy of guaranteed delivery is the atomicity of messages. Messages can take the form of transactions, meaning that one message can contain information to update a database and send a message to a host process. These transaction messages will act as an atomic unit. Should either the update fail or the target message queue be unavailable, both processes will wait until they can be completed successfully. Transaction messages are also guaranteed to arrive in order and not more than once to the destination queue.

Messages can be one of three types:

- *Guaranteed delivery*—The message is guaranteed to reach either the next intermediate message queue or destination message queue, even if a machine or machines crash along the route.
- *Express delivery*—Referred to as in-memory store and forward messaging. The message is guaranteed to be delivered, except in the case of a machine crash.
- *Transactional delivery*—The message is guaranteed to be delivered to the destination message queue not more than once, even in the case of a machine crash. The messages will arrive in order in the form of an atomic update.

It is also possible to receive confirmation from the destination queue that the message was received successfully. The responses can be one of three types.

The following is a summary of the three response types supported by MSMQ:

- *Full acknowledgment*—The acknowledgment message is placed in the response queue by MSMQ as designated by the source application by MSMQ. For mission-critical messaging, this approach might be necessary.
- *Negative acknowledgment*—MSMQ sends a message to the response queue of the sending application only if an error occurs. This can also be used with mission-critical messaging, if the user does not need confirmation that the message was delivered. This approach would be beneficial in situations where full acknowledgment might overload the message queues, causing unnecessary delays.
- *No notification*—No acknowledgments or error messages are delivered to the source application. For non-mission-critical applications this might be appropriate, but typically you will want at least an error message returned if a problem occurs; therefore, this approach is used less frequently.

Remote users are becoming not just more common, but a standard for some positions within many organizations. The obvious example is that of a salesperson who might spend days, weeks, or even months traveling to promote a product. For this distributed, disconnected user, MSMQ provides connectionless messaging. Applications utilizing MSMQ do not need to be directly connected to the receiving application. Applications that are not connected can use a local MSMQ intermediate queue to store messages until the user is connected to either the receiving application or an intermediate queue that will be able to deliver the messages to the receiving application. This allows a user to work offline and then transmit data in the form of transactional messages at a later time.

MSMQ security for messaging is based on the Windows NT security framework and the Crypto API for encryption and digital signatures. Maintaining a high level of security and working within the existing Windows NT security framework will ease some of the development pains for creating MSMQ applications. This will also allow the security administrator to sleep at night when an organization uses remote clients to distribute and collect sensitive data.

MSMQ comes with an SDK that contains MSMQ ActiveX components that can be used by Visual Basic, Internet Information Server Active Server Pages, or any other ActiveX container. MSMQ ships with MSMQ Servers that handle the routing services and host the information store that holds configuration data. Each MSMQ queue is assigned a Globally Unique Identifier (GUID) when it is created. This ensures that no matter where a message queue exists on a network, an application using this GUID will be able to find the associated message queue. MSMQ also has a Message Queue Explorer for monitoring and managing messages. Another feature of MSMQ is that the dynamic configuration of disparate networks does not come at the cost of major application changes. This is due to the availability of the MSMQ API on a variety of platforms. This means that one set of application code will work across all supported platforms.

MSMQ API allows developers to do the following:

- Create and register MSMQ queues
- Retrieve status information about queues
- Locate queues
- Close and remove queues
- Send messages to and receive messages from queues
- Encapsulate messages and database transactions into a single atomic transaction message
- Manage messages within queues

NOTE It should be pointed out here that MSMQ can theoretically function transparently. In nearly all cases, however, you will need to make use of the MSMQ API. By determining message queue status and taking an active role in the management of messages and the message queues, your applications will function in a much more consistent manner. ■

MSMQ has two components that must be installed. The MSMQ Server can be installed on an existing Windows NT Server without dedicating a machine solely for MSMQ. The MSMQ Client runtime needs to be configured on every machine that will be using MSMQ-based communications.

MSMQ gives organizations the ability to leverage their legacy and distributed applications and move forward with new technology initiatives. For organizations that are moving away from mainframe or host-based systems, MSMQ allows this migration to be done in a piecemeal fashion. These reasons can provide significant benefits to IT development efforts and the business units that pay for them.

ON THE WEB

For more information on MSMQ, visit the Microsoft Developer Network web site at **www.microsoft.com/msdn** and search on *MSMQ* or *Falcon*.

Limited Bandwidth Strategies

A common challenge for distributed applications is the need to support connected and disconnected clients. This refers to the way in which the application uses and disseminates information. If the application is connected to the database or network the entire time it is in use, then it is called a *connected client*. If there are periods of time when the application will be in use but not connected to either a database or network, then it is called a *disconnected client*.

Based purely on numbers, most client/server applications are of the connected client flavor. However, corporate cultures have been undergoing some changes in recent years that have allowed them to embrace telecommuting. There are also situations that demand the use of disconnected client architectures, such as systems used by traveling salespeople. It quickly becomes very clumsy and awkward to ask a potential customer for the use of a phone line while preparing for a sales pitch. Allowing salespeople to retrieve data, process it with a customer, and then send the updated or new data back to the office for processing is a viable alternative to this situation.

The Connected Client Architecture

A *connected client application* is one that maintains a constant connection to either a database or a network. This is the most common type of client/server computing. A large part of this book and this chapter is dedicated to technologies that are expanding the connected client architecture and client/server computing in general. Connected client applications are usually built to support some type of online process. They also will typically push some of the functionality or business logic onto the Relational Database Management System (RDBMS) that is being used as a data store.

Connected client applications are typically of the On-Line Transaction Processing (OLTP) variety. Users work at client workstations entering transaction information into a database, such as sales data. These applications offer real-time response to user requests for information and are typically designed around one business process, such as sales. In this way, you see the development of departmentalized computing.

The task of data resolution usually falls to the RDBMS, such as Microsoft's SQL Server. Managing concurrent updates and simultaneous requests for data from multiple users is one fundamental job of the RDBMS. It is also worth noting that the business rules pertinent to these applications are often maintained within the RDBMS in the form of stored procedures, grants and privileges, and user roles.

The Disconnected Client Architecture

A *disconnected client application* is one that is used offline, allowing the user to process data and not be directly connected to a network or corporate data store. This also implies that data must be resolved by some means other than using real-time transactions. It is very common to find the business rules for how the data is managed to be in the form of stored procedures, which allow for batch processing of data received over a given period of time.

Security for transactions must be handled by the local data store, which must be robust enough to handle some form of replication. The replication or dissemination of data, from remote users to corporate data stores, is typically done by periodically connecting to a corporate network by modem and transmitting data. The transmission is usually handled by application logic, making use of automated replication or messaging.

When to Use Connected and Disconnected Clients

The primary factors in choosing a connected or disconnected architecture are workflow analysis and cost. Workflow analysis helps determine the need for connectivity; cost analysis determines feasibility. Remember that additional implementation costs can be offset by reduced workflow costs. The choice of a connected or disconnected approach should be weighed for each system interface.

Workflow Analysis The first step in selecting a connected or disconnected approach should be an analysis of tasks in which the software will play a role. For each task, identify the role of the computer, the data required, and the available connectivity. For a freight dispatcher on a loading dock, a computer can track the assignment of loads to trucks; up-to-the-minute status on shipments can be valuable to customer service staff, and the fixed location makes a connected application the best choice. Customers reasonably expect to know whether their order has shipped. For a truck driver, daily updates on location of a shipment add value for customer service; mile-by-mile updates add substantially less. On a truck traveling at sixty miles per hour, a disconnected (laptop) application is the only feasible choice. Such information as that the shipment left the loading dock yesterday and left Abilene this morning will satisfy most customer inquiries.

Each new application must fit into a unique workflow. However, don't overlook opportunities to improve the workflow. For example, most organizations produce sets of reports from legacy data just because they always have. Many of these reports are obsolete and no more than recyclable waste. The costs of pushing hard copy reports can result in millions of dollars in extra expense, not just in materials but in the personnel to distribute them. The concept of a totally paperless environment is overly idealistic, but a little common sense regarding the sharing of online information between departmental systems can potentially save thousands of dollars annually.

Remember that the workflow (and the associated costs) will be different depending on the selection of a connected or disconnected architecture.

Cost Analysis It's important to understand the costs of implementing a connected or disconnected application. Costs include infrastructure (hardware, networks, and systems software), communications, support, training, administration, and of course application development (initial and maintenance). It takes time for an organization to deploy and assimilate a robust network architecture. Application design should never target a more robust network than currently exists. If branch offices have local area networks, but no wide area network exists to link branches, then choose a disconnected architecture for interbranch communications. If plans are afoot to implement a wide area network, consider that in plans for version 2.

Communication costs are a factor in the disconnected client implementation. One cost that might be incurred is the cost to upgrade or implement remote access to the corporate network. If the organization is running Window 95 or Windows NT, the use of Remote Access Server (RAS) makes this a much simpler process. RAS allows for a remote dial-in connection to a network and provides excellent support for disconnected applications. This utility is included as part of the Windows 95 and NT operating systems. For information regarding the configuration, use, and management of RAS devices, you can consult *Special Edition Using Microsoft BackOffice*, Volume 1, ISBN 0-7897-1142-7, from Que Corporation.

Long distance connection fees represent another communications cost. Some nationwide Internet Service Providers (ISPs) allow for the use of a single phone number, accessed nationwide and billed at a single rate. Still other ISPs allow for connection to a local number, regardless of city, and the use of the Point-To-Point Tunneling Protocol (PPTP). PPTP establishes a Virtual Private Network (VPN), which allows you to log on to your corporate network. The advantage to this is that you can use a lower cost national ISP and still have connectivity from a remote destination.

One last comment on the topic of communication costs involves the inability to connect. This could represent real dollar costs in the form of late or lost orders. This usually results from one of three things. One is user error; when this happens, it is beneficial to have some form of remote control software that will allow a technical support person to dial in to the user's machine to correct the problems. The second factor is network problems that result in the RAS server's being unavailable; all the organization can do is create a set of policies regarding technical hardware support and have parts on hand. The last factor is an inadequate or antiquated phone line at the remote user location. Many older hotels have old phone lines that work well for voice but have too much crosstalk or attenuation for data communications. The only resolution for this problem is to search out another phone line.

Don't overlook support and training costs in this analysis. Ongoing support of a RAS server for a disconnected application requires time, attention, and money. Poorly trained users can make expensive mistakes and generally don't make the most of the available software.

Data Integrity as a Common Goal

Data integrity should be at the heart of every OLTP or batch application, whether connected or disconnected. Many of the technologies that have been discussed have features to help developers in this task. Data integrity becomes particularly challenging when the disconnected client model is used. Handling concurrent updates, hardware failures, and disparate technologies are issues that nearly all development staffs will face at some point.

The next two sections of this chapter discuss in more detail the challenges faced—and some possible solutions—with the connected and disconnected client models. The examples presented make use of the technologies discussed earlier.

Connected Client Applications

Connected client computing is the common case for client/server development. Client machines are connected by a network to some departmental or corporate data store. This does not mean that the data store is necessarily shared among departments. Many organizations, as they evolved into specialized units, created systems that focused on departmental needs. These systems were typically designed and implemented in as short a time frame as possible. The fact that these systems and their data stores were not tied together created pockets, or silos, of departmental information. As the organization continues to grow and struggles to survive in the marketplace, the need for shared data becomes more evident. Things such as time to market and customer service are measurements that, given localized data stores, are hard to get a grasp on. Many organizations and their leaders might feel that their customer service is exemplary, but presented with data compiled from all departments, they find out that the rate of customer dissatisfaction is actually growing. Being able to see these facts before they become problems can create competitive advantages.

The following example presents a similar situation. In this case, departmentalized data must be shared to gain some measure of synergy and efficiency between different departments or business units.

A Real-World Connected Client Example

Most organizations have a product that is sold or produced. Many organizations probably do both—manufacture and sell. This section uses an example with the organizational model of a manufacturer. The systems specifications and expected results are also listed.

Figure 21.1 offers a visual representation of this organization and the disparate systems it uses. Local sales representatives sell a product to a customer. The sales information must then be used by the manufacturing department to load level production and distribution of the product. The problem domain used in Figure 21.1 is as follows: The salesperson reads a report of customers to call, and the report is generated from a legacy Customer file in VSAM format. The report is based on customer demographics, which are determined by customer address and size of customer. When the salesperson makes a sale, the order and quantity are entered into a SQL Server database used by the Sales department. An order ticket is generated and sent to the order entry department, where the order and quantity are entered into the manufacturing SQL Server database to allow for planning of production. Once the product is through the manufacturing process, the distribution department must get the address from the Customer system, residing on the mainframe; then the product is shipped, and the salesperson is notified by paper report.

FIG. 21.1
Three separate systems: One is for sales users, one is for manufacturing, and one is a legacy customer VSAM file residing on a mainframe.

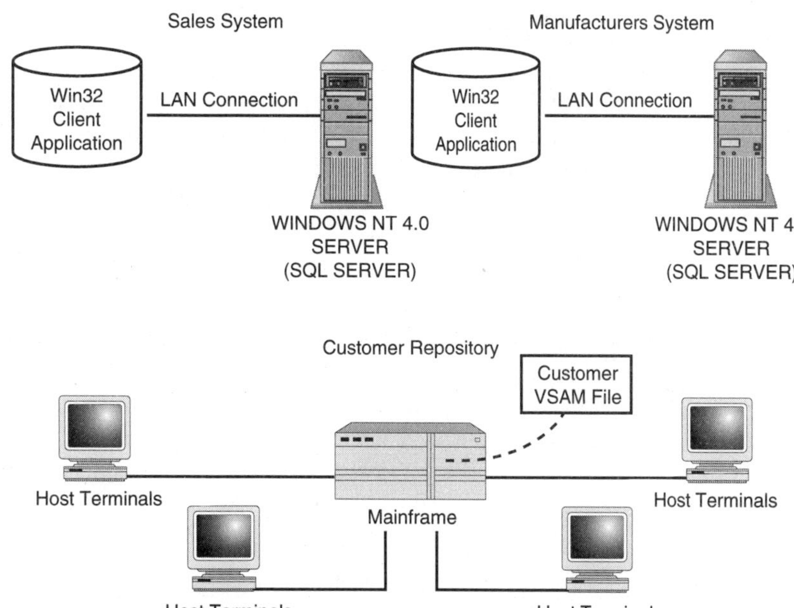

Figure 21.1 shows the complexity of disparate systems. The example might be far-fetched or might seem a little too fictitious, but it is a safe bet that most large companies have pockets of data that are not shared between systems. Department A generates a report, which is sent to Department B, and so on. It should be obvious that the systems in Figure 21.1 need to share data more effectively and efficiently.

The requirements you are handed, as the project leader, are as follows. Resolve the bottleneck resulting from the paper flow to the order entry department. The entry of order information into the manufacturing system should come as a result of the salesperson entering a sale into the Sales department database. Another fundamental change to this system is in regard to customer service. If a customer calls the salesperson, probably their only point of contact, and wants to find out order status information, how does the salesperson provide this? The salesperson doesn't have this information available. This is primarily a result of the manufacturing system not communicating with the sales system. Another goal is to make better use of the Customer repository residing on the mainframe. Instead of producing reports, the information should be available to both the salesperson and the distribution department electronically, as needed.

The problem has been established and the requirement handed down, and now you must design and implement a solution. In the next section you will see how the key technologies discussed earlier can be implemented to provide this solution.

The Role of Key Technologies

The focal point of this system is the two SQL Server databases. The fact that they need to communicate has been established. This communication could be handled in two ways, one no more correct than the other. The first is by replication, setting up a replication server to move data from one to the other, based on distributed database updates. The second alternative is to change the applications to send updates to both databases. For the sake of discussion, both will be explained.

The replication scenario for this solution would probably involve database changes and some minor application changes to take advantage of the new information. This solution dictates the use of either transaction-based or scheduled replication, depending on the requirements of the applications. Is data that is 30 minutes old too old? If so, then transaction-based replication is necessary; if 30 minutes is sufficient, then you could implement scheduled replication. Scheduled replication would free some of the network resources, whereas transactional replication would ensure a more consistent view of the data. Replicated information would probably be horizontally partitioned, taking only selected rows based on a last update timestamp.

As in the replication scenario, distributed transaction processing would require some application changes. The applications would need to send update transactions to the Distributed Transaction Coordinator to ensure the atomicity of the transactions. Remember that atomic transactions ensure that either both databases are updated correctly or both transactions roll back, thus ensuring data integrity between the databases. With this in mind, you would need to install and configure MTS on a Windows NT server, potentially on one of the database servers.

By implementing replication or MTS and DTC, you have resolved the communications bottleneck between the two SQL Server databases. You have also allowed visibility to the order status information by the salesperson. The increase in the organization's ability to service its customers should result in additional sales and, at a minimum, allow the organization to maintain its current level of sales and service. The last requirement to fulfill is the integration of the legacy customer information.

For the task of legacy integration, you can use Cedar. This will require some additional development on both the sales and manufacturing systems to take advantage of the new legacy components. With DCOM installed on the mainframe, you can begin to develop your mainframe components, specifying the inputs and outputs and registering the components with MTS and the client machines. Cedar itself will reside on a Windows NT server. The server could be either of the two SQL Server servers. The server must have Microsoft's SNA Server version 3.0 or later to allow for communication between the platforms.

Using the DCOM components, the sales and manufacturing applications can be altered to allow visibility and update capabilities to the legacy system. This not only helps to eliminate the paper flow from the systems, but will also create a synergistic environment out of disparate technologies.

Figure 21.2 shows the finished product using replication, while Figure 21.3 uses distributed database transactions. These three disparate systems now communicate with each other to transfer data seamlessly. This creates not only a more efficient organization, but also the foundation for a new development methodology. The next time a project such as this one lands in your lap, you now have the knowledge and expertise to implement a distributed and integrated solution.

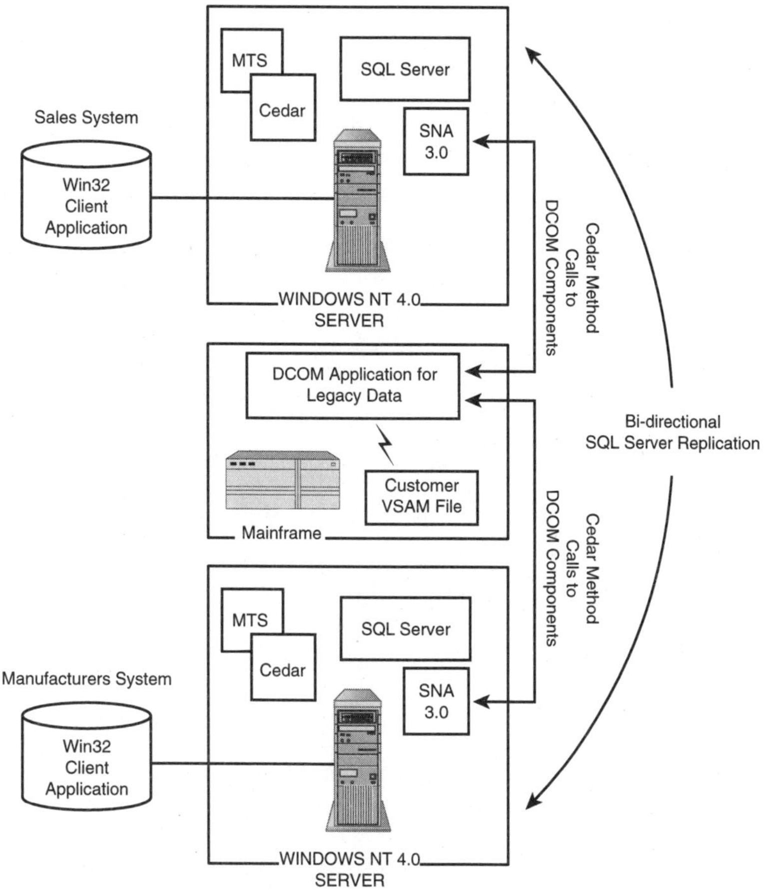

FIG. 21.2
The same three disparate systems are using a replication scenario that will allow for the successful sharing of information between the isolated departments.

Given the approaches in Figures 21.2 and 21.3, I prefer the distributed database transaction method. As a developer I prefer to have control over the data movement because it allows me to respond to error messages or use queuing to help alleviate slow response. I also prefer to rely on the database server as little as possible. In large OLTP applications, it is easy to overburden your database server, so remember that scalability should be a primary concern on every project. By separating the distributed transactions from the database server, you can gain some scalability options. In n-tier architectures, you can scale your middle-tier servers or your database server(s) for your individual application needs.

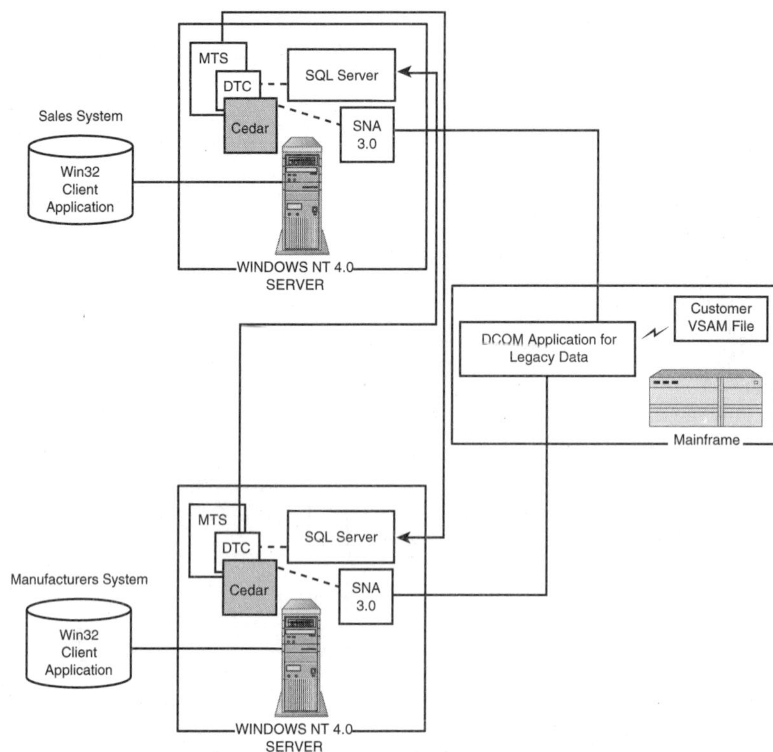

FIG. 21.3
A distributed transactions-based system will now move data between isolated groups of users, creating a more synergistic environment.

Keys to Success

The key to successfully implementing this type of solution is the proper utilization of technology to link and merge disparate systems. It would be nice to have unlimited time and resources so that all applications could be rewritten to a common platform within an organization, but this is rarely the case. Developers are often judged on what they can do in as little time and with as few resources as possible. The preceding discussion showed one alternative to the problems presented, but this is by no means the only solution. Using the technology available and leveraging existing assets within an organization, you can create a win-win scenario. The users get the system they desire, and the IT staff responsible gets credit for delivering it. This can help to build a good relationship between the IT staff and the business that it serves.

Disconnected Client Applications

Disconnected client computing is substantially more difficult than connected client computing. Client machines are not connected to a network full-time. Thus, you must allow for offline usage while allowing for connection at the user's convenience. Much like connected clients, the application architecture can be focused on departmental concerns, having the same issues with respect to data sharing and flexibility. This architecture can produce significant benefits by placing salespeople in the environment of the customer.

The following example presents a situation similar to the one used in the connected client example. Departmentalized data must also be shared, but this example has the added complexity of remote users and a DB2 legacy database.

A Real-World Disconnected Client Example

Many organizations are realizing the benefit of having sales people in the field, visiting customers. The appropriate term is *face time*. This yields significant sales and profit increases but is also much more challenging to you, as the developer. As you have seen, Microsoft provides a plethora of tools to handle these development efforts. This section deals with an example similar to the one in the previous section. The noticeable differences are a disconnected client and the use of DB2 as not just a legacy data store but as a central repository, similar to a data warehouse.

The user requirements are also similar. The disconnected client data needs to flow into the sales system's SQL Server database. This data needs to be pushed to a data warehouse residing on a host system running DB2 as the RDBMS. As in the previous example, the manufacturing system needs visibility to this data for planning purposes. In this example, the assumption is made that the disconnected client application will be implemented during this development effort.

Figure 21.4 illustrates the proposed disconnected client system, the current legacy system—which will become the data warehouse—and the manufacturing system.

The Role of Key Technologies

There are many challenges to the disconnected client approach. The first is the design and implementation of the disconnected client sales application. After the sales application is built, you then must deliver the data to the data warehouse in a reliable and timely manner. Finally, the data from the data warehouse must be delivered to the manufacturing system in adequate timeliness for planning. The distribution of data in this manner is done to separate the OLTP environments from the Decision Support (warehouse) environment. This will help to alleviate any potential bottlenecks and segregate the data by usage.

In building the sales application, many issues must be addressed. One such decision is which development tool to use. Another decision will be the data store necessary to store user data, including modified data, which can then be sent to the sales system database. The last major decision is the mechanism of transmitting data between the disconnected client and the sales system database.

In choosing the development tool for the sales client application, Visual Basic and Visual C++ are both highly rated options. Both of these provide the flexibility necessary to use COM and DCOM components while still rapidly building applications. Database connectivity is also fairly easy using these tools.

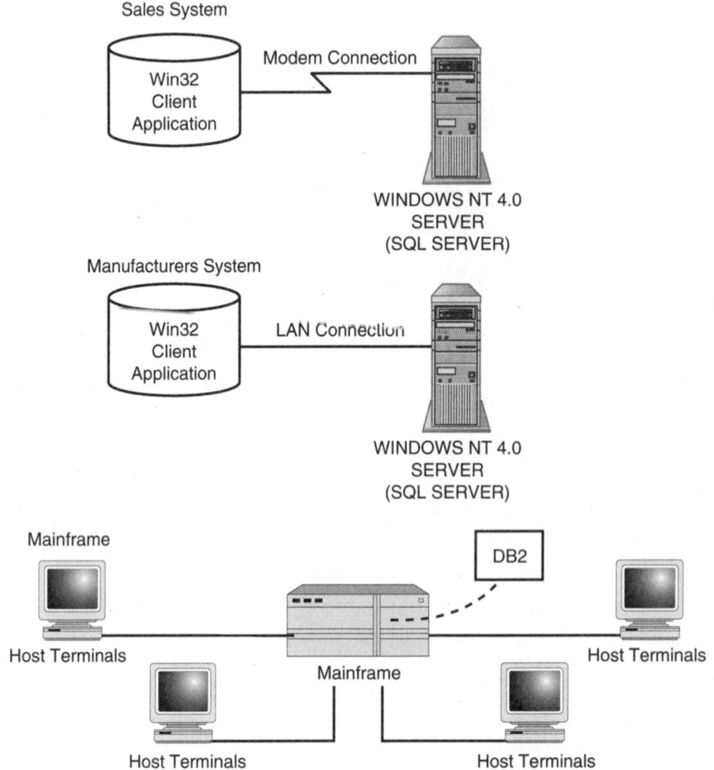

FIG. 21.4
The proposed disconnected client system; the current legacy system, which will become our data warehouse; and the manufacturing system as separate entities within the organization.

The next decision is the local data store. Microsoft Access has been proven to work effectively in these situations. Properties such as size of footprint and ease of program connectivity make it a viable solution. One note of caution is to pay careful attention to the amount of data that will be transferred to the user. Supplying the users with all the data that they might need, given any situation, is costly and time-consuming. The better alternative is to allow the user to determine what data will be needed for a given period of time. For instance, if the user is going to visit three customers and will then be transmitting data back to the office, supplying the user with the data necessary for just these three customers might be sufficient.

CAUTION

Pay particular attention to the amount of data that will be transferred to the user on a periodic basis. Large sets of data will increase communication costs. It will also increase the costs associated with a user waiting for data to be loaded. One approach is to send only changed information. Another approach is to let the users select what data they need for a given period of time. This allows them to select as little or as much data as they want.

One reason for selecting a robust development tool, such as Visual Basic or Visual C++, is that you can programmatically control the messaging architecture. Using MSMQ, the client application can update a local database with changes and write the transactions to a local MSMQ message queue to be transmitted at some later time. After the user connects by modem to the corporate network, the messages in the queue can be transmitted to the internal message queue, routing to the proper queue by referencing the GUID of the destination queue. Once in the destination queue, the transactions can be processed, making updates to the SQL Server database as necessary. Any in-doubt transactions or the collision of concurrent updates will need to be handled by an internal administrator or processed by some predetermined rules, possibly implemented using SQL Server stored procedures.

Transactions in the destination queue can also update the DB2 warehouse using the OLE DB/DDM driver over an SNA Server connection to the host environment. These transactions not only update the warehouse and the SQL Server database, but they can act as an atomic transaction (either both updates are posted or neither is posted). This allows distributed applications to maintain a reliable level of data integrity, one of the key challenges in disconnected client computing.

Thus far the discussion has covered receiving data from distributed users, but MSMQ will also allow you to transmit transactions to the user. These transactions, once processed, will load the client database with current data for processing. The creation of the data subset, to be sent to the user, can be done using stored procedures, based on user requests for specific pieces of data.

For communicating data from the DB2 warehouse to the manufacturing SQL Server database, you could use the Host Data Replicator. The data, as in the connected client replication discussion, can be horizontally partitioned and used as a recurring scheduled replication. This should provide timely data to the manufacturing system, assuming that real-time data is not absolutely necessary. Given the nature of disconnected client computing, real-time data is usually not an option. Day-old data is inherent in the disconnected client approach because users will typically communicate once or twice a day. There might also be situations where users can choose to send every other day or so. The issue of communication frequency is one that should be resolved by a good set of business rules and guidelines set forth during the design stage.

One added piece of information regarding communications has to do with phone lines and services. Users who are fairly geographically centered might be able to communicate from the same location, such as their home, for every transmission. For users who spend a larger part of their time on the road, it is prudent to experiment with various phone lines because the quality can never be guaranteed. Some services allow dialing through a national or local Internet Service Provider (ISP) regardless of location, using one phone number.

During the establishment of business rules and the design of the system, factor in the inability of users to communicate for varying periods of time. Determine the impact that this lack of communication has on the business and the system. Then present solutions to the users during formal training sessions.

Figure 21.5 shows the final solution using the disconnected client architecture.

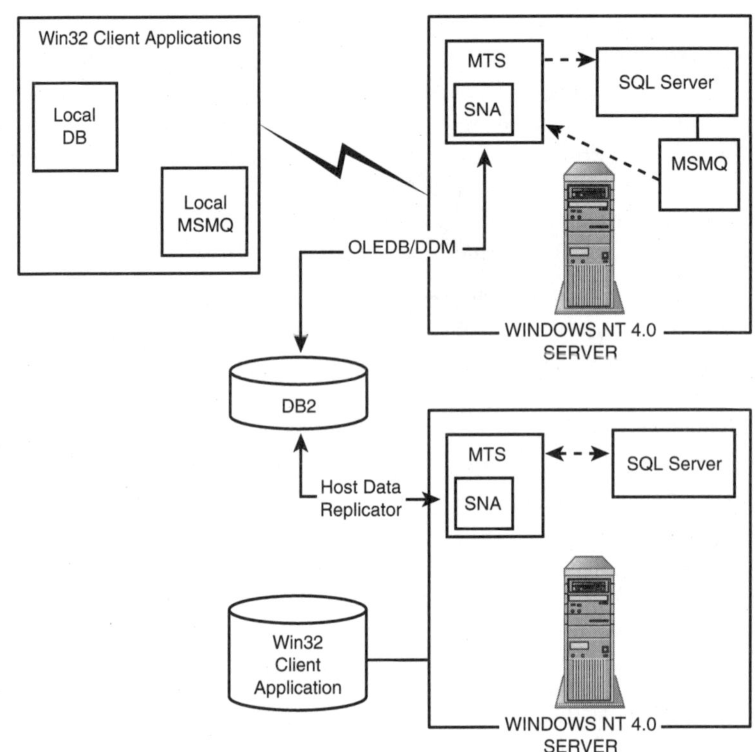

FIG. 21.5
These three disparate systems can now communicate with each other to transfer data seamlessly, and the salesperson can now spend time in front of the customer.

Keys to Success

The most important key to success with the disconnected client is a good set of business rules. Things such as which user wins on concurrent updates and specifics regarding the timeliness of data transmissions can make huge differences in the development cycle. All user requirements and rules should be thoroughly documented and even signed by the users. This gives everyone a clear definition of what is to be delivered. Good business rules can also ease support of such systems, which can be costly and time-consuming. Another key is the successful implementation of the technologies discussed.

NOTE One of the most important factors, often understated during any development project, is the clear definition of business rules. It will behoove you to get, in writing, a detailed set of business rules. By taking an afternoon and brainstorming as many potential pitfalls or gaps in a proposed system and getting specific answers to those questions in writing, you will save yourself a great deal of time and headache.

Internet/Intranet Alternatives

Internet/intranet (I-net) technologies present some very real opportunities to extend the classical client/server model. Microsoft has, as this book discusses, delivered an exceptional suite of tools for developing both Internet- and intranet-based solutions. The ability to use the thin client model versus the fat client model and the use of Java are two topics of interest when discussing distributed applications.

The *thin* client is one in which the application runs on the server with users accessing it through an Internet browser, such as Microsoft's Internet Explorer. This is in contrast to the *fat* client, which is the more traditional application architecture that uses executable files and has a fairly large amount of information stored on the client. Two advantages to the thin client are the ease of maintenance (all the application files are located on the server) and the simplification of data access compared to the disconnected client architecture. One downside is that the user must be connected, which as mentioned earlier might be prohibitive due to the nature of the business.

Java is more than a buzzword or just a lot of hype. This programming concept has the power to significantly change the way developers approach application development and the way organizations approach the purchasing of hardware. Through the use of a Java virtual machine (JVM), the developer can write one set of application code that can run on any platform that has a supported JVM. Microsoft has extended pure Java and allowed for some of the advanced controls available to the Windows environment.

▶ **See** "The Scoop on Java-Based Technologies," **p. 110**

▶ **See** "Creating a Java Applet or Application," **p. 222**

▶ **See** "Java Applets," **p. 325**

▶ **See** "JScript," **p. 327**

This section is just a cursory discussion of the benefits of Internet technologies and Java to raise your awareness of the options available to you. For more detail on the specific benefits and implementation of these tools, refer to the other chapters throughout this book that deal with web-based application development.

▶ **See** "The Web Browser as a Client Framework," **p. 314**

▶ **See** "The I-net Architecture," **p. 301**

▶ **See** "Component-Based Systems in I-net Environments," **p. 531**

From Here...

In this chapter, you learned about the products that Microsoft has delivered for building and integrating distributed applications. You learned of the two basic types of client/server computing, connected and disconnected, and some of the challenges that are inherent in these approaches.

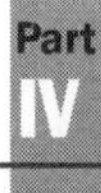

For more information regarding the topics covered in this chapter, see the following additional chapters:

- To learn more about database development in Visual Studio, see Chapter 3, "Creating Database-Aware Applications with Visual Studio."
- For more information on the development of web-based solutions, see Chapter 11, "An Inside Look at Web-Based Applications"; Chapter 8, "Using ActiveX Client Components in an I-net Environment"; and Chapter 7, "Creating Components with Visual J++."
- For additional information on distributed applications, see Chapter 25, "Using Microsoft Transaction Server to Enable Distributed Applications."

CHAPTER 22

Building Client Front Ends with Visual Basic and RDO

by Kevin D. Runnels

Over the past few years, the term *client/server computing* has changed substantially since it was first introduced. Chapter 10, "Clients, Servers, and Components: Web-Based Applications," gives a complete overview of the newer uses of this term.

This chapter focuses on the classic, two-tier client/server paradigm. Also, the server component described in this chapter is Microsoft SQL Server, which ships with the Enterprise Edition of Visual Studio 97. Although the concepts and examples given in this chapter are built around Microsoft SQL Server, they also apply generally to other database servers. Keep in mind, however, that even though the standardization developed around Structured Query Language (SQL) and Open Database Connectivity (ODBC) has made development for diverse database platforms much easier, you'll still find subtle differences in feature implementation and non-conformance to published standards (typically referred to as *enhancements*) that occasionally will cause problems.

Client and server roles and responsibilities

Discover the common concepts necessary for success in using all current data access methods.

Client/server computing concepts

See where security, data integrity, error checking, and so on are performed and why. Get an overview of client/server concepts such as stored procedures, synchronous versus asynchronous queries, and DSNs.

The role of Open Database Connectivity

Examine the structure and role of Microsoft's premier data access solution for database access. See how ODBC is the supporting foundation for RDO.

Latest changes to the RDO library

Learn about the new dissociated objects and batch update capabilities of RDO2. Learn about the importance of cursors and cursor types.

The RDO object hierarchy

Get a conceptual overview of the entire RDO object hierarchy. Find out about how much of the hard work of accessing database servers has been done for you.

You can gain access to information on the database server from a VB program in many ways:

- The Data Access Objects (DAO) library is usually used to manipulate data in a local Microsoft Access database (.mdb) file.
- You can use extensions on the DAO theme, such as ODBCDirect, which allows access to remote servers without the overhead of the Access library.
- The newest data access method, alternatively known as the Active or ActiveX Data Objects (ADO), holds much future promise but is slightly less complete than other data access object models at the current time.

Today, the most complete and robust model for use in the traditional client/server architecture when accessing a database is the Remote Data Objects (RDO) object model. This chapter introduces you to some of the key concepts necessary to understand RDO, as well as shows you the details of the RDO object model and how to use it successfully in your Visual Basic applications. ■

Classic Two-Tier Client/Server Architecture

The classic two-tier definition of client/server computing essentially describes a process model where a single process is distributed along functional lines between two separate computers. Each computer communicates over a network with the other to coordinate the execution of the process. The roles carried out by each computer are described as a *client or server process.*

Client/Server Basics

The client computer sends requests to the server, and the server carries out the requests. The request could be for the server to retrieve some information and send the information back to the client computer. The request could also be for the server to carry out some action on behalf of the client and to notify the client when the action is complete.

This model is seen within networks where print servers receive data from client computers and print the data on behalf of the client. Some other instances of this type of model are as follows:

- *File servers* are frequently found on networks and store information for client computers.
- *Mail servers* store and service requests involving electronic mail.
- *Communication servers* are used to provide access to communications devices such as faxes or modems.
- *Database servers* might be the most common implementation of the client/server process model in enterprise computing and provides services related to the storage and retrieval of information stored in a database.

Figure 22.1 shows an example of client/server architecture.

As you can see, a common process division in application development is to segment the process into functional components referred to as the Data, Rules, and Presentation components:

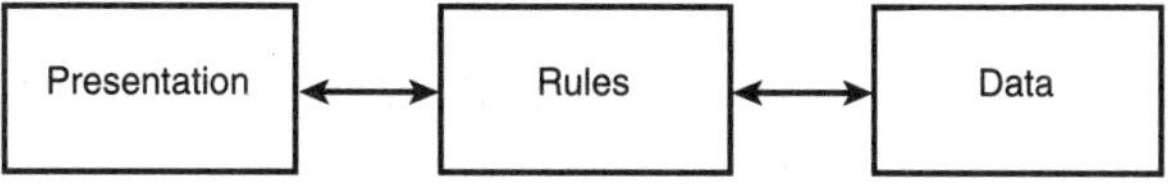

FIG. 22.1
A typical client/server application architecture consists of three distinct processing entities.

- The Data component is a server function that involves physical storage and retrieval of data. Microsoft SQL Server represents the Data component because it's responsible for the storage and manipulation of the data.
- The Rules component processes and manipulates the data and transforms the data into information. Rules can be implemented as a server process or a client process, depending on the application; however, applying the Rules function at the server is usually more efficient. Stored procedures could represent the Rules function by manipulating the data in user-defined ways and returning the data to the client as information in the form of resultsets.
- The Presentation component is a client function that displays or "presents" the information to end users. A client computer running a program created with VB5 would represent the Presentation function by transforming the result set returned by SQL Server into information displayed in controls or on hard-copy printouts.

Server-Side Responsibilities

Because the division of the process typically places more of the processing intensive burden on the server component, a more powerful computer is used on the server side. The server could be a large multiprocessing machine running Microsoft Windows NT Server, or perhaps a machine running a UNIX derivative. At any rate, the server platform will be running some type of database server software, the most popular type of which is the relational database management system (RDBMS). An RDBMS such as SQL Server stores data in tables and columns and relates the rows of one table to those of another by using *joins*.

NOTE A full discussion of the relational data model is beyond the scope of this chapter. It's assumed that you understand the basic design issues involved when using an RDBMS such as data integrity, data normalization, joins, indexing, and so forth. For more information regarding RDBMSs and design issues, see Chapter 3, "Creating Database-Aware Applications with Visual Studio."

The following sections discuss these important server responsibilities: data management, security, error handling, and query processing.

Data Management The server takes responsibility for the integrity of the data it stores. If your client application attempts to enter data into a table column that has been defined as a numeric field with a value such as `Laurie Ann`, an error will be raised and the information won't be written into the table.

The server is also responsible for maintaining relationships between defined tables. For instance, if a table has been defined with an EmployeeID field that's a foreign key to the Employee table, you won't be permitted to insert data that doesn't have a matching EmployeeID from the Employee table. Also, you can design triggers that "fire" when you add or change data in a table; these triggers will run special stored procedures to perform complex user-defined error checking and validation.

Another aspect of data management handled by the server is concurrency. Because many users are accessing the database at the same time, the server must be able to handle potential conflicts. The database typically handles concurrency by using transactions.

Security The server restricts access to the database based on user IDs and passwords. This access mechanism permits various degrees of access depending on how your account was set up on the server. You might have access to only some of the tables in the database. Your access might include only certain columns from tables in the database. You might even have no permissions at all on tables, but are restricted to accessing the data based on predefined views. The server also keeps track of all the activities against the data in the database and stores them in a transaction log for possible later review by a utility program.

Query Processing One primary responsibility of the server is to process requests that your client program sends to it. The server will accept the request that you give and analyze it to see how it can be most effectively executed. This will involve syntax checking, analyzing for redundancies, determining what indexes can be used, and so on. The server might select information and return it to the client, or it might execute some action on the data in the database without sending information back to the client.

Stored procedures, which are like small programs with several processing steps to be executed, can also be executed on the server. Also, the server might have to keep track of cursors if you've opened up a resultset by using server-side cursors.

Client-Side Responsibilities

The client program has to handle certain responsibilities, no matter which data access method is used. These responsibilities include initializing the data access interface, making the connection to the server, sending requests to the server, responding to server errors, manipulating the results of a query, presenting query results, and closing the database connection.

These key responsibilities, discussed in the following sections, are just the specific responsibilities that deal with being a client process to the server. Of course, your program will have myriad other responsibilities that can include execution of business logic ("rules"), error handling, additional security, and so on.

Initializing the Data Access Interface The client program initiates communication with the database server. To initiate communication, the client program has to set up the interface to the server, a task commonly referred to as *establishing a connection to the database*. All communication to the server takes place through this connection. Different aspects to this connection must be initialized to provide the ground rules for the communication that will take place. This includes establishing timeout values for connections and queries, and identifying the cursor library to be used.

Sending Requests to the Server When communication is established with the server and the data access interface is initialized, data access and manipulation requests can be sent to the server. These requests can be for the server to perform some action on behalf of the client, such as deleting rows that meet a specific criteria. The request might instruct the server to identify rows that meet a specific criteria and return those rows to the client process in the form of a resultset.

Responding to Server Errors Occasionally, the server might be unable to carry out instructions sent by the client process. The problem could be a lost connection, or perhaps the instruction to modify data can't be completed because another process had locked the data for its own purposes. It's important to identify where errors are likely to occur in the client process due to common server errors and then gracefully trap those errors. Unhandled errors are ugly and frequently fatal to the client program.

Manipulating Resultsets When a query has instructed the server to return rows of data in a resultset, the client program can then edit the resultset. Depending on the cursor type being used, the amount of time spent manipulating a resultset can adversely affect data concurrency in a multiuser environment. As a result, minimizing the amount of time the client holds open a resultset and cursor is usually a good idea.

Presenting Query Results Because the server simply responds to requests made by the client program, the client program takes all responsibility for presenting the results of the data access to users. In some instances, using data-bound controls might provide an effective simple solution. Most likely, however, the client program will need to deal with storing information returned by the server in resultsets by transferring the data to a grid, list box, text box, or a specially created object. Again, concurrency issues involved with maintaining an open resultset most likely will dictate how the information is presented to users.

Closing the Database Connection After the client program completes its data-manipulation functions, the connection to the database is closed.

Common Concepts

No matter which data access method is used, certain concepts apply equally across those methods. The following sections cover these concepts, which include synchronous versus asynchronous operations, row-returning queries, action queries, stored procedures, standard Windows Data Source Names (DSNs), and the various cursor types.

Synchronous Versus Asynchronous Operation

You can establish connections and execute queries synchronously or asynchronously. Synchronous queries execute on the database server, and your program *blocks* or waits for the server to return a response or timeout. Asynchronous queries continue processing while the server works on returning data, and the application must check to see whether the processing is complete, or respond to the `QueryComplete` event. Asynchronous queries provide for a more responsive user interface but require slightly more complex programming. Programmers must make sure that the query has executed and returned a resultset, for instance, before attempting cursor operations on the resultset.

If you want to code for events within the RDO library, you must use the `withevents` keyword when declaring your RDO object. See the Visual Basic online help for more information regarding event usage within your Visual Basic program.

Resultsets Versus Action Queries

Queries can return information from the database or instruct the database to perform some action on the data on behalf of the client program. Information is returned from the database in the form of resultsets. These resultsets can be the results of dynamic SQL constructed by the client program, or it could be the result of a predefined query or stored procedure. Because action queries don't return resultsets, they are commonly used to update or delete rows in the database.

Stored Procedures

Stored procedures are compiled collections of SQL statements stored and executed by the database server that are called by a client program. Stored procedures allow user-declared variables, conditional logic, cursors, and other powerful programmatic features. Because stored procedures are compiled and executed on the database server, they're very fast. They can also accept parameters, call other stored procedures, and return information in the form of return codes, resultsets, or output parameters.

Use stored procedures whenever possible because of the speed advantages. You sometimes can also use them to implement business logic that's more accessible and easier to modify than your Visual Basic program. Stored procedures can be changed to provide different information to clients without forcing code changes and recompilation of the client program.

Data Source Names

Data Source Names (DSNs) are used as sources of connection information—they describe the connection and its options. The DSN information is stored in ODBC.INI or in the Registry, depending on which version of Windows is used. When ODBC needs to make the connection, connection information can simply be retrieved from the DSN rather than all the detailed connection information be specified again. DSNs aren't required to be used, however, and all the detailed connection information can be specified at runtime by using a non-DNS connection strategy.

Standard Cursors

Cursors provide a mechanism for maintaining a "current row" in a resultset. This concept harkens back to file-based ISAM systems, where you maneuvered through a file based on the file pointer. Several common types of cursors include forward-only, static, keyset, and dynamic, which are all contained in the standard ODBC cursor library. VB5 and RDO2 have introduced a new client batch cursor library that has some real advantages over the older ODBC library.

The most important thing to understand about cursors—at least the cursors as defined by the standard ODBC library—is that you should avoid them whenever possible. They're extremely expensive in terms of system resources and are very slow. Cursors allow you to access data in a row-by-row format, which is counter to the set-based processing nature of SQL. If you find yourself in a position where you're about to use a cursor, stop and rethink your design and consider how to accomplish what you need to do without using a cursor. Nevertheless, you might find a situation where the only viable answer is to use a cursor. Occasionally, you might need to execute a series of complex function calls and processing steps for each row of a resultset. Cursors allow you to keep track of which row of the resultset on which it's positioned.

In situations where you feel you absolutely have to use a cursor, consider a couple of alternatives:

- Copy the data in the resultset to a temporary table and cursor through the data in the new temporary table. Because the temporary table is visible only to your application, you won't have to worry about contention issues with other users.
- Read the data with a forward-only cursor (the fastest cursor type available) and load the data returned into an object. When the data is loaded, write your own logic to traverse a "current pointer" through the object and issue dynamic SQL against the database if changes to the data are required. This is faster and causes less database contention with other users.

The following section discuss various cursor types and some pros and cons of using them.

Forward-Only Cursors Forward-only cursors are less painful to implement than the other standard cursor types. These cursors aren't scrollable, meaning that you can't freely move forward or backward within the resultset; you can only move forward (hence the name). These cursors are sometimes updatable, but not always.

Keyset Cursors Keyset cursors store pointers to the rows in the tables you're accessing and not the actual data. You're free to move forward or backward through these pointers, meaning that you're essentially reselecting each row of the resultset as you move through your cursored resultset. This also means that the data your cursor points to is visible to other database users. As you move through your resultset, you'll see any modifications to the data that other users have made. If another user deletes a row that you've contained in your cursor, a trappable error results. If a user adds a row that would have been included in your resultset when you created the cursor, you won't see the added data because the rows pointed to are "fixed" at the time the cursor was opened.

Snapshot/Static Cursors Static cursors, unlike keyset cursors, move all the data that you've selected to your client. As you move through the resultset, the data you see is coming from the cached copy of the data created on your computer. As a result, you won't see any changes made by any other database users. You've created a *snapshot* of the data at the specific time you created the cursor. Static cursors are sometimes updatable, depending on the implementation of the device driver.

Dynamic Cursors Like keyset cursors, dynamic cursors store pointers to the rows contained in your resultset. Unlike keysets, their membership isn't fixed, and the resultsets shrink or grow depending on the actions of other users. They requery the server as you move through the resultset so that you have the most recent updates and membership information. As you can guess, this is extremely resource-intensive, and you should limit its use accordingly.

RDO's New Approach to Offline Data Editing

RDO2 offers a new and different approach to editing data that promises to be very useful in helping reduce data-contention issues. The new batch cursor library and optimistic batch updates allow your application to be connected to the data source only while it's actually retrieving or sending information to the server. If this sounds similar to a web page access metaphor, where the browser client is connected to the web server only while actually retrieving a web page, you have the right picture.

VB5 and the Client Batch Cursor Library

VB5 and RDO2 have introduced a new cursor library, the client batch cursor library, that provides more flexibility in environments where data concurrency is an issue and offline updates to data can be made and "posted" to the database all at once. This diminishes problems associated with database locks in a multiuser environment.

In the past, VB programmers frequently implemented this type of data access approach by querying the database to acquire a resultset, and then immediately copying each row of the resultset into an object collection that mimicked the structure of the original resultset. Once the collection was built, the original resultset was closed and any database locks were released. Changes then could be made to the data contained in the collection, and updates to the data would be made by using action queries against the database as the data changed, or when the changes that were being made to the data were complete. Although effectively minimizing database contention, the construction of the collection and creation of the SQL contained in the action queries created substantial programming overhead.

The introduction of the client batch library in VB5 means that this work is done for you automatically. Essentially, the client batch library allows for the creation of resultsets that can be *dissociated* from their connection to the database. After the resultset is dissociated, it can be edited by using the standard RDO `Edit` method. When the edits are complete, the resultset is reassociated to the connection to the database, and a `BatchUpdate` method causes all the edits to be made against the database.

Dissociated Resultsets and Optimistic Batch Updates with RDO2

Dissociated resultsets and optimistic batch updates are totally new to VB5 and RDO2. This new concurrency option is extremely useful when the data being manipulated is unlikely to be modified by another user (such as batch-oriented data).

Assume that the data being accessed is batch-oriented data, and more than one person can't edit a batch at the same time. A resultset can be opened against a specific set of data based on `BatchID`, but data from another batch could be adversely affected because of the page-locking mechanisms used by some database server. SQL Server locks pages in 2KB increments. If your batch data makes up 11KB of data, you'll still set a page lock on 12KB to edit your data. This means that 1KB of data that doesn't belong to your batch is also locked. In the past, programmers would frequently create a forward-only read-only cursor, quickly read in the data, and load a special data structure that mimics the layout of the resultset. As soon as the structure was loaded, the resultset was closed. Any edits to the structure resulted in SQL Action queries to update the remote database.

The `rdUseClientBatch` cursor library, written as a replacement for the ODBC cursor library, can relieve much of the drudgery from the process of creating and loading special data structures to release any locks on the server. Using dissociated `rdoResultsets` and the `rdUseClientBatch` library allows users to retrieve the `rdoResultset` and then disconnect from the database without losing the ability to edit the data in the `rdoResultset`. Changes made to the resultset use the standard RDO `Edit`, `AddNew`, and `Delete` methods and a special `BatchUpdate` method to commit all the changes *en masse* after the `rdoResultset` is reconnected to the data source.

Optimistic Batch Update Features

The approach in using the optimistic batch update features is very similar to standard data manipulation using RDO, but a few things need to be done a little differently to be successful. The following steps outline what's necessary to take advantage of this new feature:

1. When the connection is made, be sure to specify `rdClientBatch` as the cursor library.
2. Open a resultset by using the `OpenResultSet` method from an `rdoQuery` object or directly from the `rdoConnection` object.
3. Specify the cursor behavior that you want in the `OpenResultSet` method, but remember that only scrollable cursors provide access to the `rdoResultset`'s `Status` property. You'll need access to the `Status` property later to determine the success of your batch update. Also, be sure to specify `rdConcurBatch` as the concurrency option of the `OpenResultSet` method.
4. After the `rdoResultset` is populated with the `OpenResultSet` method, disconnect from the server by setting the `ActiveConnection` property to `Nothing`. This causes the `WillDissociate` event of the `rdoResultset` object to fire.
5. Modify your data by using the standard RDO data-manipulation methods: `AddNew`, `Edit`, `Update`, and so on. When you modify the data in the `rdoResultset`, the `Update` method copies your changes into the local copy of the resultset, but the changes to the database are deferred until you re-establish a connection.
6. After all the edits to the data are made, reassociate the connection by setting the `ActiveConnection` property to an open `rdoConnection`. The `rdoResultset` is now "reconnected" to the database, but the changes you made haven't yet been sent to the server.

7. Perform the final batch update by invoking the `BatchUpdate` method. If an error occurred during execution of `BatchUpdate`, check the `rdoErrors` collection to determine the cause. Also inspect the `BatchCollisionCount` and `BatchCollisionRows` properties. The `Status` property of the individual rows of the `rdoResultset` tells you if any specific rows failed to be updated.

RDO and Open Database Connectivity

Although RDO is fairly new, it relies on an old standby to accomplish much of its work. The RDO object hierarchy is sometimes referred to as a "thin wrapper" over the ODBC API. Thus, some people claim that RDO is slower than using direct ODBC calls. This is true in the absolute sense, but isn't really noticeable. Also, the ease of use in accessing the different features provided by ODBC when using RDO saves development time and results in code that's easier to maintain and debug.

ODBC Fundamentals

Using servers that utilize products from different manufacturers has been made easier because of the industry acceptance of several standards set forth by Microsoft. Examples of these interfaces include Mail Application Programming Interface (MAPI), Telephony Application Programming Interface (TAPI), and ODBC. All these standards commonly provide a uniform interface that allows a client process to work transparently with disparate server products. The MAPI interface standard supplies a generic interface to use many different mail servers, such as Microsoft Exchange and Lotus cc:Mail. The TAPI interface standard provides uniform access to many different types of telephony equipment. The ODBC standard provides a generic approach to data access.

ODBC is implemented as a two-layer interface between the client and the database server. The first layer, to which your client application interfaces, is the Driver Manager. The Driver Manager loads the appropriate database driver, initializes the interface, provides an interface to the ODBC features that the database driver will support, and does some error checking and parameter validation. The second layer of the ODBC interface is the actual database driver, in the form of a vendor-specific DLL, that communicates with the database server. The vendor-specific ODBC driver is responsible for implementing as many ODBC functions as the server natively supports, but it can also include extra code to provide for ODBC-specific functionality itself if the database server doesn't support some particular features. The driver is also responsible for establishing connections, submitting requests to the server, returning information from the server, managing transactions, handling server-side cursors, and providing for error checking.

Although ODBC provides a common API, not all ODBC drivers provide all ODBC functionality. There are conformance levels for drivers that categorize them as providing core, level 1, or level 2 services. The drivers also must support SQL grammar and are categorized by the degree to which the full SQL grammar is supported. Figure 22.2 shows the different conformance levels and their corresponding feature requirements.

FIG. 22.2
To be fully compliant with their conformance level, ODBC drivers frequently implement some additional functionality that the data source doesn't implement natively.

ODBC API Conformance Levels

Level	Functionality
Core	Connect and disconnect from data sources Prepare and execute SQL statements Allow multiple statements per data source Manage memory and handles for connections and statements Send and retrieve data with the data source Manage transactions Retrieve error information
Level 1	All Core Functionality Provide a dialog box for connections Allow storage of connection options Allow storage of statement options Allow for handling Binary Large Object (BLOB) data types Retrieve partial catalog information Retrieve ODBC driver capabilities
Level 2	All Core and Level 1 functionality Provide list of available datasources Support for arrays as parameters and resultsets Scrollable cursors Retrieve full catalog information Manage indexes Retrieve native SQL Allow for multilingual dll's

ODBC SQL Grammar Conformance Levels

Minimum	Core	Extended
CREATE and DROP TABLE SELECT and INSERT UPDATE SEARCHED DELETE SEARCHED Simple expressions Limited data type support	All Minimum functionality Alter Table CREATE and DROP INDEX CREATE and DROP VIEW GRANT and REVOKE Full SELECT Support Set functions Subqueries Extended data type support	All Minimum and Core Functionality Positioned UPDATE Positioned DELETE SELECT FOR UPDATE Unions Outer Joins Date/Time functions String functions Stored Procedure calls Batch Statement Processing Full data type support

ODBC makes it possible for a single client application to use many different kinds of database servers. The problem for VB5 developers is that the ODBC API was designed primarily for interfacing to programs written in C/C++. Although you can directly call ODBC API functions from within VB5, it's a skill that requires a high level of expertise and a high tolerance for general protection faults (GPFs). Microsoft has developed a Component Object Model (COM) interface for use by VB developers that acts as a wrapper around ODBC. This COM interface, referred to as Remote Data Objects, is now in its second incarnation with VB5 and is commonly called RDO or RDO2. The RDO2 method of database access is the most commonly used client/server access method used by VB5 developers and offers high performance as well as an easily accessible interface to the database server. Figure 22.3 shows the relationship of the RDO2 library to the underlying ODBC layer.

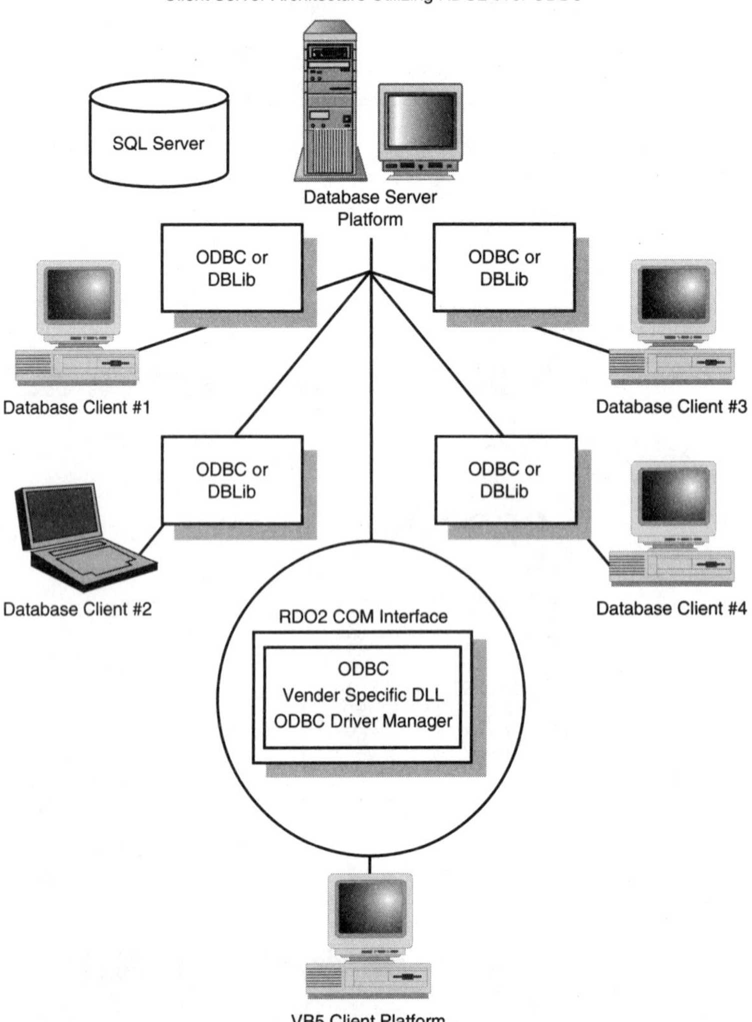

FIG. 22.3 RDO2 encapsulates ODBC in a COM object so that ODBC's functionality can be made available to the broadest range of Microsoft language products.

An Overview of RDO2

In Figure 22.4, the RDO2 object library is implemented as a hierarchy, with the `rdoEngine` as the topmost object. With the exception of the single `rdoEngine` object, all the other objects actually exist in collections. The `rdoResultset` object is a member of the `rdoResultsets` collection, etc. This collection structure was first introduced in VB4 with RDO1. In addition to this behavior, RDO2 also now allows for standalone objects that aren't part of a collection.

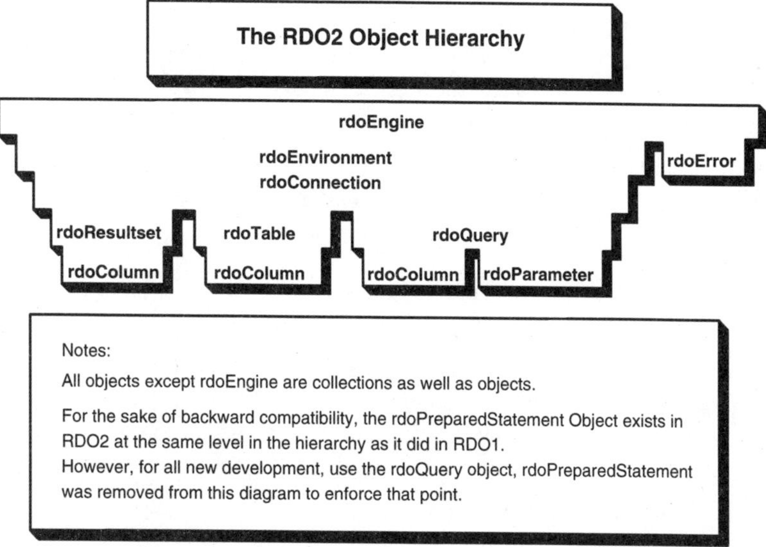
The RDO2 Object Hierarchy
rdoEngine
rdoEnvironment
rdoConnection
rdoError
rdoResultset
rdoColumn
rdoTable
rdoColumn
rdoQuery
rdoColumn
rdoParameter
Notes:
All objects except rdoEngine are collections as well as objects.
For the sake of backward compatibility, the rdoPreparedStatement Object exists in RDO2 at the same level in the hierarchy as it did in RDO1.
However, for all new development, use the rdoQuery object, rdoPreparedStatement was removed from this diagram to enforce that point.

FIG. 22.4
The RDO2 object hierarchy is an abstract model of a data source and provides a COM interface to manipulating the data source.

NOTE Before the RDO2 library can be addressed from within your VB code, remember to add the library to your current project. Choose Project, References, and select Microsoft Remote Data Objects 2.0 from the list.

The RDO2 Object Hierarchy

The RDO object hierarchy is rather large, with several high-level objects with many methods, events, and properties. The Visual Basic online help system provides excellent topical access to individual features and elements of RDO. It doesn't, however, provide convenient access to learn when you aren't sitting at your computer with a specific question in mind. The rest of this chapter gives you a complete breakdown of the RDO2 object library and offers a look at each object and its associated methods, events, and properties, with some examples of how they're used. If you need more information regarding a specific topic, check the Visual Basic online help system, using the topic that you have a question about as the search key.

The *rdoEngine* Object

Methods: `rdoCreateEnvironment`, `rdoRegisterDataSource`

Events: `InfoMessage`

Properties: `rdoDefaultCursorDriver`, `rdoDefaultErrorThreshold`, `rdoDefaultLoginTimeOut`, `rdoDefaultPassword`, `rdoDefaultUser`, `rdoLocalID`, `rdoVersion`

The top object in the RDO2 hierarchy, the `rdoEngine` is an abstract representation of the remote data source. The `rdoEngine` isn't declared and isn't explicitly instantiated from within VB code. Those steps are handled for you the first time an `rdoEnvironment` object is created. The properties of the `rdoEngine` object that begin with the word `rdoDefault` provide the default settings for newly instantiated `rdoEnvironment` objects.

As a COM object, the `rdoEngine` object supports various methods, events, and properties. All other RDO objects are a component of the `rdoEngine`.

The *rdoCreateEnvironment* Method

```
Set MyrdoEnv = rdoCreateEnvironment ( Name, User, Password )
```

The `rdoCreateEnvironment` method is used to create a new `rdoEnvironment` object and add it to the `rdoEnvironments` collection. There will always be a default `rdoEnvironment` with a collection index of 0 created when the `rdoEngine` is first initialized. If you need to add more `rdoEnvironment` objects—perhaps to manage transaction scopes—you can use this method to create the object. The *`Name`*, *`User`*, and *`Password`* arguments are all required arguments.

The *rdoRegisterDataSource* Method

```
rdoRegisterDataSource DSN, Driver, Silent, Attributes
```

The `rdoRegisterDataSource` method is used to store information about a connection in the Windows Registry. *`DSN`* is a descriptive string that describes the data source. The *`Driver`* argument specifies the name of the ODBC driver. *`Silent`* is a Boolean value that enables or suppresses the display of the ODBC dialog boxes. If *`Silent`* is `True`, the *`Attributes`* property must contain all the vendor-specific ODBC keyword attributes as specified by the ODBC vendor.

The *InfoMessage* Event The `InfoMessage` event is fired when informational messages are received from the ODBC Driver Manager. The messages are stored in the `rdoErrors` collection.

The *rdoDefaultCursorDriver* Property The `rdoDefaultCursorDriver` specifies the cursor library to implement by seeding the `CursorDriver` property of `rdoEnvironment` objects. The valid settings are `rdUseIfNeeded`, `rdUseODBC`, `rdUseServer`, `rdUseClientBatch`, and `rdUseNone`. `rdUseIfNeeded` is the default setting, and RDO will choose what it feels is the most appropriate driver for the cursor. `rdUseODBC` uses the ODBC cursor library.

> **CAUTION**
>
> The ODBC cursor library is notorious for leaking memory. Use it at your own risk.

ON THE WEB

Check **http://www.microsoft.com** for new updates to the ODBC cursor library that can solve some of the problems.

`rdUseServer` directs the `rdoEnvironment` to use server-side cursors. A server-side cursor is available for SQL Server but might not be available for your database.

New to RDO2, `rdUseClientBatch` is a cursor library that allows batch-mode operations and dissociated `rdoResultsets`. This cursor library is extremely useful in many situations and was covered more fully in the earlier section "VB5 and the Client Batch Cursor Library." `rdUseNone` doesn't create a cursor at all, but provides the functionality of a forward-only, read-only resultset.

The *rdoDefaultErrorThreshold* Property The `rdoDefaultErrorThreshold` property exists only to provide backward compatibility with RDO1. The property specifies a default value for the `ErrorThreshold` property for `rdoQuery` objects. It allows you to specify a value for non-fatal messaging from stored procedures. RDO2 uses the `InfoMessage` event for this functionality.

The *rdoDefaultLoginTimeout* Property The `rdoDefaultLoginTimeout` property specifies how long to wait while a connection is being established before an error is generated. This property seeds the `LoginTimeout` property of `rdoEnvironment` objects. Don't confuse this with the `QueryTimeout` property of an `rdoConnection` object, which specifies how long to wait for a resultset to be returned from a query. The `rdoDefaultLoginTimeout` is specified in the number of seconds to wait; 15 seconds is the default if no value is specified. When the time has expired, the `rdoEnvironment`'s `ConnectionTimeout` event will fire. To cancel the timeout behavior, specify a value of zero to have the `rdoEnvironment` wait forever.

The *rdoDefaultUser* and *rdoDefaultPassword* Properties The `rdoDefaultUser` and `rdoDefaultPassword` properties seed the `rdoEnvironment` object's `UserName` and `Password` properties. Setting these properties in code is a good idea if security isn't a major concern, or if the account you specify has limited access rights on the database. You'll almost always explicitly set these properties when creating your `rdoConnection` object. The default property values are a zero-length string (`""`).

The *rdoLocaleID* and *rdoVersion* Properties The `rdoLocaleID` specifies the language to use when generating RDO error messages and is defaulted to the Windows system locale. The `rdoVersion` property returns a value that represents the version of the RDO library in use.

The following code instantiates the `rdoEngine` and sets various properties:

```
Dim MyRdoEnv as rdoEnvironment     'Automatically instantiates rdoEngine object
With rdoEngine
    .rdoDefaultLoginTimeout = 30            'Sets timeout on login to 30 seconds
    .rdoDefaultCursorLibrary = rdUseNone    'Specifies forward-only, read-only
                                            'functionality
    .rdoDefaultUser = "Default"             'Specifies default user, should be
                                            'low security account
    .rdoDefaultPassword = "LowSecurity"       'Specifies the default password
End With
```

The *rdoError* Object

Methods: None

Events: None

Properties: `Description`, `HelpContext`, `HelpFile`, `Number`, `Source`, `SQLRetcode`, `SQLState`

The `rdoErrors` collection is a property of the `rdoEngine` object. This collection of `rdoError` objects acts as a repository of errors and informational messages returned from ODBC. When an operation generates an error or a series of errors, they're added to this collection. If another operation generates an error, the prior errors are automatically cleared.

Not all errors are fatal; many times messages or warnings are generated from stored procedures and are captured in this collection. The `rdoEngine` `InfoMessage` event is fired when one of these messages arrives, and you can examine the message in the `rdoErrors` collection. This collection automatically prioritizes its members from the most detailed to the most general. This means that the most detailed error will be placed at `rdoErrors(0)` and the most general error will be last in the index. The `rdoError` object has no methods or events, but consists of a set of properties as shown in the following sections.

The *Description* Property The `Description` property is a string that describes the error or informational message.

The *HelpContext* and *HelpFile* Properties The `HelpContext` property specifies a Long value that corresponds to a Help topic in a standard Windows Help file. The `HelpFile` property is a string that specifies the name of the help file to be used.

Help files and error handling are commonly the last things added to a program but are some of the most important aspects of programming. If your practice is to add error-handling code after a routine is written, at least comment the code to remind yourself of errors that need to be trapped. Maintenance programmers will also appreciate this practice.

The *Number* Property The `Number` property is error number returned from the database server or ODBC. This number can represent a built-in error, such as a type mismatch in a convert function in a stored procedure. The error number can also be generated by design from within a stored procedure by using a mechanism such as the `RAISERROR` command used by Microsoft SQL Server and Sybase.

The *Source* Property The `Source` property is a string value that identifies the source of the error. Errors beginning with `MSRDO20` occurred within RDO. Other strings are unique to the application/class that generated the error.

The *SQLRetCode* Property `SQLRetCode` returns a Long value that indicates the return code from the last RDO operation. Possible values are `rdSQLSuccess`, `rdSQLSuccessWithInfo`, `rdSQLNoDataFound`, `rdSQLError`, and `rdSQLInvalidHandle`.

The *SQLState* Property The `SQLState` property is a string value that represents a type of error as defined by the X/Open and SQL Access Group. It's rather cryptic, consisting of a two-character class value and a three-character subclass value. Because this property is rather arcane, it's doubtful you'll use it under most circumstances. For now, rely on the `SQLRetCode`, `Number`, and `Description` properties for information regarding your `rdoErrors`.

The *rdoEnvironment* Object

Methods: `BeginTrans`, `Close`, `CommitTrans`, `OpenConnection`, `RollbackTrans`

Events: `BeginTrans`, `CommitTrans`, `RollbackTrans`

Properties: `CursorDriver`, `hEnv`, `LoginTimeout`, `Name`, `Password`, `UserName`

The `rdoEnvironments` property is a collection of `rdoEnvironment` objects. The first entry in the collection, `rdoEnvironments(0)`, is created automatically. The `BeginTrans`, `CommitTrans`, and `RollbackTrans` methods allow fine control over synchronizing different data-manipulation operations that span different connections in the same `rdoEnvironment`. For example, you could invoke the `BeginTrans` method of an `rdoEnvironment` object, and then issue an update command against a table on one connection and a delete command against a table in another connection. If those two sequences were logically tied together and you encountered an error during one of the sequences, you could invoke the `RollBack` environment method to cancel both operations.

The transaction methods also fire `BeginTrans`, `CommitTrans`, and `RollbackTrans` events with RDO2. Those events fire immediately after the respective method completes its operation and are used primarily to synchronize other processes.

Before RDO2, this collection was the sole source of connection objects via the `OpenConnection` method. As the `OpenConnection` method is invoked, a new `rdoConnection` object is created and added to the `rdoConnections` collection. By specifying a zero-length string for the `Connect` string, the `rdoConnection` object will use the `rdoEnvironment`'s default user name and password. You must, however, specify a Data Source Name (DSN) if you use this technique.

The *BeginTrans* Method The `BeginTrans` method has no arguments and acts as a marker that identifies where a transaction begins. SQL statements executed after `BeginTrans` is invoked are part of a single transaction that can be committed or rolled back.

The *Close* Method The `Close` method has no parameters and can be used to close an `rdoEnvironment` object. This method will also close any `rdoConnection` objects belonging to the `rdoEnvironment`. The default `rdoEnvironments(0)` can't be closed.

The *CommitTrans* Method The `CommitTrans` method has no parameters. It's used to commit a transaction and cause the actions taken by the SQL contained in that transaction to be applied against the data source. By definition, the transaction is concluded when this method is invoked, and can't be rolled back.

The *OpenConnection* Method

```
Set MyConnection = MyrdoEnv.OpenConnection(DSN[,Prompt[,
➥ReadOnly[,Connect[,Options]]]])
```

The `OpenConnection` method opens a connection and creates an `rdoConnection` object.

The *DSN* argument is a string that specifies the name of a registered ODBC data source name. This argument can be a zero-length string if the optional parameters are provided.

The optional *Prompt* parameter has a default value of `rdDriverComplete`, which means that if the *DSN* argument is present, use the *Connect* argument to connect to the data source without displaying the ODBC Data Sources dialog box. The value of `rdDriverPrompt` would specify that the ODBC Data Sources dialog box be displayed. `RdDriverNoPrompt` specifies that the ODBC Data Sources dialog box not be displayed and that the values from *DSN* and *Connect* are used. `RdDriverCompleteRequired` specifies that the same behavior as `rdDriverComplete` is used, except that the controls in the ODBC Data Sources dialog box are disabled for any information not required to complete the connection.

The *RollbackTrans* Method The `RollbackTrans` method specifies that the SQL statements since the last `BeginTrans` method was invoked should be *rolled back*, or canceled.

The *BeginTrans*, *CommitTrans*, and *RollbackTrans* Events The `BeginTrans` event is fired after the `BeginTrans` method is completed. The `CommitTrans` event is fired after the `CommitTrans` method is completed. The `RollbackTrans` event is fired after the `RollbackTrans` method is completed.

The *CursorDriver* Property The `CursorDriver` property specifies what type of cursor to use against the data source:

- `rdUseIfNeeded` is the default. The ODBC driver chooses the cursor type, preferring server-side cursors, if available.
- `rdUseOdbc` specifies the ODBC cursor library.
- `rdUseServer` directs the data control to use server-side cursors. Server-side cursors are very fast but not available with some data sources. Each database driver vendor will support different features, so check with the driver documentation to see whether server-side cursors are available on your platform. Server-side cursors are available for Microsoft SQL Server.
- `rdUseClientBatch` specifies the optimistic batch cursor library.
- `rdUseNone` is essentially a single-row forward-only resultset.

The *hEnv* Property The `hEnv` property returns a Long that's the ODBC environment handle. This isn't needed for RDO2 programming, but can be used if you're making direct ODBC API calls.

The *LoginTimeout* Property The `LoginTimeout` property specifies the amount of time, in milliseconds, that the `rdoEnvironment` object uses to seed the `rdoConnection.LoginTimeout` property. This will specify how long the `rdoConnection` object waits for success when attempting to establish a connection.

The *Name* Property The `Name` property specifies the name of the `rdoEnvironment`.

The *Password* Property The `Password` property is the default password to be used by subsequent `rdoConnection` objects. Remember the security concerns in supplying a default user and password.

The *Username* Property The Username property is the default user name to be used by subsequent rdoConnection objects. Remember the security concerns in supplying a default user and password.

The *rdoConnection* Object

Methods: BeginTrans, Cancel, Close, CommitTrans, CreateQuery, EstablishConnection, Execute, OpenResultset, RollbackTrans

Events: BeforeConnect, Connect, Disconnect, QueryComplete, QueryTimeout, WillExecute

Properties: AsyhcCheckInterval, Connect, CursorDriver, hDbc, LastQueryResults, LoginTimeout, LogMessages, Name, QueryTimeout, rdoQueries, rdoResultsets, rdoTables, RowsAffected, StillConnecting, StillExecuting, Transactions, Updateable, Version

By using the rdoEnvironment object's OpenConnection method, you establish an open connection and add an rdoConnection object to the rdoEnvironment's rdoConnections collection. The newly created rdoConnection object inherits the parent rdoEnvironment object's CursorDriver and LoginTimeOut values. If a zero-length string was used in the ConnectString argument of the OpenConnection method, the parent rdoEnvironment's UserName and Password values are used.

A new feature of RDO2 now allows you to create an unopened connection by instantiating the rdoConnection object with the New keyword. After the object is instantiated, you can use the EstablishConnection method to open the connection. With this technique, the created rdoConnection object isn't part of any collection. This allows you to break the hierarchical nature of the RDO library somewhat to create "free-standing" connection objects. As you've probably noticed, many methods and properties are duplicated between parent and child objects in the hierarchy. By allowing you to create a standalone "child" object, you still have the functionality you need without the overhead of the parent object. The standalone rdoConnection object also provides a convenient connection source when used with optimistic batch updates and the batch cursor library.

The following code is an example of how to use a standalone rdoConnection object:

```
Dim myRdoC as New rdoConnection
Dim ConnectString as String
ConnectString = "UID=Laurie;PWD=Sister;Database=Sales;Server=EntServ;
                ➥Driver={SQL Server};DSN="";"

With myRdoC
     .Connect = ConnectString
     .LoginTimeout  = 30
     .CursorDriver = rdUseNone
     .EstablishConnection rdDriverNoPromopt, False, False
end with
```

The *BeginTrans*, *CommitTrans*, and *RollbackTrans* Methods The BeginTrans, CommitTrans, and RollbackTrans methods provide client-side transaction management in a similar way as the same methods of the rdoEnvironment object, except that at the rdoConnection object level the methods affect only the `rdoQuery` and `rdoResultset` objects instantiated under the `rdoConnection`. The `BeginTrans`, `CommitTrans`, and `RollbackTrans` methods have no parameters.

The *Cancel* Method The `Cancel` method, when used at the `rdoConnection` object level with `rdAsynchOption` enabled, allows you to cancel the attempted asynchronous connection to the server before it's completed.

The *Close* Method The `Close` method of the `rdoConnection` object closes the connection to the server and destroys any child objects, such as `rdoResultsets` objects, that were instantiated under the connection. If the `rdoConnection` object is a member of an `rdoEnvironment` object's `rdoConnections` object, the `rdoConnection` object whose method is invoked is closed but not removed from the collection. You must use the `rdoConnections` collection's `Remove` method to remove the object from the collection.

The *CreateQuery* Method

```
MyRdoC.CreateQuery QueryName[, SQLString]
```

This method creates a new `rdoQuery` object and adds it to the `rdoQueries` collection. Like dissociated `rdoResultsets`, `rdoQuery` objects can also be instantiated as standalone objects with the `New` keyword. The `rdoQuery` object created with the `CreateQuery` method provides a mechanism for using stored procedures and accessing input/output parameters.

The required *`QueryName`* parameter specifies the name of the query. The name acts as a key to reference the specific `rdoQuery` object in the `rdoQueries` collection. Input/output parameters associated with the query are stored in the `rdoParameters` collection of the `rdoQuery` object.

The optional *`SQLString`* parameter specifies the SQL query for the new prepared statement.

The *EstablishConnection* Method

```
MyRdoC.EstablishConnection [Prompt][, Readonly][,Options]
```

The `EstablishConnection` method is used to connect to the data source. It can also be used when reconnecting an existing `rdoConnection` object that was disconnected through the `Close` method. The `EstablishConnection` method can also be used to create standalone `rdoConnection` objects. The `EstablishConnection` method doesn't automatically add a `rdoConnectionObject` to the `rdoConnections` collection, as does the `rdoEnvironment` object's `OpenConnection` method.

The optional *`Prompt`* argument acts the same way as the `rdoEnvironment's OpenConnection` method by specifying how the ODBC Driver Manager manages prompting for missing connection information. The optional *`Readonly`* argument is a Boolean that can be set to `True` to enable read-only access. The *`Options`* argument is the same integer as the `rdoEnvironment OpenConnection` *`Options`* argument.

The *Execute* Method

```
MyRdoC.Execute SQLActionQuery, Options
```

The `Execute` method executes SQL statements that don't return rows. An example would be to execute a `Delete` action query against a table accessible through a specific connection. The

SQLActionQuery string is the actual SQL action query or the name of an `rdoQuery` object. The *Options* value is either `rdAsyncEnable` or `rdExecDirect`.

The following query deletes all the rows from the Orders table where the order amount was less than $1:

```
Dim sDeleteActionQuery as String
sDeleteActionQuery = "Delete Orders Where OrderAmount < 1"
MyRdoC.Execute sDeleteActionQuery
```

You can append optional parameters to this example for added functionality. The `rdAsyncEnable` option allows the query to run asynchronously and immediately returns control back to the calling program. The `rdExecDirect` option provides slightly faster performance by not setting up a temporary stored procedure, but executing the query directly. To use both options, simply `AND` the values together.

The *OpenResultSet* Method The `OpenResultSet` method is used to execute SQL queries that return rows and then stores those rows in a new `rdoResultset` object, which becomes part of the `rdoConnection`'s `rdoResultsets` collection:

```
Set MyRdoR = MyRdoC.OpenResultset(Source[,CursorType[LockType[,Options]]])
```

The *Source* argument is generally a string that contains one or more row-returning SQL statements, or the name of an `rdoQuery`. You can also include SQL action queries in the string, but there must also be at least one row returning query—otherwise, a trappable error results.

The *CursorType* argument specifies the cursor type to use. The default is `rdOpenForwardOnly`, but `rdOpenKeyset`, `rdOpenDynamic`, and `rdOpenStatic` are also valid values.

The `LockType` argument specifies what type of locking to use. `RdConcurReadOnly` is the default, but `rdConcurLock` (pessimistic concurrency), `rdConcurRowVer` (optimistic based on row ID), `rdConcurValues` (optimistic based on row values), and `RdConcurBatch` (optimistic using batch mode updates) are also valid values.

The *Options* are the now familiar `rdAsyncEnable` and `rdExecDirect`.

The *BeforeConnect*, *Connect*, and *Disconnect* Events The `BeforeConnect` event is fired just before a connection is made to a data source. The `Connect` event is fired just after a connection is made to a data source. The `Disconnect` event is fired after a connection is closed.

The *QueryComplete* Event This event is fired after the query of an `rdoResultset` returns a resultset. This event fires for all queries executed by `OpenResultSet` or `Execute` methods of the `rdoConnection` or `rdoQuery` objects. It's much cleaner to use this event rather than poll the `StillExecuting` property.

The *QueryTimeout* Event This event is fired when the execution time of a query exceeds the time limit set in the `QueryTimeout` property. The event handler passes the query and a Boolean `Cancel` argument. The `Cancel` argument is defaulted to `True`, so if this value isn't overridden, the query will be canceled when the event handler executes. By setting this value to `False`, the query isn't canceled, and the application will wait for another time period equal to the `QueryTimeout` value before the `QueryTimeout` event is fired again.

The *WillExecute* Event This event is fired just before a query is executed. It doesn't matter whether the query is an action query or a row-returning query. If you trap this event and examine the `rdoQuery` object, you can set the default *`Cancel`* argument from `False` (allow the query to proceed) to `True` (cancel the query). Certain queries can be disallowed or modified.

The *AsynchCheckInterval* Property The `AsynchCheckInterval` property is used when the connection was made with the `rdAsynchOption` to set a time interval, in milliseconds, used to check whether a query has completed processing. The default value is 1,000 milliseconds (1 second). More frequent polling can be detrimental to the performance of your application, whereas a longer polling period can delay how quickly results are available to users.

This setting normally isn't changed, unless foreground processing is very intensive and you need to devote more resources to it than to checking the status of your query. In that case, set `AsynchCheckInterval` to a longer time period. The `QueryComplete` event will eventually fire at the end of one of the `AsynchCheckInterval` time periods. If you set this value to 10,000, you'll be informed that the query has been completed only after at least 10 seconds elapse.

The *Connect* Property The `Connect` property is read-only after a connection is made and is a string representing the ODBC connect string. Depending on the *`Prompt`* argument of the `rdoEnvironments OpenConnection` method or the `rdoConnection` object's `EstablishConnection` method, the connect string can be fully constructed in code by the application or partially provided by the ODBC Login dialog box. A typical connect string might look something like this:

```
"DSN=AcctSrvr;UID=Laurie;PWD=Sis;DATBASE=AcctRec"
```

The *CursorDriver* Property The `CursorDriver` property of the `rdoConnection` object is necessary because of dissociated `rdoConnection` objects. Before RDO2, this connection information was stored at the `rdoEnvironment` level only, because all `rdoConnections` were part of an `rdoEnvironment` object. Because `rdoConnections` can now be a standalone object, this property has been added to the object. It's seeded from the `rdoEngine`'s `rdoDefaultCursorDriver` property.

The *hDbc* Property The `hDbc` property is a Long that represents the ODBC connection handle. Although this property isn't needed for RDO2 programming, it can be useful if you need to make direct ODBC API calls.

The *LastQueryResults* Property If the `rdoConnections`'s `rdoResultsets` collection contains any members, the `LastQueryResults` property returns a reference to the last added `rdoResultset`. If no `rdoResultsets` are available, nothing is returned. This property was added because you can now invoke `rdoQueries` as methods of the `rdoConnection` object. Because many queries provide return codes captured when the query is executed as a method, a different way of referencing the resultset returned by the query is necessary. The following code illustrates `LastQueryResults` in use:

```
Dim lReturnCode as Long
Dim MyRdoRS as rdoResultset
lReturnCode = MyRdoC.MyRdoQuery(arg1, arg2)
Set MyRdoRS = MyRdoC.LastQueryResults
```

The *LoginTimeout* Property Another property added as a result of the new standalone capabilities of the `rdoConnection` object is `LoginTimeout`. This property specifies the amount of time, in seconds, that the connection object waits for success when attempting to establish a connection.

The *LogMessages* Property The `LogMessages` property specifies the location of a log file and enables the logging of ODBC operations. If the property is set to a file location (for example, C:\Logs\MyApp.Log), ODBC operations are written to the file. If the property is set to an empty string, logging is disabled. If you set this property, be aware that the file can become very large very quickly. You'll probably want to use this only for debugging purposes.

The *Name* Property The `Name` property is the name given to the `rdoConnection` object.

The *QueryTimeout* Property This property specifies the number of seconds to wait before a timeout error occurs when a query is executed. The time is specified in seconds, like the `LoginTimeout` property, not in milliseconds like the `AsynchCheckInterval` property. The default timeout for queries is 30 seconds.

The *rdoQueries* Property The `rdoQueries` property is a collection of `rdoQuery` objects.

The *rdoResultsets* Property This property is a collection of `rdoResultset` objects that represent rows returned from one or more invocations of the `rdoConnection`'s `OpenResultSets` method.

The *rdoTables* Property The `rdoTables` collection is an obsolete property typically used to examine the structure of the tables making up a database. There are easier and faster ways of retrieving this information, such as applying a standard query against the system tables. Most likely, this collection will disappear in future versions of VB. Microsoft discourages its use.

The *RowsAffected* Property The `RowsAffected` property provides access to the count of the number of rows affected by the last `Execute` statement. Assume that you want to delete all orders of less than $1 from a table you're accessing. When you execute the SQL to accomplish this, the set-based nature of SQL will delete a set of rows based on the criteria of the order amount less than $1. You don't know how many rows were deleted until you check the `RowsAffected` property. After the `Execute` statement is executed, the `RowsAffected` property provides access to that information. The following code illustrates this example:

```
Dim MySQL as String
Dim MyrdoCon as rdoConnection
Set cn = rdoEnvironments(0).OpenConnection(dsname := "Accting",
        ➥Prompt:=rdDriverCompleteRequired)
MySQL = "DELETE FROM Orders WHERE OrderAmount < 1"
myrdoCon.Execute
Debug.Print "Rows Deleted = " & MyrdoCon.RowsAffected
```

The *StillConnecting* Property This property returns a Boolean representing whether a connection attempt is in progress against a remote data source. `True` indicates that the connection attempt is in progress; `False` indicates that the connection is established. If the progress of the connection attempt needs to be determined so that some specific action can be taken, it's easier to use the `Connect` event handler to get the same result.

You also don't have to create a busy wait loop to check the `StillConnecting` property if you rely on the `Connect` event. The following code snippet shows a busy wait loop that would execute until the connection was established. This is used when using asynchronous connections:

```
While MyCon.StillConnecting
    DoEvents
Wend
```

The *StillExecuting* Property This property returns a Boolean value representing whether a query has returned any results. Like with the `StillConnecting` method, a `True` value represents that the query is still attempting to retrieve a resultset, whereas `False` means that the query is ready to return the resultset. If the query returns no results, an empty resultset is returned. The `QueryComplete` event will also fire.

The *Transactions* Property The `Transactions` property specifies whether the `rdoConnection` supports the actions of the transaction-management functions `BeginTrans`, `CommitTrans`, and `RollBackTrans`. If transactions aren't supported, the transaction-management functions won't cause errors but simply won't work.

The *Updatable* Property The `Updatable` property specifies whether changes can be made to the object.

The *Version* Property The `Version` property specifies the RDO library version in use.

The *rdoResultsets* Object

Methods: `AddNew`, `BatchUpdate`, `Cancel`, `CancelBatch`, `CancelUpdate`, `Close`, `Delete`, `Edit`, `GetClipString`, `GetRows`, `MoreResults`, `Move`, `MoveFirst`, `MoveLast`, `MoveNext`, `MovePrevious`, `Requery`, `Resync`, `Update`

Events: `Associate`, `Dissociate`, `ResultsChanged`, `RowCurrencyChange`, `rowStatusChanged`, `WillAssociate`, `WillDissociate`, `WillUpdateRows`

Properties: `AbsolutePosition`, `ActiveConnection`, `BatchCollisionCount`, `BatchCollisionRows`, `BatchSize`, `BOF`, `Bookmark`, `Bookmarkable`, `EditMode`, `EOF`, `hStmt`, `Lastmodified`, `LockEdits`, `LockType`, `Name`, `PercentPosition`, `rdoColumns`, `Restartable`, `RowCount`, `Status`, `StillExecuting`, `Transactions`, `Type`, `Updatable`, `UpdateCriteria`, `UpdateOperation`

Information returned in an `rdoResultset` is generated by writing a SQL query. The SQL statement can return data from one table, such as

```
Select * from Sales where Amount > 1000
```

or you can return information from multiple tables by specifying the join condition, such as

```
Select Sales.ProductName, Sales.ProductAmount, SalesForce.SalespersonName from
Sales, SalesForce Where Sales.Amount > 1000 and SalesForce.SalespersonID =
Sales.SalespersonID
```

The *AbsolutePosition* Property The `AbsolutePosition` property is used to determine or set the ordinal position of the current row within a keyset or static `rdoResultset`. It's tempting to think of this as a row number, but this is unwise if the `rdoResultset` is repopulated.

The *AddNew* Method The `AddNew` method creates a new row in the `rdoResultset` that you can use to edit and add to the remote data source by using the `Update` method. If you attempt to add a record by using the `AddNew` method against a non-updatable `rdoResultset`, an error isn't generated until the `Update` method is invoked. If you need to undo an added record and haven't invoked the `Update` method, use the `CancelUpdate` method to retract the addition. The `AddNew` method has no parameters.

The *BatchUpdate* Method

```
MyrdoResultset.BatchUpdate([SingleRow][, Force])
```

The `BatchUpdate` method performs an optimistic batch update and sends the appropriate SQL to the server to synchronize the data on the remote data source with the changes made to the `rdoResultset`. The *`SingleRow`* parameter overrides the batch update and sends only the current row back to the database. The *`Force`* option is essentially a *dirty write*, where the local version of the data overwrites the data on the server, even if collisions occur. Setting *`SingleRow`* to `False` and *`Force`* to `True` causes the modifications made in the local `rdoResultset` to overwrite the data in the server, even if collisions occur. The default values of *`SingleRow`* and *`Force`* are both `False`.

The *Cancel* Method The `Cancel` method has no parameters and cancels an asynchronous query, or flushes any remaining resultset rows.

The *CancelBatch* Method The `CancelBatch` method is analogous to the `CancelUpdate` method in that any modifications made to the `rdoResultset` since the last `BatchUpdate` will be discarded.

The *CancelUpdate* Method The `CancelUpdate` method destroys any changes made to the current row that exist in the edit buffer and haven't yet been committed to the remote data source. You can use the `EditMode` property to determine whether any changes exist in the edit buffer. If the edit buffer is empty (the `EditMode` property is set to `rdEditNone`), no error is generated.

The *Close* Method The `Close` method has no parameters and closes the resultset to release resources. Always remember to call it after you complete any data-manipulation methods.

NOTE In RDO1, reusing the same `rdoResultset` object without invoking the `Close` method would result in open cursors and resources. RDO2 now automatically closes the `Close` method if an object is reused.

The *Delete* Method The `Delete` method has no parameters and deletes the current row from the `rdoResultset`; if there is no current row, a trappable error results. The deleted row remains the current row after `Delete` is invoked, so you must move the current record pointer before trying to retrieve any data from the next row. Depending on your cursor type, you might be able to maneuver to a row deleted by another user. If this happens, a trappable error results.

The *Edit* Method The `Edit` method has no parameters and allows changes to be made in the current row of an `rdoResultset` object. The `Edit` method creates a memory buffer and copies the contents of the current record into the buffer. Changes made to the buffer can then be written back to the `rdoResultset` by using the `Update` method. If you execute `Edit` and subsequently move the current record pointer to another row before `Update` is executed, any pending changes are lost. The following code shows this method in use, with and without the `Update` method:

```
MyrdoRS.Edit
MyrdoRS.rdoColumns(0) = "Changed Value Row 1"
MyrdoRS.MoveNext 'Changes are lost!
MyrdoRS.Edit
MyrdoRS.rdoColumns(0) = "Changed Value Row 2"
myrdoRS.Update 'Changes are saved!
```

The *GetClipString* Method

```
MyString = MyRDOR.GetClipString(NumRows [,ColumnDelim] [,RowDelim] [,NullExpr])
```

The `GetClipString` method returns a delimited string that represents the rows of data in a resultset. This is very handy for adding information to a grid or to some other object. The required *`NumRows`* argument specifies the number of rows to return. The *`ColumnDelim`* argument specifies a column delimiter to separate columns. The *`RowDelim`* argument specifies a row delimiter to separate rows. The *`NullExpr`* argument allows a specified character to take the place of the default empty string value that represents a `NULL` value.

The *GetRows* Method The `GetRows` method retrieves multiple rows from a recordset object and stores them in a two-dimensional array. The *`NoOfRows`* argument specifies the number of rows to retrieve from the `rdoResultset`. The following code lines show the method and argument in use:

```
Dim MyArray as Variant
MyArray = MyRdoResultset.GetRows(NoOfRows)
```

The values in the array can be referenced by using the first dimension as the column number and the second dimension as the row number. Remember that arrays are base 0. The following piece of code returns the value of the first column (0) from the second row (1):

```
Fieldvalue = MyArray(0,1)
```

If a larger *`NoOfRows`* is specified than actually exists in the `rdoResultset`, the entire `rdoResultset` is returned.

The *MoreResults* Method Because a query can return multiple resultsets, this method is used to clear the current resultset and returns a Boolean value to indicate whether more resultsets are available.

NOTE Not all ODBC drivers support multiple resultsets, so this method might be unavailable to you. Check with your ODBC driver documentation to see if this functionality is supported.

The *Move* Method

```
MyRdoRS.Move NoOfRows, [StartPosition]
```

The `Move` method moves the current pointer in the `rdoResultset` object a specified number of rows. If *`NoOfRows`* is positive, the current pointer moves forward for *`NoOfRows`* from its position. If the number is negative, the current pointer moves backward from its position. If the pointer is directed to a row beyond the beginning of the file or the end of the file, the `BOF` or `EOF` properties are set to `True`.

If the *`StartPosition`* is specified, it is to be a variant that identifies a bookmark. Also, moving the current pointer after using `Edit` or `AddNew`, but before invoking the `Update` method, causes any changes that were made to be lost. This method also fires the `RowCurrencyChange` event.

The *MoveFirst*, *MoveLast*, *MoveNext*, and *MovePrevious* Methods The `MoveFirst` method positions the current pointer to the first record in the `rdoResultset`. The `MoveLast` method positions the current pointer to the last record. `MoveNext` moves the current pointer forward one record, and `MovePrevious` moves it backward one record. Monitor the `BOF` and `EOF` properties to determine when the end of a recordset has been reached.

The *Requery* Method

```
MyrdoResultset.Requery [options]
```

The `Requery` method ensures that you have the most current data available in the resultset by re-executing the query and refreshing the data in the resultset. If the `rdAsyncEnable` option is used, check the `StillExecuting` property or wait for the `QueryCompleted` event to fire before attempting to examine the `rdoResultset`.

The *Resync* Method The `Resync` method has no parameters and is valid only when using client batch cursors. `Resync` resynchronizes the columns in the current row with the current data on the server.

The *Update* Method The `Update` method has no parameters and saves changes in the copy buffer by updating the `rdoResultset` object.

The *Associate* Event The `Associate` event is fired immediately after a new connection is associated with an `rdoResultset`.

The *Dissociate* Event The `Dissociate` event is fired after the `ActiveConnection` property is set to nothing and the `rdoResultset` is dissociated from a connection.

The *ResultsChanged* Event After the `MoreResults` method closes the current resultset and returns the next available resultset, the `ResultsChanged` event is fired. If there are no other resultsets to return, the `BOF` and `EOF` properties of the `rdoResultset` are set to `True`.

The *RowCurrencyChange* Event This event is fired whenever the current pointer is moved, including moving the current pointer to `BOF` or `EOF`.

The *RowStatusChange* Event This event is fired when the state of the current row changes due to an edit, a delete, or an insert. The current status for a specific row can be determined by moving the current pointer to that row and examining the `rdoRecordSets` `Status` property.

The *WillAssociate* Event The `WillAssociate` event is raised after a valid connection is set to the `ActiveConnection` property but before the actual connection is made. The `Cancel` parameter can be set to `True` to abort the attempted connection.

The *WillDissociate* Event The `WillDissociate` event is raised when the `ActiveConnection` property is set to nothing, but before actually disconnecting form the data source. The `Cancel` parameter can be set to `True` to abort the attempt to disconnect from the data source.

The *WillUpdateRows* Event The `WillUpdateRows` event fires before the updated data from an `rdoResultset` is sent to the remote data source. The update process can be overridden by some special code implemented for a specific purpose.

The *`ReturnCode`* specifies to RDO2 if the update was handled by another process, what the result was of the update by the other process, or whether it should handle the update itself. The default value, `rdUpdateNotHandled`, directs RDO to handle updates itself. The `rdUpdateSuccessful` value tells RDO2 that another process handled the update and was successful. The `rdUpdateWithCollisions` value, used only in batch mode, specifies that another process handled the update, but that some data collisions were encountered. `rdUpDateFailed` specifies that another process failed while attempting to complete the update.

The *ActiveConnection* Property The `ActiveConnection` property is a reference to an `rdoConnection` object to which the `rdoResultset` is associated.

The *BatchCollisionCount* Property The `BatchCollisionCount` property returns a count of the number of rows that weren't updated successfully during the execution of the last `UpdateBatch` method. A zero means that all rows were updated successfully.

The *BatchCollionsRows* Property The `BatchCollisionRows` property is a variant array of bookmarks that specify which rows in the `rdoResultset` weren't successfully updated. The count of this collection is the `BatchCollisionCount` property.

The *BatchSize* Property The `BatchSize` property refers to the number of SQL statements sent together as a batch to the remote data source. The default value is 15. Not all data sources support multiple SQL statements in a batch, so this value can be set to 1 to send a single SQL statement at a time.

The *BOF* Property The Beginning Of File (`BOF`) property indicates whether the current row of the `rdoResultset` is before the first row. A `True` value is typically what's seen when an `rdoResultset` is first retrieved, but is empty. This property is also used if the `MovePrevious` method is being used to move the cursor backward through an `rdoResultset`. When the `BOF` property becomes `True` during this activity, there are no more rows beyond the current position.

The *BookMark* Property This method is used to uniquely identify the current row in an `rdoResultset` object. You can save the value of a row's `Bookmark` property by assigning it to a variant data type. To move to that specific row at a later time when the current pointer is anywhere within the `rdoResultset`, simply set the `rdoResultset` object's `Bookmark` property to the value of the saved variant variable. You can retrieve the `Bookmark` for a row only when the current pointer is positioned on that row. If the `rdoResultset` doesn't support `Bookmarks`, a trappable error results.

The *Bookmarkable* Property This property determines whether an `rdoResultset` supports the use of `Bookmarks`.

The *EditMode* Property The `EditMode` property identifies whether the current row has values copied to the edit buffer. The values returned are `rdEditNone`, which means the row isn't being edited; `rdEditInProgress`, which means a copy of the row exists in the edit buffer; and `rdEditAdd`, which means that a new row exists in the edit buffer but hasn't yet been written to the remote data source.

The *EOF* Property The analog to the `BOF` property, the End Of File (`EOF`) property indicates whether the current row of the `rdoResultset` is after the last row. The `EOF` value is also set to `True` if an `rdoResultset` is empty. This property is frequently used when using the `MoveNext` method to move forward through an `rdoResultset`. When the `EOF` property becomes true, there are no more rows in the `rdoResultset` beyond the current position.

The *hStmt* Property This property is a pointer to an ODBC statement handle. It's not used in RDO2 programming but can be used when making direct ODBC API calls.

The *LastModified* Property The `LastModified` property is a variant that represents a bookmark to the last modified row in the resultset.

The *LockEdits* Property The `LockEdits` property is a Boolean value set to `True` when pessimistic locking is being used and `False` (the default) when optimistic locking is in effect.

The *LockType* Property The `LockType` property specifies the type of concurrency handling the `rdoQuery` object implements. Possible `LockType` values are

- `rdoConcurReadOnly`, which disallows any data modification
- `rdConcurLock`, which specifies a pessimistic concurrency type where a lock is put on the data when the `Edit` method is executed
- `rdConcurRow`, which specifies an optimistic concurrency type based on row ID
- `rdConcurValues`, which specifies an optimistic concurrency option based on the values of the rows in the resultset
- `rdConcurBatch`, which is used for optimistic batch updates

The *Name* Property The `Name` property is the name given to the `rdoResultset` and used to reference the object in code.

The *PercentPosition* Property The `PercentPosition` property represents an approximate position of the current pointer as a percentage of the number of rows in the resultset.

NOTE The PercentPosition property can be used only with keyset and dynamic cursor types. If the property is examined when some other cursor type is used, a value of 50 is returned.

The *rdoColumns* Property The rdoColumns property is a collection of rdoColumn objects that make up the fields of the resultset.

The *Restartable* Property The Restartable property returns True or False, which determines whether the rdoResultset supports the Requery method. If the property is False, the rdoResultset should be closed and the OpenResultSet method must be used to refresh the data.

The *RowCount* Property The RowCount property returns the number of rows accessed by an rdoResultset object. This is different than returning how many total rows are in the rdoResultset. To get a total row count, the last record has to have been accessed.

NOTE Some drivers can't return a RowCount value and return -1 if the value is unavailable.

The *Status* Property The Status property is a value of the rdoResultset object, which represents the status of the current row. The possible values are

- rdRowUnmodifed, which means that the row hasn't been changed since it was retrieved
- rdRowModified, which means the row has been modified but the database hasn't
- rdRowNew, which means the AddNew method was used to add a new row, but that row doesn't yet exist on the remote database
- rdRowDeleted, which means the Delete method was used to delete a row from the rdoResultset, but the remote database hasn't yet been updated
- rdRowDBDeleted, which means the row has been deleted in the local rdoResultset and the remote database

The *StillExecuting* Property Used with asynchronous operations, the StillExecuting property is True if the query is still being processed by the server and False if the resultset is available.

The *Transactions* Property The Transactions property of the rdoResultset object functions like the property of the same name that belongs to the rdoConnection object. It merely tells you whether the rdoResultset will support transactions.

The *Type* Property The Type property returns a value that specifies the data type of the rdoResultset object.

The *Updatable* Property This property is True when the rdoResultset can be updated and False when it can't be updated.

The *UpDateCriteria* Property The UpDateCriteria property is used to specify or determine how the WHERE clause is constructed for each row in an optimistic batch update. The default value is rdCriteriaKey, which specifies that just the key columns are used. The rdCriteriaUpdCols value uses the key columns and all updated columns. The rdCriteriaAllCols value uses the key columns and all the other columns in the rdoResultset. The rdCriteriaTimeStamp value specifies that a timestamp column be used, if available; if no timestamp column is available, a trappable runtime error results.

The *UpDateOperation* Property The UpdateOperation specifies how UPDATE statements sent to the remote database are represented. The default value, rdOperationUpdate, species that an UPDATE statement is used. The alternative value, rdOperationDelIns, specifies that DELETE and ADD statements be substituted for the UPDATE statement. This property is used to provide some flexibility in performance tuning when different triggers are attached to the ADD, UPDATE, and DELETE actions on the database.

The *rdoColumn* Object

Methods: AppendChunk, ColumnSize, GetChunk

Events: DataChanged, WillChangeData

Properties: AllowZeroLength, Attributes, BatchConflictValue, ChunkRequired, KeyColumn, Name, OrdinalPosition, Required, Size, SourceColumn, SourceTable, Status, Type, Updatable, Value

The rdoColumn object represents a column from an rdoTable or a column from an rdoResultset. The name of the column comes from the name defined by the Data Definition Language (DDL) that created the underlying table of an rdoTable object, or by the column name as aliased by a SQL query in an rdoResultset.

The *AppendChunk* Method The AppendChunk method is used to handle Binary Large Objects (BLOBs) and appends data from a Variant expression to an rdoColumn object with a data type rdTypeLONGVARBINARY or rdTypeLONGVARCHAR to the database column. Because the data is appended to the column, AppendChunk is used to write out successive blocks of data, one portion at a time.

The *ColumnSize* Method The ColumnSize method returns the bytes in an rdoColumn object with a data type of rdTypeLONGVARBINARY or rdTypeLONGVARCHAR. A value of –1 is returned if the size isn't available.

The *GetChunk* Method The GetChunk method returns all or a portion of an rdoColumn object with a data type of rdTypeLONGVARBINARY or rdTypeLONGVARCHAR.

The *DataChanged* Event The DataChanged event occurs after the value of a column changes.

The *WillChangeData* Event The WillChangeData event is fired before data is changed in the column. The event handler for this event provides a cancel parameter that defaults to False, which will allow the change to occur, but can be set to True, which will disallow the pending change.

The *AllowZeroLength* Property The `AllowZeroLength` property is used to determine if zero-length strings (`""`) are valid for data types of `rdTypeCHAR`, `rdTypeVARCHAR`, and `rdTypeLONGVARCHAR`. A value of `True` indicates null strings are accepted, whereas `False` indicates that they're unacceptable.

The *Attributes* Property The `Attributes` property returns a value representing the characteristics of an `rdoColumn` object:

- `rdFixedColumn` indicates that the column size is fixed.
- `rdVariableColumn` specifies that the column is a variable (`VarChar`, `VarBinary`, and so on).
- `rdAutoIncrColumn` indicates that the underlying column is an identity column.
- `rdUpdatableColumn` indicates that the value of the column can be changed.
- `rdTimeStampColumn` identifies a column that contains a timestamp value.

A column can have more than one of these values, so you must `AND` them to determine whether their bits are represented in the value of `Attributes`.

The *BatchConflictValue* Property In an optimistic batch update, it's possible that another process changed a value on the remote database between the time it was originally fetched and the time the `BatchUpdate` method was executed. The `BatchConflictValue` property represents the value of the column as it exists on the remote data source at the time `BatchUpdate` was executed.

The *ChunkRequired* Property Some column values can be too large to be fetched all at once and must be retrieved in *chunks*. The `ChunkRequired` property returns a Boolean value set to `True` when data must be accessed by using the `GetChunk` method and `False` if the value can be retrieved directly.

The *KeyColumn* property The `KeyColumn` property returns `True` if the column is part of the primary key and `False` if it isn't. This read/write property uses the `rdClientBatch` cursor library and helps build the `WHERE` clauses for the data-modification statements in an optimistic batch update.

The *Name* Property The `Name` property is the name of the column as defined in the DDL that created the underlying table in `rdoTable` objects, or possibly aliased name used in the `SELECT` statement used to create an `rdoResultset` object.

The *OrdinalPosition* Property The `OrdinalPosition` property represents the position of column in an `rdoTable` or `rdoResultset`. The position is base 0, so the `OrdinalPosition` of the first column equals 0.

The *OriginalValue* Property The `OriginalValue` property returns the value of the column as it was originally fetched from the database. You can resolve conflicts during optimistic batch updates by comparing this value with the value the batch update supplies.

The *Required* Property The `Required` property returns a `True` value if null values aren't allowed as a valid entry to the column. `False` specifies that nulls are allowed.

The *Size* Property The `Size` property returns the maximum number of characters in an `rdoColumn` object that contains text or the number of bytes of an `rdoColumn` object that contains numeric values.

The *SourceColumn* Property The `SourceColumn` property contains the name of the data source column.

The *SourceTable* Property The `SourceTable` property contains the name of the table that's the underlying source of the data.

The *Status* Property See "The *Status* Property" section under the earlier section "The *rdoResultsets* Object."

The *Type* Property The `Type` property returns a value that specifies the underlying data type of an `rdoColumn` object. There are many possible values, but a quick way to differentiate between numeric or string is that numeric values are between 2 (`rdTypeNumeric`) and 8 (`rdTypeDouble`), strings are 1 (`rdTypeChar`) and 12 (`rdTypeVarChar`), and Date/Time values are between 9 (`rdTypeDate`) and 11 (`rdTypeTimeStamp`). Negative numbers –1 through –7 are more esoteric binary or BLOB types.

The *Updatable* Property `Updatable` returns a `True` value indicating that the column can be updated, and a `False` value if the column can't be updated.

NOTE Be careful about identity columns, as they will be `Updatable`, but the `Attribute` property will be `rdAutoIncrColumn` and not `rdUpdatableColumn`.

The *Value* Property The `Value` property returns a string variant that represents the value in the current row of the underlying `rdoColumn`.

The *rdoQuery* Object

Methods: `Cancel`, `Close`, `Execute`, `OpenResultset`

Events: None

Properties: `ActiveConnection`, `BindThreshold`, `CursorType`, `hStmt`, `KeysetSize`, `LockType`, `MaxRows`, `Name`, `Prepared`, `QueryTimeout`, `rdoColumns`, `rdoParameters`, `RowsAffected`, `RowsetSize`, `SQL`, `SillExecuting`, `Type`

The `rdoQuery` object is used to define SQL queries that use input and output parameters and acts as a compiled SQL statement. The object is useful when a single query is executed repeatedly with changes to its parameters. This object replaces the `rdoPreparedStatement` object used in RDO1.

The *Cancel* Method The `Cancel` method requests the remote data source to cancel the processing of a query. Depending on the state of the query processing by the server, the query might be able to be canceled.

The *Close* Method The `Close` method closes the `rdoQuery` object, releases it from the `rdoQueries` collection, and frees resources in use by the object.

The *Execute* Method The `Execute` method is used to execute a query that doesn't return any rows, such as an action query.

The *OpenResultSet* Method The `OpenResultSet` method executes the row returning SQL that defines the `rdoQuery` object.

The *ActiveConnection* Property The `ActiveConnection` property represents the current connection to a remote data source. It's the conduit for information exchanged between the remote data source and the `rdoQuery`. `rdoQuery` objects can be set to nothing and "disconnected" from a connection, and then reused by setting the `ActiveConnection` property to another `rdoConnection` object.

The *BindThreshold* Property The `BindThreshold` property sets the largest column size that ODBC will automatically bind. Some BLOB type data is too large to handle by using standard methods. By setting this property, you identify the threshold where if the data is less than the value, standard RDO techniques can be used to manipulate the data. If the column size is larger than the value of this property, `GetChunk` and `AppendChunk` must be used. The default `BindThreshold` value is 1,024 bytes.

The *CursorType* Property The `CursorType` property specifies the cursor type that will be used. The default is `rdOpenForwardOnly`, but `rdOpenKeyset`, `rdOpenDynamic`, and `rdOpenStatic` are also valid values.

The *hStmt* Property This property represents a pointer to an ODBC statement. It's not used in RDO2 programming but can be used when making direct ODBC API calls.

The *KeysetSize* Property The `KeysetSize` property specifies the number of rows used in the keyset buffer for keyset or dynamic cursors. `KeysetSize` must be larger than the `RowsetSize` property. The default keyset size, 0, specifies a true keyset-driven cursor; a value greater than 0 actually results in a mixed-cursor type.

NOTE Not all ODBC drivers support keyset cursors.

The *LockType* Property The `LockType` property specifies the type of concurrency handling that the `rdoQuery` object implements:

- `rdoConcurReadOnly` disallows any data modification.
- `rdConcurLock` specifies a pessimistic concurrency type, where a lock is put on the data when the `Edit` method is executed.
- `rdConcurRow` value specifies an optimistic concurrency type based on row ID.
- `rdConcurValues` specifies an optimistic concurrency option based on the values of the rows in the resultset.
- `rdConcurBatch` is used for optimistic batch updates.

The *MaxRows* Property The MaxRows property defaults to 0 (return all rows), but any positive value can be used to specify the maximum number of rows a query can return.

The *Name* Property This property is used to give a name to the rdoQuery object.

The *Prepared* Property The Prepared property accepts a Boolean True or False value that specifies whether the query is to create a stored procedure (True, the default) or to execute the query directly as dynamic SQL. Creating the query as a stored procedure results in compilation of the SQL and an execution plan created by the remote data source that specifies the most efficient way to access the data. This results in faster access time during the actual operation of the query, but some time is used to create the stored procedure itself. In general, if a query will be used many times, create a stored procedure for greater throughput.

The *QueryTimeOut* Property The QueryTimeOut property specifies the number of seconds to wait if rows haven't been returned before the operation is canceled by the ODBC driver manager.

The *rdoColumns* Property The rdoColumns property is a collection of rdoColumn objects.

The *rdoParameters* Property The rdoParameters property is a collection of rdoParameter objects.

The *RowsAffected* Property The RowsAffected property returns the count of the number of rows modified by the SQL executed by the most recent Execute method.

The *RowsetSize* Property The RowsetSize property specifies how many rows will be "active" at any one time during the creation of a resultset. If a query returns 300 rows and RowsetSize is set to 100, only 100 rows at a time will populate the resultset. This way, the application can bring in subsets of the data and ease contention at the remote data source. Rows not included in the resultset aren't buffered by the application and remain unaffected on the server.

The *SQL* Property The SQL property is a string that makes up the actual Structured Query Language (SQL) to be executed by the rdoQuery.

The *StillExecuting* Property The StillExecuting property specifies whether an asynchronous query is still executing or has completed.

The *Type* Property The Type property returns a value that specifies the underlying data type of an rdoColumn object. There are many possible values, but a quick way to differentiate between numeric or string is that numeric values are between 2 (rdTypeNumeric) and 8 (rdTypeDouble), strings are 1 (rdTypeChar) and 12 (rdTypeVarChar), and Date/Time values are between 9 (rdTypeDate) and 11 (rdTypeTimeStamp). Negative numbers –1 through –7 are more esoteric binary or BLOB types.

The *rdoParameters* Object

Methods: AppendChunk

Events: None

Properties: Direction, Name, Type, Value

The `rdoParameters` property is a collection of `rdoParameter` objects that make up those variables to be passed to the stored procedure.

The *AppendChunk* Method The `AppendChunk` method is used to add large data elements in manageable sections referred to as *chunks*.

The *Direction* Property The `Direction` property specifies whether a parameter is considered an input or output parameter. The possible values include the following:

- The default, `rdParamInput`, specifies an input parameter.
- `rdParamInputOutput` specifies that the parameter be used to pass a piece of data to the query and be changed by the query, and that the changed value be read back from the query.
- `rdParamOutput` identifies an output parameter.
- `rdParamReturnValue` indicates that the parameter is used to return the status value from the stored procedure.

The *Name* Property This is the name that will represent the `rdoParameter` object.

The *Type* Property The `Type` property returns a value that specifies the underlying data type of an `rdoColumn` object. There are many possible values, but a quick way to differentiate between numeric or string is that numeric values are between 2 (`rdTypeNumeric`) and 8 (`rdTypeDouble`), strings are 1 (`rdTypeChar`) and 12 (`rdTypeVarChar`), and Date/Time values are between 9 (`rdTypeDate`) and 11 (`rdTypeTimeStamp`). Negative numbers –1 through –7 are more esoteric binary or BLOB types.

The *Value* Property The `Value` property returns or sets the actual value of the `rdoParameter`.

Obsolete Objects

To be complete, a short discussion is included on some objects that exist in RDO2 but have been deemed obsolete. They exist primarily to provide backward compatibility with RDO1 code.

The *rdoTable* Object The `rdoTable` object is used to examine the structure of tables within a database or to examine the data contained in a table. The `rdoTable` object can be used to determine whether a table is updatable or not, or the columns can be examined to determine their data type, and so on. If the `OpenResultset` method is used against the `rdoTable` object, a `Select * from MyTable` SQL command is executed, using the specified cursor library.

Needless to say, this can wreak havoc on multiuser databases, so its use isn't advised. In fact, Microsoft warns that the `rdoTable` object might not be supported in future versions of RDO. If detailed information is needed about a table, simply querying the system tables for the information is simpler and requires less overhead.

The *rdoPreparedStatement* Object The `rdoPreparedStatement` object has been replaced by the `rdoQuery` object. Use the `rdoQuery` object for situations where stored procedures with input/output parameters are used.

From Here...

In this chapter, you learned about the "classic" two-tier client/server architecture and the roles of each component of that architecture. You were introduced to the common concepts in client/server programming, such as stored procedures, cursors and cursor types, DSNs, row-returning and action queries, and asynchronous versus synchronous operations. You also were exposed to the RDO2 object hierarchy, and examined each object, method, property, and event of that object model.

Although RDO2 is now the best choice available for two-tier client/server database access, it will eventually be displaced by the Active Data Objects (ADO) library. RDO is tied very closely to ODBC. ODBC is tied very closely to the relational data model and SQL. ADO promises to provide access to heterogeneous data sources by using a consistent data access method to the client program. This way, you can query databases, phone lists, mail systems, and so forth—all using the same code! This will be a wonderful thing, but ADO is a very young product and requires some maturing. For now, RDO is your best access method to corporate RDBMSs.

- For more information about client/server architectures, see Chapter 20, "Clients, Servers, and Components: Design Strategies for Distributed Applications," and Chapter 21, "Creating Distributed Applications."
- Chapter 23, "Building Client Front Ends with Visual Basic and ADO," gives you a complete overview of ADO and explains when it might be a better choice than RDO2.

CHAPTER 23

Building Client Front Ends with Visual Basic and ADO

by Kevin D. Runnels and Eric Brown

Universal Data Access

Discover the advantages of Microsoft's new Universal Data Access architecture. Learn how this new technology has an impact on application development.

The pieces of the data access architecture

Learn how data providers, service providers, and data consumers work together to provide access to heterogeneous data sources.

The object model

Uncover the complete ActiveX Data Objects library and explore the underlying object model. Review the main objects and their properties and methods, and see how ADO's features are used.

Putting ADO to use in your applications

Use your knowledge of the object model to simplify data management and discover how it's easier than ever to access data with the help of VB and COM.

The Remote Data Objects (RDO) library has been the mainstay of Visual Basic programmers for traditional client/server development since it premiered with VB4. This robust object model is still appropriate for many client/server projects for many reasons (see Chapter 22, "Building Client Front Ends with Visual Basic and RDO"). Unfortunately, the underlying architecture of RDO 2.0 (RDO2) is too closely tied to accessing relational database management systems (RDBMSs) and doesn't provide the flexibility needed to access the many different data stores in use in today's corporate environment.

To address this problem, Microsoft has debuted the Active Data Objects, or ActiveX Data Objects (ADO) library, as the VB programmer's gateway into the world of Universal Data Access and OLE DB. ADO doesn't ship with Visual Basic 5.0 but is part of Visual Studio by virtue of its inclusion with Visual InterDev and Visual C++. That ADO didn't ship with VB 5.0 was a result of the timing of the releases of the two products, not a comment by Microsoft that the library didn't apply to VB programming. In fact, ADO can be used by VB, Visual C++, Visual J++, and Visual Basic for Applications (VBA).

This chapter introduces you to ADO's features and capabilities. Along the way you'll learn about the ADO object model and how to use its properties and methods in your applications. According to Microsoft, ADO is the preferred method of accessing data from any arbitrary data source. Due to the relative immaturity of ADO, however, there are some caveats. Guidance to help you decide between RDO and ADO during this maturation period is offered at the end of the chapter. ■

The Elusive Search for Data Access Perfection

One of the first tasks that computers were given was the management of large amounts of data. It's a natural application for a computer system, with its rapid information retrieval and sorting and searching capabilities. It's understandable, then, that a primary area of research and development in the computing community has been the development of powerful yet easy-to-use tools for data management and retrieval.

The development of the relational database management system (RDBMS) has had a huge impact on the software development industry and has spawned the growth of many tools and related technologies. In Chapter 22 you learned about using Visual Basic with RDO2, a Microsoft technology providing object-based mechanisms for handling relational data. But data isn't always stored in a relational system. The growth of the Internet, in particular, has dramatically increased the need to manage a wide array of unstructured data types stored in many different formats on myriad devices. Clearly, a mechanism is needed that addresses this problem.

Universal Data Access and OLE DB

OLE DB is Microsoft's technology to provide what Microsoft terms as *Universal Data Access.* This technology provides a common data interface to many different data sources. Users frequently need access to data that might exist in spreadsheets, phone lists, email, and so on. Programmatic access to this wide range of data types, formats, architectures, APIs, and so forth has been complex and error-prone. However, the OLE DB API was designed to address how different types of data are accessed and used, and emphasizes the commonality in data access and manipulation such as opening the data source, requesting information, and navigating through the information.

For example, on any typical project, users will store some information in a database. The database is ideally suited for well structured, easily classified things such as parts lists and accounting information. Not all data fits well in a database, however, and users will also have phone lists or to-do lists in Microsoft Exchange or Outlook. They might use Microsoft Project to keep track of complex projects and subprojects. They might need to keep track of certain information that other users are entering into Microsoft Excel spreadsheets on the corporate network. OLE DB was designed to allow access to all this information stored in disparate file types and by different applications through a single API.

Data Providers, Service Providers, and Data Consumers

OLE DB, at its most basic level, is organized into an architecture described by data providers, service providers, and data consumers and their roles as users or providers of the OLE DB interface (see Figure 23.1):

- A *data provider* owns its own data and can expose that data, via a driver, in tabular form through OLE DB interfaces.
- A *service provider* is a data consumer and data provider in that it encapsulates some type of service, such as a query engine, that exposes OLE DB interfaces but doesn't own the data that it operates against. For instance, a query engine service provider uses the OLE DB interface to retrieve information from a data provider and then, in turn, provides the manipulated queried data to the data consumer.
- The *data consumer* is any application, such as a VB program, that retrieves data through the OLE DB interface.

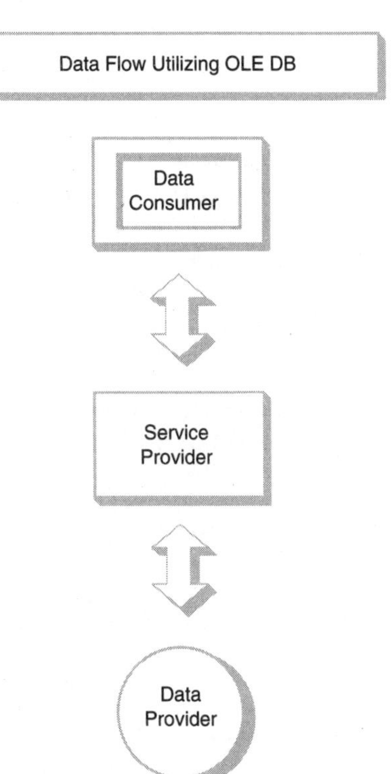

FIG. 23.1
The data provider/service provider/data consumer architecture provides the flexibility to extend the capabilities of a data access scheme by enhancing the capabilities of any of these components.

Now that these different applications and different data types can all be accessed the same way through OLE DB, seemingly impossible things—such as relating joins between a spreadsheet, a database, and an email system—are now possible.

NOTE Remember that virtually any application–spreadsheets, word processors, mail systems, and even the upcoming Windows NT 5.0 file system–can be an OLE DB Data Provider. Specialized service providers can then be developed to creatively extend the accessibility and usability of these data providers. ■

Active Data Objects

Unfortunately for VB programmers, OLE DB is implemented as a set of low-level C/C++ functions. This means that the calling language needs to be able to handle pointers, memory-management routines, specialized data structures, and other details that most VB programmers would rather avoid. To open this technology to a larger audience, Microsoft has wrapped the OLE DB API in a pointerless, language-neutral COM interface called *Active Data Objects (ADO)*.

NOTE Remember that the ADO library must be added to your project before you can address it from within your VB code. Choose Project, References, and select Microsoft ActiveX Data Objects 1.5 Library from the list. ■

ADO encapsulates OLE DB much as RDO encapsulates ODBC. ADO provides the access point for relational and ISAM-based databases, as well as access to data sources that aren't even considered databases but can provide row/column (tabular) results to queries. In ADO 1.5's current incarnation, several important features available for database access using RDO 2.0 haven't yet been implemented, including the use of asynchronous operations, queries as methods, and events. Chapter 22 provides for more information regarding RDO2 and synchronous versus asynchronous operations.

As you can see in Figure 23.2, the ADO object model is smaller than RDO2's, and its objects are generally more self-contained than those in RDO2. This deemphasis of the hierarchical approach allows greater reuse of the individual objects. Microsoft has taken what was good from the Data Access Objects (DAO) library and the RDO library and put them in ADO. As a result, VB programmers instantly feel at home with this new data access method.

NOTE One feature lacking in the ADO model that programmers will miss is events. This is likely to change with the next release of ADO. ■

Because OLE DB and ADO are so new, a limited number of data providers and service providers can be accessed. This will no doubt change in the near future; many companies are working feverishly to get into this new paradigm first and establish a presence. Microsoft has eased the situation for ODBC database access by supplying a provider code-named Kagera, which translates OLE DB to ODBC when communicating to an ODBC driver. Kagera works with any ODBC 2.0 driver that provides level-1 conformance.

▶ **See** "RDO and Open Database Connectivity," **p. 612**

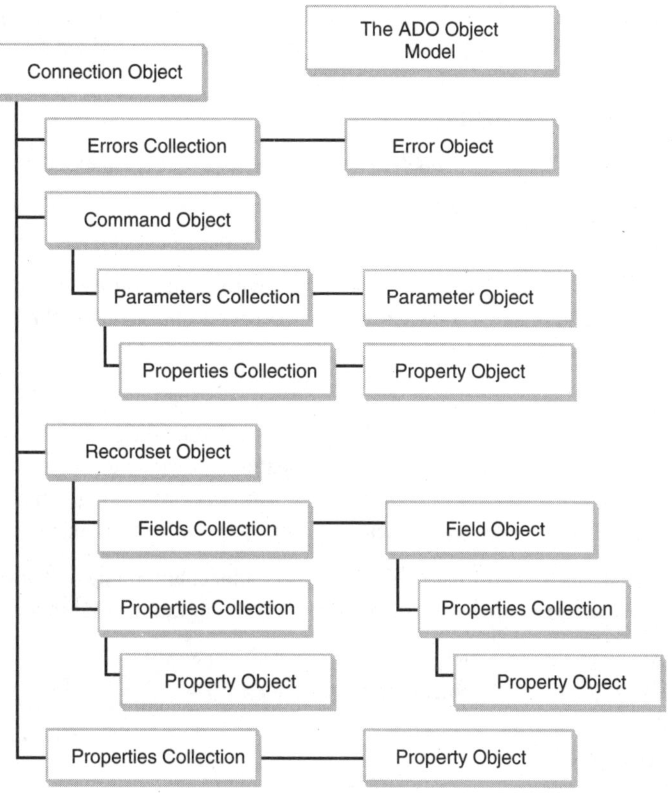

FIG. 23.2
The ADO object model is much more modular and free-standing than RDO, where the hierarchical structure of the object library is much more prevalent.

Three main objects in the ADO model do most of the work: `Connection`, `Command`, and `Recordset`. These objects encompass more functionality than the single objects of the RDO2 model in that they provide enough features and functions to operate by themselves in many cases. The RDO2 objects rely heavily on other objects to provide some functionality, and the hierarchical structure enforces this interdependency between the objects. By contrast, with ADO, the `Recordset` object alone can connect to a database, retrieve results, manipulate the results, and save the data back to the server, all without relying on other objects to handle part of the task. Many times ADO will create objects for you, such as `Connection` objects, and use the object without you ever having to address the object yourself. However, for maximum flexibility in defining transactions, managing cursor types, and so on, you should become familiar with all the ADO objects and the functionality each of them encapsulates.

The ADO Object Model

The key to using an object-based or object-oriented library is to understand the exposed object model. The details of implementation are encapsulated so that you don't need to worry about them (most of the time, at least). Although investigating the inner workings of the library is appropriate on some occasions, most of the time you need nothing more than a solid understanding of the exposed objects, including their properties and methods.

The following sections discuss the various ADO objects, along with suggestions on how best to use them in your applications. Several code samples are provided demonstrating their usage.

The *Connection* Object

Methods: `Open`, `BeginTrans`, `RollbackTrans`, `CommitTrans`, `Execute`, `Close`

Properties: `Attributes`, `CommandTimeout`, `ConnectionString`, `ConnectionTimeout`, `DefaultDatabase`, `IsolationLevel`, `Mode`, `Provider`, `Version`

The `Connection` object represents a session with a data source and is used primarily to execute commands and manage transactions. This object is analogous to the `rdoConnection` object in the RDO2 model.

▶ **See** "The `rdoConnection` Object," **p. 621**

`Connection` objects can be created and then shared by different `Recordset` objects, resulting in large performance gains, as opposed to creating and closing connections individually for each `Recordset` object you might require. Also, your DBA won't bug you about the impact your code is having on the server at large and the other users of the database.

The code in Listing 23.1 uses the `Connection` object and many of its properties. The `Error` object provides detailed information about error conditions that might arise during execution.

Listing 23.1 A *Connection* Object Example

```
Attribute VB_Name = "Module1"
Option Explicit

Sub ConnectionTest()
   Dim oDB As New ADODB.Connection
   Dim oError As ADODB.Error, strTemp As String
   oDB.Open "TimeBill"

   Debug.Print "ConnectionString = " & oDB.ConnectionString
   Debug.Print "ConnectionTimeOut = " & oDB.ConnectionTimeout
   Debug.Print "CommandTimeOut = " & oDB.CommandTimeout
   Debug.Print "DefaultDatabase = " & oDB.DefaultDatabase
   Debug.Print "Attributes = " & oDB.Attributes
   Debug.Print "IsolationLevel = " & oDB.IsolationLevel
   Debug.Print "Mode = " & oDB.Mode
   Debug.Print "Properties = " & oDB.Properties.Count
   Debug.Print "Provider = " & oDB.Provider
   Debug.Print "State = " & oDB.State
   Debug.Print "Version = " & oDB.Version

   On Error Resume Next
   oDB.BeginTrans ' begin a transaction
   oDB.Execute ("INSERT INTO Employee (FirstName,LastName)
              ➥VALUES('D.', 'Veloper')")
   If Err.Number > 0 Or oError.Number > 0 Then
      oDB.RollbackTrans
      For Each oError In oDB.Errors
```

```
            strTemp = oError.Number & Space(3) & oError.Description & Space(3) &
                  ➥oError.NativeError
        Next
        MsgBox strTemp
    Else
        oDB.CommitTrans
    End If
    oDB.Close
    Set oDB = Nothing
    Set oError = Nothing
End Sub
```


The *Open* Method You can invoke the `Open` method if the `ConnectionString`, `UserID`, and `Password` properties are set. If those properties aren't set, you can pass the values as parameters to the method.

The *BeginTrans* Method The `BeginTrans` method marks the starting point of a transaction that can later be committed or rolled back. This method has a return value that specifies the level of nesting. If a second `BeginTrans` method is invoked before `CommitTrans` or `RollbackTrans` is called, the level of nesting would cause the second invocation to return a value of 2. Calling `CommitTrans` or `RollbackTrans` affects all the data changes made since the last `BeginTrans` call.

The *RollbackTrans* Method The `RollbackTrans` method cancels the data-manipulation methods that have been invoked since the last `BeginTrans`.

The *CommitTrans* Method The `CommitTrans` method *commits* or finalizes the data-manipulation methods that have been invoked since the last `BeginTrans`.

The *Execute* Method The `Execute` method executes a statement passed in the *`CommandText`* argument. The *`CommandText`* argument is interpreted based on the value of the *`Options`* parameter. The *`CommandText`* argument is specific to the provider, but can be standard SQL if the data source is a relational database.

Specifying the *`Options`* parameter speeds up the call to the method because the method doesn't need to determine the type of the *`CommandText`* argument.

If the data source is a relational database, use this method to execute SQL strings and stored procedures that don't return a recordset or other return value. If the query returns rows, the results are stored in a new recordset object. If the query doesn't return rows, a closed recordset object is returned. For row-returning queries, using the `Open` method of the `Recordset` object might be easier.

The *Close* Method The `Close` method closes the connection to the data source. Any associated `Recordset` objects are also rolled back (if edits haven't been committed) and closed.

CAUTION

Be careful of scoping issues involving `Connection` objects. If a `Connection` object falls out of scope, any non-committed transactions are rolled back automatically.

The *Attributes* Property You can set the `Attributes` property to `adXactCommitRetaining` or `adXactAbortRetaining`. `adXactCommitRetaining` causes a new transaction to begin anytime a `CommitTrans` method is invoked. `adXactAbortRetaining` causes a new transaction to begin anytime a `RollbackTrans` method is invoked. Both values can be set by summing the two values.

The *CommandTimeout* Property The `CommandTimeout` property specifies how long the `Connection` object will wait, in seconds, before a timeout error is generated. A 0 value causes `Connection` to wait forever. An error is generated if the object times out. A timeout doesn't mean the server is unreachable, just that the command didn't finish in less time than the `CommandTimeout` period.

The *ConnectionString* Property The `ConnectionString` property specifies the information required to connect to a data source. This can be a standard data source name (DSN) or a fully qualified connection string consisting of *`argument = value`* separated by semicolons. Five reserved arguments are processed by ADO:

- The *`Provider`* argument specifies the name of the provider to use.
- *`DataSource`* specifies the name of the data source.
- *`User`* specifies the username.
- *`Password`* is the password associated with the username.
- *`FileName`* is the name of a provider-specific file containing connection information.

Any arguments other than these aren't processed by ADO and are sent directly to the provider.

NOTE The *`Provider`* and *`FileName`* arguments in a `ConnectionString` property are mutually exclusive. The provider-specific *`FileName`* overrides any manually specified *`Provider`* argument.

Use `ConnectionString` in the open method to not require a user to have previously set up an ODBC data source.

The *ConnectionTimeout* Property The `ConnectionTimeout` property specifies how long, in seconds, the `Connection` object waits after attempting to establish a connection before a timeout error is generated. A timeout error doesn't mean that the server isn't available; it means only that a connection couldn't be established before a connection timeout occurred.

The *DefaultDatabase* Property The `DefaultDatabase` property specifies the default database name. A provider populates this property when a connection is established. Any data access methods are automatically applied against this default database, unless object names are fully qualified with another available database name.

The *IsolationLevel* Property The `IsolationLevel` property specifies the visibility of data during transactions. The default value, `adXactCursorStability`, indicates that pending changes aren't visible to other transactions until after they're committed. The other values for this property include the following:

- `adXactUnspecified` is returned if ADO can't determine the isolation level used by the provider.
- `adXactChaos` indicates that pending changes made from more highly isolated transactions can't be overwritten.
- `adXactBrowse` and `adXactReadUncommitted` indicate that pending changes in other transactions are visible to other transactions.
- `adXactReadCommitted` is the same as the default `adXactCursorStability`.
- `adXactRepeatableRead` indicates that pending changes aren't visible to other transactions, but requerying can bring in new recordsets.
- `adXactIsolated` and `adXactSerializable` specify that all transactions are isolated from all other transactions.

The *Mode* Property The `Mode` property specifies the permissions available in modifying data. The default value, `adModeUnknown`, indicates that ADO can't determine the permissions. Other values include the following:

- `adModeRead` specifies read-only permissions.
- `adModeWrite` specifies write-only permissions.
- `adModeReadWrite` specifies read/write permissions.
- `adModeShareDenyRead` specifies that read permissions are denied to others.
- `adModeShareDenyWrite` denies write permissions to others.
- `adModeShareExclusive` specifies that read/write permissions are denied to others.
- `adModeShareDenyNone` specifies that all permissions are denied to others.

The *Provider* Property The `Provider` property specifies the name of the provider. The default provider is `MSDASQL` (Microsoft ODBC Provider for OLE DB). You can set this property through the `ConnectString` property or the *`ConnectionString`* argument to `Connection.Open`.

The *Version* Property The `Version` property returns the ADO version implementation number.

The *Command* Object

Methods: `CreateParameter`, `Execute`

Properties: `ActiveConnection`, `CommandText`, `CommandTimeout`, `CommandType`, `Prepared`

The `Command` object is a description of a command that's executed against a data source. It defines the text and type of the command, manages command arguments, executes the command, and creates `Recordset` objects. It contains a `Parameters` collection of `Parameter` objects and a `Properties` collection of `Property` objects. Use this object if you want to execute a query or stored procedure with input and output parameters. This object is similar to the `rdoQuery` object in the RDO2 library.

▶ **See** "The `rdoQuery` Object," **p. 635**

The code in Listing 23.2 is an example of using the `Command` object.

Listing 23.2 Using the *Command* and *Parameter* Objects

```
Attribute VB_Name = "Module4"
Option Explicit

Sub TestCommand()
   Dim oCommand As ADODB.Command
   Dim oParameterID As ADODB.Parameter

   oCommand.ActiveConnection = "TimeBill"
   oCommand.CommandText = "sp_GetEmployee"
   oCommand.CommandTimeout = 0
   oCommand.CommandType = adCmdStoredProc
   oCommand.Prepared = True
   oCommand.Name = "sp_GetEmployeeFromID"

   ' Add a parameter this way
   oParameterID.Direction = adParamInput
   oParameterID.Name = "ID"
   oParameterID.NumericScale = 0
   oParameterID.Type = adInteger
   oParameterID.Value = 15

   oCommand.Parameters.Append oParameterID    ' add this item to the list
   ' can also add a parameter this way
   oCommand.CreateParameter "Name", adVarChar, adParamOutput, 255, ""

   oCommand.Execute  ' execute the command object

   Debug.Print "Name of the person with this ID is:  " &
             ➥oCommand.Parameters("Name").Value
   Set oCommand = Nothing
   Set oParameterID = Nothing
End Sub
```

The *CreateParameter* Method The `CreateParameter` method instantiates a new `Parameter` object that's populated with properties specified by the arguments to the `CreateParameter` method:

- *`Name`* specifies the name of the `Parameter` object.
- *`Type`* specifies the data type of the `Parameter` object.
- *`Direction`* specifies the direction of the `Parameter` object.
- *`Size`* specifies the maximum size of the `Parameter` object in characters or bytes.
- *`Value`* seeds the value of the `Parameter` object.

The `Parameter` object isn't automatically added to the `Parameters` collection but must be added by using the `Parameters.Add` method. This allows for data validation of the various parameter properties before the object is added to the collection.

The *Execute* Method The `Execute` method executes the command stored in the `CommandText` property. The *`RecordsAffected`* argument is a Long that the provider uses to return the number of records affected by the command. The *`Parameters`* argument is Variant array of parameter values passed with a SQL statement.

Don't rely on output parameters from a stored procedure contained in the `Parameters` array. Values from output parameters should be obtained from the `Value` property of `Parameter` objects.

The *`Options`* argument is a constant that helps the provider determine how to handle the `CommandText` property. The possible values are as follows:

- `adCmdText` specifies that `CommandText` property should be treated as a textual definition of a command.
- `adCmdTable` specifies that the value is a table name.
- `adCmdStoredProc` specifies that the value is a stored procedure.
- `adCmdUnknown` specifies that the value is undefined.

The *ActiveConnection* Property The `ActiveConnection` property specifies to which `Connection` object the `Command` object belongs. The value can be a string containing the definition of the connection (as in `ConnectString`) or can be a `Connection` object. Setting the value to nothing disassociates the `Command` object from a connection. The property value can then be set to a different connection object, and the command can be re-executed.

The *CommandText* Property The `CommandText` property specifies the text of a command to be executed by a provider. The contents of this string are provider-specific and can be SQL or any special command the provider supports.

The *CommandTimeout* Property The `CommandTimeout` property specifies the length of time, in seconds, that the `Command` object waits for a provider to execute the command before a timeout error is generated.

The *CommandType* Property The `CommandType` property is the equivalent of and has the same values as the *`Options`* argument of the `Execute` method.

The *Prepared* Property The `Prepared` property specifies whether a temporary prepared statement is constructed from the command before it's executed. If the provider doesn't support the concept of precompiled prepared statements, this property is ignored.

The *Parameter* Object

Methods: `AppendChunk`

Properties: `Attributes`, `Direction`, `Name`, `NumericScale`, `Precision`, `Size`, `Type`, `Value`

The `Parameter` object represents a parameter or argument associated with a `Command` object. The parameter is typically used to represent input/output arguments of stored procedures. The `Parameter` object is a member of the `Parameters` collection and can be referenced as *`command`*`.Parameters(`*`index`*`)` or *`command`*`.Parameters("`*`name`*`")`. Because the `Parameters` collection is the default property of the `Command` object, `Parameter` objects can even more simply be referenced as *`command`*`(`*`index`*`)`, *`command`*`![`*`name`*`]`, or *`command`*`("`*`name`*`")`. (Refer to Listing 23.2 for an example of using the `Parameter` object.)

The *AppendChunk* Method The `AppendChunk` method appends data, typically BLOB (Binary Large Object) data, to a `Parameter` object. When memory is limited, you can use `AppendChunk` to assign data in chunks rather than all at once. This method can be used only if the `adFldLong` bit in the `Attributes` property is `True`.

The *Attributes* Property The `Attributes` property specifies one or more characteristics of the `Parameter` object. Individual values can be logically `AND`'ed to determine whether a certain attribute is present. Multiple values can be set by adding the values together. The possible values consist of the default value, `adParamSigned`, which specifies that the parameter accepts signed values, as well as `adParamNullable` and `adParamLong`, which indicates that the parameter accepts Null and Long binary data, respectively.

The *Direction* Property The `Direction` property specifies whether the parameter is used for input, output, or both. The parameter can also be a return value from a stored procedure. The default value, `adParamInput`, indicates an input parameter. `adParamOutput` indicates an output parameter. `adParamInputOutput` indicates an input/output parameter. `adParamReturnValue` specifies that the parameter is a return value.

The *Name* Property The `Name` property specifies the name used to identify the `Parameter` object.

The *NumericScale* Property The `NumericScale` property specifies the number of decimal places to which numeric values will be represented.

The *Precision* Property The `Precision` property specifies the maximum number of digits used to represent a value.

The *Size* Property The `Size` property specifies the maximum size of a `Parameter` object, in characters or bytes.

The *Type* Property The `Type` property specifies the data type of a `Parameter` object. Table 23.1 shows the possible values.

Table 23.1 *Type* Property Values

Constant	Description
`adBigInt`	8-byte signed integer
`adBinary`	Binary value
`adBoolean`	Boolean value
`adBSTR`	Null-terminated character string (Unicode B-String)

Constant	Description
adChar	A string value
adCurrency	A currency value (8-byte signed integer scaled by 10.000)
adDate	A date value
adDBDate	A date value (*yyymmdd*)
adDBTime	A time value (*hhmmss*)
adDBTimeStamp	A date/time stamp (*yyyymmddhhmmss* plus a fraction in billionths)
adDecimal	An exact numeric value with a fixed precision and scale
adDouble	A double-precision floating-point value
adEmpty	No specified value
adError	32-bit error code
adGUID	Globally Unique Identifier
adIDispatch	Pointer to OLE object `IDispatch` interface
adInteger	4-byte signed integer
adIUnknown	Pointer to OLE object `IUnknown` interface
*adLongVarBinary	Long binary value
*adLongVarChar	Long string value
adLongVarWChar	Long string value
adNumeric	Exact numeric value with fixed precision and scale
adSingle	Single-precision floating-point value
adSmallInt	2-byte signed integer
adTinyInt	1-byte signed integer
adUnsignedbigInt	8-byte unsigned integer
adUnsignedInt	4-byte unsigned integer
adUnsignedSmallInt	2-byte unsigned integer
adUnsignedTinyInt	1-byte unsigned integer
adUserDefined	User-defined value
*adVarBinary	Binary value
*adVarChar	String value
adVariant	Variant value
*adVarWchar	Null-terminated Unicode character string
adWchar	Null-terminated Unicode character string

**Denotes values applicable only to* `Parameter` *objects*

The *Value* Property The `Value` property specifies the value of the `Parameter` object.

The *Property* Object

Methods: None

Properties: `Attributes`, `Name`, `Type`, `Value`

The `Property` object represents a provider-defined dynamic property. ADO predefines normal properties, such as `Parameter.Precision` or `Connection.Timeout`. Although these predefined properties can be accessed, they can't be changed or deleted. Also, some data sources will have unique data-source–specific properties associated with them. These dynamic properties will appear as `Property` objects in the `Properties` collection of associated `Connection`, `Command`, `RecordSet`, or `Field` objects.

The *Attributes* Property The `Attributes` property specifies one or more of the following values:

- `adPropNotSupported` indicates that the provider doesn't support the property.

NOTE Because the `adPropNotSupported` value is contained in a dynamic property created by the provider, it might seem strange that it's created in the first place if it isn't supported. It remains to be seen how this will be used, but it might be used for backward compatibility by newer versions of a data provider to indicate properties that are no longer supported.

- `adPropRequired` indicates that the property must be assigned a value before the data source is initialized.
- `adPropOptional` specifies an optional property.
- `adPropRead` and `adPropWrite` specify that the property can be read from or written to, respectively.

The *Name* Property The `Name` property specifies the name to be used for the `Property` object.

The *Type* Property This property is the same as the `Type` property of the `Parameter` object. Table 23.1 in the earlier section "The `Parameter` Object" lists possible values.

The *Value* Property The `Value` property specifies the value assigned to the `Property` object.

The *Recordset* Object

Methods: `AddNew`, `CancelBatch`, `CancelUpdate`, `Clone`, `Close`, `Delete`, `GetRows`, `Move`, `MoveFirst`, `MoveLast`, `MoveNext`, `MovePrevious`, `NextRecordset`, `Open`, `Requery`, `Resync`, `Supports`, `Update`, `UpdateBatch`

Properties: `AbsolutePage`, `AbsolutePosition`, `ActiveConnection`, `BOF`, `EOF`, `Bookmark`, `CacheSize`, `CursorType`, `EditMode`, `Filter`, `LockType`, `MaxRecords`, `PageCount`, `RecordCount`, `PageSize`, `Source`, `Status`

The Recordset object represents your cursor of data that has been returned from a data source. This object allows iteration through the rows and allows data modification to occur. The Recordset object is very similar to the RDO rdoResultset object.

▶ **See** "The rdoResultsets Object," **p. 626**

One interesting aspect of ADO is that any cursors created—such as keyset, static, dynamic, or forward-only cursors—are always built on the server. Another interesting and useful feature of ADO is that the Recordset object doesn't have an Edit method. Essentially, the recordset is always in "edit mode," and the Update method can be used to send any data modifications to the server. The Update method also can be skipped if you simply move the cursor to a new row. Any changes made to the data will be made at that time. This makes processing records in a While loop easy to write and to debug. The code in Listing 23.3 gives an example of using the Recordset object.

Listing 23.3 Basic Usage for the *Recordset* Object

```
Attribute VB_Name = "Module2"
Option Explicit

Sub RecordSetTest()
   Dim oRS As New ADODB.Recordset
   Dim vntBookmark As Variant

   oRS.LockType = adLockOptimistic
   oRS.ActiveConnection = "TimeBill"
   oRS.CursorType = adOpenStatic

   oRS.Open "sp_GetEmployee (13)", Options:=adCmdStoredProc

   oRS.MoveLast
   oRS.MoveFirst

   Debug.Print "RecordCount = " & oRS.RecordCount
   Debug.Print "AbsolutePosition =" & oRS.AbsolutePosition
   Debug.Print "AbsolutePage = " & oRS.AbsolutePage
   Debug.Print "EditMode" & oRS.EditMode
   Debug.Print "MaxRecords = " & oRS.MaxRecords
   Debug.Print "State = " & oRS.State
   Debug.Print oRS.Filter
   Debug.Print oRS.Fields(0).Value

   oRS.Close
   Set oRS = Nothing
End Sub
```

The *AddNew* Method The AddNew method creates new rows in the resultset. The *Fields* optional parameter is a variant or variant array containing the names of the fields to be added. The *Values* argument is a variant or variant array containing the values of the *Fields* that have been specified.

The AddNew method works in immediate mode or batch update mode:

- In immediate mode, if the AddNew method is invoked without parameters, the EditMode property is set to adEditAdd and the Update method must be invoked to send the new record to the data source. After the new record is sent to the data source, the EditMode property is set to adEditNone. If the AddNew method was invoked in immediate mode and the optional *Fields* and *Values* arguments were passed, the update is done immediately without invoking the Update method.
- In batch update mode, if the AddNew method is invoked without arguments, the process is the same as immediate mode, except that the new record isn't added to the data source until the BatchUpdate method is called. If the optional *Fields* and *Values* arguments are passed, the BatchUpdate method must still be called to pass the new record to the data source.

The *CancelBatch* Method The CancelBatch method cancels a pending batch update. The *AffectRecords* argument specifies the records that will be canceled. The possible values are adAffectCurrent, where only the current record is canceled; adAffectGroup, where only records that satisfy the Filter property are canceled; and the default, adAffectAll, where all data modifications since the last batch update method was invoked are canceled.

The *CancelUpdate* Method The CancelUpdate method discards any changes made to the current record since the last update method was invoked.

The *Clone* Method The Clone method creates a new instance of a recordset and assigns it to a variable. These recordsets still represent the same entity in terms of their row content, so changes made to one clone are visible to the other. However, the Close method must be called for each clone individually.

Use this method if you want to be able to maintain more than one current record in a recordset. Cloning a recordset is faster than opening another recordset based on the recordset definition.

The *Close* Method The Close method closes the cursor on the recordset and releases its resources.

The *Delete* Method This method deletes records in the recordset. Depending on the value of *AffectRecords*, it will delete all the records or just the current record. If this statement is located inside a transaction, the delete can be rolled back.

The *GetRows* Method The GetRows method retrieves and stores multiple rows of a Recordset object in a two-dimensional array. The optional *Rows* argument is a Long that specifies the number of records to retrieve. The optional *Start* argument is a String or Variant that specifies the bookmark at which the retrieval will begin. The optional *Fields* argument is a Variant that can be one of three values:

- A field name specified as a string indicates the field from which the value will be stored.
- A numeric value indicates the ordinal position of a field within the Recordset that specifies the source of the field data to be stored.
- A variant string array of field names allows for the storage of more than one field value.

Use the `GetRows` method to convert the retrieved `Recordset` object into an array.

The *Move* Method The `Move` method moves the current record pointer in a `Recordset`.

The *`NoOfRecords`* argument is a Long that specifies the number of records to move the current record pointer. The optional *`Start`* argument is a String or Variant that specifies a bookmark. If *`NoOfRecords`* is a positive number, the cursor moves forward by the specified number of rows. A negative number moves the cursor backward the specified number of rows. Moving beyond the first or last record in the `Recordset` sets the `BOF` or `EOF` property to `True`.

Using the `CacheSize` property with a value lower than the number of eligible rows of a `Resultset` provides a mechanism for locally buffering data. The `Move` method can be used to fetch additional rows from the provider by specifying a `NoOfRecords` that exceeds the `CacheSize` property.

The *MoveFirst*, *MoveLast*, *MoveNext*, and *MovePrevious* Methods This group of methods provides for moving the current pointer in a `Resultset` to the first record, the last record, the next record, or the previous record, respectively.

The *NextRecordset* Method The `NextRecordset` method provides a mechanism for moving through multiple recordsets generated from a single command. Each time the `NextRecordset` method is invoked, the next `Recordset` object available is returned. If no further `Recordsets` are available, the object returns nothing.

The *Open* Method The `Open` method opens a cursor of data. The data source doesn't already need to be open. The parameters to the open method are as follows:

- *`Source`* specifies a `Command` object, table name, or SQL statement.
- *`ActiveConnection`* specifies a `Connection` object or *`CommandString`*.
- *`CursorType`* specifies the type of cursor to open. The default value is `adOpenForwardOnly`, whereas `adOpenKeyset`, `adOpenDynamic`, and `adOpenStatic` are also valid.
- *`LockType`* specifies the concurrency option. `adLockReadOnly`, `adLockPessimistic`, `adLockOptimistic`, and `adLockBatchOptimistic` are the valid values.
- *`Options`* specifies how to interpret the *`Source`* argument. `adCmdText` specifies that the *`Source`* argument is a textual definition of a command. `adCmdTable` specifies that the *`Source`* argument is a table name. `adCmdStoredProc` indicates that it's a stored procedure name, whereas `adCmdUnknown` specifies that the type of the *`Source`* argument isn't known.

The *Requery* Method The `Requery` method re-executes the query that generated the recordset. This method is equivalent to closing the recordset and reopening it.

The *Resync* Method Similar to the `Requery` method, the `Resync` method refreshes its data from the underlying data source. Unlike the `Requery` method, `Resync` won't retrieve any new records, but simply refreshes the rows that already exist.

The optional *`AffectRecords`* argument determines how many records are affected by the method; the default value is `adAffectAll`. `adAffectCurrent` specifies that only the current record is refreshed; `adAffectGroup` specifies that records that satisfy the `Filter` property are affected.

Use the `Resync` method if you don't want to have a dynamic cursor defined but want to refresh data in your recordset, and your database exists in a multiuser environment.

The *Supports* Method The `Supports` method specifies whether a `Recordset` object can support specific types of functionality. The *`CursorOptions`* argument is a Long that specifies whether any one or more of the functionality options listed in Table 23.2 are available.

Table 23.2 *Supports* Cursor Options

Value	Functionality
`adAddNew`	The `AddNew` method is available.
`adApproxPosition`	`AbsolutePosition` and `AbsolutePage` properties are available.
`adBookMark`	The `Bookmark` property is available.
`adDelete`	The `Delete` method is available.
`adHoldRecords`	Pending changes can be held while more records are retrieved.
`adMovePrevious`	The recordset can be traversed backward without bookmarks.
`adResync`	The `Resync` method is available.
`adUpdate`	The `Update` method is available.
`adUpdateBatch`	The `BatchUpdate` method is available.

NOTE The `Supports` method isn't always correct; it simply indicates whether a given type of functionality is generally available. It doesn't guarantee that the function is always available under any circumstances.

The *Update* Method The `Update` method saves any changes made to a cursor. A single field can be updated by assigning a value to the `Field` object and invoking the `Update` method, or the `Update` method can be called and the `Field` name and value can be passed. Multiple fields can be updated at one time by passing a variant array of field names and a variant array of values.

The *UpdateBatch* Method The `UpdateBatch` method writes all pending batch updates to the data source. The optional *`AffectRecords`* argument has a default value of `adAffectAll`. `adAffectCurrent`, which specifies that only the current record is updated, and `adAffectGroup`, which specifies that all records that meet the current `Filter` property are affected, are also valid entries.

The *AbsolutePage* Property The `Recordset` object can be divided into a set of "pages" by using the `PageSize` property. The `AbsolutePage` property specifies which page to move for a new current record.

The *AbsolutePosition* Property The `AbsolutePosition` property specifies the ordinal position of the current pointer within a `Recordset` object.

The *ActiveConnection* Property The `ActiveConnection` property specifies the `Connection` object to which the `Recordset` belongs.

The *BOF* and *EOF* Properties The `BOF` and `EOF` properties indicate that the current pointer is before the first record or after the last record of a recordset.

The *Bookmark* Property The `Bookmark` property uniquely identifies the current record or sets the current record to the record identified by a bookmark. You can use bookmarks to position the current pointer in a resultset without using the `Move` methods. To save the bookmark for the current pointer, simply assign the value of the `Bookmark` property to a variable. The current pointer can be moved to the same record at a later time by setting the `Bookmark` property equal to the previously saved variable.

The *CacheSize* Property The `CacheSize` property specifies how many records are held in a local memory cache.

The *CursorType* Property The `CursorType` property indicates the type of cursor used by the `Recordset` object. The default value is `adOpenForwardOnly`. `adOpenKeyset`, `adOpenDynamic`, and `adOpenStatic` are also valid values.

The *EditMode* Property The `EditMode` property specifies the edit status of the current record. The property will return `adEditNone` when editing isn't being done. `adEditInProgress` specifies that the current record has been modified but the change hasn't yet been committed. The `adEditAdd` value indicates that the `AddNew` method has added a row to the recordset, but the new row hasn't yet been committed to the data source.

The *Filter* Property The `Filter` property specifies a filter for data contained in a recordset. This value can be configured several ways:

- You can set the property to an array of bookmarks, to make only the bookmarked records visible to the cursor.
- You can set the property to one of four predefined values:
  - `adFilterNone` turns off any filtering.
  - `adFilterPendingRecords` makes only records with pending edits visible to the cursor.
  - `adFilterAffectedRecords` makes only records affected by the last `Delete`, `Resync`, `UpdateBatch`, or `CancelBatch` invocation visible to the cursor.
  - `adFilterFetchedRecords` makes the last records fetched from the data source visible to the cursor.
- For the most complex filter type, you can supply a *criteria string* made up of conditions separated by `AND`. For example, a valid criteria string would be

  ```
  "FirstName = 'Laurie' AND MiddleName = 'Ann' AND Salary >= $100000"
  ```

  The clauses consist of a field name, an operator, and a value. The operator can be `>`, `>=`, `<`, `<=`, `<>`, `=`, or `LIKE`. The `LIKE` operator can use ANSI SQL wildcard characters.

The *LockType* Property The `LockType` property specifies the lock type to use when records are being edited. Applicable values consist of `adLockReadOnly`, a read-only setting; `adLockPessimistic` for pessimistic locks; `adLockOptimistic` for optimistic locks; and `adLockBatchUpdate` for batch updates. When optimistic locking is used, the record is locked in the database only when the `Update` method is called. When pessimistic locking is used, the record is locked whenever editing begins.

The *MaxRecords* Property The `MaxRecords` property puts a limit on the number of records returned from a query. The default value of 0 means that all records are returned. Use this property to limit the number of rows returned, especially in a low-memory situation.

The *PageCount* Property The `PageCount` property indicates how many pages of data the `Recordset` object contains. Pages are sized to equal the `PageSize` value. The number of rows in the `Recordset` divided by the `PageSize` property will equal the `PageCount` property.

The *RecordCount* Property The `RecordCount` property specifies the number of records in a `Recordset` object. If ADO can't determine the value, `adUnknown` is returned. In situations where the `Recordset` doesn't support bookmarks or approximate positioning, the entire recordset object has to be retrieved from the data source for the `RecordCount` property to be determined.

The `RecordCount` property isn't always reliable until all records in the recordset are accessed. To force this to occur, call `MoveLast` and then `MoveFirst` on the `Recordset` object.

The *PageSize* Property The `PageSize` property specifies how many rows of data make up a single page. The `PageSize` property multiplied by the `PageCount` property equals the number of rows in the recordset.

The *Source* Property The `Source` property indicates the source of the data contained in the recordset. This can be a `Command` object, SQL statement, stored procedure name, or table name.

The *Status* Property The `Status` property indicates the status of the current record. This examines the results of rows after batch updates. A value of `adRecOK` means the record was successfully saved. `adRecNew` indicates the record is new. `adRecModified` indicates that the record was modified. `adRecDeleted` indicates that the record was deleted. `adRecUnmodified` indicates that the record wasn't modified. Any other value indicates that the record wasn't saved for some reason. The values shown in Table 23.3 specify the different reasons the record wasn't saved.

Table 23.3 *Status* Property Values for Failure Conditions

Value	Description
`adRecInvalid`	The record has an invalid bookmark.
`adRecMultipleChanges`	The record modification would affect multiple records.
`adRecPendingChanges`	The record refers to a pending insert.

Value	Description
adRecCanceled	The operation was canceled.
adRecCantRelease	The record lock is in contention.
adRecConcurrencyViolation	Optimistic concurrency was in use.
adRecIntegrityViolation	Integrity constraints were violated.
adRecMaxChangesExceeded	Too many changes are pending.
adRecObjectOpen	Conflict with an open storage object has occurred.
adRecOutOfMemory	Computer ran out of memory.
adRecPermissionDenied	User had insufficient permissions.
adRecSchemaViolation	Relational integrity or schema violation error has occurred.
adRecDBDeleted	Record was already deleted.

The *Field* Object

Methods: AppendChunk, GetChunk

Properties: ActualSize, Attributes, DefinedSize, Name, NumericScale, OriginalValue, Precision, Type, Underlying Value, Value

The Field object contains information about the columns of a recordset and is analogous to the rdoColumn object in the RDO2 object library. The code in Listing 23.4 shows an example of using the Field object.

▶ **See** "The rdoColumn Object," **p. 633**

Listing 23.4 *Field* and *Property* Objects Examples

```
Attribute VB_Name = "Module2"
Option Explicit

Sub RecordSetTest()
   Dim oRS As New ADODB.Recordset
   Dim vntBookmark As Variant

   oRS.LockType = adLockOptimistic
   oRS.ActiveConnection = "TimeBill"
   oRS.CursorType = adOpenStatic

   oRS.Open "sp_GetEmployee (13)", Options:=adCmdStoredProc

   oRS.MoveLast
   oRS.MoveFirst
```

continues

Listing 23.4 Continued

```
    Debug.Print "RecordCount = " & oRS.RecordCount
    Debug.Print "AbsolutePosition =" & oRS.AbsolutePosition
    Debug.Print "AbsolutePage = " & oRS.AbsolutePage
    Debug.Print "EditMode" & oRS.EditMode
    Debug.Print "MaxRecords = " & oRS.MaxRecords
    Debug.Print "State = " & oRS.State
    Debug.Print oRS.Filter
    Debug.Print oRS.Fields(0).Value

    oRS.Close
    Set oRS = Nothing
End Sub
```

The *AppendChunk* Method The `AppendChunk` method adds large amounts of data (such as BLOB data) to a field object in small chunks. The first time `AppendChunk` is invoked, it overwrites any data in the field. Subsequent invocations append data to the field.

The *GetChunk* Method The `GetChunk` method returns large amounts of data (such as BLOB data or data in a text/memo field) from a field in small chunks. The `adFldLong` bit in the `Attributes` property must be set to `True` to use the `GetChunk` method.

The *ActualSize* Property The `ActualSize` property indicates size of the data contained in the field. The `DefinedSize` property specifies a maximum size for data, whereas the `ActualSize` property specifies the size of the data actually contained in the field. This is especially useful for variable-length character data.

The *Attributes* Property The `Attributes` property specifies the characteristics of the field and can be a sum of any of the following values:

- `adFldMayDefer` indicates that the field isn't populated within a recordset until specifically referenced.
- `adFldUpdatable` indicates that the field can be modified.
- `adFldUnknownUpdatable` specifies that the data source can't determine whether the field can be modified.
- `adFldFixed` indicates that the field contains fixed-length data.
- `adFldIsNullable` indicates that Null values are accepted.
- `adFldMayBeNull` indicates that Null values can be read from the field.
- `adFldLong` indicates that the field is a long binary field, suitable for `GetChunk` and `AppendChunk` access.
- `adFldRowID` indicates that a unique row identifier is contained in the field.
- `adFldRowVersion` indicates that the field contains a time or date stamp used to track updates.
- `adFldCacheDeferred` specifies that the provider caches field values.

The *DefinedSize* Property The `DefinedSize` property specifies the defined maximum size of a `Field` object and can be used to determine the capacity of a field.

The *Name* Property The `Name` property specifies the name that identifies the `Field` object.

The *NumericScale* Property The `NumericScale` property specifies how many decimal places numeric values are represented.

The *OriginalValue* Property The `OriginalValue` property specifies the value of the field since the last `Update` method. This acts as a buffer to allow retrieval of the original value of the field before data modification.

The *Precision* Property The `Precision` property specifies the maximum total number of digits used to represent numeric values.

The *Type* Property The `Type` property specifies the data type of `Field` object. Table 23.1 earlier in this chapter shows the possible values.

The *Underlying Value* Property (Variant) The `Underlying Value` property specifies the current value in the data store of a `Field` object's value. This value might be stale if another process has modified it since it was retrieved by the current transaction.

The *Value* Property The `Value` property indicates the current value of the field.

The *Error* Object

Methods: None

Properties: `Description`, `HelpContext`, `HelpFile`, `NativeError`, `Number`, `Source`, `SQLState`

The `Error` object contains information about errors encountered in a single operation. The `Error` object's properties contain specific details about each error, describing such things as where the error originated, help file information, and so on. Provider errors are placed in the `Errors` collection of the `Connection` object. If the errors are generated without the use of a `Connection` object, the error is located in Visual Basic's `Err` object. Multiple errors can be generated from a single ADO operation. (For an example of using the `Error` object, see Listing 23.1 earlier in this chapter.)

NOTE Some `Error` objects can actually be warnings or informational messages returned from data sources.

The *Description* Property The `Description` property is a string that specifies a textual description of the error. The string can come from ADO or from a provider.

The *HelpContext* Property The `HelpContext` property is a Long value that's the help context ID for a topic in a standard Windows help file.

The *HelpFile* Property The `HelpFile` property is a string that specifies a fully qualified path name to a standard Windows help file.

The *NativeError* Property The `NativeError` property specifies the error code assigned by a provider-specific error.

The *Number* Property The `Number` property specifies the number that uniquely identifies an `Error` object.

The *Source* Property The `Source` property specifies the name of the object or application that generated the error. This value can be the object's class name or programmatic ID. ADODB errors are identified by the format `ADODB.`*`ObjectName`*.

The *SQLState* Property The `SQLState` property is a read-only string that's the five-character ANSI SQL standard error code.

ADO Versus RDO2: Which Access Method Should You Use?

This is a transition period for RDO2 and Active Data Objects. According to Microsoft, with the release of Visual Basic 5.0 Enterprise Edition and ADO 1.0, RDO2 is a superset of ADO. At the time of this writing, ADO 1.5 has been released but still doesn't offer all the features and functionality in RDO2. In the future, ADO will become a superset of RDO. Those features of RDO2 not currently found in ADO are asynchronous connections, asynchronous queries, events, integration with Transact-SQL Debugger and Connection Query Designer, and queries as methods.

At this time, if you're working with data that comes just from a database server and you need features not found in ADO and described earlier, RDO2 is the choice to make. If, however, you don't need the missing features that ADO doesn't yet implement, and you see the need to access data from multiple data providers, you should choose ADO. In today's I-net paradigm, it's also important to note that ADO is free-threaded whereas RDO2 isn't. This improves its scalability in high-performance, multiuser environments. You can easily use ADO to provide web access in a middle tier or server component, whereas you cannot with RDO.

If you choose to use RDO2 now, the later conversion to ADO will be a time-consuming activity. The object models are different in design and operation. Converting can even require changes in application design. One way to minimize the effect of changing from one library to another can be to write a COM object that hides the actual library being used. This buys you flexibility, but you might have some difficulty implementing functions available in RDO but not in ADO.

From Here...

In this chapter, you learned about Microsoft's new architecture, Universal Data Access, that promises to provide a consistent, easy-to-use interface to many different data types. You were introduced to the ActiveX Data Objects library and walked through a breakdown of the objects and their associated properties and methods. You also evaluated when ADO is preferable over RDO2 for data access.

- For more information about Microsoft's COM-based object technologies and object-oriented software development, see Chapter 4, "Using Microsoft's Object Technologies."
- For more information about client/server architectures, see Chapter 20, "Clients, Servers, and Components: Design Strategies for Distributed Applications."
- For a detailed treatment of important issues you should consider when designing and developing distributed applications, see Chapter 21, "Creating Distributed Applications."
- To learn how to use Visual Basic with RDO2, see Chapter 22, "Building Client Front Ends with Visual Basic and RDO."

CHAPTER 24

Deploying Distributed Applications

by Don Benage and Larry Millett

This chapter explores the subject of distributed transaction processing. Microsoft is creating a growing number of tools and technologies to help manage applications that execute on multiple computers. This distributes the processing load and provides a collection of other benefits. For example, distributed systems can cost less than the monolithic systems they replace. They also can be easier to maintain and update in response to changing business conditions, if properly designed. Not every application requires distributed transaction services. This area of computing technology is rapidly growing, however, and many businesses and organizations can benefit from these tools, even if they aren't yet aware of the benefits.

Some of these techniques have existed for a while, but were available only on large, expensive platforms costing hundreds of thousands or even millions of dollars. Part of the attraction of these tools is that they're now available on low-cost, commodity-priced computing platforms, putting the technology within the reach of much smaller organizations.

Transactions

A *transaction* is a series of updates that must be applied "all or nothing." See how Microsoft Transaction Server manages transactions involving a single system or many systems.

Two-phase commits

Discover how Transaction Server supports complex two-phase commit transactions.

The Distributed Transaction Coordinator

Find out about a key element of MTS that's also a part of SQL Server 6.5 (and later). The Distributed Transaction Coordinator (DTC) helps you implement transactions that access and update databases on more than one server. See how to monitor distributed transactions and use new tools to resolve problem transactions.

Transaction Server Explorer

Look at Transaction Server in action. See how to use the Transaction Server Explorer to manage the elements of a distributed application environment more easily.

Transaction Server's features

Learn about the capabilities that Transaction Server can provide. See the programming tools it supports, its application architecture, and its strengths.

This chapter provides an overview of two key components Microsoft offers for distributed transaction processing: the Distributed Transaction Coordinator (DTC) and Transaction Server. The DTC, introduced with SQL Server 6.5, greatly simplifies the process of developing and deploying distributed applications. Transaction Server 1.0 built on the functionality offered by DTC. Transaction Server 2.0, now available as part of the Windows NT Option Pack, is a standard part of Windows NT Server 4.0 Enterprise Edition. It provides a COM-based programming model and forms the basis of an entirely new computing architecture that you can use to build state-of-the-art distributed systems. ■

The Growth of Distributed Processing

In May 1997, Microsoft announced that a distributed transaction processing system based on a Microsoft platform (Windows NT Server, SQL Server, and Microsoft Transaction Server) had achieved a billion transactions per day. The day before, IBM announced a similar result, using Windows NT Server, DB2, and Transarc Encina. Each company touted the event as a major milestone in the development of high-volume, highly scalable distributed systems based on relatively inexpensive off-the-shelf hardware and software. In both cases, a transaction processing (TP) monitor was a critical piece.

A *TP monitor* is a software system designed to foster the creation, management, and execution of transactional applications. This is done, in general, by providing tools that make it easier to build scalable applications. The tools provided, which vary from one implementation to another, can include language extensions, a runtime environment, management consoles, and other useful elements.

The salient feature of applications created in TP monitor environments is that they can grow to meet the needs of an organization without experiencing disproportionate increases in costs. In other words, if the processing capacity of the system must double, the costs for the system should be of the same order of magnitude.

Microsoft introduced its TP monitor, Microsoft Transaction Server (MTS), in January 1997. As its name implies, MTS provides support for distributed applications to preserve transactional integrity. The distributed transaction services build on the Distributed Transaction Coordinator service shipped with Microsoft SQL Server 6.5. However, MTS also provides many other services typically provided by an object request broker (ORB), including security, concurrency, multithreading, shared state, and resource pooling. Both types of services are essential for scalable component-based software development.

Microsoft claims that for many distributed applications, MTS can dramatically reduce complexity and development time. In theory, a component can be developed as a single-user standalone; MTS provides the necessary infrastructure for integrated multiuser deployment. At first glance, it's a remarkable claim, and on closer examination, the difficulties seem truly overwhelming. Still, MTS version 1.0 substantially fulfills Microsoft's claims.

Microsoft has two goals for MTS: provide a robust, scalable infrastructure for component-based applications and simplify development of such applications. The component architecture of choice is, of course, ActiveX. Because MTS manages security, transaction processing, concurrency, and resource pooling, developers can concentrate on correctly implementing business logic.

Microsoft very explicitly designed MTS to support mid-tier components for a distributed three-tier application. MTS documents use special terms to identify various components:

- *Base client.* The application running on a user desktop. The base client corresponds to the user services layer in the three-tier model.
- *MTS component* (or *application component*). A COM component that executes in the MTS environment. An MTS component must be a dynamic link library (DLL), must provide a type library, and must implement a class factory. An MTS component can correspond to the business services layer in the three-tier model and can be invoked by a base client or by another application component.
- *Resource dispenser.* A service that manages nonpersistent data, such as the Microsoft ODBC 3.0 Driver Manager and the MTS Shared Property Manager. A resource dispenser corresponds to the data-management layer in the three-tier model.
- *Resource manager.* A system service that manages durable data, such as Microsoft SQL Server. A resource manager can cooperate with the DTC to implement distributed transactions. A resource manager corresponds to the data-management layer in the three-tier model.

▶ **See** "The Three-Tier Model," **p. 562**

Figure 24.1 shows various interactions among base clients, MTS components, resource dispensers, and resource managers. Base clients invoke MTS components, which can invoke resource dispensers, which can invoke resource managers.

FIG. 24.1
Base Client 1 interacts with a single application component. Base Client 2 invokes one application component, which in turn invokes two others. The secondary components implement a distributed transaction spanning two resource managers. Base Client 3 uses two mid-tier components: one updates a database, and both share data via a resource dispenser.

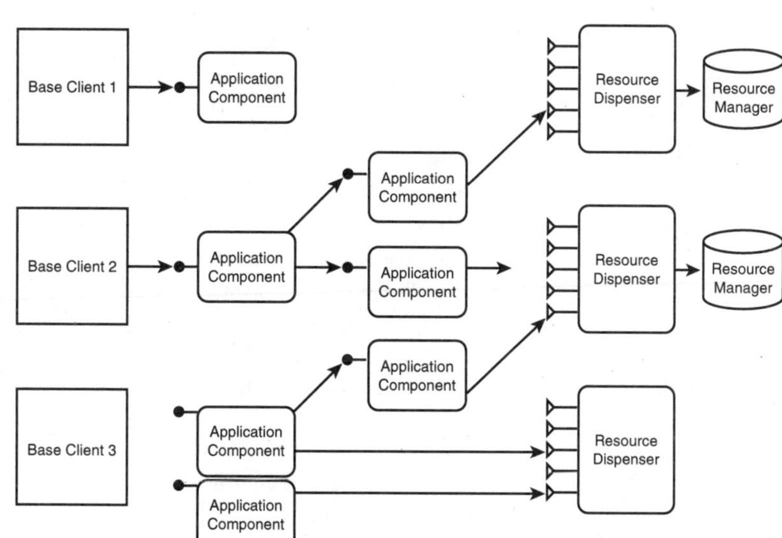

In addition to Visual Studio, MTS is included with Windows NT Server Enterprise Edition. According to Microsoft, MTS will be standard part of Windows NT Server after release of Internet Information Server (IIS) 4.0.

ON THE WEB

Microsoft maintains a list of answers to frequently asked questions about MTS at **http://www.microsoft.com/support/transaction/content/faq/**.

What Is a Transaction?

A *transaction* is a permanent series of updates to persistent data, which guarantees that all updates occur or none. If the data is consistent before the update, it will be consistent after the series of updates. For example, a program might implement a transfer of funds between two bank accounts. The program must ensure that the proper amount is transferred out of one account and transferred into the other account. Before the transfer, each account is internally consistent (all transactions sum to the current balance), and all accounts are collectively consistent (account balances for a depositor sum to his total balance with the bank). The transfer must preserve both consistencies. This means either that both parts of the transfer succeed, or that if any part fails, no change is made to either account. The ability to guarantee this sort of consistency is sometimes called *transactional integrity*. In 1983, Andreas Reuter identified four criteria for transactional integrity:

- *Atomicity*. The transaction succeeds as a single unit or fails as a single unit. If the transaction succeeds, all data sets consistently reflect the result. If the transaction fails, all data sets should consistently reflect the state before the transaction.
- *Consistency*. The transaction preserves internal consistency (as defined by the application) for each data set. Processing might temporarily generate an inconsistent state, but reestablishes consistency before the end of the transaction.
- *Isolation*. Other applications accessing data involved in a transaction see the prior state or the end state, but not any intermediate state. When a transaction begins, other applications are blocked from accessing data until the transaction completes.
- *Durability*. When a transaction completes, the updates to the data sets are permanent and aren't affected by hardware or software failure. In general, this means that when a transaction completes, all results have been physically written to disk (not just to cache).

Collectively, these criteria for transactional integrity are known as the *ACID test*.

The atomicity and isolation criteria have important implications for application developers. Because the intermediate states of a transaction aren't visible outside the transaction and because each transaction is "all or nothing," transactions appear to execute separately and sequentially. This means that an application using transactions can ignore concurrency issues, which can be a substantial simplification.

Transactional Integrity in SQL

Every major database management system (DBMS) includes transaction-management functions. For the DBMS application, each table is a separate data set, and updates to multiple tables frequently require transactional integrity. The Transact-SQL language in Microsoft SQL Server includes many transaction-management commands. These three are fundamental:

- `BEGIN TRANSACTION` (often shortened to `BEGIN TRAN`)
- `ABORT TRANSACTION` (often shortened to `ABORT TRAN`)
- `COMMIT TRANSACTION` (often shortened to `COMMIT TRAN`)

NOTE In theory, any persistent data storage mechanism can implement transactions. The best known implementations today are the major database servers such as Microsoft SQL Server, Oracle, Sybase, and Informix. For simplicity, the rest of this chapter discusses transactions as implemented in Microsoft SQL Server.

The `BEGIN TRANSACTION` command marks the beginning of a sequence of operations that must satisfy the ACID test; `COMMIT TRANSACTION` marks the end. The `ABORT TRANSACTION` command indicates that the transaction has failed, and all operations back to the `BEGIN TRANSACTION` command should be undone (rolled back). The `COMMIT TRANSACTION` command indicates that the transaction has succeeded, and all operations should be made permanent (committed). Sometimes, it's appropriate to nest transactions.

Assume two tables for a bank example: an AccountActivity table, listing each deposit, withdrawal, or transfer for each account; and a BankAccount table listing each account (including a current balance). Then the Transact-SQL commands to transfer $1,000 from account 11111 to account 22222 might look like Listing 24.1.

Listing 24.1 An Example Involving Two Accounts in Two Bank Branches

```
BEGIN TRANSACTION

    BEGIN TRANSACTION

    INSERT AccountActivity (AccountNumber, ActivityType, ActivityDate, Amount)
    VALUES ('11111', 'Transfer', getdate(), -1000.00)

    IF @@error != 0 ABORT TRANSACTION

    UPDATE BankAccount
    SET CurrentBalance = CurrentBalance - 1000.00
    WHERE AccountNumber = '11111'

    IF @@error != 0 ABORT TRANSACTION

    COMMIT TRANSACTION
```

continues

Listing 24.1 Continued

```
    BEGIN TRANSACTION

    INSERT AccountActivity (AccountNumber, ActivityType, ActivityDate, Amount)
    VALUES ('22222', 'Transfer', getdate(), 1000.00)

    IF @@error != 0 ABORT TRANSACTION

    UPDATE BankAccount
    SET CurrentBalance = CurrentBalance + 1000.00
    WHERE AccountNumber = '22222'

    IF @@error != 0 ABORT TRANSACTION

    COMMIT TRANSACTION

COMMIT TRANSACTION
```

Although it's admittedly oversimplified, this scenario does show basic transaction management. The `BEGIN TRANSACTION` and `COMMIT TRANSACTION` commands mark the beginning and end of a group of operations (inserts, updates, or nested transactions) that must collectively satisfy the ACID test. If any one operation fails due to an error condition, the entire transaction rolls back to the state at the `BEGIN TRANSACTION` command. This is implemented by the conditional `ABORT TRANSACTION` command after each operation.

NOTE Database servers implement transactions through logs. Every physical write to the data is accompanied by a log entry. Because a series of physical writes is generally required to take a database from one consistent state to another, the log also records consistent checkpoints. If the system should crash in the middle of a sequence of physical writes, the server (on restart) reverses the updates recorded in the log back to the last recorded consistent checkpoint. The `BEGIN TRANSACTION` and `COMMIT TRANSACTION` instructions force the database server to establish a new consistent checkpoint in the log; the `ABORT TRANSACTION` instruction forces the server to roll back to a specific checkpoint. After a server determines that it won't need to roll back beyond a given checkpoint, it discards all entries before that checkpoint.

If a single program can execute the funds transfer, and if all tables involved reside on a single server, the DBMS can provide all necessary transaction management services. In fact, creating a stored procedure makes sense to improve performance and encapsulate the function. When a transaction spans multiple database servers or multiple applications participate in a transaction, however, some middleware is required to coordinate the transactions. MTS fulfills that role.

Two-Phase Commit

Sometimes an application must update two or more distinct data sets, and the updates must satisfy the ACID test. Suppose that a bank customer wants to transfer funds between accounts at two different branches and that each branch maintains separate account databases. In this case, the standard transaction management provided by SQL Server won't suffice.

Suppose that account 11111 resides at Branch A and account 22222 resides at Branch B. The funds-transfer application can issue the `BEGIN TRANSACTION`, `INSERT AccountActivity`, and `UPDATE BankAccount` commands separately at Branch A and Branch B. The application can send a commit instruction to Branch A, wait for confirmation, and then send a commit to Branch B. On a good day, everything works just fine. But if the network connection to Branch B fails after Branch A is committed and before Branch B gets the commit message, Branch A is updated and committed, whereas Branch B is in an inconsistent state. The application won't meet the atomicity (all or nothing) criteria of the ACID test.

The solution is a protocol known as *two-phase commit (2PC)*. This protocol adds an extra state: ready to commit. A database in this state can durably commit or roll back a sequence of operations. Before issuing a commit transaction, the application issues a prepare-to-commit instruction to each database. When all databases involved achieve the ready-to-commit state, the application issues a final commit instruction. Figure 24.2 shows a successful 2PC transaction.

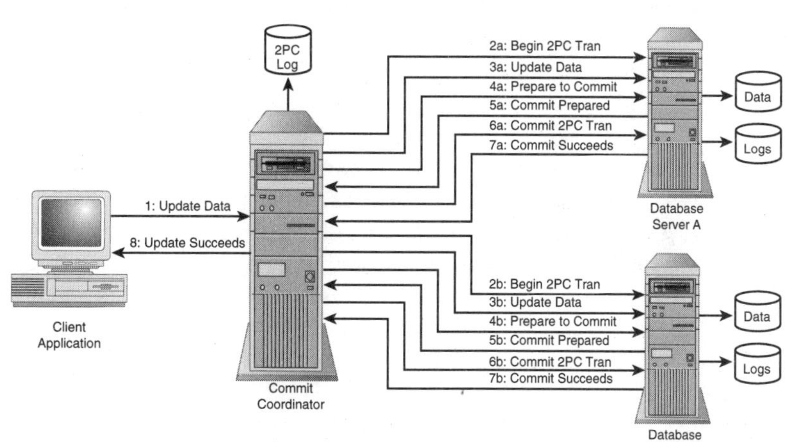

FIG. 24.2
A two-phase commit for a successful transaction involving two database servers, a commit coordinator, and a client application. The commit coordinator doesn't issue the `Commit 2PC Tran` instruction until it receives a `Commit Prepared` message from each database server.

Normally, everything succeeds. However, if one database server experiences a hardware failure or network connection failure before the final commit instruction, data can be restored to the ready-to-commit state, still ready to commit or roll back.

By using the prepare-to-commit instruction, the bank transfer application acts as its own *commit coordinator*. In the uncomplicated example where everything succeeds, it's not a major task. However, a transaction involving multiple operations on multiple databases and using multiple 2PC protocols can fail in a bewildering variety of ways:

- Normal application logic causes a database server to abort a local transaction. A database server can also abort a local transaction because it can't achieve a ready-to-commit state.
- A database server fails to respond to a `Commit 2PC Tran` instruction.
- The commit coordinator fails after issuing a `Prepare to Commit` or `Commit 2PC Tran` instruction.

- A database server or network connection can fail at any time during the 2PC transaction.
- Some combination of faults occurs.

Coping with all the various ways in which a 2PC transaction might fail requires sophisticated design and programming. Because distributed applications must often support transactional integrity, it makes sense to encapsulate the commit coordinator functions in a server—a TP monitor such as MTS.

NOTE Theoretically, no protocol can guarantee that every transaction commits or rolls back without intervention. 2PC is probably the best possible protocol, but occasionally an administrator will have to manually force transactions to abort or commit.

Although you need a basic understanding of 2PC to take advantage of MTS, a full analysis of Microsoft's implementation is beyond the scope of this book. Suffice it to say that the 2PC mechanisms described reliably provide transactional integrity with automatic problem resolution in most failure situations. However, a few conditions still require human intervention. This means that an application that uses the 2PC features in MTS will require knowledgeable administrators.

NOTE The MTS component that acts as a 2PC commit coordinator, the Distributed Transaction Coordinator, originally shipped as a component of Microsoft SQL Server 6.5. Microsoft DTC can interact with other TP monitors by using OLE transactions (the native 2PC protocol for MTS) or X/Open XA (natively supported by many UNIX databases, including Informix, Oracle, and DB2). For details of Microsoft's implementation of 2PC, see the *Microsoft SQL Server Programmer's Toolkit, Guide to Microsoft Distributed Transaction Coordinator.*

Database Access in MTS

An MTS component accessing a database uses ODBC. Microsoft provides a number of class hierarchies encapsulating the ODBC API, including Remote Data Objects (RDO), ActiveX Data Objects (ADO), OLE DB, and Remote Data Service (RDS; formerly known as the Advanced Data Connector). Different tools suit different purposes. Still, as shown in Figure 24.3, all database access methods lead to ODBC.

NOTE With its Universal Data Access initiative, Microsoft is trying to correct the assumption that every persistent data store is a relational database. ADO, OLE DB, and RDS are all designed for Universal Data Access, although, of course, they work quite well with relational databases.

MTS provides two important functions beyond basic database access: distributed transaction support and database connection pooling. The ODBC 3.0 Driver Manager plays an important role in both functions. ODBC has always used a driver manager; with MTS it takes on new responsibilities. Figure 24.4 shows how the ODBC Driver Manager fits between an application and an ODBC driver.

FIG. 24.3
All data access methods from MTS lead to ODBC, including Remote Data Service (RDS), ActiveX Data Objects (ADO), Remote Data Objects (RDO), or OLE DB.

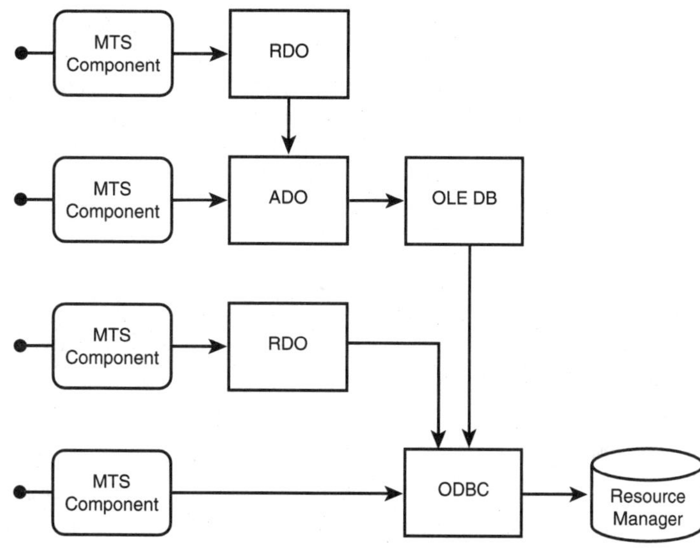

FIG. 24.4
The ODBC Driver Manager loads ODBC drivers on behalf of an application (such as an MTS component). In MTS, it also supports connection pooling and transaction enlistment.

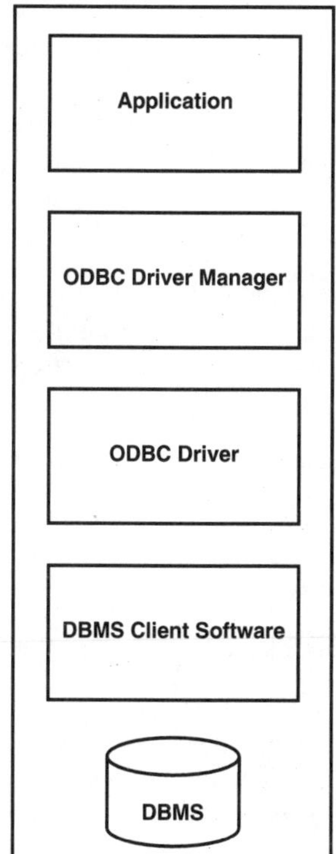

NOTE The ODBC 3.0 Driver Manager DLL is installed with Transaction Server. ■

To support distributed transactions from MTS, an ODBC driver must meet three requirements:

- The driver must be fully *thread safe*—it must be able to handle concurrent calls from any thread at any time.
- The driver must not have *thread affinity*—that is, it must allow one thread to establish a connection, another thread to use the connection, and another thread to disconnect.
- The driver must support the `SQL_ATTR_ENLIST_IN_DTC` connection attribute (used to enlist a connection on a transaction).

CAUTION

Thread safety is uncommon and thread affinity is common among popular ODBC drivers. These problems can manifest as a memory-access violation in the mtx.exe process from within the driver when the ODBC Driver Manager begins to close inactive connections.

For database access from an MTS component, choose ADO or RDO. Direct ODBC seems to offer efficiency (by eliminating an intermediate layer), but in most cases developers end up implementing their own class hierarchy. A lot of focused effort went into the development of ADO and RDO; it makes sense to use what's there. OLE DB is another low-level interface for access to any tabular (rows and columns) data source; ADO encapsulates access to OLE DB and is usually a better choice.

Microsoft introduced RDO with Visual Basic 4.0. RDO is a lightweight encapsulation of the ODBC API, designed specifically for access to a remote DBMS. With Visual Studio 97, Microsoft released RDO 2.0, a substantial revision. RDO 2.0 includes several features not available in ADO 1.0:

- Events on the `Engine`, `Connection`, `Resultset`, and `Column` objects
- Asynchronous queries
- Queries as methods
- Robust batch mode
- Close integration with Visual Basic and related tools such as the Connection Designer and T-SQL Debugger

ADO encapsulates the OLE DB interface. Although not specifically designed for DBMS access, ADO can access relational databases, ISAM, text, hierarchical, or any tabular data source, as long as a data access provider exists. ODBC turns out to be an excellent data access provider. ADO is an Automation-based component, so any Automation-capable application or language can use it.

Microsoft is clearly encouraging developers to move from RDO to ADO. The company claims that future versions of ADO will provide a superset of RDO 2.0, a more sophisticated interface, and an easier programming model. ADO also supports web page data access via RDS.

Successful pooling of database connections in MTS requires attention to two details: connection state and security. Server-side connection state can cause side effects that are difficult to reproduce and eliminate. Connection pooling requires a trade-off between database security and application scalability.

Many database servers maintain a substantial amount of state for each connection. For example, an application might create a connection local temporary table (`CREATE TABLE #MyTemporaryTable ...`). If an MTS component creates a temporary table and doesn't drop it before releasing the connection, a subsequent component using the connection and trying to create or use the same temporary table might fail. Another pitfall is changing the current database (`USE ThatDatabase`); MTS can't detect this context change and will reuse the connection as though the original database were still current. Many servers also maintain connection local system variables (such as `@@rowcount`).

Shared database connections require a trade-off between security and scalability. The user account is an inherent attribute of a connection and can't be changed. Using multiple accounts for ODBC connections will effectively prevent reuse. One approach might be to have users enter a valid account and log in from the base client, but use a common account within MTS. This approach provides user authentication but doesn't enforce access polices. This limitation can be overcome by defining user roles for an MTS component.

The Role of the DTC in Transaction Processing

SQL Server has included support for the 2PC protocol in the past. Application programmers using the C/C++ programming languages could access 2PC functionality by using the DB-Library interface provided by Microsoft for developing SQL Server applications. Procedures were provided on servers that allowed them to take on the role of commit coordinator.

The inclusion of DTC in MTS adds important new components to help implement distributed transactions and make the management of 2PC a more practical undertaking. Each server has a full DTC service that coordinates transactions with other servers. By using the DTC, a server can take on the role of commit coordinator for certain transactions. Also, the DTC can help resolve problem (or in-doubt) transactions by communicating with other DTC services that run on other servers involved in a transaction.

A client-side interface to DTC is available for Windows NT and Windows 95 computers. This interface allows developers to create applications using distributed transactions and leverage the facilities provided by the full DTC service running on SQL Servers. The client components of DTC don't include a full DTC service, even on Windows NT clients. Also, the DTC client is available only for 32-bit versions of Windows (Windows 95 and Windows NT).

A stored procedure running on a SQL Server can possibly launch a distributed transaction on behalf of a 16-bit client. Therefore, older Windows clients can still benefit from DTC functionality.

Also, a set of management utilities has been added to the Microsoft Transaction Server Explorer (MTX) and the SQL Enterprise Manager (a pair of administrative utilities). The utilities include graphical tools that allow you to dynamically monitor the state of transactions on servers running the DTC service. You can open multiple windows to monitor transactions occurring on multiple servers from a single workstation. An administrator also can manually resolve problem transactions arising from equipment or application failure.

Most developers prefer the use of MTX, although database-centric developers find the SQL Enterprise Manager to be very useful as well. There's overlapping functionality between these two tools.

Many application developers haven't seen much need for administrative utilities in the past. The MTX is an exception—it's designed specifically to configure the MTS application environment, as well as make specific settings for your application components. It's used far more often by a lead developer than by a network administrator in typical enterprise network environments, although there are clear benefits if these two groups coordinate with one another.

NOTE Although SQL Enterprise Manager can be run on Windows 95, the DTC utilities are available only when using SQL Enterprise Manager on a Windows NT computer. ■

Managing DTC with SQL Enterprise Manager

The DTC server components are installed automatically when you set up SQL Server 6.5 or upgrade SQL Server 6.0 to version 6.5. They're also installed when you set up Microsoft Transaction Server. You can start the DTC service just like any other service: by using the Control Panel on the local computer or by using the Services dialog box in the Server Manager utility provided with Windows NT Server. You also can start the service by using SQL Service Manager, SQL Enterprise Manager, or MTX.

The rest of this section focuses on the DTC capabilities added to SQL Enterprise Manager. This administrative tool has been enhanced with functionality to completely monitor and manage DTC capabilities.

The DTC Configuration dialog box allows you to control the behavior of the DTC service. You can configure parameters that affect viewing transactions in the Transactions window, the tracing information sent to the Trace window, and the location and size of the DTC log file. To configure the DTC service, follow these steps:

1. Start SQL Enterprise Manager.
2. In the Server Manager window, open a server group and select the server you want to manage. If SQL Server and the DTC service aren't running, start the services.
3. Right-click the DTC icon and select Configure from the pop-up menu. The DTC Configuration dialog box appears (see Figure 24.5).

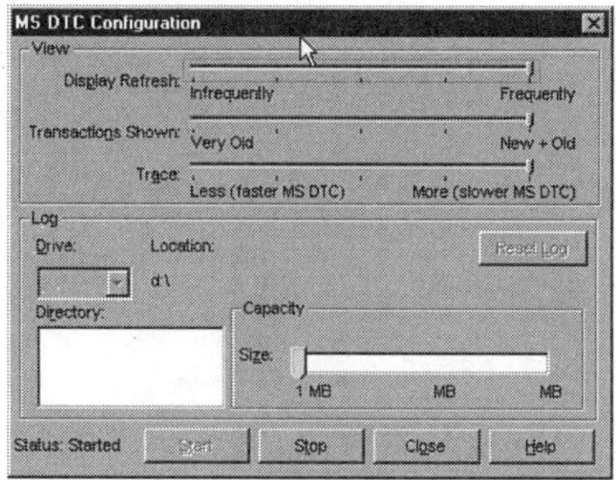

FIG. 24.5 Use this dialog box to configure the displays that monitor the Distributed Transaction Coordinator service and its behavior.

4. By using the Display Refresh slider bar, you can configure DTC to update the display at intervals from 1 to 20 seconds with a default value of 5 seconds. Updating the display more frequently adds administrative overhead to transaction processing and can cause reduced performance.
5. The older a transaction, the more likely it is having difficulty completing. The Transactions Shown slider controls how old a transaction must be before being displayed in the Transactions window. You can set values from 1 second to 5 minutes.
6. The Trace slider controls how much trace information is sent to the Trace window. You can specify no tracing, increasing levels of error, warning and informational traces, or all trace information.
7. You can change view settings while the DTC service is running. To change log settings, you must stop the DTC service. You can then change the location and size of the log.

To view the status of active transactions, follow these steps:

1. Start SQL Enterprise Manager.
2. In the Server Manager window, open a server group and select the server you want to manage. If SQL Server and the DTC service aren't running, start the services.
3. Right-click the DTC icon and select Transaction from the pop-up menu. A DTC Transactions window for the selected server appears (see Figure 24.6).
4. To manually resolve in-doubt transactions, right-click the transaction in the Transactions window and select the appropriate action (see Figure 24.7).

TIP You can select another server and open a transactions window for it as well. You can monitor transactions on a number of servers simultaneously by using tiled or cascaded windows.

CAUTION

You shouldn't manually force transactions until you thoroughly understand the interaction of all members of a DTC system. Review the *Guide to Microsoft Distributed Transaction Coordinator* carefully before using this utility to resolve transactions.

Part IV

Ch 24

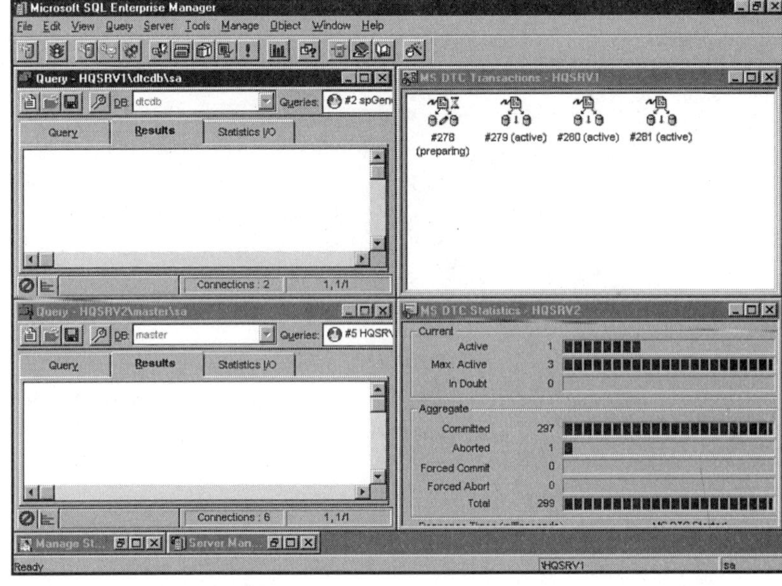

FIG. 24.6
A DTC Transactions window for the server HQSRV1 that has three active transactions and one preparing to commit.

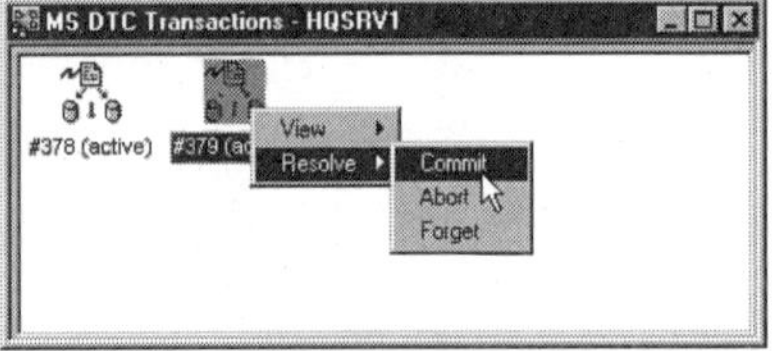

FIG. 24.7
In the Transactions window, you can monitor transaction states and manually resolve in-doubt transactions.

To view the traces being sent (at the level you configured DTC to provide), follow these steps:

1. Start SQL Enterprise Manager.
2. In the Server Manager window, open a server group and select the server you want to manage. If SQL Server and the DTC service aren't running, start the services.
3. Right-click the DTC icon and select Trace from the pop-up menu. A DTC Traces window for the selected server appears.

You can select another server and open a Traces window for it also. You can monitor traces from a number of servers simultaneously by using tiled or cascaded windows.

A DTC service maintains statistical information about its performance. To view the statistics that have accumulated for a DTC service, follow these steps:

1. Start SQL Enterprise Manager.
2. In the Server Manager window, open a server group and select the server you want to manage. If SQL Server and the DTC service aren't running, start the services.

3. Right-click the DTC icon and select Statistics from the pop-up menu. A DTC Statistics window for the selected server appears (see Figure 24.8).

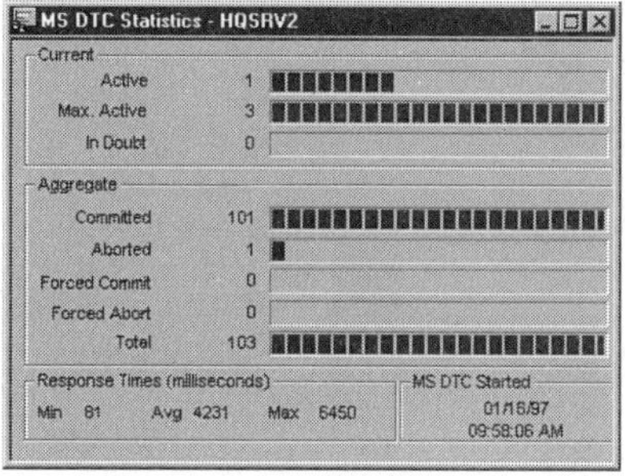

FIG. 24.8 A DTC Statistics window for the server HQSRV2.

NOTE The statistics for a DTC service are cleared and restarted whenever the DTC service is stopped and restarted.

Microsoft Transaction Server

Microsoft Transaction Server 1.0, released in January 1997, builds on the functionality offered by DTC. MTS 2.0 is now available as part of the Windows NT Option Pack and is included as a standard part of Windows NT Server 4.0 Enterprise Edition.

MTS 2.0 provides a COM-based programming model with a relatively simple Application Programming Interface (API) that makes it easy for developers to create powerful, distributed applications. Applications are created largely as though they were designed for a single user to execute on a desktop computer. With minor additions, these applications can be invoked in a Transaction Server environment. Transaction Server provides all the needed additional capabilities to make the application multiuser and leverages DTC to provide distributed transaction processing. Transaction Server therefore forms the basis for a powerful three-tiered distributed computing architecture.

Figure 24.9 shows a simple example of the way an MTS environment might be set up. Desktop PC clients might be so-called "fat" Win32 systems (running Windows 95 or Windows NT) or "thin" clients running a web browser.

Although the example in Figure 24.9 describes three tiers, nothing inherent in the design of MTS limits it to this structure. You can break a computing system into more than three logical tiers, and MTS's design makes implementing various system architectures, including multi-tiered designs, straightforward. The three-tiered model is natural in some respects and is starting to be widely used, but need not be the only deployment alternative with MTS.

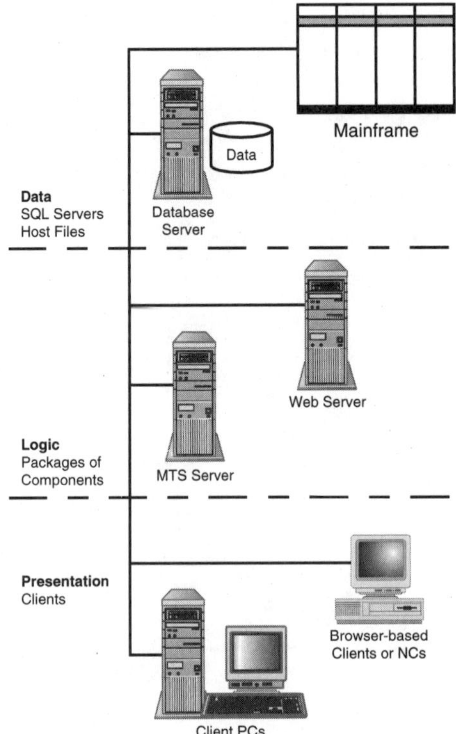

FIG. 24.9
This sample MTS environment shows various elements of a three-tiered architecture.

NOTE The operating systems and applications installed on PCs have become much larger as they've grown in sophistication. With the advent of the HTTP-based web browser, application developers started exploring the capability of using this relatively "thin" tool as the basis for server-based applications. The traditional application architecture with its executable files and dynamic link libraries (DLLs) has been characterized as "fat" because of the amount of information (programs, configuration files, and data) that must be stored on the client.

Browsers (from Netscape, Microsoft, and others) continue to get "fatter" as more features are added, however. Also, browser-based applications haven't yet reached the level of performance and sophistication offered by the more traditional Win32 client. It remains to be seen how fat the thin client will need to become to match the functionality offered by Win32 clients.

The next few sections provide an introduction to Transaction Server. You get a quick tour of MTS in action and review the product's features.

Transaction Server's Features

Transaction Server is used to deploy mid-tier logic implemented in the form of ActiveX components. These objects receive requests from clients, apply some sort of logic (for example, business rules) to the requests, and then call on appropriate resource managers to resolve the requests. The ActiveX components can be written with a variety of languages, including those listed in Table 24.1 later in the section "Packages of Components." These components can be developed in-house or purchased from third-party software vendors.

After these components are written or acquired, they're combined to form *packages* that you can deploy as a unit sharing resources (for example, memory) and security settings. MTS also manages a shared pool of ODBC data connections to various data providers, which can be traditional database servers or files on a mainframe. The packages are then deployed, usually on Windows NT servers, to act as intermediaries for clients wanting to access shared resources.

Because of MTS's capability to manage links among many clients accessing many resource managers (for example, databases) while applying application logic, the application architecture you can create with these building blocks has some very desirable characteristics:

- *Scalable.* Applications can be implemented by using one server or scaled to many multiprocessor servers handling hundreds of users.
- *Distributed.* Applications that span multiple machines are coded in a manner almost identical to an application designed to run on a single computer.
- *Multiuser.* MTS automatically provides thread management, assists with shared memory management, and offers other capabilities that make it easier to take existing single-user components and run them safely in a multiuser environment.
- *Reliable.* Through the use of transactional technologies such as the DTC and OLE TX (a COM-based protocol used by software vendors to create resource dispensers), the MTS environment ensures that discrete units of work are always done completely or not at all. Atomicity is always maintained. The data accessed through MTS resource managers remains in a consistent state, even with many users accessing diverse resources on multiple machines. By using the latest SQL Server products, you also can achieve a high degree of concurrence and processing throughput.

Much of the distributed nature of the MTS product comes as a direct result of the use of the Component Object Model (COM) and Distributed Component Object Model (DCOM) as the basis for MTS component building. Chapter 4, "Using Microsoft's Object Technologies," provides a thorough introduction to these technologies.

Packages of Components

After you purchase off-the-shelf components, write your own, or both, you can create collections of components called *packages*. The programming techniques required for creating these components are described in the Chapter 25, "Using Microsoft Transaction Server to Enable Distributed Applications."

You can manage a package of components as a unit. The components in the package can share security settings and can access other shared resources through the use of MTS's Shared Property Manager (SPM). They also can share a pool of ODBC connections to database resources. Allocating memory and processing on a one-to-one basis with clients becomes inefficient when handling large numbers of clients. A shared pool is more efficient and scales better as the number of clients grows.

▶ **See** "The Shared Property Manager," **p. 700**

When access to distributed database resources is required, the services of Microsoft's DTC (described earlier in this chapter) are used to efficiently provide a message-based architecture that can maintain the atomic nature of transactions across machine boundaries. Communications with database resource dispensers are handled by using various protocols:

- OLE TX
- Transaction Internet Protocol (TIP)
- XA
- SNA LU 6.2 (through a product code-named Cedar)

The MTS development environment provides a very flexible programming environment. As already noted, the focus of most developers is on creating components designed for single-user environments without regard for distributed applications issues. They can work in various languages, including those listed in Table 24.1.

Table 24.1 Languages Supported for MTS Development

Language	Manufacturer
Delphi	Borland
C++Builder	Borland
Visual Basic	Microsoft
Visual C++	Microsoft
Visual J++	Microsoft
PowerBuilder	PowerSoft

After components are created, they're packaged to facilitate setting security and deploying on a particular machine. Packages can be managed effectively by using the Transaction Server Explorer. You can even split a package for deployment across server boundaries by partitioning the package for multiple-machine installation. The following section describes the use of Transaction Server Explorer.

Using MTX

Microsoft Transaction Server Explorer (MTX) is the tool used to package components and then deploy the packages. This administrative console is a graphics utility that lets you manipulate and control the components that build a multitiered MTS architecture. In addition to these component-based activities, you also can use Transaction Server Explorer to start and stop the DTC, change the service account settings, or perform other administrative tasks.

The MTX included with MTS 2.0 is one of the first tools delivered by Microsoft that makes use of Microsoft's new administrative tool known as the Microsoft Management Console (MMC). Specific tools are created as *snap-ins*, which are actually just ActiveX controls written according to specific guidelines.

ON THE WEB

You can download a paper describing the MMC and its extensibility from Microsoft's web site at **http://www.microsoft.com/msdn/sdk/techinfo/default.htm**.

To use MTX, follow these steps:

1. Launch MTX from the Start menu or by double-clicking the appropriate icon. The basic Explorer interface appears (see Figure 24.10).

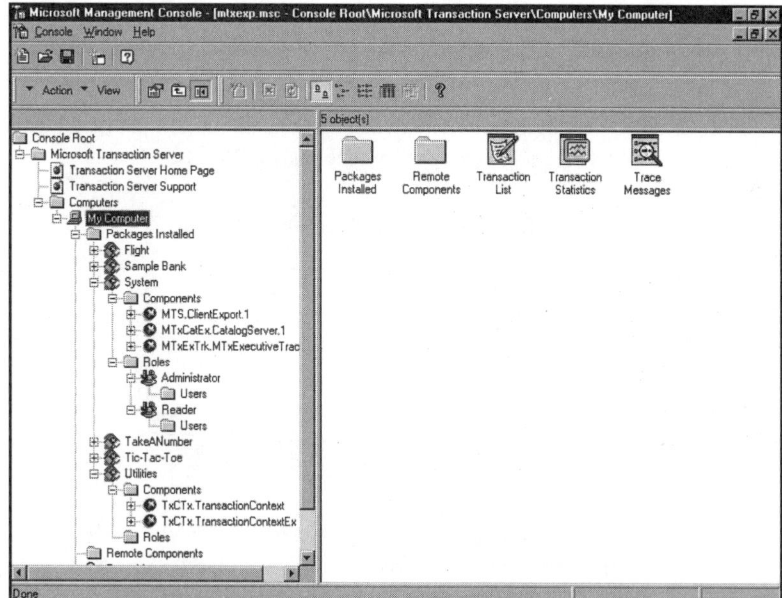

FIG. 24.10
The Transaction Server Explorer with My Computer selected in the left pane and the contents of My Computer in the right pane.

Transaction Server Explorer uses a two-pane display. The left pane is presented in hierarchical fashion, showing the computers being managed. If you select an object in the left pane, its contents appear in the right pane.

TIP Right-clicking an object generally opens a context-sensitive menu with choices pertinent to the object selected.

2. Click the plus sign (+) to the left of an object to open the hierarchical display of its contents in the left pane.
3. To add other computers to the display (after MTS is installed on the machine), click the Computers folder and choose New, Computer from the Action menu. Enter the name of the computer you want to manage and click OK.
4. To create a new package, click the Packages Installed folder in the left pane and choose New, Package from the Action menu. The Package Wizard starts.
5. Click the large button labeled Create an Empty Package.
6. In the next dialog box, enter a name for the new package and click Next.
7. Select the account context under which this package will be run. It can execute with the same status as the currently logged-on user, or it can be run by using a different account, such as a service account, for its security status. Select an account and click Finish. The new package is created.
8. To add a component to a package, highlight the Components folder within the package hierarchy in the left pane and choose New, Component from the Action menu. The opening dialog box for the Component Wizard, which is very similar to the Package Wizard, appears. You can Import Component(s) already installed on this computer and added to your system Registry. For this example, however, click Install New Component(s).
9. The Install Components dialog box appears. Click the Add Files button. The Select Files to Install dialog box appears (see Figure 24.11).

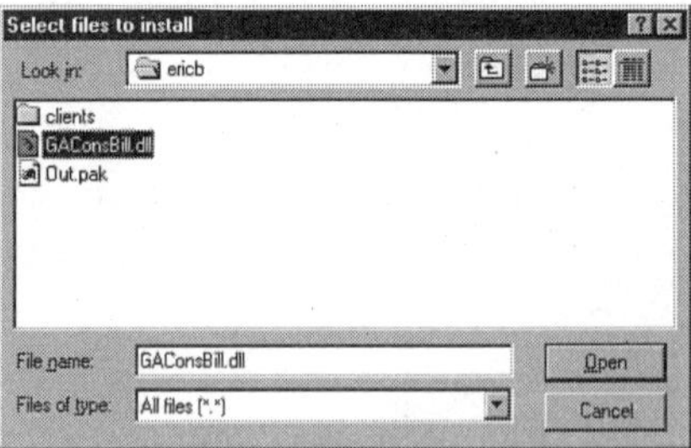

FIG. 24.11
ActiveX components created with a variety of languages can be integrated into a single package for deployment on this computer, or to be exported to other machines.

10. Select the component you want to install and click the Open button. Then click Finish to complete the wizard. The component is added to your package and appears in the right pane of the display when the package is selected in the left pane.

After you create a package that includes the appropriate components, you need to set various properties to control the package's behavior. There are properties for the package as a whole, and properties that pertain only to a particular component within the package. To set package and component properties, follow these steps:

1. Launch MTX.
2. To set properties for a package, click the Packages Installed folder in the left pane; then right-click the package in the right pane. Choose Properties from the pop-up menu.
3. A five-tabbed dialog box of package properties displays. On the General page you can enter a description of the package or view the package's unique Package ID.
4. Click the Security tab, which allows you to select the authorization level to be used for this package (see Figure 24.12). Use the Authentication Level for Calls drop-down list and click the Enable Authorization Checking checkbox to use this feature.

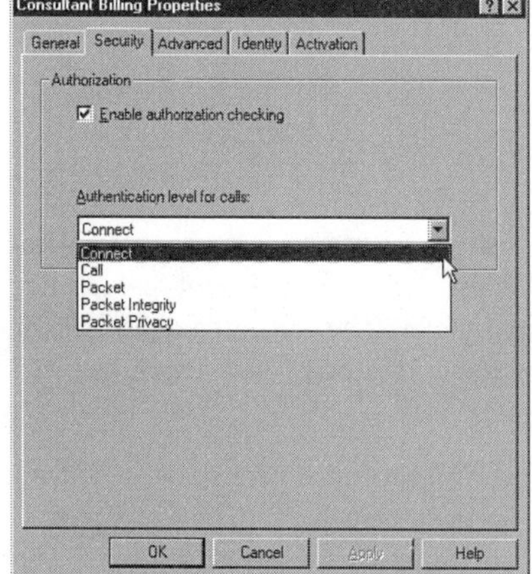

FIG. 24.12
The Security tab allows you to set more stringent authorization requirements for components in this package.

5. Use the Advanced page to set Server Process Shutdown options. Either select Leave Running When Idle or specify a number of minutes of idle time before you shut down components in this package.
6. Use the Identity page to select the account ID that will be used when executing components in this package. Choose Interactive User or This User and select a user account from the Set Package Identity dialog box.
7. Use the Activation page to control how this package is activated. You can choose to run this package's components In the Creator's Process or In a Dedicated Server Process. Make the appropriate selection and click OK.
8. You can also set component properties. Select the components folder for your package in the left pane. In the right pane, right-click a particular component and choose properties from the pop-up menu. A Properties dialog box for the component appears. Click the Transaction tab (see Figure 24.13).
9. Select one of the four choices for transaction support and click OK.

The four choices for transaction support bear further discussion. After you break up your application into component parts, you need to control their participation in transactions. To achieve the highest level of reusability and flexibility, these decisions aren't made when the code is being written, but when the components are deployed with MTX.

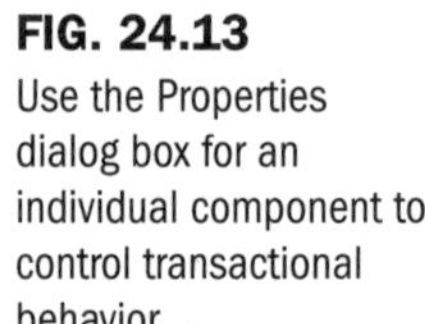

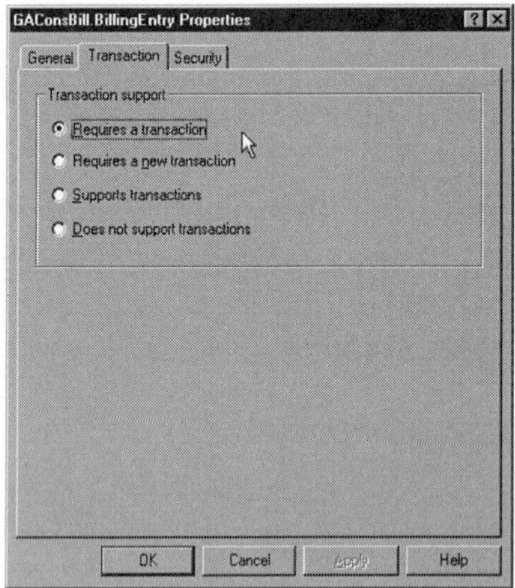

FIG. 24.13
Use the Properties dialog box for an individual component to control transactional behavior.

If a component is flagged as Requires a Transaction, it will automatically be executed within a transaction at runtime. If it's called by another component that has already begun a transaction, it will participate in that same transaction. If it's executed on its own outside the scope of any other transactions, a new transaction is created to ensure that the work done by this component is completed or rolled back.

A component that Requires a New Transaction always spawns its own transactional boundaries. A situation that might call for such behavior can be a component that writes audit information to a log. In such a case, you might want the work of this component to be durable, even if the work of a calling component must be rolled back.

A component that Supports Transactions can go either way with respect to transactional behavior. If it's called within a transaction, it participates. If the calling process isn't using a transaction, no transaction is started by this component. This varies from the previous two choices in that it's possible for this component to execute outside transactional boundaries—something that never happens with the first two choices.

The final choice, Does Not Support Transactions, is used primarily in cases where the underlying work being done is simply not transactional in nature. Some actions can't be rolled back, and some resources might be required that were never designed to support transactional behavior. These can still be used in a component, but without the benefit of transactional integrity.

Another important operation you perform with MTX is to configure role-based security. The need for this type of security is easy to understand when you reflect on an environment where many clients are sharing mid-tier business logic. If you want to control access to these components or the behavior of the components depending on the calling process, role-based security becomes an obvious choice.

To establish roles for a package, follow these steps:

1. Launch MTX.
2. Select the package you want to configure in the left pane. Choose New, Role from the Action menu. The New Role dialog box appears (see Figure 24.14).

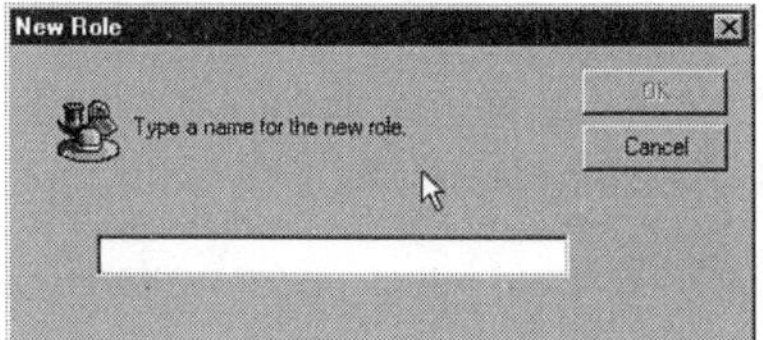

FIG. 24.14
Role-based security is a powerful feature of MTS that has been used in large mainframe-based systems for years.

3. Enter a name for the role (for example, **`Administrators`**) and click OK.
4. A new role appears within the Roles folder for the package. Select the Roles folder in the left pane and choose New, User from the Action menu. The Add Users and Groups to Role dialog box appears.
5. Select the users or groups you want to add to this role and click the Add button. To select individual users, you must first click the Show Users button. Click OK.

A common practice—recommended by Microsoft for most situations—is to create a few standard roles and then assign groups from a Windows NT domain to those roles. For example, if you have a Consultant Billing application, you might create a group called Consultant Billing Admins and another called Consultant Billing Users. This could be done by a network administrator with User Manager for Domains rights or another equivalent method. Then, by using MTX, a lead developer for the application could create roles for the application called Admin and User following the preceding steps.

After you assign the Consultant Billing Admins group to the Admin role and the Consultant Billing Users group to the Users role, it becomes very easy to control access to particular functionality within the application. Users assigned administrative responsibility for the application are simply added to the Windows NT group Consultant Billing Admins. Any code within the component restricted to the Admin role is available only to this group of people.

Microsoft plans to continue evolving MTS into the future, where it will become a key component of multimachine architectures. Microsoft has publicly announced plans to add data-dependent message routing (useful in partitioning large applications) and durable queues, which would maintain the queue of messages even in the event of catastrophic failure. These and other features will likely be delivered by, or derived from, the Microsoft Message Queue (MSMQ) Server (code-named Falcon). It will be interesting to see how these technologies are combined to extend and improve the powerful features already included in the current release of MTS.

From Here...

In this chapter, you learned about distributed database applications. You also learned about a component included in MTS and SQL Server, the Distributed Transaction Coordinator, which simplifies the process of managing distributed transactions. The various tools for monitoring the status of distributed transactions and resolving problem transactions were described. You also were introduced to Microsoft Transaction Server, a powerful tool for implementing multiuser, distributed applications.

See the following chapters for related information:

- For a review of COM and DCOM technologies, see Chapter 4, "Using Microsoft's Object Technologies."
- For information on the overall architecture of I-net environments, see Chapter 10, "Clients, Servers, and Components: Web-Based Applications."
- For information on the overall architecture of traditional client/server environments, see Chapter 20, "Clients, Servers, and Components: Design Strategies for Distributed Applications."
- To learn about how distributed applications are designed, see Chapter 21, "Creating Distributed Applications."
- For information on creating applications specifically designed for Microsoft Transaction Server, see Chapter 25, "Using Microsoft Transaction Server to Enable Distributed Applications."

CHAPTER 25

Using Microsoft Transaction Server to Enable Distributed Applications

by Larry Millett

The Shared Property Manager

The Shared Property resource dispenser allows multithreaded applications to share global variables safely.

Distributed security management

Transaction Server uses a resource-oriented role-based security scheme.

Using Transaction Server with I-net applications

Learn how I-net applications can interact with Transaction Server.

Programming tips and pitfalls

Review programming tips for developing Transaction Server components. Plan to avoid some pitfalls.

In Chapter 24, you were introduced to the Microsoft Transaction Server (MTS), the Distributed Transaction Coordinator (DTC), and distributed transaction-processing concepts. This chapter explores the techniques used to create applications for MTS and delves more deeply into the features that support distributed applications.

Creating distributed transactions isn't an easy task. With applications components running on multiple machines connected over a network, many complicated types of error scenarios can occur. Trying to foresee these possibilities and building your application to deal with them appropriately is a monumental task. Microsoft has provided an infrastructure for these applications that greatly simplifies the job of application developers.

To get the most out of this chapter, you need a basic understanding of Microsoft's Component Object Model (COM) and Distributed COM (DCOM). You also need to understand the basic concepts underlying distributed transactions and the two-phase commit transaction protocol.

▶ **See** "COM/DCOM Architecture Basics," **p. 112**

▶ **See** Chapter 24, "Deploying Distributed Applications," **p. 667** ■

Managing Transactions in MTS

MTS's primary function is automated support for transactions. Based on transaction requirements declared for each component, MTS automatically begins, commits, and aborts transactions, enlisting database connections and other components as needed. A component's transaction requirements may take one of four values:

- `Requires a Transaction`. The component's objects must always execute within a transaction. A new object may enlist in its creator's transaction; if the creator isn't executing in a transaction, MTS will create a transaction for the new object.
- `Requires a New Transaction`. The component's objects must execute within an independent transaction. Even if a new object's creator is already in a transaction, MTS will create a new, independent transaction for the new object. This value might be useful for implementing an audit trail component, which records work done on behalf of its creator's transaction regardless of the outcome of the original transaction.
- `Supports Transactions`. A new object can be enlisted in its creator's transaction, if any. If the creator isn't executing in a transaction, MTS won't create a transaction for the new object.
- `Does Not Support Transactions`. The component's objects shouldn't be included in a transaction, even when the creator is executing in a transaction. This value should be used only for older components that predate MTS.

A component's support for transactions is declared in Microsoft Transaction Explorer (MTX) when a component is added to a package.

▶ **See** Chapter 24, "Deploying Distributed Applications," **p. 667**, for more information about adding components to packages with the MTX.

To provide automatic transaction support, MTS associates an *object context* with each object created in its runtime environment. The object context includes information about the identity of the object's creator and the transaction (if any) in which the object executes. The object context exposes the `IObjectContext` interface. All newly developed MTS components should at least support transactions. At a minimum, this means that each of the component's objects will use the `SetComplete` and `SetAbort` methods of the `IObjectContext` interface. The next section discusses the object context in more detail.

Any object that includes a `Begin Tran` statement, or executes SQL that includes a `Begin Tran` statement, should be declared as `Requires a Transaction` or `Requires a New Transaction`. When a component is declared as requiring a transaction or a new transaction, you don't need to include `Begin Tran` statements in the object; MTS automatically provides transaction support.

As an alternative to its automatic management of transactions, MTS allows a base client to directly control transactions with the `ITransactionContextEx` interface. Discussion of the `ITransactionContext` interface, and the corresponding transaction context object, follows discussion of the object context.

Using the Object Context

The object context is central to MTS's implementation of automatic transactions, security, and object pooling. Every object executing in MTS has an object context and can obtain a reference to its context with the `GetObjectContext` function. Proper use of the object context is essential for automatic transaction management.

Include a private member variable of type `ObjectContext` in every MTS object. This reference must never be passed outside the object and must be explicitly released when the object is deactivated.

The `GetObjectContext` returns a reference to an `ObjectContext` object (interface `IObjectContext`). This object has a number of methods for transaction control:

- `CreateInstance` instantiates a new MTS object. Caller and transaction information for the new object's object context is derived from the current object context.
- `SetAbort` indicates that the object has completed its work and may be deactivated, but the transaction in which it executed should be aborted.
- `SetComplete` indicates that the object has successfully completed its work and may be deactivated.
- `DisableCommit` transactional updates performed by this object can't be committed in their current form.
- `EnableCommit` indicates that the object has successfully completed its transactional updates but isn't yet ready to be deactivated.
- `IsInTransaction` returns `True` if the current object is executing within a transaction; otherwise, it returns `False`.
- `SafeRef` returns a reference to the current object (not the object context) that may be passed to other objects.

A transaction can't be committed while any participating object is executing a method. MTS will behave as though `COMMIT` is disabled until all method calls return.

The work of a transaction can be divided among several MTS objects. In such cases, your first instinct might be to control the transaction and each subsidiary object from the base client. This approach, however, doesn't effectively exploit the automatic transaction support provided by MTS. A better approach would be to develop one master object that creates instances of the subsidiary objects from its object context. Because the subsidiary objects are created from the master object's context, MTS automatically enlists those objects in the transaction.

A base client creates an MTS object, which uses its object context to create two subsidiary objects, each of which uses its object context to create another subsidiary object. If the first MTS object requires a transaction and the subsidiary objects support transactions, all are automatically enlisted in the same transaction (see Figure 25.1).

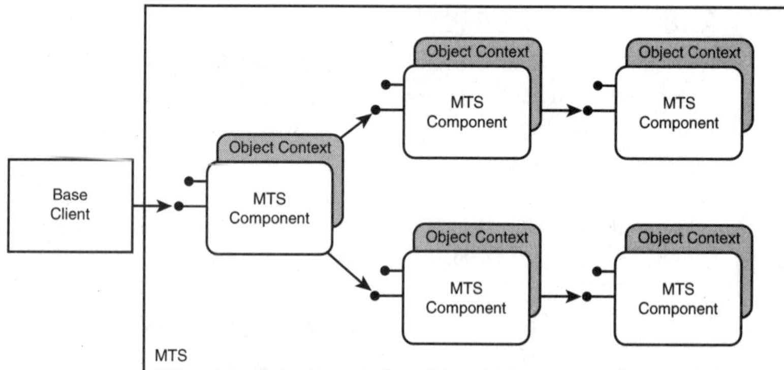

FIG. 25.1 The object context used to enlist subsidiary objects in a transaction.

NOTE Don't use `CoCreateInstance` to create a subsidiary MTS object from within another MTS object. You must use `ObjectContext.CreateInstance` so that the new object's context can inherit properties from its client's context and enlist in the client's transaction.

Suppose that an application needs to include in a single transaction work performed by two MTS components: `Walk` and `Wind`. Suppose also that each component is defined as `Requires a Transaction`. A base client implemented in Visual Basic might include the following code:

```
Public Sub WalkToSchoolAndWindWatch()

Dim objObjectContext As ObjectContext
Dim objWalk As Component1.Walk
Dim objWind As Compnent2.Wind

' Create an instance of Walk, and get a reference to the object context
Set objWalk = CreateObject("Component1.Walk")
Set objObjectContext = objWalk.GetObjectContext

' Use Object Context to create instances of Wind within the same transaction
Set objWind = objObjectContext.CreateInstance("Component2.Wind")

' do work - each component must call ObjectContext.SetComplete or SetAbort
objWalk.Walk("School")
objWind.Wind("Watch")

' Clean up
Set objWalk = Nothing
Set ObjWind = Nothing
Set objObjectContext = Nothing

End Sub
```

Using the Transaction Context

The `TransactionContext` object (`ITransactionContextEx` interface) allows a base client to control enlistment of MTS objects in a transaction. Each new instance of `TransactionContext` initiates a new transaction. The base client creates a transaction context and uses that object's methods to control the transaction:

- `CreateInstance` instantiates an MTS component. If the component supports or requires a transaction, the new object is enlisted in the transaction of the `TransactionContextEx` object.
- `Commit` attempts to commit the work of all MTS components enlisted in the current transaction. If any component has called `SetAbort` or `DisableCommit`, or a system error has occurred, the transaction aborts; otherwise, the transaction commits.
- `Abort` aborts the work of all MTS components enlisted in the current transaction.

Using a transaction context to control a transaction from the base client imposes a number of limitations on an application:

- The business logic for composing the transaction is implemented in the base client and isn't reusable.
- To actually enlist subsidiary objects in the transaction, you must create them by using the `CreateInstance` method of the transaction context object. This subtle requirement is easily overlooked and leads to sporadic failures that are difficult to isolate.
- The transaction context object must run in-process with the base client, which means that MTS must run on the same machine with the base client.

A base client creates a transaction context object and then uses it to create three subsidiary objects, one of which creates its own subsidiary object. The base client controls enlistment of subsidiary objects in the transaction (see Figure 25.2).

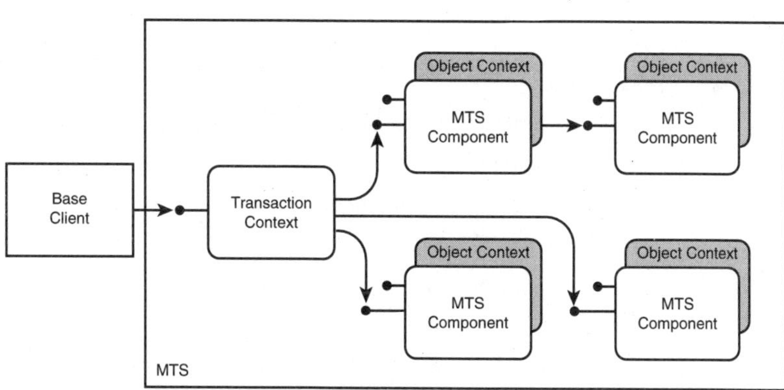

FIG. 25.2
The transaction context used to control subsidiary objects in a transaction from the base client.

Suppose that an application needs to include in a single transaction work performed by two MTS components: `Walk` and `Wind`. Each component must be defined as `Supports Transactions`. A base client implemented in Visual Basic might include the following code:

```
Public Sub WalkToSchoolAndWindWatch()

Dim objTransactionContext As TransactionContext
Dim objWalk As Component1.Walk
Dim objWind As Compnent2.Wind

' Create an instance of TransactionContext
Set objTransactionContext = CreateObject("TxCtx.TransactionContext")

' Use objTransactionContext to create instances of Walk and Wind within a
' transaction
Set objWalk = objTransactionContext.CreateInstance("Component1.Walk")
Set objWind = objTxCtx.CreateInstance("Component2.Wind")

' do work - each component must call ObjetContext.SetComplete or SetAbort
objWalk.Walk("School")
objWind.Wind("Watch")

' Commit the transaction
objTransactionContext.Commit

' Clean up
Set objWalk = Nothing
Set ObjWind = Nothing
Set objTransactionContext = Nothing

End Sub
```

To use the `TransactionContext` object in a Visual Basic project, include a reference to the Transaction Context 1.x Type Library. This library includes `TransactionContext` and `TransactionContextEx` objects. The `CreateInstance` method of the `TransactionContext` object takes a string program identifier ("*Appname.Classname*"); the `CreateInstance` method of the `TransactionContextEx` object requires the corresponding GUID strings.

Understanding MTS Component Integration Services

In addition to its support for transactions, MTS provides several features for enhanced scalability, security, and efficient administration:

- Process and thread management
- Just-in-time object activation
- Database connection pooling
- The Shared Property Manager
- Distributed security service to control object invocation and use
- A graphical tool for system administration and component management

Process and Thread Management

The MTS Executive provides an execution environment for MTS components. An MTS *package* consists of one or more ActiveX components that share an execution context (a process). Because all components in a package share a process, execution is more efficient. When components execute inside an MTS process, MTS can provide two important performance benefits: just-in-time object activation and resource pooling.

An MTS application component can execute in one of three basic scenarios: in-process, out-of-process, and remote.

NOTE Some Microsoft documents seem to imply that with MTS, all components run in-process with the base client. This isn't true. An MTS component may run in-process with the base client, but for most enterprise applications, the remote server model makes the best sense. The in-process confusion probably arose because every MTS component must be built as an in-process server (a DLL) and because all components in an MTS package execute in a common process.

Figure 25.3 illustrates in-process execution. The application component runs inside the base client's process. This method provides optimum performance but no process isolation: On any internal error in a component, MTS immediately shuts down the base client and all its active components.

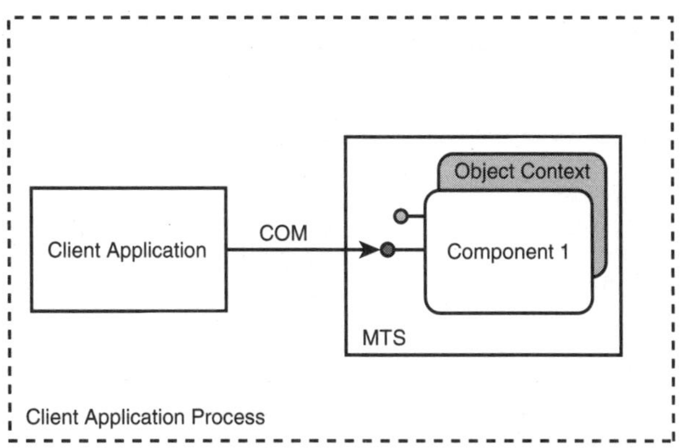

FIG. 25.3 An in-process MTS component uses the base client application's execution context.

To run MTS components in-process, the base client must run on a Windows NT Server system with MTS running and all components installed locally.

CAUTION

Although running MTS components in-process with the base client provides optimum performance, this approach may compromise security. When a base client successfully invokes a component, MTS doesn't revalidate security for calls between components within the same server process. When MTS components run in-process with the base client, the base client gains access to all components within that server process.

A local Transaction Server component executes on the same computer as the client application, but in a separate process managed by the Transaction Server Executive (see Figure 25.4). The client communicates with the component through the COM proxy/stub mechanism. Each message from a base client to an MTS component must cross a process boundary, which incurs some overhead, but this model allows MTS to provide full security and fault isolation. Scalability, however, is limited to the number of base clients and MTS components that can run on the same, single server.

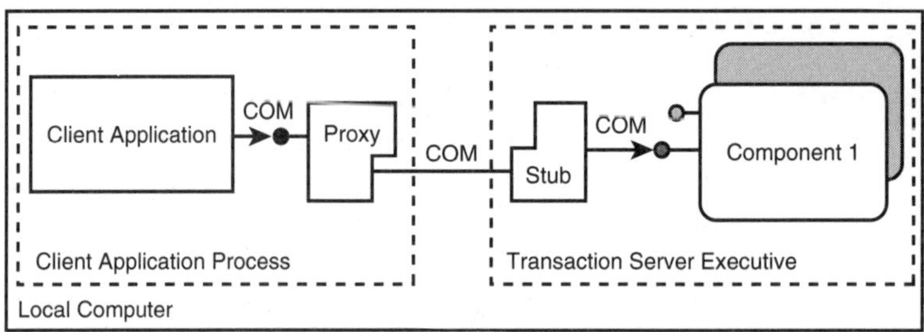

FIG. 25.4 MTS components can also run on the same computer as the base client, but in a separate process.

Finally, an MTS component might run on a separate computer from the base client, using DCOM. The client communicates with the component through the DCOM proxy/stub mechanism. Communication between the base client and MTS components takes place at network speeds—milliseconds rather than microseconds. This model, shown in Figure 25.5, provides the best scalability for large numbers of base clients.

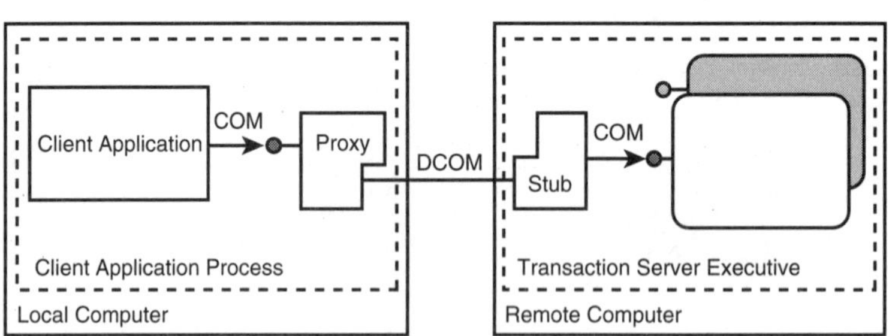

FIG. 25.5 A remote Transaction Server component executes on a separate computer from the client application, in an execution context provided by the Transaction Server Executive.

ON THE WEB

For a base client running on Windows 95, in-process and local execution aren't an option. (MTS isn't available for Windows 95.) MTS does support Windows 95 base clients for remote execution, but Windows 95 may need an upgrade for DCOM support. For the latest information on DCOM for Windows 95, see **http://www.microsoft.com/oledev**.

NOTE You might have to configure DCOM security settings (impersonation and authentication levels) on both client and server computers. The default values for these settings—`Identify` for impersonation, `Connect` for authentication—work properly for MTS but might not be appropriate for your application. Impersonation must be set to `Identify` or higher.

Microsoft recommends using MTX rather than the DCOM configuration utility (dcomcnfg) to change security settings at the package level. Using MTX ensures consistent security settings for all components in a package.

Object Pooling and Just-in-Time Object Activation

In a typical high-volume transaction-processing environment, a large number of base clients invoke a large number of transactions. In MTS, each transaction requires a new instance of a component. Unfortunately, object instantiation takes a long time. It's as though you had to assemble your car before driving to work each day, disassemble it (and put the pieces away) on arrival, reassemble the car to drive home, and take it apart again on your safe return. It's much simpler just to park, lock the car, and take the keys.

Unfortunately, when a large number of people drive to work and park their personal automobiles, parking becomes scarce and traffic becomes dense. Similarly, if every base client maintains its own instance of a component, server resources are strained and performance suffers.

Microsoft's solution to this problem is *object pooling* and *just-in-time activation*. In the ActiveX programming model, a client doesn't explicitly destroy a server component; it just releases the server. Normally, after a server is released by all clients, it destroys itself. However, MTS can deactivate and then reactivate the application component on demand. In fact, MTS can even deactivate an object while a client maintains a reference (provided that the object isn't involved in an active transaction) and doesn't need to maintain any private state information.

To let MTS know when an object isn't involved in a transaction and has no private state to maintain, you must use the `IObjectContext.SetComplete` and `IObjectContext.SetAbort` functions. When a component calls one of these functions, it indicates that it has completed its work and doesn't need to maintain any private state for its client.

To perform some action on object activation or deactivation, implement the `ObjectControl` interface (`IObjectControl` for Visual C++ and Visual J++ and `ObjectControl` for Visual Basic). This interface includes three functions:

- `Activate()` allows an object to perform context-specific initialization at each activation (fetching Registry settings, for example). MTS calls this method before any other methods are called on the object.
- `Deactivate()` allows an object to perform any necessary cleanup before it's recycled or destroyed. MTS calls this method at object deactivation.
- `CanBePooled()` returns `True` if the component supports pooling; otherwise, it returns `False`. MTS calls `CanBePooled()` immediately after the `Deactivate` method.

The following Visual Basic 5.0 (VB5) code example implements `ObjectControl`:

```
Option Explicit

Implements ObjectControl
```

```
Private Sub ObjectControl_Activate()
     'Initialize member variable for object context
     Set m_oContext = GetObjectContext()
     'A good place to fetch registry entries
End Sub

Private Sub ObjectControl_Deactivate()
     'Explicitly release reference to object context
     Set m_oContext = Nothing
     ' Deallocate any objects created since activation
End Sub

Private Function CanBePooled() As Boolean
     CanBePooled = True
End Function
```

NOTE According to Microsoft, object pooling and recycling isn't implemented for custom components in MTS 1.x. MTS invokes the `CanBePooled` function but ignores the result. Implementing the function now, however, allows a component to take advantage of resource pooling and recycling when MTS implements this feature.

The `ObjectControl` interface requires Windows NT 4.0 Service Pack 2.

When a base client initially creates an MTS component (by calling `CreateObject` or `CoCreateInstance`), MTS checks for an inactive instance of that object. If an inactive instance is available, MTS returns a reference to that object; if no inactive objects are available, MTS initializes the object in a deactivated state. When the client invokes a method on a deactivated object, MTS first invokes `ObjectControl.Activate`.

NOTE In Visual C++, calls to `QueryInterface`, `AddRef`, or `Release` won't activate an object.

MTS deactivates an object when the object calls `SetComplete` or `SetAbort` and returns to the caller, or when the last reference from an external client is dropped.

The Shared Property Manager

The Shared Property Manager (SPM) is one of two resource dispensers included with MTS. SPM allows safe multithreaded access to application-defined processwide variables. Possible applications include a web page hit counter or shared state for a multiuser application.

Traditional global variables aren't safe for use in a multithreaded or multiuser application because concurrent access may lead to inconsistent results. Figure 25.6 shows how use of a simple global variable can lead to inconsistent results. SPM provides a locking mechanism that allows safe concurrent access to shared state.

NOTE SPM doesn't provide transactions for shared properties because properties are non-durable data.

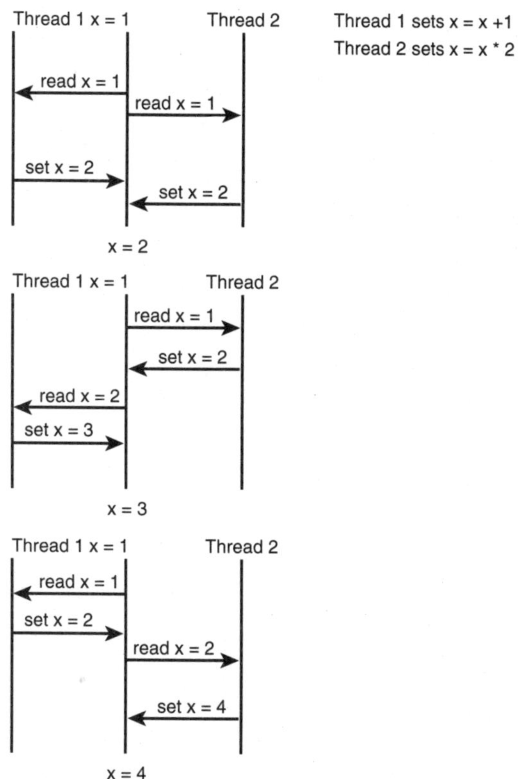

FIG. 25.6
Thread 1 and Thread 2 update a global variable x. Thread 1 sets x = x + 1; Thread 2 sets x = x * 2. Depending on the sequence of reads and writes, the result may be 2, 3, or 4. The case in which the result is 2 is clearly incorrect: Thread 2 reads x while Thread 1 updates x–a dirty read.

As shown in Figure 25.7, SPM uses a simple hierarchy of three classes:

- `SharedPropertyGroupManager` (interface `ISharedPropertyGroupManager`) supports allocation and deallocation of `SharedPropertyGroup` objects, and indexed, keyed, or enumerated (for each) access to `SharedPropertyGroups`. A process can have only one instance of `SharedPropertyGroupManager`.
- `SharedPropertyGroup` (interface `ISharedPropertyGroup`) supports allocation and deallocation of individual `SharedProperty` objects, and indexed, keyed, or enumerated (for each) access to `SharedProperty` objects.
- `SharedProperty` (interface `ISharedProperty`) provides thread-safe access to the value of an individual shared property.

The object-creation methods for SPM include features intended to simplify programming. An attempt to create an instance of `SharedPropertyGroupManager` when one is already active in the process will succeed, but will return a reference to the existing instance without creating a new one. For example, the following VB code will never fail due to a prior instance of `SharedPropertyGroupManager`, but will never create a second instance:

```
Dim spmMgr As Object

Set spmMgr = CreateObject("MTxSpm.SharedPropertyGroupManager.1")
```

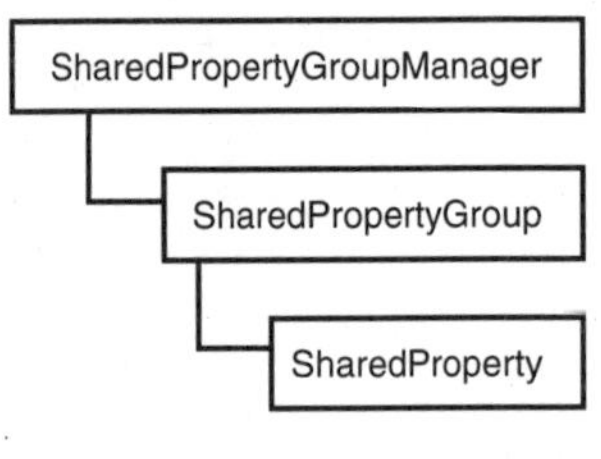

FIG. 25.7
Each process may have one instance of a `SharedPropertyGroupManager`, which contains a collection of `SharedPropertyGroups`. Each `SharedPropertyGroup` contains a collection of `SharedProperty` objects. Each `SharedProperty` contains a value (a variant).

For `SharedPropertyGroup` and `SharedProperty` objects, the create method behaves similarly, but sets a flag (out parameter) to indicate whether a new instance was created or a reference was returned for an existing instance. This flag can be used to conditionally set an initial value:

```
Dim spmGroupCounter as Object
Dim spmPropertyCounter as Object
Dim bPriorInstance as Boolean

'Create shared property group spmGroupCounter
Set spmGroupCounter = _
 spmMgr.CreatePropertyGroup("Counter", LockSetGet, Process, bPriorInstance)

' Create the counter SharedProperty.
Set spmPropertyCounter = spmGroupCounter.CreateProperty("Next", bPriorInstance)

' Set the initial value to 0 if this is a new instance
If bPriorInstance = False Then
 spmPropertyCounter.Value = 0
End If
```

Notice that the `SharedPropertyGroupManager` method `CreatePropertyGroup` takes two additional parameters: isolation mode and release mode. Setting isolation mode to `LockSetGet` ensures thread-safe concurrency for all properties in the group. By setting release mode to `Process`, `SharedPropertyGroupManager` will maintain the `SharedPropertyGroup` until the creating server process terminates.

TIP All objects sharing a property must run in the same server process with the SharedPropertyGroupManager. One way to accomplish this would be to limit use of a shared property group to objects created by the same component, or to objects created by components implemented within the same DLL. Remember that an MTS package generally equates to an MTS process. If two DLLs use the same shared property group and an administrator installs the DLLs in separate packages, the two packages couldn't share properties.

TIP SPM objects should be created only from within an MTS component, never from the base client.

NOTE The Receipt component of the sample bank application included in MTS 1.x illustrates a simple application of shared properties.

SPM provides a solution to the problem of shared variables in a multithreaded environment. This is one more way in which MTS allows you to focus on business logic by simplifying multiuser programming issues.

Distributed Security Service

MTS 1.1 uses role-based security to control application security. The security model is resource-based—each package has its own list of roles (basically groups) and users. Roles for a package are defined, renamed, and deleted by using MTX, but the role names must be hard-coded into components. An MTS component can limit access to resources or functions based on roles and can determine at runtime whether a client has access to that role.

CAUTION

For MTS objects running in-process with the base client, security is effectively disabled.

A *role* is a symbolic name for a group of users. You define and associate roles to MTS components, whereas the MTS administrator defines roles for a package and assigns users to the roles. It's important that the MTS administrator uses the same role names (spelled correctly!) as you.

See "Using MTX," **p. 684**

NOTE Roles and security information for a package can't be modified or defined while an instance of that package is running in MTS.

Security in MTS 1.1 uses only three methods from the IObjectContext interface (ObjectContext object):

- GetObjectContext returns a reference to an MTS object's object context. The object context includes the identity of the caller.

- `IsSecurityEnabled` returns `False` if the MTS object is loaded in-process with the base client.
- `IsCallerInRole` returns true if the identity of the direct caller of the object is associated to a specific role. If security isn't enabled (the MTS object is loaded in-process with the base client), `IsCallerInRole` returns `True`. If security is enabled and the identity of direct caller of the object isn't associated to a specific role, `IsCallerInRole` returns `False`.

NOTE When an MTS component runs in-process with the base client, `IsCallerInRole` always returns `True`. The `IsSecurityEnabled` method determines whether security checking is enabled. This method returns `False` when running in-process. Always call `IsSecurityEnabled` before using `IsCallerInRole`.

The Microsoft Transaction Explorer

The Microsoft Transaction Explorer (MTX) is a graphics administrative tool for creating and deploying packages, managing security, and monitoring transaction execution. As the developer, however, you'll use MTX frequently during development and unit testing. Each time an MTS component's interface changes during development, for example, the component has to be removed from any MTS packages and reinstalled.

▶ **See** Chapter 24, "Deploying Distributed Applications," **p. 667**

Using Existing Components with MTS

A COM DLL that doesn't implement any specific MTS functions can still gain substantial benefits from running in the MTS environment:

- The capability to run as an in-process server, a local server, or a remote server
- Database connection pooling through the ODBC 3.0 resource dispenser
- Improved fault isolation for out-of-process servers
- Simplified deployment through MTX

Installing an existing component to run under MTS is as easy as creating a new package and adding the component to that package. Set the `Transaction Support` property for the component to `Does Not Support Transactions`.

MTS support for legacy components can even be leveraged for non-ActiveX code. It's often quite simple to develop an ActiveX "wrapper" for a legacy application; that ActiveX component can then be added to MTS. The simple MTS programming requirements for transaction support make it possible to create a wrapper that supports transactions. For more information, see the section "Managing Transactions in MTS," earlier in this chapter.

▶ **See** "Strategies for Using Object Technology with Legacy Applications," **p. 120**

Using MTS with I-net Applications

This discussion focuses on interactions between Microsoft Internet Explorer (MSIE) and Microsoft Internet Information Server (IIS). Although a wide variety of browsers and servers exist in the market today, the MSIE/IIS combination provides the richest interaction. However, many of these interactions are proprietary extensions to WWW standards. After you commit to features available only in MSIE or IIS, there may be some loss of function or substantial expense to move to a different platform.

An I-net application may use the Hypertext Transfer Protocol (HTTP) to invoke an MTS component in two ways:

- Call an Active Server Page (ASP), which calls the MTS component using DCOM
- Call the MTS component from ActiveX components executing in the web browser using Remote Data Streams (previously known as Advanced Data Connector, or ADC), which in turn uses HTTP

Either approach works well for a thin client, with the limitation that result sets are read-only. Figure 25.8 shows the ASP scenario.

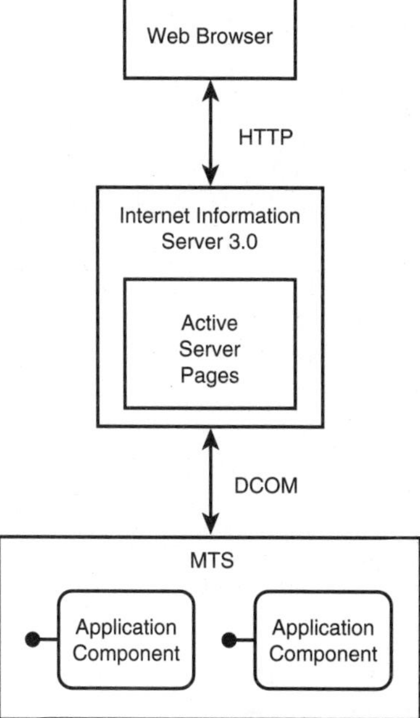

FIG. 25.8
An I-net application can use MTS components via Active Server Pages.

NOTE Microsoft VBScript embedded in a web page can't by itself access MTS components.

Using Active Server Pages

An Active Server Page can access MTC components via COM or DCOM. Although you can run the MTS components as an in-process server, any internal error in the MTS component causes MTS to terminate and may crash IIS. For reliability, it's better to run MTS components out-of-process.

By default, IIS doesn't allow out-of-process servers. To enable out-of-process components for IIS, use the Registry Editor (REGEDT32). Go to the following Registry key and set the key AllowOutOfProcCmpnts to 1:

HKEY_LOCAL_MACHINE\SYSTEM\CurrentControlSet\Services\W3SVC\ASP\Parameters

Using Browser-Side ActiveX Components

An ActiveX component executing inside a web browser can call an MTS component, provided that the component is registered on the web browser machine. Use the HTML `<OBJECT>` tag to invoke the MTS component.

NOTE The HTML script needs no special modifications to invoke an MTS component; the component just needs to be registered on the browser machine as an MTS component. Often, the same ActiveX component can be registered as a standalone (without MTS). In that case, the same script will invoke the standalone.

You can also use the `<OBJECT>` tag to load an MTS component in-process with the browser client (requires MTS installed on the web browser computer). Figure 25.9 shows an ActiveX component running in a web browser and invoking a remote MTS component.

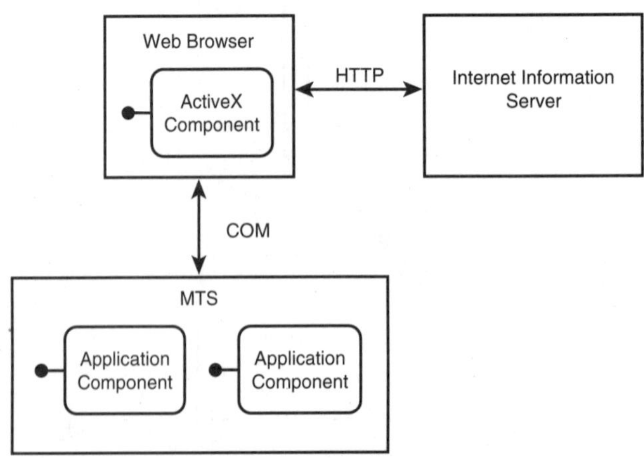

FIG. 25.9 An ActiveX component running in a browser can invoke MTS components just like any other process.

Using Remote Data Streams

Microsoft Remote Data Streams (RDS) allow an ActiveX component running in a web browser to retrieve (read-only) data sets from a Microsoft Internet Information Server via ADO. RDS supports a number of protocols:

- HTTP
- HTTP over Secure Sockets Layer (HTTPS)
- DCOM
- In-process server

NOTE RDS was previously known as the Advanced Data Connector (ADC). Microsoft changed the name to Remote Data Streams on bringing the technology into its Universal Data Access initiative. 

ON THE WEB

For more information about Remote Data Streams, visit **http://www.microsoft.com/adc**.

Unless your application uses the HTTPS protocol (Secure Sockets Layer), IIS password authorization settings must include Allow Anonymous for RDS to successfully retrieve data with the HTTP protocol. Follow these steps to modify this IIS setting (requires stop and restart for the web service):

1. Run Microsoft Internet Service Manager.
2. Double-click the web service.
3. At the bottom of the Properties dialog box, select the Allow Anonymous option for Password Authentication and click OK.
4. Stop the web service (click the black square) and then start the web service (click the black forward arrow) so that the new settings take effect.
5. Close Internet Service Manager.

Accessing MTS Components via DCOM and HTTP

Sometimes you may want to access the same MTS component on the same machine via DCOM (over a local area network) and via HTTP (remote web users). Accessing the component via DCOM simply requires adding it to a package in MTS. To make the same MTS component accessible from IIS, follow these steps:

1. Use Transaction Server Explorer to view properties for the MTS component.
2. Choose the Activation tab.
3. Select In the Creator's Process… and click OK.

Developing MTS Components with Visual Basic

One of the best features of VB is the source-level debugger. A developer can single-step through code, set breakpoints, and examine the call stack and any variable. In VB4, you could run multiple instances of the VB Integrated Development Environment (IDE), load a COM component into one session and a base client into the other, and interactively debug the two applications simultaneously.

It's not obvious how to achieve simultaneous interactive debugging for an MTS component. You would really like to debug the MTS component in the MTS environment, but the VB IDE is an EXE and won't run in the MTS runtime environment. It's not a reasonable test to comment out all MTS-specific functions. Microsoft seems to have a reasonable solution—an `ObjectContext` stub enabled with a Registry setting.

CAUTION

Use the stub `ObjectContext` only for debugging. An `ObjectContext` stub installed on a production system disables all transactioning and security for that system.

To enable the `ObjectContext` stub, log in as a member of the administrators group for the local machine and use REGEDT32 to add the following Registry key:

HKEY_LOCAL_MACHINE\SOFTWARE\Microsoft\Transaction Server\Debug\RunWithoutContext

The `ObjectContext` stub provides degenerate behavior for the most frequently used MTS functions:

- `GetObjectContext` returns a reference to the `ObjectContext` stub.
- `ObjectContext.CreateInstance` invokes `CoCreateInstance`. No information about context or caller identity is provided.
- `ObjectContext.SetComplete`, `ObjectContext.SetAbort`, `ObjectContext.EnableCommit`, and `ObjectContext.DisableCommit` all have no effect.
- `ObjectContext.IsInTransaction` and `ObjectContext.IsSecurityEnabled` return `False`.
- `IsCallerInRole` returns `True`.

NOTE Using the `ObjectContext` stub allows `ObjectContext` methods to execute. However, the debugging session does *not* run in the MTS environment.

TIP For other MTS objects, such as `ObjectControl` and `TransactionContext`, use conditional compile blocks (`#If MTS... #End If`) to disable the objects during debugging.

NOTE Another area where debug behavior will vary from MTS runtime behavior is OLE Automation Errors (`Error.Raise vbObjectError + SomeConstant`). MTS 1.x doesn't support OLE Automation exceptions. MTS components built with Visual Basic (VB) can't use the `Error` object to notify callers of error conditions.

CAUTION

Single-threaded, stateful components are prone to deadlocks. To eliminate this problem, use stateless objects and call `SetComplete` before returning from any method.

CAUTION

VB-developed server components that use RDO may be subject to deadlock. To avoid deadlock, always explicitly close and deallocate `rdoConnection` and `rdoResultset` objects. If an open `rdoResultset` is allowed to go out of scope, the ODBC calls to close and deallocate the object might not occur before the ODBC resource dispenser reuses the connection. Deadlock may follow.

Each time you recompile an OLE DLL project in VB4, VB rewrites all Registry entries for interfaces (classes) included in that DLL. Depending on project settings, VB may generate new GUIDs for the components in that DLL. The end result is that you might have to reinstall components with MTX after each compile.

One alternative is to choose Tools, Refresh All Components from the MTX menu. Another option is the MtxServer RegRefresh VB add-in optionally included with the developer install of MTS. This add-in automates the MTX refresh after each compile.

The standard developer install for MTS doesn't install the VB add-in. Select the VB Addin checkbox in the Select Components dialog box during the MTS install.

CAUTION

Any recompile that changes the CLSID and IID for a component, such as changing the `ProgID` (*`Project.Classname`*), requires a complete reinstall of all components (including associated roles) for the project into MTX. If the application is deployed, you have to re-export the packages and reinstall all clients.

In VB4, use the Project, Options, Compatible OLE Server setting to ensure that each recompile preserves CLSID and IID for each class. Preserving the IID allows MTX to preserve associated roles and client installations.

When instantiating MTS objects from VB, always use the `GetObject` and `CreateObject` functions, even if the class instantiated is part of the current project. You can use the `New` keyword for classes not part of the current project. When you want a new MTS object to enlist in an existing transaction, use `CreateInstance` with the `ObjectContext` from an object already enlisted in the transaction.

Developing MTS Components with Visual C++

This section identifies tricks and pitfalls unique to developing MTS components with Visual C++ 5.0.

NOTE To run a Visual C++ (VC++) MTS component in-process, you must call

- `CoInitialize(NULL)` before requesting services from MTS or creating an MTS object.
- `CoInitializeSecurity` to initialize process-specific security. MTS security is disabled when loading an MTS object in-process.
- `CoUninitialize` only after you finish using MTS or MTS objects, preferably just before terminating your application. You can't call `CoInitialize` again and invoke more MTS services. After `CoUninitialize` is called, your application is no longer executing in the MTS runtime environment.

MTS supports the COM transparent remote debugging infrastructure. A debugging session is automatically started on the server process if necessary. Similarly, single-stepping past the return address of code in a server object automatically stops just past the corresponding call site in the client's process.

Visual C++ 5.0 and MTS both support transparent remote debugging via OLE RPC. When enabled, transparent remote debugging allows a step-into server process code even if the server is on a different computer. To enable OLE RPC debugging in the Visual Studio IDE, choose Tools, Options, Debug, OLE RPC Debugging.

If you prefer, you can enable debugging in the Visual Studio IDE for out-of-process component DLLs:

1. Shut down server processes with MTX by right-clicking My Computer and then selecting Shutdown Server Process from the context menu.
2. Find the GUID for the MTS package in which your component is installed. You can find this information in MTX on the package's General property sheet page. To copy this text string, select the string and press Ctrl+C.
3. In the Visual Studio IDE, choose Project, Settings, Debug, General. Set the program arguments to /p:{YourPackageGUIDHere}, and set the full path to MTX.Exe (typically C:\MTX\MTX.EXE).

To enable debugging for in-process components, go to the Visual Studio IDE and enter the DLL name under Project, Settings, Debug, Additional DLLs.

NOTE MTS 1.x doesn't support OLE Automation exceptions. Visual C++ components that implement `ISupportErrorInfo` will appear not to implement this interface, even if they do. Microsoft plans to correct this omission in a future release.

NOTE Don't build MTS components as MFC extension DLLs. These applications can be loaded only by other MFC applications. Because an MTS component is a COM component, it should be loadable into any process, regardless of the type of application that started the process.

When instantiating MTS objects from Visual C++, always use `CoCreateInstance`, even if the class instantiated is part of the current project. You can use the `New` keyword for classes not part of the current project. When you want a new MTS object to enlist in an existing transaction, use `CreateInstance` with the `ObjectContext` from an object already enlisted in the transaction. To control the transaction from the base client (not necessarily a good idea), use the `ITransactionContext` interface to create a `TransactionContext` object, and then use `CreateInstance` with the `ObjectContext` for the `TransactionContext` (`MyObj = GetTransactionContextEx().GetObjectContext.CreateInstance(IID)`).

NOTE The context object isn't available during calls to a constructor or destructor. For access to the context object during activation or deactivation, implement `IObjectControl`.

From Here...

This chapter gives you a developer's tour of Microsoft Transaction Server. After looking at the programming model for managing transactions, you looked at other services the system provides, including security, database connection pooling, the Shared Property Manager, and just-in-time object activation. After seeing how I-net applications can interact with MTS, you reviewed some programming strategies and pitfalls.

- For a discussion of COM and DCOM, see Chapter 4, "Using Microsoft's Object Technologies."
- For details on using Visual Studio to build software components, see Chapter 5, "Creating ActiveX Components with Visual Basic"; Chapter 6, "Creating Components with Visual C++"; and Chapter 7, "Creating Components with Visual J++."
- Chapter 24, "Deploying Distributed Applications," looks at the graphics administrative tool included with MTS, reviewing component deployment, transaction resolution, and security issues.

PART V

Team Development with Visual Studio

CHAPTER 26

Using Visual SourceSafe

Why use Visual SourceSafe?

Learn what Visual SourceSafe is about and why and when to use it.

Administering Visual SourceSafe

Learn how to install Visual SourceSafe and use the Visual SourceSafe administration program to maintain and configure the installation.

Using SourceSafe to manage code

Learn how to use Visual SourceSafe Explorer to manage your project source code with various source control and version tracking tools.

Using SourceSafe to manage web content

Learn how to use source control and version tracking tools in Visual SourceSafe to help manage and develop a large-scale web site just like any other software development project. You will also learn how to use several new web-specific features available in Visual SourceSafe version 5.

Many large software development projects involve teamwork and last over an extended period of time. Developers involved might come and go through the course of a project, and the person who coded a particular section of the program might not even be around later on. Additionally, many large projects are developed on a phased basis, and various versions of the software are released over time. One of the biggest challenges in managing a development project with such complexity and coordinating large teams of developers working together is keeping track of the changes made to the source code. The larger the project is, the more difficult the task. The following are some typical problems a development team often has to deal with:

- They cannot tell who worked on a module or whether certain changes have been made unless they manually keep a history log. This can be extremely time-consuming and thus impractical.
- Files are sometimes accidentally deleted.
- Two developers working on the same file might inadvertently overwrite each other's work, and it is difficult to negotiate turnover of control.

Microsoft Visual SourceSafe provides just the right tools for solving these problems. Its source control mechanism offers the advantages of easy and efficient team coordination and version tracking without adding a new burden to developers, and it will be useful to any team development environment. This chapter describes the fundamentals of using Visual SourceSafe 5.0.

Introduction to Visual SourceSafe

Visual SourceSafe is a project-oriented version control system. It provides two primary benefits to your software development process:

- Source control
- Version tracking

When multiple developers are working on one project, it is important to have a source control mechanism. It helps ensure that only one developer is working on a particular piece of source code at any given time so that one developer does not overwrite another developer's work. Alternatively, you can have simultaneous editing and let Visual SourceSafe automatically merge the changes made by different developers and keep the developers in sync with each other's changes.

With versioning capability, anyone can re-create an earlier version of the software, as needed. This becomes necessary when you need to re-create an old build or to create a new branch of the application.

In addition to the standard benefits of using Visual SourceSafe for source control and version tracking in software development for any size team, Visual SourceSafe offers some new web features for managing web site development projects.

You can work with Visual SourceSafe in one of the following three ways:

- Visual SourceSafe Explorer—the graphical user interface in Windows 95 or Windows NT.
- The command-line interface in Windows 95 or Windows NT. You can use the Visual SourceSafe command line to run batch files and macros. In addition, you can use the command line to perform all Visual SourceSafe Explorer commands.
- Direct integration with Microsoft Visual Test, Microsoft Access, and Microsoft Visual FoxPro, and inside the Visual Basic and Visual C++ integrated development environments.

This chapter focuses only on the graphical user interface.

NOTE For Visual Basic, Visual C++, Access, Visual J++, FrontPage, Visual InterDev, and Visual FoxPro, SourceSafe works directly integrated into the environment. You can check files in and out of Visual SourceSafe by using menus inside the IDE. For more information, see the documentation and online Help for those products.

▶ For detailed information about using Visual SourceSafe with Visual InterDev, **see** "Managing Visual InterDev Projects," **p. 443**

Why Use Visual SourceSafe?

Compared to older, UNIX-based version control systems, Visual SourceSafe has two unique features. First, its architecture is project-oriented rather than file-oriented. It keeps track of not only the changes made to each and every file but also the relationships among files. The key concept in understanding how to work with Visual SourceSafe is the idea of a project. A *project* is a collection of interrelated files that you store in Visual SourceSafe. You can add, delete, edit, and share files within and among projects. Second, its Windows 95 Explorer–like interface makes it easy to use. So Visual SourceSafe actually helps the developers spend less time doing source code "bookkeeping" and more time programming.

Visual SourceSafe uses the "reverse delta" technique to keep track of project changes. That is, it stores only the latest and greatest version of each source file in the project as one complete version plus all the changes required to go back to the previous versions. This ensures that storing old versions takes only a minimum of disk space and you can access the current version immediately. Because the changes are not stored as files, there is no way to delete them, thus making Visual SourceSafe more reliable.

SourceSafe stores its contents like a database in its DATA directory, but only SourceSafe has access. Two files are created for each file and each project in SourceSafe, and they are stored in a subdirectory of the DATA directory. One of the two files is called the "Log" file. It does not have an extension. This is where SourceSafe information and differences between one version of the file and the next are stored. The other file is called the "Data" or "Tip" file. It has an extension of either .A or .B, and it stores the most recent version of the file or the project.

A Visual SourceSafe Network

A Visual SourceSafe network typically consists of a centralized Visual SourceSafe database on a server and several client workstations. The shared Visual SourceSafe database is where you store and track your code. To actually work on a file within Visual SourceSafe, you must obtain a copy of the file from Visual SourceSafe and place it in a working folder of your own. The Visual SourceSafe database is organized into a project tree with various projects and subprojects under a root project ($/). Visual SourceSafe associates every project with a working folder. You cannot choose a different working folder for each file in a project. However, each individual user can, and should, have a separate working folder for each project. This is a user-by-user setting.

Administering Visual SourceSafe

As the administrator of a Visual SourceSafe installation, you are responsible for setting up, configuring, and maintaining the installation. This section describes how to install Visual SourceSafe and use the Visual SourceSafe administration program for basic configuration and maintenance.

Setting Up and Installing Visual SourceSafe

The program SETUP.EXE is provided with the Visual Studio 97 CD-ROM to install Visual SourceSafe 5.0. During the installation, the Setup program checks your system and asks what type of installation you want to have. The typical way of setting up Visual SourceSafe is to have a server installation on a network drive and a client installation on each workstation. Although the server setup is all that is actually required, having only a server setup can generate large volumes of network traffic. Figure 26.1 shows the Setup program installation choice screen.

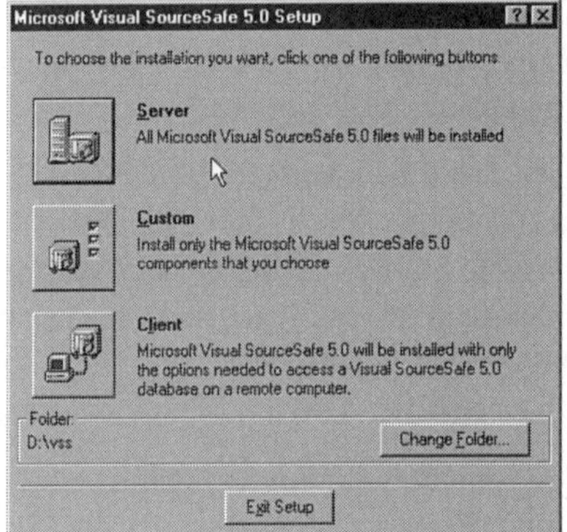

FIG. 26.1
Three options are available from the Visual SourceSafe installation choice screen: Server, Custom, or Client setup.

When you install Visual SourceSafe, you need two components—the Visual SourceSafe Explorer interface and the Visual SourceSafe database, which holds your project files and version information. Both are needed to use Visual SourceSafe. The following are the three installation options:

- Server—The Server option is used by an administrator to install Visual SourceSafe to a server computer that is accessible to all users. The folder name on the same screen can be changed to whatever folder is accessible to all Visual SourceSafe users on the network. If an older version of Visual SourceSafe exists on the server, it will be upgraded to the new version automatically. However, be sure to back up the existing SourceSafe database before upgrading.
- Custom—This option allows you to omit parts of the Server installation and install only the parts you need from the following:
    - Create SourceSafe Database
    - Client Programs (Intel 32-bit)
    - Administrative Programs (Intel 32-bit)

- Enable SourceSafe Integration
- Help files
- Conversion utilities
- Network Client Setup
- Books Online

NOTE The Custom option is the only way to install Visual SourceSafe database on your hard drive and then have it accessible for integration with Visual Basic and Visual C++. Also, you can use this option to add administrative programs such as Visual SourceSafe Administrator to a client installation.

- Client—A Visual SourceSafe user—not an administrator—usually does client installation. This setup choice installs, on the hard disk of a client computer, only the files necessary to run Visual SourceSafe. The Visual SourceSafe database or support files are not installed. The client installation must follow a server installation and cannot be used by itself. You should perform a client installation in the following situations:
  - You have heavy traffic on your network.
  - You need to integrate Visual SourceSafe with Microsoft Access, Visual Basic, Visual C++, Visual FoxPro, or Visual Test.

During a server installation, the setup program puts a copy of the NETSETUP program in the folder in which Visual SourceSafe is installed on the server. You can double-click NETSETUP to perform a network client installation instead of a client setup from disk.

CAUTION

Visual SourceSafe installation places all the Visual SourceSafe files and several subdirectories (for example, WIN32, USERS, and DATA) under the main Visual SourceSafe directory, as in a database. Only the Visual SourceSafe program can create, modify, and delete files in those directories. Users should never manually change anything in those directories. All file storage is in proprietary Visual SourceSafe formats, and any change could cause unpredictable results or loss of data.

Running Visual SourceSafe Administrator

Visual SourceSafe Administrator is the administration program provided for configuring and maintaining the Visual SourceSafe installation.

To start Visual SourceSafe Administrator,

1. Click the Start button.
2. Point to Programs.
3. Click the Visual SourceSafe 5.0 Admin.

The Visual SourceSafe Administrator main window displays as shown in Figure 26.2.

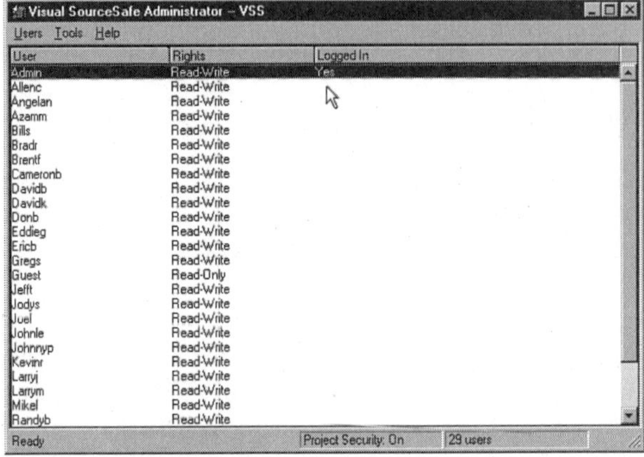

FIG. 26.2
The Visual SourceSafe Administrator program allows the administrator to configure and maintain the Visual SourceSafe installation.

In a new installation, no password is set for the administrator. Because Visual SourceSafe security is controlled from inside Visual SourceSafe Administrator and any user who can access that program can basically do anything within Visual SourceSafe, one of the first tasks of the administrator should be to assign a password to the Admin user. You can do this by using the Change Password command on the Users menu as shown in the section "Maintaining the User List" later in this chapter.

> **CAUTION**
>
> Write the password down in a safe place! If you forget the administrator's password, contact Microsoft Technical Support Services for help. You cannot reassign a new password by running Visual SourceSafe Administrator without knowing the old one.

Maintaining the User List

As a Visual SourceSafe administrator, you are responsible for maintaining the list of Visual SourceSafe users. You can use the Users menu in the Visual SourceSafe Administrator window to add, edit, or delete users and to change a user's password.

To add users,

1. Select Users, Add Users from the menu.

   Visual SourceSafe Administrator displays the Add User dialog box, as shown in Figure 26.3.

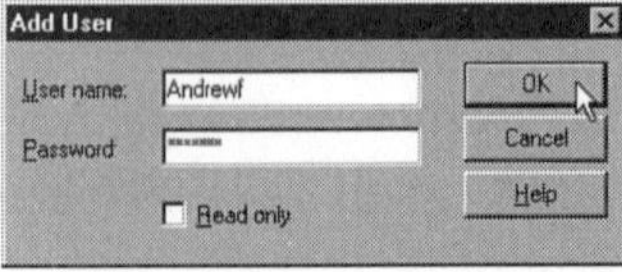

FIG. 26.3
To add a user to the database, use the Visual SourceSafe Administrator Add User dialog box.

2. Type a name in the User Name box and a password in the Password box.

   Usernames can be up to 31 characters long, cannot begin or end with a space, and cannot include any of the special characters such as $, @, *, !, ?, ^, =.

   Passwords can be up to 15 characters long and can contain any characters. Usually, they are initially set to something simple, such as the username, and the user is instructed to create a new password from within Visual SourceSafe.

3. To give the new user read-only rights, check the Read Only box. If this box is unchecked, the new user has read-write rights by default.
4. Click OK.

When you add a new user, Visual SourceSafe automatically creates an SS.INI file for that user based on the default SS.INI template in the \VSS\USERS\ADMIN folder. You can modify this template file to create a different default SS.INI file for each new user. For information on how to set security by user and by project, see the section "Setting Up Rights for Project Security," later in this chapter.

NOTE The Visual SourceSafe database is the central database in which all master copies, history, project structures, and user information are stored. A project is always contained within one database; multiple projects can be stored in one database, and multiple Visual SourceSafe databases can exist to store multiple projects. Each database is associated with a SRCSAFE.INI file. For security reasons, Visual SourceSafe's list of users and passwords is stored with a particular Visual SourceSafe database. This can be an advantage if security is the reason you want to install separate SourceSafe databases; however, to add a user to multiple Visual SourceSafe databases, you must add the user to each individual database.

To change a user's password,

1. Select a user from the Visual SourceSafe Administrator user list.
2. Choose Users, Change Password from the menu.

   Visual SourceSafe Administrator displays the Change Password dialog box, as shown in Figure 26.4.

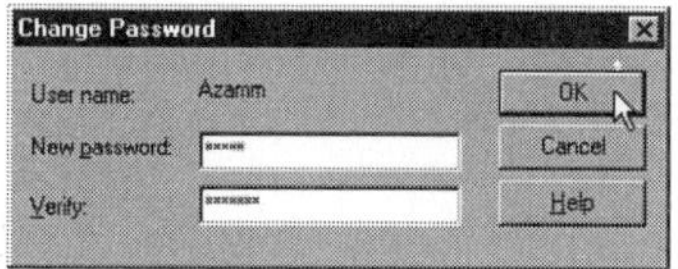

FIG. 26.4 The Visual SourceSafe Administrator Change Password dialog box is used when a user forgets his Visual SourceSafe password.

3. In the New Password box, type a new password. (You do not need to know a user's old password to assign a new one, and Visual SourceSafe passwords are not case sensitive.)
4. In the Verify box, type the new password again to verify it.
5. Click OK.

   Visual SourceSafe Administrator changes the password.

NOTE If a user forgets his or her Visual SourceSafe password, the administrator can use this dialog box to assign a new password, but cannot recover the old one. Visual SourceSafe does not prohibit you from reassigning a previously used password. Keep in mind that the Visual SourceSafe password is not meant to replace or augment your operating system or network operating system password.

As the administrator, you have a special password that is used to run Visual SourceSafe Administrator.

NOTE As the administrator, you are responsible for controlling the location of the Visual SourceSafe database, the user list, and the access rights of each user, and for performing setup and backup duties on the database. So be careful with your password.

To change the Admin user's password,

1. Select the Admin user from the Visual SourceSafe Administrator user list.
2. Choose Users, Change Password from the menu.

   Visual SourceSafe Administrator displays the Change Password dialog box, as shown in Figure 26.5. The administrator's username is always Admin.

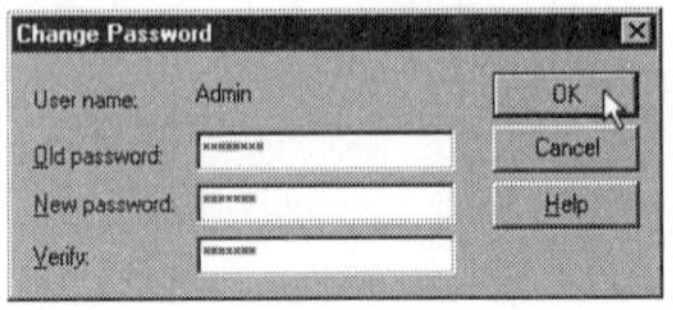

FIG. 26.5 You can change your password in the Visual SourceSafe Administrator Change Password dialog box.

3. In the Old Password box, type the old password.

   You must know the old password in order to change it.
4. In the New Password box, type a new password.
5. In the Verify box, type the new password again to verify it.
6. Click OK.

Visual SourceSafe Administrator changes the Administrator password.

To delete users,

1. Select the user(s) to be deleted from the Visual SourceSafe Administrator user list.
2. Choose Users, Delete Users from the menu.

   Visual SourceSafe Administrator displays the warning message "Are you sure you want to delete?" (see Figure 26.6).

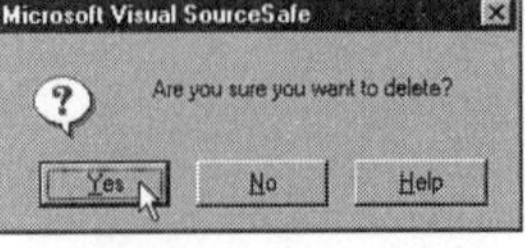

FIG. 26.6 The Administrator Delete Users dialog box enables you to delete users.

3. Click OK.

   Visual SourceSafe deletes the selected user(s).

If the deleted user has files checked out, a warning is not generated. To unlock those files, run Visual SourceSafe as the Admin user and use the Undo Check Out command.

To edit users,

1. Select the username to be edited from the Visual SourceSafe Administrator user list.
2. Choose Users, Edit User from the menu.

   Visual SourceSafe Administrator displays the Edit User dialog box, as shown in Figure 26.7. A shortcut for displaying the Edit User dialog box is to select the username in the Visual SourceSafe Administrator user list and then press Enter.

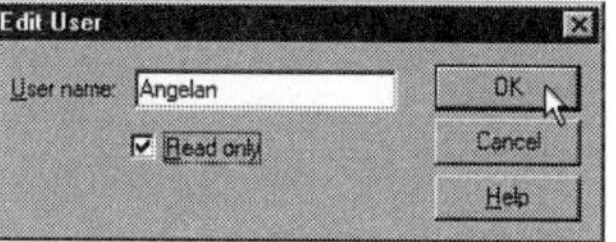

FIG. 26.7
The Visual SourceSafe Administrator Edit User dialog box is used to change the username and access rights of the selected user.

3. Check/Uncheck the Read Only box to give the user Read-Only or Read-Write rights. You can also change the user login name by typing a new one.
4. Click OK.

   Visual SourceSafe changes the selected user's rights and/or login name.

Setting Up Rights for Project Security

Security in Visual SourceSafe is based on user access rights. Default security in a Visual SourceSafe installation offers only two levels of access rights for the new users:

- Read-only rights.

  Users can see all files in all projects in the Visual SourceSafe database, but cannot change anything.

- Read-write rights.

  Users can see and change any file in any project in the Visual SourceSafe database.

If these two default levels of access rights are adequate for your installation, you do not need to go further. However, some Visual SourceSafe installations require more levels of security control. For these installations, you can enable project security and customize it to allow only specific users to have access to certain projects and certain commands. Four levels of access rights are available in Visual SourceSafe as described in Table 26.1.

Table 26.1 User Access Rights in Visual SourceSafe

Rights	Description
Read (R)	Read-only access. Users can view files by using commands such as View and Get.
Check Out (C)	Read-only plus Check in/out access. Users can modify files by using commands such as Check In, Check Out, and Undo Check Out.
Add (A)	Read-only plus Check in/out plus Add access. Users can add files to project and modify the contents of a project using the Add, Delete, and Rename commands.
Destroy (D)	Read-only plus Check in/out plus Add plus Destroy access. Users can roll back, purge, or destroy project contents.

To enable project security,

1. Select Tools, Options from the menu in the Visual SourceSafe Administrator window.

   Visual SourceSafe Administrator displays the Visual SourceSafe Options dialog box.
2. Click the Project Security tab.

   Visual SourceSafe Administrator displays the Project Security tab, as shown in Figure 26.8.

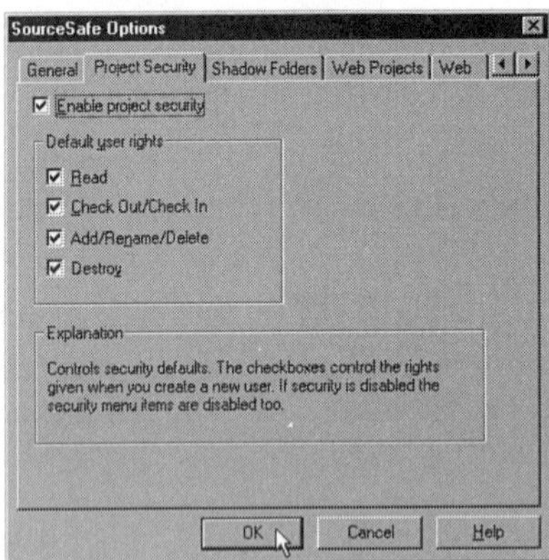

FIG. 26.8 To enable project security, use the Project Security tab in Visual SourceSafe Administrator.

3. Click the Enable Project Security checkbox to enable project security.
4. Under Default User Rights, clear the checkboxes next to the access rights you do not want to grant to the new users.
5. Click OK.

When you activate project security, you enable the security-related commands on the Tools menu: Rights by Project, Rights Assignments for User, and Copy User Rights. You can then assign rights in one of these three ways.

NOTE When you add a new user and set that user's rights for a particular project, you create an assignment in the Visual SourceSafe database. Any assignment will automatically propagate down the project list until another assignment is reached. When you first add a user, he is given rights in the root project based on the default rights that you have established on the Project Security tab. So a user's rights in the root project ($/) form a set of default rights for that user. These default rights apply to all projects in which you do not explicitly set assignments.

- Rights by Project—Shows all the users who have rights in each project and the effects of rights propagation. You can add and delete users' rights from any project and even add and delete users from the project.
- Assignments for User—Shows all the projects a user has explicit assignments in, and what rights she has in each. You can add and delete new assignments. However, the effect of propagation down the project list is not shown in this view.
- Copy User Rights—Acts as a template and copies one user's access rights to another user. After you copy rights, the two users have identical access rights in every project. You can, however, then individually change their access rights in specific projects.

To assign access rights by user,

1. In the Visual SourceSafe Administrator user list, click a user.
2. Select Tools, Rights Assignments for User from the menu.

   Visual SourceSafe Administrator displays the Assignments for User dialog box, as shown in Figure 26.9. This dialog box shows all the projects the selected user has explicit assignments in, and what rights he has in each. The effect of propagation down the project list is, however, not shown in this view.

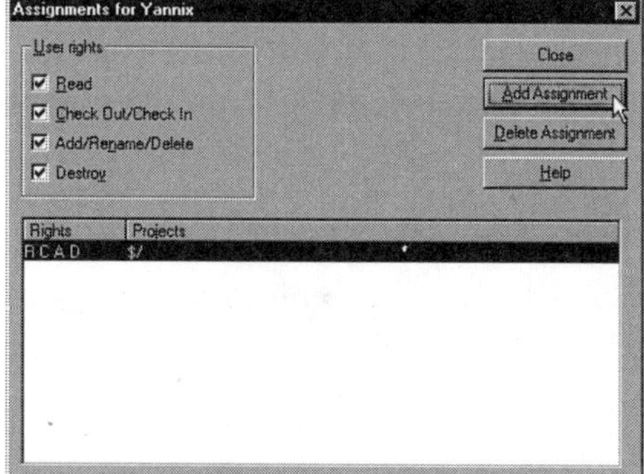

FIG. 26.9 To assign access rights by user, use the Assignments for User dialog box in Visual SourceSafe Administrator.

3. Under Projects, click a project.
4. Click the checkboxes for the access rights you want to assign to the user.
5. Click Add Assignments to display a list of projects to add the users to, or click Delete Assignments to delete rights for the user in the selected project.
6. Click Close.

To assign access rights by project,

1. Select Tools, Rights by Project from the menu.

   Visual SourceSafe Administrator displays the Project Rights dialog box, as shown in Figure 26.10.

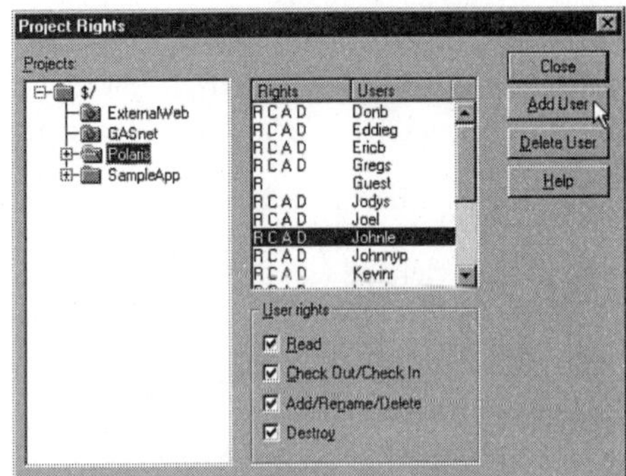

FIG. 26.10
To assign access rights by project, use the Project Rights dialog box in Visual SourceSafe Administrator.

2. Under Projects, click a project.
3. Under Users, click a user.

   Visual SourceSafe Administrator displays the current rights assigned to the selected users in the selected project.
4. Add or delete rights by clicking the appropriate User Rights checkboxes.
5. Click Add User to add a user to the currently selected project. Visual SourceSafe Administrator displays the Add Users for Project dialog box, which contains a list of users who currently do not have rights in the selected project. Click the checkbox next to each right you want to assign the user. Then click OK.

   Or click Delete User to delete a user's access to the selected project.
6. Click Close.

To copy one user's access rights to another user,

1. In the Visual SourceSafe Administrator user list, select the user to which you want to copy rights assignments.
2. Choose Tools, Copy User Rights from the menu.

   Visual SourceSafe Administrator displays the Copy Rights Assignments dialog box, shown in Figure 26.11.
3. Select the user you want to copy rights assignments from.
4. Click Copy.

After you copy rights, the two users have identical access rights in every project. If you then change one user's access rights in a specific project, these changes are not duplicated for the other user, unless you use the Copy Rights Assignments command to copy user rights again.

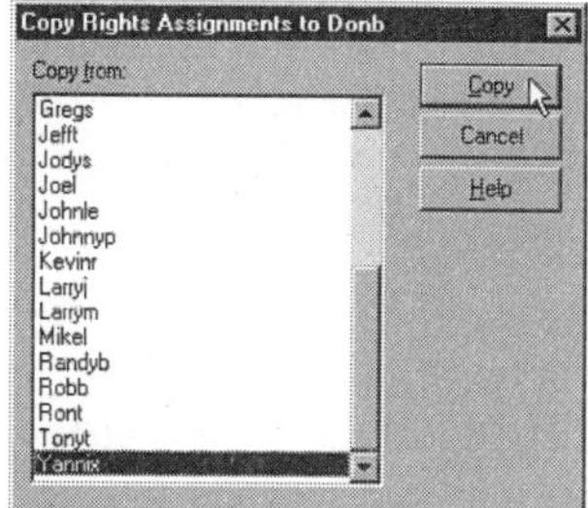

FIG. 26.11
You can use the Copy Rights Assignments dialog box in Visual SourceSafe Administrator to copy one user's access rights to another user.

Using SourceSafe to Manage Code

Your source code is a precious resource, and you need to manage this resource properly and effectively. If you are working on a team-based project or a complex system for a customer, it is important to have a source control and version tracking mechanism to help you achieve these goals. Visual SourceSafe provides you with the right tools.

Using Visual SourceSafe Explorer

Many of the actions in Visual SourceSafe take place in the Visual SourceSafe Explorer. Its graphical user interface is modeled after the Windows 95 Explorer for ease of use and logical representation of your project files.

To start Visual SourceSafe,

1. Click the Start button.
2. Point to Programs.
3. Click Visual SourceSafe 5.0.

   The Visual SourceSafe Explorer window displays, as shown in Figure 26.12. By default, the window is made up of two panes—the left project pane and the right file pane—as well as the toolbar, status bar, menus, and so on.

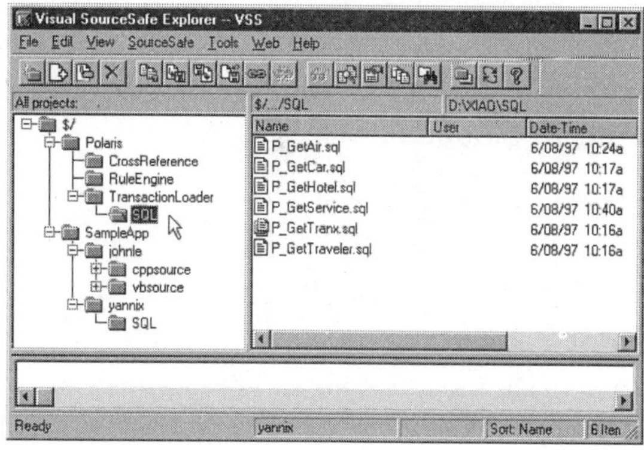

FIG. 26.12
The Visual SourceSafe Explorer window is the main user interface of the Visual SourceSafe program.

The left side of the Visual SourceSafe Explorer window shows the project tree with a root project ($/) at the top of the tree. It lists all the projects and subprojects currently under version control and gives a hierarchical display of them represented as folders. Of course, the tree list is expandable and collapsible. A plus sign (+) or a minus (-) sign next to a project indicates the existence of subprojects.

When you select a project on the list, the right side of the Visual SourceSafe Explorer window displays all the files contained in that project and the status information of those files. The Name column displays the names of all files in the project and a file icon next to each file, which provides a visual clue as to whether it is shared by two or more projects or whether it is checked out, and so on. The User column shows the name of the user if the file is checked out. The Date-Time column displays the date/time of the last modification if it is checked in or the date/time when the file was checked out. For checked-out files, the Check Out Folder column gives the folder to which the file was checked out. The current project and working folder fields are shown at the top. Below the project list and file list is the results window for some operations.

Organizing Your Files into Visual SourceSafe Projects

Visual SourceSafe is not only for source code but also for any other files (for example, DLLs, graphics, documentation, executables) you want to keep track of. To use Visual SourceSafe for source control and version tracking, you should store all your files in Visual SourceSafe and organize them into Visual SourceSafe projects.

Visual SourceSafe is project-oriented. Before you can do anything with files, you must have a project in which to place the files. Therefore, when you begin working with Visual SourceSafe, the first thing to do is to create one or more projects and subprojects. For example, you are developing a system called Polaris, and various developers on your team are working on three subsystems: CrossReference, RuleEngine, and TransactionLoader. Under each subdirectory, you might also have several different groups of files. Under TransactionLoader, for instance, you might have two other subdirectories: SQL and Documentation. When you are setting up your projects, it is always a good idea to mirror this directory structure in a Visual SourceSafe project tree. In Visual SourceSafe, you would create a project called $/Polaris. Under it, you would create three subprojects: CrossReference, RuleEngine, and TransactionLoader. Under $/Polaris/TransactionLoader, you would create two subprojects: SQL and Documentation.

To create a new project in Visual SourceSafe,

1. Select the project under which the new project will be created.
2. Choose File, Create Project from the menu in Visual SourceSafe.

   Visual SourceSafe displays the Create Project dialog box, shown in Figure 26.13.
3. Type a name for the new project.
4. Type a comment and describe why you are creating this project.
5. Click OK.

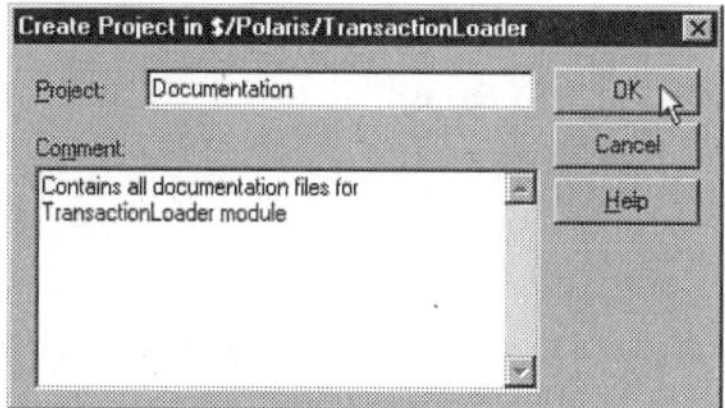

FIG. 26.13
The Create Project dialog box in Visual SourceSafe enables you to define projects.

After you create the project tree, you can add your files to the appropriate project or subproject by using the Add Files command.

To add files to a Visual SourceSafe project,

1. Select the project to which the files will be added.
2. Choose File, Add Files from the menu in Visual SourceSafe Explorer.

   Visual SourceSafe displays the Add File dialog box, shown in Figure 26.14.

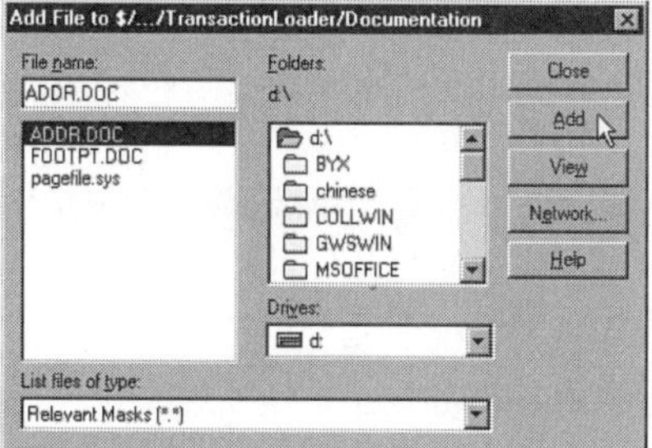

FIG. 26.14
You can add files to your project in the Add File dialog box.

3. Select the files to be added to the project. You can specify a file on any drive and folder, and that file is copied into the current Visual SourceSafe project. You must have the Add access right to use this command.
4. Click Add.

   Visual SourceSafe pops up another Add File dialog box for the comment. After you click OK, the files you added no longer appear in the File Name box because they are already part of a Visual SourceSafe project.
5. Click Close.

Don't keep executable files in Visual SourceSafe projects unless they take a long time to build. Do not take up space in Visual SourceSafe when you can compile and link to build an executable on demand.

Visual SourceSafe associates every project with a working folder. To actually work on a file within a Visual SourceSafe project, you must obtain a copy of the file from Visual SourceSafe and place it in a working folder of your own for that project. Your working folder can be a directory on your hard disk or on a network drive, and it can be an existing folder or a new folder that Visual SourceSafe creates for you. When you set a working folder for a project, you make an assignment for the entire project list, including all subprojects under that project. You can, however, explicitly set a working folder for any subproject. A working folder is set per user, per project.

To set a working folder for a Visual SourceSafe project,

1. Select the project from the project tree.
2. Choose File, Set Working Folder from the menu in the Visual SourceSafe Explorer window.

   Visual SourceSafe displays the Set Working Folder dialog box, shown in Figure 26.15.

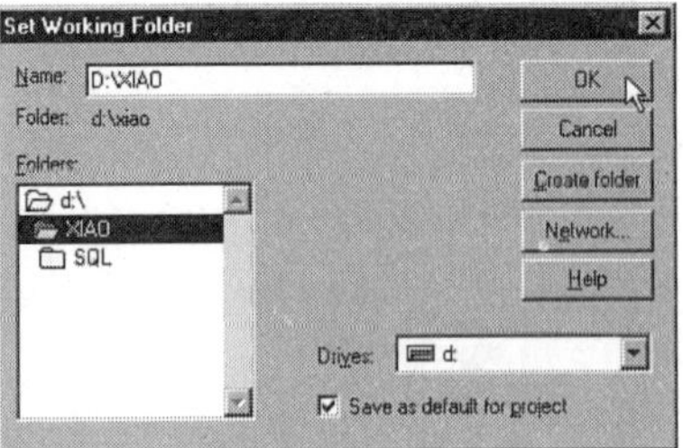

FIG. 26.15 You must designate a working folder before you can start working on any files in a Visual SourceSafe project.

3. Click the Drives arrow and click a drive. In the Folders box, double-click an existing folder.

   If you want to create a new folder, type the new folder name in the Name box and click Create Folder.
4. Click OK.

Visual SourceSafe Explorer displays your working folder path above the file list.

NOTE You must specify a working folder to perform any action that takes a file out of Visual SourceSafe, including the Check Out, Get Latest Version, and Merge commands. When you attempt to use any of these commands without a working folder, Visual SourceSafe displays a message asking if you would like to set a working folder. Click OK to set a working folder. Visual SourceSafe displays the Set Working Folder dialog box.

Basic Operations in Visual SourceSafe

As a developer on a project under source control, you will use the following four basic commands on a daily basis. They are available from the SourceSafe menu in the Visual SourceSafe Explorer window, as seen in Figure 26.16.

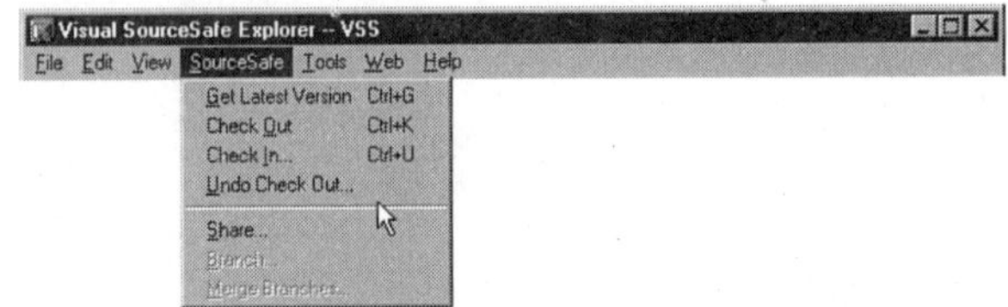

FIG. 26.16 Four basic operations in Visual SourceSafe are Get Latest Version, Check Out, Check In, and Undo Check Out.

- Get Latest Version—This command enables you to copy one or more files into your working folder as read-only so you can compile or view them.
- Check Out—This command enables you to copy one or more files into your working folder as writable so you can edit them.
- Check In—This command copies one or more files you checked out back to Visual SourceSafe with all the changes you made.
- Undo Check Out—This command enables you to revert back to the state of the file before you checked it out instead of using Check In.

To get the most recent version of a file,

1. In Visual SourceSafe Explorer, select the file(s) in the file list.
2. Choose SourceSafe, Get Latest Version from the menu.

   Visual SourceSafe copies the file(s) from the current project into your working folder for read-only access.

To check out a file,

1. In Visual SourceSafe Explorer, select the file(s) in the file list.
2. Choose SourceSafe, Check Out from the menu.

   The Check Out command creates a writable copy of the file from the project in your working folder.

CAUTION

Never use the `Get` command to fetch files on which you plan to make changes. First of all, the files on your local computer will be read-only, so you will have to change their properties, and then you will not be able to check them back in when you are finished (because Visual SourceSafe doesn't know you were planning to change them—they are not checked out to you).

To check in one or more files to Visual SourceSafe project,

1. In Visual SourceSafe Explorer, select the file(s) in the file list.
2. Choose SourceSafe, Check In from the menu.

   Visual SourceSafe displays the Check In dialog box, shown in Figure 26.17.

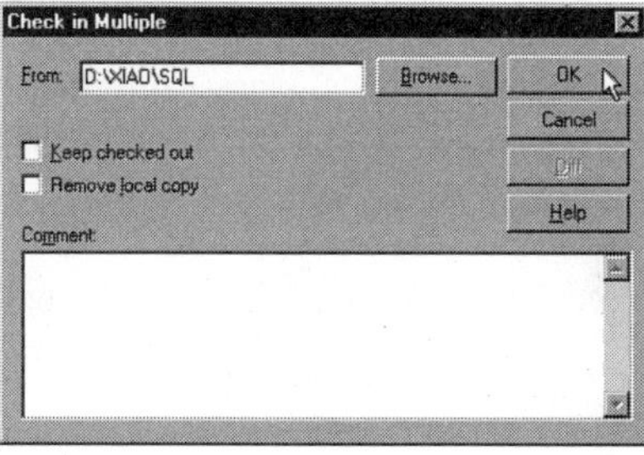

FIG. 26.17 The Check In dialog box is used to copy your changes into the Visual SourceSafe database and create a new version of the file.

3. Type a comment in the Comment box.
4. Other options.

   If you want to continue working on the file(s) after you check in your changes, click Keep checked out. If you want to remove the copy of the file(s) in your working folder after the check-in is complete, click Remove Local Copy. By default, Visual SourceSafe leaves a read-only copy of the file in your working folder when you check in a file. If you want to see the differences between the version of the file you are checking in and the version you checked out, click Diff. This option is only for checking in a single file.
5. Click OK.

In any multiuser project, no file should be checked out for longer than it takes to make and test the changes to the file. If a file is kept checked out for several days by one programmer, other programmers might not receive the benefit of changes that have been made to it.

Sharing Codes Between Projects

Sharing is a feature that enables the user to access the same file from multiple projects. This is useful for users who have several different projects that share common components. Changes made to the component in one project will be reflected in all other projects sharing this component. This feature saves time and resources by avoiding duplication of effort and storage.

To share the current version of a file with another project using a drag-and-drop operation,

1. In Visual SourceSafe Explorer, click the project containing the file or files you want to share with another project.
2. Click the file or files you want to share.
3. Drag the file from its location in the file list to a different project in the project list.

   Visual SourceSafe performs the share operation with no confirmation message. Visual SourceSafe does not allow you to share a file with a project that already contains that file.

Alternatively, you can use the Share command:

1. In Visual SourceSafe Explorer, click the project you want to share files into.
2. Choose SourceSafe, Share from the menu.

   Visual SourceSafe displays the Share dialog box, shown in Figure 26.18.

NOTE Inside the Visual SourceSafe database, there is only one copy, the master copy, of the shared file; each project to which the file belongs simply has a pointer to it. When you change the file in any one project, Visual SourceSafe immediately updates it in all the projects that share it.

3. In the Share dialog box project list, click the project containing the files you want to share.

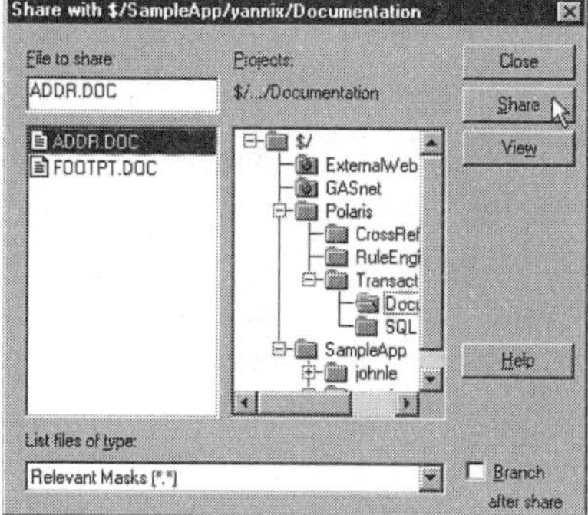

FIG. 26.18
The Visual SourceSafe Share dialog box has options for sharing files.

4. Under File to Share, click the file(s) you want to share.
5. Click Share.

   The file you share becomes part of the current project. All subsequent changes you make to the file are immediately part of the file in all projects that share it.

> **CAUTION**
>
> You cannot share files among multiple databases. For this reason, you should always organize your files into projects within a single database whenever possible.

NOTE If a file is shared by multiple projects, destroying or purging it in one project does not delete the file from the Visual SourceSafe database, and therefore will not free any disk space.

You can share any file from any project with any other project to which you have access. When a file is shared by multiple projects, the icon for that file in the file list changes from a single file to overlapping files, as shown in Figure 26.19.

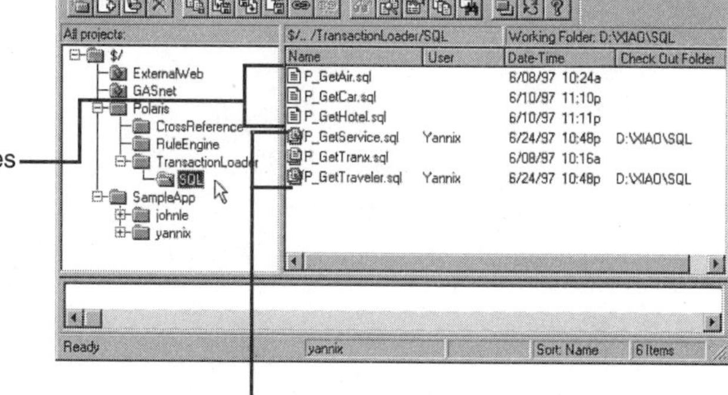

FIG. 26.19
The file icons representing unshared (top three) and shared (bottom three) files are different.

NOTE You can use the command-line Links command to show a list of all projects that are sharing a file.

There is only one master copy of a shared file; thus, any changes actually checked in propagate to all of the projects that share the file. *Branching* is like a shared file but without the dynamic link. Changes made to the file in one project will not be reflected in other projects. This feature is used when you must have a snapshot of all the files in a project at a particular moment for testing purposes or to create customized or parallel versions of a project. Visual SourceSafe tracks branches by making each development path a different project. Different project names keep the branches distinct.

To share and branch a file using the Share command,

1. In Visual SourceSafe Explorer, click the project you want to share and branch the file into.
2. Choose SourceSafe, Share from the menu to display the Share dialog box as shown in Figure 26.20.

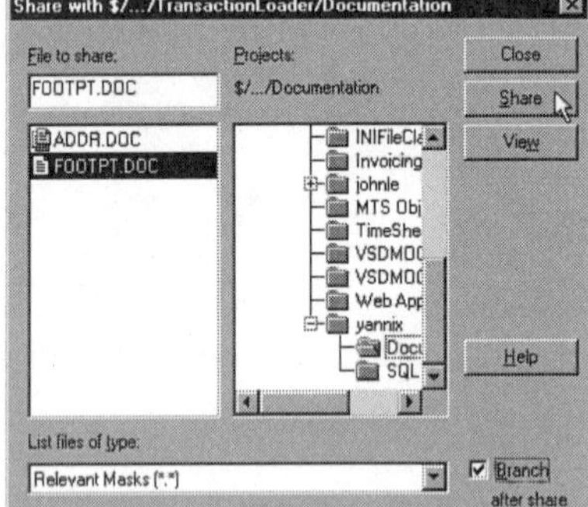

FIG. 26.20 Using the Share dialog box to share and branch a file for separate use in another project.

3. In the Share dialog box project list, click the project containing the file you want to share and branch.
4. Under File to Share, click the file you want to share and branch.
5. Click the Branch After Share checkbox.
6. Click Share.

Alternatively, you can use the file branching pop-up menu.

1. In Visual SourceSafe Explorer, right-click the file to be branched and drag it to the new project.
2. Release the mouse button and select Share and Branch from the pop-up menu.

NOTE Don't add the same file separately to multiple projects. Instead, share the file among projects.

Sometimes, a fix made to a branched file needs to be updated with the original project. The Merge Branches command allows you to combine any changes between separated files. The merge always goes in one direction, from the project in which the file was changed into the project or projects in which you want the changes to appear.

To merge branched files,

1. In Visual SourceSafe Explorer, click the file into which you want to merge the changes.
2. Choose SourceSafe, Merge Branches from the menu.

   Visual SourceSafe displays the Merge dialog box, shown in Figure 26.21.

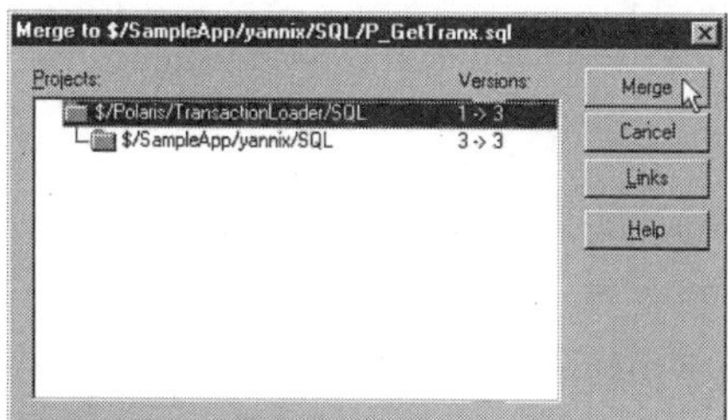

FIG. 26.21
The Merge dialog box copies all the changes made in one branch of a file to another branch.

3. In the Merge dialog box, click the project containing the version of the file from which you want to merge the changes. You can then enter a comment when Visual SourceSafe prompts for one.
4. Click Merge.

After you complete the merge operation, changes merged into a file are immediately part of any project sharing the file.

NOTE Only ASCII and ANSI text files can be merged. You must have the Check Out access right in the project being merged into, and the Read access right in the project being merged from, to use the Merge Branches command.

Version Tracking in Visual SourceSafe

In addition to various source control capabilities of Visual SourceSafe, version tracking capability is another primary benefit of using Visual SourceSafe in your software development process.

Visual SourceSafe tracks versions not only of files, but also of projects. Whenever developers check out files, make changes to them, and check them back into a Visual SourceSafe project, Visual SourceSafe tracks all the details of changes made on a file and project level. This history tracking feature enables developers to do a number of things:

- Compare two versions of a file or project and find out the differences.
- Track the history of any changes made to each file or project, when the changes were made, who did it, and what comments were made.

- Retrieve previous project versions for bug fixes or other purposes. By tracking project history, Visual SourceSafe enables you to readily retrieve previous versions of an entire application. This can help you resolve bugs reported from older versions and make sure they have been fixed in the current version.

NOTE The number of versions of a given file that Visual SourceSafe can store is limited to 32,767.

Visual SourceSafe tracks versions of files and projects by showing version numbers, labels, and date/time. You can label a specific version of a project with a descriptive string as a way to freeze a moment in the development cycle. This way, you can easily find and work with a project that has been identified as significant in the development cycle.

To label a project,

1. In Visual SourceSafe Explorer, click a project.
2. Select File, Label from the menu.

   Visual SourceSafe displays the Label dialog box, shown in Figure 26.22.

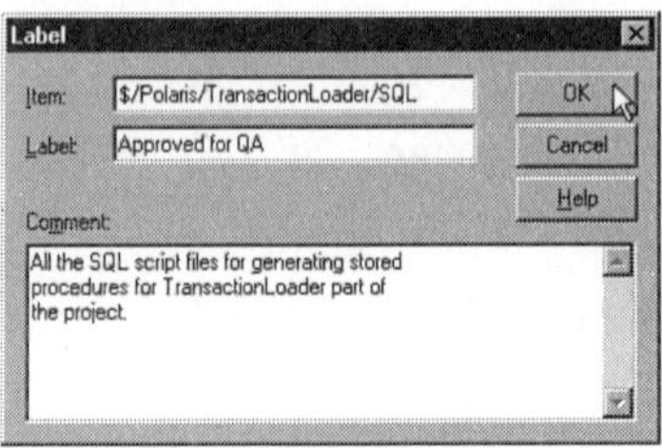

FIG. 26.22 The Label dialog box is used to assign a label to the specified version or current version of a file or project.

3. In the Label box, type a descriptive string of up to 31 characters.
4. Type a comment.
5. Click OK.

NOTE It is not recommended to label a file. When you label a project with a string, all the files in that project are labeled with that string.

You can view the history of changes to any file or project by using the Show History command on the Tools menu. From the history dialog boxes, you can access a variety of other functions such as View, Get, and Share. You can also see details and print reports on the history of files and projects.

To show the file or project history,

1. Select the file (project) of which you want to see the history from the file (project) list.
2. Choose Tools, Show History from the menu in Visual SourceSafe, or click the right mouse button and select Show History from the pop-up menu.

   Visual SourceSafe displays the History dialog box, shown in Figure 26.23.

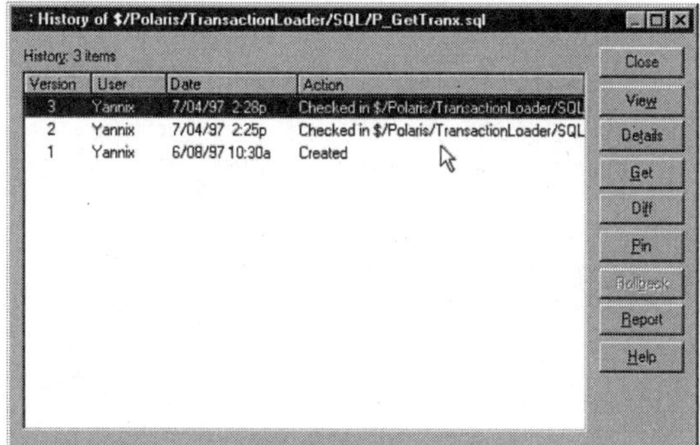

FIG. 26.23
The History dialog box lists the versions starting with the most recent.

3. Click a command button in the History dialog box.
4. Click Close.

You can use the Show Differences command in Visual SourceSafe to compare the differences between two text files. You can compare two files on your computer; a file on your computer and a file stored in Visual SourceSafe; or versions of the same file both stored in Visual SourceSafe projects. The following procedure describes how to determine the differences between versions of the same file both stored in Visual SourceSafe projects.

To display differences between versions of the same file,

1. In Visual SourceSafe Explorer, select the file in the file list.
2. Choose Tools, Show History from the menu.
3. Select two versions in the History dialog box.
4. Click Diff.

   Figure 26.24 shows file differences in Visual format, which is the default view. You can choose three different formats to view the differences: Visual, SourceSafe, or UNIX.

   Visual SourceSafe displays the "Compare" file in the left pane of the display and the "To" file in the right pane of the display. Lines that differ between two versions are displayed in several contrasting colors. By default, for example, deleted lines are shown in blue, changed lines are shown in red, and inserted lines are displayed in green.
5. Click Close.

TIP You can set the colors in the Difference tab of the SourcesSafe Options dialog box.

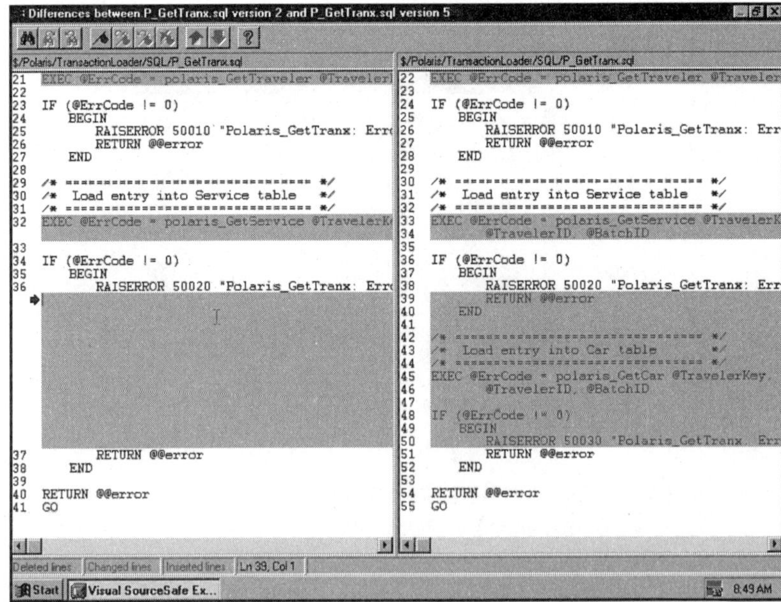

FIG. 26.24 The File Differences dialog box uses the Visual format as the default.

Using SourceSafe to Manage Web Content

Developing and managing a large-scale World Wide Web site involves a lot more than just writing HTML syntax. A large number of documents (for example, HTML files, script language files, and graphic format files), many developers, and lots of updates are normally involved in the process for submitting and updating web page content. Typical source control and version tracking features of Visual SourceSafe can help webmasters and web administrators manage the task just like any other software development project. Visual SourceSafe 5.0, however, introduces several new web features specifically designed to aid in managing web sites. These new web features include

- Check Hyperlinks—Checks a collection of web pages and reports any broken links.
- Deploy—Publishes web content to a live web server.
- Site map—Generates a site map based on a collection of web pages stored in the Visual SourceSafe project.

This section outlines these new web features in Visual SourceSafe in addition to the standard benefits of using Visual SourceSafe for source control and version tracking in web site development projects.

Organizing a Web Site into a Project Tree

To use Visual SourceSafe as a web site management tool, you need to first organize your web site into a logical hierarchy of projects as in any other projects. Then you can create the projects and subprojects in Visual SourceSafe Explorer and add your web files to the project tree. By organizing the web site into a Visual SourceSafe project tree, you get the standard benefits that version control has to offer to software developers. That is, it helps manage and coordinate the team by keeping track of changes and file versions and archiving your files.

For example, G. A. Sullivan has two web site projects: $/ExternalWeb and $/GASnet. The former is for external purposes, and the latter is for internal purposes. The "internal web site" is available only to G. A. Sullivan employees. These two projects build completely different web sites hosted on completely different servers. Some of the files between the two web sites are different, but some are the same. When an HTML file is changed, this change might affect only one site, or it might affect both sites. It is important to copy the modified file to the right places. The sharing feature in Visual SourceSafe can help track and manage multiple webs automatically just like any other projects. If a file is used on both sites, it can be shared between both web projects. So whenever a change is made to this file in either project, that change is automatically reflected in both.

In addition to all the standard benefits of using Visual SourceSafe for source control and version tracking, some special benefits exist for web projects. The next several sections describe how to designate a project as a web project and how to use the three new web features in Visual SourceSafe.

Designating Web Projects

In order to use the new web features in Visual SourceSafe 5.0, the project first needs to be designated as a web site project. Your Visual SourceSafe administrator can do this by using the Visual SourceSafe Administrator program.

To designate a project as a web project,

1. Select Tools, Options from the menu in the Visual SourceSafe Administrator main window.

   The Visual SourceSafe Administrator displays the SourceSafe Options dialog box.

2. Click the Web Projects tab on the SourceSafe Options dialog box.

   The Web Projects tab displays, as shown in Figure 26.25.

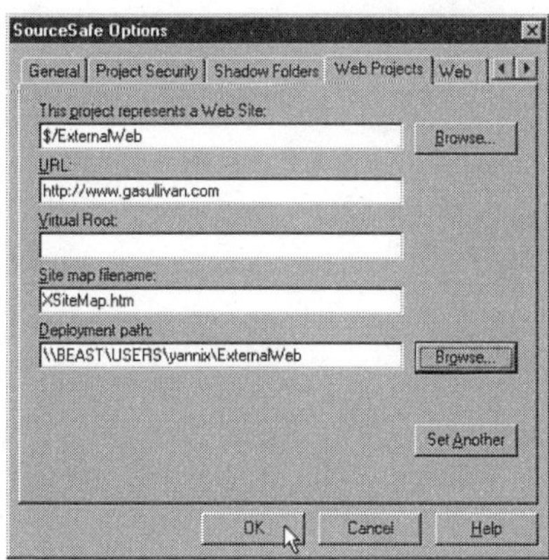

FIG. 26.25
The Web Projects tab in the SourceSafe Options dialog box is used for designating a project as a web project.

This Web Projects tab contains the following five text input fields:

- This Project Represents a Web Site—Type the name of the project into this field, or use the Browse button next to the field to select the project. All the other settings specified in the fields below apply to this project. This field must be filled in before you can designate the project as a web project.
- URL—Type the URL (Uniform Resource Locator) address for the web site into this field. Either this field or the next field must be filled in.
- Virtual Root—Some web server software supports this. If you have specified a virtual root in your server software, you should specify it here, without an initial slash.
- Site map filename—Type the name of the file you want Visual SourceSafe to use when it creates a site map. This field is optional. The site map file created by Visual SourceSafe will be an HTML file with links to all the HTML files in your web project. With some minor customization, you can then add the resulting site map file to your web site.
- Deployment path—Specify one or more deployment locations for your web site. A deployment location can be local or remote. You must specify a deployment path in order to deploy your project as a web site, but you do not need to do so in order to designate the project as a web project. You can use the Browse button next to this field to search for servers on your network. See the section "Testing and Deploying Web Content" later in the chapter for more details on deployment paths.

Once a project is designated as a web project and you restart the Visual SourceSafe program, Visual SourceSafe Explorer displays the designated project with a special icon to indicate that it is a web project. The web project icon has a small global image superimposed on it. Whenever a web project is selected, the commands on the Visual SourceSafe Web menu become enabled. Visual SourceSafe can then quickly check broken links among the project files, create a site map of the HTML files in the project and its subprojects, and automatically deploy the files to an Internet server location when they are ready. See Figure 26.26 for the Web menu in Visual SourceSafe.

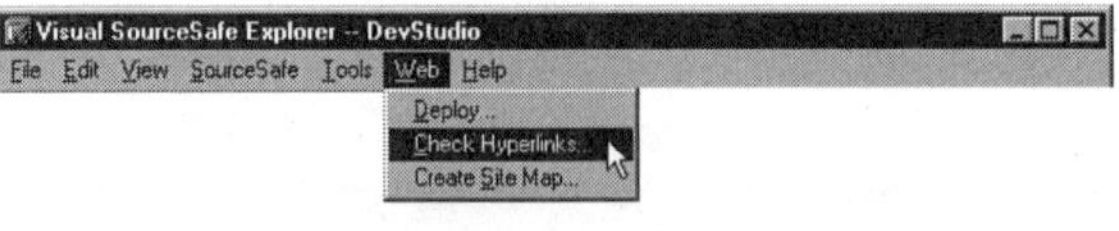

FIG. 26.26 The commands on the Visual SourceSafe Web menu are enabled whenever a web project is selected.

NOTE You can also remove a web project designation by using the Web Projects tab in the SourceSafe Options dialog box. Simply clear the URL and Virtual Root fields and then click OK.

Checking Hyperlink Integrity

As a webmaster or web administrator, you want to make sure not to publish your web page content with broken links to a live web server. One of the new web features available in Visual SourceSafe—Check Hyperlinks—makes it easy to test for bad links before you publish your web page content to the server. You can choose to check the files in your working folder or those in the Visual SourceSafe project. Visual SourceSafe provides you with a report of any internal broken hyperlinks. You can access the Check Hyperlinks dialog box by choosing Web, Check Hyperlinks from the menu in Visual SourceSafe (see Figure 26.27). The broken links report is shown in Figure 26.28.

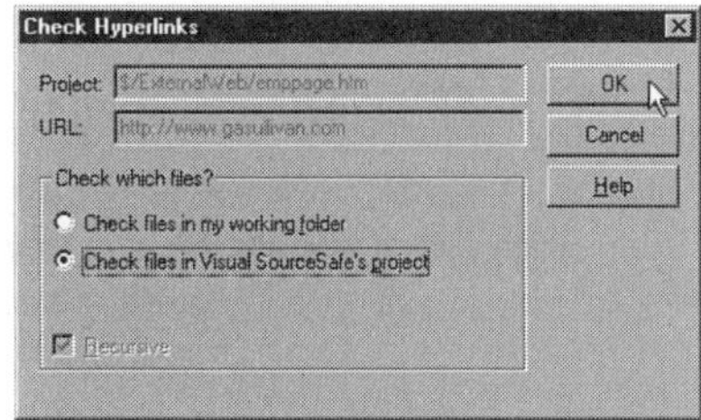

FIG. 26.27 In the Check Hyperlinks dialog box, you can request a report of any internal broken hyperlinks.

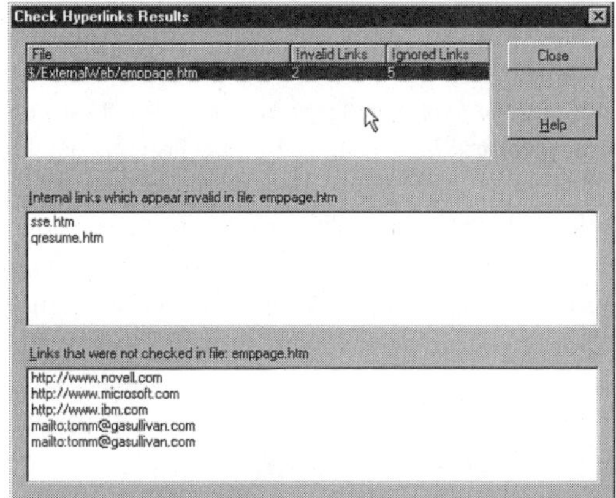

FIG. 26.28 The Check Hyperlinks command reports internal broken hyperlinks.

Visual SourceSafe differentiates between internal and external hyperlinks. *Internal links* are those within your web site in the same Visual SourceSafe project tree. Visual SourceSafe checks all local links among your HTML files and displays any potential problems. For example, the file frmain.htm in the project $/ExternalWeb/ refers to another file stlouis.htm, but this file does not exist in the same project. This hyperlink is, therefore, listed as invalid. *External hyperlinks* are jumps to sites on the World Wide Web that are not in your project tree. Visual SourceSafe does not check these external hyperlinks but only lists them in the bottom list of the Check Hyperlinks result window, as shown in Figure 26.28.

Creating a Site Map

Another new web feature available in Visual SourceSafe 5.0 is creating site maps. Site maps are often useful to the web users. They provide a list of hyperlinks to the web site's contents to help the users with the navigation. Visual SourceSafe can create a site map for your web site easily by generating a new HTML file and writing out a list of links to all the HTML files within your web site project. The name of this new site map HTML file was set by your Visual SourceSafe administrator, when the project was initially designated as a web project (refer to Figure 26.25 in the section "Designating Web Projects"). The Create Site Map dialog box displays when you choose Web, Site Map from the menu in Visual SourceSafe (see Figure 26.29).

FIG. 26.29
The Create Site Map dialog box enables you to create a site map.

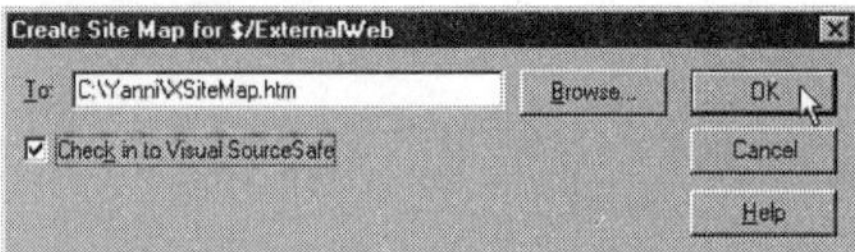

Category names in the site map file are taken directly from your Visual SourceSafe project name, so you should use unique and descriptive strings as names for your web site projects. Once the HTML site map file is created, you can add it into your project by using the Add Files command. If you add the file to your web site project, be sure to check it out before running the Create Site Map command.

Testing and Deploying Web Content

Deploy is another new web feature in Visual SourceSafe 5.0. It can be used to send a web project to one or more test servers or live web servers that have been designated by the Visual SourceSafe administrator. Servers can reside on either local networks or on the Internet. If a server is outside the local network, it is reached by File Transfer Protocol (FTP). The deployment path was specified by your Visual SourceSafe administrator when the project was initially designated as a web project (refer to Figure 26.25 in the section "Designating Web Projects"). Because this command can potentially publish a web project to the entire World Wide Web, Visual SourceSafe requires you to have Destroy-level (D) access rights in the project in order to use it. Figure 26.30 shows the Deploy dialog box in Visual SourceSafe, which you can access by choosing Web, Deploy.

FIG. 26.30
The Deploy dialog box enables you to send a web project to a server.

NOTE You can deploy any project that has been designated as a web project, regardless of the types of files it contains. That is, it does not necessarily have to be an actual web site. A single command then sends the entire project to the local or remote locations you have specified. You can only deploy an entire project, not specific files that are not designated as a project.

From Here...

Visual SourceSafe provides easy-to-use, project-oriented version control for managing software and web site development. In addition to basic source control and versioning capabilities, Visual SourceSafe provides advanced functionality that includes branching and merging to support customization and parallel development. Visual SourceSafe 5.0 also introduces some new web features for managing web site contents. Most features in Visual SourceSafe are easily executed through its graphical interface—Visual SourceSafe Explorer. The configuration and maintenance of Visual SourceSafe installation are also straightforward using its administrative program—Visual SourceSafe Administrator. Visual SourceSafe can definitely help the developers spend less time doing source code "bookkeeping" and more time coding. It fills a critical need in any team-based software and web site development environment.

The Visual Studio 97 suite is specifically designed for the team-oriented software development environment and contains many features supporting a team and its individual software developers. Refer to the following chapters for more information related to team development with Visual Studio 97:

- To learn about using Visual SourceSafe with Visual InterDev, see Chapter 15, "Advanced Visual InterDev Concepts."
- To learn about the new object-modeling tool from Microsoft, the Microsoft Visual Modeler, see Chapter 27, "System Modeling and Microsoft Visual Modeler."
- To learn about the Microsoft Repository, a new product from Microsoft for organizing software components, see Chapter 28, "The Microsoft Repository."

CHAPTER 27

System Modeling and Microsoft Visual Modeler

by David O'Leary and Don Benage

- **The value of modeling**
  See why modeling is important and how it can be used to improve the quality of your software development efforts.
- **Why use Visual Modeler?**
  See why Visual Modeler is necessary and how it helps you develop better applications in less time.
- **What is the UML?**
  Learn about the Unified Modeling Language (UML), the de facto industry standard language for representing software systems.
- **Visual Modeler's integration with Visual Basic**
  Because Visual Modeler is tightly integrated with Visual Basic, you keep your code and model synchronized throughout the development life cycle.
- **How to use Visual Modeler**
  Discover how to use Visual Modeler to design powerful, well-built enterprise systems.

Although the software development industry has many unique characteristics that distinguish it from other endeavors, an on-going attempt is being made to adapt ideas from other engineering disciplines to advance the speed and reliability with which you can build complex software solutions. In some other engineering fields, such as mechanical or chemical engineering, a more rigorous scientific approach has been adopted. Although the software development industry is still in relative infancy, it has the opportunity to build and use tools to improve itself like no other industry has before, due to the nature of software development.

Just as a carpenter would never build a sizable project without first drawing up a plan, most software development efforts are complex enough to require a general plan of system parts and how those parts should interact. Creating a model that represents a complex system allows you to better understand the individual components of the system, the relationships between components, and the ways in which they interact. The model allows you to focus on these important design decisions before getting too involved in the myriad details that must eventually be addressed. It can also help the project participants understand the modeled system more quickly and easily.

Microsoft is promoting Visual Studio as an important step in the evolution of software development tools. The core idea behind this message isn't new and unique to Microsoft: Instead of crafting an application as a single entity, most applications are built by assembling existing components (ActiveX controls, COM/DCOM objects, OLE-enabled applications, and so forth) together to create a custom application. Just as a car is made up of various parts (frame, engine, fuel system, exhaust system, drive train, and suspension) and some of these parts can be interchanged between different models of cars, it should be possible to design interchangeable software components.

This elusive concept dates back to good programming practices introduced with the development of procedural structured programming. These practices were then extended by other innovations, such as object-oriented programming, the use of dynamic link libraries (DLLs) and Visual Basic custom controls (VBXs), and the various object systems such as COM/DCOM, SOM, and OpenDoc. What Visual Studio adds to this concept is a suite of tools, each with its own strengths, designed to work together. Potentially, these tools can maximize the capability to create applications quickly by assembling pieces developed by using the various tools.

Visual Modeler is a fairly easy tool to use. (In fact, getting the tool may prove more difficult than using the tool, but that will be explained.) The difficult part isn't the tool, but the underlying language on which it's based—the Unified Modeling Language (UML)—and the concepts on which the UML was built. For that reason, this chapter focuses more on what Visual Modeler does and why, rather than how to do particular tasks. ■

What Is Visual Modeler?

Microsoft designed Visual Modeler as an entry-level modeling tool. In this, its first release, Visual Modeler offers support for only a subset of the UML. It's an appropriate tool for those of you new to modeling. If you're an experienced designer, you can choose (or already might be using) a more fully featured modeling tool. Visual Modeler allows you to create the equivalent of blueprints for software systems. It uses a standard set of symbols and icons that you can use to represent an application or group of applications at various levels of detail.

Introduction to Visual Modeler

Visual Modeler was created for Microsoft by Rational Software Corporation, with some additions made by Microsoft for better integration with Visual Basic. Rational offers Rational Rose, a full-featured modeling tool that provides support for several languages, including Visual Basic, C++, and Java. Overall, Visual Modeler provides a subset of the functionality in the Rational Rose/Visual Basic product. Rational Rose supports the full UML, whereas Visual Modeler doesn't. (This is discussed in more detail later in the section "The UML.") If you start with Visual Modeler and later decide to buy Rational Rose, you can open any models created with the Visual Modeler tool directly in Rational Rose/VB because they use the same file format.

NOTE Rational Rose was designed for use with many different languages, development environments, and operating systems. For integration with a particular language, you buy an Analyzer program that handles code generation and reverse/round-trip engineering for that language. Current languages supported by Rational Rose include C++, Forte, Java, PowerBuilder, Smalltalk, SQLWindows, and Visual Basic.

For various reasons, including license restrictions between Microsoft and Rational, you must have Visual Basic installed on your computer to be able to run Visual Modeler. Also, Visual Modeler supports only code generation for and reverse engineering from Visual Basic, although this shouldn't restrict you to using Visual Modeler only on Visual Basic applications. Any sizable software development process can benefit greatly from using a visual-modeling tool. Whether it's designing classes and controls in C++ or Java, or defining the interface of a DLL, Visual Modeler is a very useful visualization tool whose benefits go well beyond its code generation and reverse-engineering capabilities. If you want the added benefit of being able to generate code for a language other than Visual Basic, you'll have to buy the full version of Rational Rose or another tool that supports the full UML and code generation in the language of your choice.

Visual Modeler is a key piece of this software development system. It allows you to design the system at several different levels so that, from a high level, you can properly see the various components needed for the application (see Figure 27.1). Then you can select existing components or choose the proper tool for developing new components.

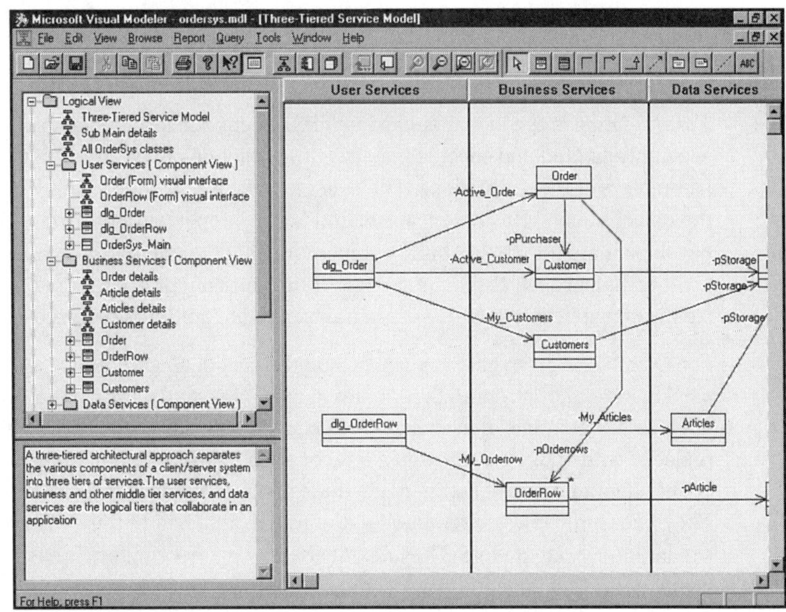

FIG. 27.1
The Visual Modeler display uses a multiple-window design to let you view your current model graphically, as well as a logical view with nested folders and a separate window for comments.

NOTE In the jargon of object-oriented software development, an *object* refers to an instance of a class. In the broader context of Visual Studio and the UML, however, you can use the term *object* to refer to a whole range of entities that contain a defined interface, actions, and attributes such as ActiveX controls, a module, or DLL. The UML defines an object as "an entity with a well-defined boundary and identity that encapsulates state and behavior. State is represented by attributes and relationships; behavior is represented by operations and methods."

How to Get Visual Modeler

You can't get Visual Modeler from the Visual Studio CD-ROMs (at least, not at the time of this writing); instead, you download it from **http://www.microsoft.com/vstudio/owner**. On this web page, follow the steps given to register Visual Basic (it must already be installed), click the `Visual Modeler` hypertext, and then follow the instructions for downloading. When it's registered, you can get a private access area from which you can download the Visual Modeler install program.

Principles of Good System Design

At the heart of Visual Modeler—and modeling tools in general—is an attempt to improve overall system design. Proper use of a modeling tool should increase the use of good programming principles such as encapsulation, abstraction, and reuse. These principles have been developed, primarily within the discipline of object-oriented software development, to help create and maintain large systems with fewer errors and better long-term cost-effectiveness.

Design Principles

Encapsulation is the idea that objects (classes, modules, and controls) should allow users to see only a limited and specific interface, the functions to be called, and the input and output parameters of those functions. The exact details of how they're implemented are hidden from the object's users. Having encapsulation is very important in software development. Without it, developers are tempted to build components that depend on the specific internal design of another (unencapsulated) component. If the component is later modified, one seemingly simple change can result in a cascading series of additional required changes.

For example, a car engine is an encapsulated part of an automotive system. One engine can be used in several different makes and models of cars, and a car can use several different types of engines (for example, four cylinder or six cylinder). That way, if one engine breaks, it can be replaced with another of the same type or even a different, but compatible, engine. The designers of other automotive components don't concern themselves with the specifics of the engine. They know only how it's mounted to the frame, attached to the exhaust system, and other similar interfacing details. They don't care how many cylinders it has, nor do they design other components that depend on a specific number of cylinders.

Abstraction is a process of focusing on certain aspects of a problem. Rather than require everyone to know and understand the implementation details of an entire system—or even a specific object within that system—with modeling you can show only the pertinent information to reduce the complexity involved in understanding a system. This makes the system easier to design and understand.

Many people may use the same object, but they need to know only the interface (the name of the functions and each function's expected input and output parameters). For example, someone who puts an engine in a car doesn't have to know about the internal workings but does have to know about the engine's interface, such as how to hook the engine to the transmission. As long as the interface requirements are known, the two objects can be designed and built separately and put together during an integration phase.

Reuse is a key concept of Visual Studio because it attempts to make software development quicker and more reliable by allowing developers to assemble already built components into a custom application rather than write from scratch. Reuse comes into play at many levels in application development from simply reusing one function to reusing components such as data combo boxes. You may even decide to reuse entire applications, such as Excel or Word, through Automation (formerly known as OLE Automation). Visual Modeler allows you to place existing elements into your model by reverse engineering them from code or their OLE interface. (See the later section "Reverse Engineering Wizard" for more details.)

Reuse is a natural byproduct of good encapsulation and abstraction. If you fail to use these principles during the design or redesign phase, you won't create reusable objects. Also, reuse tends to work from the micro level to the macro level. In other words, if you focus on the smaller objects, functions, modules, and abstracting generic functions out into separate general utility classes, what is and isn't reusable at the larger module level will become much clearer.

To maximize code reuse at the micro level, look for places where the same code is used several times in different places. If you find yourself cutting and pasting a piece of code, look for ways to move that code to a single function or even a class. If it's something that could be used in several applications, you might consider creating a DLL or an ActiveX control that exports this function and possibly other related functions.

Encapsulation, abstraction, and reuse are all very closely related, and together they lead to easier modification and maintenance as well as quicker and more reliable system development. Using thoroughly tested, prebuilt objects won't save you an immense amount of time during development; to use a prebuilt object, you must first find an object appropriate for your needs and then learn how it's properly used. Where you'll save time is during the testing and maintenance stages, and for the next project you'll already know the object's capabilities.

Encapsulation, abstraction, and reuse also make larger teams possible because of the reduced dependencies between objects. If objects aren't properly encapsulated, a team's members will constantly step on each other's toes as they try to integrate their individual system parts.

The Role of Modeling

Preliminary design work results in better code. It also saves time in the long run by greatly increasing the encapsulation of the various objects of the system, resulting in easier maintenance, reduced complexity, and an increase in the amount of reusable code produced. On many projects, especially where budgets are tight, there's pressure to begin coding immediately. Although many organizations have learned the folly of this decision, it's shocking how often this still happens. There's no substitute for good design, and taking the time to do so will save money and time in the long run.

Modeling is one of the most effective tools for creating a good design. Modeling a system allows you to step away from implementation details, so you can clearly see how a system should be broken into components and how those components need to interact. When working directly with code, you easily can get stuck in the details and not see the big picture of the overall software system. If you forgo preliminary design work and then require continual redesign throughout the project, the system begins to develop a "bubble-gum-and-bailing-wire" character, which makes changes to the system very difficult.

The UML

The Unified Modeling Language defines a graphical notation to be used in designing and representing a software system. This graphical notation helps developers visualize the problem and its solution without getting overly involved in the implementation details. Just as an outline gives a higher level view of a document, or an architectural plan gives an overview of a building, the UML can be used to give a higher level view of a software system. This higher level view proves useful throughout the software development life cycle—through analysis, design, implementation, and maintenance. Figure 27.2 summarizes the evolution of the UML.

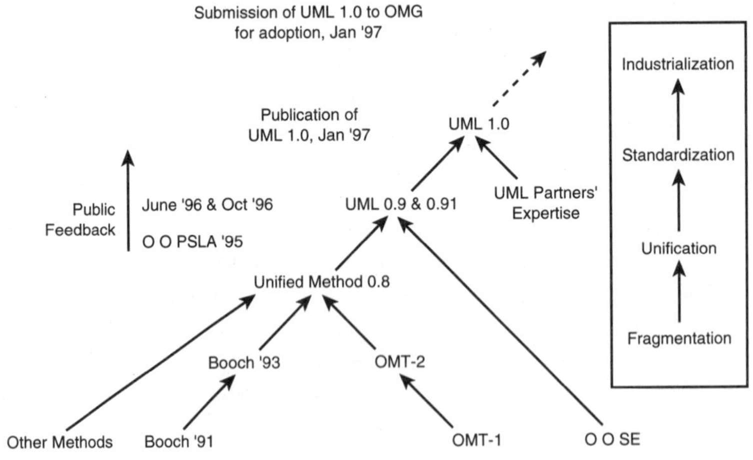

FIG. 27.2
The evolution of the UML, taken from the UML Summary document (with permission).

Developed by a consortium of individuals and companies, the UML is an attempt to bring together the most useful parts of the best modeling languages and combine them into a single language that can be used throughout the industry.

NOTE The UML isn't a methodology–it's only a modeling language. A *modeling language* defines a way to graphically express a system model, whereas a *methodology* defines a method to use in designing and developing software. The UML should generally be used within the context of a methodology such as Booch, OMT, or one of the forthcoming UML-based methodologies.

The UML is ultimately the product of a long history of ideas in the computer science and software engineering area. However, three men did much of the development and unification work: James Rumbaugh, Grady Booch, and Ivar Jacobson. These three joined forces when they all began working at Rational Software Corporation and are now commonly referred to as the Three Amigos. Each worked independently or with another team to develop a software development methodology and a complementary modeling language to describe the various elements of the methodology and their interactions. Each methodology—or at least a part of each methodology—is still being widely used throughout the industry today.

ON THE WEB

Rational Software Corporation provides a complete range of software development tools, including tools for modeling, testing, and project management. Visit Rational's web site at **http://www.rational.com/** for more information.

- James Rumbaugh—in collaboration with Michael Blaha, William Premerlani, Frederick Eddy, and William Lorensen—developed the Object Modeling Technique (OMT). OMT uses three main diagrams to define a system: the object model (which is quite similar in form and function to the object model in Visual Modeler and the UML), state diagrams, and data-flow diagrams.
- Grady Booch developed a methodology and diagramming technique bearing his name appended with the year that it was released. The latest version is Booch '93. Booch defined an object model that's quite similar to OMT's object model in terms of function and the data stored, but the icons used to represent the elements are different.
- Ivar Jacobson's main contribution to the UML is his concept of, and representation for, *use cases*. Use cases are an important part of the UML but aren't supported in Visual Modeler. Use cases allow you to capture the uses of the system in a model. You can specify who will perform an action (known as the *actor*) and what object or module will be responsible for handling that action. To use this UML technique, you need to buy a full version of Rational Rose or another product that supports the full UML.

NOTE Several tools support the full UML (including use cases, object interaction diagrams, and so on), including

- Rational Rose by Rational Software (**www.rational.com**)
- Select OMT by Select Software Corporation (**www.select.com**)
- Paradigm Plus by Platinum Software (**www.platinum.com**)

The UML Diagrams

Just as a building blueprint can contain several different diagrams, each describing various aspects of the building, different types of diagrams can be used together to describe the many aspects of a software system. Before modeling a system, it's important to have an idea of who you're producing the model for and how it will be used. Different audiences often require vastly different views of the system. The diagram produced for developers will be quite different from the model produced for a client. Management will be interested in a much higher view of the system than a class implementer.

Visual Modeler provides for a variety of views into the system. Not only does Visual Modeler have a number of different diagram types, but it also has varieties of each diagram type. Each diagram allows you to describe different aspects of the system for various audiences and purposes. Some systems require only a few of the diagrams to be defined, whereas others use all of them.

The UML defines the following graphical diagrams:

Use-case diagram*	Sequence diagram
Class diagram	Collaboration diagram
Behavior diagrams	Implementation diagrams
State diagram*	Component diagram
Activity diagram	Deployment diagram

**Not supported by Visual Modeler*

Visual Modeler adds two more diagram types to this list, both of which are variations on the class diagram: the *three-tier diagram* and the *package overview*. The three-tier diagram is used for the highest level view of the system and its architecture. The package overview is used for low-level details. The following sections provide an overview of a few key diagram types supported by Visual Modeler, when to use them, and what the various elements describe.

The Three-Tier Diagram

The three-tier diagram is a form of class diagram and is used as the highest level (see Figure 27.3). It separates the class diagram into three tiers, allowing you to view and better understand the separation between tiers in a multitiered architecture.

NOTE *Multitier architecture* is a paradigm used to complement other modeling techniques. A three-tier architecture is often used, although more tiers are possible. This architecture frequently has a direct correspondence to the physical location of components: desktop computers for client components, middle-tier servers with business-rule objects, and database servers.

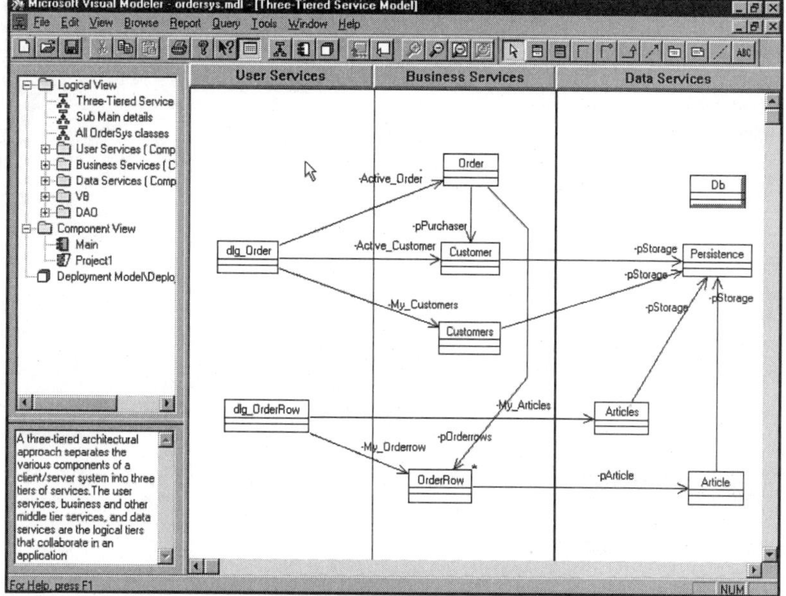

FIG. 27.3
The three-tier diagram makes it easier to understand the components that make up an application's various tiers.

Visual Modeler describes the three tiers as follows:

- *User services* provide the visual interface for presenting information and gathering data in an application. User services connect users with the application and request the business or data services needed by users to execute business tasks.
- *Business services* respond to requests from users (or other business services) to execute a business task. They accomplish this by requesting the data services needed and applying formal procedures and business rules to the relevant data. This protocol insulates users from direct interaction with the database. Because business rules tend to change more frequently than the specific business tasks they support, they're ideal candidates for encapsulating into components physically separate from the application logic itself.
- *Data services* maintain, access, and update data. They also manage and satisfy requests to manipulate data initiated by business services. Separating data services allows the data structure and access mechanisms to be maintained, modified, or, if necessary, even redesigned without affecting business or user services.

Class Diagram

Class diagrams came from the object models of OMT and Booch (see Figure 27.4). They show the classes of the system and their relationships, and optionally, each class's attributes and operations. Representing the system through class diagrams comes with a great deal of flexibility. You can show every class in the system with all its attributes and operations, or you can break the system into many different packages, each with their own class diagrams.

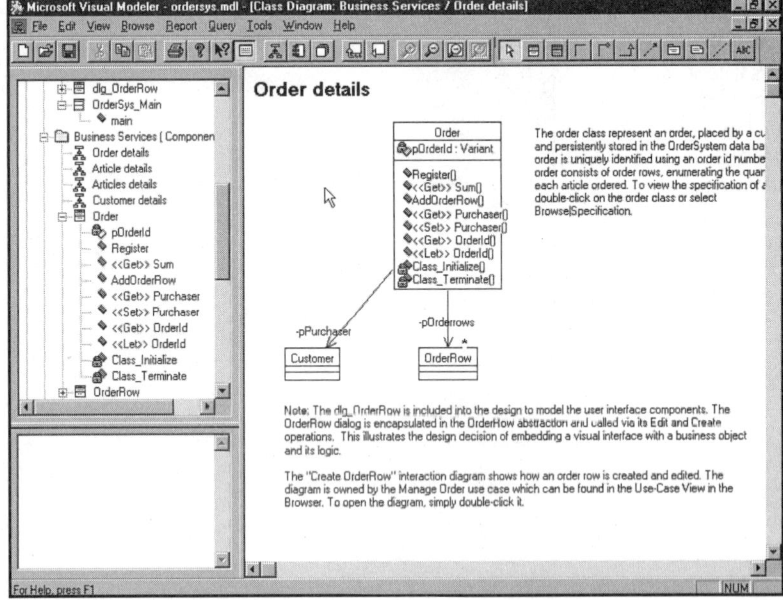

FIG. 27.4
Class diagrams provide details about a particular class and its relationship to other classes.

How you decide to represent the system depends on the intended audience and the intention behind the model. If you're preparing a class diagram to be used by the developers who will write the code, your model will contain a high level of detail. You would prepare a model with less detail, using class diagrams for only the major elements of the system, to present an overview to management.

Package Overview

When constructing a model, as with many other activities, being able to group elements based on a variety of criteria is useful. This grouping then allows you to more conveniently work with and manage the elements of the group. Visual Modeler has such a grouping mechanism known as a *package*, which is a collection of classes with a strong relationship to one another. Therefore, a package represents a logical *chunk*, or piece of, the entire system. Packages may be nested within other packages. To avoid confusion with component packages (described in the following section), it's best to refer to this type of package as a *logical package* if it's not already clear from the context in which it's being used.

A package overview is created and updated automatically when you create a package. As classes are added to the package, they're also added to the corresponding package overview. Although packages don't correspond directly to any construct in Visual Basic, they're frequently used to represent OLE Automation servers.

Component Diagram

Whereas packages represent logical chunks of the system, *components* are the physical elements of the system. Whereas packages don't correspond directly to Visual Basic constructs, components correspond directly to code modules. Components include executable applications (EXE files) and application extensions (DLLs). A *component package* is a group of related components. The role of component packages is similar to that of the logical package introduced in the preceding section, but it's a grouping of physical components rather than logical classes (or class diagrams).

A *component diagram*, therefore, represents a view of the various physical pieces of a system. It depicts the individual components, component packages, and the relationships between these elements. Component diagrams are sometimes referred to as *module diagrams*, although the newer term *component diagram* is now preferred.

Each component and component package has a corresponding *specification* that contains its properties. While the properties are viewed and edited in textual form in Visual Modeler, some of this information can be displayed inside the icons representing the components and component packages in component diagrams. When you edit a specification, Visual Modeler automatically updates all diagrams containing the icon for that component or component package. You can also directly edit the diagram, and the corresponding specification will be revised.

Through a combination of the logical and component views, it's easy to define the responsibilities and interfaces of classes and components of the system. Each developer can then begin his or her design, knowing the expected inputs and outputs of any given module.

Deployment Diagram

Each model contains a single deployment diagram. This diagram takes another step toward the actual physical implementation of the system by showing the *nodes*, or actual hardware units that will run the system, and the connections between the various nodes. Each node and connection has a corresponding specification, which can be edited directly in the icons of the deployment diagram or in more detail by directly accessing the specification itself. As with component diagrams, edits made in either fashion are reflected throughout the model in any view.

The deployment diagram, by modeling the actual physical environment where the system will run, can provide important information regarding potential time delays introduced by slow links connecting the various nodes, and other real-world artifacts of the intended environment. Although this information may be implicitly reflected in the physical partitioning represented by component diagrams, it's not directly depicted in any other diagram and is an important addition to help provide an overall understanding of how the finished system will function.

Diagram Elements

A handful of elements are used to create all the diagrams in Visual Modeler. They may take on a slightly different form or meaning depending on how they're used, but the same elements are still used. This way, it's easier to learn how to use Visual Modeler and to understand the created diagrams, much as the consistent use of visual elements such as toolbars and menus has made other computer software easier to learn and use.

The following sections describe the major elements common to the various diagrams: classes, objects, attributes, operations, and relationships.

Classes

A *class*—one of the fundamental elements of object-oriented analysis and design—is an important concept to understand when using Visual Modeler. It's one of those fundamental concepts that's easier to grasp and use than it is to describe. Although a complete description of the term *class* is beyond the scope of this book, in its most basic form a class is nothing more than the description of a group of like objects, with similar properties and behaviors. It's easy to think of many real-world object types that may be represented by a class—cars, humans, invoices, a car loan, and the manufacturer of a car are all examples. In addition to tangible things, processes also can be represented by a class.

A class is represented on an object model as a hard (square-cornered) rectangle, called a class *compartment*. A class compartment can display up to three sections, depending on the view options you select. There's always a section for class name, and it may also have sections for attributes (properties) or operations (behaviors).

Objects

In object-oriented terms, an *object* is an instance of a class. For example, `Joe Smith` is an object and a member of the class `Person`. He is also a member of many other classes, such as `male`, `human`, `mammal`, and so on. All the classes of which he is a member are related by what's called *inheritance*, described later in the section "Generalization (Inheritance)." An object is represented with a soft (round-cornered) rectangle.

NOTE As mentioned earlier in this chapter, an object can also be used to generically reference an instance (or occurrence) of several different element types, including ActiveX controls or components. As a rule, the word *object* refers to a particular element rather than that element's type or class.

Attributes

The term *attribute* is used to designate a characteristic of an object or a class. For any given instance of a particular class, a given attribute takes on a specific value. For example, color is an attribute of the class car. A specific car might be the color blue. With characteristics like color, it's generally easy to determine that they should be modeled as attributes. The color of a car should almost always be modeled as an attribute.

In some cases, however, it's not so straightforward. The engine can be viewed as an attribute or as another object with a defined relationship to the car object. If the engine's details are important in describing the system to your audience, the engine should be modeled as its own object and should have a component relationship to car. If you care only what type of engine it is (for example, four cylinder), as you would for the car's invoice, the engine can be modeled as an attribute. It all depends on the level of detail you're trying to communicate to the users of the model.

An item should never be an attribute and a component object. Attributes appear in Visual Modeler as descriptive text on the various icons in the model.

Operations

An *operation* is defined within the UML as "a service that can be requested from an object to effect behavior. An operation has a signature, which may restrict the actual parameters that are possible." Unfortunately, because of the large scope of objects that this definition applies to, this definition isn't very workable. In general, think of an operation as a function. Whether it's in VB, C++, Java, JavaScript, or an exposed function in the API of a DLL, an operation is something you call on to perform an action or get information.

Within class diagrams, operations appear in the bottom (third) section of a class.

Relationships

Relationships between classes are a key part of class diagrams. Knowing how and when objects will interact has a major effect on how classes are designed and implemented. Just as objects in the real world must have a variety of relationship types, objects in a software system must interact in various ways to perform their responsibilities. For example, if you were to model a car by using the UML, the car would be composed of parts or systems such as the engine, fuel system, electrical system, and so on, and it would have a relationship with several other objects, such as a driver (driven by), gasoline (consumes), and a mechanic (is fixed by). Cars also have a special relationship with other vehicles, in that all vehicles have common attributes. This type of relationship is referred to as *inheritance* and is discussed in further detail later in the section "Generalization (Inheritance)."

NOTE Since the release of UML 1.0, quite a bit of controversy has occurred as to the actual meaning and implementation semantics of the different types of relationships. The definitions are intentionally somewhat vague to allow for application to various languages and tools and to keep the language from being overly restrictive.

The UML defines five fundamental kinds of relationships: association, generalization, dependency, transition, and link. The two primary types of relationships, association and generalization, are described in the following sections.

Association An *association* is the most general form of a relationship. Aggregation and composition are both forms of association. If a class has any knowledge of another class, whether it's passed in as a parameter or is a member of the class, there should be an association between those classes.

An *aggregation* is a special form of association that shows a relationship between a whole (the *aggregate*) and its parts. Aggregation implies a strong dependency of the aggregate on the part, but not as strong of a dependency of the part on the aggregate. For example, a car needs an engine to be useful, but an engine can have a life outside of a particular car; they're independent entities, yet there's a definite dependency. Aggregation is represented in the UML (and Visual Modeler) by a hollow diamond.

Composition involves a stronger dependency between the whole and the part than aggregation. For example, consider a car and its frame; a car must have a frame to be considered a car, but a car without an engine is still thought of as a car. Composition is represented in the UML by a solid filled diamond.

Constraints allow you to further restrict or specify relationships. The most common type of constraint, *multiplicity*, allows you to define an exact number of associations between two objects. You can also specify multiplicity in terms of ranges. You also can add textual constraints to any relationship. A *textual* constraint can be any text that specifies a relationship, but most often is a verb that describes the interaction between the objects.

Generalization (Inheritance) *Generalization*, a specialized type of association, is also known as *inheritance* or *specialization*. Unfortunately, the definitions of *generalization* and *inheritance* are more confusing than helpful to novices:

- *Inheritance.* The mechanism by which more specific elements incorporate structure and behavior of more general elements related by behavior.
- *Generalization.* A taxonomic (class) relationship between a more general element and a more specific element. The more specific element is fully consistent with the more general element and contains additional information.

Inheritance is useful as an abstraction concept and for reducing the amount of code that needs to be written and maintained. Inheritance, a concept of object-oriented programming, isn't truly supported by object-based languages such as Visual Basic.

Object-Oriented Versus Object-Based

Inheritance is the main concept that separates object-oriented languages such as Smalltalk, C++, and Java from object-based languages such as Visual Basic. Inheritance makes a considerable difference in the way a language is used and how reuseable objects and classes are written. With Visual Basic, creating controls or modules to perform certain functions extends the language. Programmers can then use those controls in a customized way, depending on what customization options were built into the control. Or, if you have the code, you can copy that code into your own class or control and customize it to meet your needs. With inheritance, you can extend an existing class by inheriting that class's operations and attributes and then specializing its behavior by overriding existing functionality and adding additional functionality. However, an inheritance change to the underlying base class affects all inherited classes that didn't directly override that modified behavior.

Just as in good database design, you want to minimize the number of places that data resides so that changes have to be made in only a few places. Code works the same way.

Inheritance is a very important concept in object-oriented development and, when used correctly, can greatly reduce development and maintenance time and frustration.

Model Versus Code

For a model to be effective, it must closely parallel the actual system that it models. In the case of computer software, the characteristics of the model(s) should align closely with the actual computer code that makes up the project. Also, as the project changes to meet new requirements or respond to real-world requirements, it's important that the model and code stay in sync when they're modified to reflect the new information. Visual Modeler provides a number of tools and techniques to help make sure that this relationship exists and is maintained throughout the life of your project.

Two tools in Visual Modeler aid the process of keeping the model of a given system in sync with the code that's written to implement that system: the Code Generation Wizard and the Reverse Engineering Wizard.

Code Generation Wizard

After you create a model, Visual Modeler can automatically generate classes, function stubs, and comments in your project. You control which elements of the model code gets generated for. You can choose to let Visual Modeler automatically generate code for your entire model or select specific elements of the model. You can also control what's generated and how it looks by configuring options in the Code Generation Wizard.

To use the Code Generation Wizard, follow these steps:

1. Make sure that Visual Basic is running; the Code Generation Wizard won't function otherwise.
2. Load your model if you haven't already done so. (Choose File, Open from the menu.)
3. Choose Tools, Code Generation Wizard from the menu. A Welcome dialog box appears. Read the overview and then click Next.
4. The Select Classes dialog box appears (see Figure 27.5). You now can select the classes for which you want to generate code. If you want to generate code for all the classes, select the Automatically setting for the Synchronize Model and Project option.

   If you want to select specific classes for which to generate code, select the Manually option and then select the classes in the Classes in Model list. Click the Add button to move the classes into the Selected Classes list.
5. Click Next. The Preview Classes dialog box appears (see Figure 27.6).
6. If you want to preview the code before it's generated (recommended), highlight a specific class and click the Preview button. You'll see a series of four dialog boxes that allow you to tune your code: Class Options, Property Options, Role Options, and Method Options. Click the Finish button to return to the Preview Classes dialog box. Repeat with another class, if desired.
7. When you're finished previewing classes, click the Next button in the Preview Classes dialog box. The General Options dialog box appears (see Figure 27.7).

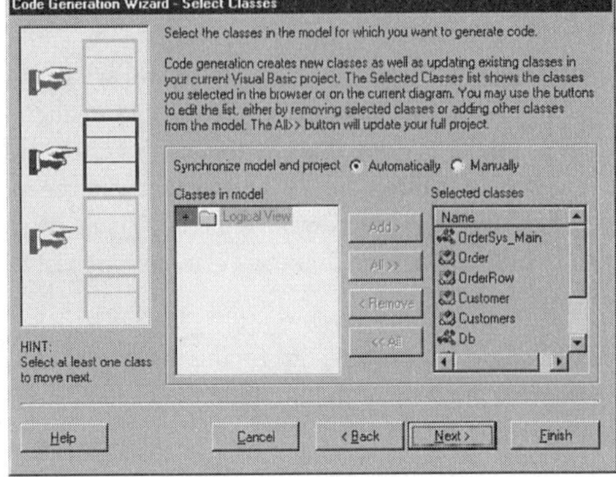

FIG. 27.5
Use the Select Classes dialog box to determine the classes for which code will be generated.

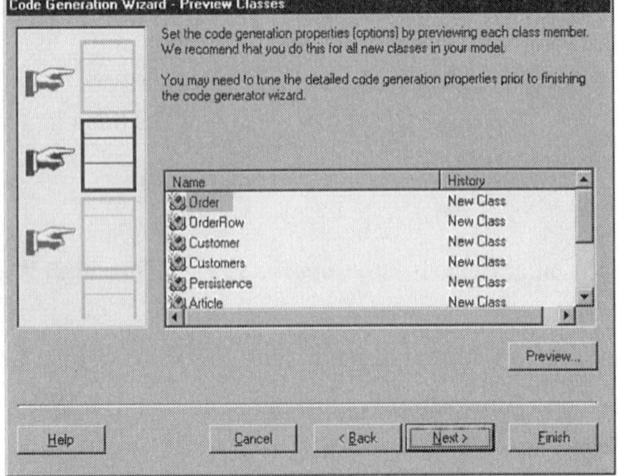

FIG. 27.6
With the Preview Classes dialog box, you can preview the code that will be generated for a specific class and change options as required, before actually generating the code.

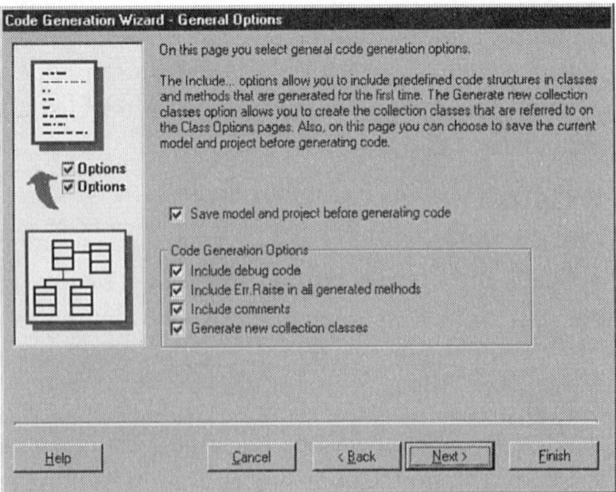

FIG. 27.7
The General Options dialog box allows you to change settings that affect the code generated for all classes in your model.

8. In the General Options dialog box, you can select options that control the generation of comments, debugging code, and other additions that may make your code easier to understand and debug. Make your selections and click Next.
9. Review the information in the Finish dialog box. At this point, you can go back and change any of your settings by clicking the Back button. When you're sure your settings are correct, click the Finish button.
10. A progress dialog box appears, to keep you apprised of the code-generation process. The Code Generation Wizard presents a Summary dialog box when finished.
11. To review the results of the process, use the Summary and Log pages to see what occurred. You can also review the generated code in Visual Basic, in addition to saving the project containing the code.
12. When you're finished reviewing the results, click the Close button.

Reverse Engineering Wizard

Even if you never performed any design work on your application, Visual Modeler can read through your code and create an object model that contains all classes, modules, controls, and relationships. This can be very useful for improving your system architecture, adding objects, doing additional design work, finding reusable code, or acquainting new people with the existing system.

Through the Reverse Engineering Wizard, you can customize what types of objects and relationships are created and drawn. To bring up the Reverse Engineering Wizard and set configuration options, follow these steps:

1. Make sure that Visual Basic is running; otherwise, the Reverse Engineering Wizard won't function.
2. Load your model, if you haven't already done so. (Choose File, Open from the menu.)
3. Choose Tools, Reverse Engineering Wizard from the menu. A Welcome dialog box appears. Read the overview and then click Next.
4. The Selection of Components dialog box appears (see Figure 27.8). In this dialog box, you can automatically generate a model that includes all your components or manually select only those components on which you want to focus.
5. Select the components you want or click the Automatically option to select them all. Click the Next button.
6. The Assignment of Components dialog box appears (see Figure 27.9). The standard Logical View includes (by default) three packages reflecting the typical three-tier model. Drag components from the Selected Components list into the desired packages in the Logical View Packages list.

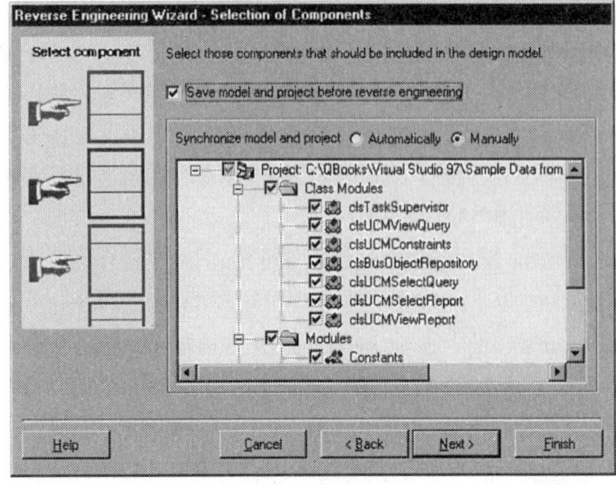

FIG. 27.8
The Selection of Components dialog box allows you to save your project and model before the reverse-engineering process as a precaution.

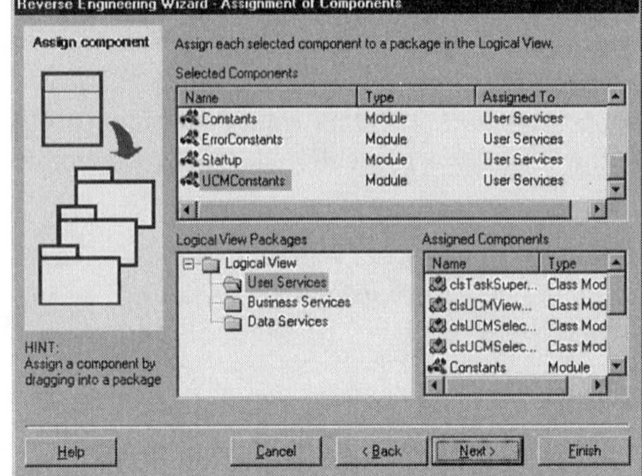

FIG. 27.9
Use the Assignment of Components dialog box to group your components into packages.

7. By highlighting a package, you can see which components have been included in that package in the Assigned Components list. When you're satisfied with your assignments, click the Next button.
8. The Finish dialog box appears, outlining the process that's about to occur (see Figure 27.10). If the information is incorrect, click the Back button to change your settings. Otherwise, click the Finish button to create a model through reverse engineering.
9. A Progress dialog box appears that provides the status of the reverse-engineering process. When it's finished, a Summary dialog box appears, allowing you to review the additions or changes made to your model.
10. Click the Close button.

After importing all the various elements from the project, Visual Modeler draws the diagram and attempts to space and group the various elements in a readable format. You'll find that you usually need to do quite a bit of reorganizing, however, to make the diagram more readable and useful.

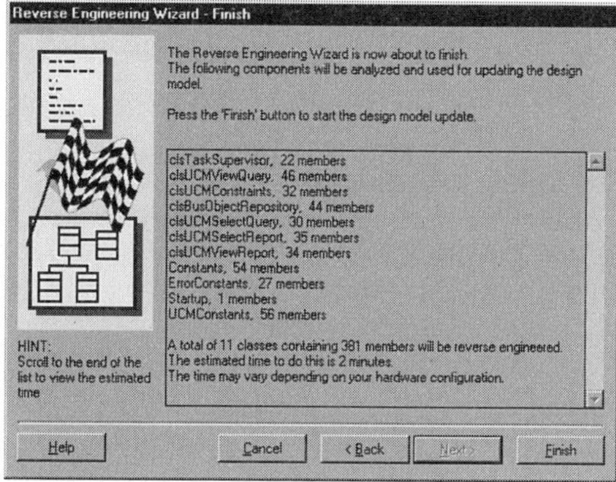

FIG. 27.10
The Finish dialog box summarizes the impending reverse-engineering process to give you the opportunity to review the outcome before it occurs.

Round-Trip Engineering

Round-trip engineering allows you to keep your model in sync with your code, and vice versa. Round-trip engineering is really just a combination of code generation and reverse engineering. With round-trip engineering, however, you get the advantage of having code and comments properly formatted by the Code Generation Wizard so that they, with any changes, can be properly imported back into the model and changes in the model can be reinserted into the code.

This is particularly necessary for keeping comments synchronized. In this way, you can completely use everything you've done from start to finish without throwing away any of your work, and yet it still allows an iterative development life cycle.

From Here...

The use of tools such as Visual Modeler is growing. After years of debate and refinement, the practice of object-oriented analysis and design is now generally accepted as being a useful way to create good software, perhaps even the best that's now available. Few modern projects created for environments with distributed databases, I-net technologies, and multitier architectures would be undertaken without these techniques. Tools such as Visual Modeler that directly support specific languages in a tightly integrated fashion are important to the success of large projects. For more information on some of the topics addressed in this chapter, see the following chapters:

- For a thorough overview of the support provided for object-oriented development by Microsoft tools, see Chapter 4, "Using Microsoft's Object Technologies."
- To learn how to web-enable existing applications, see Chapter 19, "Enabling Existing Applications for I-net Environments."

- For information on another tool that supports teams of developers who must work effectively together, see Chapter 28, "The Microsoft Repository."

ON THE WEB

For a look at multimedia creation tools for I-net applications, see "Web Content Creation Tools and Utilities" on the G. A. Sullivan web site at **http://www.gasullivan.com/vs97book/**.

CHAPTER 28

The Microsoft Repository

by Jody C. Socha

Over the years, there have been several attempts to develop software products to streamline the development process. Examples of these tools range from compilers to modeling tools to full suites of CASE tools. What has been missing from these tools, however, is a vehicle to tie all the information together so that it can be shared from one tool to another. This missing tool is the repository.

This chapter introduces the Microsoft Repository. It presents the various components of the repository and discusses how those components are used. It also discusses how your development environment needs to be changed to support using the repository. ■

The architecture of the Microsoft Repository

The components of the repository are presented and their functions discussed in detail. Also, a discussion of how the components work together is provided.

A structure for planning a repository-based environment

A discussion is provided to explain how the development environment will operate in a repository-based environment, including the team members needed to operate the repository.

How to model your information systems needs to use the repository

The concept of the metamodel is covered along with the role it plays in the repository environment.

Examples of how coding should be structured to better utilize the repository

Using the repository will not be as simple as just connecting to the repository from development tools. Some examples highlighting the challenges of capturing information in the repository are provided.

NOTE The Microsoft Repository is included with Visual Studio 97 and Visual Basic 5.0. It is installed automatically when you install Visual Basic from either of those sources. ■

Introduction to the Microsoft Repository

The word *repository* by itself is insufficient to describe what the Microsoft Repository is about. The definition of repository in the dictionary is a place to store things. The repository's technical architecture is made up of a database with a set of interfaces that can be used to access the data in the database, which describes just about every database application in existence. Thus, with some careful planning, the repository could be used to store just about anything.

On the other hand, the Microsoft Repository (and its competitors) is meant to serve a more specific purpose. Namely, that purpose is to store information describing applications and information systems. For example, suppose you have a Visual Basic application that uses ODBC to access an MS SQL Server database to manage a store's inventory. The repository could be used to store the various Visual Basic forms, classes, methods, and properties that comprise the code. Another portion of the repository would describe the SQL Server database tables, columns, stored procedures, and triggers. In addition, the repository could be used to organize any requirements and design documents used in developing the system. Thus, the repository would contain a complete description of the application in one central location.

Together, these two perspectives combine to create a potentially powerful effect. The flexible architecture of a repository should allow you to store nearly any information about a system that you want:

- *Lifecycle phases*—You could store requirements documents, design documents and models, and implemented code structures.
- *System components*—You could store code structures, database layouts, and hardware and networking configurations.
- *Project management*—You could store project plans, task and "to do" lists, and possibly even cost estimates.
- *Miscellaneous*—You could even store the information on project team members and important project contacts.

However, simply storing all this information does not unlock the true power of using a repository. The real benefit is not derived until the various pieces of data stored in the repository are integrated together to form a single, complete picture of the system. Now, you can determine which sections of code will be impacted if you change the name of a column in the database. Alternatively, you can see which parts of the Visual Basic application utilize the interface into the C++ OLE server that you want to rewrite. Theoretically, you could see what would happen to the accounting application used in the Atlanta office if a change is made to the inventory maintenance application in the Detroit office. It is this ability to measure the impact of a change across a system or systems that makes the repository so potentially powerful.

A repository is not a Computer Aided Software Engineering (CASE) tool. CASE tools provide various modeling and analysis techniques for developing software. A repository provides only the storage mechanism for information about your development environment. What a repository can do is work together with a CASE tool to store the results of an analysis effort. That information then can be shared with other analysts or developers. Alternatively, the information can be related to the results of other CASE tools to provide an integrated view of the entire environment.

Given its flexibility, the repository can also play a role in a data warehousing environment. The repository stores the structure of the data in each of the operational systems and the target warehouse system as well as the relationship map between the two sets of structures. This setup can greatly reduce the complexity of updating the warehouse when one of the operational systems is modified. In addition, if a more detailed analysis is required than the data warehouse provides, a pointer to the appropriate operational system data is available through the repository.

Now for the bad news. Very little of this potential power is available by simply starting the Microsoft Repository application. The Microsoft Repository in its basic form provides little more than a generic database structure and set of interfaces that serve no specific purpose. Only by developing a series of additional interfaces, plug-ins, and programs can the repository be truly utilized, and this requires quite a bit of work.

The remainder of this chapter is divided into three sections. The first deals with how the repository is structured. The second moves on to cover how to configure and use the repository. Finally, the third discusses how to reengineer your development process to take advantage of the repository.

Repository Architecture

The following section describes how the Microsoft Repository is organized. Consider the repository to be a series of layers controlling access to the repository's data at the center. The following discusses each of those layers and the function each serves.

Overview

The repository itself is organized into three basic components. The following list describes those components, and Figure 28.1 illustrates them:

- *Database*—A relational database where the information about applications and projects is stored.
- *Repository Engine*—The driver that enforces consistency of the database's information.
- *Tool Information Model (TIM)*—A set of unique interfaces designed to pass specific types of data into and out of the repository. One special Tool Information Model is the Type Information Model.

FIG. 28.1
The Microsoft Repository is organized into several layers designed to give specific applications access to a generic interface.

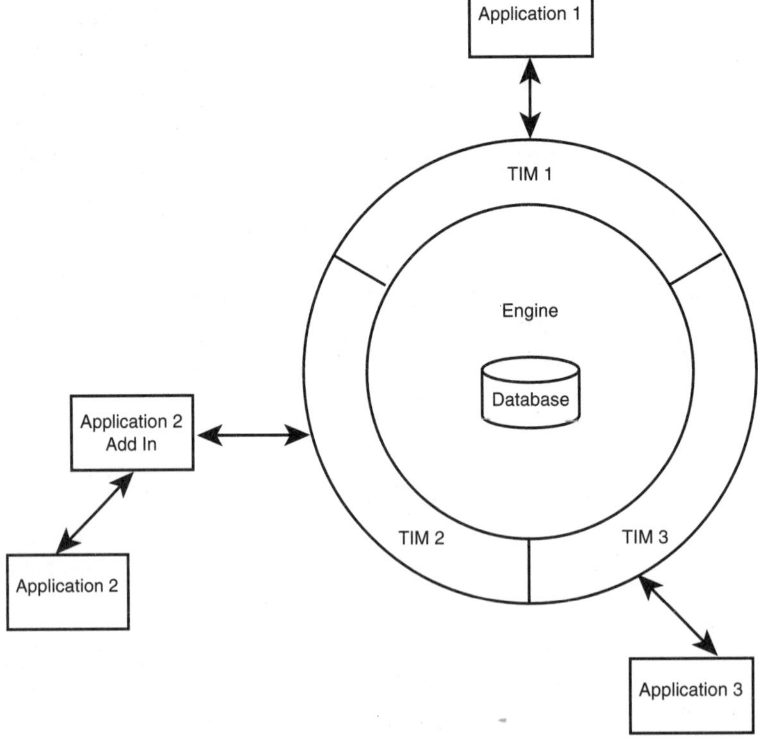

There are three basic methods for communicating with the repository, depending on your purpose:

- *Data input/output*—Around the outside of the repository are the various applications that utilize it. Each of these applications share information with the Repository by communicating with the appropriate Tool Information Models. (Note: It is possible for an application to talk to more than one TIM to store its data.) The TIM then talks to the engine through the API, which, in turn, stores and retrieves information in the database.
- *Setting up the repository structure*—You may need to configure the repository structure to expand or change its information content. In this case, you will add a new Tool Information Model to the database. This TIM will be defined in terms of Microsoft's Type Information Model. The TIM then instructs the engine what new classes, interfaces, properties, and so on to create or modify. When this step is accomplished, you will then need to write an application to interact with this new TIM to actually store the data.
- *Reporting*—For most reporting, the standard TIMs to control access to repository data will be used. However, a second method that may be more efficient is to establish a connection to the database itself and run a series of SQL queries to retrieve the desired

information. (Note: Although you can read data from the database through a direct connection, you are strongly discouraged from writing to the database in this manner. Writing to the database directly bypasses all of the logic and integrity checking provided by the TIMs and the engine itself.)

Each of the repository's components and its functions are discussed in more detail in the following sections.

Database

The heart of the repository is a standard database. The default database for the repository is created when the repository is installed on the computer. The default location is C:\Windows\MSApps\repostry\repostry.mdb.

The Microsoft Repository uses either its Jet database engine or SQL Server to store the data. The repository engine then talks to this central database through an ODBC connection. It is your choice which platform to use. Whenever you utilize the repository, you need to establish a connection to the appropriate database and then pass that connection to the repository engine. Then, through the engine, you can either set up the repository's data structure, or use the information stored in the repository.

There are basically two sets of tables in the database. The first are the tables that the engine uses to store the repository's structural information. These tables store the information that describes the various TIMs that have been created. The second set of tables is used to actually store the data you are interested in storing. These are the tables to which the TIMs allow access.

The primary method for accessing the repository is through the TIMs and the engine. However, this does not mean that the only way to pull information out of the repository is through the engine. You can establish an ODBC connection to the database if you desire. You can then query the repository tables directly, thus simplifying obtaining data for reporting purposes. However, you are strongly encouraged to only read information out of the database. Sticking information into the database circumvents the engine's consistency-checking capabilities and can lead to unpredictable results.

Repository Engine

The engine manages data in the repository. Together the engine and the database form the repository itself. All of the other components are a series of interfaces used to access the information in the repository. However, unless you are writing one of the intermediate extract applications, you will not interact with the engine itself. Thus, while you want to be familiar with its basic purpose, there is not much about the engine that you really need to know.

The engine provides the main control mechanism for the repository. It controls how data is written and read to/from the database, and it controls the basic repository structure. It provides the necessary consistency checking to ensure the integrity of the data.

The engine provides a set of classes and methods that can be called to perform various functions such as connecting to the repository database. This set of interfaces is documented in Microsoft's *Repository Programmer's Guide.*

Tool Information Models and the Type Information Model

Tool Information Models (TIM) are the definition of what information you would like to store in the repository. The word "Tool" is slightly misleading because a TIM can be used to store information from more than one tool. You have the option of creating your own TIMs or using any predefined TIMs that are available.

There is an initial TIM that Microsoft provides called the Microsoft Development Object Model (MDO Model) for use with Visual Basic. This model is created for you on the repository when the repository add-in for Visual Basic is activated. The repository add-in is provided when you install Visual Basic either from Visual Studio 97 or the Visual Basic 5.0 Enterprise Edition.

MDO is the only predefined TIM available from Microsoft when this book went to press. However, Microsoft has announced plans for releasing its Open Information Model (OIM), which promises a non-tool–specific structure for repository storage. Microsoft is working hard with third-party vendors to share the OIM concept.

There are some third-party vendors that offer predefined TIMs although they should be moving towards using the OIM.

ON THE WEB

See the Microsoft web site, **http://www.Microsoft.com/repository**, for more information on the repository including information on the latest status of the open information model and sample applications.

If you intend to write your own TIMs, then you need to become familiar with the Type Information Model. The Type Information Model is a special model that is used by a TIM to describe itself to the repository. The type information model provides the following basic concepts:

- *Class*—A thing about which you want the repository to store information
- *Interface*—The exposition of the classes, properties, collections, and behaviors to the outside world
- *Properties*—A piece of data about a class
- *Methods*—A function or service that a class performs
- *Relationship*—An association between two or more classes
- *Relationship Origin Collection*—The classes that form the parent of a relationship or initiate the action in a relationship
- *Relationship Destination Collection*—The classes that are the child in a relationship or receive the action of a relationship

The type information model is sufficiently general to allow you to describe any structure to the repository. For example, imagine you wanted to keep track of the team members assigned to a project. The following steps explain how the type information model could be used to describe this information. More information on the type information model can be obtained from Microsoft's *Repository Programmer's Reference Guide.*

1. Start by creating two new classes: `team member` and `project`.
2. Next, define interfaces for the two classes as well as any other interfaces you want to expose.
3. After defining the interfaces, define properties for the classes that you want to track, and assign them to the interfaces. Examples of properties include `name` for the `team member` class or `start date` and `stop date` for `project`.
4. Next, define the relationship for how a team member is associated with a class. For example, create a relationship named `assigned to`.
5. Finally, assign the start and stop classes to the relationships. You would assign the `team member` class as a source for the `assigned to` class and assign `project` as a destination of the relationship.

ON THE WEB

See the Microsoft web site, **http://www.Microsoft.com/repository**, for more information on the repository including the *Repository Programmer's Reference Guide*.

An example of a predefined TIM is the Microsoft Definition Object (MDO) model that is provided for use with Visual Basic. More information on the type information model can be obtained from Microsoft's *Repository Programmer's Reference Guide.*

Also, the type information model makes it possible to extend predefined TIMs by simply adding new classes, relationships, properties, methods, and interfaces to the existing model. You could also establish relationships between two different TIMs by adding a new relationship and assigning a class in one model as the relationship's source and a class in the other model as the relationship's destination. Be careful, however, not to change the meaning of a predefined TIM's components. Outside tools may use the TIM to store data and may not store it the way you want.

Microsoft has also announced that it is developing its Open Information Model for the repository. This model is supposed to provide the foundation for all third-party vendors to use so they populate the repository in a common manner. For those people unsure about implementing a repository, it would be a good idea to wait until this new model is released.

Applications

Around the outside of the repository are the various applications that use it. These applications generally fall into three categories:

- The first group of applications is the various tools you use in your development environment. These include tools such as Visual Basic, Visual C++, Visual Modeler, or even Microsoft Word. These tools do not interact with the repository directly.
- The second group is the applications that examine your development tools and extract the required information into the repository. An example of this type of tool is the repository add-in for Visual Basic, which stores Visual Basic information into the repository using Microsoft's MDO Model.
- The third group is the applications used to browse the repository to do reporting or to perform impact analysis. An example of this type of tool is the browser tool that is provided with the repository on installation.

The Open Repository Concept

In an ideal environment, the repository configuration should enable you to truly open up your development environment. Of course, the world is not ideal, and there will be limitations in Microsoft's ability to support the open concept.

The first level of openness comes at the database layer. Because the repository uses an ODBC connection to a standard relational database, any commercially available database could be used for repository data storage. However, Microsoft advertises that the repository only works with its Jet database engine or SQL server.

The second level of openness deals with sharing data between tools. For example, information about classes in a design tool could be extracted to automatically create classes in a development tool. At the present time, this type of information sharing will be difficult due to the lack of maturity of commercially available TIMs and applications. In the future, this capability should grow continuously stronger. For example, the Microsoft Open Information Model promises to solve many of these problems.

The third level of openness deals with the ability to actually replace tools. Theoretically, the repository should be capturing your tools data in such a way that that tool could be pulled out and replaced with another similar tool. Naturally, this level of openness is impossible. Vendors are not going to freely give away proprietary information just so you can switch to a competitor's tool. However, if similar tools all reference the same TIMs, then transitioning to a new tool can be greatly simplified. Again, maturation of the TIMs and TIM applications will go a long way to helping with this problem.

Planning the Repository

Utilizing a repository-based development environment takes planning to configure the pieces. You need to examine your current development process, identify resource needs, and assemble the various components that you need.

Reexamining the Development Process

Setting up your environment to use a repository is not much different than any other software development effort you will embark upon. You need to lay out the requirements to identify what information should be captured in the repository, and how you will analyze that data. Then, you need to design the repository by identifying what plug-ins, Tool Information Models, and analysis tools need to be obtained or built. Finally, you will need to build and test the repository once all the components are ready.

You also need to consider who will be responsible for maintaining the repository. People will be needed for system administration, developing any additional applications, and analyzing the repository's contents.

You will need to reexamine many of your development conventions. At what points in the development process will information need to be stored in the repository? How often will it need to be updated? What role will the repository play in managing change requests? Are there any coding conventions that should be revisited to allow better information transfer?

You will need to examine your environment to understand your development needs. Figure 28.2 shows the development lifecycle according to the standard "waterfall" approach. The waterfall method consists of a series of steps in which one step does not begin until the first had completely ended.

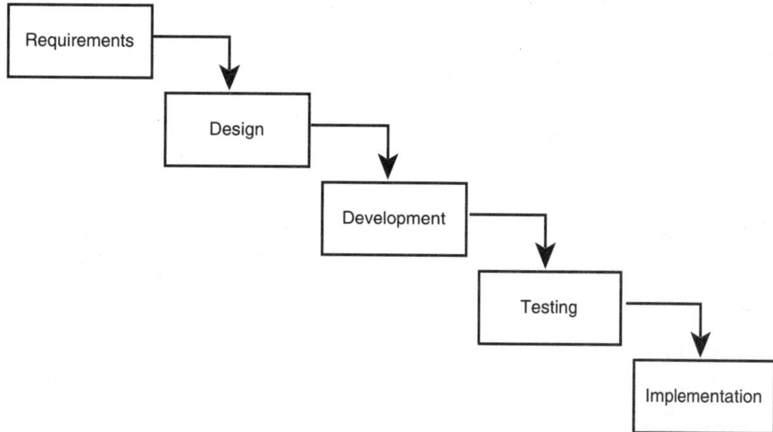

FIG. 28.2
A traditional view of the software development process is the waterfall method.

Moving to a repository-based environment means that you want to enable sharing of information between each phase of the lifecycle through centralized data storage. This new information-centered environment is shown in Figure 28.3.

Repository Team Members

Naturally, using a repository in your development environment will require additional manpower. Whether that manpower need is filled on a full-time or part-time basis depends on how extensive the repository system will be. You will have to experiment to understand how much of a strain the repository will put on development.

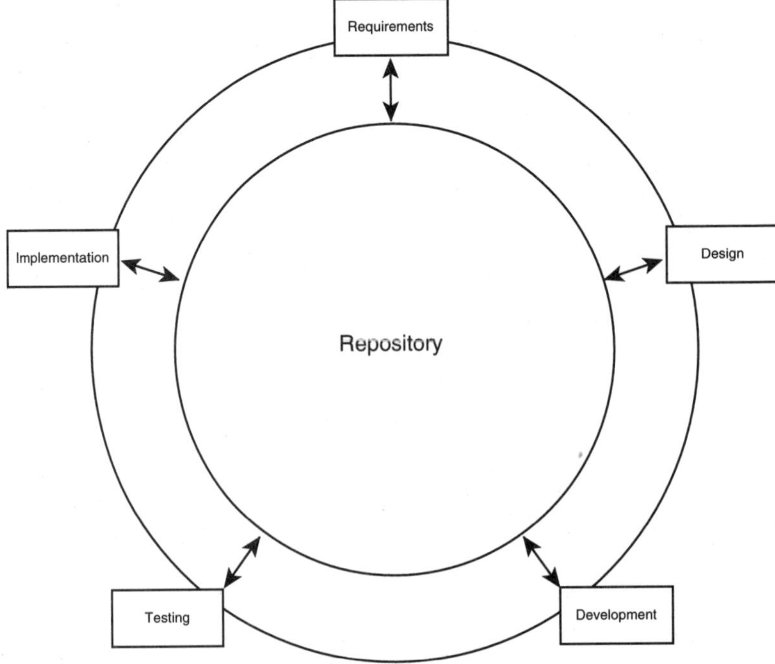

FIG. 28.3
When the repository is added to the development process, it assumes the role of a centralized, information-sharing manager.

Several roles need to be performed in a repository environment.

System Manager As with any system, someone will need to perform administration on the system. A security scheme may need to be established. The database will need to be configured and maintained. Software tools that share data with the repository will need to be configured and maintained.

Modelers/Analysts One or more individuals will need to provide the foundation of the repository by building and assembling the various TIMs. These individuals will need strong analytical skills because they will be determining what data needs to be stored in the repository and how that data should be obtained from the various tools. A well-designed TIM should be able to accommodate more than one tool. In addition, this team will need to analyze any commercially available TIMs, such as the MDO Model for Visual Basic, to determine if the necessary data is being captured and how that model integrates with the rest of the repository model.

Developers Once the TIMs are in place, a group of programmers is required to build the software needed to actually use the repository. One set of software will be built to extract the information out of the various software development tools into the repository. A second set will be built to browse and manipulate the data as well as produce analysis reports.

Alternatively, team members can research the various prebuilt components available. For example, there is already a Visual Basic add-on for populating the MDO Model, and Microsoft provides a default browser. In addition, several other vendors are already developing repository interface software. It would be worth the effort to research these commercial offerings before embarking on a time-consuming development effort.

Users The user of the repository is your organization's software development team. Because the repository stores information about the development environment, the repository will eventually prove invaluable in analyzing your application's structure, tracking the use and reuse of software components, and analyzing the impact of change on the application or applications. Thus, everyone from the project manager to coders to quality assurance could utilize information contained in the repository.

Regardless of how an organization wants to staff the repository team, the organization definitely wants to assign their most competent and experienced personnel. If you have a goal of a repository-based development environment, then consider that faulty data in the repository will lead to faulty development decisions, leading to faulty software, leading to errors in operations. Moreover, repository data management will be more complex and abstract than any other form of development effort you are undertaking.

Assembling the Repository Components

The components that you need to assemble the repository are dependent on your development environment. Thus, you will need to examine each phase of your development environment and determine how a repository should be utilized in each phase.

Define the Overall Structure The first and simplest component to identify is the repository itself. For it, you will need to identify what database server you want to use, which is based on how much information you think will be stored in the database. Then, you need to configure the database and install the repository engine.

The challenging part is to develop the various TIMs and extraction applications that surround the repository and provide the interface for the various lifecycle phases. You can use Table 28.1 as a high-level planning tool for understanding your repository needs.

Table 28.1 Methodologies and Tools Used in the Development Lifecycle

Development Phase	Products	Toolset
Requirements	Requirements Documents	Word 97
Design	Object-Oriented Design Design Documents	Visual Modeler Word 97
Development	User Interface Code Business Rule Code Database	Visual Basic 5.0 Visual C++ 5.0 SQL Server 3.1

continues

Table 28.1 Continued

Development Phase	Products	Toolset
Testing	Test Plans and Procedures Test Results	Word 97 Word 97, Excel 97
Implementation	Installation Procedures	Word 97
Project Management	Project Plan Issues Log	Project Excel 97

NOTE The tools listed in the table all happen to be Microsoft products. However, there is no reason that tools from other vendors cannot be used. ■

Notice that for any development phase, several methodologies and tools may be used. Likewise, more than one tool may be used to implement a product, or the same tool may be used in preparing more than one product. Notice, also, that some of the tools are specifically geared toward producing the specified product (such as Visual Modeler or SQL Server), whereas others are more general and have been adapted to fill a need (for example, Word and Excel).

Identify Information Requirements After identifying these products and tool sets, the next step is to identify your information requirements. At this step, you need to ask the question, "What information about this product needs to be shared?" Notice that you need to capture information about the product, not the tool itself. The tool will be utilized in determining how to capture the information, not what information needs to be captured.

The information that can be extracted from the product may be dependent on how well organized its contents are, and you always have the option not to capture any information. For example, suppose that an analysis of several requirements documents reveals several pages of simple paragraphs in no particular order, describing in general what you want the proposed system to do. Because there would be limited benefit in placing any of this information into the repository, you choose to store nothing. Placing the document into a centralized directory accomplishes the same thing much easier.

On the other hand, if the document is subdivided into subject areas and the requirements are numbered, named, and prioritized, there may be benefit from pulling in this information. The repository could provide a simple mechanism for browsing and reporting on the requirements. Furthermore, the potential to cross-reference the requirements to the system's various design components exists to provide requirements traceability throughout systems development. You probably will also want to capture the name of the document as well as file/directory information.

In the design phase, you identified that your project is developing an object-oriented design (OOD) with supporting design documents. Because OODs utilize a structured methodology, it simplifies identifying information requirements. An OOD generally includes classes, attributes, methods, and associations. Several more conventions are also available depending on which specific methodology you are using. You probably also will want to capture filenames because a design will probably be spread across several files. This information is useful in identifying what class modules need to be developed in the code as well as how those classes should work together. The design documents contain definitions of the classes in the design that were created by exporting reports from the design tool that are formatted with Microsoft Word.

The same step of identifying information requirements is repeated for the other development phases. Be sure to include support processes such as project management and quality assurance in the analysis. Table 28.2 shows some of the results.

Table 28.2 Types of Information That Should Be Stored in the Repository for Each Product

Development Phase	Products	Information Requirements
Requirements	Requirements Documents	Document Name, File, Requirement (Priority)
Design	Object-Oriented Design Design Documents	Class (Method, Property) Association not used
Project Management	Project Plan	Developers, Milestones, Issues, Develop to Issue Association

Using the Repository

Installing and setting up the repository is a fairly simple process, mainly because it's installed and configured for you when you install Visual Basic 5.0 using either the Enterprise Edition or Visual Studio. The remainder of this section discusses how you can configure the various components of a repository.

Building and Using Tool Information Models

The TIMs define what information the repository will store. You have the option of building your own TIMs or using predefined TIMs. Building your own TIM gives you more control over what information is stored in the repository. It will also make it easier for you to relate how information in different tool sets relates to each other. However, building your own TIM will involve a lot more work. Using the predefined TIM simplifies the process, and you can extend the existing model if you have special needs. Plus, vendors will provide their own extractor applications for use with their TIMs, further reducing the amount of work you need to do.

Using Existing TIMs versus Building Your Own For the time being, you should probably not write your own TIM unless you have a special need. There are several reasons for this. First, the repository is in its earliest stages. Second, Microsoft has announced the OIM, which is intended to provide the foundation model that other vendors will tie their models into. Thus, give the repository and the OIM time to mature before you invest heavily into developing your own models. Keep checking the Microsoft repository web site for information on the OIM and a list of third-party vendors.

This does not mean that you should not learn how TIMs are built. Most likely, the TIMs provided to you will not meet all of your needs. At some point in time, you will probably need to extend a TIM that involves the same basic techniques as building a complete TIM.

Using Existing TIMs Using an existing TIM is an easier exercise. Typically, the vendor should supply the application needed to install its particular TIM onto the repository. For example, the Microsoft MDO Model is installed on the repository automatically when the repository add-in for Visual Basic is used. You should become familiar with the model and the information it stores.

Building a TIM If you want to build your own TIM, first make sure you become more familiar with the type information model and its components. This step is important because when you lay out the design of your TIM, you will need to classify the design components into the type information model categories. You also will need to identify which items in the design relate back to the repository root object.

After you have developed your design, you will need to develop a program that will configure the TIM on the repository. An example of a program to create a TIM can be found on the Microsoft web site as the Create Simple Database TIM download. The program should perform the following basic actions in order.

NOTE The file Reputil.bas is installed with the repository and provides several useful functions for building TIMs and Extractor applications. The functions help you to determine whether a TIM already exists, retrieve a TIM from the repository, create and retrieve repository objects, and extend the `ReposRoot` class to implement a new interface for a TIM. ■

CAUTION

Whenever you are populating the repository with data that should be treated as a set, use the transaction `begin`, `commit`, and `rollback` methods. Otherwise, each transaction will get committed individually, and, if a fatal error occurs, an easy method to remove the corrupt data will exist. For example, when creating a TIM, wrap the entire TIM creation in a transaction so that the TIM will not be partially implemented in case of a failure.

1. Establish a connection to the appropriate repository database. This can be accomplished by creating a repository object and calling the `open` or `create` method as necessary. The method will return the repository root object to use.
2. Start a transaction on the repository so that you can save or reject the changes as necessary. This step can be accomplished by calling the `Begin` method on the transaction class for the repository object.

3. Now, create the type library for the TIM. This step is accomplished by referencing the IManageReposTypeLib interface and calling the `CreateTypeLib` method. As part of this method call, the TIM name and class ID will be assigned. This method will return the resulting `TypeLib` object. The code should check to ensure the TIM is not already implemented on the repository by using the `HasTypeLib` method. Also, the code should check the `TypeLib` object returned to make sure it was initialized successfully.
4. The code will then create each of the TIM components: interfaces, classes, properties, methods, and relationships.
5. Finally, assuming there are no errors, commit the work and the TIM is now in the repository. Otherwise, rollback the work. Call either the `Commit` or `Rollback` methods on the transaction object.

ON THE WEB

In addition to the example program available at the Microsoft web site (**http://www.Microsoft.com/repository**), you also can find full code examples for the preceding procedures at **http://www.gasullivan.com/vs97book**.

The preceding discussion outlines how to create a TIM but does not aid you in identifying the structure of the TIM. As an example of what the structure would be, reconsider Table 28.2 and start laying out your model. Use the list of development processes and products to identify subject areas for your model. From there, identify the classes, interfaces, relationships, properties, and methods needed to implement your identified requirements using the Type Information Model as the main structure. Be sure to identify which classes refer back to the repository root object for browsing purposes.

For example, based on Table 28.2, you would probably want a separate TIM for your requirements documents. Within that, you would create the following items:

- *Classes*—Document, File, Requirement
- *Interfaces*—Document, File, Requirement
- *Relationships*—Contains (a document contains requirements), Stores (a file stores a document)
- *Properties*—For Document (name, date, author); For File (storage path and name, creation date); For Requirement (text, priority, number)
- *Methods*—For Document (list requirements, list requirements with priority)

Look for opportunities to reuse classes, if possible. For example, almost all tools utilize files to store data. So, a File class could be reused across all TIMs to capture filename, directory location, and last modification date.

Identify relationships across subject areas. These relationships eventually will provide the real power behind the repository for analyzing cross-product change impacts. For example, a requirement in the design document could be related to the design class that implements it, such as an `employee` class that implements the requirement "The system will allow employees to store their timesheets online."

Building and Using Extractor Applications

Although the repository structure is in place through the TIMs, your work is not done yet. You need to develop and assemble the various extraction applications that will populate the repository. Alternatively, you need to configure any predeveloped extractor applications that you want to use.

Building the Extractor An example of a program to populate a TIM can be found on the Microsoft web site (**www.microsoft.com/repository**) as the Populate Simple Database TIM download. See the earlier section "Building a TIM" for more information on the sample applications. The program should perform the following basic actions in order:

1. Establish a connection to the appropriate repository database. This can be accomplished by creating a repository object and calling the `open` or `create` method as necessary. The method will return the repository root object to use.
2. Start a transaction on the repository so that changes can be saved or rejected as necessary. This step is accomplished by calling the `Begin` method on the transaction class for the repository object.
3. Get the type library for the TIM the extractor will populate. This step is accomplished by referencing the `ReposTypeLibs` property of the `Root` object. As part of this call, the name of the TIM to be used will be designated.
4. Next, either connect to or open the source of the data you want to load into the repository. Sources of the data could be a file, a database, the registry, or you could even prompt the user to provide the necessary information.
5. You can now begin loading the data into the repository. Grab the first piece of necessary data from the source. Create an instance of the repository object you want to load. Use the `CreateReposObject` method in the RepUtil.Bas file and specify the name of the object to use. Finally, for the object you created, reference the interface and property you want to use and set it equal to its resulting value, for example `Database.Interface("IDatabase").Name = strDBName`.
6. When all data has been loaded, assuming there are no errors, commit your work and the TIM is now in the repository. Otherwise, rollback your work. You can call either the `Commit` or `Rollback` methods on the transaction object.

NOTE The method for referencing an object for data storage depends on how the TIM's interfaces are structured. For example, a requirement in a requirements document has been rewritten, and you want to update the requirement in the repository. Making the change will involve identifying first the requirements document and then the requirement itself. ■

Extractor Considerations At this point, your main concern is with the tool used to produce the product than with the product itself. For example, you will want to know if the tool in question stores its information in a proprietary format. In this case, you need to research the tool's exporting and reporting mechanisms. Hopefully, you can dump the tool's information into a simple text file that can easily be parsed by an import routine. Otherwise, your only other choices are to add the information manually or get another tool.

Consider a requirements document written in Microsoft Word. You probably cannot gain information on Word's storage format, which will change from version to version anyway. Instead, you could write a Word macro to dump the desired information to a presorted text file, and then letting the extractor application move this information to the repository. You could, of course, simply prepare your requirements in a text document, but then you would lose sophisticated formatting capabilities such as bolding, headings, and so on. A developer should not have to give up these capabilities in order to use the repository.

Your second item of concern should be examining how the development products are organized to determine how easy it is to obtain the information required. For example, if the Word documents are just a series of standard paragraphs, your ability to pull out specific information is limited. You are better off placing the document in a centralized directory. On the other hand, imagine a document organized into a series of tables with columns labeled as Requirements ID, Name, Description, and Priority. In this case, code could more easily be written to sort through the file and pull out the data in its individual pieces.

CAUTION

This does not mean you should run and reorganize all of your products into well-defined structures. This type of activity could strangle the flexibility and creativity of the development team. Of course, a total lack of structure makes the products hard to read and use. Some type of balance between the extremes needs to be reached.

Once again, you have the option of using vendor-supplied applications or writing your own. The choice at this time is easier. Basically, if you have written your own TIM, you need to write your own extractor. Otherwise, if you have used a vendor-supplied TIM, you should use their application for populating the repository. The same rules apply in a hybrid situation. If you have extended the vendor-supplied TIM, you will need to write an application to fill in those extended portions.

Building Reporting Applications

The final piece of the repository puzzle that you will need is a set of reporting and analysis applications. Again, you have the choice of using predeveloped applications such as Microsoft's Repository Browser to do the work for you or building your own.

An example of a program to analyze the repository can be found on the Microsoft web site (**www.microsoft.com/repository**) as the Use Simple Database TIM download. See the section "Building a TIM" for more information on the sample applications. The program should perform the following basic actions in order:

1. Establish a connection to the appropriate repository database. This can be accomplished by creating a repository object and calling the `open` or `create` method as necessary. The method will return the repository root object to use.

2. Next, create and/or display the destination of the analysis data. For example, the program could display an onscreen dialog box or open a Word document for preparing a report.
3. Next, the data from the repository is obtained. Create an instance of the repository object to use. Use the `CreateReposObject` method in the RepUtil.Bas file and specify the name of the object to use. Finally, for the object you created, reference the interface and property you want retrieve its value—for example, `WordDoc.Content.InsertAfter Chr(10) & "Table:  " & Tables(I).Name & Chr(10)`.

Using the Browser

The browser is a basic analysis tool that is provided with the repository. It usually can be found in the bin directory in the repository directory in the Visual Basic installation area. Its name is Repbrows.exe.

The browser will initially connect to the default repository database, although you can connect to other databases as required (see Figure 28.4). You will either be prompted for an Access type file or ODBC connect data if you are looking for a SQL server database.

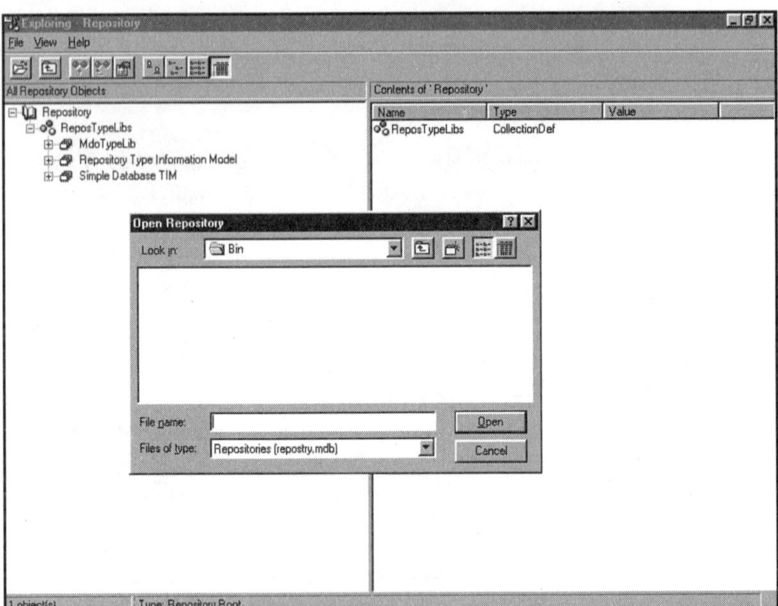

FIG. 28.4 The browser can connect to other repository databases.

Once connected, the browser uses the standard windows tree view to show the repository structure. Figures 28.5 and 28.6 show the structures of two TIMs and how they show up in the browser.

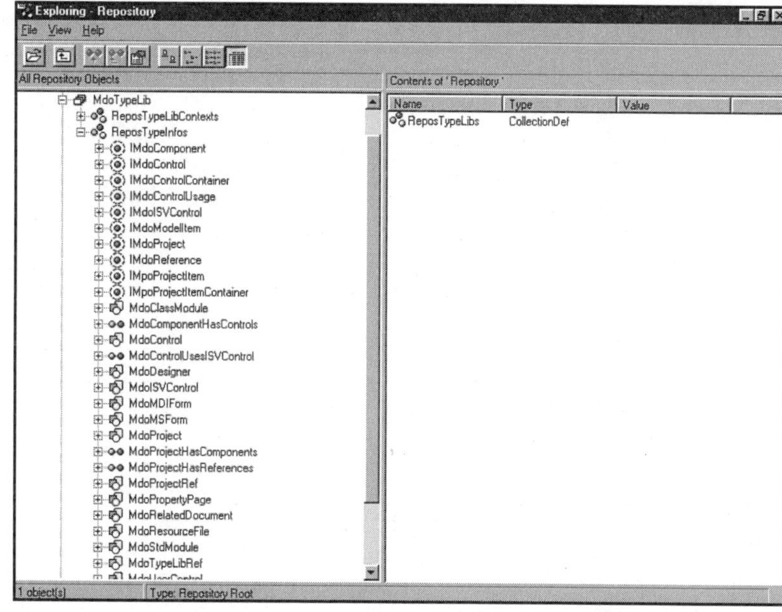

FIG. 28.5
The browser can be used to view the MDO Model components.

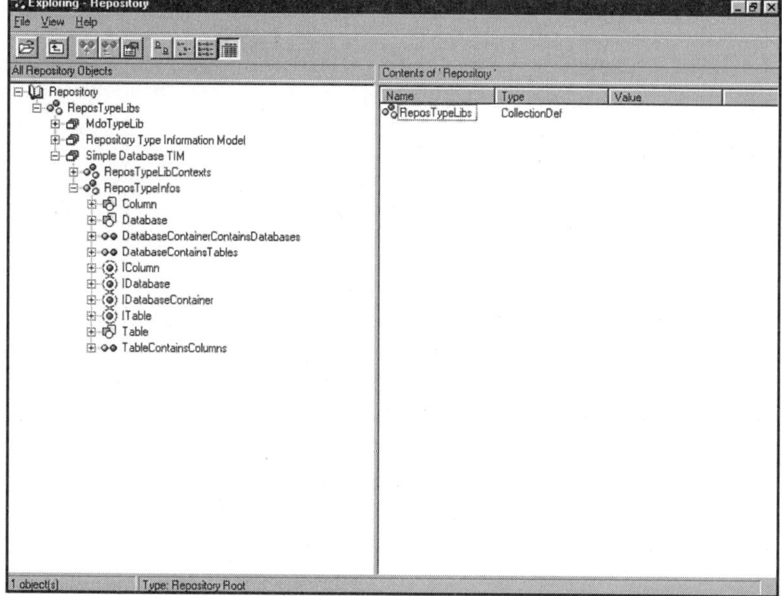

FIG. 28.6
The browser can be used to view the Simple Database Model components.

Rethinking Design and Coding Conventions

The following examples are intended to get you thinking about the complexities of a repository-based environment. Remember, the repository is just another piece of software, and, as such, it cannot "think" for you. When parsing a text file, for example, the search tool will expect certain information in certain positions or highlighted by specific keywords. If the file is not set up correctly, then errors will be reported or, worse, a large amount of corrupted data will be stored in the repository. Using the repository in a sloppy development environment, where coding standards are not enforced and coding is "quick and dirty," will produce little to no benefit. However, disciplined development can make the transition with relative ease.

For the following "Variable Declaration Example" and "Comment Formatting" sections, assume that the repository has been set up to extract information out of a Visual Basic application about its classes.

Variable Declaration Example

The following example of a variable declaration in Visual Basic is simple. In it, a `Course` class needs access to the assigned instructor information through an `Instructor` class. In the header portion of the file, the following code appears:

```
'Set up the instructor
     Private mvarInstructor as Object
```

Now, suppose that you want the repository to track the relationship between classes in your application. One way to do this is to have the tool-repository extraction application scan through the public and private variables to find those that reference other classes.

Unfortunately, in the preceding code there is no direct way to tell which class the member variable represents, so there is no way to build the `Course`-to-`Instructor` relationship. A quick solution is to avoid this form of vague data typing and declare the variable specifically:

```
'Set up the instructor
     Private mvarInstructor as New Instructor
```

Now, the extraction application can immediately relate the `Course` class to the `Instructor` class. An alternative could be that, when a variable defined as an object is encountered, the extraction application would immediately look for that variable's assignment operation elsewhere in the file:

```
'Set up the Instructor object (in Class_Initialize)
     Set mvarInstructor = new Instructor
```

Unfortunately, there are problems with this approach. First, the parsing algorithm will be slower the more searching that needs to be done. Second, simply finding the word `Set` and an equal sign in the code does not mean that you have found what the class is being set equal to. The following is a better alternative:

```
'Get the Course's Instructor from the collection (in Class_Initialize).
     Set mvarInstructor = mvarInstructors.Item(iInstructorID)
```

At this point, the extraction application can still determine that the `mvarInstructor` variable is an `Instructor` class by interrogating the data type of the return parameter of the `Item` method on the `Instructors` collection class (unless, of course, the return parameter is also declared as an Object).

A second alternative could be to use a special comment above or after the variable declaration:

```
Private mvarInstructor as Object      'Datatype: Instructor class
```

Alternatively, you could access the repository through a special browsing tool and add the relationship manually. However, a lot of work could be avoided by simply declaring variables as their specific types wherever possible, which you should be doing anyway. A similar set of arguments could make for avoiding the variant data type when possible, also.

Comment Formatting

The method that you use to format comments in the code determines how easily that comment information can be stored in the repository. Information is extracted about each class's public variables, methods, and properties. It is also safe to assume that, if the information is available, you would want to store any descriptions or definitions about classes, variables, methods, and properties.

A good candidate for a source of descriptions is the code itself, if comments are provided. Then, as the extraction application is parsing the file, the comments could be sucked up at the same time the descriptions are obtained. Sounds easy at first, but there are always problems.

First, if you are on one of those projects that do not comment the code, then this option is not even available. You will either need to find an alternative source of descriptions, such as from a design document or a class dictionary document, or add the descriptions to the database manually, or not capture descriptions at all. Actually, it is doubtful that an organization that does not comment code will find much benefit from using the repository in the first place.

Second, even if your organization does comment code, the comments are not necessarily readable or even useful. Consider this simple example:

```
''''''''''''''''''''''''''''''''''''''''''''''''''''''''''''''''''''''''''''''''
      '      This file implements the Instructor class.
''''''''''''''''''''''''''''''''''''''''''''''''''''''''''''''''''''''''''''''''
```

Yes, there is a comment there, but it contains so little information, it's not even worth extracting. Here is another, more correct header comment:

```
''''''''''''''''''''''''''''''''''''''''''''''''''''''''''''''''''''''''''''''''
      '      This file implements the Instructor class. An Instructor is a person
      '      who teaches one or more classes. This class is actually derived from
      '      the Person class. It has the following public properties and methods:
      '      Name, instructor, ExamineClassSchedule
''''''''''''''''''''''''''''''''''''''''''''''''''''''''''''''''''''''''''''''''
```

A quick read of the comments reveals that much more information is available. However, parsing it into subcomponents is impossible. Examining the comments reveals that

- The first sentence contains redundant information and does not need to be accepted.
- The second sentence actually contains a description of an instructor.
- The third sentence contains useful information. However, in its present form, you can only include it as part of the description. If you want a way to identify class derivations in the repository, another mechanism will need to be found.
- The fourth sentence merely repeats the properties and methods that will be captured anyway.

What you might actually need is a standard comment header template that can be easily parsed for all relevant information. The point is that the following commenting style is much easier to parse through and separate the data into specific components. On the other hand, your programmers may resent having their "hands tied" and fail to provide adequate comments. Of course, using a more rigid commenting style makes the code easier to read for humans as well as the computer. On the other hand, you do not want to require 500 different categories of information for people to fill in, either. One of your jobs in implementing a repository will be to strike a balance between these two extremes.

```
''''''''''''''''''''''''''''''''''''''''''''''''''''''''''''''''''''''''''''''''''''''''''
'       File:      Instruct.cls
'
'       Class:      Instructor
'
'       Description:
'            An Instructor is a person who teaches one or more classes.
'
'       Derived From: Person (virtual)
'
'       Public Properties:
'            Name             The full name of the Instructor.
'            InstructorID        Number assigned to the Instructor by the
'                                college.
'
'       Public Methods:
'             ExamineClassSchedule     Analyzes the times the instructor is
'                 scheduled to teach and identifies any scheduling conflicts.
''''''''''''''''''''''''''''''''''''''''''''''''''''''''''''''''''''''''''''''''''''''''''
```

Of course, even a standard template can have problems. Each of the following two comments would require a slightly different parsing technique. The extraction application will need to include adaptable parsing algorithms, your developers will have to impose discipline in their commenting styles, or you do not get the information stored into the repository.

```
'Description:     The description goes here.
'Description:
'     The description goes here.
```

Database Integration Considerations

One use of the repository is to store basic information describing the structure of a database you are using or developing. Extracting this information from a database should be a relatively straightforward task. A simple TIM can be created to store information about tables and their associated columns. Then, an extraction application can be built to access the database's data dictionary tables and read out the table and column data.

However, extracting such data by itself will not provide a great deal of useful information, especially because this type of information is generally tracked by organizations through various data-modeling tools and dictionaries.

More useful information is available by identifying which portions of an application's code access which tables and columns in the database, or to identify which stored procedures reference those tables and columns. With this kind of data, you can quickly assess the potential impact on your development environment if a change is made to the database's structure.

As usual, saying that you want this information and actually obtaining it are not the same thing. Consider the following sample code for your fictitious `Instructor` class module. The `Instructor` class uses a class called `Database` with a variable name of `mvarDatabase` that provides a mechanism for executing queries and maintaining any result sets. The `Database` object to use is passed to the `Instructor` class through a property.

```
'This function gathers information about a specified instructor from the
'database.
     Public Sub Load_By_Instructor_ID(lInstructID as Long)
     Dim strSelect as String
     Dim objDatabase as New Database
     Dim bSuccess as Boolean
     strSelect  = "Select Instr_ID, Name from tblInstructor where Instr_ID = " & _
                    CStr(lInstructID)
     bSuccess = mvarDatabase.ExecuteQuery(strSelect)
     If bSuccess
          'Code for manipulating the result set in the mvarDatabase object
     Else
          'Code for handling errors
     End If
     End Sub
```

Your goal at this point is to store in the repository the fact that the Visual Basic `Instructor` class references the tblInstructor table and the Instr_ID and Name columns in the database. So, how do you do that? You can use various options. The following three options are possible but have significant limitations:

- You could build an extractor that would search through the code looking for SQL-like strings and capture the key words from the string. For example, you could look for things like `"Select` or `"Update` in the code and then parse through the SQL statement appropriately. Of course, you have to be careful of phrases like `Select I.Instr_ID as ID...`, which are not as easy to parse. You will, in effect, have to become an SQL expert and know the meaning of all keywords and conventions. Furthermore, you will have to hope that something like this text string does not appear in the code:

```
MsgBox "Select the option you want from the list provided."
```

- You could create an extractor that could load up the list of table and column names from the database and look for where they are used in the code. Of course, when you search for a word like `Name`, you will probably get a ton of hits that are completely irrelevant.
- You could create a browser tool for the repository that displays a list of class modules and a second list of database tables. Then, the tool would enable you to manually relate classes to tables. This approach enables the coding to be performed any way the developer wants. However, it requires a large amount of manual, error-prone data entry.

As noted, each of these options has considerable drawbacks. On the other hand, you could redesign the code to allow for automatic identification of tables and columns used by a class. Naturally, you should not redesign the code just to take advantage of the repository. However, this approach has a few other advantages that may make it worthwhile.

The redesign is relatively straightforward. To start with, declare a set of member variables to hold the table and column data. A new class should have been created to hold the column data. Next, the values are set when the class is initialized. Finally, the various functions for the class are rewritten to use these variables instead of writing complete SQL statements.

The following code is in the declaration section of the module:

```
'Variable declaration section
'Table name
Private mvarTableName as String
'Column data
Private mvarColumns as New Collection
Private mvarInstr_ID() as New Column
Private mvarName as New Column
```

The following code is in the `Class_Initialize` subroutine and is used to initialize the variable's values. First, you initialize the table name:

```
mvarTableName = "tblInstructor"
```

Then, the `Instr_ID` column:

```
mvarInstr_ID.Name = "Instr_ID"
mvarInstr_ID.Required = True
mvarColumns.Add Item:=mvarInstr_ID Key:= mvarInstr_ID.Name
```

Finally, the `Name` column:

```
mvarName.Name = "Name"
mvarName.Required = True
mvarName.Length = 30
mvarColumns.Add Item:= mvarName Key:= mvarName.Name
```

The following code shows how the Load_By_Instructor_ID is rewritten using the new design:

```
'This function gathers information about a specified
'instructor from the database.
     Public Sub Load_By_Instructor_ID(lInstructID as Long)
          Dim strSelect as String
          Dim objDatabase as New Database
          Dim bSuccess as Boolean
          'Generic code for building the select statement
          strSelect  = "Select "
          Dim Field as Variant
          For Each Field in mvarColumns
               strSelect = strSelect & Field.Name & ", "
          Next Field
          strSelect = strSelect & " From " & mvarTableName
          'Build the unique where clause
          strSelect = strSelect & " Where "
          strSelect = strSelect & mvarInstr_ID.Name
          strSelect = strSelect & " = "
          strSelect = strSelect & mvarInsr_ID.Value
          bSuccess = mvarDatabase.ExecuteQuery(strSelect)
          If bSuccess
               'Code for manipulating the result set in
               'the mvarDatabase object
          Else
               'Code for handling errors
          End If
     End Sub
```

The following things have been accomplished in this basic redesign:

- The table-related data could be easily retrieved into the repository. All the extraction application needs to do is parse through the various class files and search for the declaration of the mvarTableName and mvarColumns variables. Then, the appropriate data can be found from there.
- The code is now easier to maintain. The save function no longer references column names directly, minimizing the impact on the code from changes to the database tables. For example, adding a column to tblInstructor would only involve adding a new member variable and initializing it in Class_Initialize. The Load_By_Instructor_ID function would not have to be changed at all.
- Additional information about the columns can be tracked as a group. Using a class to store column information allows names, maximum lengths, and any other special information together in one location. Special versions of the Column class should even be created to enforce proper datatyping such as LongColumn and StringColumn.
- Functions and portions of functions are reusable. The Load_By_Instructor_ID format can easily be used by other table access classes with minor modifications. With some additional modifications, classes could even be created to access views and joins in the database.

Coding Summary

Very few, if any, software developers have spent the last several years writing code so that its information can be easily imported into a repository. Nor should you or anyone undertake a massive redesign effort just to get data into the repository. Therefore, for the time being, the type of data and the amount of detail you can collect will be somewhat restricted. However, by implementing good coding practices, as discussed in the preceding examples, information can be more easily analyzed in the future.

The good news is that, if you are already using good coding practices, not only is your code easy to maintain, easy to read, and reusable, but the key information about your code can now be more easily imported into the repository. You certainly will not be able to import everything you want to know, but you will be able to import more detailed and more reliable data.

Reengineering the Development Process

Why a section on reengineering your development processes? Because the repository is like any other software: it will only do what you tell it to do.

In other words, the repository is meant to capture information describing your development environment. If you utilize sloppy development practices, and your code is disorganized, undocumented, and hard to read, the resulting data in the repository will be disorganized, undescribed, and hard to explain (if it can be obtained at all). Whereas if you utilized disciplined development practices and the resulting code is well organized, well documented, and easy to read, the data in the repository will reflect that. Furthermore, it will be much easier for the repository to automatically identify those cross-application relationships and dependencies that make the repository truly useful.

Consider a widget factory that wants to implement an automated control system. Near the end of the assembly line, the design team decides to insert a sensor to measure the weight of widgets before they are packaged. However, for some reason, workers are randomly removing widgets to paint and pack in separate boxes. Now the sensor will not be able to measure the weight of these special widgets. Even if it could, the design team has not taken into account the added weight from the paint in calibrating the sensor. Thus, the benefit of the automated system has been undercut by a lack of documentation on the widget process and inconsistency in how that process works. The same sorts of problems can easily occur when pulling information out of your applications and into the repository.

Quite often in a development environment several applications will be built to serve as test cases and may be thrown away when completed. Whether you want to store information about these test cases, or prototypes, depends on your development environment. On the one hand, storing the prototype information allows you to query the structure of the prototype and analyze its interdependencies with other applications. On the other hand, you could mistake prototype components for real application components if you don't pay attention. In general, you probably want to store prototype information in the repository, but you want to ensure that the prototype and its associated components are labeled as such. Be careful not to accidentally label real application components that the prototype is using as a prototype, however.

Building the Metamodel

Earlier sections have provided general guidelines on building and using TIMs and have discussed the mechanics of building the TIM. This section attempts to tie the concepts together to show how to integrate these components into a single model of your development environment's information requirements.

The metamodel is a fairly abstract concept, and a repository can be implemented without understanding the concept. However, in order to truly understand what the repository is all about, the metamodel concept needs to be understood.

The Concepts

The *metamodel* is simply a description of all the information that you need to store in the repository. It provides an abstract outline of information that is required about your applications. The TIMs that were discussed earlier are used to implement the various components of the metamodel. Thus, technically a TIM is a metamodel for its particular tool. The metamodel also identifies the relationships from one TIM to another.

A metamodel is used to store metadata. The definition of *metadata* is "data about data." For example, a database stores the names and phone numbers of employees in a company. The names and phone numbers are data. On the other hand, the repository stores the names of the database's tables: company and employee. Company and employee are metadata.

Figure 28.7 provides an example of these concepts. At the bottom layer are various processes involved in providing transportation. At the next layer are the systems that store the data needed to perform their day-to-day business. At the next layer is the metadata that describes how the system data is organized. Thus, metadata is data about data. Moving up one more layer shows the meta-meta data that describes how the metadata is organized.

The Metamodel Simplified

Fortunately, you do not need to grasp these concepts completely to implement them. Microsoft has provided mechanisms for implementing the metamodel, and has taken care of the meta-meta model for you. TIMs that are required encapsulate the metamodel concept. In addition, the repository engine and the Type Information Model encapsulate the meta-meta layer for you, so you do not have to worry about it at all.

Your main concern should be building an integrated view of the entire development environment and not just individual tools. To accomplish this goal, you need to get organized. Divide your organization along two different axes. The first axis focuses on the steps involved in developing software from requirements to design to implementation. Examples of this division were discussed in previous sections. The second axis focuses on the different aspects of the system, namely data, process, and technology. For example, a typical computer system consists of a database and several applications, each of which runs on some type of computer.

FIG. 28.7
Diagram showing the various levels of data abstraction.

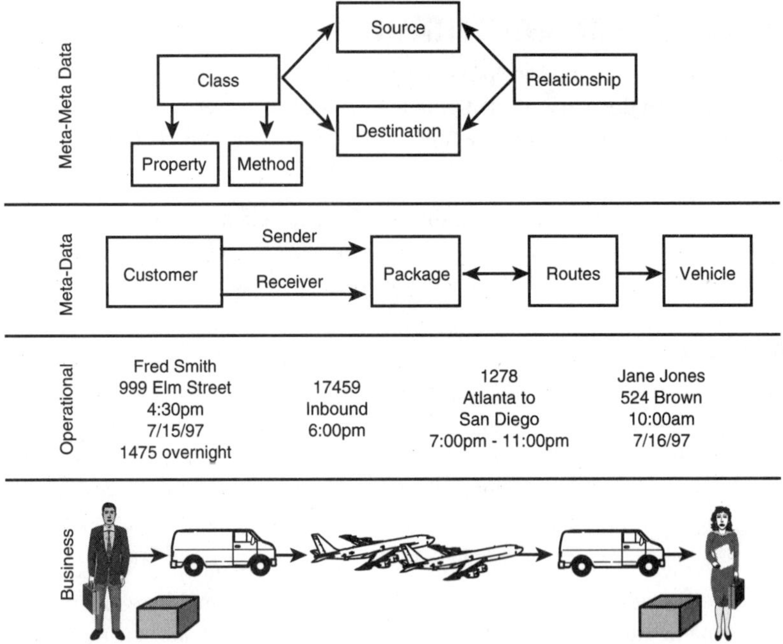

These concepts will be discussed in the following examples. The first shows how a logical concept can be related to an implementation of that concept in code. The second discusses how applications can be linked to the database.

Relating Logical Concepts to Physical Concepts

Typically, in a development effort, you will lay out a design before you begin writing code. A common methodology for laying out a design is to use an object-oriented design (OOD). A basic unit of OOD is the concept of a class. Another major concept in OOD is that classes can be derived from other classes. These concepts could be captured in the metamodel as shown in the Figure 28.8.

FIG. 28.8
A class can inherit its structure from one other class. The inherited class will have the same functions and attributes as the base class.

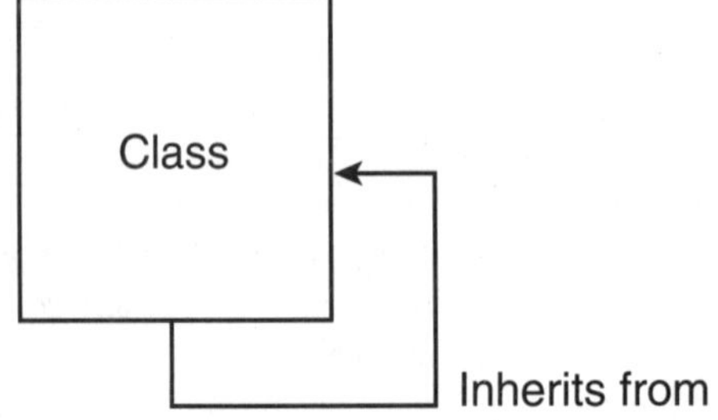

At this point, to store data about classes from an OOD software tool, you would create a TIM with a class of `class`. You would also designate the `class` class as the source and destination in the `Inheritance` relationship. You would also need to expose a `class` interface to access the data through any extraction or analysis tools.

After the design is complete, the next step is to implement the design concepts in the code. If you have a software tool that supports object-oriented programming, you will want to implement your design classes as classes in the code. This concept of a *design class* is shown in Figure 28.9. The relationship shown indicates there might be many implemented classes for every design class because the same design concept may need to be repeated in several different projects.

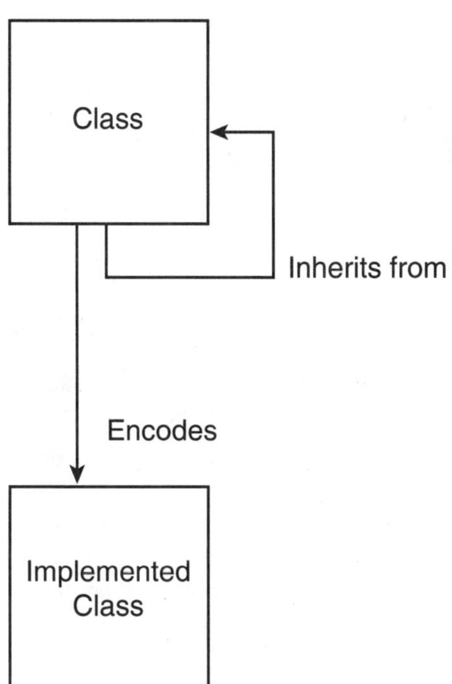

FIG. 28.9
An implemented class is a software module that physically implements the conceptual class from the system's design.

At this point, however, you are not ready to store data. Unfortunately, not all code implements classes the same way, nor do they all implement the concept of inheritance the same way. For example, Visual Basic does not provide true inheritance, but, rather, provides a different version where one class "implements" another class. On the other hand, Visual C++ provides inheritance and includes the slightly more advanced concepts of virtual and pure virtual functions to define the inherited characteristics. Another difference is that Visual Basic classes support the concept of properties, whereas Visual C++ does not. These new ideas are captured in Figure 28.10. Visual Basic only allows inheritance of the names of the functions while Visual C++ allows inheritance of the implementation of the function.

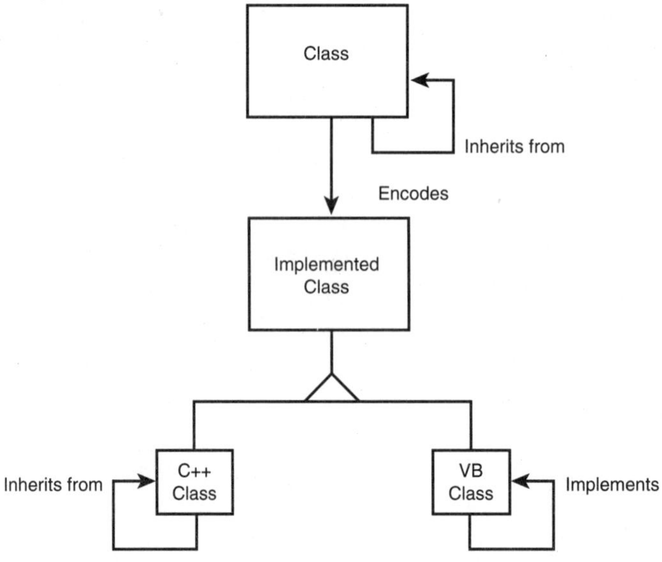

FIG. 28.10
The concept of inheritance is implemented differently in Visual Basic and Visual C++.

At this point, you can now expand the TIM discussed earlier to include the new classes and relationships. Note that when defining the TIM, the Type Information Model does not directly support the concept of inheritance. Therefore, there is no easy way to say that a Visual C++ class is derived from your `Implemented` class. Instead, create a new relationship type called `is a type of`. Make the `Implemented` class a source for the relationship, and make the Visual Basic and Visual C++ classes a destination of the relationship.

As a final consideration, assume that you are currently using the MDO model. You now need to expand that model to fit into the metamodel concepts diagrammed in the figures. Because the MDO Class Module portion of the MDO model is basically the same concept as the Visual Basic Class, you can consider them the same thing. Figure 28.11 demonstrates this concept. After that, you will need to expand the MDO Model in the repository because it does not currently capture enough information to show implement concepts.

You have now created a path for identifying which parts of your design are implemented by which applications.

Relating Applications to Data

Another piece of information you might want to capture is which portions of a database are accessed by what portions of a program. Assume that your applications are written in Visual Basic. The structure of the MDO model that is used for capturing Visual Basic information is shown in Figure 28.12.

The other item you need to track is the database itself. Figure 28.13 shows a simple model for tracking the database information including the name of the database and its basic data dictionary information.

FIG. 28.11
The MDO model for Visual Basic implements the concept of classes in the MDO Class Module class.

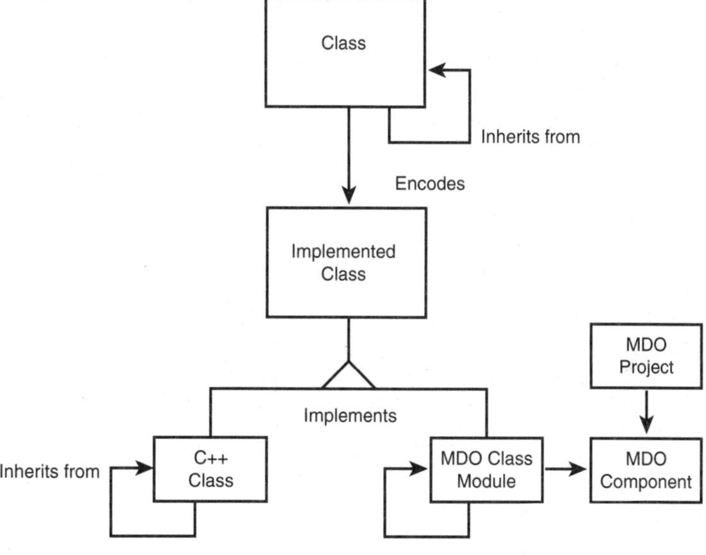

FIG. 28.12
These components of the MDO model store information about a project, its components, and references to other projects.

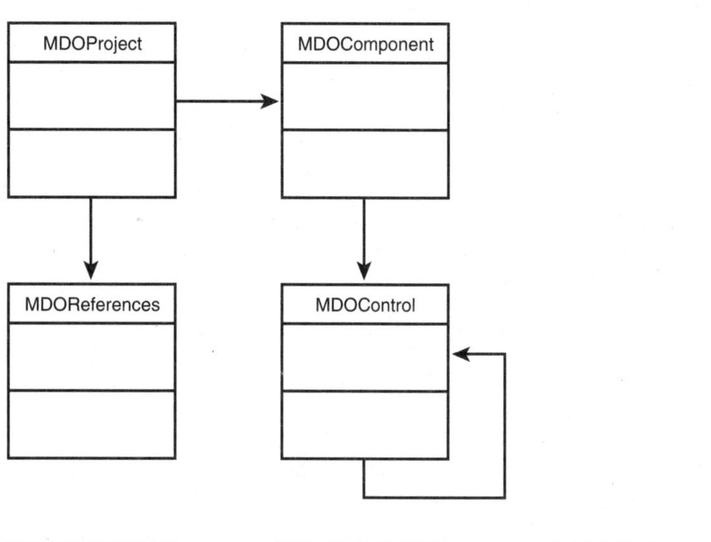

FIG. 28.13
A database consists of the database itself and one or more tables. The tables in turn consist of one or more columns.

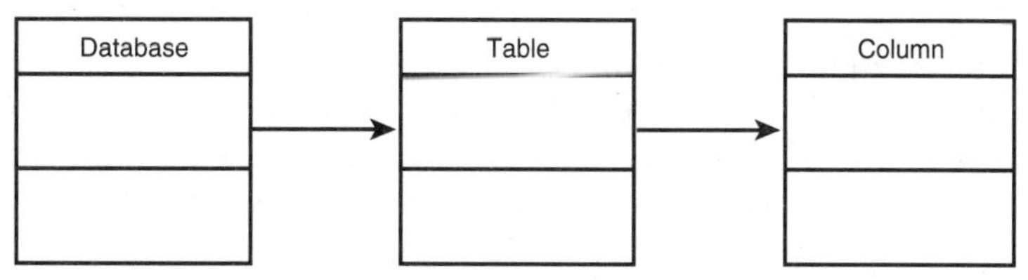

Now you are ready to show how the application and the database are interrelated. However, you have a decision to make because several alternatives are available. Two of those alternatives are shown in Figures 28.14 and 28.15.

Figure 28.14 simply shows a relationship that allows tracking of which databases are used by which applications. This information is high level and relatively easy to gather and maintain. On the other hand, this information is of limited usefulness for any analysis that needs to be done.

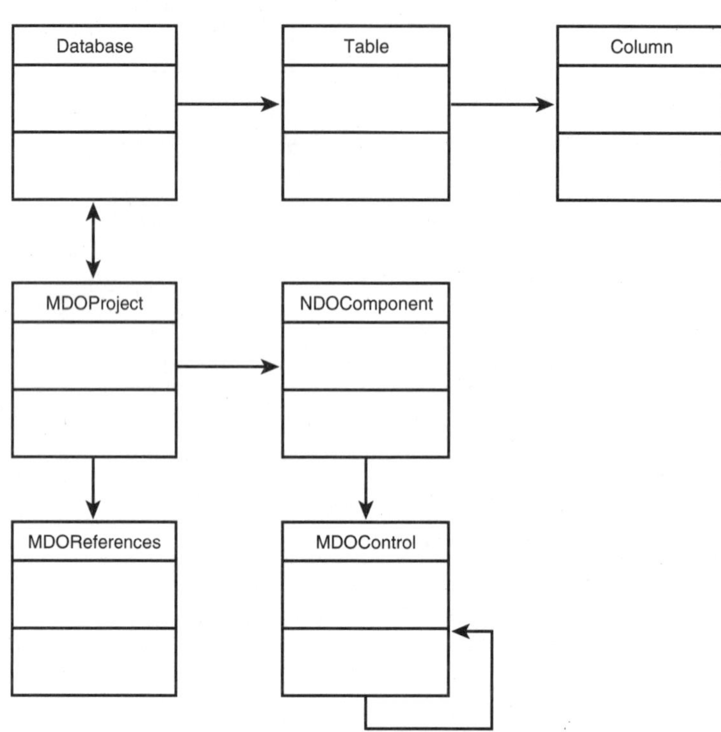

FIG. 28.14 One way to show interrelationships between a Visual Basic project and a database is to simply relate the name of the database to the Visual Basic Project.

Figure 28.15 shows each module of the application and the associated database table or tables that it interacts with. This information is more detailed and will be much harder to collect and maintain. On the other hand, the added detail will allow production of higher quality reports.

The answer to the question of which technique to pick depends on what you want. Do you need detail or just high-level concepts? Is this your first repository project? How hard will it be to gather detailed information versus the high level? Do not take these questions lightly. They will have a major impact on the usefulness of your repository system.

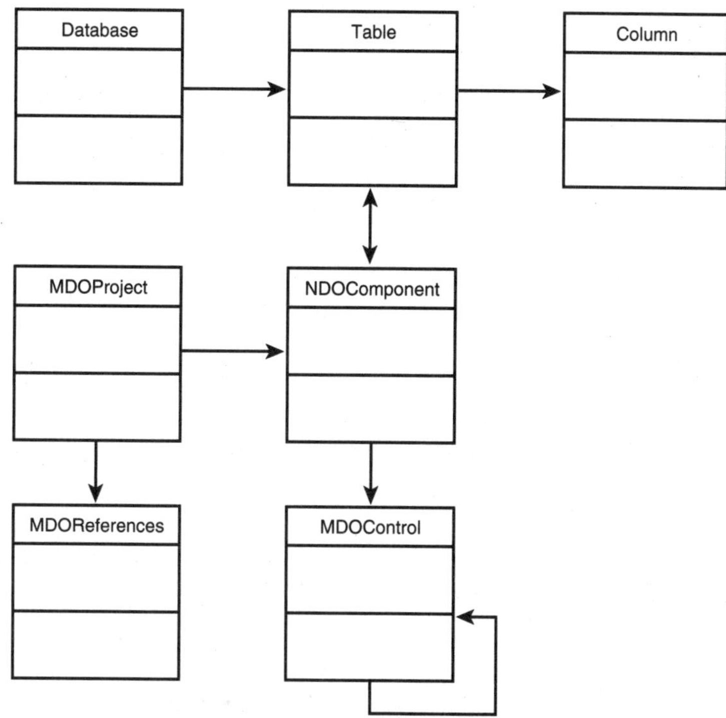

FIG. 28.15
A second method of showing the relationship is to capture which tables are accessed by which modules of code.

As a final note of consideration, the diagrams are used to show what database structure an application uses to gather data. The actual connection of an application to a database is handled through some type of data source such as an ODBC driver. The sample figures do not include the concept of a data source and would have to be expanded to include it. The point is that the metamodel plays a major role in defining what the repository can and cannot do.

Summary

Before running out and using the Microsoft Repository, bear a couple of things in mind. First, the repository is only at version 1.0. Second, as of this writing, Microsoft has announced the development of its Open Information Model, which vendors are to use as a foundation for connecting to the repository. Unless you have a specific need in mind, you may want to wait until the tool and the models have stabilized before using them. However, the tool will only do so much for you. You should be examining how your development environment will be impacted by the tool in the future. ●

Index

Symbols

A

D

E

F

G

J

K

L

M

N

O

P

Q

R

W-Z

Technical Support

If you need assistance with the information provided by Macmillan Computer Publishing, please access the information available on our web site at **http://www.mcp.com/feedback.** Our most Frequently Asked Questions are answered there. If you do not find the answers to your questions on our web site, you may contact Macmillan User Services at **(317) 581-3833** or email us at **support@mcp.com**.